THE OFFICIAL PRICE GUIDE TO RECORDS

BY
THE HOUSE OF COLLECTIBLES

We have compiled the information contained herein through a *patented computerized process* which relies primarily on a nationwide sampling of information provided by noteworthy collectible experts, auction houses and specialized dealers. This unique retrieval system enables us to provide the reader with the most current and accurate information available.

EDITOR
THOMAS E. HUDGEONS III

SEVENTH EDITION
THE HOUSE OF COLLECTIBLES, WESTMINSTER, MARYLAND 21157

PHOTOGRAPHIC RECOGNITION

Cover Photograph: Photographer — TJ. Hudgeons, Orlando, FL 32809;
Courtesy of: Steve Keith, Orlando, FL 32809.

©1985 The House of Collectibles
All rights reserved under International and Pan-American Copyright Conventions.

Published by: The House of Collectibles
P.O. Box 149
Westminster, Maryland 21157
Phone: (301) 583-6959

Distributed by Ballantine Books, a division of Random House, Inc., New York and simultaneously in Canada by Random House of Canada Limited, Toronto.

Manufactured in the United States of America

Library of Congress Catalog Card Number: 82-82256

ISBN: 0-87637-288-4

10 9 8 7 6 5 4 3

TABLE OF CONTENTS

Market Review ... 1
History of Rock as a Music Influence ... 2
Beginning A Collection ... 6
Collecting Independent Labels ... 8
Buying ... 10
Investing ... 12
Selling ... 13
Care and Storage ... 14
Record Shows and Conventions ... 14
Will Current Records
Become Valuable? ... 16
Glossary ... 17
Fan Clubs ... 19
How To Use This Book ... 22
LISTINGS
Abba ... 23
Academics ... 23
Johnny Ace ... 23
Nicky Addeo ... 23
Ad-Libs ... 23
Admirations ... 24
Aladdins ... 24
Steve Alaimo and
The Redcoats ... 24
Arthur Alexander ... 24
Davie Allen and
The Arrows ... 24
Jimmy Allen ... 25
Lee Allen and His Band ... 25
Richie Allen ... 25
Arvee Allens (Ritchie Valens) ... 25
Alley Cats ... 25
Allman Brothers ... 25
American Spring (Honeys) ... 26
Lee Andrews and The Hearts ... 26
Angels ... 26
Animals ... 27
Paul Anka ... 28
Paul Anka, Johnny Nash,
George Hamilton IV ... 30
Annette ... 30
Ann-Margret ... 32
Paul Anthony ... 33
Aqua-Nites ... 33
Aquatones ... 33
The Archies ... 33
Vance Arnold (Joe Cocker) ... 33
Arrogants ... 34
Del Ashley (David Gates) ... 34
Astronauts ... 34
Attila-Album ... 34
Audrey ... 34
The Autumns ... 34
Frankie Avalon ... 34
Average White Band ... 38
Baby Dolls ... 38
Baby Ray and the Ferns
(Frank Zappa) ... 38
Badfinger ... 39
Joan Baez ... 39
Marty Balin ... 40
Florence Ballard ... 40
Hank Ballard and The Midnighters ... 40
The Band ... 41
Barbarians ... 41
Annette Bard (Carol Connors) ... 42
Bobby Bare ... 42
Baritones ... 42
J.J. Barnes and The Delfis ... 42
Steve Barri ... 42
Barries ... 42
Barry and The Tamerlanes ... 42
Jeff Barry ... 43
Joe Barry ... 43
Bay City Rollers ... 43
Baysiders ... 43
B. Bumble and The Stingers ... 44
Beach Boys ... 44
Beach Bums ... 47
Beatles ... 47
Beau Brummels ... 53
Beau-Marks ... 54
Jimmy Beaumont ... 54
Beefeaters (Byrds) ... 54
Bee Gees ... 54
Bel-Aires ... 56
Archie Bell and The Drells ... 56
Madeline Bell ... 56
Bell Notes ... 56
Belmonts ... 56
Jesse Belvin ... 58
Boyd Bennett ... 59
Joe Bennett and The
Sparkletones ... 59
Ron Bernard ... 60
Chuck Berry ... 60
Jan Berry ... 62
Lou Berry & The Bel Raves ... 63
Mike Berry ... 63
Richard Berry ... 63
Rod Berry and The Bel Raves ... 64
Peter Best ... 64
Big Bopper ... 64
Big Brother & The Holding Company ... 64
Billy and Lillie ... 66
Cilla Black ... 66
The Black Hawks ... 66
Billy Bland ... 66
Marcie Blane ... 68
Blazons ... 68
Michael Blessing (Mike Nesmith) ... 68
Blondie (with Debby Harry) ... 68
Blossoms ... 68
Blue Cheer ... 69
Blue Jays ... 69
Blue Lites ... 69
Blue Ridge Rangers ... 69
Blues Magoos ... 69
Bluesology ... 70
Bob and Sheri ... 70
Bob B. Soxx and Blue Jeans ... 70
Bobbettes ... 70
Bobsled and The Toboggans ... 71
Bon-Aires ... 71
Gary U.S. Bonds ... 71
Bon Bons (Shangri-Las) ... 72
Bonnie and The Treasures ... 72
Sonny Bono and Little Tootsie ... 72
Bab Boon ... 72
Pat Boone ... 72
Bop-Chords ... 76
The Bottom Line ... 76
Jimmy Bowen ... 76
David Bowie ... 76
Boyfriends (5 Discs) ... 78
Jan Bradley ... 78
Brave Belt (Pre-Bachman Turner
Overdrive) ... 78
Bread ... 78
Ronnie Brent ... 79
Brewer & Shipley ... 79
Brooklyn Bridge ... 79
James Brown ... 79
Bruce and Jerry ... 81
Bruce and Terry ... 81
Billy Bryan (Gene Pitney) ... 81
Bubble Puppy ... 81
Buchanan and Goodman ... 82
Buckinghams ... 82
Buddies (Tokens) ... 83
Buddy and The Fads ... 83
Buffalo Rebels (Rockin' Rebels) ... 83
Buffalo Springfield ... 83
Tommy Burk & The Counts ... 83
Solomon Burke ... 83
Dorsey Burnette ... 85
Johnny Burnette ... 85
Johnny Burnette Trio ... 86
Jerry Butler ... 86
Byrds ... 88
Edward "Kookie" Byrnes ... 89
Cadets ... 89
Cadillacs ... 90
Caesar and Cleo (Sonny and Cher) ... 91
Aubry Cagle ... 91
California Music ... 91
Dudley Callicut & The Go Boys ... 91
Calveys ... 91
Glen Campbell ... 91
Jo-Ann Campbell ... 92
Camps ... 93
Canadian Squires (The Band) ... 93
Cannibal and The Headhunters ... 93
Freddy Cannon ... 93
Jerry Capehart ... 95
Capitols ... 95
John Capri ... 95
Capris ... 95
Captain and Tennille ... 95
Cardinals ... 95
Carlo ... 96
Kim Carnes ... 96
Karen Carpenter (Pre-Carpenters) ... 96
Wayne Carroll ... 96
Cascades ... 96
Eddie Cash ... 98
Johnny Cash ... 98
Shaun Cassidy ... 100
Castells ... 100
Joey Castle ... 100
Vince Castro ... 100
Casuals (Original Casuals) ... 101
Centuries (Buckinghams) ... 101
Chad and Jeremy ... 101
Challengers ... 102
Champs ... 102
Larry Chance ... 103
Gene Chandler ... 103
Bruce Channel ... 103
Chantays ... 104
Chantels ... 104
Chanters ... 105
Chants ... 105
Chaperones ... 105
Harry Chapin ... 105
Charlatan ... 106
Ray Charles ... 106
Charms ... 108
Chubby Checker ... 110
Cher ... 114
Cherilyn (Cher) ... 114
Chesters (Little Anthony and
The Imperials) ... 114
Chevrons ... 114
Artie Chicago (Ernie Maresca) ... 114
Chiffons ... 114
Chimes ... 115
The Chips ... 115
Chocolate Watch Band ... 115
Choir (Raspberries) ... 116
Chords ... 116
Lou Christie ... 116
Lou Christie and The Classics ... 117
Chic Christy ... 118
Don Christy (Sonny Bono) ... 118
Church Street Five ... 118
City ... 118
C.L. and The Pictures ... 118
Jimmy Clanton ... 118
Eric Clapton ... 119
Claudine Clark ... 120
Dave Clark Five ... 120
Dee Clark ... 122
Petula Clark ... 124
Sanford Clark ... 125
Class-Airs ... 126
Classics ... 126
Classics (Featured Lou Christie) ... 126
Classmates ... 126
Joe Clay ... 126
Cleftones ... 126
Patsy Cline ... 128
Clovers ... 128
Coasters ... 130
Eddie Cochran ... 131
Cochran Brothers ... 132
Joe Cocker ... 132
Colonials ... 132
Comic Books ... 132
Bobby Comstock ... 132
Carol Connors ... 133
Consorts ... 133
Contours ... 133
Sam Cooke ... 134
Cookies ... 135
Edddie Cooley and The Dimples ... 136
Rita Coolidge ... 136
Alice Cooper ... 136
Ken Copeland ... 136
Cordells ... 138
Cordials ... 138
Cornells ... 138
Count Five ... 138
Buddy Covelle ... 138
Cowsills ... 138
Craftsmen (Johnny and The
Hurricanes) ... 138
Johnny Crawford ... 138
Cream ... 139
Creedence Clearwater Revival ... 139
Crescendos ... 140
Crests ... 140
Crew Cuts ... 141
Crickets (Buddy Holly) ... 142
Crickets ... 142
Cross Country (Tokens) ... 144
Crossfires (Turtles) ... 144
Crows ... 144
Cruisers ... 144
Crystals ... 144
Johnny Cymbal ... 145
Bertell Dache (Tony Orlando) ... 145
Dakotas ... 145
Dick Dale ... 145
Jimmy Dale (Jimmy Clanton) ... 146
Roger Daltry ... 146
Danleers ... 146
Danny and The Juniors ... 147
Danny and The Memories ... 147
Dante and The Evergreens ... 147
Darchaes ... 147
Bobby Darin ... 148
Darrel and The Oxfords (Tokens) ... 151
James Darren ... 152
Dartells ... 153
David and Jonathan ... 153
David & Lee ... 153
Andrea Davis (Minnie Riperton) ... 153
Dave Davies ... 153
Spencer Davis Group ... 153

Darlene Day 154
Terry Day (Terry Melcher) 154
Bobby Dean 154
Janet Deane 154
Dave Dee, Dozy, Beaky, Mick and Tich 154
Jackie Dee (Jackie DeShannon) 154
Joey Dee 154
Joey Dee and The Starliters 154
Johnny Dee (John D. Loudermilk) . . . 155
Tommy Dee 155
Deep Purple 155
Tony Dell 156
Dells 156
Dell-Vikings 157
Eddie Delmar 157
Demensions 157
Dennis and The Explorers 158
Denny and The Dedications 158
Lee Denson 158
John Denver 158
Derek (Johnny Cymbal) 159
Jackie DeShannon 159
Desires (Regents) 161
Detergents 161
Devotions 161
Diablos 161
Dialtones (Randy and The Rainbows) 162
Neil Diamond 162
Diamonds 164
Diatones 166
Dick and DeeDee 166
Bo Diddley 167
Danny Dill 168
Ding Dongs (Rinky-Dinks) 168
Dino & The Gee-Chords 168
Dino and The Heartspinners 168
Dion 168
Dion and The Belmonts 171
Dion and The Timberlanes (Before Belmonts) 171
Dixie Cups 172
Mickey Dolenz 172
Fats Domino 172
Dominoes 177
Don and Dewey 178
Ral Donner 178
Donnie and The Del-Chords 179
Donnie and The Dreamers 179
Donovan 179
Dickey Doo and The Don'ts 180
Doors 182
Harold Dorman 182
Gerry Dorsey (Englebert Humperdinck) 183
Lee Dorsey 183
Steve Douglas 183
Ronnie Dove 183
Dovells 183
Dovers 184
Dickie Doyle 184
Dreamers 184
Dreamlovers 184
Drifters 184
Duals 188
Dubs 188
Dukays 189
Duponts (Little Anthony and The Imperials) 189
Dupress 189
Huelyn Duvall 190
Earls 190
Easybeats 190
Echoes 191
Echoes (Innocents) 191
Eddie and The Showmen 191
Duane Eddy 191
Edsels 193
El Dorados 193
Electric Prunes 194
Elegants 194
Elements of Life 194
Cass Elliot (Mama Cass) 194
El-Rays (Dells) 195
Embers 195
Emerson, Lake & Palmer 195
Enchantments 195
England Dan & John Ford Coley 195
Scott English 196
Episode Six (Deep Purple) 196
Essex 196
Paul Evans 196
Betty Everett 197
Vince Everett 198
Everly Brothers 198
The Excellons 201
Exiles 201
Extremes 201
Shelly Fabares 202
Fabian 202
Fabian and Frankie Avalon 204
Fabulous Pearl Devines 204
Adam Faith 204
Marianne Faithfull 204
Falcons 204
Falling Pebbles (Buckinghams) 206
Fantastic Baggies 206
Chris Farlowe and The Thunderbirds 206
Fascinators 206
Felix and The Escorts (Young Rascals) 208
Narvel Felts 208
Freddy Fender 208
Fendermen 208
Sally Field 208
Fifth Dimension 208
Fireballs 209
Fireflies 209
Five Americans 209
Five Blobs 210
Five Coachmen 210
Five Discs 210
The Five Embers 210
Five Gents 210
The Five Jades 210
Five Keys 210
The Five Owls 212
Five Reasons 212
Five Satins 212
Five Scripts 214
Five Trojans 214
Flamingos 214
Flares (Cadets) 215
Fleetwood Mac 216
Fleetwoods 216
Fluorescents 218
Tommy Fogerty and The Blue Velvets 218
Wayne Fontana and The Mindbenders 218
Fontane Sisters 219
Frankie Ford 219
4 After 5's (Rivingtons) 220
Four Blades 220
Four Cal-Quettes 220
Four Directions 220
Four Dots (With Jewel Akens) 220
Four Ekkos 220
Four Graduates (Happenings) 220
Four Horsemen 220
Four Jokers 220
Four Lovers (Four Seasons) 220
Fourmost 221
Four Pennies (Chiffons) 221
Four Preps 221
Four Seasons 222
Four Sevilles 225
The Four Shades 225
Four Speeds 225
Four Teens 225
Four Tops 226
Four Winds (Tokens) 227
Kim Fowley 227
Norman Fox and The Rob Roys 227
Peter Frampton 227
Connie Francis 227
Freddie and The Dreamers 232
Freddy & The Fat Boys 232
Bobby Freeman 232
Don French 233
Frogmen 233
Bobby Fuller Four 233
Gabriel & The Angels 234
Galaxies 234
Gales 234
Gamblers 234
Frank Gari 234
Johnny Garner 234
Artie Garr (Art Garfunkel) 234
Gary and Clyde (Skip and Flip) 234
Gary and The Nite Lites (American Breed) 234
David Gates 235
Marvin Gaye 235
Gene and Eunice 237
G-Clefs 237
Gee Cees 237
Gentrys 237
Germz 238
Gerry and The Pacemakers 238
Gestics 240
Steve Gibson and The Red Caps 240
Gigolos 240
Ronnie Gill 240
Mickey Gilley 240
Jimmy Gilmer and The Fireballs 243
Lou Giordano 243
Gladiolas 243
Cliff Gleaves 243
Golliwogs 243
Peter Goon 244
Lesley Gore 244
Sammy Gowans 246
Charlie Gracie 246
Gerry Granaham 246
Janie Grant 247
Guy Grants 247
Grass Roots 247
Great Society 248
Guess Who? 248
The Guise (and Their Mod Squad) . . . 249
Gulliver 249
Arlo Guthrie 249
Bob Guy (Frank Zappa) 250
Sammy Hagan 250
Ronnie Haig 250
Hale & The Hushabyes 250
Bill Haley and The Comets 250
Hall and Oates 254
Larry Hall 254
Roy Hall 254
George Hamilton IV 256
Happenings 256
Harbor Lights (Jay and The Americans) 257
Billy Harlan 257
Harmony 257
Harptones 257
Emmylou Harris 258
George Harrison 258
Bobby Hart 260
Rocky Hart 260
Phil Harvey (Spector) 260
Ali Hassan 260
Hassles 260
The Hawk (Jerry Lee Lewis) 260
Dale Hawkins 260
Ronnie Hawkins 261
Dean Hawley 262
Ron Haydock 262
Roy Head 262
Heart 264
Heartbeats 264
Heartbreakers 264
Heartbreakers (Frank Zappa) 264
Bobby Helms 264
Jimi Hendrix 266
Herd 267
Herman's Hermits 267
Ersel Hickey 268
Hi-Fives 268
High Numbers (Who) 268
Joel Hill 270
Eddie Hodges 270
Ron Holden 270
Eddie Holland 270
Hollies 271
Buddy Holly 272
Hollyhawks 274
Hollywood Argyles 274
Hollywood Saxons 276
Hollywood Tornadoes 276
The Hondells 276
Honeybees 276
Honeycombs 276
Honeys 277
Honorables 277
Honor Society (Happenings) 277
Hotlegs 277
Hot-Toddys (Rockin' Rebels) 277
Gregory Howard 277
Hullabaloos 277
Human Beinz 277
Ivory Joe Hunter 278
Tab Hunter 278
Danny Hutton (Of Three Dog Night) . 278
Brian Hyland 278
Janis Ian 280
Ideals 280
Frank Ifield 280
Impalas 282
Impressions 282
Infatuators 282
Innocence 282
Innocents 284
Intervals (Fifth Dimension) 284
Isley Brothers 284
Ivan (Jerry Allison) 284
Iveys (Badfinger) 284
Ivy Three 286
Jackson 5 286
Jacks 286
Chuck Jackson 287
Python Lee Jackson 288
Wanda Jackson 288
Tommy James 290
Tommy James and The Shondells . . 290
Jamie and Jane 292
Jan and Arnie 292
Jan and Dean 292
Jarmels 296
Javalons 296
Jay and The Americans 296
Jay and The Deans 298
Jayhawks 298
Jaynetts 298
Cathy Jean and The Roomates 298
Cathy Jean 298
Jefferson Airplane 298
Jelly Beans 299

Waylon Jennings 299
Waylon Jennings and Willie Nelson . 299
Jerry and Jeff 299
Jesters 299
Jewel and Eddie (With Jewel Akens) . 299
Jill and Ray 299
Jive Five 300
Jivetones 300
Jivin' Gene and The Jokers 300
Marcy Joe 300
Billy Joel 300
Joey & The Lexingtons 302
Elton John 302
Johnnie and Joe 302
Johnny and The Hurricanes 304
Marv Johnson 304
Bruce Johnston 306
David Jones 306
Jimmy Jones 308
Joe Jones 308
John Paul Jones 308
Tom Jones 308
Janis Joplin 308
Josie and The Pussycats 309
J.R. & The Attractions 309
Jumpin' Tones 309
Bill Justis 309
Kac-Ties 309
Kalin Twins 309
Paul Kane (Paul Simon) 310
Ernie K-Doe 310
Keith 310
Kelly Four 312
Chris Kenner 312
Kenny and The Cadets (Beach Boys) 312
Kenny & The Socialites 312
Carole King 312
King Lizard (Kim Fowley) 312
Kingsmen 312
Kingsmen (Featured Bill Haley's Comets) 313
Kingston Tio 313
Kinks 314
Kiss 316
Knickerbockers 316
Gladys Knight and The Pips 317
Sonny Knight 317
Buddy Knox 317
Kodoks 318
Kokomo 318
Billy J. Kramer and The Dakotas 320
Kris Kristofferson 320
Bob Kuban and The In Men 320
Patti Labelle and The Blue-Belles 321
Cheryl Ladd 321
Denny Laine 322
Larry Lance & The Sky Riders 322
Major Lance 322
Jerry Landis (Paul Simon) 322
Richard Lanham 322
The Larados 324
Laughing Gravy 324
Johnny Law Four 324
Leaves 324
Les Ledo 324
Led Zeppelin 324
Billy Lee and The Rivieras 324
Brenda Lee 326
Curtis Lee 329
Dickie Lee 329
Left Banke 330
Lendells 330
John Lennon 330
Lettermen 332
Levees 334
Levon and The Hawks (The Band) 334
Bobby Lewis 335
Gary Lewis and The Playboys 335
Jerry Lee Lewis 336
Ramsey Lewis 339
Smiley Lewis 340
Wally Lewis 340
Gordon Lightfoot 341
Lil' June and The Januarys 341
Kathy Linden 341
Little Anthony and The Imperials 341
Little Beats 342
Little Caesar and The Romans 342
Little Clydie and The Teens 342
Little David 342
Little Eva 342
Little Joe and The Thrillers 344
Little Richard 344
Lively Ones 345
Jackie Lloyd 346
Lobo 346
Lonnie and The Crisis 346
Trini Lopez 346
Love 346
Darlene Love 346
Love Letters 347
Ronnie Love 347
Lovers 347
Lovin' Spoonful 347
Lugee and The Lions 348
Robin Luke 348
Lulu 348
Bob Luman 348
Larry Lurex (Queen) 349
Lyme and Cybelle 349
Frankie Lymon 349
Frankie Lymon and The Teenagers 349
Louis Lymon and The Teenchords 350
Loretta Lynn 350
Madisons 354
Mad Milo 354
Johnny Maestro 354
Magnificents 354
Majors 354
Mamas and Papas 355
Manhattan Transfer 355
Manchesters 356
Barry Mann 356
Carl Mann 357
Manfred Mann 357
Manuel and The Renegades 358
Marathons 358
Marcels 358
(Little) Peggy March 359
Lee Mareno 359
Ernie Maresca 359
Tony Maresco & The Dynamics 360
Mar-Kets 360
Marksmen (Ventures) 360
Ritchie Marsh (Sky Saxon) 360
Martha and The Vandellas 360
Janis Martin 362
Marvelettes 362
Marvels 363
Mascots 363
Bonnie Jo Mason (Cher) 364
Sammy Masters 364
Matadors 364
Johnny Mathis 364
Dino Matthews 368
Nathaniel Mayer 368
MC-5 368
Paul McCartney 368
McCoys 370
Gene McDaniels 370
Don McLean 372
Clyde McPhatter 372
Larry Meadows 374
Melanie 374
Mello-Kings 374
Mello-Tones 374
The Mellows 374
Memories 374
Merseybeats 374
Jim Messina and The Jesters 375
Metros 375
Micky and Sylvia 375
Midnighters 376
Mike and The Utopians 378
Garry Miles 378
Garry Mills 378
Hayley Mills 378
Ronnie Milsap 378
Mindbenders 378
Sal Mineo 379
Miracles 379
Misfits 381
Joni Mitchell 381
Pat Moliterri 381
Monkees 381
Monotones 382
Chris Montez 382
Montgomerys 382
Moody Blues 382
Moonglows 384
Harv Moore 385
Van Morrison 385
Mothers of Invention 385
Motor City Five 386
Mudcrutch (Tom Petty and The Heartbreakers) 386
Muddy Waters 386
Maria Muldaur 388
Murmaids 388
Music Explosion 388
Music Machine 389
Mysterians 389
Mystics 389
Nashville Teens 389
Jerry Naylor 389
Nazz 389
Jerry Neal (Capehart) 389
Neil and Jack 390
Ricky Nelson 390
Sandy Nelson 394
Willie Nelson 396
Neons 401
Nervous Norvus 401
Mike Nesmith 401
Newbeats 401
Nicky & The Nacks 401
Nickie and The Nitelites 401
Nicky and The Nobles 401
Nightcrawlers 402
Nino and The Ebb Tides 402
Nitty Gritty Dirt Band 402
Jack Nitzsche 402
Nobells 403
Nutmegs 403
Nylons 403
Oasis 403
Octaves 403
Olympics 403
Yoko Ono 404
Roy Orbison 404
Orioles 407
Tony Orlando 408
Tony Orlando and Dawn 410
Orlons 411
Milt Oshins 411
Gilbert O'Sullivan 411
Our Gang 411
Outsiders 412
Oxford Circle 412
Jimmy Page 412
Pageants 412
Palisades 412
Paragons 412
Paramounts 414
Paul and Paula 414
Gary Paxton 414
Penguins 414
Pentagons 415
Pepe and The Astros 416
Carl Perkins 416
Persians 418
Personalities 418
The Persuasions 418
Peter and Gordon 419
Paul Peterson 419
Ray Peterson 420
Norman Petty Trio 421
Tom Petty and The Heartbreakers 421
Phaetons 422
Pharoahs 422
Pharos 422
Phil Phillips 422
Bobby "Boris" Picket 422
Wilson Pickett 422
Vito Picone 422
Piltdown Men 423
Pink Floyd 423
Gene Pitney 423
Planets 425
Robert Plant 425
Platters 425
Playmates 428
Pledges 429
Poni-Tails 429
Portraits 430
Sandy Powell 430
Premiers 430
Elvis Presley 430
Johnny Preston 436
Lloyd Price 436
Primettes (Supremes) 438
Prisonaires 438
P. J. Proby 438
Rod Prince 439
Pyramids 439
Suzi Quatro 439
Queen 439
? and The Mysterians 440
Quick 440
Quin-Tones 440
Eddie Quinteros 440
Quotations 440
Rachel and The Revolvers 441
Rainbo 441
Raindrops 441
Rainy Daze 441
Rajahs (Nutmegs) 441
Rally Packs 441
Ran-Dells 441
Randy and The Rainbows 442
Ken Rank 442
Rascals 442
Raspberries 442
Rationals 442
Lou Rawls 442
Ray and The Darchaes 443
Rays 443
Rebels 443
Eivets Rednow (Stevie Wonder) 443
Redwoods 443
Denny Reed 443
Reflections 443
Regents 444
Relations 444
Keith Relf 444
Renegades 444
Reparta and The Delrons 444
Reunion 444
Revelations 444

Paul Revere and The Raiders 444
Jody Reynolds 446
Charlie Rich 446
Cliff Richard 447
Righteous Brothers 450
Rinky-Dinks 452
Billy Riley 452
Rip Chords 452
Rituals 453
Johnny Rivers 453
Rivieras 454
Rivingtons 455
Robbins and Paxton 455
Robert and Johnny 455
Robins 455
Rock-A-Teens 456
Rockatones With Larry Dowd 456
Rockin' Rebels 456
Rockin' Ronald and The Rebels 456
Jimmie Rodgers 456
Tommy Roe 458
Roemans 460
Kenneth Rogers (Kenny Rogers) 460
Kenny Rogers and The First Edition . 460
Timmy Rogers 461
Rogues 461
Rollers 461
Rolling Stones 461
Ron Roman (Frank Zappa) 464
Ronettes 464
Ronnie & The Delaires 464
Ronnie and The Relatives (Ronnettes) 466
Ronny and The Daytonas 466
Roomates 466
Linda Ronstadt 466
Rosie and The Originals 469
Roxy & The Day Chords 469
Royal Drifters 469
Royals 469
Royal Teens 469
Ruben and The Jets 470
Rumblers 470
Runarounds (Regents) 470
Todd Rundgren 470
Leon Russell 472
Bobby Rydell 472
Bobby Rydell and Chubby Checker . 473
Mitch Ryder and The Detroit Wheels 473
Mitch Ryder 474
Johnny Saber & The Passions 474
Safaris 474
Sagittarius 474
Doug Sham 475
Sam The Sham and The Pharoahs . . 475
Bobby Sanders 476
Tommy Sands 476
Santo and Johnny 478
Sapphires 478
Mike Sarne 480
Peter Sarstedt 480
Sky Saxson 480
Scarlets (Pre-Five Satins) 480
Jack Scott 480
Joel Scott 481
Linda Scott 481
Rodney Scott 482
Walter Scott 482
Seals and Crofts 482
Jimmy Seals (Pre-Seals and Crofts) . 482
Seachers 483
Neil Sedaka 483
Seeds 485
Bob Seger 485
Bob Seger System 485
Ronnie Self 486
Tommy Sena 486
Shadows of Knight 486
Sha Na Na 486
Shangri-Las 486
Del Shannon 487
Jackie Shannon (Jackie DeShannon) 488
The Sharks Quintet 488
Sharon Marie 489
Dee Dee Sharp 489
Shells 489
Gary Shelton 490
Shep and The Limelites 490
Bobby Sheridan (Charlie Rich) 490
Mike Sheridan 490
Tony Sheridan and The Beat Brothers (Beatles) 490
Sherrys 491
Sherwoods 491
Shields 491
Billy Shields (Tony Orlando) 491
Shirelles 491
Shirley and Lee 493
Paul Simon 493
Simon and Garfunkel 494
Simon Sisters 494
Sir Douglas Quintet 495
Sixpence (Strawberry Alarm Clock) . 495
Six Teens 495
Skarlettones 495
Skip and Flip 495
Skyliners 496
Slades 496
Small Faces 496
Smile (Pre-Queen) 497
Huey "Piano" Smith and The Clowns 497
Patti Smith 497
Ray Smith 498
Warren Smith 498
Ronny Sommers (Sonny Bono) 499
Solitaires 499
Sonny 500
Sonny and Cher 500
David Soul 500
Jimmy Soul 501
Spaniels 501
Sparrow (Steppenwolf) 502
The Sparrows Quartet 502
Ronnie Spector 502
Spectors Three 502
Spiders 502
Spirals 502
Spring (Honeys) 502
Springfields 504
Bruce Springsteen 504
Terry Stafford 504
Standells 504
Ray Stanley 505
Ringo Starr 505
Statens 505
Steppenwolf 505
Cat Stevens 506
Connie Stevens 506
Ray Stevens 507
Rod Stewart 508
Stone Poneys 508
Gale Storm 510
Storytellers 510
Strangeloves 510
Strawberry Alarm Clock 510
Barrett Strong 511
Gene Summers 511
Sundials 511
Sunny & The Horizons 511
Sunrays 511
Supremes 512
Surfaris 513
Surfettes 514
Survivors (Beach Boys) 514
Swallows 514
Sweet 514
Swinging Blue Jeans 515
Swingin' Medallions 515
Syndicate of Sound 515
Marc Tanno 516
Tassels 516
James Taylor 516
True Taylor (Paul Simon) 516
Teardrops (Four Preps) 516
Teddy Bears 516
Teenagers 517
Teen Angels 517
Temptations 517
Temptations 519
Tendertones 519
Terrace Tones 519
Tex & The Chex 519
Chuck Tharp 519
Vic Thomas 519
Thyme 519
Tico and The Triumphs 519
Johnny Tillotson 520
Timetones 521
Today & Tommorow 521
Tom and Jerry (Simon and Garfunkel) 521
Tony and The Raindrops 522
Tornadoes 522
Townsmen 522
Trade Winds (Videls) 522
Trashmen 522
Treble Chords 523
Tremeloes 523
Triumphs 523
Troggs 523
Trophies 524
Turbans 524
Joe Turner 524
Sammy Turner 525
Turtles 525
Conway Twitty 526
Underdogs 529
Unit Four Plus Two 529
Untouchables 529
Gary Usher 529
Val-Chords 529
Ritchie Valens 529
Frankie Valley (Valli) 530
Franky Valley and The Travelers (Valli) 530
Frankie Valle and The Romans (Four Seasons) 530
Frankie Vally (Valli) 530
Bobby Vee 530
Ventures 533
Verdicts 535
Videls 535
Gene Vincent 535
Bobby Vinton 536
Virtues 538
Viscounts 539
Visuals 539
Vito and The Salutations 539
Vogues 539
Wailers 540
Walker Brothers 540
Billy Ward and His Dominoes 541
Dale Ward 541
Walter Ward and The Challengers (Olympics) 542
Dionne Warwick 542
Thomas Wayne 542
Webs 542
Mary Wells 542
Wheelers 543
Whirlwinds 543
Ian Whitcomb 543
Who 543
Whyte Boots 544
Ann Wilson and The Daybreaks 544
Brian Wilson 544
Jackie Wilson 545
J. Frank Wilson 547
Peanuts Wilson 547
Winds In The Willow 548
Wind 548
Stevie Wonder 548
Yardbirds 550
Yesterdays Today 551
Young Rascals 551
Youngtones 552
John Zacherle 552
Zager and Evans 553
Frank Zappa 553
Zebulons 553
Ben Zeppa 553
Ziggy and The Zeu 553
The Zircons 554
Zombies 554
The Motown Singles Discography . . 554
The Philles Records Discography . . . 565
Sun Records Singles Discography . . 568
Rock Memorabilia 583

NOTE TO READERS

All advertisements appearing in this book have been accepted in good faith, but the publisher assumes no responsibility in any transactions that occur between readers and advertisers.

MARKET REVIEW

This is the right time and the right place for record collecting enthusiasts. Beginning collectors are digging through their piles of dusty, old records and discovering that dealers are willing to pay handsomely for them. The more professional collectors are seeing their initial investments turn to solid profit and this upward trend, it seems, will continue. For a long time, a lot of people failed to realize the significance of investing in records but now there seems to be a swing back to nostalgia for the records of years ago and a whole new generation of collectors has been born. This is evident in the number of rare record auctions, conventions and shows taking place practically every day across the nation.

A recent Texas show last Spring drew over 100 rare record dealers and 2,000 collecting enthusiasts from all over the Southwest, the East Coast, Canada and Europe to the one day event. Dealers reported their biggest sales in 1950s and 1960s rock and roll but rare 78s, blues, Big Band hits and more recent artists fared well, also. Roky Erickson, a member of the 1960s group Thirteenth Floor Elevators was on hand to sign copies of his new book and the show was deemed an overall success.

It has been more than twenty years since the Beatles invaded America but their influence will never be forgotten. The group has reached and practically surpassed cult figure status along with Elvis. They are the most discussed, most copied and most collected music influences of all time. A show held in a Boston suburb this past summer confirmed this fact even more when rare Beatles and Elvis recordings sold in the $300 and $400 range. The show boasted an array of over 200,000 rare recordings for the attending 2,000 collectors to buy or trade. Dealers reported their most consistent sales in old 45s in the $2 range and LPs in the $6 to $8 range.

The big news of the past year, however, was the auction held last summer in New York City. The auction was dedicated to music memorabilia, especially those items belonging to The Beatles and John Lennon, in particular. The gold LP of The Beatles "Help" sold for $5,000 to the highest bidder and $3,500 was paid for the gold disc of "Something." Other memorabilia belonging to artists such as Elvis Presley, Frank Sinatra, Count Basie, Jimi Hendrix, Buddy Holly, Louis Armstrong, Cliff Richard, Eddie Cochran, the Beach Boys, David Bowie and The Who sold for substantial prices.

At a separate auction, a Jimi Hendrix album sold for over $1,000 and a record of the late 1960s group The Stone Poneys featuring Linda Ronstadt went for $100.

To cash in on the nostalgia craze, groups of the 1960s and 1970s are reuniting for concerts all across the world, such as, Mitch Ryder and the Detroit Wheels, Aerosmith and Herman's Hermits. Even Bob Dylan and Joan Baez came together for a European concert tour. But it is The Jacksons who stole the headlines last summer as they completed their spectacular and controversial Victory tour. Their popularity is due in large part to younger brother Michael. Michael Jackson, with his phenomenal success of the past two years, has breathed new life into the once floundering music industry. His "Thriller" LP surpassed all other records in sales and prompted record companies to reissue vintage Jackson Five LPs for higher prices due to the enormous collector demand.

In addition, music videos have influenced the buying market greatly and artists are finding the time ripe for experiments in older sounds. For example, Billy Joel's recent "Innocent Man" LP was clearly an ode to 1950s and 1960s rock and roll while Tracy Ullman and Cyndi Lauper are reviving the frivolity of the girl groups of the 1960s.

In recent years, the babies of the baby boom generation have grown up and discovered the records their parents once collected. Frank Sinatra is once again enjoying commercial success with his "L.A. Is My Lady" LP and accompanying music video. His older recordings are consistently high priced collector's items as well. Plus, Johnny Mathias is enjoying renewed popularity on the charts.

Collectors cannot ignore, however, the other music influences that are making the current and secondary markets so competitive. Country music has been enjoying a broader audience in recent years and has become a powerful influence with its wide ranging appeal. Carl Perkins and Patsy Cline continue to be collector favorites while the older recordings of Dolly Parton and Charley Pride, among others, are garnering collector interest. In addition, the invigorating tones of Jazz have become a force to reckon with and has brought many new artists such as Wynton Marsalis to the forefront while the late Count Basie and Thelonius Monk are among collector favorites.

Record values have so many factors that it is almost impossible to discuss them. First, record collectors and what they collect are so different that one must consider these variables before pricing records of particular interest. Prices are influenced by the personal interest of the collector or dealer as well as the fluctuating trends of the record industry. Collectors can be comforted, however, that there are still bargains to be found in the bins at local flea markets and garage sales. The word is — hurry.

HISTORY OF ROCK AS A MUSIC INFLUENCE

When did rock-and-roll begin? Anyone compiling a thorough history of rock would have to begin with primitive forms of music. Music is one of the oldest means of expression and probably predates spoken language. Manufactured instruments weren't available so our distant ancestors improvised by beating upon hollow logs or clacking shells together. Animal bones served as forerunners of the modern drumstick.

The development of music followed many paths, governed by geography and technology and the changing taste of man. As each instrument was invented, it sent music off in another direction. Even in ancient Rome there were stringed and wind instruments. The only major instrument today which had no direct relative or ancestor is the piano.

Music in the civilized world tended to reflect national cultures and became more artistic and complex with the passing of time. This was because music patrons were wealthy and wanted grandiose music. Chamber music developed as the ultimate marriage of art and instrument. But all the while, even into the gaudy Baroque era, a native music more closely allied with the common people existed everywhere. In the Middle Ages (especially c. 1200-1500), it was personalized by the "wandering minstrel" who strolled the land singing ballads and accompanying himself on lute or lyre. Later the minstrel show developed, taking quite a different form but becoming extremely popular as a public entertainment. Rock music owes much to minstrel shows. Minstrel shows reached their height of popularity in America shortly after the Civil War. Companies still toured in the early 20th century as part of vaudeville troupes. The huge numbers of minstrel records pressed by Edison, Victor Talking Machine and Columbia in the phonograph's early days attest to their public appeal. While minstrel music did not depend upon a repetitive beat, as does rock, there are close associations. The premise of minstrel music, as presented for theatrical entertainment, was that it represented unfettered emotions set to music. The tunes had been originated by slaves, for whom music was a major recreation. By the time they reached the stage, where often they were performed by white companies, they bore little trace of authenticity. Some black minstrel companies toured, too, and they were hailed as a great novelty in the north. Gradually, black musicians abandoned minstrelry and took up instruments besides the traditional banjo and guitar. By the early 1900s, another native American form of black music had been born: jazz. In an amazingly short time, black jazz became a nationwide fad and its chief exponents found themselves in heavy demand as club entertainers. New Orleans became the jazz capital of America; New York's Harlem was not far behind.

Rock was more of an indirect outgrowth of jazz. From jazz came the blues, and blues — after becoming a recognized art form in itself — contributed to the development of rock. Jazz bands traditionally had blues vocalists. By the later 1940s, it was becoming commonplace for blues singers to make 78 r.p.m. recordings for an audience that was not strictly oriented toward jazz. Smaller bands were used. Fresh material was selected, often written by the performers themselves. There was no hope at first of gaining national airplay for such records.

In a sense these were "black alternative" records for record-buyers not interested in current Top 10 hits, just as country was "white alternative" music. Both were regional and thrived in the same part of the country. But just as some country hits worked their way north, record shops in other parts of the nation gradually began stocking Southern black recordings, referring to them as "rhythm-and-blues." They were played on black stations and they sold fairly well in the North in cities with extensive black populations.

These discs gradually gained greater attention from the trade publications. Lists were prepared of the best-selling rhythm-and-blues tunes. Harlem's Apollo Theatre booked the top rhythm-and-blues stars, and their acts were occasionally given reviews in the press. By 1950, rhythm-and-blues records were being pressed in increasing numbers and more artists were emerging on the scene. Sales improved, and it was not unusual by 1950 for a top rhythm-and-blues hit to achieve sales in the 250,000-300,000 range.

Large Northern record companies hesitated to sign artists or include such music in their catalogs in the belief that such a musical style would never become fully accepted nationwide by record buyers.

The first rhythm-and-blues record to break the barrier and achieve heavy airplay on white radio stations was "Sixty Minute Man" by the Dominoes in 1951. Various black artists (such as Nat King Cole) had become top sellers in the record industry, and radio stations featured their discs as frequently as any others. The problem was not color but music. While rhythm-and-blues pleased some listeners, it offended those to whom music meant dreamy ballads and show tunes. Country records were not played by Northern stations for the same reason, even though the artists were white. The long held belief, in radio industry, was that fans of any kind of specialized music should turn to a specialized station to hear it. But fans of rhythm-and-blues were increasing in numbers, and losing them to specialized stations was not a happy prospect for major radio outlets, so the larger stations inserted an occasional rhythm-and-blues side.

Major record labels did not immediately begin to produce rhythm-and-blues discs. They wanted more proof that such a musical form could be successfully marketed to white audiences. They wondered if the fans of Perry Como, Bing Crosby, Vaughn Monroe and other million selling vocalists would buy such a drastic change in style.

The crooners continued to sell, but top rhythm-and-blues hits were selling almost as well. All that remained for rhythm-and-blues to become the dominant music was for a successful "invasion" of the field by white artists. Also, rhythm-and-blues needed to develop superstars, the way pop music had done.

In 1953 Bill Haley and the Comets reached the top 20 with "Crazy Man Crazy." It was what the Northern record companies had been dreaming of. Some people called it "hip music." Then the term "rock and roll" came into prominence. But for a long while, examples of rock music were still classified as "rhythm-and-blues" in the trade papers and even in record company advertisements. The general feeling was that discs by black artists should be termed rhythm-and-blues, and rhythm-and-blues flavored tunes by whites ought to be called "rock and roll." Eventually, the term rhythm-and-blues became less frequently used, but this did not happen until late in the 1950s.

When Ed Sullivan put Bill Haley and the Comets on his TV show, it certified the arrival of rock-and-roll as a part of mainstream culture. But in those early days (1955/56) rock was regarded by the media in a far different light. Mainly, TV networks and national magazines such as Time and Newsweek covered rock from the standpoint of giving adults an insight into the world of their teenagers. Rock and its performers were treated as novelties and/or curiosities. The newly created stars were given attention because they were making news, not necessarily because the media thought such artists were talented or significant. All of this changed within a few years, when it became obvious that rock was going to plant some firm roots. In 1956, Jackie Gleason signed 21-year-old Elvis Presley to a series of appearances on his live network TV show. Presley, who had established a reputation in the South and was just beginning to hit the national charts, created a sensation. Ratings of the Gleason show suddenly soared. Presley's rock was country-flavored and new to many audiences. Now, three varieties of rock co-existed: the country strain (Southern white), the rhythm-and-blues strain (Southern black) and Big City Northern (typified by Bill Haley).

Before the year 1956 was finished, rock had become the top-selling type of music in the country. Record companies sent scouts across the country in search of talented unknowns. When one was found, fortunes were spent on promoting him (women artists were not considered). A number of overnight superstars were created — some failed, others went on to enjoy lengthy careers. Tommy Sands was typical of the former.

Paul Anka, who for a short while was second only to Presley in sales volume, later became a headliner at Las Vegas clubs and played to audiences of a different age group. Pat Boone was the All-American Boy working his way through college; he achieved stardom while still an undergraduate at Columbia University.

The mid-to-late 1950s was an important era for rock in establishing solid credentials for rock-and-roll stars as money-makers. Since then, rock has surprised its critics by developing in various ways, proving it could change with the times. The six basic periods of rock evolution have been:

PRE-1955. Identified as rhythm-and-blues concentrated in South, artists almost exclusively black, labels small, distribution regional. Melodies commonly copied or borrowed from one group to another. Ivory Joe Hunter, Joe Williams, Dominoes.

1955-58. National TV exposure, rise of expression "rock-and-roll," million selling rock discs, advent of 45 r.p.m., first rock albums, teenage rock idols. Audiences largely 12-16 age group. Bill Haley, Elvis Presley, Buddy Holly, Chuck Berry, Everly Brothers, Fats Domino, Paul Anka, Pat Boone, Frankie Avalon, Ricky Nelson, Little Richard, Bo Diddley, Sam Cooke, the Coasters, the Diamonds.

1959-63. Some early stars remain successful. The Beach Boys introduce surf vocals. Dance crazes abound. Experimentation increases. Black artists stress harder rock and gradually, the "Motown sound" evolves. Bobby Vee, Del Shannon, Four Seasons, Jan and Dean, Freddy Cannon, Bobby Darin, Dion, Roy Orbison, Neil Sedaka, Shirelles, Chubby Checker, Miracles, Phil Spector artists.

1964-70. Age of the Beatles. Their introduction to America in 1964 revitalizes rock and the "Liverpool sound" quickly takes over. Vietnam War brings protest songs. McCartney death rumor. More emphasis on lyrics than in the past. The "poet/singer" emerges, and rock-and-roll acquires the flavor of folk music. Bob Dylan, Rolling Stones, Monkees, Simon & Garfunkel, Who, Animals, Kinks, Supremes, Dave Clark Five, Yardbirds, Led Zeppelin, Lovin' Spoonful, Doors, Jimi Hendrix, Bee Gees, Buffalo Springfield, Janis Joplin, Cream, Creedence Clearwater Revival.

1971-76. Beatles on their own, each successful. British influence continues. Bizarre stars (Kiss, David Bowie) appear. Disco emerges. Strong emphasis on experimentation, originality, poetical expression in lyrics and style. More use of electronic instruments. Guess Who, Elton John, Rod Stewart, Carole King, Fleetwood Mac, Heart, Eagles, Alice Cooper, Olivia Newton-John, ELO, Pink Floyd, Sweet, Queen, Bruce Springsteen.

1977-1982. Rise of New Wave and "punk rock." More cross-over from country into rock (and vice-versa). Death of Elvis Presley. Continued experimentation, less influence from Britain but more from continental Europe (Germany, Scandinavia). Saturday Night Fever sells 27 million albums. Renewed emphasis on stage shows. John Lennon murdered. Blondie, Elvis Costello, ABBA, Foreigner, Tom Petty and the Heartbreakers, Suzi Quatro, Pat Benatar, Kim Carnes.

1983-PRESENT. Another British invasion. Revitalized interest in ballads and older artists. Heavy Metal tries for a comeback. Influence of the movie Flashdance, MTV and the phenomenal success of Michael Jackson in every aspect of the entertainment field. Deaths include Dennis Wilson, Jackie Wilson, Karen Carpenter and Marvin Gaye. Boy George and Culture Club, Duran Duran, Cyndi Lauper, Eurythmics, Billy Joel, Jacksons, Quiet Rock, Julio Iglesias, Menundo.

· BEGINNING A COLLECTION

Rock-record collecting is what you make of it. You can spend much or little. You can make hunting expeditions to thrift shops, garage sales, antique stores and charity bazaars or you can order records from a dealer's list. You can regard rock-and-roll as a significant art form or simply a curious chapter in the history of American culture.

This hobby has drawn enthusiasts from all social spheres and all parts of the world. The magic is evident by its appeal to persons born after the Golden Age of Rock. Rock music has had a potent influence on society for more than a quarter century now. It not only has fans but cultists and followers. It has acted as a catalyst for millions to realize the powers of the music. For some, it has become a way of life. Collecting old and (sometimes) rare rock is, history. Even if the beat does *not* go on, as it once did, these recordings serve as documents of our time.

Rock record collecting has boundless possibilities. This should be treated as AN introduction only, and the collector should not hesitate to call upon his imagination (or personal feelings) to suggest other ways of collecting. There is no right and wrong, no good and bad. There are no artists unworthy of collecting, no rock forms that do not merit the collector's attention. The only "bad" thing is to be uninformed and pay too much, or to have low standards with regard to condition.

General collecting is certainly a possibility in this hobby, and is followed by many. A "general collection" is one that does not attempt to focus upon a particular artist, group of artists, record label or type of rock-and-roll. The goal is to present as diverse as possible a selection of vintage rock music and rock stars. But general collecting does have more drawbacks than specialized collecting. It tends to have a "catch-all" character, even if it grows to a large size. Often the scarcest (and most valuable) discs of each artist are omitted, as the collector can be more interested in quantity than in spending a substantial sum for a single worthy record. A general collection is harder to keep track of, in terms of what you have and what you don't. Worse, a general collection is likely to be less appealing to a dealer, if and when the time comes to sell your records. If you have any leanings toward a general collection, think first of what you want to accomplish. If you have an ambition of building a really representative collection of rock's many important artists and different styles and types of rock music, be forewarned that this is vast territory.

Many of the earlier rock collectors *did* take a general approach. They perhaps did not realize the extent of material available or the advantages offered by specialized collecting. 50s and 60s rock records were not well cataloged then.

The trend since that time has been *away from general collecting.* Today's collector is more of a connoisseur. He knows what the wants, and will perhaps forego the pleasures of having a quantity-based collection for the sake of high grade, and scarce material.

Specialized collecting has many attractions. Without spending a substantial sum of money, one can complete the discography of most mainstream rock artists. Such a collection becomes valid since you cannot do better than own one specimen of every recording by an artist or group. The mere fact that a specialized collection can be worked up to *completeness* is a strong recommendation for many hobbyists. A general collection is impossible to complete, no matter *how* large it grows.

If your own tastes and motivations do not suggest a mode of approach, we would advise a specialized collection built around specific artists. Such a collection can grow at a manageable pace yet rapidly enough to maintain interest. The artist's more recent, less valuable recordings will probably be acquired with no trouble at all. This gives the collection a foundation and it then becomes a matter of filling in the scarcer singles and albums. Unless the artist did very little recording, there will be dozens of records to get and you will undoubtedly be kept busy on your collection. In the case of Superstars whose careers spanned two decades or more (Elvis, Rolling Stones, etc.), this kind of specialized collection is a monumental undertaking — but a very rewarding one. No matter how scarce or little-known, the records of every rock artist are available and you *will* find the ones you need, sooner or later. You *will* succeed in completing an artist's discography, if you persevere.

The obvious question is: what happens when you complete an artist collection? Though this is the collector's goal, he may fear reaching a "dead end" when achieving his goal. When that time arrives and you've acquired that one last disc needed to complete your collection, rest assured you will *not* be asking "Where do I go from here?" The contacts you've made in the hobby, and your research will no doubt have suggested *other* areas of specialization. You will very likely start a second collection before the first is completed. Many "one-artist-only" collectors go into memorabilia, an intriguing and practically limitless field. But quite a few of these "one-artist-only" collectors find, as they progress, that other artists appeal to them too.

Specialization need not be a single artist or group or even several artists groups. A specialized collection could be assembled around the origins of rock concentrating, for example, on rhythm-and-blues discs from the early 1950s. Another area of specialty might be the Liverpool Sound, or collecting records that were contemporary with the early days of the Beatles. Some specialties will require more effort than others, because of the subject's scope or the material rarity. In choosing a specialty, you must take into account these considerations, but the most important point is to collect the kind of music that appeals most to you — as a listener, a historian, and a hobbyist. You must have a sense of personal involvement to be a successful collector and for the hobby to be meaningful to you. A number of fine collections have been built around little-known artists of the 50s. Artists who made one or two records and then slipped into obscurity. But because of their rarity, these records rate high and some are quite valuable. Even if they did not play much role in the development of rock, they show efforts to popularize different forms of the music. The history-minded collector is as interested in studying those which failed as those which succeeded.

Another specialized approach is collecting by label or record company. Hundreds of labels have appeared over the years and nearly every record company has recorded some rock. An intelligently compiled label collection can be informative. Of course, it would be fruitless to attempt a complete collection of all records issued by the larger companies such as RCA or Columbia. We do, however, list complete Sun and Phillies listings and early Motown.

Some collectors confine themselves to #1 or Top 10 hits — records that reached the peak of the popularity charts. This would be a suitable approach for someone on a modest budget. A rather large collection could be built without much expense, as the top-selling discs are *usually* the most plentiful and sell the cheapest. No rarities or obscure artists would need to be included in a collection of Top 10 hits!

In any case, you should have a plan or goal that you wish to accomplish with your collecting. It should be something achievable, but the goal itself should not get in the way of enjoying the hobby as you proceed. In other words, your philosophy need not be, "I'll have a good collection when I'm finished." Starting from scratch and gradually building a collection should be no less enjoyable than having the completed collection. Much of the pleasure in any hobby derives from legwork and brainwork: circulating among other collectors and dealers, "playing detective," exploring, and never knowing what will turn up. Most collectors delight in their experiences as much as in their collections.

It is important that you maintain high standards. Some people get into rare-rock collecting by chance or accident. Rediscovery of vintage records occasionally kindles the collecting spark. Potential collectors might begin by rummaging through records at a flea market or garage sale. A few purchases are made, the chemistry interacts, and another collector is born. The problem is that when a collection begins in this manner, the early purchases are often made without regard to condition. Later, the collector finds himself having to replace these early acquisitions with better items in order to upgrade his holdings. If you're reading this book without ever having bought a rare rock-and-roll record, make at least one resolution before starting out in this hobby: be fussy about condition. Don't buy a record (or swap for one, either) that ranks under Very Good condition. An exception, of course, would be a desirable, obscure disc.

There is no standard way to begin, but you must have reliable reference material at your fingertips. We have prepared *The Official Price Guide to Collectible Records,* for both the beginner and advanced collectors. We feel it is the most useful one-volume publication on the market, and certainly contains more information for the price than could be obtained anywhere else. In time you will doubtlessly add other volumes to your library — discographies, biographies of your favorite stars, or histories of the rock sound.

COLLECTING INDEPENDENT LABELS

Some hobbyists search for records that are relatively obscure and produced by small or independent companies.

These companies often produce new talent and new kinds of music. The independent labels served as a major influence for folk music in the sixties and New Wave in the seventies. But even if the songs and artists weren't successful, collectors still flock to buy their discs when they can be found.

Hobbyists are attracted by the scarcity of the label, being an exclusive owner, and owning something out of the ordinary.

There is no standard definition of "independent label," which is why the alternative designation "small label" is often used. Any recording company whose owner was also the arranger, producer and publicity person were very tiny indeed — they existed only as a concept. There was no office, no staff, no production facility; their address was the home address of the owner, or possibly a post office box number. Often they went into business for the purpose of pressing a single disc by a single artist — hoping it would take off and establish both the company and the artist. On rare occasions that happened. More frequently, lack of sufficient capital or misjudgment of the artist's talent kept these companies from getting off the ground. Even if the artist was talented and the record was good, it might flop because of poor distribution or promotion. For one thing, radio stations tend to air discs on known labels ahead of those on unknown labels. Every station is bombarded with 45's on unknown labels, and they usually get tossed aside, until a rival station starts playing one of them. But, as you will see in this book, the small label flops sometimes became big label hits.

Rarity is an important factor as in most fields of collecting. However, the number of records pressed is only complemented by the availability in a particular area. Because many obscure records were only distributed locally, it may be very hard to find them in places other than that area. Finding one of these discs in a miscellaneous stack is a chance find and a lucky one at that. If you tried to locate that record in another area, it may cost more than twice as much, and only if it can be found.

Becoming an exclusive owner of an object has for years attracted and encouraged collectors to purchase bizarre items. Many independent labels were limited on finances and therefore the number of pressings made may be minimal. The fewer pressed, generally, the more attractive it becomes to the hobbyists who want to be exclusive owners.

Some collectors accumulate albums or singles that have something unique or unusual about the paper label or cover or sleeves. Many times, these hobbyists don't care about the producer or artist.

Some relatively obscure singles are not worth more than $2 or $3, but others, because of collector interest in a particular label or artist, have become fairly valuable in today's market. This is an odd occurrence in the market, however, this does happen and here are a few examples:

• Lou Berry and the Bel Raves had a single called "What A Dolly." It was produced under the *Dreem* label. The flip side was called "Hot Rod." It is valued today in mint condition at $65.

• "Heart Trouble" and "Get Ready Baby" is a *DC* release by Dudley Callicut and the Go Boys. This record is worth between $20 and $44.

• Under the *Ritz* label, the Enchantments made a record, numbered 17003, called "Pains in My Heart." This single, valued today at $10 to $25, featured a song called "I Love My Baby" on the reverse.

• Ronnie Gill came out with number 129 on the *Rio* label. It was called "Geraldin." On the back was "Standing On the Mountain." This record may sell for as much as $40 in mint condition.

• "Be Bop-A-Jean" was produced by *CHA-CHA* with either a red or white label. Ron Haydock is the artist who solo sang "99 Chicks" on the flip side. The red label is worth only up to $8, but the white label can sell for about $50.

•Gene Norman, under the *Snag* label, released a single called "Long Gone Night Train." The reverse song was titled "Snaggle Tooth Ann" and is valued in the market today at between $70 and $150.

Some difficulties arise when trying to fill a collection with these type records. Locating them is a problem, and trying to distinguish those that are rare is the most difficult aspect to tackle. Even the companies in the past have helped make this more difficult for the hobbyist. They would try to camouflage their small size by using large serial numbers. A low serial number means that the record is one of a few produced. Be careful and don't be misled.

Also be careful when choosing your records that they are not obscure songs picked up by a larger company. If a company re-released a single that was originally produced on an independent label, the smaller label will always be more valuable.

Another obstacle is the chance of buying repressed singles. Bootlegs and fakes may be hard to catch because you will most likely not be familiar with what the label, color, format and type usually used looked like.

Many times, the values of unknown labels fluctuate more than those of established artists. The records by well-known performers are traded more often and acquire an established value. However, obscure discs may not have a record or sale to stand on and prices may vary greatly from one store to another and from one area of the country to another.

It's a good idea to play the record and check the audio quality. If there is surface noise, it could mean that it was recorded on inefficient equipment. But it could also mean that the record has been played a lot, which also brings down the value.

If you want to join this aspect of collecting, carry this price guide with you when you buy. You will have knowledgeable experts at your fingertips to help you make a decision.

BUYING

There are many sources of collectible records. The hobby's rapid growth in the past few years has brought numerous dealers into business. Records can also be found at auctions, shows and often at such locations as Salvation Army outlets, thrift shops and flea markets.

Dealers are established across the country selling old, rare and used records. They can be found in nearly every city and even in some rural locations. Many dealers sell by mail-order in addition to operating their shop. There are also dealers who conduct business exclusively by mail. The typical dealer is an ex-collector or current aficionado. Without experience in collecting, few people would be aware of the size and scope of this hobby and the profit potential it offers a skilled dealer. Most dealers start out by using their own collections as stock or they use duplicates from it. These dealers are up-to-date on current values and do not make the mistake of buying too high or selling too low.

The rare record business operates as any other business. The dealer buys his stock at the best prices and marks up his records to cover operating costs and profit.

When a dealer is buying records that he thinks can be sold immediately, he will pay more. For instance, whenever a popular music star dies (such as John Lennon), there is usually an immediate rush to purchase his or her recordings. This can cause values to double in a matter of weeks. When the dealer buys for stock, however, without any immediate prospects of sale, he is tying up capital and this becomes a consideration in the price.

Every collector ought to be on mailing lists of dealers. The selection available by mail is considerable because the collector can do business with dealers around the world. Most needed records appear on a dealer's list at one time or another and then it is up to the collector to acquire it before another buyer does. Some items from a list are still available long after the list has been circulated. Some will sell out instantly. Most dealers accept phone reservations, with the provision that the customer's check arrives within five business days of the phone call. If it does not, the record is usually then taken off reservation and the dealer sends it out to another customer who might also have shown interest in it.

There are some ways to reduce the risks of buying by mail. A large order should not be placed until at least one or two records from the dealer's stock have been inspected. Also, the size of the dealer's ad and the size and character of his list will offer some clue to his intentions. A dealer running large ads, and putting out a well organized list with hundreds of records on it is obviously serious about the business. It is a favorable sign if the dealer's ads run month after month in the same publication. The inclusion of the dealer's phone number in his ad or on his lists is most encouraging. Any dealer who openly solicits phone calls is likely to be honest and businesslike.

Selling by auction is becoming more widespread in the record business. These are usually mail bid affairs. Auctions are held not only by dealers but also collectors disposing of their unwanted discs. There is the slight possibility of getting a record at auction for less than the normal retail value. The fact that dealers do much of their buying at auction should be encouraging for any hobbyist seeking the best market.

The opposite sometimes occurs, too. Records can sell for more than the usual retail value at an auction. A collector who has been hunting for a given record might give a very high bid to make certain he will not be disappointed.

Collectors who buy records through mail auctions are accustomed to the same general rules from one sale to the next. Such an arrangement is not only convenient to customers but profitable to the auctioneers because it encourages more collectors to do their bidding at auctions.

The principle of an auction is that all items are sold to the highest bidders. The seller is not under any obligation to accept an absurdly low bid. Many sales are conducted with "minimum bids" terms. These are the lowest bids that the auctioneer will accept.

An increasingly popular method of buying collectible records, especially rare items, is to run a classified ad in collector's magazines. These ads consist of a list of desired records usually accompanied by price offers. Some collectors who run such ads use this as a "last resort" approach. Others simply do not care to send for or to look through dealer's lists. The cost of such ads is comparatively low and there is a good chance of being offered copies of all or most of the needed records.

In addition, collectible rock records are apt to turn up wherever secondhand merchandise is sold. Often discs end up in flea markets, secondhand shops, charity bazaars and Salvation Army centers among other places. The condition is not, generally, equal to the dealer's stock. The original owners, in most cases, looked upon the records as something to be played and enjoyed, not as collector's items. Many records that turn up at such sources are piled in cartons and without jackets. It is possible that a rare bargain or two is waiting in that pile.

INVESTING

Vintage discs are sound financial investments. The 79¢ or 89¢ spent on many historic discs of the 1950s, has ballooned up to a hundred dollars or more — an increase of better than 10,000%! *Every single* disc in good condition has gone up in value from its original retail price. Many people became rare record investors decades ago without knowing it. They bought discs for no purpose other than playing and enjoying them.

The purchase of rare record investment articles has begun. It's a relatively new endeavor and accounts for only a minor proportion of overall sales. The majority of collectible record transactions are still in the nature of sales to collectors. But investment interest is unquestionably increasing. Collectors are becoming more aware of investments. They're still buying the artists who appeal most to them but they're paying more attention to *condition*. And they're giving higher prices for desirable discs in very good to mint state. Along with satisfying their collecting interests, these people are acquiring items that should pay a healthy return on the cash spent for them. The fact that records as investments now demonstrate an established growth pattern has removed much hesitation on the part of buyers.

A well-assembled collection, brought together by a knowledgeable collector is probably the best possible investment. If, for example, you collect such artists as Elvis, the Beatles or the Rolling Stones, and employ keen collector judgment in selecting your purchases, you are likely to end up with a good investment.

Specialized collections tend to receive higher prices when sold than a batch of records of different artists. They can be sold to a specialized dealer, who will appreciate the quality and be willing to offer a higher buying price. He will recognize it as a "collector's collection" and this will boost its sales appeal. If you have a personal interest in vintage rock music, for instance, learn the market and polish your expertise.

If you choose to invest in rare records, our recommendation is to put your main thrust behind already popular and heavily collected artists. There may be potential investors who shy away from an Elvis Sun single at $200 in the belief that it cannot be expected to go much higher. Instead, they may purchase an inexpensive record of a lesser star, in hopes that a groundswell of interest will develop for that artist and disc. That *could* happen, but you will probably not make investment money on inexpensive records. The early, valuable discs of major greats draw the most collector attention. Though initially high-priced today, they should actually increase in value faster — overall — than most other discs. The current values for scarce early discs by music immortals are low compared to the musical interest and collector interest of these recordings. ' the most desirable coins and stamps now sell for $100,000 and more, 'e most noteworthy monuments of rock history should at least be in the thousand-dollar zone (and a few already are). The chief reason why prices are relatively low on some of the great discs is the newness of the hobby. Not too many stamps and/or coins went from an original value of 79¢ to $200 in less than thirty years.

Some collectors overestimate the availability of these records. They hesitate to pay high prices in the belief that even the earliest, most sought after records are really reasonably common. They know that some of these records were also moderate hits. The attrition rate on phonograph records, even "unbreakable" vinyls, is high. Almost every original owner was a listener or fan, not a collector who took special pains about care and storage. Many specimens were "played to death," or knocked around, or used as Frisbees in the street. The simple fact is that the vast majority of these now-collectible records are not in very good condition. There may have been 500,000 mint specimens originally, but how many have emerged mint? Obviously, just a few, and these few are genuinely scarce.

When collectors realize the actual scarcity of mint oldies, they are going to stop objecting to high prices. The competition will become more heated. Today's sums could eventually look like bargains. We believe that the scarcer classics, now in the $100-and-up range, should all be very worthwhile investments, especially in mint condition.

As far as lesser-valued records are concerned, many of these will also turn profits for those who buy at the current price levels. However, you need to be selective in purchasing. One area that might be lucrative for speculation is recordings of The Greats that were made fairly early in their careers but which are not regarded as scarce — at the moment. For example, the very first pressings of Elvis Presley on RCA-Victor, after switching over from Sun, was "Mystery Train"/"I Forgot to Remember." This was only a minor hit and not of the proportions of later Elvis hits. The Sun specimen deserves to be worth considerably more than the RCA-Victor issue, but Elvis's first single for Victor should be more of a collector's item than the current price suggests.

Potential investors could also profit by buying the first records of artists on the current music scene who are just coming into popularity. This calls for some strategy because you should get the records while they're still being sold at manufacturers' list prices. After the artist achieves popularity, there will be a run on his records and the music shops won't have his early efforts on the original label.

SELLING

Buying and selling collectibles are as different as night and day. The casual buying approach is usually incorrect for selling. To obtain the top dollar for a record collection, a seller should study all options carefully. The options include selling to a dealer, another collector or at auction. If the collection is very large and valuable, a collector could even become a full or part-time dealer. Which route a collector takes is determined by one's business skills and knowledge of the market, the amount of time devoted to the project and accuracy in grading and pricing the collection.

Selling to the dealer. Many collectors sell to dealers because this is the easiest way to dispose of a collection. Unfortunately, the dealer will usually not offer a collector the best price simply because of his overhead costs. If a collection only contains one recording artist, then a dealer who specializes in that same artist is recommended. For example, a dealer who specializes in Elvis Presley or Beatles records will probably offer a better value for a Beatles record collection than a general antique dealer.

Selling to another collector. A simple method of attracting collectors is running an ad in a collector magazine. The ad should be specific and professionally typeset to attract attention. Handwritten ads are discouraged. The seller usually receives a good response from ads if his prices are fair and the items valuable. Sometimes a collector must run several ads in different magazines to receive a desired response. One must determine if the cost of the ads is justified with the type of collection being offered for sale.

Selling at auction. Usually a hobbyist will sell through an auction house if the collection is large with several valuable pieces. Because of the cost involved to sell at an auction, a very worthwhile collection would have to be offered to justify the extra expense of the auctioneer or auction house fee.

CARE AND STORAGE

Condition is one of the primary factors affecting value. To maintain record quality, do not play them excessively. Either tape the records or obtain a more inexpensive copy for personal use.

Since records need cleaning from time to time, a soft cloth and rubbing alcohol will usually handle the situation. Use a lint free cloth and rub it in a circular motion with the grooves, not against them. Then place the cleaned record in either a paper or mylar sleeve. Insert the sleeve into the record jacket. The record is now ready for storage.

Always store records upright. The most dangerous substance to records is heat. Store records in a cool, dry place away from fireplaces, sunny windows or other heat sources.

RECORD SHOWS AND CONVENTIONS

Whether you're a seasoned hobbyist or just starting out as a collector, you may want to attend record collector shows. Not only are they fun, but they offer an opportunity to meet other collectors and dealers. You may find discs at shows that you had long searched for on dealers' lists. You may also encounter bargains. Some collectors prefer buying at shows because of the huge quantities of collectible records offered. Usually no single shop can stock as many records as you'll find at a show, where dozens of dealers and collector/dealers can exhibit. In addition to records, record collector shows are sources of hard-to-get memorabilia.

"Oldie" record shows began a few years ago but have grown tremendously. At first critics doubted that the public had sufficient interest in old records to make the events worthwhile. Today, there is an established show circuit which most major dealers attend. More shows in larger cities are being added each year, and show trade is now booming. Some dealers do more turnover in two days at a show than in a month of sending out lists! This is undoubtedly because the excitement of a show generates buying fever. Collectors often come well-equipped with cash, and many of them end up spending it all. Some shows are sponsored by record-collecting clubs, but most are commercial ventures. A promoter rents a hall for the show. He rents booth or table space to exhibitors and makes his profit from these rentals as well as the entrance admission. Most shows are held on weekends, usually running for two days and sometimes three (Friday, Saturday, Sunday). The admission charge for the public varies, depending on the show's size and location.

There may be any number of exhibitors at the larger record shows. The majority will be dealers, but some collectors exhibit at such gatherings, selling or trading their duplicates. In some localities the exhibitors are required to obtain sales tax numbers and collect local sales taxes on any sales they make. In that event, collector-exhibitors must collect sales tax, too.

Though records are the chief items featured, you will also find other merchandise. Exhibitors may also sell photographs, posters and tee shirts. Some tables or booths will be taken by publishers of collector periodicals, who have stocks of their magazines on display and will take subscription orders.

Shows are places for buyer to meet seller and swapper to meet swapper. Everyone going to a show usually has *something* he wants to buy or sell, and the odds are that he will find a willing buyer or seller — probably several of them, and therefore obtain the best possible price. At shows, stacks of scarce discs change hands for multi-digit sums, often amid bargaining. It is not unusual for the same record to be sold and resold half a dozen times in a single day, passing from exhibitor to exhibitor and going higher in price or trade each time. This is not necessarily because it was underpriced originally; it might have carried the full book value, but each buyer along the line wanted it and perhaps saw the chance to turn it over for a profit to someone who wanted it even more. Price trends are often influenced at shows. Dealers put the "message" of the show into their next *price list,* adjusting prices up and down. If they do this, other dealers may also take notice and raise the prices of their stock. If the trend lasts and the dealers are successful at selling their copies for the higher figure — it is reflected in the next book price. The prices given in this edition are compiled from many dealer and auction-sale transactions. A record is worth what it will bring in open competition. If enough buyers are willing to pay more than the book value, the record is then automatically worth more, and the book value will go up.

You will find records selling for as little as 50¢ and as much as hundreds of dollars. The 50¢ discs are generally "junkers," good for playing but not for collecting. Shows dispose of "junkers," because the heavy traffic is certain to bring people who are interested in obtaining inexpensive "players."

Many dealers who also exhibit at a show bring their best material. A dealer often goes into a show under the assumption that he can get more for his *better* records there than on his lists. He may use prices that are 25-50% higher than he would affix to these discs on a mailing list. If no sales are registered, he will mark prices down somewhat before the show closes or accept reasonable counter offers. The advice that "half an hour before closing time is the best time to buy" is partly true. By then, many of the best discs are gone. In fact, some dealers sell out and leave the show long before it closes.

Do not get so caught up in the excitement of a show that you let your guard down. Transactions are often made at a much faster pace than in a shop. Don't fail to make sure you're getting the right record and that the price is in line with the condition.

WILL CURRENT RECORDS BECOME VALUABLE?

Anyone who had the foresight to buy an abundance of rock singles, EPs and albums at their original selling prices back in the 1950s and 1960s, and preserve them in mint condition, is now sitting on a goldmine. The question is will it happen again?

There is no clear-cut "yes" or "no." *Some* currently made records will become valuable, but their numbers will probably be fewer than rock discs of bygone decades.

Part of the reason rock classics have attained such lofty values is that rock music itself made such an impact. The 1950s and 1960s rock records represent early and experimental efforts in a new form of music. If rock had withered and died, if it had not spawned superstar after superstar, if it had not become a major social force, there would perhaps not be such collector interest in vintage rock. It represents the developing stages of a significant style of music, as does the first postage stamp or automobile or any other collector's items. There are various "new" forms of rock — Heavy Metal, New Wave, Punk Rock — but these are merely offspring of the movement.

Fans and hobbyists do not follow predictable paths. Their interests can shift. But there are no important new types of music on the current scene which would spawn the kind of eventual collecting interest that now belongs to rare rock. Possibly, collectors of the 1990s will seek the earliest relics of New Wave, Punk or some other strain of late 1970s or early 1980s music. Even if the music is not making a commercial impact *right now,* there's the chance it *could* become highly collectible. Possibly some significant new form of music will grow out of the experimental efforts now being conducted (mainly by European groups). If so, collectors are certain to hunt down — and eventually pay premium sums for — the earliest fledgling examples. Or the current experimental styles could disappear without a trace to make way for yet another novelty.

There probably is a way that you can buy at least *some* of tomorrow's valuable records *before* they become valuable. Unless collecting trends go off in divergent directions, record buffs of the future are reasonably safe to be seeking the early, little-known discs of current superstars. (Tom Petty and the Heartbreakers first recorded as Mudcrutch. Billy Joel was lead vocalist of the Hassles and Atilla. Debby Harry once sang with Wind in the Willows.) Also, any well-stocked new record shop currently has on hand discs by artists who will become household words within a year or two. Few want these records now, but after the artists become established, their early efforts *will be in demand.* You will notice, in this book, that the first singles made by each well-known recording star are usually the most valuable. As popular as they are now, they were once unknown, sometimes even recording under a different name. If you can get the *first records* of artists who have soared into stardom, you will undoubtedly find these early items becoming valuable with the passing years. If the artist is the type who may attract "cult" interest, there is even more likelihood that his pioneer discs will one day attain a high value.

As to the possibility of today's hit chart records becoming valuable collectors' items in the future, that question can be answered by flipping through the listings in this book. Hundreds of million-selling discs are listed, and in many cases the values, even for records twenty years or older, are low. Even big hits by heavily collected stars are not worth very much, except in the case of pressings that did not sell originally but became hits when re-released (which occasionally happens). In the 1950s, gold discs (50,000 LPs or 1,000,000 singles) were not as common as today. Today, well over a hundred 45 r.p.m. singles reach the million-dollar sales mark each year. On the other hand, records that do not sell well have considerably smaller output. When a company (especially a minor label) is giving a new artist a try, it might press just 10,000 copies of his first record, and many of these may fail to be distributed if the record does not gain needed airplay.

GLOSSARY

ACAPPELLA — A vocal group that sings without instrumental accompaniment. This style emerged in the 50s in concentrated urban areas.

AUCTION — A sale of records when bidding determines prices. The highest bidder buys the record. Mail bids are usually used for record auctions.

BLANK LABEL — A label without a title, serial number, artist, etc. A blank label usually indicates a bootleg. A handwritten or typed label also indicates a bootleg.

BLUES — Music that expresses hard times and troubles in music and lyrics. Played country style with stringed instruments, or with wind instruments to produce a more sophisticated sound.

BOOTLEG — Recording of a concert, radio or television broadcast, or demo issued by a manufacturer who has no legal rights to the material.

COUNTRY & WESTERN — Music derived from southern and western folk styles.

DEMO — Demonstration record. Used by artists seeking contracts — manufacturing costs are paid by the artist or a manager, not by a recording company.

DISC — Record.

DISCOGRAPHY — Listing of recordings made by an artist.

DOO WOP — 50s style music that is popular today.

ERROR RECORD — A record with a label that is blank, misprinted, or switched to the wrong side.

GARAGE BAND — Emerged in the 60s — part of the psychedelic era.

HEAT DAMAGE — Usually caused by leaving records in a hot car or on a radiator, heat damage warps records. (See section on cleaning and storage for remedies.)

INDEPENDENT LABEL — Usually a small operation, an independent label is produced by a company whose owner is also manager, producer, arranger, and publicity person. Records on independent labels are very collectible. These companies could afford to press only a few records, making them quite valuable.

INSERT — Anything included with an LP along with the record and sleeve. Collector value increases when an insert is still intact.

LABEL VARIATIONS — Occurs mostly with 45s — tracks are identical but the label coloring or printing varies. Many Beatles' Capitol records have three label variations. Market values vary.

LINER NOTES — The text on the album cover or sleeve that contains information about the artist or songs.

LISTENING COPY — A record that is not in collector condition, but is suitable for listening. Most collectors play their mint discs once and record them on tape.

LIVERPOOL SOUND — Emerged in 1964 with the Beatles arrival in America. British groups became popular in America and heavily influenced music. (The British Invasion.)

LP — Long Play. A 12 inch record with fine grooves for more playing time.

LP SINGLE — Single records on a 12-inch LP. This began in the 70s, mostly with rock records. LP singles come in a soft sleeve and the cost is close to an LP album.

MAIL BID — Used in record auctions. Record listings are published and those interested send a list of the records they want along with the highest price they will pay. The person running the auction matches bids to determine buyers. Buyers are notified by mail.

MASTER DISC — The disc used in pressing copies of a record. They receive good prices when and if they reach the collector market.

MINT CONDITION — A record in perfect condition. Very hard to find, but highly collectible and valuable. Most collectors settle for near-mint or very good condition records.

MIX — The blend of vocal track with musical track when making a record. Experimentation is done with mixes to get the best results for the final sound.

NEW MUSIC — What began as punk in the late 70s is often referred to now as new music.

NEW WAVE — The punk style of music that emerged in England in the late 70s.

PICTURE DISC — The whole disc, label included, is printed with a picture. This dates to 50 years ago and 78 r.p.m.s. It has become popular again in recent years.

PICTURE SLEEVE — A 45 r.p.m. sleeve with a picture of the artist. Sleeves are more scarce than the records and are worth more.

PIRACY — Unauthorized reproduction of commercially-released records and tapes. These are sold to retailers for less than distributor's prices.

PLUG SIDE — The side of a single that the manufacturer hopes will be a hit. Disc jockeys are encouraged to play the plug side.

PROMO — Promotional copy distributed to radio stations for advance air play.

REGGAE — Originated in Jamaica, this music has a cool rhythmic sound.

RHYTHM AND BLUES — A mixture of jazz and blues, this music emerged in the 50s by black musicians.

ROCKABILLY — A cross between rock and country and western. Usually it is rock and roll sung with a country sound.

ROCK AND ROLL — Popular, fast-moving music with a definite beat. Influenced by rhythm and blues, rock and roll evolved in the 50s by such artists as Elvis Presley, Bill Haley and Chuck Berry.

SERIAL NUMBER — The manufacturer's identifying number for a record, placed on the label. Each company has a serial numbering system. Serial numbers usually tell the chronological sequence that records were released or manufactured.

VINTAGE — What is considered to be the best of a certain era.

WAX RECORD — 78 r.p.m.s were made of hard pressed wax coated with shellac. They were made until the mid 50s and vinyl.

FAN CLUBS

The following is a partial list of recording artists' fan clubs. They are listed alphabetically by state and then by artist. In most cases, the fan club president's name is included. Most clubs are soliciting for new members. Please don't forget a SASE when sending for information.

ARIZONA
Tom Jones Fan Club
Linda Burt
2234 N. 52nd Street
Phoenix, AZ 85008

ARKANSAS
Willie Nelson Fan Club
6600 Baseline Road
Little Rock, AR 72209

CALIFORNIA
Bee Gees Fan Club
P.O. Box 9488
N. Hollywood, CA 91606

John Denver Fan Club
5219 Alhama Dr.
Woodland Hills, CA 91364

Devo Fan Club
9120 Sunset Blvd.
Los Angeles, CA 90069

Neil Diamond Fan Club
P.O. Box 3357
Hollywood, CA 90028

Michael Jackson Fan Club
P. O. Box 9488
North Hollywood, CA 91609

Johnny Mathis Fan Club
P.O. Box 69278
Hollywood, CA 90069

Rick Nelson Fan Club
1626 N. Wilcox Ave.
Hollywood, CA 90028

Elvis Presley Fan Club
324 Centra Ave. #B
Alameda, CA 94501

Paul Revere And The Raiders Fan Club
P. O. Box 19254
Oakland, CA 94619

Mary Wells Fan Club
12522 Roslind Drive
Orange, CA 92699

COLORADO
Loretta Lynn Fan Club
Box 177
Wild Horse, CO 80862

CONNECTICUT
Add Some Music
Beach Boys Fan Club
Box 10405
Elmwood, CT 06110

Good Day Sunshine Beatles
Fan Club
397 Edgewood Avenue
New Haven, CT 06511

FLORIDA
Elvis Presley Fan Club
P.O. Box 6104
Orlando, FL 32803

ILLINOIS
Lou Christie Fan Club
Lightning Strikes
1645 E. 50th Street, #10-11
Chicago, IL 60615

INDIANA
Guitar Duane Eddy Fan Club
2910 Yeager Road
W. Lafayette, IN 47906

Lettermen International Fan
Club
P. O. Box 9283
Fort Wayne, IN 46899

Elvis Presley Fan Club
2550 Mars Hill Street
Indianapolis, IN 46241

LOUISIANA
Connie Francis Fan Club
P.O. Box 9317
Bridge City, LA 70094

MARYLAND
National Rick Nelson Fan Club
2654 Dublin Road
Street, MD 21154

Connie Stevens Fan Club
2500 Gaither St. SE
Hillcrest Heights, MD 20031

MASSACHUSETTS
Patsy Cline Fan Club
Box 244
Dorchester, MA 02125

Sgt. Pepper's Lonely
Hearts Fan Club
2 Birch Hill Ave.
Wakefield, MA 01880

MINNESOTA
Hoyt Axton Fan Club
1603 N. St. Albans
St. Paul, MN 55117

The Write Thing Beatles
Fan Club
3310 Roosevelt Court NE
Minneapolis, MN 55418

NEW JERSEY
Bob Dylan Fan Club
9 Northampton Dr.
Willingsboro, NJ 08046

David Bowie Bulletin
P.O. Box 1606
Bloomfield, NJ 07003

Dion Fan Club
15 Drummond Ave.
Fords, NJ 08863

Duane Eddy Fan Club
P.O. Box 8105
Jersey City, NJ 07306

Lesley Gore Fan Club
141 Vernon Avenue
Paterson, NJ 07503

Elvis Presley Tribute
P. O. Box 1124
Bloomfield, NJ 07003

Linda Ronstadt Fan
Appreciation Society
Get Closer
P.O. Box 11
Rochelle Park, NJ 07662

NEW YORK

Paul Anka Fan Club
124 Terryville Road
Port Jefferson Station, NY 11776

Jimi Hendrix Fan Club
Box 1142
1204 Avenue U
Brooklyn, NY 11229

In Appreciation of the Hollies
14 Buckly Dr.
Rochester, NY 14624

Jack Jones Fan Club
500 Mountainview Avenue
Staten Island, NY 10314

Johnny Mathis East Coast Fan Club
200 E. 33rd. St., #61
New York, NY 10016

Rolling Stones Fan Club
P. O. Box 6152
New York, NY 10128

OHIO

Tony Orlando Fan Club
4041 Rocky River Dr. #3
Cleveland, OH 44135

Bobby Vee Fan Club
Box 443
Girard, OH 44420

OKLAHOMA

Roy Clark Fan Club
3225 S. Norwood
Tulsa, OK 74135

Freddie Fender Fan Club
Rt. 1, Box 251
Muskogee, OK 74401

PENNSYLVANIA

Connie Francis Fan Club
1975 Howard Ave.
Pottsville, PA 17901

TENNESSEE

Badfinger Fan Club
5126 Creekbend Circle
Cleveland, TN 37311

The Carter Family Fan Club
P.O. Box 1371
Hendersonville, TN 37075

Roy Orbison Fan Club
P.O. Box 1257
Hendersonville, TN 37077

Elvis Presley Fan Club
Box 16948
Memphis, TN 38116

TEXAS

Bobby Fuller Four-Ever International Fan Club
720 Quinta Luz Circle
El Paso, TX 79922

Mickey Gilley Fan Club
4500 Spencer HSY.
Pasadena, TX 77504

The Buddy Holly Memorial Society
3022 56th St.
Lubbock, TX 79413

Kris Kristofferson Fan Club
200 Crescent Dr.
Littlefield, TX 79337

FOREIGN

Dave Clark Five Fan Club
Commanderjstr 25
4209 AP Schulluinen
Holland, The Netherlands

International Petula Clark Fan Club
38 Elmley Way
Margate, Kent
CT94ES, United Kingdom

Elvis Costello Information Service
Primulastr. 46
1441 HC Purmerend
Holland, The Netherlands

Creedence Fan Club
Ruurloseweg
7251 LR Vorden
Holland, The Netherlands

Everly Brothers International
15 Drygrounds La.,
Felpham, Bognor Regis
Sussex PO22
8PS, United Kingdom

HOW TO USE THIS BOOK

This is a guide to the current retail values of 45 r.p.m., EP (extended play) and LP (album) recordings. Values are given for each listed recording in two different grades of condition: VG (Very Good) and MINT. These are the prices you would probably have to pay a dealer. The third price column provides last year's mint prices for the records. At a glance you can determine how the prices have changed in a year.

The arrangement is alphabetical by artist. Individuals are alphabetized by their last name (David Bowie under B). Groups are alphabetized by the first word in the group name (the Five Satins under F). The word "The" preceding a group name is disregarded in alphabetizing. In the case of duos using actual names — such as Simon and Garfunkel — alphabetizing is by the first name.

Recordings of each artist are grouped by 45 r.p.m., then EP (if any), then LP (if any). Recordings are arranged by label (record company); the intent is for chronological order. Thus, the first labels for which an artist recorded are listed in order according to their issue numbers. This does not insure that every recording of an artist is placed in chronological order. It can happen, because of uncertainties in record companies' release schedules, that a disc with a *lower* issue number reached the market before one with a *higher* number. These numbers are assigned far in advance of the actual release of the records. It also happens that a record company will revamp its numbering system. This practice makes determining chronological order more difficult. Our feeling is that the least confusion is apt to result from following the label numbers in numerical sequence, even if this is not always the chronological order in which the records were issued.

When you look up the value of a record, be sure your record agrees with *all* the details given in our listing. There are instances of the same songs (front and flip side) by the same artist issued under two different labels. One could be more valuable than the other, even though the artist and selections are the same, *and even though* both discs are roughly of the same age. Usually this "duplication" happened when a big company bought the contract of an artist recording for a small company. The big company would sometimes "pick up" works the artist had already recorded, and issue it under their label. The *small original label* version is the more desirable and valuable to collectors.

Values of 45 r.p.m. singles are for records only, not including sleeves. If a record was issued in a picture sleeve, the specimen has added collector value. Beware of reprint or other non-original sleeves (although the bootlegging of picture sleeves is an uncommon practice).

Values of EP and LP recordings are for specimens in the original jackets as issued. With very few exceptions, EP and LP recordings have been issued in jackets of heavy card stock with glossy lithographed covers. There should be no serious jacket damage, such as tears, heavy stains, etc., for the item to be worthwhile. A jacket in excellent condition adds to the record's overall value, more so in the case of scarce or rare albums dating before 1964.

A

			Current Price Range		P/Y AVG
ABBA					
☐3035	*ATLANTIC*	WATCH OUT/WATERLOO.	2.00	5.00	3.00
☐3209		DANCE WHILE THE MUSIC STILL GOES ON/HONEY HONEY.	2.00	5.00	3.00
☐3240		RING RING/HASTA MANANA.	2.00	5.00	3.00
☐3265		MAN IN THE MIDDLE/S.O.S.	2.00	5.00	3.00
☐3310		I DO, I DO, I DO/ BANG A BOOMERANG.	2.00	5.00	3.00
LATER ATLANTIC SINGLES ARE WORTH UP TO $3.00 MINT					
ABBA—ALBUMS					
☐SD-18146 (S)	*ATLANTIC*	ABBA.	4.00	12.00	10.00
☐SD18207 (S)		ARRIVAL	4.00	12.00	10.00
ACADEMICS					
☐100	*ANCHO*	AT MY FRONT DOOR/ DARLA MY DARLIN'.	8.00	18.00	15.00
☐101		HEAVENLY LOVE/ TOO GOOD TO BE TRUE.	9.00	20.00	18.00
JOHNNY ACE					
☐1015	*FLAIR*	MIDNIGHT HOURS JOURNEY/ TROUBLE AND ME.	25.00	60.00	35.00
☐102	*DUKE*	MY SONG/FOLLOW THE RULE.	6.00	12.00	6.00
☐107		CROSS MY HEART/ANGEL.	6.00	12.00	6.00
☐112		THE CLOCK/ACES WILD	6.00	12.00	6.00
☐118		SAVING MY LOVE FOR YOU/ YES BABY.	5.50	11.00	5.75
☐128		PLEASE FORGIVE ME/ YOU'VE BEEN GONE SO LONG.	5.50	11.00	5.75
☐132		NEVER LET ME GO/ BURLEY CUTIE.	5.50	11.00	5.75
☐136		PLEDGING MY LOVE/NO MONEY.	5.50	11.00	5.75
☐144		ANYMORE/ HOW CAN YOU BE SO MEAN.	5.50	11.00	5.75
☐148		SO LONELY/I'M CRAZY BABY.	5.50	11.00	5.75
☐154		DON'T YOU KNOW/ STILL LOVE YOU SO.	5.50	11.00	5.75
JOHNNY ACE—EPs					
☐80	*DUKE*	JOHNNY ACE	18.00	35.00	23.00
☐81		JOHNNY ACE	18.00	35.00	23.00
JOHNNY ACE—ALBUMS					
☐70	*DUKE*	JOHNNY ACE MEMORIAL ALBUM (10").	80.00	185.00	120.00
☐71 (M)		JOHNNY ACE MEMORIAL ALBUM.	22.00	55.00	34.00
☐71 (S)		JOHNNY ACE MEMORIAL ALBUM (reissue)	7.00	14.00	8.50
NICKY ADDEO					
☐200	*SAVOY*	GLORIA/ BRING BACK YOUR HEART.	13.00	23.00	15.00
☐200		GLORIA/BRING BACK YOUR HEART (colored wax)	23.00	42.00	27.00
☐104	*SELSOM*	OVER THE RAINBOW/FOOL #2.	23.00	42.00	27.00
AD-LIBS					
☐102	*BLUE CAT*	THE BOY FROM NEW YORK/ KICKED AROUND.	2.00	5.00	3.00
☐114		HE AIN'T NO ANGEL/ ASK ANYBODY.	2.00	5.00	3.50

			Current Price Range		P/Y AVG
☐ 119		ON THE CORNER/			
		OO-WEE, OH ME, OH MY.	2.00	5.00	3.50
☐ 123		JOHNNY MY BOY/			
		JUST A DOWN HOME GIRL.	2.00	5.00	3.50

ADMIRATIONS

☐ 45-107	**KELWAY**	IN MY YOUNGER DAYS/			
		OVER THE RAINBOW.	5.00	8.50	7.00
☐ 12871	**ATOMIC**	MEMORIES ARE HERE TO STAY/			
		DEAR LADY.	5.00	12.00	10.00
☐ 71521	**MERCURY**	THE BELLS OF ROSA RITA/			
		LITTLE BO-PEEP.	8.00	15.00	12.50
☐ 71883		TO THE AISLE/HEY SENORITA. . . .	20.00	35.00	30.00

ALADDINS

☐ 6	**FRANKIE**	MY CHARLENE/DOT, MY LOVE. . .	65.00	110.00	70.00

STEVE ALAIMO AND THE REDCOATS

☐ 6064	**MARLIN**	I WANT YOU TO LOVE ME/			
		BLUE SKIES.	8.00	15.00	12.50
☐ 6067		SHE'S MY BABY/SHOULD I CALL.	7.00	13.00	12.00
☐ 6445	**DICKSON**	BLUE FIRE/MY			
		HEART NEVER SAID GOODBYE. .	7.00	13.00	12.00

ARTHUR ALEXANDER

☐ 16309	**DOT**	YOU BETTER MOVE ON/A SHOT			
		OF RHYTHM AND BLUES	3.00	6.00	3.75
☐ 16357		WHERE HAVE YOU BEEN (ALL MY			
		LIFE)/SOLDIER OF LOVE	3.00	6.00	3.75
☐ 16387		ANNA/I HANG MY HEAD AND CRY	3.00	6.00	3.75
☐ 16425		YOU'RE THE REASON/			
		GO HOME GIRL	2.50	5.50	3.50
☐ 16454		DREAM GIRL/I WONDER			
		WHERE YOU ARE TONIGHT	2.50	5.50	3.50
☐ 16509		PRETTY GIRLS EVERYWHERE/			
		BABY BABY	2.50	5.50	3.50
☐ 16554		KEEP HER GUESSIN'/			
		WHERE DID SALLY GO?	2.50	5.50	3.50
☐ 16616		BLACK KNIGHT/OLE JOHN AMOS	2.50	5.50	3.50
☐ 16737		DETROIT CITY/YOU DON'T CARE .	2.50	5.50	3.50
		ARTHUR ALEXANDER—ALBUMS			
☐ 3434 (M)	**DOT**	YOU BETTER MOVE ON	11.00	21.00	13.00
☐ 25434 (S)		YOU BETTER MOVE ON	10.00	25.00	22.50

DAVIE ALLEN AND THE ARROWS

☐ 101	**CUDE**	WAR PATH/BEYOND THE BLUE			
		(Davie Allen)	12.00	22.00	15.00
☐ 3223	**MARC**	WAR PATH/BEYOND THE BLUE			
		(Davie Allen)	4.00	7.00	6.00
☐ 1	**SIDEWALK**	APACHE '65/BLUE GUITAR	3.00	6.00	4.00
☐ 116	**TOWER**	APACHE '65/BLUE GUITAR	3.00	6.00	4.00
☐ 133		MOON DAWG '65/			
		DANCE THE FREDDIE	3.00	6.00	4.00
☐ 142		BABY RUTH/I'M LOOKING OVER A			
		FOUR LEAF CLOVER	2.50	5.50	3.50
☐ 150		SPACE HOP/GRANNY GOOSE	2.50	5.50	3.50
☐ 267		THEME FROM THE WILD ANGELS/			
		U. F. O.	2.50	5.50	3.50
☐ 295		BLUE'S THEME/BONGO PARTY . .	2.50	5.50	3.50
☐ 341		DEVIL'S ANGELS/CODY'S THEME .	2.50	5.50	3.50
☐ 381		BLUE RIDES AGAIN/CYCLE-DELIC	2.50	5.50	3.50
		DAVIE ALLEN AND THE ARROWS—ALBUMS			
☐ 5002 (M)	**TOWER**	APACHE '65	6.00	14.00	12.00

			Current Price Range		P/Y AVG
☐5002 (S)		APACHE '65	8.00	20.00	18.00
☐5078 (M)		BLUE'S THEME	6.00	14.00	12.00
☐5078 (S)		BLUE'S THEME	8.00	20.00	18.00
☐5094 (M)		THE CYCLE-DELIC SOUNDS OF DAVIE ALLEN AND THE ARROWS	5.00	14.00	12.00
☐5094 (S)		THE CYCLE-DELIC SOUNDS OF DAVIE ALLEN AND THE ARROWS	8.00	18.00	15.00

JIMMY ALLEN

☐1200	**AL-BRITE**	FORGIVE ME MY DARLING/ MY GIRL IS A PEARL	22.00	45.00	30.00

LEE ALLEN AND HIS BAND

☐1027	**EMBER**	WALKIN' WITH MR. LEE/ PROMENADE	3.00	5.00	2.00
☐1031		STROLLIN' WITH MR. LEE/ BOPPIN' AT THE HOP	3.00	5.00	4.00
☐1039		TIC TOC/CHUGGIN'	3.00	5.00	4.00
☐1047		JIM JAM/SHORT CIRCUIT	3.00	5.00	4.00
☐1057		CAT WALK/CREOLE ALLEY	3.00	5.00	4.00

LEE ALLEN AND HIS BAND—EP

☐103	**EMBER**	WALKIN' WITH MR. LEE	8.00	20.00	15.00

LEE ALLEN AND HIS BAND—ALBUM

☐200 (M)		WALKIN' WITH MR. LEE	23.00	55.00	50.00

RICHIE ALLEN

☐5683	**IMPERIAL**	STRANGER FROM DURANGO/ REDSKIN	3.00	5.00	3.50
☐5720		HAUNTED GUITAR/ IN A PERSIAN WORLD	3.00	5.00	3.50
☐5846		COMIN' BACK TO YOU/ MR. HOBBS THEME	3.00	5.00	3.50
☐5917		BUTTERSCOTCH/SUNDAY PICNIC	3.00	5.00	3.50
☐5984		BALLAD OF THE SURF/ THE QUIET SIDE	3.00	5.00	3.50

RICHIE ALLEN—ALBUMS

☐9229 (M)	**IMPERIAL**	THE RISING SURF	10.00	25.00	22.50
☐9243 (M)		SURFER'S SLIDE	10.00	25.00	22.50

ARVEE ALLENS (RITCHIE VALENS)

☐4111	**DEL-FI**	FAST FREIGHT/BIG BABY BLUES	7.00	13.00	8.00

ALLEY CATS

☐108	**PHILLES**	PUDDIN' 'N TAIN/FEEL SO GOOD.	5.00	7.00	6.00

ALLMAN BROTHERS

☐35066	**VANGUARD**	PICK A GRIPE/ SANDCASTLES	2.00	5.00	3.00
☐56002	**LIBERTY**	HEARTBEAT/ NOTHING BUT TEARS (billed as ''Hour Glass'')	6.00	12.00	7.50
☐8003	**CAPRICORN**	BLACK HEARTED WOMAN/ EVERY HUNGRY WOMAN	2.50	5.50	3.50
☐8011		REVIVAL/	2.50	5.50	3.50
☐8014		WHIPPING POST/ MIDNIGHT RIDER	2.50	5.50	3.50
☐0003		MELISSA/AIN'T WASTIN' TIME NO MORE	2.50	5.50	3.50
☐0007		MELISSA/BLUE SKY	2.50	5.50	3.50
☐0014		STAND BACK/ONE WAY OUT	2.50	5.50	3.50
☐0027		PONY BOY/RAMBLIN' MAN	2.50	5.50	3.50
☐0036		JESSICA/COME & GO BLUES	2.50	5.50	3.50
☐0053		MIDNIGHT RIDER/ DON'T MESS UP A GOOD THING.	2.50	5.50	3.50

LATER CAPRICORN SINGLES ARE WORTH UP TO $3.00 MINT

			Current Price Range		P/Y AVG
		ALLMAN BROTHERS—ALBUMS			
☐ SD2-805 (S)	**ATCO**	BEGINNINGS	13.00	32.00	21.00
☐ SD33-308 (S)		THE ALLMAN BROTHERS	15.00	38.00	24.00
☐ SD33-342 (S)		IDLEWILD SOUTH	11.00	24.00	16.00
☐ 2CX-0177 (S)					
	CAPRICORN	WIPE THE WINDOWS	6.00	16.00	12.50
☐ CP-0156 (S)		WIN, LOSE OR DRAW	6.00	16.00	12.50
☐ 2CP-0164 (S)		ROAD GOES ON FOREVER	6.00	16.00	12.50
☐ CX4-0131 (QUAD)		AT FILLMORE EAST	7.00	19.00	16.50

AMERICAN SPRING (HONEYS)
PRODUCER: BRIAN WILSON

☐ 45834	**COLUMBIA**	SHYIN' AWAY/FALLIN' IN LOVE. .	10.00	20.00	18.00
☐ 4-45834		SHYIN' AWAY/SHYIN' AWAY			
		(PROMO)	15.00	30.00	25.00
		(PICTURE SLEEVE)	10.00	30.00	20.00

LEE ANDREWS AND THE HEARTS

☐ 252	**RAINBOW**	MAYBE YOU'LL BE THERE/ BABY COME BACK.	90.00	175.00	120.00
☐ 256		WHITE CLIFFS OF DOVER/ MUCH TOO MUCH.	90.00	175.00	120.00
☐ 259		THE BELLS OF ST. MARY'S/ FAIREST.	90.00	175.00	120.00
☐ 318	**GOTHAM**	BLUEBIRD OF HAPPINESS/ SHOW ME THE MERENGUE. . .	30.00	55.00	36.00
☐ 320		LONELY ROOM/LEONA	30.00	55.00	36.00
☐ 321		JUST SUPPOSE/IT'S ME	30.00	55.00	36.00
☐ 156	**GRAND**	TEARDROPS/ THE GIRL AROUND THE CORNER	30.00	55.00	36.00
☐ 157		LONG LONELY NIGHTS/ THE CLOCK.	30.00	55.00	36.00
☐ 102	**MAINLINE**	LONG LONELY NIGHTS/ THE CLOCK.	25.00	45.00	30.00
☐ 1665	**CHESS**	LONG LONELY NIGHTS/ THE CLOCK.	4.00	7.00	4.75
☐ 1675		TEAR DROPS/ THE GIRL AROUND THE CORNER	3.50	5.50	4.00
☐ 1000	**ARGO**	TEAR DROPS/ THE GIRL AROUND THE CORNER	6.00	11.00	7.00
☐ 110	**CASINO**	I WONDER/BABY COME BACK. . . .	11.00	18.00	13.00
☐ 452		TRY THE IMPOSSIBLE/ NOBODY'S HOME.	11.00	18.00	13.00
☐ 123	**UNITED ARTISTS**	TRY THE IMPOSSIBLE/ NOBODY'S HOME.	3.50	5.50	4.00
☐ 136		WHO DO I/GLAD TO BE HERE.	4.00	6.50	4.50
☐ 151		ALL I ASK IS LOVE/ MAYBE YOU'LL BE THERE. . . .	4.00	6.50	4.50
☐ 162		JUST SUPPOSE/BOOM	4.00	6.50	4.50

ANGELS

☐ 107	**CAPRICE**	'TIL/A MOMENT AGO	3.00	5.50	3.50
☐ 112		CRY BABY CRY/ THAT'S ALL I ASK OF YOU.	3.00	5.50	3.50
☐ 116		EVERBODY LOVES A LOVER/ BLOW, JOE.	3.00	5.50	3.50
☐ 118		I'D BE GOOD FOR YOU/ YOU SHOULD HAVE TOLD ME. .	3.00	5.50	3.50
☐ 121		A MOMENT AGO/COTTON FIELDS.	3.00	5.50	3.50
☐ 1834	**SMASH**	MY BOYFRIEND'S BACK/ (LOVE ME) NOW.	2.50	5.50	3.00
☐ 1854		I ADORE HIM/ THANK YOU AND GOODNIGHT. .	2.50	5.50	3.00
☐ 1870		WOW WOW WEE/ SNOWFLAKES AND TEARDROPS	2.50	4.50	3.00

			Current Price Range		P/Y AVG
☐ 1885		LITTLE BEATLE BOY/JAVA.	2.50	4.50	3.00
☐ 1915		DREAM BOY/JAMAICA JOE.	2.50	4.50	3.00
☐ 1931		THE BOY FROM 'CROSS TOWN/			
		A WORLD WITHOUT LOVE. . . .	2.50	4.50	3.00
☐ 47-9541	**RCA VICTOR**	THE MEDLEY/IF I DIDN'T LOVE			
		YOU.	2.50	4.50	3.00

ANGELS—ALBUMS

☐ 1001 (M)	**CAPRICE**	AND THE ANGELS SING.	9.00	20.00	18.00
☐ 1001 (S)		AND THE ANGELS SING.	12.00	30.00	25.00
☐ 27039 (M)	**SMASH**	MY BOYFRIEND'S BACK.	8.00	18.00	15.00
☐ 67039 (S)		MY BOYFRIEND'S BACK.	10.00	25.00	22.50
☐ 27048 (M)		A HALO TO YOU	8.00	18.00	15.00
☐ 67048 (S)		A HALO TO YOU	10.00	25.00	22.50
☐ 13009 (M)	**ASCOT**	12 OF THEIR GREATEST HITS. . . .	8.00	18.00	15.00

ANIMALS

☐ 13242	**MGM**	GONNA SEND YOU BACK TO WALKER/BABY LET ME TAKE YOU HOME.	3.50	6.00	4.25
☐ 13264		HOUSE OF THE RISING SUN/ TALKING 'BOUT YOU.	2.75	5.25	3.75
☐ 13274		I'M CRYING/TAKE IT EASY BABY.	2.75	5.25	3.75
☐ 13298		BOOM BOOM/BLUE FEELING.	2.75	5.25	3.75
☐ 13311		DON'T LET ME BE MISUNDERSTOOD/ CLUB A GO GO.	2.75	5.25	3.75
☐ 13339		BRING IT ON HOME/ FOR MISS CAULKER.	2.75	5.25	3.75
☐ 13382		WE GOTTA GET OUT OF THIS PLACE/I CAN'T BELIEVE IT. . . .	2.25	5.00	3.50
☐ 13414		IT'S MY LIFE/I'M GOING TO CHANGE THE WORLD.	2.25	5.00	3.50
☐ 13468		INSIDE-LOOKING OUT/ YOU'RE ON MY MIND.	2.25	5.00	3.50
☐ 13514		DON'T BRING ME DOWN/ CHEATING.	2.25	5.00	3.50
☐ 13582		SEE SEE RIDER/ SHE'LL RETURN IT.	2.25	5.00	3.50
☐ 13636		HELP ME GIRL/ THAT AIN'T WHERE IT'S AT. . . .	2.25	5.00	3.50
☐ 13721		WHEN I WAS YOUNG/ A GIRL NAMED SANDOZ.	2.25	5.00	3.50
☐ 13769		SAN FRANCISCAN NIGHTS/ GOOD TIMES.	2.25	5.00	3.50
☐ 13868		MONTEREY/AIN'T THAT SO.	2.25	5.00	3.50
☐ 13917		ANYTHING/IT'S ALL MEAT.	2.25	5.00	3.50
☐ 13939		SKY PILOT (PT. 1)/(PT. 2)	2.25	5.00	3.50
☐ 14013		WHITE HOUSES/RIVER DEEP-MOUNTAIN HIGH.	2.25	5.00	3.50

ANIMALS—ALBUMS

☐ 4264 (M)	**MGM**	THE ANIMALS	9.00	20.00	12.00
☐ 4264 (S)		THE ANIMALS	12.00	27.00	17.50
☐ 4281 (M)		THE ANIMALS ON TOUR	7.00	16.00	11.00
☐ 4281 (S)		THE ANIMALS ON TOUR	10.00	22.00	14.00
☐ 4305 (M)		ANIMAL TRACKS	7.00	16.00	11.00
☐ 4305 (S)		ANIMAL TRACKS	10.00	22.00	14.00
☐ 4324 (M)		THE BEST OF THE ANIMALS. . . .	6.00	14.00	9.00
☐ 4324 (S)		THE BEST OF THE ANIMALS. . . .	10.00	22.00	14.00
☐ 4384 (M)		ANIMALIZATION	7.00	16.00	10.00
☐ 4384 (S)		ANIMALIZATION	10.00	22.00	13.00
☐ 4414 (M)		ANIMALISM	7.00	16.00	10.00
☐ 4414 (S)		ANIMALISM	10.00	22.00	13.00
☐ 4433 (M)		ERIC IS HERE	7.00	16.00	10.00
4433 (S)		ERIC IS HERE	8.00	19.00	12.00

			Current Price Range		P/Y AVG
☐ 4454 (M)		BEST OF ERIC BURDON AND THE ANIMALS, VOL. II............	7.00	16.00	10.00
☐ 4454 (S)		BEST OF ERIC BURDON AND THE ANIMALS, VOL. II............	9.00	20.00	13.00
☐ 4484 (M)		WINDS OF CHANGE............	5.50	12.00	10.00
☐ 4484 (S)		WINDS OF CHANGE............	5.50	12.00	10.00
☐ 4537 (M)		THE TWAIN SHALL MEET........	5.50	12.00	10.00
☐ 4537 (S)		THE TWAIN SHALL MEET........	5.50	12.00	10.00
☐ 4553 (M)		EVERY ONE OF US.............	5.50	12.00	10.00
☐ 4553 (S)		EVERY ONE OF US.............	5.50	12.00	10.00
☐ 4591 (S)		LOVE IS.....................	5.50	12.00	10.00
☐ 4602 (S)		GREATEST HITS OF ERIC BURDON AND THE ANIMALS...........	5.50	12.00	10.00

PAUL ANKA

			Current Price Range		P/Y AVG
☐ 472	**RPM**	I CONFESS/BLAU-WILE DEVEEST FONTAINE (with the Jacks)....	25.00	50.00	36.00
☐ 2027	**BARNABY RECORDS**	WHY ARE YOU LEANING ON ME SIR/YOU'RE SOME KIND OF FRIEND..................	12.00	21.00	14.00
☐ 9831	**ABC-PARAMOUNT**	DIANA/ DON'T GAMBLE WITH LOVE...	3.50	5.50	4.50
☐ 9855		I LOVE YOU BABY/ TELL ME THAT YOU LOVE ME..	3.50	5.50	4.00
☐ 9880		YOU ARE MY DESTINY/ WHEN I STOP LOVING YOU....	3.50	5.00	4.00
☐ 9907		CRAZY LOVE/LET THE BELLS KEEP RINGING..............	3.50	5.00	4.00
☐ 9937		MIDNIGHT/VERBOTEN.........	3.50	5.00	4.00
☐ 9956		JUST YOUNG/SO IT'S GOODBYE.	3.50	5.50	4.00
☐ 9987		MY HEART SINGS/THAT'S LOVE.	3.50	6.00	4.00
☐ 10011		I MISS YOU SO/LATE LAST NIGHT	3.50	6.00	4.00
☐ 10022		LONELY BOY/YOUR WAY.......	3.50	6.00	4.00
☐ 10040		PUT YOUR HEAD ON MY SHOULDER/DON'T EVER LEAVE ME................	3.50	6.00	4.00
☐ 10064		IT'S TIME TO CRY/ SOMETHING HAS CHANGED ME	3.50	6.00	4.00
☐ 10082		PUPPY LOVE/ADAM AND EVE...	3.50	6.00	4.00
☐ 10106		MY HOME TOWN/ SOMETHING HAPPENED......	3.50	6.00	4.00
☐ 10132		HELLO YOUNG LOVERS/I LOVE YOU IN THE SAME OLD WAY..	3.50	6.00	4.00
☐ 10147		SUMMER'S GONE/ I'D HAVE TO SHARE.........	3.50	6.00	4.00
☐ 10163		I SAW MOMMY KISSING SANTA CLAUS/RUDOLPH THE RED-NOSED REINDEER..........	4.00	6.50	4.50
☐ 10168		THE STORY OF MY LOVE/ DON'T SAY YOU'RE SORRY...	3.00	5.00	3.50
☐ 10169		IT'S CHRISTMAS EVERYWHERE/ RUDOLPH THE RED-NOSED REINDEER..................	4.00	6.50	4.50
☐ 10194		TONIGHT MY LOVE TONIGHT/ I'M JUST YOUR FOOL ANYWAY	3.00	5.00	3.50
☐ 10220		DANCE ON LITTLE GIRL/ I TALK TO YOU............	3.00	5.00	3.50
☐ 10239		CINDERELLA/ KISSIN' ON THE PHONE......	3.00	5.00	3.50
☐ 10279		LOVELAND/ THE BELLS AT MY WEDDING..	3.00	5.00	3.50
☐ 10282		THE FOOL'S HALL OF FAME/FAR FROM THE LIGHTS OF TOWN..	3.00	5.00	3.50

			Current Price Range		P/Y AVG
☐ 10311		I'D NEVER FIND ANOTHER YOU/ UH HUH	3.00	5.00	3.50
☐ 10338		I'M COMING HOME/CRY	3.00	5.00	3.50
☐ 7977	**RCA**	LOVE ME WARM AND TENDER/ I'D LIKE TO KNOW	2.00	4.50	3.00
☐ 8030		A STEEL GUITAR AND A GLASS OF WINE/I NEVER KNEW YOUR NAME	2.25	4.75	3.25
☐ 8068		EVERY NIGHT/THERE YOU GO	2.25	4.75	3.25
☐ 8097		ESO BESO/GIVE ME BACK MY HEART	2.25	4.75	3.25
☐ 8115		LOVE/CRYING IN THE WIND	2.25	4.75	3.25
☐ 8170		REMEMBER DIANA/AT NIGHT	2.25	4.75	3.25
☐ 8195		HELLO JIM/YOU'VE GOT THE NERVE TO CALL THIS LOVE	2.25	4.75	3.25
☐ 8237		WONDROUS ARE THE WAYS OF LOVE/HURRY UP AND TELL ME	2.25	4.75	3.25
☐ 8272		DID YOU HAVE A HAPPY BIRTHDAY?/FOR NO GOOD REASON AT ALL	2.25	4.75	3.25
☐ 8311		FROM ROCKING HORSE TO ROCKING CHAIR/CHEER UP	2.25	4.75	3.25
☐ 8349		BABY'S COMING HOME/NO, NO	2.25	4.75	3.25
☐ 8396		IT'S EASY TO SAY/ IN MY IMAGINATION	2.25	4.75	3.25
☐ 8441		CINDY GO HOME/OGNI VOLTA	2.25	4.75	3.25
☐ 8493		BEHIND MY SMILE/SYLVIA	2.25	4.75	3.25
☐ 8595		THE LONELIEST BOY IN THE WORLD/DREAM ME HAPPY	2.25	4.75	3.25
☐ 8662		AS IF THERE WERE NO TOMORROW/EVERY DAY A HEART IS BROKEN	2.25	4.75	3.25
☐ 8764		OH, SUCH A STRANGER/ TRULY YOURS	2.25	4.75	3.25
☐ 8839		I WENT TO YOUR WEDDING/ I WISH	2.25	4.75	3.25
☐ 8893		CAN'T GET ALONG VERY WELL WITHOUT HER/I CAN'T HELP LOVING YOU	2.25	4.75	3.25
☐ 9032		POOR OLD FOOL/ I'D RATHER BE A STRANGER	2.25	4.75	3.25
☐ 9128		UNTIL IT'S TIME FOR YOU TO GO/ WOULD YOU STILL BE MY BABY?	2.25	4.75	3.25
☐ 9228		THAT'S HOW LOVE GOES/ A WOMAN IS A SENTIMENTAL THING	2.25	4.75	3.25
☐ 9457		CAN'T GET YOU OUT OF MY MIND/ WHEN WE GET THERE	2.25	4.75	3.25
☐ 9648		GOODNIGHT MY LOVE/ THIS CRAZY WORLD	2.25	4.75	3.25
☐ 9767		HAPPY/CAN'T GET YOU OUT OF MY MIND	2.25	4.75	3.25
☐ 9846		MIDNIGHT MISTRESS/BEFORE IT'S TOO LATE — THIS LAND IS YOUR LAND	2.25	4.75	3.25
☐ 0126		IN THE STILL OF THE NIGHT/ PICKIN' UP THE PIECES	2.25	4.75	3.25
☐ 0164		SINCERELY/NEXT YEAR	2.25	4.75	3.25
		PAUL ANKA—EPs			
☐ 296-1	**ABC- PARAMOUNT**	MY HEART SINGS	10.00	19.00	12.00
☐ 296-2		MY HEART SINGS	10.00	19.00	12.00
☐ 296-3		MY HEART SINGS	10.00	19.00	12.00

			Current Price Range		P/Y AVG

PAUL ANKA—ALBUMS

☐ 240 (M)	ABC-				
	PARAMOUNT	PAUL ANKA	20.00	42.00	29.00
☐ 240 (S)		PAUL ANKA	26.00	59.00	39.00
☐ 296 (M)		MY HEART SINGS	14.00	30.00	20.00
☐ 296 (S)		MY HEART SINGS	22.00	48.00	33.00
☐ 323 (M)		PAUL ANKA SINGS HIS BIG 15 . . .	15.00	37.00	25.00
☐ 323 (S)		PAUL ANKA SINGS HIS BIG 15 . . .	22.00	48.00	33.00
☐ 347 (M)		SWINGS FOR YOUNG LOVERS . . .	12.00	27.00	18.00
☐ 347 (S)		SWINGS FOR YOUNG LOVERS . . .	20.00	42.00	29.00
☐ 353 (M)		ANKA AT THE COPA	11.00	26.00	18.00
☐ 353 (S)		ANKA AT THE COPA	15.00	37.00	25.00
☐ 360 (M)		IT'S CHRISTMAS EVERYWHERE .	11.00	26.00	18.00
☐ 360 (S)		IT'S CHRISTMAS EVERYWHERE .	15.00	37.00	25.00
☐ 371 (M)		STRICTLY INSTRUMENTAL	10.00	21.00	15.00
☐ 371 (S)		STRICTLY INSTRUMENTAL	13.00	30.00	20.00
☐ 390 (M)		PAUL ANKA SINGS HIS BIG 15, VOL. II	11.00	26.00	18.00
☐ 390 (S)		PAUL ANKA SINGS HIS BIG 15, VOL. II	16.00	37.00	24.00
☐ 409 (M)		PAUL ANKA SINGS HIS BIG 15, VOL. III	11.00	26.00	18.00
☐ 409 (S)		PAUL ANKA SINGS HIS BIG 15, VOL. III	15.00	35.00	24.00
☐ 420 (M)		DIANA	10.00	22.00	15.00
☐ 420 (S)		DIANA	10.00	25.00	17.00
☐ 2502 (M)	RCA	YOUNG, ALIVE AND IN LOVE	10.00	22.00	15.00
☐ 2502 (S)		YOUNG, ALIVE AND IN LOVE	10.00	25.00	17.00
☐ 2575 (M)		LET'S SIT THIS ONE OUT	10.00	22.00	15.00
☐ 2575 (S)		LET'S SIT THIS ONE OUT	10.00	25.00	17.00
☐ 2614 (M)		OUR MAN AROUND THE WORLD . .	7.00	17.00	15.00
☐ 2614 (S)		OUR MAN AROUND THE WORLD . .	9.00	20.00	18.00
☐ 2691 (M)		21 GOLDEN HITS (redone)	6.50	15.00	13.50
☐ 2691 (S)		21 GOLDEN HITS (redone)	7.00	17.00	15.00
☐ 2744 (M)		SONGS I WISH I'D WRITTEN	7.00	17.00	15.00
☐ 2744 (S)		SONGS I WISH I'D WRITTEN	9.00	20.00	18.00
☐ 2966 (M)		EXCITEMENT ON PARK AVENUE . .	7.00	17.00	15.00
☐ 2966 (S)		EXCITEMENT ON PARK AVENUE . .	9.00	20.00	18.00
☐ 3580 (M)		STRICTLY NASHVILLE	6.50	15.00	13.50
☐ 3580 (S)		STRICTLY NASHVILLE	7.00	15.00	15.00
☐ 4142 (S)		GOODNIGHT MY LOVE	6.50	15.00	13.50
☐ 4250 (S)		LIFE GOES ON	6.50	15.00	13.50

PAUL ANKA, JOHNNY NASH, GEORGE HAMILTON IV

☐ 9974	ABC-				
	PARAMOUNT	THE TEEN COMMANDMENTS/ IF YOU LEARN TO PRAY	4.50	7.00	5.50

ANNETTE

☐ 102	DISNEYLAND	HOW WILL I KNOW MY LOVE/ DON'T JUMP TO CONCLUSIONS	5.50	10.00	8.00
☐ 114		THAT CRAZY PLACE FROM OUTER SPACE/GOLD DUBLOONS AND PIECES OF EIGHT	5.50	8.50	7.00
☐ 118		TALL PAUL/MA, HE'S MAKING EYES AT ME	3.50	5.00	4.00
☐ 758		HOW WILL I KNOW MY LOVE/ ANNETTE (Jimmy Dodd)	4.50	7.00	5.50
☐ 786		THAT CRAZY PLACE IN OUTER SPACE/HAPPY GLOW	5.50	8.50	7.00
☐ 336	VISTA	JO-JO THE DOG-FACED BOY/ LOVE ME FOREVER	3.50	6.00	4.00
☐ 339		LONELY GUITAR/WILD WILLIE . .	3.50	6.00	4.00

			Current Price Range		P/Y AVG
☐ 344		MY HEART BECAME OF AGE/ ESPECIALLY FOR YOU	3.50	6.00	4.00
☐ 349		FIRST NAME INITIAL/MY HEART BECAME OF AGE	3.50	6.00	4.00
☐ 354		O DIO MIO/IT TOOK DREAMS	3.50	6.00	4.00
☐ 359		TRAIN OF LOVE/TELL ME WHO'S THE GIRL	3.25	5.25	4.00
☐ 362		PINEAPPLE PRINCESS/ LUAU CHA CHA CHA	3.25	5.25	4.00
☐ 369		TALK TO ME BABY/ I LOVE YOU BABY	3.25	5.25	4.00
☐ 374		DREAM BOY/PLEASE, PLEASE SIGNORE	3.25	5.25	4.00
☐ 375		INDIAN GIVER, MAMA, MAMA ROSA	3.25	5.25	4.00
☐ 384		HAWAIIAN LOVE TALK/ BLUE MUU MUU	3.25	5.25	4.00
☐ 388		DREAMIN' ABOUT YOU/ THE STRUMMIN' SONG	3.25	5.25	4.00
☐ 392		THAT CRAZY PLACE FROM OUTER SPACE/SEVEN MOONS	3.25	5.25	4.00
☐ 394		THE TRUTH ABOUT YOUTH/ I CAN'T DO THE SUM	3.75	5.25	4.25
☐ 400		MY LITTLE GRASS SHACK/ HUKILAU SONG	3.75	5.25	4.25
☐ 405		HE'S MY IDEAL/MR. PIANO MAN	3.75	5.25	4.25
☐ 407		BELLA BELLA FLORENCE/ CANZONE D'AMORE	3.75	5.25	4.25
☐ 414		TEENAGE WEDDING/ WALKING AND TALKING	3.75	5.25	4.25
☐ 427		TREAT HIM NICELY/ PROMISE ME ANYTHING	3.75	5.25	4.25
☐ 431		MERLIN JONES/ THE SCRAMBLED EGGHEAD ...	3.75	5.25	4.25
☐ 432		CUSTOM CITY/REBEL RIDER	3.75	5.25	4.25
☐ 433		MUSCLE BEACH PARTY/ I DREAM ABOUT FRANKIE	3.75	5.25	4.25
☐ 436		BIKINI BEACH PARTY/THE CLYDE	3.75	5.25	4.25
☐ 437		THE WAH WATUSI/THE CLYDE ..	3.75	5.25	4.25
☐ 438		SOMETHING BORROWED, SOMETHING BLUE/HOW WILL I KNOW MY LOVE	3.75	5.25	4.25
☐ 440		THE MONKEY'S UNCLE/HOW WILL I KNOW MY LOVE	6.00	12.00	7.50
	VISTA 440 FEATURES BACKUP BY THE BEACH BOYS				
☐ 442		BOY TO LOVE/ NO ONE COULD BE PROUDER ..	4.00	7.00	4.25
☐ 450		NO WAY TO GO BUT UP/ CRYSTAL BALL	4.00	7.00	4.25
☐ 802		LET'S GET TOGETHER/ THE PARENT TRAP	4.00	7.00	4.25
☐ 9828	*EPIC*	BABY NEEDS ME NOW/ MOMENT OF SILENCE	6.00	10.00	5.75
☐ 326	*TOWER*	WHAT'S A GIRL TO DO/WHEN YOU GET WHAT YOU WANT	6.00	10.00	5.75
		ANNETTE—EPs			
☐ 04	*DISNEYLAND*	TALL PAUL	10.00	25.00	22.50
☐ 69		MICKEY MOUSE CLUB-ANNETTE .	8.50	20.00	18.00
☐ 3301	*VISTA*	LONELY GUITAR	8.50	20.00	18.00
		ANNETTE—ALBUMS			
☐ 3301 (M)	*VISTA*	ANNETTE	20.00	45.00	45.00
☐ 3302 (M)		ANNETTE SINGS ANKA	12.00	29.00	25.00
☐ 3303 (M)		HAWAIIANETTE	12.00	29.00	25.00
☐ 3304 (M)		ITALIANETTE	12.00	29.00	25.00

			Current Price Range		P/Y AVG
☐3305 (M)		DANCE ANNETTE	10.00	25.00	22.50
☐3309 (M)		THE PARENT TRAP	10.00	25.00	22.50
☐3312 (M)		ANNETTE-THE STORY OF MY TEENS	10.00	25.00	22.50
☐3313 (M)		TEEN STREET	15.00	34.00	30.00
☐3314 (M)		MUSCLE BEACH PARTY	12.00	29.00	25.00
☐3316 (M)		ANNETTE'S BEACH PARTY	12.00	29.00	25.00
☐3320 (M)		ANNETTE ON CAMPUS	9.00	20.00	18.00
☐3324 (M)		ANNETTE AT BIKINI BEACH	10.00	15.00	12.50
☐3325 (M)		ANNETTE'S PAJAMA PARTY	9.00	20.00	18.00
☐3325 (S)		ANNETTE'S PAJAMA PARTY	10.00	25.00	22.50
☐3327 (M)		ANNETTE SINGS GOLDEN SURFIN' HITS	9.00	20.00	18.00
☐3328 (M)		SOMETHING BORROWED, SOMETHING BLUE	9.00	20.00	18.00
☐3906 (M)		SNOW WHITE AND THE SEVEN DWARFS	9.00	20.00	18.00
☐4037 (M)		ANNETTE FUNICELLO	9.00	20.00	18.00
☐24 (M)	**MICKEY MOUSE**	SONGS FROM ANNETTE	10.00	25.00	22.50

ANN-MARGRET

			Current Price Range		P/Y AVG
☐7857	**RCA**	LOST LOVE/I AIN'T GOT NOBODY	4.00	7.50	5.00
☐7894		I JUST DON'T UNDERSTAND/ I DON'T HURT ANYMORE	3.50	5.50	4.00
☐7952		IT DO ME SO GOOD/GIMMIE LOVE	3.50	5.50	4.00
☐7986		WHAT AM I SUPPOSED TO DO/ LET'S STOP KIDDING EACH OTHER	3.50	5.50	4.00
☐8061		JIM DANDY/I WAS ONLY KIDDING	3.50	5.50	4.00
☐8130		SO DID I/NO MORE	3.50	5.50	4.00
☐8168		TAKE ALL THE KISSES/ BYE BYE BIRDIE	3.50	5.50	4.00
☐8295		HEY LITTLE STAR/ MAN'S FAVORITE SPORT	3.50	5.50	4.00
☐8446		SOMEDAY SOON/HE'S MY MAN	3.50	5.50	4.00
☐8734		WHAT DID I HAVE THAT I DON'T HAVE?/MR. KISS KISS BANG BANG	3.50	5.50	4.00
☐9013		YOU CAME A LONG WAY FROM ST. LOUIS/THE SWINGER	3.50	5.50	4.00
☐1	**LHI**	IT'S A NICE WORLD TO VISIT/ TURNED MY HEAD AROUND	3.50	5.50	4.00
☐2		SLEEP IN THE GRASS/CHICO	3.50	5.50	4.00
☐5		DARK END OF THE STREET/ VICTIMS OF THE NIGHT	3.50	5.50	4.00
☐11		HANGIN' ON/ WALK ON OUT OF MY MIND	3.50	5.50	4.00

LEE HAZELWOOD FEATURED ON ALL LHI RELEASES

ANN-MARGRET—ALBUMS

			Current Price Range		P/Y AVG
☐2399 (M)	**RCA**	AND HERE SHE IS!	12.00	28.00	18.00
☐2399 (S)		AND HERE SHE IS!	15.00	35.00	21.00
☐2453 (M)		ON THE WAY UP	11.00	23.00	15.00
☐2453 (S)		ON THE WAY UP	13.00	30.00	18.00
☐2551 (M)		THE VIVACIOUS ONE	8.00	18.00	12.00
☐2551 (S)		THE VIVACIOUS ONE	11.00	23.00	15.00
☐2659 (M)		BACHELOR'S PARADISE	8.00	18.00	12.00
☐2659 (S)		BACHELOR'S PARADISE	11.00	23.00	15.00
☐2690 (M)		BEAUTY AND THE BEARD (with Al Hirt)	7.00	16.00	11.00
☐2690 (S)		BEAUTY AND THE BEARD (with Al Hirt)	8.00	18.00	12.00
☐3710 (M)		THE SWINGER (soundtrack)	7.00	16.00	11.00

			Current Price Range		P/Y AVG
☐ 3710 (S)		THE SWINGER (soundtrack)	8.00	18.00	12.00
☐ 12007 (S)	*LHI*	THE COWBOY AND THE LADY			
		(with Lee Hazelwood)	8.00	18.00	12.00

PAUL ANTHONY

☐ 1003	*METRO INTERNATIONAL*	STEP UP/LOOK AT ME NOW	15.00	30.00	21.00
☐ 1103	*GAMBIT*	ANGEL FACE/HELLO TEARDROPS	15.00	30.00	21.00
☐ 4099	*ROULETTE*	MY PROMISE TO YOU/			
		BOP BOP BOP	7.00	15.00	8.50

AQUA-NITES

☐ 1000	*ASTRA*	LOVER DON'T YOU WEEP/			
		CARIOCA	20.00	37.00	22.00
☐ 2001		LOVER DON'T YOU WEEP/CHRISTI.	15.00	28.00	16.00

AQUATONES

☐ 1001	*FARGO*	YOU/SHE'S THE ONE FOR ME ...	3.50	6.00	4.50
☐ 1002		SAY YOU'LL BE MINE/SO FINE ..	4.50	8.00	6.00
☐ 1003		OUR FIRST KISS/THE DRIVE-IN .	4.50	8.00	6.00
☐ 1005		MY ONE DESIRE/MY TREASURE .	4.50	8.00	6.00
☐ 1015		EVERY TIME/THERE'S A LONG			
		LONG TRAIL	4.50	8.00	6.00
☐ 1016		CRAZY FOR YOU/WANTED	4.50	8.00	6.00
☐ 1022		MY TREASURE/			
		SAY YOU'LL BE MINE	4.50	8.00	4.00
☐ 1111		MY DARLING/FOR YOU, FOR YOU	4.50	8.00	6.00

AQUATONES—ALBUM

☐ 3001 (M)	*FARGO*	THE AQUATONES SING	28.00	66.00	60.00

THE ARCHIES
FEATURED: RON DANTE

☐ 1006	*CALENDAR*	BANG SHANG A LANG/			
		TRUCK DRIVER	2.00	3.50	2.50
☐ 1007		FEELIN' SO GOOD/LOVE LIGHT ..	2.00	3.50	2.50
☐ 1008		SUGAR SUGAR/MELODY HILL ...	2.00	3.50	2.50
☐ 5002	*KIRSHNER*	JINGLE JANGLE/JUSTINE	1.50	3.00	1.75
☐ 5003		WHO'S YOUR BABY?/			
		SENORITA RITA	1.50	3.00	1.75
☐ 1009		SUNSHINE/OVER AND OVER	1.50	3.00	1.75
☐ 5009		TOGETHER WE TWO/			
		EVERYTHING'S ALRIGHT	1.50	3.00	1.75
☐ 5011		THIS IS LOVE/			
		THROW A LITTLE LOVE MY WAY .	1.50	3.00	1.75
☐ 5014		MAYBE I'M WRONG/			
		A SUMMER PRAYER FOR PEACE	1.50	3.00	1.75
☐ 5018		LOVE IS LIVING IN YOU/			
		HOLD ON TO LOVIN'	1.50	3.00	1.75
☐ 5021		PLUMB CRAZY/			
		STRANGERS IN THE MORNING .	1.50	3.00	1.75

THE ARCHIES — ALBUMS

☐ 101	*CALENDAR*	THE ARCHIES	8.00	15.00	12.00
☐ 103		EVERYTHING'S ARCHIE	8.00	15.00	12.00
☐ 103	*KIRSHNER*	SUGAR SUGAR	4.00	11.00	8.50
☐ 105		JINGLE JANGLE	4.00	11.00	8.50
☐ 107		SUNSHINE	4.00	11.00	8.50
☐ 109		THE ARCHIES' GREATEST HITS ..	4.00	11.00	8.50
☐ 110		THIS IS LOVE	4.00	11.00	8.50
☐ 0221	*RCA SPECIAL PRODUCTS*	THE ARCHIES	5.00	12.00	10.00

VANCE ARNOLD (JOE COCKER)

☐ 40255	*PHILLIPS*	I'LL CRY INSTEAD/			
		THOSE PRECIOUS WORDS	5.00	9.00	7.00

			Current Price Range		P/Y AVG

ARROGANTS

☐6226	**LUTE**	CANADIAN SUNSET/ MIRROR MIRROR	3.00	14.00	12.00
☐200	**VANESS**	TAKE LIKE EASY/STONE BROKE .	6.50	12.00	10.00
☐12184	**BIG "A"**	MAKE UP YOUR MIND/TOMBOY .	5.50	12.00	10.00

DEL ASHLEY (DAVID GATES)
SEE: BREAD

☐103	**PLANETARY**	LITTLE MISS STUCK-UP/ THE BRIGHTER SIDE	5.00	9.00	7.00

ASTRONAUTS

☐459	**JAN ELL**	GENEVA TWIST/TAKE 17	4.25	7.00	5.50
☐100	**LUNEY**	RIDGE ROUTE/BLAST OFF	4.25	7.00	5.20
☐1000	**VANRUS**	SKI LIFT/BLUES BEAT	4.25	7.00	5.20
☐8194	**RCA**	BAJA/ KUK	3.50	5.50	4.00
☐8224		HOT DOGGIN'/EVERYONE BUT ME	3.00	5.00	3.50
☐8298		SURF PARTY/ COMPETITION COUPE	3.00	5.00	3.50
☐8364		SWIM LITTLE MERMAID/ GO FIGHT FOR HER	3.00	5.00	3.50
☐8419		RIDE THE WILD SURF/ AROUND AND AROUND	3.00	5.00	3.50
☐8463		I'M A FOOL/CAN'T YOU SEE I DO	3.00	5.00	3.50
☐8499		ALMOST GROWN/ MY SIN IS PRIDE	3.00	5.00	3.50
☐8628		IT DOESN'T MATTER ANYMORE/ THE LA LA LA SONG	3.00	5.00	3.50

ASTRONAUTS—ALBUMS

☐183 (M)	**RCA**	ROCKIN' WITH THE ASTRONAUTS	15.00	34.00	30.00
☐2760 (M)		SURFIN' WITH THE ASTRONAUTS	9.00	20.00	18.00
☐2760 (S)		SURFIN' WITH THE ASTRONAUTS	12.00	29.00	25.00
☐2782 (M)		EVERYTHING IS A-OK	9.00	20.00	18.00
☐2782 (S)		EVERYTHING IS A-OK	9.50	25.00	22.50
☐2858 (M)		COMPETITION COUPE	9.00	20.00	18.00
☐2858 (S)		COMPETITION COUPE	10.00	14.00	12.50
☐2903 (M)		THE ASTRONAUTS ORBIT CAMPUS	7.00	17.00	15.00
☐2903 (S)		THE ASTRONAUTS ORBIT CAMPUS	9.00	20.00	18.00
☐3307 (M)		GO GO GO....................	7.00	17.00	15.00
☐3307 (S)		GO GO GO....................	9.00	20.00	18.00
☐3359 (M)		FAVORITES FOR YOU	7.00	17.00	15.00
☐3359 (S)		FAVORITES FOR YOU	9.00	20.00	18.00
☐3454 (M)		DOWN THE LINE	7.00	17.00	15.00
☐3454 (S)		DOWN THE LINE	9.00	20.00	18.00
☐3733 (M)		TRAVELIN' MEN	7.00	17.00	15.00
☐3733 (S)		TRAVELIN' MEN	9.00	20.00	18.00

ATTILA—ALBUM
FEATURED: BILLY JOEL

☐30030 (S)	**EPIC**	ATTILA....................	22.00	45.00	29.00

AUDREY

☐104	**PLUS**	DEAR ELVIS (PAGE 1)/(PAGE 2) ..	20.00	40.00	29.00

THE AUTUMNS

☐856	**AMBER**	NEVER/EXODUS	2.00	3.50	2.50
☐208	**MEDIEVAL**	DEAREST LITTLE ANGEL/ MAUREEN	3.00	5.00	4.00

FRANKIE AVALON

☐0006	**X**	TRUMPET SORRENTO/THE BOOK	11.00	19.00	14.00

ABC-PARAMOUNT, 10040, 45 RPM

CAPITOL, DKAP 2893, LP

			Current Price Range		P/Y AVG
0026		TRUMPET TARANTELLA/ DORMI, DORMI	11.00	19.00	14.00
		X LABELS READ "BY 11 YEAR OLD FRANKIE AVALON"			
1004	CHANCELLOR	CUPID/JIVIN' WITH THE SAINTS	6.50	11.50	9.00
1006		TEACHER'S PET/SHY GUY	5.00	9.00	7.50
1011		DEDE DINAH/OOH LA LA	3.25	6.00	4.25
1016		YOU EXCITE ME/DARLIN'	3.25	6.00	4.25
1021		GINGERBREAD/BLUE BETTY	3.25	6.00	4.25
1026		I'LL WAIT FOR YOU/ WHAT LITTLE GIRL	3.25	5.50	4.00
1031		VENUS/I'M BROKE	3.25	5.50	4.00
1036		BOBBY SOX TO STOCKINGS/ A BOY WITHOUT A GIRL	3.25	5.50	4.00
1040		JUST ASK YOUR HEART/ TWO FOOLS	3.25	5.50	4.00
1045		WHY/SWINGIN' ON A RAINBOW	3.25	5.50	4.00
1048		DON'T THROW AWAY ALL THOSE TEARDROPS/TALK TALK TALK	3.25	5.50	4.00
1052		WHERE ARE YOU/ TUXEDO JUNCTION	3.25	5.50	4.00
1056		TOGETHERNESS/DON'T LET LOVE PASS ME BY	3.25	5.50	4.00
1065		A PERFECT LOVE/ THE PUPPET SONG	3.25	5.50	4.00
1071		ALL OF EVERYTHING/ CALL ME ANYTIME	3.25	5.50	4.00
1077		GOTTA GET A GIRL/ WHO ELSE BUT YOU	3.25	5.50	4.00
1081		THE SUMMER OF '61/VOYAGE TO THE BOTTOM OF THE SEA	3.25	5.50	4.00
1087		TRUE TRUE LOVE/MARRIED	3.25	5.50	4.00
1095		SLEEPING BEAUTY/ THE LONELY BIT	3.25	5.50	4.00
1101		AFTER YOU'VE GONE/IF YOU DON'T THINK I'M LEAVING	3.25	5.50	4.00
1107		YOU ARE MINE/PONCHINELLA	3.25	5.50	4.00
1114		VENUS/I'M BROKE (reissue)	3.25	5.00	3.25
1115		A MIRACLE/DON'T LET ME STAND IN YOUR WAY	3.25	5.50	4.00
1125		WELCOME HOME/ DANCE BOSSA NOVA	3.25	5.50	4.00
1131		MY EX-BEST FRIEND/ FIRST LOVE NEVER DIES	3.25	5.50	4.00
1134		COME FLY WITH ME/ GIRL BACK HOME	3.25	5.50	4.00
1135		CLEOPATRA/HEARTBEATS	3.25	5.50	4.00
1139		BEACH PARTY/DON'T STOP NOW	3.25	5.50	4.00
FX-1		CHRISTMAS HOLIDAY/ DEAR GESU BAMBINO	3.00	5.00	3.50
0697	REPRISE	BUT I DO/ DANCING ON THE STARS	2.00	4.50	3.00
0826		FOR YOU LOVE/WHY DON'T THEY UNDERSTAND	2.00	4.50	3.00
728	UNITED ARTISTS	AGAIN/DON'T MAKE FUN OF ME	2.00	4.50	3.00
748		MY LOVE IS HERE TO STAY/NEW FANGLED JINGLE JANGLE SWIMMING SUIT FROM PARIS	2.00	4.50	3.00
800		MOON RIVER/EVERY GIRL SHOULD GET MARRIED	2.00	4.50	3.00
895		THERE'LL BE RAINBOWS AGAIN/ I'LL TAKE SWEDEN	2.00	4.50	3.00
20	X	A VERY YOUNG MAN WITH A HORN	14.00	24.00	20.00

FRANKIE AVALON

Frankie Avalon (real name Avalonne) first saw life in Philadelpha on September 18, 1940. Originally he wished to someday become a reknowned boxer. Then he saw a movie entitled "Young Man With a Horn". That did it. Avalon switched his future ambition to that of trumpeteer. His father purchased a trumpet, and Avalon cut a pair of 1952 singles on which he played his trumpet. He was eleven years old at the time.

As a teenager Avalon signed with Chancellor Records. His first two singles bombed, but his third attempt was a smash hit — and somewhat of a fluke. Frankie held his nose and sang while horsing around, waiting for the final rehearsal of "DeDe Dinah". The producer correctly sensed that the gimmick might provide Chancellor with a novelty hit.

After No. 1 singles like "Venus" and "Why" Frankie's career faded; however, he later resurfaced in several beach-party movies during the 1960s. Today he, his wife (a former dental assistant) and their eight children live in Hollywood. A disco version of "Venus" pumped some temporary life into Avalon's career in 1976.

			Current Price Range		P/Y AVG
		FRANKIE AVALON—EPs			
A-5001	*CHANCELLOR*	FRANKIE AVALON. VOL. I	6.50	11.50	9.00
B-5001		FRANKIE AVALON. VOL. II	6.50	11.50	9.00
C-5001		FRANKIE AVALON. VOL. III	6.50	11.50	9.00
A-5002		THE YOUNG FRANKIE AVALON	6.50	11.50	9.00
B-5002		THE YOUNG FRANKIE AVALON	6.50	11.50	9.00
C-5002		THE YOUNG FRANKIE AVALON	6.50	11.50	9.00
A-5004		SWINGIN' ON A RAINBOW	5.00	8.50	7.00
B-5004		SWINGIN' ON A RAINBOW	5.00	8.50	7.00
C-5004		SWINGIN' ON A RAINBOW	5.00	8.50	7.00
A-5011		SUMMER SCENE	8.00	13.00	11.00
B-5011		SUMMER SCENE	8.00	13.00	11.00
C-5011		SUMMER SCENE	8.00	13.00	11.00
A-5012		THE GOOD OLD SUMMERTIME	8.00	13.00	11.00
B-5012		THE GOOD OLD SUMMERTIME	8.00	13.00	11.00
C-5012		THE GOOD OLD SUMMERTIME	8.00	13.00	11.00
302		GUNS OF THE TIMBERLAND	8.50	14.00	12.00
303		BALLAD OF THE ALAMO	8.50	13.00	11.00
		FRANKIE AVALON—ALBUMS			
5001 (M)	*CHANCELLOR*	FRANKIE AVALON	14.00	34.00	30.00
5002 (M)		THE YOUNG FRANKIE AVALON	12.00	29.00	25.00
5004 (M)		SWINGIN' ON A RAINBOW	12.00	29.00	25.00
5009 (M)		AVALON AND FABIAN	12.00	29.00	25.00
5011 (M)		SUMMER SCENE	9.50	25.00	22.50
5018 (M)		A WHOLE LOTTA FRANKIE (greatest hits)	9.50	25.00	22.50
5022 (M)		AND NOW. ABOUT MR. AVALON	9.00	20.00	18.00
5022 (S)		AND NOW. ABOUT MR. AVALON	12.00	29.00	25.00
5025 (M)		ITALIANO	9.00	20.00	18.00
5025 (S)		ITALIANO	12.00	29.00	25.00
5027 (M)		YOU ARE MINE	9.00	20.00	18.00
5027 (S)		YOU ARE MINE	12.00	29.00	25.00
5031 (M)		FRANKIE AVALON'S CHRISTMAS ALBUM	9.00	20.00	18.00
5031 (S)		FRANKIE AVALON'S CHRISTMAS ALBUM	12.00	29.00	25.00
5032 (M)		FRANKIE AVALON SINGS CLEOPATRA	7.00	17.00	15.00
5032 (S)		FRANKIE AVALON SINGS CLEOPATRA	9.00	20.00	18.00

AVERAGE WHITE BAND

			Current Price Range		P/Y AVG
40196	*MCA*	HOW CAN YOU GO HOME	2.50	5.00	3.50
3229	*ATLANTIC*	WORK TO DO/PICK UP THE PIECES	2.00	4.50	3.00
3261		PERSON TO PERSON/ CUT THE CAKE	2.00	4.50	3.00
3285		IF I EVER LOSE THIS HEAVEN/ HIGH FLYIN' WOMAN	2.00	4.50	3.00
3354		WOULD YOU STAY/ QUEEN OF MY SOUL	2.00	4.50	3.00
3363		SOUL SEARCHING/ A LOVE OF YOUR OWN	2.00	4.50	3.00

B

BABY DOLLS

			Current Price Range		P/Y AVG
021	*ELGIN*	BOYFRIEND/IS THIS THE END?	9.00	18.00	16.00

BABY RAY AND THE FERNS (FRANK ZAPPA)

			Current Price Range		P/Y AVG
1378	*DONNA*	THE WORLD'S GREATEST SINNER/ HOW'S YOUR BIRD	11.00	20.00	13.00

			Current Price Range		P/Y AVG

BADFINGER
SEE: IVEYS

☐ 1815	**APPLE**	COME AND GET IT/			
		ROCK OF ALL AGES	2.50	5.00	3.00
☐ 1822		NO MATTER WHAT/			
		CARRY ON UNTIL TOMORROW .	2.50	5.00	3.00
☐ 1841		DAY AFTER DAY/MONEY	2.50	5.00	3.00
☐ 1844		BABY BLUE/FLYING	2.50	5.00	3.00
☐ 1864		APPLE OF MY EYE/BLIND OWL ..	2.50	5.00	3.50
☐ 7801	**WARNER BROTHERS**	I MISS YOU/SHINE ON	3.00	5.50	4.00

BADFINGER—ALBUMS

☐ 3364 (S)	**APPLE**	MAGIC CHRISTIAN MUSIC	9.00	20.00	18.00
☐ 3367 (S)		NO DICE	7.00	17.00	15.00
☐ 3387 (S)		STRAIGHT UP	7.00	17.00	15.00
☐ 3411 (S)		ASS	7.00	17.00	15.00
☐ 2762 (S)	**WARNER BROTHERS**	BADFINGER	6.00	15.00	13.50
☐ 2827 (S)		WISH YOU WERE HERE	6.00	15.00	13.50

JOAN BAEZ

☐ 35012	**VANGUARD**	BANKS OF THE OHIO/OLD BLUE .	3.50	7.00	5.50
☐ 35013		PAL OF MINE/LONESOME ROAD .	3.00	5.50	4.50
☐ 35023		WE SHALL OVERCOME/WHAT HAVE THEY DONE TO THE RAIN	2.00	5.00	3.50
☐ 35031		DADDY YOU BEEN ON MY MIND/ THERE BUT FOR FORTUNE	2.00	5.00	3.50
☐ 35040		SWALLOW SONG/ PACK UP YOUR SORROWS	2.00	5.00	3.50
☐ 35055		NORTH/BE NOT TOO HARD	2.00	5.00	3.50
☐ 35092		ROCK SALT & NAILS/IF I KNEW ..	2.00	4.50	3.00
☐ 35138		NIGHT THEY DROVE OLD DIXIE DOWN/WHEN TIME IS STOLEN	2.00	4.50	3.00
☐ 35145		LET IT BE/ POOR WAYFARING STRANGER .	2.00	4.50	3.00
☐ 32890	**DECCA**	SILENT RUNNING/ REJOICE IN THE SUN	2.00	4.50	3.00
☐ 1334	**A&M**	SONG OF BANGLADESH/ PRISON TRILOGY	2.00	4.50	3.00
☐ 1362		IN THE QUIET MORNING/ TO BOBBY	3.00	5.00	3.50
☐ 1393		LOVE SONG TO A STRANGER/ TUMBLEWEED	2.00	4.50	3.00
☐ 74-0568	**RCA**	BALLAD OF SACCO & VANZETTI/ HERE'S TO YOU	3.00	5.50	4.00
☐ 700006	**PORTRAIT**	ALTAR BOY & THE THIEF/ I'M BLOWIN' AWAY	2.00	5.00	3.00

JOAN BAEZ—ALBUMS

☐ VSD-2077 (S)	**VANGUARD**	JOAN BAEZ	12.00	35.00	32.00
☐ VSD7-9160 (S)		JOAN BAEZ	7.00	20.00	18.00
☐ VSD-2097 (S)		JOAN BAEZ, VOL. II	12.00	35.00	32.00
☐ VSD-2122 (S)		IN CONCERT, VOL. I	7.00	20.00	18.00
☐ VSD-2123 (S)		IN CONCERT, VOL. II	7.00	20.00	18.00
☐ VSD-49/50 (S)		COMTEMPORARY BALLAD BOOK .	5.00	15.00	13.50
☐ VSD7-9230 (S)		NOEL	6.50	20.00	18.00
☐ VSD7-9310 (S)		ONE DAY AT A TIME	5.00	15.00	13.50
☐ VSD7-9320 (S)		MILAN	5.00	15.00	13.50
☐ VS-6560/61 (S)		THE FIRST 10 YEARS	10.00	30.00	28.00
		A TWO-DISC ALBUM WITH ACCOMPANYING BOOKLET			
☐ VD57-9313 (S)		CARRY IT ON	5.00	15.00	13.50
☐ VS-6570 (S)		BLESSED ARE	5.00	15.00	13.50
☐ VS07-9275 (S)		BAPTISM	4.00	14.00	12.50

			Current Price Range		P/Y AVG
☐ 5015 (M)	*FANTASY*	JOAN BAEZ IN SAN FRANCISCO ..	10.00	29.00	25.00
☐ SP-3614 (S)	*A&M*	GRACIAS A LA VIDA............	5.00	15.00	13.50
☐ SP-3704 (S)		FROM EVERY STAGE	5.00	15.00	13.50
☐ SP-4339 (S)		COME FROM THE SHADOWS	5.00	15.00	13.50
☐ QU-54339 (QUAD)		COME FROM THE SHADOWS	7.00	20.00	18.00

MARTY BALIN
SEE: JEFFERSON AIRPLANE

☐ 9146	*CHALLENGE*	NOBODY BUT YOU/			
		YOU MADE ME FALL	10.00	20.00	11.00
☐ 9156		I SPECIALIZE IN LOVE/			
		YOU'RE ALIVE WITH LOVE	10.00	20.00	11.00

FLORENCE BALLARD
SEE: SUPREMES

☐ 11074	*ABC*	GOIN' OUT OF MY HEAD/IT			
		DOESN'T MATTER HOW I SAY IT	3.00	5.50	4.00
☐ 11144		LOVE AIN'T LOVE/			
		FOREVER FAITHFUL	3.00	5.50	4.00

HANK BALLARD AND THE MIDNIGHTERS
SEE: MIDNIGHTERS, ROYALS

☐ 5171	*KING*	THE TWIST/			
		TEARDROPS ON YOUR LETTER .	3.50	5.50	4.00
☐ 5195		KANSAS CITY/			
		I'LL KEEP YOU HAPPY	3.50	5.50	4.00
☐ 5215		SUGAREE/RAIN DOWN TEARS ...	3.50	5.50	4.00
☐ 5245		CUTE LITTLE WAYS/			
		HOUSE WITH NO WINDOWS ...	3.50	5.50	4.00
☐ 5275		NEVER KNEW/I COULD LOVE YOU	3.50	5.50	4.00
☐ 5289		LOOK AT LITTLE SISTER/			
		I SAID I WOULDN'T BEG	3.50	5.50	4.00
☐ 5312		THE COFFEE GRIND/WAITING ...	3.50	5.50	4.00
☐ 5341		FINGER POPPIN' TIME/			
		I LOVE YOU. I LOVE YOU SO-0-0	3.50	5.50	4.00
☐ 5400		LET'S GO. LET'S GO. LET'S GO/			
		IF YOU'D FORGIVE ME	3.50	5.50	4.00
☐ 5430		THE HOOCHI COOCHI COO/			
		I'M THINKING OF YOU	3.50	5.50	4.00
☐ 5449		ROCK JUNCTION/SPONGIE ...	3.50	5.50	4.00
☐ 5459		LET'S GO AGAIN/DEEP BLUE SEA	3.50	5.50	4.00
☐ 5491		THE CONTINENTAL WALK/			
		WHAT'S THIS I SEE?	3.50	5.50	4.00
☐ 5510		THE SWITCH-A-ROO/THE FLOAT .	3.50	5.50	4.00
☐ 5535		NOTHING BUT GOOD/			
		KEEP ON DANCING	3.50	5.50	4.00
☐ 5550		CAN'T YOU SEE — I NEED A			
		FRIEND/BIG RED SUNSET	3.50	5.50	4.00
☐ 5578		I'M GONNA MISS YOU/			
		DO YOU REMEMBER?	3.50	5.50	4.00
☐ 5593		DO YOU KNOW HOW TO TWIST?/			
		BROADWAY	3.50	5.50	4.00

LATER KING SINGLES ARE WORTH UP TO $1.75 MINT

HANK BALLARD AND THE MIDNIGHTERS—EPs

☐ 435	*KING*	SINGIN' AND SWINGIN'. VOL. I ..	11.00	23.00	15.00
☐ 451		SINGIN' AND SWINGIN'. VOL. II .	11.00	23.00	15.00
☐ 793		JUMPIN'	9.00	20.00	12.00

HANK BALLARD AND THE MIDNIGHTERS—ALBUMS

☐ 541 (M)	*KING*	THEIR GREATEST JUKE BOX HITS	22.00	55.00	35.00
☐ 581 (M)		HANK BALLARD AND THE			
		MIDNIGHTERS	16.00	38.00	24.00
☐ 618 (M)		SINGIN' AND SWINGIN'	14.00	31.00	21.00
☐ 674 (M)		THE ONE AND ONLY	14.00	31.00	21.00
☐ 700 (M)		MR. RHYTHM AND BLUES	14.00	31.00	21.00

			Current Price Range		P/Y AVG
☐740 (M)		SPOTLIGHT ON HANK BALLARD ..	14.00	31.00	21.00
☐748 (M)		LET'S GO AGAIN	14.00	31.00	21.00
☐759 (M)		DANCE ALONG...............	11.00	26.00	18.00
☐781 (M)		THE TWISTIN' FOOLS	10.00	22.00	15.00
☐793 (M)		JUMPIN' HANK BALLARD AND THE MIDNIGHTERS	10.00	22.00	15.00
☐815 (M)		THE 1963 SOUND OF HANK BALLARD AND THE MIDNIGHTERS	8.00	19.00	12.00
☐867 (M)		BIGGEST HITS	8.00	19.00	12.00
☐896 (M)		A STAR IN YOUR EYES	8.00	19.00	12.00
☐913 (M)		THOSE LAZY, LAZY DAYS	8.00	19.00	12.00
☐927 (M)		GLAD SONGS, SAD SONGS	8.00	19.00	12.00
☐950 (M)		24 HIT TUNES	8.00	19.00	12.00

THE BAND
SEE: CANADIAN SQUIRES, RONNIE HAWKINS AND THE HAWKS, LEVON AND THE HAWKS

☐2041	**CAPITOL**	JABBERWOCKY/ NEVER TOO MUCH LOVE	3.00	5.00	3.50
☐2269		THE WEIGHT/ I SHALL BE RELEASED	2.00	4.50	3.00
☐2635		UP ON CRIPPLE CREEK/ THE NIGHT THEY DROVE OLD DIXIE DOWN	2.00	4.50	3.00
☐2705		RAG MAMA RAG/ UNFAITHFUL SERVANT	2.00	4.50	3.00
☐2870		TIME TO KILL/THE SHAPE I'M IN	2.00	4.50	3.00
☐3199		LIFE IS A CARNIVAL/ THE MOON STRUCK ONE	2.00	4.50	3.00
☐3249		WHEN I PAINT MY MASTERPIECE/ WHERE DO WE GO FROM HERE .	2.00	4.50	3.00
☐3433		DON'T DO IT/RAG MAMA RAG ...	2.00	4.50	3.00
☐3500		CALEDONIA MISSION/HANG UP MY ROCK 'N ROLL SHOES	2.00	4.50	3.00
☐3758		AIN'T GOT NO HOME/ GET UP JAKE	2.00	4.50	3.00
☐3828		THIRD MAN THEME/W. S. WALCOTT MEDICINE SHOW ...	2.00	4.50	3.00
☐4316		THE TWILIGHT/ ACADIAN DRIFTWOOD	2.00	4.50	3.00

THE BAND—ALBUMS

☐2955 (S)	**CAPITOL**	MUSIC FROM BIG PINK	5.50	14.00	12.00
☐132 (S)		THE BAND	5.00	12.00	10.00
☐425 (S)		STAGE FRIGHT...............	5.00	12.00	10.00
☐651 (S)		CAHOOTS..................	5.00	12.00	10.00
☐11045 (S)		ROCK OF AGES	5.00	12.00	10.00
☐11214 (S)		MOONDOG MATINEE	5.00	12.00	10.00
☐11440 (S)		NORTHERN LIGHTS, SOUTHERN LIGHTS	5.00	12.00	10.00

BARBARIANS

☐290	**JOY**	HEY LITTLE BIRD/ YOU'VE GOT TO UNDERSTAND .	4.50	7.50	6.50
☐3308	**LAURIE**	ARE YOU A BOY OR ARE YOU A GIRL/TAKE IT OR LEAVE IT	3.00	5.00	3.50
☐3321		SUSIE Q/ WHAT THE NEW BREED SAY ...	3.00	5.00	3.50
☐3326		MOULTY/ I'LL KEEP ON SEEING YOU	3.00	5.00	3.50

BARBARIANS—ALBUM

☐2033 (M)		THE BARBARIANS	17.00	38.00	35.00
☐2033 (S)		THE BARBARIANS	20.00	49.00	45.00

			Current Price Range		P/Y AVG

ANNETTE BARD (CAROL CONNORS)
SEE: TEDDY BEARS

☐5643	IMPERIAL	WHAT DIFFERENCE DOES IT MAKE?/ALIBI	5.50	11.00	9.00

BOBBY BARE

☐835	FRATERNITY	THE ALL AMERICAN BOY/RUBBER DOLLY (by Bill Parsons on label)	3.00	5.50	4.00
☐838		EDUCATED ROCK AND ROLL/ THE CAREFREE WANDERER (by Bill Parsons on label)	3.50	6.00	4.50
☐861		I'M HANGING UP MY RIFLE/ THAT'S WHERE I WANT TO BE.	3.00	8.50	7.00
☐867		MORE THAN A POOR BOY COULD GIVE/SWEET SINGIN' SAM	3.50	6.00	4.50
☐871		NO LETTER FROM MY BABY/ LYNCHIN' PARTY	3.00	5.50	4.00
☐878		BOOK OF LOVE/LORENA	3.50	6.00	4.50
☐885		ISLAND OF LOVE/SAILOR MAN	3.00	5.50	4.00
☐890		ZIG ZAG/BROOKLYN BRIDGE	3.50	6.00	4.50
☐892		THAT MEAN OLD CLOCK/ THE DAY MY RAINBOW FELL	3.00	5.50	4.00

BARITONES

☐501	DORE	AFTER SCHOOL ROCK/ SENTIMENTAL BABY	17.00	29.00	19.00

J. J. BARNES AND THE DELFIS

☐913	RICH	MY LOVE CAME TUMBLING DOWN/ WON'T YOU LET ME KNOW	18.00	33.00	22.00

THE DELFIS WERE MARTHA AND THE VANDELLAS

STEVE BARRI
SEE: FANTASTIC BAGGIES

☐1003	RONA	DOWN AROUND THE CORNER/ PLEASE LET IT BE YOU	5.50	8.50	7.00
☐1004		THE STORY OF THE RING/ I WANT YOUR LOVE	5.50	8.50	7.00
☐1005		TWO DIFFERENT WORLDS/DON'T RUN AWAY FROM LOVE	5.50	8.50	7.00
☐1006		WHENEVER YOU KISS ME/ NEVER BEFORE	5.50	8.50	7.00

BARRIES

☐102	VERNON	WHY DON'T YOU WRITE ME/ MARY-ANN	9.50	17.00	15.00
☐1101	EMBER	TONIGHT TONIGHT/MARY-ANN	8.50	14.00	12.00

BARRY AND THE TAMERLANES
FEATURED: BARRY DeVORZON

☐6034	VALIANT	I WONDER WHAT SHE'S DOING TONIGHT/DON'T GO	3.00	5.00	3.50
☐6040		ROBERTA/BUTTERFLY	3.00	5.00	3.50
☐6046		LUCKY GUY/I DON'T WANT TO BE YOUR CLOWN	3.00	5.00	3.50
☐6050		A DATE WITH JUDY/ PRETTY THINGS	3.00	5.00	3.50
☐6059		DON'T CRY CINDY/GEE	3.00	5.00	3.50

BARRY AND THE TAMERLANES—ALBUM

☐406 (M)	VALIANT	I WONDER WHAT SHE'S DOING TONIGHT	9.50	17.00	15.00

			Current Price Range		P/Y AVG

JEFF BARRY
SEE: RAINDROPS

☐ 7477	**RCA**	IT'S CALLED ROCK AND ROLL/ HIP COUPLES	11.00	20.00	18.00
☐ 7797		LONELY LIPS/ FACE FROM OUTER SPACE	11.00	20.00	18.00
☐ 7821		ALL YOU NEED IS A QUARTER/ TEEN QUARTET	8.50	14.00	12.00
☐ 31037	**DECCA**	IT WON'T HURT/NEVER NEVER . .	8.50	14.00	12.00
☐ 31089		WHY DOES THE FEELING GO AWAY/LENORE	8.50	14.00	12.00

JEFF BARRY—ALBUM

☐ 4393 (S)		WALKING IN THE SUN	7.50	17.00	15.00

JOE BARRY

☐ 144	**JIN**	I'M A FOOL TO CARE/ I GOT A FEELING	5.50	11.00	9.00
☐ 1702	**SMASH**	I'M A FOOL TO CARE/ I GOT A FEELING	2.50	5.00	3.00
☐ 1710		TEARDROPS IN MY HEART/ FOR YOU. SUNSHINE	2.50	5.00	3.00
☐ 1745		WHY DID YOU SAY GOODBYE?/ LITTLE PAPOOSE	2.50	5.00	3.00
☐ 1762		JUST BECAUSE/LITTLE JEWEL OF THE VEAUX CARRE	2.50	5.00	3.00

BAY CITY ROLLERS

☐ 45169	**BELL**	KEEP ON DANCING/ALRIGHT	3.25	5.50	4.00
☐ 45274		MANANA/(DJ)	3.25	5.50	4.00
☐ 45481		SHANG A LANG/(DJ)	3.25	5.50	4.00
☐ 45607		SUMMER LOVE SENSATION/(DJ)	3.25	5.50	4.00
☐ 45618		ALL OF ME LOVES YOU/(DJ)	3.25	5.50	4.00
☐ 120	**ARISTA**	BYE BYE BABY/IT'S FOR YOU . . .	3.25	5.50	4.00
☐ 149		SATURDAY NIGHT/MARLINA	2.00	4.50	2.50
☐ 170		MONEY HONEY/MARYANNE	2.00	4.50	2.50
☐ 185		ROCK AND ROLL LOVE LETTER/ SHANGHAI'D IN LOVE	2.00	4.50	2.50
☐ 193		DON'T STOP THE MUSIC (Disco)/ DON'T STOP THE MUSIC (Short)	2.00	4.50	3.50
☐ 205		I ONLY WANT TO BE WITH YOU/ WRITE A LETTER	2.00	3.50	2.50
☐ 216		YESTERDAY'S HERO/MY LISA . .	2.00	3.50	2.50
☐ 233		DEDICATION/ROCK 'N ROLLER	2.00	3.50	2.50
☐ 256		YOU MADE ME BELIEVE IN MAGIC/ DANCE DANCE DANCE	2.00	3.50	2.50
☐ 272		THE WAY I FEEL TONIGHT/ LOVE POWER	2.00	3.50	2.50
☐ 363		WHERE WILL I BE NOW/ IF YOU WERE MY WOMAN	2.00	3.50	2.50
☐ 476		TURN ON THE RADIO/HELLO AND WELCOME HOME (Rollers) . . .	2.00	3.50	2.50

ARISTA ALBUMS ARE WORTH UP TO $10.00 MINT

BAYSIDERS

☐ 19366	**EVEREST**	OVER THE RAINBOW/MY BONNIE	3.00	5.50	4.00
☐ 19386		LOOK FOR THE SILVER LINING/ TREES	3.00	5.50	4.00
☐ 19393		THE BELLS OF ST. MARY'S/ COMIN' THROUGH THE RYE . . .	3.00	5.50	4.00

BAYSIDERS—ALBUM

☐ 5124 (M)	**EVEREST**	OVER THE RAINBOW	17.00	39.00	35.00

			Current Price Range		P/Y AVG

B. BUMBLE AND THE STINGERS

			Current Price Range		P/Y AVG
☐ 140	*RENDEZVOUS*	BUMBLE BOOGIE/SCHOOL DAY ..	3.00	5.00	3.50
☐ 151		BOOGIE WOOGIE/NEAR YOU	3.00	5.00	3.50
☐ 160		BEE HIVE/CARAVAN	3.00	5.00	3.50
☐ 166		NUT ROCKER/NAUTILUS	3.00	5.00	3.50
☐ 174		ROCKIN' ON-'N'-OFF/MASHED #5 .	3.00	5.00	3.50
☐ 179		APPLE KNOCKER/ THE MOON AND THE SEA	3.00	5.00	3.50
☐ 182		DAWN CRACKER/SCALES.......	3.00	5.00	3.50
☐ 192		BABY MASH/ NIGHT TIME MADNESS	3.00	5.00	3.50

BEACH BOYS

			Current Price Range		P/Y AVG
☐ 301	*X*	SURFIN'/LUAU	95.00	165.00	105.00
☐ 301	*CANDIX*	SURFIN'/LUAU (without ''Era Sales'' on label)	40.00	70.00	44.00
☐ 301		SURFIN'/LUAU (with ''Era Sales'' on label)	40.00	70.00	44.00
☐ 331		SURFIN'/LUAU	40.00	70.00	44.00
☐ 4777	*CAPITOL*	SURFIN' SAFARI/409	3.50	6.00	4.50
☐ 4880		TEN LITTLE INDIANS/ COUNTY FAIR	5.00	10.00	5.75
☐ 4932		SURFIN' U.S.A./SHUT DOWN ...	3.00	6.00	4.00
☐ 5009		SURFER GIRL/ LITTLE DEUCE COUPE	3.00	6.00	4.00
☐ 5069		BE TRUE TO YOUR SCHOOL/ IN MY ROOM	3.00	6.00	4.00
☐ 5096		LITTLE SAINT NICK/ THE LORD'S PRAYER	7.00	15.00	8.25
☐ 5118		FUN, FUN, FUN/WHY DO FOOLS FALL IN LOVE	3.00	5.00	3.50
☐ 5174		I GET AROUND/ DON'T WORRY BABY	3.00	5.00	3.50
☐ 5245		WHEN I GROW UP/SHE KNOWS ME TOO WELL	3.00	5.00	3.50
☐ 5306		DANCE, DANCE, DANCE/ THE WARMTH OF THE SUN	3.00	5.00	3.50
☐ 5312		THE MAN WITH ALL THE TOYS/ BLUE CHRISTMAS	6.00	11.00	7.00
☐ 5372		DO YOU WANNA DANCE?/ PLEASE LET ME WONDER	3.00	5.00	3.50
☐ 5395		HELP ME RHONDA/KISS ME BABY.	3.00	5.00	3.50
☐ 5464		CALIFORNIA GIRLS/ LET HIM RUN WILD	3.00	5.00	3.50
☐ 5540		THE LITTLE GIRL I ONCE KNEW/ THERE'S NO OTHER	3.00	5.00	3.50
☐ 5561		BARBARA ANN/ GIRL DON'T TELL ME	3.00	5.00	3.50
☐ 5602		SLOOP JOHN B/ YOU'RE SO GOOD TO ME	3.00	5.00	3.50
☐ 5676		GOOD VIBRATIONS/LET'S GO AWAY FOR AWHILE	3.00	5.00	3.50
☐ 5706		WOULDN'T IT BE NICE/ GOD ONLY KNOWS	3.00	5.00	3.50
☐ 2028		WILD HONEY/WIND CHIMES	3.00	5.00	3.50
☐ 2068		DARLIN'/HERE TODAY	3.00	5.00	3.50
☐ 2160		FRIENDS/LITTLE BIRD	3.00	4.50	4.00
☐ 2239		DO IT AGAIN/WAKE THE WORLD .	3.00	4.50	4.00
☐ 2360		BLUEBIRDS OVER THE MOUNTAIN/ NEVER LEARN NOT TO LOVE ...	3.50	6.00	4.50
☐ 2432		I CAN HEAR MUSIC/ ALL I WANT TO DO	3.00	5.50	4.00
☐ 2530		BREAK AWAY/ CELEBRATE THE NEWS	7.00	12.00	10.00

BEACH BOYS

It was initally a family affair — Brian Wilson formed a rock group with brothers Dennis and Carl and first-cousin Mike Love. Neighbor Larry Marks was then brought in but he was soon replaced by another neighbor, aspiring folk singer Al Jardine.

Brian called his group Kenny and the Cadets and cut an unpolished single called "Barbee", which went nowhere. He then changed the group's name to the Pendletons for another original song, "Surfin'." The song was recorded for Los Angeles' small Candix label. At that session, Dennis Wilson drummed on the bottom of a plastic garbage pail.

When the single was released, though, Candix had redubbed the group the Beach Boys. "We hated that name," Brian later grumbled," but we had to go with it." "Surfin' Safari" became a big Los Angeles hit, but it took "Surfin' Safari" to get things really rolling for the Hawthrone, CA hotshots.

By the end of 1963, the Beach Boys had dropped their successful surf/hot-car formula but stayed basically in the teen vein until their masterpiece of "Good Vibrations". It took four months and $50,000 to produce the Beach Boys' last number-one hit.

They remain today as America's longest-surviving rock group, carrying on without mentor Brian Wilson on a regular basis, but still playing to sellout crowds everywhere.

			Current Price Range		P/Y AVG
☐ 2765		COTTON FIELDS/ THE NEAREST FARAWAY PLACE.	8.50	17.00	15.00
☐ 2937		SALT LAKE CITY/AMUSEMENT PARKS U.S.A. (promotional) . . .	120.00	225.00	140.00
☐	*CAPITOL CUSTOM*	BOOGIE WOODIE/ SPIRIT OF AMERICA	75.00	140.00	80.00
☐ 1001	*BROTHER*	HEROES AND VILLAINS/ YOU'RE WELCOME	3.00	5.00	3.50
☐ 1002		GETTIN' HUNGRY/ DEVOTED TO YOU	3.50	5.50	4.50
☐ 0894	*REPRISE*	ADD SOME MUSIC TO YOUR DAY/ SUSIE CINCINATTI	3.00	5.50	4.00
☐ 0929		THIS WHOLE WORLD/ SLIP ON THROUGH	3.50	5.50	4.50
☐ 0957		TEARS IN THE MORNING/ IT'S ABOUT TIME	3.50	5.50	4.50
☐ 0998		COOL, COOL WATER/FOREVER . .	3.50	5.50	4.50
☐ 1015		LONG PROMISED ROAD/DEIRDRE	3.50	5.50	4.50
☐ 1047		LONG PROMISED ROAD/TILL I DIE	3.50	5.50	4.00
☐ 1058		SURF'S UP/DON'T GO NEAR THE WATER	3.50	5.50	4.50
☐ 1091		CUDDLE UP/YOU NEED A MESS OF HELP TO STAND ALONE	10.00	20.00	11.00
☐ 1101		MARCELLA/ HOLD ON, DEAR BROTHER	4.50	7.00	6.00
☐ 1138		SAIL ON SAILOR/ONLY WITH YOU	4.50	7.00	6.00
☐ 1156		CALIFORNIA SAGA/ FUNKY PRETTY	4.50	7.00	6.00
☐ 1321		CHILD OF WINTER/ SUSIE CINCINATI	11.00	22.00	11.50
☐ 1325		SAIL ON SAILOR/ONLY WITH YOU	3.50	5.50	4.00
☐ 66016	*ODE*	WOULDN'T IT BE NICE/THE TIMES THEY ARE A-CHANGIN'	9.00	17.00	10.50
		BEACH BOYS—EP			
☐ 5267	*CAPITOL*	FOUR BY THE BEACH BOYS	12.00	20.00	18.00
		BEACH BOYS—ALBUMS			
☐ 1808 (M)	*CAPITOL*	SURFIN' SAFARI	8.50	20.00	18.00
☐ 1890 (M)		SURFIN' U.S.A.	7.50	17.00	15.00
☐ 1981 (M)		SURFER GIRL.	7.50	17.00	15.00
☐ 1998 (M)		LITTLE DEUCE COUPE	7.50	17.00	15.00
☐ 2027 (M)		SHUT DOWN, VOL. II	7.50	17.00	15.00
☐ 2110 (M)		ALL SUMMER LONG	7.50	17.00	15.00
☐ 2164 (M)		THE BEACH BOYS' CHRISTMAS ALBUM	8.50	20.00	18.00
☐ 2198 (M)		THE BEACH BOYS' CONCERT	6.50	15.00	13.50
		STEREO VERSIONS OF THE ABOVE HAVE THE SAME VALUE			
☐ 2269 (M)		THE BEACH BOYS TODAY!	7.50	17.00	15.00
☐ 2269 (S)		THE BEACH BOYS TODAY!	6.50	15.00	13.50
☐ 2354 (M)		SUMMER DAYS (AND SUMMER NIGHTS)	7.50	17.00	15.00
☐ 2354 (S)		SUMMER DAYS (AND SUMMER NIGHTS)	6.50	15.00	13.50
☐ 2398 (M)		THE BEACH BOYS' PARTY	6.50	15.00	13.50
☐ 2398 (S)		THE BEACH BOYS' PARTY	5.50	14.00	12.00
☐ 2458 (M)		PET SOUNDS	7.50	17.00	15.00
☐ 2458 (S)		PET SOUNDS	6.50	15.00	13.50
☐ 2545 (S)		BEST OF THE BEACH BOYS, VOL. I .	5.00	13.00	11.50
☐ 2706 (S)		BEST OF THE BEACH BOYS, VOL. II	5.00	13.00	11.50
☐ 2859 (S)		WILD HONEY	7.50	17.00	15.00
☐ 2891 (S)		SMILEY SMILE (black Capitol label)	85.00	190.00	130.00
☐ 2893 (S)		STACK-O-TRACKS (with book) . . .	40.00	85.00	58.00
☐ 2893 (S)		STACK-O-TRACKS (without book)	33.00	70.00	46.00

			Current Price Range		P/Y AVG
☐ 2895 (S)		FRIENDS	6.50	15.00	13.50
☐ 2945 (S)		BEST OF THE BEACH BOYS.			
		VOL. III	6.50	15.00	13.50
☐ 9001 (S)	*BROTHER*	SMILEY SMILE			
		(reissue of rare Capitol album)	7.50	17.00	15.00

BEACH BUMS
FEATURED: BOB SEGER

☐ 1010	*ARE YOU KIDDING ME?*	BALLAD OF THE YELLOW BERET/ FLORIDA TIME	12.00	20.00	17.50

BEATLES
SEE: PETER BEST, GEORGE HARRISON, JOHN LENNON, PAUL McCARTNEY, YOKO ONO, TONY SHERIDAN AND THE BEAT BROTHERS, RINGO STARR

☐ 0462	*POLYDOR*	WHAT'D I SAY?/YA YA	475.00	1000.00	690.00
☐ 24-673		MY BONNIE/THE SAINTS	485.00	1025.00	680.00
		Tony Sheridan and the Beat Brothers (picture sleeve with only Tony Sheridan)	900.00	2100.00	1400.00
		(picture sleeve/twist songs) ...	950.00	2300.00	1450.00
☐ 24-849		YOU ARE MY SUNSHINE/SWANEE	250.00	650.00	410.00
		Tony Sheridan and the Beat Brothers (picture sleeve)	750.00	1850.00	1200.00
☐ 24-948		MADISON KID/LET'S DANCE	275.00	680.00	420.00
		Tony Sheridan and the Beat Brothers (picture sleeve)	800.00	1950.00	1225.00
☐ 52-025		RUBY BABY?/WHAT'D I SAY? ...	310.00	650.00	430.00
		Tony Sheridan and the Beat Brothers (picture sleeve)	650.00	1400.00	950.00
☐ 52-273		MY BONNIE/THE SAINTS			
		(red label)	35.00	80.00	50.00
		(picture sleeve)	90.00	210.00	135.00
☐ 52-317		AIN'T SHE SWEET?/ IF YOU LOVE ME. BABY (German release) (red label with picture)	55.00	130.00	85.00
		(red label/no picture sleeve) ...	28.00	65.00	42.00
☐ 52-317		AIN'T SHE SWEET?/TAKE OUT SOME INSURANCE (picture sleeve).	55.00	130.00	85.00
☐ 52-324		SWEET GEORGIA BROWN/ SKINNY MINNY	40.00	90.00	53.00
		(picture sleeve)	110.00	250.00	140.00
☐ 66-833		MY BONNIE/THE SAINTS Tony Sheridan and the Beatles .	1700.00	3500.00	2200.00
		(MOST VALUABLE BEATLES' 45)			
☐ 6061	*CAPITOL STARLINE*	TWIST & SHOUT/ THERE'S A PLACE	10.00	24.00	14.00
☐ 6063		PLEASE PLEASE ME/ FROM ME TO YOU	10.00	24.00	14.00
☐ 6064		DO YOU WANT TO KNOW A SECRET?/THANK YOU GIRL ...	10.00	24.00	14.00
☐ 6065		MISERY/ROLL OVER. BEETHOVEN (green label)................	10.00	24.00	14.00
		(red and orange bullseye label) .	8.00	17.00	10.50
☐ 6066		KANSAS CITY/BOYS (green label)	10.00	24.00	14.00
		(red and orange bullseye label) .	8.00	17.00	11.00
☐ 9008		LOVE ME DO/P.S. I LOVE YOU ...	10.00	24.00	14.00
☐ 9-31382	*DECCA*	MY BONNIE/THE SAINTS Tony Sheridan and the Beat Brothers (promo. pink label) ...	425.00	975.00	575.00
		(commercial)	1600.00	3100.00	2100.00
		(silver and black label)	850.00	1800.00	1100.00

			Current Price Range		P/Y AVG
☐498	**VEE JAY**	PLEASE PLEASE ME/ASK ME WHY (promo)	145.00	335.00	200.00
		PLEASE PLEASE ME/ASK ME WHY (Beattles/thin letters)	850.00	1750.00	1085.00
☐522		PLEASE PLEASE ME/ASK ME WHY (Beattles/thick letters)	150.00	340.00	205.00
		FROM ME TO YOU/THANK YOU GIRL (promo)	30.00	70.00	42.00
		FROM ME TO YOU/THANK YOU GIRL (label name in brackets)	6.00	12.00	8.00
☐581		FROM ME TO YOU/THANK YOU GIRL (label name in oval)	9.00	21.00	14.00
		FROM ME TO YOU/PLEASE PLEASE ME (promo)	40.00	85.00	55.00
		FROM ME TO YOU/PLEASE PLEASE ME (label name in brackets)	7.00	15.00	9.50
		FROM ME TO YOU/PLEASE PLEASE ME (label name in brackets/picture sleeve)	60.00	125.00	80.00
		FROM ME TO YOU/PLEASE PLEASE ME (label name in oval)	15.00	32.00	20.00
☐587		FROM ME TO YOU/PLEASE PLEASE ME (label name in oval/picture sleeve)	65.00	135.00	85.00
		DO YOU WANT TO KNOW A SECRET?/THANK YOU GIRL (label name in brackets)	7.00	15.00	9.50
		DO YOU WANT TO KNOW A SECRET?/THANK YOU GIRL (label name in brackets/picture sleeve)	29.00	62.00	40.00
		DO YOU WANT TO KNOW A SECRET?/THANK YOU GIRL (label name in oval)	9.00	19.00	12.00
☐587		DO YOU WANT TO KNOW A SECRET?/THANK YOU GIRL (label name in oval/picture sleeve)	29.00	63.00	41.00
		DO YOU WANT TO KNOW A SECRET?/THANK YOU GIRL (promo)	24.00	50.00	33.00
☐4152	**SWAN**	SHE LOVES YOU/I'LL GET YOU (white label)	35.00	75.00	47.00
☐4152-1		SHE LOVES YOU/I'LL GET YOU (black label)	4.00	7.00	4.50
☐4182		I'LL GET YOU (uniface, promo)	90.00	210.00	125.00
☐9001	**TOLLIE**	SIE LIEBT DICH	30.00	65.00	40.00
		TWIST AND SHOUT/THERE'S A PLACE	5.00	11.00	7.00
☐9008		LOVE ME DO/P.S., I LOVE YOU (promo)	35.00	85.00	50.00
		LOVE ME DO/P.S., I LOVE YOU (commercial)	4.00	8.00	5.50
☐K-13213	**MGM**	LOVE ME DO/P.S., I LOVE YOU (picture sleeve)	18.00	38.00	24.00
		MY BONNIE/THE SAINTS (promo)	42.00	95.00	60.00
☐K-13227		MY BONNIE/THE SAINTS	7.00	15.00	7.50
		WHY/CRY FOR A SHADOW (promo)	42.00	90.00	58.00
		WHY/CRY FOR A SHADOW	13.00	25.00	15.00
		MGM RELEASES ARE LISTED AS TONY SHERIDAN AND THE BEATLES			
☐6302	**ATCO**	SWEET GEORGIA BROWN/TAKE OUT SOME INSURANCE (promo)	40.00	85.00	52.00

BEATLES

Fascinated with Elvis Presley, John Lennon formed a rock band called the Quarrymen in 1956. (All attended Quarry Bank High School at the time.) As certain members drifted out, others came in, most notably cherubic Paul McCartney, whom Lennon initially felt was too young. He later allowed Paul entrance into the group when he felt McCartney bore a resemblance to Elvis, John's idol.

They became a quintet, with Pete Best on drums and Stu Sutcliffe on bass. Sutcliffe knew just three chords and always played with his back to the audience. Stu left the group and died soon afterwards — at age 21 — of a brain tumor. Pete Best was fired, supposedly because of jealousy from Lennon and McCartney. (Best was said to have had the best rapport with the Liverpool ladies.) Today Best works in a Liverpool employment office.

Manager Brian Epstein saw great potential in this scruffy bar band who had gone by such names as the Four Everlys, Rainbows, Merseymen, Johnny and the Moondogs, Beat Brothers and Silver Beatles. (The final name for the Beatles was gleaned from Buddy Holly's Crickets group.)

"Love Me Do" became the Beatles' first English hit in 1962, and two years later they arrived full-force in America with "I Want to Hold Your Hand". The rest, as says the chiche, is history.

			Current Price Range		P/Y AVG
		SWEET GEORGIA BROWN/TAKE OUT SOME INSURANCE	11.00	22.00	14.00
☐6308		NOBODY'S CHILD/AIN'T SHE SWEET? (promo)	35.00	75.00	45.00
		NOBODY'S CHILD/AIN'T SHE SWEET?	4.00	8.00	5.50
☐5112	CAPITOL	I WANT TO HOLD YOUR HAND/ I SAW HER STANDING THERE ..	5.00	10.00	5.75
☐5150		CAN'T BUY ME LOVE/YOU CAN'T DO THAT	5.00	10.00	5.00
☐5222		A HARD DAY'S NIGHT/I SHOULD HAVE KNOWN BETTER	2.00	4.50	3.25
☐5234		I'LL CRY INSTEAD/I'M HAPPY JUST TO DANCE WITH YOU ...	2.00	4.50	3.25
☐5235		AND I LOVE HER/IF I FELL	2.00	4.50	3.25
☐5255		SLOW DOWN/MATCHBOX	2.00	4.50	3.25
☐5327		I FEEL FINE/SHE'S A WOMAN ...	2.00	4.50	3.25
☐5371		EIGHT DAYS A WEEK/I DON'T WANT TO SPOIL THE PARTY ...	5.00	9.00	5.00
☐5407		TICKET TO RIDE/YES IT IS	5.00	9.00	5.00
☐5476		HELP/I'M DOWN	2.00	4.50	3.00
☐5498		YESTERDAY/ACT NATURALLY ..	2.00	4.50	3.00
☐5555		WE CAN WORK IT OUT/DAY TRIPPER	2.00	4.50	3.00
☐5587		NOWHERE MAN/WHAT GOES ON .	2.00	4.50	3.00
☐5651		PAPERBACK WRITER/RAIN	2.00	4.50	3.00
☐5715		YELLOW SUBMARINE/ELEANOR RIGBY	2.00	4.50	3.00
☐5810		PENNY LANE/STRAWBERRY FIELDS FOREVER	2.00	4.50	3.00
☐5964		ALL YOU NEED IS LOVE/BABY YOU'RE A RICH MAN (promo) ..	40.00	90.00	58.00
		ALL YOU NEED IS LOVE/BABY YOU'RE A RICH MAN	2.00	4.50	3.00
☐4506		GIRL/YOU'RE GONNA LOSE THAT GIRL (promo)	35.00	75.00	48.00
		GIRL/YOU'RE GONNA LOSE THAT GIRL (promo)	42.00	95.00	59.00
☐2056		HELLO GOODBYE/I AM THE WALRUS (promo)	45.00	100.00	60.00
		HELLO GOODBYE/I AM THE WALRUS	2.00	4.50	3.00
☐2138		LADY MADONNA/THE INNER LIGHT (promo)	40.00	95.00	61.00
		LADY MADONNA/THE INNER LIGHT	2.00	4.50	3.00
☐2490		GET BACK/DON'T LET ME DOWN .	2.00	4.00	3.00
☐4274		HELTER SKELTER (both sides) (promo)	9.00	19.00	11.50
☐4274		HELTER SKELTER/GOT TO GET YOU INTO MY LIFE (promo)	9.00	19.00	11.50
☐4347		OB-LA-DI OB-LA-DA/JULIA (promo)	7.00	15.00	9.50
		OB-LA-DI OB-LA-DA/JULIA (commercial)	2.50	5.50	4.00
		OB-LA-DI OB-LA-DA/JULIA	4.00	9.50	5.50
		SERGEANT PEPPER'S LONELY HEARTS CLUB BAND/A DAY IN THE LIFE	2.00	4.00	3.00
☐2764		LET IT BE/YOU KNOW MY NAME LONG AND WINDING ROAD/ FOR YOU BLUE..............	2.00	4.00	3.00
☐5112	APPLE	I WANT TO HOLD YOUR HAND/ I SAW HER STANDING THERE ..	2.50	5.50	3.50

			Current Price Range		P/Y AVG
☐ 5150		CAN'T BUY ME LOVE/ YOU CAN'T DO THAT	3.00	5.50	3.50
☐ 5222		HARD DAY'S NIGHT/I SHOULD HAVE KNOWN BETTER	2.50	5.50	3.50
☐ 5234		I'LL CRY INSTEAD/I'M HAPPY JUST TO DANCE WITH YOU ...	2.50	5.50	3.50
☐ 5235		AND I LOVE HER/IF I FELL	2.50	5.50	3.50
☐ 5255		SLOW DOWN/MATCHBOX	2.00	4.50	3.00
☐ 5327		I FEEL FINE/SHE'S A WOMAN ...	2.50	5.50	3.50
☐ 5371		EIGHT DAYS A WEEK/I DON'T WANT TO SPOIL THE PARTY ...	2.50	5.50	3.50
☐ 5407		TICKET TO RIDE/YES IT IS	2.50	5.50	3.50
☐ 5476		HELP/I'M DOWN	2.50	5.50	3.50
☐ 5498		YESTERDAY/ACT NATURALLY ..	2.50	5.50	3.50
☐ 5555		WE CAN WORK IT OUT/DAY TRIPPER	2.50	5.50	3.50
☐ 5587		NOWHERE MAN/WHAT GOES ON .	2.00	4.00	3.00
☐ 5651		PAPERBACK WRITER/RAIN	2.00	4.00	3.00
☐ 5715		YELLOW SUBMARINE/ ELEANOR RIGBY	2.50	5.50	3.50
☐ 5810		PENNY LANE/STRAWBERRY FIELDS FOREVER	2.00	4.00	3.00
☐ 5964		ALL YOU NEED IS LOVE/ BABY, YOU'RE A RICH MAN ...	2.00	4.00	3.00
☐ 2056		HELLO GOODBYE/I AM THE WALRUS	2.50	5.50	3.50
☐ 2138		LADY MADONNA/THE INNER LIGHT....................	2.50	5.50	3.50
☐ 2276		HEY JUDE/REVOLUTION	3.00	6.50	4.00
☐ 2490		GET BACK/DON'T LET ME DOWN .	3.00	6.50	4.50
☐ 2531		THE BALLAD OF JOHN AND YOKO/ OLD BROWN SHOE	2.50	5.50	3.50
☐ 2654		COME TOGETHER/SOMETHING...	2.50	5.50	3.50
☐ 2764		LET IT BE/YOU KNOW MY NAME .	2.50	5.50	3.50
☐ 2832		THE LONG AND WINDING ROAD/ FOR YOU BLUE..............	2.50	5.50	3.50
☐ 149	OLDIES	DO YOU WANT TO KNOW A SECRET?/THANK YOU, GIRL ..	4.00	9.00	5.50
☐ 150		PLEASE PLEASE ME/ FROM ME TO YOU	4.00	9.00	5.50
☐ 151		LOVE ME DO/P.S. I LOVE YOU ...	4.00	9.00	5.50
☐ 152		TWIST AND SHOUT/ THERE'S A PLACE	4.00	9.00	5.50
		BEATLES—EPs			
☐ 18901	VEE JAY	SOUVENIR OF THEIR VISIT TO AMERICA	23.00	58.00	30.00
☐ 2121	CAPITOL	FOUR BY THE BEATLES	45.00	125.00	85.00
☐ 5365		FOUR BY THE BEATLES	36.00	90.00	50.00
		BEATLES—ALBUMS			
☐ 24-4504 (S)	POLYDOR	IN THE BEGINNING	6.00	13.00	8.00
☐ 27001	LINGASONG	LIVE AT THE STAR CLUB	9.00	19.00	11.00
☐ unnumbered	R.P.N.	THE BEATLES AMERICAN TOUR WITH ED RUBY, #2	40.00	85.00	56.00
☐ unnumbered	R.P.N.	THE BEATLES AMERICAN TOUR WITH ED RUBY, #3	28.00	65.00	42.00
☐ DX 30 (M)	VEE JAY	BEATLES VS. THE FOUR SEASONS	26.00	60.00	40.00
☐ DX 30 (S)		BEATLES VS. THE FOUR SEASONS	60.00	142.00	100.00
☐ PRO 202 (M)		HEAR THE BEATLES TELL ALL ...	28.00	65.00	42.00
☐ 1062 (M)		INTRODUCING THE BEATLES	50.00	120.00	80.00
(S)		INTRODUCING THE BEATLES	100.00	250.00	150.00
		(ALBUM PHOTOS ON BACK)			
(M)		INTRODUCING THE BEATLES (with Love Me Do)	18.00	38.00	25.00
(S)		INTRODUCING THE BEATLES (with Love Me Do)	27.00	60.00	40.00

			Current Price Range		P/Y AVG
(M)		INTRODUCING THE BEATLES (with Please Please Me)	12.00	25.00	18.00
(S)		INTRODUCING THE BEATLES (with Please Please Me)	27.00	60.00	40.00
□1085 (M)		THE BEATLES AND FRANK IFIELD	170.00	350.00	230.00
(S)		THE BEATLES AND FRANK IFIELD	325.00	650.00	415.00
		(BOTH ALBUMS FEATURED A PAINTED BEATLE PORTRAIT)			
(M)		THE BEATLES AND FRANK IFIELD	14.00	32.00	21.00
(S)		THE BEATLES AND FRANK IFIELD	28.00	60.00	40.00
		(BOTH ALBUMS FEATURE A DRAWING OF AN OLD MAN)			
□1092 (M)		SONGS, PICTURES AND STORIES OF THE BEATLES	11.00	25.00	18.00
□4215 (M)	MGM	THE BEATLES WITH TONY SHERIDAN AND GUESTS	11.00	25.00	18.00
(S)		THE BEATLES WITH TONY SHERIDAN AND GUESTS	28.00	64.00	40.00
□601 (M)	CLARION	THE AMAZING BEATLES	11.00	25.00	18.00
(S)		THE AMAZING BEATLES	17.00	38.00	25.00
□69 (M)	SAVAGE	SAVAGE YOUNG BEATLES	14.00	31.00	21.00
□563 (M)	METRO	THIS IS WHERE IT STARTED	11.00	25.00	16.00
(S)		THIS IS WHERE IT STARTED	11.00	25.00	16.00
□11638 (S)	CAPITOL	LIVE AT HOLLYWOOD BOWL	5.00	11.00	8.00
□2047 (S)		MEET THE BEATLES (green label)	8.00	17.00	10.00
□2047 (S)		MEET THE BEATLES (black label)	10.00	25.00	15.00
□SXA-2080		THE BEATLES SECOND ALBUM (compact 33 r.p.m. for jukeboxes)	75.00	160.00	110.00
□2080 (S)		THE BEATLES SECOND ALBUM (green label)	12.00	26.00	17.50
		THE BEATLES SECOND ALBUM (black label)	9.00	20.00	13.00
□2108 (S)		SOMETHING NEW (green label)	6.00	13.00	7.50
		SOMETHING NEW (black label)	9.00	20.00	13.50
□2222 (S)		THE BEATLES STORY (green label)	15.00	35.00	22.00
		THE BEATLES STORY (black label)	9.00	20.00	14.00
□2228 (S)		BEATLES '65 (green label)	6.00	13.00	8.00
		BEATLES '65 (black label)	8.00	19.00	13.50
□2309 (S)		THE EARLY BEATLES (green label)	7.00	13.00	9.00
		THE EARLY BEATLES (black label)	8.00	17.00	11.00
□2358 (S)		BEATLES VI	4.00	8.50	6.00
		BEATLES VI (sleeve has "See label for correct playing order)	11.00	23.00	15.00
□2386 (S)		HELP (green label)	6.00	13.00	8.00
		HELP (black label)	7.50	16.00	9.50
□2442 (S)		RUBBER SOUL (green label)	6.00	13.00	8.00
		RUBBER SOUL (black label)	7.00	16.00	9.00
		MONO VERSIONS OF THE ABOVE ALBUMS HAVE SIMILAR VALUES			
□2553 (M)		YESTERDAY AND TODAY (butcher cover)	165.00	330.00	220.00
		YESTERDAY AND TODAY (revised cover)	100.00	225.00	135.00
□2553 (S)		YESTERDAY AND TODAY (butcher cover)	310.00	625.00	420.00
		YESTERDAY AND TODAY (revised cover)	150.00	325.00	210.00
□2553 (M)		YESTERDAY AND TODAY (new cover)	9.00	21.00	14.50
(S)		YESTERDAY AND TODAY (new cover)	9.00	21.00	14.50
□2576 (M)		REVOLVER (green label)	6.00	13.00	8.00
(S)		REVOLVER (black label)	7.00	16.00	9.00
(S)		REVOLVER (green label)	6.00	13.00	8.00
(S)		REVOLVER (black label)	7.00	16.00	9.00

			Current Price Range		P/Y AVG
☐ 2652 (S)		SERGEANT PEPPER'S LONELY HEARTS CLUB BAND (green label)	6.00	13.00	8.00
		SERGEANT PEPPER'S LONELY HEARTS CLUB BAND (black label)	7.00	15.00	9.00
(M)		SERGEANT PEPPER'S LONELY HEARTS CLUB BAND	9.00	25.00	13.00
☐ 28355 (S)		MAGICAL MYSTERY TOUR (green label)	8.00	20.00	11.00
		MAGICAL MYSTERY TOUR (black label)	6.00	13.00	8.00
(M)		MAGICAL MYSTERY TOUR	9.00	20.00	11.00
☐ 6366 (S)	*UNITED ARTISTS*	A HARD DAY'S NIGHT (tan label) . .	5.00	11.00	7.00
		A HARD DAY'S NIGHT (black label)	7.00	16.00	9.00
		A HARD DAY'S NIGHT (salmon label)	6.00	13.00	8.00
(M)		A HARD DAY'S NIGHT	12.00	25.00	16.00
☐ 1171 (S)		LOVE SONGS	5.00	11.00	7.00
☐ 2047 (S)	*APPLE*	MEET THE BEATLES	4.00	9.00	6.00
☐ 2080 (S)		THE BEATLES SECOND ALBUM . .	4.00	9.00	6.00
		THE BEATLES SECOND ALBUM (with Apple and Capitol markings)	6.00	13.00	8.00
☐ 2108 (S)		SOMETHING NEW	5.00	11.00	7.00
☐ 2222 (S)		THE BEATLES STORY	6.00	13.00	8.00
☐ 2228 (S)		BEATLES '65	5.00	11.00	7.00
☐ 2309 (S)		THE EARLY BEATLES	5.00	11.00	7.00
☐ 2358 (S)		BEATLES VI	7.00	16.00	9.00
		BEATLES VI (with Apple and Capitol markings)	5.00	11.00	7.00
☐ 2386 (S)		HELP	4.00	9.00	6.00
☐ 2442 (S)		RUBBER SOUL	5.00	11.00	7.00
☐ 2553 (S)		YESTERDAY AND TODAY	15.00	35.00	21.00
☐ 2576 (S)		REVOLVER	5.00	11.00	7.00
☐ 2652 (S)		SERGEANT PEPPER'S LONELY HEARTS CLUB BAND	5.00	11.00	7.00
☐ 2853 (S)		MAGICAL MYSTERY TOUR	6.00	13.00	8.00
☐ 100 (S)		CHRISTMAS FAN CLUB ALBUM . .	40.00	90.00	54.00
☐ 101 (S)		THE BEATLES	16.00	35.00	21.00
☐ 153 (S)		YELLOW SUBMARINE	4.00	9.00	6.00
☐ 383 (S)		ABBEY ROAD	8.00	20.00	10.00
☐ 385 (S)		HEY JUDE	4.00	9.00	6.00
☐ 34001 (S)		LET IT BE	4.00	9.00	6.00
☐ 3403 (S)		THE BEATLES 1962-1966	6.00	13.00	8.00
☐ 3404 (S)		THE BEATLES 1967-1970	6.00	13.00	8.00

BEAU BRUMMELS

☐ 8	*AUTUMN*	LAUGH LAUGH/STILL IN LOVE WITH YOU BABY	3.25	5.50	4.00
☐ 10		JUST A LITTLE/ THEY'LL MAKE YOU CRY	3.25	5.50	4.00
☐ 16		YOU TELL ME WHY/I WANT YOU .	3.25	5.50	4.00
☐ 20		DON'T TALK TO STRANGERS/ IN GOOD TIME	3.25	5.50	4.00
☐ 24		GOOD TIME MUSIC/ SAD LITTLE GIRL	3.25	5.50	4.00

BEAU BRUMMELS—ALBUMS

☐ 103 (M)	*AUTUMN*	INTRODUCING THE BEAU BRUMMELS	8.50	20.00	18.00
☐ 104 (M)		THE BEAU BRUMMELS, VOL. II . .	8.50	20.00	18.00

			Current Price Range		P/Y AVG

BEAU-MARKS

			Current Price Range		P/Y AVG
☐ 1032	*TIME*	ROCKIN' BLUES/OH JOAN	3.50	6.00	4.50
☐ 5017	*SHAD*	CLAP YOUR HANDS/DADDY SAID	3.00	5.50	4.00
☐ 5021		'CAUSE WE'RE IN LOVE/			
		BILLY WENT A-WALKING	3.00	5.50	4.00
☐ 1370	*QUALITY*	LOVELY LITTLE LADY/			
		LITTLE MISS TWIST	3.50	6.00	4.50
☐ 5035	*RUST*	CLASSMATE/SCHOOL IS OUT	3.00	5.50	4.00
☐ 5051		TENDER YEARS/			
		I'LL NEVER BE THE SAME	3.00	5.50	4.00

JIMMY BEAUMONT
SEE: SKYLINERS

☐ 112	*MAY*	EV'RYBODY'S CRYIN'/CAMERA	3.50	6.00	4.50
☐ 115		I SHOULDA LISTENED TO MAMA/			
		JUAREZ	3.25	5.50	4.25
☐ 120		NEVER SAY GOODBYE/			
		I'M GONNA TRY MY WINGS	3.25	5.50	4.25
☐ 136		I'LL ALWAYS BE IN LOVE WITH			
		YOU/GIVE HER MY BEST	3.25	5.50	4.25
☐ 3007	*GALLANT*	PLEASE SEND ME SOMEONE TO			
		LOVE/THERE IS NO			
		OTHER LOVE	3.25	5.50	4.25
☐ 607	*COLPIX*	THE END OF A STORY/			
		BAION RHYTHMS	3.25	5.50	4.25
☐ 510	*BANG*	TELL ME/			
		I FEEL I'M FALLING IN LOVE	3.25	5.50	4.25
☐ 525		I NEVER LOVED HER ANYWAY/			
		YOU GOT TOO MUCH GOIN'			
		FOR YOU	3.25	5.50	4.25

BEEFEATERS (BYRDS)

☐ 45013	*ELEKTRA*	PLEASE LET ME LOVE YOU/			
		DON'T BE LONG	30.00	55.00	32.00

BEE GEES

☐ 6487	*ATCO*	NEW YORK MINING DISASTER-			
		1941/I CAN'T SEE NOBOBY	3.00	5.00	3.00
☐ 6503		TO LOVE SOMEBODY/			
		CLOSE ANOTHER DOOR	3.00	5.00	3.00
☐ 6521		HOLIDAY/EVERY CHRISTIAN LION			
		HEARTED MAN WILL SHOW YOU	3.00	5.00	3.00
☐ 6532		(THE LIGHTS WENT OUT IN)			
		MASSACHUSETTS/SIR			
		GEOFFREY SAVED THE WORLD	3.00	5.00	3.00
☐ 6548		WORDS/SINKING SHIPS	3.00	5.00	3.00
☐ 6570		JUMBO/			
		THE SINGER SANG HIS SONG	3.00	5.00	3.00
☐ 6603		I'VE GOTTA GET A MESSAGE TO			
		YOU/KITTY CAN	3.00	5.00	3.00
☐ 6639		I STARTED A JOKE/			
		KILBURN TOWERS	2.50	4.00	3.00
☐ 6657		FIRST OF MAY/LAMPLIGHT	2.50	4.00	2.50
☐ 6682		TOMORROW TOMORROW/			
		SUN IN THE MORNING	2.50	4.00	2.50
☐ 6702		DON'T FORGET TO REMEMBER/			
		THE LORD	2.50	4.00	2.50
☐ 6702		DON'T FORGET TO REMEMBER/			
		I LAY DOWN AND DIE	2.50	4.00	2.50
☐ 6741		IF I ONLY HAD MY MIND ON			
		SOMETHING ELSE/			
		SWEETHEART	2.50	4.00	2.50
☐ 6752		I.O.I.O./THEN YOU LEFT ME	2.50	4.00	2.50

BEE GEES

British-born Barry Gibb and younger twin brothers Robin and Maurice formed a singing trio before any of them was 10 years old. Most people viewed the youngsters as a novelty trio but the boys always took their music seriously. They quickly developed a tight, distinctive harmony. At first, they called themselves the Rattlesnakes, later changing to the name Bluecats.

In 1958, the Gibb family moved to Australia. In that year, the trio took on a third name, the Bee Gees, for Brothers Gibb. In Australia, they became a top-notch group, successful in clubs and on TV, but going nowhere on Australia's Festival Records label. Hugh Gibb then decided to return his family to England. Just before they left, the Bee Gees' final outing of "Spicks and Specks" hit number one in Australia.

Within a week after arriving in London, the Bee Gees had signed with producer Robert Stigwood, who today heads RSO Records. The Bee Gees' first Atco single was "New York Mining Disaster - 1941," a song written in 20 minutes on a darkened stairway when the power in the recording studio had failed temporarily.

From 1977 to 1979, the Bee Gees grossed $150,000,000 from records, tapes and concerts. It was a radical departure for their former days of Festival failure, to be sure.

			Current Price Range		P/Y AVG
☐6795		LONELY DAYS/			
		MAN FOR ALL SEASONS	2.50	4.00	2.50
☐6824		HOW CAN YOU MEND A BROKEN			
		HEART?/COUNTRY WOMAN . . .	2.50	4.00	2.50
☐6847		DON'T WANT TO LIVE INSIDE			
		MYSELF/WALKING BACK TO			
		WATERLOO	2.50	4.00	2.50
☐6871		MY WORLD/ON TIME	2.50	4.00	2.50
☐6896		RUN TO ME/ROAD TO ALASKA . . .	2.50	4.00	2.50
☐6909		ALIVE/PAPER MACHE',			
		CABBAGES AND KINGS	2.50	4.00	2.50

BEE GEES—ALBUMS

			Current Price Range		P/Y AVG
☐223 (M)	ATCO	BEE GEES' 1ST	12.00	28.00	17.00
☐223 (S)		BEE GEES' 1ST	8.00	19.00	12.00
☐233 (M)		HORIZONTAL	11.00	25.00	14.50
☐233 (S)		HORIZONTAL	8.00	19.00	12.00
☐253 (S)		IDEA	8.00	19.00	12.00
☐264 (S)		RARE, PRECIOUS AND BEAUTIFUL.	11.00	25.00	14.50
☐292 (S)		BEST OF THE BEE GEES	8.00	19.00	12.00
☐321 (S)		RARE, PRECIOUS AND BEAUTIFUL,			
		VOL. II	11.00	25.00	14.50
☐327 (S)		CUCUMBER CASTLE	8.00	19.00	12.00
☐353 (S)		TWO YEARS ON	8.00	19.00	12.00
☐702 (S)		ODESSA	15.00	35.00	21.00
☐7003 (S)		TRAFALGAR	8.00	19.00	12.00
☐7012 (S)		TO WHOM IT MAY CONCERN	8.00	19.00	12.00

BEL-AIRES

			Current Price Range		P/Y AVG
☐30631	DECCA	MY YEARBOOK/			
		ROCKIN' AND STROLLIN'	9.50	17.00	15.00
☐5034	ARVEE	MR. MOTO/LITTLE BROWN JUG .	3.00	5.50	4.00
☐54	TRIUMPH	KAMI-KAZE/VAMPIRE	3.00	5.50	4.00
☐107	LUCKY TOKEN	BAGGIES/CHARLIE CHAN	3.00	5.50	4.00

ARCHIE BELL AND THE DRELLS

			Current Price Range		P/Y AVG
☐228	OVIDE	TIGHTEN UP(PT. 1)/(PT. 2)	12.00	20.00	18.00

MADELINE BELL

			Current Price Range		P/Y AVG
☐2180	ASCOT	DAYTIME/DON'T CRY, MY HEART	3.00	5.50	4.00
☐1007	MOD	I'M GONNA MAKE YOU LOVE ME/			
		PICTURE ME GONE	4.00	7.00	6.00
☐40517	PHILIPS	I'M GONNA MAKE YOU LOVE ME/			
		PICTURE ME GONE	2.50	5.00	3.00
☐40539		FINDING YOU, LOVING YOU/			
		DOING THINGS TOGETHER			
		WITH YOU	2.50	5.00	3.00

MADELINE BELL—ALBUM

			Current Price Range		P/Y AVG
☐600-271 (S)	PHILIPS	I'M GONNA MAKE YOU LOVE ME .	7.00	17.00	15.00

BELL NOTES

			Current Price Range		P/Y AVG
☐1004	TIME	I'VE HAD IT/BE MINE	3.00	5.50	4.00
☐1010		OLD SPANISH TOWN/			
		SHE WENT THAT-A-WAY	3.00	5.50	4.00
☐1013		THAT'S RIGHT/BETTY DEAR	3.00	5.50	4.00
☐1015		YOU'RE A BIG GIRL NOW/			
		DON'T ASK ME WHY	3.00	5.50	4.00
☐1017		WHITE BUCKSKIN SNEAKERS AND			
		CHECKERBOARD SOCKS/			
		NO DICE	3.00	5.50	4.00

BELL NOTES—EP

			Current Price Range		P/Y AVG
☐100	TIME	I'VE HAD IT	8.50	14.00	12.00

BELMONTS

			Current Price Range		P/Y AVG
☐3080	LAURIE	WE BELONG TOGETHER/			
		SUCH A LONG WAY	8.50	14.00	12.00

ATKO, SD33-233, LP

CHESS, 5121, EP

			Current Price Range		P/Y AVG
☐ 1000	**SURPRISE**	TELL ME WHY/SMOKE FROM YOUR CIGARETTE	15.00	32.00	22.00
☐ 500	**SABRINA**	TELL ME WHY/SMOKE FROM YOUR CIGARETTE	3.00	5.50	4.00
☐ 501		DON'T GET AROUND MUCH ANYMORE/SEARCHING FOR A NEW LOVE	3.00	5.50	4.00
☐ 502	**SABINA**	I NEED SOMEONE/ THAT AMERICAN DANCE	3.00	5.50	4.00
☐ 503		I CONFESS/HOMBRE	3.00	5.50	4.00
☐ 505		COME ON LITTLE ANGEL/ HOW ABOUT ME?	3.00	5.50	4.00
☐ 507		DIDDLE-DEE-DUM/FAREWELL . . .	3.00	5.50	4.00
☐ 509		ANN-MARIE/ACCENTUATE THE POSITIVE	3.00	5.50	4.00
☐ 513		WALK ON BY/ LET'S CALL IT A DAY	3.00	5.50	4.00
☐ 517		MORE IMPORTANT THINGS TO DO/ LET'S CALL IT A DAY	3.00	5.50	4.00
☐ 519		C'MON EVERYBODY/WHY	8.50	14.00	12.00
☐ 521		NOTHING IN RETURN/ SUMMERTIME TIME	8.50	14.00	12.00
☐ 809	**UNITED ARTISTS**	I DON'T KNOW WHY/ SUMMERTIME	4.50	7.00	6.00
☐ 904		(THEN) I WALKED AWAY/TODAY MY LOVE HAS GONE AWAY . . .	5.00	8.50	7.00
☐ 966		I GOT A FEELING/TO BE WITH YOU .	5.00	8.50	7.00
☐ 5007		COME WITH ME/ YOU'RE LIKE A MYSTERY	5.00	8.50	7.00
☐ 17173	**DOT**	SHE ONLY WANTS TO DO HER OWN THING/REMINISCENCES .	4.50	7.00	4.50
☐ 17257		HAVE YOU HEARD/ ANSWER ME, MY LOVE	4.50	7.00	4.50
☐ 17257		THE WORST THAT COULD HAPPEN/ ANSWER ME, MY LOVE	4.50	7.00	4.50
		BELMONTS—ALBUMS			
☐ 5001 (M)	**SABINA**	CARNIVAL OF HITS	15.00	35.00	24.00
☐ 25949 (S)	**DOT**	SUMMER LOVE	8.00	20.00	18.00
☐ 5123 (S)	**BUDDAH**	CIGARS, ACAPELLA AND CANDY .	7.00	17.00	15.00

JESSE BELVIN

☐ 5115	**IMPERIAL**	ALL THAT WINE IS GONE/ DON'T CRY BABY	55.00	90.00	85.00
☐ 120	**HOLLYWOOD**	DREAM GIRL/HANG YOUR TEARS OUT TO DRY	44.00	74.00	70.00
☐ 1059		DEAR HEART/BETTY MY DARLING .	75.00	125.00	120.00
☐ 435	**SPECIALTY**	CONFUSIN' BLUES/ BABY DON'T GO	10.00	17.00	15.00
☐ 447		DREAM GIRL/DADDY LOVES BABY (Jesse and Marvin)	10.00	17.00	15.00
☐ 550		GONE/ONE LITTLE BLESSING . . .	7.00	12.00	10.00
☐ 559		WHERE'S MY GIRL/ LOVE LOVE OF MY LIFE	7.00	12.00	10.00
☐ 12237	**FEDERAL**	SO FINE/SENTIMENTAL HEART (Shieks)	33.00	51.00	48.00
☐ 208	**MONEY**	I'M ONLY A FOOL/ TROUBLE AND MISERY	11.00	20.00	18.00
☐ 1056	**CASH**	BEWARE/DRY YOUR EYES	7.50	13.00	11.00
☐ 987	**MODERN**	GIRL OF MY DREAMS/ I WANNA KNOW WHY (Cliques)	4.50	7.00	6.00
☐ 1005		GOODNIGHT MY LOVE/I WANT YOU WITH ME CHRISTMAS . . .	4.50	7.00	6.00

			Current Price Range		P/Y AVG
☐ 1005		GOODNIGHT MY LOVE/LET ME LOVE YOU TONIGHT	4.50	7.00	6.00
☐ 1013		SENORITA/I NEED YOU SO	4.50	7.00	6.00
☐ 1015		DON'T CLOSE THE DOOR/ BY MY SIDE	4.50	7.00	6.00
☐ 1020		SAD AND LONESOME/ I'M NOT FREE	4.50	8.00	6.00
☐ 1025		YOU SEND ME/SUMMERTIME ...	4.50	7.00	6.00
☐ 1027		JUST TO SAY HELLOW/ MY SATELLITE	5.00	7.50	6.00
☐ 326	**KENT**	SENTIMENTAL REASONS/ SENORITA	3.00	5.50	4.00
☐ 267	**CLASS**	DEEP IN MY HEART/ I'M CONFESSIN'	3.50	6.00	4.50
☐ 3431	**ALADDIN**	SUGAR DOLL/LET ME DREAM ...	3.50	6.00	4.50
☐ 7310	**RCA**	EVER SINCE WE MET/VOLARE ...	3.00	5.50	4.00
☐ 7387		FUNNY/PLEDGING MY LOVE.....	3.00	5.50	4.00
☐ 7469		GUESS WHO/MY GIRL IS JUST ENOUGH WOMAN FOR ME	3.00	5.50	4.00
☐ 7543		IT COULD'VE BEEN WORSE/ HERE'S A HEART	3.00	5.50	4.00
☐ 7596		GIVE ME LOVE/ I'LL NEVER BE LONELY AGAIN .	3.00	5.50	4.00

JESSE BELVIN—ALBUMS

☐ 2089 (M)	**RCA**	JUST JESSE BELVIN	14.00	34.00	30.00
☐ 2089 (S)		JUST JESSE BELVIN	19.00	48.00	45.00
☐ 2105 (M)		MR. EASY	12.00	27.00	25.00
☐ 2105 (S)		MR. EASY	17.00	38.00	35.00
☐ 5145 (M)	**CROWN**	THE CASUAL JESSE BELVIN	7.00	17.00	15.00
☐ 5187 (M)		THE UNFORGETTABLE JESSE BELVIN	7.00	17.00	15.00
☐ 1058 (M)	**CUSTOM**	GONE BUT NOT FORGOTTEN	7.00	17.00	15.00
☐ 960 (M)	**CAMDEN**	JESSE BELVIN'S BEST	7.00	17.00	15.00

BOYD BENNETT

☐ 1413	**KING**	WATERLOO/I'VE HAD ENOUGH ..	9.50	17.00	15.00
☐ 1432		POISON IVY/YOU UPSET ME BABY	8.50	17.00	15.00
☐ 1443		BOOGIE AT MIDNIGHT/ EVERLOVIN'	8.50	17.00	15.00
☐ 1470		SEVENTEEN/LITTLE OLD YOU-ALL.	6.00	8.50	7.00
☐ 1475		TENNESSEE ROCK AND ROLL/ 00-00-00	4.50	7.50	6.00
☐ 1494		MY BOY FLAT-TOP/ BANJO ROCK AND ROLL	4.50	7.50	6.00

PRICES ABOVE ARE FOR MAROON LABELS;
SECOND-PRESS BLUE LABELS ARE WORTH HALF

BOYD BENNETT—EPs

☐ 337	**KING**	ROCK AND ROLL WITH BOYD BENNETT	25.00	60.00	40.00
☐ 383		ROCK AND ROLL WITH BOYD BENNETT	25.00	60.00	40.00

BOYD BENNETT—ALBUM

☐ 594 (M)	**KING**	BOYD BENNETT	30.00	75.00	45.00

JOE BENNETT AND THE SPARKLETONES

☐ 9837	**ABC-PARAMOUNT**	BLACK SLACKS/ BOPPIN' ROCK BOOGIE	3.50	5.50	4.00
☐ 9867		PENNY LOAFERS AND BOBBY SOCKS/ROCKET	3.50	5.50	4.00
☐ 9885		COTTON PICKIN' ROCKER/ I DIG YOU BABY	8.50	14.00	12.00
☐ 9929		WE'VE HAD IT/LITTLE TURTLE ..	3.00	5.00	3.50
☐ 9959		LATE AGAIN/DO THE STOP	3.00	5.00	3.50

			Current Price Range		P/Y AVG
☐ 10659		RUN RABBIT RUN/			
		WELL-DRESSED MAN	3.00	5.00	3.50
☐ 537	**PARIS**	WHAT THE HECK/BOYS DO CRY .	3.00	5.50	4.00
☐ 542		ARE YOU FROM DIXIE?/			
		BEAUTIFUL ONE	3.00	5.50	4.00

RON BERNARD

☐ 105	**JIN**	THIS SHOULD GO ON FOREVER/			
		PARDON, MR. GORDON	8.50	14.00	12.00
☐ 5327	**ARGO**	THIS SHOULD GO ON FOREVER/			
		PARDON, MR. GORDON	3.00	5.00	3.50

RON BERNARD—ALBUM

☐ 4007 (M)	**JIN**	RON BERNARD	10.00	25.00	22.50

CHUCK BERRY

☐ 1604	**CHESS**	MAYBELLENE/WEE WEE HOURS .	5.50	9.00	7.00
☐ 1610		THIRTY DAYS/TOGETHER	6.50	11.00	9.00
☐ 1615		NO MONEY DOWN/			
		THE DOWNBOUND TRAIN	6.50	11.00	9.00
☐ 1626		ROLL OVER BEETHOVEN/			
		DRIFTING HEART	5.50	9.00	7.00
☐ 1635		TOO MUCH MONKEY BUSINESS/			
		BROWN EYED HANDSOME MAN	6.50	11.00	9.00
☐ 1645		YOU CAN'T CATCH ME/			
		HAVANA MOON	5.50	9.00	7.00
☐ 1653		SCHOOL DAY/DEEP FEELING	4.00	6.00	4.50
☐ 1664		OH BABY DOLL/LAJUNDA	4.00	6.00	4.50

ABOVE ISSUES FEATURED THE SILVER-AND-BLUE CHESS-TOP LABELS

☐ 1671		ROCK AND ROLL MUSIC/			
		BLUE FEELING	4.00	6.50	5.00
☐ 1683		SWEET LITTLE SIXTEEN/			
		REELIN' AND ROCKIN'	4.00	6.50	5.00
☐ 1691		JOHNNY B. GOODE/			
		AROUND AND AROUND	4.00	6.50	5.00
☐ 1697		BEAUTIFUL DELILAH/			
		VACATION TIME	3.00	5.50	4.00
☐ 1700		CAROL/HEY PEDRO............	3.00	5.50	4.00
☐ 1709		SWEET LITTLE ROCK AND ROLL/			
		JOE JOE GUN	3.00	5.50	4.00
☐ 1714		MERRY CHRISTMAS BABY/			
		RUN RUDOLPH RUN	3.00	5.50	4.00
☐ 1716		ANTHONY BOY/			
		THAT'S MY DESIRE	3.50	6.00	4.25
☐ 1722		LITTLE QUEENIE/ALMOST GROWN	3.25	5.50	4.00
☐ 1729		BACK IN THE U.S.A./			
		MEMPHIS, TENNESSEE	3.25	5.50	4.00
☐ 1736		CHILDHOOD SWEETHEART/			
		BROKEN ARROW	3.25	5.50	4.00
☐ 1747		TOO POOPED TO POP/LET IT ROCK	3.25	5.50	4.00
☐ 1754		BYE BYE JOHNNY/			
		WORRIED LIFE BLUES	3.25	5.50	4.00
☐ 1763		MAD LAD/I GOT TO FIND MY BABY	3.25	5.50	4.00
☐ 1767		JAGUAR AND THE THUNDERBIRD/			
		OUR LITTLE RENDEZVOUS	3.00	5.25	3.75
☐ 1779		LITTLE STAR/			
		I'M TALKING ABOUT YOU	3.00	5.25	3.75
☐ 1799		GO GO GO/COME ON	3.00	5.25	3.75
☐ 1853		I'M TALKING ABOUT YOU/			
		DIPLOMA FOR TWO	3.00	5.25	3.75
☐ 1866		SWEET LITTLE SIXTEEN/			
		MEMPHIS (reissue)	3.00	5.25	3.75
☐ 1883		NADINE/ORANGUTANG	3.00	5.25	3.75
☐ 1898		NO PARTICULAR PLACE TO GO/			
		YOU TWO	3.00	5.25	3.75

CHUCK BERRY

Rock critic Lillian Roxon once said, "Chuck Berry may be the single most important name in the history of rock."

He was born Charles Edward Anderson Berry in St. Louis on October 18, 1926. Chuck was one of six children who grew up surrounded by music. He also discovered the guitar, embracing an electric instrument shortly after an initial stint with a Spanish acoustic.

Chuck attended Poro Junior College and later took a degree in cosmetology. He went to school at night, toiling during the day as an assembly-line worker at a car factory.

On a 1955 vacation, Chuck went to Chicago and sat in with blues master Muddy Waters. Muddy was so impressed that he insisted Chuck look up Leonard Chess the very next day. Berry signed with Chess Records and cut "Maybellene", a song he had originally composed as "Ida Red".

During his sporadic career, Chuck Berry left behind some of the most durable classics of the early rock-and-roll period. However, not once did he hit number one on the charts until 1972 when he lifted Davie Bartholemew's 1952 song "My Ding-a-Ling", took the writing credit for it and played the novelty tune at a London concert. The hit single — Berry's final chart success — was called from that session.

			Current Price Range		P/Y AVG
☐1906		YOU NEVER CAN TELL/			
		BRENDA LEE	3.00	5.25	3.75
☐1912		LITTLE MARIE/GO BOBBY SOXER	3.00	5.25	3.75
☐1916		PROMISED LAND/			
		THINGS I USED TO DO	3.00	5.25	3.75
☐1926		DEAR DAD/LONELY SCHOOL DAYS	3.00	5.25	3.75
☐1943		IT WASN'T ME/WELCOME BACK			
		PRETTY BABY	3.00	5.25	3.75
☐1963		LONELY SCHOOL DAYS/			
		RAMONA, SAY YES`	3.00	5.25	3.75
☐2090		TULANE/HAVE MERCY JUDGE ...	3.00	5.25	3.75
☐2131		MY DING-A-LING/			
		JOHNNY B. GOODE	3.00	5.25	3.75
☐2136		REELIN' AND ROCKIN'/			
		LET'S BOOGIE	3.00	5.25	3.75
☐2140		BIO/ROLL 'EM PETE	3.00	5.25	3.75
☐2169		SHAKE, RATTLE AND ROLL/BABY			
		WHAT YOU WANT ME TO DO ...	3.00	5.25	3.75
☐72643	*MERCURY*	LAUGH AND CRY/			
		CLUB NITTY GRITTY	2.50	4.75	3.25
☐72680		BACK TO MEMPHIS/			
		I DO REALLY LOVE YOU	2.50	4.75	3.25
☐72748		FEELIN' IT/IT HURTS ME TOO ...	2.50	4.75	3.25
☐72840		LOUIE TO FRISCO/MA DEAR	2.50	4.75	3.25
☐72963		GOOD LOOKING WOMAN/			
		IT'S TOO DARK IN THERE	2.50	4.75	3.25

CHUCK BERRY—EPs

☐5118	*CHESS*	AFTER SCHOOL SESSION	10.00	17.00	15.00
☐5119		ROCK AND ROLL MUSIC	10.00	17.00	15.00
☐5121		SWEET LITTLE SIXTEEN	8.50	14.00	12.00
☐5124		PICKIN' BERRIES..............	8.50	14.00	12.00
☐5126		JOHNNY B. GOODE	8.50	14.00	12.00

ADD $5.00 PER EP FOR SILVER-TOP LABELS

CHUCK BERRY—ALBUMS

☐1426 (M)	*CHESS*	AFTER SCHOOL SESSION	17.00	39.00	24.00
☐1432 (M)		ONE DOZEN BERRYS	12.00	28.00	18.00
☐1435 (M)		CHUCK BERRY IS ON TOP	11.00	23.00	14.00
☐1448 (M)		ROCKIN' AT THE HOPS	11.00	23.00	14.00
☐1456 (M)		MORE JUKE BOX HITS	11.00	23.00	14.00
☐1465 (M)		MORE CHUCK BERRY	11.00	23.00	14.00
☐1485 (M)		CHUCK BERRY'S GREATEST HITS	11.00	23.00	14.00
☐1488 (M)		ST. LOUIS TO LIVERPOOL	11.00	23.00	14.00
☐1495 (M)		CHUCK BERRY IN LONDON	11.00	23.00	14.00
☐1498 (M)		FRESH BERRY'S	9.00	19.00	13.00
☐1514 (S)		CHUCK BERRY'S GOLDEN DECADE.	6.00	12.00	8.25
☐1550 (S)		BACK HOME	6.00	12.00	8.25
☐21103 (M)	*MERCURY*	GOLDEN HITS	6.00	12.00	8.25
☐61103 (S)		GOLDEN HITS	6.00	12.00	8.25
☐21123 (M)		IN MEMPHIS	6.00	12.00	8.25
☐61123 (S)		IN MEMPHIS	6.00	12.00	8.25
☐21138 (M)		LIVE AT FILLMORE AUDITORIUM .	6.00	12.00	8.25
☐61138 (S)		LIVE AT FILLMORE AUDITORIUM .	6.00	12.00	8.25
☐61176 (S)		FROM ST. LOUIS TO FRISCO	6.00	12.00	8.25
☐61223 (S)		CONCERTO IN B. GOODE	6.00	12.00	8.25

JAN BERRY
SEE: JAN AND DEAN

☐6101	*RIPPLE*	TOMORROW'S TEARDROPS/			
		MY MIDSUMMER NIGHT'S			
		DREAM (by Jan Berry)	25.00	50.00	31.00
☐66023	*ODE*	MOTHER EARTH/			
		BLUE MOON SHUFFLE	8.50	14.00	12.00
☐66034		DON'T YOU JUST KNOW IT/			
		BLUE MOON SHUFFLE (Jan) ...	9.50	17.00	15.00

			Current Price Range		P/Y AVG
☐ 66050		TINSELTOWN/BLOW UP MUSIC (1 Jan 1)	5.50	8.50	7.00
☐ 66111		FUN CITY/TOTALLY WILD (Jan and Dean)	5.50	8.50	7.00
☐ 66120		SING SANG A SONG/SING SANG A SONG (SINGALONG VERSION) (Jan Berry)	3.50	6.00	4.50
☐ 1957	**A & M**	LITTLE QUEENIE/ THAT'S THE WAY IT IS	3.50	6.00	4.00
☐ 2020		SKATEBOARD SURFIN' U.S.A./ HOW-HOW I LOVE HER	3.50	6.00	4.00

LOU BERRY & THE BEL RAVES

☐ 1001	**DREEM**	WHAT A DOLLY/HOT ROD	33.00	69.00	65.00

MIKE BERRY

☐ 62341	**CORAL**	TRIBUTE TO BUDDY HOLLY/ EVERY LITTLE KISS	9.50	17.00	15.00
☐ 62357		DON'T YOU THINK IT'S TIME/ LONELINESS	3.00	5.50	4.00
☐ 62483		IT COMES AND GOES/ GONNA FALL IN LOVE	3.00	5.50	4.00

RICHARD BERRY

☐ 1016	**FLAIR**	I'M STILL IN LOVE WITH YOU/ ONE LITTLE PRAYER	5.50	11.00	9.00
☐ 1052		BYE BYE/AT LAST	5.50	11.00	9.00
☐ 1055		THE BIG BREAK/ WHAT YOU DO TO ME	9.50	17.00	15.00
☐ 1058		BABY DARLING/DADDY-DADDY	5.50	8.00	7.00
☐ 1064		PLEASE TELL ME/OH OH, GET OUT OF THE CAR	8.00	14.00	12.00
☐ 1068		GOD GAVE ME YOU/DON' CHA GO	5.50	9.00	7.00
☐ 1071		NEXT TIME/CRAZY LOVE	5.50	9.00	7.00
☐ 1075		JELLY ROLL/TOGETHER	5.50	9.00	7.00
☐ 448	**RPM**	BIG JOHN/ROCKIN' MAN	5.50	11.00	9.00
☐ 452		I AM BEWILDERED/ PRETTY BROWN EYES	8.50	14.00	12.00
☐ 465		YAMA YAMA PRETTY MAMA/ ANGEL OF MY LIFE	5.50	11.00	9.00
☐ 477		GOOD LOVE/WAIT FOR ME	4.50	7.00	6.00
☐ 318	**FLIP**	TAKE THE KEY/ NO KISSIN' AND A-HUGGIN'	5.50	9.00	7.00
☐ 321		LOUIE LOUIE/ROCK ROCK ROCK	5.50	9.00	7.00
☐ 321		LOUIE LOUIE/ YOU ARE MY SUNSHINE	4.50	7.00	6.00
☐ 327		SWEET SUGAR YOU/ ROCK ROCK ROCK	4.50	7.00	6.00
☐ 331		YOU'RE THE GIRL/ YOU LOOK SO GOOD	3.00	5.50	4.00
☐ 336		THE MESS AROUND/ HEAVEN ON WHEELS	3.00	5.50	4.00
☐ 339		BESAME MUCHO/DO I, DO I	3.00	5.50	4.00
☐ 349		HAVE LOVE, WILL TRAVEL/ NO ROOM	3.50	6.00	4.50
☐ 352		I'LL NEVER LOVE AGAIN/ SOMEWHERE THERE'S A RAINBOW	3.00	5.50	4.00
☐ 360		YOU ARE MY SUNSHINE/ YOU LOOK SO GOOD	3.00	5.50	4.00

RICHARD BERRY—ALBUMS

☐ 1001 (M)	**PAM**	LIVE AT THE CENTURY CLUB	16.00	26.00	24.00
☐ 1002 (M)		WILD BERRY	12.00	20.00	18.00
☐ 5371 (M)	**CROWN**	RICHARD BERRY AND THE DREAMERS	12.00	20.00	18.00

			Current Price Range		P/Y AVG

ROD BERRY AND THE BEL RAVES

| ☐ 1001 | DREEM | WHAT A DOLLY/HOT ROD (Lou Berry) | 90.00 | 175.00 | 100.00 |
| ☐ 169 | 20TH FOX | WHAT A DOLLY/HOT ROD (Lou Berry) | 55.00 | 90.00 | 60.00 |

PETER BEST (EX-BEATLE)

☐ 1118	HAPPENING	THE WAY I FEEL ABOUT YOU/ IF YOU CAN'T GET HER	16.00	30.00	19.00
☐ 800	ORIGINAL BEATLES DRUMMER	(I'LL TRY) ANYWAY/ I WANNA BE THERE	14.00	25.00	16.00
☐ 711	MR. MAESTRO	I CAN'T DO WITHOUT YOU/ KEYS TO MY HEART	14.00	25.00	16.00
☐ 712		I'M BLUE/CASTING MY SPELL	14.00	25.00	16.00
☐ 391	CAMEO	BOYS/KANSAS CITY	11.00	20.00	13.00
☐ 2092	CAPITOL	CAROUSEL OF LOVE/WANT YOU	9.00	17.00	11.00

PETER BEST—ALBUM

| ☐ 71 (M) | SAVAGE | BEST OF THE BEATLES | 30.00 | 55.00 | 30.00 |

BIG BOPPER
SEE: JAPE RICHARDSON

☐ 1008	D	CHANTILLY LACE/PURPLE PEOPLE EATER MEETS THE WITCH DOCTOR	45.00	95.00	51.00
☐ 71343	MERCURY	CHANTILLY LACE/PURPLE PEOPLE EATER MEETS THE WITCH DOCTOR	3.25	5.50	4.00
☐ 71375		BIG BOPPER'S WEDDING/ LITTLE RED RIDING HOOD	3.25	5.50	4.00
☐ 71416		WALKING THROUGH MY DREAMS/ SOMEONE WATCHING OVER YOU	6.00	11.00	7.25
☐ 71451		IT'S THE TRUTH, RUTH/THAT'S WHAT I'M TALKING ABOUT	6.00	11.00	7.25
☐ 71482		PINK PETTICOATS/THE CLOCK	6.00	11.00	7.25

BIG BOPPER—ALBUM

| ☐ 20402 (M) | MERCURY | CHANTILLY LACE | 65.00 | 125.00 | 73.00 |

BIG BROTHER & THE HOLDING COMPANY
VOCALS BY JANIS JOPLIN
SEE: JANIS JOPLIN

☐ 657	MAINSTREAM	BLINDMAN/ALL IS LONLINESS	4.00	8.00	6.50
☐ 662		CALL ON ME/DOWN ON ME	4.00	8.00	6.50
☐ 666		INTRUDER/BYE BYE BABY	4.00	8.00	6.50
☐ 675		WOMEN IS LOSERS/LIGHT IS FASTER THAN SOUND	4.00	8.00	6.50
☐ 678		LAST TIME/COO COO	4.00	8.00	6.50
☐ 44626	COLUMBIA	TURTLE BLUES/ PIECE OF MY HEART	3.00	6.50	5.00
☐ 45502		NU BUGALOO JAM/ BLACK WIDOW SPIDER	2.50	5.50	4.00

COLUMBIA #45502 WAS RECORDED WITHOUT JANIS JOPLIN, WHICH ALMOST CERTAINLY ACCOUNTS FOR THE REDUCED COLLECTOR INTEREST

BIG BROTHER & THE HOLDING COMPANY—ALBUMS

☐ S-6099 (S)	MAINSTREAM	BIG BROTHER & THE HOLDING COMPANY	8.00	24.00	20.00
☐ C-30631 (S)	COLUMBIA	BIG BROTHER & THE HOLDING COMPANY	6.50	17.00	15.00
☐ C-30222 (S)		BE A BROTHER	3.50	12.00	10.00
☐ C-30738 (S)		HOW HARD IT IS	4.50	13.00	11.00
☐ KCS-9700 (S)		CHEAP THRILLS	4.50	13.00	11.00

BIG BOPPER

The Big Bopper, whose real name was Jape Richardson, had just turned 24 when he died in 1959. That accident in an Iowa pasture ended his life but established the Big Bopper forever in rock-and-roll history. Though he had only one Top 10 hit—"Chantilly Lace"—Jape Richardson was a man of many talents, including that of a songwriter for others. "Running Bear" by Johnny Preston was a No. 1 hit penned by Richardson, who is heard making the Indian calls on the record.

A native of Sabine Pass, Texas, where he was born on October 24, 1934, Richardson went by the initial J. P. as he disliked his real name. While in college he found work as a part-time disc jockey. He became an instant success with his jovial bass delivery and soon became a top name on Beaumont's station KTRM.

He cut the single of "Chantilly Lace" on the Texas-based D label. The master was then released to Mercury Records, which had a larger distribution budget. When the single rocketed to the Top 10, Richardson took a leave of absence to go on a midwestern winter tour with Buddy Holly, Ritchie Valens, Dion and the Belmonts, and Frankie Sardo. The rest is history.

			Current Price Range		P/Y AVG

BILLY AND LILLIE

☐4002	SWAN	LA DEE DAH/THE MONSTER	3.25	5.50	4.00
☐4005		HAPPINESS/CREEPIN'. CRAWLIN', CRAWLIN'	3.25	5.50	4.00
☐4011		HANGIN' ON TO YOU/ THE GREASY SPOON	3.25	5.50	4.00
☐4020		LUCKY LADYBUG/I PROMISE YOU	3.25	5.50	4.00
☐4030		TUMBLED DOWN/ALOYSIUS HORATIO THOMAS THE CAT ...	3.25	5.50	4.00
☐4036		BELLS. BELLS. BELLS/ HONEYMOONIN'	3.25	5.50	4.00
☐4042		TERRIFIC TOGETHER/SWAMPY ..	3.25	5.50	4.00
☐4051		FREE FOR ALL/ THE INS AND OUTS (OF LOVE) .	3.25	5.50	4.00
☐4058		OVER THE MOUNTAIN, ACROSS THE SEA/THAT'S THE WAY THE COOKIE CRUMBLES	3.25	5.50	4.00
☐4069		AIN'T COMIN' BACK TO YOU/ BANANAS	3.25	5.50	4.00
☐10421	ABC- PARAMOUNT	LOVE ME SINCERELY/ WHIP IT TO ME BABY	3.25	6.00	4.25
☐10489		CARRY ME 'CROSS THE THRESHOLD/WHY I LOVE BILLY	3.25	6.00	4.25
☐412	CAMEO	OVER AND OVER AGAIN/ TWO OF US	3.25	6.00	4.25
☐435		YOU GOT ME BY THE HEART/ HEAR. YOU BETTER HEAR	3.25	6.00	4.25

CILLA BLACK

☐5196	CAPITOL	YOU'RE MY WORLD/ SUFFER NOW I MUST	3.00	5.00	3.50
☐5258		IT'S FOR YOU/HE WON'T ASK ME	3.00	5.00	3.50
☐5373		IS IT LOVE/ONE LITTLE VOICE ...	3.00	5.00	3.50
☐5414		I'VE BEEN WRONG BEFORE/ MY LOVE COME HOME	3.00	5.00	3.50
☐5595		YESTERDAY/LOVE'S JUST A BROKEN HEART	3.00	5.00	3.50
☐5674		ALFIE/NIGHT TIME IS HERE	3.00	5.00	3.50
☐5763		DON'T ANSWER ME/ THE RIGHT ONE IS LEFT	2.50	4.50	3.00
☐5782		A FOOL AM I/FOR NO ONE	2.50	4.50	3.00

CILLA BLACK—ALBUMS

☐2308 (M)	CAPITOL	IS IT LOVE?	7.00	17.00	15.00
☐2308 (S)		IS IT LOVE?	9.00	25.00	22.50

THE BLACK HAWKS

☐RH-1000	PROMO COPY ROADHOUSE	BEATRICE MY DARLING/ LOVE ME WHEN I'M OLD	20.00	40.00	27.00

BILLY BLAND

☐708	TIP TOP	CHICKEN HOP/ CHICKEN IN A BASKET	10.00	17.50	15.00
☐1016	OLD TOWN	CHICKEN IN THE BASKET/ THE FAT MAN	9.50	17.00	15.00
☐1022		CHICKEN HOP/OH. YOU FOR ME .	3.00	14.00	12.00
☐1035		IF I COULD BE YOUR MAN/ I HAD A DREAM	4.00	6.50	5.00
☐1076		LET THE LITTLE GIRL DANCE/ SWEET THING	3.00	5.00	3.50
☐1082		PARDON ME/YOU WERE BORN TO BE LOVED	3.00	5.00	3.50
☐1088		HARMONY/MAKE BELIEVE LOVER .	3.00	5.00	3.50

BLONDIE

By now everyone knows that Debbie Harry is Blondie. She was born in 1945 in Miami, Fl. Debbie never knew her real parents but was adopted at age three months by a New Jersey couple named Harry.

As a child, Debbie Harry played piano and took ballet lessons. Junior-high found her before her bedroom mirror, experimenting with a variety of hair colors and styles. "I wore ten or twelve different hair colors to school!" she laughs.

She later attended Hawthorne High in Hawthorne, New Jersey. She twirled baton but balked at the idea of joining a beauty contest. ("I've got no talent!") Still, she was named Best Looking Senior Girl before graduating in 1963.

Junior college proved boring, so Debbie split for the flashy magnet called New York City. There Ms. Harry toiled in a beauty shop, typed in an office and even worked as a cocktail waitress for the New York City Playboy Club. She also became involved with a local rock drummer. They took drugs together until he overdosed one day. "I died a couple of times, too," she admits. She curtailed her own drug use.

She joined an eight-piece folk-rock group, Wind in the Willows. Their one LP flopped, so Debbie drifted into the Stilettoes. This was a three-girl rock outfit who dressed in Stone Age costumes and sang oldies. The Stilettoes later disbanded, and Debbie and boyfriend Chris Stein formed Blondie. "The name had nothing to do with my hair," Ms. Harry claims. "We just wanted our future albums racked next to the Beatles!"

			Current Price Range		P/Y AVG
☐ 1093		KEEP TALKIN' THAT SWEET TALK/ EVERYTHING THAT SHINES AIN'T GOLD	3.00	5.00	3.50
☐ 1098		STEADY KIND/I CROSS MY HEART	3.00	5.00	3.50
☐ 1105		MY HEART'S ON FIRE/CAN'T STOP HER FROM DANCING . . .	3.00	5.00	3.50
☐ 1109		UNCLE BUD/ DO THE BUG WITH ME	3.00	5.00	3.50
☐ 1114		ALL I WANT TO DO IS CRY/ BUSY LITTLE BOY	3.00	5.00	3.50
☐ 1124		MAMA STOLE THE CHICKEN/ I SPENT MY LIFE LOVING YOU .	3.00	5.00	3.50
☐ 1128		DARLING WON'T YOU THINK OF ME/HOW MANY HEARTS	3.00	5.00	3.50
☐ 1143		DOING THE MULE/ FARMER IN THE DELL	3.00	5.00	3.50

MARCIE BLANE

☐ 120	**SEVILLE**	BOBBY'S GIRL/TIME TO DREAM .	2.50	4.50	3.00
☐ 123		WHAT DOES A GIRL DO/ HOW CAN I TELL HIM	2.50	4.50	3.00
☐ 126		LITTLE MISS FOOL/ RAGTIME SOUND	2.50	4.50	3.00
☐ 128		YOU GAVE MY NUMBER TO BILLY/ TOLD YOU SO	2.50	4.50	3.00
☐ 133		BOBBY DID/AFTER THE LAUGHTER	2.50	4.50	3.00
☐ 137		SHE'LL BREAK THE STRING/ THE HURTIN' KIND	2.50	4.50	3.00

BLAZONS
SEE: MONKEES

☐ 5001	**BRAVURA**	LITTLE GIRL/MAGIC LAMP	9.00	20.00	18.00

MICHAEL BLESSING (MIKE NESMITH)

☐ 787	**COLPIX**	THE NEW RECRUIT/A JOURNEY . .	9.50	17.00	15.00
☐ 792		UNTIL IT'S TIME FOR YOU TO GO/ WHAT'S THE TROUBLE. OFFICER?	8.50	14.00	12.00

BLONDIE (WITH DEBBIE HARRY)
SEE: WIND IN THE WILLOWS

☐ 45097	**PRIVATE STOCK**	X-OFFENDER/IN THE SUN	5.00	10.00	6.00
☐ 45141		IN THE FLESH/MAN OVERBOARD	5.00	10.00	6.00
☐ 2220	**CHRYSALIS**	DENIS/I'M ONE	4.00	7.00	4.00
☐ 2251		I'M GONNA LOVE YOU TOO/ JUST GO AWAY	4.00	7.00	4.25
☐ 2271		HANGING ON THE TELEPHONE/ FADE AWAY AND RADIATE	3.50	6.00	4.00

BLONDIE—ALBUM

☐ 2023 (S)	**PRIVATE STOCK**	BLONDIE	12.00	25.00	14.00

BLOSSOMS
FEATURED: DARLENE LOVE

☐ 3822	**CAPITOL**	HE PROMISED ME/MOVE ON . . .	3.00	5.00	3.50
☐ 3878		HAVE FAITH IN ME/LITTLE LOUIE	3.00	5.00	3.50
☐ 4072		BABY DADDY-O/NO OTHER LOVE .	3.00	5.00	3.50
☐ 9109	**CHALLENGE**	SON-IN-LAW/I'LL WAIT	2.50	4.50	3.00
☐ 108	**ODE**	WONDERFUL/ CRY LIKE A BABY	2.50	4.50	3.00
☐ 0436	**REPRISE**	GOOD GOOD LOVIN'/THAT'S WHEN THE TEARS START	2.50	4.50	3.00
☐ 13964	**MGM**	TWEEDLE DEE/ YOU GOT ME HUMMIN'	2.50	4.50	3.00

			Current Price Range		P/Y AVG

BLOSSOMS—ALBUM

| ☐ 1007 (M) | *LION* | SHOCK WAVE .... | 7.00 | 17.00 | 15.00 |

BLUE CHEER

☐ 40516	*PHILLIPS*	SUMMERTIME BLUES/ OUT OF FOCUS	3.00	5.00	3.50
☐ 40541		JUST A LITTLE BIT/GYPSY BALL .	3.00	5.00	3.50
☐ 40561		FEATHERS FROM YOUR TREE/ SUN CYCLE	3.00	5.00	3.50
☐ 40602		WEST COAST CHILD OF SUNSHINE/WHEN IT ALL GETS OLD	3.00	5.00	3.50
☐ 40651		ALL NIGHT LONG/FORTUNES ...	3.00	5.00	3.50
☐ 40664		NATURAL MEN/HELLO L.A., BYE BYE BIRMINGHAM	3.00	5.00	3.50
☐ 40682		FOOL/AIN'T THAT THE WAY	3.50	5.50	4.00
☐ 40691		FOOL/PILOT	3.00	5.00	3.50
☐ 40691		PILOT/BABAJAI...............	3.00	5.00	3.50

BLUE CHEER—ALBUMS

☐ 264 (M)	*PHILIPS*	VINCEBUS ERUPTUM	6.00	15.00	13.50
☐ 264 (S)		VINCEBUS ERUPTUM	7.00	17.00	15.00
☐ 278 (S)		OUTSIDE INSIDE	6.00	15.00	13.50
☐ 305 (S)		NEW! IMPROVED!	7.00	17.00	15.00
☐ 333 (S)		BLUE CHEER	6.00	15.00	13.50
☐ 347 (S)		THE ORIGINAL HUMAN BEING ...	6.00	15.00	13.50
☐ 350 (S)		OH! PLEASANT HOPE	6.00	15.00	13.50

BLUE JAYS

☐ 113472	*ROADHOUSE*	COULD I ADORE YOU/ SWEET PAULINE	4.00	7.50	5.00
☐ 2008	*MILESTONE*	LOVER'S ISLAND/ YOU'RE GONNA CRY	3.25	6.00	4.25
☐ 2009		TEARS ARE FALLING/ TREE TOP LEN	3.25	6.00	4.25
☐ 2010		LET'S MAKE LOVE/ ROCK ROCK ROCK	3.25	6.00	4.25
☐ 2012		THE RIGHT TO LOVE/ ROCK ROCK ROCK	3.25	6.00	4.25
☐ 2014		VENUS, MY LOVE/TALL LEN	3.25	6.00	4.25
☐ 2021		ROCK ROCK ROCK/ THE RIGHT TO LOVE	3.25	5.50	4.00

BLUE LITES

| ☐ 67003 | *BAY SOUND* | THEY DON'T KNOW MY HEART/ FOREVER .... | 13.00 | 27.00 | 16.00 |
| ☐ 67007 | | BONEY MARONEY/ LONEY MAN'S PRAYER ...... | 8.50 | 17.00 | 15.00 |

BLUE RIDGE RANGERS
FEATURED: JOHN FOGERTY

☐ 683	*FANTASY*	BLUE RIDGE MOUNTAIN BLUES/ HAVE THINE OWN WAY	2.75	4.50	3.25
☐ 689		JAMBALAYA (ON THE BAYOU)/ WORKIN' ON A BUILDING	2.75	4.50	3.25
☐ 700		HEARTS OF STONE/SOMEWHERE LISTENING (FOR MY NAME) ...	2.75	4.50	3.25
☐ 710		BACK IN THE HILLS/ YOU DON'T OWE ME A THING ..	2.75	4.50	3.25

BLUES MAGOOS

| ☐ 1000 | *GANIM* | WHO DO YOUR LOVE/ LET YOUR LOVE RIDE .... | 4.00 | 6.00 | 5.00 |
| ☐ 5006 | *VERVE FOLKWAYS* | SO I'M WRONT & YOU ARE RIGHT/PEOPLE HAD NO FACES | 4.00 | 6.00 | 5.00 |

			Current Price Range		P/Y AVG
☐ 5044		SO I'M WRONG & YOU ARE RIGHT/PEOPLE HAD NO FACES (reissue)	4.00	6.00	4.00
☐ 72590	**MERCURY**	TOBACCO ROAD/SOMETIMES	3.00	5.00	4.00
☐ 72622		(WE AIN'T GOT) NOTHIN' YET GOTTA GET AWAY	3.00	5.00	4.00
☐ 72660		PIPE DREAM/THERE'S A CHANCE WE CAN MAKE IT	3.00	5.00	4.00
☐ 72692		ONE BY ONE/DANTE'S INFERNO	2.50	4.50	3.75
☐ 72707		I WANNA BE THERE/ SUMMER IS THE MAN	2.50	4.50	3.75
☐ 72729		THERE SHE GOES/LIFE IS JUST A CHER O'BOWLIES	2.50	4.50	3.75
☐ 72762		JINGLE BELLS/SANTA CLAUS IS COMING TO TOWN	3.00	5.00	4.00
☐ 72838		I CAN HEAR THE GRASS GROW/ YELLOW ROSE	2.00	4.00	2.75
☐ 11250	**ABC**	NEVER GOIN' BACK TO GEORGIA/ FELLIN' TIME (I CAN FEEL IT)	2.00	4.00	2.75
		BLUES MAGOOS—ALBUMS			
☐ 61096	**MERCURY**	PSYCHEDELIC LOLLIPOP	7.50	12.50	9.00
☐ 61104		ELECTRIC COMIC BOOK	10.00	20.00	15.00
☐ 61167		BASIC BLUES MAGOOS	8.00	16.00	12.00
☐ 697	**ABC**	NEVER GOIN' BACK TO GEORGIA	6.00	9.00	7.00
☐ 710		GULF COAST BOUND	5.00	9.00	7.00

BLUESOLOGY
FEATURED: ELTON JOHN

☐ 594	**FONTANA**	COME BACK BABY/ TIMES ARE GETTING TOUGHER	23.00	40.00	27.00
☐ 668		EVERY DAY I HAVE THE BLUES/ MR. FRANTIC	23.00	40.00	27.00
☐ 56195	**POLYDOR**	JUST A LITTLE BIT/ SINCE I FOUND YOU BABY	20.00	34.00	23.00

ALL OF THE ABOVE ARE BRITISH RELEASES

BOB AND SHERI

☐ 101	**SAFARI**	THE SURFER MOON/ HUMPTY DUMPTY	290.00	625.00	415.00

THIS WAS BRIAN WILSON'S FIRST PRODUCTION - 1961

BOB B. SOXX AND THE BLUE JEANS

☐ 107	**PHILLIES**	ZIP-A-DEE-DOO-DAH/ FLIP AND NITTY	3.00	5.50	4.00
☐ 110		WHY DO LOVERS BREAK EACH OTHER'S HEARTS/ DR. KAPLAN'S OFFICE	3.00	5.50	4.00
☐ 113		NOT TOO YOUNG TO GET MARRIED/ANNETTE	3.00	5.50	4.00

BOBBETTES

☐ 1144	**ATLANTIC**	MR. LEE/LOOK AT THE STARS	3.25	5.50	4.00
☐ 1159		COME-A COME-A/SPEEDY	3.25	5.50	4.00
☐ 1181		ZOOMY/ROCK AND REE-AH-ZOLE	3.25	5.50	4.00
☐ 1194		THE DREAM/UM BOW BOW	3.25	5.50	4.00
☐ 2027		DON'T SAY GOODNIGHT/ YOU ARE MY SWEETHEART	3.25	5.50	4.00
☐ 2069		I SHOT MR. LEE/UNTRUE LOVE	6.00	12.00	6.75
☐ 104	**TRIPLE-X**	I SHOT MR. LEE/BILLY	3.25	5.50	4.00
☐ 106		HAVE MERCY BABY/ DANCE WITH ME. GEORGIE	3.25	5.50	4.00
☐ 1093	**END**	TEACH ME TONIGHT/ MR. JOHNNY Q	3.25	5.50	4.00
☐ 1095		I DON'T LIKE IT LIKE THAT (PT. 1)/(PT. 2)	3.25	5.50	4.00

			Current Price Range		P/Y AVG

			Current Price Range		P/Y AVG
☐5112	*GONE*	I DON'T LIKE IT LIKE THAT/			
		MR. JOHNNY Q	3.25	5.50	4.00
☐5490	*KING*	OH MEIN PAPA/			
		DANCE WITH ME GEORGIE	3.25	5.50	4.00
☐5551		LOOKING FOR A LOVER/ARE YOU			
		SATISFIED (WITH YOUR LOVE?)	3.25	5.50	4.00
☐5623		MY DEAREST/			
		I'M STEPPING OUT TONIGHT . .	3.25	5.50	4.00
☐5427	*JUBILEE*	OVER THERE (STANDS MY BABY)/			
		LONELINESS	3.25	5.50	4.00
☐5442		BROKEN HEART/MAMA PAPA . . .	3.25	5.50	4.00
☐133	*DIAMOND*	TEDDY/ROW, ROW, ROW	3.25	5.50	4.00
☐142		CLOSE YOUR EYES/SOMEBODY			
		BAD STOLE DE WEDDING BELL .	3.25	5.50	4.00
☐156		MY MAMA SAID/SANDMAN	3.25	5.50	4.00
☐166		IN PARADISE/			
		I AM CLIMBING A MOUNTAIN . .	3.25	5.50	4.00
☐181		YOU AIN'T SEEN NOTHIN' YET/			
		I'M CLIMBING A MOUNTAIN . .	3.25	5.50	4.00
☐189		LOVE IS BLIND/TEDDY	3.25	5.50	4.00
☐1006	*GALLIANT*	I CRIED/OH MY PAPA	3.25	5.50	4.00
☐8832	*RCA*	I'VE GOTTA FACE THE WORLD/			
		HAVING FUN	3.25	5.50	4.00
☐8983		IT'S ALL OVER/			
		HAPPY-GO-LUCKY ME	3.25	5.50	4.00

BOBSLED AND THE TOBOGGANS
FEATURED: BRUCE JOHNSTON

☐400	*CAMEO*	HERE WE GO/SEA AND SKI	4.50	8.00	6.50

BON-AIRES

☐TR3	*RUST*	BLUE BEAT	16.00	37.00	24.00
☐5077		MY LOVE MY LOVE/BYE BYE	7.00	15.00	8.75
☐5097		SHRINE OF ST. CECELIA/			
		JEANIE BABY	7.00	15.00	8.75

GARY U.S. BONDS

☐1003	*LEGRAND*	NEW ORLEANS/			
		PLEASE FORGIVE ME	3.25	5.50	4.00
☐1005		NOT ME/			
		GIVE ME ONE MORE CHANCE . .	5.00	10.00	6.00
☐1008		QUARTER TO THREE/			
		TIME OLD STORY	3.25	5.50	4.00
☐1009		SCHOOL IS OUT/			
		ONE MILLION TEARS	3.25	5.50	4.00
☐1012		SCHOOL IS IN/			
		TRIP TO THE MOON	3.25	5.50	4.00
☐1015		DEAR LADY TWIST/			
		HAVIN' SO MUCH FUN	3.25	5.50	4.00
☐1018		TWIST TWIST SENORA/			
		FOOD OF LOVE	3.25	5.50	4.00
☐1019		SEVEN DAY WEEKEND/			
		GETTIN' A GROOVE	3.25	5.50	4.00
☐1020		COPY CAT/			
		I'LL CHANGE THAT TOO	3.25	5.50	4.00
☐1022		I DIG THIS STATION/			
		MIXED UP FACULTY	3.25	5.50	4.00
☐1025		DO THE LIMBO WITH ME/WHERE			
		DID THAT NAUGHTY GIRL GO . .	3.25	5.50	4.00
☐1027		I DON'T WANNA WAIT/			
		WHAT A DREAM	3.25	5.50	4.00
☐1029		NO MORE HOMEWORK/			
		SHE'S ALRIGHT	3.25	5.50	4.00
☐1030		PERDIDO (PT. 1)/(PT. 2)	3.25	5.50	4.00

			Current Price Range		P/Y AVG
☐ 1031		MY SWEET RUBY ROSE/			
		KING KONG'S MONKEY	3.25	5.50	4.00
☐ 1035		OH YEAH, OH YEAH/			
		LET ME GO LOVER	3.25	5.50	4.00
☐ 1039		DO THE BUMPSIE/			
		BEACHES, U.S.A.	3.25	5.50	4.00
☐ 1040		TAKE ME BACK TO NEW ORLEANS/			
		I'M THAT KIND OF GUY	3.25	5.50	4.00
☐ 1043		SEND HER BACK TO ME/			
		WORKIN' FOR MY BABY	3.25	5.50	4.00
☐ 1045		CALL ME FOR CHRISTMAS/			
		MIXED UP FACULTY	3.25	5.50	4.00
☐ 1046		WHAT A CRAZY WORLD/			
		SARAH JANE	3.25	5.50	4.00
		GARY U.S. BONDS—ALBUMS			
☐ 3001 (M)	**LEGRAND**	DANCE TILL QUARTER TO THREE	14.00	33.00	20.00
☐ 3002 (M)		TWIST UP CALYPSO	14.00	33.00	20.00
☐ 3003 (M)		GREATEST HITS OF			
		GARY U.S. BONDS	18.00	40.00	24.00

BON BONS (SHANGRI-LAS)

			Current Price Range		P/Y AVG
☐ 62402	**CORAL**	WHAT'S WRONG WITH RINGO?/			
		COME ON BABY	6.00	11.00	9.00
☐ 62435		EVERYBODY WANTS MY			
		BOYFRIEND/EACH TIME	4.50	7.50	6.00

BONNIE AND THE TREASURES

			Current Price Range		P/Y AVG
☐ 5005	**PHI DAN**	HOME OF THE BRAVE/OUR SONG	3.50	5.50	4.50

SONNY BONO AND LITTLE TOOTSIE

SEE: DON CHRISTY, RONNY SOMMERS, SONNY, SONNY AND CHER, CAESAR AND CLEO

			Current Price Range		P/Y AVG
☐ 733	**SPECIALTY**	COMIN' DOWN THE CHIMNEY/			
		ONE LITTLE ANSWER	4.50	7.50	6.00

BAB BOON

			Current Price Range		P/Y AVG
☐ 100	**POLEESE**	SONG TITLES/WHISTLER	14.00	34.00	30.00

THE SECOND SIDE OF THIS DISC WAS NOT BY BAB BOON.

PAT BOONE

			Current Price Range		P/Y AVG
☐ 7062	**REPUBLIC**	REMEMBER TO ME MINE/			
		HALFWAY CHANCE WITH YOU	9.50	17.00	15.00
☐ 7084		I NEED SOMEONE/			
		LOVING YOU MADLY	8.50	14.00	12.00
☐ 7119		I NEED SOMEONE/			
		MY HEART BELONGS TO YOU	5.50	11.00	9.00
☐ 15338	**DOT**	TWO HEARTS/TRA LA LA	3.50	6.50	4.25
☐ 15377		AIN'T THAT A SHAME/			
		TENNESSEE SATURDAY NIGHT	3.50	6.50	4.25
☐ 15422		AT MY FRONT DOOR/			
		NO OTHER ARMS	3.50	6.50	4.25
☐ 15435		GEE WHITTAKERS/			
		TAKE THE TIME	3.50	6.50	4.25
☐ 15443		TUTTI FRUITTI/I'LL BE HOME	3.50	6.50	4.25
☐ 15457		LONG TALL TALLY/JUST AS LONG			
		AS I'M WITH YOU	3.50	6.50	4.25
☐ 15472		I ALMOST LOST MY MIND/			
		I'M IN LOVE WITH YOU	3.50	6.00	4.00
☐ 15490		FRIENDLY PERSUASION/			
		CHAINS OF LOVE	3.50	6.00	4.00

FIRST PRESSES OF ABOVE DOT SINGLES WERE ON A MAROON LABEL

			Current Price Range		P/Y AVG
☐ 15521		DON'T FORBID ME/ANASTASIA	2.75	5.00	3.50
☐ 15545		WHY BABY WHY/			
		I'M WAITING JUST FOR YOU	2.75	5.00	3.50
☐ 15570		LOVE LETTERS IN THE SAND/			
		BERNADINE	2.75	5.00	3.50

		Current Price Range		P/Y AVG
☐ 15602	REMEMBER YOU'RE MINE/ THERE'S A GOLD MINE IN THE SKY	2.75	5.00	3.50
☐ 15660	APRIL LOVE/ WHEN THE SWALLOWS COME BACK TO CAPISTRANO	2.75	5.00	3.50
☐ 15690	A WONDERFUL TIME UP THERE/ IT'S TOO SOON TO KNOW	2.75	5.00	3.50
☐ 15750	SUGAR MOON/ CHERIE I LOVE YOU	2.75	5.00	3.50
☐ 15785	IF DREAMS CAME TRUE/THAT'S HOW MUCH I LOVE YOU	2.75	5.00	3.50
☐ 15825	FOR MY GOOD FORTUNE/ GEE BUT IT'S LONELY	2.75	5.00	3.50
☐ 15840	I'LL REMEMBER TONIGHT/ THE MARDI GRAS MARCH	2.75	5.00	3.50
☐ 15888	WITH THE WIND AND THE RAIN IN YOUR HAIR/GOOD ROCKING TONIGHT	2.75	5.00	3.50
☐ 15914	FOR A PENNY/THE WANG DANG TAFFY APPLE TANGO	2.75	5.00	3.50
☐ 15955	TWIXT TWELVE AND TWENTY/ ROCK BOLL WEEVIL	2.75	5.00	3.50
☐ 15982	FOOL'S HALL OF FAME/THE BRIGHTEST WISHING STAR ...	2.75	5.00	3.50
☐ 16006	BEYOND THE SUNSET/ MY FAITHFUL HEART	2.75	5.00	3.50
☐ 16048	(WELCOME) NEW LOVERS/ WORDS	2.75	5.00	3.50
☐ 16073	WALKING THE FLOOR OVER YOU/ SPRING RAIN	2.75	5.00	3.50
☐ 16122	DELIA GONE/CANDY SWEET	2.75	5.00	3.50
☐ 16152	DEAR JOHN/ALABAM	2.75	5.00	3.50
☐ 16176	THE EXODUS SONG/THERE'S A MOON OUT TONIGHT	2.75	5.00	3.50
☐ 16209	MOODY RIVER/ A THOUSAND YEARS	2.75	5.00	3.50
☐ 16244	BIG COLD WIND/ THAT'S MY DESIRE	2.75	5.00	3.50
☐ 16284	JOHNNY WILL/ JUST LET ME DREAM	2.75	5.00	3.50
☐ 16312	I'LL SEE YOU IN MY DREAMS/ PICTURES IN THE FIRE	2.75	5.00	3.50
☐ 16349	QUANDO, QUANDO, QUANDO/ WILLING AND EAGER	2.75	5.00	3.50
☐ 16368	SPEEDY GONZALES/THE LOCKET	2.75	5.00	3.50
☐ 16391	TEN LONELY GUYS/ LOVER'S ISLAND	2.75	5.00	3.50
☐ 16406	BLUES STAY AWAY FROM ME/ EVERY STEP OF THE WAY	2.75	5.00	3.50
☐ 16416	MEXICAN JOE/IN THE ROOM	2.75	5.00	3.50
☐ 16439	MEDITATION/ THE DAYS OF WINE AND ROSES	2.75	5.00	3.50
☐ 16474	ALWAYS YOU AND ME/ MAIN ATTRACTIONS	2.75	5.00	3.50
☐ 16494	TIE ME KANGAROO DOWN SPORT/ I FEEL LIKE CRYING	2.75	5.00	3.50
☐ 16498	MAIN ATTRACTION/SI, SI, SI ...	2.75	5.00	3.50
☐ 16525	MISTER MOON/LOVE ME	2.75	5.00	3.50
☐ 16559	SOME ENCHANTED EVENING/ THAT'S ME	2.75	5.00	3.50
☐ 16576	I LIKE WHAT YOU DO/ NEVER PUT IT IN WRITING	2.75	5.00	3.50

		Current Price Range		P/Y AVG
☐ 16598	I UNDERSTAND/ROSEMARIE	2.75	5.00	3.50
☐ 16626	SIDE BY SIDE/			
	I'LL NEVER BE FREE	2.75	5.00	3.50
☐ 16641	SINCERELY/			
	DON'T YOU JUST KNOW IT	4.00	7.00	4.00
☐ 16658	BEACH GIRL/LITTLE HONDA	5.00	10.00	6.00

DOT 16658 IS A BRIAN WILSON PRODUCTION
LATER DOT SINGLES ARE WORTH UP TO $1.75 MINT

PAT BOONE—EPs

☐ 1049	*DOT*	PAT BOONE	6.00	11.00	7.25
☐ 1053		PAT ON MIKE	6.00	11.00	7.25
☐ 1054		FRIENDLY PERSUASION	6.00	11.00	7.25
☐ 1055		A DATE WITH PAT BOONE	4.75	9.00	6.25
☐ 1056		A CLOSER WALK WITH THEE	4.75	9.00	6.25
☐ 1057		FOUR BY PAT	4.75	9.00	6.25
☐ 1062		MERRY CHRISTMAS	4.75	9.00	6.25
☐ 1064		TUTTI FRUITTI	4.75	9.00	6.25
☐ 1069		STAR DUST	4.30	9.00	6.25
☐ 1075		MARDI GRAS	4.50	9.00	6.25
☐ 1076		SIDE BY SIDE.............	4.50	9.00	6.25
☐ 1082		TENDERLY	4.50	9.00	6.25
☐ 1083		PAT'S GREATEST HITS	4.50	9.00	6.25
☐ 1086		I'M IN THE MOOD FOR LOVE	4.25	7.50	5.50
☐ 1090		BEYOND THE SUNSET	4.25	7.50	5.50
☐ 1091		JOURNEY TO THE CENTER			
		OF THE EARTH	4.25	7.50	5.50
☐ 1096		MOONGLOW	4.25	7.50	5.50

PAT BOONE—ALBUMS

☐ 3012 (M)	*DOT*	PAT BOONE	8.50	20.00	18.00
☐ 3030 (M)		HOWDY	7.50	17.00	15.00
☐ 3050 (M)		PAT	7.50	17.00	15.00
☐ 3068 (M)		HYMNS WE LOVE	7.50	17.00	15.00
☐ 3071 (M)		PAT'S GREAT HITS	5.50	14.00	12.00
☐ 25071 (S)		PAT'S GREAT HITS	7.50	17.00	15.00
☐ 3077 (M)		PAT BOONE SINGS IRVING BERLIN.	5.50	14.00	12.00
☐ 25077 (S)		PAT BOONE SINGS IRVING BERLIN.	7.50	17.00	15.00
☐ 3118 (M)		STAR DUST	5.50	14.00	12.00
☐ 25118 (S)		STAR DUST	7.50	17.00	15.00
☐ 3121 (M)		YES INDEED...............	5.50	14.00	12.00
☐ 25121 (S)		YES INDEED...............	7.50	17.00	15.00
☐ 3158 (M)		PAT BOONE SINGS...........	5.50	14.00	12.00
☐ 25158 (S)		PAT BOONE SINGS...........	7.50	17.00	15.00
☐ 3180 (M)		TENDERLY	5.50	14.00	12.00
☐ 25180 (S)		TENDERLY	7.50	17.00	15.00
☐ 3181 (M)		GREAT MILLIONS	5.50	14.00	12.00
☐ 25181 (S)		GREAT MILLIONS	7.50	17.00	15.00
☐ 3222 (M)		WHITE CHRISTMAS............	5.50	14.00	12.00
☐ 25222 (S)		WHITE CHRISTMAS............	7.50	17.00	15.00
☐ 3261 (M)		PAT'S GREATEST HITS. VOL. II ..	5.50	14.00	12.00
☐ 25261 (S)		PAT'S GREATEST HITS. VOL. II ..	7.50	17.00	15.00
☐ 3270 (M)		MOONGLOW	5.50	14.00	12.00
☐ 25270 (S)		MOONGLOW	7.50	17.00	15.00
☐ 3285 (M)		THIS AND THAT	5.50	14.00	12.00
☐ 25285 (S)		THIS AND THAT	7.50	17.00	15.00
☐ 3346 (M)		GREAT. GREAT. GREAT	4.50	12.00	10.00
☐ 25346 (S)		GREAT. GREAT. GREAT	5.50	14.00	12.00
☐ 3384 (M)		MOODY RIVER	5.50	12.00	10.00
☐ 25384 (S)		MOODY RIVER	5.50	15.00	13.50
☐ 3399 (M)		I'LL SEE YOU IN MY DREAMS ...	4.50	12.00	10.00
☐ 25399 (S)		I'LL SEE YOU IN MY DREAMS ...	5.50	14.00	12.00
☐ 3455 (M)		PAT BOONE GOLDEN HITS	4.50	12.00	10.00
☐ 25455 (S)		PAT BOONE GOLDEN HITS	5.50	14.00	12.00
☐ 3501 (M)		GUESS WHO (Presley hits)	8.50	20.00	18.00
☐ 25501 (S)		GUESS WHO (Presley hits)	9.00	25.00	22.50

PAT BOONE

While less a legend than Presley, Charles Boone (Pat is a middle name) is still a 1950s institution. He was born in Nashville, Tennessee, on June 1, 1934. Pat is a direct descendant of Daniel Boone and was a three-letter athlete as well as student-body president during his high-school days. Shortly after graduation he married another Nashville native, Shirley Foley, a daughter of country star Red Foley.

As a teenager, Boone won a recording contract with Nashville's small Republic label. Nothing from those studio dates was a success. Boone later enrolled in a Nashville college but soon transfered to North Texas State. During that time he won first place on "Ted Mack's Amateur Hour." A disc-jockey pal of Boone's introduced the clean-cut college student to Dot Records owner Randy Wood. While Boone prefered ballads — his real forte — Wood insisted that Boone "cover" r & b hits of the day. Those insipid singles made Boone's name known, and his record sales rivaled Presley's during the later 1950s. Pat was later allowed the shift to ballads, where he found even greater success.

			Current Price Range		P/Y AVG

BOP-CHORDS

			Current	Price Range	P/Y AVG
☐2601	HOLIDAY	CASTLE IN THE SKY/			
		MY DARLING, TO YOU	17.00	29.00	25.00
☐2603		WHEN I WOKE UP THIS MORNING/			
		I REALLY LOVE HER	14.00	24.00	20.00
☐2608		BABY/SO WHY	12.00	20.00	18.00

THE BOTTOM LINE
FEATURED: TONY ORLANDO

☐15556	A&M	WHEN I WAS KING/			
		SHOW ME THE WORLD OF			
		WONDER	3.50	6.00	4.50

JIMMY BOWEN

☐797	TRIPLE D	I'M STICKIN' WITH YOU/			
		PARTY DOLL (Buddy Knox)	75.00	150.00	90.00
☐4001	ROULETTE	I'M STICKIN' WITH YOU/			
		EVER-LOVIN' FINGERS	3.25	4.50	4.00
☐4010		WARM UP TO ME BABY/			
		I TRUSTED YOU	3.25	4.50	4.00
☐4017		DON'T TELL ME YOUR TROUBLES/			
		EVER SINCE THAT NIGHT	3.25	4.50	4.00
☐4023		CROSS OVER/IT'S SHAMEFUL ..	3.25	4.50	4.00
☐4083		BY THE LIGHT OF THE SILVERY			
		MOON/THE TWO-STEP	3.00	5.00	3.50
☐4102		MY KIND OF WOMAN/BLUE MOON	3.00	5.00	3.50
☐4122		ALWAYS FAITHFUL/			
		WISH I WERE TIED TO YOU	3.00	5.00	3.50
☐4175		YOU'RE JUST WASTING YOUR			
		TIME/WALKING ON AIR	3.00	5.00	3.50
☐4224		YOUR LOVING ARMS/			
		OH YEAH, OH YEAH	3.00	5.00	3.50

JIMMY BOWEN—EP

☐302	ROULETTE	JIMMY BOWEN	9.50	17.00	15.00

JIMMY BOWEN—ALBUM

☐25004 (M)	ROULETTE	JIMMY BOWEN	25.00	60.00	38.00

DAVID BOWIE

☐5815	WARNER BROTHERS	CAN'T HELP THINKING ABOUT ME/			
		AND I SAY TO MYSELF	25.00	42.00	27.00
☐85009	DERAM	RUBBER BAND/			
		THE LONDON BOYS	17.00	33.00	20.00
☐85009		RUBBER BAND/			
		THERE IS A HAPPY LAND	14.00	25.00	16.00
☐85016		LOVE YOU TILL TUESDAY/			
		DID YOU EVER HAVE A DREAM?	14.00	25.00	16.00
☐72949	MERCURY	SPACE ODDITY/WILD-EYED BOY			
		FROM FREECLOUD	10.00	18.00	12.00
☐73075		MEMORY OF A FREE FESTIVAL			
		(PT. 1)/(PT. 2)..............	11.00	20.00	13.00
☐0605	RCA	CHANGES/ANDY WARHOL	3.50	6.00	4.00
☐0719		STARMAN/SUFFRAGETTE CITY ..	3.50	6.00	4.00
☐0838		THE JEAN GENIE/			
		HANG ON TO YOURSELF	3.50	6.00	4.00
☐0876		SPACE ODDITY/THE MAN			
		WHO SOLD THE WORLD	2.25	4.00	2.50
		LATER RCA SINGLES ARE WORTH UP TO $3.00 MINT			

DAVID BOWIE—ALBUMS

☐16003 (M)	DERAM	DAVID BOWIE	28.00	62.00	39.00
☐18003 (S)		DAVID BOWIE	35.00	75.00	47.00
☐61246 (M)	MERCURY	MAN OF WORDS, MAN OF MUSIC	28.00	62.00	39.00
☐61325 (S)		THE MAN WHO SOLD THE WORLD			
		(with rare drag photo cover)	215.00	480.00	320.00

DAVID BOWIE

His real name is David Robert Jones, but he later became David Bowie in order to avoid confusion with Monkee Davey Jones. David Jones/Bowie first saw life on January 8, 1947, in Brixton, England.

He attended Bromley Technical School in Kent where his art teacher, Mr. Frampton, introduced David to son Peter. Future superstars David Bowie and Peter Frampton then played a Bromley Christmas assembly. Frampton played guitar, Bowie an old, leaky saxophone.

Bowie quit school shortly afterwards. Even though he possessed a super IQ, he was passing just two classes — art and wood shop. He then worked as a commercial artist and a male model for shirts.

Bowie played in groups like George and the Dragons and the Conrads but later headed his own outfit called the Lower Third. His band traveled from gig to gig in an old white ambulance that Bowie owned. (He later sold it for $25.00.)

His "straight" act went nowhere so David Bowie became an outrageous drag/glitter artist. "It was the only way I could get recognition." he later admitted.

After years of English popularity, David Bowie finally earned American acceptance during the early 1970s.

			Current Price Range		P/Y AVG
☐ 61325 (S)		THE MAN WHO SOLD THE WORLD	9.00	20.00	12.00
☐ 50007 (S)	LONDON	STARTING POINT	9.00	20.00	12.00
☐ 61829 (S)		IMAGES	9.00	20.00	12.00
☐ 4623 (S)	RCA	HUNKY DORY	9.00	20.00	12.00
☐ 4702 (S)		THE RISE AND FALL OF ZIGGY STARDUST AND THE SPIDERS FROM MARS	8.00	18.00	11.00
☐ 4813 (S)		SPACE ODDITY	7.00	16.00	9.00
☐ 4816 (S)		THE MAN WHO SOLD THE WORLD	6.00	14.00	8.50

LATER RCA ALBUMS ARE WORTH UP TO $9.00 MINT

BOYFRIENDS (5 DISCS)

☐ 569	KAPP	LET'S FALL IN LOVE/OH LANA . .	17.50	30.00	25.00

JAN BRADLEY

☐ 1044	FORMAL	MAMA DIDN'T LIE/ LOVERS LIKE ME	8.25	14.00	12.00
☐ 1845	CHESS	MAMA DIDN'T LIE/ LOVERS LIKE ME	2.50	5.00	3.00
☐ 1851		THESE TEARS/ BABY, WHAT CAN I DO?	2.50	5.00	3.00
☐ 1884		PACK MY THINGS/ CURFEW BLUES	2.50	5.00	3.00
☐ 1897		PLEASE MR. DJ/TWO OF A KIND .	2.50	5.00	3.00
☐ 1919		I'M OVER YOU/THE BRUSH OFF .	2.50	5.00	3.00
☐ 1975		JUST A SUMMER MEMORY/ HE'LL WAIT FOR ME	2.50	5.00	13.00
☐ 2023		YOUR KIND OF LOVE/ IT'S JUST YOUR WAY	2.50	5.00	3.00
☐ 2043		YOU HAVE ME, WHAT'S MISSING/ NIGHTS IN NEW YORK CITY . . .	2.50	5.00	3.00

BRAVE BELT (PRE-BACHMAN TURNER OVERDRIVE)

☐ 1023	REPRISE	ROCK AND ROLL BAND/ ANYDAY MEANS TOMORROW .	3.50	5.50	4.00
☐ 1039		CRAZY ARMS, CRAZY EYES/ HOLY TRAIN	3.50	5.50	4.00
☐ 1061		NEVER COMIN' HOME/ CAN YOU FEEL IT?	3.50	5.50	4.00
☐ 1083		ANOTHER WAY OUT/ DUNROBIN'S GONE	3.50	5.50	4.00

BREAD
FEATURED: DAVID GATES
SEE: DEL ASHLEY

☐ 45365	ELEKTRA	CHANGE OF HEART/ LOST WITHOUT YOUR LOVE . . .	2.25	4.50	3.00
☐ 45666		ANY WAY YOU WANT ME/ DISMAL DAY	3.50	6.50	5.00
☐ 45668		COULD/ I CAN'T MEASURE THE COST . .	3.50	6.50	5.00
☐ 45686		(I WANNA) MAKE IT WITH YOU/ WHY DO YOU KEEP ME WAITING	2.00	5.00	3.00
☐ 45701		IT DON'T MATTER TO ME/ CALL ON ME	2.00	5.00	3.00
☐ 45711		TOO MUCH LOVE/ LET YOUR LOVE GO	2.50	5.00	3.00
☐ 45720		IF/TAKE COMFORT	2.50	5.00	3.00
☐ 45740		LIVE IN YOUR LOVE/ MOTHER FREEDOM	2.50	5.00	3.00
☐ 45751		BABY I'M-A WANT YOU/ TRUCKIN'	2.50	5.00	3.00

			Current Price Range		P/Y AVG

| ☐45784 | | (I FOUND HER) DIARY/ | | | |
| | | DOWN ON MY KNEES . . . . | 2.50 | 5.00 | 3.00 |

DAVID GATES, LEAD SINGER OF BREAD, LATER SCORED A HUGE SUCCESS ON HIS OWN WITH HIS RECORD OF "THE GOODBYE GIRL," A MOVIE THEME

RONNIE BRENT

☐108	*UNITED ARTISTS*	LOVE/MY SEET VERLENA	17.00	37.00	24.00

BREWER & SHIPLEY

☐905	*A&M*	I CAN'T SEE HER/			
		KEEPER OF THE KEYS	3.50	7.00	5.00
☐938		GREEN BAMBOO/TRULY RIGHT . .	3.50	7.00	5.00
☐996		TIME & CHANGES/			
		DREAMIN' IN THE SHADE	3.50	7.00	5.00
☐516	*KAMA SUTRA*	ONE TOKE OVER THE LINE/			
		OH MOMMY	2.25	5.00	3.00
☐524		SEEMS LIKE A LONG TIME/			
		TARKIO ROAD	2.50	4.25	3.75
☐539		INDIAN SUMMER/			
		SHAKE OFF THE DEMON	2.50	4.25	3.75
☐547		YANKEE LADY/NATURAL CHILD .	2.50	4.25	3.75

BREWER & SHIPLEY'S "ONE TOKE OVER THE LINE," PRESSED IN 1971, WAS THE FIRST RECORD ABOUT MARIJUANA SMOKING THAT RECEIVED WIDESPREAD AIRPLAY IN THE U.S.

BROOKLYN BRIDGE
FEATURED: JOHNNY MAESTRO

☐60	*BUDDAH*	FROM MY WINDOW/LITTLE RED			
		BOAT BY THE RIVER	4.00	7.00	4.50
☐75		WORST THAT COULD HAPPEN/			
		YOUR KITE. MY KITE	3.00	5.25	3.75
☐95		BLESSED IS THE RAIN/			
		WELCOME ME LOVE	3.00	5.25	3.75
☐126		YOUR HUSBAND - MY WIFE/			
		UPSIDE DOWN	3.00	5.25	3.75
☐139		YOU'LL NEVER WALK ALONE/			
		MINSTREL LADY	3.00	5.25	3.75
☐162		FREE AS THE WIND/			
		HE'S NOT A HAPPY MAN	3.00	5.25	3.75
☐179		DOWN BY THE RIVER/LOOK AGAIN	3.00	5.25	3.75
☐193		DAY IS DONE/OPPOSITES	3.00	5.25	3.75
☐199		NIGHTS IN WHITE SATIN/			
		CYNTHIA	3.00	5.25	3.75
☐201		NEVER KNEW THIS KIND OF HURT			
		BEFORE/THEN RAIN CAME			
		(Johnny Maestro)	3.00	5.25	3.75

BROOKLYN BRIDGE—ALBUMS

☐5034 (S)	*BUDDAH*	BROOKLYN BRIDGE	7.50	17.00	15.00
☐5042 (S)		SECOND	7.50	17.00	15.00
☐5065 (S)		THE BROOKLYN BRIDGE	7.50	17.00	15.00
☐5107 (S)		BRIDGE IN BLUE	7.50	17.00	15.00

JAMES BROWN

☐12258	*FEDERAL*	PLEASE PLEASE PLEASE/			
		WHY DO YOU DO ME	5.50	9.00	7.00
☐12277		HOLD MY BABY'S HAND/			
		NO. NO. NO. NO	8.50	14.00	12.00
☐12289		JUST WON'T DO RIGHT/			
		LET'S MAKE IT	8.50	14.00	12.00
☐12290		I WON'T PLEAD NO MORE/			
		CHONNIE ON CHON	8.50	14.00	12.00
☐12292		GONNA TRY/CAN'T BE THE SAME	8.50	14.00	12.00
☐12295		MESSING WITH THE BLUES/			
		GONNA TRY	8.50	14.00	12.00

			Current Price Range		P/Y AVG
☐ 12300		I WALKED ALONE/			
		YOU'RE MINE, YOU'RE MINE ..	8.50	14.00	12.00
☐ 12311		THAT DOOD IT/			
		BABY CRIES OVER THE OCEAN .	8.50	14.00	12.00
☐ 12316		BEGGING, BEGGING/THAT'S			
		WHEN I LOST MY HEART	8.50	14.00	12.00
☐ 12337		TRY ME/			
		TELL ME WHAT I DID WRONG ..	5.00	9.00	5.75
☐ 12348		I WANT YOU SO BAD/			
		THERE MUST BE A REASON ...	5.00	9.00	5.75
☐ 12352		I'VE GOT TO CHANGE/			
		IT HURTS TO TELL YOU	5.00	9.00	5.75
☐ 12361		GOOD GOOD LOVIN'/			
		DON'T LET IT HAPPEN TO ME ..	5.00	9.00	5.75
☐ 12364		IT WAS YOU/GOT TO CRY	5.00	9.00	5.75
☐ 12369		I'LL GO CRAZY/			
		I KNOW IT'S TRUE	5.00	9.00	5.75
☐ 12370		THINK/YOU'VE GOT THE POWER .	5.00	9.00	5.75
☐ 12378		THIS OLD HEART/WONDER WHEN			
		YOU'RE COMING HOME	5.00	9.00	5.75
☐ 5423	KING	THE BELLS/			
		AND I DO WHAT I WANT	5.00	9.00	5.75
☐ 5438		HOLD IT/THE SCRATCH	5.00	9.00	5.75
☐ 5442		BEWILDERED/IF YOU WANT ME .	5.00	9.00	5.75
☐ 5466		I DON'T MIND/			
		LOVE DON'T LOVE NOBODY ...	5.00	9.00	5.75
☐ 5485		STICKY SUDS (PT. 1)/PT. 2)	5.00	9.00	5.75
☐ 5524		BABY YOU'RE RIGHT/			
		I'LL NEVER LET YOU GO	5.00	9.00	5.75
☐ 5547		I LOVE YOU, YES I DO/			
		JUST YOU AND ME, DARLING ..	5.00	9.00	5.75
☐ 5573		LOST SOMEONE/CROSS FIRING .	5.00	9.00	5.75
☐ 5614		NIGHT TRAIN/WHY DOES			
		EVERYTHING HAPPEN TO ME? .	5.00	9.00	5.75
☐ 5657		SHOUT AND SHIMMY/			
		COME OVER HERE	5.00	9.00	5.75
☐ 5672		MASHED POTATOES U.S.A./			
		YOU DON'T HAVE TO GO	5.00	9.00	5.75
☐ 5701		THREE HEARTS IN A TANGLE/			
		I'VE LOST MONEY	5.00	9.00	5.75
☐ 5710		EVERY BEAT OF MY HEART/			
		LIKE A BABY	5.00	9.00	5.75
☐ 5739		PRISONER OF LOVE/CHOO-CHOO	5.00	9.00	5.75
☐ 5767		THESE FOOLISH THINGS/			
		FEEL IT (PT. 1)	5.00	9.00	5.75
☐ 5803		SIGNED, SEALED AND DELIVERED/			
		WAITING IN VAIN	5.00	9.00	5.75
☐ 5829		I'VE GOT TO CHANGE/THE BELLS	5.00	9.00	5.75
☐ 5842		OH BABY DON'T YOU WEEP			
		(PT. 1)/(PT. 2)	5.00	9.00	5.75
☐ 5853		PLEASE PLEASE PLEASE/			
		IN THE WEE WEE HOURS	5.00	9.00	5.75
☐ 5876		HOW LONG DARLING/AGAIN	4.50	6.00	5.00
☐ 5899		SO LONG/DANCIN' LITTLE THING	4.50	7.00	5.00
☐ 5956		FINE OLD FOXY SELF/MEDLEY ..	4.50	7.00	5.00
☐ 5968		HAVE MERCY BABY/			
		JUST WON'T DO RIGHT	4.50	7.00	5.00
☐ 5999		PAPA'S GOT A BRAND NEW BAG/			
		(PT. 2)	3.00	5.00	3.50
☐ 6015		I GOT YOU (I FEEL GOOD)/			
		I CAN'T HELP IT	3.00	5.00	3.50
☐ 6020		I'LL GO CRAZY/LOST SOMEONE .	3.00	5.00	3.50
☐ 6025		AIN'T THAT A GROOVE/(PT. 2) ..	3.00	5.00	3.50

			Current Price Range		P/Y AVG
☐6032		COME OVER HERE/TELL ME WHAT YOU'RE GONNA DO	3.00	5.00	3.50
☐6035		IT'S A MAN'S MAN'S MAN'S MAN'S WORLD/IS IT YES OR IS IT YOU?	3.00	5.00	3.50

LATER KING SINGLES WORTH UP TO $3.00 MINT

JAMES BROWN—EPs

☐430	*KING*	PLEASE, PLEASE, PLEASE	5.50	10.00	8.50
☐826		LIVE AT THE APOLLO	4.50	9.00	7.25

JAMES BROWN—ALBUMS

☐610 (M)	*KING*	PLEASE, PLEASE, PLEASE	17.00	38.00	35.00
☐635 (M)		TRY ME	14.50	34.00	30.00
☐683 (M)		THINK	14.50	34.00	30.00
☐743 (M)		THE ALWAYS AMAZING JAMES BROWN AND THE FAMOUS FLAMES	12.00	28.00	25.00
☐771 (M)		JUMP AROUND	12.00	28.00	25.00
☐780 (M)		THE EXCITING JAMES BROWN ...	10.00	25.00	22.50
☐804 (M)		TOUR THE U.S.A.	10.00	25.00	22.50
☐826 (M)		THE JAMES BROWN SHOWN	10.00	25.00	22.50
☐851 (M)		PRISONER OF LOVE	10.00	25.00	22.50
☐883 (M)		PURE DYNAMITE	8.50	20.00	18.00
☐909 (M)		PLEASE, PLEASE, PLEASE	8.50	20.00	18.00
☐919 (M)		THE UNBEATABLE 16 HITS	8.50	20.00	18.00
☐938 (M)		PAPA'S GOT A BRAND NEW BAG .	7.50	17.00	15.00
☐946 (M)		I GOT YOU (I FEEL GOOD)	7.50	17.00	15.00
☐985 (M)		SOUL BROTHER #1	6.50	15.00	13.50

LATER KING ALBUMS ARE WORTH UP TO $8.00 MINT

BRUCE AND JERRY
FEATURED: BRUCE JOHNSTON

☐1003	*ARWIN*	I SAW HER FIRST/ TAKE THIS PEARL	6.00	7.50	9.00

BRUCE AND TERRY
FEATURED: BRUCE JOHNSTON, TERRY MELCHER

☐42956	*COLUMBIA*	CUSTOM MACHINE/ MAKAHA AT MIDNIGHT	4.50	7.50	6.00
☐43055		SUMMER MEANS FUN/YEAH! ...	3.50	5.50	4.50
☐43238		I LOVE YOU MODEL T/CARMEN ..	4.50	7.50	6.00
☐43378		FOUR STRONG WINDS/ RAINING IN MY HEART	4.50	7.50	6.00
☐43479		COME LOVE/THANK YOU BABY ..	4.50	7.50	6.00
☐43582		DON'T RUN AWAY/ IT'S ALRIGHT NOW	4.50	7.50	6.00

BILLY BRYAN (GENE PITNEY)

☐351	*BLAZE*	GOING BACK TO MY LOVE/ CRADLE OF MY ARMS	5.50	8.50	7.00

BUBBLE PUPPY

☐128	*INTERNATIONAL ARTISTS*	HOT SMOKE AND SASSAFRASS/ LONELY	3.50	5.50	3.50
☐133		IF I HAD A REASON/BEGINNINGS	3.50	5.50	3.50
☐136		DAYS OF OUR TIME/ THINKIN' ABOUT THINKIN' ...	3.50	5.50	3.50
☐138		WHAT DO YOU SEE/ HURRY SUNDOWN	3.50	5.50	3.50

BUBBLE PUPPY—ALBUM

☐10 (M)	*INTERNATIONAL ARTISTS*	A GATHERING OF PROMISES	15.00	32.00	21.00

			Current Price Range		P/Y AVG

BUCHANAN AND GOODMAN

☐101	*RADIOACTIVE*	THE FLYING SAUCER (PT. 1)/ (PT. 2)	16.00	29.00	19.00
☐101	*LUNIVERSE*	THE FLYING SAUCER (PT. 1)/ (PT. 2)	6.00	11.00	7.00
☐102		BUCHANAN AND GOODMAN ON TRIAL/CRAZY	8.00	14.00	10.00
☐103		THE BANANA BOAT STORY/ THE MYSTERY	9.00	17.00	11.00
☐105		FLYING SAUCER THE 2ND/ MARTIAN MELODY	6.00	11.50	8.50
☐107		SANTA AND THE SATELLITE (PT. 1)/(PT. 2)	6.00	11.50	8.50
☐108		THE FLYING SAUCER GOES WEST/ SAUCER SERENADE	9.00	17.00	11.00
☐500	*COMIC*	FLYING SAUCER THE 3RD/ THE CHA CHA LESSON	9.00	17.00	11.00
☐301	*NOVELTY*	FRANKENSTEIN OF '59/ FRANKENSTEIN RETURNS	6.00	11.50	8.50

BUCHANAN AND GOODMAN—ALBUM

☐716 (M)	*BUCHANAN AND GOODMAN*	THE FLYING SAUCER STORY, VOL. 1	35.00	75.00	46.00

BUCKINGHAMS

SEE: CENTURIES, FALLING PEBBLES

☐4618	*SPECTRA-SOUND*	SWEETS FOR MY SWEET/ BEGINNER'S LOVE	5.50	11.00	9.00
☐844	*U.S.A.*	DON'T WANT TO CRY/ I'LL GO CRAZY	3.50	5.50	4.00
☐848		I CALL YOUR NAME/ MAKIN' UP AND BREAKIN' UP	3.50	5.50	4.00
☐860		KIND OF A DRAG/ YOU MAKE ME FEEL SO GOOD	2.50	5.00	3.00
☐869		LAWDY MISS CLAWDY/ MAKIN' UP AND BREAKIN' UP	2.75	5.25	3.75
☐44053	*COLUMBIA*	DON'T YOU CARE/ WHY DON'T YOU LOVE ME	2.75	5.25	3.75
☐44182		MERCY, MERCY, MERCY/ YOU ARE GONE	2.75	5.25	3.75
☐44254		HEY BABY (THEY'RE PLAYING OUR SONG)/AND OUR LOVE	2.75	5.25	3.75
☐44378		SUSAN/FOREIGN POWER	2.75	5.25	3.75
☐44533		BACK IN LOVE AGAIN/ YOU MISUNDERSTAND ME	2.75	5.25	3.75
☐44672		WHERE DID YOU COME FROM/ SONG OF THE BREEZE	2.75	5.25	3.75
☐44790		THIS IS HOW MUCH I LOVE YOU/ CAN'T FIND THE WORDS	2.75	5.25	3.75
☐44923		IT'S A BEAUTIFUL DAY/ DIFFERENCE OF OPINION	2.75	5.25	3.75
☐3258	*LAURIE*	GONNA SAY GOODBYE/ MANY TIMES	2.75	5.25	3.75

BUCKINGHAMS—ALBUMS

☐107 (M)	*U.S.A.*	KIND OF A DRAG	14.50	34.00	30.00
☐107 (S)		KIND OF A DRAG	8.50	20.00	18.00
☐2669 (M)	*COLUMBIA*	TIME AND CHARGES	8.50	20.00	18.00
☐9469 (S)		TIME AND CHARGES	7.00	17.00	15.00
☐2798 (M)		PORTRAITS	8.50	20.00	18.00
☐9589 (S)		PORTRAITS	7.00	17.00	15.00
☐2903 (M)		IN ONE EAR AND GONE TOMORROW	8.50	20.00	18.00

			Current Price Range		P/Y AVG
☐9703 (S)		IN ONE EAR AND GONE TOMORROW	7.00	20.00	18.00
☐3012 (M)		THE BUCKINGHAMS' GREATEST HITS	9.00	25.00	22.50
☐9812 (S)		THE BUCKINGHAMS' GREATEST HITS	6.50	15.00	13.50

BUDDIES (TOKENS)

☐102	*SWING*	ON THE GO/MY ONLY FRIEND ...	4.50	7.50	6.00

BUDDY AND THE FADS

☐1001	*MOROCCO*	WON'T YOU LOVE ME?/ IS IT JUST A GAME?	9.50	17.00	15.00

BUFFALO REBELS (ROCKIN' REBELS)

☐0095	*MAR-LEE*	DONKEY WALK/BUFFALO BLUES	4.50	7.50	6.00
☐0096		THEME FROM REBEL/ ANY WAY YOU WANT ME	4.50	7.50	6.00

BUFFALO SPRINGFIELD

☐6428	*ATCO*	NOWADAYS CLANCY CAN'T EVEN SING/GO AND SAY GOODBYE ..	3.50	6.00	4.25
☐6452		BURNED/EVERBODY'S WRONG ..	3.50	6.00	4.25
☐6459		FOR WHAT IT'S WORTH/ DO I HAVE TO COME RIGHT OUT AND SAY IT	2.75	5.25	3.75
☐6499		BLUEBIRD/MR. SOUL	2.75	5.25	3.75
☐6519		ROCK 'N' ROLL WOMAN/ A CHILD'S CLAIM TO FAME ...	2.75	5.25	3.75
☐6545		EXPECTING TO FLY/EVERYDAYS .	2.75	5.25	3.75
☐6572		UNO-MUNDO/MERRY-GO-ROUND	2.75	5.25	3.75
☐6602		KIND WOMAN/SPECIAL CARE ...	2.75	5.25	3.75
☐6615		ON THE WAY HOME/ FOUR DAYS GONE	2.75	5.25	3.75

BUFFALO SPRINGFIELD—ALBUMS

☐200 (S)	*ATCO*	BUFFALO SPRINGFIELD (without "For What It's Worth")	17.00	38.00	24.00
☐200 (S)		BUFFALO SPRINGFIELD (with "For What It's Worth") ..	9.00	20.00	12.00
☐226 (S)		BUFFALO SPRINGFIELD AGAIN ..	9.00	20.00	12.00
☐256 (S)		LAST TIME AROUND	9.00	20.00	12.00
☐283 (S)		RETROSPECTIVE (THE BEST OF BUFFALO SPRINGFIELD)	7.00	17.00	11.00

TOMMY BURK & THE COUNTS

☐1003	*RICH-ROSE*	SHE TOLD A LIE/ YOU TOOK MY HEART	11.00	34.00	30.00

SOLOMON BURKE

☐485	*APOLLO*	CHRISTMAS PRESENTS/ WHEN I'M ALL ALONE	5.00	10.00	8.00
☐487		WHY DO ME THAT WAY/ I'M IN LOVE	5.00	10.00	8.00
☐500		WALKING IN A DREAM/ NO MAN WALKS ALONE	5.00	10.00	8.00
☐505		YOU CAN RUN BUT YOU CAN'T HIDE/A PICTURE OF YOU	5.00	10.00	8.00
☐511		I NEED YOU TONIGHT/ THIS IS IT	5.00	10.00	8.00
☐522		THEY ALWAYS SAY/ DON'T CRY	5.00	8.00	6.50
☐527		MY HEART IS A CHAPEL/ THIS IS IT	5.00	8.00	6.50

			Current Price Range		P/Y AVG
☐2114	**ATLANTIC**	JUST OUT OF REACH/ BE BOP GRANDMA	5.00	8.00	6.50
☐2131		CRY TO ME/ I ALMOST LOST MY MIND	5.00	8.00	6.50
☐2147		I'M HANGING UP MY HEART FOR YOU/DOWN IN THE VALLEY	5.00	8.00	6.50
☐2157		TONIGHT MY HEART SHE IS CRYING/I REALLY DON'T WANT TO KNOW	4.00	7.00	5.50
☐2170		GO ON BACK TO HIM/ I SAID I WAS SORRY	4.00	7.00	5.50
☐2180		HOME IN YOUR HEART/WORDS	3.00	5.00	4.00
☐2185		IF YOU NEED ME/ YOU CAN MAKE IT IF YOU TRY	3.00	5.00	4.00
☐2196		CAN'T NOBODY LOVE YOU/ STUPIDITY	3.00	5.00	4.00
☐2205		YOU'RE GOOD FOR ME/ BEAUTIFUL BROWN EYES	3.00	5.00	4.00
☐2218		HE'LL HAVE TO GO/ ROCKIN' SOUL	3.00	5.00	4.00
☐2226		GOODBYE BABY, BABY GOODBYE/ SOMEONE TO LOVE ME	3.00	5.00	4.00
☐2241		EVERYBODY NEEDS SOMEBODY TO LOVE/LOOKING FOR MY BABY	3.00	5.00	4.00
☐2254		WON'T YOU GIVE HIM ONE MORE CHANCE/YES I DO	3.00	5.00	4.00
☐2259		THE PRICE/MORE ROCKIN' SOUL	3.00	5.00	4.00
☐2276		GOT TO GET YOU OFF/ PEEPIN'	3.00	5.00	4.00
☐2288		TONIGHT'S THE NIGHT/ MAGGIE'S FARM	3.00	5.00	4.00
☐2299		SOMEONE IS WATCHING/ DANCE, DANCE, DANCE	3.00	5.00	4.00
☐2308		ONLY LOVE (CAN SAVE ME NOW)/ LITTLE GIRL THAT LOVES ME	3.00	5.00	4.00
☐2314		BABY COME ON HOME/ CAN'T STOP LOVIN' YOU NOW	3.00	5.00	4.00
☐2327		I FEEL A SIN COMING ON/ MOUNTAIN OF PRIDE	3.00	5.00	4.00
☐2345		LAWDY MISS CLAUDY/ SUDDENLY	3.00	5.00	4.00
☐2349		KEEP LOOKING/I DON'T WANT YOU NO MORE	3.00	5.00	4.00
☐2359		WOMAN HOW DO YOU MAKE ME LOVE YOU LIKE I DO/ WHEN SHE TOUCHES ME	3.00	5.00	4.00
☐2369		PRESENTS FOR CHRISTMAS/ A TEAR FELL	3.00	5.00	4.00
		SOLOMAN BURKE — ALBUMS			
ALP498	**APOLLO**	SOLOMON BURKE	14.00	25.00	20.00
☐8067	**ATLANTIC**	SOLOMON BURKE'S GREATEST HITS	10.00	15.00	12.00
☐8096		ROCK 'N' SOUL	10.00	15.00	13.00
☐8109		THE BEST OF SOLOMON BURKE	5.00	9.00	7.50
☐8158		THE SOUL SOUNDS OF SOLOMON BURKE - KING SOLOMON	5.00	9.00	7.50
☐8185		I WISH I KNEW	5.00	9.00	7.50
☐LPS6033	**BELL**	PROUD MARY	4.00	8.00	6.00
☐SE4767	**MGM**	ELECTRONIC MAGNETISM	4.00	8.00	6.00
☐4830		WE'RE ALMOST HOME	4.00	8.00	6.00
☐35ST		COOL BREEZE	4.00	8.00	6.00
☐60042	**CHESS**	MUSIC TO MAKE LOVE BY	4.00	8.00	6.00
☐AMX1018	**AMHERST**	PLEASE DON'T SAY GOODBYE TO ME	4.00	8.00	6.00

			Current Price Range		P/Y AVG
☐ SL14717	**SAVOY**	TAKE ME, SHAKE ME	4.00	8.00	6.00
☐ 2042/43	**ROUNDER**	SOULD ALIVE (2 LP LIVE SET) ...	4.00	8.00	6.00

DORSEY BURNETTE

☐ 188	**ABBOTT**	THE DEVIL'S QUEEN/			
		LET'S FALL IN LOVE	4.50	7.50	6.00
☐ 16	**CEE JAM**	BERTHA LOU/			
		'TIL THE LAW SAYS STOP	4.50	7.50	6.00
☐ 5561	**IMPERIAL**	TRY/YOU CAME AS A MIRACLE ..	3.25	5.50	4.00
☐ 5597		LONELY TRAIN/MISERY	3.25	5.50	4.00
☐ 5668		WAY IN THE MIDDLE OF THE			
		NIGHT/YOUR LOVE	3.25	5.50	4.00
☐ 5987		CIRCLE ROCK/			
		HOUSE WITH A TIN ROOFTOP ..	3.25	5.50	4.00
☐ 3012	**ERA**	TALL OAK TREE/JUAREZ TOWN ..	3.00	5.00	3.50
☐ 3019		HEY LITTLE ONE/			
		BIG ROCK CANDY MOUNTAIN ..	3.00	5.00	3.50
☐ 3025		THE GHOST OF BILLY MALOO/			
		RED ROSES	3.00	5.00	3.50
☐ 3033		THE RIVER AND THE MOUNTAIN/			
		THIS HOTEL	3.00	5.00	3.50
☐ 3041		(IT'S NO) SIN/HARD ROCK MINE .	3.00	5.00	3.50
☐ 3045		GREAT SHAKIN' FEVER/			
		THAT'S ME WITHOUT YOU	3.00	5.00	3.50

DORSEY BURNETTE—ALBUM

☐ 102 (M)	**ERA**	TALL OAK TREE	8.00	23.00	20.00

JOHNNY BURNETTE

☐ 44001	**FREEDOM**	I'M RESTLESS/KISS ME	6.00	12.00	8.00
☐ 44011		GUMBO/ME AND THE BEAR	6.00	12.00	8.00
☐ 44017		SWEET BABY DOLL/			
		I'LL NEVER LOVE AGAIN	6.00	12.00	8.00
☐ 55222	**LIBERTY**	SETTIN' THE WOODS ON FIRE/			
		KENTUCKY WALTZ	3.50	7.00	4.75
☐ 55243		DON'T DO IT/PATRICK HENRY ...	3.50	7.00	4.75
☐ 55258		DREAMIN'/CINCINNATI FIREBALL.	3.50	7.00	4.75
☐ 55285		YOU'RE SIXTEEN/			
		I BEG YOUR PARDON	3.50	7.00	4.75
☐ 55298		LITTLE BOY SAD/			
		I GO DOWN TO THE RIVER	3.50	7.00	4.75
☐ 55318		BIG BIG WORLD/BALLAD			
		OF THE ONE-EYED JACKS	3.50	7.00	4.75
☐ 55345		GIRLS/I'VE GOT A			
		LOT OF THINGS TO DO	3.50	7.00	4.75
☐ 55379		GOD, COUNTRY AND MY BABY/			
		HONESTLY I DO	3.50	7.00	4.75
☐ 55416		WHY AM I/CLOWN SHOES	3.50	7.00	4.75
☐ 55448		THE FOOL OF THE YEAR/			
		POOREST BOY IN TOWN	3.50	7.00	4.75
☐ 55489		DAMN THE DEFIANT/			
		LONESOME WATERS	3.50	7.00	4.75
☐ 1116	**CHANCELLOR**	I WANNA THANK YOUR FOLKS/			
		THE GIANT	3.50	7.00	4.75
☐ 1123		TAG ALONG/PARTY GIRL	3.50	7.00	4.75
☐ 1129		REMEMBER ME/			
		TIME IS NOT ENOUGH	3.50	7.00	4.75

JOHNNY BURNETTE—EPs

☐ 1004	**LIBERTY**	DREAMIN'	10.50	20.00	18.00
☐ 1011		JOHNNY BURNETTE HITS	9.50	17.00	15.00

JOHNNY BURNETTE—ALBUMS

☐ 3179 (M)	**LIBERTY**	DREAMIN'	11.50	28.00	25.00
☐ 7179 (S)		DREAMIN'	17.50	39.00	35.00
☐ 3183 (M)		JOHNNY BURNETTE	11.50	28.00	25.00
☐ 7183 (S)		JOHNNY BURNETTE	17.50	39.00	35.00

			Current Price Range		P/Y AVG
☐3190 (M)		JOHNNY BURNETTE SINGS	11.50	28.00	25.00
☐7190 (S)		JOHNNY BURNETTE SINGS	17.00	39.00	35.00
☐3206 (M)		HITS AND OTHER FAVORITES	12.00	28.00	25.00
☐7206 (S)		HITS AND OTHER FAVORITES	17.00	39.00	35.00
☐3255 (M)		ROSES ARE RED	10.00	25.00	22.50
☐7255 (S)		ROSES ARE RED	14.50	33.00	30.00
☐3389 (M)		THE JOHNNY BURNETTE STORY .	10.00	25.00	22.50
☐7389 (S)		THE JOHNNY BURNETTE STORY .	14.50	33.00	30.00

JOHNNY BURNETTE TRIO

☐61651	CORAL	TEAR IT UP/YOU'RE UNDECIDED .	30.00	40.00	42.00
☐61675		MIDNIGHT TRAIN/OH BABY BABE	20.00	35.00	30.00
☐61719		THE TRAIN KEPT A ROLLIN'/			
		HONEY HUSH	25.00	50.00	40.00
☐61758		LONESOME TRAIN/			
		I JUST FOUND OUT	14.00	23.00	20.00
☐61829		EAGER BEAVER BABY/			
		IF YOU WANT IT ENOUGH	14.00	23.00	20.00
☐61918		DRINKIN' WINE SPO-DEE-O-DEE/			
		ROCK BILLY BOOGIE	14.00	23.00	20.00

JOHNNY BURNETTE TRIO—ALBUM

☐57080 (M)	CORAL	JOHNNY BURNETTE AND THE			
		ROCK 'N ROLL TRIO	90.00	235.00	155.00

JERRY BUTLER
SEE: IMPRESSIONS

☐1024	ABNER	ONE BY ONE/LOST	3.50	6.00	4.35
☐1028		HOLD ME MY DARLING/			
		RAINBOW VALLEY	3.50	6.00	4.35
☐1030		I WAS WRONG/			
		COULDN'T GO TO SLEEP	3.50	6.00	4.35
☐1035		A LONELY SOLDIER/			
		I FOUND A LOVE	4.50	7.00	5.25
☐354	VEE JAY	HE WILL BREAK YOUR HEART/			
		THANKS TO YOU	3.25	5.50	4.00
☐371		O HOLY NIGHT/SILENT NIGHT . . .	4.50	7.00	5.25
☐375		FIND ANOTHER GIRL/			
		WHEN TROUBLE CALLS	3.25	5.50	4.00
☐390		I'M A TELLING YOU/I SEE A FOOL	3.25	5.50	4.00
☐396		FOR YOUR PRECIOUS LOVE/			
		SWEET WAS THE WINE	3.25	5.50	4.00
☐405		MOON RIVER/AWARE OF LOVE . .	3.00	5.00	3.50
☐426		CHI TOWN/ISLE OF SIRENS	3.00	5.00	3.50
☐451		MAKE IT EASY ON YOURSELF/			
		IT'S TOO LATE	3.00	5.00	3.50
☐463		YOU CAN RUN/I'M THE ONE	3.00	5.00	3.50
☐475		WISHING STAR (TARUS BULBA			
		THEME)/YOU GO RIGHT			
		THROUGH ME	3.00	5.00	3.50
☐486		WHATEVER YOU WANT/			
		YOU WON'T BE SORRY	3.00	5.00	3.50
☐526		I ALMOST LOST MY MIND/			
		STRAWBERRIES	3.00	5.00	3.50
☐534		WHERE'S THE GIRL/			
		HOW BEAUTIFUL YOU LIE	3.00	5.00	3.50
☐556		A WOMAN WITH SOUL/			
		JUST A LITTLE BIT	3.00	5.00	3.50
☐567		NEED TO BELONG/			
		GIVE ME YOUR LOVE	3.00	5.00	3.50
☐588		GIVING UP ON LOVE/			
		I'VE BEEN TRYING	3.00	5.00	3.50
☐598		STAND ACCUSED/I DON'T WANT			
		TO HEAR ANYMORE	3.00	5.00	3.50

MERCURY, MG 20402, LP

CAPITOL, ST 2851, LPN

			Current Price Range		P/Y AVG
☐613		LET IT BE ME/AIN'T THAT LOVING YOU BABY (with Betty Everett)..	2.50	5.00	3.25
☐633		SMILE/LOVE IS STRANGE (with Betty Everett)	3.00	5.00	3.50
☐651		GOOD TIMES/I'VE GROWN ACCUSTOMED TO HER FACE ..	3.00	5.00	3.50
☐676		SINCE I DON'T HAVE YOU/JUST BE TRUE (with Betty Everett) ...	3.00	5.00	3.50
☐696		I CAN'T STAND TO SEE YOU CRY/ NOBODY NEEDS YOUR LOVE ...	3.00	5.00	3.50
☐707		BELIEVE IN ME/JUST FOR YOU ..	3.00	5.00	3.50
☐715		FOR YOUR PRECIOUS LOVE/ GIVE IT UP	3.00	5.00	3.50

MERCURY SINGLES ARE WORTH UP TO 2.00 MINT

JERRY BUTLER—ALBUMS

☐2001 (M)	**ABNER**	JERRY BUTLER, ESQUIRE	17.00	39.00	35.00
☐1027 (M)	**VEE JAY**	JERRY BUTLER, ESQUIRE	12.00	28.00	25.00
☐1029 (M)		HE WILL BREAK YOUR HEART ...	10.00	25.00	22.50
☐1034 (M)		LOVE ME	10.00	25.00	22.50
☐1038 (M)		AWARE OF LOVE	10.00	25.00	22.50
☐1038 (S)		AWARE OF LOVE	15.50	34.00	30.00
☐1046 (M)		MOON RIVER	10.00	25.00	22.50
☐1046 (S)		MOON RIVER	14.50	34.00	30.00
☐1048 (M)		THE BEST OF JERRY BUTLER	9.00	20.00	18.00
☐1048 (S)		THE BEST OF JERRY BUTLER	12.00	29.00	25.00
☐1057 (M)		FOLK SONGS	7.50	17.00	15.00
☐1057 (S)		FOLK SONGS	8.50	20.00	18.00
☐1075 (M)		FOR YOUR PRECIOUS LOVE	7.50	17.00	15.00
☐1075 (S)		FOR YOUR PRECIOUS LOVE	8.50	20.00	18.00
☐1076 (M)		GIVING UP ON LOVE	7.50	17.00	15.00
☐1076 (S)		GIVING UP ON LOVE	8.50	20.00	18.00
☐1099 (M)		DELICIOUS TOGETHER (with Betty Everett)	7.50	17.00	15.00
☐1099 (S)		DELICIOUS TOGETHER (with Betty Everett)	8.50	20.00	18.00
☐1119 (M)		MORE OF THE BEST OF JERRY BUTLER	7.50	17.00	15.00
☐1119 (S)		MORE OF THE BEST OF JERRY BUTLER	8.50	20.00	18.00

BYRDS
SEE: BEEFEATERS

☐43271	**COLUMBIA**	MR. TAMBOURINE MAN/ I KNEW I'D WANT YOU	2.75	5.50	3.75
☐43332		ALL I REALLY WANT TO DO/ I'LL FEEL A WHOLE LOT BETTER	3.00	5.50	3.85
☐43424		TURN! TURN! TURN!/ SHE DON'T CARE ABOUT TIME .	2.75	5.50	3.75
☐43501		IT WON'T BE WRONG/ SET YOU FREE THIS TIME	2.75	5.50	3.75
☐43578		EIGHT MILES HIGH/WHY	2.75	5.50	3.75
☐43702		5D (FIFTH DIMENSION)/ CAPTAIN SOUL	2.75	5.50	3.75
☐43766		MR. SPACEMAN/ WHAT'S HAPPENING	2.75	5.50	3.75
☐43987		SO YOU WANT TO BE A ROCK 'N' ROLL STAR/EVERYBODY'S BEEN BURNED	2.75	5.50	3.75
☐44054		MY BACK PAGES/ RENAISSANCE FAIR	2.75	5.50	3.75
☐44157		HAVE YOU SEEN HER FACE/ DON'T MAKE WAVES	2.75	5.50	3.75
☐44230		LADY FRIEND/ OLD JOHN ROBERTSON	2.75	5.50	3.75

			Current Price Range		P/Y AVG
☐ 44362		GOIN' BACK/CHANGE IS NOW ...	2.75	5.50	3.75
☐ 44499		YOU AIN'T GOIN' NOWHERE/ ARTIFICIAL ENERGY	2.75	5.50	3.75
☐ 44643		PRETTY BOY FLOYD/ I AM A PILGRIM	2.75	5.50	3.75
☐ 44746		BAD NIGHT AT THE WHISKEY/ DRUG STORE TRUCK DRIVIN' MAN	2.50	5.00	3.00
☐ 44868		LAY LADY LAY/OLD BLUE	2.50	5.00	3.00
☐ 44990		BALLAD OF EASY RIDER/ OIL IN MY LAMP	3.00	5.50	3.50
☐ 44990		BALLAD OF EASY RIDER/ WASN'T BORN TO FOLLOW ...	2.75	5.00	3.00
☐ 45071		JESUS IS JUST ALRIGHT/IT'S ALL OVER NIGHT, BABY BLUE	2.75	5.00	3.00
☐ 45259		CHESTNUT MARE/ JUST A SEASON	2.75	5.00	3.00
☐ 45440		GLORY GLORY/CITIZEN KANE ...	2.75	5.00	3.00

BYRDS—ALBUMS

☐ 2372 (M)	COLUMBIA	MR. TAMBOURINE MAN	6.50	15.00	13.50
☐ 9172 (S)		MR. TAMBOURINE MAN	8.00	20.00	18.00
☐ 2454 (M)		TURN, TURN, TURN	6.50	15.00	13.50
☐ 9254 (S)		TURN, TURN, TURN	8.00	20.00	18.00
☐ 2549 (M)		FIFTH DIMENSION.............	6.50	15.00	13.50
☐ 9349 (S)		FIFTH DIMENSION.............	8.00	20.00	18.00
☐ 2642 (M)		YOUNGER THAN YESTERDAY	6.50	15.00	13.50
☐ 9442 (S)		YOUNGER THAN YESTERDAY	8.00	20.00	18.00
☐ 2716 (M)		THE BYRDS' GREATEST HITS	7.50	17.00	15.00
☐ 9516 (S)		THE BYRDS' GREATEST HITS	6.50	15.00	13.50
☐ 2775 (M)		THE NOTORIOUS BYRD BROTHERS.	7.50	17.00	15.00
☐ 9575 (S)		THE NOTORIOUS BYRD BROTHERS.	6.50	15.00	13.50
☐ 9670 (S)		SWEETHEART OF THE RODEO	6.50	15.00	13.50
☐ 9755 (S)		DR. BYRDS AND MR. HYDE	6.50	15.00	13.50
☐ 9942 (S)		BALLAD OF EASY RIDER	6.50	15.00	13.50

EDWARD "KOOKIE" BYRNES

☐ 5047	WARNER BROTHERS	KOOKIE, KOOKIE (LEND ME YOUR COMB)/YOU'RE THE TOP	3.50	6.00	4.00
☐ 5087		LIKE I LOVE YOU/ KOOKIE'S MAD PAD	3.50	6.00	4.00
☐ 5114		KOOKIE'S LOVE SONG (PT. 1)/(PT. 2)	3.50	6.00	4.00
☐ 5121		YULESVILLE/ LONELY CHRISTMAS	3.50	6.00	4.00

EDWARD "KOOKIE" BYRNES—EP

☐ 1309	WARNER BROTHERS	EDD "KOOKIE" BYRNES	6.00	11.00	7.00
☐ 1309 (M)	WARNER BROTHERS	KOOKIE	11.00	20.00	13.00
☐ 1309 (S)		KOOKIE	17.00	29.00	19.00

C

CADETS
SEE: FLARES, JACKS

☐ 956	MODERN	DON'T BE ANGRY/I CRIED	17.00	31.00	19.00
☐ 960		ROLLIN' STONE/ FINE LOOKIN' WOMAN	17.00	31.00	19.00
☐ 961		MARY LOU/I THINK I WILL	17.00	31.00	19.00
☐ 963		I CRIED/FINE LOOKIN' WOMAN ..	14.00	27.00	16.00
☐ 969		ANNIE MET HENRY/SO WILL I ...	14.00	27.00	16.00

			Current Price Range		P/Y AVG
☐971		DO YOU WANNA ROCK?/			
		IF IT IS WRONG	28.00	52.00	31.00
☐985		CHURCH BELLS MAY RING/			
		HEARTBREAK HOTEL	6.00	10.00	7.00
☐994		STRANDED IN THE JUNGLE/			
		I WANT YOU	6.00	10.00	7.00
☐1000		DANCIN' DAN/I GOT LOADED	5.00	9.00	6.00
☐1006		I'LL BE SPINNING/			
		FOOLS RUSH IN	5.00	9.00	6.00
☐1012		HEAVEN HELP ME/LOVE BANDIT .	5.00	9.00	6.00
☐1017		YOU BELONG TO ME/			
		WIGGIE WAGGIE WOO	5.00	9.00	6.00
☐1019		PRETTY EVEY/RUM, JAMAICA RUM	5.00	9.00	6.00
☐1024		HANDS ACROSS THE TABLE/LOVE			
		CAN DO MOST ANYTHING	5.00	9.00	6.00
☐1026		RING CHIMES/BABY YA KNOW . .	5.00	9.00	6.00
☐211	**SHERWOOD**	ONE MORE CHANCE/			
		I'M LOOKING FOR A JOB	3.50	6.00	4.30
		CADETS—ALBUMS			
☐5015 (M)	**CROWN**	ROCKIN' AND REELIN'	35.00	75.00	47.00
☐370 (S)		THE CADETS	15.00	32.00	20.00

CADILLACS

			Current Price Range		P/Y AVG
☐765	**JOSIE**	GLORIA/I WONDER WHY	65.00	130.00	78.00
☐769		WISHING WELL/			
		I WANT TO KNOW ABOUT LOVE	80.00	155.00	95.00
☐773		NO CHANCE/SYMPATHY	37.00	70.00	41.00
☐778		DOWN THE ROAD/WIDOW LADY .	25.00	48.00	27.00
☐785		SPEEDOO/LET ME EXPLAIN	11.00	16.00	12.00
☐792		ZOOM/YOU ARE	12.00	20.00	14.00
☐798		BETTY MY LOVE/WOE IS ME	12.00	20.00	14.00
☐805		THE GIRL I LOVE/			
		THAT'S ALL I NEED	15.00	25.00	16.00
☐807		SHOCK-A-DOO/RUDOLPH			
		THE RED-NOSED REINDEER . . .	10.00	15.00	11.00
☐812		SUGAR SUGAR/			
		ABOUT THAT GAL NAMED LOU .	11.00	16.00	12.00
☐820		MY GIRL FRIEND/BROKEN HEART	15.00	25.00	16.00
☐821		LUCY/HURRY HOME	11.00	16.00	11.00
☐829		BUZZ BUZZ BUZZ/YEA YEA BABY	11.00	16.00	12.00
☐836		SPEEDO IS BACK/A LOOKA HERE .	11.00	16.00	12.00
☐842		I WANT TO KNOW/			
		HOLY SMOKE, BABY	9.00	14.00	9.00
☐846		PEEK-A-BOO/ OH OH LOLITA	9.00	14.00	9.00
☐857		JAY WALKER/COPY CAT	9.00	14.00	9.00
☐861		COOL IT FOOL/			
		PLEASE MR. JOHNSON	9.00	14.00	9.00
☐866		ROMEO/ALWAYS MY DARLING . .	9.00	14.00	9.00
☐870		BAD DAN McGOON/DUMBELL . . .	9.00	14.00	9.00
☐883		THE BOOGIE MAN/THAT'S WHY .	9.00	14.00	9.00
☐915		I'LL NEVER LET YOU GO/			
		WAYWARD WANDERER	9.00	14.00	9.00
		CADILLACS—ALBUMS			
☐1045 (M)	**JUBILEE**	THE FABULOUS CADILLACS			
		(blue label)	50.00	115.00	72.00
☐1045 (M)		THE FABULOUS CADILLACS			
		(black label)	32.00	65.00	43.00
☐1045 (M)		THE FABULOUS CADILLACS			
		(multi-color label)	23.00	45.00	29.00
☐1089 (M)		THE CRAZY CADILLACS			
		(black label)	32.00	65.00	43.50
☐1089 (M)		THE CRAZY CADILLACS			
		(multi-color label)	17.00	32.00	20.00
☐5009 (M)		TWISTING WITH THE CADILLACS .	20.00	40.00	23.00

			Current Price Range		P/Y AVG

CAESAR AND CLEO (SONNY AND CHER)

			Current Price Range		P/Y AVG
☐916	VAULT	THE LETTER/SPRING FEVER	6.00	10.00	8.00
☐0308	REPRISE	LOVE IS STRANGE/			
		DO YOU WANT TO DANCE?	4.50	6.50	5.00
☐0419		LOVE IS STRANGE/			
		LET THE GOOD TIMES ROLL ...	4.50	6.50	5.00

AUBREY CAGLE

☐100	GLEE	JUST FOR YOU/BE-BOP BLUES ..	8.50	20.00	18.00
☐1958		BLUE LONELY WORLD/			
		COME ALONG LITTLE GIRL	8.50	20.00	18.00
☐10013		BOP 'N' STROLL/	8.50	20.00	18.00
☐104	HOUSE OF SOUND	REAL COOL/	5.00	10.00	7.50

CALIFORNIA MUSIC

FEATURED: BRIAN WILSON, BRUCE JOHNSTON, TERRY MELCHER

☐10120	EQUINOX	DON'T WORRY BABY/			
		TEN YEARS HARMONY	5.00	9.50	8.00
☐10363		DON'T WORRY BABY/			
		WHY DO FOOLS FALL IN LOVE .	4.50	8.00	7.50
☐10572		CALIFORNIA MUSIC/			
		JAMAICA FAREWELL	4.50	8.00	7.50

DUDLEY CALLICUT & THE GO BOYS

☐0412	DC	HEART TROUBLE/			
		GET READY BABY	22.00	47.00	44.00

CALVEYS

☐84349	COMMA	I NEED LOVE/THE WIND	14.00	34.00	30.00

GLEN CAMPBELL

SEE: GEE CEES, SAGITTARIUS

☐1324	CENECO	DREAMS FOR SALE/			
		I'VE GOT TO WIN	7.00	12.00	10.00
☐1087	CREST	TURN AROUND. LOOK AT ME/			
		BRENDA	3.50	5.50	4.00
☐1096		MIRACLE OF LOVE/ONCE MORE .	3.50	5.50	4.00
☐4783	CAPITOL	TOO LATE TO WORRY.			
		TOO BLUE TO CRY	3.25	5.25	4.00
☐4856		LONG BLACK LIMOUSINE/			
		HERE I AM	3.25	5.25	4.00
☐4867		KENTUCKY MEANS PARADISE/			
		TRUCK DRIVING MAN	3.25	5.25	4.00
☐4925		PRIMA DONNA/OH MY DARLING .	3.25	5.25	4.00
☐4990		DARK AS A DUNGEON/			
		DIVORCE ME C.O.D.			
		(with Green River Boys)	3.25	5.25	4.00
☐5037		AS FAR AS I'M CONCERNED/			
		SAME OLD PLACES	3.25	5.25	4.00
☐5172		THROUGH THE EYES OF A CHILD/			
		LET ME TELL YOU 'BOUT MARY	3.25	5.25	4.00
☐5279		SUMMER. WINTER. SPRING AND			
		FALL/HEARTACHES CAN BE			
		FUN	3.25	5.25	4.00
☐5360		TOMORROW NEVER COMES/			
		WOMAN'S WORLD	3.25	5.25	4.00
☐5441		GUESS I'M DUMB/THAT'S ALL			
		RIGHT (Brian Wilson composition			
		and production)	12.00	19.00	17.50
☐5504		THE UNIVERSAL SOLDIER/			
		SPANISH SOLDIER	2.50	5.00	3.00
☐5545		LESS OF ME/PRIVATE JOHN Q. ...	3.00	5.00	3.00
☐5638		SATISFIED MIND/CAN'T YOU SEE			
		I'M TRYING?	3.00	5.00	3.00

			Current Price Range		P/Y AVG
☐5773		BURNING BRIDGES/ ONLY THE LONELY	3.00	5.00	3.00
☐5854		I GOTTA HAVE MY BABY BACK/ JUST TO SATISFY YOU	3.00	5.00	3.00

LATER CAPITOL SINGLES ARE WORTH UP TO 1.50 EACH

GLEN CAMPBELL—ALBUMS

			Current Price Range		P/Y AVG
☐1810 (M)	CAPITOL	BIG BLUE GRASS SPECIAL	5.50	13.00	11.00
☐1810 (S)		BIG BLUE GRASS SPECIAL	7.50	17.00	15.00
☐1881 (M)		TOO LATE TO WORRY - TOO BLUE TO CRY	5.50	13.00	11.00
☐1881 (S)		TOO LATE TO WORRY - TOO BLUE TO CRY	7.50	17.00	15.00
☐2023 (M)		THE ASTOUNDING 12-STRING GUITAR OF GLEN CAMPBELL . .	4.50	12.00	10.00
☐2023 (S)		THE ASTOUNDING 12-STRING GUITAR OF GLEN CAMPBELL . .	5.50	14.00	12.00

LATER CAPITOL ALBUMS ARE WORTH UP TO $5.00 MINT

JO-ANN CAMPBELL

			Current Price Range		P/Y AVG
☐504	ELDORADO	COME ON BABY/FOREVER YOUNG	5.50	8.50	7.00
☐509		FUNNY THING/I CAN'T GIVE YOU ANYTHING BUT LOVE	5.50	8.50	7.00
☐4	POINT	WHEREVER YOU GO/I'M COMING HOME LATE TONIGHT	5.00	8.00	6.00
☐5014	GONE	WAIT A MINUTE/ I'M IN LOVE WITH YOU	5.00	8.00	6.00
☐5021		ROCK AND ROLL LOVE/ YOU'RE DRIVING ME MAD	5.00	8.00	6.00
☐5027		WASSA MATTER WITH YOU?/ YOU-OO	5.00	8.00	6.00
☐5037		I'M NOBODY'S BABY NOW/ I REALLY REALLY LOVE YOU . .	5.00	8.00	6.00
☐5049		TALL BOY/ HAPPY NEW YEAR BABY	5.00	8.00	6.00
☐5055		MAMA (CAN I GO OUT TONIGHT)/ NERVOUS	5.00	8.00	6.00
☐5068		I AIN'T GOT NO STEADY DATE/ BEACHCOMBER	5.00	8.00	6.00
☐10134	ABC-PARAMOUNT	A KOOKIE LITTLE PARADISE/ BOBBY BOBBY BOBBY	3.50	6.00	4.00
☐10172		CRAZY DAISY/ BUT MAYBE THIS YEAR	3.50	6.00	4.00
☐10200		MOTORCYCLE MICHAEL/ PUKA PUKA PANTS	3.50	6.00	4.00
☐10224		EDDIE MY LOVE/ IT WASN'T RIGHT	3.50	6.00	4.00
☐10258		MAMA DON'T WANT/DUANE	3.50	6.00	4.00
☐10300		YOU MADE ME LOVE YOU/ I CHANGED MY MIND	3.50	6.00	4.00
☐10335		I WISH IT WOULD RAIN ALL SUMMER/AMATEUR NIGHT . . .	3.50	6.00	4.00
☐223	CAMEO	(I'M THE GIRL ON) WOLVERTON MOUNTAIN/SLOPPY JOE	3.50	6.00	4.00
☐237		MR. FIX-IT MAN/ LET ME DO IT MY WAY	3.50	6.00	4.00
☐249		MOTHER, PLEASE/ WAITIN' FOR LOVE	3.50	6.00	4.00

JO-ANN CAMPBELL—ALBUMS

			Current Price Range		P/Y AVG
☐306 (M)	END	I'M NOBODY'S BABY	17.00	37.00	24.00
☐393 (M)	ABC-PARAMOUNT	TWISTIN' AND LISTENIN'	12.00	28.00	25.00
☐199 (M)	CORONET	STARRING JO-ANN CAMPBELL . .	10.00	25.00	22.50

			Current Price Range		P/Y AVG
☐ 1026 (M)	*CAMEO*	ALL THE HITS OF JO-ANN CAMPBELL	8.50	20.00	18.00
☐ 1026 (S)		ALL THE HITS OF JO-ANN CAMPBELL	12.00	28.00	25.00

CAMPS
FEATURED: SONNY CURTIS

☐974	*PARKWAY*	BALLAD OF BATMAN/BATMOBILE	7.50	17.00	15.00

CANADIAN SQUIRES (THE BAND)

☐76964	*APEX*	UH-UH-UH/LEAVE ME ALONE ...	8.50	14.00	12.00
☐6002	*WARE*	UH-UH-UH/LEAVE ME ALONE ...	8.50	14.00	12.00

CANNIBAL AND THE HEADHUNTERS

☐1001	*AIRES*	DANCE BY THE LIGHT/ MEANS SO MUCH	4.50	7.50	6.00
☐642	*RAMPART*	LAND OF 1000 DANCES/I'LL SHOW YOU HOW TO LOVE ME .	3.50	6.00	3.50
☐644		HERE COMES LOVE/ NAU NINNY NAU	3.50	6.00	3.50
☐646		FOLLOW THE MUSIC/ I NEED YOUR LOVING	3.50	6.00	3.50
☐654		PLEASE BABY PLEASE/ OUT OF SIGHT	3.50	6.00	3.50
☐1516	*DATE*	ZULU KING/LA BAMBA	3.50	6.00	3.50
☐1525		LAND OF 1000 DANCES/ LOVE BIRD	2.50	4.50	3.00

CANNIBAL AND THE HEADHUNTERS—ALBUMS

☐3302 (M)	*RAMPART*	LAND OF 1000 DANCES	8.50	20.00	18.00
☐3302 (S)		LAND OF 1000 DANCES	8.50	20.00	18.00
☐3001 (S)	*DATE*	LAND OF 1000 DANCES	7.50	17.00	15.00

FREDDY CANNON

☐201	*AMHEARST*	MEAN REBEL ROUSER/ DANCE TO THE BOP	4.00	7.50	5.00
☐4031	*SWAN*	TALLAHASSEE LASSIE/ YOU KNOW	3.25	5.50	4.00
☐4038		OKEFENOKEE/KOOKIE HAT	3.50	6.00	4.35
☐4043		WAY DOWN YONDER IN NEW ORLEANS/FRACTURED ..	3.25	5.50	4.00
☐4050		CHATTANOOGA SHOE SHINE BOY/ BOSTON	3.25	5.50	4.00
☐4053		THE URGE/JUMP OVER	3.25	5.50	4.00
☐4057		HAPPY SHADES OF BLUE/ CUERNAVACA CHOO CHOO	3.25	5.50	4.00
☐4061		HUMDINGER/MY BLUE HEAVEN .	3.25	5.50	4.00
☐4066		MUSKRAT RAMBLE/ TWO THOUSAND-88	3.25	5.50	4.00
☐4071		BUZZ BUZZ A DIDDLE-IT/ OPPORTUNITY	3.25	5.50	4.00
☐4078		TRANSISTOR SISTER/ WALK ON THE MOON	3.25	5.50	4.00
☐4083		FOR ME AND MY GAL/ BLUE PLATE SPECIAL	3.25	5.50	4.00
☐4096		TEEN QUEEN OF THE WEEK/ WILD GUY	3.25	5.50	4.00
☐4106		PALISADES PARK/ JUNE, JULY AND AUGUST	3.25	5.50	4.00
☐4117		WHAT'S GONNA HAPPEN WHEN SUMMER'S DONE/BROADWAY	3.25	5.50	4.00
☐4122		IF YOU WERE A ROCK AND ROLL RECORD/THE TRUTH, RUTH ...	3.25	5.50	4.00
☐4132		FOUR LETTER MAN/ COME ON AND LOVE ME	3.25	5.50	4.00

			Current Price Range		P/Y AVG
☐ 4139		PATTY BABY/BETTY JEAN	3.25	5.50	4.00
☐ 4149		EVERYBODY MONKEY/OH GLORIA	3.25	5.50	4.00
☐ 4155		DO WHAT THE HIPPIES DO/ THAT'S THE WAY THE GIRLS ARE	3.25	5.50	4.00
☐ 4168		SWEET GEORGIA BROWN/ WHAT A PARTY	3.25	5.50	4.00
☐ 4178		THE UPS AND DOWNS OF LOVE/ IT'S BEEN NICE	3.25	5.50	4.00
☐ 5409	WARNER BROTHERS	ABIGAIL BEECHER/ ALL AMERICAN GIRL	3.25	5.50	4.00
☐ 5434		OK WHEELER THE USED CAR DEALER/ODIE COLOGNE	3.25	5.50	4.00
☐ 5448		SUMMERTIME U.S.A./ GOTTA GOOD THING GOIN'	3.25	5.50	4.00
☐ 5487		TOO MUCH MONKEY BUSINESS/ LITTLE AUTOGRAPH SEEKER	3.25	5.50	4.00
☐ 5616		LITTLE MISS A-GO-GO/ IN THE NIGHT	3.25	5.50	4.00
☐ 5645		ACTION/BEACHWOOD CITY	3.25	5.50	4.00
☐ 5666		LET ME SHOW YOU WHERE IT'S AT/THE OLD RAG MAN	3.00	5.00	3.50
☐ 5673		SHE'S SOMETHIN' ELSE/ LITTLE BITTY CORRINE	3.00	5.00	3.50
☐ 5693		THE DEDICATION SONG/ COME ON, COME ON	3.00	5.00	3.50
☐ 5810		THE GREATEST SHOW ON EARTH/ HOKIE POKIE GAL	3.00	5.00	3.50
☐ 5832		NATALIE/THE LAUGHING SONG	3.00	5.00	3.50
☐ 5859		RUN FOR THE SUN/ USE YOUR IMAGINATION	3.00	5.00	3.50
☐ 5876		IN MY WILDEST DREAM/ A HAPPY CLOWN	3.00	5.00	3.50
☐ 7019		MAVERICK'S FLATS/ RUN TO THE POET MAN	3.00	5.00	3.50
☐ 7075		20TH CENTURY FOX/ CINCINNATI WOMAN	3.50	5.50	3.75
☐ 1601	WE MAKE ROCK 'N ROLL RECORDS	ROCK AROUND THE CLOCK/ SOCK IT TO THE JUDGE	3.00	5.00	3.50
☐ 1604		SEA CRUISE/ SHE'S A FRIDAY NIGHT FOX	3.00	5.00	3.50
☐ 2	ROYAL AMERICAN	CHARGED-UP, TURNED-UP ROCK AND ROLL SINGER/I AIN'T MUCH BUT I'M YOURS	3.00	5.00	3.50
☐ 288		BLOSSOM DEAR/ STRAWBERRY WINE	3.00	5.00	3.50
☐ 4102	SIRE	IF YOU GIVE ME A TITLE/ BEAUTIFUL DOWNTOWN BURBANK	3.00	5.00	3.50
☐ 40269	MCA	ROCK AND ROLL ABC'S/ SUPERMAN	2.50	4.50	3.00
		FREDDY CANNON—ALBUMS			
☐ 502 (M)	SWAN	THE EXPLOSIVE FREDDY CANNON	23.00	55.00	50.00
☐ 504 (M)		HAPPY SHADES OF BLUE	17.00	39.00	35.00
☐ 505 (M)		SOLID GOLD HITS	17.00	39.00	35.00
☐ 507 (M)		PALISADES PARK	14.50	34.00	30.00
☐ 511 (M)		FREDDY CANNON STEPS OUT	14.50	34.00	30.00
☐ 511 (S)		FREDDY CANNON STEPS OUT	17.00	39.00	35.00
☐ 1544 (M)	WARNER BROTHERS	FREDDY CANNON	8.50	20.00	18.00
☐ 1544 (S)		FREDDY CANNON	12.00	28.00	25.00

			Current Price Range		P/Y AVG
☐ 1612 (M)		ACTION!	7.50	17.00	15.00
☐ 1612 (S)		ACTION!	9.50	25.00	22.50
☐ 1628 (M)		GREATEST HITS	7.50	17.00	15.00
☐ 1628 (S)		GREATEST HITS	9.50	25.00	22.50

JERRY CAPEHART
GUITAR: EDDIE COCHRAN

☐ 1021	CASH	WALKIN' STICK BOOGIE/ROLLIN'	8.50	14.00	12.00
☐ 1101	CREST	SONG OF NEW ORLEANS/ THE YOUNG AND BLUE	7.00	13.00	11.00

CAPITOLS

☐ 721	GATEWAY	DAY BY DAY/LITTLE THINGS	26.00	46.00	42.00
☐ 807	PET	ANGEL OF LOVE/ 'CAUSE I LOVE YOU	20.00	34.00	30.00
☐ 3002	CINDY	ROSEMARY/MILLIE	20.00	34.00	30.00

JOHN CAPRI

☐ 306	BOMARC	LOVE FOR ME/WHEN I'M LONELY	12.00	31.00	28.00

CAPRIS

☐ 1010	PLANET	THERE'S A MOON OUT TONIGHT/ INDIAN GIRL	44.00	76.00	72.00
☐ 101	TROMMERS	THERE'S A MOON OUT TONIGHT/ INDIAN GIRL	5.50	11.00	9.00
☐ 101	LOST NIGHT	THERE'S A MOON OUT TONIGHT/ INDIAN GIRL (pink label)	12.00	20.00	18.00
☐ 1094	OLD TOWN	THERE'S A MOON OUT TONIGHT/ INDIAN GIRL	3.50	5.50	4.00
☐ 1099		WHERE I FELL IN LOVE/ SOME PEOPLE THINK	4.50	7.50	6.00
☐ 1103		TEARS IN MY EYES/ WHY DO I CRY	5.50	8.50	7.00
☐ 1107		GIRL IN MY DREAMS/ MY ISLAND IN THE SUN	4.50	7.50	6.00
☐ 118	MR. PEEKE	LIMBO/FROM THE VINE CAME THE GRAPE	4.50	7.50	6.00

CAPTAIN AND TENNILLE

☐ 001	BUTTERSCOTCH CASTLE	THE WAY I WANT TO TOUCH YOU/ DISNEY GIRLS	32.00	60.00	36.00
☐ 101	JOYCE	THE WAY I WANT TO TOUCH YOU/ DISNEY GIRLS	14.00	25.00	13.50

CARDINALS

☐ 938	ATLANTIC	SHOULDN'T I KNOW/ PLEASE DON'T LEAVE ME	60.00	110.00	69.00
☐ 952		I'LL ALWAYS LOVE YOU/ PRETTY BABY BLUES	60.00	110.00	69.00
☐ 958		WHEEL OF FORTUNE/ KISS ME BABY	60.00	110.00	69.00
☐ 972		THE BUMP/SHE ROCKS	55.00	95.00	61.00
☐ 995		LOVELY DARLING/ YOU ARE MY ONLY LOVE	55.00	95.00	61.00
☐ 1025		PLEASE BABY/ UNDER A BLANKET OF BLUE	27.00	45.00	31.00
☐ 1054		THE DOOR IS STILL OPEN/ MISERLOU	15.00	28.00	16.00
☐ 1067		COME BACK MY LOVE/ TWO THINGS I LOVE	13.00	24.00	13.00
☐ 1079		LOVELY GIRL/HERE GOES MY HEART TO YOU	10.00	19.00	11.00

FIRST-PRESSES OF THE ABOVE WERE ON THE YELLOW-AND-BLACK LABEL

			Current Price Range		P/Y AVG
☐ 1090		OFF SHORE/CHOO CHOO	5.50	11.00	9.00
☐ 1103		THE END OF THE STORY/I WON'T			
		MAKE YOU CRY ANYMORE	5.00	8.50	7.00
☐ 1126		ONE LOVE/NEAR YOU	4.50	7.50	6.00

CARLO

☐ 3151	*LAURIE*	WRITE ME A LETTER/BABY DOLL	10.00	23.00	14.00
☐ 3157		LITTLE ORPHAN GIRL/			
		MAIRZY DOATS	10.00	23.00	14.00
☐ 3175		FIVE MINUTES MORE/			
		STORY OF MY LOVE	10.00	23.00	14.00
☐ 3227		STRANGER IN MY ARMS/			
		RING-A-LING	15.00	30.00	16.50

KIM CARNES

☐ 166	*AMOS*	TO LOVE SOMEBODY/			
		I FELL IN LOVE WITH A POET ..	4.00	8.00	4.00
☐ 1767	*A & M*	YOU'RE A PART OF ME/(DJ)	4.00	8.00	4.00
☐ 1807		BAD SEED/(DJ)	4.00	8.00	4.00
☐ 1902		LET YOU LOVE COME EASY/			
		THE LAST THING YOU EVER			
		WANTED TO DO	4.00	8.00	4.00
☐ 1943		SAILIN'/HE'LL COME HOME	4.00	8.00	4.00

KIM CARNES—ALBUMS

☐ 7016 (S)	*AMOS*	REST ON ME	11.00	24.00	14.00
☐ 4548 (S)		KIM CARNES	9.00	20.00	12.00
☐ 4606 (S)		SAILIN'	9.00	20.00	12.00

KAREN CARPENTER (PRE-CARPENTERS)

☐ 704	*MAGIC LAMP*	I'LL BE YOURS/			
		LOOKING FOR LOVE	30.00	60.00	36.00

WAYNE CARROLL

☐ 1018	*DOMAIN*	CINDY LEE/CHICKEN OUT	7.50	17.00	15.00

CASCADES

☐ 6021	*VALIANT*	SECOND CHANCE/			
		THERE'S A REASON	3.50	6.00	4.00
☐ 6026		RHYTHM OF THE RAIN/LET ME BE	3.50	6.00	4.00
☐ 6028		THE LAST LEAF/SHY GIRL	3.50	6.00	4.00
☐ 6032		MY FIRST DAY ALONE/			
		I WANNA BE YOUR LOVER	3.50	6.00	4.00
☐ 8206	*RCA*	A LITTLE LIKE LOVIN'/			
		CINDERELLA	3.50	6.00	4.00
☐ 8268		FOR YOUR SWEET LOVE/JEANNIE	3.50	6.00	4.00
☐ 8321		LITTLE BITTY FALLING STAR/			
		THOSE WERE THE GOOD			
		OLD DAYS	3.50	6.00	4.00
☐ 132	*ARWIN*	CHERYL'S GOIN' HOME/			
		TRULY JULIE'S BLUES	3.00	5.00	3.50
☐ 134		ALL'S FAIR IN LOVE AND WAR/			
		MIDNIGHT LACE	3.00	5.00	3.50
☐ 2083	*SMASH*	HEY LITTLE GIRL OF MINE/			
		BLUE HOURS	3.00	5.00	3.50
☐ 2101		FLYING ON THE GROUND/			
		MAIN STREET	3.00	5.50	3.75
☐ 55152	*UNI*	MAYBE THE RAIN WILL FALL/			
		NAGGIN' CRIES	3.00	5.00	3.50
☐ 55169		BIG CITY COUNTRY BOY/			
		INDIAN RIVER	3.00	5.00	3.50
☐ 55200		BUT FOR LOVE/			
		HAZEL AUTUMN COCOA BROWN	3.00	5.00	3.50
☐ 55231		APRIL. MAY. JUNE AND JULY/			
		BIG UGLY SKY	3.00	5.00	3.50

JOHNNY CASH

Johnny Cash is a true country-music legend of this century. He first saw life on February 26, 1932, in Kingsland, Arkansas. Johnny picked cotton on his parents' farm and wrote songs and poems. During high school he sang on a local radio station. He later graduated and joined the air force.

Following his military obligation, Cash went to work door-to-door in Memphis as an appliance salesman. Cash said he often greeted people with, "You don't want to buy anything, do you?" He also attended a disc-jockey training school. In the meantime Johnny formed a backup team, the Tennessee Two, with Luther Perkins (Carl's brother) and Marshall Grant. After two rejections Sam Phillips signed Cash and his duo to Sun Records. Johnny Cash soon became a local favorite. In 1955 he toured the South with a hot young local named Elvis Presley, then also a Sun artist.

Cash's first major hit was "I Walk the Line" and it has been smooth sailing ever since for Johnny in terms of recording success. Drug problems plagued him during the early 1960s, though. He was salvaged in part by his present wife, June Carter Cash, who encouraged Johnny to enroll at a health clinic.

Today the Cash family lives in a $3,000,000 mansion overlooking Old Hickory Lake near Nashville.

			Current Price Range		P/Y AVG
		CASCADES—ALBUMS			
☐ 405 (M)	*VALIANT*	RHYTHM OF THE RAIN	14.00	34.00	30.00
☐ 273069 (S)	*UNI*	MAYBE THE RAIN WILL FALL	8.50	20.00	18.00
☐ 6820 (S)	*CASCADES*	WHAT GOES ON INSIDE THE CASCADES	7.50	17.00	15.00
		EDDIE CASH			
☐ 1001	*PEAK*	LAND OF PROMISES/ DOING ALL RIGHT	35.00	75.00	48.00
		JOHNNY CASH			
☐ 221	*SUN*	HEY PORTER/CRY! CRY! CRY! . . .	5.50	8.50	7.00
☐ 232		FOLSOM PRISON BLUES/ SO DOGGONE LONESOME	5.00	8.00	6.00
☐ 241		I WALK THE LINE/GET RHYTHM .	3.50	5.25	3.75
☐ 258		TRAIN OF LOVE/THERE YOU GO . .	3.50	5.25	3.75
☐ 266		NEXT IN LINE/ DON'T MAKE ME GO	3.50	5.25	3.75
☐ 279		HOME OF THE BLUES/ GIVE MY LOVE TO ROSE	3.50	5.25	3.75
☐ 283		BALLAD OF A TEENAGE QUEEN/ BIG RIVER	3.00	5.00	3.50
☐ 295		GUESS THINGS HAPPEN THAT WAY/COME IN STRANGER	3.25	5.25	4.00
☐ 302		THE WAYS OF A WOMAN IN LOVE/ YOU'RE THE NEAREST THING TO HEAVEN	3.25	5.25	4.00
☐ 309		IT'S JUST ABOUT TIME/I JUST THOUGHT YOU'D LIKE TO KNOW	3.25	5.25	4.00
☐ 316		THANKS A LOT/ LUTHER PLAYED THE BOOGIE . .	3.25	5.25	4.00
☐ 321		KATY TOO/I FORGOT TO REMEMBER TO FORGET	3.25	5.25	4.00
☐ 331		GOODBYE, LITTLE DARLING/ YOU TELL ME	3.25	5.25	4.00
☐ 334		STRAIGHT A'S IN LOVE/ I LOVE YOU BECAUSE	3.25	5.25	4.00
☐ 343		DOWN THE STREET TO 301/THE STORY OF A BROKEN HEART . .	3.25	5.25	4.00
☐ 347		MEAN EYED CAT/ PORT OF LONELY HEARTS	3.25	5.25	4.00
☐ 355		OH, LONESOME ME/ LIFE GOES ON	3.25	5.25	4.00
☐ 363		MY TREASURE/SUGAR TIME	3.25	5.25	4.00
☐ 376		BLUE TRAIN/BORN TO LOSE	3.25	5.25	4.00
☐ 392		WIDE OPEN ROAD/BELSHAZAR . .	3.25	5.25	4.00
		COLUMBIA SINGLES ARE WORTH UP TO $2.50 MINT			
		JOHNNY CASH—EPs			
☐ 111	*SUN*	JOHNNY CASH SINGS HANK WILLIAMS	10.50	18.00	10.00
☐ 112		JOHNNY CASH	10.50	18.00	10.00
☐ 113		I WALK THE LINE	10.50	18.00	10.00
☐ 114		HIS TOP HITS	10.50	18.00	10.00
☐ 116		HOME OF THE BLUES	10.50	18.00	10.00
☐ 117		JOHNNY CASH	10.50	18.00	10.00
		JOHNNY CASH—ALBUMS			
☐ 1220 (M)	*SUN*	JOHNNY CASH WITH HIS HOT AND BLUE GUITAR	12.00	28.00	25.00
☐ 1235 (M)		JOHNNY CASH SINGS THE SONGS THAT MADE HIM FAMOUS	10.00	25.00	22.50
☐ 1240 (M)		JOHNNY CASH - GREATEST	10.00	25.00	22.50
☐ 1245 (M)		JOHNNY CASH SINGS HANK WILLIAMS	9.00	20.00	18.00
☐ 1255 (M)		NOW HERE'S JOHNNY CASH	9.00	20.00	18.00

SUN, 1220, LP

CBS, S 63316, LP

			Current Price Range		P/Y AVG
1270 (M)		ALL ABOARD THE BLUE TRAIN ...	9.00	20.00	18.00
1275 (M)		THE ORIGINAL SUN SOUND OF JOHNNY CASH	9.00	20.00	18.00

SHAUN CASSIDY

8365	**WARNER BROS.**	DA DOO RON RON/HOLIDAY	2.50	4.75	3.35
8423		I WANNA BE WITH YOU/ THAT'S ROCK & ROLL	2.50	4.75	3.35
8488		STRANGE SENSATION/ HEY DEANIE	2.50	4.75	3.35
8533		TEEN DREAM/ DO YOU BELIEVE IN MAGIC ...	2.50	4.75	3.35

LATER WARNER BROS. SINGLES ARE WORTH UP TO $1.50 MINT

SHAUN CASSIDY—ALBUM

BS-3067 (S)	**WARNER BROS.-CURB**	SHAUN CASSIDY	7.00	14.00	8.50

CASTELLS

3038	**ERA**	LITTLE SAD EYES/ROMEO	3.75	6.00	4.50
3048		SACRED/I GET DREAMY	3.00	5.00	3.50
3057		MAKE BELIEVE WEDDING/ MY MIRACLE	3.00	5.00	3.50
3064		THE VISION OF YOU/ STIKI DE BOOM BOOM	3.00	5.00	3.50
3073		SO THIS IS LOVE/ ON THE STREET OF TEARS	3.00	5.00	3.50
3083		OH! WHAT IT SEEMED TO BE/ STAND THERE MOUNTAIN	3.00	5.00	3.50
3089		ECHOES IN THE NIGHT/ONLY ONE	2.50	4.50	3.00
3098		ETERNAL LOVE. ETERNAL SPRING/ CLOWN PRINCE	2.50	4.50	3.00
3102		INITIALS/LITTLE SAD EYES	2.50	4.50	3.00
3107		SOME ENCHANTED EVENING/ WHAT DO LITTLE GIRLS DREAM OF?	2.50	4.50	3.00
5421	**WARNER BROTHERS**	I DO/TEARDROPS	10.50	22.50	15.00

BRIAN WILSON PRODUCTION ON WARNER BROTHERS 5421

5445		COULD THIS BE YOU/ SHINNY UP YOUR OWN SIDE	2.50	4.50	3.00
5486		LOVE FINDS A WAY/ TELL HER IF I COULD	2.50	4.50	3.00
31834	**DECCA**	AN ANGEL CRIED/ JUST WALK AWAY	3.50	6.00	4.50
31967		LIFE GOES ON/I THOUGHT YOU'D LIKE THAT	3.50	6.00	4.50
50324	**UNITED ARTISTS**	TWO LOVERS/JERUSALEM	3.00	5.00	3.50
3444	**LAURIE**	ROCK RIDGES/I'D LIKE TO KNOW	3.00	5.00	3.50
1351	**SOLOMON**	IN A LETTER TO ME/ WE BETTER SLOW DOWN	3.00	5.00	3.50

CASTELLS—ALBUMS

109 (M)	**ERA**	SO THIS IS LOVE	10.00	25.00	22.50
109 (S)		SO THIS IS LOVE	14.50	34.00	30.00

JOEY CASTLE

1008	**HEADLINE**	ROCK & ROLL DADDY/WILD LOVE	30.00	65.00	42.00

VINCE CASTRO

102	**DOE**	YOU'RE MY GIRL/BONG BONG ...	10.00	17.00	15.00
25007	**APT**	YOU'RE MY GIRL/BONGO TWIST	4.50	6.50	4.50
25025		CAUSE I LOVE YOU/ TOO PROUD TO CRY	4.50	6.50	4.50
25047		YOU'RE MY GIRL/BONGO TWIST	4.50	6.50	4.50

			Current Price Range		P/Y AVG

CASUALS (ORIGINAL CASUALS)

☐ 503	BACK BEAT	SO TOUGH/MY DARLING	3.50	5.50	4.00
☐ 15557		MY LOVE SONG FOR YOU/			
		SOMEBODY HELP ME	3.50	5.50	4.00
☐ 15671		TILL YOU COME BACK TO ME/			
		HELLO LOVE	3.50	5.50	4.00

CASUALS (ORIGINAL CASUALS)—EP

☐ 40	BACK BEAT	THE ORIGINAL CASUALS	8.50	14.00	12.00

CENTURIES (BUCKINGHAMS)

☐ 641	SPECTRA-SOUND	IT'S ALRIGHT/			
		I LOVE YOU NO MORE	7.00	11.00	9.00

CHAD AND JEREMY
SEE: CHAD STUART

☐ 1021	WORLD ARTISTS	YESTERDAY'S GONE/			
		LEMON TREE	3.50	6.00	4.00
☐ 1027		A SUMMER SONG/			
		NO TEARS FOR JOHNNY	3.50	6.00	4.00
☐ 1034		WILLOW WEEP FOR ME/			
		IF SHE WAS MINE	3.50	6.00	4.00
☐ 1041		IF I LOVED YOU/DONNA DONNA .	3.50	6.00	4.00
☐ 1052		WHAT DO YOU WANT WITH ME?/			
		VERY GOOD YEAR	3.50	6.00	4.00
☐ 1056		FROM A WINDOW/			
		MY COLOURING BOOK	3.50	6.00	4.00
☐ 1060		SEPTEMBER IN THE RAIN/			
		ONLY FOR THE YOUNG	3.50	6.00	4.00
☐ 43277	COLUMBIA	BEFORE AND AFTER/			
		FARE THEE WELL	3.00	5.00	3.50
☐ 43339		I DON'T WANNA LOSE YOU BABY/			
		PENNIES	3.00	5.00	3.50
☐ 43414		I HAVE DREAMED/SHOULD I	3.00	5.00	3.50
☐ 43490		TEENAGE FAILURE/			
		EARLY MORNING RAIN	3.00	5.00	3.50
☐ 43682		DISTANT SHORES/LAST NIGHT . .	3.00	5.00	3.50
☐ 43807		YOU ARE SHE/I WON'T CRY	3.00	5.00	3.50
☐ 44379		PAINTED DAYGLOW SMILE/			
		EDITORIAL	3.00	5.00	3.50
☐ 44525		SISTER MARIE/REST IN PEACE . .	3.00	5.00	3.50
☐ 44660		PASTOR QUIGLEY/YOU NEED FEET	3.00	5.00	3.50

CHAD AND JEREMY—ALBUMS

☐ 2002 (M)	WORLD ARTISTS	YESTERDAY'S GONE	7.50	17.00	15.00
☐ 3002 (S)		YESTERDAY'S GONE	9.50	25.00	22.50
☐ 2005 (M)		CHAD AND JEREMY SING FOR YOU	7.50	17.00	15.00
☐ 3005 (S)		CHAD AND JEREMY SING FOR YOU	9.50	25.00	22.50
☐ 2374 (M)	COLUMBIA	BEFORE AND AFTER	6.50	15.00	13.50
☐ 9174 (S)		BEFORE AND AFTER	8.50	20.00	18.00
☐ 2398 (M)		I DON'T WANT TO LOSE YOU BABY	6.50	15.00	13.50
☐ 9198 (S)		I DON'T WANT TO LOSE YOU BABY	8.50	20.00	18.00
☐ 2564 (M)		DISTANT SHORES	6.50	15.00	13.50
☐ 9364 (S)		DISTANT SHORES	8.50	20.00	18.00
☐ 2657 (M)		OF CABBAGES AND KINGS	6.50	15.00	13.50
☐ 9457 (S)		OF CABBAGES AND KINGS	8.50	20.00	18.00
☐ 2899 (M)		THE ARK	7.50	17.00	15.00
☐ 9699 (S)		THE ARK	7.50	17.00	15.00

			Current Price Range		P/Y AVG
☐ 2470 (M)	*CAPITOL*	THE BEST OF CHAD AND JEREMY	6.00	14.00	12.00
☐ 2470 (S)		THE BEST OF CHAD AND JEREMY	6.50	15.00	13.50
☐ 2546 (M)		MORE CHAD AND JEREMY	6.00	14.00	12.00
☐ 2546 (S)		MORE CHAD AND JEREMY	6.50	15.00	13.50

CHALLENGERS

☐ 900	*VAULT*	TORQUAY/BULLDOG	3.50	6.00	4.00
☐ 902		MOONDOG/TIDAL WAVE	3.50	6.00	4.00
☐ 904		FOOT TAPPER/ON THE MOVE	3.50	6.00	4.00
☐ 910		HOT ROD HOOTENANNY/ MAYBELLENE	3.50	6.00	4.00
☐ 913		HOT ROD SHOW (PT. 1)/ HOT ROD SHOW (PT. 2)	3.50	6.00	4.00
☐ 918		CHANNEL NINE/ CAN'T SEEM TO GET OVER YOU	3.50	6.00	4.00
☐ 53	*PRINCESS*	MR. MOTO '65/CHIEFLADO	3.50	6.00	4.00
☐ 376	*GNP-CRESCENDO*	WIPEOUT/NORTH BEACH	3.50	6.00	4.00
☐ 400		COLOR ME IN/BEFORE YOU	3.50	6.00	4.00

CHALLENGERS—ALBUMS

☐ 101 (M)	*VAULT*	SURFBEAT	8.00	19.00	12.00
☐ 101-A (M)		SURFING WITH THE CHALLENGERS	9.00	22.00	14.00
☐ 102 (M)		THE CHALLENGERS ON THE MOVE	8.00	19.00	12.00
☐ 107 (M)		K-39	∖8.00	19.00	12.00
☐ 109 (M)		SURF'S UP	8.00	19.00	12.00
☐ 110 (M)		THE CHALLENGERS A-GO GO	8.00	19.00	12.00
☐ 2010 (M)	*GNP-CRESCENDO*	THE CHALLENGERS AT THE TEENAGE FAIR	8.00	19.00	12.00
☐ 2018 (M)		THE MAN FROM U.N.C.L.E.	8.00	19.00	12.00
☐ 2025 (M)		CALIFORNIA KICKS	8.00	19.00	12.00
☐ 2031 (M)		WIPEOUT	8.00	19.00	12.00
☐ 2045 (M)		LIGHT MY FIRE	8.00	19.00	12.00
☐ 2056 (M)		VANILLA FUNK	8.00	19.00	12.00
☐ 100 (M)	*TRIUMPH*	THE CHALLENGERS GO SIDEWALK SURFING	17.00	38.00	24.00

CHAMPS

☐ 1016	*CHALLENGE*	TEQUILA/TRAIN TO NOWHERE	3.50	5.50	4.00
☐ 59007		EL RANCHO ROCK/MIDNIGHTER	3.50	5.50	4.00
☐ 59018		CHARIOT ROCK/SUBWAY	3.50	5.50	4.00
☐ 59026		ROCKIN' MARY/TURNPIKE	3.50	5.50	4.00
☐ 59035		GONE TRAIN/BEATNIK	3.50	5.50	4.00
☐ 59043		CARAMBA!/MOONLIGHT BAY	3.50	5.50	4.00
☐ 59049		NIGHT TRAIN/THE RATTLER	3.50	5.50	4.00
☐ 59053		DOUBLE EAGLE ROCK/SKY HIGH	3.50	5.50	4.00
☐ 59063		TOO MUCH TEQUILA/ TWENTY THOUSAND LEAGUES	3.50	5.50	4.00
☐ 59076		RED EYE/THE LITTLE MATADOR	3.50	5.50	4.00
☐ 59086		ALLEY CAT/COCONUT GROVE	3.50	5.50	4.00
☐ 59097		TOUGH TRAIN/THE FACE	3.50	5.50	4.00
☐ 59103		HOKEY POKEY/JUMPING BEAN	3.50	5.50	4.00
☐ 9113		SOMBRERO/ THE SHODDY SHODDY	3.50	5.50	4.00
☐ 9116		CANTINA/PANIC BUTTON	3.50	5.50	4.00
☐ 9131		LIMBO ROCK/TEQUILA TWIST	3.00	5.00	3.50
☐ 9140		LA CUCARACHA/ EXPERIMENT IN TERROR	3.00	5.00	3.50
☐ 9143		I'VE JUST SEEN HER/ WHAT A COUNTRY	3.00	5.00	3.50
☐ 9162		LIMBO DANCE/LATIN LIMBO	3.00	5.00	3.50
☐ 9174		VARSITY ROCK/THAT DID IT	3.00	5.00	3.50
☐ 9180		MR. COOL/3/4 MASH	3.00	5.00	3.50

			Current Price Range		P/Y AVG
☐9189		SHADES/NIK NAK	3.00	5.00	3.50
☐9199		CACTUS JUICE/ROOTS	3.00	5.00	3.50
☐59219		SAN JUAN/JALISCO	3.00	5.00	3.50
☐59236		ONLY THE YOUNG/SWITZERLAND	3.00	5.00	3.50
☐59263		KAHLUA/FRATERNITY WALTZ ...	3.00	5.00	3.50
☐59277		BRIGHT LIGHTS, BIG CITY/ FRENCH 75	3.00	5.00	3.50
☐59314		THE MAN FROM DURANGO/ RED PEPPER	3.00	5.00	3.50
☐59322		BUCKAROO/ANNA	3.00	5.00	3.50
		CHAMPS—EPs			
☐7100	**CHALLENGE**	TEQUILA	8.50	14.00	12.00
☐7101		CARAMBA!	7.50	13.00	11.00
		CHAMPS—ALBUMS			
☐601 (M)	**CHALLENGE**	GO CHAMPS GO	12.00	29.00	25.00
☐605 (M)		EVERYBODY'S ROCKIN' WITH THE CHAMPS	10.00	25.00	22.50
☐605 (S)		EVERYBODY'S ROCKIN' WITH THE CHAMPS	14.50	34.00	30.00
☐613 (M)		GREAT DANCE HITS	8.50	21.00	18.00
☐613 (S)		GREAT DANCE HITS	12.00	25.00	22.50
☐614 (M)		ALL AMERICAN MUSIC FROM THE CHAMPS	8.50	21.00	18.00
☐614 (S)		ALL AMERICAN MUSIC FROM THE CHAMPS	12.00	25.00	25.00

LARRY CHANCE

☐110	**BARRY**	PROMISE HER ANYTHING/ LET THEM TALK	12.50	29.00	25.00

GENE CHANDLER
SEE: DUKAYS

☐416	**VEE JAY**	DUKE OF EARL/ KISSIN' IN THE KITCHEN	3.00	5.00	3.50
☐440		WALK ON WITH THE DUKE/ LONESOME TOWN (Duke of Earl)	3.25	5.50	4.00
☐450		DADDY'S HOME/THE BIG LIE (Duke of Earl)	3.25	5.50	4.00
☐455		YOU LEFT ME/I'LL FOLLOW YOU (Duke of Earl)	3.00	5.00	3.50
☐461		TEAR FOR TEAR/ MIRACLE AFTER MIRACLE	3.00	5.00	3.50
☐468		RAINBOW/ YOU THREW A LUCKY PUNCH	3.00	5.00	3.50
☐511		CHECK YOURSELF/FORGIVE ME	3.00	5.00	3.50
☐536		MAN'S TEMPTATION/ BABY THAT'S LOVE	3.00	5.00	3.50
		GENE CHANDLER—ALBUMS			
☐1040 (M)	**VEE JAY**	THE DUKE OF EARL	14.50	34.00	30.00
☐1040 (S)		THE DUKE OF EARL	19.50	49.00	45.00

BRUCE CHANNEL

☐601	**TEEN AGER**	RUN ROMANCE RUN/ DON'T LEAVE ME	6.00	11.00	9.00
☐1035	**MANCO**	RUN ROMANCE RUN/ DON'T LEAVE ME	5.50	8.50	7.00
☐953	**LE CAM**	HEY! BABY/DREAM GIRL	12.00	20.00	18.00
☐122		GOING BACK TO LOUISIANA/ FORGET ME NOT	3.50	6.00	4.00
☐125		BLUE MONDAY/MY BABY	3.50	6.00	4.00
☐579	**MALA RECORDS**	MR. BUS DRIVER/IT'S ME	3.50	6.00	4.00
☐1731	**SMASH**	HEY! BABY/DREAM GIRL	3.00	5.25	3.65
☐1752		NUMBER ONE MAN/ IF ONLY I HAD KNOWN	3.00	5.25	3.65

			Current Price Range		P/Y AVG
☐ 1769		COME ON BABY/			
		MINE EXCLUSIVELY	3.00	5.25	3.65
☐ 1780		SOMEWHERE IN THIS TOWN/			
		STAND TOUGH	3.00	5.25	3.65
☐ 1792		LET'S HURT TOGETHER/OH BABY	3.00	5.25	3.65
☐ 1826		NIGHT PEOPLE/NO OTHER BABY .	3.00	5.25	3.65
☐ 1838		SEND HER HOME/DIPSY DOODLE	3.00	5.25	3.65
		BRUCE CHANNEL—ALBUMS			
☐ 27008 (M)	**SMASH**	HEY! BABY	8.25	14.00	12.00
☐ 67008 (S)		HEY! BABY	12.00	20.00	18.00

CHANTAYS

☐ 104	**DOWNEY**	PIPELINE/MOVE IT	4.50	7.50	6.00
☐ 108		MONSOON/SCOTCH HIGH'S	3.75	5.00	4.50
☐ 116		SPACE PROBE/			
		CONTINENTAL MISSLE	3.75	5.00	4.50
☐ 120		BEYOND/I'LL BE BACK SOMEDAY	3.75	5.00	4.50
☐ 16440	**DOT**	PIPELINE/MOVE IT	3.00	5.00	3.50
☐ 16492		MONSOON/SCOTCH HIGH'S	3.00	5.00	3.50
		CHANTAYS—ALBUMS			
☐ 1002 (M)	**DOWNEY**	PIPELINE	45.00	100.00	65.00
☐ 1002 (S)		PIPELINE	55.00	130.00	87.00
☐ 3516 (M)	**DOT**	PIPELINE	12.00	28.00	17.00
☐ 25516 (S)		PIPELINE	16.00	38.00	24.00
☐ 3771 (M)		TWO SIDES OF THE CHANTAYS ..	10.00	23.00	13.00
☐ 25771 (S)		TWO SIDES OF THE CHANTAYS ..	14.00	32.00	21.00

CHANTELS

☐ 1001	**END**	HE'S GONE/THE PLEA	4.50	7.50	6.00
☐ 1005		MAYBE/COME MY LITTLE BABY .	3.75	6.00	4.50
☐ 1015		EVERY NIGHT (I PRAY)/			
		WHOEVER YOU ARE	3.75	6.00	4.50
☐ 1020		I LOVE YOU SO/			
		HOW COULD YOU CALL IT OFF .	3.50	5.50	4.00
☐ 1026		PRAYEE/SURE OF LOVE	3.50	5.50	4.50
☐ 1030		CONGRATULATIONS/IF YOU TRY	3.50	5.50	4.00
☐ 1037		I CAN'T TAKE IT/			
		NEVER LET YOU GO	3.50	5.50	4.00
☐ 1048		I'M CONFESSIN'/			
		GOODBYE TO LOVE	3.50	5.50	4.00
☐ 1069		WHOEVER YOU ARE/			
		HOW COULD YOU CALL IT OFF?	3.25	5.25	4.00
☐ 1105		THERE'S OUR SONG AGAIN/			
		I'M THE GIRL	3.25	5.25	4.00
☐ 5056	**GONE**	COME SOFTLY TO ME/WALKING			
		THROUGH DREAMLAND	3.75	6.00	4.50
☐ 5060		SUMMER'S LOVE/			
		ALL IS FORGIVEN	3.75	5.00	4.50
☐ 555	**CARLTON**	LOOK IN MY EYES/			
		GLAD TO BE BACK	3.25	5.25	4.00
☐ 564		WELL I TOLD YOU/I STILL	3.25	5.25	4.00
☐ 569		HERE IT COMES AGAIN/			
		SUMMERTIME	3.25	5.25	4.00
☐ 3073	**BIG TOP**	LOVE. LOVE. LOVE/HE KNOWS I			
		LOVE HIM TOO MUCH	3.25	5.25	4.00
☐ 101	**LUDIX**	ETERNALLY/SWAMP WATER	3.25	5.25	4.00
☐ 106		SOME TEARS FALL DRY/			
		THAT'S WHY YOU'RE HAPPY ..	3.25	5.25	4.00
☐ 10387	**VERVE**	SOUL OF A SOLDIER/YOU'RE			
		WELCOME TO MY HEART	3.25	5.25	4.00
☐ 10435		IT'S JUST ME/INDIAN GIVER	3.25	5.25	4.00
		CHANTELS—EP			
☐ 201	**END**	I LOVE YOU SO	14.00	24.00	20.00
☐ 202		C'EST SI BON	12.00	21.00	18.00

			Current Price Range		P/Y AVG
		CHANTELS—ALBUMS			
☐301 (M)	**END**	WE ARE THE CHANTELS (group cover)	80.00	190.00	120.00
☐301 (M)		WE ARE THE CHANTELS (juke box cover)	20.00	40.00	27.00
☐301 (S)		WE ARE THE CHANTELS (reissue)	6.00	12.00	10.00
☐312 (M)		THERE'S OUR SONG AGAIN	15.00	35.00	24.00
☐312 (S)		THERE'S OUR SONG AGAIN (reissue)	7.00	15.50	13.50
☐144 (M)	**CARLTON**	THE CHANTELS ON TOUR	14.50	34.00	30.00
☐144 (S)		THE CHANTELS ON TOUR	19.00	49.00	45.00
		CHANTERS			
☐6162	**DELUXE**	MY MY DARLING/ I NEED YOUR TENDERNESS	12.00	20.00	18.00
☐6166		STARS IN THE SKIES/ ROW YOUR BOAT	12.00	20.00	18.00
☐6172		FIVE LITTLE KISSES/ ANGEL DARLING	12.00	20.00	18.00
☐6177		NO, NO, NO/OVER THE RAINBOW	9.50	17.00	15.00
☐6191		NO, NO, NO/I MAKE THIS PLEDGE	9.50	17.00	15.00
☐6194		AT MY DOOR/MY MY DARLING	9.50	17.00	15.00
☐6200		NO, NO, NO/ROW YOUR BOAT	8.25	14.00	12.00
		CHANTS			
☐277	**CAMEO**	COME GO WITH ME/I DON'T CARE	5.50	8.50	7.00
☐297		A THOUSAND STARS/ I COULD WRITE A BOOK	5.50	8.50	7.00
☐7703	**INTERPHON**	SHE'S MINE/THEN I'LL BE HOME	5.00	7.50	6.00
		CHAPERONES			
☐880	**JOSIE**	DANCE WITH ME/ CRUISE TO THE MOON	5.50	8.50	7.00
☐885		SHINING STAR/ MY SHADOW AND ME	5.50	8.50	7.00
☐891		THE MAN FROM THE MOON/ BLUEBERRY SWEET	5.50	8.50	7.00
		HARRY CHAPIN			
☐45203	**ELEKTRA**	CAT'S IN THE CRADLE/VACANCY	3.75	5.75	4.00
☐45236		SHE SINGS SONGS/ I WANNA LEARN A LOVE SONG	3.75	5.75	4.00
☐45264		DREAMS GO BY/SANDY	3.50	6.00	4.75
☐45285		DIRT GETS UNDER THE FINGERNAILS/TANGLED UP PUPPET	3.50	6.00	4.75
☐45327		BETTER PLACE TO BE (PT. 1)/ PT. 2)	3.50	6.00	4.75
☐45368		COREY'S COMING	3.75	5.75	5.00
☐45426		I WONDER WHAT HAPPENED TO HIM/DANCE BAND ON THE TITAC	3.75	5.75	4.00
☐45445		MY OLD LADY/ I DO IT FOR YOU, JANE	3.75	5.75	4.00
☐45497		IF YOU WANT TO FEEL/I WONDER WHAT WOULD HAPPEN	3.50	6.00	4.50
☐45770		TAXI/EMPTY	3.50	6.00	4.50
☐45792		ANY OLD KIND OF DAY/ COULD YOU PUT YOUR LIGHT ON, PLEASE	3.50	6.00	4.50
☐45811		SUNDAY MORNING SUNSHINE/ BURNING YOURSELF	3.25	5.00	3.50
☐45828		BETTER PLACE TO BE (reissue)	3.25	5.00	3.50

			Current Price Range		P/Y AVG

CHARLATAN

☐ 779	**KAPP**	THIRTY-TWO TWENTY/			
		THE SHADOW KNOWS	7.00	17.00	15.00
☐ 40610	**PHILLIPS**	HIGH COIN/WHEN I GO SAILIN' BY	7.00	12.00	10.00

RAY CHARLES

☐ 250	**SWING TIME**	BABY. LET ME HOLD YOUR HAND/			
		LONELY BOY	20.00	34.00	30.00
☐ 274		KISS ME. BABY/			
		I'M GLAD FOR YOUR SAKE	14.00	27.00	24.00
☐ 976	**ATLANTIC**	ROLL WITH MY BABY/			
		THE MIDNIGHT HOUR	17.00	27.00	24.00
☐ 984		THE SUN'S GONNA SHINE AGAIN/			
		JUMPIN' IN THE MORNIN'	14.00	24.00	20.00
☐ 999		MESS AROUND/FUNNY	14.00	24.00	20.00
☐ 1008		FEELIN' SAD/HEARTBREAKER ...	14.00	24.00	20.00
☐ 1021		IT SHOULD'VE BEEN ME/			
		SINNER'S PRAYER	12.00	20.00	18.00
☐ 1037		DON'T YOU KNOW?/			
		LOSING HAND	12.00	20.00	18.00
☐ 1050		I'VE GOT A WOMAN/COME BACK	9.50	17.00	15.00
☐ 1063		THIS LITTLE GIRL OF MINE/			
		A FOOL FOR YOU	9.50	17.00	15.00
☐ 1076		GREENBACKS/BLACKJACK	8.25	14.00	12.00

FIRST-PRESSES OF THE ABOVE ARE ON THE YELLOW-AND-BLACK LABEL

☐ 1085		DROWN IN MY OWN TEARS/			
		MARY ANN	5.00	8.00	6.50
☐ 1096		HALLELUJAH. I LOVE HER SO/			
		WHAT WOULD I DO WITHOUT			
		YOU	5.00	8.00	6.50
☐ 1108		LONELY AVENUE/			
		LEAVE MY WOMAN ALONE	5.00	8.20	6.70
☐ 1124		AIN'T THAT LOVE/			
		I WANT TO KNOW	5.00	8.00	6.50
☐ 1143		IT'S ALL RIGHT/GET ON THE			
		RIGHT TRACK BABY	5.00	8.00	6.50
☐ 1154		SWANEE RIVER ROCK/			
		I WANT A LITTLE GIRL	3.50	5.50	4.00
☐ 1172		TALKIN' 'BOUT YOU/WHAT KIND			
		OF MAN ARE YOU?	3.75	6.00	4.50
☐ 1180		YES INDEED/I HAD A DREAM	3.75	6.00	4.50
☐ 1196		YOU BE MY BABY/MY BONNIE ..	3.75	6.00	4.50
☐ 2006		ROCKHOUSE (PT. 1)/(PT. 2)	3.50	5.50	4.00
☐ 2010		THE RIGHT TIME/TELL ALL THE			
		WORLD ABOUT YOU	3.50	5.50	4.00
☐ 2022		THAT'S ENOUGH/			
		TELL ME HOW YOU FEEL	3.50	5.50	4.00
☐ 2031		WHAT'D I SAY (PT. 1)/(PT. 2) ...	3.00	5.00	3.50
☐ 2043		I'M MOVIN' ON/			
		I BELIEVE TO MY SOUL	3.00	5.00	3.50
☐ 2047		LET THE GOOD TIMES ROLL/			
		DON'T LET THE SUN CATCH			
		YOU CRYING	3.25	5.50	4.00
☐ 2055		JUST FOR A THRILL/			
		HEARTBREAKER	3.25	5.50	4.00
☐ 2068		TELL THE TRUTH/			
		SWEET SIXTEEN	3.00	5.00	3.50
☐ 2084		COME RAIN OR COME SHINE/			
		TELL ME YOU'LL WAIT FOR ME	3.00	5.00	3.50
☐ 2094		EARLY IN THE MORNING/			
		A BIT OF SOUL	3.00	5.00	3.50
☐ 2106		IT SHOULD'VE BEEN ME/			
		AM I BLUE?	3.00	5.00	3.50
☐ 2118		HARD TIMES/I WONDER WHO ...	3.00	5.00	3.50

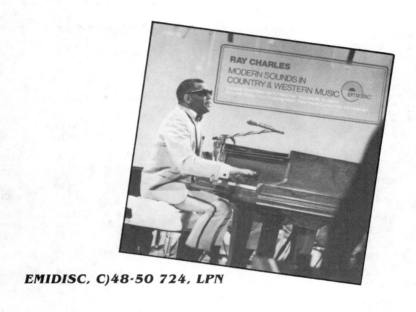

EMIDISC, C)48-50 724, LPN

ABC, ABCX 755 / TRC, LPN

			Current Price Range		P/Y AVG
☐2174		CARRYING THAT LOAD/ FEELIN' SAD	3.00	5.00	3.50
☐2239		IN A LITTLE SPANISH TOWN/ TALKIN' 'BOUT YOU	3.00	5.00	3.50
☐2470		COME RAIN OR COME SHINE/ YOU'LL WAIT FOR ME	3.00	5.00	3.50

ABC-PARAMOUNT SINGLES ARE WORTH UP TO $2.50 MINT

RAY CHARLES—EPs

☐587	*ATLANTIC*	RAY CHARLES	6.50	11.00	9.00
☐597		THE GREAT RAY CHARLES	6.00	11.00	9.00
☐607		ROCK WITH RAY CHARLES	6.00	11.00	9.00

RAY CHARLES—ALBUMS

☐8006 (M)	*ATLANTIC*	ROCK AND ROLL	17.00	39.00	35.00
☐8025 (M)		YES, INDEED!	14.00	34.00	30.00
☐8029 (M)		WHAT'D I SAY	14.00	34.00	30.00
☐8039 (M)		RAY CHARLES IN PERSON	12.00	29.00	25.00
☐8052 (M)		GENIUS SINGS THE BLUES	10.00	24.00	20.00
☐8054 (M)		DO THE TWIST WITH RAY CHARLES	9.50	20.00	18.00
☐8063 (M)		THE RAY CHARLES STORY, VOL. I	7.00	17.00	15.00
☐8064 (M)		THE RAY CHARLES STORY, VOL. II	7.00	17.00	15.00
☐8094 (M)		THE RAY CHARLES STORY, VOL. III	7.00	17.00	15.00
☐8094 (S)		THE RAY CHARLES STORY, VOL. III	7.00	17.00	15.00
☐1256 (M)		THE GREAT RAY CHARLES	6.00	15.00	13.50
☐1256 (S)		THE GREAT RAY CHARLES	6.00	15.00	13.50
☐1279 (M)		SOUL BROTHERS (with Milt Jackson)	6.00	15.00	13.50
☐1279 (S)		SOUL BROTHERS (with Milt Jackson)	6.00	15.00	13.50
☐1289 (M)		RAY CHARLES AT NEWPORT	6.00	15.00	13.50
☐1289 (S)		RAY CHARLES AT NEWPORT	6.00	15.00	13.50
☐1312 (M)		THE GENIUS OF RAY CHARLES	5.50	14.00	12.00
☐1312 (S)		THE GENIUS OF RAY CHARLES	5.50	14.00	12.00
☐1369 (M)		GENIUS AFTER HOURS	5.50	14.00	12.00
☐1369 (S)		GENIUS AFTER HOURS	5.50	14.00	12.00

LATER ATLANTIC ALBUMS ARE WORTH UP TO $9.00 MINT

CHARMS
FEATURED: OTIS WILLIAMS

☐516	*ROCKIN'*	HEAVEN ONLY KNOWS/ LOVING BABY	75.00	150.00	98.00
☐6000	*DELUXE*	HEAVEN ONLY KNOWS/ LOVING BABY	60.00	125.00	72.00
☐6014		HAPPY ARE WE/WHAT DO YOU KNOW ABOUT THAT?	60.00	125.00	72.00
☐6034		PLEASE BELIEVE IN ME/ BYE BYE BABY	40.00	90.00	50.00
☐6050		QUIET PLEASE/55 SECONDS	32.00	65.00	32.00
☐6056		MY BABY DEAREST DARLING/ COME TO ME BABY	32.00	65.00	32.00
☐6062		HEARTS OF STONE/WHO KNOWS?	17.00	35.00	19.00
☐6065		TWO HEARTS/ THE FIRST TIME WE MET	17.00	35.00	19.00
☐6072		CRAZY, CRAZY LOVE/ MAMBO SH-MAMBO	17.00	35.00	19.00
☐6076		LING TING TONG/BAZOOM (I NEED YOUR LOVIN')	17.00	35.00	19.00
☐6080		KO KO MO/WHADAYA WANT?	15.00	30.00	16.00
☐6082		CRAZY, CRAZY LOVE/ WHADAYA WANT?	12.00	25.00	13.50
☐6087		WHEN WE GET TOGETHER/ LET THE HAPPENINGS HAPPEN	10.00	20.00	11.00

CHUBBY CHECKER

During the 1950s he was known to his friends as Ernest Evans. He was a young (born October 3, 1941) unknown then, undistinguished from many other South Philadelphia kids. Ernie worked after school plucking chickens at a local market. To while away the time, Evans amused himself by loudly belting out the latest rock-and-roll hits. The market's owner was a friend of Kal Mann, who worked at nearby Parkway Records. Mann liked Ernest and signed him.

Dick Clark's wife later came up with the novelty name of Chubby Checker after Chubby's idol, Fats Domino. His first Parkway disc in 1959 was called "The Class", a novelty on which Chubby — then eighteen — imitated several other singers. Three singles later Checker mimicked Hank Ballard's "The Twist" which squirmed up the charts to No. 1, and Chubby Checker, former chicken-plucker, was on his way to a long string of dance hits.

In 1963 he married Catharina Lodders, a former Miss World. He and his family still live in Philadelphia, and Chubby tours as a headliner at rock shows around the world.

			Current Price Range		P/Y AVG
☐6088		MISS THE LOVE/TELL ME NOW ..	10.00	20.00	11.00
☐6089		ONE FINE DAY/			
		IT'S YOU, YOU, YOU	10.00	20.00	11.00
☐6090		GUM DROP/SAVE ME. SAVE ME .	10.00	20.00	11.00
☐6091		THAT'S YOUR MISTAKE/			
		TOO LATE I LEARNED	7.00	14.00	9.50
☐6092		ROLLING HOME/DO BE YOU	7.00	14.00	9.50
☐6093		IVORY TOWER/IN PARADISE	6.00	11.00	7.25
☐6095		IT'S ALL OVER/ONE NIGHT ONLY	6.00	11.00	7.25
☐6097		WHIRLWIND/I'D LIKE TO			
		THANK YOU, MR. D. J.	6.00	11.00	7.25
☐6098		GYPSY LADY/			
		I'LL REMEMBER YOU	6.00	11.00	7.25
☐6105		BLUES STAY AWAY FROM ME/			
		PARDON ME	6.00	11.00	7.25
☐6115		I'M WAITING JUST FOR YOU/			
		WALKIN' AFTER MIDNIGHT ...	6.00	11.00	7.25
☐6130		NOWHERE ON EARTH/			
		NO GOT DE WOMAN	6.00	11.00	7.25
☐6137		ONE KIND WORD FROM YOU/			
		TALKING TO MYSELF	6.00	11.00	7.25
☐6138		UNITED/DON'T DENY ME	6.00	11.00	7.25
☐6149		DYNAMITE DARLING/			
		WELL OH WELL	4.00	7.00	4.75
☐6158		COULD THIS BE MAGIC/OH JULIE	4.00	7.00	4.75
☐6160		LET SOME LOVE IN YOUR HEART/			
		BABY-O	4.00	7.00	4.75
☐6165		BURNIN' LIPS/RED HOT LOVE ...	4.00	7.00	4.75
☐6174		YOU'LL REMAIN FOREVER/			
		DON'T WAKE UP THE KIDS	4.00	7.00	4.75
☐6178		MY FRIENDS/THE SECRET	4.00	7.00	4.75
☐6181		WELCOME HOME/PRETTY LITTLE			
		THINGS CALLED GIRLS	3.75	6.00	4.50
☐6183		MY PRAYER TONIGHT/			
		WATCH DOG	3.75	6.00	4.50
☐6185		I KNEW IT ALL THE TIME/			
		TEARS OF HAPPINESS	3.75	6.00	4.50
☐6186		IN PARADISE/WHO KNOWS	3.75	6.00	4.50
☐6187		BLUES STAY AWAY FROM ME/			
		FUNNY WHAT TRUE LOVE			
		CAN DO	3.75	6.00	4.50
		CHARMS—EPs			
☐357	*KING*	HITS BY THE CHARMS	18.00	35.00	23.00
☐364		THE CHARMS. VOL. II	18.00	35.00	23.00
☐385		HITS	18.00	35.00	23.00
		CHARMS—ALBUMS			
☐570 (M)	*KING*	OTIS WILLIAMS AND			
		THE CHARMS	75.00	160.00	100.00
☐614 (M)		THIS IS OTIS WILLIAMS			
		THE CHARMS	35.00	75.00	47.00

CHUBBY CHECKER

☐006	*PARKWAY*	THE JET/RAY CHARLES-TON	5.50	8.50	7.00
☐804		THE CLASS/SCHOOLDAYS,			
		OH, SCHOOLDAYS	5.50	8.50	7.00
☐808		SAMSON AND DELILAH/			
		WHOLE LOTTA LAUGHIN'	8.50	14.00	12.00
☐810		DANCING DINOSAUR/			
		THOSE PRIVATE EYES	8.50	14.00	12.00
☐811		THE TWIST/TOOT (1960 release) .	4.00	7.00	4.50
☐811		THE TWIST/TWISTIN' U.S.A.			
		(1961 release)	3.50	6.00	4.00
☐813		THE HUCKLEBUCK/WHOLE LOTTA			
		SHAKING GOIN' ON	3.50	6.00	4.00

DELUXE, DEP 385, EP

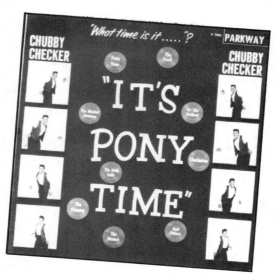

PARKWAY, P 7003, LP

			Current Price Range		P/Y AVG
☐818		PONY TIME/OH, SUSANNAH	3.50	6.00	4.00
☐822		DANCE THE MESS AROUND/			
		GOOD, GOOD LOVIN'	3.50	6.00	4.00
☐824		LET'S TWIST AGAIN/			
		EVERYTHING'S GONNA BE			
		ALL RIGHT	3.50	6.00	4.00
☐830		THE FLY/			
		THAT'S THE WAY IT GOES	3.50	6.00	4.00
☐835		SLOW TWISTIN'/			
		LA PALOMA TWIST	3.50	6.00	4.00
☐842		DANCIN' PARTY/GOTTA GET			
		MYSELF TOGETHER	3.50	6.00	4.00
☐849		LIMBO ROCK/POPEYE			
		(THE HITCH-HIKER)	3.50	6.00	4.00
☐862		TWENTY MILES/			
		LET'S LIMBO SOME MORE	3.50	6.00	4.00
☐873		BIRDLAND/BLACK CLOUD	3.00	5.00	3.70
☐879		TWIST IT UP/SURF PARTY	3.00	5.00	3.70
☐890		LODDY LO/HOOKA TOOKA......	3.00	5.00	3.70
☐907		HEY BOBBA NEEDLE/SPREAD JOY	3.00	5.00	3.70
☐920		LAZY ELSIE MOLLY/ROSIE	3.00	5.00	3.70
☐922		SHE WANT T'SWIM/YOU BETTER			
		BELIEVE IT, BABY	3.00	5.00	3.70
☐936		LOVELY, LOVELY/			
		THE WEEKEND'S HERE	3.00	5.00	3.70
☐949		LET'S DO THE FREDDIE/			
		(AT THE) DISCOTEQUE	3.00	5.00	3.70
☐959		EVERYTHING'S WRONG/			
		CU MA LA BE-STAY	3.00	5.00	3.70
☐989		HEY YOU! LITTLE BOO-GA-LOO/			
		PUSSY CAT	3.00	5.00	3.70
☐105		YOU GOT THE POWER/			
		LOOKING AT TOMORROW	3.00	5.00	3.70
☐112		KARATE MONKEY/HER HEART ..	3.00	5.00	3.70
☐70E		BLUEBERRY HILL/I COULD HAVE			
		DANCED ALL NIGHT	3.00	5.00	3.70
CHUBBY CHECKER—ALBUMS					
☐5001 (M)	**PARKWAY**	CHUBBY CHECKER	15.00	28.00	16.00
☐7001 (M)		TWIST WITH CHUBBY CHECKER .	9.00	16.00	11.00
☐7002 (M)		FOR TWISTERS ONLY	9.00	16.00	11.00
☐7003 (M)		IT'S PONY TIME.............	9.00	16.00	11.00
☐7004 (M)		LET'S TWIST AGAIN	9.00	16.00	11.00
☐7007 (M)		YOUR TWIST PARTY	9.00	16.00	11.00
☐7008 (M)		TWISTIN' ROUND THE WORLD ...	9.00	16.00	11.00
☐7009 (M)		FOR TEEN TWISTERS ONLY	9.00	16.00	11.00
☐7011 (M)		DON'T KNOCK THE TWIST			
		(movie soundtrack)	9.00	16.00	11.00
☐7014 (M)		ALL THE HITS	9.00	16.00	11.00
☐7020 (M)		LIMBO PARTY	9.00	16.00	11.00
☐7020 (S)		LIMBO PARTY	9.00	16.00	11.00
☐7022 (M)		BIGGEST HITS	6.50	11.00	9.00
☐7022 (S)		BIGGEST HITS	8.50	14.00	12.00
☐7026 (M)		IN PERSON.................	6.50	11.00	9.00
☐7026 (S)		IN PERSON.................	8.50	14.00	12.00
☐7027 (M)		LET'S LIMBO SOME MORE	6.50	11.00	9.00
☐7027 (S)		LET'S LIMBO SOME MORE	8.50	14.00	12.00
☐7030 (M)		BEACH PARTY	6.50	11.00	9.00
☐7030 (S)		BEACH PARTY	8.60	14.00	12.00
☐7040 (M)		CHUBBY'S FOLK ALBUM	6.50	11.00	9.00
☐7040 (S)		CHUBBY'S FOLK ALBUM	8.50	14.00	12.00
☐7045 (M)		CHUBBY CHECKER DISCOTEQUE .	6.50	11.00	9.00
☐7045 (S)		CHUBBY CHECKER DISCOTEQUE .	8.50	14.00	12.00

CHER

Cherilyn LaPierre was born on May 20, 1946, in the parched farming town of El Centro, CA.

At sixteen, Cher dropped out of a strict church school and took off for Hollywood on a bus. She was determined to become a movie star but found all doors closed once she arrived in Tinseltown.

Cher soon became friends with a girl who worked part time as a background singer for some Los Angeles sessions. Cher was with her one day at Gold Star Studios where Phil Spector was recording. Cher was told (not asked) to go in and sing because "we need some noise in here." (She had never sung before.) On that day, Cher became a professional singer. Also on that day she met Salvatore (Sonny) Bono, a truck-driver-turned-songwriter. He was bursting with clever ideas but possessed a dreadful voice. Somehow, the chemistry was right.

They worked together, got married, bombed as Caesar and Cleo, then tore up the music world as rock's first married couple.

Later, when their marriage ended, Cher landed her own TV show and stayed on the charts throughout the mid-1970s. In 1979 she began her career anew with the disco-flavored hit "Take Me Home."

			Current Price Range		P/Y AVG

CHER
SEE: CHERILYN, BONNIE JO MASON, SONNY AND CHER, CAESAR AND CLEO

☐66114	IMPERIAL	ALL I REALLY WANT TO DO/			
		I'M GONNA LOVE YOU	3.00	5.25	3.85
☐66136		WHERE DO YOU GO?/			
		SEE SEE BLUES	3.00	5.25	3.85
☐66160		BANG BANG/OUR DAY WILL COME	3.00	5.25	3.85
☐66192		ALFIE/			
		SHE'S NOT BETTER THAN ME	3.00	5.25	3.85
☐66217		BEHIND THE DOOR/			
		MAGIC IN THE AIR	3.00	5.25	3.85
☐66223		DREAM BABY/MAMA (WHEN MY			
		DOLLIES HAVE BABIES)	3.00	5.25	3.85
☐66252		HEY JOE/OUR DAY WILL COME	3.00	5.25	3.85
☐66261		YOU BETTER SIT DOWN, KIDS/			
		ELUSIVE BUTTERFLY	3.00	5.25	3.85
☐66282		BUT I CAN'T LOVE YOU MORE/			
		CLICK SONG, NUMBER ONE	3.00	5.25	3.85
☐6658	ATCO	YOURS UNTIL TOMORROW/			
		THE THOUGHT OF LOVING YOU	2.75	4.75	3.50
☐6704		FOR WHAT IT'S WORTH/			
		HANGIN' ON	2.75	4.75	3.50
☐6713		YOU MADE ME SO VERY HAPPY/			
		THE FIRST TIME	2.75	4.75	3.50
☐6793		SUPERSTAR/THE FIRST TIME	2.75	4.75	3.50

CHER—ALBUMS

☐9292 (M)	IMPERIAL	ALL I REALLY WANT TO DO	6.50	11.00	9.00
☐12292 (S)		ALL I REALLY WANT TO DO	8.25	14.00	12.00
☐9301 (M)		THE SONNY SIDE OF CHER	6.50	11.00	9.00
☐12301 (S)		THE SONNY SIDE OF CHER	8.25	14.00	12.00
☐9320 (M)		CHER	6.50	11.00	9.00
☐12320 (S)		CHER	8.25	14.00	12.00
☐9358 (M)		WITH LOVE	6.50	11.00	9.00
☐12358 (S)		WITH LOVE	8.25	14.00	12.00
☐12373 (S)		BACKSTAGE	6.50	11.00	9.00
☐12406 (S)		GOLDEN GREATS	6.50	11.00	9.00
☐298 (S)	ATCO	3614 JACKSON HIGHWAY	5.50	10.00	8.00

CHERILYN (CHER)
SEE: BONNIE JO MASON

☐66081	IMPERIAL	DREAM BABY/STAN QUENTZAL	5.50	10.00	8.00

CHESTERS (LITTLE ANTHONY AND THE IMPERIALS)

☐521	APOLLO	THE FIRES BURN NO MORE/			
		LIFT UP YOUR HEAD	8.25	14.00	12.00

CHEVRONS

☐1	TIME	COME GO WITH ME/I'M IN LOVE			
		AGAIN - ALL SHOOK UP	3.75	6.50	4.00
☐7007	BRENT	THE DAY AFTER FOREVER/			
		LULLABYE	3.75	6.50	4.00
☐7015		LITTLE STAR/LITTLE DARLING	3.75	6.50	4.00
☐94	INDEPENDENCE	MINE FOREVER MORE/			
		IN THE DEPTHS OF MY SOUL	3.00	5.00	3.50

CHEVRONS—ALBUM

☐1008 (M)	TIME	SING-A-LONG ROCK AND ROLL	10.00	17.00	15.00

ARTIE CHICAGO (ERNIE MARESCA)

☐3424	LAURIE	THE WANDERER/			
		PLEASE DON'T PLAY ME A-7	4.50	7.50	6.00

CHIFFONS
SEE: FOUR PENNIES

☐6003	BIG DEAL	TONIGHT'S THE NIGHT/			
		DO YOU KNOW	8.50	14.00	12.00

			Current Price Range		P/Y AVG
☐ 20103	**REPRISE**	AFTER LAST NIGHT/			
		DOCTOR OF HEARTS	5.50	8.50	7.00
☐ 3152	**LAURIE**	HE'S SO FINE/OH MY LOVER	3.00	5.00	3.50
☐ 3166		WHY AM I SO SHY/LUCKY ME ...	3.75	6.00	4.50
☐ 3179		ONE FINE DAY/WHY AM I SO SHY	3.50	5.50	4.00
☐ 3195		A LOVE SO FINE/			
		ONLY MY FRIEND	3.50	5.50	4.00
☐ 3212		I HAVE A BOYFRIEND/			
		I'M GONNA DRY MY EYES	3.50	5.50	4.00
☐ 3224		TONIGHT I MET AN ANGEL/			
		EASY TO LOVE	3.50	5.50	4.00
☐ 3262		SAILOR BOY/			
		WHEN SUMMER IS THROUGH .	3.50	5.50	4.00
☐ 3275		WHAT AM I GONNA DO WITH YOU,			
		BABY/STRANGE, STRANGE			
		FEELING	3.50	5.50	4.00
☐ 3301		NOBODY KNOWS WHAT'S GOIN'			
		ON/THE REAL THING	3.50	5.50	4.00
☐ 3318		TONIGHT I'M GONNA DREAM/			
		HEAVENLY PLACE	3.50	5.50	4.00
☐ 3340		SWEET TALKIN' GUY/DID YOU			
		EVER GO STEADY	3.00	5.00	3.65
☐ 3350		OUT OF THIS WORLD/JUST A BOY	3.00	5.00	3.65
☐ 3357		STOP, LOOK, LISTEN/MARCH ...	3.00	5.00	3.65
☐ 3364		MY BOYFRIEND'S BACK/			
		I GOT PLENTY OF NUTTIN'	3.00	5.00	3.65
☐ 3377		KEEP THE BOY HAPPY/			
		IF I KNEW THEN	3.00	5.00	3.65
☐ 3423		JUST FOR TONIGHT/			
		TEACH ME HOW	3.00	5.00	3.65
☐ 3460		UP ON THE BRIDGE/MARCH	3.00	5.00	3.65
☐ 3497		LOVE ME LIKE YOU'RE GONNA			
		LOSE ME/THREE DIPS OF			
		ICE CREAM	3.00	5.00	3.65
☐ 3630		MY SWEET LORD/MAIN NERVE ..	3.00	5.00	3.65
☐ 3648		DREAM, DREAM, DREAM/			
		OH MY LOVER	3.00	5.00	3.65
☐ 558	**B. T. PUPPY**	MY SECRET LOVE/			
		STRANGE STRANGE FEELING ..	3.25	5.50	4.00
☐ 601	**WILD CAT**	NO MORE TOMORROWS/			
		NEVER NEVER	3.25	5.50	4.00
		CHIFFONS—ALBUMS			
☐ 2018 (M)	**LAURIE**	HE'S SO FINE	14.00	24.00	20.00
☐ 2020 (M)		ONE FINE DAY	12.00	20.00	18.00
☐ 2036 (M)		SWEET TALKIN' GUY	10.00	14.00	12.00
☐ 2036 (S)		SWEET TALKIN' GUY	12.00	20.00	18.00
☐ 1011 (S)	**B. T. PUPPY**	MY SECRET LOVE	10.00	14.00	12.00

CHIMES

☐ 444	**TAG**	ONCE IN A WHILE/			
		SUMMER NIGHT	3.00	5.00	3.50
☐ 445		I'M IN THE MOOD FOR LOVE/			
		ONLY LOVE	3.00	5.00	3.50
☐ 447		LET'S FALL IN LOVE/DREAM GIRL.	3.00	5.00	3.50
☐ 450		PARADISE/MY LOVE	3.00	5.00	3.50

THE CHIPS

☐ 45-54	**CLIFTON**	WHEN I'M WITH YOU/			
		EVERYONE'S LAUGHING	35.00	75.00	48.00

CHOCOLATE WATCH BAND

☐ 740	**UPTOWN**	BABY BLUE/			
		SWEET YOUNG THING	5.50	8.50	7.00
☐ 749		MISTY LANE/			
		SHE WEAVES A TENDER TRAP .	4.50	7.50	6.00

			Current Price Range		P/Y AVG
☐373	**TOWER**	NO WAY OUT/			
		ARE YOU GONNA BE THERE? ..	4.50	7.50	6.00

CHOCOLATE WATCH BAND—ALBUMS

☐5096 (M)	**TOWER**	NO WAY OUT	8.25	14.00	12.00
☐5096 (S)		NO WAY OUT	12.00	20.00	18.00
☐5106 (M)		THE INNER MYSTIQUE	8.25	14.00	12.00
☐5106 (S)		THE INNER MYSTIQUE	12.00	20.00	18.00
☐5153 (S)		ONE STEP BEYOND	10.00	17.00	15.00

CHOIR (RASPBERRIES)
FEATURED: ERIC CARMEN

☐203	**CANADIAN-AMERICAN**	IT'S COLD OUTSIDE/			
		I'M GOING HOME	18.00	35.00	19.50
☐4738	**ROULETTE**	IT'S COLD OUTSIDE/			
		I'M GOING HOME	5.00	9.00	5.50
☐4760		NO ONE HERE TO PLAY WITH/			
		DON'T YOU FEEL A LITTLE			
		SORRY FOR ME	5.00	9.00	5.50
☐7005		CHANGIN' MY MIND/			
		WHEN YOU WERE WITH ME ...	5.00	9.00	5.50

CHORDS

☐104	**CAT**	SH-BOOM/			
		CROSS OVER THE BRIDGE	17.00	34.00	30.00
☐104		SH-BOOM/LITTLE MAIDEN	8.25	14.00	12.00
☐109		ZIPPITY ZUM/BLESS YOU	9.50	17.00	15.00
☐112		A GIRL TO LOVE/HOLD ME BABY .	12.00	20.00	18.00
☐117		COULD IT BE/PRETTY WILD	12.00	20.00	18.00
☐0295	**VIK**	LULU/I DON'T WANT TO SET THE			
		WORLD ON FIRE	8.25	14.00	12.00

LOU CHRISTIE
SEE: CHIC CHRISTY, CLASSICS, MARCY JOE, LUGEE AND THE LIONS

☐102	**C & C**	THE GYPSY CRIED/			
		RED SAILS IN THE SUNSET	25.00	45.00	30.00
☐4457	**ROULETTE**	THE GYPSY CRIED/			
		RED SAILS IN THE SUNSET ...	3.50	6.00	4.00
☐4481		TWO FACES HAVE I/			
		ALL THAT GLITTER ISN'T GOLD	3.50	6.00	4.00
☐4504		HOW MANY TEARDROPS?/			
		YOU AND I	3.50	6.00	4.00
☐4527		SHY BOY/IT CAN HAPPEN	3.50	6.00	4.00
☐4545		STAY/THERE THEY GO	3.50	6.00	4.00
☐4554		WHEN YOU DANCE/			
		MAYBE YOU'LL BE THERE	3.50	6.00	4.00
☐13412	**MGM**	LIGHTNIN' STRIKES/			
		CRYIN' IN THE STREETS	3.00	5.00	3.50
☐13473		RHAPSODY IN THE RAIN/TRAPEZE.	3.00	5.00	3.50
☐13533		PAINTER/DU RONDA	3.00	5.00	3.50
☐13576		IF MY CAR COULD ONLY TALK/			
		SONG OF LITA	3.00	5.00	3.50
☐13623		SINCE I DON'T HAVE YOU/			
		WILD LIFE'S IN SEASON	3.00	5.00	3.50
☐235	**CO & CE**	OUTSIDE THE GATES OF HEAVEN/			
		ALL THAT GLITTERS ISN'T GOLD	3.00	5.00	3.50
☐735	**COLPIX**	MERRY GO ROUND/			
		GUITARS AND BONGOS	3.00	5.50	3.75
☐753		HAVE I SINNED?/POT OF GOLD ..	3.00	5.50	3.75
☐770		MAKE SUMMER LAST FOREVER/			
		WHY DID YOU DO IT, BABY? ...	3.00	5.50	3.75
☐778		A TEENAGER IN LOVE/			
		BACKTRACK	3.00	5.50	3.75

			Current Price Range		P/Y AVG
☐799		BIG TIME/CRYIN' ON MY KNEES .	3.00	5.50	3.75
☐44062	COLUMBIA	SHAKE HANDS AND WALK AWAY CRYIN'/ESCAPE	3.00	5.50	3.75
☐44177		SELF EXPRESSION/BACK TO THE DAYS OF THE ROMANS	3.00	5.50	3.75
☐44240		GINA/ESCAPE	3.00	5.50	3.75
☐44338		DON'T STOP ME/BACK TO THE DAYS OF ROMANS	3.00	5.50	3.75
☐65	BUDDAH	GENESIS AND THE THIRD VERSE/ RAKE UP THE LEAVES	3.00	5.50	3.75
☐76		SAINTS OF AQUARIUS/ CANTERBURY ROAD	3.00	5.50	3.75
☐116		I'M GONNA MAKE YOU MINE/ I'M GONNA GET MARRIED	3.00	5.50	3.75
☐149		ARE YOU GETTING ANY SUNSHINE?/IT'LL TAKE TIME .	3.00	5.50	3.75
☐163		SHE SOLD ME MAGIC/ LOVE IS OVER	3.00	5.50	3.75
☐192		INDIAN LADY/GLORY RIVER	3.00	5.50	3.75
☐235		WACO/LIGHTHOUSE	3.00	5.50	3.75
☐257		MICKEY'S MONKEY/ WONDERFUL DREAM	3.00	5.50	3.75
☐285		SING ME, SING ME/ THE PAPER SONG	3.00	5.50	3.75
☐312		SHUFFLE ON DOWN TO PITTSBURGH/I'M GONNA GET MARRIED	3.00	5.50	3.75
☐400	THREE BROTHERS	BLUE CANADIAN ROCKY DREAM/ WILMA LEE AND STONY	3.00	5.50	3.75
☐402		BEYOND THE BLUE HORIZON/ SADDLE THE WIND	3.00	5.50	3.75
☐403		YOU WERE THE ONE/GOOD MORNIN' ZIP A DEE DOO DAH ..	3.00	5.50	3.75
☐405		SUNBEAM/HEY YOU CAJUN	3.00	5.50	3.75

LOU CHRISTIE—ALBUMS

☐25208 (M)	ROULETTE	LOU CHRISTIE	8.50	20.00	18.00
☐25208 (S)		LOU CHRISTIE	12.00	29.00	25.00

ABOVE ISSUED WITH TWO DIFFERENT COVERS

☐25332 (M)		LOU CHRISTIE STRIKES AGAIN ..	7.50	17.00	15.00
☐25332 (S)		LOU CHRISTIE STRIKES AGAIN ..	9.50	25.00	22.50
☐4360 (M)	MGM	LIGHTNIN' STRIKES	7.50	17.00	15.00
☐4360 (S)		LIGHTNIN' STRIKES	8.50	20.00	18.00
☐4394 (M)		PAINTER OF HITS	7.50	17.00	15.00
☐4394 (S)		PAINTER OF HITS	8.50	20.00	18.00
☐1231 (M)	CO & CE	LOU CHRISTIE STRIKES BACK ...	7.50	17.00	15.00
☐1231 (S)		LOU CHRISTIE STRIKES BACK ...	8.50	20.00	18.00
☐4001 (M)	COLPIX	LOU CHRISTIE STRIKES AGAIN ..	7.50	17.00	15.00
☐4001 (S)		LOU CHRISTIE STRIKES AGAIN ..	8.50	20.00	18.00

SONGS OF THE ABOVE TWO LPs ARE DIFFERENT

☐5052 (S)	BUDDAH	I'M GONNA MAKE YOU MINE	7.00	15.50	13.50
☐5073 (S)		PAINT AMERICA LOVE	7.00	15.50	13.50
☐2000 (S)	THREE BROTHERS	LOU CHRISTIE	7.00	15.50	13.50

LOU CHRISTIE AND THE CLASSICS

☐207	ALCAR	CLOSE YOUR EYES/FUNNY THING.	8.25	14.00	12.00
☐208		YOU'RE WITH IT/ TOMORROW WILL COME	8.25	14.00	12.00
☐1002	WORLD	THE JURY/LITTLE DID I KNOW (Lou Christie)	5.50	10.50	9.00
☐006	AMERICAN MUSIC MAKERS	THE JURY/LITTLE DID I KNOW (Lou Christie)	4.50	7.50	6.00

			Current Price Range		P/Y AVG

CHIC CHRISTY
FEATURED: LOU CHRISTIE

☐103	**HAC**	WITH THIS KISS/ MY BILLET-DOUX TO YOU	4.50	7.50	6.00

DON CHRISTY (SONNY BONO)

☐672	**SPECIALTY**	ONE LITTLE ANSWER/ WEARING BLACK	4.50	7.50	6.00

CHURCH STREET FIVE

☐1004	**LEGRAND**	A NIGHT WITH DADDY G (PT. 1)/(PT. 2)	3.00	5.50	3.50
☐1010		EVERYBODY'S HAPPY/ FALLEN ARCHES	3.00	5.50	3.50
☐1014		CHURCH STREET WALK/ I'M GONNA SUE	3.00	5.50	3.50
☐1021		DADDY G RIDES AGAIN/HEY NOW	3.00	5.50	3.50

CITY
FEATURED: CAROLE KING

☐113	**ODE**	PARADISE ALLEY/SNOW QUEEN	3.75	6.00	4.50
☐119		THAT OLD SWEET ROLL/ WHY ARE YOU LEAVING?	3.75	6.00	4.50

CITY—ALBUM

☐244012 (S)	**ODE**	NOW THAT EVERYTHING'S BEEN SAID	12.00	20.00	18.00

C. L. AND THE PICTURES
FEATURED: CURTIS LEE

☐2010	**DUNES**	LET'S TAKE A RIDE/ I'M ASKING FORGIVENESS	3.50	5.50	4.00
☐2017		AFRAID/MARY GO ROUND	3.50	5.50	4.00
☐2023		I'M SORRY/ THAT'S WHAT'S HAPPENING ..	3.50	5.50	4.00

JIMMY CLANTON
SEE: JIMMY DALE

☐537	**ACE**	I TRUSTED YOU/ THAT'S YOU BABY	4.25	7.50	6.00
☐546		JUST A DREAM/ YOU AIM TO PLEASE	3.25	5.50	4.00
☐551		A LETTER TO AN ANGEL/ A PART OF ME	3.25	5.50	4.00
☐560		A SHIP ON A STORMY SEA/ MY LOVE IS STRONG	3.25	5.50	4.00
☐567		MY OWN TRUE LOVE/ LITTLE BOY IN LOVE	3.25	5.50	4.00
☐575		GO JIMMY GO/I TRUSTED YOU ..	3.00	5.50	3.50
☐585		ANOTHER SLEEPLESS NIGHT/ I'M GONNA TRY	3.00	5.00	3.50
☐600		COME BACK/WAIT	3.00	5.00	3.50
☐607		WHAT AM I GONNA DO/IF I	3.00	5.00	3.50
☐616		DOWN THE AISLE/NO LONGER BLUE (with Mary Ann Mobley) ..	3.00	5.00	3.50
☐622		I JUST WANNA MAKE LOVE/ DON'T LOOK AT ME	3.00	5.00	3.50
☐634		LUCKY IN LOVE WITH YOU/ NOT LIKE A BROTHER	3.00	5.00	3.50
☐641		TWIST ON LITTLE GIRL/ WAYWARD LOVE	3.00	5.00	3.50
☐655		JUST A MOMENT/BECAUSE I DO .	3.00	5.00	3.50
☐664		VENUS IN BLUE JEANS/ HIGHWAY BOUND	4.50	7.50	6.00
☐668		HEART HOTEL/MANY DREAMS ..	3.00	5.00	3.50

			Current Price Range		P/Y AVG
☐ 8001		VENUS IN BLUE JEANS/ HIGHWAY BOUND	3.00	5.00	3.50
☐ 8005		DARKEST STREET IN TOWN/ DREAMS OF A FOOL	3.00	5.00	3.50
☐ 8006		ENDLESS NIGHT/ANOTHER DAY, ANOTHER HEARTACHE	3.00	5.00	3.50
☐ 8007		CINDY/I CARE ENOUGH	3.00	5.00	3.50
☐ 1028	*VIN*	WHAT AM I LIVING FOR?/ WEDDING BLUES	2.75	4.50	3.00
☐ 40181	*PHILIPS*	ALL THE WORDS IN THE WORLD/ RED DON'T GO WITH BLUE	2.75	4.50	3.00
☐ 40181		I'LL STEP ASIDE/ I WON'T CRY ANYMORE	2.75	4.50	3.00
☐ 40208		IF I'M A FOOL FOR LOVING YOU/ A MILLION DRUMS	2.75	4.50	3.00
☐ 40219		FOLLOW THE SUN/LOCK THE WINDOWS, LOCK THE DOORS	2.75	4.50	3.00

JIMMY CLANTON—EPs

☐ 101	*ACE*	THINKING OF YOU	10.00	17.00	15.00
☐ 102		THINKING OF YOU	10.00	17.00	15.00
☐ 103		I'M ALWAYS CHASING RAINBOWS	10.00	17.00	15.00
☐ 642	*ACE*	TEENAGE MILLIONAIRE	8.25	14.00	12.00
☐ 10087	*TOP RANK*	JIMMY'S BIG FOUR	8.25	14.00	12.00

JIMMY CLANTON—ALBUMS

☐ 1001 (M)	*ACE*	JUST A DREAM	17.00	39.00	35.00
☐ 1007 (M)		JIMMY'S HAPPY	14.50	34.00	30.00
☐ 1008 (M)		JIMMY'S BLUE	14.50	34.00	30.00
☐ 1011 (M)		MY BEST TO YOU	14.50	34.00	30.00
☐ 1014 (M)		TEENAGE MILLIONAIRE	14.50	34.00	30.00
☐ 1026 (M)		VENUS IN BLUE JEANS	10.00	25.00	22.50
☐ 100 (M)	*PHILIPS*	JIMMY'S HAPPY/JIMMY'S BLUE	8.50	20.00	18.00
☐ 154 (M)		THE BEST OF JIMMY CLANTON	8.50	20.00	18.00
☐ 154 (S)		THE BEST OF JIMMY CLANTON	10.00	25.00	22.50

ERIC CLAPTON
SEE: CREAM

☐ 6738	*ATCO*	TEASING/SOULING (First side with King Curtis; second side by King Curtis alone)	3.00	6.00	4.00
☐ 15049	*POLYDOR*	EASY NOW/LET IT RAIN	3.00	6.00	4.00
☐ 15056		BELL BOTTOM BLUES/ LITTLE WING	3.00	6.00	4.00
☐ 409	*RSO*	I SHOT THE SHERIFF/ GIVE ME STRENGTH	2.75	5.25	3.75
☐ 500		I SHOT THE SHERIFF/ GIVE ME STRENGTH	2.75	5.25	3.75
☐ 509		PRETTY BLUE EYES/ SWING LOW SWEET CHARIOT	2.75	5.25	3.75
☐ 513		KNOCKIN' ON HEAVEN'S DOOR/ SOMEONE LIKE YOU	2.75	5.25	3.75
☐ 861		ALL OUR PASTIMES/ HELLO OLD FRIEND	2.75	5.25	3.75
☐ 868		HUNGRY/CARNIVAL	2.75	5.25	3.75
☐ 886		LAY DOWN SALLY/ NEXT TIME YOU SEE HER	2.75	5.25	3.75

LATER RSO SINGLES ARE WORTH UP TO $2.50 MINT

ERIC CLAPTON—ALBUMS

☐ 1009 (S)	*RSO*	BACKLESS (LIMITED) (colorless vinyl)	16.00	45.00	30.00
☐ 035 (S)		SLOWHAND (colorless vinyl)	16.00	45.00	30.00

BOTH OF THE ABOVE WERE PROMOTIONAL ISSUES, MARKED AS SUCH AND NOT DISTRIBUTED FOR STORE SALE

☐ 3004 (S)		NO REASON TO CRY (with Bob Dylan)	5.00	12.00	10.00

			Current Price Range		P/Y AVG
☐3008 (S)		ERIC CLAPTON	6.75	17.00	15.00
☐3023 (S)		461 OCEAN BOULEVARD	3.75	11.00	9.00
☐4801 (S)		461 OCEAN BOULEVARD	3.75	11.00	9.00
☐QD-4801 (QUAD)		461 OCEAN BOULEVARD	5.00	15.00	13.50
☐SO-877 (S)		RAINBOW CONCERT	3.75	11.00	9.00
☐4809 (S)		E. C. WAS HERE	3.75	11.00	9.00
☐803 (S)	*ATCO*	HISTORY OF ERIC CLAPTON	5.00	15.00	13.50

CLAUDINE CLARK

☐521	*HERALD*	ANGEL OF HAPPINESS/			
		TEENAGE BLUES	6.00	11.00	9.00
☐1113	*CHANCELLOR*	PARTY LIGHTS/DISAPPOINTED	3.00	5.00	3.50
☐1124		TELEPHONE GAME/WALKIN'			
		THROUGH A CEMETERY	3.00	5.00	3.50
☐1130		WALK ME HOME/			
		WHO WILL YOU HURT?	3.00	5.00	3.50

CLAUDINE CLARK—ALBUM

☐5029 (M)	*CHANCELLOR*	PARTY LIGHTS	12.00	29.00	25.00

DAVE CLARK FIVE

☐212	*CONGRESS*	I KNEW IT ALL THE TIME/			
		THAT'S WHAT I SAID	5.00	9.00	6.00
☐5078	*RUST*	I WALK THE LINE/FIRST LOVE	6.00	12.00	8.25
☐3188	*LAURIE*	I WALK THE LINE/FIRST LOVE	6.00	12.00	8.25
☐5476	*JUBILEE*	CHAQUITA/IN YOUR HEART	5.50	10.00	8.25
☐9656	*EPIC*	GLAD ALL OVER/I KNOW YOU	3.25	5.50	4.00
☐9671		BITS AND PIECES/			
		ALL OF THE TIME	3.25	5.50	4.00
☐9678		DO YOU LOVE ME/CHAQUITA	3.25	5.50	4.00
☐9692		CAN'T YOU SEE THAT SHE'S			
		MINE/NO TIME TO LOSE	3.25	5.50	4.00
☐9704		BECAUSE/			
		THEME WITHOUT A NAME	3.25	5.50	4.00
☐9722		EVERYBODY KNOWS/OL' SOL	3.25	5.50	4.00
☐9739		ANY WAY YOU WANT IT/			
		CRYING OVER YOU	3.25	5.50	4.00
☐9763		COME HOME/YOUR TURN TO CRY	3.25	5.50	4.00
☐9786		REELIN' AND ROCKIN'/			
		I'M THINKING	3.25	5.50	4.00
☐9811		I LIKE IT LIKE THAT/			
		HURTIN' INSIDE	3.25	5.50	4.00
☐9833		CATCH US IF YOU CAN/			
		ON THE MOVE	3.25	5.50	4.00
☐9863		OVER AND OVER/			
		I'LL BE YOURS (MY LOVE)	3.25	5.50	4.00
☐9882		AT THE SCENE/I MISS YOU	3.25	5.50	4.00
☐10004		TRY TOO HARD/ALL NIGHT LONG	3.25	5.50	4.00
☐10031		PLEASE TELL ME WHY/			
		LOOK BEFORE YOU LEAP	3.25	5.50	4.00
☐10053		SATISFIED WITH YOU/			
		DON'T LET ME DOWN	3.25	5.50	4.00
☐10076		NINETEEN DAYS/			
		SITTING HERE BABY	3.25	5.50	4.00
☐10114		I'VE GOT TO HAVE A REASON/			
		GOOD TIME BABY	3.25	5.50	4.00
☐10144		YOU GOT WHAT IT TAKES/			
		DOCTOR RHYTHM	3.00	5.00	3.50
☐10179		YOU MUST HAVE BEEN A			
		BEAUTIFUL BABY/MAN IN THE			
		PIN-STRIPE SUIT	3.00	5.00	3.50
☐10209		A LITTLE BIT NOW/			
		YOU DON'T PLAY ME AROUND	3.00	5.00	3.50
☐10244		RED AND BLUE/			
		CONCENTRATION BABY	3.00	5.00	3.50

DAVE CLARK FIVE

They originally began as a group of British school pals who often played sports in the gymnasium after regular school hours. Clark and his associates decided to form a band in order to raise money for the school's soccer club. Seeing success on the local level, the Dave Clark Five later raised their sights when the Beatles struck 1964 gold in America.

Never pretending to be in the music business for anything but the money, the DC-5 ran up an impressive string of Epic hits (eight made the American Top 10) while earning the plaudits of such influential straights as Ed Sullivan. While openly disdaining the Beatles (although he did sign them to draw high ratings), Sullivan featured the Dave Clark Five on his popular show many times.

Dave Clark was the quintet's mediocre drummer who did little singing. Rather, those chores were left to Mike Smith, a handsome lad with an agressive grating voice that many at first interpreted as belonging to a black singer.

After the hits ended late in 1967, the Dave Clark Five disbanded, but not after first ringing up over $250,000,000 in worldwide record sales.

			Current Price Range		P/Y AVG
☐ 10265		EVERYBODY KNOWS/			
		INSIDE AND OUT	3.00	5.00	3.50
☐ 10325		PLEASE STAY/FORGET	3.00	5.00	3.50
☐ 10375		THE RED BALLOON/			
		MAZE OF LOVE	3.00	5.00	3.50
☐ 10474		PARADISE/34-06	3.00	5.00	3.50
☐ 10509		IF SOMEBODY LOVES YOU/			
		BEST DAY'S WORK	3.00	5.50	3.80
☐ 10547		BRING IT ON HOME TO ME/			
		DARLING, I LOVE YOU	3.00	5.50	3.80
☐ 10635		HERE COMES SUMMER/			
		FIVE BY FIVE	3.00	5.00	3.50
☐ 10684		BLUEBERRY HILL-MY BLUE			
		HEAVEN/ONE NIGHT-LAWDY			
		MISS CLAWDY	3.00	5.00	3.50
☐ 10704		SOUTHERN MAN/			
		IF YOU WANNA SEE ME CRY	3.00	5.50	3.50
☐ 10768		WON'T YOU BE MY LADY?/			
		INTO YOUR LIFE	3.00	5.50	3.50
☐ 10894		RUB IT IN/I'M SORRY BABY	3.00	5.50	3.50
		DAVE CLARK FIVE—ALBUMS			
☐ 24093 (M)		GLAD ALL OVER	10.00	23.00	14.00
☐ 24104 (M)		THE DAVE CLARK FIVE RETURN	8.00	18.00	12.00
☐ 24117 (M)		AMERICAN TOUR	8.00	18.00	12.00
☐ 24128 (M)		COAST TO COAST	8.00	18.00	12.00
☐ 24139 (M)		WEEKEND IN LONDON	8.00	18.00	12.00
☐ 24162 (M)		HAVING A WILD WEEKEND	8.00	18.00	12.00
☐ 24178 (M)		I LIKE IT LIKE THAT	8.00	18.00	12.00
☐ 24185 (M)		DAVE CLARK FIVE'S			
		GREATEST HITS	8.00	18.00	12.00
		STEREO VERSIONS OF THE ABOVE HAVE THE SAME VALUE			
☐ 24198 (M)		TRY TOO HARD	8.00	18.00	12.00
☐ 26198 (S)		TRY TOO HARD	7.00	16.00	11.00
☐ 24212 (M)		SATISFIED WITH YOU	8.00	18.00	12.00
☐ 26212 (S)		SATISFIED WITH YOU	7.00	16.00	11.00
☐ 24221 (M)		MORE GREATEST HITS	8.00	18.00	12.00
☐ 26221 (S)		MORE GREATEST HITS	7.00	16.00	11.00
☐ 24236 (M)		5 X 5	8.00	18.00	12.00
☐ 26236 (S)		5 X 5	6.50	15.00	13.50
☐ 24312 (M)		YOU GOT WHAT IT TAKES	7.50	17.00	15.00
☐ 26312 (S)		YOU GOT WHAT IT TAKES	6.50	15.00	13.50
☐ 24354 (M)		EVERYBODY KNOWS	7.50	17.00	15.00
☐ 26354 (S)		EVERYBODY KNOWS	6.50	15.00	13.50
		DEE CLARK			
☐ 1002	*FALCON*	GLORIA/KANGAROO HOP	12.00	20.00	18.00
☐ 1005		24 BOY FRIENDS/SEVEN NIGHTS	14.00	24.00	20.00
☐ 1019	*ABNER*	NOBODY BUT YOU/			
		WHEN I CALL ON YOU	3.50	6.00	4.00
☐ 1026		JUST KEEP IT UP/			
		WHISPERING GRASS	3.50	6.00	4.00
☐ 1029		HEY LITTLE GIRL/			
		IF IT WASN'T FOR LOVE	3.50	6.00	4.00
☐ 1032		HOW ABOUT THAT/			
		BLUES, GET OFF MY SHOULDER	3.50	6.00	4.00
☐ 1037		AT MY FRONT DOOR/			
		CLING A LING	3.50	6.00	4.00
☐ 355	*VEE JAY*	YOU'RE LOOKING GOOD/GLORIA	3.00	5.00	3.50
☐ 372		YOUR FRIENDS/			
		BECAUSE I LOVE YOU	3.00	5.00	3.50
☐ 383		RAINDROPS/I WANT TO LOVE YOU	2.75	4.50	3.00
☐ 409		DON'T WALK AWAY FROM ME/			
		YOU'RE TELLING OUR SECRETS	2.75	4.50	3.00
☐ 428		YOU ARE LIKE THE WIND/			
		DRUMS IN MY HEART	2.75	4.50	3.00

DEE CLARK

His real name is Delectus Clark but (not surprisingly) he has always preferred to be called Dee. Blythsville, AR. was Clark's hometown; he was born there on November 7, 1938.

The Clarks moved north to the Windy City when Dee was young. At age 14, Dee began singing with some other Chicago boys who called themselves the Hambone Kids. They were good enough to be signed to Okeh Records, where they recorded a song called "Hambone". It didn't sell.

Two years later, in 1955, Dee entered - and won - a talent contest. A disc jockey named Herb Kent was highly impressed with Clark's strong tenor voice. Kent then provided the connections Dee needed for a second shot at recording. Clark signed with Vee Jay Records. They issued his first singles on their subsidiary Falcon label, which later became Abner Records.

Dee Clark saw no major success on Falcon, but he scored again and again on Abner. Vee Jay then pushed Clark "upstairs" and he became a Vee Jay artist.

Dee's biggest hit was the number-two chart smash of "Raindrops" in the spring of 1961. Later he went to the Constellation label, but was never able to duplicate his Abner or Vee Jay success.

			Current Price Range		P/Y AVG
☐ 443		DANCE ON LITTLE GIRL/FEVER ..	2.75	4.50	3.00
☐ 462		I'M GOING BACK TO SCHOOL/ NOBODY BUT YOU	2.75	4.50	3.00
☐ 487		I'M A SOLDIER BOY/ SHOOK UP OVER YOU	2.75	4.50	3.00
☐ 532		HOW IS HE TREATING YOU?/ THE JONES BROTHERS	2.75	4.50	3.00
☐ 548		NOBODY BUT ME/ WALKING MY DOG	2.75	4.50	3.00
		DEE CLARK—EP			
☐ 1900	**VEE JAY**	DEE CLARK	7.50	12.00	10.00
		DEE CLARK—ALBUMS			
☐ 2000 (M)	**ABNER**	DEE CLARK	12.00	29.00	25.00
☐ 2000 (S)		DEE CLARK	17.00	39.00	35.00
☐ 2002 (M)		HOW ABOUT THAT	12.00	29.00	25.00
☐ 2002 (S)		HOW ABOUT THAT	17.00	39.00	35.00
☐ 1019 (M)	**VEE JAY**	YOU'RE LOOKING GOOD	12.00	29.00	25.00
☐ 1028 (M)		DEE CLARK	10.00	25.00	22.50
☐ 1037 (M)		HOLD ON - IT'S DEE CLARK......	10.00	25.00	22.50
☐ 1047 (M)		THE BEST OF DEE CLARK	10.00	25.00	22.50
		PETULA CLARK			
☐ 12049	**MGM**	THE PENDULUM SONG/ ROMANCE IN ROME	7.00	13.00	7.75
☐ 9142	**EPIC**	THERE IS NO CURE FOR L'AMOUR/ HOTTER 'N A PISTOL	7.00	13.00	7.75
☐ 10504	**LONDON**	WITH ALL MY LOVE/ MY FRIEND THE SEA	4.00	7.00	4.85
☐ 10510		I'M COUNTING ON YOU/ SOME OTHER WORLD	4.00	7.00	4.85
☐ 10516		WHISTLIN' FOR THE MOON/ TENDER LOVE	4.00	7.00	4.85
☐ 652	**WARWICK**	ROMEO/ ISN'T THIS A LOVELY DAY	4.00	7.00	4.85
☐ 5582	**IMPERIAL**	BABY LOVER/ EVER BEEN IN LOVE?	3.75	6.00	4.00
☐ 5655		WHERE ARE YOU (NOW THAT I NEED YOU?)/I LOVE A VIOLIN .	3.50	5.50	4.00
☐ 3143	**LAURIE**	THE ROAD/JUMBLE SALE	3.75	6.00	4.50
☐ 3156		I WILL FOLLOW HIM/ DARLING CHERI	3.25	5.25	4.00
☐ 3316		IN LOVE/DARLING CHERI	3.25	5.25	4.00
☐ 5494	**WARNER BROTHERS**	DOWNTOWN/ YOU'D BETTER LOVE ME	3.00	5.00	3.65
☐ 5612		I KNOW A PLACE/JACK AND JOHN.	3.00	5.00	3.65
☐ 5643		YOU'D BETTER COME HOME/ HEART	3.00	5.00	3.65
☐ 5661		ROUND EVERY CORNER/ TWO RIVERS	3.00	5.00	3.65
☐ 5684		MY LOVE/WHERE AM I GOING? ..	3.00	5.00	3.65
☐ 5802		A SIGN OF THE TIMES/ TIME FOR LOVE	3.00	5.00	3.65
☐ 5835		I COULDN'T LIVE WITHOUT YOUR LOVE/YOUR WAY OF LIFE	3.00	5.00	3.65
☐ 5863		WHO AM I/ LOVE IS A LONG JOURNEY	3.00	5.00	3.65
☐ 5882		COLOR MY WORLD/ TAKE ME HOME AGAIN	3.00	5.00	3.65
☐ 7002		THIS IS MY SONG/HIGH	3.00	5.00	3.65
☐ 7049		DON'T SLEEP IN THE SUBWAY/ HERE COMES THE MORNING ..	3.00	5.00	3.65
☐ 7073		THE CAT IN THE WINDOW/ FANCY DANCIN' MAN	3.00	5.00	3.65

			Current Price Range		P/Y AVG
☐ 7097		THE OTHER MAN'S GRASS IS ALWAYS GREENER/			
		AT THE CROSSROADS	3.00	5.00	3.65
☐ 7170		KISS ME GOODBYE/			
		I'VE GOT LOVE GOING FOR ME	3.00	5.00	3.65
☐ 7216		DON'T GIVE UP/EVERYTIME I SEE A RAINBOW	3.00	5.00	3.65
☐ 7244		AMERICAN BOYS/			
		LOOK TO THE SKY	3.00	5.00	3.65
☐ 7275		HAPPY HEART/			
		LOVE IS THE ONLY THING	3.00	5.00	3.65
☐ 7310		LOOK AT MINE/YOU AND I	3.00	5.00	3.65
☐ 7343		NO ONE BETTER THAN YOU/ THINGS BRIGHT AND BEAUTIFUL	3.00	5.00	3.65
☐ 7422		THE SONG IS LOVE/ BEAUTIFUL SOUNDS	3.00	5.00	3.65
☐ 7467		THE SONG OF MY LIFE/ COULDN'T SLEEP	3.00	5.00	3.65
☐ 7484		I DON'T KNOW HOW TO LOVE HIM/ MAYBE	3.00	5.00	3.65
		PETULA CLARK—ALBUMS			
☐ 2032 (S)	*LAURIE*	IN LOVE!	10.00	25.00	22.50
☐ 2043 (S)		PETULA CLARK SINGS FOR EVERYBODY (reissue of 2032)	7.50	17.00	15.00
☐ 9079 (M)	*IMPERIAL*	PET CLARK	7.50	17.00	15.00
☐ 12027 (S)		PET CLARK	7.50	17.00	15.00
☐ 9281 (M)		UPTOWN WITH PET CLARK	7.50	17.00	15.00
☐ 12281 (S)		UPTOWN WITH PET CLARK	8.50	20.00	18.00
☐ 1590 (M)	*WARNER BROTHERS*	DOWNTOWN	6.50	15.00	13.50
☐ 1590 (S)		DOWNTOWN	7.50	17.00	15.00
☐ 1598 (M)		I KNOW A PLACE	6.50	15.00	13.50
☐ 1598 (S)		I KNOW A PLACE	7.50	17.00	15.00
☐ 1608 (M)		THE WORLD'S GREATEST INTERNATIONAL HITS	6.50	15.00	13.50
☐ 1608 (S)		THE WORLD'S GREATEST INTERNATIONAL HITS	7.50	17.00	15.00
☐ 1630 (M)		MY LOVE	5.50	14.00	12.00
☐ 1630 (S)		MY LOVE	6.50	15.00	13.50
☐ 1645 (M)		I COULDN'T LIVE WITHOUT YOUR LOVE	5.50	14.00	12.00
☐ 1645 (S)		I COULDN'T LIVE WITHOUT YOUR LOVE	6.50	15.00	13.50
☐ 1673 (M)		COLOR MY WORLD/WHO AM I?	5.50	14.00	12.00
☐ 1673 (S)		COLOR MY WORLD/WHO AM I?	6.50	15.00	13.50
☐ 1698 (M)		THESE ARE MY SONGS	5.50	14.00	12.00
☐ 1698 (S)		THESE ARE MY SONGS	6.50	15.00	13.50
☐ 1719 (M)		THE OTHER MAN'S GRASS IS ALWAYS GREENER	5.50	14.00	12.00
☐ 1719 (S)		THE OTHER MAN'S GRASS IS ALWAYS GREENER	6.50	15.00	13.50
☐ 1743 (S)		PETULA	5.50	12.00	10.00
☐ 1765 (S)		PETULA CLARK'S GREATEST HITS, VOL. 1	5.50	12.00	10.00
☐ 1789 (S)		PORTRAIT OF PETULA	5.50	12.00	10.00
☐ 1823 (S)		JUST PET	5.50	12.00	10.00
☐ 1862 (S)		MEMPHIS	5.50	12.00	10.00
☐ 1885 (S)		WARM AND TENDER	5.50	12.00	10.00
		SANFORD CLARK			
☐ 1003	*MCI*	THE FOOL/ LONESOME FOR A LETTER	12.00	20.00	18.00
☐ 15481	*DOT*	THE FOOL/ LONESOME FOR A LETTER	3.75	6.00	4.50

			Current Price Range		P/Y AVG
15516		A CHEAT/USTA BE MY BABY	3.50	5.50	4.00
15534		9 LB. HAMMER/OOO BABY	3.00	5.00	3.50
15556		THE GLORY OF LOVE/ DARLING DEAR	3.00	5.00	3.50
15585		LOVE CHARMS/LOU BE DOO	3.00	5.00	3.50

CLASS-AIRS

unnumbered	**HONEY BEE**	MY TEARS START TO FALL/ TOO OLD TO CRY	16.00	48.00	30.00

CLASSICS

1015	**DART**	CINDERELLA/SO IN LOVE	5.50	8.50	7.00
1032		ANGEL ANGELA/ EENIE, MEENIE, MINIE AND MO	8.00	12.00	10.00
1038		LIFE IS BUT A DREAM/ THAT'S THE WAY	8.00	12.00	10.00
71829	**MERCURY**	LIFE IS BUT A DREAM/ THAT'S THE WAY	3.75	6.00	4.50
1114	**MUSICTONE**	CINDERELLA/SO IN LOVE	4.50	7.50	6.00
1116	**MUSICNOTE**	TILL THEN/ EENIE, MEENIE, MINIE AND MO	3.00	5.00	3.50
1118		P.S. I LOVE YOU/WRAP YOUR TROUBLES IN DREAMS	3.00	5.00	3.50

CLASSICS
FEATURED: LOU CHRISTIE

508	**STARR**	CLOSE YOUR EYES/FUNNY THING.	32.00	60.00	36.00

CLASSMATES

101	**MARQUEE**	DON'T MAKE ME CRY/ HIGH SCHOOL	6.50	12.00	10.00
102		UNTIL THEN/PRETTY LITTLE PET	8.50	23.00	20.00

JOE CLAY

0211	**VIK**	DUCK TAIL/SIXTEEN CHICKS . . .	25.00	50.00	30.00

CLEFTONES

1000	**GEE**	YOU BABY YOU/I WAS DREAMING.	6.50	11.00	9.50
1011		LITTLE GIRL OF MINE/ YOU'RE DRIVING ME MAD	5.50	10.50	9.00
1016		CAN'T WE BE SWEETHEARTS?/ NIKI-HOKEY	5.25	8.50	7.00
1025		STRING AROUND MY HEART/ HAPPY MEMORIES	5.25	8.50	7.00
1031		I LIKE YOUR STYLE OF MAKING LOVE/WHY DO YOU DO ME LIKE YOU DO?	5.25	8.50	7.00
1038		SEE YOU NEXT YEAR/ TEN PAIRS OF SHOES	4.50	7.50	6.00
1041		HEY BABE/WHAT DID I DO THAT WAS WRONG?	4.50	7.50	6.00
1048		LOVER BOY/BEGINNERS AT LOVE	4.50	7.50	6.00
1064		HEART AND SOUL/ HOW DO YOU FEEL	3.25	5.50	4.00
1067		FOR SENTIMENTAL REASONS/ DEED I DO	3.25	5.50	4.00
1074		EARTH ANGEL/ BLUES IN THE NIGHT	3.25	5.50	4.00
1077		DO YOU/AGAIN	3.25	5.50	4.00
1079		LOVER COME BACK TO ME/ THERE SHE GOES	3.25	5.50	4.00
1080		HOW DEEP IS THE OCEAN/ SOME KIND OF BLUE	3.25	5.50	4.00

CLEFTONES—ALBUMS

705 (S)	**GEE**	HEART AND SOUL	20.00	41.00	28.00
707 (S)		FOR SENTIMENTAL REASONS . . .	24.00	55.00	32.00

EPIC, 5-9704, LP

ATLANTIC, 8009, LP

			Current Price Range		P/Y AVG

PATSY CLINE
PATSY CLINE—ALBUMS

			Current Price Range		P/Y AVG
☐ 8611	DECCA	PATSY CLINE	10.00	23.00	14.00
☐ 4202/74202		PATSY CLINE SHOWCASE	10.00	23.00	14.00
☐ 4282/74282		SENTIMENTALLY YOURS	8.00	20.00	12.00
☐ 176/7176		THE PATSY CLINE STORY	8.00	20.00	12.00
☐ 4508/74508		A PORTRAIT OF PATSY CLINE	8.00	20.00	12.00
☐ 4586/74586		THAT'S HOW A HEARTACHE BEGINS	9.00	22.00	13.00
☐ 73753	VOCALION	HERE'S PATSY CLINE	10.00	23.00	14.00
☐ 73872		COUNTRY GREAT	10.00	23.00	14.00
☐ 6001	HILLTOP	TODAY, TOMORROW AND FOREVER	10.00	23.00	14.00
☐ 6016		I CAN'T FORGET YOU	10.00	23.00	14.00
☐ 6039		STOP THE WORLD AND LET ME OFF	10.00	23.00	14.00
☐ 6954		MISS COUNTRY MUSIC	10.00	23.00	14.00
☐ 6072	PICKWICK	IN CARE OF THE BLUES	10.00	23.00	14.00
☐ 2019		THE LEGEND	10.00	23.00	14.00
☐ 6148		COUNTRY MUSIC HALL OF FAME	7.00	19.00	12.50
☐ 540	METRO	GOTTA LOT OF RHYTHM IN MY SOUL	10.00	23.00	14.00
☐ 102	SEARS	WALKING AFTER MIDNIGHT	10.00	23.00	14.00
☐ 112		I CAN'T FORGET YOU	7.00	19.00	12.50
☐ 93489	LONGINES SYMPHONETTE	THE HEART YOU BREAK	10.00	23.00	14.00
☐ 93488		STOP THE WORLD	8.00	18.00	9.50
☐ 87	MCA	PATSY CLINE SHOWCASE	8.00	18.00	9.50
☐ 90		SENTIMENTALLY YOURS	8.00	18.00	9.50
☐ 2-4038		THE PATSY CLINE STORY	8.00	18.00	9.50
☐ 224		A PORTRAIT OF PATSY CLINE	8.00	18.00	9.50
☐ 12		PATSY CLINE'S GREATEST HITS	8.00	18.00	9.50
☐ 3263		ALWAYS	8.00	18.00	9.50
☐ 5319		PATSY CLINE/JIM REEVES REMEMBERING	8.00	18.00	9.50
☐ 2600	BRITISH MCA	THE PATSY CLINE STORY	7.00	13.00	8.00
☐ 8077		COUNTRY HALL OF FAME	7.00	13.00	8.00
☐ 2725		HAVE YOU EVER BEEN LONELY	7.00	13.00	8.00
☐ 20107	MCA CORAL	COUNTRY GREAT	7.00	13.00	8.00
☐ 5200/1200	EVEREST	PATSY CLINE'S GOLDEN HITS	7.00	13.00	8.00

CLOVERS

			Current Price Range		P/Y AVG
☐ 122	RAINBOW	YES SIR, THAT'S MY BABY/ WHEN YOU COME BACK TO ME	160.00	285.00	190.00
☐ 934	ATLANTIC	DON'T YOU KNOW I LOVE YOU/ SKYLARK	43.00	65.00	60.00
☐ 944		FOOL FOOL FOOL/NEEDLESS	22.00	39.00	36.00
☐ 963		ONE MINT JULEP/ MIDDLE OF THE NIGHT	18.00	34.00	30.00
☐ 969		TING-A-LING/WONDER WHERE MY BABY'S GONE	15.00	26.00	24.00
☐ 977		HEY MISS FANNIE/ I PLAYED THE FOOL	15.00	26.00	24.00
☐ 989		CRAWLIN'/YES IT'S YOU	15.00	26.00	24.00
☐ 1000		GOOD LOVIN'/ HERE COMES A FOOL	18.00	34.00	30.00
☐ 1010		COMIN' ON/ THE FEELING IS SO GOOD	10.00	17.00	15.00
☐ 1022		LOVEY DOVEY/LITTLE MAMA	10.00	17.00	15.00
☐ 1035		YOUR CASH AIN'T NOTHIN' BUT TRASH/I'VE GOT MY EYES ON YOU	8.50	17.00	15.00
☐ 1046		I CONFESS/ ALL RIGHTIE. OH SWEETIE	8.50	14.00	12.00

COASTERS

The Robin's first real taste of success came on the small rhythm-and-blues label called Spark. It was a Los Angeles outfit owned and run by a pair of energetic and idealistic young songwriters named Jerry Leiber and Mike Stoller.

Before their Spark signing, the Robins had had limited success. However, under the Leiber-Stoller tutelage, they scored time and time again in the rhythm-and-blues market.

But a myriad of differences soon developed. Some of the Robins wanted to stay and develop their newly successful rhythm-and-blues format; others within the group wished to exploit the growing rock-and-roll market.

The group divided and the Robins signed with another rhythm-and-blues label, Whippet. Those remaining behind took on a new name, the Coasters. (They were all from the West Coast, chiefly the Los Angeles area.)

"Down in Mexico" got things rolling for the Coasters, and "One Kiss Led to Another" did even better. Their next release was a two-sided smash, "Searchin' "/Young Blood", which became Atco's biggest single ever up to that time.

The Coasters were the biggest novelty act of the 1950s, scoring five Top hits. They even stayed on the charts into the 1960s, always employing their successful blend of slapstick and clever vocalizing.

			Current Price Range		P/Y AVG
☐ 1052		BLUE VELVET/IF YOU LOVE ME . .	9.75	17.00	15.00
☐ 1060		LOVE BUG/IN THE MORNING TIME.	8.50	14.00	12.00
☐ 1073		NIP SIP/			
		IF I COULD BE LOVED BY YOU .	8.50	14.00	12.00
☐ 1083		DEVIL OR ANGEL/HEY DOLL BABY.	8.50	14.00	12.00
	FIRST-PRESSES OF	THE ABOVE WERE ON THE YELLOW-AND-BLACK LABEL			
☐ 1094		LOVE, LOVE, LOVE/			
		YOUR TENDER LIPS	4.00	6.50	4.85
☐ 1107		FROM THE BOTTOM OF MY			
		HEART/BRING ME LOVE	5.00	8.50	6.00
☐ 1118		BABY BABY OH MY DARLING/			
		A LONELY FOOL	5.00	8.50	6.00
☐ 1129		HERE COMES ROMANCE/			
		YOU GOOD LOOKING WOMAN . .	5.00	8.50	6.00
☐ 1139		I-I-I LOVE YOU/SO YOUNG	5.00	8.50	6.00
☐ 1152		DOWN IN THE VALLEY/			
		THERE'S NO TOMORROW	5.00	8.50	6.00
☐ 1175		WISHING FOR YOUR LOVE/			
		ALL ABOUT YOU	6.00	10.00	6.70
☐ 110	*POPLAR*	PLEASE COME ON TO ME/			
		THE GOSPEL WHEEL	5.50	9.00	6.75
☐ 111		THE GOOD OLD SUMMERTIME/			
		IDAHO	5.50	9.00	6.75
☐ 139		THE GOOD OLD SUMMERTIME/			
		IDAHO	4.50	7.50	6.00
☐ 174	*UNITED ARTISTS*	OLD BLACK MAGIC/			
		ROCK AND ROLL TANGO	4.50	7.50	6.00
☐ 180		LOVE POTION #9/STAY AWHILE .	3.75	6.00	4.50
☐ 209		ONE MINT JULEP/LOVEY	3.75	6.00	4.50
☐ 227		EASY LOVIN'/I'M CONFESSIN'			
		THAT I LOVE YOU	3.75	6.00	4.50
☐ 263		YES IT'S YOU/BURNING FIRE . . .	3.50	5.50	4.00
☐ 307		THE HONEY DRIPPER/HAVE GUN .	3.50	5.50	4.00
		CLOVERS—EPs			
☐ 504	*ATLANTIC*	THE CLOVERS SING			
		"ONE MINT JULEP"	10.00	17.00	15.00
☐ 537		THE CLOVERS SING			
		"GOOD LOVIN'"	8.50	14.00	12.00
☐ 590		THE CLOVERS	8.50	14.00	12.00
		CLOVERS—ALBUMS			
☐ 1248 (M)	*ATLANTIC*	THE CLOVERS	34.00	80.00	75.00
☐ 8009 (M)		THE CLOVERS	22.00	55.00	50.00
☐ 8034 (M)		THE CLOVERS' DANCE PARTY . . .	22.00	55.00	50.00
☐ 1001 (M)	*POPLAR*	IN CLOVER	20.00	49.00	45.00
☐ 3033 (M)	*UNITED ARTISTS*	IN CLOVER	17.00	39.00	35.00
☐ 3099 (M)		LOVE POTION NUMBER NINE	12.00	29.00	25.00
☐ 6099 (S)		LOVE POTION NUMBER NINE	17.00	39.00	35.00

COASTERS

SEE: ROBINS

			Current Price Range		P/Y AVG
☐ 2-1607	*DATE RECORDS*	SHE CAN/EVERYBODY'S			
		WOMAN (Radio Station copy) . .	12.00	19.00	17.00
☐ 6064	*ATCO*	DOWN IN MEXICO/			
		TURTLE DOVIN' (maroon label) .	10.00	17.00	15.00
☐ 6073		ONE KISS LED TO ANOTHER/			
		BRAZIL (maroon label)	8.50	14.00	12.00
☐ 6087		SEARCHIN'/			
		YOUNG BLOOD (maroon label) . .	5.00	7.50	6.00
☐ 6087		SEARCHIN'/YOUNG BLOOD			
		(yellow-and-white label)	3.50	5.50	4.00
☐ 6098		IDOL WITH THE GOLDEN HEAD/			
		MY BABY COMES TO ME	3.50	5.50	4.00

			Current Price Range		P/Y AVG
6104		SWEET GEORGIA BROWN/WHAT'S THE SECRET OF YOUR SUCCESS	3.50	5.50	4.00
6111		GEE GOLLY/DANCE	8.50	14.00	12.00
6116		YAKETY YAK/ZING! WENT THE STRINGS OF MY HEART	3.50	5.50	4.00
6126		THE SHADOW KNOWS/SORRY BUT I'M GONNA HAVE TO PASS	4.50	7.50	6.00
6132		CHARLIE BROWN/ THREE COOL CATS	3.50	5.50	4.00
6141		ALONG CAME JONES/ THAT IS ROCK 'N' ROLL	3.50	5.50	4.00
6146		POISON IVY/I'M A HOG FOR YOU	3.50	5.50	4.00
6153		RUN RED RUN/WHAT ABOUT US	3.25	5.25	4.00
6163		BESAME MUCHO (PT. 1)/(PT. 2)	3.25	5.25	4.00
6168		WAKE ME, SHAKE ME/STEWBALL	3.25	5.25	4.00
6178		SHOPPIN' FOR CLOTHES/ SNAKE AND THE BOOKWORM	3.25	5.25	4.00
6186		WAIT A MINUTE/ THUMBIN' A RIDE	3.25	5.25	4.00
6192		LITTLE EGYPT/KEEP ON ROLLING	3.25	5.25	4.00
6204		GIRLS, GIRLS, GIRLS (PT. 1)/ (PT. 2)	3.25	5.25	4.00
6210		JUST LIKE ME/BAD BLOOD	3.25	5.25	4.00
6219		RIDIN' HOOD/ TEACH ME HOW TO SHIMMY	3.25	5.25	4.00
6234		THE CLIMB/THE CLIMB (instrumental)	3.25	5.25	4.00
6251		THE PTA/BULL TICK WALTZ	3.25	5.25	4.00
6287		T'AIN'T NOTHING TO ME/ SPEEDOO'S BACK IN TOWN	3.25	5.25	4.00
6300		BAD DETECTIVE/LOVEY DOVEY	3.25	5.25	4.00
6321		WILD ONE/I MUST BE DREAMING	3.25	5.25	4.00
6341		HONGRY/LADY LIKE	3.25	5.25	4.00
6356		LET'S GO GET STONED/ MONEY HONEY	3.25	5.25	4.00
6379		BELL BOTTOM SLACKS/ CRAZY BABY	3.25	5.25	4.00
6407		SHE'S A YUM YUM/ SATURDAY NIGHT FISH FRY	3.25	5.25	4.00
		COASTERS—EPs			
4501	**ATCO**	ROCK AND ROLL WITH THE COASTERS	15.50	30.00	25.50
4502		KEEP ROCKIN' WITH THE COASTERS	15.50	30.00	25.50
4506		THE COASTERS	15.50	30.00	25.50
4507		TOP HITS	15.50	30.00	25.50
		COASTERS—ALBUMS			
101 (M)	**ATCO**	THE COASTERS	17.00	39.00	35.00
111 (M)		THE COASTERS' GREATEST HITS	15.00	34.00	30.00
123 (M)		ONE BY ONE	12.00	29.00	25.00
123 (S)		ONE BY ONE	17.00	39.00	35.00
135 (M)		COAST ALONG WITH THE COASTERS	12.00	29.00	25.00
135 (S)		COAST ALONG WITH THE COASTERS	17.00	39.00	35.00
371		THE COASTERS: THE EARLY YEARS-THEIR GREATEST RECORDINGS	7.50	10.00	8.75

EDDIE COCHRAN

SEE: JERRY CAPEHART, COCHRAN BROTHERS, LEE DENSON, GALAXIES, CEE GEES, JEWEL AND EDDIE, KELLY FOUR, JERRY NEAL, PAT STANLEY

1026	**CREST**	SKINNY JIM/HALF LOVED	45.00	76.00	72.00
55056	**LIBERTY**	SITTIN' IN THE BALCONY/ DARK LONELY STREET	4.50	7.50	6.00

			Current Price Range		P/Y AVG
55070		MEAN WHEN I'M MAD/ONE KISS	6.50	11.00	9.00
55087		DRIVE-IN SHOW/AM I BLUE	6.00	10.00	7.25
55112		TWENTY FLIGHT ROCK/ CRADLE BABY	6.00	10.00	7.25
55123		JEANNIE JEANNIE JEANNIE/ POCKETFUL OF HEARTACHES	6.00	10.00	7.25
55138		PRETTY GIRL/THERESA	6.00	10.00	7.25
55144		SUMMERTIME BLUES/ LOVE AGAIN	3.50	5.50	4.00
55166		C'MON EVERYBODY/ DON'T EVER LET ME GO	3.50	5.50	4.00
55177		TEENAGE HEAVEN/I REMEMBER	4.50	7.50	6.00
55203		SOMETHIN' ELSE/ BOLL WEEVIL SONG	3.75	6.00	4.50
55217		HALLELUJAH. I LOVE HER SO/ LITTLE ANGEL	5.00	9.00	7.00
55242		THREE STEPS TO HEAVEN/ CUT ACROSS SHORTY	5.00	9.00	7.00
55278		SWEETIE PIE/LONELY	4.50	7.50	6.00
55389		WEEKEND/LONELY	4.50	7.50	6.00
		EDDIE COCHRAN—EPs			
3061	*LIBERTY*	SINGIN' TO MY BABY. (PT. 1)	14.00	24.00	20.00
3061		SINGIN' TO MY BABY. (PT. 2)	14.00	24.00	20.00
3061		SINGIN' TO MY BABY. (PT. 3)	14.00	24.00	20.00
		EDDIE COCHRAN—ABLUMS			
3061 (M)	*LIBERTY*	SINGIN' TO MY BABY	37.00	96.00	90.00
3172 (M)		EDDIE COCHRAN	34.00	79.00	75.00
3220 (M)		NEVER TO BE FORGOTTEN	24.00	54.00	50.00
1123 (M)	*SUNSET*	SUMMERTIME BLUES	8.50	20.00	18.00

COCHRAN BROTHERS
FEATURED: EDDIE COCHRAN

1003	*EKKO*	MR. FIDDLE/ TWO BLUE SINGING STARS	45.00	76.00	72.00
1005		GUILTY CONSCIENCE/YOUR TOMORROWS NEVER COME	45.00	76.00	72.00
3001		TIRED AND SLEEPY/ FOOL'S PARADISE	51.00	97.00	90.00

JOE COCKER

40255	*PHILLIPS*	I'LL CRY INSTEAD/ PRECIOUS WORDS	4.50	7.50	6.00

COLONIALS

127	*TRU-LITE*	LITTLE MISS MUFFET/DO POP SI	15.00	30.00	22.00

COMIC BOOKS

6199	*NEW PHOENIX*	BLACK MAGIC & WITCHCRAFT/ MANUEL	17.00	34.00	30.00

BOBBY COMSTOCK

602	*TRIUMPH*	JEALOUS FOOL/ZIG ZAG	5.00	9.00	6.00
349	*BLAZE*	TENNESSEE WALTZ/SWEET TALK	3.50	6.00	4.15
2051	*ATLANTIC*	JAMBALAYA/LET'S TALK IT OVER	3.25	5.50	4.00
124	*MOHAWK*	WAYWARD WIND/ EVERYDAY BLUES	3.25	5.50	4.00
25000	*FESTIVAL*	GARDEN OF EDEN/ A PIECE OF PAPER	3.25	5.50	4.00
5392	*JUBILEE*	BONY MARONIE/ DO THAT LITTLE THING	3.25	5.50	4.00
5396		JEZEBEL/YOUR BIG BROWN EYES	3.25	5.50	4.00
202	*LAWN*	LET'S STOMP/I WANT TO DO IT	3.25	5.50	4.00
210		SUSIE BABY/TAKE A WALK	3.25	5.50	4.00
219		YOUR BOYFRIEND'S BACK/ THIS LITTLE LOVE OF MINE	3.25	5.50	4.00

			Current Price Range		P/Y AVG
☐224		I CAN'T HELP MYSELF/ RUN MY HEART	3.25	5.50	4.00
☐229		THE BEATLE BOUNCE/ SINCE YOU'VE BEEN GONE	3.25	5.50	4.00
☐232		AIN'T THAT JUST LIKE ME/ CAN IT BE TRUE?	3.25	5.50	4.00
☐2164	ASCOT	RIGHT HAND MAN/ALWAYS	3.25	5.50	4.00
☐2175		I'M A MAN/I'LL MAKE YOU GLAD	3.25	5.50	4.00
☐2193		SHOT GUN SALLY/ THIS MAGIC MOMENT	3.25	5.50	4.00
☐2216		OUT OF SIGHT/ CAN'T JUDGE A BOOK	3.25	5.50	4.00
		BOBBY COMSTOCK—ALBUMS			
☐1000 (M)	BLAZE	ROCKIN' WITH BOBBY	14.50	34.00	30.00
☐13026 (M)	ASCOT	OUT OF SIGHT	9.00	21.00	18.00
☐16026 (S)		OUT OF SIGHT	10.00	25.00	22.50

CAROL CONNORS
SEE: ANNETTE BARD, TEDDY BEARS, SURFETTES

☐3084	ERA	BIG BIG LOVE/TWO RIVERS	6.00	13.00	8.25
☐3096		TOMMY, GO AWAY/ I WANNA KNOW	6.00	13.00	8.25
☐5152	CAPITOL	NEVER/ANGEL, MY ANGEL	5.50	10.00	7.00
☐41976	COLUMBIA	MY DIARY/YOU ARE MY ANSWER	5.50	1.00	7.00
☐42155		MY SPECIAL BOY/ LISTEN TO THE BEAT	5.50	10.00	7.00
☐42337		WHAT DO YOU SEE IN HIM?/ THAT'S ALL IT TAKES	5.50	10.00	7.00
☐2005	DUNES	DEAR ONE/JOHNNY OH JOHNNY (Carol Collins)	5.00	9.00	6.00

CONSORTS

☐1004	COUSINS	PLEASE BE MINE/ TIME AFTER TIME	26.00	39.00	36.00
☐25066	APT	PLEASE BE MINE/ TIME AFTER TIME	4.50	7.50	6.00

CONTOURS

☐1008	MOTOWN	WHOLE LOTTA WOMAN/ COME ON AND BE MINE	7.50	13.00	11.00
☐1012		THE STRETCH/FUNNY	5.50	11.00	9.00
☐7005	GORDY	DO YOU LOVE ME/MOVE ME, MAN	3.00	5.50	3.85
☐7012		SHAKE SHERRY/ YOU BETTER GET IN LINE	3.00	5.50	3.85
☐7016		DON'T LET HER BE YOUR BABY/ IT MUST BE LOVE	3.00	5.50	3.85
☐7019		YOU GET UGLY/PA, I NEED A CAR	3.00	5.50	3.85
☐7029		CAN YOU DO IT/ I'LL STAND BY YOU	3.00	5.50	3.85
☐7037		CAN YOU JERK LIKE ME?/THE DAY WHEN SHE NEEDED ME	3.00	5.50	3.85
☐7044		FIRST I LOOK AT THE PURSE/ SEARCHING FOR A GIRL	3.00	5.50	3.85
☐7052		JUST A LITTLE MISUNDERSTANDING/ DETERMINATION	3.00	5.50	3.85
☐7059		IT'S SO HARD BEING A LOSER/ YOUR LOVE GROWS MORE PRECIOUS EVERY DAY	3.00	5.50	3.85
		CONTOURS—ALBUM			
☐901 (M)	GORDY	DO YOU LOVE ME?	14.00	34.00	30.00

			Current Price Range		P/Y AVG
		SAM COOKE			
596	SPECIALTY	LOVEABLE/FOREVER (Dale Cooke)	5.00	9.00	6.00
619		I'LL COME RUNNING BACK TO YOU/FOREVER	5.00	9.00	6.00
627		THAT'S ALL I NEED TO KNOW/ I DON'T WANT TO CRY	4.00	7.00	4.85
667		HAPPY IN LOVE/I NEED YOU NOW	4.00	7.00	4.85
4002	KEEN	FOR SENTIMENTAL REASONS/ DESIRE ME	4.00	7.00	4.85
4009		LONELY ISLAND/ YOU WERE MADE FOR ME	4.00	7.00	4.85
4013		YOU SEND ME/SUMMERTIME	4.00	7.00	4.85
2003		FOR SENTIMENTAL REASONS/ DESIRE ME	3.75	6.00	4.50
2005		ALL OF MY LIFE/ STEALING KISSES	3.75	6.00	4.50
2006		WIN YOUR LOVE FOR ME/LOVE SONG FROM "HOUSEBOAT"	3.50	5.75	4.35
2008		LOVE YOU MOST OF ALL/ BLUE MOON	3.50	5.75	4.35
2018		EVERYBODY LIKES TO CHA-CHA-CHA/LITTLE THINGS YOU DO	3.50	5.75	4.35
2022		ONLY SIXTEEN/ LET'S GO STEADY AGAIN	3.50	5.75	4.35
2101		SUMMERTIME (PT. 1)/(PT. 2)	3.50	5.75	4.35
2105		THERE. I'VE SAID IT AGAIN/ONE HOUR AHEAD OF THE POSSE	3.50	5.75	4.35
2111		NO ONE/ IT AIN'T NOBODY'S BIZNESS	3.50	5.75	4.35
2112		WONDERFUL WORLD/ ALONG THE NAVAJO TRAIL	3.50	5.75	4.35
2117		WITH YOU/I THANK GOD	3.50	5.75	4.35
2118		STEAL AWAY/SO GLAMOROUS	3.50	5.75	4.35
2122		MARY. MARY LOU/ EE-YI-EE-YI-OH	3.50	5.75	4.35
7701	RCA	TEENAGE SONATA/ IF YOU WERE THE ONLY GIRL	3.25	5.50	4.00
7730		YOU UNDERSTAND ME/ I BELONG TO YOUR HEART	3.25	5.50	4.00
7783		CHAIN GANG/I FALL IN LOVE EVERY DAY	3.25	5.50	4.00
7816		SAD MOOD/LOVE ME	3.25	5.50	4.00
7853		THAT'S IT. I QUIT. I'M MOVIN ON/DO WHAT YOU SAY	3.25	5.50	4.00
7883		CUPID/FAREWELL. MY DARLING	3.25	5.50	4.00
7927		FEEL IT/IT'S ALL RIGHT	3.25	5.50	4.00
7983		TWISTIN' THE NIGHT AWAY/ ONE MORE TIME	3.25	5.50	4.00
8036		BRING IT ON HOME TO ME/ HAVING A PARTY	3.25	5.50	4.00
8088		NOTHING CAN CHANGE THIS LOVE/SOMEBODY HAVE MERCY	3.25	5.50	4.00
8129		SEND ME SOME LOVIN'/ BABY. BABY. BABY	3.25	5.50	4.00
8164		ANOTHER SATURDAY NIGHT/ LOVE WILL FIND A WAY	3.25	5.50	4.00
8215		FRANKIE AND JOHNNY/ COOL TRAIN	3.25	5.50	4.00
8247		LITTLE RED ROOSTER/ YOU'VE GOTTA MOVE	3.25	5.50	4.00
8299		GOOD NEWS/ BASIN STREET BLUES	3.25	5.50	4.00
8368		GOOD TIMES/TENNESSEE WALTZ	3.25	5.50	4.00

			Current Price Range		P/Y AVG
8426		COUSIN OF MINE/ THAT'S WHERE IT'S AT	3.00	5.00	3.85
8486		SHAKE/ A CHANGE IS GONNA COME ...	3.00	5.00	3.65
8539		IT'S GOT THE WHOLE WORLD SHAKIN'/EASE MY TROUBLIN' MIND	3.00	5.00	3.65
8586		WHEN A BOY FALLS IN LOVE/ THE PIPER	3.00	5.00	3.65
8631		SUGAR DUMPLING/ BRIDGE OF TEARS	3.00	5.00	3.65
8751		FEEL IT/THAT'S ALL	3.00	5.00	3.65
8803		LET'S GO STEADY AGAIN/ TROUBLE BLUES	3.00	5.00	3.65
8934		IF I HAD A HAMMER/ MEET ME AT MARY'S PLACE ..	3.00	5.00	3.65
		SAM COOKE—EPs			
2001	*KEEN*	SAM COOKE.................	6.50	13.00	8.50
2002		SAM COOKE.................	6.50	13.00	8.50
2003		SAM COOKE.................	6.50	13.00	8.50
2006		ENCORE. VOL. I.............	6.50	13.00	8.50
2007		ENCORE. VOL. II	6.50	13.00	8.50
2008		ENCORE. VOL. III..........	6.50	13.00	8.50
2012		TRIBUTE TO THE LADY. VOL. I ...	6.00	12.00	7.00
2013		TRIBUTE TO THE LADY. VOL. II ..	6.00	12.00	7.00
2014		TRIBUTE TO THE LADY. VOL. III .	6.00	12.00	7.00
4372	*RCA*	ANOTHER SATURDAY NIGHT	6.00	12.00	7.00
		SAM COOKE—ALBUMS			
2001 (M)	*KEEN*	SAM COOKE.................	12.00	24.00	20.00
2003 (M)		ENCORE	10.00	18.00	13.25
2004 (M)		TRIBUTE TO THE LADY	10.00	18.00	13.25
86101 (M)		HIT KIT	10.00	18.00	13.25
86103 (M)		I THANK GOD	10.00	18.00	13.25
86106 (M)		WONDERFUL WORLD OF SAM COOKE	12.00	24.00	20.00
502 (M)	*FAMOUS*	SAM'S SONGS...............	8.50	15.00	12.00
505 (M)		ONLY SIXTEEN	8.50	14.00	12.00
508 (M)		SO WONDERFUL	8.50	14.00	12.00
512 (M)		CHA-CHA-CHA.............	8.50	14.00	12.00
2221 (M)	*RCA*	COOKE'S TOUR	9.50	18.00	15.00
2236 (M)		HITS OF THE 50'S	9.50	18.00	15.00
2293 (M)		SWING LOW	9.50	18.00	15.00
2392 (M)		MY KIND OF BLUES	8.50	21.00	18.00
2555 (M)		TWISTIN' THE NIGHT AWAY	8.00	18.00	12.00
2625 (M)		THE BEST OF SAM COOKE	8.00	18.00	12.00
2673 (M)		MR. SOUL	8.00	18.00	12.00
2709 (M)		NIGHT BEAT...............	8.00	18.00	12.00
2899 (M)		AIN'T THAT GOOD NEWS	8.00	18.00	12.00
2970 (M)		AT THE COPA	8.00	18.00	12.00
3367 (M)		SHAKE	8.00	18.00	12.00
3373 (M)		BEST OF SAM COOKE. VOL. 2 ...	8.00	18.00	12.00
3435 (M)		TRY A LITTLE LOVE	8.00	18.00	12.00
3517 (M)		UNFORGETTABLE SAM COOKE ...	8.00	18.00	12.00
3991 (M)		THE MAN WHO INVENTED SOUL .	8.00	18.00	12.00
		STEREO VERSIONS OF RCA ALBUMS ARE WORTH 25% LESS THAN THOSE IN MONO			
2110 (M)	*SPECIALTY*	TWO SIDES OF SAM COOKE	7.50	17.00	15.00
105 (M)	*SAR*	SOUL STIRRERS FEATURING SAM COOKE	7.50	17.00	15.00

COOKIES

1002	*DIMENSION*	CHAINS/STRANGER IN MY ARMS	3.25	5.50	4.00
1008		DON'T SAY NOTHIN' BAD/ SOFTLY IN THE NIGHT	3.25	5.50	4.00

			Current Price Range		P/Y AVG
☐1012		WILL POWER/I WANT A BOY FOR MY BIRTHDAY	3.25	5.50	4.00
☐1020		GIRLS GROW UP FASTER THAN BOYS/ONLY TO OTHER PEOPLE	3.25	5.50	4.00
☐1032		I NEVER DREAMED/ THE OLD CROWD	3.25	5.50	4.00

EDDIE COOLEY AND THE DIMPLES

☐621	ROYAL ROOST	PRISCILLA/GOT A LITTLE WOMAN	3.75	6.00	4.50
☐626		A SPARK MET A FLAME/ DRIFTWOOD	3.50	5.50	4.00
☐628		HEY YOU/PULL. PULL	3.50	5.50	4.00

RITA COOLIDGE

☐442	PEPPER	SECRET PLACES/RAINBOW CHILD	3.00	5.50	4.00
☐443		WALKIN' IN THE MORNIN / TURN AROUND & LOVE YOU	3.50	5.50	4.00
☐1256	A&M	MUD ISLAND/I BELIEVE IN YOU	2.50	4.50	2.50
☐1271		MOUNTAINS/CRAZY LOVE	2.50	4.50	2.50
☐1324		LAY MY BURDEN DOWN/ NICE FEELIN	2.50	4.50	2.50

ALICE COOPER
SEE: NAZZ, SPIDERS

☐101	STRAIGHT	REFLECTED/LIVING	12.00	22.00	20.00
☐7141	WARNER BROTHERS	EIGHTEEN/CAUGHT IN A DREAM	3.75	6.00	4.50
☐7398		RETURN OF THE SPIDERS/ SHOE SALESMAN	3.50	5.50	4.00
☐7449		EIGHTEEN/BODY	3.00	5.25	3.85
☐7490		CAUGHT IN A DREAM/ HALLOWED BE MY NAME	3.00	5.25	3.85
☐7529		UNDER MY WHEELS/DESPERADO	3.00	5.25	3.85
☐7568		BE MY LOVER/YEAH. YEAH. YEAH	3.00	5.25	3.85
☐7596		SCHOOL S OUT/GUTTER CAT	2.75	5.00	3.50
☐7631		ELECTED/LUNEY TUNE	2.75	5.00	3.50
☐7673		HELLO HURRAY/ GENERATION LANDSLIDE	2.75	5.00	3.50
☐7691		NO MORE MR. NICE GUY/ RAPED AND FREEZIN	2.75	5.00	3.50
☐7724		BILLION DOLLAR BABIES/ MARY ANN	2.75	5.00	3.50
☐7762		TEENAGE LAMENT 74/ HARD HEARTED ALICE	2.75	5.00	3.50
☐7783		MUSCLE OF LOVE/ CRAZY LITTLE CHILD	3.00	5.50	3.85

ALICE COOPER—ALBUMS

1845 (S)	STRAIGHT	EASY ACTION	17.00	39.00	35.00
1051 (S)		PRETTIES FOR YOU	10.00	25.00	22.50
1883 (S)	WARNER BROTHERS	LOVE IT TO DEATH	6.00	15.00	10.00
2567 (S)		KILLER	6.00	15.00	10.00
2623 (S)		SCHOOL S OUT	5.50	13.00	8.75
2685 (S)		BILLION DOLLAR BABIES	5.50	13.00	8.75
2748 (S)		MUSCLE OF LOVE	5.50	13.00	8.75
2803 (S)		ALICE COOPER S GREATEST HITS	5.50	13.00	8.75

KEN COPELAND

5008	LIN	PLEDGE OF LOVE/NIGHT AIR (Mints)	5.50	11.00	9.00
5432	IMPERIAL	PLEDGE OF LOVE/NIGHT AIR (Mints)	3.50	5.50	4.00

ALICE COOPER

As a boy, Vincent Furnier carried a briefcase and wore a suit-and-tie to school. He was teased about being a preacher's kid, and he found solace cheifly in front of his family's TV set. There Vincent imitated the stars who flickered before him. And Furnier dreamed of one day, too, performing before people and gaining attention and acceptance.

He attended Cortez High in Phoenix, AZ. Wanting to impress girls with a sports letter, he was too thin (130 pounds) to play football, so he turned to track. On tryout day, the school's track star laughed aloud at Vincent Furnier. Vincent became so enraged he outran the Cortez star. Furnier later set a state high-school record for track.

He also wrote a column called "Get Outta My Hair!" for the school newspaper. Vincent himself was expelled eight times for having hair half-an-inch too long for the Cortez codes.

He and some fellow track runners formed a "band" as a joke for a father-son sports banquet. Impressed by the reaction they got (they mimicked the Beatles), the group decided to actually learn to play! They called themselves the Spiders, cut a record, became the Nazz, made a second record, and finally became Alice Cooper. (The real Alice Cooper was an English woman accused of being a witch. She committed suicide before being brought to trial, and is said to walk the earth to this day, seeking refuge in living souls . . .)

			Current Price Range		P/Y AVG

CORDELLS
☐ 1017	*BULLSEYE*	PLEASE DON'T GO/BELIEVE IN ME	12.00	22.00	20.00

CORDIALS
☐ 276	*WHIP*	LISTEN MY HEART/ MY HEART'S DESIRE	20.00	34.00	30.00
☐ 106	*REVEILLE*	ETERNAL LOVE/ THE INTERNATIONAL TWIST	14.00	24.00	20.00

CORNELLS
☐ 102	*GAREX*	MALIBU SURF/AGUA CALIENTE	3.50	5.50	4.00
☐ 201		BEACH BOUND/ LONE STAR STOMP	3.50	5.50	4.00
☐ 206		SURF FEVER/DO THE SLAUSON	3.50	5.50	4.00

CORNELLS—ALBUM
☐ 100 (M)		BEACH BOUND	9.50	17.00	15.00

COUNT FIVE
☐ 104	*DOUBLE SHOT*	PSYCHOTIC REACTION/ THEY'RE GONNA GET YOU	3.00	5.25	3.85
☐ 106		PEACE OF MIND/ THE MORNING AFTER	3.00	5.25	3.85
☐ 110		YOU MUST BELIEVE ME/TEENY BOPPER, TEENY BOPPER	3.00	5.25	3.85
☐ 115		CONTRAST/MERRY-GO-ROUND	3.00	5.25	3.85

COUNT FIVE—ALBUMS
☐ 1001 (M)	*DOUBLE SHOT*	PSYCHOTIC REACTION	7.00	17.00	15.00
☐ 5001 (S)		PSYCHOTIC REACTION	9.00	25.00	22.50

BUDDY COVELLE
9-55151	*BRUNSWICK*	SHOW ME HOW/BILLY BOY	26.00	70.00	64.00
		BILLED AS BY "VALINE HACKERT"			

COWSILLS
☐ 103	*JODA*	ALL I REALLY WANT TO BE IS ME/ AND THE NEXT DAY, TOO	3.75	6.00	4.50
40282	*PHILIPS*	MOST OF ALL/SIAMESE CAT	3.50	5.50	4.00
40406		PARTY GIRL/ WHAT'S IT GONNA BE LIKE?	3.50	5.50	4.00

CRAFTSMEN (JOHNNY AND THE HURRICANES)
538	*WARWICK*	GOOFUS/ROCK ALONG	4.50	7.50	6.00
586		TWEEDLE DEE/ WALKIN' WITH MR. LEE	4.50	7.50	6.00

JOHNNY CRAWFORD
124	*WYNNE*	DANCE WITH THE DOLLY/ASK	5.00	9.00	7.00
4162	*DEL-FI*	DAYDREAMS/ SO GOES THE STORY	3.25	6.00	4.00
4165		YOUR LOVE IS GROWING COLD/ TREASURE	3.75	6.00	4.50
4172		PATTI ANN/DONNA	3.25	6.00	4.00
4178		CINDY'S BIRTHDAY/ SOMETHING SPECIAL	3.25	6.00	4.00
4181		YOUR NOSE IS GONNA GROW/ MR. BLUE	3.25	6.00	4.00
4188		RUMORS/NO ONE REALLY LOVES A CLOWN	3.25	6.00	4.00
4193		PROUD/LONESOME TOWN	3.25	6.00	4.00
4203		WHEN I FALL IN LOVE/ CRY ON MY SHOULDER	3.25	6.00	4.00
4215		WHAT HAPPENED TO JANIE?/ PETITE CHANSON	3.25	6.00	4.00

			Current Price Range		P/Y AVG
4221		CINDY'S GONNA CRY/DEBBIE ...	3.25	6.00	4.00
4229		SANDY/OL' SHORTY	3.25	6.00	4.00
4231		JUDY LOVES ME/			
		LIVING IN THE PAST	3.75	6.00	4.50
		PRODUCER: JAN BERRY (DEL-FI 4231)			
4242		THE GIRL NEXT DOOR/			
		SITTIN' AND A WATCHIN	3.00	5.00	3.50
		JOHNNY CRAWFORD—ALBUMS			
1220 (M)	**DEL-FI**	THE CAPTIVATING			
		JOHNNY CRAWFORD	12.00	29.00	25.00
1223 (M)		A YOUNG MAN'S FANCY	7.00	17.00	15.00
1223 (S)		A YOUNG MAN'S FANCY	9.00	25.00	22.50
1224 (M)		RUMORS	7.00	17.00	15.00
1224 (S)		RUMORS	9.00	25.00	22.50
1229 (M)		HIS GREATEST HITS	7.00	17.00	15.00
1229 (S)		HIS GREATEST HITS	9.00	25.00	22.50
1248 (M)		GREATEST HITS. VOL. II	8.00	20.00	18.00
1248 (S)		GREATEST HITS. VOL. II	12.00	29.00	25.00

CREAM
FEATURED: ERIC CLAPTON

591-007	**POLYDOR**	WRAPPING PAPER/			
		CAT'S SQUIRREL	6.00	12.00	8.50
		(British release)			
6462	**ATCO**	I FEEL FREE/N.S.U.	3.50	6.50	4.35
6488		STRANGE BREW/			
		TALES OF BRAVE ULYSSES ...	3.50	6.50	4.35
6522		SPOONFUL (PT. 1)/(PT. 2)	3.50	6.50	4.35
6544		SUNSHINE OF YOUR LOVE/			
		S.W.L.A.B.R.	3.00	6.00	3.85
6575		ANYONE FOR TENNIS?/			
		PRESSED RAT AND WARTHOG .	3.00	6.00	3.85
6617		WHITE ROOM/			
		THOSE WERE THE DAYS	3.00	6.00	3.85
6646		CROSSROADS/PASSING THE TIME	3.00	6.00	3.85
6668		BADGE/WHAT A BRINGDOWN .	3.00	6.00	3.85
6708		SWEET WINE/LAWDY MAMA	3.00	6.00	3.85
		CREAM—ALBUMS			
206 (S)	**ATCO**	FRESH CREAM	5.50	14.00	12.00
232 (S)		DISRAELI GEARS	5.50	14.00	12.00
700 (S)		WHEELS OF FIRE.............	5.50	14.00	12.00
7001 (S)		GOODBYE CREAM	5.50	14.00	12.00

CREEDENCE CLEARWATER REVIVAL
SEE: BLUE RIDGE RANGERS, TOMMY FOGERTY
AND THE BLUE VELVETS, GOLLIWOGS

412	**SCORPIO**	PORTERVILLE/			
		CALL IT PRETENDING	15.00	29.00	19.00
616	**FANTASY**	SUSIE Q (PT. 1)/(PT. 2)	3.50	6.00	4.00
617		I PUT A SPELL ON YOU/			
		WALK ON THE WATER	3.00	5.00	3.85
619		PROUD MARY/			
		BORN ON THE BAYOU	3.00	5.00	3.85
622		BAD MOON RISING/LODI	3.00	5.00	3.65
625		GREEN RIVER/COMMOTION	3.00	5.00	3.65
634		DOWN ON THE CORNER/			
		FORTUNATE SON	3.00	5.00	3.65
637		TRAVELIN BAND/			
		WHO'LL STOP THE RAIN?	3.00	5.00	3.65
641		UP AROUND THE BEND/			
		RUN THROUGH THE JUNGLE ..	3.00	5.00	3.65
645		LOOKIN' OUT MY BACK DOOR/			
		LONG AS I CAN SEE THE LIGHT	3.00	5.00	3.65
655		HAVE YOU EVER SEEN THE RAIN?/			
		HEY TONIGHT	3.00	5.00	3.65

			Current Price Range		P/Y AVG
L 665		SWEET HITCH-HIKER/ DOOR TO DOOR	3.00	5.00	3.65
L 676		SOMEDAY NEVER COMES/ TEARIN' UP THE COUNTRY	3.00	5.00	3.65
L 759	FANTASY	HEARD IT THROUGH THE GRAPEVINE/GOOD GOOLY	2.75	4.50	3.00
		CREEDENCE CLEARWATER REVIVAL—ALBUMS			
L 8382 (S)	FANTASY	CREEDENCE CLEARWATER REVIVAL	7.00	17.00	11.00
L 8387 (S)		BAYOU COUNTRY	6.50	15.00	10.00
L 8393 (S)		GREEN RIVER	6.50	15.00	10.00
L 8397 (S)		WILLY AND THE POOR BOYS	6.50	15.00	10.00
L 8402 (S)		COSMO'S FACTORY	6.50	15.00	10.00
L 8410 (S)		PENDULUM	6.50	15.00	10.00
L 9404 (S)		MARDI GRAS	6.50	15.00	10.00
L 9418 (S)		CREEDENCE GOLD	6.00	13.00	8.75
L 9430 (S)		MORE CREEDENCE GOLD	6.00	13.00	8.75

CRESCENDOS
FEATURED: DALE WARD

L 7027	TAP	OH JULIE/MY LITTLE GIRL	12.00	24.00	20.00
L 6005	NASCO	OH JULIE/MY LITTLE GIRL	3.75	6.00	4.50
L 6009		SCHOOL GIRL/CRAZY HOP	3.75	6.00	4.50
L 6021		YOUNG AND IN LOVE/ RAINY SUNDAY	3.75	6.00	4.50
		CRESCENDOS—ALBUM			
L 1453 (M)	GUEST STAR	OH JULIE	12.00	29.00	25.00

CRESTS
SEE: JOHNNY MAESTRO

L 103	JOYCE	SWEETEST ONE/MY JUANITA	20.00	34.00	30.00
L 105		NO ONE TO LOVE/ WISH SHE WAS MINE	26.00	45.00	40.00
L 501	COED	PRETTY LITTLE ANGEL/ I THANK THE MOON	17.00	24.00	20.00
L 506		SIXTEEN CANDLES/BESIDE YOU	3.75	6.00	4.50
L 509		SIX NIGHTS A WEEK/I DO	3.75	6.00	4.50
L 511		FLOWER OF LOVE/MOLLY MAE	3.75	6.00	4.50
L 515		THE ANGELS LISTENED IN/ I THANK THE MOON	3.75	6.00	4.50
L 521		A YEAR AGO TONIGHT/ PAPER CROWN	3.75	6.00	4.50
L 525		STEP BY STEP/GEE	3.75	6.00	4.50
L 531		TROUBLE IN PARADISE/ ALWAYS YOU	3.75	6.00	4.50
L 535		JOURNEY OF LOVE/IF MY HEART COULD WRITE A LETTER	3.75	6.00	4.50
L 537		ISN'T IT AMAZING/MOLLY ME	3.75	6.00	4.50
L 543		IN THE STILL OF THE NIGHT/ GOOD GOLLY MISS MOLLY	3.75	6.00	4.50
L 561		LITTLE MIRACLES/ BABY I GOTTA KNOW	3.75	6.00	4.50
L 696	TRANS ATLAS	THE ACTOR/ THREE TEARS IN A BUCKET	3.75	6.00	4.50
L 311	SELMA	GUILTY/NUMBER ONE WITH ME	3.75	6.00	4.50
L 400		TEARS WILL FALL/ DID I REMEMBER	3.75	6.00	4.50
L 987	PARKWAY	TRY ME/HEARTBURN	3.75	6.00	4.50
L 999		I CARE ABOUT YOU/COME SEE ME	3.75	6.00	4.50
L 118		MY TIME/IS IT YOU?	3.75	6.00	4.50
L 2	TIMES SQUARE	NO ONE TO LOVE/ WISH SHE WAS MINE	4.00	7.00	4.85
L 6		BABY/I LOVE YOU SO	4.00	7.00	4.85
L 97		BABY/I LOVE YOU SO	3.75	6.00	4.50

			Current Price Range		P/Y AVG
12112	SCEPTER	I'M STEPPING OUT OF THE PICTURE/AFRAID OF LOVE	3.75	6.00	4.50
62403	CORAL	YOU BLEW OUT THE CANDLES/ A LOVE TO LAST A LIFETIME ..	6.00	12.00	8.25
256	CAMEO	I'LL BE TRUE/ OVER THE WEEKEND	3.75	6.00	4.75
305		LEAN ON ME/MAKE UP MY MIND	3.75	6.00	4.50
		CRESTS—EP			
101	COED	THE ANGELS LISTENED IN	23.00	37.00	27.00
		CRESTS—ALBUMS			
901 (M)	COED	THE CRESTS SING ALL BIGGIES ..	39.00	90.00	58.00
904 (M)		THE BEST OF THE CRESTS	39.00	90.00	58.00
904 (S)		THE BEST OF THE CRESTS	55.00	126.00	120.00

CREW CUTS

			Current Price Range		P/Y AVG
70341	MERCURY	CRAZY 'BOUT YOU, BABY/ ANGELA MIA	3.75	6.00	4.50
70404		SH BOOM/I SPOKE TOO SOON ...	3.75	6.00	4.50
70443		OOP SHOOP/DO ME GOOD BABY .	3.75	6.00	4.50
70490		ALL I WANNA DO/ THE BARKING DOG	3.75	6.00	4.50
70491		DANCE MR. SNOWMAN DANCE/ TWINKLE TOES	3.75	6.00	4.50
70494		THE WHIFFENPOOF SONG/ VARSITY DRAG	3.75	6.00	4.50
70527		EARTH ANGEL/KO KO MO	3.50	5.50	4.00
70597		DON'T BE ANGRY/ CHOP CHOP BOOM	3.50	5.50	4.00
70598		UNCHAINED MELODY/ TWO HEARTS. TWO KISSES ...	3.50	5.50	4.00
70634		A STORY UNTOLD/ CARMEN'S BOOGIE	3.50	5.50	4.00
70668		GUM DROP/SONG OF THE FOOL ..	3.50	5.50	4.00
70668		GUM DROP/PRESENT ARMS	3.50	5.50	4.00
70710		SLAM BAM/ ARE YOU HAVING ANY FUN? ..	3.50	5.50	4.00
70741		ANGELS IN THE SKY/ MOSTLY MARTHA	3.00	5.00	3.65
70782		SEVEN DAYS/ THAT'S YOUR MISTAKE	3.00	5.00	3.65
70840		OUT OF THE PICTURE/ HONEY HAIR. SUGAR LIPS. EYES OF BLUE	3.00	5.00	3.65
70890		TELL ME WHY/REBEL IN TOWN ..	3.00	5.00	3.65
70922		THIRTEEN GOING ON FOURTEEN/ BEI MIR BIST DU SCHOEN	3.00	5.00	3.65
70977		LOVE IN A HOME/ KEEPER OF THE FLAME	3.00	5.00	3.65
70988		HALLS OF IVY/VARSITY DRAG ..	3.00	5.00	3.65
71022		YOUNG LOVE/LITTLE BY LITTLE .	3.00	5.00	3.65
71076		ANGELUS/WHATEVER. WHENEVER. WHOEVER	3.00	5.00	3.65
71125		SUSIE-Q/SUCH A SHAME	3.00	5.00	3.65
71168		I SIT IN MY WINDOW/ HEY YOU FACE	3.00	5.00	3.65
71223		BE MY ONLY LOVE/ I LIKE IT LIKE THAT	3.00	5.00	3.65
558	WARWICK	OVER THE MOUNTAIN/SEARCHIN	3.00	5.00	3.65
623		NUMBER ONE WITH ME/ LEGEND OF GUNGA DIN	3.00	5.00	3.65
		CREW CUTS—EPs			
13261	MERCURY	CRAZY 'BOUT YOU BABY	7.00	12.00	10.00
13274		THREE CHEERS FOR THE CREW CUTS	7.00	12.00	10.00

			Current Price Range		P/Y AVG
13275		THREE CHEERS FOR THE CREW CUTS	7.00	12.00	10.00
13290		TOPS IN POPS	7.00	12.00	10.00
13325		THE CREW CUTS GO LONGHAIR	5.50	11.00	9.00
13326		LONGHAIR SWING WITH THE CREW CUTS	5.50	11.00	9.00
13327		SWING THE MASTERS	5.50	11.00	9.00
		CREW CUTS—ALBUMS			
20067 (M)	**MERCURY**	THE CREW CUTS GO LONGHAIR	9.00	25.00	22.50
20140 (M)		ON THE CAMPUS	9.00	25.00	22.50
20143 (M)		CREW CUT CAPERS	9.00	25.00	22.50
21044 (M)		ROCK AND ROLL BASH	9.00	25.00	22.50
20199 (M)		MUSIC ALA CARTE	8.00	20.00	18.00

CRICKETS
FEATURED: BUDDY HOLLY

55009	**BRUNSWICK**	THAT'LL BE THE DAY/ I'M LOOKING FOR SOMEONE TO LOVE	5.50	11.00	9.00
55035		OH BOY!/NOT FADE AWAY	5.50	11.00	9.00
55053		MAYBE BABY/TELL ME HOW	5.50	11.00	9.00
55072		THINK IT OVER/FOOL'S PARADISE	5.50	11.00	9.00
55094		IT'S SO EASY/LONESOME TEARS	8.25	14.00	12.00
		CRICKETS—EPs			
71036	**BRUNSWICK**	THE "CHIRPING" CRICKETS	40.00	75.00	55.00
71038		THE SOUND OF THE CRICKETS	27.00	45.00	40.00
		CRICKETS—ALBUM			
54038	**BRUNSWICK**	THE "CHIRPING" CRICKETS	55.00	135.00	90.00

CRICKETS

55124	**BRUNSWICK**	LOVE'S MADE A FOOL OF YOU/ SOMEONE, SOMEONE	7.50	14.00	12.00
55153		WHEN YOU ASK ABOUT LOVE/ DEBORAH	5.00	9.00	7.00
62198	**CORAL**	MORE THAN I CAN SAY/ BABY MY HEART	5.50	11.00	9.00
62238		PEGGY SUE GOT MARRIED/ DON'T CHA KNOW	9.00	17.00	15.00
55392	**LIBERTY**	I'M FEELING BETTER/HE'S OLD ENOUGH TO KNOW BETTER	4.00	7.00	4.85
55441		DON'T EVER CHANGE/ I'M NOT A BAD GUY	4.00	7.00	4.85
55495		LITTLE HOLLYWOOD GIRL/ PARISIAN GIRL	4.00	7.00	4.85
55540		TEARDROPS FALL LIKE RAIN/ MY LITTLE GIRL	4.00	7.00	4.85
55603		APRIL AVENUE/ DON'T SAY YOU LOVE ME	4.00	7.00	4.85
55668		PLEASE PLEASE ME/ FROM ME TO YOU	4.00	7.00	4.85
55696		ALL OVER YOU/LA BAMBA	4.00	7.00	4.85
55742		I THINK I'VE CAUGHT THE BLUES/ WE GOTTA GET TOGETHER	4.00	7.00	4.85
55767		NOW HEAR THIS/EVERYBODY'S GOT A LITTLE PROBLEM	4.00	7.00	4.85
415	**MILLION**	MILLION DOLLAR MOVIE/ A MILLION MILES APART	3.50	6.00	4.00
2061	**BARNABY**	TRUE LOVE WAYS/ROCKIN' 50'S ROCK AND ROLL	3.50	6.00	4.00
		CRICKETS—ALBUMS			
57320 (M)	**CORAL**	IN STYLE WITH THE CRICKETS	22.00	55.00	50.00
3272 (M)	**LIBERTY**	SOMETHING OLD, SOMETHING NEW, SOMETHING BLUE, SOMETHIN' ELSE!	12.00	29.00	25.00

ATCO, 33-101, LP

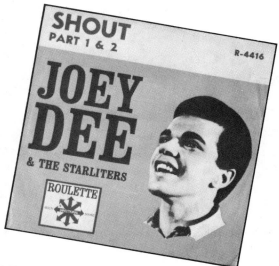

ROULETTE, R-4416, 45

			Current Price Range		P/Y AVG
7272 (S)		SOMETHING OLD. SOMETHING NEW.SOMETHING BLUE. SOMETHIN' ELSE!	17.00	40.00	35.00
3351 (M)		CALIFORNIA SUN	12.00	29.00	25.00
7351 (S)		CALIFORNIA SUN	17.00	40.00	35.00

CROSS COUNTRY (TOKENS)

6932	ATCO	ROCK AND ROLL MUSIC/ JUST A THOUGHT	3.00	5.50	4.00
6934		IN THE MIDNIGHT HOUR/ A SMILE SONG	2.50	4.00	2.50
6947		TASTES SO GOOD TO ME/ A BALL SONG	2.50	4.00	2.50
7009		PENNY WHISTLE BAND/ LORD CAN'T SING A SOLO	2.50	4.00	2.50

CROSS COUNTRY—ALBUM

7024 (S)	ATCO	CROSS COUNTRY	6.00	15.00	13.50

CROSSFIRES (TURTLES)

104	CAPCO	FIBERGLASS JUNGLE/ DR. JEKYLL AND MR. HYDE	5.50	11.00	9.00
112	LUCKY TOKEN	THAT'LL BE THE DAY/ ONE POTATO. TWO POTATO	5.00	9.00	7.00

CROSSFIRES (TURTLES)—ALBUM

1083 (M)	STRAND	LIMBO ROCK	8.00	20.00	18.00

CROWS

3	RAMA	SEVEN LONELY DAYS/ NO HELP WANTED	100.00	165.00	108.00
5		GEE/I LOVE YOU SO	10.00	20.00	13.00
5		GEE/I LOVE YOU SO (red wax)	28.00	50.00	32.00
10		HEARTBREAKER/CALL A DOCTOR	50.00	90.00	60.00
29		UNTRUE/BABY	50.00	90.00	60.00
30		MISS YOU/I REALLY. REALLY LOVE YOU	50.00	90.00	60.00
50		SWEET SUE/BABY DOLL	50.00	90.00	60.00

CRUISERS

119	ZEBRA	FOOLISH ME/THERE'S A GIRL	25.00	46.00	42.00

CRYSTALS

100	PHILLES	THERE'S NO OTHER/ OH YEAH. MAYBE BABY	4.50	7.50	6.00
102		UPTOWN/WHAT A NICE WAY TO TURN SEVENTEEN	4.50	7.50	6.00
105		HE HIT ME (AND IT FELT LIKE A KISS)/NO ONE EVER TELLS YOU	5.50	11.00	9.00
106		HE'S A REBEL/I LOVE YOU EDDIE	3.25	5.50	4.00
109		HE'S SURE THE BOY I LOVE/ WALKIN' ALONG	3.25	5.50	4.00
111		DO THE SCREW (PT. 1)/(PT. 2) (DJ copies only)	210.00	375.00	350.00
112		DA DOO RON RON/GIT IT	3.25	5.50	4.00
115		THEN HE KISSED ME/ BROTHER JULIUS	3.25	5.50	4.00
119		LITTLE BOY/HARRY AND MILT	3.75	6.00	4.70
122		ALL GROWN UP/IRVING	3.75	6.00	4.50
927	UNITED ARTISTS	MY PLACE/YOU CAN'T TIE A GOOD GIRL DOWN	4.50	8.00	6.00
994		I GOT A MAN/ARE YOU TRYING TO GET RID OF ME. BABY?	4.50	8.00	6.00

CRYSTALS—ALBUMS

4000 (M)	PHILLES	TWIST UPTOWN	30.00	68.00	47.00
4001 (M)		HE'S A REBEL	30.00	68.00	47.00

			Current Price Range		P/Y AVG
4003 (M)		THE CRYSTALS SING THE GREATEST HITS. VOL. 1	25.00	55.00	50.00

JOHNNY CYMBAL

12935	*MGM*	IT'LL BE ME/ALWAYS	5.00	9.00	7.00
503	*KAPP*	MR. BASS MAN/ SACRED LOVER'S VOW	3.00	5.00	3.50
524		TEENAGE HEAVEN/ CINDERELLA BABY	3.75	6.00	4.50
539		DUM DUM DEE DUM/TIJUANA ..	3.00	5.00	3.50
556		HURDY GURDY MAN/ MARSHMALLOW	3.00	5.00	3.50
576		THERE'S GOES A BAD GIRL/ REFRESHMENT TIME	3.00	5.00	3.50
614		LITTLE MISS LONELY/CONNIE	3.00	5.00	3.50

JOHNNY CYMBAL—ALBUMS

1324 (M)	*KAPP*	MR. BASS MAN	7.00	17.00	15.00
3324 (S)		MR. BASS MAN	9.00	25.00	22.50

D

BERTELL DACHE (TONY ORLANDO)
FEATURED: CAROLE KING

☐260		ALL THE WORLD LOVES A LOVER/ HAVE CHICKS	2.00	21.00	18.00
☐260	*UNITED ARTISTS*	ALL THE WORLD LOVES A LOVER/ YOU GOTTA HAVE CHICKS	12.00	21.00	18.00
☐290		LOVE EYES/NOT JUST TOMORROW BUT ALWAYS	12.00	21.00	18.00

DAKOTAS
SEE: BILLY J. KRAMER AND THE DAKOTAS

☐55618	*LIBERTY*	THE CRUEL SURF/ THE MILLIONAIRE	5.00	9.00	7.00

DICK DALE
FEATURED: THE DEL-TONES

☐5012	*DELTONE*	OH WHEE MARIE/ BREAKING HEART	9.50	17.00	15.00
☐5013		STOP TEASIN'/ WITHOUT YOUR LOVE	9.50	17.00	15.00
☐5014		JESSIE PEARL/ST. LOUIS BLUES	20.00	34.00	30.00
☐5017		LET'S GO TRIPPIN'/ DEL-TONES ROCK	5.00	9.00	6.00
☐5018		SHAKE 'N' STOMP/ JUNGLE FEVER	5.00	9.00	6.00
☐5019		MISERLOU/EIGHT TILL MIDNIGHT.	5.00	9.00	6.00
☐5020		SURF BEAT/PEPPERMINT MAN ..	5.00	9.00	6.00
☐5028		LOVIN' ON MY BRAIN/ RUN FOR YOUR LIFE	14.00	24.00	20.00
☐106	*CUPID*	WE'LL NEVER HEAR THE END OF IT/FAIREST OF THEM ALL	8.25	14.00	12.00
☐371	*CONCERT ROOM*	WE'LL NEVER HEAR THE END OF IT/FAIREST OF THEM ALL	7.00	12.00	10.00
☐401	*SATURN*	WE'LL NEVER HEAR THE END OF IT/FAIREST OF THEM ALL	7.00	12.00	10.00
☐7014	*YES*	WE'LL NEVER HEAR THE END OF IT/FAIREST OF THEM ALL	4.50	7.50	6.00
☐4939	*CAPITOL*	MISERLOU/EIGHT TILL MIDNIGHT.	3.50	6.00	4.35
☐4940		SURF BEAT/PEPPERMINT MAN ..	3.50	6.00	4.35

			Current Price Range		P/Y AVG
☐ 4963		KING OF THE SURF GUITAR/ HAVA NAGILA	3.50	6.00	4.35
☐ 5010		SECRET SURFIN' SPOT/ SURFIN' AND A SWINGIN'	3.50	6.00	4.35
☐ 5048		THE SCAVENGER/WILD IDEAS	3.50	6.00	4.35
☐ 5098		THE WEDGE/NIGHT RIDER	3.50	6.00	4.35
☐ 5140		MR. ELIMINATOR/THE VICTOR	3.50	6.00	4.35
☐ 5187		GRUDGE RUN/ WILD, WILD MUSTANG	3.50	6.00	4.35
☐ 5225		GLORY WAVE/NEVER ON SUNDAY	3.50	6.00	4.35
☐ 5290		WHO CAN HE BE/OH MARIE	3.50	6.00	4.35
☐ 5389		LET'S GO TRIPPIN' '65/ WATUSI JOE	3.50	6.00	4.35
		DICK DALE—ALBUMS			
☐ 1001 (M)	*DELTONE*	SURFER'S CHOICE	19.00	49.00	45.00
☐ 1886 (M)	*CAPITOL*	SURFER'S CHOICE (reissue)	10.00	25.00	22.50
☐ 1886 (S)		SURFER'S CHOICE (reissue)	14.00	35.00	30.00
☐ 1930 (M)		KING OF THE SURF GUITAR	10.00	25.00	22.50
☐ 1930 (S)		KING OF THE SURF GUITAR	14.00	35.00	30.00
☐ 2002 (M)		CHECKERED FLAG	8.00	21.00	18.00
☐ 2002 (S)		CHECKERED FLAG	12.00	29.00	25.00
☐ 2052 (M)		MR. ELIMINATOR	8.00	21.00	18.00
☐ 2053 (S)		MR. ELIMINATOR	12.00	29.00	25.00
☐ 2111 (M)		SUMMER SURF	8.00	21.00	18.00
☐ 2111 (S)		SUMMER SURF	12.00	29.00	25.00
☐ 2293 (M)		LIVE AT CIRO'S	8.00	21.00	18.00
☐ 2292 (S)		LIVE AT CIRO'S	10.00	25.00	22.50
☐ 2095 (S)	*GNP-CRESCENDO*	GREATEST HITS	7.00	17.00	15.00

JIMMY DALE (JIMMY CLANTON)

☐ 1003	*DREW-BLAN*	EMMA LEE/MY PRIDE AND JOY	7.00	13.00	11.00

ROGER DALTRY
SEE: THE WHO

☐ 066040	*ODE*	UNDERTURE/I'M FREE	2.50	5.00	3.35
☐ 40053	*TRACK*	GIVING IT ALL AWAY/ WAY OF THE WORLD	2.50	5.00	3.35
☐ 40084		THINKING	2.50	5.00	3.35
☐ 40453	*MCA-GOLDHAWKE*	HEART'S RIGHT/ COME & GET YOUR LOVE	2.50	5.00	3.35
☐ 40512		FEELING/OCEANS AWAY	2.50	5.00	3.35
☐ 40765		SAY IT AIN'T SO, JOE/ SATIN & LACE	2.50	5.00	3.35
☐ 40800		THE PRISONER/AVENGING ANNIE	2.50	5.00	3.35
		ROGER DALTRY—ALBUMS			
☐ 328 (S)	*MCA*	DALTRY	6.00	17.00	15.00
☐ 2147 (S)		RIDE A ROCK HORSE	4.50	12.00	10.00

DANLEERS

☐ 3	*AMP*	ONE SUMMER NIGHT/ WHEELIN' AND A DEALIN'	15.00	29.00	18.50
☐ 71322	*MERCURY*	ONE SUMMER NIGHT/ WHEELIN' AND A DEALIN'	4.00	7.00	4.50
☐ 71356		MY FLAMING HEART/ I REALLY LOVE YOU	4.00	7.00	4.50
☐ 71401		A PICTURE OF YOU/ PRELUDE TO LOVE	4.00	7.00	4.50
☐ 71441		I CAN'T SLEEP/YOUR LOVE	4.00	7.00	4.50
☐ 9367	*EPIC*	IF YOU DON'T CARE/ HALF A BLOCK FROM AN ANGEL	3.50	6.00	4.00
☐ 9421		I'LL ALWAYS BE IN LOVE WITH YOU/LITTLE LOSER	3.50	6.00	4.00

			Current Price Range		P/Y AVG
☐ 1872	*SMASH*	IF/WERE YOU THERE?	3.50	6.00	4.00
☐ 1895		WHERE IS LOVE?/			
		THE ANGELS SENT YOU	3.50	6.00	4.00
☐ 19412	*EVEREST*	FOOLISH/I'M LOOKIN' AROUND .	3.50	6.00	4.00
☐ 005	*LEMANS*	THE TRUTH HURTS/			
		BABY YOU'VE GOT IT	3.50	6.00	4.00
☐ 008		I'M SORRY/			
		THIS THING CALLED LOVE	3.50	6.00	4.00

DANNY AND THE JUNIORS

☐ 711	*SINGULAR*	AT THE HOP/SOMETIMES	39.00	65.00	42.00
☐ 9871	*ABC-*				
	PARAMOUNT	AT THE HOP/SOMETIMES	3.75	6.00	4.50
☐ 9888		ROCK AND ROLL IS HERE TO STAY/			
		SCHOOL BOY ROMANCE	3.75	6.00	4.50
☐ 9926		DOTTIE/IN THE MEANTIME	3.75	6.00	4.50
☐ 9953		CRAZY CAVE/A THIEF	3.75	6.00	4.50
☐ 9978		I FEEL SO LONELY/SASSY FRAN .	3.75	6.00	4.50
☐ 10004		DO YOU LOVE ME?/			
		SOMEHOW I CAN'T FORGET . . .	3.75	6.00	4.50
☐ 10052		PLAYING HARD TO GET/OF LOVE .	3.75	6.00	4.50
☐ 4060	*SWAN*	TWISTIN' U.S.A./			
		A THOUSAND MILES AWAY . . .	3.00	5.00	3.50
☐ 4064		O HOLY NIGHT/			
		CANDY CANE, SUGARY PLUM .	4.00	7.00	4.85
☐ 4068		PONY EXPRESS/DAY DREAMER . .	3.50	5.50	4.00
☐ 4072		CHA CHA GO-GO/MR. WHISPER .	3.50	5.50	4.00
☐ 4082		BACK TO THE HOP/			
		CHARLESTON FISH	3.50	5.50	4.00
☐ 4092		TWISTIN' ALL NIGHT LONG/			
		SOME KIND OF NUT	3.50	5.50	4.00
☐ 4100		DOIN' THE CONTINENTAL WALK/			
		DO THE MASHED POTATO	3.50	5.50	4.00
☐ 4113		WE GOT SOUL/FUNNY	3.50	5.50	4.00
☐ 2076	*GUYDEN*	OO-LA-LA-LIMBO/NOW AND THEN	3.50	5.50	4.00
☐ 72240	*MERCURY*	SAD GIRL/LET'S GO SKIING	3.50	5.50	4.00
☐ 24	*RONN*	I CAN'T SEE NOBODY/MR. 'REEN	4.00	7.00	4.50
☐ 604	*TOP RANK*	TWISTIN' ALL NIGHT LONG/			
		TWISTIN' ENGLAND	3.00	5.00	3.50
☐ 18001	*CRUNCH*	LET THE GOOD TIMES ROLL/			
		AT THE HOP	3.00	5.00	3.50

DANNY AND THE JUNIORS—EP

☐ 11	*ABC-PARAMOUNT*	AT THE HOP	20.00	35.00	30.00

DANNY AND THE JUNIORS—ALBUM

☐ 506 (M)	*SWAN*	TWISTIN' ALL NIGHT LONG	29.00	65.00	60.00

DANNY AND THE MEMORIES
FEATURED: NEIL YOUNG

☐ 6049	*VALIANT*	DON'T GO/CAN'T HELP LOVIN'			
		THAT GIRL OF MINE	10.00	17.00	15.00

DANTE AND THE EVERGREENS
PRODUCERS: JAN AND DEAN

☐ 130	*MADISON*	ALLEY-OOP/THE RIGHT TIME . . .	4.00	7.00	4.50
☐ 135		TIME MACHINE/DREAM LAND . . .	4.00	7.00	4.50
☐ 143		WHAT ARE YOU DOING NEW			
		YEAR'S EVE/YEAH BABY	4.00	7.00	4.50
☐ 154		THINK SWEET THOUGHTS/			
		DA DOO	4.00	7.00	4.50

DANTE AND THE EVERGREENS—ALBUM

☐ 1002 (M)	*MADISON*	DANTE AND THE EVERGREENS . . .	25.00	58.00	35.00

DARCHAES

7001	*NOBELL*	DANNY BOY/PAIN IN MY HEART . . .	5.00	10.00	7.50

			Current Price Range		P/Y AVG

BOBBY DARIN
SEE: RINKY-DINKS

☐29883	*DECCA*	ROCK ISLAND LINE/TIMBER	15.00	29.00	18.50
☐29922		SILLY WILLIE/			
		BLUE EYED MERMAID	11.00	20.00	13.50
☐30031		HEAR THEM BELLS/			
		THE GREATEST BUILDER	11.00	20.00	13.50
☐30225		DEALER IN DREAMS/HELP ME . . .	11.00	20.00	13.50
☐30737		SILLY WILLIE/			
		DEALER IN DREAMS	9.00	16.00	11.00
☐6092	*ATCO*	I FOUND A MILLION DOLLAR			
		BABY/TALK TO ME	4.00	7.00	4.85
☐6103		PRETTY BABY/			
		DON'T CALL MY NAME	4.00	7.00	4.85
☐6109		JUST IN CASE YOU CHANGE YOUR			
		MIND/SO MEAN	4.00	7.00	4.85
☐6117		SPLISH SPLASH/			
		JUDY, DON'T BE MOODY	3.75	6.00	4.50
☐6127		QUEEN OF THE HOP/LOST LOVE .	3.75	6.00	4.50
☐6133		PLAIN JANE/WHILE I'M GONE . . .	3.75	6.00	4.50
☐6140		DREAM LOVER/BULL MOOSE . . .	3.75	6.00	4.50
☐6147		MACK THE KNIFE/			
		WAS THERE A CALL FOR ME . .	3.50	5.50	4.00
☐6158		BEYOND THE SEA/			
		THAT'S THE WAY LOVE IS	3.50	5.50	4.00
☐6161		CLEMENTINE/TALL STORY	3.50	5.50	4.00
☐6167		WON'T YOU COME HOME BILL			
		BAILEY/I'LL BE THERE	3.50	5.50	4.00
☐6173		BEACHCOMBER/AUTUMN BLUES	3.50	5.50	4.00
☐6179		ARTIFICIAL FLOWERS/			
		SOMEBODY TO LOVE	3.50	5.50	4.00
☐6183		CHRISTMAS AULD LANG SYNE/			
		CHILD OF GOD	3.50	5.50	4.00
☐6188		LAZY RIVER/OO-EE-TRAIN	3.50	5.50	4.00
☐6196		NATURE BOY/			
		LOOK FOR MY TRUE LOVE	3.50	5.50	4.00
☐6200		COME SEPTEMBER/			
		WALK BACK WITH ME	3.50	5.50	4.00
☐6206		YOU MUST HAVE BEEN A			
		BEAUTIFUL BABY/			
		SORROW TOMORROW	3.50	5.50	4.00
☐6211		AVE MARIA/			
		O COME, ALL YE FAITHFUL . . .	3.50	5.50	4.00
☐6214		IRRESISTABLE YOU/			
		MULTIPLICATION	3.50	5.50	4.00
☐6221		WHAT'D I SAY (PT. 1)/(PT. 2) . . .	3.50	5.50	4.00
☐6229		THINGS/			
		JAILER, BRING ME WATER	3.50	5.50	4.00
☐6236		BABY FACE/YOU KNOW HOW . . .	3.50	5.50	4.00
☐6244		I FOUND A NEW BABY/			
		KEEP A WALKIN'	3.50	5.50	4.00
☐6297		MILORD/GOLDEN EARRINGS	3.50	5.50	4.00
☐6316		SWING LOW, SWEET CHARIOT/			
		SIMILAU	3.50	5.50	4.00
☐6334		HARD HEARTED HANNAH/			
		MINNIE THE MOOCHER	3.50	5.50	4.00
☐4837	*CAPITOL*	IF A MAN ANSWERS/			
		TRUE TRUE LOVE	3.00	5.00	3.65
☐4897		YOU'RE THE REASON I'M LIVING/			
		NOW YOU'RE GONE	3.00	5.00	3.65
☐4970		EIGHTEEN YELLOW ROSES/			
		NOT FOR ME	3.00	5.00	3.65
☐5019		TREAT MY BABY GOOD/			
		DOWN SO LONG	3.00	5.00	3.65

BOBBY DARIN

He failed to win success on the Decca label and initial singles for Atco weren't doing any better. One night, Bobby Darin had some friends visit his New York City apartment. He told the wife of DJ Murray the K that he was trying for a catchy novelty rocker to get his career going. Murray's wife jokingly said, "Why not write something like 'splish splash, take a bath'?" Darin then sat down at his piano and composed "Splish Splash" — his first hit — in ten minutes.

His real name was Walden Robert Cassoto (his stage name was picked at random from a phone book). He was born to impoverished parents in the Bronx on May 14, 1936. Darin spent his first year of life using a dresser drawer for a bed.

As a youngster, Bobby contracted scarlet fever and suffered irreparable heart damage. As a teenager, he learned to play guitar, piano and drums. Darin attended New York's Hunter College but soon dropped out to make records.

Bobby's "Mack the Knife" became 1959's best-selling single and he was rarely off the hit charts during the late 1950s and early-to-mid 1960s.

On December 20, 1973, Bobby Darin - just 37 - died in a Los Angeles hospital during his second open-heart surgery.

150 / BOBBY DARIN

			Current Price Range		P/Y AVG
☐ 5079		BE MAD LITTLE GIRL/ SINCE YOU'VE BEEN GONE	3.00	5.00	3.65
☐ 5126		I WONDER WHO'S KISSING HER NOW/AS LONG AS I'M SINGING	3.00	5.00	3.65
☐ 5257		THE THINGS IN THIS HOUSE/ WAIT BY THE WATER	3.00	5.00	3.65
☐ 5359		HELLO, DOLLY!/ GOLDEN EARRINGS	3.00	5.00	3.65
☐ 5399		A WORLD WITHOUT YOU/VENICE	3.00	5.00	3.65
☐ 5443		WHEN I GET HOME/LONELY ROAD.	3.00	5.00	3.65
☐ 5481		THAT FUNNY FEELING/ GYP THE CAT	3.00	5.00	3.65
☐ 2305	**ATLANTIC**	FUNNY WHAT LOVE CAN DO/ WE DIDN'T ASK TO BE BROUGHT HERE	2.75	4.50	3.25
☐ 2317		THE BREAKING POINT/ SILVER DOLLAR	2.75	4.50	3.25
☐ 2329		MAME/WALKING IN THE SHADOW OF LOVE	2.75	4.50	3.25
☐ 2341		MERCI, CHERI/WHO'S AFRAID OF VIRGINIA WOOLF?	2.75	4.50	3.25
☐ 2350		IF I WERE A CARPENTER/RAININ'	2.75	4.50	3.25
☐ 2367		THE GIRL THAT STOOD BESIDE ME/REASON TO BELIEVE	2.75	4.50	3.25
☐ 2376		LOVIN' YOU/AMY	2.75	4.50	3.25
☐ 2395		THE LADY CAME FROM BALTIMORE/I AM	2.75	4.50	3.25
☐ 2420		DARLING BE HOME SOON/ HELLO, SUNSHINE	2.75	4.50	3.25
☐ 2433		SHE KNOWS/ TALK TO THE ANIMALS	2.75	4.50	3.25
☐ 2433		AFTER TODAY/ TALK TO THE ANIMALS	2.75	4.50	3.25
☐ 350	**DIRECTION**	LONG LINE RIDER/CHANGE	2.75	4.50	3.25
☐ 351		SONG FOR A DOLLAR/ ME AND MR. HOHNER	2.75	4.50	3.25
☐ 352		DISTRACTIONS/JIVE	2.75	4.50	3.25
☐ 4001		BABY MAY/SWEET REASON	2.75	4.50	3.25
☐ 4002		MAYBE WE CAN GET IT TOGETHER/ RX PYRO	2.75	4.50	3.25
☐ 1183	**MOTOWN**	SOMEDAY WE'LL BE TOGETHER/ MELODIE	2.75	4.50	3.25
☐ 1193		SIMPLE SONG OF FREEDOM/ I'LL BE YOUR BABY TONIGHT ..	2.75	4.50	3.25
☐ 1203		SAIL AWAY/ SOMETHING IN HER LOVE	2.75	4.50	3.25
☐ 1212		AVERAGE PEOPLE/ SOMETHING IN HER LOVE	2.75	4.50	3.25
☐ 1217		HAPPY/SOMETHING IN HER LOVE	2.75	4.50	3.25
		BOBBY DARIN—EPs			
☐ 2676	**DECCA**	BOBBY DARIN	20.00	35.00	30.00
☐ 4502	**ATCO**	BOBBY DARIN	8.25	14.00	12.00
☐ 4504		THAT'S ALL................	7.00	13.00	11.00
☐ 4505		BOBBY DARIN	7.00	13.00	11.00
☐ 4508		THIS IS DARIN	6.00	12.00	10.00
☐ 4512		DARIN AT THE COPA	6.00	12.00	10.00
☐ 4513		FOR TEENAGERS ONLY	6.00	12.00	10.00
		BOBBY DARIN—ALBUMS			
☐ 102 (M)	**ATCO**	BOBBY DARIN	19.00	50.00	45.00
☐ 104 (M)		THAT'S ALL................	12.00	29.00	25.00
☐ 104 (S)		THAT'S ALL................	18.00	40.00	35.00
☐ 115 (M)		THIS IS DARIN	12.00	29.00	25.00
☐ 115 (S)		THIS IS DARIN	17.00	40.00	35.00
☐ 122 (M)		DARIN AT THE COPA	10.00	25.00	22.50

			Current Price Range		P/Y AVG
☐ 122 (S)		DARIN AT THE COPA	15.00	35.00	30.00
☐ 125 (M)		25TH DAY OF DECEMBER	10.00	25.00	22.50
☐ 125 (S)		25TH DAY OF DECEMBER	15.00	35.00	30.00
☐ 126 (M)		TWO OF A KIND (with Johnny Mercer)	9.00	25.00	22.50
☐ 126 (S)		TWO OF A KIND (with Johnny Mercer)	14.00	35.00	30.00
☐ 131 (M)		THE BOBBY DARIN STORY (greatest hits)	9.00	25.00	22.50
☐ 131 (S)		THE BOBBY DARIN STORY (greatest hits)	14.00	35.00	30.00
		FIRST PRESSES FEATURE A WHITE ALBUM COVER ON 131			
☐ 134 (M)		LOVE SWINGS	8.00	21.00	18.00
☐ 134 (S)		LOVE SWINGS	9.00	25.00	22.50
☐ 138 (M)		TWIST WITH BOBBY DARIN	8.00	21.00	18.00
☐ 138 (S)		TWIST WITH BOBBY DARIN	9.00	25.00	22.50
☐ 140 (M)		BOBBY DARIN SINGS RAY CHARLES	8.00	21.00	18.00
☐ 140 (S)		BOBBY DARIN SINGS RAY CHARLES	9.00	25.00	22.50
☐ 146 (M)		THINGS AND OTHER THINGS	8.00	21.00	18.00
☐ 146 (S)		THINGS AND OTHER THINGS	9.00	25.00	22.50
☐ 167 (S)		BOBBY DARIN WINNERS	8.00	21.00	18.00
☐ 1001 (M)		FOR TEENAGERS ONLY	12.00	29.00	25.00
☐ 1791 (M)	*CAPITOL*	OH! LOOK AT ME NOW	7.00	17.00	15.00
☐ 1791 (S)		OH! LOOK AT ME NOW	8.00	21.00	18.00
☐ 1826 (M)		EARTHY	7.00	17.00	15.00
☐ 1826 (S)		EARTHY	8.00	21.00	18.00
☐ 1866 (M)		YOU'RE THE REASON I'M LIVING	7.00	17.00	15.00
☐ 1866 (S)		YOU'RE THE REASON I'M LIVING	8.00	21.00	18.00
☐ 1942 (M)		18 YELLOW ROSES	7.00	17.00	15.00
☐ 1942 (S)		18 YELLOW ROSES	8.00	21.00	18.00
☐ 2007 (M)		GOLDEN FOLK HITS	7.00	17.00	15.00
☐ 2007 (S)		GOLDEN FOLK HITS	8.00	21.00	18.00
☐ 2194 (M)		FROM HELLO DOLLY TO GOODBYE CHARLIE	7.00	17.00	15.00
☐ 2194 (S)		FROM HELLO DOLLY TO GOODBYE CHARLIE	8.00	21.00	18.00
☐ 2322 (M)		VENICE BLUE	7.00	17.00	15.00
☐ 2322 (S)		VENICE BLUE	8.00	21.00	18.00
☐ 2571 (M)		BEST OF BOBBY DARIN	6.00	17.00	15.00
☐ 2571 (S)		BEST OF BOBBY DARIN	7.00	21.00	18.00
☐ 8121 (M)	*ATLANTIC*	THE SHADOW OF YOUR SMILE . . .	5.50	14.00	12.00
☐ 8121 (S)		THE SHADOW OF YOUR SMILE . . .	7.00	17.00	15.00
☐ 8126 (M)		IN A BROADWAY BAG	5.50	14.00	12.00
☐ 8126 (S)		IN A BROADWAY BAG	7.00	17.00	15.00
☐ 8135 (M)		IF I WERE A CARPENTER	5.50	12.00	10.00
☐ 8135 (S)		IF I WERE A CARPENTER	6.00	15.00	13.50
☐ 8142 (M)		INSIDE OUT	5.00	12.00	10.00
☐ 8142 (S)		INSIDE OUT	6.00	15.00	13.50
☐ 8154 (M)		BOBBY DARIN SINGS DOCTOR DOLITTLE	5.00	12.00	10.00
☐ 8154 (S)		BOBBY DARIN SINGS DOCTOR DOLITTLE	6.00	15.00	13.50
☐ 1936 (S)	*DIRECTION*	BOBBY DARIN	5.00	12.00	10.00
☐ 1937 (S)		COMMITMENT	5.00	12.00	10.00
☐ 753 (S)	*MOTOWN*	BOBBY DARIN	5.00	12.00	10.00
☐ 813 (S)		DARIN: 1936-1973	5.00	12.00	10.00

DARREL AND THE OXFORDS (TOKENS)

☐ 4174	*ROULETTE*	PICTURE IN MY WALLET/ ROSES ARE RED	6.00	12.00	10.00
☐ 4230		CAN'T YOU TELL?/ YOUR MOTHER SAID NO	6.00	12.00	10.00

			Current Price Range		P/Y AVG
		JAMES DARREN			
☐102	**COLPIX**	THERE'S NO SUCH THING/			
		MIGHTY PRETTY TERRITORY ..	4.00	7.00	4.85
☐113		GIDGET/YOU	3.50	6.00	4.35
☐119		ANGEL FACE/			
		I DON'T WANNA LOSE YA	3.50	6.00	4.35
☐128		LOVE AMONG THE YOUNG/			
		I AIN'T SHARIN' SHARON	3.25	5.50	4.00
☐130		TEENAGE TEARS/			
		LET THERE BE LOVE	3.25	5.50	4.00
☐138		YOU ARE MY DREAM/			
		YOUR SMILE	3.25	5.50	4.00
☐142		BECAUSE THEY'RE YOUNG/			
		TEARS IN MY EYES	3.25	5.50	4.00
☐145		TRAVELING DOWN A LONESOME			
		ROAD/P.S., I LOVE YOU	3.25	5.50	4.00
☐168		MAN ABOUT TOWN/			
		COME ON MY LOVE	3.25	5.50	4.00
☐189		GIDGET GOES HAWAIIAN/			
		WILD ABOUT THAT GIRL	3.25	5.50	4.00
☐609		GOODBYE CRUEL WORLD/			
		VALERIE	3.00	5.00	3.65
☐622		HER ROYAL MAJESTY/IF I COULD			
		ONLY TELL YOU	3.00	5.00	3.65
☐630		CONSCIENCE/DREAM BIG	3.00	5.00	3.65
☐644		MARY'S LITTLE LAMB/			
		THE LIFE OF THE PARTY	3.00	5.00	3.85
☐655		HAIL TO THE CONQUERING HERO/			
		TOO YOUNG TO GO STEADY . . .	3.00	5.00	3.85
☐664		HEAR WHAT I WANT TO HEAR/			
		I'LL BE LOVING YOU	3.00	5.00	3.85
☐672.		PIN A MEDAL ON JOEY/			
		DIAMOND HEAD	3.00	5.00	3.85
☐685		THEY SHOULD HAVE GIVEN YOU			
		THE OSCAR/BLAME IT ON			
		MY YOUTH	3.00	5.00	3.85
☐696		GEGETTA/			
		GRANDE LUNA, ITALIANO	3.00	5.00	3.85
☐708		UNDER THE YUM YUM TREE/			
		BACKSTAGE	3.00	5.00	3.85
☐758		JUST THINK OF TONIGHT/			
		PUNCH AND JUDY	3.00	5.00	3.85
☐765		A MARRIED MAN/			
		BABY, TALK TO ME	3.00	5.00	3.85
☐5648	**WARNER BROTHERS**	BECAUSE YOU'RE MINE/			
		MILLIONS OF ROSES	3.00	5.00	3.85
☐5689		I WANT TO BE LONELY/			
		TOMMY HAWK	3.00	5.00	3.85
☐5812		WHERE DID WE GO WRONG?/			
		COUNTING THE CRACKS	3.00	5.00	3.85
☐5838		CRAZY ME/THEY DON'T KNOW ..	3.00	5.00	3.85
☐5874		ALL/MISTY MORNING EYES	3.00	5.00	3.85
☐7071		THE HOUSE SONG/			
		THEY DON'T KNOW	3.00	5.00	3.85
☐7152		CHERIE/WAIT UNTIL DARK	3.00	5.00	3.85
		JAMES DARREN—ALBUMS			
☐406 (M)	**COLPIX**	ALBUM NO. 1	9.00	25.00	22.50
☐418 (M)		GIDGET GOES HAWAIIAN	6.00	15.00	13.50
☐418 (S)		GIDGET GOES HAWAIIAN	8.00	21.00	18.00
☐424 (M)		JAMES DARREN SINGS			
		FOR ALL SIZES	7.00	17.00	15.00
☐428 (M)		LOVE AMONG THE YOUNG	7.00	17.00	15.00

			Current Price Range		P/Y AVG
☐ 1688 (M)	**WARNER BROTHERS**	ALL	6.00	15.00	13.50
☐ 1688 (S)		ALL	7.00	17.00	15.00
		DARTELLS			
☐ 509	**ARLEN**	HOT PASTRAMI/DARTELL STOMP	5.50	11.00	9.00
☐ 513		DANCE, EVERYBODY, DANCE/			
		THE SCOOBIE SONG	4.50	7.50	6.00
☐ 16453	**DOT**	HOT PASTRAMI/DARTELL STOMP	2.75	5.00	3.00
☐ 16502		DANCE, EVERYONE, DANCE/			
		THE SCOOBIE SONG	2.75	5.00	3.00
		DARTELLS—ALBUM			
☐ 3522 (M)	**DOT**	HOT PASTRAMI	7.00	17.00	15.00
☐ 25522 (S)		HOT PASTRAMI	9.00	25.00	22.50
		DAVID AND JONATHAN			
☐ 5563	**CAPITOL**	MICHELLE/HOW BITTER THE			
		TASTE OF LOVE	2.75	5.00	3.00
☐ 5625		SPEAK HER NAME/I KNOW	2.75	5.00	3.00
☐ 5700		LOVERS OF THE WORLD UNITE/			
		OH MY WORD	2.75	5.00	3.00
☐ 5777		TIME/THE MAGIC BOOK	2.75	5.00	3.00
☐ 5870		LOOKIN' FOR MY LIFE/			
		TEN STORIES HIGH	2.75	5.00	3.00
☐ 5934		SHE'S LEAVING HOME/			
		ONE MORE EVERY MINUTE	2.75	5.00	3.00
		DAVID AND JONATHAN—ALBUM			
☐ 2473 (M)	**CAPITOL**	MICHELLE	8.00	21.00	18.00
☐ 2473 (S)		MICHELLE	9.00	25.00	22.50
		DAVID & LEE			
		FEATURED: DAVID GATES			
☐ 1	**GSP**	SAD SEPTEMBER/THINKING OF			
		YOU	5.00	15.00	13.50
		ANDREA DAVIS (MINNIE RIPERTON)			
☐ 1980	**CHESS**	LONELY GIRL/			
		YOU GAVE ME SOUL	6.00	10.00	7.50
		DAVE DAVIES			
		SEE: KINKS			
☐ 0614	**REPRISE**	DEATH OF A CLOWN/LOVE ME			
		TILL THE SUN SHINES	5.00	8.50	7.00
☐ 0660		SUSANNAH'S STILL ALIVE/			
		FUNNY FACE	5.00	8.50	7.00
		SPENCER DAVIS GROUP			
		FEATURED: STEVIE WINWOOD			
☐ 6400	**ATCO**	KEEP ON RUNNIN'/			
		HIGH TIME BABY	3.25	5.50	4.00
☐ 6416		SOMEBODY HELP ME/			
		STEVIE'S BLUES	3.25	5.50	4.00
☐ 50108	**UNITED ARTISTS**	GIMMIE SOME LOVIN'/			
		BLUES IN F	3.00	5.25	3.85
☐ 50144		I'M A MAN/			
		CAN'T GET ENOUGH OF IT	3.00	5.25	3.85
☐ 50162		SOMEBODY HELP ME/			
		ON THE GREEN LIGHT	3.00	5.25	3.85
☐ 50202		TIME SELLER/			
		DON'T WANT YOU NO MORE ...	3.00	5.25	3.85
☐ 50286		AFTER TEA/LOOKING BACK	3.00	5.25	3.85

			Current Price Range		P/Y AVG
SPENCER DAVIS GROUP—ALBUMS					
☐3578 (M)	**UNITED ARTISTS**	GIMMIE SOME LOVIN'	7.00	17.00	15.00
☐6578 (S)		GIMMIE SOME LOVIN'	9.00	25.00	22.50
☐3589 (M)		I'M A MAN	7.00	17.00	15.00
☐6589 (S)		I'M A MAN	9.00	25.00	22.50
☐3641 (M)		SPENCER DAVIS GREATEST HITS	6.00	15.00	13.50
☐6641 (S)		SPENCER DAVIS GREATEST HITS	8.00	21.00	18.00
☐3652 (M)		WITH THEIR NEW FACE ON	6.00	15.00	13.50
☐6652 (S)		WITH THEIR NEW FACE ON	8.00	21.00	18.00
☐6691 (S)		HEAVIES	6.00	15.00	13.50
DARLENE DAY					
☐106	**MUSIC MAKERS**	I LOVE YOU SO/WILL	14.00	29.00	25.00
TERRY DAY (TERRY MELCHER)					
		SEE: BRUCE AND TERRY			
☐42427	**COLUMBIA**	THAT'S ALL I WANT/ I WAITED TOO LONG	6.00	11.00	7.00
☐42678		BE A SOLDIER/I LOVE YOU BETTY	6.00	11.00	7.00
BOBBY DEAN					
☐4006	**PROFILE**	JUST BETWEEN TEENS/ IT'S A FAD	9.50	22.00	20.00
☐1710	**CHESS**	GO MR. DILLON/I'M READY	6.00	13.00	11.00
JANET DEANE					
		FEATURED: SKYLINERS			
☐719	**GATEWAY**	ANOTHER NIGHT ALONE/ I'M GLAD I WAITED	5.00	9.00	7.00
DAVE DEE, DOZY, BEAKY, MICK AND TICH					
☐1537	**FONTANA**	YOU MAKE IT MOVE/NO TIME	3.00	5.00	3.50
☐1545		HOLD TIGHT/ YOU KNOW WHAT I WANT	3.00	5.00	3.50
☐1553		HIDEAWAY/HERE'S A HEART	3.00	5.00	3.50
☐1569		BEND IT/SHE'S SO GOOD TO ME	3.00	5.00	3.50
☐1591		OKAY/MASTER LLEWELLYN	3.00	5.00	3.50
☐66270	**IMPERIAL**	ZABADAK/THE SUN GOES DOWN	2.75	5.00	3.00
☐66287		LEGEND OF XANADU/PLEASE	2.75	5.00	3.00
☐66319		BREAKOUT/MRS. THURSDAY	2.75	5.00	3.00
☐66339		MARGARITA LIDMAN/ WRECK OF THE ANTOINETTE	2.75	5.00	3.00
DAVE DEE, DOZY, BEAKY, MICK AND TICH—ALBUMS					
☐27567 (M)	**FONTANA**	GREATEST HITS	8.25	14.00	12.00
☐67567 (S)		GREATEST HITS	12.00	22.00	20.00
☐12402 (M)	**IMPERIAL**	TIME TO TAKE OFF	7.00	13.00	11.00
☐15402 (S)		TIME TO TAKE OFF	9.50	17.00	15.00
JACKIE DEE (JACKIE DeSHANNON)					
☐5008	**GONE**	I'LL BE TRUE/HOW WRONG WAS I	6.00	12.00	10.00
☐55148	**LIBERTY**	BUDDY/STROLYPSO DANCE	4.50	7.50	6.00
JOEY DEE					
☐7009	**BONUS**	LORRAINE/ THE GIRL I WALK TO SCHOOL	5.00	9.00	6.00
☐1210	**SCEPTER**	THE FACE OF AN ANGEL/ SHIMMY BABY	5.00	9.00	6.00
JOEY DEE AND THE STARLITERS					
☐5539	**JUBILEE**	DANCIN' ON THE BEACH/ GOOD LITTLE YOU	5.00	9.00	6.00
☐5554		SHE'S SO EXCEPTIONAL/ IT'S GOT YOU	5.00	9.00	6.00

			Current Price Range		P/Y AVG
☐5566		YOU CAN'T SIT DOWN/			
		PUT YOUR HEART IN IT	5.00	9.00	6.00
☐4401	ROULETTE	PEPPERMINT TWIST (PT. 1)/			
		(PT. 2)	3.50	6.00	4.00
☐4408		HEY, LET'S TWIST/ROLY POLY	3.50	6.00	4.00
☐4416		SHOUT (PT. 1)/(PT. 2)	3.50	6.00	4.00
☐4431		EVERYTIME (PT. 1)/(PT. 2)	3.50	6.00	4.00
☐4438		WHAT KIND OF LOVE IS THIS?/			
		WING DING	3.50	6.00	4.00
☐4456		I LOST MY BABY/KEEP YOUR			
		MIND ON WHAT YOU'RE DOIN'	3.50	6.00	4.00
☐4467		BABY, YOU'RE DRIVING ME			
		CRAZY/HELP ME PICK UP			
		THE PIECES	3.50	6.00	4.00
☐4488		HOT PASTRAMI WITH MASHED			
		POTATOES (PT. 1)/(PT. 2)	3.50	6.00	4.00
☐4503		DANCE, DANCE, DANCE/			
		LET'S HAVE A PARTY	3.50	6.00	4.00
☐4525		FANNIE MAE/YA YA	3.50	6.00	4.00
☐4539		DOWN BY THE RIVERSIDE/			
		GETTING NEARER	3.50	6.00	4.00
	JOEY DEE AND THE STARLITERS—ALBUMS				
☐503 (M)	SCEPTER	PEPPERMINT TWISTERS	9.00	25.00	22.50
☐25166 (M)	ROULETTE	DOIN' THE TWIST AT THE			
		PEPPERMINT LOUNGE	7.00	17.00	15.00
☐25166 (S)		DOIN' THE TWIST AT THE			
		PEPPERMINT LOUNGE	9.00	25.00	22.50
☐25168 (M)		HEY, LET'S TWIST	7.00	17.00	15.00
☐25168 (S)		HEY, LET'S TWIST	9.00	25.00	22.50
☐25171 (M)		ALL THE WORLD IS TWISTIN'	6.00	15.00	13.50
☐25171 (S)		ALL THE WORLD IS TWISTIN'	8.00	21.00	18.00
☐25173 (M)		BACK AT THE PEPPERMINT			
		LOUNGE	6.00	15.00	13.50
☐25173 (S)		BACK AT THE PEPPERMINT			
		LOUNGE	7.00	21.00	18.00
☐25182 (M)		TWO TICKETS TO PARIS			
		(soundtrack)	7.00	17.00	15.00
☐25182 (S)		TWO TICKETS TO PARIS			
		(soundtrack)	9.00	25.00	22.50
☐25197 (M)		JOEY DEE	6.00	15.00	13.50
☐25197 (S)		JOEY DEE	8.00	21.00	18.00
☐25221 (M)		DANCE, DANCE, DANCE	6.00	15.00	13.50
☐25221 (S)		DANCE, DANCE, DANCE	8.00	21.00	18.00
	JOHNNY DEE (JOHN D. LOUDERMILK)				
☐430	COLONIAL	SITTIN' IN THE BALCONY/			
		A-PLUS IN LOVE	7.50	15.00	10.00
☐433		TEENAGE QUEEN/			
		IT'S GOTTA BE YOU	6.00	10.50	9.00
	TOMMY DEE				
☐1057	CREST	THREE STARS/			
		I'LL NEVER CHANGE	3.75	6.00	4.50
☐1067		ANGEL OF LOVE/			
		MERRY CHRISTMAS, MARY	3.50	5.50	4.00
☐5905	PIKE	LOOK HOMEWARD DEAR ANGEL/			
		A LITTLE DOG CRIED	3.50	5.50	4.00
☐59087	CHALLENGE	BALLAD OF A DRAG RACE/			
		THE STORY OF SUSIE	3.00	5.00	3.50
☐1061	CREST	THE CHAIR/HELLO LONESOME	3.00	5.00	3.50
	DEEP PURPLE				
	SEE: EPISODE SIX				
☐1503	TETRA-GRAMMATON	HUSH/ONE MORE RAINY DAY	3.00	5.50	3.85

			Current Price Range		P/Y AVG
☐ 1508		KENTUCKY WOMAN/HARD ROAD	3.00	5.50	3.85
☐ 1514		RIVER DEEP-MOUNTAIN HIGH/ LISTEN, LEARN, READ ON	3.00	5.50	3.85
☐ 1519		THE BIRD HAS FLOWN/ EMMARETTA	3.00	5.50	3.85
☐ 1537		HALLELUJAH (I AM THE PREACHER)/APRIL (PT. 1)	3.00	5.50	3.85
☐ 7504	**WARNER BROTHERS**	BLACK NIGHT/INTO THE FIRE ...	3.50	6.00	4.00
☐ 7528		FIREBALL/I'M ALONE	3.50	6.00	4.00
☐ 7572		WHEN A BLIND MAN CRIES/ NEVER BEFORE	3.50	6.00	4.00
☐ 7595		STRANGE KIND OF WOMAN/ I'M ALONE	3.50	6.00	4.00
☐ 7634		HIGHWAY STAR/HIGHWAY STAR (Long Version)	3.50	6.00	4.00
☐ 7672		WOMAN FROM TOKYO/ SUPER TROUPER	2.75	5.00	3.00
☐ 7710		SMOKE ON THE WATER/ SMOKE ON THE WATER (Live) ..	2.50	4.50	2.50
☐ 7737		WOMAN FROM TOKYO/ SUPER TROUPER	2.75	5.00	3.00
☐ 7784		MIGHT JUST TAKE YOUR LIFE/ CORONARIES REDIG	2.75	5.00	3.00
☐ 7809		BURN/CORONARIES REDIG	2.75	5.00	3.00
☐ 8049		HIGHBALL SHOOTER/ YOU CAN'T DO IT RIGHT	2.75	5.00	3.00
☐ 8069		STORMBRINGER/ LOVE DON'T MEAN A THING ...	2.75	5.00	3.00
☐ 8182		GETTING TIGHTER/(DJ)	2.75	5.00	3.00

WARNER BROTHERS ALBUMS ARE WORTH UP TO $9.00 MINT

DEEP PURPLE—ALBUMS

☐ 102 (S)	**TETRA- GRAMMATON**	SHADES OF DEEP PURPLE	7.00	17.00	10.00
☐ 107 (S)		BOOK OF TALIESYN	7.00	17.00	10.00
☐ 119 (S)		DEEP PURPLE	7.00	17.00	10.00

TONY DELL

☐ 5766	**KING**	MAGIC WAND/MY GIRL	17.00	35.00	30.00

DELLS
SEE: EL-RAYS

☐ 134	**VEE JAY**	TELL THE WORLD/ FLIP BY COUNT MORRIS	110.00	200.00	125.00
☐ 166		DREAMS ON CONTENTMENT/ ZING ZING ZING	45.00	90.00	52.00
☐ 204		OH WHAT A NITE/JO JO	9.00	17.00	11.00
☐ 230		MOVIN' ON/I WANNA GO HOME .	9.00	17.00	11.00
☐ 236		WHY DO YOU HAVE TO GO?/ DANCE DANCE DANCE	9.00	17.00	11.00
☐ 251		A DISTANT LOVE/O-BOP SHE-BOP	9.00	17.00	11.00
☐ 258		PAIN IN MY HEART/ TIME MAKES YOU CHANGE ...	7.25	14.00	12.00
☐ 274		WHAT YOU SAY BABY/ THE SPRINGER	8.25	14.00	12.00
☐ 292		I'M CALLING/JEEPERS CREEPERS.	9.50	17.00	15.00
☐ 300		MY BEST GIRL/WEDDING DAY ...	9.50	17.00	15.00
☐ 324		DRY YOUR EYES/ BABY OPEN UP YOUR HEART ..	8.25	14.00	12.00
☐ 338		OH WHAT A NITE/ I WANNA GO HOME	5.50	11.00	9.00
☐ 376		SWINGIN' TEENS/HOLD ON TO WHAT YOU'VE GOT	5.50	11.00	9.00
☐ 595		SHY GIRL/WHAT DO WE PROVE? .	5.00	9.00	7.00

			Current Price Range		P/Y AVG
☐615		OH WHAT A GOOD NIGHT/ WAIT 'TIL TOMORROW	5.00	9.00	7.00
☐674		STAY IN MY CORNER/ IT'S NOT UNUSUAL	4.00	9.00	7.00
☐712		HEY SUGAR (DON'T GET SERIOUS)/POOR LITTLE BOY ..	5.00	9.00	7.00
☐5415	ARGO	GOD BLESS THE CHILD/ I'M GOING HOME	3.75	6.00	4.50
☐5428		THE (BOSSA NOVA) BIRD/ ETERNALLY	3.75	6.00	4.50
☐5442		IF IT AIN'T ONE THING IT'S ANOTHER/HI DIDDLEY DEE DUM DUM	3.75	6.00	4.50
☐5456		AFTER YOU/GOODBYE MARY ANN	3.75	6.00	4.50
		DELLS—ALBUMS			
☐1010 (M)	VEE JAY	OH WHAT A NITE	20.00	50.00	45.00
☐1141 (M)		IT'S NOT UNUSUAL............	10.00	25.00	22.50
		DELL-VIKINGS			
☐106	LUNIVERSE	OVER THE RAINBOW/ HEY SENORITA	17.00	30.00	25.00
☐114		GIRL, GIRL/THERE I GO	15.00	25.00	22.00
☐205	FEE BEE	COME GO WITH ME/ HOW CAN I FIND TRUE LOVE ..	40.00	65.00	60.00
☐210		TRUE LOVE/UH UH BABY	8.25	14.00	12.00
☐214		WHISPERING BELLS/ DON'T BE A FOOL	26.00	45.00	40.00
☐66	ALPINE	PISTOL PACKIN' MAMA/THE SUN	8.25	14.00	12.00
☐15538	DOT	COME GO WITH ME/ HOW CAN I FIND TRUE LOVE ..	4.00	7.00	4.85
☐15571		WHAT MADE MAGGIE RUN/ LITTLE BILLY BOY	4.00	7.00	4.85
☐15592		WHISPERING BELLS/ DON'T BE A FOOL	4.00	7.00	4.85
☐15636		I'M SPINNING/ WHEN I COME HOME	4.00	7.00	4.85
☐71132	MERCURY	COOL SHAKE/JITTERBUG MARY .	3.75	6.00	4.50
☐71880		COME ALONG WITH ME/ WHAT 'CHA GOTTA LOSE	3.75	6.00	4.50
☐71241		YOUR BOOK OF LOVE/ SNOWBOUND	3.75	6.00	4.50
☐71266		THE VOODOO MAN/CAN'T WAIT .	3.75	6.00	4.50
		DELL-VIKINGS—EPs			
☐1058	DOT	COME GO WITH US	16.00	29.00	19.00
☐3362	MERCURY	THEY SING - THEY SWING	16.00	29.00	19.00
		DELL-VIKINGS—ALBUMS			
☐1000 (M)	LUNIVERSE	COME GO WITH THE DELL- VIKINGS	65.00	160.00	150.00
☐1003 (M)	DOT	BEST OF THE DELL-VIKINGS	44.00	115.00	110.00
☐20314 (M)	MERCURY	THEY SING - THEY SWING	55.00	145.00	135.00
		EDDIE DELMAR			
☐168	MADISON	BLANCHE/LOVE BELLS	14.00	26.00	24.00
		DEMENSIONS			
☐116	MOHAWK	OVER THE RAINBOW/ NURSERY RHYME ROCK	4.00	7.00	4.75
☐120		DON'T TAKE YOUR LOVE FROM ME/ZING! WENT THE STRINGS OF MY HEART	4.00	7.00	4.75
☐121		AVE MARIA/GOD'S CHRISTMAS .	4.00	7.00	4.75
☐123		A TEAR FELL/THERESA	4.00	7.00	4.75
☐62277	CORAL	COUNT YOUR BLESSINGS INSTEAD OF SHEEP/AGAIN ...	3.50	5.50	4.00

			Current Price Range		P/Y AVG
☐ 62293		AS TIME GOES BY/ SEVEN DAYS A WEEK	3.50	5.50	4.00
☐ 62323		YOUNG AT HEART/ YOUR CHEATIN' HEART	3.50	5.50	4.00
☐ 62344		MY FOOLISH HEART/ JUST ONE MORE CHANCE	3.50	5.50	4.00
☐ 62359		FLY ME TO THE MOON/ YOU'LL NEVER KNOW	3.00	5.25	3.85
☐ 62382		JUST A SHOULDER TO CRY ON/ DON'T WORRY ABOUT BOBBY .	3.00	5.25	3.85
☐ 62392		DON'T CRY PRETTY BABY/ A LITTLE WHITE GARDENIA ...	3.00	5.25	3.85
☐ 62432		THIS TIME NEXT YEAR/ MY OLD GIRL FRIEND	3.00	5.25	3.85
☐ 62444		ONCE A DAY/ TING-A-LING-TING-TOY	3.00	5.25	3.85
		DEMENSIONS—ALBUM			
☐ 57430 (M)	*CORAL*	MY FOOLISH HEART	30.00	65.00	55.00

DENNIS AND THE EXPLORERS

☐ 62147	*CORAL*	ON A CLEAR NIGHT/ VISION OF LOVE	8.25	17.00	15.00
☐ 62295		EVERY ROAD/REMEMBER	5.50	12.00	10.00

DENNY AND THE DEDICATIONS

☐ 45-111	*SUSAN*	LOST LOVE/I'LL SHOW YOU HOW TO LOVE ME	5.00	10.00	7.50

LEE DENSON
GUITAR: EDDIE COCHRAN

☐ 0281	*VIK*	NEW SHOES/ CLIMB LOVE MOUNTAIN	8.25	14.00	12.00

JOHN DENVER

☐ 74-0275	*RCA*	I WISH I KNEW/DAYDREAM	5.00	9.00	7.00
☐ SPS-45-217		JIMMY NEWMAN (promotion release, not for sale)	6.00	12.00	10.00
☐ 74-0305		ANTHEM (REVELATION)	4.00	8.00	6.00
☐ 74-0332		ISABEL/FOLLOW ME...........	4.00	8.00	6.00
☐ 74-0376		SAIL AWAY HOME/I WISH I COULD HAVE BEEN THERE	5.00	9.00	7.00
☐ 74-0391		MR. BOJANGLES/ WHOSE GARDEN WAS THIS? ..	3.75	7.00	5.50
☐ 74-0445		TAKE ME HOME COUNTRY ROADS/ POEMS, PRAYERS, PROMISES .	2.75	6.00	4.00
☐ 74-0567		STARWOOD IN ASPEN/ FRIENDS WITH YOU	2.75	6.00	4.00
☐ 74-0647		CITY OF NEW ORLEANS/ EVERYDAY	3.50	6.50	5.00
☐ 74-0737		THE EAGLE & THE HAWK/ GOODBYE AGAIN	3.50	6.50	5.00
☐ 74-0829		ROCKY MOUNTAIN HIGH/SPRING	2.75	5.50	4.00
☐ APBO-0067		FAREWELL ANDROMEDA/ WHISKEY BASIN BLUES	2.75	5.50	4.00
☐ APBO-0182		ROCKY MOUNTAIN SUITE/ PLEASE DADDY	2.75	5.50	4.00
☐ 74-0801		LATE WINTER, EARLY SPRING/ HARD LIFE, HARD TIMES	3.50	6.50	5.00
☐ 74-0955		SUNSHINE ON MY SHOULDERS/ I'D RATHER BE A COWBOY	4.00	8.00	6.50
☐ PB-10065		IT'S UP TO YOU/ BACK HOME AGAIN	2.75	6.00	4.00
☐ PB-10148		SUMMER/SWEET SURRENDER ..	2.75	6.00	4.00

			Current Price Range		P/Y AVG
APBO-0213		SUNSHINE ON MY SHOULDERS/ AROUND & AROUND	2.75	6.00	4.00
APBO-0295		ANNIE'S SONG/COOL AN' GREEN	2.75	6.00	4.00
DJBO-0213		SUNSHINE ON MY SHOULDERS (DJ pressing)	4.50	8.50	7.00

LATER RCA SINGLES ARE WORTH UP TO $4.00 MINT

JOHN DENVER—ALBUMS

			Current Price Range		P/Y AVG
66 (S)	HJD	JOHN DENVER SINGS	19.00	65.00	60.00
DLJ1-0683 (S)	RCA	JOHN DENVER (DJ issue)	7.00	24.00	20.00
AQL1-3075 (S)		JOHN DENVER	4.00	11.00	9.00
LSP-4207 (S)		RHYMES & REASONS	5.00	15.00	13.50
LSP-4278 (S)		TAKE ME TO TOMORROW	5.00	15.00	13.50
LSP-4414 (S)		WHOSE GARDEN WAS THIS?	4.50	12.00	10.00
LSP-4499 (S)		POEMS, PRAYERS & PROMISES	5.00	15.00	13.50
LSP-4607 (S)		AERIE	5.00	15.00	13.50
LSP-4731 (S)		ROCKY MOUNTAIN HIGH	4.50	12.00	10.00
RS-1050 (S)		LIVE IN LONDON	4.50	12.00	10.00
APL1-1183 (S)		WINDSONG	5.00	14.00	12.00
APL1-1201 (S)		ROCKY MOUNTAIN CHRISTMAS	4.50	12.00	10.00
APL1-1694 (S)		SPIRIT	4.50	12.00	10.00
APL2-1263 (S)		ROCKY MOUNTAIN CHRISTMAS/ WINDSONG	4.50	12.00	10.00

DEREK (JOHNNY CYMBAL)

558	BANG	CINNAMON/THIS IS MY STORY	2.50	4.50	2.50
566		BACK DOOR MAN/ SELL YOUR SOUL	2.50	4.50	2.50
571		INSIDE OUT - OUTSIDE IN/ SELL YOUR SOUL	2.50	4.50	2.50

JACKIE DeSHANNON
SEE: JACKIE DEE, JACKIE SHANNON

416	EDISON INTERNATIONAL	I WANNA GO HOME/SO WARM	5.00	9.00	6.25
418		PUT MY BABY DOWN/ THE FOOLISH ONE	5.00	9.00	6.25
55288	LIBERTY	LONELY GIRL/TEACH ME	3.75	6.50	4.75
55342		THINK ABOUT YOU/HEAVEN IS BEING WITH YOU	3.75	6.50	4.75
55358		WISH I COULD FIND A BOY/ I WON'T TURN YOU DOWN	3.75	6.50	4.75
55387		BABY (WHEN YA KISS ME)/ AIN'T THAT LOVE	3.50	6.50	4.60
55425		THE PRINCE/I'LL DROWN IN MY OWN TEARS	3.50	6.50	4.60
55425		THE PRINCE/THAT'S WHAT BOYS ARE MADE OF	3.25	5.50	4.00
55484		JUST LIKE IN THE MOVIES/ GUESS WHO	3.25	5.50	4.00
55497		YOU WON'T FORGET ME/I DON'T THINK SO MUCH OF MYSELF	3.50	6.25	4.65
55526		FADED LOVE/ DANCING SILHOUETTES	3.50	6.25	4.65
55563		NEEDLES AND PINS/DID HE CALL TODAY, MAMA?	3.50	6.25	4.65
55602		LITTLE YELLOW ROSES/ OH SWEET CHARIOT	3.50	6.25	4.65
55602		LITTLE YELLOW ROSES/ 500 MILES	3.50	6.25	4.65
55645		WHEN YOU WALK IN THE ROOM/ TILL YOU SAY YOU'RE MINE	3.50	6.25	4.65
55678		OH BOY!/I'M LOOKIN' FOR SOMEONE TO LOVE	3.50	6.25	4.65

			Current Price Range		P/Y AVG
☐ 55705		SHE DON'T UNDERSTAND HIM LIKE I DO/ HOLD YOUR HEAD HIGH	3.50	6.25	4.65
☐ 55730		HE'S GOT THE WHOLE WORLD IN IN HIS HANDS/IT'S LOVE BABY	3.50	6.25	4.65
☐ 55735		OVER YOU/WHEN YOU WALK IN THE ROOM	3.50	6.25	4.65
☐ 56187		IT'S SO NICE/ MEDITERRANEAN SKY	3.50	6.25	4.65
☐ 13349	MGM	LOVE AND LEARN/ I'M GLAD IT'S YOU	3.25	5.50	4.00
☐ 66110	IMPERIAL	WHAT THE WORLD NEEDS NOW IS LOVE/REMEMBER THE BOY ...	3.00	5.25	3.85
☐ 66132		A LIFETIME OF LONELINESS/ DON'T TURN YOUR BACK ON ME	3.00	5.25	3.85
☐ 66171		COME AND GET ME/ SPLENDOR IN THE GRASS	3.00	5.25	3.85
☐ 66202		I CAN MAKE IT WITH YOU/ TO BE MYSELF	3.00	5.25	3.85
☐ 66224		COME ON DOWN/FIND ME LOVE .	3.00	5.25	3.85
☐ 66236		WHERE DOES THE SUN GO?/ THE WISHING DOLL	3.00	5.25	3.85
☐ 66251		IT'S ALL IN THE GAME/ CHANGIN' MY MIND	3.00	5.25	3.85
☐ 66281		ME ABOUT YOU/ I KEEP WANTING YOU	3.00	5.25	3.85
☐ 66301		NOBODY'S HOME TO GO HOME TO/NICOLE	3.00	5.25	3.85
☐ 66312		I DIDN'T WANT TO HAVE TO DO IT/SPLENDOR IN THE GRASS ..	3.00	5.25	3.85
☐ 66313		THE WEIGHT/ EFFERVESCENT BLUE	3.00	5.25	3.85
☐ 66342		LAUREL CANYON/HOLLY WOULD	3.00	5.25	3.85
☐ 66370		TRUST ME/WHAT IS THIS?	3.00	5.25	3.85
☐ 66385		PUT A LITTLE LOVE IN YOUR HEART/ALWAYS TOGETHER ..	3.00	5.25	3.85
☐ 66419		LOVE WILL FIND A WAY/ COMPLETELY	3.00	5.25	3.85
☐ 66430		ONE CHRISTMAS/DO YOU KNOW HOW CHRISTMAS TREES ARE GROWN?	3.00	5.25	3.85
☐ 66438		BRIGHTON HILL/ YOU CAN COME TO ME	3.00	5.25	3.85
☐ 66452		YOU KEEP ME HANGIN' ON - HURT SO BAD/WHAT WAS YOUR DAY LIKE?	3.00	5.25	3.85

JACKIE DeSHANNON—ALBUMS

☐ 3320 (M)	LIBERTY	JACKIE DeSHANNON	8.00	21.00	18.00
☐ 7320 (S)		JACKIE DeSHANNON	12.00	29.00	25.00
☐ 3390 (M)		BREAKIN' IT UP ON THE BEATLES TOUR	15.00	25.00	22.50
☐ 7390 (S)		BREAKIN' IT UP ON THE BEATLES TOUR	20.00	30.00	25.00
☐ 3430 (M)		C'MON, LET'S LIVE A LITTLE (soundtrack)	8.00	21.00	18.00
☐ 7430 (S)		C'MON, LET'S LIVE A LITTLE (soundtrack)	12.00	29.00	25.00
☐ 9286 (M)	IMPERIAL	THIS IS JACKIE DeSHANNON	7.00	17.00	15.00
☐ 12286 (S)		THIS IS JACKIE DeSHANNON	8.00	21.00	18.00
☐ 9294 (M)		YOU WON'T FORGET ME	7.00	17.00	15.00
☐ 12294 (S)		YOU WON'T FORGET ME	8.00	21.00	18.00
☐ 9296 (M)		IN THE WIND	6.00	15.00	13.50
☐ 12296 (S)		IN THE WIND	7.00	17.00	15.00

			Current Price Range		P/Y AVG
☐ 9328 (M)		ARE YOU READY FOR THIS?	6.00	15.00	13.50
☐ 12328 (S)		ARE YOU READY FOR THIS?	7.00	17.00	15.00
☐ 9344 (M)		NEW IMAGE	6.00	15.00	13.50
☐ 12344 (S)		NEW IMAGE	7.00	17.00	15.00
☐ 9352 (M)		FOR YOU	6.00	15.00	13.50
☐ 12352 (S)		FOR YOU	7.00	17.00	15.00
☐ 12386 (S)		ME ABOUT YOU	5.50	14.00	12.00
☐ 12404 (S)		WHAT THE WORLD NEEDS NOW IS LOVE	5.50	14.00	12.00
☐ 12415 (S)		LAUREL CANYON	5.50	14.00	12.00
☐ 12442 (S)		PUT A LITTLE LOVE IN YOUR HEART	5.50	14.00	12.00
☐ 12453 (S)		TO BE FREE	5.50	14.00	12.00

DESIRES (REGENTS)

☐ 118	*SEVILLE*	STORY OF LOVE/I ASK YOU	5.00	9.00	7.00

DETERGENTS

☐ 4590		LEADER OF THE LAUNDROMAT/ ULCERS	3.00	5.00	3.50
☐ 4603		DOUBLE-O-SEVEN/ THE BLUE KANGAROO	3.00	5.00	3.50
☐ 4616		LITTLE DUM-DUM/SOLDIER GIRL	3.00	5.00	3.50

DETERGENTS—ALBUMS

☐ 25308 (M)	*ROULETTE*	THE MANY FACES OF THE DETERGENTS	7.00	17.00	15.00
☐ 25308 (S)		THE MANY FACES OF THE DETERGENTS	9.00	25.00	22.50

DEVOTIONS

☐ 1001	*DELTA*	RIP VAN WINKLE/FOR SENTIMENTAL REASONS	12.00	25.00	27.00
☐ 4406	*ROULETTE*	RIP VAN WINKLE/I LOVE YOU FOR SENTIMENTAL REASONS	6.00	12.00	10.00
☐ 4541		RIP VAN WINKLE/I LOVE YOU FOR SENTIMENTAL REASONS	3.75	6.00	4.50
☐ 4556		A SUNDAY KIND OF LOVE/ TEARS FROM A BROKEN HEART	4.50	7.50	6.00
☐ 4580		ZINDY LOU/SNOW WHITE	4.50	7.50	6.00

DIABLOS

☐ 509	*FORTUNE*	(I WANT) AN OLD FASHIONED GIRL/ADIOS MY DESERT LOVE .	12.00	21.00	18.00
☐ 511		THE WIND/BABY. BE MINE	9.50	17.00	15.00
☐ 514		HOLD ME UNTIL ETERNITY/ ROUTE 16	12.00	21.00	18.00
☐ 516		DADDY ROCKING STRONG/ DO YOU REMEMBER WHAT YOU DID?	12.00	21.00	18.00
☐ 518		THE WAY YOU DOG ME AROUND/ JUMP. SHAKE AND MOVE	9.50	17.00	15.00
☐ 519		YOU ARE/YOU'RE THE ONLY GIRL. DOLORES	9.00	16.00	11.00
☐ 522		A TEARDROP FROM HEAVEN/ TRY ME ONE MORE TIME	9.00	16.00	11.00
☐ 525		CAN'T WE TALK THIS OVER?/ THE MAMBO OF LOVE	9.00	16.00	11.00
☐ 529		FOR OLD TIME'S SAKE/MY HEART WILL ALWAYS BELONG TO YOU	9.00	16.00	11.00
☐ 531		I AM WITH YOU/ GOODBYE MATILDA	9.00	16.00	11.00
☐ 532		IF I COULD BE WITH YOU/ I WANNA KNOW	9.00	16.00	11.00

			Current Price Range		P/Y AVG
☐536		SINCE YOU'RE GONE/			
		WHAT YOU GONNA DO?	9.00	16.00	11.00
☐544		BLUE MOON/I DON'T CARE	6.00	13.00	8.00
☐546		MIND OVER MATTER/BESIDE YOU	6.00	13.00	8.00
☐553		I REALLY LOVE YOU/			
		YOU'RE MY LOVE	6.00	13.00	8.00
☐556		YOU'RE EVERY BEAT OF MY			
		HEART/IT'S BECAUSE OF YOU	6.00	13.00	8.00
☐563		VILLAGE OF LOVE/			
		REAL TRUE LOVE	5.00	9.00	7.00
☐564		ARE YOU MAKING A FOOL OUT OF			
		ME/I WANT TO BE YOUR			
		HAPPINESS	5.00	9.00	7.00
☐569		ALI COOCHIE/			
		YOU'RE PRESENTABLE	5.00	9.00	7.00
☐841		HARRIET/			
		COME HOME, LITTLE GIRL	4.50	8.00	6.00

DIALTONES (RANDY AND THE RAINBOWS)

☐3005	GOLDISC	TILL I HEARD IT FROM YOU/			
		JOHNNY	5.00	9.00	7.00
☐3020		TILL I HEARD IT FROM YOU/			
		JOHNNY	4.50	8.00	6.00

NEIL DIAMOND
SEE: NEIL AND JACK

☐42809	COLUMBIA	CLOWN TOWN/AT NIGHT	20.00	35.00	22.50
☐519	BANG	SOLITARY MAN/DO IT	3.50	6.00	4.00
☐528		CHERRY CHERRY/			
		I'LL COME RUNNING	3.00	5.00	3.65
☐536		I GOT THE FEELIN' (OH NO NO)/			
		THE BOAT THAT I ROW	3.00	5.00	3.65
☐540		YOU GOT TO ME/SOMEDAY, BABY	3.00	5.00	3.65
☐542		GIRL, YOU'LL BE A WOMAN SOON/			
		YOU'LL FORGET	3.00	5.00	3.65
☐547		I THANK THE LORD FOR THE			
		NIGHT TIME/			
		THE LONG WAY HOME	3.00	5.00	3.65
☐551		KENTUCKY WOMAN/			
		THE TIME IS NOW	3.00	5.00	3.65
☐554		NEW ORLEANS/HANKY PANKY	3.00	5.00	3.65
☐556		RED RED WINE/			
		RED RUBBER BALL	3.00	5.00	3.65
☐561		SHILO/LA BAMBA	3.00	5.00	3.65
☐575		SHILO/LA BAMBA	3.00	5.00	3.65
☐578		SOLITARY MAN/			
		THE TIME IS NOW	3.00	5.00	3.65
☐580		DO IT/HANKY PANKY	3.00	5.00	3.65
☐586		I'M A BELIEVER/			
		CROOKER STREET	3.00	5.00	3.65
☐703		MONDAY MONDAY/			
		THE LONG WAY HOME	3.00	5.00	3.65
☐55065	UNI	BROOKLYN ROADS/HOLIDAY INN	2.75	4.50	3.25
☐55075		TWO BIT MANCHILD/			
		BROAD OLD WOMAN	2.75	4.50	3.25
☐55084		SUNDAY SUN/			
		HONEY DRIPPIN' TIME	2.75	4.50	3.25
☐55109		BROTHER LOVE'S TRAVELING			
		SALVATION SHOW/MODERN			
		DAY VERSION OF LOVE	2.75	4.50	3.25
☐55136		SWEET CAROLINE/DIG IN	2.75	4.50	3.25
☐55175		HOLLY HOLY/HURTIN' YOU			
		DON'T COME EASY	2.75	4.50	3.25

NEIL DIAMOND

Neil Diamond's first Bang release of "Solitary Man" in 1966 put him on the road to stardom. He scored half-a-dozen Bang winners before shifting to MCA's Uni subsidiary, where he realized even more success. But things didn't always go so well for Neil Diamond.

He was born on January 21, 1939, in Brooklyn, NY. Neil's father was a restless dry cleaner and moved his family from tenement to tenement. (Neil attended nine schools before he was 16.) Diamond was a shy, withdrawn and sullen child, finding solace chiefly in music (he sang in the same glee club as Barbra Streisand) and fencing. His latter talents earned him a scholarship to college. Four years later, Neil quit eight credits short of a pre-med degree to write songs for $50 a week. Diamond was so broke that for a time he spent 33 cents a day for food — 23 cents for a cheap sandwich and a dime for a soft drink.

Today he records for Columbia Records, ironically his first label (he did the failed "Clown Town" in 1963). Neil Diamond ranks as one of the highest-paid and most successful recording artists of the day.

			Current Price Range		P/Y AVG
☐55204		UNTIL IT'S TIME FOR YOU TO GO/			
		THE SINGER SINGS HIS SONG .	2.75	4.50	3.25
☐55224		SOOLAIMON/AND THE GRASS			
		WON'T PAY NO MIND	2.75	4.50	3.25
☐55250		CRACKLIN' ROSIE/LORDY	2.75	4.50	3.25
☐55264		HE AIN'T HEAVY. HE'S MY			
		BROTHER/FREE LIFE	2.75	4.50	3.25
☐55278		I AM . . . I SAID/DONE TOO SOON	2.75	4.50	3.25
☐55310		STONES/			
		CRUNCHY GRANOLA SUITE . . .	2.75	4.50	3.25
☐55326		SONG SUNG BLUE/			
		GITCHY GOOMY	2.75	4.50	3.25
☐55346		PLAY ME/PORCUPINE PIE	2.75	4.50	3.25
☐55352		WALK ON WATER/			
		HIGH ROLLING MAN	2.75	4.50	3.25
☐40017	**MCA**	CHERRY CHERRY/MORNINGSIDE	2.75	4.50	3.25
☐40092		THE LAST THING ON MY MIND/			
		CANTA LIBRA	2.75	4.50	3.25

SINGLES ON COLUMBIA ARE WORTH UP TO $2.00 MINT

NEIL DIAMOND—ALBUMS

☐214 (M)	**BANG**	THE FEEL OF NEIL DIAMOND	7.00	17.00	15.00
☐214 (S)		THE FEEL OF NEIL DIAMOND	9.00	25.00	22.50
☐217 (M)		JUST FOR YOU	6.00	15.00	13.50
☐217 (S)		JUST FOR YOU	8.00	21.00	18.00
☐219 (M)		GREATEST HITS	6.00	15.00	13.50
☐219 (S)		GREATEST HITS	8.00	21.00	18.00
☐221 (S)		SHILO	6.00	15.00	13.50
☐224 (S)		DO IT!	6.00	15.00	13.50
☐227 (S)		DOUBLE GOLD NEIL DIAMOND . . .	6.00	15.00	13.50
☐73030 (S)	**UNI**	VELVET GLOVES AND SPIT	4.50	14.00	12.00
☐73047 (S)		BROTHER LOVE'S TRAVELING			
		SALVATION SHOW	5.00	12.00	10.00
☐73071 (S)		TOUCHING YOU. TOUCHING ME . .	5.00	12.00	10.00
☐73084 (S)		NEIL DIAMOND - GOLD	6.00	13.00	8.50
☐73092 (S)		TAP ROOT MANUSCRIPT	6.00	13.00	8.50
☐93106 (S)		STONES	6.00	13.00	8.50
☐93136 (S)		MOODS	6.00	13.00	8.50

DIAMONDS

☐61502	**CORAL**	BLACK DENIM TROUSERS AND			
		MOTORCYCLE BOOTS/NIP SIP .	5.00	9.00	6.00
☐61577		BE MY LOVIN' BABY/SMOOCH ME	5.00	9.00	6.00
☐70790	**MERCURY**	WHY DO FOOLS FALL IN LOVE/			
		YOU BABY YOU	3.50	7.00	4.65
☐70835		THE CHURCH BELLS MAY RING/			
		LITTLE GIRL OF MINE	3.50	7.00	4.65
☐70889		LOVE. LOVE. LOVE/			
		EV'RY NIGHT ABOUT THIS TIME.	3.50	7.00	4.65
☐70934		SOFT SUMMER BREEZE/			
		KA-DING-DONG	3.50	7.00	4.65
☐71021		A THOUSAND MILES AWAY/			
		EV'RY MINUTE OF THE DAY	3.50	7.00	4.65
☐71060		LITTLE DARLIN' /			
		FAITHFUL AND TRUE	3.50	7.00	4.65
☐71128		WORDS OF LOVE/			
		DON'T SAY GOODBYE	3.25	5.50	4.00
☐71165		ZIP ZIP/OH. HOW I WISH	3.25	5.50	4.00
☐71197		SILHOUETTES/DADDY COOL	3.25	5.50	4.00
☐71242		THE STROLL/LAND OF BEAUTY . .	3.25	5.50	4.00
☐71291		HIGH SIGN/CHICK-LETS			
		(DON'T LET ME DOWN)	3.25	5.50	4.00
☐71330		KATHY-O/HAPPY YEARS	3.25	5.50	4.00
☐71366		WALKING ALONG/			
		ETERNAL LOVERS	3.25	5.50	4.00

DIAMONDS

The Diamonds came from Ontario, Canada. Their first gigs were at local clubs and churches. Later a Cleveland, Ohio, disc jockey saw the Diamonds perform and suggested they go on record. With the disc jockey's assistance the quartet signed a contract with Mercury Records a few days later.

Their hits were chiefly "cover" versions of r & b hits, usually proving to be inferior to the originals (as were most "covers"). They sang such black hits as "Why Do Fools Fall In Love", "Church Bells May Ring" and "Ka-Ding Dong" before cutting one of the 1957's best-selling singles.

"Little Darlin' " had been originally done by the Gladiolas, a Southern group led by Maurice Williams. (The group would resurface in 1960 as Maurice Williams and the Zodiacs.) The Diamonds' manager insisted that the group sing the Gladiolas' song. Legend has it that the Diamonds, tired of the song after practicing it all night in a hotel room, intended their version of "Little Darlin' " to be a satire, with the falsetto and bass parts highly exaggerated in comparison with the original. The result was a single that sold 4,000,000 copies, with the buying public unaware of the joke.

			Current Price Range		P/Y AVG
71404		SHE SAY (OOM DOOBY DOOM)/ FROM THE BOTTOM OF MY HEART	3.25	5.50	4.00
71449		GRETCHEN/A MOTHER'S LOVE	3.25	5.50	4.00
71468		HOLDING YOUR HAND/ SNEAKY ALLIGATOR	3.25	5.50	4.00
71831		ONE SUMMER NIGHT/ IT'S A DOGGONE SHAME	3.25	5.50	4.00
		DIAMONDS—EPs			
71031	**BRUNSWICK**	THE DIAMONDS	8.25	14.00	12.00
3356	**MERCURY**	THE DIAMONDS	5.50	11.00	9.00
3357		THE DIAMONDS	5.50	11.00	9.00
3358		THE DIAMONDS	5.50	11.00	9.00
3367		THE DIAMONDS	5.50	11.00	9.00
3390		THE STROLL	5.00	9.00	7.00
4038		GOLDEN HITS	5.50	11.00	9.00
		DIAMONDS—ALBUMS			
20213 (M)	**MERCURY**	COLLECTION OF GOLDEN HITS	17.00	39.00	35.00
20309		THE DIAMONDS	14.00	34.00	30.00
20368 (M)		THE DIAMONDS MEET PETE RUGULO	17.00	39.00	35.00
60076 (S)		THE DIAMONDS MEET PETE RUGULO	19.00	50.00	45.00
		DIATONES			
2509	**BANDERA**	OH BABY. COME DANCE WITH ME/RUBY BE GONE	9.00	18.00	16.00
		DICK AND DEEDEE			
7778	**LAMA**	THE MOUNTAIN'S HIGH/ I WANT SOMEONE	20.00	21.00	18.00
7780		GOODBYE TO LOVE/SWING LOW	8.25	14.00	12.00
7783		TELL ME/WILL YOU ALWAYS LOVE ME?	9.50	17.00	15.00
55350	**LIBERTY**	THE MOUNTAIN'S HIGH/ I WANT SOMEONE	3.50	6.00	4.00
55382		GOODBYE TO LOVE/SWING LOW	3.50	6.00	4.00
55412		TELL ME/WILL YOU ALWAYS LOVE ME?	3.50	6.00	4.00
55478		ALL I WANT/LIFE'S JUST A PLAY	3.50	6.00	4.00
5320	**WARNER BROTHERS**	THE RIVER TOOK MY BABY/ MY LONELY SELF	3.50	6.00	4.00
5342		YOUNG AND IN LOVE/SAY TO ME	3.00	5.00	3.65
5364		LOVE IS A ONCE IN A LIFETIME THING/CHUG-A-CHUG-A-CHOO-CHOO	3.00	5.00	3.65
5383		WHERE DID THE GOOD TIMES GO/ GUESS OUT LOVE MUST SHOW	3.00	5.00	3.65
5396		TURN AROUND/DON'T LEAVE ME	3.00	5.00	3.65
5411		ALL MY TRIALS/DON'T THINK TWICE, IT'S ALL RIGHT	3.00	5.00	3.65
5426		THE GIFT/NOT FADE AWAY	3.00	5.00	3.65
5451		YOU WERE MINE/ REMEMBER THEN	3.00	5.00	3.65
5470		WITHOUT YOUR LOVE/ THE RIDDLE SONG	3.00	5.00	3.65
5482		THOU SHALT NOT STEAL/JUST 'ROUND THE RIVER BEND	3.00	5.00	3.65
5608		BE MY BABY/ROOM 404	3.00	5.00	3.65
5627		WHEN BLUE TURNS TO GRAY/ SOME THINGS JUST STICK IN YOUR MIND	3.00	5.00	3.65
5652		THE WORLD IS WAITING/VINI VINI	3.00	5.00	3.65

			Current Price Range		P/Y AVG
☐5680		NEW ORLEANS/			
		USE WHAT YOU'VE GOT	3.00	5.00	3.65
☐5699		SHA-LA/TILL.................	3.00	5.00	3.65
☐5860		MAKE UP BEFORE WE BREAK UP/			
		CAN'T GET ENOUGH OF			
		YOUR LOVE	3.00	5.00	3.65
☐7017		LONG LONELY NIGHTS/			
		I'LL ALWAYS BE AROUND	3.00	5.00	3.65
☐7069		ONE IN A MILLION/			
		BABY, I NEED YOU	3.00	5.00	3.65
		DICK AND DEEDEE—ALBUMS			
☐3236 (M)	*LIBERTY*	TELL ME	8.00	21.00	18.00
☐7236 (S)		TELL ME	12.00	29.00	25.00
☐1500 (M)	*WARNER*				
	BROTHERS	YOUNG AND IN LOVE	7.00	17.00	15.00
☐1500 (S)		YOUNG AND IN LOVE	9.00	25.00	22.50
☐1538 (M)		TURN AROUND	7.00	17.00	15.00
☐1538 (S)		TURN AROUND	9.00	25.00	22.50
☐1586 (M)		THOU SHALT NOT STEAL	7.00	17.00	15.00
☐1586 (S)		THOU SHALT NOT STEAL	9.00	25.00	22.50
☐1623 (M)		SONGS WE'VE SUNG ON SHINDIG	7.00	17.00	15.00
☐1623 (S)		SONGS WE'VE SUNG ON SHINDIG	9.00	25.00	22.50

BO DIDDLEY

☐814	*CHECKER*	BO DIDDLEY/I'M A MAN	5.50	11.00	9.00
☐819		DIDDLEY DADDY/			
		SHE'S FINE, SHE'S MINE	5.50	10.00	7.00
☐827		PRETTY THING/			
		BRING IT TO JEROME	5.50	10.00	7.00
☐832		DIDDY WAH DIDDY/			
		I'M LOOKING FOR A WOMAN ..	5.50	10.00	7.00
☐842		WHO DO YOU LOVE/I'M BAD	5.50	10.00	7.00
☐850		COPS AND ROBBERS/			
		DOWN HOME SPECIAL	5.50	10.00	7.00
☐860		HEY, BO DIDDLEY/MONA	5.50	10.00	7.00
☐878		SAY, BOSS MAN/			
		BEFORE YOU ACCUSE ME	5.50	10.00	7.00
☐896		HUSH YOUR MOUTH/			
		DEAREST DARLING	5.50	10.00	7.00
☐907		WILLIE AND LILLIE/			
		BO MEETS THE MONSTER	5.50	10.00	7.00
☐914		I'M SORRY/OH YEA	5.00	9.00	6.25
☐924		CRACKIN' UP/			
		THE GREAT GRANDFATHER ...	5.00	9.00	6.25
☐931		SAY MAN/			
		THE CLOCK STRIKES TWELVE .	5.00	9.00	6.25
☐936		SAY MAN, BACK AGAIN/			
		SHE'S ALRIGHT	5.00	9.00	6.25
☐942		ROAD RUNNER/MY STORY	5.00	9.00	6.25
☐951		WALKIN' AND TALKIN'/CRAWDAD	3.15	6.00	4.50
☐965		GUNSLINGER/SIGNIFYING	4.50	8.00	6.00
☐976		NOT GUILTY/AZTEC	3.75	6.00	4.50
☐985		CALL ME/PILLS	3.50	6.00	4.00
☐997		BO DIDDLEY/I'M A MAN	3.00	5.00	3.50
☐1019		YOU CAN'T JUDGE A BOOK BY ITS			
		COVER/I CAN TELL	3.00	5.00	3.50
☐1045		SURFER'S LOVE CALL/GREATEST			
		LOVER IN THE WORLD	3.00	5.00	3.50

LATER CHECKER SINGLES ARE WORTH UP TO $2.75 MINT

BO DIDDLEY—ALBUMS

☐1431 (M)	*CHECKER*	BO DIDDLEY..................	17.00	40.00	35.00
☐1436 (M)		GO BO DIDDLEY	14.00	35.00	30.00
☐2974 (M)		HAVE GUITAR WILL TRAVEL	12.00	29.00	25.00
☐2976 (M)		IN THE SPOTLIGHT	12.00	29.00	25.00

			Current Price Range		P/Y AVG
☐ 2977 (M)		BO DIDDLEY IS A GUNSLINGER . .	12.00	29.00	25.00
☐ 2980 (M)		BO DIDDLEY IS A LOVER	12.00	29.00	25.00
☐ 2982 (M)		BO DIDDLEY IS A TWISTER	12.00	29.00	25.00
☐ 2984 (M)		BO DIDDLEY.	10.00	25.00	16.00
☐ 2985 (M)		BO DIDDLEY AND COMPANY	9.00	21.00	14.00
☐ 2987 (M)		SURFIN' WITH BO DIDDLEY	9.00	21.00	14.00
☐ 2988 (M)		BO DIDDLEY'S BEACH PARTY . . .	9.00	21.00	14.00
☐ 2989 (M)		16 ALL TIME GREATEST HITS . . .	10.00	25.00	17.00
☐ 2992 (M)		HEY GOOD LOOKIN'.	9.00	21.00	14.00
☐ 2996 (M)		500% MORE MAN	9.00	21.00	14.00
☐ 3001 (M)		THE ORIGINATOR.	8.00	17.00	12.00
☐ 3013 (M)		BLACK GLADIATOR	8.00	17.00	12.00

DANNY DILL

☐ 9734	**ABC-PARAMOUNT**	HUNGRY FOR YOUR LOVIN'	12.00	35.00	30.00

DING DONGS (RINKY-DINKS)
FEATURED: BOBBY DARIN

☐ 55073	**BRUNSWICK**	EARLY IN THE MORNING/			
		NOW WE'RE ONE	25.00	50.00	31.00

DINO & THE GEE-CHORDS

☐ 152	**ROBIN HOOD**	BABY CAN I TAKE YOU HOME/			
		DARLING	12.00	25.00	19.00

DINO AND THE HEARTSPINNERS

⌐ SR-45-9	**STARLIGHT RECORDS**	I WILL BELIEVE IN YOU/GEE	4.50	9.00	5.50
⌐ SR-45-11		THE LOVER'S PLEA/MEXICO	4.50	9.00	5.50
⌐ SR-45-13		THE BELLS OF LOVE/DINO			
		AND THE HEARTSPINNERS	4.50	9.00	5.50
⌐ 164	**PYRAMID RECORDS**	FLAMES/SHIRLEY	4.50	9.00	5.50
⌐ 108	**BAM BOOM RECORDS**	CRY LIKE I CRIED/			
		THAT'S MY GIRL	2.50	4.50	3.30
⌐ 112		I LOVE YOU SO/TWO			
		KINDS OF PEOPLE IN THE			
		WORLD	2.50	4.50	3.00
⌐ 45-141	**ROBIN HOOD**	ZOOM/LET'S GO BACK			
		TO YESTERDAY	2.50	4.50	3.00
⌐ 45-142		WHO DO YOU THINK YOU ARE/			
		A THOUSAND MILES AWAY . . .	2.50	4.50	3.00

DINO AND THE HEARTSPINNERS—ALBUMS

⌐ 8300	**FIRST BORN**	BELIEVE IT OR NOT!	6.00	10.00	7.50

DION

⌐ 3070	**LAURIE**	LONELY TEENAGER/			
		LITTLE MISS BLUE	3.00	5.00	3.50
. 3081		HAVIN' FUN/NORTHEAST END			
		OF THE CORNER	3.00	5.00	3.50
. 3090		KISSIN' GAME/HEAVEN HELP ME	3.00	5.00	3.50
. 3101		SOMEBODY NOBODY WANTS/			
		COULD SOMEBODY TAKE			
		MY PLACE TONIGHT?	3.25	6.00	4.00
3110		RUNAROUND SUE/			
		RUNAWAY GIRL	3.00	5.00	3.50
3115		THE WANDERER/THE MAJESTIC .	3.00	5.00	3.50
3123		LOVERS WHO WANDER/			
		(I WAS) BORN TO CRY	3.00	5.00	3.50
3134		LITTLE DIANE/LOST FOR SURE . .	3.00	5.00	3.50
3145		LOVE CAME TO ME/LITTLE GIRL .	3.00	5.00	3.50
3153		SANDY/FAITH	3.00	5.00	3.50

DION

In 1968, the Smothers Brothers introduced Dion as "an exciting new folk talent" on their weekly TV show. That night, Dion sang what would become his last major hit, "Abraham, Martin and John". Of course, those in the know recognized him not as a "new talent" but a major superstar of the late 1950s and early 1960s who had sold 22 million records before his demise in popularity late in 1963.

Dion DiMucci was born in 1939 on July 18th. A rough-and-tumble child of the Bronx streets, Dion formed the Belmonts with Freddie Milano, Carlo Mastrangelo and Angelo D'Aleo (who left in 1959).

In 1960, at the height of the Belmonts' popularity, Dion departed to become a solo act. On his own, DiMucci racked up several classic hits such as "Runaround Sue", "The Wanderer" and "Ruby Baby". These established Dion as one of the gutsiest, high-energy rockers of the early 1960s.

Drug problems and a dissatisfaction with recording material led to a withdrawl from the recording world after "Drip Drop" late in 1963. Five years later, Dion emerged victoriously from his personal battles to become a fairly successful folk singer. He now records gospel music.

			Current Price Range		P/Y AVG
☐ 3171		COME GO WITH ME/ KING WITHOUT A QUEEN	3.00	5.00	3.50
☐ 3187		LONELY WORLD/TAG ALONG	3.25	6.00	4.00
☐ 3225		THEN I'LL BE TIRED OF YOU/ AFTER THE DANCE	3.25	6.00	4.00
☐ 3240		SHOUT/LITTLE GIRL	3.25	6.00	4.00
☐ 3303		I GOT THE BLUES/ (I WAS) BORN TO CRY	3.25	6.00	4.00
☐ 3464		ABRAHAM, MARTIN AND JOHN/ DADDY ROLLIN'	2.75	5.00	3.00
☐ 3478		PURPLE HAZE/THE DOLPHINS . . .	2.75	5.00	3.00
☐ 3495		BOTH SIDES NOW/SUN FUN SONG	3.25	6.00	4.00
☐ 3504		LOVING YOU IS SWEETER THAN EVER/HE LOOKS A LOT LIKE ME.	3.25	6.00	3.00
☐ 42662	COLUMBIA	RUBY BABY/ HE'LL ONLY HURT YOU	2.75	5.00	3.00
☐ 42776		THIS LITTLE GIRL/THE LONELIEST MAN IN THE WORLD	3.00	5.00	3.50
☐ 42810		BE CAREFUL OF STONES THAT YOU THROW/I CAN'T BELIEVE .	3.00	5.00	3.50
☐ 42852		DONNA THE PRIMA DONNA/ YOU'RE MINE	3.00	5.00	3.50
☐ 42917		DRIP DROP/ NO ONE'S WAITING FOR ME . . .	3.00	5.00	3.50
☐ 42977		I'M YOU HOOCHIE COOCHI MAN/ THE ROAD I'M ON	3.00	5.00	3.50
☐ 43096		JOHNNY B. GOODE/ CHICAGO BLUES	3.00	5.00	3.50
☐ 43213		UNLOVED. UNWANTED ME/ SWEET SWEET BABY	3.00	5.00	3.50
☐ 43293		SPOONFUL/KICKIN' CHILD	3.00	5.00	3.50
☐ 43423		TOMORROW WON'T BRING THE RAIN/YOU MOVE ME BABE . . .	3.25	5.50	4.00
☐ 43483		TIME IN MY HEART FOR YOU/ WAKE UP BABY	3.00	5.00	3.50
☐ 43692		TWO TON FEATHER/ SO MUCH YOUNGER	3.00	5.00	3.50
☐ 44719		SOUTHERN TRAIN/ I CAN'T HELP BUT WONDER WHERE I'M BOUND	3.00	5.00	3.50
☐ 7356	WARNER BROTHERS	NATURAL MAN/ IF WE ONLY HAVE LOVE	3.25	5.50	4.00
☐ 7401		YOUR OWN BACK YARD/ SIT DOWN OLD FRIEND	3.00	5.25	3.85
☐ 7469		CLOSE TO IT ALL/LET IT BE	3.00	5.25	3.85
☐ 7491		JOSIE/SUNNILAND	3.00	5.25	3.85
☐ 7537		SANCTUARY/ BRAND NEW MORNING	3.00	5.25	3.85
☐ 7663		RUNNING CLOSE BEHIND YOU/ SEAGULL	3.00	5.25	3.85
☐ 7704		DOCTOR ROCK AND ROLL/ SUNSHINE LADY	3.00	5.25	3.85
☐ 7793		NEW YORK CITY SONG/RICHER THAN A RICH MAN	3.00	5.25	3.85
☐ 8234		LOVER BOY SUPREME/ HEY MY LOVE	3.00	5.25	3.85
☐ 8258		THE WAY YOU DO THE THINGS YOU DO/LOVER BOY SUPREME	3.00	5.25	3.85
☐ 8293		THE QUEEN OF '59/ OH. THE NIGHT	3.00	5.25	3.85
☐ 8406		YOUNG VIRGIN EYES/ OH. THE NIGHT	3.00	5.25	3.85

			Current Price Range		P/Y AVG
		DION—ALBUMS			
☐ 2004 (M)	*LAURIE*	ALONE WITH DION	14.00	29.00	25.00
☐ 2009 (M)		RUNAROUND SUE	11.00	26.00	17.50
☐ 2012 (M)		LOVERS WHO WANDER	11.00	26.00	17.50
☐ 2013 (M)		DION SINGS HIS GREATEST HITS	11.00	26.00	17.50
☐ 2015 (M)		LOVE CAME TO ME	11.00	26.00	17.50
☐ 2017 (M)		DION SINGS TO SANDY	11.00	26.00	17.50
☐ 2019 (M)		DION SINGS THE 15 MILLION SELLERS	11.00	26.00	17.50
☐ 2022 (M)		MORE OF DION'S GREATEST HITS	11.00	26.00	17.50
☐ 2047 (S)		DION	7.00	17.00	15.00
☐ 2010 (M)	*COLUMBIA*	RUBY BABY	4.00	17.00	15.00
☐ 8810 (S)		RUBY BABY	8.00	21.00	18.00
☐ 2107 (M)		DONNA THE PRIMA DONNA	9.00	17.00	15.00
☐ 8907 (S)		DONNA THE PRIMA DONNA	8.00	21.00	18.00
☐ 9773 (S)		WONDER WHERE I'M BOUND	7.00	17.00	15.00
☐ 1826 (S)	*WARNER BROTHERS*	SIT DOWN OLD FRIEND	7.00	17.00	15.00
☐ 1872 (S)		YOU'RE NOT ALONE	6.00	13.00	10.50
☐ 1945 (S)		SANCTUARY	6.00	15.00	13.50
☐ 2642 (S)		SUITE FOR LATE SUMMER	6.00	15.00	13.50
☐ 2954 (S)		STREETHEART	5.00	12.00	10.00

DION AND THE BELMONTS
SEE: DION, BELMONTS

☐ 106	*MOHAWK*	TEENAGE CLEMENTINE/ SANTA MARGARITA	20.00	34.00	30.00
☐ 107		WE WENT AWAY/TAG ALONG	20.00	34.00	30.00
☐ 3013	*LAURIE*	I WONDER WHY/TEEN ANGEL	3.75	6.00	4.50
☐ 3015		NO ONE KNOWS/I CAN'T GO ON (ROSALIE)	3.75	6.00	4.50
☐ 3021		DON'T PITY ME/JUST YOU	3.75	6.00	4.50
☐ 3027		A TEENAGER IN LOVE/ I'VE CRIED BEFORE	3.00	5.00	3.50
☐ 3035		EVERY LITTLE THING I DO/ A LOVER'S PRAYER	3.00	5.00	3.50
☐ 3044		WHERE OR WHEN/ THAT'S MY DESIRE	3.00	5.00	3.50
☐ 3052		WHEN YOU WISH UPON A STAR/ WONDERFUL GIRL	3.00	5.00	3.50
☐ 3059		IN THE STILL OF THE NIGHT/ A FUNNY FEELING	3.00	5.00	3.50
☐ 10868	*ABC*	MY GIRL, THE MONTH OF MAY/ BERIMBAU	3.75	6.00	4.50
☐ 10896		MOVIN' MAN/FOR BOBBY	3.75	6.00	4.50
		DION AND THE BELMONTS—EPs			
☐ 301	*LAURIE*	THEIR HITS	8.25	14.00	12.00
☐ 302		WHERE OR WHEN	8.25	14.00	12.00
		DION AND THE BELMONTS—ALBUMS			
☐ 2002 (M)	*LAURIE*	PRESENTING DION AND THE BELMONTS	12.00	29.00	25.00
☐ 2006 (M)		WISH UPON A STAR	10.00	25.00	22.50
☐ 2016 (M)		BY SPECIAL REQUEST	10.00	25.00	22.50
☐ 599 (M)	*ABC*	TOGETHER AGAIN	8.00	21.00	18.00
☐ 599 (S)		TOGETHER AGAIN	10.00	25.00	22.50
☐ 2664 (S)	*WARNER BROTHERS*	REUNION	7.00	17.00	15.00

DION AND THE TIMBERLANES (BEFORE BELMONTS)

☐ 105	*MOHAWK*	THE CHOSEN FEW/ OUT IN COLORADO	22.00	40.00	35.00
☐ 5294	*JUBILEE*	THE CHOSEN FEW/ OUT IN COLORADO	17.00	29.00	25.00

			Current Price Range		P/Y AVG

DIXIE CUPS

☐ 10-001	**RED BIRD**	CHAPEL OF LOVE/			
		AIN'T THAT NICE	3.25	5.50	4.00
☐ 10-006		PEOPLE SAY/GIRLS CAN TELL ...	3.25	5.50	4.00
☐ 10-012		YOU SHOULD HAVE SEEN THE			
		WAY HE LOOKED AT ME/			
		NO TRUE LOVE	3.25	5.50	4.00
☐ 10-017		LITTLE BELL/			
		ANOTHER BOY LIKE MINE	3.25	5.50	4.00
☐ 10-024		IKO IKO/GEE BABY GEE	3.25	5.50	4.00
☐ 10-032		GEE THE MOON IS SHINING			
		BRIGHT/I'M GONNA GET			
		YOU YET	3.25	5.50	4.00

DIXIE CUPS—ALBUMS

☐ 100 (M)	**RED BIRD**	CHAPEL OF LOVE..............	8.00	21.00	18.00
☐ 100 (S)		CHAPEL OF LOVE..............	12.00	29.00	25.00
☐ 103 (M)		IKO IKO	7.00	17.00	15.00
☐ 103 (S)		IKO IKO	9.00	25.00	22.50
☐ 525 (M)	**ABC-**				
	PARAMOUNT	RIDING HIGH	7.00	17.00	15.00
☐ 525 (S)		RIDING HIGH	9.00	25.00	22.50

MICKEY DOLENZ
SEE: MONKEES

☐ 59353	**CHALLENGE**	DON'T DO IT/			
		PLASTIC SYMPHONY III	3.50	5.50	4.00
☐ 59372		HUFF PUFF/(THE OBVIOUS) FATE	3.50	5.50	4.00
☐ 14309	**MGM**	EASY ON YOU/OH, SOMEONE ...	3.50	5.50	4.00
☐ 14395		A LOVER'S PRAYER/UNATTENDED			
		IN THE DUNGEON	3.50	5.50	4.00
☐ 710	**ROMAR**	DAYBREAK/LOVE WAR	3.50	5.50	4.00
☐ 715		BUDDY HOLLY TRIBUTE/			
		OOH SHE'S YOUNG	5.00	10.00	6.85

FATS DOMINO

☐ 5058	**IMPERIAL**	THE FAT MAN/			
		DETROIT CITY BLUES	27.00	46.00	42.00
☐ 5065		BOOGIE WOOGIE BABY/			
		LITTLE BEE	27.00	46.00	42.00
☐ 5077		SHE'S MY BABY/			
		HIDEAWAY BLUES	27.00	46.00	42.00
☐ 5085		HEY LA BAS BOOGIE/			
		BRAND NEW BABY	27.00	46.00	42.00

THE FIRST FOUR RELEASES WERE ISSUED ONLY ON 78 RPM
THE FOLLOWING REFLECT PRICES FOR 45 RPM DISCS

☐ 5099		KOREA BLUES/EVERY NIGHT			
		ABOUT THIS TIME	34.00	48.00	44.00
☐ 5114		TIRED OF CRYING/			
		WHAT'S THE MATTER, BABY? .	25.00	45.00	31.50
☐ 5123		DON'T YOU LIE TO ME/			
		SOMETIMES I WONDER	25.00	45.00	31.50
☐ 5138		NO, NO BABY/			
		RIGHT FROM WRONG	25.00	45.00	31.50
☐ 5145		ROCKIN' CHAIR/CARELESS LOVE	25.00	45.00	31.50
☐ 5167		YOU KNOW I MISS YOU/			
		I'LL BE GONE	17.00	29.00	25.00
☐ 5180		GOIN' HOME/			
		REELING AND ROCKING	17.00	29.00	25.00
☐ 5197		POOR POOR ME/TRUST IN ME ...	17.00	29.00	25.00
☐ 5209		HOW LONG?/DREAMING........	14.00	25.00	20.00
☐ 5220		NOBODY LOVES ME/CHEATIN' ..	12.00	21.00	18.00
☐ 5231		GOING TO THE RIVER/			
		MARDI GRAS IN NEW ORLEANS	12.00	21.00	18.00

FATS DOMINO

Antoine "Fats" Domino came from New Orleans, Louisiana, where he was born on February 26, 1928. One of nine children, Fats showed an early interest in the piano and played it daily after school. He departed the halls of learning at fifteen, first to drive an ice cream truck, then to toil in a bedspring factory to support his family. One day at the factory a heavy bedspring fell across Fats' hands. Doctors at first told the burly teenager that he would never again be able to write or play the piano. Fats didn't listen and, through determination and constant exercise, he eventually regained the use of his hands.

By the end of the 1940s Fats was playing regularly at New Orleans clubs. He signed a contract with Imperial Records and began a working partnership with the sax player Dave Bartholomew. Domino's first single was "The Fat Man". An instant r & b hit, it was followed by two dozen more winners. Fats finally "crossed over" to the rock charts in 1955 with the rocking "Ain't That A Shame".

During his recording career he earned nineteen gold records, including one for his biggest hit, "Blueberry Hill". Today Domino—still a New Orleans resident—appears in Las Vegas showrooms and headlines various oldies shows.

		Current Price Range		P/Y AVG
☐ 5240	PLEASE DON'T LEAVE ME/			
	THE GIRL I LOVE	10.00	19.00	13.50
☐ 5251	ROSE MARY/			
	YOU SAID YOU LOVED ME	10.00	19.00	13.50
☐ 5262	DON'T LEAVE ME THIS WAY/			
	SOMETHING'S WRONG	10.00	19.00	13.50
☐ 5272	LITTLE SCHOOL GIRL/			
	YOU DONE ME WRONG	10.00	19.00	13.50
☐ 5283	BABY, PLEASE/			
	WHERE DID YOU STAY?	10.00	19.00	13.50
☐ 5301	YOU CAN PACK YOUR SUITCASE/			
	I LIVED MY LIFE	10.00	19.00	13.50
☐ 5313	DON'T YOU HEAR ME CALLING			
	YOU/LOVE ME	8.25	14.00	12.00
☐ 5323	I KNOW/THINKING OF YOU	7.00	12.00	10.00
☐ 5340	DON'T YOU KNOW/			
	HELPING HAND	5.50	11.00	9.00
☐ 5348	AIN'T IT A SHAME/LA LA	5.00	9.00	7.00
☐ 5357	ALL BY MYSELF/			
	TROUBLES OF MY OWN	5.00	9.00	7.00
☐ 5369	POOR ME/I CAN'T GO ON	4.50	8.00	6.00
☐ 5375	BO WEEVIL/			
	DON'T BLAME IT ON ME	4.50	8.00	6.00
☐ 5386	I'M IN LOVE AGAIN/			
	MY BLUE HEAVEN	3.75	6.00	4.50
☐ 5396	WHEN MY DREAMBOAT COMES			
	HOME/SO-LONG	3.75	6.00	4.50
☐ 5407	BLUEBERRY HILL/HONEY CHILE .	3.75	6.00	4.50
☐ 5417	BLUE MONDAY/WHAT'S THE			
	REASON I'M NOT PLEASING			
	YOU	3.50	6.00	4.65
☐ 5428	I'M WALKIN'/			
	I'M IN THE MOOD FOR LOVE . . .	3.50	6.00	4.65
☐ 5442	VALLEY OF TEARS/			
	IT'S YOU I LOVE	3.50	6.00	4.65
☐ 5454	WHEN I SEE YOU/			
	WHAT WILL I TELL MY HEART .	3.50	6.00	4.65
☐ 5467	WAIT AND SEE/I STILL LOVE YOU	3.50	6.00	4.65
☐ 5477	THE BIG BEAT/			
	I WANT YOU TO KNOW	3.25	5.50	4.00
☐ 5492	YES, MY DARLING/DON'T YOU			
	KNOW I LOVE YOU	3.25	5.50	4.00
☐ 5515	SICK AND TIRED/NO, NO	3.25	5.50	4.00
☐ 5526	LITTLE MARY/PRISONER'S SONG	3.25	5.50	4.00
☐ 5537	YOUNG SCHOOL GIRL/			
	IT MUST BE LOVE	3.25	5.50	4.00
☐ 5553	WHOLE LOTTA LOVING/COQUETTE	3.25	5.50	4.00
☐ 5569	WHEN THE SAINTS GO MARCHING			
	IN/TELLING LIES	3.25	5.50	4.00
☐ 5585	I'M READY/MARGIE	3.25	5.50	4.00
☐ 5606	I WANT TO WALK YOU HOME/			
	I'M GONNA BE A WHEEL			
	SOMEDAY	3.25	5.50	4.00
☐ 5629	BE MY GUEST/I'VE BEEN AROUND	3.25	5.50	4.00
☐ 5645	COUNTRY BOY/IF YOU NEED ME .	3.25	5.50	4.00
☐ 5660	TELL ME THAT YOU LOVE ME/			
	BEFORE I GROW TOO OLD	3.25	5.50	4.00
☐ 5675	WALKING TO NEW ORLEANS/			
	DON'T COME KNOCKING	3.25	5.50	4.00
☐ 5687	THREE NIGHTS A WEEK/PUT			
	YOUR ARMS AROUND ME			
	HONEY	3.25	5.50	4.00
☐ 5704	MY GIRL JOSEPHINE/			
	NATURAL BORN LOVER	3.25	5.50	4.00

			Current Price Range		P/Y AVG
☐ 5723		WHAT A PRICE/AIN'T THAT JUST LIKE A WOMAN	3.25	5.50	4.00
☐ 5734		SHU RAH/FELL IN LOVE ON MONDAY	3.25	5.50	4.00
☐ 5753		IT KEEPS RAININ'/I JUST CRY . . .	3.25	5.50	4.00
☐ 5764		LET THE FOUR WINDS BLOW/ GOOD HEARTED MAN	3.25	5.50	4.00
☐ 5779		WHAT A PARTY/ROCKIN' BICYCLE	3.25	5.50	4.00
☐ 5796		JAMBALAYA (ON THE BAYOU)/ I HEAR YOU KNOCKING	3.25	5.50	4.00
☐ 5816		YOU WIN AGAIN/IDA JANE	3.25	5.50	4.00
☐ 5833		MY REAL NAME/ MY HEART IS BLEEDING	3.25	5.50	4.00
☐ 5863		NOTHING NEW (SAME OLD THING)/ DANCE WITH MR. DOMINO	3.25	5.50	4.00
☐ 5875		DID YOU EVER SEE A DREAM WALKING?/STOP THE CLOCK .	3.25	5.50	4.00
☐ 5895		WON'T YOU COME ON BACK/ HANDS ACROSS THE TABLE . . .	3.25	5.50	4.00
☐ 5909		THOSE EYES/HUM DIDDY DOO . .	3.25	5.50	4.00
☐ 5937		YOU ALWAYS HURT THE ONE YOU LOVE/TROUBLED BLUES	3.25	5.50	4.00
☐ 5959		ISLE OF CAPRI/ I CAN'T GO ON THIS WAY	3.25	5.50	4.00
☐ 5980		ONE NIGHT/ I CAN'T GO ON THIS WAY	3.25	5.50	4.00
☐ 66005		I CAN'T GIVE YOU ANYTHING BUT LOVE/GOIN' HOME	3.25	5.50	4.00
☐ 66016		YOUR CHEATIN' HEART/ WHEN I WAS YOUNG	3.25	5.50	4.00
☐ 10444	**ABC-PARAMOUNT**	THERE GOES (MY HEART AGAIN)/ CAN'T GO ON WITHOUT YOU . .	3.00	5.25	3.85
☐ 10475		WHEN I'M WALKING/ I'VE GOT A RIGHT TO CRY	3.00	5.25	3.85
☐ 10484		RED SAILS IN THE SUNSET/ SONG FOR ROSEMARY	3.00	5.25	3.85
☐ 10512		WHO CARES/ JUST A LONELY MAN	3.00	5.25	3.85
☐ 10531		LAZY LADY/I DON'T WANT TO SET THE WORLD ON FIRE	3.00	5.25	3.85
☐ 10545		SOMETHING YOU GOT. BABY/ IF YOU DON'T KNOW WHAT LOVE IS	3.00	5.25	3.85
☐ 10567		MARY OH MARY/PACKIN' UP . . .	3.00	5.25	3.85
☐ 10584		SALLY WAS A GOOD OLD GIRL/ FOR YOU	3.00	5.25	3.85
☐ 10596		HEARTBREAK HILL/KANSAS CITY	3.00	5.25	3.85
☐ 10631		WHY DON'T YOU DO RIGHT?/ WIGS	3.00	5.25	3.85
☐ 10644		LET ME CALL YOU SWEETHEART/ GOODNIGHT SWEETHEART	3.00	5.25	3.85
☐ 10902		I DON'T WANT TO SET THE WORLD ON FIRE/I'M LIVIN' RIGHT	3.00	5.25	3.85
☐ 72463	**MERCURY**	I LEFT MY HEART IN SAN FRANCISCO/ I DONE GOT OVER IT	3.00	5.25	3.85
☐ 72485		WHAT'S THAT YOU GOT/ IT'S NEVER TOO LATE	3.00	5.25	3.85
☐ 0696	**REPRISE**	ONE FOR THE HIGHWAY/ HONEST PAPAS LOVE THEIR MAMAS BETTER	3.00	5.25	3.85
☐ 0763		LADY MADONNA/ ONE FOR THE HIGHWAY	3.00	5.25	3.85

			Current Price Range		P/Y AVG
☐0775		LOVELY RITA/WAIT TILL IT HAPPENS TO YOU	3.00	5.25	3.85
☐0810		EVERYBODY'S GOT SOMETHING TO HIDE EXCEPT ME AND MY MONKEY/SO SWELL WHEN YOU'RE WELL	3.00	5.25	3.85
☐0891		HAVE YOU SEEN MY BABY?/ LET ME BELONG TO YOU	3.00	5.25	3.85
☐0944		NEW ORLEANS AIN'T THE SAME/ SWEET PATOOTIE	3.00	5.25	3.85
		FATS DOMINO—EPs			
☐127	**IMPERIAL**	FATS DOMINO	27.00	45.00	30.00
☐139		ROCK AND ROLLIN' WITH FATS DOMINO	20.00	35.00	23.00
☐141		FATS DOMINO: ROCK AND ROLLIN'	20.00	35.00	23.00
☐142		FATS DOMINO: ROCK AND ROLLIN'	20.00	35.00	23.00
☐143		FATS DOMINO: ROCK AND ROLLIN'	20.00	35.00	23.00
☐146		THIS IS FATS DOMINO	20.00	35.00	23.00
☐147		HERE COMES FATS	20.00	35.00	23.00
☐148		HERE STANDS FATS DOMINO	15.00	27.00	19.00
☐149		HERE STANDS FATS DOMINO	15.00	27.00	19.00
☐150		HERE STANDS FATS DOMINO	15.00	27.00	19.00
☐151		COOKIN' WITH FATS	13.00	23.00	17.00
☐152		ROCKIN' WITH FATS	13.00	23.00	17.00

PRICES SHOWN ARE FOR BLOCK-LETTER LABELS; EPs WITH SCRIPT
LETTERING WOULD BE WORTH TWICE THE AMOUNT SHOWN

		FATS DOMINO—ALBUMS			
☐9004 (M)	**IMPERIAL**	ROCK AND ROLLIN' WITH FATS DOMINO	27.00	66.00	60.00
☐9009 (M)		ROCK AND ROLLIN'	23.00	55.00	50.00
☐9028 (M)		THIS IS FATS DOMINO	23.00	55.00	50.00
☐9038 (M)		HERE STANDS FATS DOMINO	23.00	55.00	50.00
☐9040 (M)		THIS IS FATS	17.00	39.00	35.00
☐9055 (M)		THE FABULOUS MR. D.	17.00	39.00	35.00
☐9062 (M)		FATS DOMINO SWINGS	14.00	34.00	30.00
☐9065 (M)		LET'S PLAY	14.00	34.00	30.00
☐9103 (M)		FATS DOMINO SINGS	12.00	29.00	25.00
☐9138 (M)		A LOT OF DOMINOS	12.00	24.00	20.00
☐9153 (M)		LET THE FOUR WINDS BLOW	12.00	24.00	20.00
☐9164 (M)		WHAT A PARTY	12.00	24.00	20.00
☐9170 (M)		TWISTIN' THE STOMP	12.00	24.00	20.00
☐9195 (M)		MILLION SELLERS	9.00	25.00	22.50
☐9208 (M)		JUST DOMINO	9.00	25.00	22.50
☐9227 (M)		WALKING TO NEW ORLEANS	9.00	25.00	22.50
☐9239 (M)		LET'S DANCE WITH DOMINO	8.00	21.00	18.00
☐9248 (M)		HERE HE COMES AGAIN	8.00	21.00	18.00
☐455 (M)	**ABC-PARAMOUNT**	HERE COMES FATS DOMINO	7.00	17.00	15.00
☐455 (S)		HERE COMES FATS DOMINO	9.00	25.00	22.50
☐479 (M)		FATS ON FIRE	7.00	17.00	15.00
☐479 (S)		FATS ON FIRE	9.00	25.00	22.50
☐510 (M)		GETAWAY WITH FATS DOMINO	7.00	17.00	15.00
☐510 (S)		GETAWAY WITH FATS DOMINO	9.00	25.00	22.50
☐21039 (M)	**MERCURY**	FATS DOMINO '65	7.00	17.00	15.00
☐61039 (S)		FATS DOMINO '65	9.00	21.00	18.00
☐21065 (M)		SOUTHLAND U.S.A.	7.00	17.00	15.00
☐61065 (S)		SOUTHLAND U.S.A.	9.00	21.00	18.00
☐6304 (S)	**REPRISE**	FATS IS BACK	7.00	21.00	18.00
☐6439 (S)		FATS	9.00	21.00	18.00

		Current Price Range		P/Y AVG

DOMINOES
SEE: BILLY WARD AND HIS DOMINOES
FEATURED: CLYDE McPHATTER, JACKIE WILSON

			Current Price Range		P/Y AVG
☐ 12001	**FEDERAL**	CHICKEN BLUES/			
		DO SOMETHING TO ME	65.00	125.00	75.00
☐ 12010		HARBOR LIGHTS/			
		NO SAYS MY HEART	180.00	325.00	215.00
☐ 12016		OTHER LIPS, OTHER ARMS/			
		THE DEACON MOVES IN	95.00	160.00	100.00
☐ 12022		SIXTY MINUTE MAN/			
		I CAN'T ESCAPE FROM YOU	43.00	85.00	51.00
☐ 12036		HEART TO HEART/			
		LOOKIN' FOR A MAN	60.00	130.00	72.00
☐ 12039		WEEPING WILLOW BLUES/			
		I AM WITH YOU	60.00	130.00	72.00
☐ 12059		WHEN THE SWALLOWS COME BACK TO CAPISTRANO/THAT'S WHAT YOU'RE DOING TO ME	60.00	130.00	72.00
☐ 12068		DEEP SEA BLUES/			
		HAVE MERCY BABY	60.00	130.00	72.00
☐ 12072		LOVE, LOVE, LOVE/THAT'S WHAT YOU'RE DOING TO ME	43.00	85.00	51.00
☐ 12105		NO ROOM/I'D BE SATISFIED	33.00	59.00	37.00
☐ 12106		YOURS FOREVER/I'M LONELY	33.00	59.00	37.00
☐ 12114		THE BELLS/PEDAL PUSHIN' PAPA	33.00	59.00	37.00
☐ 12129		THESE FOOLISH THINGS/DON'T LEAVE ME THIS WAY	33.00	59.00	37.00
☐ 12139		WHERE NOW, LITTLE HEART?/YOU CAN'T KEEP A GOOD MAN DOWN	33.00	59.00	37.00
		FIRST PRESSES OF THE ABOVE FEATURE A GOLD TOP			
☐ 12162		MY BABY'S 3-D/UNTIL THE REAL THING COMES ALONG	17.00	29.00	25.00
☐ 12165		MERCY ME/ALL IS FORGIVEN	17.00	29.00	25.00
☐ 12178		I'M GONNA MOVE TO THE OUTSKIRTS OF TOWN/TOOTSIE ROLL	17.00	29.00	25.00
☐ 12184		ONE MOMENT WITH YOU/HANDWRITING ON THE WALL	17.00	29.00	25.00
☐ 12193		LITTLE BLACK TRAIN/ABOVE JACOB'S LADDER	17.00	29.00	25.00
		FIRST PRESSES OF THE ABOVE FEATURE A SILVER TOP			
☐ 12209		CAN'T DO 60 NO MORE/IF I NEVER GET TO HEAVEN	14.00	24.00	20.00
☐ 12218		CAVE MAN/LOVE ME NOW OR LET ME GO	12.00	21.00	18.00
☐ 12263		BOBBY SOX BABY/HOW LONG, HOW LONG BLUES	12.00	21.00	18.00
☐ 12300		ONE MOMENT WITH YOU/LOVE, LOVE, LOVE	10.00	19.00	13.50
☐ 12301		ST. LOUIS BLUES/ONE MOMENT WITH YOU	10.00	19.00	13.50
☐ 12308		HAVE MERCY BABY/LOVE, LOVE, LOVE	10.00	19.00	13.50
☐ 1280	**KING**	RAGS TO RICHES/DON'T THANK ME	12.00	21.00	18.00
☐ 1281		CHRISTMAS IN HEAVEN/RINGING IN A BRAND NEW YEAR	17.00	30.00	25.00
☐ 1342		TENDERLY/A LITTLE LIE	12.00	21.00	18.00
☐ 1364		THREE COINS IN THE FOUNTAIN/LONESOME ROAD	10.00	19.00	13.50
☐ 1368		LITTLE THINGS MEAN A LOT/I REALLY DON'T WANT TO KNOW	10.00	19.00	13.50

			Current Price Range		P/Y AVG
☐1492		LEARNING THE BLUES/			
		I MAY NEVER LOVE AGAIN	10.00	19.00	13.50
☐1502		OVER THE RAINBOW/			
		GIVE ME YOU	8.25	14.00	12.00
☐5322		HAVE MERCY BABY/			
		SIXTY MINUTE MAN	5.50	11.00	9.00
☐5463		LAY IT ON THE LINE/THAT'S HOW			
		YOU KNOW WHEN YOU'RE			
		GROWING OLD	5.50	11.00	9.00
☐5163	JUBILEE	COME TO ME BABY/			
		GIMMIE GIMMIE GIMMIE	8.00	16.00	11.50
☐5213		SWEETHEARTS IN PARADISE/			
		TAKE ME BACK TO HEAVEN ...	8.00	16.00	11.50
		DOMINOES—EPs			
☐212	KING	ALL-TIME HIT STANDARDS	10.00	20.00	17.50
☐262		ALL-TIME HIT STANDARDS	10.00	20.00	17.50
☐269		ALL-TIME HIT STANDARDS	10.00	20.00	17.50
		DOMINOES—10" ALBUM			
☐94	FEDERAL	BILLY WARD AND HIS DOMINOES	175.00	500.00	450.00
		DOMINOES—ALBUMS			
☐548 (M)	FEDERAL	BILLY WARD AND HIS DOMINOES	80.00	190.00	180.00
☐559 (M)		CLYDE McPHATTER WITH			
		THE DOMINOES	40.00	100.00	90.00
☐548 (M)	KING	BILLY WARD AND HIS DOMINOES	9.00	25.00	22.50
☐559 (M)		CLYDE McPHATTER WITH			
		BILLY WARD	17.00	40.00	35.00
☐733 (M)		BILLY WARD AND HIS DOMINOES	8.00	21.00	18.00

DON AND DEWEY

☐599	SPECIALTY	JUNGLE HOP/A LITTLE LOVE	4.50	7.50	6.00
☐610		LEAVIN' IT ALL UP TO YOU/			
		JELLY BEAN	4.50	7.50	6.00
☐617		JUST A LITTLE LOVIN'/WHEN THE			
		SUN HAS BEGUN TO SHINE ...	3.75	6.00	4.50
☐631		JUSTINE/BIM BAM	3.75	6.00	4.50
☐639		THE LETTER/JUSTINE	3.75	6.00	4.50
☐659		BIG BOY PETE/FARMER JOHN ...	3.75	6.00	4.50
☐691		ANNIE LEE/GET YOUR HAT	3.25	6.00	4.00
		DON AND DEWEY—ALBUM			
☐2131 (S)	SPECIALTY	THEY'RE ROCKIN' TILL			
		MIDNIGHT, ROLLIN' TILL DAWN .	5.00	12.00	10.00

RAL DONNER

☐1310	SCOTTIE	TELL ME WHY/			
		THAT'S ALL RIGHT WITH ME ..	14.00	24.00	20.00
☐5102	GONE	GIRL OF MY BEST FRIEND/			
		IT'S BEEN A LONG LONG TIME .	8.25	14.00	12.00
		THE ABOVE PRICE IS FOR THE BLACK LABEL VERSION			
☐5102		GIRL OF MY BEST FRIEND/			
		IT'S BEEN A LONG LONG TIME .	3.00	5.00	3.50
☐5108		YOU DON'T KNOW WHAT YOU'VE			
		GOT/SO CLOSE TO HEAVEN ...	3.00	5.00	3.50
☐5114		PLEASE DON'T GO/I DIDN'T			
		FIGURE ON HIM TO COME BACK	3.00	5.00	3.50
☐5119		SCHOOL OF HEARTBREAKERS/			
		BECAUSE WE'RE YOUNG	8.25	14.00	12.00
☐5121		SHE'S EVERYTHING/WILL YOU			
		LOVE ME IN HEAVEN	5.50	11.00	9.00
☐5121		SHE'S EVERYTHING/			
		BECAUSE WE'RE YOUNG	3.00	5.00	3.50
☐5125		TO LOVE SOMEONE/			
		WILL YOU LOVE ME IN HEAVEN	3.00	5.00	3.50
☐5129		LOVELESS LIFE/BELLS OF LOVE .	4.50	8.00	6.00
☐5133		TO LOVE/SWEETHEART	4.50	8.00	6.00

			Current Price Range		P/Y AVG
☐ 105	**TAU**	LONELINESS OF A STAR/			
		AND THEN	5.50	11.00	9.00
☐ 20135	**REPRISE**	SECOND MIRACLE/			
		CHRISTMAS DAY	5.00	9.00	7.00
☐ 20141		I GOT BURNED/A TEAR IN MY EYE	4.00	9.00	7.00
☐ 20176		I WISH THIS NIGHT WOULD NEVER			
		END/DON'T PUT YOUR HEART			
		IN HIS HAND	5.50	10.00	7.00
☐ 20192		RUN LITTLE LINDA/			
		BEYOND THE HEARTBREAK ...	5.50	10.00	7.00
☐ 1502	**FONTANA**	POISON IVY LEAGUE/YOU			
		FINALLY SAID SOMETHING GOOD	5.50	10.00	7.00
☐ 1502		POISON IVY LEAGUE/			
		TEAR IN MY EYE	5.50	10.00	7.00
☐ 1515		GOOD LOVIN'/OTHER SIDE OF ME	5.50	10.00	7.00
☐ 10-051	**RED BIRD**	LOVE ISN'T LIKE THAT/IT WILL			
		ONLY MAKE YOU LOVE			
		ME MORE	5.50	10.00	7.00
☐ 10-057		LOVE ISN'T LIKE THAT/IT WILL			
		ONLY MAKE YOU LOVE			
		ME MORE	4.50	8.00	6.00
		RAL DONNER—ALBUM			
☐ 5012 (M)	**GONE**	TAKIN' CARE OF BUSINESS	35.00	82.00	75.00

DONNIE AND THE DEL-CHORDS

☐ 352	**TAURUS**	WHEN YOU'RE ALONE/			
		SO LONELY	5.00	9.00	7.00
☐ 357		I DON'T CARE/I'LL BE WITH YOU			
		IN APPLE BLOSSOM TIME	5.00	9.00	7.00
☐ 361		THAT OLD FEELING/			
		TRANSYLVANIA MIST	5.00	9.00	7.00
☐ 363		I FOUND HEAVEN/BE WITH YOU .	7.00	13.00	11.00
☐ 364		I'M IN THE MOOD FOR LOVE/			
		I'VE GOT A WOMAN	4.50	8.00	6.00

DONNIE AND THE DREAMERS

☐ 500	**WHALE**	COUNT EVERY STAR/DOROTHY ..	3.25	6.00	4.00
☐ 505		MY MEMORIES OF YOU/			
		TEENAGE LOVE	3.25	6.00	4.00

DONOVAN

☐ 1309	**HICKORY**	CATCH THE WIND/WHY DO YOU			
		TREAT ME LIKE YOU DO	3.25	6.00	4.00
☐ 1324		COLOURS/JOSIE	3.25	6.00	4.00
☐ 1338		UNIVERSAL SOLDIER/			
		DO YOU HEAR ME NOW?	3.25	6.00	4.00
☐ 1402		TO TRY FOR THE SUN/TURQUOISE	3.25	6.00	4.00
☐ 1417		THE WAR DRAGS ON/HEY GYP ..	3.25	6.00	4.00
☐ 1470		SUNNY GOODGE STREET/			
		SUMMER DAY REFLECTION			
		SONG	3.25	5.25	3.50
☐ 10045	**EPIC**	SUNSHINE SUPERMAN/THE TRIP	3.00	5.25	3.85
☐ 10098		MELLOW YELLOW/			
		SUNNY SOUTH KENSINGTON ..	3.00	5.25	3.85
☐ 10127		EPISTLE TO DIPPY/			
		PREACHIN' LOVE	3.00	5.25	3.85
☐ 10212		THERE IS A MOUNTAIN/			
		SAND AND FOAM	3.00	5.25	3.85
☐ 10253		WEAR YOUR LOVE LIKE HEAVEN/			
		OH GOSH	3.00	5.25	3.85
☐ 10300		JENNIFER JUNIPER/POOR COW ..	3.00	5.25	3.85
☐ 10345		HURDY GURDY MAN/TEEN ANGEL.	3.00	5.25	3.85
☐ 10393		LALENA/AYE MY LOVE	3.00	5.25	3.85

			Current Price Range		P/Y AVG
☐ 10434		ATLANTIS/TO SUSAN ON THE WEST COAST WAITING	3.00	5.25	3.85
☐ 10510		GOO GOO BARABAJAGAL/TRUDI .	3.00	5.25	3.85
☐ 10649		RIKI TIKI TAVI/ROOTS OF OAK . . .	3.00	5.25	3.85
☐ 10694		CELIA OF THE SEALS/SONG OF THE WANDERING AENGUS	3.00	5.25	3.85
☐ 10983		I LIKE YOU/EARTH SIGN MAN . . .	3.00	5.25	3.85
☐ 11023		MARIA MAGENTA/ INTERGALACTIC LAXATIVE	3.00	5.25	3.85
☐ 11108		SAILING HOMEWARD/ YELLOW STAR	3.00	5.25	3.85
☐ 50016		ROCK 'N ROLL WITH ME/DIVINE DAZE OF DEATHLESS DELIGHT .	3.00	5.25	3.85
☐ 50077		ROCK AND ROLL SOULIER/ HOW SILLY	3.00	5.25	3.85
		DONOVAN—ALBUMS			
☐ 123 (M)	**HICKORY**	CATCH THE WIND	7.00	18.00	15.00
☐ 127 (M)		FAIRYTALES	6.00	15.00	13.50
☐ 127 (S)		FAIRYTALES	7.00	18.00	15.00
☐ 135 (M)		THE REAL DONOVAN	6.00	15.00	13.50
☐ 135 (S)		THE REAL DONOVAN	7.00	18.00	15.00
☐ 143 (M)		LIKE IT IS, WAS AND EVERMORE SHALL BE	6.00	15.00	13.50
☐ 143 (S)		LIKE IT IS, WAS AND EVERMORE SHALL BE	7.00	18.00	15.00
☐ 147 (S)		THE BEST OF DONOVAN	6.00	15.00	13.50
☐ 24217 (M)	**EPIC**	SUNSHINE SUPERMAN	5.00	12.00	10.00
☐ 26217 (S)		SUNSHINE SUPERMAN	7.00	18.00	15.00
☐ 24239 (M)		MELLOW YELLOW	5.00	12.00	10.00
☐ 26239 (S)		MELLOW YELLOW	7.00	18.00	15.00
☐ 24349 (M)		WEAR YOUR LOVE LIKE HEAVEN .	5.00	12.00	10.00
☐ 26349 (S)		WEAR YOUR LOVE LIKE HEAVEN .	7.00	18.00	15.00
☐ 24350 (M)		FOR LITTLE ONES	5.00	12.00	10.00
☐ 26350 (S)		FOR LITTLE ONES	7.00	18.00	15.00
☐ 6071 (M)		A GIFT FROM A FLOWER TO A GARDEN (box set)	8.00	21.00	18.00
☐ 171 (S)		A GIFT FROM A FLOWER TO A GARDEN	7.00	18.00	15.00
☐ 26386 (S)		IN CONCERT	6.50	17.00	11.00
☐ 26420 (S)		THE HURDY GURDY MAN	6.50	17.00	11.00
☐ 26439 (S)		GREATEST HITS.	6.50	17.00	11.00
☐ 26481 (S)		BARABAJAGAL	6.50	17.00	11.00
☐ 30125 (S)		OPEN ROAD	6.50	17.00	11.00
☐ 32156 (S)		COSMIC WHEELS	6.50	17.00	11.00
☐ 32800 (S)		ESSENCE TO ESSENCE	6.50	17.00	11.00
☐ 33245 (S)		7-TEASE	6.50	17.00	11.00
☐ 33945 (S)		SLOW DOWN WORLD.	6.50	17.00	11.00

DICKEY DOO AND THE DON'TS
FEATURED: GERRY GRANAHAN

			Current Price Range		P/Y AVG
☐ 4001	**SWAN**	CLICK CLACK/DID YOU CRY? . . .	3.50	7.00	4.65
☐ 4006		NEE NEE NA NA NA NA NU NU/ FLIP TOP BOX	3.50	7.00	4.65
☐ 4014		LEAVE ME ALONE (LET ME CRY)/ WILD PARTY	3.50	7.00	4.65
☐ 4025		TEARDROPS WILL FALL/ COME WITH US	3.50	7.00	4.65
☐ 4033		DEAR HEART, DON'T CRY/ BALLAD OF A TRAIN	3.50	7.00	4.65
☐ 4046		WABASH CANNONBALL/THE DRUMS OF RICHARD-A-DOO . . .	3.50	7.00	4.65
☐ 238	**UNITED ARTISTS**	TEEN SCENE/PITY, PITY	3.00	5.00	3.50
☐ 362		THE JUDGE/A LITTLE DOG CRIED .	3.00	5.00	3.50

DOORS

Jim Morrison was the Doors. Born in Melbourne, Florida, to a naval submarine commander and his wife, Morrison became a handsome, withdrawn and brilliant high school student. After graduation in 1961, Jim headed west to UCLA, where he had won a scholarship in the film arts department.

While at UCLA Morrison fell in with a trio of UCLA musicians. They invited Jim to become the lead singer of a group they were forming. A name was needed. Morrison, long an expert on English poetry, came up with the title Doors, based on a William Blake poem.

The Doors quit UCLA and soon developed an L. A. cult following. A contract was signed with Elektra Records. After an initial single bombed, the Doors saw instant success with a second offering, "Light My Fire". The Doors became a national phenomenon and scored five Top 10 hits during the late 1960s.

Jim Morrison died in Paris, France, on July 3, 1971, shortly after the Doors had earned a sixth major hit with "Love Her Madly". No autopsy was performed, and Morrison's death was attributed to a heart attack. Though she denied Jim's drug usage, Morrison's wife died one year later of a heroin overdose.

			Current Price Range		P/Y AVG

DICKEY DOO AND THE DON'TS—ALBUMS

☐ 3094 (M)	*UNITED ARTISTS*	MADISON	14.00	35.00	30.00
☐ 6094 (S)		MADISON	19.00	50.00	45.00
☐ 3097 (M)		TEEN SCENE	12.00	29.00	25.00
☐ 6097 (S)		TEEN SCENE	17.00	40.00	35.00

DOORS
FEATURED: JIM MORRISON

☐ 45611	*ELEKTRA*	BREAK ON THROUGH/ END OF THE NIGHT	4.50	7.50	6.00
☐ 45615		LIGHT MY FIRE/CRYSTAL SHIP	2.75	5.00	3.50
☐ 45621		PEOPLE ARE STRANGE/ UNHAPPY GIRL	3.00	5.50	3.85
☐ 45624		LOVE ME TWO TIMES/ STARLIGHT DRIVE	3.00	5.50	3.85
☐ 45628		UNKNOWN SOLDIER/WE COULD BE SO GOOD TOGETHER	3.00	5.50	3.85
☐ 45635		HELLO, I LOVE YOU/LOVE STREET	3.00	5.50	3.85
☐ 45646		TOUCH ME/WILD CHILD	3.00	5.50	3.85
☐ 45656		WISHFUL, SINFUL/ WHO SCARED YOU	3.00	5.50	3.85
☐ 45663		TELL ALL THE PEOPLE/EASY RIDE	3.00	5.50	3.85
☐ 45675		RUNNIN' BLUE/DO IT	3.00	5.50	3.85
☐ 45685		YOU MAKE ME REAL/ ROADHOUSE BLUES	3.00	5.50	3.85
☐ 45726		LOVE HER MADLY/ DON'T GO NO FURTHER	3.00	5.50	3.85
☐ 45738		RIDERS ON THE STORM/ CHANGELING	3.00	5.50	3.85

THE FOLLOWING SINGLES DO NOT FEATURE JIM MORRISON

☐ 757	*ELEKTRA*	TIGHTROPE RIDE/VARIETY IS THE SPICE OF LIFE	2.75	5.00	3.00
☐ 768		IN THE EYE OF THE SUN/ SHIPS WITH SAILS	2.75	5.00	3.00
☐ 793		GET UP AND DANCE/TREE TRUNK	2.75	5.00	3.00
☐ 807		THE MOSQUITO/ IT SLIPPED MY MIND	2.75	5.00	3.00
☐ 825		GOOD ROCKING/THE PIANO BIRD	2.75	5.00	3.00

DOORS—ALBUMS

☐ 4007 (M)	*ELEKTRA*	DOORS	7.00	18.00	15.00
☐ 74007 (S)		DOORS	6.00	15.00	13.50
☐ 4014 (M)		STRANGE DAYS	7.00	18.00	15.00
☐ 74007 (S)		STRANGE DAYS	6.00	15.00	13.50
☐ 74024 (S)		WAITING FOR THE SUN	6.00	15.00	13.50
☐ 74079 (S)		13 (greatest hits)	5.75	14.00	10.00
☐ 9002 (S)		ABSOLUTELY LIVE	5.75	14.00	10.00
☐ 75005 (S)		SOFT PARADE	5.75	14.00	10.00
☐ 75007 (S)		MORRISON HOTEL	5.75	14.00	10.00
☐ 75011 (S)		L. A. WOMAN	5.75	14.00	10.00

THE FOLLOWING ALBUMS DO NOT FEATURE JIM MORRISON

☐ 75017 (S)		OTHER VOICES	5.50	14.00	12.00
☐ 75038 (S)		FULL CIRCLE	5.50	14.00	12.00

HAROLD DORMAN

☐ 362	*SUN*	THERE THEY GO/ I'LL STICK BY YOU	4.00	7.00	4.85
☐ 370		UNCLE JOHAN'S PLACE/ JUST ONE STEP	4.00	7.00	4.85
☐ 377		WAIT TIL' SATURDAY NIGHT/ IN THE BEGINNING	4.00	7.00	4.85
☐ 1003	*RITA*	MOUNTAIN OF LOVE/ TO BE WITH YOU	3.50	6.00	4.00
☐ 1008		RIVER OF TEARS/ I'LL COME RUNNING	3.50	5.50	3.50

			Current Price Range		P/Y AVG
☐ 1012		MOVED TO KANSAS CITY/			
		TAKE A CHANCE ON ME	3.00	5.50	3.30
☐ 2092	*TOP RANK*	MOVED TO KANSAS CITY/			
		TAKE A CHANCE ON ME	2.75	5.00	3.00
☐ 1002	*TINCE*	RIVER OF TEARS/			
		I'LL COME RUNNING	2.75	5.00	3.00

GERRY DORSEY (ENGLEBERT HUMPERDINCK)

☐ 1337	*HICKORY*	BABY TURN AROUND/			
		DO THE THINGS	5.00	9.00	7.00

LEE DORSEY

☐ 1053	*FURY*	YA YA/GIVE ME YOU	3.25	5.50	4.00
☐ 1056		DO-RE-MI/			
		PEOPLE ARE GONNA TALK	3.25	5.50	4.00
☐ 1061		EENIE MEENIE MINY MOE/			
		BEHIND THE EIGHT BALL	3.25	5.50	4.00
☐ 1066		YOU ARE MY SUNSHINE/			
		GIVE ME YOUR LOVE	3.25	5.50	4.00
☐ 1074		HOODLUM JOE/			
		WHEN I MET MY BABY	3.25	5.50	4.00
		SINGLES ON AMY ARE WORTH UP TO $2.50 MINT			

LEE DORSEY—ALBUM

☐ 1002 (M)	*FURY*	YA YA	13.00	24.00	20.00

STEVE DOUGLAS

☐ 104	*PHILLES*	YES SIR, THAT'S MY BABY/			
		COLONEL BOGEY'S PARADE ...	5.50	11.00	9.00
☐ 601	*GRAPEVINE RECORDS*	ROCKING GREEN SLEEVES/HAD .	5.50	11.00	9.00

RONNIE DOVE

☐ 1406	*JALO*	SADDEST SONG (OF THE YEAR)/			
		NO GREATER LOVE	4.50	7.50	6.00
☐ 4231	*SWAN*	(HEY HEY HEY) ALRIGHT/HAPPY .	3.50	6.00	4.00

DOVELLS
FEATURED: LEN BARRY

☐ 819	*PARKWAY*	NO NO NO/LETTERS OF LOVE ...	5.00	9.00	7.00
☐ 827		BRISTOL STOMP/OUT IN THE			
		COLD AGAIN	4.50	7.50	6.00
☐ 827		BRISTOL STOMP/			
		LETTERS OF LOVE	3.25	5.50	4.00
☐ 833		DOIN' THE NEW CONTINENTAL/			
		MOPE-ITTY MOPE STOMP	3.25	5.50	4.00
☐ 838		BRISTOL TWISTIN' ANNIE/			
		THE ACTOR	3.25	5.50	4.00
☐ 845		HULLY GULLY BABY/			
		YOUR LAST CHANCE	3.25	5.50	4.00
☐ 855		THE JITTERBUG/			
		KISSIN' IN THE KITCHEN	3.25	5.50	4.00
☐ 861		YOU CAN'T RUN AWAY FROM			
		YOURSELF/HELP ME BABY ...	3.25	5.50	4.00
☐ 867		YOU CAN'T SIT DOWN/			
		STOMPIN' EVERYWHERE	3.25	5.50	4.00
☐ 867		YOU CAN'T SIT DOWN/			
		WILDWOOD DAYS	3.25	5.50	4.00
☐ 882		BETTY IN BERMUDAS/			
		DANCE THE FROOG	3.25	5.50	4.00
☐ 889		STOP MONKEYIN' AROUN'/			
		NO NO NO	3.25	5.50	4.00
☐ 901		BE MY GIRL/			
		DRAGSTER ON THE PROWL	3.25	5.50	4.00
☐ 911		HAPPY BIRTHDAY JUST THE SAME/			
		ONE POTATO, TWO POTATO ...	3.25	5.50	4.00

			Current Price Range		P/Y AVG
☐ 925		WATUSI WITH LUCY/WHAT IN THE WORLD'S COME OVER YOU?	3.25	5.50	4.00
☐ 4231	*SWAN*	(HEY HEY HEY) ALRIGHT/HAPPY .	3.25	5.50	4.00
☐ 1369	*JAMIE*	ONE WINTER LOVE/BLUE	3.25	5.50	4.00
☐ 13628	*MGM*	THERE'S A GIRL/ LOVE IS EVERYWHERE	3.25	5.50	4.00
☐ 13946		HERE COMES THE JUDGE/ GIRL (Magistrates)	3.25	5.50	4.00
☐ 14568		MARY'S MAGIC SHOW/ DON'T VOTE FOR LUKE McCABE .	3.25	5.50	4.00
☐ 3310	*EVENT*	ROLL OVER BEETHOVEN/ SOMETHING ABOUT YOU BOY .	3.25	5.50	4.00
☐ 216		DANCING IN THE STREET/ BACK ON THE ROAD AGAIN	3.25	5.50	4.00
		DOVELLS—ALBUMS			
☐ 7006 (M)	*PARKWAY*	BRISTOL STOMP	9.00	25.00	22.50
☐ 7021 (M)		FOR YOUR HULLY GULLY PARTY .	8.00	21.00	18.00
☐ 7025 (M)		YOU CAN'T SIT DOWN	8.00	21.00	18.00
		DOVERS			
☐ 1000	*VALENTINE*	ALICE MY LOVE/LONELY HEART .	9.50	25.00	22.00
		DICKIE DOYLE			
☐ 1009	*WYE*	DREAMLAND LAST NIGHT/ MY LITTLE ANGEL	17.00	35.00	30.00
		DREAMERS			
☐ 1005	*COUSINS*	BECAUSE OF YOU/LITTLE GIRL ..	12.00	21.00	18.00
☐ 133	*MAY*	BECAUSE OF YOU/LITTLE GIRL ..	4.50	8.00	6.00
☐ 3015	*GOLDISC*	NATALIE/ TEENAGE VOWS OF LOVE	4.50	8.00	6.00
		DREAMLOVERS			
☐ 102	*HERITAGE*	WHEN WE GET MARRIED/ JUST BECAUSE	3.50	6.00	4.00
☐ 104		WELCOME HOME/LET THEM LOVE	3.50	6.00	4.00
☐ 107		ZOOM ZOOM ZOOM/ WHILE WE WERE DANCING	3.50	6.00	4.00
☐ 1114	*END*	IF I SHOULD LOSE YOU/ I MISS YOU	3.50	6.00	4.00
☐ 1308	*CASINO*	TOGETHER/ AMAZONS AND COYOTES	3.50	6.00	4.00
☐ 5619	*SWAN*	TOGETHER/ AMAZONS AND COYOTES	3.25	5.50	4.00
☐ 42698	*COLUMBIA*	SAD SAD BOY/ IF I WERE A MAGICIAN	3.25	5.50	4.00
☐ 42752		SAD SAD BOY/BLACK BOTTOM ..	3.25	5.50	4.00
☐ 42842		PRETTY LITTLE GIRL/ I'M THROUGH WITH YOU	3.25	5.50	4.00
☐ 326	*CAMEO*	THESE WILL BE THE GOOD OLD DAYS/OH BABY MINE	3.25	5.50	4.00
☐ 72595	*MERCURY*	BAD TIMES MAKE THE GOOD TIMES/BLESS YOUR SOUL ...	3.25	5.50	4.00
☐ 72630		CALLING JO-ANN/YOU GAVE ME SOMEBODY TO LOVE	3.25	5.50	4.00
		DREAMLOVERS—ALBUM			
☐ 2020 (M)	*COLUMBIA*	THE BIRD	12.00	21.00	18.00
☐ 8820 (S)		THE BIRD	17.00	28.00	25.00
		DRIFTERS			
☐ 1006	*ATLANTIC*	MONEY HONEY/THE WAY I FEEL .	17.00	40.00	25.00
☐ 1019		SUCH A NIGHT/LUCILLE	17.00	35.00	25.00
☐ 1029		HONEY LOVE/WARM YOUR HEART	15.00	35.00	20.00
☐ 1043		BIP BAM/SOMEDAY YOU'LL WANT ME TO WANT YOU	10.00	17.00	15.00

DRIFTERS

In 1953, Clyde McPhatter left the successful Dominoes group. He then fell in with the Civitones, a gospel outfit. Clyde convinced two Civitones to join him and a friend in the formation of a new rhythm-and-blues group.

They often joked about drifting from one group to another, so they took on the name Drifters. In the summer of 1953, they auditioned for (and won a contract from) Atlantic Records. That fall they cut "Money Honey". It was an immediate hit and was later "covered" by Elvis Presley. Then came bouncy, raunchy songs like "Bip Bam" and "Honey Love", as well as the satin-smooth "White Christmas".

McPhatter left for the Army in 1954. His third replacement was Bobby Hendricks (who later did "Itchy Twitchy Feeling"). After minor hits like "Drip Drop" (later a Dion winner), the original Drifters split up.

Their manager then signed the Five Crowns (led by Ben E. King) as the Drifters. The "new" Drifters hit big with their first waxing, the now-classic "There Goes My Baby". It was the first rock record to employ a full orchestra. "There Goes My Baby" became the first of many fine Drifters hits. They made a dozen trips to the Top 30 before falling on less successful times.

		Current Price Range		P/Y AVG
☐ 1048	WHITE CHRISTMAS/			
	THE BELLS OF ST. MARY'S ...	8.25	14.00	12.00
☐ 1055	GONE/WHAT 'CHA GONNA DO? ...	8.25	14.00	12.00
	FEATURED ABOVE: CLYDE McPHATTER			
☐ 1078	ADORABLE/STEAMBOAT	7.00	13.00	11.00
	FIRST PRESSES OF ABOVE WERE ON THE YELLOW-AND-BLACK LABEL			
☐ 1089	RUBY BABY/			
	YOUR PROMISE TO BE MINE ...	7.00	13.00	11.00
☐ 1101	SOLDIER OF FORTUNE/I GOTTA			
	GET MYSELF A WOMAN	7.00	13.00	11.00
☐ 1123	FOOLS FALL IN LOVE/			
	IT WAS A TEAR	4.50	8.00	6.00
☐ 1141	HYPNOTIZED/			
	DRIFTING AWAY FROM YOU ...	4.50	8.00	6.00
☐ 1161	I KNOW/YODEE YAKEE	4.50	8.00	6.00
☐ 1187	DRIP DROP/MOONLIGHT BAY ...	3.75	6.00	4.50
☐ 2025	THERE GOES MY BABY/			
	OH MY LOVE	3.75	6.00	4.00
☐ 2038	THERE YOU GO/YOU WENT			
	BACK ON YOUR WORD	4.50	7.50	6.00
☐ 2040	DANCE WITH ME/			
	TRUE LOVE, TRUE LOVE	3.50	6.50	4.65
☐ 2050	THIS MAGIC MOMENT/			
	BALTIMORE	3.50	6.50	4.65
☐ 2062	LONELY WINDS/HEY SENORITA .	3.50	6.50	4.65
☐ 2071	SAVE THE LAST DANCE FOR ME/			
	NOBODY BUT ME	3.50	6.50	4.65
☐ 2087	I COUNT THE TEARS/			
	SUDDENLY THERE'S A VALLEY	3.50	6.50	4.65
☐ 2096	SOME KIND OF WONDERFUL/			
	HONEY BEE	3.50	6.50	4.65
☐ 2105	PLEASE STAY/NO SWEET LOVIN'	3.50	6.50	4.65
☐ 2117	SWEETS FOR MY SWEET/			
	LONELINESS OR HAPPINESS ..	3.25	6.00	4.00
☐ 2127	ROOM FULL OF TEARS/			
	SOMEBODY NEW DANCIN'			
	WITH YOU	3.25	6.00	4.00
☐ 2134	WHEN MY LITTLE GIRL IS			
	SMILING/MEXICAN DIVORCE ..	3.25	6.00	4.00
☐ 2143	STRANGER ON THE SHORE/			
	WHAT TO DO	3.25	6.00	4.00
☐ 2151	SOMETIMES I WONDER/JACKPOT	3.25	6.00	4.00
☐ 2162	UP ON THE ROOF/ANOTHER			
	NIGHT WITH THE BOYS	3.25	6.00	4.00
☐ 2182	ON BROADWAY/			
	LET THE MUSIC PLAY	3.25	6.00	4.00
☐ 2191	RAT RACE/			
	IF YOU DON'T COME BACK	3.25	6.00	4.00
☐ 2201	I'LL TAKE YOU HOME/			
	I FEEL GOOD ALL OVER	3.25	6.00	4.00
☐ 2216	VAYA CON DIOS/IN THE			
	LAND OF MAKE BELIEVE	3.25	6.00	4.00
☐ 2225	ONE WAY LOVE/DIDN'T IT	3.25	6.00	4.00
☐ 2237	UNDER THE BROADWALK/I DON'T			
	WANT TO GO ON WITHOUT YOU	3.25	6.00	4.00
☐ 2253	I'VE GOT SAND IN MY SHOES/			
	HE'S JUST A PLAYBOY	3.00	5.50	3.85
☐ 2260	SATURDAY NIGHT AT THE			
	MOVIES/SPANISH LACE	3.00	5.50	3.85
☐ 2261	THE CHRISTMAS SONG/			
	I REMEMBER CHRISTMAS	3.00	5.50	3.85
☐ 2268	AT THE CLUB/			
	ANSWER THE PHONE	3.00	5.50	3.85
☐ 2285	COME ON OVER TO MY PLACE/			
	CHAINS OF LOVE	3.00	5.50	3.85

MERCURY, MG 20314, LP

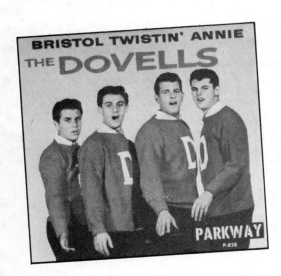

PARKWAY, P-838, 45

			Current Price Range		P/Y AVG
☐ 2292		FOLLOW ME/ THE OUTSIDE WORLD	3.00	5.50	3.85
☐ 2298		I'LL TAKE YOU WHERE THE MUSIC'S PLAYING/FAR FROM THE MADDENING CROWD	3.00	5.50	3.85
☐ 2310		WE GOTTA SING/ NYLON STOCKINGS	3.00	5.50	3.85
☐ 2325		MEMORIES ARE MADE OF THIS/ MY ISLANDS IN THE SUN	3.00	5.50	3.85
☐ 2336		UP IN THE STREETS OF HARLEM/ YOU CAN'T LOVE THEM ALL . .	3.00	5.50	3.85
☐ 2366		BABY WHAT I MEAN/ARETHA . . .	3.00	5.50	3.85
☐ 2426		AIN'T IT THE TRUTH/ UP JUMPED THE DEVIL	3.00	5.50	3.85
☐ 2471		STILL BURNING IN MY HEART/ I NEED YOU NOW	3.00	5.50	3.85
☐ 2624		STEAL AWAY/YOUR BEST FRIEND .	3.00	5.50	3.85
☐ 2746		BLACK SILK/YOU GOT TO PAY YOUR DUES	3.00	5.50	3.85
☐ 2786		BE MY LADY/A ROSE BY ANY OTHER NAME	3.00	5.50	3.85
		DRIFTERS—EPS			
☐ 534	*ATLANTIC*	THE DRIFTERS FEATURING CLYDE McPHATTER	12.00	21.00	18.00
☐ 592		THE DRIFTERS	9.50	17.00	15.00
		DRIFTERS—ALBUMS			
☐ 8003 (M)		CLYDE McPHATTER AND THE DRIFTERS	19.00	50.00	45.00
☐ 8022 (M)		ROCKIN' AND DRIFTIN'	17.00	40.00	35.00
☐ 8041 (M)		GREATEST HITS	17.00	40.00	35.00
☐ 8059 (M)		SAVE THE LAST DANCE FOR ME .	9.00	25.00	22.50
☐ 8059 (S)		SAVE THE LAST DANCE FOR ME .	14.00	35.00	30.00
☐ 8073 (M)		UP ON THE ROOF	9.00	25.00	22.50
☐ 8073 (S)		UP ON THE ROOF	14.00	35.00	30.00
☐ 8093 (M)		OUR BIGGEST HITS	8.00	21.00	18.00
☐ 8093 (S)		OUR BIGGEST HITS	12.00	29.00	25.00
☐ 8099 (M)		UNDER THE BOARDWALK	8.00	21.00	18.00
☐ 8099 (S)		UNDER THE BOARDWALK	12.00	29.00	25.00
☐ 8102 (M)		THE GOOD LIFE WITH THE DRIFTERS	8.00	17.00	15.00
☐ 8102 (S)		THE GOOD LIFE WITH THE DRIFTERS	9.00	25.00	22.50
☐ 8113 (M)		I'LL TAKE YOU WHERE THE MUSIC'S PLAYING	7.00	17.00	15.00
☐ 8113 (S)		I'LL TAKE YOU WHERE THE MUSIC'S PLAYING	9.00	25.00	22.50
☐ 8153 (M)		THE DRIFTERS' GOLDEN HITS . . .	7.00	17.00	15.00
☐ 8153 (S)		THE DRIFTERS' GOLDEN HITS . . .	9.00	25.00	22.50
		DUALS			
☐ 1031	*STAR REVUE*	STICK SHIFT/CRUISIN'	5.50	11.00	9.00
☐ 745	*SUE*	STICK SHIFT/CRUISIN'	3.00	5.00	3.50
		DUALS—ALBUM			
☐ 2002 (M)		STICK SHIFT	8.00	21.00	18.00
		DUBS			
☐ 102	*JOHNSON*	DON'T ASK ME (TO BE LONELY)/ DARLING	40.00	75.00	48.00
☐ 5002	*GONE*	DON'T ASK ME (TO BE LONELY)/ DARLING	7.00	12.00	10.00
☐ 5011		COULD THIS BE MAGIC?/ SUCH LOVIN'	6.00	12.00	8.00
☐ 5020		BESIDE MY LOVE/ GONNA MAKE A CHANGE	6.00	12.00	8.00

			Current Price Range		P/Y AVG
☐ 5034		BE SURE (MY LOVE)/ SONG IN MY HEART	6.00	12.00	8.00
☐ 5046	/	CHAPEL OF DREAMS/ IS THERE A LOVE FOR ME?	6.00	12.00	8.00
☐ 5069		CHAPEL OF DREAMS/ IS THERE A LOVE FOR ME?	5.00	9.00	7.00
		FIRST-PRESS SINGLES WERE ON THE BLACK LABEL			
☐ 5138		YOU'RE FREE TO GO/ IS THERE A LOVE FOR ME	5.00	9.00	7.00
☐ 8008	MARK-X	BE SURE (MY LOVE)/ SONG IN MY HEART	5.50	11.00	9.00
☐ 9771	ABC-PARAMOUNT	I WON'T HAVE YOU BREAKING MY HEART/JUMP ROCK AND ROLL (Marvels)	6.00	10.00	6.00
☐ 10056		EARLY IN THE MORNING/NO ONE	5.00	10.00	6.00
☐ 10100		DON'T LAUGH AT ME/ YOU'LL NEVER BELONG TO ME	5.00	10.00	6.00
☐ 10150		FOR THE FIRST TIME/ AIN'T THAT SO	5.00	10.00	6.00
☐ 10198		IF I ONLY HAD MAGIC/ JOOGIE BOOGIE	5.00	10.00	6.00
☐ 10269		DOWN. DOWN. DOWN I GO/ LULLABY	5.00	10.00	6.00
☐ 1108	END	NOW THAT WE BROKE UP/ THIS TO ME IS LOVE	8.25	13.00	12.00
☐ 911	JOSIE	THIS IS SWEAR/ WISDOM OF A FOOL	8.25	13.00	12.00
		DUBS—ALBUM			
☐ 4001 (M)	JOSIE	DUBS MEET THE SHELLS ..	19.00	49.00	45.00

DUKAYS
FEATURED: GENE CHANDLER

☐ M-102	MONOGRAM	THE BIG LIE/NIGHT OWL	4.00	7.50	5.00
☐ 4001	NAT	THE GIRL'S A DEVIL/THE BIG LIE	3.75	6.00	4.50
☐ 4002		NITE OWL/FESTIVAL OF LOVE ...	3.75	6.00	4.50
☐ 430	VEE JAY	NITE OWL/FESTIVAL OF LOVE ...	3.00	5.00	3.50
☐ 442		I'M GONNA LOVE YOU SO/ PLEASE HELP	3.00	5.00	3.50
☐ 460		I FEEL GOOD ALL OVER/ I NEVER KNEW	3.00	5.00	3.50
☐ 491		COMBINATION/EVERY STEP	3.00	5.00	3.50

DUPONTS (LITTLE ANTHONY AND THE IMPERIALS)

☐ 212	WINLEY	MUST BE FALLING IN LOVE/YOU	20.00	35.00	30.00
☐ 527	ROYAL ROOST	PROVE IT TONIGHT/SOMEBODY .	17.00	29.00	25.00

DUPREES

☐ 569	COED	YOU BELONG TO ME/ TAKE ME AS I AM	3.25	5.50	4.00
☐ 571		MY OWN TRUE LOVE/GINNY	3.25	5.50	4.00
☐ 574		I'D RATHER BE HERE IN YOU ARMS/I WISH I COULD BELIEVE YOU	3.25	5.50	4.00
☐ 576		GONE WITH THE WIND/ LET'S MAKE LOVE AGAIN	3.25	5.50	4.00
☐ 580		I GOTTA TELL HER NOW/ TAKE ME AS I AM	3.25	5.50	4.00
☐ 584		WHY DON'T YOU BELIEVE ME/ THE THINGS I LOVE	3.50	7.00	4.65
☐ 584		WHY DON'T YOU BELIEVE ME/ MY DEAREST ONE	3.25	5.50	4.00
☐ 585		HAVE YOU HEARD?/LOVE EYES .	3.25	5.50	4.00

			Current Price Range		P/Y AVG
☐587		(IT'S NO) SIN/			
		THE SAND AND THE SEA	3.25	5.50	4.00
☐591		WHERE ARE YOU/			
		PLEASE LET HER KNOW	3.25	5.50	4.00
☐593		SO MANY HAVE TOLD YOU/			
		UNBELIEVABLE	3.25	5.50	4.00
☐595		IT ISN'T FAIR/SO LITTLE TIME ..	3.25	5.50	4.00
☐596		I'M YOURS/WISHING RING	3.25	5.50	4.00
☐4-44078	COLUMBIA	I UNDERSTAND/BE MY LOVE	3.25	5.50	4.00
		DUPREES—ALBUMS			
☐905 (M)	COED	YOU BELONG TO ME	19.00	49.00	45.00
☐906 (M)		HAVE YOU HEARD?	17.00	39.00	35.00

HUELYN DUVALL

☐1012	CHALLENGE	TEEN QUEEN/COMIN' OR GOIN' ..	9.50	19.00	15.00
☐59002		HUM-DINGER/			
		YOU KNOCK ME OUT	8.25	15.00	12.00
☐59014		LITTLE BOY BLUE/			
		THREE MONTHS TO KILL	5.00	9.00	4.00
☐59025		FRIDAY NIGHT ON A DOLLAR			
		BILL/JULIET	5.00	9.00	7.00

E

EARLS

☐101	ROME	LIFE IS BUT A DREAM/IT'S YOU .	8.25	14.00	12.00
☐101		LIFE IS BUT A DREAM/			
		WITHOUT YOU	5.50	11.00	9.00
☐102		LOOKIN' FOR MY BABY/			
		CROSS MY HEART	5.00	9.00	7.00
☐111		STORMY WEATHER/COULD THIS			
		BE MAGIC (Pretenders)	4.50	7.50	6.00
☐112		LITTLE BOY AND GIRL/LOST LOVE.	4.50	7.50	6.00
☐113		WHOEVER YOU ARE/LOST LOVE .	4.50	7.50	6.00
☐114		ALL THROUGH OUR TEENS/			
		WHOEVER YOU ARE	5.50	7.50	6.00
☐114		ALL THROUGH OUR TEENS/			
		WHOEVER YOU ARE			
		(colored wax)	8.25	14.00	12.00
☐1130	OLD TOWN	REMEMBER THEN/LET'S WADDLE	3.50	6.00	4.35
☐1133		NEVER/KEEP A-TELLIN' YOU	3.50	6.00	4.35
☐1141		LOOK MY WAY/EYES	4.00	7.00	4.85
☐1145		CRY, CRY, CRY/KISSIN'	4.00	7.00	4.85
☐1149		I BELIEVE/DON'T FORGET	4.00	7.00	4.85
☐1169		ASK ANYBODY/OH WHAT A TIME	4.00	7.00	4.85
☐1182		REMEMBER ME. BABY/AMOR ...	4.00	7.00	4.85
☐801	MR. G	IF I COULD DO IT OVER AGAIN/			
		PAPA	4.50	7.50	6.00
☐11109	ABC	MY LONELY LONELY ROOM/			
		LONG TIME COMING	3.75	6.00	4.50
☐10225	COLUMBIA	GOIN' UPTOWN/MRS. WOMEN ..	3.25	6.00	4.00
☐100	HARVEY	A SUNDAY KIND OF LOVE/			
		DREAM COME TRUE	3.25	6.00	4.00
☐101	WOODBURY	TONIGHT (COULD BE THE NIGHT)/			
		MEDITATION	3.25	6.00	4.00
		EARLS—ALBUM			
☐104 (M)	OLD TOWN	REMEMBER ME. BABY	24.00	45.00	40.00

EASYBEATS

☐2214	ASCOT	WOMEN/IN MY BOOK	4.50	7.50	6.00

			Current Price Range		P/Y AVG
☐ 50106	UNITED ARTISTS	FRIDAY ON MY MIND/ MADE MY BED	3.50	5.50	4.00
☐ 50187		PRETTY GIRL/HEAVEN AND HELL	3.50	5.50	4.00
☐ 50206		FALLING OFF THE EDGE OF THE WORLD/SAM	3.50	5.50	4.00
☐ 50289		HELLO. HOW ARE YOU/COME IN. YOU'LL GET PNEUMONIA	3.50	5.50	4.00
☐ 50488		GOOD TIMES/ LAY ME DOWN AND DIE	3.50	5.50	4.00
☐ 5009	RARE EARTH	ST. LOUIS/CAN'T FIND LOVE	3.50	5.50	4.00

EASYBEATS—ALBUMS

☐ 3588 (M)	UNITED ARTISTS	FRIDAY ON MY MIND	7.00	18.00	15.00
☐ 6588 (S)		FRIDAY ON MY MIND	9.00	25.00	22.50
☐ 6667 (S)		FALLING OFF THE EDGE OF THE WORLD	8.00	21.00	18.00

ECHOES

☐ 101	SRG	BABY BLUE/BOOMERANG	10.00	18.00	15.00
☐ 102	SEG-WAY	ANGEL OF MY HEART/GEE OH GEE	4.50	7.50	6.00
☐ 103		BABY BLUE/BOOMERANG	3.00	5.00	3.50
☐ 106		SAD EYES/IT'S RAININ'	3.00	5.00	3.50

ECHOES (INNOCENTS)

☐ 22102	ANDEX	TIME/DEE DEE DI OH	5.50	11.00	9.00

EDDIE AND THE SHOWMEN

☐ 55566	LIBERTY	TOES ON THE NOSE/ BORDER TOWN	4.00	7.00	4.85
☐ 55608		SQUAD CAR/SCRATCH	4.00	7.00	4.85
☐ 55659		MR. REBEL/MOVIN'	4.00	7.00	4.85
☐ 55695		LANKY BONES/ FAR AWAY PLACES	4.00	7.00	4.85
☐ 55720		YOUNG AND LONELY/ WE ARE THE YOUNG	4.00	7.00	4.85

DUANE EDDY

☐ 500	FORD	RAMROD/CARAVAN	20.00	37.00	23.00
☐ 1101	JAMIE	MOVIN' 'N' GROOVIN'/ UP AND DOWN	4.00	7.00	4.35
☐ 1104		REBEL-ROUSER/STALKIN'	3.25	5.25	4.00
☐ 1109		RAMROD/THE WALKER	3.25	5.25	4.00
☐ 1111		CANNONBALL/ MASON DIXON LINE	3.25	5.25	4.00
☐ 1117		THE LONELY ONE/DETOUR	3.25	5.25	4.00
☐ 1122		YEP!/DETOUR	3.25	5.25	4.00
☐ 1126		FORTY MILES OF BAD ROAD/ THE QUIET THREE	3.25	5.25	4.00
☐ 1130		SOME KIND-A EARTHQUAKE/ FIRST LOVE. FIRST TEARS	3.25	5.25	4.00
☐ 1144		BONNIE CAME BACK/ LOST ISLAND	3.25	5.25	4.00
☐ 1151		SHAZAM!/THE SECRET SEVEN	3.25	5.25	4.00
☐ 1156		BECAUSE THEY'RE YOUNG/ REBEL WALK	3.25	5.25	4.00
☐ 1158		THE GIRL ON DEATH ROW/ WORDS MEAN NOTHING	3.25	5.25	4.00
☐ 1163		KOMOTION/ THEME FOR MOON CHILDREN	3.25	5.25	4.00
☐ 1168		PETER GUNN/ ALONG THE NAVAJO TRAIL	3.25	5.25	4.00
☐ 1175		PEPE/LOST FRIEND	3.25	5.25	4.00
☐ 1183		THEME FROM DIXIE/ GIDGET GOES HAWAIIAN	3.25	5.25	4.00

			Current Price Range		P/Y AVG
☐ 1187		RING OF FIRE/BOBBIE	3.25	5.25	4.00
☐ 1195		DRIVIN' HOME/TAMMY	3.25	5.25	4.00
☐ 1200		MY BLUE HEAVEN/ ALONG CAME LINDA	3.25	5.25	4.00
☐ 1206		THE AVENGER/ LONDONBERRY AIR	3.25	5.25	4.00
☐ 1209		THE BATTLE/TROMBONE	3.25	5.25	4.00
☐ 1224		RUNAWAY PONY/JUST BECAUSE	3.25	5.25	4.00
☐ 7999	*RCA*	DEEP IN THE HEART OF TEXAS/ SAINTS AND SINNERS	3.00	5.00	3.50
☐ 8047		THE BALLAD OF PALADIN/ THE WILD WESTERNERS	3.00	5.00	3.50
☐ 8087		(DANCE WITH THE) GUITAR MAN/ STRETCHIN' OUT	3.00	5.00	3.50
☐ 8131		BOSS GUITAR/THE DESERT RAT .	3.00	5.00	3.50
☐ 8180		LONELY BOY, LONELY GUITAR/ JOSHIN'	3.00	5.00	3.50
☐ 8214		YOUR BABY'S GONE SURFIN'/ SHUCKIN'	3.00	5.00	3.50
☐ 8276		THE SON OF REBEL ROUSER/ THE STORY OF THREE LOVES ..	3.00	5.00	3.50
☐ 8335		GUITAR CHILD/JERKY JALOPY ..	3.00	5.00	3.50
☐ 8376		THEME FROM A SUMMER PLACE/ WATER SKIING	3.00	5.00	3.50
☐ 8442		GUITAR STAR/THE IGUANA	3.00	5.00	3.50
☐ 8507		MOONSHOT/ROUGHNECK.......	3.00	5.00	3.50
☐ 779	*COLPIX*	TRASH/SOUTH PHOENIX	3.00	5.00	3.50
☐ 788		DON'T THINK TWICE, IT'S ALRIGHT/HOUSE OF THE RISING SUN	3.00	5.00	3.50
☐ 795		EL RANCHO GRANDE/POPPA'S MOVIN' ON (I'M MOVIN' ON) ..	3.00	5.00	3.50
☐ 0504	*REPRISE*	DAYDREAM/THIS GUITAR WAS MADE FOR TWANGIN'	3.00	5.00	3.50
☐ 0557		MONSOON/ROARIN'	3.00	5.00	3.50
☐ 0622		GUITAR ON MY MIND/WICKED WOMAN FROM WICKENBURG ..	3.00	5.00	3.50
☐ 0662		THIS TOWN/ THERE IS A MOUNTAIN	3.00	5.00	3.50
☐ 0690		VELVET NIGHT/NIKI HOKEY	3.00	5.00	3.50
		DUANE EDDY—EPs			
☐ 100	*JAMIE*	DUANE EDDY	8.25	14.00	12.00
☐ 301		DETOUR....................	8.00	12.00	10.00
☐ 302		YEP!......................	8.00	12.00	10.00
☐ 303		SHAZAM!...................	8.00	12.00	10.00
☐ 304		BECAUSE THEY'RE YOUNG	8.00	12.00	10.00
		DUANE EDDY—ALBUMS			
☐ 3000 (M)	*JAMIE*	HAVE TWANGY GUITAR, WILL TRAVEL	12.00	19.00	17.50
☐ 3000 (S)		HAVE TWANGY GUITAR, WILL TRAVEL	19.00	34.00	30.00
☐ 3006 (M)		ESPECIALLY FOR YOU	12.00	19.00	17.50
☐ 3006 (S)		ESPECIALLY FOR YOU	17.00	28.00	25.00
☐ 3009 (M)		THE TWANG'S THE THING	12.00	19.00	17.50
☐ 3009 (S)		THE TWANG'S THE THING	17.00	28.00	25.00
☐ 3011 (M)		SONGS OF OUR HERITAGE	10.00	17.00	15.00
☐ 3011 (S)		SONGS OF OUR HERITAGE	14.00	23.00	20.00
☐ 3014 (M)		$1,000,000 WORTH OF TWANG ..	10.00	17.00	15.00
☐ 3014 (S)		$1,000,000 WORTH OF TWANG ..	14.00	23.00	20.00
☐ 3019 (M)		GIRLS, GIRLS, GIRLS	10.00	17.00	15.00
☐ 3019 (S)		GIRLS, GIRLS, GIRLS	14.00	23.00	20.00
☐ 3021 (M)		$1,000,000 WORTH OF TWANG, VOL. II	10.00	17.00	15.00

			Current Price Range		P/Y AVG
☐ 3021 (S)		$1.000.000 WORTH OF TWANG. VOL. II	12.00	19.00	17.50
☐ 3022 (M)		TWISTING WITH DUANE EDDY . . .	8.00	20.00	18.00
☐ 3022 (S)		TWISTING WITH DUANE EDDY . . .	9.00	25.00	22.50
☐ 3024 (M)		SURFIN'	8.00	20.00	18.00
☐ 3024 (S)		SURFIN'	9.00	25.00	22.50
☐ 3025 (M)		IN PERSON	7.00	17.00	15.00
☐ 3025 (S)		IN PERSON	9.00	25.00	22.50
☐ 3026 (M)		16 GREATEST HITS	7.00	17.00	15.00
☐ 3026 (S)		16 GREATEST HITS	8.00	20.00	18.00
☐ 2525 (M)	**RCA**	TWISTIN' AND TWANGIN'	7.00	17.00	15.00
☐ 2525 (S)		TWISTIN' AND TWANGIN'	8.00	20.00	18.00
☐ 2576 (M)		TWANGY GUITAR. SILKY STRINGS.	6.00	15.00	13.50
☐ 2576 (S)		TWANGY GUITAR. SILKY STRINGS.	8.00	20.00	18.00
☐ 2648 (M)		DANCE WITH THE GUITAR MAN . .	6.00	15.00	13.50
☐ 2648 (S)		DANCE WITH THE GUITAR MAN . .	8.00	20.00	18.00
☐ 2681 (M)		TWANG A COUNTRY SONG	6.00	15.00	13.50
☐ 2681 (S)		TWANG A COUNTRY SONG	7.00	17.00	15.00
☐ 2700 (M)		TWANGIN' UP A STORM	6.00	15.00	13.50
☐ 2700 (S)		TWANGIN' UP A STORM	7.00	17.00	15.00
☐ 2798 (M)		LONELY GUITAR	6.00	15.00	13.50
☐ 2798 (S)		LONELY GUITAR	7.00	17.00	15.00
☐ 2918 (M)		WATER SKIING	6.00	15.00	13.50
☐ 2918 (S)		WATER SKIING	7.00	17.00	15.00
☐ 2993 (M)		TWANGIN' THE GOLDEN HITS . . .	6.00	15.00	13.50
☐ 2993 (S)		TWANGIN' THE GOLDEN HITS . . .	7.00	17.00	15.00
☐ 3432 (M)		TWANGSVILLE	6.00	15.00	13.50
☐ 3432 (S)		TWANGSVILLE	7.00	17.00	15.00
☐ 3477 (M)		THE BEST OF DUANE EDDY	6.00	15.00	13.50
☐ 3477 (S)		THE BEST OF DUANE EDDY	7.00	17.00	15.00
☐ 490 (M)	**COLPIX**	A-GO-GO	6.00	15.00	13.50
☐ 490 (S)		A-GO-GO	7.00	17.00	15.00
☐ 494 (M)		DUANE EDDY DOES BOB DYLAN . .	6.00	15.00	13.50
☐ 490 (S)		DUANE EDDY DOES BOB DYLAN . .	7.00	17.00	15.00
☐ 6218 (M)	**REPRISE**	BIGGEST TWANG OF THEM ALL . .	5.50	14.00	12.00
☐ 6218 (S)		BIGGEST TWANG OF THEM ALL . .	7.00	17.00	15.00
☐ 6240 (M)		ROARING TWANGIES	5.50	14.00	12.00
☐ 6240 (S)		ROARING TWANGIES	7.00	17.00	15.00

EDSELS

☐ 2843	**DUB**	LAMA RAMA DING DONG/ BELLS (original title)	13.50	22.50	18.50
☐ 2843		RAMA LAMA DING DONG/ BELLS (revised title)	8.00	14.00	11.50
☐ 700	**TWIN**	RAMA LAMA DING DONG/BELLS .	4.00	7.00	6.00

EL DORADOS

☐ 115	**VEE JAY**	MY LOVING BABY/ BABY I NEED YOU	35.00	69.00	42.00
☐ 115		MY LOVING BABY/ BABY I NEED YOU (red wax) . . .	75.00	135.00	95.00
☐ 118		ANNIE'S ANSWER/ LIVING WITH VIVIAN	30.00	60.00	38.00
☐ 127		ONE MORE CHANCE/ LITTLE MISS LOVE	25.00	42.00	38.00
☐ 147		AT MY FRONT DOOR/ WHAT'S BUGGIN' YOU BABY . .	10.00	15.00	13.00
☐ 165		I'LL BE FOREVER LOVING YOU/ I BEGAN TO REALIZE	14.00	22.00	19.00
☐ 180		NOW THAT YOU'VE GONE/ ROCK 'N' ROLL'S FOR ME	14.00	22.00	19.00
☐ 197		A FALLEN TEAR/CHOP LING SOON.	14.00	22.00	19.00
☐ 211		BIM BAM BOOM/ THERE IN THE NIGHT	14.00	22.00	19.00

			Current Price Range		P/Y AVG
☐ 250		TEARS ON MY PILLOW/			
		A ROSE FOR MY DARLING	14.00	22.00	19.00
☐ 263		THREE REASONS WHY/			
		BOOM DIDDLE BOOM	19.00	30.00	27.00
☐ 302		LIGHTS ARE LOW/			
		OH, WHAT A GIRL	25.00	45.00	38.00
		EL DORADOS—ALBUM			
☐ 1001 (M)	*VEE JAY*	CRAZY LITTLE MAMA	40.00	100.00	92.00

ELECTRIC PRUNES

☐ 0473	*REPRISE*	AIN'T IT HARD/LITTLE OLIVE ...	3.50	5.50	4.00
☐ 0532		I HAD TOO MUCH TO DREAM LAST			
		NIGHT/LOVIN'	3.00	5.00	3.85
☐ 0564		GET ME TO THE WORLD ON TIME/			
		ARE YOU LOVIN' ME MORE? ..	3.00	5.00	3.85
☐ 0594		DR. DO GOOD/HIDEAWAY	3.00	5.00	3.65
☐ 0607		WIND-UP TOYS/			
		THE GREAT BANANA HOAX	3.00	5.00	3.65
☐ 0652		YOU NEVER HAD IT BETTER/			
		EVERYBODY KNOWS YOU'RE			
		NOT IN LOVE	3.00	5.00	3.65
☐ 0833		VIOLENT ROSE/SELL	3.00	5.00	3.65
		ELECTRIC PRUNES—ALBUMS			
☐ 6248 (M)	*REPRISE*	THE ELECTRIC PRUNES.........	8.00	21.00	18.00
☐ 6248 (S)		THE ELECTRIC PRUNES.........	7.00	17.00	15.00
☐ 6262 (M)		UNDERGROUND...............	10.00	25.00	22.50
☐ 6262 (S)		UNDERGROUND...............	8.00	21.00	18.00
☐ 6275 (S)		MASS IN F MINOR.............	7.00	17.00	15.00
☐ 6316 (S)		RELEASE OF AN OATH..........	7.00	17.00	15.00
☐ 6342 (S)		JUST GOOD OLD ROCK N' ROLL ..	7.00	17.00	15.00

ELEGANTS

☐ 25005	*APT*	LITTLE STAR/GETTING DIZZY			
		(black label)	8.25	14.00	12.00
☐ 25005		LITTLE STAR/GETTING DIZZY			
		(colored label)	4.50	7.50	6.00
☐ 25017		PLEASE BELIEVE ME/GOODNIGHT	4.50	7.50	6.00
☐ 25029		TRUE LOVE AFFAIR/PAYDAY	4.50	7.50	6.00
☐ 732	*HULL*	LITTLE BOY BLUE/			
		GET WELL SOON	12.00	21.00	18.00
☐ 230	*UNITED ARTISTS*	LET MY PRAYERS BE WITH YOU/			
		SPEAK LOW	5.50	10.00	6.75
☐ 295		HAPPINESS/SPIRAL HAPPINESS .	5.50	10.00	6.75
☐ 10219	*ABC*	I'VE SEEN EVERYTHING/			
		TINY CLOUD	5.50	10.00	6.75
☐ 2662	*PHOTO*	A DREAM CAN COME TRUE/			
		DRESSIN' UP	5.50	10.00	6.75
☐ 10160	*IPG*	PATH IN THE WILDERNESS/			
		GET ON THE RIGHT TRACK	5.50	10.00	6.75
☐ 3283	*LAURIE*	BARBARA, BEWARE/			
		A LETTER FROM VIETNAM	4.50	7.50	6.00
☐ 3298		BRING BACK WENDY/WAKE UP ..	5.00	8.50	7.00
☐ 3324		BELINDA/LAZY LOVE	4.50	7.50	6.00

ELEMENTS OF LIFE

☐ 14 A & B	*STARLIGHT*	IN A FAIRY TALE/			
		DISCO MAMA, DISCO MAN	17.00	36.00	24.00

CASS ELLIOT (MAMA CASS)

☐ 4145	*DUNHILL*	DREAM A LITTLE DREAM OF ME/			
		MIDNIGHT VOYAGE	2.75	5.50	4.00
☐ 4166		TALKIN' TO YOUR TOOTHBRUSH/			
		CALIFORNIA EARTHQUAKE	3.00	6.00	4.50

			Current Price Range		P/Y AVG
☐4184		ALL FOR ME/MOVE IN A LITTLE CLOSER, BABY	3.00	6.00	4.50
☐4195		WHO'S TO BLAME/ IT'S GETTING BETTER	2.75	5.50	4.00
☐4214		LADY LOVE/MAKE YOUR OWN KIND OF MUSIC	2.75	5.50	4.00
☐4225		NEW WORLD COMING/ BLOW ME A KISS	3.00	6.00	4.50
☐4226		NEXT TO YOU/SOMETHING TO MAKE YOU HAPPY	2.75	5.50	4.00
☐4244		I CAN DREAM, CAN'T I?/A SONG THAT NEVER COMES TRUE	2.75	5.50	4.00
☐4253		WELCOME TO THE WORLD/ GOOD TIMES ARE COMING	2.75	5.50	4.00
☐4264		DON'T LET THE GOOD LIFE PASS YOU BY/SONG THAT NEVER COMES TRUE	2.75	5.00	4.00
☐0764	RCA	BREAK ANOTHER HEART/ DISNEY GIRLS	2.75	5.50	4.00
☐0957		I THINK A LOT ABOUT YOU/ LISTEN TO THE WORLD	2.75	5.50	4.00

EL-RAYS (DELLS)

☐794	CHECKER	DARLING I KNOW/CHRISTINE	50.00	100.00	69.00

EMBERS

☐101	EMBER	PARADISE HILL/SOUND OF LOVE	48.00	95.00	61.00
☐410	HERALD	PARADISE HILL/SOUND OF LOVE	10.00	20.00	13.50
☐101	EMPRESS	SOLITAIRE/I'M FEELING ALL RIGHT AGAIN	3.00	6.00	4.25
☐107		ABIGAIL/I WAS TOO CAREFUL	3.00	6.00	4.25

EMERSON, LAKE & PALMER

☐44106	COTILLION	KNIFE'S EDGE/LUCKY MAN	3.00	6.00	4.00
☐44131		A TIME & A PLACE/ STONE OF YEARS	3.50	6.25	4.50
☐44151		GREAT GATES OF KIEV/ NUTROCKER	2.75	4.50	3.50
☐44158		FROM THE BEGINNING/ LIVING SIN	2.75	4.50	3.50
☐2003	MANTICORE	STILL YOU TURN ME ON/ BRAIN SALAD SURGERY	3.25	6.00	4.50
☐3405	ATLANTIC	JEREMY BENDER/C'EST LA VIE	2.75	4.50	3.50

ON ATLANTIC #3405, THE SIDE "C'EST LA VIE" IS BY GREG LAKE ALONE, NOT WITH EMERSON AND PALMER

ENCHANTMENTS

☐17003	RITZ	PAINS IN MY HEART/ I LOVE MY BABY	12.00	29.00	25.00

ENGLAND DAN & JOHN FORD COLEY

☐1278	A&M	TELL HER HELLO/NEW JERSEY	3.00	5.50	4.00
☐1354		SIMONE/CASEY	3.50	6.50	5.00
☐1369		FREE THE PEOPLE/CAROLINA	3.50	6.50	5.00
☐1465		MISS YOU SONG/ I HEAR THE MUSIC	3.00	5.00	4.00
☐16069	BIG TREE	IT'S NOT THE SAME/I'D REALLY LOVE TO SEE YOU TONIGHT	2.75	5.00	3.50
☐16079		SHOWBOAT GAMBLER/NIGHTS ARE FOREVER WITHOUT YOU	2.75	5.00	3.50
☐16088		THE TIME HAS COME/ IT'S SAD TO BELONG	2.75	5.00	3.50
☐16102		WHERE DO I GO FROM HERE/ GONE TOO FAR	2.75	5.00	3.50

			Current Price Range		P/Y AVG
☐16110		CALLING FOR YOU/WE'LL NEVER HAVE TO SAY GOODBYE AGAIN	2.75	5.00	3.50
☐16117		WANTING YOU DESPERATELY/ YOU CAN'T DANCE	2.75	5.00	3.50
☐16125		IF THE WORLD RAN OUT OF LOVE TONIGHT	2.75	5.00	3.50
☐16130		WESTWARD WIND/SOME THINGS DON'T COME EASY	2.50	4.50	2.50
☐16131		LOVE IS THE ANSWER/ RUNNING AFTER YOU	2.50	4.50	2.50
☐16135		ROLLING FEVER/ HOLLYWOOD HECKLE	2.50	4.50	2.50

LATER BIG TREE SINGLES ARE WORTH UP TO $2.00 MINT

SCOTT ENGLISH

☐16099	DOT	THE WHITE CLIFFS OF DOVER/ 4.000 MILES AWAY	4.50	7.50	6.00
☐4003	SULTAN	HIGH ON A HILL/WHEN	5.50	11.00	9.00
☐5500		RAGS TO RICHES/ WHERE CAN I GO?	3.25	5.50	4.00
☐4003	SPOKANE	HIGH ON A HILL/WHEN	3.00	5.00	3.50
☐4007		HERE COMES THE PAIN/ ALL I WANT IS YOU	2.75	4.50	3.00

EPISODE SIX (DEEP PURPLE)

☐45617	ELEKTRA	LOVE-HATE-REVENGE/ BABY BABY BABY	5.00	9.00	7.00
☐7007	COMPASS	MORNING DEW/SUNSHINE GIRL .	5.50	11.00	9.00

ESSEX

☐4494	ROULETTE	EASIER SAID THAN DONE/ ARE YOU GOING MY WAY?	3.00	5.25	3.65
☐4515		A WALKIN' MIRACLE/WHAT I DON'T KNOW WON'T HURT ME	3.00	5.25	3.65
☐4530		SHE'S GOT EVERYTHING/OUT OF SIGHT. OUT OF MIND	3.00	5.25	3.65
☐4542		WHAT DID I DO?/CURFEW LOVER	3.00	5.25	3.65
☐537	BANG	MOONLIGHT. MUSIC AND YOU/ THE EAGLE	3.00	5.25	3.65

ESSEX—ALBUMS

☐25234 (M)	ROULETTE	EASIER SAID THAN DONE	7.00	17.00	15.00
☐25234 (S)		EASIER SAID THAN DONE	9.00	25.00	22.50
☐25235 (M)		A WALKIN' MIRACLE.	6.00	15.00	13.50
☐25235 (S)		A WALKIN' MIRACLE.	8.00	21.00	18.00

PAUL EVANS

☐6906	RCA	WHAT DO YOU KNOW/DOROTHY .	4.50	7.50	6.00
☐6992		CAUGHT/POOR BROKEN HEART . .	4.50	7.50	6.00
☐6138	ATCO	AT MY PARTY/BEAT GENERATION	3.25	5.50	4.00
☐6170		LONG GONE/MICKEY. MY LOVE .	3.25	5.50	4.00
☐200	GUARANTEED	SEVEN LITTLE GIRLS SITTING IN THE BACK SEAT/ WORSHIPPING AN IDOL	3.00	5.50	3.50
☐205		MIDNIGHT SPECIAL/ SINCE I MET YOU BABY	3.00	5.50	3.50
☐208		HAPPY-GO-LUCKY-ME/ FISH IN THE OCEAN	3.00	5.00	3.50
☐210		THE BRIGADE OF BROKEN HEARTS/TWINS	3.00	5.00	3.50
☐213		HUSHABYE LITTLE GUITAR/ BLIND BOY	3.00	5.00	3.50
☐539	CARLTON	SHOW FOLK/I LOVE TO MAKE LOVE TO YOU	3.00	5.00	3.50
☐543		NOT ME/AFTER THE HURRICANE	3.00	5.00	3.50

			Current Price Range		P/Y AVG

PAUL EVANS—ALBUMS

□ 1000 (M)	GUARANTEED	FABULOUS TEENS............	8.00	21.00	18.00
□ 1000 (S)		FABULOUS TEENS............	12.00	29.00	25.00
□ 129 (M)	CARLTON	HEAR PAUL EVANS IN YOUR HOME TONIGHT	7.00	17.00	15.00
□ 129 (S)		HEAR PAUL EVANS IN YOUR HOME TONIGHT	9.00	25.00	22.50
□ 130 (M)		FOLK SONGS OF MANY LANDS ..	7.00	17.00	15.00
□ 130 (S)		FOLK SONGS OF MANY LANDS ..	9.00	25.00	22.50
□ 3346 (M)	KAPP	21 YEARS IN A TENNESSEE JAIL .	6.00	15.00	13.50
□ 3346 (S)		21 YEARS IN A TENNESSEE JAIL .	8.00	21.00	18.00
□ 3475 (M)		ANOTHER TOWN, ANOTHER JAIL .	6.00	15.00	13.50
□ 3475 (S)		ANOTHER TOWN, ANOTHER JAIL .	8.00	21.00	18.00

BETTY EVERETT

□ 5019	COBRA	MY LIFE DEPENDS ON YOU/ MY LOVE	7.00	13.00	8.50
□ 5024		AIN'T GONNA CRY/KILLER DILLER	7.00	13.00	8.50
□ 5031		TELL ME DARLING/ I'LL WEEP NO MORE	7.00	13.00	8.50
□ 1126	DOTTIE	TELL ME DARLING/ I'LL WEEP NO MORE	4.50	7.50	6.00
□ 619	C.J.	YOUR LOVING ARMS/ HAPPY I LONG TO BE	4.50	7.50	6.00
□ 4806	ONE-DER-FUL	YOUR LOVE IS IMPORTANT TO ME/ I'VE GOT A CLAIM ON YOU	3.25	5.50	4.00
□ 4823		I'LL BE THERE/PLEASE LOVE ME	3.25	5.50	4.00
□ 513	VEE JAY	BY MY SIDE/PRINCE OF PLAYERS	3.25	5.50	4.00
□ 566		YOU'RE NO GOOD/ CHAINED TO YOUR LOVE	3.25	5.50	4.00
□ 585		THE SHOOP SHOOP SONG (IT'S IN HIS KISS)/HANDS OFF	3.25	5.50	4.00
□ 599		I CAN'T HEAR YOU/ CAN I GET TO KNOW YOU	3.25	5.50	4.00
□ 610		IT HURTS TO BE IN LOVE/ UNTIL YOU WERE GONE	3.25	5.50	4.00
□ 628		GETTING MIGHTY CROWDED/ CHAINED TO A MEMORY	3.25	5.50	4.00
□ 683		THE REAL THING/ GONNA BE READY	3.25	5.50	4.00
□ 699		TOO HOT TO HOLD/ I DON'T HURT ANYMORE	3.25	5.50	4.00
□ 716		TROUBLE OVER THE WEEKEND/ MY SHOE WON'T FIT	3.25	5.50	4.00
□ 10829	ABC	IN YOUR ARMS/ NOTHING I WOULDN'T DO	3.00	5.00	3.65
□ 10861		YOUR LOVE IS IMPORTANT TO ME/BYE BYE BABY	3.00	5.00	3.65
□ 10919		PEOPLE AROUND ME/ LOVE COMES TUMBLING DOWN .	3.00	5.00	3.65
□ 10978		MY BABY/ LOVING MY BEST FRIEND	3.00	5.00	3.65
□ 55100	UNI	THERE'LL COME A TIME/TAKE ME	2.75	4.50	3.25
□ 55122		I CAN'T SAY NO TO YOU/BETTER TOMORROW THAN TODAY	2.75	4.50	3.25
□ 55141		MAYBE/1900 YESTERDAY	2.75	4.50	3.25
□ 55174		IT'S BEEN A LONG TIME/ JUST A MAN'S WAY	2.75	4.50	3.25
□ 55189		SUGAR/JUST ANOTHER WINTER .	2.75	4.50	3.25

BETTY EVERETT—ALBUMS

□ 1077 (M)	VEE JAY	IT'S IN HIS KISS	9.00	25.00	22.50
□ 1077 (S)		IT'S IN HIS KISS	14.00	34.00	30.00
□ 1122 (M)		THE VERY BEST OF BETTY EVERETT	9.00	25.00	22.50

			Current Price Range		P/Y AVG
☐1122 (S)		THE VERY BEST OF BETTY EVERETT	14.00	34.00	30.00

VINCE EVERETT

☐1964	**TOWN**	BUTTERCUP/LAND OF NO RETURN	9.00	17.00	11.25
☐10313	**ABC-**				
	PARAMOUNT	SUCH A NIGHT/DON'T GO	9.00	17.00	11.25
☐10360		I AIN'T GONNA BE YOUR LOW DOWN DOG NO MORE/ SUGAR BEE	9.00	17.00	11.25
☐10472		BABY LET'S PLAY HOUSE/ LIVIN' HIGH	11.00	20.00	13.50
☐10624		TO HAVE, TO HOLD, AND LET GO/ BIG BROTHER	6.00	12.00	8.00

EVERLY BROTHERS

☐21496	**COLUMBIA**	KEEP A-LOVING ME/ THE SUN KEEPS SHINING	20.00	34.00	30.00
☐1315	**CADENCE**	BYE BYE LOVE/I WONDER IF I CARE AS MUCH	4.00	7.00	4.75
☐1337		WAKE UP LITTLE SUZIE/ MAYBE TOMORROW	4.00	7.00	4.75
☐1342		THIS LITTLE GIRL OF MINE/ SHOULD WE TELL HIM?	4.00	7.00	4.75
☐1348		ALL I HAVE TO DO IS DREAM/ CLAUDETTE	3.50	6.00	4.00
☐1350		BIRD DOG/DEVOTED TO YOU	3.50	6.00	4.00
☐1355		PROBLEMS/LOVE OF MY LIFE ...	3.50	6.00	4.00
☐1364		TAKE A MESSAGE TO MARY/ POOR JENNY	3.50	6.00	4.00
☐1369		('TIL) I KISSED YOU/ OH. WHAT A FEELING	3.50	6.00	4.00
☐1376		LET IT BE ME/ SINCE YOU BROKE MY HEART .	3.50	6.00	4.00
☐1380		WHEN WILL I BE LOVED?/ BE BOP A LULA	3.50	6.00	4.00
☐1388		LIKE STRANGERS/ A BRAND NEW HEARTACHE ...	3.50	6.00	4.00
☐1429		I'M HERE TO GET MY BABY OUT OF JAIL/LIGHTNING EXPRESS .	4.00	7.00	4.75
☐5151	**WARNER**				
	BROTHERS	CATHY'S CLOWN/ ALWAYS IT'S YOU	3.50	6.00	4.00
☐5163		SO SAD/ LUCILLE	3.50	6.00	4.00
☐5199		EBONY EYES/WALK RIGHT BACK	3.50	6.00	4.00
☐5220		TEMPTATION/ STICK WITH ME BABY	3.50	6.00	4.00
☐5250		CRYING IN THE RAIN/ I'M NOT ANGRY	3.50	6.00	4.00
☐5273		THAT'S OLD FASHIONED/ HOW CAN I MEET HER?	3.50	6.00	4.00
☐5297		DON'T ASK ME TO BE FRIENDS/ NO ONE CAN MAKE MY SUNSHINE SMILE	3.00	5.50	3.85
☐5346		NANCY'S MINUET/ SO IT ALWAYS WILL BE	3.00	5.50	3.85
☐5362		IT'S BEEN NICE/I'M AFRAID	3.00	5.50	3.85
☐5389		THE GIRL SANG THE BLUES/ LOVE HER	3.00	5.50	3.85
☐5422		HELLO AMY/AIN'T THAT LOVING YOU BABY	3.00	5.50	3.85
☐5441		THE FERRIS WHEEL/ DON'T FORGET TO CRY	3.00	5.50	3.85

RCA, LSP-4620

EMBER, 100, EP

			Current Price Range		P/Y AVG
☐ 5466		YOU'RE THE ONE I LOVE/ RING AROUND MY ROSIE	3.00	5.25	3.85
☐ 5478		GONE, GONE, GONE/TORTURE ...	3.00	5.25	3.85
☐ 5600		YOU'RE MY GIRL/DON'T LET THE WHOLE WORLD KNOW	3.00	5.25	3.85
☐ 5611		THAT'LL BE THE DAY/ GIVE ME A SWEETHEART	3.00	5.25	3.85
☐ 5628		THE PRICE OF LOVE/ IT ONLY COSTS A DIME	3.00	5.25	3.85
☐ 5639		FOLLOW ME/ I'LL NEVER GET OVER YOU	3.00	5.25	3.85
☐ 5649		LOVE IS STRANGE/ A MAN WITH MONEY	3.00	5.25	3.85
☐ 5682		IT'S ALL OVER/ I USED TO LOVE YOU	3.00	5.25	3.85
☐ 5698		THE DOLL HOUSE IS EMPTY/ LOVELY KRAVEZIT	3.00	5.25	3.85
☐ 5808		LEAVE MY GIRL ALONE/(YOU GOT) THE POWER OF LOVE	3.00	5.25	3.85
☐ 5833		SOMEBODY HELP ME/ HARD, HARD YEAR	3.00	5.25	3.85
☐ 5857		LIKE EVERYTIME BEFORE/ FIFI THE FLEA	3.00	5.25	3.85
☐ 5901		THE DEVIL'S CHILD/ SHE NEVER SMILES ANYMORE	3.00	5.25	3.85
☐ 7020		BOWLING GREEN/ I DON'T WANT TO LOVE YOU ..	3.00	5.25	3.85
☐ 7062		MARY JANE/ TALKING TO THE FLOWERS ...	3.00	5.25	3.85
☐ 7088		VOICE WITHIN/ LOVE OF THE COMMON PEOPLE	3.00	5.25	3.85
☐ 7121		ALL I HAVE TO DO IS DREAM/ BYE BYE LOVE	3.00	5.25	3.85
☐ 7192		EMPTY BOXES/IT'S MY TIME ...	3.00	5.25	3.85
☐ 7226		MILK TRAIN/ LORD OF THE MANOR	3.00	5.25	3.85
☐ 7262		I WONDER IF I CARE AS MUCH/ T FOR TEXAS	3.00	5.25	3.85
☐ 7290		I'M ON MY WAY HOME AGAIN/ CUCKOO BIRD	3.00	5.25	3.85
☐ 7326		CAROLINA ON MY MIND/ MY LITTLE YELLOW BIRD	3.00	5.25	3.85
☐ 7425		YVES/THE HUMAN RACE	3.00	5.25	3.85
		EVERLY BROTHERS—EPs			
☐ 104	*CADENCE*	THE EVERLY BROTHERS	10.00	20.00	13.00
☐ 105		THE EVERLY BROTHERS	10.00	20.00	13.00
☐ 107		THE EVERLY BROTHERS	10.00	20.00	13.00
☐ 108		SONGS OUR DADDY TAUGHT US .	9.00	18.00	11.50
☐ 109		SONGS OUR DADDY TAUGHT US .	9.00	18.00	11.50
☐ 110		SONGS OUR DADDY TAUGHT US .	9.00	18.00	11.50
☐ 111		THE EVERLY BROTHERS	9.00	18.00	11.50
☐ 118		THE EVERLY BROTHERS	9.00	18.00	11.50
☐ 121		THE VERY BEST OF THE EVERLY BROTHERS	8.00	15.00	10.00
☐ 333		ROCKIN' WITH THE EVERLY BROTHERS	8.00	15.00	10.00
☐ 334		DREAM WITH THE EVERLY BROTHERS	8.00	15.00	10.00
☐ 1381-1	*WARNER BROTHERS*	FOREVERLY YOURS............	6.00	11.00	7.00
☐ 1381-2		ESPECIALLY FOR YOU	6.00	11.00	8.50
☐ 5501		THE EVERLY BROTHERS TWO OLDIES	3.50	6.00	4.50

			Current Price Range		P/Y AVG

EVERLY BROTHERS—ALBUMS

			Current Price Range		P/Y AVG
☐ 3003 (M)	*CADENCE*	THE EVERLY BROTHERS	24.00	56.00	50.00
☐ 3016 (M)		SONGS OUR DADDY TAUGHT US	19.00	49.00	45.00
☐ 3025 (M)		THE EVERLY BROTHERS' BEST	17.00	38.00	35.00
☐ 3040 (M)		THE FABULOUS STYLE OF THE EVERLY BROTHERS	17.00	38.00	35.00
☐ 3059 (M)		FOLK SONGS	12.00	29.00	25.00
☐ 25029 (S)		FOLK SONGS	17.00	38.00	35.00
☐ 3062 (M)		15 EVERLY HITS	10.00	25.00	22.50
☐ 25062 (S)		15 EVERLY HITS	14.00	34.00	30.00
☐ 1381 (M)	*WARNER BROTHERS*	IT'S EVERLY TIME	7.00	14.00	12.00
☐ 1381 (S)		IT'S EVERLY TIME	10.00	25.00	22.50
☐ 1395 (M)		A DATE WITH THE EVERLY BROTHERS	7.00	17.00	15.00
☐ 1395 (S)		A DATE WITH THE EVERLY BROTHERS	10.00	25.00	22.50
☐ 1418 (M)		THE EVERLY BROTHERS	7.00	17.00	15.00
☐ 1418 (S)		THE EVERLY BROTHERS	10.00	25.00	22.50
☐ 1430 (M)		INSTANT PARTY	7.00	17.00	15.00
☐ 1430 (S)		INSTANT PARTY	10.00	25.00	22.50
☐ 1471 (M)		GOLDEN HITS OF THE EVERLY BROTHERS	6.00	15.00	13.50
☐ 1471 (S)		GOLDEN HITS OF THE EVERLY BROTHERS	8.00	21.00	18.00
☐ 1483 (M)		CHRISTMAS WITH THE EVERLY BROTHERS	7.00	17.00	15.00
☐ 1483 (S)		CHRISTMAS WITH THE EVERLY BROTHERS	8.00	21.00	18.00
☐ 1513 (M)		THE EVERLY BROTHERS SING GREAT COUNTRY HITS	6.00	15.00	13.50
☐ 1513 (S)		THE EVERLY BROTHERS SING GREAT COUNTRY HITS	8.00	21.00	18.00
☐ 1554 (M)		THE VERY BEST OF THE EVERLY BROTHERS	6.00	15.00	13.50
☐ 1554 (S)		THE VERY BEST OF THE EVERLY BROTHERS	7.00	17.00	15.00
☐ 1578 (M)		ROCK'N SOUL	6.00	15.00	13.50
☐ 1578 (S)		ROCK'N SOUL	7.00	17.00	15.00
☐ 1585 (M)		GONE, GONE, GONE	6.00	15.00	13.50
☐ 1585 (S)		GONE, GONE, GONE	7.00	17.00	15.00
☐ 1605 (M)		BEAT'N SOUL	6.00	15.00	13.50
☐ 1605 (S)		BEAT'N SOUL	7.00	17.00	15.00
☐ 1620 (M)		IN OUR IMAGE	6.00	15.00	13.50
☐ 1620 (S)		IN OUR IMAGE	7.00	17.00	15.00
☐ 1646 (M)		TWO YANKS IN LONDON	6.00	15.00	13.50
☐ 1646 (S)		TWO YANKS IN LONDON	7.00	17.00	15.00
☐ 1708 (M)		THE EVERLY BROTHERS SING	6.00	15.00	13.50
☐ 1708 (S)		THE EVERLY BROTHERS SING	7.00	17.00	15.00
☐ 1752 (M)		ROOTS	5.50	14.00	12.00
☐ 1752 (S)		ROOTS	6.00	15.00	13.50
☐ 1858 (S)		THE EVERLY BROTHERS SHOW	5.50	14.00	12.00

THE EXCELLONS

☐ B601	*BOBBY*	HELEN (YOUR WISH CAME TRUE)/SUNDAY KIND OF LOVE	3.00	7.50	5.00

EXILES
FEATURED: DICK DALE

☐ 1111	*CAMPUS*	TAKE IT OFF/TEN LITTLE INDIANS	14.00	24.00	20.00

EXTREMES

☐ 733	*PARO*	THAT'S ALL I WANT/THE BELLS	17.00	35.00	30.00

F

			Current Price Range		P/Y AVG

SHELLY FABARES

☐ 621	COLPIX	JOHNNY ANGEL/ WHERE'S IT GONNA GET ME ..	3.25	5.50	4.00
☐ 638		JOHNNY LOVES ME/ I'M GROWING UP	3.25	5.50	4.00
☐ 654		THE THINGS WE DID LAST SUMMER/BREAKING UP IS HARD TO DO	3.25	5.50	4.00
☐ 667		BIG STAR/TELEPHONE (WON'T YOU RING)	3.25	5.50	4.00
☐ 682		RONNIE. CALL ME WHEN YOU GET A CHANCE/I LEFT A NOTE TO SAY GOODBYE	3.25	5.50	4.00
☐ 705		WELCOME HOME/BILLY BOY ...	3.25	5.50	4.00
☐ 721		FOOTBALL SEASON'S OVER/ HE DON'T LOVE ME	3.25	5.50	4.00
☐ 632	VEE JAY	LOST SUMMER LOVE/I KNOW YOU'LL BE THERE	3.50	6.00	4.50
☐ 4001	DUNHILL	MY PRAYER/PRETTY PLEASE ...	3.25	5.50	4.00

SHELLEY FABARES—ALBUMS

☐ 426 (M)	COLPIX	SHELLEY	10.00	20.00	13.50
☐ 431 (M)		THE THINGS WE DID LAST SUMMER	10.00	20.00	13.50

FABIAN

☐ 1020	CHANCELLOR	SHIVERS/I'M IN LOVE	5.50	11.00	9.00
☐ 1024		LILLY LOU/BE MY STEADY DATE	5.00	9.00	7.00
☐ 1029		I'M A MAN/HYPNOTIZED	3.25	5.50	4.00
☐ 1033		TURN ME LOOSE/STOP THIEF ...	3.00	5.00	3.50
☐ 1037		TIGER MIGHTY COLD (TO A WARM. WARM HEART)	3.00	5.00	3.50
☐ 1041		COME ON AND GET ME/ GOT THE FEELING	3.00	5.00	3.50
☐ 1044		HOUND DOG MAN/ THIS FRIENDLY WORLD	3.00	5.00	3.50
☐ 1047		ABOUT THIS THING CALLED LOVE/STRING ALONG	2.75	4.50	3.00
☐ 1051		STROLLIN' IN THE SPRINGTIME/ I'M GONNA SIT RIGHT DOWN AND WRITE MYSELF A LETTER	2.75	4.50	3.00
☐ 1055		TOMORROW/KING OF LOVE	3.00	5.00	3.50
☐ 1061		KISSIN' AND TWISTIN'/ LONG BEFORE	2.50	5.00	3.00
☐ 1067		YOU KNOW YOU BELONG TO SOMEBODY ELSE/HOLD ON ...	2.50	5.00	3.00
☐ 1072		GRAPEVINE/DAVID AND GOLIATH	2.50	5.00	3.00
☐ 1079		THE LOVE THAT I'M GIVING TO YOU/YOU'RE ONLY YOUNG ONCE	2.50	5.00	3.00
☐ 1084		A GIRL LIKE YOU/ DREAM FACTORY	2.50	5.00	3.00
☐ 1086		KANSAS CITY/TONGUE-TIED	2.50	5.00	3.00
☐ 1092		WILD PARTY/THE GOSPEL TRUTH	2.50	5.00	3.00
☐ 1092		WILD PARTY/MADE YOU	2.50	5.00	3.00

FABIAN—EPs

☐ A-5003	CHANCELLOR	HOLD THAT TIGER	9.00	17.00	11.00
☐ B-5003		HOLD THAT TIGER	9.00	17.00	11.00
☐ C-5003		HOLD THAT TIGER	9.00	17.00	11.00
☐ A-5005		THE FABULOUS FABIAN	7.00	13.00	11.00

FABIAN

Frankie Avalon's manager was seeking another Avalon—handsome, young and ready for "American Bandstand". Avalon spoke highly of Fabian Forte, a fellow student at Southern High in Philadelphia, Pennsylvania. Fabian, it seemed, was fifteen, sophomore class president, and thought to be the best-looking lad on campus. Avalon's manager was interested.

He found Fabian sitting on the doorstep of his home. The boy was upset as his father, a Philadelphia detective, had just had a heart attack and had been rushed away by ambulance. Fabian was in no mood to talk and dismissed the possibility of his becoming a singer.

He later changed his mind, although three voice teachers ended up walking out of Chancellor Records' office, saying that Fabian couldn't carry a tune in a bucket. No matter. A loud backup group drowned out most of Fabian's growls. Fabian was also given good material to sing and made frequent "Bandstand" appearances.

He scored three 1959 Top 10 singles and became that year's hottest teen idol. Fabian turned to movies after his recording career declined and starred in a few low-budget teen films.

			Current Price Range		P/Y AVG
☐ B-5005		THE FABULOUS FABIAN	7.00	13.00	11.00
☐ C-5005		THE FABULOUS FABIAN	7.00	13.00	11.00
☐ 301		HOUND DOG MAN	7.00	13.00	11.00
		FABIAN—ALBUMS			
☐ 5003 (M)	*CHANCELLOR*	HOLD THAT TIGER	12.00	29.00	25.00
☐ 5003 (S)		HOLD THAT TIGER	17.00	39.00	35.00
☐ 5005 (M)		THE FABULOUS FABIAN	12.00	29.00	25.00
☐ 5005 (S)		THE FABULOUS FABIAN	17.00	39.00	35.00
☐ 5012 (M)		THE GOOD OLD SUMMERTIME ...	10.00	25.00	22.50
☐ 5012 (M)		THE GOOD OLD SUMMERTIME ...	14.00	34.00	30.00
☐ 5019 (M)		ROCKIN' HOT	12.00	29.00	25.00
☐ 5024 (M)		FABIAN'S 16 FABULOUS HITS ...	12.00	29.00	25.00

FABIAN AND FRANKIE AVALON—ALBUM

☐ 5009 (M)	*CHANCELLOR*	THE HIT MAKERS	17.00	37.00	24.00

FABULOUS PEARL DEVINES

☐ 101	*ARCO*	SO LONELY/YOU'VE BEEN GONE	17.00	34.00	30.00

ADAM FAITH

☐ 9061	*CUB*	WHAT DO YOU WANT?/ FROM NOW UNTIL FOREVER	3.50	6.00	4.00
☐ 9068		POOR ME/THE REASON	3.50	6.00	4.00
☐ 9074		I DID WHAT YOU TOLD ME/ JOHNNY COMES MARCHING HOME	3.50	6.00	4.00
☐ 16405	*DOT*	DON'T THAT BEAT ALL/ MIX ME A PERSON	3.50	6.00	4.00
☐ 895	*AMY*	SO LONG BABY/THE FIRST TIME	3.50	6.00	4.00
☐ 899		WE ARE IN LOVE/WHAT NOW?	3.50	6.00	4.00
☐ 913		IT'S ALRIGHT/ I JUST DON'T KNOW	3.50	6.00	4.00
☐ 922		TALK ABOUT LOVE/STOP FEELING SORRY FOR YOURSELF	3.50	6.00	4.00
		ADAM FAITH—ALBUMS			
☐ 3951 (M)	*MGM*	ENGLAND'S TOP SINGER	8.00	21.00	18.00
☐ 8005 (M)	*AMY*	ADAM FAITH	8.00	21.00	18.00

MARIANNE FAITHFULL

☐ 9697	*LONDON*	AS TEARS GO BY/GLEENSLEEVES	3.25	5.50	4.00
☐ 9731		COME AND STAY WITH ME/ WHAT HAVE I DONE WRONG?	3.25	5.50	4.00
☐ 9759		THIS LITTLE BIRD/MORNING SUN	3.25	5.50	4.00
☐ 9780		SUMMER NIGHTS/ THE SHA-LA-LA SONG	3.25	5.50	4.00
☐ 9802		GO AWAY FROM MY WORLD/ OH. LOOK AROUND YOU	3.25	5.50	4.00
☐ 1022		SISTER MORPHINE/ SOMETHING BETTER	5.50	11.00	9.00
		MARIANNE FAITHFULL—ALBUMS			
☐ 3423 (M)	*LONDON*	MARIANNE FAITHFUL	7.00	17.00	15.00
☐ 423 (S)		MARIANNE FAITHFUL	10.00	25.00	22.50
☐ 3452 (M)		GO AWAY FROM MY WORLD	7.00	17.00	15.00
☐ 452 (S)		GO AWAY FROM MY WORLD	10.00	25.00	22.50
☐ 3482 (M)		FAITHFULL FOREVER	7.00	17.00	15.00
☐ 482 (S)		FAITHFULL FOREVER	10.00	25.00	22.50
☐ 3547 (M)		GREATEST HITS	7.00	17.00	15.00
☐ 547 (S)		GREATEST HITS	8.00	21.00	18.00

FALCONS

☐ 70940	*MERCURY*	BABY THAT'S IT/THIS DAY	14.00	24.00	20.00
☐ 1006	*FALCON*	MY ONLY LOVE/ NOW THAT IT'S OVER	20.00	34.00	30.00

FREDDY FENDER

San Benito, TX, was Freddy's birthplace on June 4, 1936. (His real name is Baldemar Huerta.) He often played an old three-string guitar and sang for his migrant-labor family. Sometimes Freddy and other lads in the labor camps would sing on their dusty street corners.

Fender was influenced greatly by country music; Saturday nights were spent listening to radio's Grand Ole Opry. In 1954, Freddy quit high school and joined the marines. While in the service, he was introduced to the music of r & b artists such as Fats Domino and Joe Turner.

Fender was busted for pot in 1960 in Louisiana and spent the next three years in prison. He often gave concerts for fellow inmates. After being paroled, he hopped a bus to New York City and spent five years singing in country-oriented clubs and bars there.

In 1969, Freddy returned to Texas to work as a mechanic (he continued singing on weekends with a small group). He even earned his high-school diploma at night. He thought of attending college to become a social worker, but fame first intervened. "Before the Next Teardrop Falls" and "Wasted Days and Wasted Nights" (the latter first recorded in 1959) established Freddy Fender as a major recording artist.

			Current Price Range		P/Y AVG
☐1006	**ABNER**	MY ONLY LOVE/			
		NOW THAT IT'S OVER	12.00	21.00	18.00
☐661	**KUDO**	THIS HEART OF MINE/ROMANITA	20.00	34.00	30.00
☐1110	**ANNA**	THIS HEART OF MINE/ROMANITA	10.00	17.00	15.00
☐1743	**CHESS**	THIS HEART OF MINE/ROMANITA	5.00	9.00	7.00
☐001	**FLICK**	YOU'RE SO FINE/			
		GODDESS OF ANGELS	20.00	34.00	30.00
☐008		THAT'S WHAT I AIM TO DO/YOU			
		MUST KNOW I LOVE YOU	8.25	14.00	12.00
☐2013	**UNART**	YOU'RE SO FINE/			
		GODDESS OF ANGELS	3.50	6.00	4.00
☐2022		YOU'RE MINE/COUNTRY SHACK .	3.50	6.00	4.00
☐229	**UNITED**				
	ARTISTS	WAITING FOR YOU/THE TEACHER	3.25	5.50	4.00
☐255		I LOVE YOU/WONDERFUL LOVE ..	3.25	5.50	4.00
☐289		WORKIN' MAN'S SONG/			
		POW! YOU'RE IN LOVE	3.25	5.50	4.00
☐1003	**LUPINE**	I FOUND A LOVE/SWIM	3.25	5.50	4.00
☐323	**BIG WHEEL**	I CAN'T HELP IT/			
		STANDING ON GUARD	3.25	5.50	4.00
		FALCONS—EP			
☐10010	**UNITED**				
	ARTISTS	THE FALCONS	12.00	21.00	18.00

FALLING PEBBLES (BUCKINGHAMS)

☐201	**ALLEY CAT**	LAWDY MISS CLAWDY/			
		VIRGINIA WOLF	8.25	14.00	12.00

FANTASTIC BAGGIES
FEATURED: STEVE BARRI

☐66047	**IMPERIAL**	TELL 'EM I'M SURFIN'/			
		SURFER BOY'S DREAM	5.00	9.00	7.00
☐66072		ANYWHERE THE GIRLS ARE/			
		DEBBIE BE TRUE	5.00	9.00	7.00
☐66092		ALONE ON THE BEACH/IT WAS I .	5.50	11.00	9.00
		FANTASTIC BAGGIES—ALBUMS			
☐9270 (M)	**IMPERIAL**	TELL 'EM I'M SURFIN'	12.00	29.00	25.00
☐12270 (S)		TELL 'EM I'M SURFIN'	17.00	39.00	35.00

CHRIS FARLOWE AND THE THUNDERBIRDS

☐13567	**MGM**	OUT OF TIME/			
		BABY, MAKE IT SOON	4.25	6.50	4.50
☐5002	**IMMEDIATE**	PAINT IT BLACK/			
		YOU'RE SO GOOD TO ME	4.00	6.00	4.00
☐5005		HANDBAGS AND GLADBAGS/			
		EVERYBODY MAKES A MISTAKE	4.00	6.00	4.00
☐5011		PAINT IT BLACK/			
		WHAT HAVE I BEEN DOING? ...	4.00	6.00	4.00
		CHRIS FARLOWE AND THE THUNDERBIRDS—ALBUMS			
☐52010 (M)	**IMMEDIATE**	PAINT IT FARLOWE	9.00	22.00	18.50
☐2593 (M)	**COLUMBIA**	THE FABULOUS CHRIS FARLOWE			
		AND THE THUNDERBIRDS	8.00	18.00	15.50
☐9393 (S)		THE FABULOUS CHRIS FARLOWE			
		AND THE THUNDERBIRDS	9.00	22.00	19.00

FASCINATORS

☐4053	**CAPITOL**	I WONDER WHO/CHAPEL BELLS .	14.00	33.00	21.00
☐4137		WHO DO YOU THINK YOU ARE/			
		PARADISE	14.00	33.00	21.00
☐4247		OH ROSE MARIE/			
		FRIED CHICKEN & MACARONI .	14.00	33.00	21.00
☐4544		I WONDER WHO/CHAPEL BELLS			
		(reissue)	8.00	18.00	16.00

FENDERMEN

The Fendermen took their name from the fact that they both played Fender guitars. Their career was brief, as they scored just one hit. But what a hit it was! The song was "Mule Skinner Blues", first sung by composer Jimmie Rodgers during the 1930s. (A mule-skinner was the driver of a mule train; the song speaks of a man's boasting of his abilities as a top-notch handler of the stubborn beasts.) The meaning of the Fendermen's version was lost amid the laughs, shouts, whoops and driving bass line that propelled the record into the Top 10 during the spring of 1960.

The Fendermen both hailed from Wisconsin. Jim Sundquist was from the town of Niagara; Bill Humphrey was born in the larger burg of Madison. Coincidentally, both share the same exact birthdate - November 26, 1937.

During their late teens, they both formed rock-and-roll bands. In time, they met and became a duo. An audition at Minneapolis' small Soma Records convinced executives there to sign the dynamic duo. (Soma was searching for another success, as star Bobby Vee had left Soma for Liberty Records a year earlier.)

The Fendermen followed their million-selling hit with a send-up of Huey "Piano" Smith's "Don't You Just Know It?" The record failed to catch on, as did a third Soma effort, and the Fendermen faded away posthaste.

			Current Price Range		P/Y AVG
FELIX AND THE ESCORTS (YOUNG RASCALS)					
☐685	*JAG*	THE SYRACUSE/SAVE	8.25	14.00	12.00
NARVEL FELTS					
☐71140	*MERCURY*	KISS-A-ME BABY/			
		FOOLISH THOUGHTS	5.25	9.50	8.00
☐71190		CRY BABY CRY/			
		LONESOME FEELING	5.00	9.00	7.00
☐71249		DREAM WORLD/ROCKET RIDE ...	5.00	9.00	7.00
☐701		CUTIE BABY/THREE THOUSAND			
		MILES	5.00	9.00	7.00
NARVEL FELTS—ALBUMS					
☐5000 (M)	*CINNAMON*	DRIFT AWAY	7.00	17.00	15.00
☐5000 (S)		DRIFT AWAY	8.00	21.00	18.00
FREDDY FENDER					
☐1000	*DUNCAN*	MEAN WOMAN/HOLY ONE	5.50	11.00	9.00
☐1001		WASTED DAYS AND WASTED			
		NIGHTS/SAN ANTONIO ROCK ..	9.50	17.00	15.00
☐1002		CRAZY BABY/			
		THE WILD SIDE OF LIFE	5.50	11.00	9.00
☐1004		SINCE I MET YOU BABY/			
		LITTLE MAMA	7.00	13.00	11.00
☐5670	*IMPERIAL*	WASTED DAYS AND WASTED			
		NIGHTS/I CAN'T REMEMBER			
		WHEN (I DIDN'T LOVE YOU) ...	5.00	9.00	7.00
☐5375	*ARGO*	YOU'RE SOMETHING ELSE/			
		A MAN CAN CRY	5.00	9.00	7.00
☐100	*NORCO*	THE NEW STROLL/			
		LOVE'S LIGHT IS AN EMBER ..	4.50	7.50	6.00
LATER HIT SINGLES ARE WORTH UP TO $2.50 MINT					
FENDERMEN					
☐1137	*SOMA*	MULE SKINNER BLUES/TORTURE	3.25	5.50	4.00
☐1142		DON'T YOU JUST KNOW IT/			
		BEACH PARTY	3.25	5.50	4.00
☐1155		CAN'T YOU WAIT?/			
		HEART BREAKIN' SPECIAL	3.25	5.50	4.00
☐102	*DAB*	RAIN DROP/			
		FAS-NACHT-KUECHEL	3.25	5.50	4.00
FENDERMEN—ALBUM					
☐1240 (M)	*SOMA*	MULE SKINNER BLUES	52.00	96.00	90.00
SALLY FIELD					
☐1008	*COLGEMS*	FELICIDAD/			
		FIND YOURSELF A RAINBOW ..	3.00	5.00	3.50
☐1014		GOLDEN DAYS/			
		YOU'RE A GRAND OLD FLAG ...	3.00	5.00	3.50
SALLY FIELD—ALBUM					
☐106 (S)	*COLGEMS*	SALLY FIELD (STAR OF			
		"THE FLYING NUN")	9.50	17.00	15.00
FIFTH DIMENSION					
☐752	*SOUL CITY*	I'LL BE LOVING YOU FOREVER/			
		TRAIN, KEEP ON MOVING	3.00	6.00	4.00
☐753		TOO POOR TO DIE/			
		GO WHERE YOU WANNA GO ...	3.00	6.00	4.00
☐755		ANOTHER DAY, ANOTHER			
		HEADACHE/ROSECRANS BLVD.	3.00	6.00	4.00
☐756		UP, UP & AWAY/			
		WHICH WAY TO NOWHERE	2.50	5.50	3.75
☐760		POOR SIDE OF TOWN/PAPER CUP	2.50	5.50	3.75
☐762		CARPET MAN/MAGIC GARDEN ..	2.50	5.50	3.75

			Current Price Range		P/Y AVG
☐766		STONED SOUL PICNIC/			
		SAILBOAT SONG	2.50	5.50	3.75
☐768		SWEET BLINDNESS/			
		BOBBY'S BLUES	2.50	5.50	3.75
☐770		CALIFORNIA SOUL/			
		IT'LL NEVER BE THE SAME . . .	2.50	5.50	3.75

FIREBALLS
SEE: JIMMY GILMER AND THE FIREBALLS

☐2008	TOP RANK	TORQUAY/CRY BABY	4.00	7.00	4.75
☐2026		BULLDOG/NEARLY SUNRISE	4.00	7.00	4.75
☐2038		FOOT PATTER/KISSIN'	4.00	7.00	4.75
☐2054		VAQUERO/CHIEF WHOOPEN KOFF	4.00	7.00	4.75
☐2081		ALMOST PARADISE/SWEET TALK	4.00	7.00	4.75
☐3003		RIK-A-TIK/YACKY DOO	4.00	7.00	4.75
☐248	KAPP	FIREBALL/I DON'T KNOW	3.50	6.00	4.00
☐630	WARWICK	RIK-A-TIK/YACKY DOO	3.50	6.00	4.00
☐644		QUITE A PARTY/GUNSHOT	3.50	6.00	4.00
☐16493	DOT	TORQUAY TWO/PEG LEG	3.50	6.00	4.00
☐16661		DUMBO/MR. REED	3.50	6.00	4.00
☐16715		MORE THAN I CAN SAY/			
		THE BEATING OF MY HEART . . .	3.50	6.00	4.00
☐16745		CAMPUSOLOGY/AHHH. SOUL . . .	3.50	6.00	4.00
☐16992		SHY GIRL/			
		I THINK I'LL CATCH A BUG	3.50	6.00	4.00

FIREBALLS—EP

☐1000	TOP RANK	THE FIREBALLS	12.00	21.00	18.00

FIREBALLS—ALBUMS

☐324 (M)	TOP RANK	THE FIREBALLS	17.00	39.00	35.00
☐343 (M)		VAQUERO	14.00	34.00	30.00
☐2042 (M)	WARWICK	HERE ARE THE FIREBALLS	9.00	25.00	22.50
☐3512 (M)	DOT	TORQUAY	7.00	17.00	15.00
☐25512 (S)		TORQUAY	9.00	25.00	22.50
☐3709 (M)		CAMPUSOLOGY	7.00	17.00	15.00
☐25709 (S)		CAMPUSOLOGY	9.00	25.00	22.50
☐3856 (M)		FIREWATER	7.00	17.00	15.00
☐25856 (S)		FIREWATER	9.00	25.00	22.50

FIREFLIES

☐6901	RIBBON	YOU WERE MINE/			
		STELLA'S GOT A FELLA	3.25	5.50	4.00
☐6904		I CAN'T SAY GOODBYE/			
		WHAT DID I DO WRONG?	3.25	5.50	4.00
☐6906		MY GIRL/BECAUSE OF MY PRIDE	3.25	5.50	4.00
☐117	CANADIAN-				
	AMERICAN	MARIANNE/			
		GIVE ALL YOUR LOVE TO ME . .	3.25	5.50	4.00
☐355	TAURUS	YOU WERE MINE FOR AWHILE/			
		ONE O'CLOCK TWIST	3.25	5.50	4.00

FIREFLIES—ALBUM

☐1002 (S)	TAURUS	YOU WERE MINE	17.00	39.00	35.00

FIVE AMERICANS

☐109	ABNAK	I SEE THE LIGHT/THE OUTCAST .	4.00	7.00	4.75
☐116		IF I COULD/NOW THAT IT'S OVER	2.50	6.00	4.50
☐118		WESTERN UNION/			
		NOW THAT IT'S OVER	3.00	5.50	3.85
☐120		SOUND OF LOVE/SYMPATHY . . .	3.00	5.50	3.85
☐123		ZIP CODE/SWEET BIRD OF YOUTH	3.00	5.50	3.85
☐125		STOP LIGHT/			
		TELL ANN I LOVE HER	3.00	5.50	3.85
☐126		7:30 GUIDED TOUR/			
		SEE-SAW MAN	3.00	5.50	3.85

			Current Price Range		P/Y AVG
☐ 128		RAIN MAKER/			
		NO COMMUNICATION	3.00	5.50	3.85
☐ 131		LOVIN' IS LOVIN'/CON MAN	3.00	5.50	3.87
☐ 132		GENERATION CAP/THE SOURCE .	3.00	5.50	3.87
☐ 142		SHE'S GOOD TO ME/			
		MOLLY BLACK	3.00	5.50	3.87
☐ 454	HBR	I SEE THE LIGHT/THE OUTCAST .	3.00	5.50	3.87
☐ 468		EVOL - NO LOVE/			
		DON'T BLAME ME	3.00	5.50	3.87
☐ 483		THE LOSING GAME/GOOD TIMES .	3.00	5.50	3.87
		FIVE AMERICANS—ALBUMS			
☐ 1967 (M)	ABNAK	WESTERN UNION.............	6.00	15.00	13.50
☐ 2067 (S)		WESTERN UNION.............	7.00	17.00	15.00
☐ 2069 (S)		PROGRESSIONS.............	6.00	15.00	13.50
☐ 2071 (S)		NOW AND THEN.............	6.00	15.00	13.50
☐ 8503 (M)	HBR	I SEE THE LIGHT	6.00	15.00	13.50

FIVE BLOBS

☐ 41250	COLUMBIA	THE BLOB/			
		SATURDAY NIGHT IN TIJUANA .	5.00	8.50	7.00

FIVE COACHMEN

☐ 100	JANSON	THIS I KNOW/OH JOAN	9.00	17.00	15.00

FIVE DISCS

☐ 45-114	CRYSTAL BALL	MIRROR MIRROR/			
		MOST OF ALL I WONDER WHY .	30.00	60.00	42.00
☐ 607	DWAIN	MY CHINESE GIRL/ROSES	20.00	34.00	30.00
☐ 803		MY CHINESE GIRL/ROSES	13.00	23.00	20.00
☐ 1002	MELLO MOOD	MY CHINESE GIRL/ROSES	13.00	23.00	20.00
☐ 1004	EMGE	I REMEMBER/THE WORLD IS A			
		BEAUTIFUL PLACE	12.00	21.00	18.00
☐ 0327	VIK	I REMEMBER/THE WORLD IS A			
		BEAUTIFUL PLACE	12.00	21.00	18.00
☐ 5027	RUST	I REMEMBER/THE WORLD IS A			
		BEAUTIFUL PLACE	4.50	7.50	6.00
☐ 240	YALE	WHEN LOVE COMES KNOCKING/			
		GO-GO	8.50	14.00	12.00
☐ 243		COME ON BABY/I DON'T KNOW			
		WHAT I'LL DO	14.00	23.00	20.00

THE FIVE EMBERS

☐ 45-6218	GEM	ALL ALONE/LOVE TEARS	45.00	75.00	50.00
☐ 45-224		PLEASE COME HOME/LOVE BIRDS .	80.00	160.00	125.00

FIVE GENTS

☐ 101	VIKING	BABY DOLL/SANDY	12.00	28.00	25.00

THE FIVE JADES

☐ 163	PYRAMID	ARE YOU SORRY/			
		LET THERE BE YOU	50.00	90.00	65.00
☐ 45-908	YOUR CHOICE	MY REVERIE/ROSEMARIE	65.00	110.00	78.00
☐ 1012		MY GIRL FRIEND/			
		HOW MUCH I LOVE YOU	60.00	100.00	70.00

FIVE KEYS

☐ 116	BIM BAM BOOM	OUT OF SIGHT. OUT OF MIND/			
		CLOSE YOUR EYES	3.00	5.00	4.00
☐ 3085	ALADDIN	WITH A BROKEN HEART/			
		TOO LATE	95.00	170.00	120.00
☐ 3099		THE GLORY OF LOVE/			
		HUCKLEBUCK WITH JIMMY ...	70.00	130.00	89.00
☐ 3113		IT'S CHRISTMAS TIME/			
		OLD MACDONALD HAD A FARM	110.00	200.00	145.00

		Current Price Range		P/Y AVG
☐3118	YES SIR, THAT'S MY BABY/OLD MACDONALD HAD A FARM	110.00	200.00	145.00
☐3119	DARLING/GOIN' DOWNTOWN ...	110.00	200.00	145.00
☐3127	RED SAILS IN THE SUNSET/ BE ANYTHING BUT BE MINE ...	120.00	230.00	145.00
☐3131	MISTAKES/HOW LONG	95.00	170.00	120.00
☐3136	I HADN'T ANYONE TILL YOU/ HOLD ME	95.00	170.00	120.00
☐3158	I CRIED FOR YOU/ SERVE ANOTHER ROUND	95.00	170.00	120.00
☐3167	CAN'T KEEP FROM CRYING/ COME GO MY BAIL, LOUISE ...	95.00	170.00	120.00
☐3175	THERE OUGHT TO BE A LAW/ MAMA (YOUR DAUGHTER TOLD A LIE ON ME)	95.00	170.00	120.00
☐3182	I'LL ALWAYS BE IN LOVE WITH YOU/OCKING AND CRYING BLUES	95.00	170.00	120.00
☐3190	THESE FOOLISH THINGS/ LONESOME OLD STORY	95.00	170.00	120.00
☐3204	TEARDROPS IN MY EYES/ I'M SO HIGH	70.00	130.00	89.00
☐3214	MY SADDEST HOUR/OH! BABE! .	70.00	130.00	89.00
☐3228	LOVE MY LOVING/ SOMEDAY SWEETHEART	70.00	130.00	89.00
☐3245	DEEP IN MY HEART/HOW DO YOU EXPECT ME TO GET IT?	70.00	130.00	89.00
☐3263	MY LOVE/WHY, OH WHY	34.00	55.00	50.00
☐3312	STORY OF LOVE/ SERVE ANOTHER ROUND	34.00	55.00	50.00
☐2945	**CAPITOL** LING, TING, TONG/I'M ALONE ...	8.50	16.00	11.00
☐3032	CLOSE YOUR EYES/ DOGGONE IT, YOU DID IT	8.50	16.00	11.00
☐3127	THE VERDICT/ ME MAKE UM POW WOW	8.50	16.00	11.00
☐3185	DON'T YOU KNOW I LOVE YOU/ I WISH I'D NEVER LEARNED TO READ	8.50	16.00	11.00
☐3267	GEE WHITTAKERS!/ 'CAUSE YOU'RE MY LOVER ...	8.50	16.00	11.00
☐3318	WHAT GOES ON/YOU BROKE THE RULES OF LOVE	5.25	10.00	7.00
☐3392	SHE'S THE MOST/I DREAMED I DWELT IN HEAVEN	5.25	10.00	7.00
☐3455	PEACE AND LOVE/ MY PIGEON'S GONE	5.25	10.00	7.00
☐3502	OUT OF SIGHT, OUT OF MIND/ THAT'S RIGHT	5.25	10.00	7.00
☐3597	WISDOM OF A FOOL/NOW DON'T THAT PROVE I LOVE YOU ...	5.25	10.00	7.00
☐3660	LET THERE BE YOU/TIGER LILY ..	5.25	10.00	7.00
☐3710	IT'S A GROOVE/FOUR WALLS ...	4.75	8.50	6.00
☐3738	THIS I PROMISE/ THE BLUES DON'T CARE	4.75	8.50	6.00
☐3786	THE FACE OF AN ANGEL/ BOOM-BOOM	4.75	8.50	6.00
☐3830	DO ANYTHING/ IT'S A CRYIN' SHAME	4.75	8.50	6.00
☐3861	FROM ME TO YOU/ WHIPPETY WHIRL	4.75	8.50	6.00
☐3948	WITH ALL MY LOVE/ YOU'RE FOR ME	4.75	8.50	6.00
☐4009	EMILY PLEASE/HANDY ANDY ...	4.75	8.50	6.00
☐4092	ONE GREAT LOVE/ REALLY-O TRULY-O	4.75	8.50	6.00

			Current Price Range		P/Y AVG
☐4828		FROM THE BOTTOM OF MY HEART/OUT OF SIGHT, OUT OF MIND	3.25	6.00	4.00
		FIVE KEYS—EPs			
☐572	**CAPITOL**	JUST FOR A THRILL	20.00	35.00	30.00
☐1-828		THE FIVE KEYS ON STAGE	15.00	32.00	22.00
☐2-828		THE FIVE KEYS ON STAGE	15.00	32.00	22.00
☐3-828		THE FIVE KEYS ON STAGE	15.00	32.00	22.00
		FIVE KEYS—ALBUMS			
☐806 (M)	**ALADDIN**	ON THE TOWN	65.00	158.00	150.00
☐808 (M)		THE FIVE KEYS, VOL. II	55.00	140.00	135.00
☐810 (M)		THE BEST OF THE FIVE KEYS	45.00	115.00	110.00
☐828 (M)	**CAPITOL**	THE FIVE KEYS ON STAGE	45.00	100.00	67.00
☐1001 (M)		THE BEST OF THE FIVE KEYS	45.00	100.00	67.00
☐1006 (M)		THE BEST OF THE FIVE KEYS	45.00	100.00	67.00
☐1769 (M)		THE FANTASTIC FIVE KEYS	40.00	90.00	58.00
☐4003 (M)	**SCORE**	ON THE TOWN	40.00	90.00	58.00
		THE FIVE OWLS			
☐327	**OWL**	THE THRILL IS GONE/LIMA BEANS.	30.00	70.00	50.00
☐1025	**VULCAN**	PLEADING TO YOU/I LIKE MOONSHINE	40.00	75.00	60.00
		FIVE REASONS			
☐9006	**CUB**	THREE O'CLOCK ROCK/ GO TO SCHOOL	12.00	29.00	25.00
		FIVE SATINS			
		SEE: SCARLETS			
☐5105	**STANDORD**	ALL MINE/ROSEMARIE	25.00	50.00	40.00
☐105		ALL MINE/ROSEMARIE	60.00	120.00	78.00
☐106		IN THE STILL OF THE NIGHT/ THE JONES GIRL	45.00	80.00	74.00
☐1005	**EMBER**	I'LL REMEMBER (IN THE STILL OF THE NITE)/THE JONES GIRL	12.00	21.00	18.00
☐1005		IN THE STILL OF THE NIGHT/ THE JONES GIRL	9.00	17.00	11.00
☐1008		WONDERFUL GIRL	9.00	17.00	11.00
☐1014		OH HAPPY DAY/ OUR LOVE IS FOREVER	9.00	17.00	11.00
☐1019		TO THE AISLE/ WISH I HAD MY BABY	6.00	12.00	8.25
☐1025		OUR ANNIVERSARY/PRETTY GIRL	6.00	12.00	8.25
☐1038		A NIGHT TO REMEMBER/ SENORITA LOLITA	6.00	12.00	8.25
☐1056		SHADOWS/TONI MY LOVE	6.00	12.00	8.25
☐1061		I'LL BE SEEING YOU/ A NIGHT LIKE THIS	6.00	12.00	8.25
☐1066		CANDLELIGHT/THE TIME	6.00	12.00	8.25
☐1070		WISHING RING/TELL ME DEAR	6.00	12.00	8.25
☐1108	**MUSICTONE**	JUST TO BE NEAR YOU/ TO THE AISLE	6.00	12.00	8.25
☐4251	**KIRSHNER**	YOU ARE LOVE/VERY PRECIOUS OLDIES	6.00	12.00	8.25
☐9071	**CUB**	YOUR MEMORY/I DIDN'T KNOW	6.00	12.00	8.25
☐1110	**CHANCELLOR**	THE MASQUERADE IS OVER/RAINING IN MY HEART	6.00	12.00	8.25
☐901	**NIGHTTRAIN**	ALL MINE/THE VOICE	6.00	12.00	8.25
		FIVE SATINS—EPs			
☐100	**EMBER**	THE FIVE SATINS SING	18.00	29.00	18.00
☐101		TO THE AISLE	9.50	17.00	15.00
☐102		OUR ANNIVERSARY	9.50	17.00	15.00

FIVE SATINS

The Five Satins initially formed as the Scarlets in 1954. The New Haven, CT, quintet signed with the small Red Robin label. After four fine (but poorly selling) singles, they moved to Klik Records for one other single that likewise bombed. Leader Fred Parris then dissolved the group and enlisted in the Army.

One night as he was walking guard duty at 3:00 A.M., Parris began creating a song in his mind. The result was "In the Still of the Night".

In 1956, Fred completed his Army stint and reformed the group as the Five Satins. They signed with a small Connecticut label called Standord. There they cut Fred's "In the Still of the Night". It did nothing on Standord, but the single was noticed by the larger Ember label. Ember purchased the Standord master outright for a paltry $1,200. However, Ember had bought the song to promote the flip side, a bouncy, risque ditty entitled "The Jones Girl". As fate would have it, though, "In the Still of the Night (first called "I'll Remember" on Ember) became a classic hit.

A year later came the only other Five Satins winner, "To the Aisle".

For a time, the group worked as a quartet (see photo).

			Current Price Range		P/Y AVG

FIVE SATINS—ALBUMS

			Current Price Range		P/Y AVG
☐ 100 (M)	EMBER	THE FIVE SATINS SING	40.00	98.00	67.00
☐ 401 (M)		FIVE SATINS: ENCORE	29.00	64.00	60.00
☐ 108 (M)	MT. VERNON	THE FIVE SATINS SING	14.00	34.00	30.00

FIVE SCRIPTS

☐ LF201	LONGFIBER	PEACE OF MIND/THE CLOCK	25.00	50.00	35.00
☐ 57-S103	SCRIPT	YOU LEFT MY HEART/MY FRIENDS TELL ME (DJ Copy)	30.00	60.00	42.00

FIVE TROJANS

☐ 410	EDISON INTERNATIONAL	CREATOR OF LOVE	12.00	46.00	42.00

FLAMINGOS

☐ 1133	CHANCE	IF I CAN'T HAVE YOU/ SOMEDAY, SOMEWAY	110.00	200.00	145.00
☐ 1140		THAT'S MY DESIRE/ HURRY HOME BABY	100.00	180.00	125.00
☐ 1140		THAT'S MY DESIRE/ HURRY HOME BABY (red wax)	150.00	275.00	170.00
☐ 1145		GOLDEN TEARDROPS/ CARRIED AWAY	100.00	180.00	125.00
☐ 1145		GOLDEN TEARDROPS/ CARRIED AWAY (red wax)	150.00	275.00	170.00
☐ 1149		PLAN FOR LOVE/ YOU AIN'T READY	150.00	275.00	170.00
☐ 1154		CROSS OVER THE BRIDGE/ LISTEN TO MY PLEA	150.00	275.00	170.00
☐ 1162		BLUES IN A LETTER/ JUMP CHILDREN	150.00	275.00	170.00
☐ 808	PARROT	DREAM OF A LIFETIME/ ON MY MERRY WAY	70.00	150.00	105.00
☐ 808		DREAM OF A LIFETIME/ ON MY MERRY WAY (red wax)	100.00	170.00	120.00
☐ 811		I REALLY DON'T WANT TO KNOW/ GET WITH IT	230.00	450.00	255.00
☐ 812		I'M YOURS/KO KO MO	90.00	150.00	105.00
☐ 384	VEE JAY	GOLDEN TEARDROPS/ CARRIED AWAY	11.00	20.00	13.50
☐ 815	CHECKER	WHEN/THAT'S MY BABY	11.00	20.00	13.50
☐ 821		PLEASE COME BACK HOME/ I WANT TO LOVE	11.00	20.00	13.50
☐ 830		I'LL BE HOME/NEED YOUR LOVE	11.00	20.00	13.50
☐ 837		A KISS FROM YOUR LIPS/ GET WITH IT	11.00	20.00	13.50
☐ 846		THE VOW/SILLY DILLY	11.00	20.00	13.50
☐ 853		WOULD I BE CRYING/ JUST FOR A KICK	11.00	20.00	13.50
☐ 915		WHISPERING STARS/ DREAM OF A LIFETIME	9.00	17.00	10.75
☐ 1084		LOVER COME BACK TO ME/ YOUR LITTLE GUY	9.00	17.00	11.00
☐ 1091		GOODNIGHT SWEETHEART/ DOES IT REALLY MATTER?	9.00	17.00	11.00
☐ 30335	DECCA	THE LADDER OF LOVE/ LET'S MAKE UP	8.00	15.00	10.00
☐ 30454		MY FAITH IN YOU/HELPLESSS	8.00	15.00	10.00
☐ 30687		WHERE DID MARY GO?/ ROCK N' ROLL MARCH	6.00	12.00	8.00
☐ 30880		EVER SINCE I MET LUCY/ KISS-A-ME	6.00	12.00	8.00
☐ 30948		JERRI-LEE/HEY NOW	6.00	12.00	8.00

			Current Price Range		P/Y AVG
☐ 1035	**END**	LOVERS NEVER SAY GOODBYE/ THAT LOVE IS YOU	8.00	15.00	10.00
☐ 1040		BUT NOT FOR ME/I SHED A TEAR AT YOUR WEDDING	8.00	15.00	10.00
☐ 1044		LOVE WALKED IN/AT THE PROM	8.00	15.00	10.00
☐ 1046		I ONLY HAVE EYES FOR YOU/ GOODNIGHT SWEETHEART	8.00	15.00	10.00
☐ 1046		I ONLY HAVE EYES FOR YOU/ AT THE PROM	5.50	10.00	7.00
☐ 1055		LOVE WALKED IN/YOURS	5.50	10.00	7.00
☐ 1062		I WAS SUCH A FOOL/ HEAVENLY ANGEL	5.50	10.00	7.00
☐ 1065		MIO AMORE/ YOU, ME AND THE SEA	5.50	10.00	7.00
☐ 1068		NOBODY LOVES ME LIKE YOU/ BESAME MUCHO	5.50	10.00	7.00
☐ 1068		NOBODY LOVES ME LIKE YOU/ BESAME MUCHO	5.00	8.00	6.00
☐ 1070		BESAME MUCHO/ YOU, ME AND THE SEA	5.00	8.00	6.00
☐ 1073		MIO AMORE/AT NIGHT	5.00	8.00	6.00
☐ 1079		WHEN I FALL IN LOVE/ BESIDE YOU	5.00	8.00	6.00
☐ 1081		YOUR OTHER LOVE/ LOVERS GOTTA CRY	5.00	8.00	6.00
☐ 1085		KOKOMO/ THAT'S WHY I LOVE YOU	5.00	8.00	6.00
☐ 1092		TIME WAS/DREAM GIRL	4.00	7.00	5.00
☐ 1099		MY MEMORIES OF YOU/ I WANT TO LOVE YOU	4.00	7.00	5.00
☐ 1111		I'M NO FOOL ANYMORE/ IT MUST BE LOVE	4.00	7.00	5.00
☐ 1116		FOR ALL WE KNOW/NEAR YOU	4.00	7.00	5.00
☐ 1121		I KNOW BETTER/FLAME OF LOVE	4.00	7.00	5.00
☐ 1124		(TALK ABOUT) TRUE LOVE/ COME ON TO MY PARTY	4.00	7.00	5.00

FLAMINGOS—EP

☐ 205	**END**	THE FLAMINGOS	12.00	21.00	18.00

FLAMINGOS—ALBUMS

☐ 304 (M)	**END**	FLAMINGO SERENADE	17.00	39.00	35.00
☐ 307 (M)		FLAMINGO FAVORITES	14.00	34.00	30.00
☐ 308 (M)		REQUESTFULLY YOURS	14.00	34.00	30.00
☐ 316 (M)		SOUND OF THE FLAMINGOS	14.00	34.00	30.00
☐ 1433 (M)	**CHECKER**	THE FLAMINGOS	12.00	29.00	25.00

FLARES (CADETS)
SEE: CADETS, JACKS

☐ 8604	**FELSTED**	LOVING YOU/ HOTCHA CHA-CHA BROWN	3.50	6.50	4.65
☐ 8607		JUMP AND BUMP/ WHAT DO YOUWANT IF YOU DON'T WANT LOVE?	3.50	6.50	4.65
☐ 8624		FOOT STOMPIN'FOOT STOMPIN' (instrumental)	3.50	6.50	4.65
☐ 2800	**PRESS**	ROCK AND ROLL HEAVEN (PT. 1)/(PT. 2)	3.25	6.00	4.00
☐ 2802		DOING THE HULLY GULLY/ TRUCK AND TRAILER	3.25	6.00	4.00
☐ 2803		MAD HOUSE/MAKE IT BE ME	3.25	6.00	4.00
☐ 2807		DO IT WITH ME/YON WE GO	3.25	6.00	4.00
☐ 2808		HAND CLAPPIN'/ SHIMMY AND STOMP	3.25	6.00	4.00
☐ 2810		THE MONKEY WALK/ DO IT IF YOU WANNA	3.25	6.00	4.00

			Current Price Range		P/Y AVG
☐ 2814		I DIDN'T LOSE A DOGGONE THING/ WRITE A SONG ABOUT ME	3.25	6.00	4.00
		FLARES—ALBUMS			
☐ 73001 (M)	**PRESS**	ENCORE OF FOOTSTOMPIN' HITS	8.00	21.00	18.00
☐ 83011 (S)		ENCORE OF FOOTSTOMPIN' HITS	12.00	29.00	25.00

FLEETWOOD MAC
FEATURED: STEVIE NICKS

			Current Price Range		P/Y AVG
☐ 10386	**EPIC**	STOP MESSIN' 'ROUND/ NEED YOUR LOVE SO BAD	3.50	6.00	4.50
☐ 10436		ALBATROSS/ JIGSAW PUZZLE BLUES	3.50	6.00	4.50
☐ 11029		ALBATROSS/ BLACK MAGIC WOMAN	3.25	5.50	4.00
☐ 0860	**REPRISE**	COMING YOUR WAY/ RATTLESNAKE SHAKE	3.25	5.50	4.00
☐ 0883		OH WELL (PT. 1)/(PT. 2)........	3.00	5.00	3.50
☐ 0925		WORLD IN HARMONY/ GREEN MANALISHI	3.00	5.00	3.50
☐ 0984		JEWEL EYED JUDY/STATION MAN.	3.00	5.00	3.50
☐ 1057		SANDS OF TIME/ LAY IT ALL DOWN	3.00	5.00	3.50
☐ 1079		OH WELL/GREEN MANALISHI ...	3.00	5.00	3.50
☐ 1093		SENTIMENTAL LADY/ SUNNY SIDE OF HEAVEN	3.25	5.50	4.00
☐ 1172		DID YOU EVER LOVE ME?/ REVELATION	3.00	5.00	3.50
		FLEETWOOD MAC—ALBUMS			
☐ 26402 (S)	**EPIC**	FLEETWOOD MAC	7.00	18.00	11.00
☐ 26446 (S)		ENGLISH ROSE	6.00	16.00	10.00
☐ 2080 (S)	**REPRISE**	BARE TREES	5.50	14.00	8.50
☐ 2138 (S)		PENGUIN	5.50	14.00	8.50
☐ 2158 (S)		MYSTERY TO ME.............	5.50	14.00	8.50
☐ 2196 (S)		HEROES ARE HARD TO FIND	5.50	14.00	8.50
☐ 2225 (S)		FLEETWOOD MAC	5.50	14.00	8.50
☐ 6368 (S)		THEN PLAY ON	5.50	14.00	8.50
☐ 6408 (S)		KILN HOUSE	5.50	14.00	8.50
☐ 6465 (S)		FUTURE GAMES	5.50	14.00	8.50

FLEETWOODS

			Current Price Range		P/Y AVG
☐ 55188	**LIBERTY**	COME SOFTLY TO ME/ I CARE SO MUCH	4.50	7.50	6.00
☐ 1	**DOLPHIN**	COME SOFTLY TO ME/ I CARE SO MUCH	3.00	5.00	3.50
☐ 3	**DOLTON**	GRADUATION'S HERE/ OH LORD, LET IT BE	3.00	5.00	3.50
☐ 5		MR. BLUE/YOU MEAN EVERYTHING TO ME	3.00	5.00	3.50
☐ 15		OUTSIDE MY WINDOW/ MAGIC STAR	2.75	4.75	3.50
☐ 22		RUNAROUND/TRULY DO	2.75	4.75	3.50
☐ 27		THE LAST ONE TO KNOW/ DORMILONA	2.75	4.75	3.50
☐ 30		CONFIDENTIAL/I LOVE YOU SO ..	2.75	4.75	3.50
☐ 40		TRAGEDY/LITTLE MISS SAD ONE	2.75	4.75	3.50
☐ 45		(HE'S) THE GREAT IMPOSTER/ POOR LITTLE GIRL	2.75	4.75	3.50
☐ 49		BILLY OLD BUDDY/TROUBLE	2.75	4.75	3.50
☐ 62		LOVERS BY NIGHT, STRANGERS BY DAY/THEY TELL ME IT'S SUMMER	2.75	4.75	3.50
☐ 74		YOU SHOULD HAVE BEEN THERE/ SURE IS LONESOME DOWNTOWN	2.75	4.75	3.50

FLEETWOODS

Two Girls And a Guy?

That was the original name of the Fleetwoods. They were classmates at Olympia High in Olympia, Washington. At first the two girls (Barbara Ellis and Gretchen Christopher) sang as a nameless duo. Then they asked school pal Gary Troxel to join them—as a trumpet player. However, the girls soon discovered that Troxel's singing talents outdistanced his trumpeting.

They finished high school in June of 1958 and signed with the Liberty Records subsidiary of Dolton. The manager of Two Girls And a Guy thought the youngsters should choose a more commercial name. They decided on their Olympia telephone prefix, FLeetwood. (Prefixes were used long before all-digit phone numbers.)

The Fleetwoods' first release was a song they had written a year earlier called "Come Softly To Me". It shot to No. 1, as did another 1959 single, "Mr. Blue". After "covering" Thomas Wayne's hit of "Tragedy" the Fleetwoods' last chart hit came in 1963 with another "cover"—a 1950s r & b hit called "Goodnight My Love", originally done by Jesse Belvin.

			Current Price Range		P/Y AVG
□75		GOODNIGHT MY LOVE/ JIMMY BEWARE	2.75	4.75	3.50
□86		WHAT'LL I DO?/BABY BYE-0	2.75	4.75	3.50
□93		LONESOME TOWN/ RUBY RED, BABY BLUE	2.75	4.75	3.50
□97		TEN TIMES BLUE/ SKA LIGHT, SKA BRIGHT	2.75	4.75	3.50
□98		MR. SANDMAN/ THIS IS MY PRAYER	2.75	4.75	3.50
□302		BEFORE AND AFTER/ LONELY IS AS LONELY DOES	2.75	4.75	3.50
□307		I'M NOT JIMMY/ COME SOFTLY TO ME	2.75	4.75	3.50
□310		RAINBOW/JUST AS I NEEDED YOU	2.75	4.75	3.50
□315		FOR LOVIN' ME/ THIS IS WHERE I SEE HER	2.75	4.75	3.50
		FLEETWOODS—EP			
□502	*DOLTON*	RUNAROUND	6.00	11.00	9.00
		FLEETWOODS—ALBUMS			
□2001 (M)	*DOLTON*	MR. BLUE	8.00	21.00	18.00
□8001 (S)		MR. BLUE	12.00	29.00	25.00
□2002 (M)		THE FLEETWOODS	8.00	21.00	18.00
□8002 (S)		THE FLEETWOODS	12.00	29.00	25.00
□2005 (M)		SOFTLY	7.00	17.00	15.00
□8005 (S)		SOFTLY	10.00	25.00	22.50
□2007 (M)		DEEP IN A DREAM	7.00	17.00	15.00
□8007 (S)		DEEP IN A DREAM	10.00	25.00	22.50
□2011 (M)		THE FLEETWOODS SING THE BEST OF THE OLDIES	7.00	17.00	15.00
□8011 (S)		THE FLEETWOODS SING THE BEST OF THE OLDIES	10.00	25.00	22.50
□2018 (M)		THE FLEETWOODS' GREATEST HITS	7.00	17.00	15.00
□8018 (S)		THE FLEETWOODS' GREATEST HITS	10.00	25.00	22.50
□2020 (M)		THE FLEETWOODS SING FOR LOVERS BY NIGHT	7.00	17.00	15.00
□8020 (S)		THE FLEETWOODS SING FOR LOVERS BY NIGHT	8.00	20.00	18.00
□2025 (M)		GOODNIGHT MY LOVE	7.00	17.00	15.00
□8025 (S)		GOODNIGHT MY LOVE	8.00	20.00	18.00
□2030 (M)		BEFORE AND AFTER	7.00	17.00	15.00
□8030 (S)		BEFORE AND AFTER	8.00	20.00	18.00
□2039 (M)		FOLK ROCK	6.00	15.00	13.50
□8039 (S)		FOLK ROCK	7.00	17.00	15.00

FLOURESCENTS

□4520	*HANOVER*	THE FACTS OF LOVE/ SHOOPY POP-A-DOO	20.00	34.00	30.00

TOMMY FOGERTY AND THE BLUE VELVETS
SEE: CREEDENCE CLEARWATER REVIVAL

□1010	*ORCHESTRA*	HAVE YOU EVEN BEEN LONELY?/ BONITA	12.00	20.00	18.00

WAYNE FONTANA AND THE MINDBENDERS

□1503	*FONTANA*	THE GAME OF LOVE/ SINCE YOU'VE BEEN GONE	3.25	5.50	4.00
□1509		THE GAME OF LOVE/ ONE MORE TIME	3.00	5.00	3.65
□1514		IT'S JUST A LITTLE BIT TOO LATE/ A LONG TIME COMIN'	3.00	5.00	3.65
□1524		SHE NEEDS LOVE/LIKE I DID	3.00	5.00	3.65

			Current Price Range		P/Y AVG
WAYNE FONTANA AND THE MINDBENDERS—ALBUMS					
☐27542 (M)	FONTANA	THE GAME OF LOVE	6.00	14.00	12.00
☐67542 (S)		THE GAME OF LOVE	8.00	21.00	18.00

FONTANE SISTERS

☐3979	RCA	TENNESSEE WALTZ/I GUESS I'LL HAVE TO	3.75	5.50	4.25
☐5524		THE KISSING BRIDGE/ SILVER BELLS	3.75	5.50	4.25
☐5612		TILL THEN/THE BEACON	3.75	5.50	4.25
☐15171	DOT	IF I DIDN'T HAVE YOU/HAPPY DAYS AND LONELY NIGHTS	3.75	5.50	4.25
☐15265		HEARTS OF STONE/ BLESS YOUR HEART	3.75	5.50	4.25
☐15333		ROCK LOVE/YOU'RE MINE	3.50	5.25	4.00
☐15352		MOST OF ALL/ PUT ME IN THE MOOD	3.50	5.25	4.00
☐15370		ROLLIN' STONE/PLAYMATES	3.50	5.25	4.00
☐15386		SEVENTEEN/ IF I COULD BE WITH YOU	3.50	5.25	4.00
☐15428		DADDY-O/ADORABLE	3.50	5.25	4.00
☐15434		NUTTIN' FOR CHRISTMAS/ SILVER BELLS	3.50	5.25	4.00
☐15450		EDDIE MY LOVE/YUM YUM	3.50	5.25	4.00
☐15462		I'M IN LOVE AGAIN/YOU ALWAYS HURT THE ONE YOU LOVE	3.00	5.00	3.65
☐15480		VOICES/ LONESOME LOVER BLUES	2.75	4.50	3.00
☐15501		PLEASE DON'T LEAVE ME/STILL	2.75	4.50	3.00
LATER DOT SINGLES ARE WORTH UP TO $1.75 MINT					
FONTANE SISTERS—EPs					
☐1019	DOT	THE FONTANE SISTERS	4.50	7.50	6.00
☐1020		THE FONTANE SISTERS	4.50	7.50	6.00
FONTANE SISTERS—ALBUMS					
☐3004 (M)	DOT	THE FONTANE SISTERS	7.00	17.00	15.00
☐3042 (M)		THE FONTANES SING	6.00	15.00	13.50
☐3531 (M)		TIPS OF MY FINGERS	5.50	14.00	12.00
☐25531 (S)		TIPS OF MY FINGERS	7.00	17.00	15.00

FRANKIE FORD

☐549	ACE	CHEATIN' WOMAN/ THE LAST ONE TO CRY	4.50	7.50	6.00
☐554		SEA CRUISE/ROBERTA	3.50	7.00	4.65
☐566		ALIMONY/CAN'T TELL MY HEART (WHAT TO DO)	3.25	5.50	4.00
☐580		TIME AFTER TIME/ I WANT TO BE YOUR MAN	3.25	5.50	4.00
☐592		CHINATOWN/WHAT'S GOIN' ON?	3.25	5.50	4.00
☐8009		OCEAN FULL OF TEARS/ HOURS OF NEED	3.00	5.00	3.65
☐5686	IMPERIAL	YOU TALK TOO MUCH/ IF YOU'VE GOT TROUBLES	3.00	5.00	3.65
☐5706		MY SOUTHERN BELLE/ THE GROOM	3.00	5.00	3.65
☐5735		SEVENTEEN/DOGHOUSE	3.00	5.00	3.65
☐5749		SATURDAY NIGHT FISH FRY/ LOVE DON'T LOVE NOBODY	3.00	5.00	3.65
☐5775		WHAT HAPPENED TO YOU?/ LET THEM TALK	3.00	5.00	3.65
☐5819		A MAN ONLY DOES/THEY SAID IT COULDN'T BE DONE	3.00	5.00	3.65
FRANKIE FORD—EP					
☐105	ACE	THE BEST OF FRANKIE FORD	7.00	13.00	11.00

			Current Price Range		P/Y AVG

FRANKIE FORD—ALBUM

| ☐1005 (M) | ACE | ON A SEA CRUISE WITH FRANKIE FORD | 17.50 | 40.00 | 25.00 |

4 AFTER 5's (RIVINGTONS)

| ☐9076 | ALL TIME | HELLO, SCHOOLTEACHER/ I GOTTA HAVE SOMEBODY | 8.50 | 14.00 | 12.00 |

FOUR BLADES

| ☐1170 | GATEWAY | I WANT YOU (TO BE MY GIRL)/ CAN YOU FIND IT | 23.00 | 52.00 | 34.00 |
| ☐1174 | | STARDUST/ CHURCH BELLS MAY RING | 23.00 | 52.00 | 34.00 |

FOUR CAL-QUETTES

☐4534	CAPITOL	SPARKLE AND SHINE/ IN THIS WORLD (Couquettes)	4.50	7.50	6.00
☐4574		STARBRIGHT/BILLY MY BILLY	3.50	6.50	4.50
☐4657		MOST OF ALL/I'M GONNA LOVE HIM ANYWAY	3.50	6.50	4.50
☐4725		I'LL NEVER COME BACK/AGAIN	3.50	6.50	4.50
☐55549	LIBERTY	I CRIED/MOVIE MAGAZINES	3.25	6.00	4.00

FOUR DIRECTIONS

| ☐62456 | CORAL | ARTHUR/TONIGHT WE LOVE | 12.00 | 29.00 | 25.00 |

FOUR DOTS (WITH JEWEL AKENS)
GUITAR: EDDIE COCHRAN

| ☐44005 | FREEDOM | DON'T WAKE UP THE KIDS/ PLEADING FOR LOVE | 7.00 | 13.00 | 11.00 |

FOUR EKKOS

| ☐55037 | BRUNSWICK | SPUTNIK/SATELLITE LOVE | 12.00 | 29.00 | 25.00 |

FOUR GRADUATES (HAPPENINGS)

| ☐5062 | RUST | A LOVELY WAY TO SPEND AN EVENING/PICTURE OF AN ANGEL | 5.00 | 9.00 | 7.00 |
| ☐5084 | | CANDY QUEEN/A BOY IN LOVE | 4.50 | 7.50 | 6.00 |

FOUR HORSEMEN

| ☐134 | UNITED ARTISTS | MY HEARTBEAT/ LONG LONG TIME | 15.00 | 33.00 | 22.00 |

FOUR JOKERS
FEATURED: NERVOUS NORVUS

| ☐3004 | DIAMOND | TRANSFUSION/YOU DID | 12.00 | 21.00 | 18.00 |

THIS WAS THE ORIGINAL VERSION OF THE NERVOUS NORVUS HIT

FOUR LOVERS (FOUR SEASONS)

☐6518	RCA	YOU'RE THE APPLE OF MY EYE/ THE GIRL IN MY DREAMS	12.00	21.00	18.00
☐6519		HONEY LOVE/ PLEASE DON'T LEAVE ME	12.00	21.00	18.00
☐6646		JAMBALAYA/BE LOVEY DOVEY	12.00	21.00	18.00
☐6768		NEVER NEVER/HAPPY AM I	14.00	24.00	20.00
☐6812		SHAKE A HAND/THE STRANGER	14.00	24.00	20.00

FOUR LOVERS (FOUR SEASONS)—EPs

| ☐869 | RCA | THE FOUR LOVERS | 90.00 | 160.00 | 150.00 |
| ☐871 | | JOYRIDE | 53.00 | 96.00 | 90.00 |

FOUR LOVERS (FOUR SEASONS)—ALBUM

| ☐1317 (M) | RCA | JOYRIDE | 75.00 | 192.00 | 185.00 |

			Current Price Range		P/Y AVG

FOURMOST

☐6280	ATCO	HELLO, LITTLE GIRL/			
		JUST IN CASE	5.00	8.50	7.00
☐6285		RESPECTABLE/I'M IN LOVE	5.00	8.60	7.00
☐6307		IF YOU CRY/			
		A LITTLE BIT OF LOVING	4.50	7.50	6.00
☐6317		HOW CAN I TELL HER?/			
		YOU GOT THAT WAY	4.50	7.50	6.00
☐5591	CAPITOL	WHY DO FOOLS FALL IN LOVE/			
		GIRLS, GIRLS, GIRLS	3.50	6.00	4.50
☐5738		HERE, THERE AND EVERYWHERE/			
		YOU'VE CHANGED	3.50	6.00	4.50

FOUR PENNIES (CHIFFONS)

☐5070	RUST	WHEN THE BOY'S HAPPY/			
		HOCKADAY, (PT. 1)	4.50	7.50	6.00
☐5071		MY BLOCK/DRY YOUR EYES	3.50	6.00	4.50

FOUR PREPS
SEE: TEARDROPS

☐3576	CAPITOL	DREAMY EYES/			
		FOOLS WILL BE FOOLS	3.50	6.00	4.35
☐3621		MOONSTRUCK IN MADRID/			
		I CRIED A MILLION TEARS	3.25	5.50	4.00
☐3699		FALLING STAR/			
		WHERE WUZ YOU?	3.25	5.50	4.00
☐3761		PROMISE ME BABY/			
		AGAIN AN' AGAIN AN' AGAIN ..	3.25	5.50	4.00
☐3775		BAND OF ANGELS/			
		HOW ABOUT THAT	3.25	5.50	4.00
☐3845		26 MILES (SANTA CATALINA)/			
		IT'S YOU	3.25	5.50	4.00
☐3960		BIG MAN/STOP BABY	3.25	5.50	4.00
☐4023		LAZY SUMMER NIGHT/			
		SUMMERTIME LIES	3.25	5.50	4.00
☐4078		CINDERELLA/GIDGET	3.25	5.50	4.00
☐4126		SHE WAS 5 AND HE WAS 10/			
		THE RIDDLE OF LOVE	3.25	5.50	4.00
☐4218		TRY MY ARMS/BIG SURPRISE ...	3.25	5.50	4.00
☐4256		I AIN'T NEVER/			
		MEMORIES, MEMORIES	3.25	5.50	4.00
☐4312		DOWN BY THE STATION/			
		LISTEN HONEY	3.25	5.50	4.00
☐4362		GOT A GIRL/(WAIT 'TIL YOU)			
		HEAR IT FROM ME	3.25	5.50	4.00
☐4400		SENTIMENTAL KID/MADELINA ..	3.25	5.50	4.00
☐4435		THE SAND AND THE SEA/			
		KAW-LIGA	3.25	5.50	4.00
☐4478		BALBOA/			
		I'VE ALREADY STARTED IN ...	3.25	5.50	4.00
☐4508		CALCUTTA/GONE ARE THE DAYS	3.25	5.50	4.00
☐4568		DREAM BOY, DREAM/GROUNDED	3.25	5.50	4.00
☐4599		MORE MONEY FOR YOU AND ME/			
		SWING DOWN CHARIOT	3.25	5.50	4.00
☐4659		ONCE AROUND THE BLOCK/			
		THE SEINE	2.75	5.00	3.50
☐4716		THE BIG DRAFT/			
		SUZY COCKROACH	2.75	5.00	3.50
☐4792		GOOD NIGHT, SWEETHEART/			
		ALICE	2.75	5.00	3.50
☐4974		CHARMAINE/			
		HI HO, ANYBODY HOME?	2.75	5.00	3.50
☐5020		DEMONS AND WITCHES/			
		OH WHERE, OH WHERE	2.75	5.00	3.50

			Current Price Range		P/Y AVG
☐5074		THE GREATEST SURFER COUPLE/ I'M FALLING IN LOVE WITH A GIRL	2.75	5.00	3.50
☐5143		A LETTER TO THE BEATLES/ COLLEGE CANNONBALL	3.50	6.00	4.35
☐5178		I'VE KNOWN YOU ALL MY LIFE/ WHAT KIND OF BIRD IS THAT?	2.50	4.50	3.00
☐5236		THE GIRL WITHOUT A TOP/TWO WRONGS DON'T MAKE A RIGHT	3.00	5.00	3.50
☐5274		MY LOVE, MY LOVE/HOW TO SUCCEED IN LOVE	2.50	4.50	3.00
☐5341		EVERLASTING/ I'LL SET MY LOVE TO MUSIC	2.50	4.50	3.00
☐5450		OUR FIRST AMERICAN DANCE/ I'LL NEVER BE THE SAME	2.50	4.50	3.00
☐5609		SOMETHING TO REMEMBER YOU BY/ANNIE IN HER GRANNY	2.50	4.50	3.00
		FOUR PREPS—EPs			
☐1015	*CAPITOL*	26 MILES	6.00	11.00	9.00
☐1064		BIG MAN	6.00	11.00	9.00
☐1090		THINGS WE DID LAST SUMMER	6.00	11.00	9.00
☐1139		LAZY SUMMER NIGHT	4.50	7.50	6.00
☐1862		DREAMY EYES	4.50	7.50	6.00
☐11064		BIG MAN	4.50	7.50	6.00
☐11090		THINGS WE DID LAST SUMMER	3.50	6.00	4.50
		FOUR PREPS—ALBUMS			
☐994 (M)	*CAPITOL*	FOUR PREPS	12.00	29.00	25.00
☐1216 (M)		DANCING AND DREAMING	10.00	25.00	22.50
☐1291 (M)		DOWN BY THE STATION	7.00	17.00	15.00
☐1291 (S)		DOWN BY THE STATION	10.00	25.00	22.50
☐1566 (M)		FOUR PREPS ON CAMPUS	6.00	15.00	13.50
☐1566 (S)		FOUR PREPS ON CAMPUS	8.00	21.00	18.00
☐1647 (M)		CAMPUS ENCORE	6.00	15.00	13.50
☐1647 (S)		CAMPUS ENCORE	8.00	21.00	18.00
☐1814 (M)		CAMPUS CONFIDENTIAL	6.00	15.00	13.50
☐1814 (S)		CAMPUS CONFIDENTIAL	8.00	21.00	18.00

FOUR SEASONS
FEATURED: FRANKIE VALLI

			Current Price Range		P/Y AVG
☐5122	*GONE*	BERMUDA/SPANISH LACE	17.00	29.00	25.00
☐456	*VEE JAY*	SHERRY/I'VE CRIED BEFORE	3.25	5.50	4.00
☐465		BIG GIRLS DON'T CRY/CONNIE-O	3.25	5.50	4.00
☐478		SANTA CLAUS IS COMING TO TOWN/CHRISTMAS TEARS	3.25	5.50	4.00
☐485		WALK LIKE A MAN/ LUCKY LADYBUG	3.25	5.50	4.00
☐512		AIN'T THAT A SHAME/SOON	3.25	5.50	4.00
☐539		CANDY GIRL/MARLENA	3.25	5.50	4.00
☐562		NEW MEXICAN ROSE/ THAT'S THE ONLY WAY	3.25	5.50	4.00
☐576		PEANUTS/STAY	4.00	7.00	4.75
☐582		STAY/GOODNIGHT MY LOVE	3.25	5.50	4.00
☐597		ALONE/LONG LONELY NIGHTS	3.25	5.50	4.00
☐608		SINCERELY/ONE SONG	3.25	5.50	4.00
☐618		HAPPY, HAPPY BIRTHDAY BABY/ YOU'RE THE APPLE OF MY EYE	4.25	7.50	5.00
☐626		I SAW MOMMY KISSING SANTA CLAUS/CHRISTMAS TEARS	4.25	7.50	5.00
☐639		NEVER ON SUNDAY/CONNIE-O	4.25	7.50	5.00
☐664		SINCE I DON'T HAVE YOU/ TONITE, TONITE	5.00	9.00	6.00
☐713		LITTLE BOY (IN GROWN-UP CLOTHES)/SILVER WINGS	3.25	5.50	4.00
☐719		MY MOTHER'S EYES/STAY	3.25	5.50	4.00

FOUR SEASONS

They originally were a New York City quartet called the Four Lovers. Under that name they scored on the East Coast with a 1956 RCA single called "The Apple of My Eye". Nationally the song failed to do well, and the Four Lovers later slipped into a half-dozen years of obscurity.

By 1962 they had added one new member, Bob Gaudio, who had recently left the Royal Teens ("Short Shorts", "Believe Me"). They had also changed their name by 1962. While working as a bowling alley lounge act at a place called the Four Seasons, the group decided to adopt the name of their place of employment.

A Gone Records single went nowhere, but the Four Seasons' first Vee Jay 45 ("Sherry") was a million-selling monster. Thanks to Frankie Valli's wailing falsetto, the Four Seasons established a distinctive sound and name for themselves. After a successful career on Vee Jay, the Four Seasons went to the Phillips label, where their hit streak continued.

In 1978 Valli left the group to concentrate on solo efforts ("Grease," etc). Without the Valli trademark, the Four Seasons eventually fell apart.

			Current Price Range		P/Y AVG
☐ 40166	**PHILIPS**	DAWN/NO SURFIN' TODAY	3.00	5.00	3.65
☐ 40185		RONNIE/BORN TO WANDER	3.00	5.00	3.65
☐ 40211		RAG DOLL/SILENCE IS GOLDEN ..	3.00	5.00	3.65
☐ 40225		SAVE IT FOR ME/FUNNY FACE ..	3.00	5.00	3.65
☐ 40238		BIG MAN IN TOWN/LITTLE ANGEL	3.00	5.00	3.65
☐ 40260		BYE, BYE, BABY/ SEARCHING WIND	3.00	5.00	3.65
☐ 40278		TOY SOLDIER/BETRAYED	3.00	5.00	3.65
☐ 40305		GIRL COME RUNNING/ CRY MYSELF TO SLEEP	3.00	5.00	3.65
☐ 40317		LET'S HANG ON/ ON BROADWAY TONIGHT	3.00	5.00	3.65
☐ 40350		WORKING MY WAY BACK TO YOU/ TOO MANY MEMORIES	3.00	5.00	3.65
☐ 40370		OPUS 17/BEGGAR'S PARADISE ..	3.00	5.00	3.65
☐ 40393		I'VE GOT YOU UNDER MY SKIN/ HUGGIN' MY PILLOW	3.00	5.00	3.65
☐ 40412		TELL IT TO THE RAIN/SNOW GIRL	3.00	5.00	3.65
☐ 40433		BEGGIN'/DODY	3.00	5.00	3.65
☐ 40460		C'MON MARIANNE/ LET'S RIDE AGAIN	3.00	5.00	3.65
☐ 40490		WATCH THE FLOWERS GROW/ RAVEN	3.00	5.00	3.65
☐ 40523		WILL YOU LOVE ME TOMORROW/ AROUND AND AROUND	3.00	5.00	3.65
☐ 40542		SATURDAY'S FATHER/ GOODBYE GIRL	3.00	5.00	3.65
☐ 40577		ELECTRIC STORIES/PITY	3.00	5.00	3.65
☐ 40597		IDAHO/ SOMETHING'S ON HER MIND ..	3.00	5.00	3.65
☐ 40661		YOU'VE GOT YOUR TROUBLES/ A DREAM OF KINGS	3.00	5.00	3.65
☐ 40662		A PATCH OF BLUE/ SHE GIVES ME LIGHT	3.00	5.00	3.65
☐ 40688		HEARTACHES AND RAINDROPS/ LAY ME DOWN (Frankie Valli and the Four Seasons)	3.00	5.00	3.65
☐ 40694		WHERE ARE MY DREAMS/ ANY DAY NOW (HAPPY DAY) ...	3.00	5.00	3.65
☐ 5026	**MOWEST**	WALK ON, DON'T LOOK BACK/ SUN COUNTRY	3.00	5.00	3.65
☐ 1255	**MOTOWN**	LIFE AND BREATH/HOW COME ..	3.00	5.00	3.65
☐ 1288		HICKORY/CHARISMA	3.00	5.00	3.65
		SINGLES ON WARNER BROTHERS ARE WORTH UP TO $2.00 EACH			
		FOUR SEASONS—EPs			
☐ 1901	**VEE JAY**	THE FOUR SEASONS SING	6.00	12.00	10.00
☐ 1902		THE FOUR SEASONS SING	6.00	12.00	10.00
		FOUR SEASONS—ALBUMS			
☐ 1053 (M)	**VEE JAY**	SHERRY AND 11 OTHERS	8.00	21.00	18.00
☐ 1053 (S)		SHERRY AND 11 OTHERS	12.00	29.00	25.00
☐ 1055 (M)		FOUR SEASONS' GREETINGS	9.00	25.00	22.50
☐ 1055 (S)		FOUR SEASONS' GREETINGS	14.00	34.00	30.00
☐ 1056 (M)		BIG GIRLS DON'T CRY	7.00	17.00	15.00
☐ 1056 (S)		BIG GIRLS DON'T CRY	8.00	25.00	22.50
☐ 1059 (M)		AIN'T THAT A SHAME	7.00	17.00	15.00
☐ 1059 (S)		AIN'T THAT A SHAME	9.00	25.00	22.50
☐ 1065 (M)		GOLDEN HITS OF THE FOUR SEASONS	7.00	17.00	15.00
☐ 1065 (S)		GOLDEN HITS OF THE FOUR SEASONS	9.00	25.00	22.50
☐ 1082 (M)		FOLK-NANNY.................	7.00	17.00	15.00
☐ 1082 (S)		FOLK-NANNY.................	9.00	25.00	22.50
☐ 1082 (M)		STAY (retitle of above)	6.00	15.00	13.50
☐ 1082 (S)		STAY (retitle of above)	8.00	21.00	18.00

			Current Price Range		P/Y AVG
☐ 1088 (M)		MORE GOLDEN HITS BY THE FOUR SEASONS	6.00	15.00	13.50
☐ 1088 (S)		MORE GOLDEN HITS BY THE FOUR SEASONS	8.00	21.00	18.00
☐ 1121 (M)		WE LOVE GIRLS	6.00	15.00	13.50
☐ 1121 (S)		WE LOVE GIRLS	8.00	21.00	18.00
☐ 1154 (M)		RECORDED LIVE ON STAGE	6.00	15.00	13.50
☐ 1154 (S)		RECORDED LIVE ON STAGE	8.00	21.00	18.00
☐ 200124 (M)	**PHILIPS**	DAWN	5.50	14.00	12.00
☐ 600124 (S)		DAWN	7.00	17.00	15.00
☐ 200129 (M)		BORN TO WANDER...........	6.00	15.00	13.50
☐ 600129 (S)		BORN TO WANDER...........	8.00	21.00	18.00
☐ 200146 (M)		RAG DOLL	5.50	14.00	12.00
☐ 200146 (S)		RAG DOLL	7.00	17.00	15.00
☐ 200150 (M)		ALL THE SONG HITS OF THE FOUR SEASONS	5.50	14.00	12.00
☐ 600150 (S)		ALL THE SONG HITS OF THE FOUR SEASONS	7.00	17.00	15.00
☐ 200164 (M)		THE FOUR SEASONS ENTERTAIN YOU	5.50	14.00	12.00
☐ 600164 (S)		THE FOUR SEASONS ENTERTAIN YOU	7.00	17.00	15.00
☐ 200193 (M)		BIG HITS BY BACHARACH-DAVID AND BOB DYLAN	5.50	14.00	12.00
☐ 600193 (S)		BIG HITS BY BACHARACH-DAVID AND BOB DYLAN	7.00	17.00	15.00
☐ 200196 (M)		GOLD VAULT OF HITS	5.50	14.00	12.00
☐ 600196 (S)		GOLD VAULT OF HITS	7.00	17.00	15.00
☐ 200201 (M)		WORKING MY WAY BACK TO YOU	5.50	14.00	12.00
☐ 600201 (S)		WORKING MY WAY BACK TO YOU	7.00	17.00	15.00
☐ 200221 (M)		2ND GOLD VAULT OF HITS	5.50	14.00	12.00
☐ 600221 (S)		2ND GOLD VAULT OF HITS	7.00	17.00	15.00
☐ 200222 (M)		LOOKIN` BACK...............	5.50	14.00	12.00
☐ 600222 (S)		LOOKIN` BACK...............	7.00	17.00	15.00
☐ 200223 (M)		CHRISTMAS ALBUM	5.50	15.00	12.00
☐ 600223 (S)		CHRISTMAS ALBUM ....·	7.00	17.00	15.00
☐ 200243 (M)		NEW GOLD HITS	5.50	14.00	12.00
☐ 600243 (S)		NEW GOLD HITS	7.00	17.00	15.00
☐ 600290 (S)		GENUINE IMITATION LIFE GAZETTE	6.50	15.00	13.50
☐ 600341 (S)		HALF AND HALF	6.50	15.00	13.50
☐ 6501 (S)		EDIZONE D`ORO.............	6.50	15.00	13.50
☐ 1081 (S)	**MOWEST**	CHAMELEON	5.50	14.00	12.00

FOUR SEVILLES

☐ SR-45-3	**STARLIGHT**	IF I/WHAT`S YOUR NAME	21.00	42.00	30.00
☐ SR-45-5		MELBA/IF YOU DIDN`T MEAN IT .	20.00	40.00	28.00
☐ SR-45-6		HEARTBEAT/YOU`RE MINE	20.00	40.00	28.00
☐ SR-45-8		HEART BREAKER/I`M NOT A KNOW IT ALL	20.00	40.00	28.00
☐ SR-45-10		OH BABY DON`T/LITTLE MAIDEN	19.00	38.00	26.00
☐ SR-45-12		IN BETWEEN TEARS/DARLING ...	19.00	38.00	26.00

THE FOUR SHADES

☐ 1000	**RACE**	YES SIR! THAT`S MY BABY/ STORMY WEATHER	32.00	65.00	41.00

FOUR SPEEDS
FEATURED: DENNIS WILSON, GARY USHER

☐ 9187	**CHALLENGE**	R.P.M./MY STING RAY..........	6.50	11.00	9.00
☐ 9202		FOUR ON THE FLOOR/ CHEATER SLICKS	8.50	14.00	12.00

FOUR TEENS

☐ 59021	**CHALLENGE**	SPARK PLUG/GO LITTLE GO CAT	24.00	50.00	45.00

			Current Price Range		P/Y AVG

FOUR TOPS

			Current Price Range		P/Y AVG
☐ 1623	**CHESS**	COULD IT BE YOU?/ KISS ME BABY	28.00	46.00	42.00
☐ 4534	**RIVERSIDE**	PENNIES FROM HEAVEN/ WHERE ARE YOU?	14.00	24.00	20.00
☐ 41755	**COLUMBIA**	AIN'T THAT LOVE/ LONELY SUMMER	8.00	14.00	12.00
☐ 43356		AIN'T THAT LOVE/ LONELY SUMMER	4.50	7.50	6.00
☐ 1062	**MOTOWN**	BABY, I NEED YOUR LOVING/ CALL ON ME	2.75	5.00	3.75
☐ 1069		WITHOUT THE ONE YOU LOVE/ LOVE HAS GONE	2.75	5.00	3.75
☐ 1073		ASK THE LONELY/ WHERE DID YOU GO?	2.75	5.00	3.75
☐ 1076		I CAN'T HELP MYSELF/ SAD SOUVENIRS	2.75	3.00	3.75
☐ 1081		IT'S THE SAME OLD SONG/ YOUR LOVE IS AMAZING	2.75	5.00	3.75
☐ 1084		SOMETHING ABOUT YOU/ DARLING, I HUM OUR SONG	2.75	5.00	3.75
☐ 1090		SHAKE ME, WAKE ME/JUST AS LONG AS YOU NEED ME	2.75	5.00	3.75
☐ 1096		LOVING YOU IS SWEETER THAN EVER/I LIKE EVERYTHING ABOUT YOU	2.75	5.00	3.75
☐ 1098		REACH OUT, I'LL BE THERE/ UNTIL YOU LOVE SOMEONE	2.75	5.00	3.75
☐ 1102		STANDING IN THE SHADOWS OF LOVE/SINCE YOU'VE BEEN GONE	2.75	5.00	3.75
☐ 1104		BERNADETTE/I GOT A FEELING	2.75	5.00	3.75
☐ 1110		7 ROOMS OF GLOOM/ I'LL TURN TO STONE	2.75	5.00	3.75
☐ 1113		YOU KEEP RUNNING AWAY/ IF YOU DON'T WANT MY LOVE	2.75	5.00	3.75
☐ 1119		WALK AWAY RENEE/ OUR LOVE IS WONDERFUL	2.75	5.00	3.75
☐ 1124		IF I WERE A CARPENTER/ WONDERFUL BABY	2.75	5.00	3.75
☐ 1127		YESTERDAY'S DREAMS/ FOR ONCE IN MY LIFE	2.75	5.00	3.75
☐ 1132		I'M IN A DIFFERENT WORLD/ REMEMBER WHEN	2.75	5.00	3.75
☐ 1147		WHAT IS A MAN/DON'T BRING BACK MEMORIES	2.75	5.00	3.75
☐ 1159		DON'T LET HIM TAKE YOUR LOVE FROM ME/THE KEY	2.75	5.00	3.75
☐ 1164		IT'S ALL IN THE GAME/ LOVE (IS THE ANSWER)	2.75	5.00	3.75
☐ 1170		STILL WATER (LOVE)/ STILL WATER (PEACE)	2.75	5.00	3.75
☐ 1175		JUST SEVEN NUMBERS/ I WISH I WERE YOUR MIRROR	2.75	5.00	3.75
☐ 1185		IN THESE CHANGING TIMES/ RIGHT BEFORE MY EYES	2.75	5.00	3.75
☐ 1189		MacARTHUR PARK/(PT. 2)	2.75	5.00	3.75
☐ 1196		A SIMPLE GAME/ L. A. (MY TOWN)	2.75	5.00	3.75
☐ 1198		I CAN'T QUIT YOUR LOVE/ HAPPY (IS A BUMPY ROAD)	2.75	5.00	3.75
☐ 1210		(IT'S THE WAY) NATURE PLANNED IT/I'LL NEVER CHANGE	2.75	5.00	3.75

SINGLES ON DUNHILL ARE WORTH UP TO $2.00 MINT

			Current Price Range		P/Y AVG
FOUR TOPS—ALBUMS					
☐ 622 (M)	*MOTOWN*	THE FOUR TOPS.............	12.00	29.00	25.00
☐ 634 (M)		FOUR TOPS, NO. 2..........	8.00	21.00	18.00
☐ 634 (S)		FOUR TOPS, NO. 2...........	12.00	29.00	25.00
☐ 647 (M)		ON TOP	8.00	21.00	18.00
☐ 647 (S)		ON TOP	12.00	29.00	25.00
☐ 654 (M)		LIVE.....................	7.00	17.00	15.00
☐ 654 (S)		LIVE.....................	8.00	21.00	18.00
☐ 669 (S)		YESTERDAY'S DREAMS	6.00	15.00	13.50
☐ 675 (S)		NOW	6.00	15.00	13.50
☐ 695 (S)		SOUL SPIN................	6.00	15.00	13.50
☐ 704 (S)		STILL WATERS RUN DEEP	6.00	15.00	13.50
☐ 740 (S)		GREATEST HITS.............	5.50	14.00	12.00
☐ 748 (S)		NATURE PLANNED IT.........	5.50	14.00	12.00
☐ 764 (S)		BEST OF THE FOUR TOPS	5.50	14.00	12.00
FOUR WINDS (TOKENS)					
☐ 102	*CRYSTAL BALL*	COME SOFTLY TO ME/DEAR JUDY.	5.50	11.00	9.00
☐ 100	*SWING*	REMEMBER LAST SUMMER/ STRANGE FEELINGS	5.00	9.00	7.00
☐ 555	*B. T. PUPPY*	LET IT RIDE/ ONE FACE IN THE CROWD	4.50	7.50	6.00
KIM FOWLEY					
		SEE: KING LIZARD, RENEGADES			
☐ 216	*CORBY*	BIG SUR/THE TRIP	5.50	11.00	9.00
☐ 209	*MIRA*	AMERICAN DREAM/THE STATUE	4.50	8.00	6.00
☐ 721	*LIVING LEGEND*	MR. RESPONSIBILITY/ MY FOOLISH HEART	4.50	8.00	6.00
☐ 725		UNDERGROUND LADY/ POP ART '66	5.00	9.00	7.00
☐ 0569	*REPRISE*	DON'T BE CRUEL/ STRANGERS FROM THE SKY ..	4.50	8.00	6.00
☐ 342	*TOWER*	LOVE IS ALIVE AND WELL/ REINCARNATION	3.75	6.00	4.50
☐ 66326	*IMPERIAL*	BORN TO BE WILD/ SPACE ODYSSEY	4.50	7.50	6.00
KIM FOWLEY—ALBUMS					
☐ 5080 (M)	*TOWER*	LOVE IS ALIVE AND WELL	8.00	21.00	18.00
☐ 12413 (M)	*IMPERIAL*	BORN TO BE WILD	7.00	17.00	15.00
☐ 12423 (M)		OUTRAGEOUS	7.00	17.00	15.00
☐ 12443 (M)		GOOD CLEAN FUN	7.00	17.00	15.00
NORMAN FOX AND THE ROB-ROYS					
☐ 501	*BACK BEAT*	TELL ME WHY/AUDREY	4.50	8.50	6.00
☐ 508		MY DEAREST ONE/ DANCE, GIRL, DANCE	5.00	9.00	7.00
☐ 4128	*CAPITOL*	DREAM GIRL/PIZZA PIE	21.00	34.00	30.00
PETER FRAMPTON					
		SEE: HERD			
☐ 1379	*A & M*	JUMPING JACK FLASH/ OH, FOR ANOTHER DAY	3.00	5.00	3.50
☐ 1506		I WANNA GO TO THE SUN/ SOMETHING'S HAPPENING ...	3.00	5.00	3.50
☐ 1693		SHOW ME THE WAY/ CRYING CLOWN	3.25	6.00	4.00
☐ 1738		BABY, I LOVE YOUR WAY/MONEY	3.25	6.00	4.00
CONNIE FRANCIS					
☐ 12015	*MGM*	FREDDY/ DIDN'T I LOVE YOU ENOUGH? .	5.00	9.00	6.00
☐ 12056		MAKE HIM JEALOUS/ GOODY GOODBYE	5.00	9.00	6.00

		Current Price Range		P/Y AVG
☐ 12122	ARE YOU SATISFIED?/			
	MY TREASURE	5.00	9.00	6.00
☐ 12191	MY FIRST REAL LOVE/			
	BELIEVE IN ME	5.00	9.00	6.00
☐ 12251	SEND FOR MY BABY/FORGETTING.	5.00	9.00	6.00
☐ 12335	MY SAILOR BOY/			
	EVERYONE NEEDS SOMEONE ..	4.00	7.00	4.85
☐ 12375	I NEVER HAD A SWEETHEART/			
	LITTLE BLUE WREN	4.00	7.00	4.85
☐ 12440	NO OTHER ONE/			
	I LEANED ON A MAN	4.00	7.00	4.85
☐ 12490	EIGHTEEN/FADED ORCHID	4.00	7.00	4.85
☐ 12555	YOU, MY DARLIN', YOU/			
	THE MAJESTY OF LOVE	4.00	7.00	4.85
☐ 12588	WHO'S SORRY NOW/			
	YOU WERE ONLY FOOLING	3.50	5.75	4.35
☐ 12647	I'M SORRY I MADE YOU CRY/			
	LOCK UP YOUR HEART	3.50	5.75	4.35
☐ 12683	STUPID CUPID/CAROLINA MOON	3.50	5.75	4.35
☐ 12713	FALLIN'/HAPPY DAYS AND			
	LONELY NIGHTS	3.50	5.75	4.35
☐ 12738	MY HAPPINESS/NEVER BEFORE .	3.50	5.75	4.35
☐ 12769	IF I DIDN'T CARE/TOWARD THE			
	END OF THE DAY	3.50	5.75	4.35
☐ 12793	LIPSTICK ON YOUR COLLAR/			
	FRANKIE	3.50	5.75	4.35
☐ 12824	YOU'RE GONNA MISS ME/			
	PLENTY GOOD LOVIN'	3.25	5.50	4.00
☐ 12841	AMONG MY SOUVENIRS/			
	GOD BLESS AMERICA	3.25	5.50	4.00
☐ 12878	MAMA/TEDDY................	3.25	5.50	4.00
☐ 12899	EVERYBODY'S SOMEBODY'S			
	FOOL/JEALOUS OF YOU	3.25	5.50	4.00
☐ 12923	MY HEART HAS A MIND OF IT			
	OWN/MALAGUENA	3.00	5.00	3.50
☐ 12964	MANY TEARS AGO/SENZA MAMA	3.00	5.00	3.50
☐ 12971	WHERE THE BOYS ARE/NO ONE .	3.00	5.00	3.50
☐ 12995	BREAKIN' IN A BRAND NEW			
	BROKEN HEART/			
	SOMEONE ELSE'S BOY	2.75	4.50	3.00
☐ 13005	SWANEE/ATASHI NO	2.75	4.50	3.00
☐ 13019	TOGETHER/TOO MANY RULES ...	2.50	4.50	2.50
☐ 13039	(HE'S MY) DREAMBOAT/			
	HOLLYWOOD	2.50	4.25	3.10
☐ 13051	WHEN THE BOY IN YOUR ARMS/			
	BABY'S FIRST CHRISTMAS ...	2.50	4.25	3.10
☐ 13059	DON'T BREAK THE HEART THAT			
	LOVES YOU/DROP IT, JOE	2.50	4.25	3.10
☐ 13074	SECOND HAND LOVE/			
	GONNA GIT THAT MAN	2.50	4.25	3.10
☐ 13087	VACATION/			
	THE BIGGEST SIN OF ALL	2.50	4.25	3.10
☐ 13096	I WAS SUCH A FOOL/			
	HE THINKS I STILL CARE	2.50	4.25	3.10
☐ 13116	I'M GONNA BE WARM THIS			
	WINTER/AL DI LA	2.50	4.25	3.10
☐ 13127	FOLLOW THE BOYS/			
	WAITING FOR BILLY	2.50	4.25	3.10
☐ 13143	IF MY PILLOW COULD TALK/			
	YOU'RE THE ONLY ONE CAN			
	HURT ME	2.50	4.25	3.10
☐ 13160	DROWNIN' MY SORROWS/			
	MALA FEMMENA	2.50	4.25	3.10

CONNIE FRANCIS

Constance Franconero first saw the light of day on December 12, 1938. Belleville, New Jersey, was her birthplace. Young Connie took up the accordian when she was four. Becoming highly adept at the instrument, she made her first professional appearance at the age of eleven. She also sang at that appearance. After a fine reaction to her singing, Connie then knew that she was destined to become a singer rather than an accordian player.

A year later — before she entered her teens — she began singing on NBC radio. Connie auditioned for "Arthur Godfrey's Talent Scouts" and earned a chance to sing on the show. It was Godfrey who suggested Connie change her name to something simpler and easier to remember.

In 1955 Connie Francis signed on with MGM Records as a sixteen-year-old vocalist. Single after single went nowhere. Connie finally hit pay dirt with her eleventh release, "Who's Sorry Now', in 1958. And that million-seller was just the beginning. During her recording career Ms. Francis scored nineteen Top 20 singles, including three that reached the No. 1 spot.

			Current Price Range		P/Y AVG
☐ 13176		YOUR OTHER LOVE/WHATEVER HAPPENED TO ROSEMARIE? . . .	2.50	4.25	3.10
☐ 13203		IN THE SUMMER OF HIS YEARS/ MY BUDDY (JFK tribute)	3.00	6.00	3.85
☐ 13214		BLUE WINTER/YOU KNOW YOU DON'T WANT ME	2.50	4.25	3.10
☐ 13237		BE ANYTHING (BUT BE MINE)/ TOMMY	2.50	4.25	3.10
☐ 13256		LOOKING FOR LOVE/THIS IS MY HAPPIEST MOMENT	2.50	4.25	3.10
☐ 13287		DON'T EVER LEAVE ME/ WE HAVE SOMETHING MORE . .	2.50	4.25	3.10
☐ 13303		WHOSE HEART ARE YOU BREAKING TONIGHT?/ C'MON JERRY	2.50	4.25	3.10
☐ 13325		FOR MAMA/SHE'LL BE COMING AROUND THE MOUNTAIN	2.50	4.25	3.10
☐ 13331		WISHING IT WAS YOU/ YOU'RE MINE	2.50	4.25	3.10
☐ 13363		FORGET DOMANI/ NO ONE SENDS ME ROSES	2.50	4.25	3.10
☐ 13389		ROUNDABOUT/ BOSSA NOVA HAND DANCE . . .	2.50	4.25	3.10
☐ 13420		JEALOUS HEART/ CAN I RELY ON YOU?	2.50	4.25	3.10
☐ 13470		LOVE IS ME. LOVE IS YOU/ I'D LET YOU BREAK MY HEART ALL OVER AGAIN	2.50	4.25	3.10
☐ 13505		IT'S A DIFFERENT WORLD/ EMPTY CHAPEL	2.50	4.25	3.10
☐ 13545		A LETTER FROM A SOLDIER/ SOMEWHERE. MY LOVE	2.50	4.25	3.10
☐ 13578		ALL THE LOVE IN THE WORLD/ SO NICE	2.50	4.25	3.10
☐ 13610		SPANISH NIGHTS AND YOU/ GAMES THAT LOVERS PLAY . . .	2.50	4.25	3.10
☐ 13665		ANOTHER PAGE/ SOUVENIR D'ITALIE	2.50	4.25	3.10
☐ 13718		TIME ALONE WILL TELL/ BORN FREE	2.50	4.25	3.10
☐ 13773		MY HEART CRIES OUT FOR YOU/ SOMEONE TOOK THE SWEETNESS OUT OF SWEETHEART	2.50	4.25	3.10
☐ 13814		LONELY AGAIN/WHEN YOU CARE A LOT FOR SOMEONE	2.50	4.25	3.10
☐ 13876		MY WORLD IS SLIPPING AWAY/ TILL WE'RE TOGETHER	2.50	4.25	3.10
☐ 13923		WHY SAY GOODBYE?/ ADIOS MI AMORE	2.50	4.25	3.10
☐ 13948		SOMEBODY ELSE IS TAKING MY PLACE/BROTHER. CAN YOU SPARE A DIME?	2.50	4.25	3.10
☐ 14004		I DON'T WANNA PLAY HOUSE/ THE WELFARE CHECK	2.50	4.25	3.10
☐ 14034		THE WEDDING CAKE/ OVER HILL. UNDER GROUND . .	2.50	4.25	3.10
☐ 14058		GONE LIKE THE WIND/AM I BLUE?	2.50	4.25	3.10
☐ 14089		INVIERNO TRISTE/ NOCHES ESPANOLAS Y TU	2.50	4.25	3.10
☐ 14091		MR. LOVE/ZINGARA	2.50	4.25	3.10

LATER MGM SINGLES ARE WORTH UP TO $2.50 MINT

CONNIE FRANCIS—EPs

☐ 1599	**MGM**	CONNIE FRANCIS	7.00	12.00	10.00

			Current Price Range		P/Y AVG
☐ 1603		WHO'S SORRY NOW	5.50	11.00	9.00
☐ 1604		WHO'S SORRY NOW	5.50	11.00	9.00
☐ 1605		WHO'S SORRY NOW	5.50	11.00	9.00
☐ 1655		MY HAPPINESS	5.50	9.50	8.00
☐ 1662		IF I DIDN'T CARE	5.50	9.50	8.00
☐ 1663		EXCITING CONNIE FRANCIS	5.00	9.00	7.00
☐ 1664		EXCITING CONNIE FRANCIS	5.00	9.00	7.00
☐ 1665		EXCITING CONNIE FRANCIS	5.00	9.00	7.00
☐ 1687		CONNIE FRANCIS	4.50	7.50	6.00
☐ 1688		CONNIE'S GREATEST HITS	4.00	6.50	4.85
☐ 1689		CONNIE'S GREATEST HITS	4.00	6.50	4.85
☐ 1690		CONNIE'S GREATEST HITS	4.00	6.50	4.85
☐ 1691		ROCK 'N ROLL MILLION SELLERS	4.00	6.50	4.85
☐ 1692		ROCK 'N ROLL MILLION SELLERS	4.00	6.50	4.85
☐ 1693		ROCK 'N ROLL MILLION SELLERS	4.00	6.50	4.85
☐ 1694		COUNTRY AND WESTERN GOLDEN HITS	4.00	6.50	4.85
☐ 1695		COUNTRY AND WESTERN GOLDEN HITS	4.00	6.50	4.85
☐ 1696		COUNTRY AND WESTERN GOLDEN HITS	4.00	6.50	4.85
☐ 1703		CONNIE FRANCIS	4.00	6.50	4.85
		CONNIE FRANCIS—ALBUMS			
☐ 3686 (M)	**MGM**	WHO'S SORRY NOW	14.00	34.00	30.00
☐ 3761 (M)		EXCITING CONNIE FRANCIS	12.00	29.00	25.00
☐ 3761 (S)		EXCITING CONNIE FRANCIS	14.00	34.00	30.00
☐ 3776 (M)		MY THANKS TO YOU	12.00	29.00	25.00
☐ 3776 (S)		MY THANKS TO YOU	14.00	34.00	30.00
☐ 3791 (M)		ITALIAN FAVORITES	8.00	21.00	18.00
☐ 3791 (S)		ITALIAN FAVORITES	12.00	29.00	25.00
☐ 3792 (M)		CHRISTMAS IN MY HEART	8.00	21.00	18.00
☐ 3792 (S)		CHRISTMAS IN MY HEART	12.00	21.00	18.00
☐ 3793 (M)		CONNIE'S GREATEST HITS	8.00	21.00	18.00
☐ 3793 (S)		CONNIE'S GREATEST HITS	12.00	21.00	18.00
☐ 3794 (M)		ROCK 'N ROLL MILLION SELLERS	7.00	17.00	15.00
☐ 3794 (S)		ROCK 'N ROLL MILLION SELLERS	10.00	25.00	22.50
☐ 3795 (M)		COUNTRY AND WESTERN GOLDEN HITS	7.00	17.00	15.00
☐ 3795 (S)		COUNTRY AND WESTERN GOLDEN HITS	10.00	25.00	22.50
☐ 3853 (M)		SPANISH AND LATIN AMERICAN FAVORITES	7.00	17.00	15.00
☐ 3853 (S)		SPANISH AND LATIN AMERICAN FAVORITES	10.00	25.00	22.50
☐ 3869 (M)		JEWISH FAVORITES	7.00	17.00	15.00
☐ 3869 (S)		JEWISH FAVORITES	10.00	25.00	22.50
☐ 3871 (M)		MORE ITALIAN FAVORITES	7.00	17.00	15.00
☐ 3871 (S)		MORE ITALIAN FAVORITES	10.00	25.00	22.50
☐ 3893 (M)		SONGS TO A SWINGIN' BAND	7.00	17.00	15.00
☐ 3893 (S)		SONGS TO A SWINGIN' BAND	10.00	25.00	22.50
☐ 3913 (M)		AT THE COPA	7.00	17.00	15.00
☐ 3913 (S)		AT THE COPA	10.00	25.00	22.50
☐ 3942 (M)		MORE GREATEST HITS	7.00	17.00	13.50
☐ 3942 (S)		MORE GREATEST HITS	8.00	21.00	18.00
☐ 3965 (M)		CONNIE FRANCIS SINGS "NEVER ON SUNDAY"	7.00	17.00	13.50
☐ 3965 (S)		CONNIE FRANCIS SINGS "NEVER ON SUNDAY"	8.00	21.00	18.00
☐ 3969 (M)		FOLK SONG FAVORITES	7.00	17.00	13.50
☐ 3969 (S)		FOLK SONG FAVORITES	8.00	21.00	18.00
☐ 4022 (M)		DO THE TWIST WITH CONNIE FRANCIS	7.00	17.00	13.50
☐ 4022 (S)		DO THE TWIST WITH CONNIE FRANCIS	8.00	21.00	18.00

			Current Price Range		P/Y AVG
☐ 4048 (M)		AWARD WINNING MOTION PICTURE HITS	7.00	17.00	13.50
☐ 4048 (S)		AWARD WINNING MOTION PICTURE HITS	8.00	21.00	18.00
☐ 4049 (M)		CONNIE FRANCIS SINGS	5.50	14.00	12.00
☐ 4049 (S)		CONNIE FRANCIS SINGS	7.00	17.00	15.00
☐ 4079 (M)		COUNTRY MUSIC CONNIE STYLE	5.50	14.00	12.00
☐ 4079 (S)		COUNTRY MUSIC CONNIE STYLE	7.00	17.00	15.00
☐ 4102 (M)		MODERN ITALIAN HITS	5.50	14.00	12.00
☐ 4102 (S)		MODERN ITALIAN HITS	7.00	17.00	15.00
☐ 4123 (M)		FOLLOW THE BOYS	5.50	14.00	12.00
☐ 4123 (S)		FOLLOW THE BOYS	7.00	17.00	15.00

LATER MGM ALBUMS ARE WORTH UP TO $12.00 MINT

FREDDIE AND THE DREAMERS

☐ 5053	CAPITOL	I'M TELLIN' YOU NOW/ WHAT HAVE I DONE TO YOU?	5.00	8.50	7.00
☐ 5137		YOU WERE MADE FOR ME/ SEND A LETTER TO ME	4.50	7.50	6.00
☐ 125	TOWER	I'M TELLING YOU NOW/ WHAT HAVE I DONE TO YOU?	2.50	5.00	3.00
☐ 127		YOU WERE MADE FOR ME/ SO FINE	2.50	5.00	3.00
☐ 72327	MERCURY	DON'T DO THAT TO ME/ JUST FOR YOU	3.00	5.00	3.50
☐ 72377		I UNDERSTAND/I WILL	2.50	5.00	3.00
☐ 72428		DO THE FREDDIE/TELL ME WHEN	2.50	5.00	3.00
☐ 72462		A LITTLE YOU/ THINGS I'D LIKE TO SAY	2.50	5.00	3.00
☐ 72487		I DON'T KNOW/WINDMILL IN OLD AMSTERDAM	2.50	5.00	3.00

FREDDIE AND THE DREAMERS—ALBUMS

☐ 5003 (M)	TOWER	I'M TELLING YOU NOW	9.00	25.00	22.50
☐ 21017 (M)	MERCURY	FREDDIE AND THE DREAMERS	7.00	17.00	15.00
☐ 61017 (S)		FREDDIE AND THE DREAMERS	8.00	21.00	18.00
☐ 21026 (M)		DO THE FREDDIE	7.00	17.00	15.00
☐ 61026 (S)		DO THE FREDDIE	8.00	21.00	18.00
☐ 21031 (M)		SEASIDE SWINGERS	7.00	17.00	15.00
☐ 61031 (S)		SEASIDE SWINGERS	8.00	21.00	18.00
☐ 21053 (M)		FRANTIC FREDDIE	7.00	17.00	15.00
☐ 61053 (S)		FRANTIC FREDDIE	8.00	21.00	18.00
☐ 21061 (M)		FUN LOVIN' FREDDIE	7.00	17.00	15.00
☐ 61061 (S)		FUN LOVIN' FREDDIE	8.00	21.00	18.00
☐ 11895 (S)	CAPITOL	THE BEST OF FREDDIE AND THE DREAMERS	5.00	12.00	10.00

FREDDY & THE FAT BOYS

☐ 101	FAT MAN	WHY DO FOOLS FALL IN LOVE/ BALLAD OF FREDDIE & RICH	9.50	24.00	20.00

BOBBY FREEMAN

☐ 835	JOSIE	DO YOU WANT TO DANCE?/ BIG FAT WOMAN	4.00	7.00	4.65
☐ 841		BETTY LOU GOT A NEW PAIR OF SHOES/STARLIGHT	3.50	6.00	4.00
☐ 844		NEED YOUR LOVE/SHAME ON YOU, MISS JOHNSON	3.25	5.50	4.00
☐ 855		WHEN YOU'RE SMILING/ A LOVE TO LAST A LIFETIME	3.25	5.50	4.00
☐ 863		MARY ANN THOMAS/LOVE ME	3.25	5.50	4.00
☐ 867		MY GUARDIAN ANGEL/ WHERE DID MY BABY GO?	3.25	5.50	4.00
☐ 872		EBB TIDE/SINBAD	3.25	5.50	4.00
☐ 879		I NEED SOMEONE/ THE FIRST DAY OF SPRING	3.00	5.25	3.85

			Current Price Range		P/Y AVG
☐886			BABY, WHAT WOULD YOU DO?/		
			I MISS YOU SO	3.00	5.25	3.85
☐887			MESS AROUND/SO MUCH TO DO .	3.00	5.25	3.85
☐889			SHE SAID SHE WANTS TO DANCE/		
			PUT YOU DOWN	3.00	5.25	3.85
☐896			LITTLE GIRL DON'T UNDERSTAND/		
			LOVE ME	3.00	5.25	3.85
☐4678	KING		BE MY LITTLE CHICK-A-		
			DEE/SOMEBODY, SOMEWHERE	3.25	5.50	4.00
☐5373	KING		(I DO THE) SHIMMY SHIMMY/		
			YOU DON'T UNDERSTAND ME .	3.25	5.50	4.00
☐1	AUTUMN		LET'S SURF AGAIN/COME TO ME	3.25	5.50	4.00
☐2			C'MON AND SWIM (PT. 1)/(PT. 2)	2.75	5.50	3.75
☐5			S-W-I-M/THAT LITTLE		
			OLD HEARTBREAKER ME	2.75	5.00	3.50
☐9			I'LL NEVER FALL IN LOVE AGAIN/		
			FRIENDS	2.75	5.00	3.50
☐25			CROSS MY HEART/THE DUCK ...	2.75	5.00	3.50
☐928	JOSIE		THE MESSAROUND/LITTLE GIRL		
			DON'T YOU UNDERSTAND	2.75	5.00	3.50

BOBBY FREEMAN—ALBUMS

☐5010 (M)	JUBILEE	TWIST WITH BOBBY FREEMAN	14.00	34.00	30.00
☐1086 (M)		DO YOU WANNA DANCE?	12.00	29.00	25.00
☐1086 (S)		DO YOU WANNA DANCE?	17.00	38.00	35.00
☐930	KING	THE LOVEABLE SIDE OF		
		BOBBY FREEMAN	10.00	25.00	22.50
☐4007 (M)	JOSIE	GET IN THE SWIM WITH		
		BOBBY FREEMAN	8.00	21.00	18.00
☐4007 (S)		GET IN THE SWIM WITH		
		BOBBY FREEMAN	9.00	25.00	22.50
☐102 (M)	AUTUMN	C'MON AND SWIM	5.00	14.00	12.00

DON FRENCH

☐104	LANCER	LONELY SATURDAY NIGHT/		
		GOLDILOCKS	4.50	7.50	6.00

FROGMEN

☐101	SCOTT	SEAHORSE FLATS/TIOGA	4.50	7.50	6.00
☐102		BEWARE BELOW/TIOGA	4.50	7.50	6.00
☐314	CANDIX	UNDERWATER/THE MAD RUSH ..	3.25	5.50	4.00
☐326		BEWARE BELOW/TIOGA	3.25	5.50	4.00
☐131	TEE JAY	SEA HUNT/DIAMOND BACK	3.25	5.50	4.00

BOBBY FULLER FOUR

☐1090	TODD	STINGER/SATURDAY NIGHT	8.00	15.00	10.00
☐345	EASTWOOD	NOT FADE AWAY/		
		NERVOUS BREAKDOWN	8.00	15.00	10.00
☐141	YUCCA	YOU'RE IN LOVE/		
		GUESS WE'LL FALL IN LOVE ..	6.00	12.00	8.00
☐144		MY HEART JUMPED/		
		GENTLY, MY LOVE	6.00	10.00	8.00
☐1403	DONNA	THOSE MEMORIES OF YOU/		
		OUR FAVORITE MARTIAN	6.00	10.00	8.00
☐124		I FOUGHT THE LAW/LITTLE		
		ANNIE LOU	10.00	25.00	20.00
☐55812	LIBERTY	LET HER DANCE/ANOTHER		
		SAD NIGHT	5.50	11.00	9.00
☐122	EXETER	KING OF THE BEACH/		
		WINE, WINE, WINE	6.00	10.00	8.00
☐3003	MUSTANG	WOLFMAN/THUNDER REEF		
		(Shindigs)	5.00	9.00	6.25
☐3004		SHE'S MY GIRL/TAKE MY WORD .	5.00	9.00	6.25
☐3006		LET HER DANCE/ANOTHER		
		SAD AND LONELY NIGHT	4.00	7.00	4.85

			Current Price Range		P/Y AVG
3011		NEVER TO BE FORGOTTEN/ YOU KISS ME	4.00	7.00	4.85
3012		LET HER DANCE/ANOTHER SAD AND LONELY NIGHT	3.25	5.50	4.00
3014		I FOUGHT THE LAW/ LITTLE ANNIE LOU	3.00	5.00	3.50
3016		LOVE'S MADE A FOOL OF YOU/ DON'T EVER LEAVE ME	3.00	5.00	3.50
3018		THE MAGIC TOUCH/ MY TRUE LOVE	3.00	5.00	3.50
		BOBBY FULLER FOUR—ALBUMS			
900 (M)	**MUSTANG**	KRLA KING OF THE WHEELS	12.00	29.00	25.00
901 (M)		I FOUGHT THE LAW	8.00	21.00	18.00

G

GABRIEL & THE ANGELS

823	**AMY**	THE ROOSTER/ZING WENT THE STRINGS OF MY HEART	14.00	30.00	26.00
S-4118	**SWAN**	THAT'S LIFE/ DON'T WANNA TWIST	4.00	7.50	5.00

GALAXIES
GUITAR: EDDIE COCHRAN

216	**GUARANTEED**	MY TATTLE TALE/ LOVE HAS ITS WAY	5.50	11.00	9.00

GALES

916	**WINN**	SQUUZE ME/I LOVE YOU	8.25	18.00	16.00

GAMBLERS

815	**WORLD PACIFIC**	MOON DAWG/LSD-25	4.50	7.50	6.00

FRANK GARI

6903	**RIBBON**	YOUR ONLY LOVE/LIL' GIRL	4.50	7.50	6.00
1020	**CRUSADE**	UTOPIA/I AIN'T GOT A GIRL	3.00	5.00	3.50
1021		LULLABY OF LOVE/ TONIGHT IS OUR LAST NIGHT ..	3.00	5.00	3.50
1022		PRINCESS/THE LAST BUS LEFT AT MIDNIGHT	3.00	5.00	3.50
1024		YOU BETTER KEEP RUNNIN'/ THERE'S LOTS MORE WHERE THIS CAME FROM	3.00	5.00	3.50

JOHNNY GARNER

5548	**IMPERIAL**	FOOL/DIDI DIDI	21.00	44.00	40.00

ARTIE GARR (ART GARFUNKEL)
SEE: SIMON AND GARFUNKEL, TOM AND JERRY

515	**WARWICK**	DREAM ALONE/BEAT LOVE	9.50	17.00	15.00
8002	**OCTAVIA**	PRIVATE WORLD/FORGIVE ME ..	9.50	17.00	15.00

GARY AND CLYDE (SKIP AND FLIP)

3523	**REV**	WHY NOT CONFESS/ JOHNNY RISK	5.50	11.00	9.00

GARY AND THE NITE LITES (AMERICAN BREED)
SEEBURG

3016	**JUKE BOX**	SWEET LITTLE SIXTEEN/ TAKE ME BACK	5.00	9.00	7.00

			Current Price Range		P/Y AVG
☐ 3017		BONY MARONIE/ GLAD YOU'RE MINE	5.00	9.00	7.00
☐ 833	**U.S.A.**	I DON'T NEED YOUR HELP/ BIG BAD WOLF	4.50	7.50	6.00

DAVID GATES
SEE: DEL ASHLEY, MANCHESTERS, BREAD

☐ 1008	**ROBBINS**	LOVIN' AT NIGHT/JO BABY	9.50	17.00	15.00
☐ 123	**EAST WEST**	SWINGIN' BABY DOLL/ WALKIN' AND TALKIN'	7.00	12.00	10.00
☐ 413	**MALA**	YOU'LL BE MY BABY/ WHAT'S THIS I HEAR	5.50	11.00	9.00
☐ 418		THE HAPPIEST MAN ALIVE/ THE ROAD LEADS TO LOVE	5.50	11.00	9.00
☐ 427		TEARDROPS IN MY HEART/ JO BABY	5.00	9.00	7.00
☐ 4206	**DEL-FI**	NO ONE REALLY LOVES A CLOWN/YOU HAVE IT COMIN' TO YOU	5.00	9.00	7.00
☐ 108	**PLANETARY**	ONCE UPON A TIME/LET YOU GO .	5.00	9.00	7.00

MARVIN GAYE
SEE: MARY WELLS

☐ 54041	**TAMLA**	LET YOUR CONSCIENCE BE YOUR GUIDE/NEVER LET YOU GO	6.00	11.00	7.00
☐ 54055		I'M YOURS. YOU'RE MINE/ SANDMAN	5.00	9.00	6.00
☐ 54063		SOLDIER'S PLEA/ TAKING MY TIME	5.00	9.00	6.00
☐ 54068		STUBBORN KIND OF FELLOW/ IT HURTS ME TOO	4.00	7.00	4.00
☐ 54075		HITCH HIKE/HELLO THERE ANGEL.	4.00	6.50	3.75
☐ 54079		PRIDE AND JOY/ ONE OF THESE DAYS	3.00	5.00	3.50
☐ 54087		CAN I GET A WITNESS/ I'M CRAZY 'BOUT MY BABY ...	3.00	5.00	3.50
☐ 54093		YOU'RE A WONDERFUL ONE/ WHEN I'M ALONE I CRY	3.00	5.00	3.50
☐ 54095		TRY IT BABY/ IF MY HEART COULD SING	3.00	5.00	3.50
☐ 54101		BABY DON'T YOU DO IT/ WALK ON THE WILD SIDE	3.00	5.00	3.50
☐ 54104		WHAT GOOD AM I WITHOUT YOU?/ I WANT YOU (with Kim Weston) .	3.00	5.00	3.50
☐ 54107		HOW SWEET IT IS (TO BE LOVED BY YOU)/FOREVER	3.00	5.00	3.50
☐ 54112		I'LL BE DOGGONE/YOU'VE BEEN A LONG TIME COMING	3.00	5.00	3.50
☐ 54117		PRETTY LITTLE BABY/ NOW THAT YOU'VE WON ME ..	3.00	5.00	3.50
☐ 54122		AIN'T THAT PECULIAR/ SHE'S GOT TO BE REAL	3.00	5.00	3.50
☐ 54129		ONE MORE HEARTACHE/ WHEN I HAD YOUR LOVE	3.00	5.00	3.50
☐ 54132		TAKE THIS HEART OF MINE/ NEED YOUR LOVIN'	3.00	5.00	3.50
☐ 54138		LITTLE DARLING. I NEED YOU/ HEY DIDDLE DIDDLE	3.00	4.50	3.25
☐ 54141		IT TAKES TWO/IT'S GOT TO BE A MIRACLE (with Kim Weston) ...	3.00	4.50	3.25
☐ 54149		AIN'T NO MOUNTAIN HIGH ENOUGH/GIVE A LITTLE LOVE (with Tammi Terrell)	3.00	4.50	3.25

		Current Price Range		P/Y AVG
☐ 54153	YOUR UNCHANGING LOVE/ I'LL TAKE CARE OF YOU	3.00	4.50	3.25
☐ 54156	YOUR PRECIOUS LOVE/ HOLD ME, OH MY DARLING (with Tammi Terrell)	3.00	4.50	3.25
☐ 54160	YOU/CHANGE WHAT YOU CAN . .	3.00	4.50	3.25
☐ 54161	IF I COULD BUILD MY WHOLE WORLD AROUND YOU/ IF THIS WORLD WERE MINE (with Tammi Terrell)	2.50	4.75	3.35
☐ 54163	AIN'T NOTHING LIKE THE REAL THING/LITTLE OLE BOY, LITTLE OLE GIRL (with Tammi Terrell) . .	2.50	4.75	3.35
☐ 54169	YOU'RE ALL I NEED TO GET BY/ TWO CAN HAVE A PARTY (with Tammi Terrell)	2.50	4.75	3.35
☐ 54170	CHAINED/AT LAST	2.50	4.75	3.35
☐ 54173	KEEP ON LOVIN' ME, HONEY/YOU AIN'T LIVIN' TILL YOU'RE LOVIN' (with Tammi Terrell) . . .	2.50	4.75	3.35
☐ 54176	I HEARD IT THROUGH THE GRAPEVINE/YOU'RE WHAT'S HAPPENING	2.50	4.75	3.35
☐ 54179	GOOD LOVIN' AIN'T EASY TO COME BY/SATISFIED FEELING (with Tammi Terrell)	2.50	4.75	3.35
☐ 54181	TOO BUSY THINKING ABOUT MY BABY/WHEREVER I LAY MY HAT	2.50	4.75	3.35
☐ 54185	THAT'S THE WAY LOVE IS/ GONNA KEEP ON	2.50	4.75	3.35
☐ 54187	WHAT YOU GAVE ME/ HOW YOU GONNA KEEP IT? (with Tammi Terrell)	2.50	4.75	3.35
☐ 54190	HOW CAN I FORGET?/GONNA GIVE HER ALL THE LOVE I GOT	2.50	4.75	3.35
☐ 54192	CALIFORNIA SOUL/THE ONION SONG (with Tammi Terrell)	2.50	4.75	3.35
☐ 54195	THE END OF OUR ROAD/ ME AND MY LONELY ROOM . . .	2.50	4.75	3.35

LATER TAMLA SINGLES ARE WORTH UP TO $2.50 MINT

MARVIN GAYE—ALBUMS

☐ 221 (M)	**TAMLA** SOUFUL MOODS OF MARVIN GAYE	20.00	42.00	28.00
☐ 239 (M)	THAT STUBBORN KINDA FELLA . .	11.00	26.00	17.00
☐ 242 (M)	MARVIN GAYE ON STAGE	10.00	24.00	14.00
☐ 251 (M)	WHEN I'M ALONE I CRY	10.00	24.00	14.00
☐ 252 (M)	MARVIN GAYE'S GREATEST HITS	10.00	24.00	14.00
☐ 258 (M)	HOW SWEET IT IS TO BE LOVED BY YOU	8.00	19.00	12.00
☐ 258 (S)	HOW SWEET IT IS TO BE LOVED BY YOU	10.00	24.00	14.00
☐ 259 (M)	HELLO BROADWAY, THIS IS MARVIN	8.00	19.00	12.00
☐ 259 (S)	HELLO BROADWAY, THIS IS MARVIN	10.00	24.00	14.00
☐ 266 (M)	MOODS OF MARVIN GAYE	8.00	19.00	12.00
☐ 266 (S)	MOODS OF MARVIN GAYE	10.00	24.00	14.00
☐ 270 (M)	MARVIN GAYE AND KIM WESTON	8.00	19.00	12.00
☐ 270 (S)	MARVIN GAYE AND KIM WESTON	10.00	24.00	14.00
☐ 278 (M)	GREATEST HITS, VOL. II	8.00	19.00	12.00
☐ 278 (S)	GREATEST HITS, VOL. II	10.00	24.00	14.00
☐ 284 (S)	YOU'RE ALL I NEED (with Tammi Terrell)	8.00	19.00	12.00
☐ 285 (S)	IN THE GROOVE (first title)	7.00	16.00	10.50

			Current Price Range		P/Y AVG
□ 285 (S)		I HEARD IT THROUGH THE GRAPEVINE (second title)	7.00	16.00	10.50
□ 299 (S)		THAT'S THE WAY LOVE IS	7.00	16.00	10.50

LATER TAMLA ALBUMS ARE WORTH UP TO $7.50 MINT

GENE AND EUNICE

□ 64	COMBO	KO KO MO/YOU AND ME	6.00	12.00	10.00
□ 3276	ALADDIN	KO KO MO/YOU AND ME	5.50	9.00	6.75
□ 3282		THIS IS MY STORY/ MOVE IT OVER, BABY	5.50	9.00	6.75
□ 3292		FLIM FLAM/CAN WE FORGET IT?	5.50	9.00	6.75
□ 3305		I GOTTA GO HOME/HAVE YOU CHANGED YOUR MIND?	5.50	9.00	6.75
□ 3315		HOOTCHY KOOTCHY/ I'LL NEVER BELIEVE IN YOU	5.50	9.00	6.75
□ 3321		LET'S GET TOGETHER/ I'M SO IN LOVE WITH YOU	5.50	9.00	6.75
□ 3351		BOM BOM LULU/ HI DIDDLE DIDDLE	5.50	9.00	6.75
□ 3374		STRANGE WORLD/THE VOW	5.50	9.00	6.75
□ 3376		DOODLE DOODLE DOO/ DON'T TREAT ME THIS WAY	5.50	9.00	6.75
□ 3414		I MEAN LOVE/THE ANGELS GAVE YOU TO ME	5.50	9.00	6.75
□ 1001	CASE	POCO LOCO/GO ON KOKOMO	3.00	5.00	3.50
□ 1002		YOU THINK I'M NOT THINKING/ AH AH	3.00	5.00	3.50
□ 1007		SUGAR BABE/ LET'S PLAY THE GAME	3.00	5.00	3.50

GENE AND EUNICE—ALBUMS

□ 4018 (M)	SCORE	ROCK AND ROLL SOCK HOP	27.00	65.00	60.00

G-CLEFS

□ 715	PILGRIM	KA-DING DONG/ DARLA MY DARLIN'	4.50	7.50	6.00
□ 720		'CAUSE YOU'RE MINE/PLEASE WRITE WHILE I'M AWAY	4.50	7.50	6.00
□ 502	PARIS	SYMBOL OF LOVE/ LOVE HER IN THE MORNIN'	3.50	6.00	4.50
□ 506		IS THIS THE WAY/ZING ZANG ZOO	3.50	6.00	4.50
□ 7500	TERRACE	I UNDERSTAND (JUST HOW YOU FEEL)/LITTLE GIRL, I LOVE YOU	3.00	5.50	3.85
□ 7503		A GIRL HAS TO KNOW/LAD	3.00	5.50	3.85
□ 7507		MAKE UP YOUR MIND/ THEY'LL CALL ME AWAY	3.00	5.50	3.85
□ 7510		LOVER'S PRAYER/ SITTING IN THE MOONLIGHT	3.00	5.50	3.85
□ 7514		ALL MY TRIALS/THE BIG RAIN	3.00	5.50	3.85

GEE CEES

FEATURED: EDDIE COCHRAN (GUITAR), GLEN CAMPBELL (VOCALS)

□ 1088	CREST	ANNIE HAD A PARTY/BUZZSAW	9.50	17.00	15.00

GENTRYS

□ 600	YOUNGSTOWN	LITTLE DROPS OF WATER/ SOMETIMES	5.50	11.00	9.00
□ 601		KEEP ON DANCING/ MAKE UP YOUR MIND	9.50	17.00	15.00
□ 1120	SUN	GODDESS OF LOVE/FRIENDS	2.50	3.50	3.00
□ 13379	MGM	KEEP ON DANCING/ MAKE UP YOUR MIND	3.00	5.50	3.85
□ 13432		SPREAD IT ON THICK/ BROWN PAPER SACK	3.00	5.50	3.85

			Current Price Range		P/Y AVG
☐ 13495		EVERY DAY I HAVE TO CRY/ DON'T LET IT BE	3.00	5.50	3.85
☐ 13561		WOMAN OF THE WORLD/THERE ARE TWO SIDES TO EVERY STORY	3.00	5.50	3.85

GENTRYS—ALBUM

☐ 4336 (M)	MGM	KEEP ON DANCING	7.00	17.00	15.00
☐ 4336 (S)		KEEP ON DANCING	9.00	25.00	22.50
☐ 4346 (M)		TIME	6.00	15.00	13.50
☐ 4346 (S)		TIME	8.00	21.00	18.00

GERMZ
FEATURED: CAROLE KING

☐ 8001	VERTIGO	BOY-GIRL LOVE/ NO EASY WAY DOWN	5.50	11.00	9.00

GERRY AND THE PACEMAKERS

☐ 3162	LAURIE	HOW DO YOU DO IT/ AWAY FROM YOU	3.50	7.00	4.65
☐ 3196		I LIKE IT/IT HAPPENED TO ME . . .	3.50	7.00	4.65
☐ 3218		IT'S ALL RIGHT/ YOU'LL NEVER WALK ALONE . .	3.50	7.00	4.65
☐ 3233		I'M THE ONE/ YOU'VE GOT WHAT I LIKE	3.25	6.00	4.00
☐ 3251		DON'T LET THE SUN CATCH YOU CRYING/I'M THE ONE	3.25	6.00	4.00
☐ 3251		DON'T LET THE SUN CATCH YOU CRYING/AWAY FROM YOU	3.00	5.50	3.85
☐ 3261		HOW DO YOU DO IT/ YOU'LL NEVER WALK ALONE . .	3.00	5.50	3.85
☐ 3271		I LIKE IT/JAMBALAYA	3.00	5.50	3.85
☐ 3279		I'LL BE THERE/YOU, YOU, YOU . .	3.00	5.50	3.85
☐ 3284		FERRY ACROSS THE MERSEY/ PRETEND	3.00	5.50	3.85
☐ 3293		IT'S GONNA BE ALRIGHT/ SKINNY MINNIE	3.00	5.50	3.85
☐ 3302		YOU'LL NEVER WALK ALONE/ AWAY FROM YOU	3.00	5.50	3.85
☐ 3313		GIVE ALL YOUR LOVE TO ME/ YOU'RE THE REASON	3.00	5.50	3.85
☐ 3323		WALK HAND IN HAND/DREAMS .	3.00	5.50	3.85
☐ 3337		LA LA LA/WITHOUT YOU	3.00	5.50	3.85
☐ 3354		GIRL ON A SWING/THE WAY YOU LOOK TONIGHT	3.00	5.50	3.85
☐ 3370		LOOKING FOR MY LIFE/ THE BIG BRIGHT GREEN PLEASURE MACHINE	3.00	5.50	3.85

GERRY AND THE PACEMAKERS—ALBUMS

☐ 2024 (M)	LAURIE	DON'T LET THE SUN CATCH YOU CRYING	7.00	17.00	15.00
☐ 2024 (S)		DON'T LET THE SUN CATCH YOU CRYING	9.00	25.00	22.50
☐ 2027 (M)		SECOND ALBUM	7.00	17.00	15.00
☐ 2027 (S)		SECOND ALBUM	9.00	25.00	22.50
☐ 2030 (M)		I'LL BE THERE	7.00	17.00	15.00
☐ 2030 (S)		I'LL BE THERE	9.00	25.00	22.50
☐ 2031 (M)		GREATEST HITS	6.00	15.00	13.50
☐ 2031 (S)		GREATEST HITS	8.00	21.00	18.00
☐ 2037 (M)		GIRL ON A SWING	6.00	15.00	13.50
☐ 2037 (S)		GIRL ON A SWING	8.00	21.00	18.00
☐ 3387 (M)	UNITED ARTISTS	FERRY ACROSS THE MERSEY (soundtrack)	6.00	15.00	13.50

GERRY AND THE PACEMAKERS

In 1963, Laurie Records of New York City signed an English group called Gerry and the Pacemakers, who had had much success in England. For a time, Laurie must have regretted their decision to take on the quartet. By the late spring of 1964, though, Laurie realized they had made the right move. Gerry and the Pacemakers scored half-a-dozen Top 30 hits on Laurie by the end of 1965.

Gerry Marsden had once delivered packages around the Liverpool area. On weekends, he played guitar with a skiffle group. He later turned to rock-and-roll and, along with older brother Fred, formed the Mars Bars. They soon added another member and changed the group's name to the Pacemakers late in 1959. Like the Beatles, Gerry and the Pacemakers (their final name) bacame a top club draw in both Liverpool and nearby Hamburg, Germany.

They signed with Beatles manager Brian Epstein in 1962. Gerry and the Pacemakers then recorded a song called "How Do You Do It?". (The Beatles had rejected the same song earlier in favor of an original, "Love Me Do".) "How Do You Do It?" went to number one in England in 1963. At this point, Laurie Records signed the group for American releases. Their first American hit was a ballad, "Don't Let the Sun Catch You Crying".

			Current Price Range		P/Y AVG
☐ 90812 (S)		FERRY ACROSS THE MERSEY (soundtrack)	8.00	21.00	18.00

GESTICS

☐ 106	**SURFER**	LET'S GO TRIPPIN'/KAHUNA	4.50	7.50	6.00
☐ 114		ROCKIN' FURY/INVASION	4.50	7.50	6.00

STEVE GIBSON AND THE RED CAPS

☐ 796	**JAY DEE**	IT HURTS ME BUT I LIKE IT/ OUCH!	5.50	11.00	9.00
☐ 9702	**ABC-PARAMOUNT**	ROCK AND ROLL STOMP/ LOVE ME TENDERLY	3.75	6.00	4.50
☐ 9856		SILHOUETTES/FLAMINGO	3.00	6.00	3.50
☐ 326	**HUNT**	BLESS YOU/CHERYL LEE	3.00	5.00	3.50
☐ 330		WHERE ARE YOU?/ SAN ANTONIO ROSE	3.00	5.00	3.50

GIGOLOS
GUITAR: DUANE EDDY

☐ 1	**DAYNITE**	SWINGIN' SAINTS/ NIGHT CRAWLERS	8.50	14.00	12.00

RONNIE GILL

☐ 129	**RIO**	GERALDINE/ STANDING ON THE MOUNTAIN .	12.00	46.00	40.00

MICKEY GILLEY

☐ 106	**MINOR**	TELL ME WHY/OOWEE BABY	25.00	40.00	35.00
☐ 15706	**DOT**	CALL ME SHORTY/ COME ON BABY	20.00	35.00	28.00
☐ 1007	**REX**	GRAPEVINE/THAT'S HOW IT'S GOT TO BE	5.00	10.00	7.50
☐ 712	**KHOURY'S**	DRIVE IN MOVIE/ GIVE ME A CHANCE	15.00	25.00	22.00
☐ 901	**POTOMAC**	IS IT WRONG/NO GREATER LOVE .	5.00	8.50	7.00
☐ 503	**LYNN**	EVERYTHING TURNED TO LOVE/YOUR SELFISH PRIDE. ..	5.00	10.00	6.50
☐ 508		TURN AROUND/MY BABY'S BEEN CHEATIN' AGAIN	4.00	8.00	7.50
☐ 512		SLIPPIN' AND SLIDIN'/(IT'S THE) END OF THE LINE	5.00	10.00	7.50
☐ 508		MY BABY'S CHEATIN' AGAIN/LONELY LONELY NIGHTS	5.00	10.00	7.50
☐ 518	**SABRA**	VALLEY OF TEARS/ I NEED YOUR LOVE	7.50	12.00	9.00
☐ 4004	**PRINCESS**	YOUR FIRST TIME/ DRIVE IN MOVIE	7.50	12.00	9.00
☐ 4006		WILD SIDE OF LIFE/ CAUGHT IN THE MIDDLE	5.00	10.00	7.50
☐ 4011		I'LL KEEP ON DREAMING/ I'LL KEEP SEARCHING	4.00	8.00	6.50
☐ 4015		WORLD OF MY OWN/I STILL CARE .	4.00	8.00	6.50
☐ 101	**SUPREME**	NOW THAT I HAVE YOU/ HAPPY BIRTHDAY	3.00	6.00	5.00
☐ 102		EVERYTHING TURNED TO LOVE/NO ONE WILL EVER KNOW	3.00	6.00	5.00
☐ 1513	**SAN**	I AIN'T NO BO DIDDLEY/ I'M TO BLAME	3.00	6.00	5.00
☐ 101	**DARYL**	WHAT HAVE I DONE/ THERE'S A CROWD	3.00	6.00	5.00

			Current Price Range		P/Y AVG
☐ 101	**ASTRO**	THE SURF SIDERS CHUG-A-LUG CHARLIE/I WANT TO LOVE YOU MY WAY	3.00	6.00	5.00
☐ 102		MICKEY GILLEY LONELY WINE/DOWN THE LINE	3.00	6.00	5.00
☐ 104		NIGHT AFTER NIGHT/SUSIE Q	3.00	6.00	5.00
☐ 106		LOTTA LOVIN'/I MISS YOU SO	3.00	6.00	5.00
☐ 110		IF I DIDN'T HAVE A DIME/ A CERTAIN SMILE	3.00	6.00	5.00
☐ 110		IF I DIDN'T HAVE A DIME/ LITTLE EGYPT	3.00	6.00	5.00
☐ 5002		EVERYTHING IS YOURS THAT ONCE WAS MINE/DON'T THROW A GOOD LOVE AWAY	3.00	6.00	5.00
☐ 5003		A TOAST TO MARY ANN/ YOU TOUCH MY LIFE	3.00	6.00	5.00
☐ 10003		SHE CALLED ME BABY/ ROOM FULL OF ROSES	3.00	6.00	5.00
☐ 1223	**GOLDBAND**	I AIN'T GOING HOME/ NO GREATER LOVE	3.00	6.00	5.00
☐ 7021	**EPIC**	FRAULEIN/WHOLE LOT OF TWISTIN' GOIN' ON	3.50	6.00	5.00
☐ 50580		HERE COMES THE HURT AGAIN	2.00	4.00	3.00
☐ 50631		THE SONG WE MADE LOVE TO/MEMPHIS MEMORIES	2.50	4.00	3.00
☐ 50672		JUST LONG ENOUGH TO SAY GOODBYE/TONIGHT I'LL HELP YOU SAY GOODBYE AGAIN	2.50	4.00	3.00
☐ 50740		MY SILVER LINING	2.50	4.00	3.00
☐ 50801		A LITTLE GETTING USED TO	2.50	4.00	3.00
☐ 50876		TRUE LOVE WAYS/THE MORE I TURN THE BOTTLE UP	2.50	4.00	3.00
☐ 50940		THAT'S ALL THAT MATTERS TO ME	2.50	4.00	3.00
☐ 50973		A HEADACHE TOMORROW (OR A HEARTACHE TONIGHT)/ MILLION DOLLAR MEMORIES	2.50	4.00	3.00
☐ 51003		MAMAS DON'T LET YOUR BABIES GROW UP TO BE COWBOYS/ BAYOU CITY BEATS COTTON EYED JOE	2.50	4.00	3.00
☐ 02172		YOU DON'T KNOW ME	2.50	4.00	3.00
☐ 02578		LONELY NIGHTS	2.50	4.00	3.00
☐ 126	**TCG-HALL**	WHEN TWO WORLDS COLLIDE/LET'S HURT TOGETHER	2.50	4.00	3.00
☐ 101	**ACT-1**	SAY NO TO YOU/ MAKE ME BELIEVE	2.50	4.00	3.00
☐ 256	**PAULA**	SAY NO TO YOU/ MAKE ME BELIEVE	2.50	4.00	3.00
☐ 269		I'M GONNA PUT MY LOVE IN THE WANT ADS/WORLD OF MY OWN	2.50	4.00	3.00
☐ 280		BLAME IT ON THE MOON/ SOUNDS LIKE TROUBLE	2.50	4.00	3.00
☐ 301		THAT HEART BELONGS TO ME/ A NEW WAY TO LIVE	2.50	4.00	3.00
☐ 1200		NOW I CAN LIVE AGAIN/ WITHOUT YOU	2.50	4.00	3.00
☐ 1208		SHE'S STILL GOT A HOLD ON YOU/THERE'S NO ONE LIKE YOU	2.50	4.00	3.00
☐ 1215		WATCHING THE WAY/IT'S JUST A MATTER OF MAKING UP MY MIND	2.50	4.00	3.00
☐ 402		NIGHT AFTER NIGHT/ I'M TO BLAME	2.50	4.00	3.00

			Current Price Range		P/Y AVG
☐27	GRT	I'M NOBODY TODAY/ SHE'S NOT YOURS ANYMORE	2.50	4.00	3.00
☐45		TIME TO TELL ANOTHER LIE/ BECAUSE I LOVE YOU	2.50	4.00	3.00
☐617	RESCO	A TOAST TO MARY ANN/ YOU TOUCH MY LIFE	2.50	4.00	3.00
☐620		QUITTIN' TIME/ SHE GIVE ME LOVE	2.50	4.00	3.00
☐50056	PLAYBOY	ROOM FULL OF ROSES/ SHE CALLED ME BABY	2.50	4.00	3.00
☐6004		I OVERLOOKED AN ORCHID/ SWINGING DOORS	2.50	4.00	3.00
☐6015		CITY LIGHTS/FRAULEIN	2.50	4.00	3.00
☐6031		WINDOW UP ABOVE	2.50	4.00	3.00
☐6041		BOUQUET OF ROSES	2.50	4.00	3.00
☐6045		ROLL YOU LIKE A WHEEL/ LET'S SING A SONG	2.50	4.00	3.00
☐6055		OVERNIGHT SENSATION	2.50	4.00	3.00
☐6063		DON'T THE GIRLS ALL GET PRETTIER AT CLOSING TIME	2.50	4.00	3.00
☐6075		BRING IT ON HOME TO ME/ HOW'S MY EX TREATING YOU	2.50	4.00	3.00
☐6089		LAWDY MISS CLAWDY	2.50	4.00	3.00
☐6095		LONELY CHRISTMAS CALL/ PRETTY PAPER	2.50	4.00	3.00
☐6100		SHE'S PULLING ME BACK AGAIN	2.50	4.00	3.00
☐5807		HONKYTONK MEMORIES/FIVE FOOT TWO EYES OF BLUE	2.50	4.00	3.00
☐5818		CHAINS OF LOVE/NO. 1 ROCK 'N' ROLL C&W BOOGIE BLUES MAN	2.50	4.00	3.00
☐5826		THE POWER OF POSITIVE DRINKING	2.50	4.00	3.00
☐46640	ASYLUM	STAND BY ME	2.50	4.00	3.00

MICKEY GILLEY—ALBUMS

☐1005		MICKEY AT GILLEY'S	7.50	12.00	10.00
☐1007		WELCOME TO GILLEY'S	7.50	12.00	10.00
☐81078		WHY ME LORD?	7.50	12.00	10.00
☐2195	PAULA	DOWN THE LINE	7.50	12.00	10.00
☐401	PLAYBOY	ROOM FULL OF ROSES	7.50	12.00	10.00
☐403		CITY LIGHTS	7.50	12.00	10.00
☐405		MICKEY'S MOVIN ON	7.50	12.00	10.00
☐408		OVERNIGHT SENSATION	7.50	12.00	10.00
☐415		GILLEY'S SMOKIN'	7.50	12.00	10.00
☐418		FIRST CLASS	7.50	12.00	10.00
☐35009		FLYIN' HIGH	7.50	12.00	10.00
☐35714	EPIC	THE SONGS WE MADE LOVE TO	5.00	10.00	7.50
☐36201		MICKEY GILLEY	5.00	10.00	7.50
☐36921		URBAN COWBOY II: MORE MUSIC FROM THE ORIGINAL SOUNDTRACK	5.00	10.00	7.50
☐37416		YOU DON'T KNOW ME	5.00	10.00	7.50
☐37595		CHRISTMAS AT GILLEY'S	5.00	10.00	7.50
☐38082		PUT YOUR DREAMS AWAY	5.00	10.00	7.50
☐38583		FOOL FOR YOUR LOVE	5.00	10.00	7.50
☐39000		YOU'VE REALLY GOT A HOLD ON ME	5.00	10.00	7.50
☐39292		MICKEY GILLEY AND CHARLY McCLAIN-IT TAKES BELIEVERS	5.00	10.00	7.50
☐90002	ASYLUM	URBAN COWBOY SOUNDTRACK	5.00	10.00	7.50

			Current Price Range		P/Y AVG
☐ 36492		THAT'S ALL THAT NATTERS TO ME	5.00	10.00	7.50
☐ 51141	**LIBERTY**	TOJGH ENOUGH ORIGINAL SOUNDTRACK	5.00	10.00	7.50

JIMMY GILMER AND THE FIREBALLS
SEE: FIREBALLS

☐ 30942	**DECCA**	LOOK ALIVE/ BECAUSE I NEED YOU	3.75	6.00	4.50
☐ 547	**WARWICK**	TRUE LOVE WAYS/WISHING	3.50	5.50	4.00
☐ 592		GOOD, GOOD LOVIN'/ DO YOU THINK	3.00	5.00	3.50
☐ 50037	**HAMILTON**	I'M GONNA GO WALKING/ WON'T BE LONG	3.75	6.00	4.50
☐ 16487	**DOT**	SUGAR SHACK/ MY HEART IS FREE	2.75	5.00	3.00
☐ 16539		DAISY PETAL PICKIN'/ WHEN MY TEARS HAVE DRIED .	2.75	5.00	3.00
☐ 16583		AIN'T GONNA TELL ANYBODY/ YOU AM I	2.75	5.00	3.00
☐ 16666		CRY BABY/ THUNDER AND LIGHTNIN'	3.00	5.00	3.50
☐ 16714		LONESOME TEARS/ BORN TO BE WITH YOU	3.00	5.00	3.50
☐ 16743		THE FOOL/SOMEBODY STOLE MY WATERMELON	2.75	5.00	3.00

JIMMY GILMER AND THE FIREBALLS—ALBUM

☐ 3577 (M)	**DOT**	BUDDY'S BUDDY	7.00	17.00	15.00
☐ 25577 (S)		BUDDY'S BUDDY	9.00	25.00	22.50

LOU GIORDANO
GUITAR: BUDDY HOLLY

☐ 55115	**BRUNSWICK**	STAY CLOSE TO ME/ DON'T CHA KNOW (DJ)	150.00	275.00	165.00
☐ 55115		STAY CLOSE TO ME/ DON'T CHA KNOW (maroon) ...	250.00	500.00	305.00

GLADIOLAS
FEATURED: MAURICE WILLIAMS

☐ 2101	**EXCELLO**	LITTLE DARLIN'/SWEETHEART PLEASE DON'T GO	6.00	12.00	8.00
☐ 2110		RUN RUN LITTLE JOE/ COMIN' HOME TO YOU	6.00	12.00	8.00
☐ 2120		HEY! LITTLE GIRL/ I WANNA KNOW	6.00	12.00	8.00
☐ 2136		SAY YOU'LL BE MINE/ SHOOP SHOOP	6.00	12.00	8.00

CLIFF GLEAVES

☐ 55263	**LIBERTY**	LONG BLACK HEARSE/ YOU AND YOUR KIND	3.25	6.00	4.00
☐ 623	**DORE**	HOLD BACK THE DAWN/TIMBER .	3.00	5.00	3.50

GOLLIWOGS
SEE: CREEDENCE CLEARWATER REVIVAL

☐ 404	**SCORPIO**	BROWN EYED GIRL/ YOU BETTER BE CAREFUL	6.00	12.00	10.00
☐ 405		FIGHT FIRE/FRAGILE GIRL	6.00	12.00	10.00
☐ 408		WALKING ON THE WATER/ YOU BETTER GET IT	7.00	14.00	12.00
☐ 412		PORTERVILLE/ CALL IT PRETENDING	6.00	12.00	10.00
☐ 590	**FANTASY**	DON'T TELL ME NO LIES/LITTLE GIRL, DOES YOU MAMA KNOW?.	8.25	14.00	12.00

			Current Price Range		P/Y AVG
☐597		YOU CAME WALKING/			
		WHERE YOU BEEN?	7.00	14.00	12.00
☐599		YOU GOT NOTHIN' ON ME/			
		YOU CAN'T BE TRUE	7.00	14.00	12.00

PETER GOON

☐100	**POLEESE**	WHISTLER/SONG TITLES	14.00	40.00	36.00

THE SECOND SIDE OF THIS DISC WAS NOT BY PETER GOON

LESLEY GORE

☐72119	**MERCURY**	IT'S MY PARTY/DANNY	3.00	5.50	3.85
☐72143		JUDY'S TURN TO CRY/			
		JUST LET ME CRY	3.00	5.50	3.85
☐72180		SHE'S A FOOL/THE OLD CROWD .	3.00	5.50	3.85
☐72206		YOU DON'T OWN ME/			
		RUN, BOBBY, RUN	3.00	5.50	3.85
☐72245		JE NE SAIS PLUS/JE N'OSE PAS .	3.00	5.50	3.85
		(French version of ''You Don't			
		Own Me'')			
☐72259		THAT'S THE WAY BOYS ARE/			
		THAT'S THE WAY THE BALL			
		BOUNCES	3.00	5.50	3.85
☐72270		I DON'T WANNA BE A LOSER/			
		IT'S GOTTA BE YOU	3.00	5.50	3.85
☐72309		MAYBE I KNOW/WONDER BOY ..	3.00	5.50	3.85
☐72352		SOMETIMES I WISH I WERE A			
		BOY/HEY NOW	3.00	5.50	3.85
☐72372		THE LOOK OF LOVE/			
		LITTLE GIRL, GO HOME	3.00	5.50	3.85
☐72412		ALL OF MY LIFE/			
		I CANNOT HOPE FOR ANYONE .	3.00	5.50	3.85
☐72433		SUNSHINE, LOLLIPOPS AND			
		ROSES/YOU'VE COME BACK ..	3.00	5.50	3.85
☐72475		MY TOWN, MY GUY AND ME/			
		A GIRL IN LOVE	3.00	5.50	3.85
☐72513		I WON'T LOVE YOU ANYMORE			
		(SORRY)/NO MATTER WHAT			
		YOU DID	3.00	5.50	3.85
☐72530		WE KNOW WE'RE IN LOVE/			
		THAT'S WHAT I'LL DO	3.00	5.50	3.85
☐72553		YOUNG LOVE/I JUST DON'T			
		KNOW IF I CAN	3.00	5.50	3.85
☐72580		OFF AND RUNNING/I DON'T CARE	3.00	5.50	3.85
☐72611		TREAT ME LIKE A LADY/			
		MAYBE NOW	3.00	5.50	3.85
☐72649		CALIFORNIA NIGHTS/			
		I'M GOING OUT	3.00	5.50	3.85
☐72683		SUMMER AND SANDY/			
		I'M FALLIN' DOWN	3.00	5.50	3.85
☐72726		BRINK OF DISASTER/			
		ON A DAY LIKE THIS	3.00	5.50	3.85
☐72759		IT'S A HAPPENING WORLD/			
		MAGIC COLORS	3.00	5.50	3.85
☐72787		SMALL TALK/SAY WHAT YOU SEE	3.00	5.50	3.85
☐72819		HE GIVES ME LOVE (LA LA LA)/			
		A BRAND NEW ME	3.00	5.50	3.85
☐72842		I CAN'T MAKE IT WITHOUT YOU/			
		WHERE CAN I GO?	3.00	5.50	3.85
☐72867		LOOK THE OTHER WAY/			
		I'LL BE STANDING BY	3.00	5.50	3.85
☐72892		TAKE GOOD CARE/			
		YOU SENT ME SILVER BELLS ..	3.00	5.50	3.85
☐72892		I CAN'T MAKE IT WITHOUT YOU/			
		TAKE GOOD CARE	3.00	5.50	3.85

LESLEY GORE

Tenafly, NJ, was the birthplace of Lesley Gore. She was born there on May 2, 1946. Music meant little to Lesley until she became interested in her cousin's jazz record collection.

Noted composer and arranger Quincy Jones later heard Ms. Gore singing with her cousin's band. Quincy told of Lesley's talents to Mercury Records executives. Later, she was called into Mercury for an audition. She soon signed a contract. Shortly after that, Quincy and Lesley sifted through a stack of demo singles that had been passed over by other singers and groups. They finally settled on one called "It's My Party".

In April of 1963, Lesley cut the teen-oriented song; it was on the charts within a month. By the summertime, "It's My Party" had gone all the way to the top. Lesley quickly followed that hit with three more Top 5 songs in a row.

Then she was faced with the choice of pursuing her career or attending college (she was an honor-student in high school). She chose the latter, eventually graduating although she continued recording hits for Mercury until the last chart success in 1967. Later singles on Crewe and Mowest did nothing.

			Current Price Range		P/Y AVG

☐72931		98.6 - SUMMER DAY/ SUMMER SYMPHONY	3.00	5.50	3.85
☐72969		WEDDING BELL BLUES/ ONE BY ONE	3.00	5.50	3.85
☐338	**CREWE**	TOMORROW'S CHILREN/ WHY DOESN'T LOVE MAKE ME HAPPY?	3.00	5.50	3.85
☐343		COME SOFTLY TO ME/ BILLY 'N SUE'S LOVE SONG (Billy and Sue)	3.50	6.00	4.00
☐344		WHEN YESTERDAY WAS TOMORROW/WHY ME, WHY YOU?	3.00	5.50	3.85
☐5029	**MOWEST**	THE ROAD I WALK/ SHE SAID THAT	2.75	5.00	3.00
☐1710	**A & M**	IMMORTALITY/GIVE IT TO ME, SWEET THING	2.75	5.00	3.00
		LESLEY GORE—ALBUMS			
☐20805 (M)	**MERCURY**	I'LL CRY IF I WANT TO	8.00	21.00	18.00
☐60805 (S)		I'LL CRY IF I WANT TO	12.00	29.00	25.00
☐20849 (M)		LESLEY GORE SINGS FOR MIXED UP HEARTS	8.00	21.00	18.00
☐60849 (S)		LESLEY GORE SINGS FOR MIXED UP HEARTS	12.00	21.00	18.00
☐20901 (M)		BOYS, BOYS, BOYS.........	7.00	17.00	15.00
☐60901 (S)		BOYS, BOYS, BOYS...........	9.00	25.00	22.50
☐20943 (M)		GIRL TALK	7.00	17.00	15.00
☐60943 (S)		GIRL TALK	9.00	25.00	22.50
☐21024 (M)		GOLDEN HITS OF LESLEY GORE ..	7.00	17.00	15.00
☐61024 (S)		GOLDEN HITS OF LESLEY GORE ..	9.00	25.00	22.50
☐21042 (M)		MY TOWN, MY GUY, AND ME ...	6.00	15.00	13.50
☐61042 (S)		MY TOWN, MY GUY, AND ME ...	8.00	21.00	18.00
☐21066 (M)		ALL ABOUT LOVE	6.00	15.00	13.50
☐61066 (S)		ALL ABOUT LOVE	8.00	21.00	18.00
☐21120 (M)		CALIFORNIA NIGHTS	6.00	15.00	13.50
☐61120 (S)		CALIFORNIA NIGHTS	8.00	21.00	18.00
☐61185 (S)		GOLDEN HITS OF LESLEY GORE, VOL. II	6.00	15.00	13.50
☐117 (S)	**MOWEST**	SOMEPLACE ELSE NOW	5.50	14.00	12.00

SAMMY GOWANS

| ☐114 | **UNITED ARTISTS** | KISSIN' AT THE DRIVE-IN/ ROCKIN' BY MYSELF .... | 29.00 | 58.00 | 36.00 |

CHARLIE GRACIE

☐105	**CAMEO**	BUTTERFLY/NINETY-NINE WAYS	3.50	6.50	4.65
☐107		FABULOUS/JUST LOOKIN'	3.50	6.50	4.65
☐111		I LOVE YOU SO MUCH IT HURTS/ WANDERIN' EYES	3.25	5.50	4.00
☐113		COOL BABY/YOU'VE GOT A HEART LIKE A ROCK	3.25	5.50	4.00
☐127		DRESSIN' UP/CRAZY GIRL	3.25	5.50	4.00
☐141		LOVE BIRD/TRYING............	3.25	5.50	4.00
☐178	**DIAMOND**	HE'LL NEVER LOVE YOU LIKE I DO/KEEP MY LOVE NEXT TO YOUR HEART	3.25	5.50	4.00

GERRY GRANAHAN
SEE: DICKEY DOO AND THE DON'TS

☐102	**SUNBEAM**	NO CHEMISE, PLEASE/ GIRL OF MY DREAMS	3.25	5.50	4.00
☐108		BABY, WAIT/COMPLETELY	3.25	5.50	4.00
☐112		AS READY AS I'LL EVER BE/ NOBODY CAN HANDLE THIS JOB	3.25	5.50	4.00

			Current Price Range		P/Y AVG
☐ 122		KING SIZE/I'M AFRAID YOU'LL NEVER KNOW	3.00	5.00	3.50
☐ 127		A RING, A BRACELET, A HEART/ ''A'' YOU'RE ADORABLE	3.00	5.00	3.50

JANIE GRANT

☐ 104	CAPRICE	TRIANGLE/SHE'S GOING STEADY WITH YOU	3.25	5.50	4.00
☐ 109		ROMEO/ROLLER COASTER	3.25	5.50	4.00
☐ 111		UNHAPPY/I WONDER WHO'S KISSING HER NOW	3.25	5.50	4.00
☐ 113		OH JOHNNY/OH, MY LOVE	3.25	5.50	4.00
☐ 115		THAT GREASY KID STUFF/ TRYING TO FORGET	3.00	5.00	3.50
☐ 119		PEGGY GOT ENGAGED/TWO'S COMPANY, THREE'S A CROWD	3.00	5.00	3.50
☐ 616	UNITED ARTISTS	TELL ME MAMA/WHOSE HEART ARE YOU BREAKING NOW	3.00	5.00	3.50

GUY GRANTS

☐ 103	LAWN	IT'S YOU/SO YOUNG	24.00	50.00	45.00

GRASS ROOTS

☐ 4013	DUNHILL	MR. JONES/ YOU'RE A LONELY GIRL	3.50	6.00	4.35
☐ 4029		WHERE WERE YOU WHEN I NEEDED YOU?/ (THESE ARE) BAD TIMES	3.00	5.00	3.65
☐ 4043		ONLY WHEN YOU'RE LONELY/ THIS IS WHAT I WAS MADE FOR.	3.25	5.50	3.75
☐ 4053		LOOK OUT, GIRL/ TIP OF MY TONGUE	3.25	5.50	4.00
☐ 4084		LET'S LIVE FOR TODAY/ DEPRESSED FEELING	3.00	5.00	3.65
☐ 4094		THINGS I SHOULD HAVE SAID/ TIP OF MY TONGUE	3.00	5.00	3.65
☐ 4105		WAKE UP, WAKE UP/NO EXIT . . .	3.00	5.00	3.65
☐ 4122		MELODY FOR YOU/HEY FRIEND .	3.00	5.00	3.65
☐ 4129		FEELINGS/ HERE'S WHERE YOU BELONG . .	3.00	5.00	3.65
☐ 4144		MIDNIGHT CONFESSIONS/WHO WILL YOU BE TOMORROW? . . .	3.00	5.00	3.65
☐ 4162		BELLA LINDA/HOT BRIGHT BLUES.	3.00	5.00	3.65
☐ 4180		LOVIN' THINGS/YOU AND LOVE ARE THE SAME	3.00	5.00	3.65
☐ 4187		THE RIVER IS WIDE/(YOU GOTTA) LIVE FOR LOVE	3.00	5.00	3.65
☐ 4198		I'D WAIT A MILLION YEARS/ FLY ME TO HAVANA	3.00	5.00	3.65
☐ 4217		HEAVEN KNOWS/ DON'T REMIND ME	3.00	5.00	3.65
☐ 4227		WALKING THROUGH THE COUNTRY/TRUCK DRIVIN' MAN.	3.00	5.00	3.65
☐ 4237		BABY HOLD ON/GET IT TOGETHER.	3.00	5.00	3.65
☐ 4249		COME ON AND SAY IT/ SOMETHING'S COMIN' OVER ME	3.00	5.00	3.65
☐ 4263		TEMPTATION EYES/ KEEPIN' ME DOWN	3.00	5.00	3.65
☐ 4279		SOONER OR LATER/I CAN TURN OFF THE RAIN	3.00	5.00	3.65
☐ 4289		TWO DIVIDED BY LOVE/LET IT GO	3.00	5.00	3.65
☐ 4302		GLORY BOUND/ONLY ONE	3.00	5.00	3.65
☐ 4316		THE RUNWAY/MOVE ALONG	3.00	5.00	3.65

			Current Price Range		P/Y AVG
☐ 4325		ANY WAY THE WIND BLOWS/ MONDAY BLUES	3.00	5.00	3.65
☐ 4335		LOVE IS WHAT YOU MAKE IT/ SOMEONE TO LOVE	3.00	5.00	3.65
☐ 4345		WHERE THERE'S SMOKE, THERE'S FIRE/LOOK BUT DON'T TOUCH	3.00	5.00	3.65
☐ 4371		WE CAN'T DANCE TO YOUR MUSIC/LOOK BUT DON'T TOUCH	3.00	5.00	3.65
☐ 15006		STEALIN' LOVE (IN THE NIGHT)/ WE ALMOST MADE IT TOGETHER	2.75	4.50	3.00
		GRASS ROOTS—ALBUMS			
☐ 50020 (M)	**DUNHILL**	LET'S LIVE FOR TODAY	6.00	17.00	15.00
☐ 50020 (S)		LET'S LIVE FOR TODAY	7.00	17.00	15.00
☐ 50027 (S)		FEELINGS	6.00	15.00	13.50
☐ 50047 (S)		GOLDEN GRASS (greatest hits)	6.00	15.00	13.50
☐ 50052 (S)		LOVIN' THINGS	6.00	15.00	13.50
☐ 50067 (S)		LEAVING IT ALL BEHIND	6.00	15.00	13.50
☐ 50087 (S)		MORE GOLDEN GRASS	6.00	15.00	13.50
☐ 50107 (S)		THEIR 16 GREATEST HITS	5.00	12.00	10.00
☐ 50112 (S)		MOVE ALONG	5.00	12.00	10.00
☐ 50137 (S)		A LOTTA MILEAGE	5.00	12.00	10.00

GREAT SOCIETY
FEATURED: GRACE SLICK
SEE: JEFFERSON AIRPLANE

☐ 1001	**NORTH BEACH**	SOMEONE TO LOVE/FREE ADVICE	17.00	29.00	25.00
☐ 44583	**COLUMBIA**	SALLY GO 'ROUND THE ROSES/ DIDN'T THINK SO	4.50	7.50	6.00
		GREAT SOCIETY—ALBUMS			
☐ 9624 (S)	**COLUMBIA**	CONSPICUOUS ONLY IN ITS ABSENCE	6.00	15.00	13.50
☐ 9702 (S)		HOW IT WAS	6.00	15.00	13.50

GUESS WHO

☐ 1295	**SCEPTER**	SHAKIN' ALL OVER/ TILL WE KISSED	3.50	6.00	4.00
☐ 12108		GOODNIGHT, GOODNIGHT/HEY, HO, WHAT YOU DID TO ME	3.50	6.00	4.00
☐ 12188		HURTING EACH OTHER/ BABY'S BIRTHDAY	3.50	6.00	4.00
☐ 12131		BABY FEELIN'/BELIEVE ME	3.50	6.00	4.00
☐ 12144		CLOCK ON THE WALL/ONE DAY	3.50	6.00	4.00
☐ 967	**AMY**	SHE'S ALL MINE/ALL RIGHT	3.50	6.00	4.00
☐ 976		HIS GIRL/IT'S MY PRIDE	3.50	6.00	4.00
☐ 1597	**FONTANA**	THIS TIME LONG AGO/THERE'S NO GETTING AWAY FROM YOU	3.50	6.00	4.00
☐ 0102	**RCA**	THESE EYES/LIGHTFOOT	3.00	5.00	3.65
☐ 0195		LAUGHING/UNDUN	3.00	5.00	3.65
☐ 0223		FRIEND OF MINE/(PT. 2)	3.00	5.00	3.65
☐ 0300		NO TIME/PROPER STRANGER	3.00	5.00	3.65
☐ 0325		AMERICAN WOMAN/ NO SUGAR TONIGHT	3.00	5.00	3.65
☐ 0367		HAND ME DOWN WORLD/ RUNNIN' DOWN THE STREET	3.00	5.00	3.65
☐ 0388		SHARE THE LAND/BUS RIDER	3.00	5.00	3.65
☐ 0414		HANG ON TO YOUR LIFE/ DO YOU MISS ME, DARLIN'	3.00	5.00	3.65
☐ 0458		ALBERT FLASHER/BROKER	3.00	5.00	3.65
☐ 0522		RAIN DANCE/ONE DIVIDED	3.00	5.00	3.65
☐ 0578		SOUR SUITE/O LIFE IN THE BLOODSTREAM	3.00	5.00	3.65

			Current Price Range		P/Y AVG
☐ 0695		HEARTBROKEN BOPPER/ ARRIVEDERCI GIRL	3.00	5.00	3.65
☐ 0708		GUNS, GUNS, GUNS/HEAVEN MOVED ONLY ONCE YESTERDAY	3.00	5.00	3.65
☐ 0803		RUNNIN` BACK TO SASKATOON/ NEW MOTHER NATURE	3.00	5.00	3.65
☐ 0880		FOLLOW YOUR DAUGHTER HOME/ BYE BYE BABY	3.00	5.00	3.65
☐ 0906		ALBERT FLASHER/BROKEN	3.00	5.00	3.65
☐ 0926		THE WATCHER/ORLY	3.00	5.00	3.65
☐ 0977		GLAMOUR BOY/LIE DOWN	2.75	4.50	2.50
☐ 0217		STAR BABY/MUSICONE	2.75	4.50	5.50
☐ 0324		CLAP FOR THE WOLFMAN/ ROAD FOOD	2.75	4.50	2.50
☐ 10075		DANCIN` FOOL/SEEMS LIKE I CAN`T LIVE WITH YOU BUT I CAN`T LIVE WITHOUT YOU	2.75	4.50	2.50
☐ 10216		LOVES ME LIKE A BROTHER/ HOEDOWN TIME	2.75	4.50	2.50
☐ 10360		ROSANNE/DREAMS	2.75	4.50	2.50
☐ 10410		WHEN THE BAND WAS SINGING ``SHAKIN` ALL OVER``/WOMEN	2.75	4.50	2.50
☐ 10716		RUNNIN` DOWN THE STREET/ SILVER BIRD	2.75	4.50	2.50
		GUESS WHO—ALBUMS			
☐ 533 (M)	**SCEPTER**	SHAKIN` ALL OVER	8.00	21.00	18.00
☐ 533 (S)		SHAKIN` ALL OVER	12.00	29.00	25.50
☐ 4141 (S)	**RCA**	WHEATFIED SOUL	5.50	14.00	12.00
☐ 4157 (S)		CANNED WHEAT	5.50	14.00	12.00
☐ 4266 (S)		AMERICAN WOMAN	5.50	14.00	12.00
☐ 4359 (S)		SHARE THE LAND	5.50	14.00	12.00
☐ 4574 (S)		SO LONG BANNATYNE.	5.50	14.00	12.00
☐ 4602 (S)		ROCKIN`	5.50	14.00	12.00
☐ 4779 (S)		LIVE AT THE PARAMOUNT	5.00	12.00	10.00
☐ 4830 (S)		ARTIFICIAL PARADISE.	5.00	12.00	10.00
☐ 1004 (S)		BEST OF THE GUESS WHO	5.00	12.00	10.00
☐ 0130 (S)		NO. 10	5.00	12.00	10.00
☐ 0269 (S)		BEST OF THE GUESS WHO, VOL. II.	5.00	12.00	10.00
☐ 0405 (S)		ROAD FOOD	5.00	12.00	10.00
☐ 0636 (S)		FLAVOURS.	5.00	12.00	10.00

THE GUISE (AND THEIR MOD SQUAD)
FEATURED: WALTER SCOTT

☐ BMI-6915/6	**MUSICLAND**	LONG HAIRED MUSIC/WHEN YOU`RE SORRY	3.00	5.00	3.50
☐ BMI-7058/9		HALF A MAN/CHUMPY McGEE . .	3.00	5.00	3.50

GULLIVER
FEATURED: DARYL HALL (HALL AND OATES)

☐ 45698	**ELEKTRA**	EVERYBODY`S LOVELY DAY/ TRULY GOOD SONG	10.00	20.00	12.00
☐ 74040 (S)		GULLIVER	8.25	13.50	12.00

ARLO GUTHRIE

☐ PRO-304	**REPRISE**	MOTORCYCLE SONG/ THE PAUSE OF MR. CLAUS . . .	4.00	7.50	6.50
☐ 0793		MOTORCYCLE SONG (PT. 1)/ (PT. 2)	3.00	6.00	4.50
☐ 0877		ALICE`S RESTAURANT/ COMING IN TO L.A.	3.00	6.00	4.50
☐ 0644		MOTORCYCLE SONG/ NOW AND THEN	3.00	6.00	4.50
☐ 0951		VALLEY TO PRAY/ GABRIEL`S MOTHER	3.00	6.00	4.50

			Current Price Range		P/Y AVG
☐1103		CITY OF NEW ORLEANS/ DAYS ARE SHORT	2.50	2.50	2.50

BOB GUY (FRANK ZAPPA)

☐1380	*DONNA*	LETTER FROM JEEPERS/ DEAR JEEPERS	12.00	24.00	20.00

H

SAMMY HAGAN

☐3772	*CAPITOL*	SMOOCHIE POOCHIE/ OUT OF YOUR HEART	12.00	25.00	22.00

RONNIE HAIG

☐10010	*NOTE*	TRAVELER OF LOVE/DON'T YOU HEAR ME CALLING, BABY	10.00	23.00	20.00
☐10014		ROCKIN' WITH RHYTHM & BLUES/ MONEY	10.00	23.00	20.00

HALE & THE HUSHABYES

☐104	*APOGEE*	YES SIR, THAT'S MY BABY/ 900 QUETZALS	17.00	34.00	30.00
☐0299	*REPRISE*	YES SIR, THAT'S MY BABY/ 900 QUETZALS	10.00	25.00	23.00

THIS WAS AN ALL-STAR GROUP OF GUEST ARTISTS, INCLUDING SONNY & CHER, ASSEMBLED FOR JUST THIS ONE RECORDING

BILL HALEY AND THE COMETS

☐303	*ESSEX*	ROCK THE JOINT/ICY HEART	23.00	40.00	27.00
☐305		DANCE WITH THE DOLLY/ ROCKING CHAIR ON THE MOON	23.00	40.00	27.00
☐310		REAL ROCK DRIVE/STOP BEATIN' 'ROUND THE MULBERRY BUSH	19.00	35.00	23.00
☐321		CRAZY MAN CRAZY/ WHATCHA GONNA DO	13.00	25.00	16.50
☐327		FRACTURED/PAT-A-CAKE	13.00	25.00	16.50
☐332		LIVE IT UP/FAREWELL, SO LONG, GOODBYE	10.00	19.00	13.50
☐340		I'LL BE TRUE/ TEN LITTLE INDIANS	9.00	16.00	11.00
☐348		STRAIGHT JACKET/ CHATTANOOGA CHOO-CHOO . .	9.00	16.00	11.00
☐374		SUNDOWN BOOGIE/ JUKEBOX CANNONBALL	10.00	20.00	13.50
☐381		ROCKET 88/GREEN TREE BOOGIE	10.00	20.00	13.50
☐399		ROCK THE JOINT/FAREWELL, SO LONG, GOODBYE	9.00	16.00	11.00
☐718	*TRANS WORLD*	REAL ROCK DRIVE/YES INDEED . .	9.00	16.00	11.00
☐29124	*DECCA*	ROCK AROUND THE CLOCK/ THIRTEEN WOMEN	5.00	9.00	6.00
☐29204		SHAKE, RATTLE AND ROLL/ A.B.C. BOOGIE	5.00	9.00	6.00
☐29317		DIM, DIM THE LIGHTS/ HAPPY BABY	4.50	7.00	5.00
☐29418		MAMBO ROCK/ BIRTH OF THE BOOGIE	4.50	7.00	5.00
☐29552		RAZZLE-DAZZLE/ TWO HOUND DOGS	4.50	7.00	5.00
☐29713		BURN THAT CANDLE/ ROCK-A-BEATIN' BOOGIE	4.50	7.00	5.00
☐29791		SEE YOU LATER ALLIGATOR/ THE PAPER BOY	4.50	7.00	5.00

BILL HALEY AND THE COMETS

Bill Haley was born on March 6, 1927, in Highland Park, MI. He was earning $1.00 a night with his guitar by age 13. At 15, he left home to tour with a country group called the Down Homers. He later formed Bill Haley and the Saddlemen. In 1952, Bill rechristened them the Comets.

Haley saw initial success in 1953 on the Essex label with "Crazy Man Crazy". (Many call this the first authentic rock-and-roll hit.) Bill Haley and the Comets then signed with the larger Decca outfit. In 1954 they cut a song called "Rock Around the Clock". It died. Haley and his men then followed up with a laundered "cover" version of Joe Turner's raunchy rhythm-and-blues hit, "Shake, Rattle and Roll". It became a winner, as did other (later) Decca offerings.

In 1955, "Rock Around the Clock" was tapped to become the theme song for "Blackboard Jungle". This was a film about high school juvenile delinquents. Suddenly the world sat up and took notice of this wild, obscure rocker. As a result, Decca reissued the former flop; it shot to number one for eight weeks. In time, "Rock Around the Clock" became the best-selling rock-and-roll single of all time. To date it has sold over 23,000,000 copies.

			Current Price Range		P/Y AVG
☐ 29870		R-O-C-K/ THE SAINTS ROCK 'N' ROLL ...	4.00	6.50	4.50
☐ 29948		HOT DOG BUDDY BUDDY/ ROCKIN' THROUGH THE RYE ..	4.00	6.50	4.50
☐ 30028		RIP IT UP/TEENAGER'S MOTHER .	4.00	6.50	4.50
☐ 30085		RUDY'S ROCK/ BLUE COMET BLUES	4.00	6.50	4.50
☐ 30148		DON'T KNOCK THE ROCK/ CHO CHO CH'BOOGIE	4.00	6.00	4.50
☐ 30214		FORTY CUPS OF COFFEE/ HOOK, LINE AND SINKER	3.25	5.25	4.00
☐ 30314		BILLY GOAT/ ROCKIN' ROLLIN' ROVER	3.25	5.25	4.00
☐ 30394		THE DIPSY DOODLE/MISS YOU ..	3.25	5.25	4.00
☐ 30461		ROCK THE JOINT/HOW MANY ...	3.25	5.25	4.00
☐ 30530		MARY, MARY LOU/IT'S A SIN ...	3.25	5.25	4.00
☐ 30592		SKINNY MINNIE/SWAY WITH ME	3.25	5.25	4.00
☐ 30681		LEAN JEAN/DON'T NOBODY MOVE	3.25	5.25	4.00
☐ Q0741		WHOA MABEL/CHIQUITA LINA ..	3.25	5.25	4.00
☐ 30781		CORRINE, CORRINA/B. B. PLENTY.	3.25	5.25	4.00
☐ 30844		I GOT A WOMAN/CHARMAINE ...	3.25	5.25	4.00
☐ 30873		A FOOL SUCH AS I/ WHERE'D YOU DO LAST NIGHT?.	3.25	5.25	4.00
☐ 30926		CALDONIA/SHAKY	3.25	5.25	4.00
☐ 30956		JOEY'S SONG/OOH! LOOK-A-THERE AIN'T SHE PRETTY!	3.25	5.25	4.00
☐ 31030		SKOKIAAN/ PUERTO RICAN PEDDLER	3.25	5.25	4.00
☐ 31080		MUSIC, MUSIC, MUSIC/ STRICTLY INSTRUMENTAL ...	3.25	5.25	4.00
☐ 31650		THE GREEN DOOR/ YEAH! SHE'S EVIL!	3.25	5.25	4.00
☐ 31677		SKINNY MINNIE/LEAN JEAN	2.75	4.50	3.50
☐ 72571		THE GREEN DOOR/CORRINE, CORRINA	2.75	4.50	3.50
☐ 5145	WARNER BROTHERS	CANDY KISSES/TAMIANI	2.75	4.50	3.50
☐ 5154		CHICK SAFARI/HAWK	2.75	4.50	3.50
☐ 5171		SO RIGHT TONIGHT/LET THE GOOD TIMES ROLL, CREOLE ...	2.75	4.50	3.50
☐ 5228		FLIP, FLOP AND FLY/ HONKY TONK	2.75	4.50	3.50
☐ 7124		ROCK AROUND THE CLOCK/ SHAKE, RATTLE AND ROLL ...	2.75	4.50	3.50
		BILL HALEY AND THE COMETS—EPs			
☐ 102	ESSEX	DANCE PARTY	25.00	42.00	31.00
☐ 117		ROCK WITH BILL HALEY AND THE COMETS	23.00	39.00	28.00
☐ 118		ROCK WITH BILL HALEY AND THE COMETS	23.00	39.00	28.00
☐ 2168	DECCA	SHAKE, RATTLE AND ROLL	16.00	30.00	19.00
☐ 2209		DIM, DIM THE LIGHTS	14.00	27.00	17.00
☐ 2322		ROCK AND ROLL	10.00	19.00	13.50
☐ 2398		HE DIGS ROCK AND ROLL	9.00	17.00	11.00
☐ 2416		ROCK AND ROLL STAGE SHOW ..	9.00	17.00	11.00
☐ 2417		ROCK AND ROLL STAGE SHOW ..	9.00	17.00	11.00
☐ 2418		ROCK AND ROLL STAGE SHOW ..	9.00	17.00	11.00
☐ 2532		ROCKIN' THE OLDIES	9.00	17.00	11.00
☐ 2533		ROCK AND ROLL PARTY	9.00	17.00	11.00
☐ 2534		ROCKIN' AND ROLLIN'	9.00	17.00	11.00
☐ 2564		ROCKIN' AROUND THE WORLD ..	9.00	17.00	11.00
☐ 2576		ROCKIN' AROUND EUROPE	7.00	13.00	11.00
☐ 2577		ROCKIN' AROUND THE AMERICAS	7.00	13.00	11.00
☐ 2615		ROCKIN' THE JOINT	6.00	11.00	8.50

MGM, 665105, LP

DECCA, ED 2168, EP

			Current Price Range		P/Y AVG
☐2616		ROCKIN' THE JOINT	6.00	11.00	8.50
☐2638		BILL HALEY'S CHICKS	6.00	11.00	8.50
☐2670		BILL HALEY AND HIS COMETS ...	6.00	11.00	8.50
☐2671		STRICTLY INSTRUMENTAL	6.00	11.00	8.50
		BILL HALEY AND THE COMETS—ALBUMS			
☐202 (M)	**ESSEX**	ROCK WITH BILL HALEY AND HIS COMETS	70.00	150.00	100.00
☐202 (M)	**TRANS WORLD**	ROCK WITH BILL HALEY AND HIS COMETS	17.00	38.00	35.00
☐5560 (M)	**DECCA**	SHAKE RATTLE AND ROLL (10" LP)....................	50.00	120.00	75.00
☐8225 (M)		ROCK AROUND THE CLOCK	14.00	34.00	30.00
☐8315 (M)		HE DIGS ROCK AND ROLL	12.00	29.00	25.00
☐8345 (M)		ROCK AND ROLL STAGE SHOW ..	12.00	29.00	25.00
☐8569 (M)		ROCKIN' THE OLDIES	10.00	25.00	22.50
☐8692 (M)		ROCKIN' AROUND THE WORLD ..	8.00	21.00	18.00
☐8692 (S)		ROCKIN' AROUND THE WORLD ..	12.00	29.00	25.00
☐8775 (M)		ROCKIN' THE JOINT	8.00	21.00	18.00
☐8775 (S)		ROCKIN' THE JOINT	12.00	29.00	25.00
☐8821 (M)		BILL HALEY'S CHICKS	7.00	17.00	15.00
☐8821 (S)		BILL HALEY'S CHICKS	9.00	25.00	22.50
☐8964 (M)		STRICTLY INSTRUMENTAL	6.00	15.00	13.50
☐8964 (S)		STRICTLY INSTRUMENTAL	8.00	21.00	18.00
☐1378 (M)	**WARNER BROTHERS**	BILL HALEY AND HIS COMETS ...	6.00	15.00	13.50
☐1378 (S)		BILL HALEY AND HIS COMETS ...	8.00	21.00	18.00
☐1391 (M)		HALEY'S JUKE BOX............	6.00	15.00	13.50
☐1391 (S)		HALEY'S JUKE BOX............	8.00	21.00	18.00

HALL AND OATES
SEE: GULLIVER

☐2922	**ATLANTIC**	GOODNIGHT AND GOOD MORNING/ (DJ) (by Whole Oates)	3.50	6.00	4.50
☐2939		I'M SORRY/(DJ)	3.25	5.50	4.00
☐3026		WHEN THE MORNING COMES ...	2.75	5.00	3.00
☐2993		SHE'S GONE/I'M JUST LIKE A KID.	2.75	5.00	3.00
☐3332		SHE'S GONE/I'M JUST LIKE A KID.	2.50	4.50	2.50
☐3397		IT'S UNCANNY/ LILY (ARE YOU UNHAPPY?)....	2.75	5.00	3.00
		HALL AND OATES—ALBUMS			
☐7242 (S)	**ATLANTIC**	WHOLE OATS.................	5.50	14.00	12.00
☐7269 (S)		ABANDONED LUNCHEONETTE ...	5.00	12.00	10.00
☐18109 (S)		WAR BABIES	5.00	12.00	10.00
☐547 (S)	**CHELSEA**	PAST TIMES BEHIND	6.00	15.00	13.50

LARRY HALL

☐1	**HOT**	SANDY/LOVIN' TREE	12.00	21.00	18.00
☐25007	**STRAND**	SANDY/LOVIN' TREE	3.00	5.00	3.50
☐25013		ROSEMARY/A GIRL LIKE YOU ...	3.00	5.00	3.50
☐25016		FOR EVERY BOY/ I'LL STAY SINGLE	2.75	4.50	3.00
☐25025		KOOL LUV/ THE GIRL I LEFT BEHIND	2.75	4.50	3.00
☐25029		SWEET LIPS/REBEL HEART	2.75	4.50	3.00
☐25048		THE ONE YOU LEFT BEHIND/ LADDER OF LOVE	2.75	4.50	3.00
		LARRY HALL—ALBUM			
☐1005 (M)	**STRAND**	SANDY AND OTHER LARRY HALL HITS	9.00	29.00	25.00

ROY HALL

☐9-29697	**DECCA**	WHOLE LOT OF SHAKIN' GOIN' ON/ALL BY MYSELF	11.00	23.00	15.00

HALL AND OATES

   One of today's most successful recording duos met by accident. Daryl Hall and John Oates were both students at Temple University in Philadelphia during the late 1960s. (Neither knew the other.) Hall was riding a school elevator one day, when an exhausted Oates entered at one of the floor stops. Oates, it turned out, was escaping a group of fraternity pranksters who had been chasing him.

   A casual conversation in the elevator ensued, and the two men discovered mutual interests in music. Hall played in a local group called the Temptones (named after Temple University). Oates was in a group named the Masters.

   When the elevator stopped, the two agreed to do some collaborating.

   Hall later drifted into a folk group called Gulliver. They made one Elektra album that flopped. Hall and Oates then teamed up as songwriter/singers during the early 1970s. Eventually, they secured a contract with Atlantic Records in New York. From their second album came the song "She's Gone." When first released, "She's Gone" became only a minor chart hit. But, after Hall and Oates switched to the RCA label in 1976, Atlantic reissued the same single — and "She's Gone" became a Top 10 smash in 1977, hot on the heels of RCA's "Sara Smile"! The Hall and Oates winning streak has continued unabated to this day.

			Current Price Range		P/Y AVG
☐9-29880		BLUE SUEDE SHOE/LUSCIOUS ..	11.00	23.00	15.00
☐9-29786		SEE YA LATER ALLIGATOR/ DON'T STOP NOW	11.00	23.00	15.00

GEORGE HAMILTON IV

☐420	**COLONIAL**	A ROSE AND A BABY RUTH/ IF YOU DON'T KNOW	14.00	24.00	20.00
☐9765	**ABC-PARAMOUNT**	A ROSE AND A BABY RUTH/ IF YOU DON'T KNOW	3.75	6.00	4.50
☐9782		ONLY ONE LOVE/IF I POSSESSED A PRINTING PRESS	3.25	5.50	4.00
☐9838		HIGH SCHOOL DANCE/ EVERYBODY'S BODY	5.00	8.50	7.00
☐9862		WHY DON'T THEY UNDERSTAND/ EVEN THO	3.00	5.00	3.50
☐9898		NOW AND FOR ALWAYS/ ONE HEART	3.00	5.00	3.50
☐9924		I KNOW WHERE I'M GOIN'/WHO'S TAKING YOU TO THE PROM? ..	3.00	5.00	3.50
☐9966		THE TWO OF US/LUCY, LUCY ...	2.75	4.50	3.00
☐10009		STEADY GAME/ CAN YOU BLAME US?	2.75	4.50	3.00
☐10028		GEE, I KNOW/YOUR SWEETHEART.	2.75	4.50	3.00
☐10059		LITTLE TOM/ONE LITTLE ACRE ..	2.75	4.50	3.00

GEORGE HAMILTON IV—ALBUMS

☐461 (M)	**ABC-PARAMOUNT**	BIG 15	9.00	25.00	22.50
☐461 (S)		BIG 15	14.00	34.00	30.00

HAPPENINGS

SEE: FOUR GRADUATES, HONOR SOCIETY

☐517	**B.T.PUPPY**	GIRLS ON THE GO-GO-GO	3.50	6.00	4.35
☐520		SEE YOU IN SEPTEMBER/ HE THINKS HE'S A HERO	3.25	5.50	4.00
☐522		GO AWAY LITTLE GIRL/TEA TIME	3.25	5.50	4.00
☐523		GOODNIGHT MY LOVE/ LILIES BY MONET	3.25	5.50	4.00
☐527		I GOT RHYTHM/ YOU'RE IN A BAD WAY	3.25	5.50	4.00
☐530		MY MAMMY/ I BELIEVE IN NOTHING	3.25	5.50	4.00
☐532		WHY DO FOOLS FALL IN LOVE/ WHEN SUMMER IS THROUGH .	3.00	5.00	3.65
☐538		MUSIC MUSIC MUSIC/ WHEN I LOCK MY DOOR	3.00	5.00	3.65
☐540		RANDY/ LOVE SONG OF MOM AND DAD .	3.00	5.00	3.65
☐542		SEALED WITH A KISS/ANYWAY .	3.00	5.00	3.65
☐543		BREAKING UP IS HARD TO DO/ ANYWAY	3.00	5.00	3.65
☐544		GIRL ON A SWING/ WHEN I LOCK MY DOOR	3.00	5.00	3.65
☐545		CRAZY RHYTHM/ LOVE SONG OF MOM AND DAD .	3.00	5.00	3.65
☐549		THAT'S ALL I WANT FROM YOU/ HE THINKS HE'S A HERO	3.00	5.00	3.65
☐5666	**JUBILEE**	WHERE DO I GO-BE IN (HARE KRISHNA)/NEW DAY COMIN' ..	3.00	5.00	3.65
☐5677		WON'T ANYBODY LISTEN?/ EL PASO COUNTY JAIL	3.00	5.00	3.65
☐5686		ANSWER ME, MY LOVE/ I NEED A WOMAN	3.00	5.00	3.65

			Current Price Range		P/Y AVG
☐5698		TOMORROW TODAY WILL BE YESTERDAY/CHAIN OF HANDS	3.00	5.00	3.65
☐5702		CRAZY LOVE/CHAIN OF HANDS ..	3.00	5.00	3.65
☐5712		LULLABY IN THE RAIN/I WISH YOU COULD KNOW ME (NAOMI)	3.00	5.00	3.65

HAPPENINGS—ALBUMS

☐1001 (M)	**B.T.PUPPY**	THE HAPPENINGS	7.00	17.00	15.00
☐1001 (S)		THE HAPPENINGS	9.00	25.00	22.50
☐1003 (M)		PSYCHLE	5.50	14.00	12.00
☐1003 (S)		PSYCHLE	8.00	21.00	18.00
☐1004 (S)		THE HAPPENINGS' GOLDEN HITS .	5.50	14.00	12.00
☐8028 (S)	**JUBILEE**	PIECE OF MIND	5.50	14.00	12.00

HARBOR LIGHTS (JAY AND THE AMERICANS)

☐422	**MALA**	ANGEL OF LOVE/ TICK-A-TICK-A-TOCK	7.00	13.00	9.00
☐77020	**JARO**	WHAT WOULD I DO WITHOUT YOU?/IS THAT TOO MUCH TO ASK?	7.00	13.00	9.00

BILLY HARLAN

☐9-55066	**BRUNSWICK**	SCHOOL HOUSE ROCK/ I WANNA BOP	30.00	70.00	66.00

HARMONY

☐SR-45-7A	**STARLIGHT**	SWEET WAS THE WINE/ GUILTY	17.00	33.00	21.00

HARPTONES

☐364	**ESSEX**	I'LL NEVER TELL/HONEY LOVE ..	20.00	34.00	30.00
☐1135	**BROADCAST**	MARIE/THAT'S THE WAY IT GOES	12.00	21.00	14.00
☐101	**BRUCE**	A SUNDAY KIND OF LOVE/ I'LL NEVER TELL	14.00	23.00	20.00
☐102		MY MEMORIES OF YOU/ IT WAS JUST FOR LAUGHS	14.00	23.00	20.00
☐104		I DEPENDED ON YOU/ MAMBO BOOGIE	20.00	34.00	30.00
☐109		FOREVER MINE/ WHY SHOULD I LOVE YOU? . . .	20.00	34.00	30.00
☐113		SINCE I FELL FOR YOU/ OBIDEE-OBIDEE-O	17.00	28.00	25.00
☐123		LOVING A GIRL LIKE YOU/ HIGH FLYING BABY	14.00	23.00	20.00
☐128		I ALMOST LOST MY MIND/ OU WEE BABY	14.00	23.00	20.00
☐101	**PARADISE**	LIFE IS BUT A DREAM/YOU KNOW YOU'RE DOING ME WRONG	14.00	23.00	20.00
☐103		IT ALL DEPENDS ON YOU/ I'VE GOT A NOTION	14.00	23.00	20.00
☐105		IT ALL DEPENDS ON YOU/ GUITAR SHUFFLE	12.00	21.00	18.00
☐100	**ANDREA**	WHAT IS YOUR DECISION?/ GIMME SOME	12.00	21.00	18.00
☐401	**TIP TOP**	MY MEMORIES OF YOU/ HIGH FLYIN' BABY	12.00	21.00	18.00
☐197	**RAMA**	THAT'S THE WAY IT GOES/ MARLEE	8.25	14.00	12.00
☐203		THREE WISHES/ THAT'S THE WAY IT GOES	8.25	14.00	12.00
☐214		ON SUNDAY AFTERNOON/ THE MASQUERADE IS OVER . . .	8.25	14.00	12.00
☐221		THE SHRINE OF ST. CECELIA/ OU WEE BABY	7.00	14.00	12.00

			Current Price Range		P/Y AVG
☐ 1029	GEE	WHAT DID I DO WRONG?/WHEN WILL I KNOW? (Carol Blades)	26.00	46.00	42.00
☐ 1045		CRY LIKE I CRIED/SO GOOD, SO FINE, YOU'RE MINE	9.50	17.00	15.00
☐ 8001	RAVEN	SUNDAY KIND OF LOVE/ MAMBO BOOGIE	9.50	17.00	15.00
☐ 9097	CUB	DEVIL IN VELVET/ YOUR LOVE IS A GOOD LOVE	5.50	11.00	9.00
☐ 540	COED	RAIN DOWN KISSES/ ANSWER ME, MY LOVE	5.50	11.00	9.00
☐ 102	COMPANION	ALL IN YOUR MIND/ THE LAST DANCE	4.50	7.50	6.00
☐ 103		WHAT WILL I TELL MY HEART/ FOOLISH ME	4.50	7.50	6.00
☐ 500	WARWICK	I REMEMBER/ LAUGHING ON THE OUTSIDE	3.50	6.00	4.50
☐ 512		LOVE ME COMPLETELY/ HIP TEENAGER	3.50	6.00	4.50
☐ 551		NO GREATER MIRACLE/ WHAT KIND OF A FOOL	3.50	6.00	4.50

EMMYLOU HARRIS

			Current Price Range		P/Y AVG
☐ 5679	JUBILEE	I'LL BE YOUR BABY TONIGHT/ I'LL NEVER FALL IN LOVE	5.50	11.00	9.00
☐ 5697		PADDY/FUGUE FOR THE OX	5.00	9.00	7.00
☐ 1326	REPRISE	TOO FAR GONE/ BOULDER TO BIRMINGHAM	3.50	6.00	4.35
☐ 1332		IF I COULD ONLY WIN YOUR LOVE/BOULDER TO BIRMINGHAM	3.25	5.50	4.00
☐ 1341		LIGHT OF THE STABLE/ BLUEBIRD WINE	3.25	5.50	4.00
☐ 1346		HERE, THERE AND EVERYWHERE/ TOGETHER AGAIN	3.25	5.50	4.00
☐ 1353		ONE OF THESE DAYS/ TILL I GAIN CONTROL AGAIN	3.25	5.50	4.00
☐ 1371		SWEET DREAMS/AMARILLO	3.25	5.50	4.00

EMMYLOU HARRIS—ALBUMS

☐ 8031 (S)	JUBILEE	GLIDING BIRD	12.00	29.00	25.00
☐ 2213 (S)	REPRISE	PIECES OF THE SKY	7.00	17.00	15.00
☐ 2236 (S)		ELITE HOTEL	7.00	17.00	15.00

GEORGE HARRISON
SEE: BEATLES

☐ 2995	APPLE	MY SWEET LORD/ISN'T IT A PITY	2.75	5.00	3.50
☐ 1828		WHAT IS LIFE?/APPLE SCRUFFS	2.75	5.00	3.50
☐ 1836		BANGLA-DESH/DEEP BLUE	2.75	5.00	3.50
☐ 1862		GIVE ME LOVE (GIVE ME PEACE ON EARTH)/MISS O'DELL	2.75	5.00	3.50
☐ 1877		DARK HORSE/ I DON'T CARE ANYMORE	2.75	5.00	3.50
☐ 1879		DING DONG, DING DONG/ HARI' ON TOUR (EXPRESS)	2.75	5.00	3.50
☐ 1884		YOU/WORLD OF STONE	2.75	5.00	3.50
☐ 1885		THIS GUITAR (CAN'T KEEP FROM CRYING)/MAYA LOVE	2.75	5.00	3.50

DARK HORSE SINGLES ARE WORTH UP TO $3.00 MINT

GEORGE HARRISON—ALBUMS

☐ 3350 (S)	APPLE	WONDERWALL MUSIC	9.00	29.00	25.00
☐ 639 (S)		ALL THINGS MUST PASS	7.00	17.00	15.00
☐ 3385 (S)		CONCERT FOR BANGLA-DESH	6.00	15.00	13.50
☐ 3410 (S)		LIVING IN THE MATERIAL WORLD	5.50	14.00	12.00
☐ 3418 (S)		DARK HORSE	5.50	14.00	12.00
☐ 3420 (S)		EXTRA TEXTURE	5.50	14.00	12.00
☐ 11578 (S)	CAPITOL	THE BEST OF GEORGE HAMILTON	5.00	12.00	10.00

GEORGE HARRISON

He was born on February 25, 1943, in the Wavertree section of Liverpool. In school, George was a rebel. He became the first in his class to grow long hair. He also took to wearing the tightest pants. (He wore tight black jeans under his standard ones, changing clothes at his school-bus stop.) He also fell in love with American rock-and-roll. Soon he got a guitar for a birthday gift. After that, he would practice by his radio each night, playing until his fingers actually bled.

Paul McCartney had once been refused a spot in John Lennon's Quarrymen band because Lennon though Paul too young. When Paul later told John about schoolmate George Harrison, Lennon had the same attitude: George was simply too young. McCartney was persistent, though, and George eventually won an audition. He was a shoo-in when he proved to John and Paul that he could outplay both of them.

During his Beatle days, Harrison was the first to show interest in the Indian sitar. He succeeded also in bringing the Beatles into his Indian religion during the late 1960s.

In 1970, George was sued for his first Apple hit of "My Sweet Lord". The melody, it seemed, was identical to that of "He's so Fine", the Chiffons' former number-one hit from 1963.

			Current Price Range		P/Y AVG

BOBBY HART

☐ 100	REEL	GIRL IN THE WINDOW/ JOURNEY OF LOVE	5.50	11.00	9.00
☐ 3039	ERA	GIRL IN THE WINDOW/ JOURNEY OF LOVE	3.25	5.50	4.00
☐ 507	BAMBOO	THE SPIDER AND THE FLY/ A GIRL I USED TO KNOW	5.00	9.00	7.00
☐ 017	INFINITY	TOO MANY TEARDROPS/ THE PEOPLE NEXT DOOR	3.75	6.00	4.50
☐ 022		LOVESICK BLUES/I THINK IT'S CALLED A HEARTACHE	3.75	5.50	4.50
☐ 1113	DCP	THAT'LL BE THE DAY/ TURN ON YOUR LOVE LIGHT	3.25	5.50	4.00
☐ 1142		BABY, LET YOUR HAIR DOWN/ JEALOUS FEELING	3.75	6.00	4.50
☐ 1152		CRY MY EYES OUT/ AROUND THE CORNER	4.50	7.50	6.00

ROCKY HART

☐ 9052	CUB	EVERYDAY/COME WITH ME	4.50	7.50	6.00
☐ 216	GLO	I PLAY THE PART OF A FOOL/ SOMEBODY STOLE MY BABY WHILE DOING THE TWIST	12.00	21.00	18.00

PHIL HARVEY (SPECTOR)

☐ 5583	IMPERIAL	BUMBERSHOOT/WILLY BOY	8.25	14.00	12.00

ALI HASSAN

☐ 103	PHILLES	MALAGUENA/CHOP STICKS	5.00	9.00	7.50

HASSLES
FEATURED: BILLY JOEL

☐ 50258	UNITED ARTISTS	EVERY STEP I TAKE (EVERY MOVE I MAKE)/I HEAR VOICES	5.50	11.00	9.00
☐ 50450		4 O'CLOCK IN THE MORNING/ LET ME BRING YOU TO THE SUNSHINE	6.00	11.50	9.50
☐ 50586		GREAT BALLS OF FIRE/ TRAVELING BAND	7.00	12.00	10.00

HASSLES—ALBUMS

☐ 6631 (S)		THE HASSLES	19.00	49.00	45.00
☐ 6699 (S)		HOUR OF THE WOLF	17.00	39.00	35.00

THE HAWK (JERRY LEE LEWIS)

☐ 3559	PHILLIPS INTERNATIONAL	IN THE MOOD/I GET THE BLUES WHEN IT RAINS	10.00	17.00	15.00

DALE HAWKINS

☐ 843	CHECKER	SEE YOU SOON, BABOON/ FOUR LETTER WORD	8.25	14.00	12.00
☐ 863		SUSIE-Q/ DON'T TREAT ME THIS WAY	3.75	6.00	4.50
☐ 876		BABY, BABY/MRS. MERGUITORY'S DAUGHTER	4.50	7.50	6.00
☐ 892		LITTLE PIG/TORNADO	4.50	7.50	6.00
☐ 900		LA-DO-DADA/CROSS TIES	3.50	6.00	4.35
☐ 906		A HOUSE, A CAR, AND A WEDDING RING/MY BABE	3.50	6.00	4.35
☐ 913		TAKE MY HEART/ SOMEDAY, ONE DAY	3.50	6.00	4.35
☐ 916		CLASS CUTTER (YEAH, YEAH)/ LONELY NIGHTS	3.50	6.00	4.35

			Current Price Range		P/Y AVG
☐923		AIN'T THAT LOVIN' YOU BABY/ MY DREAM	3.50	6.00	4.35
☐929		OUR TURN/LIFEGUARD MAN	3.50	6.00	4.35
☐934		LIZA JANE/ BACK TO SCHOOL BLUES	3.50	6.00	4.35
☐940		HOT DOG/DON'T BREAK YOUR PROMISE TO ME	3.50	6.00	4.35
☐944		EVERY LITTLE GIRL/ POOR LITTLE RHODE ISLAND	3.50	6.00	4.35
☐962		LINDA/WHO	3.50	6.00	4.35
☐970		GRANDMA'S HOUSE/ I WANT TO LOVE YOU	3.50	6.00	4.35
		DALE HAWKINS—ALBUM			
☐1429 (M)	**CHESS**	OH! SUZY-Q	39.00	110.00	100.00

RONNIE HAWKINS
FEATURED: HAWKS (THE BAND)

☐6128	**QUALITY**	HEY BO DIDDLEY/ LOVE ME LIKE YOU CAN	10.00	17.00	15.00
☐4154	**ROULETTE**	FORTY DAYS/ ONE OF THESE DAYS	3.50	6.00	4.35
☐4177		MARY LOU/NEED YOUR LOVIN'	3.50	6.00	4.35
☐4209		SOUTHERN LOVE/ LOVE ME LIKE YOU CAN	3.50	6.00	4.35
☐4228		LONELY HOURS/CLARA	3.50	6.00	4.35
☐4231		THE BALLAD OF CARYL CHESSMAN/DEATH OF FLOYD COLLINS	4.50	7.50	6.00
☐4249		RUBY BABY/HAYRIDE	3.50	6.00	4.35
☐4267		SUMMERTIME/ MISTER AND MISSISSIPPI	3.50	6.00	4.35
☐4311		COLD, COLD HEART/ NOBODY'S LONESOME FOR ME	3.50	6.00	4.35
☐4400		COME, LOVE/I FEEL GOOD	3.50	6.00	4.35
☐4483		BO DIDDLEY/WHO DO YOU LOVE	3.50	6.00	4.35
☐4503		HIGH BLOOD PRESSURE/ THERE'S A SCREW LOOSE	3.50	6.00	4.35
☐45016	**YORKVILLE**	WILL THE CIRCLE BE UNBROKEN HOME FROM THE FOREST	3.50	6.00	4.35
☐45019		REASON TO BELIEVE/MARY JANE	3.50	6.00	4.35
☐002	**HAWK**	GOT MY MOJO WORKIN'/ LET THE GOOD TIMES ROLL	3.50	6.00	4.35
☐106		BLUEBIRDS OVER THE MOUNTAIN/ DIDDLEY DADDY	3.50	6.00	4.35
☐301		MATCHBOX/LITTLE BIRD	3.50	6.00	4.35
☐302		DOWN IN THE ALLEY/ HOME FROM THE FOREST	3.50	6.00	4.35
☐305		FORTY DAYS/BITTER GREEN	3.50	6.00	4.35
☐1205		BLACK SHEEP BOY/PATRICIA	3.50	6.00	4.35
☐44060	**COTILLION**	DOWN IN THE ALLEY/MATCHBOX	3.25	5.50	4.00
☐44067		FORTY DAYS/BITTER GREEN	3.25	5.50	4.00
☐44076		ONE MORE NIGHT/LITTLE BIRD	3.25	5.50	4.00
☐8548	**MONUMENT**	LAWDY MISS CLAWDY/ CORA MAE	3.25	5.50	4.00
☐8561		LONESOME TOWN/KINKY	3.25	5.50	4.00
☐8571		DIDDLEY DADDY/CORA MAE	3.25	5.50	4.00
☐8573		BO DIDDLEY/LONELY HOURS	3.25	5.50	4.00
		RONNIE HAWKINS—ALBUMS			
☐25078 (M)	**ROULETTE**	RONNIE HAWKINS	14.00	35.00	30.00
☐25078 (S)		RONNIE HAWKINS	18.00	50.00	45.00
☐25102 (M)		MR. DYNAMO	12.00	29.00	25.00
☐25102 (S)		MR. DYNAMO	17.00	39.00	35.00
☐25120 (M)		FOLK BALLADS OF RONNIE HAWKINS	12.00	29.00	25.00

			Current Price Range		P/Y AVG
☐ 25120 (S)		FOLK BALLADS OF RONNIE HAWKINS	17.00	39.00	35.00
☐ 25137 (M)		THE SONGS OF HANK WILLIAMS .	8.00	21.00	18.00
☐ 25137 (S)		THE SONGS OF HANK WILLIAMS .	9.00	25.00	22.50
☐ 25255 (M)		THE BEST OF RONNIE HAWKINS .	8.00	21.00	18.00
☐ 25255 (S)		THE BEST OF RONNIE HAWKINS .	9.00	25.00	22.50
☐ 9019 (S)	COTILLION	RONNIE HAWKINS	6.00	14.00	12.00
☐ 9039 (S)		THE HAWK...................	6.00	14.00	12.00
☐ 31330 (S)	MONUMENT	ROCK AND ROLL RESURRECTION .	5.00	12.00	10.00
☐ 32940 (S)		THE GIANT OF ROCK AND ROLL ..	5.00	12.00	10.00

DEAN HAWLEY

			Current Price Range		P/Y AVG
☐ 524	DORE	PRETTY LITTLE MARY/NEW FAD .	3.25	5.50	4.00
☐ 536		GOOD MORNING MR. SUN/ BOSSMAN	3.25	5.50	4.00
☐ 543		I'LL NEVER BE A FOOL AGAIN/ WHERE IS MY ANGEL?	3.25	5.50	4.00
☐ 554		LOOK FOR A STAR/BOSSMAN ...	3.00	5.00	3.50
☐ 569		LIKE A FOOL/ STAY AT HOME BLUES	3.00	5.00	3.50
☐ 577		RAINBOW/HEY THERE	3.00	5.00	3.50
☐ 55359	LIBERTY	POCKETFUL OF RAINBOWS/ THAT DREAM COULD NEVER BE	3.00	5.00	3.50
☐ 55446		QUEEN OF THE ANGELS/ YOU CONQUERED	3.25	5.50	4.00

RON HAYDOCK

			Current Price Range		P/Y AVG
☐ 701	CHA-CHA	BE-BOP-A-JEAN/99 CHICKS (white label)	27.00	56.00	50.00
☐		BE-BOP-A-JEAN/99 CHICKS (red label)	5.00	10.00	8.00

ROY HEAD

			Current Price Range		P/Y AVG
☐ 194	TNT	ONE MORE TIME/DON'T BE BLUE	5.00	9.00	7.00
☐ 12116	SCEPTER	JUST A LITTLE BIT/ TREAT ME RIGHT	3.25	5.50	4.00
☐ 12124		GET BACK (PT. 1)/(PT. 2)	3.25	5.50	4.00
☐ 543	BACK BEAT	TEENAGE LETTER/PAIN	3.50	5.75	4.35
☐ 546		TREAT HER RIGHT/ SO LONG, MY LOVE	3.00	5.00	3.65
☐ 555		APPLE OF MY EYE/ I PASS THE DAY	3.00	5.00	3.65
☐ 560		MY BABE/PAIN	3.00	5.00	3.65
☐ 563		DRIVING WHEEL/ WIGGLIN' AND GIGGLIN'	3.00	5.00	3.65
☐ 571		TO MAKE A BIG MAN CRY/ DON'T CRY NO MORE	3.00	5.00	3.65
☐ 576		YOU'RE (ALMOST) TUFF/ TUSH HOG	3.00	5.00	3.65
☐ 583		NOBODY BUT ME/A GOOD MAN IS HARD TO FIND	3.00	5.00	3.65
☐ 257 9000	TMI RECORDS	PUFF OF SMOKE	4.00	7.00	4.50
		RADIO STATION COPY			
☐ 72799	MERCURY RECORDS	BROADWAY WALK/TURN OUT THE LIGHTS	4.00	7.00	4.50
		NOT ORIGINALLY FOR SALE			
☐ 72848		AIN'T GOING DOWN RIGHT/ LOVIN' MAN ON YOUR HANDS .	4.00	7.00	4.50
		ROY HEAD—ALBUMS			
☐ 101 (M)	TNT	ROY HEAD AND THE TRAITS	17.00	40.00	35.00
☐ 532 (M)	SCEPTER	TREAT ME RIGHT.............	7.00	17.00	15.00
☐ 532 (S)		TREAT ME RIGHT.............	8.00	25.00	22.50

HEARTBEATS

Jamaica, Queens, NY, was the origin of the Heartbeats. They left behind one of the finest rhythm-and-blues ballads of the mid-1950s...and a fine early 1960s rhythm-and-blues ballad under another name!

Jim "Shep" Sheppard formed the group. As with many New York City outfits, rehearsals were often confined to street corners. They eventually auditioned for Hull Records and were accepted. Their audition song of "Crazy For You" became their first Hull release.

Three singles later came "A Thousand Miles Away". (Shep wrote it about his girl friend; she had just moved to Texas.) Rama Records released the Hull master and "A Thousand Miles Away" became an instant rhythm-and-blues classic. Later Rama releases didn't do as well, though, and the Heartbeats drifted to other labels. As always, their songs were excellent. A good example is "Down on My Knees" on the Roulette label.

In 1961, Shep formed a new group called Shep and the Limelites. They recorded an "answer" song to "A Thousand Miles Away". "Daddy's Home" became a million-seller.

Shep Sheppard was later beaten to death and robbed. On January 24, 1970, his battered corpse was found in his parked car on the Long Island Expressway.

			Current Price Range		P/Y AVG

HEART

SEE: ANN WILSON AND THE DAYBREAKS

			Current Price Range		P/Y AVG
☐ 7011	**MUSHROOM**	MAGIC MAN/HOW DEEP IT GOES .	2.50	4.00	2.50
☐ 7021		CRAZY ON YOU/			
		DREAMBOAT ANNIE	2.50	4.00	2.50
☐ 7023		DREAMBOAT ANNIE/SING CHILD	2.50	4.00	2.50
☐ 7031		HEARTLESS/JUST THE WINE ...	2.50	4.00	2.50
☐ 7035		WITHOUT YOU/HERE SONG	2.75	4.50	3.00
☐ 7043		MAGAZINE/DEVIL DELIGHT	2.75	4.50	3.00

HEARTBEATS

SEE: SHEP AND THE LIMELITES

☐ 71200	**NETWORK**	TORMENTED/			
		AFTER EVERYBODY'S GONE ...	20.00	35.00	30.00
☐ 711	**HULL**	CRAZY FOR YOU/			
		ROCKIN'-N'-ROLLIN'-			
		N'-RHYTHMIN'-N'-BLUESIN' ..	20.00	35.00	30.00
☐ 713		DARLING HOW LONG?/			
		HURRY HOME BABY	20.00	35.00	30.00
☐ 716		YOUR WAY/PEOPLE ARE TALKING	17.00	29.00	25.00
☐ 720	**HULL**	A THOUSAND MILES AWAY/			
		OH BABY DON'T	22.00	39.00	35.00
☐ 216	**RAMA**	A THOUSAND MILES AWAY/			
		OH BABY DON'T	6.00	12.00	8.00
☐ 222		I WON'T BE THE FOOL ANYMORE/			
		WEDDING BELLS	6.00	12.00	8.00
☐ 231		EVERYBODY'S SOMEBODY'S			
		FOOL/I WANT TO KNOW	6.00	12.00	8.00
☐ 2011	**GUYDEN**	ONE MILLION YEARS/DARLING,			
		I WANT TO GET MARRIED	6.00	12.00	8.00
☐ 1043	**GEE**	WHEN I FOUND YOU/			
		HANDS OFF MY BABY	6.00	12.00	8.00
☐ 1047		AFTER NEW YEAR'S EVE/			
		500 MILES TO GO	6.00	12.00	8.00
☐ 1061		YOUR WAY/PEOPLE ARE TALKING	6.00	12.00	8.00
☐ 1062		DARLING HOW LONG?/			
		HURRY HOME BABY	5.00	8.50	7.00
☐ 4054	**ROULETTE**	DOWN ON MY KNEES/			
		I FOUND A JOB	4.50	7.50	6.00
☐ 4091		ONE DAY NEXT YEAR/			
		SOMETIMES I WONDER	4.50	7.50	6.00
☐ 4194		CRAZY FOR YOU/			
		DOWN ON MY KNEES	3.25	6.00	4.00

HEARTBEATS—ALBUMS

☐ 25107 (M)	**ROULETTE**	A THOUSAND MILES AWAY	19.00	50.00	45.00
☐ 25107 (S)		A THOUSAND MILES AWAY	28.00	65.00	60.00

HEARTBREAKERS

☐ 1381	**VIK**	1. 2. I LOVE YOU/			
		WITHOUT A CAUSE	14.00	24.00	20.00

HEARTBREAKERS (FRANK ZAPPA)

SEE: MOTHERS OF INVENTION

☐ 1381	**DONNA**	EVERYTIME I SEE YOU/			
		CRADLE ROCK	8.25	14.00	12.00

BOBBY HELMS

☐ 29947	**DECCA**	TENNESSEE ROCK AND ROLL/			
		I DON'T OWE YOU NOTHING ...	14.00	24.00	20.00
☐ 30194		FRAULEIN/HEARTSICK FEELING .	3.00	5.00	3.50
☐ 30423		MY SPECIAL ANGEL/STANDING			
		AT THE END OF THE WORLD ...	3.00	5.00	3.50
☐ 30513		JINGLE BELL ROCK/			
		CAPTAIN SANTA CLAUS	3.00	5.00	3.50

JIMI HENDRIX

On the night of September 18, 1970, an ambulance screamed to a stop before a London hotel. Moments later, the comatose body of James Marshall Hendrix was wheeled out. But Jimi Hendrix died before reaching the hospital. The cause of death was suffocation; he choked to death on his vomit when he regurgitated in his sleep. An autopsy showed that he had been smoking pot and ingesting alcohol and sleeping pills.

His birthdate was November 27, 1942, in Seattle, WA. Jimi paid $5.00 for his first guitar. His first gigs involved playing intermissions for a local dance.

He quit school at 16, toiled as a gardener for his father, joined the Army and became a paratrooper. (He broke his ankle on his 26th jump.) Hendrix returned to Seattle but soon left to go on the road with the likes of Little Richard and, later, the Isley Brothers.

In 1965, he formed Jimmy James and the Blue Flames in New York City. A year later, he went to England and began the Jimi Hendrix Experience. Hendrix then returned to American to tour briefly as a warmup act for the Monkees (!).

Jimi Hendrix was a flambouyant showman and a true pioneer in the world of psychedelic music during the late 1960s.

			Current Price Range		P/Y AVG
☐ 30557		JUST A LITTLE LONESOME/ LOVE MY LADY	2.75	4.75	3.50
☐ 30619		JACQUELINE/LIVING IN THE SHADOW OF THE PAST	2.75	4.75	3.50
☐ 30682		BORROWED DREAMS/ SCHOOLBOY CRUSH	2.75	4.75	3.50
☐ 30749		THE FOOL AND THE ANGEL/ A HUNDRED HEARTS	2.75	4.75	3.50
☐ 30831		NEW RIVER TRAIN/ MISS MEMORY	2.75	4.75	3.50
☐ 30886		I GUESS I'LL MISS THE PROM/ SOON IT CAN BE TOLD	2.75	4.75	3.50
☐ 30928		NO OTHER BABY/ YOU'RE NO LONGER MINE	2.75	4.75	3.50
☐ 30976		MY LUCKY DAY/HURRY BABY	2.75	4.75	3.50
☐ 31041		SOMEONE WAS ALREADY THERE/ TO MY SORROW	2.75	4.75	3.50
☐ 31103		LET ME BE THE ONE/ I WANT TO BE WITH YOU	2.75	4.75	3.50
☐ 31148		GUESS WE THOUGHT THE WORLD WOULD END/THE LONELY RIVER RHINE	2.75	4.75	3.50
☐ 31230		SAD-EYED BABY/ YOU'RE THE ONE	2.75	4.75	3.50
☐ 31287		MY GREATEST WEAKNESS/ HOW CAN YOU DIVIDE A LITTLE CHILD?	2.75	4.75	3.50
☐ 31356		ONE DEEP LOVE/ ONCE IN A LIFETIME	2.75	4.75	3.50
☐ 31403		YESTERDAY'S CHAMPAGNE/ THEN CAME YOU	2.75	4.75	3.50
		BOBBY HELMS—EPs			
☐ 2555	*DECCA*	SINGS TO MY SPECIAL ANGEL	5.50	11.00	9.00
☐ 2586		TONIGHT'S THE NIGHT	5.00	9.00	7.00
☐ 2629		BOBBY HELMS WITH THE ANITA KERR SINGERS	4.50	7.50	6.00
		BOBBY HELMS—ALBUM			
☐ 8638 (M)	*DECCA*	SINGS TO MY SPECIAL ANGEL	9.00	25.00	22.50

JIMI HENDRIX

			Current Price Range		P/Y AVG
☐ 167	*AUDIO FIDELITY*	NO SUCH ANIMAL (PT. 1)/(PT. 2)	9.50	17.00	15.00
☐ 0572	*REPRISE*	HEY JOE/51ST ANNIVERSARY	5.00	9.00	7.00
☐ 0597		PURPLE HAZE/ THE WIND CRIES MARY	3.25	5.50	4.00
☐ 0641		FOXEY LADY/HEY JOE	3.25	5.50	4.00
☐ 0665		UP FROM THE SKIES/ ONE RAINY WISH	3.25	5.50	4.00
☐ 0767		ALL ALONG THE WATCHTOWER/ BURNING OF THE MIDNIGHT LAMP	2.75	4.50	3.00
☐ 0792		CROSSTOWN TRAFFIC/ GYPSY EYES	2.75	4.50	3.00
☐ 0853		IF 6 WAS 9/STONE FREE	3.00	5.00	3.50
☐ 1000		FREEDOM/ANGEL	2.75	4.50	3.00
☐ 1044		STAR-SPANGLED BANNER/ DOLLY DAGGER	3.00	5.00	3.50
☐ 1082		JOHNNY B. GOODE/LOVER MAN	3.00	5.00	3.50
		JIMI HENDRIX—ALBUMS			
☐ 6261 (M)	*REPRISE*	ARE YOU EXPERIENCED?	8.00	21.00	18.00
☐ 6261 (S)		ARE YOU EXPERIENCED?	6.00	15.00	13.50
☐ 6281 (S)		AXIS: BOLD AS LOVE	6.00	15.00	13.50
☐ 6307 (S)		ELECTRIC LADYLAND	6.00	15.00	13.50
☐ 2025 (S)		SMASH HITS	6.00	15.00	13.50
☐ 2034 (S)		THE CRY OF LOVE	5.50	11.00	9.00

			Current Price Range		P/Y AVG
☐ 2049 (S)		HENDRIX IN THE WEST	5.50	11.00	9.00
☐ 2204 (S)		CRASH LANDING	5.50	11.00	9.00
☐ 2229 (S)		MIDNIGHT LIGHTNING	5.50	11.00	9.00

HERD
FEATURED: PETER FRAMPTON

☐ 1588	**FONTANA**	I CAN FLY/UNDERSTAND ME	4.00	7.00	4.75
☐ 1602		FROM THE UNDERGROUND/ SWEET WILLIAM	4.00	7.00	4.75
☐ 1610		COME ON, BELIEVE ME/ PARADISE LOST	4.00	7.00	4.75
☐ 1618		I DON'T WANT OUR LOVING TO DIE/OUR FAIRY TALE	4.00	7.00	4.75
		HERD—ALBUM			
☐ 67579 (S)	**FONTANA**	LOOKIN' THROUGH YOU	12.00	21.00	18.00

HERMAN'S HERMITS

☐ 13280	**MGM**	I'M INTO SOMETHING GOOD/ YOUR HAND IN MINE	3.00	5.00	3.65
☐ 13310		CAN'T YOU HEAR MY HEARTBEAT/ I KNOW WHY	3.00	5.00	3.65
☐ 13332		SILHOUETTES/ WALKIN' WITH MY ANGEL	3.00	5.00	3.65
☐ 13341		MRS. BROWN, YOU'VE GOT A LOVELY DAUGHTER/ I GOTTA DREAM ON	3.00	5.00	3.65
☐ 13354		WONDERFUL WORLD/ TRAVELING LIGHT	3.00	5.00	3.65
☐ 13367		I'M HENRY VIII I AM/ THE END OF THE WORLD	3.00	5.00	3.65
☐ 13398		JUST A LITTLE BIT BETTER/ SEA CRUISE	3.00	5.00	3.65
☐ 13437		A MUST TO AVOID/ THE MAN WITH THE CIGAR	3.00	5.00	3.65
☐ 13462		LISTEN PEOPLE/GOT A FEELING	3.00	5.00	3.65
☐ 13500		LEANING ON THE LAMP POST/ HOLD ON	3.00	5.00	3.65
☐ 13548		THIS DOOR SWINGS BOTH WAYS/ FOR LOVE	3.00	5.00	3.65
☐ 13603		DANDY/MY RESERVATIONS HAVE BEEN CONFIRMED	3.00	5.00	3.65
☐ 13639		EAST WEST/WHAT IS WRONG, WHAT IS RIGHT	3.00	5.00	3.65
☐ 13681		THERE'S A KIND OF HUSH/ NO MILK TODAY	3.00	5.00	3.65
☐ 13761		DON'T GO OUT INTO THE RAIN/ MOONSHINE MEN	3.00	5.00	3.65
☐ 13787		MUSEUM/THE LAST BUS HOME	3.00	5.00	3.65
☐ 13885		I CAN TAKE OR LEAVE YOUR LOVING/MARCELS	3.00	5.00	3.65
☐ 13934		SLEEPY JOE/JUST ONE GIRL	3.00	5.00	3.65
☐ 13973		SUNSHINE GIRL/ NOBODY NEEDS TO KNOW	3.00	5.00	3.65
☐ 13994		THE MOST BEAUTIFUL THING IN LIFE/OOH! SHE'S DONE IT AGAIN!	3.00	5.00	3.65
☐ 14035		SOMETHING'S HAPPENING/ LITTLE MISS SORROW, CHILD OF TOMORROW	3.00	5.00	3.65
☐ 14060		MY SENTIMENTAL FRIEND/ MY LADY	3.00	5.00	3.65
☐ 14100		IT'S ALRIGHT NOW/THE STAR	3.00	5.00	3.65
		HERMAN'S HERMITS—ALBUMS			
☐ 4282 (M)	**MGM**	INTRODUCING HERMAN'S HERMITS	7.00	17.00	15.00

			Current Price Range		P/Y AVG
☐ 4282 (S)		INTRODUCING HERMAN'S HERMITS	9.00	25.00	22.50
☐ 4295 (M)		ON TOUR	6.00	15.00	13.50
☐ 4295 (S)		ON TOUR	8.00	21.00	18.00
☐ 4315 (M)		THE BEST OF HERMAN'S HERMITS	6.00	15.00	13.50
☐ 4315 (S)		THE BEST OF HERMAN'S HERMITS	8.00	21.00	18.00
☐ 4342 (M)		HOLD ON!	6.00	15.00	13.50
☐ 4342 (S)		HOLD ON!	8.00	21.00	18.00
☐ 4386 (M)		BOTH SIDES OF HERMAN'S HERMITS	6.00	15.00	13.50
☐ 4386 (S)		BOTH SIDES OF HERMAN'S HERMITS	8.00	21.00	18.00
☐ 4416 (M)		THE BEST OF HERMAN'S HERMITS, VOL. II	5.50	14.00	12.00
☐ 4416 (S)		THE BEST OF HERMAN'S HERMITS, VOL. II	7.00	17.00	15.00
☐ 4438 (M)		THERE'S A KIND OF HUSH ALL OVER THE WORLD	5.50	14.00	12.00
☐ 4438 (S)		THERE'S A KIND OF HUSH ALL OVER THE WORLD	7.00	17.00	15.00
☐ 4478 (M)		BLAZE	5.50	14.00	12.00
☐ 4478 (S)		BLAZE	7.00	17.00	15.00
☐ 4505 (M)		THE BEST OF HERMAN'S HERMITS, VOL. III	7.00	17.00	15.00
☐ 4505 (S)		THE BEST OF HERMAN'S HERMITS, VOL. III	5.50	14.00	12.00
☐ 4548 (M)		MRS. BROWN, YOU'VE GOT A LOVELY DAUGHTER	7.00	17.00	15.00
☐ 4548 (S)		MRS. BROWN, YOU'VE GOT A LOVELY DAUGHTER	5.50	14.00	12.00

ERSEL HICKEY

☐ 9263	*EPIC*	BLUEBIRDS OVER THE MOUNTAIN/ HANGIN' AROUND	3.25	6.00	4.00
☐ 9278		GOIN' DOWN THE ROAD/ LOVER'S LAND	5.50	11.00	9.00
☐ 9298		YOU NEVER CAN TELL/ WEDDING DAY	3.25	6.00	4.00
☐ 9309		DON'T BE AFRAID OF LOVE/ YOU THREW A DART	3.00	5.00	3.50
☐ 9357		WHAT DO YOU WANT?/ LOVE IN BLOOM	3.00	5.00	3.50
☐ 602	*TOOT*	TRYIN' TO GET TO YOU/ BLUE SKIES	3.00	5.00	3.50
☐ 3165	*LAURIE*	SOME ENCHANTED EVENING/ PUT YOUR MIND AT EASE	3.00	5.00	3.50
☐ 151	*JANUS*	BLUEBIRDS OVER THE MOUNTAIN/ SELF MADE MAN	2.75	4.50	3.00

HI-FIVES

☐ 30576	*DECCA*	MY FRIEND/HOW CAN I WIN? . . .	9.50	17.00	15.00
☐ 30657		DOROTHY/ JUST A SHOULDER TO CRY ON .	5.50	11.00	9.00
☐ 30744		WHAT'S NEW, WHAT'S NEW/ LONELY	5.00	9.00	7.00

HIGH NUMBERS (WHO)
FEATURED: ROGER DALTRY

☐ 480	*FONTANA*	ZOOT SUIT/I'M THE FACE (British Release)	160.00	300.00	210.00

ERSEL HICKEY

Ersel Hickey was born in the South during the late 1930s. As did many boys in that area and during that time, he grew into adolescence listening to the black r & b sound as well as country music. He also learned to play the guitar—first a Spanish six-string, then an electric.

He worked after school as a locksmith and planned on entering that profession. But Hickey became restless and quit school during his sophomore year. Only fifteen, Ersel Hickey left home to tour and sing with a carnival. He felt he had musical talent, as he had earlier won $500 imitating crooner Johnny Ray in a talent contest.

Ersel wrote "Bluebirds Over the Mountain" and approached Epic Records with it early in 1958. Singing in a style much like Elvis Presley and Gene Vincent, "Bluebirds Over the Mountain" by Ersel Hickey proved most impressive to Epic. The song, one of the shortest records in rock history, was only a minor chart single. Later songs—including the great "Goin' Down the Road"—failed to establish Hickey's name as anything other than a "one-shot" artist.

			Current Price Range		P/Y AVG

JOEL HILL

			Current Price Range		P/Y AVG
☐519	TRANS-AMERICAN	I THOUGHT IT OVER/ LITTLE LOVER	14.00	35.00	30.00

EDDIE HODGES

☐1397	CADENCE	I'M GONNA KNOCK ON YOUR DOOR/AIN'T GONNA WASH FOR A WEEK	3.00	5.00	3.50
☐1410		BANDIT OF MY DREAMS/ MUGMATES	3.00	5.00	3.50
☐1421		(GIRLS, GIRLS, GIRLS) MADE TO LOVE/I MAKE BELIEVE IT'S YOU	3.00	5.00	3.50
☐42649	COLUMBIA	SEEIN' IS BELIEVIN'/SECRET ...	2.75	4.50	3.00
☐42811		RAININ' IN MY HEART/HALFWAY	3.00	5.00	3.50
☐52697		TOO SOON TO KNOW/ WOULD YOU COME BACK	2.75	4.50	3.00
☐13219	MGM	JUST A KID IN LOVE/AVALANCHE	2.75	4.50	3.00
☐153	AURORA	NEW ORLEANS/HARD TIMES FOR YOUNG LOVERS	2.75	4.50	3.00
☐156		LOVE MINUS ZERO/ THE WATER IS OVER MY HEAD .	2.75	4.50	3.00
☐161		HITCH HIKE/OLD RAG MAN	2.75	4.50	3.00

RON HOLDEN
PRODUCER: BRUCE JOHNSTON

☐10	NITE OWL	LOVE YOU SO/MY BABE	22.00	40.00	36.00
☐1315	DONNA	LOVE YOU SO/MY BABE	3.50	6.00	4.35
☐1324		GEE BUT I'M LONESOME/ SUSIE JANE	3.50	6.00	4.35
☐1328		TRUE LOVE CAN BE/ EVERYTHING'S GONNA BE ALRIGHT	3.50	6.00	4.35
☐1331		YOUR LINE IS BUSY/WHO SAYS THERE AIN'T NO SANTA CLAUS	3.50	6.00	4.35
☐1335		LET NO ONE TELL YOU/ THE BIG SHOE	3.50	6.00	4.35
☐1338		SO DEARLY/BRING ME HAPPINESS (Rosie and Ron) ...	3.50	6.00	4.35

RON HOLDEN—ALBUM

| ☐2111 (M) | DONNA | LOVE YOU SO .... | 14.00 | 34.00 | 30.00 |

EDDIE HOLLAND

☐102	TAMLA	MERRY-GO-ROUND/IT MOVES ME	34.00	54.00	48.00
☐172	UNITED ARTISTS	MERRY-GO-ROUND/IT MOVES ME	4.50	7.50	6.00
☐1021	MOTOWN	JAMIE/TAKE A CHANCE ON ME ..	3.25	5.50	4.00
☐1026		YOU DESERVE WHAT YOU GOT/ LAST NIGHT I HAD A VISION ...	3.25	5.50	4.00
☐1030		WHAT ABOUT ME?/ IF CLEOPATRA TOOK A CHANCE	3.25	5.50	4.00
☐1031		IF IT'S LOVE/IT'S NOT TOO LATE	3.25	5.50	4.00
☐1036		DARLING, I HUM OUR SONG/ JUST A FEW MORE DAYS	3.25	5.50	4.00
☐1043		BRENDA/BABY SHAKE	3.25	5.50	4.00
☐1049		I'M ON THE OUTSIDE LOOKING IN/ I COULDN'T CRY IF I WANTED TO	3.25	5.50	4.00
☐1052		LEAVING HERE/BRENDA........	3.25	5.50	4.00
☐1058		JUST AIN'T ENOUGH LOVE/ LAST NIGHT I HAD A VISION ...	3.25	5.50	4.00
☐1063		CANDY TO ME/IF YOU DON'T WANT MY LOVE	3.25	5.50	4.00

			Current Price Range		P/Y AVG

EDDIE HOLLAND—ALBUM

□604 (M)	*MOTOWN*	EDDIE HOLLAND	9.00	25.00	22.50

HOLLIES

□55674	*LIBERTY*	STAY/NOW'S THE TIME	8.25	14.00	12.00
□66026	*IMPERIAL*	JUST ONE LOOK/KEEP OFF			
		THAT FRIEND OF MINE	3.50	6.00	4.35
□66044		HERE I GO AGAIN/LUCILLE	3.50	6.00	4.35
□66070		COME ON BACK/WE'RE THROUGH .	3.50	6.00	4.35
□6099		NOBODY/YES I WILL	3.50	6.00	4.35
□66119		I'M ALIVE/YOU KNOW HE DID . . .	3.50	6.00	4.35
□66134		LOOK THROUGH ANY WINDOW/			
		SO LONELY	3.25	5.50	4.00
□66158		I CAN'T LET GO/			
		I'VE GOT A WAY OF MY OWN . .	3.25	5.50	4.00
□66186		BUS STOP/DON'T RUN AND HIDE	3.25	5.50	4.00
□66214		STOP STOP STOP/IT'S YOU	3.25	5.50	4.00
□66231		ON A CAROUSEL/			
		ALL THE WORLD IS LOVE	3.00	5.00	3.50
□66240		PAY YOU BACK WITH INTEREST/			
		WHATCHA GONNA DO 'BOUT IT	3.00	5.00	3.50
□66258		JUST ONE LOOK/			
		RUNNING THROUGH THE NIGHT	3.00	5.00	3.50
□66271		IF I NEED SOMEONE/			
		I'LL BE TRUE TO YOU	3.00	5.00	3.50
□50079	*UNITED ARTISTS*	AFTER THE FOX/THE FOX TROT			
		(with Peter Sellers)	5.50	11.00	9.00
□10180	*EPIC*	CARRIE-ANNE/SIGNS THAT			
		WILL NEVER CHANGE	3.00	5.00	3.65
□10234		KING MIDAS IN REVERSE/			
		WATER ON THE BRAIN	3.00	5.00	3.65
□10251		DEAR ELOISE/WHEN YOUR			
		LIGHTS TURNED ON	3.00	5.00	3.65
□10298		JENNIFER ECCLES/TRY IT	3.00	5.00	3.65
□10361		DO THE BEST YOU CAN/			
		ELEVATED OBSERVATIONS . . .	3.00	5.00	3.65
□10400		LISTEN TO ME/			
		EVERYTHING IS SUNSHINE . . .	3.00	5.00	3.65
□10454		SORRY SUZANNE/			
		NOT THAT WAY AT ALL	3.00	5.00	3.65
□10532		HE AIN'T HEAVY, HE'S MY			
		BROTaER/COS YOU LIKE			
		TO LOVE ME	3.00	5.00	3.65
□10613		I CAN'T TELL THE BOTTOM FROM			
		THE TOP/MAD PROFESSOR			
		BLYTHE	3.00	5.00	3.65
□10677		GASOLINE ALLEY BRED/			
		DANDELION WINE	3.00	5.00	3.65
□10716		MAN WITHOUT A HEART/			
		SURVIVAL OF THE FITTEST . . .	3.00	5.00	3.65
□10754		HEY WILLIE/			
		ROW THE BOAT ASHORE	3.00	5.00	3.65
□10842		OH, GRANNY/THE BABY	3.00	5.00	3.65
□10871		LONG COOL WOMAN (IN A BLACK			
		DRESS)/LOOK WHAT			
		WE'VE GOT	3.00	5.00	3.65
□10920		LONG DARK ROAD/INDIAN GIRL .	3.00	5.00	3.65
□10951		MAGIC WOMAN TOUCH/			
		BLUE IN THE MORNING	3.00	5.00	3.65
□10989		JESUS WAS A CROSSMAKER/			
		I HAD A DREAM	3.00	5.00	3.65
□11025		SLOW DOWN/			
		WON'T WE FEEL GOOD	3.00	5.00	3.65

			Current Price Range		P/Y AVG
□ 11051		BORN A MAN/THE DAY CURLY BILLY SHOT DOWN CRAZY SAM McGEE	3.00	5.00	3.65
□ 11100		THE AIR THAT I BREATHE/ NO MORE RIDERS	3.00	5.00	3.65
□ 50029		DON'T LET ME DOWN/ LAY INTO THE MUSIC	3.00	5.00	3.65
□ 50086		SANDY/ SECOND-HAND HANG-UPS	3.00	5.00	3.65
□ 50110		ANOTHER NIGHT/ TIME MACHINE JIVE	3.00	5.00	3.65
□ 50144		I'M DOWN/LOOK OUT JOHNNY ..	3.00	5.00	3.65
□ 50204		WRITE ON/CROCODILE WOMAN .	3.00	5.00	3.65
□ 50359		SANDY/ SECOND-HAND HANG-UPS	3.00	5.00	3.65
□ 50422		DRAGGIN' MY HEELS/ I WON'T MOVE OVER	3.00	5.00	3.65

HOLLIES—ALBUMS

□ 9265 (M)	IMPERIAL	HERE I GO AGAIN	9.00	25.00	22.50
□ 12265 (S)		HERE I GO AGAIN	14.00	34.00	30.00
□ 9299 (M)		HEAR! HEAR!.................	8.00	21.00	18.00
□ 12299 (S)		HEAR! HEAR	11.00	29.00	25.00
□ 9312 (M)		THE HOLLIES	8.00	21.00	18.00
□ 12312 (S)		THE HOLLIES	12.00	29.00	25.00
□ 9330 (M)		BUS STOP	7.00	17.00	15.00
□ 12330 (S)		BUS STOP	9.00	25.00	22.50
□ 9339 (M)		STOP! STOP! STOP!	7.00	17.00	15.00
□ 12339 (S)		STOP! STOP! STOP!	9.00	25.00	22.50
□ 9350 (M)		GREATEST HITS..............	6.00	15.00	13.50
□ 12350 (S)		GREATEST HITS..............	8.00	21.00	18.00
□ 24315 (M)	EPIC	EVOLUTION	6.00	15.00	13.50
□ 26315 (S)		EVOLUTION	7.00	17.00	15.00
□ 24344 (M)		DEAR ELOISE/ KING MIDAS IN REVERSE	6.00	15.00	13.50
□ 26344 (S)		DEAR ELOISE/ KING MIDAS IN REVERSE	7.00	17.00	15.00
□ 26447 (S)		WORDS AND MUSIC BY BOB DYLAN	6.00	15.00	10.00
□ 26538 (S)		HE AIN'T HEAVY, HE'S MY BROTHER	6.00	15.00	10.00
□ 30255 (S)		MOVING FINGER	6.00	15.00	10.00
□ 30958 (S)		DISTANT LIGHT	6.00	15.00	10.00
□ 31992 (S)		ROMANY	6.00	15.00	10.00
□ 33387 (S)		ANOTHER NIGHT	6.00	15.00	10.00

BUDDY HOLLY

SEE: CRICKETS, LOU GIORDANO, IVAN, WAYLON JENNINGS, NORMAN PETTY TRIO

□ 29854	DECCA	LOVE ME/ BLUE DAYS, BLACK NIGHTS ..	35.00	65.00	40.00
□ 30166		MODERN DON JUAN/ YOU ARE MY ONE DESIRE	28.00	48.00	33.00
□ 30534		THAT'LL BE THE DAY/ROCK AROUND WITH OLLIE VEE	45.00	90.00	58.00
□ 30543		LOVE ME/ YOU ARE MY ONE DESIRE	25.00	45.00	31.00
□ 30650		GIRL ON MY MIND/TING-A-LING .	29.00	53.00	35.00
□ 61852	CORAL	WORDS OF LOVE/MAILMAN, BRING ME NO MORE BLUES ...	65.00	120.00	78.00
□ 61885		PEGGY SUE/EVERYDAY	7.00	11.00	8.00
□ 61947		I'M GONNA LOVE YOU TOO/ LISTEN TO ME	8.00	14.00	9.00
□ 61985		RAVE ON/TAKE YOUR TIME	8.00	14.00	9.00
□ 62006		EARLY IN THE MORNING/ NOW WE'RE ONE	8.00	14.00	9.00

BUDDY HOLLY

He began life as Charles Hardin Holley. His birthdate was September 7, 1936, and he was born in Lubbock, TX. Buddy (his school nickname) began playing the violin, but soon switched to guitar. Later, he and classmate Bob Montgomery formed the Buddy and Bob duo. They landed a Sunday afternoon radio show in Lubbock during their high school days.

Buddy and Bob opened shows for Bill Haley and the Comets and Elvis Presley when they played Lubbock. At one such show, a Decca Records scout signed Holley. Buddy's name was misspelled as Holly on his Decca contract; the mistake remained.

Two country-rock singles evolved from a trio of Nashville sessions. Both failed to sell. Buddy then formed a hometown quartet. They journeyed to Clovis, NM, and came under the aegis of Norman Petty.

As a solo artist, Buddy had one major hit with "Peggy Sue". It was originally "Cindy Lou", written for Buddy's four-year-old niece. (Peggy Sue Garrow was drummer Jerry Allison's girl friend at the time.)

In 1958, Buddy married Maria Elena Santiago after a two-week courtship. He split with the Crickets, set up residence in New York City and later died tragically in a plane crash on February 3, 1959, outside of Mason City, IA.

			Current Price Range		P/Y AVG
☐ 62051		HEARTBEAT/WELL . . . ALL RIGHT .	8.00	14.00	9.00
☐ 62074		IT DOESN'T MATTER ANYMORE/ RAINING IN MY HEART	8.00	14.00	9.00
☐ 62134		PEGGY SUE GOT MARRIED/ CRYING, WAITING, HOPING	21.00	38.00	24.00
☐ 62210		TRUE LOVE WAYS/ THAT MAKES IT TOUGH	21.00	38.00	24.00
☐ 62283		YOU'RE SO SQUARE/VALLEY OF TEARS (Canadian Release)	21.00	38.00	24.00
☐ 62329		REMINISCING/WAIT TILL THE SUN SHINES NELLIE	13.00	25.00	15.00
☐ 62352		TRUE LOVE WAYS/BO DIDDLEY . . .	10.00	18.00	11.00
☐ 62369		BROWN EYED HANDSOME MAN/ WISHING	10.00	18.00	11.00
☐ 62390		I'M GONNA LOVE YOU TOO/ ROCK AROUND WITH OLLIE VEE .	10.00	18.00	11.00
☐ 62448		SLIPPIN' AND SLIDIN'/ WHAT TO DO	17.00	32.00	20.00
☐ 62554		RAVE ON/EARLY IN THE MORNING .	13.00	21.00	14.00
☐ 62558		LOVE IS STRANGE/ YOU'RE THE ONE	12.00	20.00	12.50
		BUDDY HOLLY—EPs			
☐ 2575	**DECCA**	THAT'LL BE THE DAY	175.00	300.00	310.00
☐ 81169	**CORAL**	LISTEN TO ME	35.00	70.00	40.00
☐ 81182		THE BUDDY HOLLY STORY	28.00	50.00	34.00
☐ 81191		PEGGY SUE GOT MARRIED	28.00	50.00	34.00
☐ 81193		BROWN EYED HANDSOME MAN . . .	28.00	50.00	34.00
		BUDDY HOLLY—ALBUMS			
☐ 8707 (M)	**DECCA**	THAT'LL BE THE DAY (flat black label)	125.00	280.00	200.00
☐ 8707 (M)		THAT'LL BE THE DAY (rainbow label)	95.00	200.00	135.00
☐ 57210 (M)	**CORAL**	BUDDY HOLLY	35.00	75.00	49.00
☐ 57279 (M)		THE BUDDY HOLLY STORY	17.00	33.00	22.00
☐ 57279 (S)		THE BUDDY HOLLY STORY	20.00	42.00	29.00
☐ 57326 (M)		THE BUDDY HOLLY STORY, VOL. II .	17.00	33.00	22.00
☐ 57326 (S)		THE BUDDY HOLLY STORY, VOL. II .	18.00	40.00	27.00
☐ 57405 (M)		BUDDY HOLLY AND THE CRICKETS	14.00	31.00	21.00
☐ 57405 (S)		BUDDY HOLLY AND THE CRICKETS	18.00	40.00	27.00
☐ 57426 (M)		REMINISCING	14.00	31.00	21.00
☐ 57426 (S)		REMINISCING	18.00	40.00	27.00
☐ 57450 (M)		SHOWCASE	11.00	26.00	17.00
☐ 57450 (S)		SHOWCASE	16.00	35.00	24.00
☐ 57463 (M)		HOLLY IN THE HILLS	11.00	26.00	17.00
☐ 57463 (S)		HOLLY IN THE HILLS	17.00	36.00	24.00
☐ 57492 (M)		GREATEST HITS	9.00	22.00	15.00
☐ 57492 (S)		GREATEST HITS	13.00	32.00	20.00

HOLLYHAWKS

☐ 5441	**JUBILEE**	I CRY ALL THE TIME/ WHEN CAME THE FALL	12.00	24.00	22.00

HOLLYWOOD ARGYLES

FEATURED: KIM FOWLEY, GARY PAXTON

☐ 5905	**LUTE**	ALLEY-OOP/ SHO KNOW A LOT ABOUT LOVE	3.50	6.00	4.35
☐ 5908		GUN TOTIN' CRITTER NAMED JACK/BUG EYE	3.50	6.00	4.35
☐ 6002		HULLY GULLY/SO FINE	3.50	6.00	4.35
☐ 752	**PAXLEY**	YOU'VE BEEN TORTURING ME/ THE GRUBBLE	3.25	5.50	4.00
☐ 691	**CHATTAHOOCHIE**	LONG HAIRED UNSQUARE DUDE NAMED JACK/OLE'	3.25	5.50	4.00

DECCA, DL8707, LP

CORAL, CRL 57492, LP

			Current Price Range		P/Y AVG
☐8674	**FELSTED**	BOSSY NOVER/			
		FIND ANOTHER WAY	3.25	5.50	4.00
☐105	**KAMMY**	ALLEY OOP '66/			
		DO THE FUNKY FOOT	3.25	5.50	4.00
		HOLLYWOOD ARGYLES—ALBUM			
☐9001 (M)	**LUTE**	ALLEY-OOP	38.00	95.00	90.00

HOLLYWOOD SAXONS

			Current Price Range		P/Y AVG
☐101	**FAN CLUB**	AGAIN (SUNDAY KIND OF LOVE)/			
		A CASUAL KISS	19.00	37.00	23.00
☐631	**SWINGIN'**	EVERYDAY'S A HOLIDAY/L.A.			
		LOVER	5.00	9.00	7.50
☐651		I'M YOUR MAN/IT'S YOU	5.00	9.50	7.50

HOLLYWOOD TORNADOES
SEE: TORNADOES

☐101	**AERTAUM**	THE GREMIE (PT. 1)/(PT. 2)	3.25	5.50	4.00
☐102		MOON DAWG/			
		THE INEBRIATED SURFER	3.25	5.50	4.00

THE HONDELLS
FEATURED: GARY USHER

☐72324	**MERCURY**	LITTLE HONDA/HOT ROD HIGH ..	3.00	5.00	3.50
☐72366		MY BUDDY SEAT/			
		YOU'RE GONNA RIDE WITH ME	3.00	5.00	3.50
☐72405		LITTLE SIDEWALK SURFER GIRL/			
		COME ON (PACK IT ON)	3.00	5.00	3.50
☐72443		SEA OF LOVE/DO AS I SAY	3.00	5.00	3.50
☐72479		YOU MEET THE NICEST PEOPLE ON			
		A HONDA/SEA CRUISE	3.00	5.00	3.50
☐72563		YOUNGER GIRL/			
		ALL-AMERICAN GIRL	2.75	5.00	3.00
		HONDELLS—ALBUMS			
☐20940 (M)	**MERCURY**	GO LITTLE HONDA	8.00	21.00	18.00
☐20940 (S)		GO LITTLE HONDA	12.00	29.00	25.00
☐20982 (M)		THE HONDELLS	7.00	17.00	15.00
☐20982 (S)		THE HONDELLS	9.00	25.00	22.50

HONEYBEES
FEATURED: CAROLE KING

☐1939	**FONTANA**	ONE WONDERFUL NIGHT/			
		SHE DON'T DESERVE YOU	5.00	15.00	12.50
☐611	**VEE JAY**	NO GUY/ONE GIRL, ONE BOY	3.00	5.00	3.75

HONEYCOMBS

☐7707	**INTERPHON**	HAVE I THE RIGHT?/			
		PLEASE DON'T PRETEND AGAIN	3.25	5.50	4.00
☐7713		I CAN'T STOP/			
		I'LL CRY TOMORROW	3.25	5.50	4.00
☐7716		THAT'S THE WAY/COLOR SLIDE .	3.25	5.50	4.00
☐5634	**WARNER BROTHERS**	I'LL SEE YOU TOMORROW/			
		SOMETHING BETTER			
		BEGINNING	3.25	5.50	4.00
☐5655		I CAN'T GET THROUGH TO YOU/			
		THAT'S THE WAY	3.25	5.50	4.00
☐5803		WHO IS SYLVIA/			
		HOW WILL I KNOW?	3.25	5.50	4.00
		HONEYCOMBS—ALBUMS			
☐88001 (M)	**VEE JAY**	HERE ARE THE HONEYCOMBS ...	18.00	49.00	45.00
☐88001 (M)	**INTERPHON**	HERE ARE THE HONEYCOMBS ...	10.00	25.00	22.50

			Current Price Range		P/Y AVG

HONEYS

SEE: AMERICAN SPRING, SPRING
PRODUCER: BRIAN WILSON

☐4952	*CAPITOL*	SURFIN' DOWN THE SWANEE RIVER/SHOOT THE CURL	22.00	40.00	36.00
☐5034		PRAY FOR SURF/ HIDE AND GO SEEK	20.00	34.00	30.00
☐5093		THE ONE YOU CAN'T HAVE/ FROM JIMMY WITH TEARS ...	20.00	34.00	30.00
☐2454		TONIGHT YOU BELONG TO ME/ GOODNIGHT MY LOVE	17.00	29.00	25.00
☐5430	*WARNER BROTHERS*	HE'S A DOLL/ LOVE OF A BOY AND GIRL	13.00	22.00	20.00

HONORABLES

☐100	*HONOR*	CASTLE IN THE SKY	12.00	29.00	25.00

HONOR SOCIETY (HAPPENINGS)

☐5703	*JUBILEE*	SWEET SEPTEMBER/ CONDITION RED	4.50	7.50	6.00

HOTLEGS

☐3043	*CAPITOL*	RUN, BABY, RUN/ HOW MANY TIMES	9.00	18.00	16.00
☐2886		NEANDERTHAL MAN/YOU DON'T LIKE IT BECAUSE YOU DIDN'T THINK OF IT	9.00	18.00	16.00

HOT-TODDYS (ROCKIN' REBELS)

☐0056	*SHAN-TODD*	ROCKIN' CRICKETS/ SHAKIN' AND STOMPIN'	3.25	6.00	4.00
☐25011	*STRAND*	HOEDOWN/NAN-JE-DI	3.25	6.00	4.00

GREGORY HOWARD

☐536	*KAPP*	SWEET PEA/WHEN IN LOVE	22.00	55.00	50.00

HULLABALOOS

☐4587	*ROULETTE*	I'M GONNA LOVE YOU TOO/ PARTY DOLL	3.00	5.00	3.50
☐4593		DID YOU EVER/BEWARE	3.00	5.00	3.50
☐4612		LEARNING THE GAME/ DON'T STOP	3.00	5.00	3.50
☐4662		I WON'T TURN AWAY NOW/ MY HEART KEEPS TELLING ME	3.00	5.00	3.50

HULLABALOOS—ALBUMS

☐25297 (M)	*ROULETTE*	ENGLAND'S NEWEST SINGING SENSATIONS	8.00	21.00	18.00
☐25297 (S)		ENGLAND'S NEWEST SINGING SENSATIONS	12.00	29.00	25.00

HUMAN BEINZ

☐828	*GATEWAY*	GLORIA/THE TIMES THEY ARE A-CHANGIN'	5.00	9.00	7.00
☐5990	*CAPITOL*	NOBODY BUT ME/SUENO	2.75	4.50	3.00
☐2119		TURN ON YOUR LOVE LIGHT/ IT'S FUN TO BE CLEAN	2.75	4.50	3.00
☐2198		EVERY TIME WOMAN/THE FACE .	2.75	4.50	3.00
☐2431		THIS LITTLE GIRL OF MINE/ I'VE GOT TO KEEP ON PUSHIN' .	2.75	4.50	3.00

HUMAN BEINZ—ALBUM

☐2906 (S)	*CAPITOL*	NOBODY BUT ME..............	7.00	14.00	12.00

			Current Price Range		P/Y AVG

IVORY JOE HUNTER

☐ 1111	ATLANTIC	SINCE I MET YOU BABY/ I CAN'T STOP THIS ROCKING AND ROLLING	3.75	6.00	4.50
☐ 1128		EMPTY ARMS/ LOVE'S A HURTIN' GAME	3.25	5.50	4.00

TAB HUNTER

☐ 15533	DOT	YOUNG LOVE/ RED SAILS IN THE SUNSET . . .	3.00	5.00	3.65
☐ 15548		NINETY-NINE WAYS/DON'T GET AROUND MUCH ANYMORE	3.00	5.00	3.65
☐ 15657		I'M ALONE BECAUSE I LOVE YOU/ DON'T GET AROUND MUCH ANYMORE	3.00	5.00	3.65
☐ 15767		I'M A RUNAWAY/ IT'S ALL OVER TOWN	3.00	5.00	3.65
☐ 16205		MY DEVOTION/WILD SIDE OF LIFE .	3.00	5.00	3.65
☐ 16264		THE WAY YOU LOOK TONIGHT/ YOU CHEATED	3.00	5.00	3.65

SINGLES ON WARNER BROTHERS ARE WORTH UP TO $3.00 MINT

TAB HUNTER—ALBUM

☐ 3370 (M)	DOT	YOUNG LOVE	13.00	27.00	17.00

DANNY HUTTON (OF THREE DOG NIGHT)

☐ 213	ALMO	WHY DON'T YOU LOVE ME ANYMORE/HOME IN PASADENA	3.25	5.50	4.00
☐ 447	HBR	ROSES AND RAINBOWS/ MONSTER SHINDIG	3.00	5.00	3.50
☐ 453		BIG BRIGHT EYES/ MONSTER SHINDIG	3.00	5.00	3.50
☐ 13502	MGM	FUNNY HOW LOVE CAN BE/ DREAMIN' ISN'T GOOD FOR YOU	2.75	4.50	3.00
☐ 13613		HANG ON TO A DREAM/ HIT THE WALL	2.75	4.50	3.00

DANNY HUTTON—ALBUM

☐ 4664 (S)	MGM	PRE-DOG NIGHT	5.00	12.00	10.00

BRIAN HYLAND

☐ 801	LEADER	ROSEMARY/ LIBRARY LOVE AFFAIR	6.00	12.00	8.00
☐ 805		ITSY BITSY TEENIE WEENIE YELLOW POLKADOT BIKINI/ DON'T DILLY DALLY, SALLY . .	3.50	6.00	4.15
☐ 342	KAPP	ITSY BITSY TEENIE WEENIE YELLOW POLKADOT BIKINI/ DON'T DILLY DALLY, SALLY . .	3.25	5.50	4.00
☐ 352		FOUR LITTLE HEELS/ THAT'S HOW MUCH	3.25	5.50	4.00
☐ 363		I GOTTA GO/ LOP-SIDED, OVERLOADED	3.25	5.50	4.00
☐ 401		LIPSTICK ON YOUR LIPS/ WHEN WILL I KNOW	3.25	5.50	4.00
☐ 10236	ABC-PARAMOUNT	LET ME BELONG TO YOU/ LET IT DIE	3.25	5.50	4.00
☐ 10262		I'LL NEVER STOP WANTING YOU/ THE NIGHT I CRIED	3.25	5.50	4.00
☐ 10294		GINNY COME LATELY/ I SHOULD BE GETTING BETTER .	3.25	5.50	4.00
☐ 10336		SEALED WITH A KISS/ SUMMER JOB	3.25	5.50	4.00
☐ 10359		WARMED OVER KISSES/ WALK A LONELY MILE	3.25	5.50	4.00

			Current Price Range		P/Y AVG
☐10374		I MAY NOT LIVE TO SEE TOMORROW/			
		IT AIN'T THAT WAY	3.25	5.50	4.00
☐10400		IF MARY'S THERE/			
		REMEMBER ME	3.25	5.50	4.00
☐10427		SOMEWHERE IN THE NIGHT/			
		I WISH TODAY WAS YESTERDAY	3.25	5.50	4.00
☐10452		I'M AFRAID TO GO HOME/			
		SAVE YOUR HEART FOR ME ...	3.25	5.50	4.00
☐10494		NOTHING MATTERS BUT YOU/LET			
		US MAKE OUR OWN MISTAKES	3.25	5.50	4.00
☐10549		OUT OF SIGHT, OUT OF MIND/			
		ACT NATURALLY	3.25	5.50	4.00
☐40179	*PHILIPS*	HERE'S TO OUR LOVE/			
		TWO KINDS OF GIRLS	3.25	5.50	4.00
☐40203		DEVOTED TO YOU/			
		PLEDGING MY LOVE	3.25	5.50	4.00
☐40221		NOW I BELONG TO YOU/ONE STEP			
		FORWARD, TWO STEPS BACK .	3.25	5.50	4.00
☐40263		HE DON'T UNDERSTAND YOU/			
		LOVE WILL FIND A WAY	3.25	5.50	4.00
☐40306		STAY AWAY FROM HER/			
		I CAN'T KEEP A SECRET	3.25	5.50	4.00
☐40354		3,000 MILES/SOMETIMES THEY			
		DO, SOMETIMES THEY DON'T .	3.25	5.50	4.00
☐40377		THE JOKER WENT WILD/			
		I CAN HEAR THE RAIN	3.00	5.00	3.65
☐40405		RUN, RUN, LOOK AND SEE/			
		WHY DID YOU DO IT?	3.00	5.00	3.65
☐40424		HUNG UP IN YOUR EYES/			
		WHY MINE	3.00	5.00	3.65
☐40444		HOLIDAY FOR CLOWNS/			
		YESTERDAY I HAD A GIRL	3.00	5.00	3.65
☐40472		GET THE MESSAGE/			
		KINDA GROOVY	3.00	5.00	3.65
☐17050	*DOT*	APOLOGIZE/WORDS ON PAPER ..	2.50	4.25	3.15
☐17176		TRAGEDY/YOU'D BETTER STOP			
		AND THINK IT OVER	2.50	4.25	3.15
☐17222		A MILLION TO ONE/			
		IT COULD ALL BEGIN AGAIN ...	2.50	4.25	3.15
☐17258		STAY AND LOVE ME ALL SUMMER/RAINY APRIL			
		MORNING	2.50	4.25	3.15
☐55240	*UNI*	GYPSY WOMAN/YOU AND ME #2	2.50	4.25	3.15
☐55272		LONELY TEARDROPS/LORRAYNE	2.50	4.25	3.15
☐55287		NO PLACE TO RUN/			
		SO LONG, MARIANNE	2.50	4.25	3.15
☐55306		OUT OF THE BLUE/			
		IF YOU COME BACK	2.50	4.25	3.15
☐55323		WITH MY EYES WIDE OPEN/ I LOVE EVERY LITTLE THING			
		ABOUT YOU	2.50	4.25	3.15
☐55334		ONLY WANNA MAKE YOU HAPPY/			
		WHEN YOU'RE LOVIN' ME	2.50	4.25	3.15
		BRIAN HYLAND—ALBUMS			
☐1202 (M)	*KAPP*	THE BASHFUL BLONDE	8.00	21.00	18.00
☐1202 (S)		THE BASHFUL BLONDE	12.00	29.00	25.00
☐400 (M)	*ABC-*				
	PARAMOUNT	LET ME BELONG TO YOU	7.00	17.00	15.00
☐400 (S)		LET ME BELONG TO YOU	9.00	25.00	22.50
☐431 (M)		SEALED WITH A KISS	7.00	17.00	15.00
☐431 (S)		SEALED WITH A KISS	9.00	25.00	22.50
☐463 (M)		COUNTRY MEETS FOLK.........	6.00	15.00	13.50
☐463 (S)		COUNTRY MEETS FOLK.........	8.00	21.00	18.00

			Current Price Range		P/Y AVG
☐ 136 (M)	**PHILLIPS**	HERE'S TO OUR LOVE	6.00	15.00	13.50
☐ 136 (S)		HERE'S TO OUR LOVE	8.00	21.00	18.00
☐ 158 (M)		ROCKIN' FOLK	6.00	15.00	13.50
☐ 158 (S)		ROCKIN' FOLK	8.00	21.00	18.00
☐ 217 (M)		THE JOKER WENT WILD	6.00	15.00	13.50
☐ 217 (S)		THE JOKER WENT WILD	8.00	21.00	18.00
☐ 25926 (S)	**DOT**	TRAGEDY	5.00	12.00	10.00
☐ 25954 (S)		STAY AND LOVE ME ALL SUMMER	5.00	12.00	10.00
☐ 73097 (S)	**UNI**	BRIAN HYLAND	5.00	12.00	10.00

I

JANIS IAN

☐ 5027	**VERVE FOLKWAYS**	SOCIETY'S CHILD/LETTER TO JON	4.00	8.00	5.50
☐ 5041	**VERVE FORECAST**	YOUNGER GENERATION BLUES/ I'LL GIVE YOU A STONE	4.00	8.00	5.50
☐ 5059		LADY OF THE NIGHT/ FRIENDS AGAIN	4.00	8.00	5.50
☐ 5072		SUNFLAKES FALL/INSANITY ...	4.00	8.00	5.50
☐ 5079		SONG FOR ALL THE SEASONS/ LONELY ONE	4.00	8.00	5.50
☐ 5099		EVERYBODY KNOWS/ JANEY'S BLUES	4.75	7.00	5.50
☐ 3107	**CAPITOL**	HERE IN SPAIN/HE'S A RAINBOW	4.75	7.00	4.50
☐ 10154	**COLUMBIA**	STARS/AT SEVENTEEN	2.25	4.50	2.50

LATER COLUMBIA SINGLES ARE WORTH UP TO $2.50 MINT

IDEALS

☐ 108	**COOL**	YOU WON'T LIKE IT/ DO I HAVE THE RIGHT	20.00	49.00	45.00

FRANK IFIELD
SEE: BEATLES

☐ 457	**VEE JAY**	I REMEMBER YOU/ I LISTEN TO MY HEART	3.25	5.50	4.00
☐ 477		LOVESICK BLUES/ANYTIME	3.25	5.50	4.00
☐ 499		THE WAYWARD WIND/ I'M SMILING NOW	3.25	5.50	4.00
☐ 525		UNCHAINED MELODY/ NOBODY'S DARLIN' BUT MINE .	3.25	5.50	4.00
☐ 553		I'M CONFESSIN' (THAT I LOVE YOU)/HEART AND SOUL	3.25	5.50	4.00
☐ 5032	**CAPITOL**	I'M CONFESSIN'/ WALTZING MATILDA	3.00	5.00	3.65
☐ 5089		PLEASE/MULE TRAIN	3.00	5.00	3.65
☐ 5134		DON'T BLAME ME/ SAY IT ISN'T SO	3.00	5.00	3.85
☐ 5170		YOU CAME A LONG WAY FROM ST. LOUIS/SWEET LORRAINE .	3.00	5.00	3.65
☐ 72055		LOVESICK BLUES/SHE TAUGHT ME HOW TO YODEL ...	3.00	5.00	3.65

FRANK IFIELD—ALBUMS

☐ 1054 (M)	**VEE JAY**	I REMEMBER YOU	10.00	23.00	14.00
☐ 1054 (S)		I REMEMBER YOU	14.00	33.00	21.00
☐ 10356 (M)	**CAPITOL**	I'M CONFESSIN' (THAT I LOVE YOU)	9.00	19.00	12.00
☐ 10356 (S)		I'M CONFESSIN' (THAT I LOVE YOU)	11.00	28.00	17.00

IMPALAS

At first three Brooklyn teenagers formed a nameless singing trio. With the cooperation of a neighbor, the boys set up a practice area in the back room of a neighborhood candy store. As they practiced and improved, they became determined to stick together and become successful. The trio later took on a fourth member, then cast about in search of a catchy and unique name for the quartet. The father of one of the boys had just purchased a new Chevrolet Impala. The boys liked the name and decided to dub their group the Impalas.

They worked hard at making as many contacts as they could. Finally they were signed to the small Hamilton label to do a single called "First Date". Sales were nil. Still determined, the boys soon met a businessman who knew Alan Freed. When Freed heard the boys, he was sufficiently impressed to recommend an audition with Cub records, an MGM subsidiary.

The Impalas recorded "(Sorry) I Ran All the Way Home" in 1959, and it sold a million. However, the Impalas proved to be a one-hit wonder. A follow-up 45 of "Oh, What A Fool" barely made the charts and later attempts failed altogether.

			Current Price Range		P/Y AVG

IMPALAS

☐50026	**HAMILTON**	FIRST DATE/I WAS A FOOL	9.25	15.00	13.00
☐9022	**CUB**	SORRY (I RAN ALL THE WAY HOME)/FOOL FOOL FOOL	4.25	7.00	5.00
☐9033		OH, WHAT A FOOL/ SANDY WENT AWAY	4.25	7.00	5.00
☐9053		PEGGY DARLING/BYE EVERYBODY	4.25	7.00	5.00
☐9066		WHEN MY HEART DOES ALL THE TALKING/ALL ALONE	4.25	7.00	5.00

IMPALAS—EP

☐5000	**CUB**	SORRY (I RAN ALL THE WAY HOME)	14.00	22.00	19.00

IMPALAS—ALBUMS

☐8003 (M)	**CUB**	SORRY (I RAN ALL THE WAY HOME)	25.00	60.00	57.00
☐8003 (S)		SORRY (I RAN ALL THE WAY HOME)	40.00	100.00	92.00

IMPRESSIONS
FEATURED: JERRY BUTLER

☐2504	**BANDERA**	LISTEN TO ME/ SHORTY'S GOTTA GO	5.50	11.00	9.00
☐107	**SWIRL**	DON'T LEAVE ME/ I NEED YOUR LOVE	5.00	9.00	7.00
☐280	**VEE JAY**	FOR YOUR PRECIOUS LOVE/ SWEET WAS THE WINE	75.00	130.00	120.00
☐424		SAY THAT YOU LOVE ME/ SENORITA, I LOVE YOU	5.00	9.00	7.00
☐575		THE GIFT OF LOVE/ AT THE COUNTY FAIR	4.50	7.50	6.00
☐621		SAY THAT YOU LOVE ME/ SENORITA, I LOVE YOU	3.25	5.00	4.00
☐1013	**FALCON**	FOR YOUR PRECIOUS LOVE/ SWEET WAS THE WINE	8.25	14.00	12.00
☐1013	**ABNER**	FOR YOUR PRECIOUS LOVE/ SWEET WAS THE WINE	4.50	7.50	6.00

SINGLES ON ABC-PARAMOUNT ARE WORTH UP TO $2.00 MINT

IMPRESSIONS—ALBUMS

☐1075 (M)	**VEE JAY**	FOR YOUR PRECIOUS LOVE	17.00	39.00	35.00
☐1075 (S)		FOR YOUR PRECIOUS LOVE	22.00	55.00	50.00

INFATUATORS

☐504	**DESTINY**	I FOUND MY LOVE/ WHERE ARE YOU?	22.00	40.00	36.00
☐395	**VEE JAY**	I FOUND MY LOVE/ WHERE ARE YOU?	5.00	9.00	7.00

INNOCENCE

☐214	**KAMA SUTRA**	THERE'S GOT TO BE A WORD/ IT'S NOT GONNA TAKE TOO LONG	3.00	5.00	3.65
☐222		MAIRZY DOATS/ A LIFETIME LOVIN' YOU	3.00	5.00	3.65
☐228		ALL I DO IS THINK ABOUT YOU/ WHENCE I MAKE THEE MINE ..	3.00	5.00	3.65
☐232		SOMEONE GOT CAUGHT IN MY EYE/YOUR SHOW IS OVER	3.00	5.00	3.65
☐237		DAY TURNS ME ON/IT'S NOT GONNA TAKE TOO LONG	3.00	.5.00	3.65

INNOCENCE—ALBUMS

☐8059 (M)	**KAMA SUTRA**	THE INNOCENCE	6.00	15.00	13.50
☐8059 (S)		THE INNOCENCE	8.00	21.00	18.00

ISLEY BROTHERS

The Isley Brothers hailed from Cincinnati, Ohio. They were raised in the church and surrounded by gospel music as children. (Ronald Isley won a spiritual-singing contest when he was three.)

They began as an r & b quartet, but Vernon — the youngest member — died in a car wreck. The three remaining Isleys then vowed to stay together. They played cheap bars and clubs around Cincinnati, then spread out through the Midwest, building a name as they went. They first recorded in 1957, singing for their first single a beautiful ballad called "The Angels Cried".

One night near the end of a 1959 stage show, one of the Isleys commanded their audience to "put up your hands and shout!" Later the request became a song and "Shout!" became an RCA hit. Their second RCA disc, "Respectable", later became a hit for the Outsiders, although it did little for the Isley Brothers.

A shift to Wand Records produced a Top 20 single of "Twist and Shout" to cash in on the dance craze at the time.

			Current Price Range		P/Y AVG

INNOCENTS
SEE: ECHOES, KATHY YOUNG

			Current Price Range		P/Y AVG
☐70001	**TRANS WORLD**	TICK TOCK/THE RAT	4.50	7.50	6.00
☐105	**INDIGO**	HONEST I DO/			
		MY BABY HULLY GULLYS	3.00	5.00	3.50
☐111		GEE WHIZ/PLEASE MR. SUN	3.00	5.00	3.50
☐116		KATHY/IN THE BEGINNING	3.25	5.50	4.00
☐124		BEWARE/BECAUSE I LOVE YOU . .	3.25	5.50	4.00
☐128		DONNA/YOU GOT ME GOIN'	3.00	5.00	3.50
☐141		TIME/DEE DEE DI OH	3.00	5.00	3.50
☐20112	**REPRISE**	OH, HOW I MISS MY BABY/			
		BE MINE	3.00	5.00	3.50
☐20125		OH, HOW I MISS MY BABY/			
		YOU'RE NEVER SATISFIED	3.00	5.00	3.50
☐31519	**DECCA**	DON'T CRY/COME ON, LOVER . . .	3.00	5.00	3.50
☐5450	**WARNER BROTHERS**	MY HEART STOOD STILL/DON'T			
		CALL ME LONELY ANYMORE . .	3.00	5.00	3.50

INNOCENTS—ALBUM

☐503 (M)	**INDIGO**	INNOCENTLY YOURS	14.00	35.00	30.00

INTERVALS (FIFTH DIMENSION)

☐304	**CLASS**	HERE'S THAT RAINY DAY/I WISH			
		I COULD CHANGE MY MIND . . .	22.00	40.00	36.00

ISLEY BROTHERS

☐1004	**TEENAGE**	THE ANGELS CRIED/THE COW			
		JUMPED OVER THE MOON	40.00	66.00	60.00
☐3009	**CINDY**	DON'T BE JEALOUS/			
		THIS IS THE END	20.00	35.00	30.00
☐5022	**GONE**	I WANNA KNOW/EVERYBODY'S			
		GONNA ROCK AND ROLL	12.00	21.00	18.00
☐5048		MY LOVE/THE DRAG	8.25	14.00	12.00
☐8000	**MARK X**	ROCKIN' MACDONALD/THE DRAG	6.00	11.00	9.00
☐7588	**RCA**	SHOUT (PT. 1)/(PT. 2)	3.25	5.50	4.00
☐7657		RESPECTABLE/WITHOUT A SONG	3.75	6.00	4.50
☐124	**WAND**	TWIST AND SHOUT/			
		SPANISH TWIST	3.00	5.00	3.50
☐127		TWISTIN' WITH LINDA/			
		YOU BETTER COME HOME	3.00	5.00	3.50
☐501	**T NECK**	TESTIFY (PT. 1)/(PT. 2)			
		(Jimi Hendrix on guitar)	5.00	8.50	7.00
☐54128	**TAMLA**	THIS OLD HEART OF MINE/			
		THERE'S NO LOVE LEFT	3.00	5.00	3.50

ISLEY BROTHERS—ALBUMS

☐2156 (M)	**RCA**	SHOUT!	14.00	35.00	30.00
☐2156		SHOUT!	24.00	58.00	50.00
☐653 (M)	**WAND**	TWIST AND SHOUT	10.00	25.00	22.50
☐269 (S)	**TAMLA**	THIS OLD HEART OF MINE	8.00	21.00	18.00

IVAN (JERRY ALLISON)
GUITAR: BUDDY HOLLY

☐62017	**CORAL**	REAL WILD CHILD/			
		OH YOU BEAUTIFUL DOLL	12.00	21.00	18.00
☐62081		FRANKIE FRANKENSTEIN/			
		THAT'LL BE ALRIGHT	20.00	34.00	30.00
☐65607		REAL WILD CHILD/			
		THAT'LL BE ALRIGHT	9.50	17.00	15.00

IVEYS (BADFINGER)

☐1803	**APPLE**	MAYBE TOMORROW/AND HER			
		DADDY'S A MILLIONAIRE	3.25	6.00	4.00

MERCURY, MG 20940, LP

MOTOWN, M6-851S1, LP

			Current Price Range		P/Y AVG

IVY THREE

			Current Price Range		P/Y AVG
☐720	SHELL	YOGI/WAS JUDY THERE?	3.00	5.00	3.50
☐723		ALONE IN THE CHAPEL/			
		HUSH LITTLE BABY	3.00	5.00	3.50
☐302		NINE OUT OF TEN/			
		I'VE CRIED ENOUGH FOR TWO .	3.00	5.00	3.50
☐306		BAGOO/SUICIDE	3.00	5.00	3.50

J

JACKSON 5

☐681	STEELTOWN	YOU'VE CHANGED/BIG BOY	17.00	28.00	18.00
☐684		YOU DON'T HAVE TO BE OVER 21			
		TO FALL IN LOVE/SOME GIRLS			
		WANT ME FOR THEIR LOVE . . .	17.00	28.00	18.00
☐1157	MOTOWN	I WANT YOU BACK/			
		WHO'S LOVING YOU	5.00	9.00	5.00
☐1163		ABC/IT'S ALL IN THE GAME	5.00	9.00	5.00
☐1166		THE LOVE YOU SAVE/			
		I FOUND THAT GIRL	5.00	9.00	5.00
☐1171		I'LL BE THERE/			
		ONE MORE CHANCE	5.00	9.00	5.00
☐1174		SANTA CLAUS IS COMING			
		TO TOWN/CHRISTMAS WON'T			
		BE THE SAME THIS YEAR	7.00	13.00	5.25
☐1177		MAMA'S PEARL/DARLING DEAR .	4.00	7.00	4.25
☐1179		NEVER CAN SAY GOODBYE/			
		SHE'S GOOD	4.00	7.00	4.25
☐1186		MAYBE TOMORROW/			
		I WILL FIND A WAY	4.00	7.00	4.25
☐1194		SUGAR DADDY/I'M SO HAPPY . . .	4.00	7.00	4.25
☐1199		LITTLE BITTY PRETTY ONE/IF I			
		HAVE TO MORE A MOUNTAIN . .	4.00	7.00	4.25
☐1205		LOOKING THROUGH THE			
		WINDOWS/LOVE SONG	4.00	7.00	4.25
☐1214		CORNER OF THE SKY/TO KNOW .	4.00	7.00	4.25
☐1224		HALLELUJAH DAY/			
		YOU MAKE ME WHAT I AM	4.00	7.00	4.25
☐1277		GET IT TOGETHER/TOUCH	4.00	7.00	4.25
☐1286		DANCING MACHINE/IT'S TOO			
		LATE TO CHANGE THE TIME . . .	4.00	7.00	4.25
☐1308		WHATEVER YOU GOT, I WANT/			
		I CAN'T QUIT YOUR LOVE	4.00	7.00	4.25
☐1310		I AM LOVE (PT. 1)/(PT. 2)	4.00	7.00	4.25
☐1356		FOREVER CAME TODAY/			
		ALL I DO IS THINK OF YOU	4.00	7.00	4.25

MOTOWN ALBUMS ARE WORTH UP TO $10.00 MINT

JACKS
SEE: CADETS, FLARES

☐428	RPM	WHY DON'T YOU WRITE ME?/			
		SMACK DAB IN THE MIDDLE . .	5.50	11.00	9.00
☐432		LOVE ME AGAIN/DOG GONE IT . . .	5.00	9.00	7.00
☐433		I'M CONFESSIN'/			
		SINCE MY BABY'S BEEN GONE	4.00	9.00	7.00
☐439		BOB-O-LINK/SINCE YOU	5.00	9.00	7.00
☐444		THIS EMPTY HEART/			
		MY CLUMSY HEART	4.00	9.00	7.00

			Current Price Range		P/Y AVG
☐454		HOW SOON/SO WRONG	5.00	9.00	7.00
☐458		WHY DID I FALL IN LOVE?/			
		SUGAR BABY	5.00	9.00	7.00
☐467		DREAM A LITTLE LONGER/			
		LET'S MAKE UP	5.00	9.00	7.00

JACKS—ALBUMS

☐3006 (M)	**RPM**	JUMPIN' WITH THE JACKS	29.00	66.00	60.00
☐5021 (M)	**CROWN**	JUMPIN' WITH THE JACKS	19.00	49.00	45.00

CHUCK JACKSON

☐1005	**BELTONE**	MR. PRIDE/HULA HULA	4.00	7.00	4.85
☐106	**WAND**	I DON'T WANT TO CRY/			
		JUST ONCE	3.25	5.50	4.00
☐108		(IT NEVER HAPPENS) IN REAL			
		LIFE/THE SAME OLD STORY ..	3.25	5.50	4.00
☐110		I WAKE UP CRYING/			
		EVERYBODY NEEDS LOVE	3.25	5.50	4.00
☐115		THE BREAKING POINT/			
		MY WILLOW TREE	3.25	5.50	4.00
☐119		ANGEL OF ANGELS/WHAT'CHA			
		GONNA SAY TOMORROW?	3.25	5.50	4.00
☐122		ANY DAY NOW/THE PROPHET ...	3.25	5.50	4.00
☐126		I KEEP FORGETTIN'/WHO'S			
		GONNA PICK UP THE PIECES? .	3.00	5.00	3.65
☐128		GETTING READY FOR THE			
		HEARTBREAK/IN BETWEEN			
		TEARS	3.00	5.00	3.65
☐132		TELL HIM I'M NOT HOME/			
		LONELY AM I	3.00	5.00	3.65
☐138		TEARS OF JOY/I WILL NEVER			
		TURN MY BACK ON YOU	3.00	5.00	3.65
☐141		ANY OTHER WAY/BIG NEW YORK	3.00	5.00	3.65
☐149		HAND IT OVER/			
		LOOK OVER YOUR SHOULDER .	3.00	5.00	3.65
☐154		BEG ME/FOR ALL TIME	3.00	5.00	3.65
☐161		SOMEBODY NEW/STAND BY ME .	3.00	5.00	3.65
☐169		SINCE I DON'T HAVE YOU/			
		HAND IT OVER	3.00	5.00	3.65
☐179		I NEED YOU/			
		SOUL BROTHER'S TWIST	3.00	5.00	3.65
☐188		IF I DIDN'T LOVE YOU/JUST A			
		LITTLE BIT OF YOUR SOUL	3.00	5.00	3.65
☐1105		GOOD THINGS COME TO THOSE			
		WHO WAIT/YEAH	3.00	5.00	3.65
☐1119		ALL IN MY MIND/			
		THAT'S SAYING A LOT	3.00	5.00	3.65
☐1129		THESE CHAINS OF LOVE/			
		THEME TO THE BLUES	3.00	5.00	3.65
☐1142		WHERE DID SHE STAY?/			
		I'VE GOT TO BE STRONG	3.00	5.00	3.65
☐1151		EVERY MAN NEEDS A DOWN			
		HOME GIRL/NEED YOU THERE .	3.00	5.00	3.65
☐1159		LOVE ME TENDER/HOUND DOG ..	4.00	7.00	4.00
☐1166		SHAME ON ME/CANDY	2.75	4.50	3.00
☐1178		MY CHILD'S CHILD/			
		THEME TO THE BLUES	2.75	4.50	3.00
☐849	**AMY**	OOH BABY/			
		COME ON AND LOVE ME	2.75	4.50	3.00
☐868		I'M YOURS/HULA LULA	2.75	4.50	3.00

CHUCK JACKSON—ALBUMS

☐650 (M)	**WAND**	I DON'T WANT TO CRY	9.00	25.00	22.50
☐654 (M)		ANY DAY NOW	8.00	21.00	18.00
☐665 (M)		ENCORE	7.00	17.00	15.00
☐667 (M)		MR. EVERYTHING	6.00	15.00	13.50

			Current Price Range		P/Y AVG
☐ 667 (S)		MR. EVERYTHING	7.00	21.00	18.00
☐ 673 (M)		TRIBUTE TO RHYTHM AND BLUES	6.00	15.00	13.50
☐ 673 (S)		TRIBUTE TO RHYTHM AND BLUES	8.00	21.00	18.00
☐ 676 (M)		TRIBUTE TO RHYTHM AND BLUES, VOL. II	6.00	15.00	13.50
☐ 676 (S)		TRIBUTE TO RHYTHM AND BLUES, VOL. II	8.00	21.00	18.00
☐ 680 (M)		DEDICATED TO THE KING (Elvis songs)	7.00	17.00	15.00
☐ 680 (S)		DEDICATED TO THE KING (Elvis songs)	8.00	21.00	18.00
☐ 683 (M)		CHUCK JACKSON'S GREATEST HITS	5.50	14.00	12.00
☐ 683 (S)		CHUCK JACKSON'S GREATEST HITS	7.00	17.00	15.00

PYTHON LEE JACKSON
FEATURED: ROD STEWART

☐ 449	**GNP-CRESCENDO**	IN A BROKEN DREAM/DOIN FINE	4.50	7.50	6.00
☐ 462		CLOUD NINE/ROD'S BLUES	5.00	8.50	7.00

PYTHON LEE JACKSON—ALBUM

☐ 2066 (S)	**GNP-CRESCENDO**	IN A BROKEN DREAM	9.50	17.00	15.00

WANDA JACKSON

☐ 3485	**CAPITOL**	I GOTTA KNOW/ HALF AS GOOD A GIRL	4.50	7.50	6.00
☐ 3575		HOT DOG. THAT MADE HIM MAD!/ SILVER THREADS AND GOLDEN NEEDLES	4.50	7.50	6.00
☐ 3637		CRYIN' THROUGH THE NIGHT/ BABY LOVES HIM	3.75	6.00	4.50
☐ 3683		LET ME EXPLAIN/DON'A WANNA	3.75	6.00	4.50
☐ 3764		COOL LOVE/DID YOU MISS ME?	4.50	7.00	5.50
☐ 3843		FUJIYAMA MAMA/NO WEDDING BELLS FOR JOE	4.50	7.00	5.50
☐ 3941		HONEY BOP/ JUST A QUEEN FOR A DAY	4.50	7.00	5.50
☐ 4026		MEAN MEAN MAN/OUR SONG	4.50	7.00	5.50
☐ 4081		ROCK YOUR BABY/SINFUL HEART.	4.50	7.00	5.50
☐ 4142		SAVIN' MY LOVE/ I WANNA WALTZ	3.75	6.00	4.50
☐ 4398		LET'S HAVE A PARTY/COOL LOVE	3.75	6.00	4.50
☐ 4553		RIGHT OR WRONG/ TUNNEL OF LOVE	3.25	5.50	4.00
☐ 4635		IN THE MIDDLE OF A HEARTACHE/ I'D BE ASHAMED	3.25	5.50	4.00
☐ 4681		A LITTLE BITTY TEAR/ I DON'T WANTA GO	3.25	5.50	4.00
☐ 4723		IF I CRIED EVERY TIME YOU HURT ME/LET MY LOVE WALK IN	3.25	5.50	4.00

LATER CAPITOL SINGLES ARE WORTH UP TO $3.50 MINT

WANDA JACKSON—ALBUMS

☐ 1041 (M)	**CAPITOL**	WANDA JACKSON	26.00	65.00	60.00
☐ 1384 (M)		ROCKIN' WITH WANDA	23.00	54.00	50.00
☐ 1511 (M)		THERE'S A PARTY GOIN' ON	17.00	59.00	55.00
☐ 1511 (S)		THERE'S A PARTY GOIN' ON	23.00	54.00	50.00
☐ 1596 (M)		RIGHT OR WRONG	12.00	29.00	25.00
☐ 1596 (S)		RIGHT OR WRONG	17.00	39.00	35.00
☐ 1776 (M)		WONDERFUL WANDA	10.00	25.00	22.50
☐ 1776 (S)		WONDERFUL WANDA	14.00	34.00	30.00
☐ 1911 (M)		LOVE ME FOREVER	10.00	25.00	22.50
☐ 1911 (S)		LOVE ME FOREVER	14.00	34.00	30.00

WANDA JACKSON

"Let's Have a Party" wasn't Wanda Jackson's biggest hit but it was that song that made her a star. *"Let's Have a Party"* was a rocker taken from Elvis Presley's *"Loving You"* film. Ironically, Wanda Jackson had once toured with Elvis when he had been a struggling unknown.

Wanda Jackson was born on October 20, 1937, in Oklahoma City, OK. Her father, a country-music fan, taught Wanda how to read and write music. He also instructed Ms. Jackson on the guitar and piano.

Wanda was a good student in high school, although her interests chiefly centered around music. She entered every talent contest she could and usually won those in which she sang.

Country singing star Hank Thompson was impressed by the talented and attractive girl and he signed Wanda to travel with him and his band.

Wanda Jackson's initial Capitol singles were good, strong rockers. *"Let's Have a Party"* put her name before the buying public. She then followed her first hit with *"Right or Wrong"* and *"In the Middle of a Heartache"*.

			Current Price Range		P/Y AVG

TOMMY JAMES

			Current Price Range		P/Y AVG
☐7084	ROULETTE	BALL AND CHAIN/CANDY MAKER	3.00	5.00	3.65
☐7093		CHURCH STREET SOUL REVIVAL/ DRAGGIN' THE LINE	3.00	5.00	3.65
☐7100		ADRIENNE/LIGHT OF DAY	3.00	5.00	3.65
☐7103		DRAGGIN' THE LINE/ BITS AND PIECES	3.00	5.00	3.65
☐7110		I'M COMIN' HOME/ SING SING SING	3.00	5.00	3.65
☐7114		NOTHING TO HIDE/ WALK A COUNTRY MILE	2.75	5.00	3.50
☐7119		TELL 'EM WILLIE BOY'S A COMIN'/40 DAYS AND 40 NIGHTS	2.75	5.00	3.50
☐7126		CAT'S EYE IN THE WINDOW/ DARK IS THE NIGHT	2.75	5.00	3.50
☐7130		LOVE SONG/KINGSTON HIGHWAY	2.75	5.00	3.50
☐7135		CELEBRATION/ THE LAST ONE TO KNOW	2.75	5.00	3.50
☐7140		BOO, BOO, DON'TCHA BE BLUE/ RINGS AND THINGS	2.75	5.00	3.50
☐7147		CALICO/HEY BABY	2.75	5.00	3.50

TOMMY JAMES—ALBUMS

			Current Price Range		P/Y AVG
☐3001 (S)	ROULETTE	CHRISTIAN OF THE WORLD	5.00	12.00	10.00
☐3007 (S)		MY HEAD, MY BED AND MY RED GUITAR	5.00	12.00	10.00
☐42051 (S)		TOMMY JAMES	5.00	12.00	10.00

TOMMY JAMES AND THE SHONDELLS

			Current Price Range		P/Y AVG
☐102	SNAP	HANKY PANKY/THUNDERBOLT (Shondells)	12.00	21.00	18.00
☐110	RED FOX	HANKY PANKY/THUNDERBOLT (Shondells)	9.50	17.00	15.00
☐4686	ROULETTE	HANKY PANKY/THUNDERBOLT	3.00	5.00	3.65
☐4695		SAY I AM (WHAT I AM)/ LOTS OF PRETTY GIRLS	3.00	5.00	3.65
☐4710		IT'S ONLY LOVE/DON'T LET MY LOVE PASS YOU BY	3.00	5.00	3.65
☐4720		I THINK WE'RE ALONE NOW/ GONE GONE GONE	3.00	5.00	3.65
☐4736		MIRAGE/RUN RUN RUN	3.00	5.00	3.65
☐4756		I LIKE THE WAY/ I CAN'T TAKE IT NO MORE	3.00	5.00	3.65
☐4762		GETTIN' TOGETHER/REAL GIRL	3.00	5.00	3.65
☐4775		OUT OF THE BLUE/ LOVE'S CLOSIN' IN ON ME	3.00	5.00	3.65
☐7000		GET OUT NOW/ WISH IT WERE YOU	3.00	5.00	3.65
☐7008		MONY MONY/ONE, TWO, THREE AND I FELL	2.75	4.50	3.25
☐7016		SOMEBODY CARES/DO UNTO ME	2.75	4.50	3.25
☐7024		DO SOMETHING TO ME/ GINGERBREAD MAN	2.75	4.50	3.25
☐7028		CRIMSON AND CLOVER/ (I'M) TAKEN	2.75	4.50	3.25
☐7039		SWEET CHERRY WINE/ BREAKAWAY	2.75	4.50	3.25
☐7050		CRYSTAL BLUE PERSUASION/ I'M ALIVE	2.75	4.50	3.25
☐7060		BALL OF FIRE/MAKIN' GOOD TIME	2.75	4.50	3.25
☐7066		SHE/LOVED ONE	2.75	4.50	3.25
☐7071		GOTTA GET BACK TO YOU/ RED ROVER	2.75	4.50	3.25
☐7076		COME TO ME/LOVED ONE	2.75	4.50	3.25

JAN AND ARNIE

Jan Berry and Arnie Ginsberg were classmates at University High in the posh L.A. suburb of Bel Air. They were also members of a car club called the Barons. One night Jan, Arnie and several other Barons took in a burlesque show in seedy downtown Los Angeles. That night they saw a stripper billed as Jennie Lee. Jan was particularly taken by the way Jennie bounced when she moved. On the way home he began a repetition of the words. ". . bomp-bomp-bomp-bomp-" in between verbalizing about the physical attributes of Ms. Lee.

Before long Jan and Arnie had set up a makeshift recording studio in Jan's garage. Using a two-track home recorder, Jan found that he could produce an echo effect with a second recorder. He and Arnie then made the tape of their original "Jennie Lee". Jan banged on an old piano and Arnie drummed on a wooden box with a pair of sticks.

The tape was later taken to the small Arwin Record Company in Beverly Hills. With added studio instruments, "Jennie Lee" was released and — surprise! — became a Top 10 winner.

			Current Price Range		P/Y AVG
TOMMY JAMES AND THE SHONDELLS—ALBUMS					
☐ 25336 (M)	*ROULETTE*	HANKY PANKY	7.00	17.00	15.00
☐ 25336 (S)		HANKY PANKY	8.00	21.00	18.00
☐ 25344 (M)		IT'S ONLY LOVE	7.00	17.00	15.00
☐ 25344 (S)		IT'S ONLY LOVE	8.00	21.00	18.00
☐ 25353 (M)		I THINK WE'RE ALONE NOW	7.00	17.00	15.00
☐ 25353 (S)		I THINK WE'RE ALONE NOW	8.00	21.00	18.00
☐ 25355 (M)		SOMETHING SPECIAL (greatest hits)	6.00	15.00	13.50
☐ 25355 (S)		SOMETHING SPECIAL (greatest hits)	7.00	17.00	15.00
☐ 25357 (M)		GETTIN' TOGETHER	7.00	17.00	15.00
☐ 25357 (S)		GETTIN' TOGETHER	6.00	15.00	13.50
☐ 42023 (S)		CRIMSON AND CLOVER	5.50	14.00	12.00
☐ 42040 (S)		THE BEST OF TOMMY JAMES AND THE SHONDELLS	5.50	14.00	12.00
☐ 42044 (S)		TRAVELIN'	5.50	14.00	12.00

JAMIE AND JANE
GENE PITNEY AND GINNY ARNELL

☐ 30862	*DECCA*	STROLLING (THRU THE PARK)/ SNUGGLE UP BABY	4.50	7.50	6.00
☐ 30934		FAITHFUL OUR LOVE/ CLASSICAL ROCK AND ROLL	4.50	7.50	6.00

JAN AND ARNIE
SEE: JAN AND DEAN, RITUALS

☐ 108	*ARWIN*	JENNIE LEE/GOTTA GET A DATE	5.00	8.50	7.00
☐ 111		GAS MONEY/BONNIE LOU	8.25	14.00	12.00
☐ 113		I LOVE LINDA/THE BEAT THAT CAN'T BE BEAT	12.00	21.00	18.00
☐ 16116	*DOT*	GAS MONEY/GOTTA GET A DATE	12.00	21.00	18.00
JAN AND ARNIE—EP					
☐ 1097	*DOT*	JAN AND ARNIE	45.00	76.00	72.00

JAN AND DEAN
SEE: JAN BERRY, LEGENDARY MASKED SURFERS, MATADORS, RALLY PACKS

☐ 522	*DORE*	BABY TALK/JEANETTE, GET YOUR HAIR DONE (listed as Jan and Arnie)	50.00	98.00	90.00
☐ 522		BABY TALK/JEANETTE GET YOUR HAIR DONE	4.50	7.50	6.00
☐ 531		THERE'S A GIRL/ MY HEART SINGS	5.00	8.50	7.00
☐ 539		CLEMENTINE/ YOU'RE ON MY MIND	5.00	8.50	7.00
☐ 548		WHITE TENNIS SNEAKERS/CINDY	5.50	11.00	9.00
☐ 555		WE GO TOGETHER/ROSIE LANE	4.50	7.50	6.00
☐ 555		WE GO TOGETHER/ROSILANE	4.50	7.50	6.00
☐ 576		GEE/SUCH A GOOD NIGHT FOR DREAMING	4.50	7.50	6.00
☐ 583		BAGGY PANTS/JUDY'S AN ANGEL	5.50	11.00	9.00
☐ 610		JULIE/DON'T FLY AWAY	8.25	14.00	12.00
☐ 9111	*CHALLENGE*	HEART AND SOUL/THOSE WORDS	12.00	21.00	18.00
☐ 9111		HEART AND SOUL/ MIDSUMMER NIGHT'S DREAM (also issued as 59111)	3.25	5.00	4.00
☐ 9120		WANTED, ONE GIRL/SOMETHING A LITTLE BIT DIFFERENT	4.50	8.00	6.50
☐ 55397	*LIBERTY*	A SUNDAY KIND OF LOVE/ POOR LITTLE PUPPET	4.50	8.00	6.00
☐ 55454		TENNESSEE/YOUR HEART HAS CHANGED ITS MIND	3.75	6.00	4.50
☐ 55496		WHO PUT THE BOMP/ MY FAVORITE DREAM	5.50	11.00	9.00

JAN AND DEAN

Jan Berry was a high school student when he and pal Arnie Ginsberg created the fluke hit of "Jennie Lee". (It was recorded in Jan's garage on a home tape recorder.) After "Jennie Lee" died out, Arnie enlisted in the Navy.

Managers Herb Alpert and Lou Adler (then struggling unknowns) insisted that Jan find another partner. Dean Torrence, a fellow football player at L.A.'s University High School, was invited to replace Arnie. Jan and Dean's "Baby Talk" (another product from Jan's garage) put them in the Top 10.

They later signed with Challenge Records and had a solitary hit with "Heart and Soul". On Liberty, they did well with "Linda". But this Top 30 single was just a fore-runner of the monster hits that would come in 1963 and 1964. Among these was the number-one winner of "Surf City" (first title: "Two Girls for Every Boy").

Making records was a part-time job for Jan and Dean; both were full-time college students. Jan was six months away from beginning his internship as a doctor when he was nearly killed in an auto accident in 1966.

Today Jan is on the mend after severe head injuries, and he and Dean are headliners on the concert circuit once again.

			Current Price Range		P/Y AVG
☐55522		SHE'S STILL TALKING BABY TALK/			
		FROSTY THE SNOWMAN	12.00	21.00	18.00
☐55531		LINDA/			
		WHEN I LEARN HOW TO CRY . .	3.00	5.00	3.50
☐55580		SURF CITY/			
		SHE'S MY SUMMER GIRL	3.00	5.50	3.85
☐55613		HONOLULU LULU/SOMEDAY			
		YOU'LL GO WALKING BY	3.00	5.50	3.85
☐55641		DRAG CITY/			
		SCHLOCK ROD.(PT. 1)	3.00	5.50	3.85
☐55672		DEAD MAN'S CURVE/			
		NEW GIRL IN SCHOOL	3.00	5.50	3.85
☐55704		THE LITTLE OLD LADY FROM			
		PASADENA/MY MIGHTY G.T.O.	3.00	5.50	3.85
☐55724		RIDE THE WILD SURF/			
		THE ANAHEIM, AZUSA AND			
		CUCAMONGA SEWING CIRCLE,			
		BOOK REVIEW AND TIMING			
		ASSOCIATION	3.00	5.50	3.85
☐55727		SIDEWALK SURFIN'/			
		WHEN IT'S OVER	3.00	5.50	3.85
☐55766		FROM ALL OVER THE WORLD/			
		FREEWAY FLYER	3.00	5.50	3.85
☐55792		YOU REALLY KNOW HOW TO HURT			
		A GUY/IT'S AS EASY AS 1, 2, 3	3.00	5.50	3.85
☐55833		I FOUND A GIRL/IT'S A			
		SHAME TO SAY GOODBYE	3.00	5.50	3.85
☐55849		FOLK CITY/BEGINNING TO AN END	3.25	5.50	4.00
☐55860		BATMAN/BUCKET ''T''	3.00	5.00	3.50
☐55886		POPSICLE/NORWEGIAN WOOD . .	2.75	4.50	3.00
☐55905		FIDDLE AROUND/			
		A SURFER'S DREAM	3.00	5.00	3.50
☐55923		SCHOOL DAY/			
		THE NEW GIRL IN SCHOOL	3.00	5.00	3.50
☐10	*JAN AND DEAN*	HAWAII/TIJUANA	40.00	70.00	45.00
☐11		FAN TAN/LOVE AND HATE	40.00	70.00	45.00
☐001	*J & D*	SUMMERTIME, SUMMERTIME/			
		CALIFORNIA LULLABY	40.00	70.00	45.00
☐401		SUMMERTIME, SUMMERTIME/			
		CALIFORNIA LULLABY	8.25	14.00	12.00
☐402		LIKE A SUMMER RAIN/			
		LOUISIANA MEN	9.50	17.00	15.00
☐401	*MAGIC LAMP*	SUMMERTIME, SUMMERTIME/			
		CALIFORNIA LULLABY	8.25	14.00	12.00
☐44036	*COLUMBIA*	YELLOW BALLOON/			
		TASTE OF RAIN	8.25	14.00	12.00
☐7151	*WARNER*				
	BROTHERS	ONLY A BOY/LOVE AND HATE . . .	14.00	24.00	20.00
☐7219		LAUREL AND HARDY/			
		I KNOW MY MIND	12.00	21.00	18.00
		JAN AND DEAN—ALBUMS			
☐101 (M)	*DORE*	JAN AND DEAN			
		(with color photo insert)	60.00	145.00	100.00
☐3248 (M)	*LIBERTY*	JAN AND DEAN'S GREATEST HITS	10.00	25.00	22.50
☐7248 (S)		JAN AND DEAN'S GREATEST HITS	14.00	34.00	30.00
☐3294 (M)		JAN AND DEAN TAKE LINDA			
		SURFING	8.00	21.00	18.00
☐7294 (S)		JAN AND DEAN TAKE LINDA			
		SURFING	12.00	29.00	25.00
☐3314 (M)		SURF CITY	7.00	17.00	15.00
☐7314 (S)		SURF CITY	9.00	25.00	22.50
☐3339 (M)		DRAG CITY	7.00	17.00	15.00
☐7339 (S)		DRAG CITY	9.00	25.00	22.50

LIBERTY, LRP-3368, LP

LIBERTY, #55727, 45

			Current Price Range		P/Y AVG
☐3361 (M)		DEAD MAN'S CURVE/ NEW GIRL IN SCHOOL	8.00	21.00	18.00
☐7361 (S)		DEAD MAN'S CURVE/ NEW GIRL IN SCHOOL	12.00	29.00	25.00
☐3368 (M)		RIDE THE WILD SURF	8.00	21.00	18.00
☐7368 (S)		RIDE THE WILD SURF	12.00	29.00	25.00
☐3377 (M)		LITTLE OLD LADY FROM PASADENA	7.00	17.00	15.00
☐7377 (S)		LITTLE OLD LADY FROM PASADENA	8.00	25.00	22.50
☐3403 (M)		COMMAND PERFORMANCE	7.00	17.00	15.00
☐7403 (S)		COMMAND PERFORMANCE	9.00	25.00	22.50
☐3414 (M)		JAN AND DEAN'S POP SYMPHONY NO. 1	8.00	21.00	18.00
☐7414 (S)		JAN AND DEAN'S POP SYMPHONY NO. 1	12.00	29.00	25.00
☐3417 (M)		JAN AND DEAN'S GOLDEN HITS, VOL. II	8.00	21.00	18.00
☐7417 (S)		JAN AND DEAN'S GOLDEN HITS, VOL. II	8.00	21.00	18.00
☐3431 (M)		FOLK 'N' ROLL	8.00	21.00	18.00
☐7431 (S)		FOLK 'N' ROLL	7.00	17.00	15.00
☐3441 (M)		FILET OF SOUL	8.00	21.00	18.00
☐7441 (S)		FILET OF SOUL	7.00	17.00	15.00
☐3444 (M)		JAN AND DEAN MEET BATMAN	8.00	21.00	18.00
☐7444 (S)		JAN AND DEAN MEET BATMAN	7.00	17.00	15.00
☐3458 (M)		POPSICLE	9.00	25.00	22.50
☐7458 (S)		POPSICLE	7.00	17.00	15.00
☐3460 (M)		JAN AND DEAN'S GOLDEN HITS, VOL. III	9.00	25.00	22.50
☐7460 (S)		JAN AND DEAN'S GOLDEN HITS, VOL. III	7.00	17.00	15.00
☐101 (M)	**J & D**	SAVE FOR A RAINY DAY	35.00	78.00	75.00

JARMELS

☐3085	**LAURIE**	LITTLE LONELY ONE/ SHE LOVES TO DANCE	4.50	7.50	6.00
☐3098		A LITTLE BIT OF SOAP/ THE WAY YOU LOOK TONIGHT	3.00	5.00	3.50
☐3116		I'LL FOLLOW YOU/GEE OH GOSH	3.50	6.00	4.00
☐3124		RED SAILS IN THE SUNSET/ LONELINESS	3.50	6.00	4.00
☐3141		ONE BY ONE/LITTLE BUG	3.50	6.00	4.00
☐3174		COME ON GIRL/ KEEP YOUR MIND ON ME	3.50	6.00	4.00

JAVALONS

☐6901	**EKO**	THAT IS WHY/I TOOK A CHANCE	5.50	14.00	12.00

JAY AND THE AMERICANS
SEE: JAY BLACK, HARBOR LIGHTS, ROCKAWAYS, JAY TRAYNOR

☐353	**UNITED ARTISTS**	TONIGHT/THE OTHER GIRLS (without Jay Black)	3.75	6.00	4.50
☐415		SHE CRIED/DAWNING	3.00	5.00	3.50
☐479		THIS IS IT/IT'S MY TURN TO CRY	3.25	5.50	4.00
☐504		TOMORROW/YES	3.25	5.50	4.00
☐566		WHAT'S THE USE/ STRANGERS TOMORROW	3.25	5.50	4.00
☐626		ONLY IN AMERICA/ MY CLAIR DE LUNE	3.00	5.00	3.65
☐669		COME DANCE WITH ME/ LOOK IN MY EYES, MARIE	3.00	5.00	3.65
☐693		TO WAIT FOR LOVE/FRIDAY	3.00	5.00	3.65

		Current Price Range		P/Y AVG
☐759	COME A LITTLE BIT CLOSER/			
	GOODBYE, BOYS, GOODBYE ...	3.00	5.00	3.65
☐805	LET'S LOCK THE DOOR/			
	I'LL REMEMBER YOU	3.00	5.00	3.65
☐845	THINK OF THE GOOD TIMES/			
	IF YOU WERE MINE, GIRL	3.00	5.00	3.65
☐881	CARA MIA/WHEN IT'S ALL OVER	3.00	5.00	3.65
☐919	SOME ENCHANTED EVENING/GIRL	3.00	5.00	3.65
☐948	SUNDAY AND ME/			
	THROUGH THIS DOORWAY	3.00	5.00	3.65
☐992	WHY CAN'T YOU BRING ME			
	HOME?/BABY, STOP YOUR			
	CRYIN'	3.00	5.00	3.65
☐50016	CRYING/I DON'T NEED A FRIEND .	3.00	5.00	3.65
☐50046	LIVIN' ABOVE YOUR HEAD/LOOK			
	AT ME, WHAT DO YOU SEE? ...	3.00	5.00	3.65
☐50086	STOP THE CLOCK/			
	BABY, COME HOME	3.00	5.00	3.65
☐50094	HE'S RAINING IN MY SUNSHINE/			
	THE REASON FOR LIVING	3.00	5.00	3.65
☐50139	NATURE BOY/YOU AIN'T AS HIP			
	AS ALL THAT, BABY	3.00	5.00	3.65
☐50196	GOT HUNG UP ALONG THE WAY/			
	YELLOW FOREST	3.00	5.00	3.65
☐50222	FRENCH PROVINCIAL/			
	SHANGHAI NOODLE FACTORY .	3.00	5.00	3.65
☐50282	NO OTHER LOVE/			
	NO, I DON'T KNOW HER	3.00	5.00	3.65
☐50448	YOU AIN'T GONNA WAKE UP			
	CRYIN'/GEMINI	3.00	5.00	3.65
☐50475	THIS MAGIC MOMENT/			
	SINCE I DON'T HAVE YOU	3.00	5.00	3.65
☐50510	WHEN YOU DANCE/			
	NO, I DON'T KNOW HER	3.00	5.00	3.65
☐50535	HUSHABYE/GYPSY WOMAN	3.00	5.00	3.65
☐50567	LEARNIN' HOW TO FLY/			
	FOR THE LOVE OF A LADY	3.00	5.00	3.65
☐50605	WALKIN' IN THE RAIN/			
	FOR THE LOVE OF A LADY	3.00	5.00	3.65
☐50654	CAPTURE THE MOMENT/			
	DO YOU EVER THINK OF ME? ..	3.00	5.00	3.65
☐50683	DO I LOVE YOU/TRICIA			
	(TELL YOUR DADDY)	3.00	5.00	3.65
☐50858	THERE GOES MY BABY/			
	SOLITARY MAN	3.00	5.00	3.65

JAY AND THE AMERICANS—ALBUMS

			Current Price Range		P/Y AVG
☐3222 (M)	UNITED ARTISTS	SHE CRIED	8.00	21.00	18.00
☐6222 (S)		SHE CRIED	12.00	29.00	25.00
☐3300 (M)		JAY AND THE AMERICANS AT THE			
		CAFE WHA?	7.00	17.00	15.00
☐6300 (S)		JAY AND THE AMERICANS AT THE			
		CAFE WHA?	7.00	25.00	22.50
☐3417 (M)		BLOCKBUSTERS	7.00	17.00	15.00
☐6417 (S)		BLOCKBUSTERS	9.00	25.00	22.50
☐3453 (M)		GREATEST HITS	6.00	15.00	13.50
☐6453 (S)		GREATEST HITS..............	8.00	21.00	18.00
☐3474 (M)		SUNDAY AND ME	6.00	15.00	13.50
☐6474 (S)		SUNDAY AND ME	8.00	21.00	18.00
☐3534 (M)		LIVIN' ABOVE YOUR HEAD	5.50	14.00	12.00
☐6534 (S)		LIVIN' ABOVE YOUR HEAD	7.00	17.00	15.00
☐3555 (M)		GREATEST HITS, VOL. II	5.50	14.00	12.00
☐6555 (S)		GREATEST HITS, VOL. II	7.00	17.00	15.00
☐3562 (M)		TRY SOME OF THIS	5.50	14.00	12.00

			Current Price Range		P/Y AVG
☐6562 (S)		TRY SOME OF THIS	5.50	14.00	12.00
☐6671 (S)		SANDS OF TIME	5.50	14.00	12.00
☐6719 (S)		WAX MUSEUM	5.50	14.00	12.00
☐6751 (S)		WAX MUSEUM, VOL. II	5.50	14.00	12.00
☐6762 (S)		CAPTURE THE MOMENT	5.50	14.00	12.00

JAY AND THE DEANS

☐5405	**WARNER BROTHERS**	BELLS ARE RINGING/ SUPER HAWK	8.25	14.00	12.00

JAYHAWKS
SEE: MARATHONS, VIBRATIONS

☐109	**FLASH**	STRANDED IN THE JUNGLE/ MY ONLY DARLING	4.50	8.00	6.50

JAYNETTS

☐1102	**GOLDIE**	WE BELONG TO EACH OTHER/ HE'S CRYING INSIDE	3.75	6.00	4.50
☐369	**TUFF**	SALLY GO 'ROUND THE ROSES (PT. 1)/(PT. 2)	3.00	5.00	3.50
☐371		KEEP AN EYE ON HER (PT. 1)/ (PT. 2)	3.00	5.00	3.50

JAYNETTS—ALBUM

☐13 (M)	**TUFF**	SALLY, GO 'ROUND THE ROSES . .	9.00	25.00	22.50

CATHY JEAN AND THE ROOMATES
SEE: CATHY JEAN, ROOMATES

☐007	**VALMOR**	PLEASE LOVE ME FOREVER/ CANADIAN SUNSET	3.50	6.00	4.35
☐009		MAKE ME SMILE AGAIN/ SUGAR CAKE	3.50	6.00	4.35
☐011		ONE LOVE/I ONLY WANT YOU . . .	3.50	6.00	4.35
☐016		PLEASE TELL ME/SUGAR CAKE . .	3.50	6.00	4.35
☐40014	**PHILIPS**	BELIEVE ME/DOUBLE TROUBLE .	3.25	5.50	4.00

CATHY JEAN AND THE ROOMATES—ALBUM

☐789 (M)	**VALMOR**	AT THE HOP	25.00	45.00	31.00

CATHY JEAN

☐40106	**PHILIPS**	MY HEART BELONGS TO ONLY YOU/I ONLY WANT YOU	3.00	5.00	3.50
☐40143		BELIEVE ME/DOUBLE TROUBLE .	3.00	5.00	3.50

JEFFERSON AIRPLANE
FEATURED: GRACE SLICK
SEE: GREAT SOCIETY

☐8769	**RCA**	RUNNIN' AROUND THIS WORLD/ IT'S NO SECRET	3.50	6.00	4.35
☐8848		COME UP THE YEARS/ BLUES FROM AN AIRPLANE . . .	3.50	6.00	4.35
☐8967		BRINGING ME DOWN/LET ME IN .	3.50	6.00	4.35
☐9063		MY BEST FRIEND/ HOW DO YOU FEEL?	3.50	6.00	4.35
☐9140		SOMEBODY TO LOVE/ SHE HAS FUNNY CARS	3.00	5.00	3.65
☐9248		WHITE RABBIT/ PLASTIC FANTASTIC LOVER . . .	3.00	5.00	3.65
☐9297		BALLAD OF YOU AND ME AND POONEIL/TWO HEADS	3.00	5.00	3.65
☐9389		WATCH HER RIDE/MARTHA	3.00	5.00	3.65
☐9496		GREASY HEART/ SHARE A LITTLE JOKE	3.00	5.00	3.65
☐9644		CROWN OF CREATION/LATHER . .	3.00	5.00	3.65

			Current Price Range		P/Y AVG
☐ 0245		VOLUNTEERS/			
		WE CAN BE TOGETHER	3.00	5.00	3.65
☐ 0150		THE OTHER SIDE OF THIS LIFE/			
		PLASTIC FANTASTIC LOVER . . .	3.00	5.00	3.65

JELLY BEANS

☐ 10-003	**RED BIRD**	I WANNA LOVE HIM SO BAD/			
		SO LONG	3.00	5.00	3.50
☐ 10-011		BABY BE MINE/THE KIND OF BOY			
		YOU CAN'T FORGET	3.00	5.00	3.50
☐ 001	**ESKEE**	I'M HIP TO YOU/YOU DON'T			
		MEAN NO GOOD TO ME	3.25	5.50	4.00

WAYLON JENNINGS

☐ 106	**TREND**	THE STAGE/			
		BABY WALKS ALL OVER ME . . .	7.50	12.00	10.00
☐ 55130	**BRUNSWICK**	JOLE BLON/WHEN SIN STOPS . . .	50.00	96.00	90.00
		GUITAR ON BRUNSWICK 55130: BUDDY HOLLY			
☐ 121639	**BAT**	CRYING/DREAM BABY	9.50	18.00	15.00
☐ 722	**A & M**	RAVE ON/LOVE DENIED	6.00	12.00	10.00

WAYLON JENNING AND WILLIE NELSON

☐ PB-10529	**RCA**	GOOD HEARTED WOMAN/			
		HEAVEN AND HELL	3.00	5.00	3.50
☐ PB-11198		MAMAS DON'T LET YOUR BABY			
		GROW UP TO BE COWBOYS/			
		I CAN GET OFF ON YOU	3.00	5.00	3.50
	WAYLON JENNINGS AND WILLIE NELSON—ALBUM				
☐ AFLI-2686	**RCA**	WAYLON AND WILLIE	5.00	10.00	7.00

JERRY AND JEFF
FEATURED: TONY ORLANDO

☐ SK101	**SUPERK**	SWEET SWEET LOVIN' YOU/			
		MR. JENSEN	13.00	25.00	18.00

JESTERS

☐ 218	**WINLEY**	SO STRANGE/			
		LOVE NO ONE BUT YOU	4.50	7.50	6.00
☐ 221		PLEASE LET ME LOVE YOU/			
		I'M FALLING IN LOVE	4.50	7.50	6.00
☐ 225		THE PLEA/OH BABY	3.75	6.00	4.50
☐ 242		THE WIND/SALLY GREEN	3.75	6.00	4.50
☐ 248		THAT'S HOW IT GOES/			
		TUTTI FRUITTI	3.75	6.00	4.50
☐ 252		COME LET ME SHOW YOU/			
		UNCLE HENRY'S BASEMENT . .	3.75	6.00	4.50
☐ 5011	**CYCLONE**	I LAUGHED/			
		NOW THAT YOU'RE GONE	9.50	17.00	15.00

JEWEL AND EDDIE (WITH JEWEL AKENS)
GUITAR: EDDIE COCHRAN

☐ 1004	**SILVER**	OPPORTUNITY/			
		DOIN' THE HULLY GULLY	6.00	11.00	7.00
☐ 1004		OPPORTUNITY/			
		STROLLIN' GUITAR	6.00	11.00	7.00
☐ 1008		SIXTEEN TONS/			
		MY EYES ARE CRYING FOR YOU	6.00	11.00	7.00

JILL AND RAY
SEE: PAUL AND PAULA

☐ 979	**LE CAM**	HEY PAULA/BOBBIE IS THE ONE .	12.00	21.00	18.00

			Current Price Range		P/Y AVG

JIVE FIVE

☐ 1006	BELTONE	MY TRUE STORY/			
		WHEN I WAS SINGLE	3.25	5.50	4.00
☐ 1014		NEVER, NEVER/PEOPLE			
		FROM ANOTHER WORLD	3.25	5.50	4.00
☐ 2019		NO, NOT AGAIN/			
		HULLY GULLY CALLIN' TIME ..	3.25	5.50	4.00
☐ 2024		WHAT TIME IS IT?/			
		BEGGIN' YOU PLEASE	3.25	5.50	4.00
☐ 2029		THESE GOLDEN RINGS/DO YOU			
		HEAR WEDDING BELLS?	3.00	5.00	3.65
☐ 2030		JOHNNY NEVER KNEW/			
		LILI MARLENE	3.00	5.00	3.65
☐ 2034		SHE'S MY GIRL/RAIN	3.00	5.00	3.65
☐ 219	SKETCH	UNITED/			
		PROVE EVERY WORD YOU SAY .	4.00	7.00	4.85
☐ 807	UNITED ARTISTS	UNITED/			
		PROVE EVERY WORD YOU SAY .	3.00	5.00	3.65
☐ 853		I'M A HAPPY MAN/			
		KISS KISS KISS	3.00	5.00	3.65
☐ 936		A BENCH IN THE PARK/			
		PLEASE BABY PLEASE	3.00	5.00	3.65
☐ 50004		MAIN STREET/GOIN' WILD	3.00	5.00	3.65
☐ 50033		IN MY NEIGHBORHOOD/			
		THEN CAME HEARTBREAK	3.00	5.00	3.65
☐ 50069		YOU'RE A PUZZLE/HA HA	3.00	5.00	3.65
☐ 50107		YOU PROMISED ME GREAT			
		THINGS/YOU	3.00	5.00	3.65
☐ 1250	MUSICOR	CRYING LIKE A BABY/			
		YOU'LL FALL IN LOVE	3.00	5.00	3.65
☐ 1270		NO MORE TEARS/			
		YOU'LL FALL IN LOVE	3.00	5.00	3.65
☐ 1305		BLUES IN THE GHETTO/SUGAR ..	3.00	5.00	3.65
☐ 32736	DECCA	I WANT YOU TO BE MY BABY/			
		IF I HAD A CHANCE TO			
		LOVE YOU	3.00	5.00	3.65

JIVE FIVE—ALBUMS

☐ 3455 (M)	UNITED ARTISTS	JIVE FIVE....................	8.00	21.00	18.00
☐ 6455 (S)		JIVE FIVE....................	12.00	29.00	25.00

JIVETONES

☐ 25020	APT	GERALDINE/DING DING DONG ...	8.50	18.00	16.00

JIVIN' GENE AND THE JOKERS

☐ 71485	MERCURY	BREAKIN' UP IS HARD TO DO/			
		MY NEED FOR LOVE	3.25	5.50	4.00
☐ 71561		YOU'RE JEALOUS/GO ON, GO ON	3.25	5.50	4.00
☐ 71751		POOR ME/			
		THAT'S WHAT IT'S LIKE	3.25	5.50	4.00

MARCY JOE
FEATURED: LOU CHRISTIE

☐ 110	ROBBEE	RONNIE/MY FIRST MISTAKE	3.00	5.00	3.50
☐ 115		WHAT I DID THIS SUMMER/SINCE			
		GARY WENT IN THE NAVY	3.25	5.50	4.00
☐ 117		JUMPING JACK/TAKE A WORD ..	3.00	5.00	3.50

BILLY JOEL
SEE: ATTILA, HASSLES

☐ 0900	FAMILY	EVERYBODY LOVES YOU NOW/			
		SHE'S GOT A WAY	4.00	7.00	4.85

BILLY JOEL

Billy Joel first saw the light of day in Hicksville, Long Island, New York, in 1949 on May 9th. Music appealed to him at an early age; by 1953 he was taking piano lessons.

Joel played in a number of local rock groups during his mid-teens. He also encountered problems with the local police. Soon non-conformist Joel had dropped out of Hicksville High School to roam the streets.

He turned to amateur boxing, entering 26 local matches during the mid-1960s and winning 23. Still, Joel preferred making music. He hooked up with a Long Island band dubbed the Hassles. They eventually cut a pair of flop albums. Billy and the Hassles' drummer then became a duo called Atilla.

In 1971, Billy made an album called Cold Spring Harbor. It achieved moderate sales, and soon Joel drifted to Los Angeles. He ended up playing two years in a L. A. Bar, performing under the name Bill Martin.

In 1973, Joel signed with Columbia (his current recording home). "Piano Man" — written about his L. A. bar experiences — became a Top 30 hit. Joel then again slipped from the charts, only to come back in a big way with "Just the Way You Are" in 1977. He hasn't looked back since.

			Current Price Range		P/Y AVG
☐0906		TOMORROW IS TODAY/			
		EVERYBODY LOVES YOU NOW .	3.50	6.00	4.35
☐45963	COLUMBIA	PIANO MAN/YOU'RE MY HOME ..	3.00	5.00	3.65
☐46055		WORSE COMES TO WORST/			
		SOMEWHERE ALONG THE LINE	3.00	5.00	3.65
☐10064		THE ENTERTAINER/			
		THE MEXICAN CONNECTION ...	3.00	5.00	3.65
☐10412		SUMMER HIGHLAND FALLS/			
		JAMES	3.00	5.00	3.65
☐10562		SAY GOODBYE TO HOLLYWOOD/			
		I'VE LOVED THESE DAYS	3.50	6.00	4.00

LATER COLUMBIA SINGLES ARE WORTH UP TO $2.00 MINT

BILLY JOEL—ALBUM

☐2700 (S)	FAMILY	COLD SPRING HARBOR	20.00	40.00	24.00

COLUMBIA ALBUMS ARE WORTH UP TO $10.00 MINT

JOEY & THE LEXINGTONS

☐2154	COMET	THE GIRL I LOVE/HEAVEN	12.00	24.00	20.00
☐2029	DUNES	BOBBIE/TEARS FROM MY EYES .	8.50	18.00	16.00

ELTON JOHN
SEE: BLUESOLOGY

☐1643	PHILIPS	I'VE BEEN LOVING YOU/HERE'S			
		TO THE NEXT TIME (British)	30.00	58.00	37.00
☐70-008	DJM	LADY SAMANTHA/			
		ALL ACROSS THE HEAVENS ...	23.00	40.00	28.00
☐6017	CONGRESS	LADY SAMANTHA/			
		IT'S ME THAT YOU NEED	23.00	40.00	28.00
☐6022		BORDER SONG/			
		BAD SIDE OF THE MOON	14.00	27.00	16.50
☐55246	UNI	BORDER SONG/			
		BAD SIDE OF THE MOON	3.00	5.00	3.50
☐55265		YOUR SONG/			
		TAKE ME TO THE PILOT	2.75	4.50	3.00
☐55277		FRIENDS/HONEY ROLL	2.75	4.50	3.00
☐55314		LEVON/GOODBYE	2.75	4.50	3.00
☐55318		TINY DANCER/RAZOR FACE	2.75	4.50	3.00
☐55328		ROCKET MAN/SUZIE (DRAMAS)..	2.75	4.50	3.00
☐55343		HONKY CAT/SLAVE	2.75	4.50	3.00

MCA SINGLES ARE WORTH UP TO $1.75 MINT

ELTON JOHN—ALBUMS

☐73090 (S)	UNI	ELTON JOHN	9.00	22.00	14.00
☐73096 (S)		TUMBLEWOOD CONNECTION	9.00	22.00	14.00
☐93105 (S)		11-17-70	9.00	22.00	14.00
☐93120 (S)		MADMAN ACROSS THE WATER ..	9.00	22.00	14.00
☐93135 (S)		HONKY CHATEAU	9.00	22.00	14.00

MCA ALBUM REISSUES HAVE HALF THE VALUE OF UNI PRESSINGS

JOHNNIE AND JOE

☐1605	J & S	TRUST IN ME/			
		WHO DO YOU LOVE?	14.00	24.00	20.00
☐1630		WARM, SOFT AND LOVELY/			
		FALSO LOVE HAS GOT TO GO ..	12.00	21.00	18.00
☐1641		I'LL BE SPINNING/FEEL ALRIGHT	12.00	21.00	18.00
☐1654		ACROSS THE SEA/			
		MY BABY'S GONE, ON, ON	27.00	46.00	42.00
☐1654		OVER THE MOUNTAIN, ACROSS			
		THE SEA/MY BABY'S GONE,			
		ON, ON (second title)	9.50	18.00	15.00
☐1659		IT WAS THERE/			
		THERE GOES MY HEART	8.25	14.00	12.00
☐1701		RED SAILS IN THE SUNSET/			
		WHERE DID SHE GO?	7.00	14.00	12.00
☐1641	CHESS	I'LL BE SPINNING/FEEL ALRIGHT	5.50	11.00	9.00

ELTON JOHN

He was born Reginald Dwight in Middlesex, England. His birthdate was March 25, 1947. Fat, withdrawn and socially rejected as a boy, Dwight built his world around the piano. He later won a full scholarship to the Royal Academy of Music in London. He quit two weeks before graduation to work as an errand boy for a music publisher.

Reg later joined Bluesology, a British rock outfit. He was still fat and often hid behind the massive speakers so as not to be seen. He eventually summoned the courage to strike out for a solo career. He dieted off fifty pounds and changed his name to Elton John. (Bluesology's sax player was Elton Dean; its leader was Long John Baldry.)

Elton met a girl, fell in love and became engaged. She then left him and John attempted suicide by sticking his head in his apartment oven with the gas turned on. Luckily, he forgot to close the kitchen windows and survived.

John was later put in touch with Bernie Taupin, a full time egg gatherer who fancied himself as a poet. Together they wrote pop tunes for a year but nobody wanted to record them. They then put their efforts into Elton's performing career. Elton John and Bernie Taupin later came up with John's first winner, "Your Song", an ode of love from Taupin to his father. With that hit, Elton John was on his way.

			Current Price Range		P/Y AVG
☐ 1654		OVER THE MOUNTAIN, ACROSS THE SEA/MY BABY'S GONE, ON, ON	5.00	9.00	7.00
☐ 1677		I WAS SO LONELY/IF YOU TELL ME YOU'RE MINE	5.50	11.00	9.00
☐ 1693		WHY OH WHY?/WHY DID SHE GO?	5.50	11.00	9.00
☐ 1706		DARLING/MY BABY'S GONE	5.00	9.00	7.00
☐ 1769		YOU SAID IT AND DON'T FORGET IT/ACROSS THE SEA	5.00	9.00	7.00
☐ 5024	GONE	WHO DO YOU LOVE?/ TRUST IN ME	9.50	18.00	15.00
☐ 379	TUFF	THAT'S THE WAY YOU GO/ HERE WE GO, BABY	4.00	9.00	7.00
☐ 237	OMEGA	WE GET THAT FEELIN'/ SPEAK SOFTLY (ANGEL)	3.25	5.50	4.00
☐ 10079	ABC-PARAMOUNT	I ADORE YOU/ I WANT YOU HERE BESIDE ME	3.25	5.50	4.00

JOHNNY AND THE HURRICANES
SEE: CRAFTSMEN

☐ 1001	TWIRL	CROSSFIRE/LAZY	14.00	24.00	20.00
☐ 502	WARWICK	CROSSFIRE/LAZY	3.50	6.00	4.35
☐ 509		RED RIVER ROCK/BUCKEYE	3.25	5.50	4.00
☐ 513		REVILLE ROCK/TIME BOMB	3.25	5.50	4.00
☐ 520		BEATNIK FLY/SAND STORM	3.25	5.50	4.00
☐ 3036	BIG TOP	DOWN YONDER/SHEBA	3.25	5.50	4.00
☐ 3051		ROCKING GOOSE/REVIVAL	3.25	5.50	4.00
☐ 3056		YOU ARE MY SUNSHINE/ MOLLY-O	3.25	5.50	4.00
☐ 3063		JA-DA/MR. LONELY	3.25	5.50	4.00
☐ 3076		OLD SMOKIE/HIGH VOLTAGE	3.00	5.00	3.65
☐ 3090		TRAFFIC JAM/ FAREWELL, FAREWELL	3.00	5.00	3.65
☐ 3103		MISERLOU/SALVATION	3.00	5.00	3.65
☐ 3113		SAN ANTONIO ROSE/ COME ON TRAIN	3.00	5.00	3.65
☐ 3125		SHIEK OF ARABY/ MINNESOTA FATS	3.00	5.00	3.65
☐ 3132		WHATEVER HAPPENED TO BABY JANE?/GREENS AND BEANS	3.00	5.00	3.65
☐ 3146		JAMES BOND THEME/ HUNGRY EYES	3.00	5.00	3.65
☐ 3159		KAW-LIGA/ROUGH ROAD	3.00	5.00	3.65
☐ 214	ATILA	I LOVE YOU/JUDY'S MOODY	3.00	5.00	3.50
☐ 215		BECAUSE I LOVE HER/ WISDOM'S FIFTH TAKE	3.00	5.00	3.50
☐ 211	JEFF	SAGA OF THE BEATLES/RENE	3.25	5.50	4.00

JOHNNY AND THE HURRICANES—EP

☐ 700	WARWICK	JOHNNY AND THE HURRICANES	12.00	21.00	18.00

JOHNNY AND THE HURRICANES—ALBUMS

☐ 5002 (M)	TWIRL	BEATNIK FLY	17.00	40.00	35.00
☐ 2007 (M)	WARWICK	JOHNNY AND THE HURRICANES	20.00	50.00	45.00
☐ 2010 (M)		STORMSVILLE	17.00	40.00	35.00
☐ 2010 (S)		STORMSVILLE	30.00	66.00	60.00
☐ 1302 (M)	BIG TOP	THE BIG SOUND OF JOHNNY AND THE HURRICANES	17.00	40.00	35.00
☐ 1030 (M)	ATILA	LIVE AT THE STAR CLUB	17.00	40.00	35.00

MARV JOHNSON

☐ 663	KUDO	MY BABY-O/ONCE UPON A TIME	17.00	40.00	35.00
☐ 101	TAMLA	COME TO ME/WHISPER	24.00	42.00	36.00
☐ 160	UNITED ARTISTS	COME TO ME/WHISPER	3.50	7.00	4.65

MCA, MCA-3007, LP

LONDON, LP

			Current Price Range		P/Y AVG
☐175		I'M COMING HOME/ RIVER OF TEARS	3.00	5.00	3.50
☐185		YOU GOT WHAT IT TAKES/ DON'T LEAVE ME	3.00	5.00	3.50
☐208		I LOVE THE WAY YOU LOVE/ LET ME LOVE YOU	3.00	5.00	3.50
☐226		ALL THE LOVE I'VE GOT/ AIN'T GONNA BE THAT WAY ...	3.00	5.00	3.50
☐241		MOVE TWO MOUNTAINS/ I NEED YOU	3.00	5.00	3.50
☐273		HAPPY DAYS/BABY, BABY	3.00	5.00	3.50
☐294		MERRY-GO-ROUND/ TELL ME THAT YOU LOVE ME ..	3.00	5.00	3.50
☐322		I'VE GOT A NOTION/ HOW CAN WE TELL HIM?	2.75	4.50	3.00
☐359		OH MARY/SHOW ME..........	2.75	4.50	3.00
☐423		MAGIC MIRROR/ WITH ALL THAT'S IN ME	2.75	4.50	3.00
☐454		THAT'S HOW BAD/ HE GAVE ME YOU	2.75	4.50	3.00
☐483		LET YOURSELF GO/ THAT'S WHERE I LOST MY BABY	2.75	4.50	3.00
☐556		KEEP TELLIN' YOURSELF/ EVERYONE WHO'S BEEN IN LOVE WITH YOU	2.75	4.50	3.00
☐590		ANOTHER TEAR FALLS/ HE'S GOT THE WHOLE WORLD IN HIS HANDS	2.75	4.50	3.00
☐617		COME ON AND STOP/ NOT AVAILABLE	2.75	4.50	3.00
☐7042	GORDY	I'M NOT A PLAYTHING/WHY DO YOU WANT TO LET ME GO	2.75	4.50	3.00
☐7051		I MISS YOU BABY/ JUST THE WAY YOU ARE	2.75	4.50	3.00
☐7077		I'LL PICK A ROSE FOR MY ROSE/ YOU GOT THE LOVE I LOVE	2.75	4.50	3.00

MARV JOHNSON—ALBUMS

☐3081 (M)	UNITED ARTISTS	MARVELOUS MARV JOHNSON ...	14.00	34.00	30.00
☐3118 (M)		MORE MARV JOHNSON	12.00	29.00	25.00
☐3187 (M)		I BELIEVE...................	9.00	25.00	22.50

BRUCE JOHNSTON

SEE: BRUCE AND TERRY, RENEGADES, SAGITTARIUS

☐1003	RONDA	DO THE SURFER STOMP (PT. 1)/(PT. 2)	8.25	14.00	12.00
☐1354	DONNA	DO THE SURFER STOMP (PT. 1)/(PT. 2)	5.50	11.00	9.00
☐4202	DEL-FI	THE ORIGINAL SURFER STOMP/ PAJAMA PARTY	5.00	9.00	7.00

BRUCE JOHNSTON—ALBUMS

☐1228 (M)	DEL-FI	SURFER'S PAJAMA PARTY	12.00	29.00	25.00
☐1228 (S)		SURFER'S PAJAMA PARTY	17.00	40.00	35.00
☐2057 (M)	COLUMBIA	SURFIN' AROUND THE WORLD ..	17.00	40.00	35.00
☐8857 (S)		SURFIN' AROUND THE WORLD ..	22.00	56.00	50.00

DAVID JONES

SEE: MONKEES

☐764	COLPIX	DREAM GIRL/ TAKE ME TO PARADISE	3.25	5.50	4.00
☐784		WHAT ARE WE GOING TO DO?/ THIS BOUQUET	3.00	5.00	3.50

JANIS JOPLIN
SEE: BIG BROTHER AND THE HOLDING COMPANY

She was born on January 19, 1943, in Port Arthur, TX. Janis Joplin was shy, overweight and the best reader in class. She skipped a grade and finished high school in 1970, a year ahead of her neighborhood peers.

Joplin enrolled at the University of Texas in Austin. But her stay there proved short when a fraternity named her Ugliest Man on Campus. She briefly took up with an Austin bluegrass group, the Waller Creek Boys.

Janis hitchhiked to San Francisco in 1963, worked in an office, then returned to Texas. She enrolled in Beaumont's Lamar University. A top student, Joplin left college forever in 1966 to return to the more liberal climes of San Francisco.

She fell in with a struggling band called Big Brother and the Holding Company. With Joplin at the mike, Big Brother tore up 1967's Monterey Pop Festival. The group signed with Mainstream Records, later shifting to the larger Columbia label.

At the end of 1968, Joplin departed Big Brother for a solo career. She returned to Port Arthur in 1970 for her high-school reunion to drunkenly chastise those who had once scorned (and now glorified) her. On October 3rd of that year, Janis Lynn Joplin died, alone in a Hollywood motel on a Saturday night, the victim of a heroin overdose.

			Current Price Range		P/Y AVG
☐789		GIRL FROM CHELSEA/ THEME FOR A NEW LOVE	3.00	5.00	3.50
		DAVID JONES—ALBUM			
☐493 (M)	**COLPIX**	DAVID JONES	8.00	21.00	18.00

JIMMY JONES

☐210	**RAMA**	PLAIN OLD LOVE/LOVER	5.00	9.00	7.00
☐4232	**ROULETTE**	PLAIN OLD LOVE/LOVER	3.75	6.00	4.50
☐9049	**CUB**	HANDY MAN/ THE SEARCH IS OVER	3.25	5.50	4.00
☐9067		GOOD TIMIN'/ MY PRECIOUS ANGEL	3.25	5.50	4.00
☐9072		THAT'S WHEN I CRIED/ I JUST GO FOR YOU	3.25	5.50	4.00
☐9076		ITCHIN'/EE-I-EE-OH	3.25	5.50	4.00
☐9082		FOR YOU/READY FOR LOVE	3.25	5.50	4.00
☐9085		I TOLD YOU SO/YOU GOT IT	3.25	5.50	4.00
☐9093		DEAR ONE/I SAY LOVE	3.25	5.50	4.00
☐9102		MR. MUSIC MAN/HOLLER HEY . .	3.25	5.50	4.00
☐9110		YOU'RE MUCH TOO YOUNG/ NIGHTS OF MEXICO	3.25	5.50	4.00
☐505	**VEE JAY**	MR. FIX-IT/NO INSURANCE	3.25	5.50	4.00
		JIMMY JONES—ALBUMS			
☐3847 (M)	**MGM**	GOOD TIMIN'	17.00	40.00	35.00
☐3847 (S)		GOOD TIMIN'	27.00	66.00	60.00

JOE JONES

☐488	**HERALD**	YOU DONE ME WRONG/ WHEN YOUR HAIR HAS TURNED TO SILVER	4.50	7.50	6.00
☐972	**RIC**	YOU TALK TOO MUCH/ I LOVE YOU STILL	3.25	5.50	4.00
☐4304	**ROULETTE**	YOU TALK TOO MUCH/ I LOVE YOU STILL	3.00	5.00	3.65
☐4316		ONE BIG MOUTH/ HERE'S WHAT YOU GOTTA DO .	3.00	5.00	3.65
☐4344		CALIFORNIA SUN/PLEASE DON'T TALK ABOUT ME	3.00	5.00	3.65
☐4377		THE BIG MULE/UH UH WIFE	3.00	5.00	3.65
		JOE JONES—ALBUMS			
☐25143 (M)	**ROULETTE**	YOU TALK TOO MUCH	8.00	21.00	18.00
☐25143 (S)		YOU TALK TOO MUCH	12.00	29.00	25.00

JOHN PAUL JONES
SEE: LED ZEPPLIN

☐915	**CAMEO/ PARKWAY**	BAJA/FOGGY DAY IN VIETNAM . .	9.50	18.00	15.00

TOM JONES

☐126	**TOWER**	LITTLE LONELY ONE/ THAT'S WHAT WE'LL ALL DO . .	4.50	7.50	6.00
☐176		I WAS A FOOL/LONELY JOE	3.75	6.00	4.50
☐190		CHILLS AND FEVER/ BABY I'M IN LOVE	4.50	7.50	6.00

JANIS JOPLIN
SEE: BIG BROTHER AND THE HOLDING COMPANY

☐45023	**COLUMBIA**	KOZMIC BLUES/ LITTLE GIRL BLUE	3.00	5.00	3.50
☐45080		ONE GOOD MAN/ TRY (A LITTLE BIT HARDER) . . .	3.25	5.50	4.00
☐45128		MAYBE/WORK ME. LORD	3.25	5.50	4.00
☐45284		KEEP ON/ HOME ON THE STRANGER	3.25	5.50	4.00

			Current Price Range		P/Y AVG
☐ 45314		ME AND BOBBY McGEE	2.25	4.00	2.50
☐ 45379		CRY BABY/MERCEDES BENZ	2.25	4.00	2.50
☐ 45433		GET IT WHILE YOU CAN/			
		MOVE OVER	2.25	4.00	2.50
☐ 45630		DOWN MON ME/BYE BYE BABY ..	2.25	4.00	2.50
		JANIS JOPLIN—ALBUMS			
☐ 9913 (S)	**COLUMBIA**	I GOT DEM OLD KOZMIC BLUES			
		AGAIN MAMA	5.00	12.00	10.00
☐ 30322 (S)		PEARL	5.00	12.00	10.00
☐ 32168 (S)		JANIS JOPLIN`S GREATEST HITS .	5.50	14.00	12.00
☐ 33160 (S)		JOPLIN IN CONCERT	5.00	11.25	9.50
☐ 33345 (S)		JANIS	5.00	11.25	9.50
☐ 713 (S)	**MEMORY**	WICKED WOMAN	5.50	14.00	12.00

JOSIE AND THE PUSSYCATS
FEATURED: CHERYL LADD

☐ 59-2	**CAPITOL**				
	CREATIVE PRODUCTS	WITH EVERY BEAT OF MY			
		HEART/JOSIE	5.00	9.00	7.00

J.R. & THE ATTRACTIONS

☐ 928	**HUNCH**	BRISTOL STOMP/I`M YOURS	12.00	25.00	22.00

JUMPIN' TONES

☐ 8004	**RAVEN**	I HAD A DREAM/I WONDER	14.00	24.00	20.00
☐ 8005		THAT ANGEL IS YOU/			
		GRANDMA`S HEARING AID	20.00	35.00	30.00

BILL JUSTIS

☐ 3519	**PHILLIPS**				
	INTERNATIONAL	RAUNCHY/MIDNIGHT MAN	3.50	6.00	4.35
☐ 3522		COLLEGE MAN/THE STRANGER ..	3.50	6.00	4.35
☐ 3525		SCROUNGIE/WILD RICE	3.25	5.50	4.00
☐ 3529		SUMMER HOLIDAY/			
		CATTYWAMPUS	3.25	5.50	4.00
☐ 3535		BOP TRAIN/STRING OF PEARLS ..	3.25	5.50	4.00
☐ 3544		CLOUD NINE/FLEA CIRCUS	3.25	5.50	4.00
		BILL JUSTIS—ALBUM			
☐ 1950 (M)	**PHILLIPS**				
	INTERNATIONAL	CLOUD NINE	16.00	38.00	25.00

K

KAC-TIES

☐ 702	**KAPE**	DONALD DUCK/			
		OVER THE RAINBOW	5.00	10.00	6.50
☐ 501		HAPPY BIRTHDAY/			
		GIRL IN MY HEART	3.00	6.00	5.00
☐ 165	**SHELLY**	OH WHAT A NIGHT/			
		LET ME IN YOUR LIFE	4.00	8.00	6.50
☐ 45-6299	**ATCO**	OH WHAT A NIGHT/			
		LET ME IN YOUR LIFE	3.50	7.50	5.50

KALIN TWINS

☐ 30552	**DECCA**	JUMPIN` JACK/			
		WALKIN` TO SCHOOL	4.50	7.50	6.00
☐ 30642		WHEN/THREE O`CLOCK THRILL .	3.25	5.50	4.00
☐ 30745		FORGET ME NOT/DREAM OF ME .	3.25	5.50	4.00
☐ 30807		IT`S ONLY THE BEGINNING/			
		OH! MY GOODNESS	3.00	5.00	3.50

			Current Price Range		P/Y AVG
☐30868		WHEN I LOOK IN THE MIRROR/			
		COOL	3.00	5.00	3.50
☐30911		SWEET SUGAR LIPS/MOODY	3.00	5.00	3.50
☐30977		WHY DON'T YOU BELIEVE ME?/			
		THE MEANING OF THE BLUES	3.00	5.00	3.50
☐31064		LONELINESS/CHICKEN THIEF	3.00	5.00	3.50
☐9-31111		TRUE TO YOU/BLUE BLUE TOWN	6.00	10.00	6.50
		KALIN TWINS—EPs			
☐2623	*DECCA*	WHEN	8.25	14.00	12.00
☐2641		FORGET ME NOT	5.50	11.00	9.00
		KALIN TWINS—ALBUMS			
☐8812 (S)	*DECCA*	THE KALIN TWINS	8.00	21.00	18.00
☐78812 (S)		THE KALIN TWINS	12.00	29.00	25.00

PAUL KANE (PAUL SIMON)

☐128	*TRIBUTE*	HE WAS MY BROTHER/			
		CARLOS DOMINGUEZ	26.00	50.00	31.00

ERNIE K-DOE

☐1050	*EMBER*	TUFF-ENUFF/MY LOVE FOR YOU			
		(Ernie Kado)	3.50	6.00	4.35
☐1075		SHIRLEY'S TUFF/			
		MY LOVE FOR YOU (Ernie Kado)	3.50	6.00	4.35
☐623	*MINIT*	MOTHER-IN-LAW/			
		WANTED: $10.000 REWARD	3.25	5.50	4.00
☐627		TE-TA-TE-TA-TA/REAL MAN	3.25	5.50	4.00
☐634		I CRIED MY LAST TEAR/			
		A CERTAIN GIRL	3.25	5.50	4.00
☐641		POPEYE JOE/COME ON HOME	3.25	5.50	4.00
☐645		HEY. HEY. HEY/			
		I LOVE YOU THE BEST	3.25	5.50	4.00
☐651		I GOT TO FIND SOMEBODY/			
		BEATING LIKE A TOM-TOM	3.25	5.50	4.00
☐656		GET OUT OF MY HOUSE/			
		LOVING YOU	3.25	5.50	4.00
☐661		EASIER SAID THAN DONE/			
		BE SWEET	3.25	5.50	4.00
		ERNIE K-DOE—ALBUM			
☐0002 (M)	*MINIT*	MOTHER-IN-LAW	18.00	38.00	25.00

KEITH

☐72596	*MERCURY*	AIN'T GONNA LIE/			
		IT STARTED ALL OVER AGAIN	3.00	5.00	3.65
☐72639		98.6/TEENIE BOPPER SONG	3.00	5.00	3.65
☐72652		TELL ME TO MY FACE/			
		PRETTY LITTLE SHY ONE	3.00	5.00	3.65
☐72695		DAYLIGHT SAVIN' TIME/			
		HAPPY WALKING AROUND	3.00	5.00	3.65
☐72715		SUGAR MAN/EASY AS PIE	3.00	5.00	3.65
☐72746		CANDY. CANDY/I'M SO PROUD	3.00	5.00	3.65
☐72794		THE PLEASURE OF YOUR			
		COMPANY/HURRY	3.00	5.00	3.65
☐74-0140	*RCA*	MARSTAND/THE PROBLEM	6.00	10.00	6.50
☐74-0222		FAIRY TALE OR TWO/			
		TRIXON'S ELECTION	6.00	10.00	6.50
		THE RCA RECORDINGS LISTED ARE PROMOS			
		KEITH—ALBUMS			
☐21102 (M)	*MERCURY*	98.6/AIN'T GONNA LIE	5.00	12.00	10.00
☐61102 (S)		98.6/AIN'T GONNA LIE	6.00	15.00	13.50
☐21129 (M)		OUT OF CRANK	5.00	12.00	10.00
☐61129 (S)		OUT OF CRANK	6.00	15.00	13.50

CAROLE KING

She was born Carole Klein in Brooklyn, New York, on February 9, 1941. Carole began singing when she was four. In a few years, she was composing. (She reportedly wrote the Drifters' "Up on the Roof" when she was 15.) Ms. King was a high school senior when neighborhood pal (and ex-boy friend) Neil Sedaka wrote and recorded "Oh! Carol" for her. (She encountered with the dismal "Oh! Neil.")

In 1959, Don Kirshner signed Carole to his stable of writers in his Nevins-Kirshner publishing organization. Ms. King soon met future husband Jerry Goffin; he was then a successful songwriter and record producer. The King-Goffin team turned out a large number of hits, including the Shirelles' "Will You Love Me Tomorrow?" and Bobby Vee's "Take Good Care of My Baby". Their baby sitter, Eva Boyd, sang their "Loco-Motion" as Little Eva in 1962. That year, after several flops, Carole King began her own recording career with "It Might As Well Rain until September".

Nothing was heard from Carole King from 1962 to 1971. In that year, though, her *Tapestry* album emerged. It is considered one of the finest LPs of the decade and for a time was the best-selling pop album in history. (*Frampton Comes Alive!* displaced it five years later.) Today Carole King reigns as the most successful female songwriter of all time.

			Current Price Range		P/Y AVG

KELLY FOUR
GUITAR: EDDIE COCHRAN

☐ 1001	**SILVER**	STROLLIN' GUITAR/GUYBO	5.50	11.00	9.00
☐ 1006		ANNIE HAD A PARTY/			
		SO FINE, BE MINE	5.50	11.00	9.00

CHRIS KENNER

☐ 5448	**IMPERIAL**	SICK AND TIRED/NOTHING WILL			
		KEEP ME FROM YOU	4.50	7.50	6.00
☐ 3229	**INSTANT**	I LIKE IT LIKE THAT (PT. 1)/			
		(PT. 2)	3.00	5.00	3.50
☐ 3234		PACKIN' UP/VERY TRUE STORY .	3.00	5.00	3.50
☐ 3237		SOMETHING YOU GOT/			
		COME SEE ABOUT ME	3.00	5.00	3.50
☐ 3244		HOW FAR/TIME	3.00	5.00	3.50
☐ 3252		LAND OF 1,000 DANCES/			
		THAT'S MY GIRL	3.00	5.00	3.50

KENNY AND THE CADETS (BEACH BOYS)

☐ 422	**RANDY**	BARBIE/WHAT IS A YOUNG GIRL			
		MADE OF (colored wax)	200.00	385.00	275.00
☐ 422		BARBIE/WHAT IS A YOUNG GIRL			
		MADE OF (black wax)	140.00	265.00	170.00

KENNY & THE SOCIALITES

☐ 001	**CROSSTOWN**	KING TUT ROCK/			
		I'LL HAVE TO DECIDE	8.25	18.00	16.00

KENNY & THE SOCIALITES "KING TUT ROCK" WAS NOT RELATED TO THE
KING TUT SONG BY STEVE MARTIN

CAROLE KING
SEE: CITY, BERTELL DACHE, GERMZ, PALISADES

☐ 9921	**ABC-PARAMOUNT**	GOIN' WILD/THE RIGHT GIRL	23.00	42.00	27.00
☐ 9986		BABY SITTIN'/UNDER THE STARS.	23.00	42.00	27.00
☐ 7560	**RCA**	QUEEN OF THE BEACH/			
		SHORT MORT	23.00	42.00	27.00
☐ 57	**ALPINE**	OH NEIL!/A VERY SPECIAL BOY .	40.00	75.00	44.00
☐ 2000	**COMPANION**	IT MIGHT AS WELL RAIN UNTIL			
		SEPTEMBER/NOBODY'S			
		PERFECT	32.00	60.00	37.00
☐ 2000	**DIMENSION**	IT MIGHT AS WELL RAIN UNTIL			
		SEPTEMBER/NOBODY'S			
		PERFECT	4.00	8.00	4.00
☐ 1004		SCHOOL BELLS ARE RINGING/			
		I DIDN'T HAVE ANY	7.00	13.00	8.00
☐ 1009		HE'S A BAD BOY/			
		WE GROW UP TOGETHER	5.00	10.00	6.00
☐ 7502	**TOMORROW**	A ROAD TO NOWHERE/			
		SOME OF YOUR LOVIN'	9.00	17.00	10.00

KING LIZARD (KIM FOWLEY)

☐ 99	**ORIGINAL SOUND**	BIG BAD CADILLAC/			
		MAN WITHOUT A COUNT	4.50	7.50	6.00

KINGSMEN

☐ 108	**JALYNNE**	LADY'S CHOICE/DIG THIS	5.00	9.00	7.00
☐ 712	**JERDEN**	LOUIE LOUIE/HAUNTED CASTLE .	21.00	35.00	30.00
☐ 143	**WAND**	LOUIE LOUIE/HAUNTED CASTLE .	2.75	4.50	3.00
☐ 150		MONEY/BENT SCEPTER	2.75	4.50	3.00
☐ 157		LITTLE LATIN LUPE LU/			
		DAVID'S MOOD	2.75	4.50	3.00
☐ 164		DEATH OF AN ANGEL/			
		SEARCHING FOR LOVE	2.75	4.50	3.00

			Current Price Range		P/Y AVG
☐172		THE JOLLY GREEN GIANT/			
		LONG GREEN	2.75	4.50	3.00
☐183		THE CLIMB/I'M WAITING	2.75	4.,50	3.00
☐189		ANNIE FANNY/GIVE HER LOVIN'.	2.75	4.50	3.00
☐1107		THE GAMMA GOOCHEE/			
		IT'S ONLY THE DOG	2.75	4.50	3.00
☐1115		KILLER JOE/LITTLE GREEN THING	2.75	4.50	3.00
		LATER WAND SINGLES ARE WORTH UP TO $1.75 MINT			
		KINGSMEN—ALBUMS			
☐657 (M)	*WAND*	IN PERSON...................	6.00	12.00	10.00
☐659 (M)		VOLUME 2	6.00	12.00	10.00
☐662 (M)		VOLUME 3	6.00	12.00	10.00
☐670 (M)		ON CAMPUS	6.00	12.00	10.00
☐674 (M)		16 GREATEST HITS	5.50	11.00	9.00

KINGSMEN
FEATURED: BILL HALEY'S COMETS

☐115	*EAST WEST*	WEEKEND/BETTER BELIEVE IT ..	3.75	5.50	4.50
☐120		THE CAT WALK/CONGA ROCK ...	4.50	7.50	6.00

KINGSTON TRIO

☐3970	*CAPITOL*	SCARLET RIBBONS/			
		THREE JOLLY COACHMEN	5.00	9.00	6.00
☐4049		TOM DOOLEY/RUBY RED	3.50	6.00	4.35
☐4114		RASPBERRIES, STRAWBERRIES/			
		SALLY	3.50	6.00	4.35
☐4167		TIJUANA JAIL/OH, CINDY	3.25	5.50	4.00
☐4221		M.T.A./ALL MY SORROWS	3.25	5.50	4.00
☐4271		A WORRIED MAN/SAN MIGUEL ..	3.25	5.50	4.00
☐4303		COO COO-U/GREEN GRASSES ...	3.50	6.00	4.35
☐4338		EL MATADOR/			
		HOME FROM THE HILL	3.25	5.50	4.00
☐4379		BAD MAN BLUNDER/THE ESCAPE			
		OF OLD JOHN WEBB	3.25	5.50	4.00
☐4441		EVERGLADES/THIS MORNIN'			
		THIS EVENIN' SO SOON	3.25	5.50	4.00
☐4536		YOU'RE GONNA MISS ME/			
		EN EL AGUA	3.25	5.50	4.00
☐4671		WHERE HAVE ALL THE FLOWERS			
		GONE/O KEN KARANGA	3.00	5.00	3.65
☐4740		SCOTCH AND SODA/			
		JANE. JANE. JANE	3.00	5.00	3.65
☐4808		OLD JOE CLARK/			
		C'MON HOME BETTY	3.50	5.50	4.00
☐4842		ONE MORE TOWN/			
		SHE WAS GOOD TO ME	3.00	5.00	3.65
☐4898		GREENBACK DOLLAR/			
		THE NEW FRONTIER	3.00	5.00	3.65
☐4951		REVEREND MR. BLACK/			
		ONE MORE ROUND	3.00	5.00	3.65
☐5005		DESERT PETE/			
		BALLAD OF THE THRESHER ...	3.00	5.00	3.65
☐5078		ALLY ALLY OXEN FREE/			
		MARCELLE VAHINE	3.00	5.00	3.65
☐5138		LAST NIGHT I HAD THE			
		STRANGEST DREAM/			
		THE PATRIOT GAME	3.50	5.50	4.00
☐5166		SEASONS IN THE SUN/			
		IF YOU DON'T LOOK AROUND ..	3.50	5.50	4.00
		KINGSTON TRIO—ALBUMS			
☐996 (M)	*CAPITOL*	THE KINGSTON TRIO	8.00	21.00	18.00
☐1107 (M)		FROM THE HUNGRY I	8.00	21.00	18.00
☐1199 (M)		THE KINGSTON TRIO AT LARGE ..	7.00	17.00	15.00
☐1199 (S)		THE KINGSTON TRIO AT LARGE ..	8.00	21.00	18.00

			Current Price Range		P/Y AVG
☐ 1258 (M)		HERE WE GO AGAIN	7.00	17.00	15.00
☐ 1258 (S)		HERE WE GO AGAIN	8.00	21.00	18.00
☐ 1352 (M)		SOLD OUT	7.00	17.00	15.00
☐ 1352 (S)		SOLD OUT	8.00	21.00	18.00
☐ 1407 (M)		STRING ALONG	7.00	17.00	15.00
☐ 1407 (S)		STRING ALONG	8.00	21.00	18.00
☐ 1183 (S)		STEREO CONCERT	7.00	17.00	15.00
☐ 1446 (S)		THE LAST MONTH OF THE YEAR	7.00	17.00	15.00
☐ 1474 (S)		MAKE WAY	7.00	17.00	15.00
☐ 1564 (S)		GOIN' PLACES	7.00	17.00	15.00
☐ 1642 (S)		THE KINGSTON TRIO CLOSE UP	7.00	17.00	15.00
☐ 1658 (S)		COLLEGE CONCERT	7.00	17.00	15.00
☐ 1705 (S)		THE BEST OF THE KINGSTON TRIO	6.00	15.00	13.50
☐ 1747 (S)		SOMETHING SPECIAL	6.00	15.00	13.50
☐ 1809 (S)		NEW FRONTIER	6.00	15.00	13.50
☐ 1871 (S)		KINGSTON TRIO #16	6.00	15.00	13.50
☐ 1935 (S)		SUNNY SIDE!	6.00	15.00	13.50
☐ 2005 (S)		SING A SONG WITH THE KINGSTON TRIO	6.00	15.00	15.00
☐ 2011 (S)		TIME TO THINK	6.00	15.00	13.50
☐ 2081 (S)		BACK IN TOWN	6.00	15.00	13.50

KINKS
SEE: DAVE DAVIES

☐ 308	**CAMEO**	LONG TALL SALLY/ I TOOK MY BABY HOME	46.00	82.00	75.00
☐ 345		LONG TALL SALLY/ I TOOK MY BABY HOME	34.00	54.00	48.00
☐ 348		YOU STILL WANT ME/ YOU DO SOMETHING TO ME	34.00	54.00	48.00
☐ 0306	**REPRISE**	YOU REALLY GOT ME/ IT'S ALL RIGHT	4.25	7.00	5.00
☐ 0334		ALL DAY AND ALL OF THE NIGHT/ I GOTTA MOVE	4.25	7.00	5.00
☐ 0347		TIRED OF WAITING FOR YOU/ COME ON NOW	4.25	7.00	5.00
☐ 0366		WHO'LL BE THE NEXT IN LINE?/ EVERYBODY IS GONNA BE HAPPY	3.25	5.50	4.00
☐ 0379		SET ME FREE/I NEED YOU	3.25	5.50	4.00
☐ 0409		SEE MY FRIENDS/NEVER MET A GIRL LIKE YOU BEFORE	3.25	5.50	4.00
☐ 0420		A WELL RESPECTED MAN/ SUCH A SHAME	3.25	5.50	4.00
☐ 0454		TILL THE END OF THE DAY/ WHERE HAVE ALL THE GOOD TIMES GONE	3.25	5.50	4.00
☐ 0471		DEDICATED FOLLOWER OF FASHION/SITTING ON MY SOFA	3.25	5.50	4.00
☐ 0497		SUNNY AFTERNOON/ I'M NOT LIKE EVERYONE ELSE	3.25	5.50	4.00
☐ 0540		DEADEND STREET/ BIG BLACK SMOKE	3.25	5.50	4.00
☐ 0587		MR. PLEASANT/HARRY RAG	3.25	5.50	4.00
☐ 0612		WATERLOO SUNSET/ TWO SISTERS	3.25	5.50	4.00
☐ 0647		AUTUMN ALMANAC/ DAVID WAITS	3.25	5.50	4.00
☐ 0691		WONDERBOY/POLLY	3.25	5.50	4.00
☐ 0743		LOLA/APEMAN	4.50	7.50	6.00
☐ 0762		SHE'S GOT EVERYTHING/DAYS	3.00	5.00	3.50
☐ 0806		STARSTRUCK/PICTURE BOOK	3.00	5.00	3.50
☐ 0847		VILLAGE GREEN PRESERVATION SOCIETY/WALTER	3.00	5.00	3.50

LONDON, PAS 71028, LP

REPRISE, 6217, LP

			Current Price Range		P/Y AVG
☐0863		VICTORIA/BRAINWASHED	3.00	5.00	3.50
☐0930		LOLA/MINDLESS CHILD OF MOTHERHOOD	2.75	4.50	3.00
☐0979		APEMAN/RATS	2.75	4.50	3.00
☐1017		THE WAY LOVE USED TO BE/ GOD'S CHILDREN	2.75	4.50	3.00
☐1094		KING KONG/WATERLOO SUNSET .	2.75	4.50	3.00

RCA SINGLES ARE WORTH UP TO $1.75 MINT

KINKS—ALBUMS

☐6143 (M)	REPRISE	YOU REALLY GOT ME	9.00	25.00	22.50
☐6143 (S)		YOU REALLY GOT ME	14.00	35.00	30.00
☐6158 (M)		KINKS SIZE	9.00	25.00	22.50
☐6158 (S)		KINKS SIZE	14.00	35.00	30.00
☐6173 (M)		KINDA KINKS .'..............	9.00	25.00	22.50
☐6173 (S)		KINDA KINKS	14.00	35.00	30.00
☐6184 (M)		KINKS KINGDOM	9.00	25.00	22.50
☐6184 (S)		KINKS KINGDOM	14.00	35.00	30.00
☐6197 (M)		KINK KONTROVERSY	9.00	25.00	22.50
☐6197 (S)		KINK KONTROVERSY	14.00	35.00	30.00
☐6217 (M)		THE KINKS' GREATEST HITS	8.00	21.00	18.00
☐6217 (S)		THE KINKS' GREATEST HITS	9.00	25.00	22.50
☐6260 (M)		LIVE KINKS	7.00	17.00	15.00
☐6280 (S)		LIVE KINKS	8.00	21.00	18.00
☐6279 (M)		SOMETHING ELSE	7.00	17.00	15.00
☐6279 (S)		SOMETHING ELSE	8.00	21.00	18.00
☐6327 (S)		THE VILLAGE GREEN PRESERVATION SOCIETY	7.00	17.00	15.00
☐6366 (S)		ARTHUR...................	7.00	17.00	15.00
☐6423 (S)		LOLA VERSUS THE POWERMAN ..	7.00	17.00	15.00
☐6454 (S)		KINK KRONIKLES	7.00	17.00	15.00
☐2127 (S)		THE GREAT LOST KINKS ALBUM .	7.00	17.00	15.00

KISS

FEATURED: GENE SIMMONS

☐931	BELL	HEY, MR. HOLY MAN/ KIDS ARE CRYING	3.75	6.00	4.50
☐0004	CASABLANCA	LOVE THEME FROM KISS/ NOTHIN' TO LOSE	3.75	5.50	4.00
☐0011		KISSIN' TIME/NOTHIN' TO LOSE .	3.00	5.00	3.50
☐0015		STRUTTER/100,000 YEARS	3.00	5.00	3.50
☐823		HOTTER THAN HELL/LET ME GO, ROCK AND ROLL	3.00	5.00	3.50
☐829		ROCK AND ROLL ALL NITE/ GETAWAY	2.75	4.50	3.00
☐841		C'MON AND LOVE ME/GETAWAY	2.75	4.50	3.00
☐850		ROCK AND ROLL ALL NITE/ROCK AND ROLL ALL NITE (LIVE)	2.50	4.00	2.50

KNICKERBOCKERS

☐59268	CHALLENGE	BITE BITE BARRACUDA/ ALL I NEED IS YOU	3.50	6.00	4.35
☐59293		JERKTOWN/ROOM FOR ONE MORE	3.50	6.00	4.35
☐59321		LIES/THE COMING GENERATION .	3.25	5.50	4.00
☐59326		ONE TRACK MIND/I MUST BE DOING SOMETHING RIGHT	3.00	5.00	3.65
☐59332		HIGH ON LOVE/STICK WITH ME ..	3.00	5.00	3.65
☐59335		CHAPEL IN THE FIELDS/ JUST ONE GIRL	3.00	5.00	3.65
☐59341		RUMORS, GOSSIP, WORDS UNTRUE/LOVE IS A BIRD	3.00	5.00	3.65
☐59348		CAN YOU HELP ME/ PLEASE DON'T LOVE HIM	3.00	5.00	3.65
☐59359		SWEET GREEN FIELDS/ WHAT DOES THAT MAKE YOU?	3.00	5.00	3.65

			Current Price Range		P/Y AVG
☐59366		COME AND GET IT/ WISHFUL THINKING	3.00	5.00	3.65
☐59380		YOU'LL NEVER WALK ALONE/ I CAN DO IT BETTER	3.00	5.00	3.65
☐59384		THEY RAN FOR THEIR LIVES/ AS A MATTER OF FACT	3.00	5.00	3.65
		KNICKERBOCKERS—ALBUMS			
☐621 (M)	*CHALLENGE*	JERK AND TWINE TIME	9.00	25.00	22.50
☐621 (S)		JERK AND TWINE TIME	12.00	29.00	25.00
☐622 (M)		LIES	9.00	25.00	22.50
☐622 (S)		LIES	12.00	29.00	25.00
☐12664 (M)		LLOYD THAXTON PRESENTS THE KNICKERBOCKERS	8.00	21.00	18.00
☐12664 (S)		LLOYD THAXTON PRESENTS THE KNICKERBOCKERS	9.00	25.00	22.50

GLADYS KNIGHT AND THE PIPS

☐55048	*BRUNSWICK*	CHING CHONG/ WHISTLE MY LOVE (Pips)	20.00	34.00	30.00
☐2510	*HUNTOM*	EVERY BEAT OF MY HEART/ ROOM IN YOUR HEART	14.00	24.00	20.00
☐386	*VEE JAY*	EVERY BEAT OF MY HEART/ ROOM IN YOUR HEART	3.50	6.00	4.35
☐545		QUEEN OF TEARS/ A LOVE LIKE MINE	3.25	5.50	4.00
☐2012	*ENJOY*	LOVE CALL/WHAT SHALL I DO	3.25	5.50	4.00
☐5035	*EVERLAST*	I HAD A DREAM LAST NIGHT/ HAPPINESS	3.25	5.50	4.00
☐1050	*FURY*	EVERY BEAT OF MYHEART/ ROOM IN YOUR HEART	3.25	5.50	4.00
☐1052		GUESS WHO/ STOP RUNNING AROUND	3.25	5.50	4.00
☐1054		LETTER FULL OF TEARS/ YOU BROKE YOUR PROMISE	3.00	5.00	3.65
☐1064		OPERATOR/I'LL TRUST IN YOU	3.00	5.00	3.65
☐1067		DARLING/LINDA	3.00	5.00	3.65
☐1073		COME SEE ABOUT ME/ I WANT THAT KIND OF LOVE (Gladys Knight)	3.00	5.00	3.65
☐326	*MAXX*	GIVING UP/MAYBE MAYBE BABY	3.00	5.00	3.65
☐329		LOVERS ALWAYS FORGIVE/ ANOTHER LOVE	3.00	5.00	3.65
☐331		EITHER WAY I LOSE/ GO AWAY, STAY AWAY	3.00	5.00	3.65
☐334		STOP AND THINK IT OVER/ WHO KNOWS	3.00	5.00	3.65
		SOUL SINGLES ARE WORTH UP TO $1.75 MINT			
		GLADYS KNIGHT AND THE PIPS—ALBUMS			
☐1003 (M)	*FURY*	LETTER FULL OF TEARS	17.00	40.00	35.00
☐3000 (M)	*MAXX*	GLADYS KNIGHT AND THE PIPS	9.00	25.00	22.50

SONNY KNIGHT

☐137	*VITA*	CONFIDENTIAL/JAIL BIRD	8.25	14.00	12.00
☐15507	*DOT*	CONFIDENTIAL/JAIL BIRD	3.75	6.00	4.50
☐1	*STARLA*	DEDICATED TO YOU/SHORT WALK	3.75	6.00	4.50
☐10		ONCE IN A WHILE/SCHOOL'S OUT	5.00	8.50	7.00
☐102	*FIFO*	COLD, COLD NIGHT/ SAVING MY LOVE	3.25	5.50	4.00

BUDDY KNOX

☐797	*TRIPLE D*	PARTY DOLL/I'M STICKIN' WITH YOU (Jimmy Bowen)	76.00	130.00	120.00
☐4002	*ROULETTE*	PARTY DOLL/MY BABY'S GONE	4.50	7.50	6.00

			Current Price Range		P/Y AVG
☐4009		ROCK YOUR LITTLE BABY TO SLEEP/DON'T MAKE ME CRY ..	3.25	5.50	4.00
☐4018		HULA LOVE/DEVIL WOMAN	3.25	5.50	4.00
☐4042		SWINGIN' DADDY/ WHENEVER I'M LONELY	3.25	5.50	4.00
☐4082		SOMEBODY TOUCHED ME/ C'MON BABY	3.25	5.50	4.00
☐4120		TEASABLE, PLEASABLE YOU/ THAT'S WHY I CRY	3.00	5.00	3.50
☐4140		I THINK I'M GONNA KILL MYSELF/ TO BE WITH YOU	3.00	5.00	3.50
☐4179		I AIN'T SHARIN' SHARON/ TASTE OF THE BLUES	3.00	5.00	3.50
☐4262		LONG LONELY NIGHTS/ STORM CLOUDS	3.00	5.00	3.50
☐55290	*LIBERTY*	LOVEY DOVEY/I GOT YOU	2.75	4.50	3.00
☐55305		LING-TING-TONG/THE KISSES ...	2.75	4.50	3.00
☐55366		ALL BY MYSELF/ THREE-EYED MAN	2.75	4.50	3.00
☐55411		CHI-HUA-HUA/OPEN	2.75	4.50	3.00
☐55473		SHE'S GONE/ NOW THERE'S ONLY ME	2.75	4.50	3.00
☐55503		THREE WAY LOVE AFFAIR/ DEAR ABBY	2.75	4.50	3.00
☐55592		TOMORROW IS A COMIN'/ SHADAROOM	2.75	4.50	3.00
☐55650		HITCH-HIKE BACK TO GEORGIA/ THANKS A LOT	2.75	4.50	3.00
☐55693		ALL TIME LOSER/GOOD LOVIN' ..	2.75	4.50	3.00
☐0395	*REPRISE*	GOOD TIME GIRL/LIVIN' IN A HOUSE FULL OF LOVE	2.75	4.50	3.00
☐0431		A LOVER'S QUESTION/ YOU SAID GOODBYE	2.75	4.50	3.00
☐0463		A WHITE SPORT COAT (AND A PINK CARNATION)/THAT DON'T DO ME NO GOOD	2.75	4.50	3.00
☐0501		LOVE HAS MANY WAYS/ 16 FEET OF PATIO	2.75	4.50	3.00
		BUDDY KNOX—EP			
☐301	*ROULETTE*	BUDDY KNOX................	14.00	24.00	20.00
		BUDDY KNOX—ALBUMS			
☐25003 (M)	*ROULETTE*	BUDDY KNOX................	34.00	88.00	80.00
☐3251 (M)	*LIBERTY*	GOLDEN HITS	8.00	21.00	18.00
☐7251 (S)		GOLDEN HITS	12.00	29.00	25.00

KODOKS

☐1007	*FURY*	TEENAGER'S DREAM/ LITTLE GIRL AND BOY	9.50	18.00	15.00
☐1015		MAKE BELIEVE WORLD/ OH GEE, OH GOSH	8.25	14.00	12.00
☐1019		MY BABY AND ME/ KINGLESS CASTLE	8.25	14.00	12.00
☐1020		GUARDIAN ANGEL/ RUNAROUND BABY	7.00	13.00	11.00
☐1683	*J & S*	DON'T WANT NO TEASING/ LOOK UP TO THE SKY	5.50	10.50	9.00
☐1004	*WINK*	LET'S ROCK/TWISTA TWISTIN' ..	4.50	7.50	6.00
☐1006		LOVE WOULDN'T MEAN A THING/ MISTER MAGOO	5.00	9.00	7.00

KOKOMO

☐1023	*FUTURE*	ASIA MINOR/ROY'S TUNE	4.50	6.50	6.00

KRIS KRISTOFFERSON

Brownsville, TX, was Kris's place of birth on June 22, 1936. When Kris was a teenager, his father — an air force major general — relocated the family in San Mateo, CA. There young Kristofferson became high-school student body president, an honor student and a varsity football star. He won a scholarship to southern California's Pomona college. He organized the school's first soccer team and did some amateur boxing.

Kris was such a brilliant student that he became a Rhodes Scholar and studied literature at Oxford University in England. While there, he wrote two (unsuccessful) novels and dabbled at composing songs. His tunes were eventually shown to the manager of British star Tommy Steele. Kris then signed a songwriting/recording contract under the name Kris Carson but found no tangible success.

He finished his work at Oxford and entered the army, where he rose to the rank of captain. He attended flight school and jump school and eventually piloted a helicopter in Vietnam.

He later returned to the States, where he flew a civilian helicopter for awhile. Still interested in show business, he went to work in Nashville as a janitor for $50 a week in order to learn production and to get his foot in the door with his songs.

In 1973, Kristofferson played L. A.'s Troubadour Club and, as a result, signed with Monument Records. Later, he entered the Hollywood world of films as a respected actor.

			Current Price Range		P/Y AVG
BILLY J. KRAMER AND THE DAKOTAS					
☐55586	*LIBERTY*	DO YOU WANT TO KNOW A SECRET?/I'LL BE ON MY WAY .	5.50	11.00	9.00
☐55626		BAD TO ME/I CALL YOUR NAME .	4.50	7.50	6.00
☐55643		I'LL KEEP YOU SATISFIED/I KNOW	4.50	7.50	6.00
☐55667		DO YOU WANT TO KNOW A SECRET?/BAD TO ME	3.25	5.50	4.00
☐66027	*IMPERIAL*	LITTLE CHILDREN/BAD TO ME . . .	3.00	5.00	3.50
☐66048		I'LL KEEP YOU SATISFIED/I KNOW	3.00	5.00	3.50
☐66051		FROM A WINDOW/ I'LL BE ON MY WAY	3.00	5.00	3.50
☐66085		IT'S GOTTA LAST FOREVER/ THEY REMIND ME OF YOU	3.00	5.00	3.50
☐66115		TRAINS AND BOATS AND PLANES/ THAT'S THE WAY I FEEL	3.00	5.00	3.50
☐66135		IRRESISTABLE YOU/ TWILIGHT TIME	3.00	5.00	3.50
☐66143		I'LL BE DOGGONE/NEON CITY . . .	3.00	5.00	3.50
☐66210		TAKE MY HAND/YOU MAKE ME FEEL LIKE SOMEONE	3.00	5.00	3.50
BILLY J. KRAMER AND THE DAKOTAS -- ALBUMS					
☐9267 (M)	*IMPERIAL*	LITTLE CHILDREN	8.00	21.00	18.00
☐12267 (S)		LITTLE CHILDREN	12.00	29.00	25.00
☐9273 (M)		I'LL KEEP YOU SATISFIED.	7.00	17.00	15.00
☐12273 (S)		I'LL KEEP YOU SATISFIED.	9.00	25.00	22.50
☐9291 (M)		TRAINS AND BOATS AND PLANES	7.00	17.00	15.00
☐12291 (S)		TRAINS AND BOATS AND PLANES	9.00	25.00	22.50
KRIS KRISTOFFERSON					
☐8525	*MONUMENT*	LOVING HER WAS EASIER (THAN ANYTHNG I'LL EVER DO AGAIN)/ EPITAPH (black and white)	2.75	4.50	3.00
☐8531		THE PILGRIM, CHAPTER 33/(DJ) .	3.00	5.00	3.50
☐8536		JOSIE/BORDER LORD	2.75	4.50	3.00
☐8558		JESUS WAS A CAPRICORN/ ONLY IN A MOMENT	3.00	5.00	3.50
☐8564		JESSE YOUNG/GIVE IT TIME TO BE TENDER	3.00	5.00	3.50
☐8571		WHY ME?/HELP ME	2.50	4.50	3.00
☐8618		THE LIGHTS OF MAGDALA/ I MAY SMOKE TO MUCH	2.75	4.50	3.00
☐8658		EASY, COME ON/ ROCKET TO STARDOM	2.75	4.50	3.50
☐8679		THE YEAR 2000 MINUS 25/(DJ) . .	2.75	4.50	3.00
☐8707		IT'S NEVER GONNA BE THE SAME AGAIN/(DJ)	2.75	4.50	3.00
MONUMENT ALBUMS ARE WORTH UP TO $10.00 MINT					
BOB KUBAN AND THE IN MEN					
LEAD SINGER: WALTER SCOTT					
☐558	*NORMAN*	TURN ON YOUR LOVE LIGHT/ JERKIN' TIME	4.50	7.50	6.00
☐20001	*MUSICLAND U.S.A.*	THE CHEATER/TRY ME, BABY . . .	2.75	4.50	3.00
☐20006		THE TEASER/ALL I WANT	2.75	4.50	3.00
☐20007		DRIVE MY CAR/THE PRETZEL. . . .	2.75	4.50	3.00
☐20013		HARLEM SHUFFLE/THEME FROM 'VIRGINIA WOLFE'	2.75	4.50	3.00
☐20017		YOU BETTER RUN, YOU BETTER HIDE/BATMAN THEME	2.75	3.00	
BOB KUBAN AND THE IN MEN -- ALBUM					
☐3500 (M)	*MUSICLAND*	LOOK OUT FOR THE CHEATER . . .	7.00	18.00	15.00
☐3500 (S)		LOOK OUT FOR THE CHEATER . . .	8.00	21.00	18.00

L

			Current Price Range		P/Y AVG
	PATTI LABELLE AND THE BLUE-BELLES				
☐1900	*RAINBOW*	YOU BETTER MOVE ON/YOU'RE JUST FOOLING YOURSELF	5.00	9.00	6.00
☐5000	*NEWTOWN*	I SOLD MY HEART TO THE JUNKMAN/ITTY BITTY TWIST (Blue-Belles)	3.25	5.50	4.00
☐5006		PITTER PATTER/ I FOUND A NEW LOVE	3.25	5.50	4.00
☐5007		GO ON (THIS IS GOODBYE)/ TEAR AFTER TEAR	3.25	5.50	4.00
☐5009		WHEN JOHNNY COMES MARCHING HOME/COOL WATER	3.25	5.50	4.00
☐5019		DECATUR STREET/ ACADEMY AWARD	3.25	5.50	4.00
☐5777		DOWN THE AISLE/C'EST LA VIE .	4.00	8.00	4.85
☐5777	*KING*	DOWN THE AISLE/C'EST LA VIE .	3.25	5.50	4.00
☐5020	*NICETOWN*	YOU'LL NEVER WALK ALONE/ DECATUR STREET	3.25	5.50	4.00
☐896	*PARKWAY*	YOU'LL NEVER WALK ALONE/ DECATUR STREET	3.25	5.50	4.00
☐913		ONE PHONE CALL/YOU WILL FILL MY EYES NO MORE	3.25	5.50	4.00
☐935		DANNY BOY/I BELIEVE	3.25	5.50	4.00
☐2311	*ATLANTIC*	ALL OR NOTHING/ YOU FORGOT HOW TO LOVE ...	3.25	5.50	4.00
☐2318		OVER THE RAINBOW/ GROOVY KIND OF LOVE	3.25	5.50	4.00
☐2333		EBB TIDE/PATTI'S PRAYER	3.25	5.50	4.00
☐2347		I'M STILL WAITING/FAMILY MAN	3.25	5.50	4.00
☐2373		TAKE ME FOR A LITTLE WHILE/ I DON'T WANT TO GO ON WITHOUT YOU	3.25	5.50	4.00
☐2390		TENDER WORDS/THERE'S ALWAYS SOMETHING THERE TO REMIND ME	3.25	5.50	4.00
☐2408		UNCHAINED MELODY/DREAMER .	3.25	5.50	4.00
☐2446		OH MY LOVE/I NEED YOUR LOVE .	3.25	5.50	4.00
☐2548		HE'S MY MAN/WONDERFUL	3.25	5.50	4.00
☐2610		DANCE TO THE RHYTHM OF LOVE/ HE'S GONE	3.25	5.50	
☐2629		PRIDE'S NO MATCH FOR LOVE/ LOVING RULES	3.25	5.50	4.00
☐2712		SUFFER/TRUSTIN' IN YOU	3.25	5.50	4.00
	PATTI LABELLE AND THE BLUE-BELLES—ALBUMS				
☐631 (M)	*NEWTOWN*	THE APOLLO PRESENTS THE BLUE-BELLES	16.00	38.00	24.00
☐632 (M)		SLEIGH BELLS. JINGLE BELLS, AND BLUE BELLES	16.00	38.00	24.00
☐8119 (M)	*ATLANTIC*	OVER THE RAINBOW	8.00	21.00	18.00
☐8119 (S)		OVER THE RAINBOW	12.00	29.00	25.00
	CHERYL LADD				
	SEE: JOSIE AND THE PUSSYCATS				
☐4599	*CAPITOL*	THINK IT OVER/HERE IS A SONG .	2.75	4.50	3.00
☐4650		GOOD GOOD LOVIN'/ SKINNY DIPPIN'	2.75	4.50	3.00

			Current Price Range		P/Y AVG

DENNY LAINE
SEE: MOODY BLUES

☐7509	**DERAM**	ASK THE PEOPLE/			
		SAY YOU DON'T MIND	3.50	6.00	4.35
☐4340	**CAPITOL**	I'M LOOKIN' FOR SOMEONE TO			
		LOVE/IT'S SO EASY-LISTEN			
		TO ME	3.25	5.50	4.00
☐4425		HEARTBEAT/MOONDREAMS	3.25	5.50	4.00

DENNY LAINE—ALBUM

☐11588 (S)		HOLLY DAYS	7.00	17.00	15.00

LARRY LANCE & THE SKY RIDERS

☐3101	**MONKSWELL**	BRIGHT ORANGE LIGHT/			
		TICKLED PINK	8.00	16.00	11.50
☐3106		PUDDIN' & PIE/ONE LONE TUGGER			
		AT THE DOCK	8.00	16.00	11.50

MAJOR LANCE

☐71582	**MERCURY**	I'VE GOT A GIRL/PHYLLIS	10.00	19.00	13.00
☐7175	**OKEH**	THE MONKEY TIME/			
		MAMA DIDN'T KNOW	3.25	5.50	4.00
☐7181		HEY LITTLE GIRL/			
		CRYING IN THE RAIN	3.25	5.50	4.00
☐7187		UM, UM, UM, UM, UM, UM/			
		SWEET MUSIC	3.25	5.50	4.00
☐7191		THE MATADOR/			
		GONNA GET MARRIED	3.25	5.50	4.00
☐7197		GIRLS/IT AIN'T NO USE	3.25	5.50	4.00
☐7203		RHYTHM/PLEASE DON'T SAY			
		NO MORE	3.25	5.50	4.00
☐7209		SOMETIMES I WONDER/			
		I'M SO LOST	3.00	5.00	3.65
☐7216		COME SEE/			
		YOU BELONG TO ME, MY LOVE	3.00	5.00	3.65
☐7223		AIN'T IT A SHAME/			
		GOTTA GET AWAY	3.00	5.00	3.65
☐7226		TOO HOT TO HANDLE/			
		DARK AND LONELY	3.00	5.00	3.65

MAJOR LANCE—ALBUMS

☐12105 (M)	**OKEH**	MONKEY TIME	7.00	17.00	15.00
☐14105 (S)		MONKEY TIME	9.00	25.00	22.50
☐12106 (M)		UM, UM, UM, UM, UM, UM	7.00	17.00	15.00
☐14106 (S)		UM, UM, UM, UM, UM, UM	9.00	25.00	22.50
☐12110 (M)		GREATEST HITS	7.00	17.00	15.00
☐14110 (S)		GREATEST HITS	9.00	25.00	22.50

JERRY LANDIS (PAUL SIMON)
SEE: SIMON AND GARFUNKEL, TOM AND JERRY

☐12822	**MGM**	ANNA BELLE/LONELINESS	17.00	29.00	25.00
☐522	**WARWICK**	SWANEE/TOOT TOOT			
		TOOTSIE GOODBYE	14.00	24.00	20.00
☐552		JUST A BOY/SHY	9.50	17.00	15.00
☐588		JUST A BOY/I'D LIKE TO BE	5.50	11.00	9.00
☐619		PLAY ME A SAD SONG/			
		IT MEANS A LOT TO THEM	5.50	11.00	9.00
☐130	**CANADIAN-**				
	AMERICAN	I'M LONELY/			
		I WISH I WEREN'T IN LOVE	12.00	21.00	18.00
☐875	**AMY**	THE LONELY TEEN RANGER/LISA	5.50	11.00	9.00

RICHARD LANHAM

☐722	**ACME**	WISHING ALL THE TIME/			
		THE DAY I MET YOU	12.00	24.00	20.00

MAJOR LANCE

Like rhythm-and-blues stars James Brown and Jackie Wilson, Major Lance had initially set his sights on becoming a pro boxer. He later turned to singing gospel songs instead. Lance joined some fellow Chicagoans in forming the Five Harmonaires. In 1959 (when Major was 18) the group disbanded.

Shortly after that, a dj friend arranged an audition for Lance with an executive at Mercury Records. He won a contract, cut a single called "I've Got a Girl" (which failed to sell) and went label-shopping a second time.

He found his niche on the Columbia subsidiary of Okeh. There Major Lance began churning out a steady stream of Curtis Mayfield-composed hits. In the summer of 1963, Major scored a Top 10 winner with a danceable "The Monkey Time". This was followed by three more Top 20 hits in a row, including Lance's biggest career hit of Mayfield's "Um, Um, Um, Um, Um" early in 1964.

By the end of 1964, though, Major Lance's recording success was nearing an end. He hit the Top 30 once more that August with "Rhythm". After that, it was a slow decline to the bottom of the charts, finally dropping off completely in mid-1965.

			Current Price Range		P/Y AVG

THE LARADOS

☐ MDG 801	**MADOG**	WILL YOU LOVE ME TOMORROW/ YOU DIDN'T CARE	10.00	19.00	13.00

LAUGHING GRAVY
PRODUCER: DEAN TORRENCE

☐ 261	**WHITE WHALE**	VEGETABLES/SNOW FLAKES	9.50	17.00	15.00

JOHNNY LAW FOUR

☐ 419	**PROVIDENCE**	THERE OUGHT TO BE A LAW/ CALL ON ME	8.25	18.00	16.00

LEAVES

☐ 202	**MIRA**	LOVE MINUS ZERO/ TOO MANY PEOPLE	5.00	9.00	6.00
☐ 207		HEY JOE, WHERE YOU GONNA GO?/BE WITH YOU	5.00	9.00	6.00
☐ 213		YOU BETTER MOVE ON/ A DIFFERENT STORY	3.75	6.50	4.35
☐ 222		HEY JOE/FUNNY LITTLE WORLD	3.25	5.50	4.00
☐ 227		GIRL FROM THE EAST/ TOO MANY PEOPLE	3.25	5.50	4.00
☐ 231		GIRL FROM THE EAST/GET OUT OF MY LIFE, WOMAN	3.00	5.00	3.65
☐ 234		YOU BETTER MOVE ON/ BE WITH YOU	3.00	5.00	3.65
☐ 5799	**CAPITOL**	TWILIGHT SANCTUARY/ LEMON PRINCESS	3.00	5.00	3.65

LEAVES—ALBUMS

☐ 3005 (M)	**MIRA**	HEY JOE	8.00	21.00	18.00
☐ 3005 (S)		HEY JOE	11.00	29.00	25.00
☐ 2368	**CAPITOL**	ALL THE GOOD THAT'S HAPPENING	7.00	17.00	15.00

LES LEDO

☐ 721	**SHELL**	SCARLET ANGEL/DON'T FIGHT	18.00	40.00	35.00

LED ZEPPELIN
SEE: JOHN PAUL JONES, JIMMY PAGE, ROBERT PLANT, YARDBIRDS

☐ 2613	**ATLANTIC**	GOOD TIMES BAD TIMES/ COMMUNICATION BREAKDOWN	3.25	5.50	4.00
☐ 2690		WHOLE LOTTA LOVE/ LIVING LOVING MAID	2.75	4.50	3.00
☐ 2777		IMMIGRANT SONG/ HEY HEY, WHAT CAN I DO	3.25	5.50	4.00
☐ 2849		BLACK DOG/ MISTY MOUNTAIN HOP	2.75	4.50	3.00
☐ 2865		ROCK AND ROLL/FOUR STICKS	2.75	4.50	3.00
☐ 2970		OVER THE HILLS AND FAR AWAY/ DANCING DAYS	2.75	4.50	3.00
☐ 2986		D'YER MAKER/THE CRUNGE	2.75	4.50	3.00
☐ PR 175		STAIRWAY TO HEAVEN/ STAIRWAY TO HEAVEN (DJ only)	20.00	35.00	30.00
☐ 70102	**SWAN SONG**	TRAMPLED UNDER FOOT/ BLACK COUNTRY WOMAN	2.75	4.50	3.00
☐ 70110		ROYAL ORLEANS/ CANDY STORE ROCK	3.00	5.00	3.50

LED ZEPPELIN ALBUMS ARE WORTH UP TO $10.00 MINT

BILLY LEE AND THE RIVIERAS
SEE: MITCH RYDER AND THE DETROIT WHEELS

☐ 3016	**HYLAND**	WON'T YOU DANCE WITH ME/ YOU KNOW	5.50	11.00	9.00

BRENDA LEE

Brenda Mae Tarpley has been singing since she was four. (She was born December 11, 1944.) At the age of six she won top honors in a children's talent contest in her hometown of Atlanta, Georgia. That win aided her in getting a regular television show in the area.

The Tarpley family later moved to Augusta, Georgia. Brenda then began singing on a local radio station. When country singing star Red Foley came to Augusta on tour, Brenda met him and showed off her singing skills. Foley was overwhelmed by the little girl's skills and gusto and asked her to open his stage show for him.

When she entered her teens, Brenda began appearing on the "Ozark Jubilee" television show. Shortly thereafter Brenda Lee (her recording name was taken from the final syllable of her last name) earned minor chart success with "One Step At A Time", and her next single ("Dynamite") gave her the nickname of "Little Miss Dynamite".

As the 1960s began, Brenda experienced her first smash hit — "Sweet Nothin's". On the charts for half a year, "Sweet Nothin's" proved to be the first of ten Top 10 single winners, two of which went all the way to No. 1.

			Current Price Range		P/Y AVG

BRENDA LEE

			Current Price Range		P/Y AVG
☐30050	DECCA	JAMBALAYA/BIGELOW-6200 ...	5.50	11.00	9.00
☐30107		CHRISTY CHRISTMAS/I'M GONNA LASSO SANTA CLAUS	5.00	9.00	7.00
☐30198		ONE STEP AT A TIME/FAIRYLAND	4.50	7.50	6.00
☐30333		DYNAMITE/LOVE YOU 'TIL I DIE .	4.50	7.50	6.00
☐30411		AIN'T THAT LOVE/ ONE TEENAGER TO ANOTHER ..	3.75	5.50	4.50
☐30535		ROCK THE BOP/ ROCK-A-BYE BABY BLUES	3.75	5.50	4.50
☐30673		RING-A MY PHONE/LITTLE JONAH.	4.50	7.50	6.00
☐30776		ROCKIN' AROUND THE CHRISTMAS TREE/PAPA NOEL	3.00	5.00	3.50
☐30806		BILL BAILEY WON'T YOU PLEASE COME HOME/ HUMMIN' THE BLUES	3.75	6.00	4.50
☐30885		LET'S JUMP THE BROOMSTICK/ SOME OF THESE DAYS	3.75	6.00	4.50
☐30967		SWEET NOTHIN'S/ WEEP NO MORE MY BABY	3.25	5.50	4.00
☐31093		I'M SORRY/THAT'S ALL YOU GOTTA DO	3.25	5.50	4.00
☐31149		I WANT TO BE WANTED/ JUST A LITTLE	3.25	5.50	4.00
☐31195		EMOTIONS/ I'M LEARNING ABOUT LOVE ...	3.00	5.00	3.65
☐31231		YOU CAN DEPEND ON ME/ IT'S NEVER TOO LATE	3.00	5.00	3.65
☐31272		DUM DUM/EVENTUALLY	3.00	5.00	3.65
☐31309		FOOL NO. 1/ANYBODY BUT ME ..	3.00	5.00	3.65
☐31348		BREAK IT TO ME GENTLY/ SO DEEP	3.00	5.00	3.65
☐31379		EVERYBODY LOVES ME BUT YOU/ HERE COMES THAT FEELIN' ...	3.00	5.00	3.65
☐31407		HEART IN HAND/IT STARTED ALL OVER AGAIN	3.00	5.00	3.65
☐31424		ALL ALONE AM I/SAVE ALL YOUR LOVIN' FOR ME	3.00	5.00	3.65
☐31454		YOUR USED-TO-BE/ SHE'LL NEVER KNOW	3.00	5.00	3.65
☐31478		LOSING YOU/HE'S SO HEAVENLY	3.00	5.00	3.65
☐31510		MY WHOLE WORLD IS FALLING DOWN/I WONDER	3.00	5.00	3.65
☐31539		THE GRASS IS GREENER/ SWEET IMPOSSIBLE YOU	3.00	5.00	3.65
☐31570		AS USUAL/ LONELY LONELY LONELY ME ..	3.00	5.00	3.65
☐31599		THINK/THE WAITING GAME	3.00	5.00	3.65
☐31628		ALONE WITH YOU/MY DREAMS .	3.00	5.00	3.65
☐31654		WHEN YOU LOVED ME/ HE'S SURE TO REMEMBER ME .	3.00	5.00	3.65
☐31687		JINGLE BELL ROCK/ WINTER WONDERLAND	3.00	5.00	3.65
☐31688		THIS TIME OF THE YEAR/ CHRISTMAS WILL BE JUST ANOTHER DAY	3.00	5.00	3.65
☐31690		IS IT TRUE?/ JUST BEHIND THE RAINBOW ..	3.00	5.00	3.65
☐31728		THANKS A LOT/ THE CRYING GAME	3.00	5.00	3.65
☐31762		TRULY. TRULY. TRUE/ I STILL MISS SOMEONE	3.00	5.00	3.65
☐31792		TOO MANY RIVERS/NO ONE	3.00	5.00	3.65
☐31849		RUSTY BELLS/IF YOU DON'T	3.00	5.00	3.65

DECCA, DL 75111, LP

SPECIALTY, SEP-400

			Current Price Range		P/Y AVG
☐ 31917		TOO LITTLE TIME/ TIME AND TIME AGAIN	3.00	5.00	3.65
☐ 31970		AIN'T GONNA CRY NO MORE/ IT TAKES ONE TO KNOW ONE . .	3.00	5.00	3.65
☐ 32018		COMING ON STRONG/YOU KEEP COMING BACK TO ME	3.00	5.00	3.65
☐ 32079		RIDE. RIDE. RIDE/LONELY PEOPLE DO FOOLISH THINGS	3.00	5.00	3.65
☐ 32119		TAKE ME/ BORN TO BE BY YOUR SIDE . . .	3.00	5.00	3.65
☐ 32161		MY HEART KEEPS HANGIN' ON/ WHERE LOVE IS	3.00	5.00	3.65
☐ 33213		WHERE'S THE MELODY?/ SAVE ME FOR A RAINY DAY . . .	3.00	5.00	3.65
☐ 32248		FANTASY/THAT'S ALL RIGHT . . .	3.00	5.00	3.65
☐ 32299		CABARET/MOOD INDIGO (with Pete Fountain)	3.00	5.00	3.65
☐ 32330		KANSAS CITY/ EACH DAY IS A RAINBOW	3.00	5.00	3.65
☐ 32428		JOHNNY ONE TIME/I MUST HAVE BEEN OUT OF MY MIND	3.00	5.00	3.65
☐ 32491		YOU DON'T NEED ME FOR ANYTHING ANYMORE/ BRING ME SUNSHINE	3.00	5.00	3.65
☐ 32560		LET IT BE ME/ YOU BETTER MOVE ON	3.00	5.00	3.65
☐ 32675		I THINK I LOVE YOU AGAIN/ HELLO LOVE	3.00	5.00	3.65
☐ 32734		SISTERS IN SORROW/DO RIGHT WOMAN. DO RIGHT MAN	3.00	5.00	3.65
☐ 32848		IF THIS IS OUR LAST TIME/ EVERYBODY'S REACHING OUT FOR SOMEONE	3.00	5.00	3.65
☐ 32918		MISTY MEMORIES/ I'M A MEMORY	3.00	5.00	3.65
☐ 32975		ALWAYS ON MY MIND/ THAT AIN'T RIGHT	3.00	5.00	3.65
		BRENDA LEE—EPs			
☐ 2661	**DECCA**	BRENDA LEE	9.00	17.00	11.00
☐ 2678		SWEET NOTHIN'S	8.00	15.00	10.50
☐ 2682		BRENDA LEE	6.00	12.00	8.00
☐ 2683		I'M SORRY	6.00	12.00	8.00
☐ 2702		BRENDA LEE	6.00	12.00	8.00
☐ 2704		LOVER. COME BACK TO ME	6.00	12.00	8.00
☐ 2712		BRENDA LEE	5.50	10.00	7.00
☐ 2716		BRENDA LEE	5.50	10.00	7.00
☐ 2725		EVERYBODY LOVES ME BUT YOU	5.50	10.00	7.00
☐ 2730		BRENDA LEE	4.50	8.00	6.00
☐ 2738		BRENDA LEE	4.50	8.00	6.00
☐ 2745		BRENDA LEE	4.50	8.00	6.00
☐ 2764		BRENDA LEE	4.50	8.00	6.00
☐ 2755		BRENDA LEE	4.50	8.00	6.00
		BRENDA LEE—ALBUMS			
☐ 4039 (M)	**DECCA**	BRENDA LEE	14.00	35.00	30.00
☐ 74039 (S)		BRENDA LEE	17.00	40.00	35.00
☐ 4082 (M)		THIS IS BRENDA	14.00	35.00	30.00
☐ 74082 (S)		THIS IS BRENDA	17.0C	40.00	35.00
☐ 4104 (M)		EMOTIONS	12.00	29.00	25.00
☐ 74104 (S)		EMOTIONS	14.00	35.00	30.00
☐ 4176 (M)		ALL THE WAY	12.00	29.00	25.00
☐ 74176 (S)		ALL THE WAY	14.00	35.00	30.00
☐ 4216 (M)		SINCERELY. BRENDA LEE	10.00	25.00	22.50
☐ 74216 (S)		SINCERELY. BRENDA LEE	12.00	29.00	25.00
☐ 4326 (M)		THAT'S ALL	10.00	25.00	22.50

			Current Price Range		P/Y AVG
☐74326 (S)		THAT'S ALL	12.00	29.00	25.00
☐4370 (M)		ALL ALONE AM I	10.00	25.00	22.50
☐74370 (S)		ALL ALONE AM I	12.00	29.00	25.00
☐4439 (M)		LET ME SING	7.00	17.00	15.00
☐74439 (S)		LET ME SING	8.00	21.00	18.00
☐4509 (M)		BY REQUEST	7.00	17.00	15.00
☐74509 (S)		BY REQUEST	8.00	21.00	18.00
☐4583 (M)		MERRY CHRISTMAS FROM BRENDA LEE	7.00	17.00	15.00
☐74583 (S)		MERRY CHRISTMAS FROM BRENDA LEE	8.00	21.00	18.00
☐4626 (M)		TOP TEEN HITS	7.00	17.00	15.00
☐74626 (S)		TOP TEEN HITS	8.00	21.00	18.00
☐4661 (M)		THE VERSATILE BRENDA LEE	7.00	17.00	15.00
☐74661 (S)		THE VERSATILE BRENDA LEE	8.00	21.00	18.00
☐4684 (M)		TOO MANY RIVERS	7.00	17.00	15.00
☐74684 (S)		TOO MANY RIVERS	8.00	21.00	18.00
☐4755 (M)		BYE BYE BLUES	6.00	15.00	13.50
☐74755 (S)		BYE BYE BLUES	7.00	17.00	15.00
☐4757 (M)		10 GOLDEN YEARS	6.00	15.00	13.50
☐74757 (S)		10 GOLDEN YEARS	7.00	17.00	15.00

LATER DECCA AND MCA ALBUMS ARE WORTH UP TO $10.00 MINT

CURTIS LEE
SEE: C. L. AND THE PICTURES

☐7	*HOT*	I NEVER KNEW LOVE COULD DO/ GOTTA HAVE YOU	14.00	24.00	20.00
☐1555	*WARRIOR*	WITH ALL MY HEART/PURE LOVE	12.00	21.00	18.00
☐517	*SABRA*	LET'S TAKE A RIDE/ I'M ASKING FORGIVENESS	5.50	11.00	9.00
☐2001	*DUNES*	SPECIAL LOVE/D- IN LOVE	5.00	9.00	7.00
☐2003		PLEDGE OF LOVE/ THEN I'LL KNOW	4.50	7.50	6.00
☐2007		PRETTY LITTLE ANGEL EYES/ GEE HOW I WISH	3.50	6.00	4.00
☐2008		UNDER THE MOON OF LOVE/ BEVERLY JEAN	3.50	6.00	4.00
☐2010		LET'S TAKE A RIDE/ I'M ASKING FORGIVENESS	3.50	6.00	4.00
☐2012		A NIGHT AT DADDY GEE'S/ JUST ANOTHER FOOL	3.50	6.00	4.00
☐2015		DOES HE MEAN THAT MUCH TO YOU?/THE WOBBLE	3.50	6.00	4.00
☐2017		MARY GO ROUND/AFRAID	3.50	6.00	4.00
☐2020		LONELY WEEKENDS/ BETTER HIM THAN ME	3.50	6.00	4.00
☐2021		PICKIN' UP THE PIECES OF MY HEART/MR. MISTAKER	3.50	6.00	4.00
☐2023		THAT'S WHAT'S HAPPENING/ I'M SORRY	3.50	6.00	4.00

DICKIE LEE
SEE: SUN DISCOGRAPHY

☐131	*TAMPA*	STAY TRUE BABY/DREAM BOY	10.00	20.00	17.50
☐16087	*DOT*	WHY DON'T YOU WRITE ME?/ LIFE IN A TEENAGE WORLD	5.00	9.00	7.00
☐1758	*SMASH*	PATCHES/MORE OR LESS	3.25	5.50	4.00
☐1791		I SAW LINDA YESTERDAY/ THE GIRL I CAN'T FORGET	3.25	5.50	4.00
☐1808		DON'T WANNA THINK ABOUT PAULA/JUST A FRIEND	3.25	5.50	4.00
☐1822		I GO LONELY/TEN MILLION FACES	3.25	5.50	4.00
☐1844		SHE WANTS TO BE BOBBY'S GIRL/ THE DAY THE SAWMILL CLOSED DOWN	3.25	5.50	4.00

			Current Price Range		P/Y AVG
☐ 1871		TO THE AISLE/MOTHER NATURE .	3.25	5.50	4.00
☐ 1913		ME AND MY TEARDROPS/			
		ONLY TRUST IN ME	3.25	5.50	4.00
☐ 102	**TCF HALL**	LAURIE (STRANGE THINGS			
		HAPPEN)/PARTY DOLL	3.00	5.00	3.65
☐ 111		THE GIRL FROM PEYTON PLACE/			
		THE GIRL I USED TO KNOW	3.00	5.00	3.65
☐ 118		GOOD GIRL GOIN' BAD/			
		PRETTY WHITE DRESS	3.00	5.00	3.65
☐ 188		STAY TRUE BABY/DREAM BOY ..	3.00	5.00	3.65
☐ 6546	**ATCO**	RED, GREEN, YELLOW &			
		BLUE/RUN RIGHT BACK	3.00	5.00	3.65
		DICKIE LEE—ALBUMS			
☐ 27020 (M)	**SMASH**	THE TALE OF PATCHES	7.00	17.00	15.00
☐ 67020 (S)		THE TALE OF PATCHES	9.00	25.00	22.50
☐ 8001 (M)	**TCF HALL**	LAURIE AND THE GIRL FROM			
		PEYTON PLACE	6.00	15.00	13.50
☐ 8001 (S)		LAURIE AND THE GIRL FROM			
		PEYTON PLACE	8.00	21.00	18.00

LEFT BANKE

☐ 2041	**SMASH**	WALK AWAY RENEE/			
		I HAVEN'T GOT THE NERVE ...	3.00	5.00	3.65
☐ 2074		PRETTY BALLERINA/LAZY DAY ..	3.00	5.00	3.65
☐ 2089		AND SUDDENLY/IVY, IVY	3.00	5.00	3.65
☐ 2119		DESIREE/I'VE GOT SOMETHING			
		ON MY MIND	3.00	5.00	3.65
☐ 2197		BARTENDERS AND THEIR WIVES/			
		SHE MAY CALL			
		YOU UP TONIGHT	3.00	5.00	3.65
		LEFT BANKE—ALBUMS			
☐ 27088 (M)	**SMASH**	WALK AWAY RENEE	8.00	21.00	18.00
☐ 67088 (S)		WALK AWAY RENEE	9.00	25.00	22.50
☐ 27113 (M)		TOO	7.00	17.00	15.00
☐ 67113 (S)		TOO	8.00	21.00	18.00

LENDELLS

☐ 2	**REACH**	MARYANN/LITTERBUG	35.00	80.00	72.00
		THIS GROUP WAS ALSO KNOWN AS THE LYDELLS			

JOHN LENNON
SEE: BEATLES, YOKO ONO

☐ 1809	**APPLE**	GIVE PEACE A CHANCE/			
		REMEMBER LOVE			
		(Plastic Ono Band)	4.00	7.00	4.75
☐ 1813		COLD TURKEY/DON'T WORRY,			
		KYOKO (Plastic Ono Band)	4.00	7.00	4.75
☐ 1818		INSTANT KARMA/			
		WHO HAS SEEN THE WIND? ...	4.00	7.00	4.75
☐ 1827		MOTHER/WHY	4.00	7.00	4.75
☐ 1830		POWER TO THE PEOPLE/			
		TOUCH ME	4.00	7.00	4.75
☐ 1840		IMAGINE/IT'S SO BAD	4.00	7.00	4.85
☐ 1846		HAPPY XMAS (WAR IS OVER)/			
		LISTEN, THE SNOW IS FALLING	6.00	11.00	6.00
☐ 1848		WOMAN IS THE NIGGER OF THE			
		WORLD/SISTERS, OH SISTERS	5.00	9.00	4.75
☐ 1868		MIND GAMES/MEAT CITY	4.00	7.00	4.85
☐ 1874		WHATEVER GETS YOU THROUGH			
		THE NIGHT/BEEF JERKY	4.00	7.00	4.85
☐ 1878		#9 DREAM/WHAT YOU GOT	4.00	7.00	4.85
☐ 1881		STAND BY ME/			
		MOVE OVER, MRS. L.	4.00	7.00	4.85

JOHN LENNON

He was born John Winston Lennon in Liverpool, England, on October 9, 1940. His father had deserted the family and John's mother died shortly afterwards. John was raised by an aunt named Mimi. At school John was bright but hot-tempered, often getting into fistfights with classmates. At home, though, John was often a paragon of politeness and manners. He preferred to be alone so he could write. (He wrote his first book at the age of seven.)

The advent of Elvis Presley in 1956 overwhelmed John Lennon. He quickly formed a rock-and-roll band with some classmates from Quarry Bank High. He called them the Quarrymen.

In time, John took on new personnel as others drifted away. By 1960, his band had become a quintet called the Beat Brothers. One member — Stu Sutcliffe — left but died shortly afterwards of a brain tumor. Lennon then adopted the name Silver Beatles and finally Beatles. With friend Paul McCartney, John led his group to worldwide fame during the mid-1960s.

John Lennon was the first married (and first divorced) Beatle, leaving first wife Cynthia for Japanese photographer Yoko Ono. (They married in 1969 on March 20th.)

Lennon went into "retirement" in 1975 after "Stand By Me" became his last Apple chart hit. On December 8, 1980, John was tragically gunned down in New York City.

			Current Price Range		P/Y AVG
		JOHN LENNON—ALBUMS			
☐8018 (S)	**ADAM VIII**	JOHN LENNON SINGS THE GREAT ROCK & ROLL HITS	32.00	78.00	50.00
☐5001 (S)	**APPLE**	TWO VIRGINS/ UNFINISHED MUSIC NO. 1	32.00	78.00	50.00
☐3361 (S)		WEDDING ALBUM	40.00	100.00	60.00
☐3362 (S)		LIVE PEACE IN TORONTO (with Plastic Ono Band)	12.00	29.00	25.00
☐3372 (S)		PLASTIC ONO BAND	10.00	22.00	14.50
☐3379 (S)		IMAGINE	8.00	22.00	14.00
☐3392 (S)		SOME TIME IN NEW YORK CITY	8.00	22.00	14.00
☐3414 (S)		MIND GAMES	8.00	22.00	14.00
☐3416 (S)		WALLS AND BRIDGES	8.00	22.00	14.00
☐3419 (S)		ROCK 'N' ROLL	8.00	22.00	14.00
☐3421 (S)		SHAVED FISH (greatest hits)	8.00	22.00	14.00
		LETTERMEN			
☐4586	**CAPITAL**	THE WAY YOU LOOK TONIGHT/THAT'S MY DESIRE	1.75	3.25	2.25
☐4658		WHEN I FALL IN LOVE/SMILE	1.75	3.25	2.25
☐4760		NOVELTY RECORD-SUN OF OLD RIVERS/DUTCHMAN'S GOLD	1.75	3.25	2.25
☐4699		COME BACK SILLY GIRL/ A SONG FOR YOUNG LOVE	1.75	3.25	2.25
☐4746		HOW IS JULIE/ TURN AROUND LOOK AT ME	1.75	3.25	2.25
☐4810		SILLY BOY (SHE DOESN'T LOVE YOU)/I TOLD THE STARS	1.75	3.25	2.25
☐4851		A TREE IN THE MEADOW/ AGAIN	1.75	3.25	2.25
☐4914		HEARTACHE, OH HEARTACHE/ NO OTHER LOVE	1.75	3.25	2.25
☐4976		ALLENTOWN JAIL/ TWO BROTHERS	1.75	3.25	2.25
☐5091		WHERE OR WHEN/ BE MY GIRL	1.75	3.25	2.25
☐5218		SEVENTH DAWN THEME/ PUT AWAY YOUR TEARDROPS	1.75	3.25	2.25
☐5273		YOU DON'T KNOW HOW LUCKY YOU ARE/WHEN SUMMER ENDS	1.75	3.25	2.25
☐5370		IT'S OVER/GIRL WITH THE LITTLE TIN HEART	1.75	3.25	2.25
☐5437		THEME FROM ''A SUMMER PLACE''/SEALED WITH A KISS	1.75	3.25	2.25
☐5499		SECRETLY/THE THINGS WE DID LAST SUMMER	1.75	3.25	2.25
☐5544		SWEET SEPTEMBER/ I BELIEVE	1.75	3.25	2.25
☐5583		YOU'LL BE NEEDIN' ME/ RUN TO MY LOVIN' ARMS	1.75	3.25	2.25
☐5649		I ONLY HAVE EYES FOR YOU/ LOVE LETTERS	1.75	3.25	2.25
☐5749		CHANSON D'AMOUR/ SHE DON'T WANT ME NOW	1.75	3.25	2.25
☐5813		OUR WINTER LOVE/WARM	1.75	3.25	2.25
☐5913		VOLARE/MR. SUN	1.75	3.25	2.25
☐6916		SOMEWHERE MY LOVE/ THEME FROM ''A SUMMER PLACE'' (This record was on Capital-Star Line)	1.75	3.25	2.25
☐2054		GOIN' OUT OF MY HEAD-CAN'T TAKE MY EYES OFF YOU/ I BELIEVE	1.75	3.25	2.25

			Current Price Range		P/Y AVG
☐ 2132		SHERRY DON'T GO/ NEVER MY LOVE	1.75	3.25	2.25
☐ 2196		ALL THE GREY HAIRED MEN/ ANYONE WHO HAD A HEART . .	1.75	3.25	2.25
☐ 2203		HOLLY/NO OTHER LOVE	1.75	3.25	2.25
☐ 2218		LOVE IS BLUE-GREEN SLEEVES/WHERE WERE YOU WHEN THE LIGHTS WENT OUT .	1.75	3.25	2.25
☐ 2254		SALLY LE ROY/ PLAYING THE PIANO	1.75	3.25	2.25
☐ 2324		PUT YOUR HEAD ON MY SHOULDERS/ MARY'S RAINBOW	1.75	3.25	2.25
☐ 2414		I HAVE DREAMED/THE PENDULIM SWINGS BOTH WAYS	1.75	3.25	2.25
☐ 2476		BLUE ON BLUES/SITTIN' PRETTY	1.75	3.25	2.25
☐ 2482		HURT SO BAD/CATCH THE WIND .	1.75	3.25	2.25
☐ 2643		SHANGRI-LA/ WHEN SUMMER ENDS	1.75	3.25	2.25
☐ 2697		TRACES-MEMORIES/ FOR ONCE IN A LIFETIME	1.75	3.25	2.25
☐ 2774		HANG ON SLOOPY/FOR LOVE . . .	1.75	3.25	2.25
☐ 2820		SHE CRIED/FOR LOVE	1.75	3.25	2.25
☐ 2938		HEY GIRL/WORLDS	1.75	3.25	2.25
☐ 3006		MORNING GIRL/HERE. THERE AND EVERYWHERE	1.75	3.25	2.25
☐ 3020		EVERYTHING IS GOOD ABOUT YOU/IT'S OVER	1.75	3.25	2.25
☐ 3097		THE GREATEST DISCOVERY/ SINCE YOU'VE BEEN GONE	1.75	3.25	2.25
☐ 3098		FEELINGS/ LOVE IS A HURTIN' THING	1.75	3.25	2.25
☐ 3192		LOVE/MAYBE TOMORROW	1.75	3.25	2.25
☐ 3285		OH MY LOVE/AN OLD FASHIONED LOVE SONG	1.75	3.25	2.25
☐ 3449		SPIN AWAY/MAYBE WE SHOULD	1.75	3.25	2.25
☐ 3512		SANDMAN/LOVE SONG	1.75	3.25	2.25
☐ 3619		MAC ARTHUR PARK/ SUMMER SONG	1.75	3.25	2.25
☐ 3810		GOODBYE/YOU PART OF ME	1.75	3.25	2.25
☐ 3912		TOUCH ME-FROM ''THE WAY WE WERE''/ISN'T IT A SHAME	1.75	3.25	2.25
☐ 4005		EASTWARD/TO LOVE AND BE LOVED-FROM ''SOME CAME RUNNING''	1.75	3.25	2.25
☐ 4096		YOU ARE MY SUNSHINE GIRL/MAKE A TIME FOR LOVIN' .	6.00	12.00	7.50
☐ 4161		LOVE ME LIKE A STRANGER/ IF YOU FEEL THE WAY I DO	1.75	3.25	2.25
☐ 4226		THE WAY YOU LOOK TONIGHT (DISCO)/STORMS OF TROUBLED TIMES	1.75	3.25	2.25
☐ 0101	*ALPHA OMEGA*	WHAT I DID FOR LOVE/ I'LL BE BACK	1.75	3.25	2.25
☐ 0102		THE PARTY'S OVER (DISCO)/BEST OF MY LOVE-BEST OF MY LOVE . .	1.75	3.25	2.25

LETTERMEN—ALBUMS

☐ ST1669	*CAPITAL*	A SONG FOR YOUNG LOVE	6.00	11.00	7.50
☐ ST1711		ONCE UPON A TIME	6.00	11.00	7.50
☐ ST1761		JIM. TONY, BOB	6.00	11.00	7.50
☐ ST1829		COLLEGE STANDARDS	6.00	11.00	7.50
☐ ST1936		LETTERMEN-IN CONCDERT	6.00	11.00	7.50

		Current Price Range		P/Y AVG
ST2013	A LETTERMEN KIND OF LOVE	6.00	11.00	7.50
ST2083	THE LETTERMEN LOOK AT LOVE .	6.00	11.00	7.50
ST2142	SHE CRIED	6.00	11.00	7.50
ST2213	YOU`LL NEVER WALK ALONE	6.00	11.00	7.50
ST2270	PORTRAIT OF MY LOVE	6.00	11.00	7.50
ST2359	HIT SOUNDS OF THE LETTERMEN	6.00	11.00	7.50
ST2428	MORE HIT SOUNDS!	6.00	11.00	7.50
ST2496	A NEW SONG FOR YOUNG LOVE ..	6.00	11.00	7.50
ST2554	THE BEST OF THE LETTERMEN ..	6.00	11.00	7.50
ST2587	FOR CHRISTMAS THIS YEAR	6.00	11.00	7.50
ST2663	WARM	6.00	11.00	7.50
ST2711	SPRING	6.00	11.00	7.50
ST2758	LETTERMEN!!! ... AND ``LIVE`` .	6.00	11.00	7.50
ST2865	GOING OUT OF MY HEAD........	6.00	11.00	7.50
ST2934	SPECIAL REQUEST	6.00	11.00	7.50
91594	LOVE LETTERS	6.00	11.00	7.50
ST147	PUT YOUR HEAD ON MY SHOULDER	6.00	11.00	7.50
SKA0138	BEST OF THE LETTERMEN VOL. II	6.00	11.00	7.50
ST202	I HAVE DREAMED	6.00	11.00	7.50
SWBB251	CLOSE-UP	6.00	11.00	7.50
ST269	HURT SO BAD	6.00	11.00	7.50
ST390	TRACES/MEMORIES	6.00	11.00	7.50
ST496	REFLECTIONS	6.00	11.00	7.50
SPC3294	THE SOFT HITS OF THE LETTERMEN	6.00	11.00	7.50
ST634	EVERYTHING IS GOOD ABOUT YOU .	6.00	11.00	7.50
SW781	FEELINGS	6.00	11.00	7.50
ST836	LOVEBOOK	6.00	11.00	7.50
SW11010	LETTERMEN ONE	6.00	11.00	7.50
SW11124	SPINAWAY	6.00	11.00	7.50
LS220-C	LETTERMEN LIVE IN JAPAN 1972 FROM LETTERMEN WITH LOVE (LONGINES SYMPHONETTE) ...	6.00	11.00	7.50
220	A TIME FOR US (LONGINES SYMPHONETTE--5 RECORDS) .	6.00	11.00	7.50
SW11183	ALIVE AGAIN NATURALLY	6.00	11.00	7.50
SW11249	LETTERMEN ALL-TIME GREATEST HITS	6.00	11.00	7.50
SW11319	NOW AND FOREVER	6.00	11.00	7.50
SW11364	THERE IS NO GREATER LOVE	6.00	11.00	7.50
SW11424	MAKE A TIME FOR LOVIN`.......	6.00	11.00	7.50
ECS67064	LIVE IN JAPAN 1975	6.00	11.00	7.50
SLB6999	THE LOVIN` TOUCH OF THE LETTERMEN	6.00	11.00	7.50
SW11470	THE TIME IS RIGHT	6.00	11.00	7.50
SW11508	LETTERMEN KIND OF COUNTRY ..	6.00	11.00	7.50
3565	WITH LOVE FROM THE LETTERMEN	6.00	11.00	7.50
ECS90016	LETTERMEN-BEST 20	6.00	11.00	7.50
AO-1001 **ALPHA OMEGA**	TO A FRIEND (LIMITED SPECIAL EDITION T.K.E. ALBUM)	4.00	12.00	5.50
AO-1002	LETTERMEN, LOVE IS	6.00	11.00	7.50

LEVEES

1004	**KAREN** WALKIE TALKIE BABY/ OUR LOVE IS A VOW	8.50	18.00	16.00

LEVON AND THE HAWKS (THE BAND)

6383	**ATCO** THE STONES I THROW/ HE DON`T LOVE YOU	6.00	10.00	6.75
6625	GO GO LISA JANE/ HE DON`T LOVE YOU	6.00	10.00	6.75

			Current Price Range		P/Y AVG
		BOBBY LEWIS			
☐ 1002	*BELTONE*	TOSSIN' AND TURNIN'/			
		OH YES. I LOVE YOU	3.25	5.50	4.00
☐ 1012		ONE TRACK MIND/			
		ARE YOU READY?	3.25	5.50	4.00
☐ 1015		WHAT A WALK/CRY NO MORE . . .	3.25	5.50	4.00
☐ 1016		MAMIE IN THE AFTERNOON/			
		YES. OH YES. IT DID	3.25	5.50	4.00
☐ 2018		A MAN'S GOTTA BE A MAN/			
		DAY BY DAY I NEED YOUR LOVE	3.25	5.50	4.00
☐ 2023		I'M TOSSIN' AND TURNIN' AGAIN/			
		NOTHIN' BUT THE BLUES	3.25	5.50	4.00
☐ 2026		LONELY TEARDROPS/			
		BOOM A CHICK CHICK	3.25	5.50	4.00
☐ 2035		INTERMISSION/			
		NOTHIN' BUT THE BLUES	3.25	5.50	4.00
		BOBBY LEWIS—ALBUM			
☐ 4000 (M)	*BELTONE*	TOSSIN' AND TURNIN'	9.00	25.00	22.50

GARY LEWIS AND THE PLAYBOYS

			Current Price Range		P/Y AVG
☐ 55756	*LIBERTY*	THIS DIAMOND RING/			
		HARD TO FIND	3.00	5.00	3.65
☐ 55756		THIS DIAMOND RING/			
		TIJUANA WEDDING	3.00	5.00	3.65
☐ 55778		COUNT ME IN/			
		LITTLE MISS GO-GO	3.00	5.00	3.65
☐ 55809		SAVE YOUR HEART FOR ME/			
		WITHOUT A WORD OF WARNING.	3.00	5.00	3.65
☐ 55818		EVERYBODY LOVES A CLOWN/			
		TIME STANDS STILL	3.00	5.00	3.65
☐ 55846		SHE'S JUST MY STYLE/I WON'T			
		MAKE THAT MISTAKE AGAIN . .	3.00	5.00	3.65
☐ 55865		SURE GONNA MISS HER/I DON'T			
		WANNA SAY GOODNIGHT	3.00	5.00	3.65
☐ 55880		GREEN GRASS/I CAN READ			
		BETWEEN THE LINES	3.00	5.00	3.65
☐ 55898		MY HEART'S SYMPHONY/TINA . .	3.00	5.00	3.65
☐ 55914		(YOU DON'T HAVE TO) PAINT ME			
		A PICTURE/LOOKING			
		FOR THE STARS	3.00	5.00	3.65
☐ 55933		WHERE WILL THE WORDS COME			
		FROM?/MAY THE			
		BEST MAN WIN	3.00	5.00	3.65
☐ 55949		THE LOSER (WITH A BROKEN			
		HEART)/ICE MELTS IN THE SUN	3.00	5.00	3.65
☐ 55971		GIRLS IN LOVE/			
		LET'S BE MORE THAN FRIENDS	3.00	5.00	3.65
☐ 55985		JILL/NEW IN TOWN	3.00	5.00	3.65
☐ 56011		HAPPINESS/HAS SHE GOT			
		THE NICEST EYES	3.00	5.00	3.65
☐ 56037		SEALED WITH A KISS/SARA JANE	3.00	5.00	3.65
☐ 56075		C. C. RIDER/MAIN STREET	3.00	5.00	3.65
☐ 56093		EVERYDAY I HAVE TO CRY/			
		MISTER MEMORY	3.00	5.00	3.65
☐ 56093		RHYTHM OF THE RAIN/			
		MISTER MEMORY	3.00	5.00	3.65
☐ 56121		HAYRIDE/GARY'S GROOVE	3.00	5.00	3.65
☐ 56144		I SAW ELVIS PRESLEY LAST			
		NIGHT/SOMETHING IS WRONG	9.00	16.00	9.50
☐ 56158		GREAT BALLS OF FIRE/			
		I'M ON THE RIGHT ROAD NOW .	3.00	5.00	3.50
		GARY LEWIS AND THE PLAYBOYS—ALBUMS			
☐ 3408 (M)	*LIBERTY*	THIS DIAMOND RING	7.00	17.00	15.00
☐ 7408 (S)		THIS DIAMOND RING	8.00	21.00	18.00

			Current Price Range		P/Y AVG
☐ 3419 (M)		A SESSION WITH GARY LEWIS AND THE PLAYBOYS	7.00	17.00	15.00
☐ 7419 (S)		A SESSION WITH GARY LEWIS AND THE PLAYBOYS	8.00	21.00	18.00
☐ 3428 (M)		EVERYBODY LOVES A CLOWN ...	7.00	17.00	15.00
☐ 7428 (S)		EVERYBODY LOVES A CLOWN ...	8.00	21.00	18.00
☐ 3435 (M)		SHE'S JUST MY STYLE	6.00	15.00	13.50
☐ 7435 (S)		SHE'S JUST MY STYLE	7.00	17.00	15.00
☐ 3452 (M)		HITS AGAIN	6.00	15.00	13.50
☐ 7453 (S)		HITS AGAIN	7.00	17.00	15.00
☐ 3468 (M)		GOLDEN GREATS	6.00	15.00	13.50
☐ 7468 (S)		GOLDEN GREATS	7.00	17.00	15.00
☐ 3519 (M)		NEW DIRECTIONS	6.00	15.00	13.50
☐ 7519 (S)		NEW DIRECTIONS	6.00	15.00	13.50
☐ 3524 (M)		LISTEN	7.00	17.00	15.00
☐ 7524 (S)		LISTEN	6.00	15.00	13.50
☐ 7568 (S)		NOW	6.00	15.00	13.50
☐ 7589 (S)		MORE GOLDEN GREATS	6.00	15.00	13.50
☐ 7606 (S)		CLOSE COVER BEFORE PLAYING .	6.00	15.00	13.50
☐ 7623 (S)		RHYTHM OF THE RAIN	6.00	15.00	13.50
☐ 7633 (S)		I'M ON THE RIGHT ROAD NOW ...	6.00	15.00	13.50

JERRY LEE LEWIS
SEE: THE HAWK

☐ 259	**SUN**	CRAZY ARMS/END OF THE ROAD	8.25	14.00	12.00
☐ 267		WHOLE LOT OF SHAKIN' GOING ON/IT'LL BE ME	4.50	7.50	6.00
☐ 281		GREAT BALLS OF FIRE/ YOU WIN AGAIN	4.50	7.50	6.00
☐ 288		BREATHLESS/DOWN THE LINE ..	4.00	6.00	4.50
☐ 296		HIGH SCHOOL CONFIDENTIAL/ FOOLS LIKE ME	4.00	6.00	4.50
☐ 301		THE RETURN OF JERRY LEE/ LEWIS BOOGIE (George and Louis)	4.50	7.50	6.00
☐ 303		BREAK-UP/ I'LL MAKE IT ALL UP TO YOU ..	3.50	6.00	4.35
☐ 312		I'LL SAIL MY SHIP ALONE/ IT HURT ME SO	3.50	6.00	4.35
☐ 317		LOVIN' UP A STORM/ BIG BLON' BABY	3.50	6.00	4.35
☐ 324		LET'S TALK ABOUT US/ BALLAD OF BILLY JOE	3.50	6.00	4.35
☐ 330		LITTLE QUEENIE/I COULD NEVER BE ASHAMED OF YOU	3.50	6.00	4.35
☐ 337		OLD BLACK JOE/ BABY. BABY BYE BYE	3.50	6.00	4.35
☐ 344		HANG UP MY ROCK AND ROLL SHOES/JOHN HENRY	3.50	6.00	4.35
☐ 352		WHEN I GET PAID/ LOVE MADE A FOOL OF ME	3.50	6.00	4.35
☐ 356		WHAT'D I SAY/ LIVIN' LOVIN' WRECK	3.25	5.50	4.00
☐ 364		IT WON'T HAPPEN WITH ME/ COLD. COLD HEART	3.25	5.50	4.00
☐ 367		SAVE THE LAST DANCE FOR ME/ AS LONG AS I LIVE	3.25	5.50	4.00
☐ 371		MONEY/BOBBIE B	3.25	5.50	4.00
☐ 374		I'VE BEEN TWISTIN'/ RAMBLIN' ROSE	3.25	5.50	4.00
☐ 379		SWEET LITTLE SIXTEEN/ HOW'S MY EX TREATING YOU?	3.25	5.50	4.00
☐ 382		GOOD GOLLY. MISS MOLLY/ I CAN'T TRUST ME (IN YOUR ARMS)	3.25	5.50	4.00

JERRY LEE LEWIS

In 1958, the conservative element of American society was shocked and repulsed by the news of Jerry Lee Lewis's marriage to his 13-year-old cousin. (He was 22 and it was his third trip to the altar!) As a result, Jerry Lee Lewis's records were dropped from a great many playlists. But, always the consummate man of confidence, Lewis simply switched to country music and became a star in that field. (He's been a major country-music star since the mid-1960s.)

Jerry Lee began life on September 29, 1935, in the Louisiana town of Ferriday. His first performance was at a local Ford dealer, where young Lewis played and sang for people who came to view the new 1949 Fords.

After a brief stint as a Bible student in Texas, Jerry Lee auditioned at Sam Phillips' Sun Records outfit in Nashville. A plodding "Crazy Arms" went nowhere. On his second attempt at stardom, though, Jerry Lee Lewis tore up the rock charts with the now-classic "Whole Lot of Shakin' Going On". It sold a million copies in just weeks. Then came "Great Balls of Fire", and his name became a household word.

In later years, Lewis' wife divorced him (he's married again) and he has encountered alcohol and drug problems. Still, he thrills audiences to this day with his wild and frantic shows and outrageous mannerisms.

			Current Price Range		P/Y AVG
☐384		TEENAGE LETTER/SEASONS OF MY HEART (with Linda Gail Lewis)	3.25	5.50	4.00
☐396		CARRY ME BACK TO OLD VIRGINIA/ I KNOW WHAT IT MEANS	3.25	5.50	4.00
☐1101		INVITATION TO YOUR PARTY/ I COULD NEVER BE ASHAMED OF YOU	3.25	5.50	4.00
☐1107		ONE MINUTE PAST ETERNITY/ FRANKIE AND JOHNNY	3.25	5.50	4.00
☐1115		I CAN'T SEEM TO SAY GOODBYE/ GOODNIGHT IRENE	3.25	5.50	4.00
☐1119		BIG LEGGED WOMAN/ WAITING FOR A TRAIN	3.25	5.50	4.00
☐1125		MATCHBOX/LOVE ON BROADWAY .	3.25	5.50	4.00
☐1128		YOUR LOVING WAYS/ I CAN'T TRUST ME IN YOUR ARMS ANYMORE	3.25	5.50	4.00
☐1130		GOOD ROCKIN' TONIGHT/ I CAN'T TRUST ME IN YOUR ARMS ANYMORE	3.25	5.50	4.00
☐1857	**SMASH**	HIT THE ROAD JACK/ PEN AND PAPER	3.00	5.00	3.65
☐1886		I'M ON FIRE/ BREAD AND BUTTER MAN	3.00	5.00	3.65
☐1906		SHE WAS MY BABY. HE WAS MY FRIEND/THE HOME HE SAID HE BUILT FOR ME	3.00	5.00	3.65
☐1930		HIGH HEEL SNEAKERS/YOU WENT BACK ON YOUR WORD	3.00	5.00	3.65
☐1969		I BELIEVE IN YOU/ BABY. HOLD ME CLOSE	3.00	5.00	3.65
☐1992		ROCKIN' PNEUMONIA AND THE BOOGIE WOOGIE FLU/ THIS MUST BE THE PLACE	3.00	5.00	3.65
☐2006		YOU'VE GOT WHAT IT TAKES/ THE GREEN. GREEN GRASS OF HOME	3.00	5.00	3.65
☐2027		STICKS AND STONES/ WHAT A HECK OF A MESS	3.00	5.00	3.65
☐2053		MEMPHIS BEAT/ IF I HAD IT TO DO ALL OVER ...	3.00	5.00	3.65
☐2103		HOLDING ON/ IT'S A HANGUP. BABY	3.00	5.00	3.65
☐2122		TURN ON YOUR LOVE LIGHT/ SHOTGUN MAN	3.00	5.00	3.65
☐2146		ANOTHER PLACE. ANOTHER TIME/ I'M WALKING THE FLOOR OVER YOU	3.00	5.00	3.65
☐2164		WHAT'S MADE MILWAUKEE FAMOUS/ALL THE GOOD IS GONE	3.00	5.00	3.65
☐2186		SHE STILL COMES AROUND/ SLIPPING AROUND	3.00	5.00	3.65
☐2202		LET'S TALK ABOUT US/TO MAKE LOVE SWEETER FOR YOU	3.00	5.00	3.65
☐2220		DON'T LET ME CROSS OVER/ WE LIVE IN TWO DIFFERENT WORLDS	3.00	5.00	3.65
☐2224		ONE HAS MY NAME/ I CAN'T STOP LOVING YOU	3.00	5.00	3.65
☐2244		SHE EVEN WOKE UP TO SAY GOODBYE/ECHOES	3.00	5.00	3.65

			Current Price Range		P/Y AVG
☐2254		ROLL OVER BEETHOVEN/ SECRET PLACES (with Linda Gail Lewis)	3.00	5.00	3.65
☐2257		ONCE MORE WITH FEELING/YOU WENT OUT OF YOUR WAY	3.00	5.00	3.65
		JERRY LEE LEWIS—EPs			
☐107	**SUN**	THE GREAT BALL OF FIRE	12.00	21.00	18.00
☐108		JERRY LEE LEWIS	9.50	17.00	15.00
☐109		JERRY LEE LEWIS	9.50	17.00	15.00
☐110		JERRY LEE LEWIS	9.50	17.00	15.00
		JERRY LEE LEWIS—ALBUMS			
☐1230 (M)	**SUN**	JERRY LEE LEWIS	17.00	40.00	35.00
☐1265 (M)		JERRY LEE'S GREATEST!	22.00	55.00	50.00
☐27010 (M)	**SMASH**	COUNTRY SONGS FOR CITY FOLKS	7.00	17.00	15.00
☐67010 (S)		COUNTRY SONGS FOR CITY FOLKS	8.00	21.00	18.00
☐27040 (M)		GOLDEN HITS OF JERRY LEE LEWIS	7.00	17.00	15.00
☐67040 (S)		GOLDEN HITS OF JERRY LEE LEWIS	8.00	21.00	18.00
☐27056 (M)		THE GREATEST LIVE SHOW ON EARTH	7.00	17.00	15.00
☐67056 (S)		THE GREATEST LIVE SHOW ON EARTH	8.00	21.00	18.00
☐27063 (M)		THE RETURN OF ROCK	6.00	15.00	13.50
☐67063 (S)		THE RETURN OF ROCK	7.00	17.00	15.00
☐27079 (M)		MEMPHIS BEAT	6.00	15.00	13.50
☐67079 (S)		MEMPHIS BEAT	7.00	17.00	15.00
☐27086 (M)		BY REQUEST	6.00	15.00	13.50
☐67086 (S)		BY REQUEST	7.00	17.00	15.00
☐27097 (M)		SOUL MY WAY	6.00	15.00	13.50
☐67097 (S)		SOUL MY WAY	7.00	17.00	15.00
☐67104 (S)		ANOTHER PLACE. ANOTHER TIME	5.50	14.00	12.00
☐67112 (S)		SHE STILL COMES AROUND	5.50	14.00	12.00
☐67118 (S)		COUNTRY HITS. VOL. I	5.50	15.00	13.50
☐67126 (S)		TOGETHER WITH LINDA GAIL LEWIS	5.50	14.00	12.00
☐67128 (S)		SHE EVEN WOKE ME UP TO SAY GOODBYE	5.50	14.00	12.00
☐67131 (S)		THE BEST OF JERRY LEE LEWIS . .	5.50	14.00	12.00

RAMSEY LEWIS
RAMSEY LEWIS—ALBUMS

☐C-32030	**COLUMBIA**	FUNKY SERENITY	5.00	7.50	6.00
☐RC-32490		RAMSEY LEWIS' GREATEST HITS	5.00	7.50	6.00
☐PC-33194		SUN GODDESS	5.00	7.50	6.00
☐PC-33800		DON'T IT FEEL GOOD	5.00	7.50	6.00
☐PC-34173		SALONGO	5.00	7.50	6.00
☐PC-35018		TEQUILA MOCKINGBIRD	5.00	7.50	6.00
☐PC-35483		LEGACY	5.00	7.50	6.00
☐JC-33815		RAMSEY	5.00	7.50	6.00
☐FC-36354		THE BEST OF RAMSEY LEWIS . . .	5.00	7.50	6.00
☐JC-36423		ROUTES	5.00	7.50	6.00
☐PC-37019		BLUES FOR THE NIGHT OWL	5.00	7.50	6.00
☐FC-37153		THREE PIECE SUIT	5.00	7.50	6.00
☐FC-37687		LIVE AT THE SAVOY	5.00	7.50	6.00
☐FC-38294		CHANCE ENCOUNTER	5.00	7.50	6.00
☐FC-39158		REUNION (WITH THE RAMSEY LEWIS TRIO)	5.00	7.50	6.00

THE RAMSEY LEWIS TRIO—ALBUMS

☐645	**CADET/ARGO**	AN HOUR WITH THE RLT	3.50	6.50	5.00
☐665		STRETCHING OUT	3.50	6.50	5.00

			Current Price Range		P/Y AVG
☐668		MUSIC FROM THE SOIL	3.50	6.50	5.00
☐671		THE RLT IN CHICAGO	3.50	6.50	5.00
☐680		MORE MUSIC FROM THE SOIL	3.50	6.50	5.00
☐686		NEVER ON SUNDAY	3.50	6.50	5.00
☐687X		THE SOUND OF CHRISTMAS	3.50	6.50	5.00
☐715		POT LUCK	3.50	6.50	5.00
☐723		BAREFOOT SUNDAY BLUES	3.50	6.50	5.00
☐732		BACH TO THE BLUES	3.50	6.50	5.00
☐741		THE RLT AT THE BOHEMIAN CAVERNS	3.50	6.50	5.00
☐745		MORE SOUNDS OF CHRISTMAS	3.50	6.50	5.00
☐755		CHOICE! THE BEST OF THE RLT	3.50	6.50	5.00
☐757		THE IN CROWD	3.50	6.50	5.00
☐761		HANG ON RAMSEY!	3.50	6.50	5.00

SMILEY LEWIS

☐5067	*IMPERIAL*	LOWDOWN/TEE-NAH-NAH	52.00	95.00	90.00
☐5072		SLIDE ME DOWN/GROWING OLD	52.00	95.00	90.00
☐5102		IF YOU EVER LOVED A WOMAN/ DIRTY PEOPLE	46.00	78.00	72.00
☐5124		MY BABY WAS RIGHT/ BEE'S BOOGIE	46.00	78.00	72.00
☐5194		THE BELLS ARE RINGING/ LILLIE MAE	40.00	66.00	60.00
☐5208		GUMBO BLUES/ IT'S SO PEACEFUL	40.00	66.00	60.00
☐5224		YOU'RE NOT THE ONE/ GYPSY BLUES	34.00	54.00	48.00
☐5234		BIG MAMOU/PLAYGIRL	17.00	29.00	25.00
☐5241		OH BABY/CALDONIA'S PARTY	17.00	29.00	25.00
☐5252		IT'S MUSIC/LITTLE FERNANDEZ	17.00	29.00	25.00
☐5268		BLUE MONDAY/DOWN THE ROAD	22.00	40.00	36.00
☐5279		I LOVE YOU FOR SENTIMENTAL REASONS/THE ROCKS	14.00	24.00	16.50
☐5296		CAN'T STOP LOVING YOU/ THAT CERTAIN DOOR	14.00	24.00	16.50
☐5316		OOH LA LA/TOO MANY DRIVERS	14.00	24.00	16.50
☐5325		JAILBIRD/FAREWELL	14.00	24.00	16.50
☐5349		REAL GONE LOVER/ NOBODY KNOWS	14.00	24.00	16.50
☐5356		I HEAR YOU KNOCKING/ BUMPITY BUMP	14.00	24.00	16.50
☐5372		COME ON/QUEEN OF HEARTS	14.00	24.00	16.50
☐5380		ONE NIGHT/AIN'T GONNA DO IT	9.00	16.00	11.00
☐5389		SHE'S GOT ME HOOK, LINE AND SINKER/PLEASE LISTEN TO ME	9.00	16.00	11.00
☐5404		DOWN YONDER WE GO BALLIN'/ SOMEDAY YOU'LL WANT ME	9.00	16.00	11.00
☐5418		SHAME SHAME SHAME/NO NO	7.00	14.00	9.00
☐5431		YOU ARE MY SUNSHINE/ SWEETER WORDS	7.00	14.00	9.00

SMILEY LEWIS—ALBUM

☐9141 (M)	*IMPERIAL*	I HEAR YOU KNOCKING	70.00	150.00	90.00

WALLY LEWIS

☐117	*TALLY*	KATHLEEN/DONNA	5.50	11.00	9.00
☐15705	*DOT*	KATHLEEN/DONNA	3.25	5.50	4.00
☐15763		WHITE BOBBY SOX/I'M WITH YOU	3.00	5.00	3.50
☐55178	*LIBERTY*	THAT'S THE WAY IT GOES/ EVERY DAY	3.00	5.00	3.50
☐55196		SALLY GREEN/ARMS OF JO-ANN	3.00	5.00	3.50
☐55211		MY BABY/LOVER BOY	3.00	5.00	3.50
☐55370		STREETS OF BERLIN/WALKING IN THE FOOTSTEPS OF A FOOL	2.75	4.50	3.00

			Current Price Range		P/Y AVG

GORDON LIGHTFOOT

☐ 10352	ABC-PARAMOUNT	(REMEMBER ME) I'M THE ONE/			
		DAISY DOO	3.75	6.00	4.50
☐ 10373		IT'S TOO LATE. HE WINS/			
		NEGOTIATIONS	3.75	6.00	4.50

LIL' JUNE AND THE JANUARYS

☐ 4009	PROFILE	OH. WHAT A FEELING/			
		OH. MY LOVE	12.00	21.00	18.00

KATHY LINDEN

☐ 106	NATIONAL	IT'S JUST MY LUCK TO BE			
		FIFTEEN/TOUCH OF LOVE	3.50	6.00	4.35
☐ 8510	FELSTED	BILLY/IF I COULD HOLD YOU			
		IN MY ARMS	3.50	6.00	4.35
☐ 8521		YOU'D BE SURPRISED/			
		WHY OH WHY	3.50	6.00	4.35
☐ 8533		OH JOHNNY OH/GEORGIE	3.50	6.00	4.35
☐ 8544		KISSIN' CONVERSATION/			
		JUST A SANDY HAIRED BOY			
		CALLED SANDY	3.50	6.00	4.35
☐ 8554		SOMEBODY LOVES YOU/			
		YOU WALKED INTO MY LIFE ...	3.50	6.00	4.35
☐ 8571		GOODBYE JIMMY GOODBYE/			
		HEARTACHES AT SWEET			
		SIXTEEN	3.50	6.00	4.35
☐ 8587		YOU DON'T KNOW GIRLS/			
		SO CLOSE TO MY HEART	3.25	5.50	4.00
☐ 8596		THINK LOVE/MARY LOU WILSON			
		AND JOHNNY BROWN	3.25	5.50	4.00

KATHY LINDEN—ALBUM

☐ 7501 (M)	FELSTED	THAT CERTAIN BOY	16.00	33.00	21.00

LITTLE ANTHONY AND THE IMPERIALS

☐ 1552	SAVOY	MUST BE FALLING IN LOVE/YOU .	9.50	17.00	15.00
☐ 1027	END	TEARS ON MY PILLOW/			
		TWO PEOPLE IN THE WORLD ...	4.50	9.00	6.00
☐ 1036		SO MUCH/OH YEAH	4.00	7.00	4.85
☐ 1038		THE DIARY/CHA CHA HENRY	4.00	7.00	4.85
☐ 1039		WISHFUL THINKING/			
		WHEN YOU WISH UPON A STAR	3.50	6.00	4.35
☐ 1047		A PRAYER AND A JUKE BOX/			
		RIVER PATH	3.50	6.00	4.35
☐ 1053		I'M ALRIGHT/			
		SO NEAR AND YET SO FAR	3.50	6.00	4.35
☐ 1060		SHIMMY. SHIMMY. KO-KO-BOP/			
		I'M STILL IN LOVE WITH YOU ..	3.50	6.00	4.35
☐ 1067		MY EMPTY ROOM/			
		BAYOU BAYOU BABY	3.25	5.50	4.00
☐ 1074		I'M TAKING A VACATION FROM			
		LOVE/ONLY SYMPATHY	3.25	5.50	4.00
☐ 1080		LIMBO (PT. 1)/(PT. 2)	3.25	5.50	4.00
☐ 1083		DREAM/FORMULA OF LOVE	3.25	5.50	4.00
☐ 1086		PLEASE SAY YOU WANT ME/			
		SO NEAR YET SO FAR	3.25	5.50	4.00
☐ 1091		TRAVELING STRANGER/			
		SAY YEAH	3.25	5.50	4.00
☐ 1104		A LONELY WAY TO SPEND AN			
		EVENING/DREAM	3.25	5.50	4.00
☐ 1104	DCP	I'M ON THE OUTSIDE (LOOKING			
		IN)/PLEASE GO	3.00	5.00	3.65
☐ 1119		GOIN' OUT OF MY HEAD/			
		MAKE IT EASY ON YOURSELF .	3.00	5.00	3.65

			Current Price Range		P/Y AVG
☐1128		HURT SO BAD/REPUTATION	3.00	5.00	3.65
☐1136		TAKE ME BACK/OUR SONG	3.00	5.00	3.65
☐1149		I MISS YOU SO/			
		GET OUT OF MY LIFE	3.00	5.00	3.65
☐1154		HURT/NEVER AGAIN	3.00	5.00	3.65
☐1241	VEEP	GOIN' OUT OF MY HEAD/			
		MAKE IT EASY ON YOURSELF .	3.00	5.00	3.65
☐1278		I'M HYPNOTIZED/			
		HUNGRY HEART	2.75	4.50	3.00
☐1283		WHAT GREATER LOVE/			
		BACK OF MY HEART	2.75	4.50	3.00
		LITTLE ANTHONY AND THE IMPERIALS—EP			
☐204	END	WE ARE THE IMPERIALS	9.50	17.00	15.00
		LITTLE ANTHONY AND THE IMPERIALS—ALBUMS			
☐303 (M)	END	WE ARE LITTLE ANTHONY AND			
		THE IMPERIALS	17.00	40.00	35.00
☐3800 (M)	DCP	GOIN' OUT OF MY HEAD	7.00	17.00	15.00
☐6800 (S)		GOIN' OUT OF MY HEAD	8.00	21.00	18.00
☐3801 (M)		I'M ON THE OUTSIDE			
		(LOOKING IN)	7.00	17.00	15.00
☐6801 (S)		I'M ON THE OUTSIDE			
		(LOOKING IN)	8.00	21.00	18.00
☐3809 (M)		THE BEST OF LITTLE ANTHONY			
		AND THE IMPERIALS	6.00	15.00	13.50
☐6809 (S)		THE BEST OF LITTLE ANTHONY			
		AND THE IMPERIALS	7.00	17.00	15.00

LITTLE BEATS

☐71155	MERCURY	LOVE IS TRUE/SOMEONE FOR ME	9.00	21.00	18.00

LITTLE CAESAR AND THE ROMANS

☐4158	DEL-FI	THOSE OLDIES BUT GOODIES/			
		FEVER	3.75	6.00	4.50
☐4158		THOSE OLDIES BUT GOODIES/			
		SHE DON'T WANNA DANCE ...	3.25	5.50	4.00
☐4164		HULLY GULLY AGAIN/			
		FRANKIE AND JOHNNY	3.25	5.50	4.00
☐4166		MEMORIES OF THOSE OLDIES BUT			
		GOODIES/FEVER	3.25	5.50	4.00
☐4170		THE TEN COMMANDMENTS OF			
		LOVE/C. C. RIDER	3.25	5.50	4.00
☐4176		POPEYE ONCE MORE/			
		YOYO YO YOYO	3.25	5.50	4.00
		LITTLE CAESAR AND THE ROMANS—ALBUM			
☐1218 (M)	DEL-FI	MEMORIES OF THOSE OLDIES BUT			
		GOODIES. VOL. I	12.00	30.00	25.00

LITTLE CLYDIE AND THE TEENS

☐462	RPM	A CASUAL LOOK/OH ME	12.00	21.00	18.00

LITTLE DAVID
FEATURED: THE REGENTS

☐40	SYMPHONY	CALL ON ME/			
		I WANT THE GOOD LIFE	8.25	14.00	12.00

LITTLE EVA

☐1000	DIMENSION	THE LOCO-MOTION/			
		HE IS THE BOY	3.25	5.50	4.00
☐1003		KEEP YOUR HANDS OFF MY BABY/			
		WHERE DO I GO?	3.25	5.50	4.00
☐1006		LET'S TURKEY TROT/			
		DOWN HOME	3.25	5.50	4.00
☐1011		OLD SMOKEY LOCOMOTION/			
		JUST A LITTLE GIRL	3.25	5.50	4.00

LITTLE RICHARD

Richard Penniman was the third of a family of 14 children. (He was born in Macon, GA, on December 5, 1935.) His shortness earned the nickname "Little Richard" from his brothers and sisters. Richard began dancing on street corners for coins. Then he decided to become a singer; he formed a vocal group called the Upsetters. Convinced his son was insane, Mr. Penniman threw Richard out of the house at age 13.

When Richard was 17, he entered — and won — an Atlanta talent show. The prize was an RCA Victor contract. Four singles there failed, as did his next four for Houston's Peacock label. Richard then became a dishwasher at the Macon Greyhound bus depot.

Specialty Records' owner Art Rupe liked Richard's style on an audition tape and decided to take a chance. Richard's first single was "Tutti Frutti", originally a stream of obscene insults aimed at Richard's bus-depot boss. It became an instant hit, the first of many for the Macon Maniac.

In 1957, Richard interpreted an airplane-engine fire as a sign from God to quit "the Devil's music". Richard later returned to the concert circuit (after becoming an ordained minister). However, he quit performing all rock-and-roll in 1975 to become a Bible salesman for a Nashville publisher.

			Current Price Range		P/Y AVG
1013		THE TROUBLE WITH BOYS/ WHAT I GOTTA DO	3.25	5.50	4.00
1019		PLEASE HURT ME/ LET'S START THE PARTY AGAIN.	3.25	5.50	4.00
1021		THE CHRISTMAS SONG/I WISH YOU A MERRY CHRISTMAS . . .	3.25	5.50	4.00
1035		RUN TO HER/ MAKIN' WITH THE MAGILLA . .	3.25	5.50	4.00
1042		WAKE UP JOHN/ TAKIN' BACK WHAT I SAID	3.25	5.50	4.00
943	AMY	STAND BY ME/THAT'S MY MAN .	3.25	5.50	4.00
		LITTLE EVA—ALBUMS			
6000 (M)	DIMENSION	L-L-L-LOCOMOTION	9.00	28.00	25.00
6000 (S)		L-L-L-LOCOMOTION	14.00	34.00	30.00

LITTLE JOE AND THE THRILLERS

7075	OKEH	THIS I KNOW/LET'S DO THE SLOP	4.50	7.50	6.00
7088		PEANUTS/LILLY LOU	3.50	6.00	4.35
7094		THE ECHOES KEEP CALLING ME/ LONESOME	3.50	6.00	4.35
7099		WHAT HAPPENED TO YOUR HALO?/DON'T LEAVE ME ALONE	3.50	6.00	4.35
7107		MINE/IT'S TOO BAD WE HAD TO SAY GOODBYE	3.50	6.00	4.35
7116		CHEERY (PT. 1/(PT. 2)	3.50	6.00	4.35
7134		EV'RY NOW AND THEN/ GOODNIGHT. LITTLE GIRL	3.50	6.00	4.35
7136		STAY/PLEASE DON'T GO	3.50	6.00	4.35
9293	EPIC	MINE/IT'S TOO BAD WE HAD TO SAY GOODBYE	3.25	5.50	4.00
1214	20TH CENTURY	FOR SENTIMENTAL REASONS/ ONE MORE TIME	3.25	5.50	4.00
715	UPTOWN	COME WHAT MAY/ THIS I KNOW. LITTLE GIRL	3.25	5.50	4.00
20142	REPRISE	PEANUTS/NO. NO. I CAN'T STOP	3.25	5.50	4.00
		LITTLE JOE AND THE THRILLERS—EP			
7198	EPIC	LITTLE JOE AND THE THRILLERS .	11.00	20.00	13.00

LITTLE RICHARD

4392	RCA	TAXI BLUES/EVERY HOUR	76.00	128.00	120.00
4582		GET RICH QUICK/ THINKIN' ABOUT MY MOTHER .	64.00	128.00	120.00
4722		WHY DID YOU LEAVE ME?/ AIN'T NOTHIN' HAPPENIN'	64.00	128.00	120.00
5025		PLEASE HAVE MERCY ON ME/ I BROUGHT IT ALL ON MYSELF	54.00	96.00	90.00
1616	PEACOCK	FOOL AT THE WHEEL/ AIN'T THAT GOOD NEWS	26.00	46.00	42.00
1628		RICE. RED BEANS AND TURNIP GREENS/ALWAYS	22.00	40.00	36.00
1658		LITTLE RICHARD'S BOOGIE/ DIRECTLY FROM MY HEART . . .	20.00	34.00	30.00
1673		MAYBE I'M RIGHT/ I LOVE MY BABY	17.00	30.00	25.00
561	SPECIALTY	TUTTI FRUTTI/ I'M JUST A LONELY GUY	4.50	7.50	6.00
572		LONG TALL SALLY/ SLIPPIN' AND SLIDIN'	4.50	7.50	6.00
579		RIP IT UP/REDDY TEDDY	4.50	7.50	6.00
584		SHE'S GOT IT/HEEBIE JEEBIES . .	5.50	11.00	9.00
591		THE GIRL CAN'T HELP IT/ ALL AROUND THE WORLD	5.00	9.00	7.00
598		LUCILLE/SEND ME SOME LOVIN'	3.75	5.50	4.50

FIRST-PRESSES OF THE ABOVE FEATURE A WAVY YELLOW CENTER LINE

			Current Price Range		P/Y AVG
☐606		JENNY JENNY/MISS ANN	3.50	5.50	4.15
☐611		KEEP A KNOCKIN'/CAN'T BELIEVE YOU WANNA LEAVE	3.50	5.50	4.15
☐624		GOOD GOLLY MISS MOLLY/ HEY HEY HEY HEY	3.50	5.50	4.15
☐633		OOH! MY SOUL/ TRUE, FINE MAMA	3.50	5.50	4.15
☐645		BABY FACE/ I'LL NEVER LET YOU GO	3.50	5.50	4.35
☐652		SHE KNOWS HOW TO ROCK/ EARLY ONE MORNING	3.25	5.50	4.00
☐660		BY THE LIGHT OF THE SILVERY MOON/WONDERIN'	3.25	5.50	4.00
☐664		KANSAS CITY/ LONESOME AND BLUE	3.25	5.50	4.00
☐670		SHAKE A HAND/ALL NIGHT LONG	3.25	5.50	4.00
☐680		WHOLE LOTTA SHAKIN' GOING ON/ MAYBE I'M RIGHT	3.25	5.50	4.00
☐681		I GOT IT/BABY	3.25	5.50	4.00
☐686		DIRECTLY FROM MY HEART/ THE MOST I CAN OFFER	3.25	5.50	4.00
☐692		BAMA LAMA BAMA LOO/ ANNIE'S BACK	3.25	5.50	4.00
☐697		KEEP A KNOCKIN'/ BAMA LAMA BAMA LOO	3.25	5.50	4.00
☐665	**VEEJAY**	WITHOUT LOVE/ DANCE WHAT YOU WANNA ...	3.25	5.50	4.00
☐71905	**MERCURY**	HE GOT WHAT HE WANTED/ WHY DON'T YOU CHANGE YOUR WAYS	3.00	5.00	3.50
☐71884		JOY, JOY, JOY/HE'S NOT JUST A SOLDIER	3.00	5.00	3.50
☐1022	**MODERN**	DIRECTLY FROM MY HEART/ I'M BACK	3.00	5.00	3.50
		LITTLE RICHARD—EPs			
☐400	**SPECIALTY**	HERE'S LITTLE RICHARD, VOL. I .	12.00	21.00	18.00
☐401		HERE'S LITTLE RICHARD, VOL. II	12.00	21.00	18.00
☐402		HERE'S LITTLE RICHARD, VOL. III	12.00	21.00	18.00
☐403		LITTLE RICHARD, VOL. I	10.00	17.00	15.00
☐404		LITTLE RICHARD, VOL. II	10.00	17.00	15.00
☐405		LITTLE RICHARD, VOL. III	10.00	17.00	15.00
		LITTLE RICHARD—ALBUMS			
☐SP-100 (M)	**SPECIALTY**	HERE'S LITTLE RICHARD (yellow-and-white label)	17.00	40.00	35.00
☐2100 (M)		HERE'S LITTLE RICHARD (gold label)	8.00	21.00	18.00
☐2103 (M)		LITTLE RICHARD, VOL. II	9.00	25.00	22.50
☐2104 (M)		THE FABULOUS LITTLE RICHARD	9.00	25.00	22.50

LIVELY ONES

☐4189	**DEL-FI**	MISERLOU/LIVIN'	3.00	5.00	3.50
☐4196		SURF RIDER/SURFER'S LAMENT	3.00	5.00	3.50
☐4205		SURFER BOOGIE/RIC-A-TIC	3.00	5.00	3.50
☐4210		GOOFY FOOT/HIGH TIDE	3.00	5.00	3.50
☐4217		SURF CITY/TELSTAR SURF	3.00	5.00	3.50
		LIVELY ONES—ALBUMS			
☐1226 (M)	**DEL-FI**	SURF-RIDER	7.00	17.00	15.00
☐1226 (S)		SURF-RIDER	9.00	25.00	22.50
☐1231 (M)		SURF DRUMS	7.00	17.00	15.00
☐1231 (S)		SURF DRUMS	8.00	21.00	18.00
☐1237 (M)		THIS IS SURF CITY	7.00	17.00	15.00
☐1237 (S)		THIS IS SURF CITY	8.00	21.00	18.00
☐1238 (M)		GREAT SURF HITS	6.00	15.00	13.50
☐1238 (S)		GREAT SURF HITS	7.00	17.00	15.00

			Current Price Range		P/Y AVG
1240 (M)		SURFIN' SOUTH OF THE BORDER	6.00	15.00	13.50
1240 (S)		SURFIN' SOUTH OF THE BORDER	7.00	17.00	15.00

JACKIE LLOYD

342	HERO	COME & GET ME/WARM LOVE ...	17.00	40.00	35.00

LOBO

112	BIG TREE	ME & YOU & A DOG NAMED BOO/ WALK AWAY	2.50	4.50	3.10
116		I'M THE ONLY ONE/ SHE DIDN'T DO MAGIC	2.50	4.50	3.10
119		A LITTLE DIFFERENT/ CALIFORNIA DID	2.50	4.50	3.10
141		DON'T EXPECT ME TO BE YOUR FRIEND/A SIMPLE MAN	2.50	4.50	3.10
147		I'D LOVE YOU TO WANT ME/ AM I TRUE TO MYSELF	2.50	4.50	3.10
158		DON'T EXPECT ME TO BE YOUR FRIEND/BIG RED KITE	2.50	4.50	3.10
15001		STONEY/STANDING AT THE END OF THE LINE	2.50	4.50	3.10

LATER SINGLES ARE WORTH UP TO $2.50 EACH MINT

LONNIE AND THE CRISIS

103	UNIVERSAL	BELLS IN THE CHAPEL/ SANTA TOWN. U.S.A.	8.25	14.00	12.00

TRINI LOPEZ

5187	KING	ROCK ON/ SINCE I DON'T HAVE YOU	4.50	7.50	6.00

TRINI LOPEZ—EP

483	KING	TEENAGE IDOL	4.50	7.50	6.00

TRINI LOPEZ—ALBUMS

863 (M)	KING	TEENAGE LOVE SONGS	8.00	21.00	18.00
877 (M)		MORE OF TRINI LOPEZ	8.00	21.00	18.00

LOVE

45603	ELEKTRA	MY LITTLE RED BOOK/ A MESSAGE TO PRETTY	3.25	5.50	4.00
45605		7 AND 7 IS/NO. FOURTEEN	3.25	5.50	4.00
45608		ORANGE SKIES/ SHE COMES IN COLORS	3.25	5.50	4.00
45613		REVELATION/QUE VIDA	3.25	5.50	4.00
45629		ALONE AGAIN OR/ A HOUSE IS NOT A MOTEL	3.25	5.50	4.00
45633		YOUR MIND AND ME BELONG TOGETHER/LAUGHING STOCK	3.25	5.50	4.00
45700		ALONE AGAIN OR/ A HOUSE IS NOT A MOTEL	3.25	5.50	4.00

LOVE—ALBUMS

4001 (M)	ELEKTRA	LOVE	8.00	21.00	18.00
74001 (S)		LOVE	7.00	17.00	15.00
4005 (M)		DA CAPO	8.00	21.00	18.00
74005 (S)		DA CAPO	7.00	17.00	15.00
74013 (S)		FOREVER CHANGES	7.00	17.00	15.00
74049 (S)		FOUR SAIL	7.00	17.00	15.00
74058 (S)		LOVE - REVISITED	7.00	17.00	15.00

DARLENE LOVE

SEE: BLOSSOMS, BOB B. SOXX AND THE BLUE JEANS

111	PHILLES	(TODAY I MET) THE BOY I'M GONNA MARRY/MY HEART BEAT A LITTLE BIT	5.50	11.00	9.00

			Current Price Range		P/Y AVG
☐ 111		(TODAY I MET) THE BOY I'M GONNA MARRY/ TAKE IT FROM ME	3.75	6.00	4.50
☐ 114		WAIT 'TIL MY BOBBY GETS HOME/ TAKE IT FROM ME	3.25	5.50	4.00
☐ 117		A FINE FINE BOY/ NINO AND SONNY	3.25	5.50	4.00
☐ 119		WINTER WONDERLAND/ CHRISTMAS BABY PLEASE COME HOME	5.50	11.00	9.00
☐ 123		HE'S A QUIET GUY/ STUMBLED AND FELL	21.00	40.00	36.00
☐ 125		WINTER WONDERLAND/ CHRISTMAS BABY PLEASE COME HOME	4.50	8.00	6.00

LOVE LETTERS

☐ 714	ACME	WALKING THE STREETS ALONE/ OWEE-NELLIE	28.00	46.00	42.00

RONNIE LOVE

☐ 5001	STARTIME	CHILLS AND FEVER/ NO USE PLEDGING MY LOVE (Johnny Love)	5.50	11.00	9.00
☐ 16144	DOT	CHILLS AND FEVER/ NO USE PLEDGING MY LOVE ..	3.00	5.00	3.50

LOVERS

☐ 2005	LAMP	DARLING IT'S WONDERFUL/ GOTTA WHOLE LOTTA LOVIN' .	4.50	7.50	6.00
☐ 2013		I WANNA BE LOVED/LET'S ELOPE	3.75	6.00	4.50

LOVIN' SPOONFUL

☐ 201	KAMA SUTRA	DO YOU BELIEVE IN MAGIC?/ ON THE ROAD AGAIN	3.00	5.00	3.65
☐ 205		YOU DIDN'T HAVE TO BE SO NICE/ MY GAL	3.00	5.00	3.65
☐ 208		DAYDREAM/NIGHTOWL BLUES ..	3.00	5.00	3.65
☐ 209		DID YOU EVER HAVE TO MAKE UP YOUR MIND?/DIDN'T WANT TO HAVE TO DO IT	3.00	5.00	3.65
☐ 211		SUMMER IN THE CITY/ BUTCHIE'S TUNE	3.00	5.00	3.65
☐ 211		SUMMER IN THE CITY/ FISHIN' BLUES	3.00	5.00	3.65
☐ 216		RAIN ON THE ROOF/POW!	3.00	5.00	3.65
☐ 219		NASHVILLE CATS/ FULL MEASURE	3.00	5.00	3.65
☐ 220		DARLING BE HOME SOON/ DARLIN' COMPANION	3.00	5.00	3.65
☐ 225		SIX O'CLOCK/THE FINALE	3.00	5.00	3.65
☐ 231		YOU'RE A BIG BOY NOW/ LONELY (AMY'S THEME)	3.50	5.50	4.00
☐ 239		SHE IS STILL A MYSTERY/ ONLY PRETTY, WHAT A PITY ..	2.75	4.75	3.50
☐ 241		MONEY/CLOSE YOUR EYES	2.75	4.75	3.50
☐ 250		NEVER GOING BACK/FOREVER ..	2.75	4.75	3.50
☐ 251		RUN WITH YOU/REVELATION: REVOLUTION '69	2.75	4.75	3.50
☐ 255		ME ABOUT YOU/AMAZING AIR ..	2.75	4.75	3.50

LOVIN' SPOONFUL—ALBUMS

☐ 8050 (M)	KAMA SUTRA	DO YOU BELIEVE IN MAGIC?	6.00	15.00	13.50
☐ 8050 (S)		DO YOU BELIEVE IN MAGIC?	8.00	21.00	18.00

			Current Price Range		P/Y AVG
☐8051 (M)		DAYDREAM	6.00	15.00	13.50
☐8051 (S)		DAYDREAM	8.00	21.00	18.00
☐8054 (M)		HUMS OF THE LOVIN' SPOONFUL	5.50	14.00	12.00
☐8054 (S)		HUMS OF THE LOVIN' SPOONFUL	7.00	17.00	15.00
☐8056 (S)		BEST OF THE LOVIN' SPOONFUL .	5.50	14.00	12.00
☐8061 (S)		EVERYTHING PLAYING	5.00	12.00	10.00
☐8064 (S)		BEST OF THE LOVIN' SPOONFUL, VOL. 2	5.00	12.00	10.00
☐8073 (S)		REVELATION REVOLUTION '69 ...	5.00	12.00	10.00
☐2608-2 (S)		BEST OF THE LOVIN' SPOONFUL .	5.00	12.00	10.00

LUGEE AND THE LIONS
FEATURED: LOU CHRISTIE

☐112	**ROBBEE**	THE JURY/LITTLE DID I KNOW ...	12.00	21.00	18.00

ROBIN LUKE

☐206	**INTERNATIONAL**	SUSIE DARLIN'/ LIVING'S LOVING YOU	14.00	21.00	20.00
☐208		MY GIRL/CHICKA CHICKA HONEY	6.00	12.00	8.00
☐210		STROLLIN' BLUES/YOU CAN'T STOP ME FROM DREAMIN'	6.00	12.00	8.00
☐212		WON'T YOU PLEASE BE MINE/ FIVE MINUTES MORE	6.00	12.00	8.00
☐15781	**DOT**	SUSIE DARLIN'/ LIVING'S LOVING YOU	3.25	5.50	4.00
☐15839		MY GIRL/CHICKA CHICKA HONEY	3.00	5.00	3.50
☐15899		STROLLIN' BLUES/YOU CAN'T STOP ME FROM DREAMIN'	3.00	5.00	3.50
☐15959		FIVE MINUTES MORE/WHO'S GONNA HOLD YOUR HAND? ...	3.00	5.00	3.50
☐16040		BAD BOY/ SCHOOL BUS LOVE AFFAIR ...	3.00	5.00	3.50

ROBIN LUKE—EP

☐1092	**DOT**	SUSIE DARLIN'	9.50	18.00	15.00

LULU

☐9678	**PARROT**	SHOUT/FORGET ME BABY	3.25	5.50	4.00
☐9714		HERE COMES THE NIGHT/ I'LL COME RUNNING	3.25	5.50	4.00
☐9778		LEAVE A LITTLE LOVE/HE DON'T WANT YOUR LOVE ANYMORE ..	3.25	5.50	4.00
☐9791		TRY TO UNDERSTAND/ NOT IN THIS WHOLE WORLD ..	3.25	5.50	4.00
☐40021		SHOUT/WHEN HE TOUCHES ME .	3.00	5.00	3.65

LULU—ALBUMS

☐61016 (M)	**PARROT**	FROM LULU WITH LOVE	6.00	15.00	13.00
☐71016 (S)		FROM LULU WITH LOVE	8.00	21.00	18.00

BOB LUMAN

☐8311	**IMPERIAL**	RED CADILLAC AND A BLACK MUSTACHE/ALL NIGHT CLEANUP	9.50	17.00	15.00
☐8313		RED HOT/ WHENEVER YOU'RE READY ...	13.00	23.00	20.00
☐8315		MAKE UP YOUR MIND, BABY/ YOUR LOVE	9.50	17.00	15.00
☐4059	**CAPITOL**	PRECIOUS/SVENGALI	5.50	11.00	9.00
☐5081	**WARNER BROTHERS**	CLASSIC OF '59/MY BABY WALKS ALL OVER ME	3.25	5.50	4.00
☐5105		BUTTERCUP/DREAMY DOLL	3.25	5.50	4.00
☐5172		LET'S THINK ABOUT LIVING/ YOU'VE GOT EVERYTHING	2.75	4.50	3.00

LATER WARNER BROTHERS SINGLES ARE WORTH UP TO $2.50 MINT
BOB LUMAN-EP

			Current Price Range		P/Y AVG
☐ 1396	**WARNER BROTHERS**	LET'S THINK ABOUT LIVING	7.00	12.50	11.00

BOB LUMAN—ALBUMS

☐ 1396 (M)	**WARNER BROTHERS**	LET'S THINK ABOUT LIVING	8.00	21.00	18.00
☐ 1396 (S)		LET'S THINK BOUT LIVING	12.00	29.00	25.00

LARRY LUREX (QUEEN)

☐ 104	**ANTHEM**	I CAN HEAR MUSIC/GOIN' BACK .	9.50	17.00	15.00

LYME AND CYBELLE
FEATURED: WARREN ZEVON

☐ 228	**WHITE WHALE**	FOLLOW ME/LIKE THE SEASONS	3.00	5.00	3.65
☐ 232		IF YOU GOT TO GO, GO ON/ I'LL GO ON	3.00	5.00	3.65
☐ 245		SONG #7/ WRITE IF YOU GET WORK	3.00	5.00	3.65

FRANKIE LYMON

☐ 4026	**ROULETTE**	MY GIRL/SO GOES MY LOVE	3.50	6.00	4.35
☐ 4035		LITTLE GIRL/ IT'S CHRISTMAS ONCE AGAIN .	3.50	6.00	4.35
☐ 4044		FOOTSTEPS/THUMB THUMB	3.50	6.00	4.35
☐ 4068		MAMA DON'T ALLOW IT/ PORTABLE ON MY SHOLDER ..	3.50	6.00	4.35
☐ 4093		ONLY WAY TO LOVE/MELINDA ..	3.50	6.00	4.35
☐ 4128		NO MATTER WHAT YOU'VE DONE/ UP JUMPED THE RABBIT	3.50	6.00	4.35
☐ 4150		WHAT MOONLIGHT CAN DO/ BEFORE I FELL ASLEEP	3.50	6.00	4.35
☐ 4257		LITTLE BITTY PRETTY ONE/ CREATION OF LOVE	3.25	5.50	4.00
☐ 4283		WAITIN' IN SCHOOL/ BUZZ BUZZ BUZZ	3.25	5.50	4.00
☐ 4310		JAILHOUSE ROCK/SILHOUETTES	3.25	5.50	4.00
☐ 4348		CHANGE PARTNERS/SO YOUNG .	3.25	5.50	4.00
☐ 4391		I PUT THE BOMP/SO YOUNG	3.25	5.50	4.00

FRANKIE LYMON—EP

☐ 304	**ROULETTE**	FRANKIE LYMON AT THE LONDON PALLADIUM	11.00	20.00	13.00

FRANKIE LYMON—ALBUMS

☐ 25013 (M)	**ROULETTE**	FRANKIE LYMON AT THE LONDON PALLADIUM	20.00	43.00	28.75
☐ 25036 (M)		ROCK AND ROLL	20.00	43.00	28.75

FRANKIE LYMON AND THE TEENAGERS
SEE: TEENAGERS

☐ 1002	**GEE**	WHY DO FOOLS FALL IN LOVE/ PLEASE BE MINE	5.00	9.00	6.00
☐ 1012		I WANT YOU TO BE MY GIRL/ I'M NOT A KNOW IT ALL	5.00	9.00	6.00
☐ 1018		I PROMISE TO REMEMBER/ WHO CAN EXPLAIN	5.00	9.00	6.00
☐ 1022		THE ABC'S OF LOVE/SHARE	5.00	9.00	6.00
☐ 1026		I'M NOT A JUVENILE DELINQUENT/ BABY BABY	6.00	11.00	7.00
☐ 1032		TEENAGE LOVE/PAPER CASTLES .	6.00	11.00	7.00
☐ 1035		LOVE IS A CLOWN/ AM I FOOLING MYSELF AGAIN?	6.00	11.00	7.00
☐ 1036		OUT IN THE COLD AGAIN/ MIRACLE OF LOVE	6.00	11.00	7.00
☐ 1039		GOODY GOODY/ CREATION OF LOVE	5.00	9.00	6.00
☐ 1046		EVERYTHING TO ME/ FLIP FLOP .	5.00	9.00	6.00

			Current Price Range		P/Y AVG
☐ 1052		GOODY GOODY GIRL/			
		I'M NOT TOO YOUNG TO DREAM	5.00	9.00	6.00
	FRANKIE LYMON AND THE TEENAGERS—ALBUMS				
☐ 701 (M)	**GEE**	THE TEENAGERS FEATURING			
		FRANKIE LYMON (red label) ...	35.00	66.00	60.00
☐ 701 (S)		THE TEENAGERS FEATURING			
		FRANKIE LYMON			
		(reissue/gray label)	5.50	14.00	12.00

LOUIS LYMON AND THE TEENCHORDS

☐ 1000	**FURY**	LYDIA/I'M SO HAPPY	22.00	40.00	25.00
☐ 1003		PLEASE TELL THE ANGELS/			
		HONEY HONEY	22.00	40.00	25.00
☐ 1006		I'M NOT TOO YOUNG TO FALL IN			
		LOVE/FALLING IN LOVE	22.00	40.00	25.00
☐ 1003	**END**	TOO YOUNG/YOUR LAST CHANCE	15.00	30.00	20.00
☐ 1007		I FOUND OUT WHY/			
		TELL ME, LOVE	22.00	40.00	20.00
☐ 101	**JUANITA**	DANCE GIRL/THEM THERE EYES .	12.00	21.00	18.00

LORETTA LYNN

☐ 107	**ZERO**	I'M A HONKY TONK GIRL/			
		WISHERING SEA	5.00	7.50	6.00
☐ 110		NEW RAINBOW/HEARTACHES			
		MEET MR. BLUES	5.00	7.50	6.00
☐ 112		THE DARKEST DAY/I'M			
		GONNA PACK MY TROUBLES ..	5.00	7.50	6.00
☐ 31323	**DECCA**	I WALKED AWAY FROM THE			
		WRECK/THE GIRL THAT I AM			
		NOW	3.00	4.50	3.75
☐ 31345		WORLD OF FORGOTTEN PEOPLE/			
		GET SET FOR A HEARTACHE ...	3.00	4.50	3.75
☐ 31384		SUCCESS/HUNDRED PROOF			
		HEARTACHE	3.00	4.50	3.75
☐ 31471		THE OTHER WOMAN/WHO'LL			
		HELP ME GET OVER YOU	3.00	4.50	3.75
☐ 31541		BEFORE I'M OVER YOU/			
		WHERE WERE YOU	3.00	4.50	3.75
☐ 31608		WINE, WOMAN AND SONG/			
		THIS HAUNTED HOUSE	3.00	4.50	3.75
☐ 31643		MR. & MRS. USED TO BE/			
		LOVE WAS RIGHT HERE ALL			
		THE TIME	3.00	4.50	3.75
☐ 31707		HAPPY BIRTHDAY/WHEN			
		LONELY HITS YOUR HEART ...	3.00	4.50	3.75
☐ 31769		BLUE KENTUCKY GIRL/			
		TWO STEPS FORWARD	3.00	4.50	3.75
☐ 31793		OUR HEARTS ARE HOLDING			
		HANDS/WE'RE NOT KIDS			
		ANYMORE	3.00	4.50	3.75
☐ 31836		THE HOME YOU'RE TEARING			
		DOWN/FARTHER TO GO	3.00	4.50	3.75
☐ 31879		WHEN I HEAR MY CHILDREN			
		PRAY/EVERYBODY WANTS TO			
		GO TO HEAVEN	3.00	4.50	3.75
☐ 31893		DEAR UNCLE SAM/			
		HURTIN' FOR CERTAIN	2.75	3.50	3.00
☐ 31966		YOU AIN'T WOMAN ENOUGH/			
		GOD GAVE ME A HEART TO			
		FORGIVE	2.75	3.50	3.00
☐ 32043		TO HECK WITH OLE' SANTA			
		CLAUS/IT WON'T SEEM LIKE			
		CHRISTMAS	2.75	3.50	3.00

		Current Price Range		P/Y AVG
☐ 32045	DON'T COME HOME A DRINKIN'/ SAINT TO A SINNER	2.75	3.50	3.00
☐ 32091	SWEET THING/BEAUTIFUL, UNHAPPY HOME	2.75	3.50	3.00
☐ 32127	IF YOU'RE NOT GONE TOO LONG/ A MAN I HARDLY KNOW	2.75	3.50	3.00
☐ 32184	WHAT KIND OF A GIRL/ BARGAIN BASEMENT DRESS	2.75	3.50	3.00
☐ 32264	FIST CITY/SLOWLY KILLING ME	2.75	3.50	3.00
☐ 32332	YOU'VE JUST STEPPED IN/ THE BOTTLE'S TAKING THE PLACE OF MY MAN	2.75	3.50	3.00
☐ 32392	YOUR SQUAW IS ON THE WAR PATH/LET ME GO YOU'RE HURTING ME	2.75	3.50	3.00
☐ 32439	WOMAN OF THE WORLD/ SNEAKIN' IN	2.75	3.50	3.00
☐ 32496	WHO'S GONNA TAKE YOUR GARBAGE OUT/SOMEWHERE BETWEEN	2.75	3.50	3.00
☐ 32513	TO MAKE A MAN/ONE LITTLE REASON	2.75	3.50	3.00
☐ 32570	IF WE PUT OUR HEADS TOGETHER/ I CHASED YOU TILL YOU CAUGHT ME	2.75	3.50	3.00
☐ 32586	WINGS UPON YOUR HORNS/ LET'S GET BACK DOWN TO EARTH	2.75	3.50	3.00
☐ 32637	I KNOW HOW/JOURNEY TO THE END OF MY WORLD	2.75	3.50	3.00
☐ 32693	YOU WANNA GIVE ME A LIFT/ WHAT'S THE BOTTLE DONE	2.75	3.50	3.00
☐ 32749	COAL MINER'S DAUGHTER/ THE MAN OF THE HOUSE	2.75	3.50	3.00
☐ 32776	AFTER THE FIRE IS GONE/THE ONE I CAN'T LIVE WITHOUT	2.75	3.50	3.00
☐ 32796	I WANNA BE FREE/IF I NEVER LOVE AGAIN	2.75	3.50	3.00
☐ 32851	YOU'RE LOOKIN' AT COUNTRY/ WHEN YOU'RE POOR	2.75	3.50	3.00
☐ 32873	LEAN ME ON/FOUR GLASS WALLS	2.75	3.50	3.00
☐ 32900	ONE'S ON THE WAY/ KINFOLKS HOLLER	2.75	3.50	3.00
☐ 32974	HERE I AM AGAIN/ MY KING OF MAN	2.75	3.50	3.00
☐ 33039	RATED X/'TILL THE PAIN OUTWEARS THE SHAME	2.75	3.50	3.00
☐ 40058	**MCA** LOVE IS THE FOUNDATION/ WHAT SUNDOWN DOES TO YOU	2.00	3.00	2.50
☐ 40079	LOUISIANA WOMAN, MISSISSIPPI MAN/LIVING TOGETHER ALONE	2.00	3.00	2.50
☐ 40150	HEY LORETTA/TURN ME ANYWAY BUT LOOSE	2.00	3.00	2.50
☐ 40228	THEY DON'T MAKE 'EM LIKE MY DADDY/NOTHIN'	2.00	3.00	2.50
☐ 40251	AS SOON AS I HANG UP THE PHONE/A LIFETIME BEFORE	2.00	3.00	2.50
☐ 40283	TROUBLE IN PARADISE/ WE'VE ALREADY TASTED LOVE	2.00	3.00	2.50
☐ 65034	SHADRACK THE BLACK REINDEER/ LET'S PUT CHRISTMAS BACK INTO CHRISTMAS	2.00	3.00	2.50
☐ 40358	THE PILL/WILL YOU BE THERE	2.00	3.00	2.50

			Current Price Range		P/Y AVG
		LORETTA LYNN—ALBUMS			
☐74457	*DECCA*	LORETTA LYNN SINGS	7.50	12.00	10.00
☐74541		BEFORE I'M OVER YOU	7.50	12.00	10.00
☐74620		SONGS FROM MY HEART	7.50	12.00	10.00
☐74639		MR. & MRS. USED TO BE	7.50	12.00	10.00
☐74665		BLUE KENTUCKY GIRL	7.50	12.00	10.00
☐74695		HYMNS	7.50	12.00	10.00
☐74744		I LIKE 'EM COUNTRY	7.50	12.00	10.00
☐74783		YOU AIN'T WOMAN ENOUGH	7.50	12.00	10.00
☐74817		COUNTRY CHRISTMAS	7.50	12.00	10.00
☐74842		DON'T COME HOME A DRINKIN' .	7.50	12.00	10.00
☐74872		ERNEST TUBB AND LORETTA LYNN SINGIN' AGAIN	7.50	12.00	10.00
☐74930		SINGIN' WITH FEELIN'	5.00	10.00	7.50
☐74928		WHO SAYS GOD IS DEAD!	5.00	10.00	7.50
☐73925		HERE'S LORETTA LYNN	5.00	10.00	7.50
☐74997		FIST CITY	5.00	10.00	7.50
☐75000		LORETTA LYNN'S GREATEST HITS .	5.00	10.00	7.50
☐75084		YOUR SQUAW IS ON THE WARPATH	5.00	10.00	7.50
☐75113		WOMAN OF THE WORLD/ TO MAKE A MAN	5.00	10.00	7.50
☐75115		IF WE PUT OUR HEADS TOGETHER WITH ERNEST TUBB	5.00	10.00	7.50
☐75163		HERE'S LORETTA LYNN SINGING WINGS UPON YOUR HORNS ...	5.00	10.00	7.50
☐75198		LORETTA LYNN WRITES 'EM AND SINGS 'EM	5.00	10.00	7.50
☐75253		COAL MINER'S DAUGHTER	5.00	10.00	7.50
☐75251		WE ONLY MAKE BELIEVE	5.00	10.00	7.50
☐75282		I WANNA BE FREE	5.00	10.00	7.50
☐75310		YOU'RE LOOKIN' AT COUNTRY ..	5.00	10.00	7.50
☐75326		LEAD ME ON (WITH CONWAY TWITTY)	5.00	10.00	7.50
☐75334		ONE'S ON THE WAY	5.00	10.00	7.50
☐75351		GOD BLESS AMERICA AGAIN	5.00	10.00	7.50
☐73925		ALONE WITH YOU	5.00	10.00	7.50
☐75381		HERE I AM AGAIN	5.00	10.00	7.50
☐300	*MCA*	ENTERTAINER OF THE YEAR	3.50	7.50	5.00
☐335		LOUISIANA WOMAN/MISSISSIPPI MAN (WITH CONWAY TWITTY) .	3.50	7.50	5.00
☐420		ERNEST TUBB AND LORETTA LYNN STORY	3.50	7.50	5.00
☐420		GREATEST HITS, VOLUME II	3.50	7.50	5.00
☐427		COUNTRY PARTNERS (WITH CONWAY TWITTY)	3.50	7.50	5.00
☐444		THEY DON'T MAKE 'EM LIKE MY DADDY	3.50	7.50	5.00
☐471		BACK TO THE COUNTRY	3.50	7.50	5.00
☐2143		FEELINGS (WITH CONWAY TWITTY)	3.50	7.50	5.00
☐2146		HOME	3.50	7.50	5.00
☐2179		WHEN THE TINGLE BECOMES A CHILL	3.50	7.50	5.00
☐2209		UNITED TALENT (WITH CONWAY TWITTY)	3.50	7.50	5.00
☐2228		SOMEBODY SOMEWHERE	3.50	7.50	5.00
☐2265		I REMEMBER PATSY	3.50	7.50	5.00
☐2278		DYNAMIC DUO	3.50	7.50	5.00
☐2330		OUT OF MY HEAD AND BACK IN MY BED	3.50	7.50	5.00
☐2372		HONKY TONK HEROES	3.50	7.50	5.00
☐3073		WE'VE COME A LONG WAY BABY	3.50	7.50	5.00

			Current Price Range		P/Y AVG
☐ 40420		FEELINGS/YOU DONE LOST YOUR BABY	2.00	3.00	2.50
☐ 40438		HOME/TAKE ME TO HEAVEN EVERY NIGHT	2.00	3.00	2.50
☐ 40484		WHEN THE TINGLE BECOMES A CHILL/ALL I WANT FROM YOU	2.00	3.00	2.50
☐ 40541		RED, WHITE AND BLUE/ SOUNDS OF A NEW LOVE	2.00	3.00	2.50
☐ 40607		SOMEBODY SOMEWHERE/ SUNDOWN TAVERN	2.00	3.00	2.50
☐ 40679		SHE'S GOT YOU/THE LADY THAT LIVED HERE BEFORE	2.00	3.00	2.50
☐ 40728		I CAN'T LOVE YOU ENOUGH/ THE BED I'M DREAMING OF ...	2.00	3.00	2.50
☐ 40747		WHY CAN'T HE BE YOU/ I KEEP PUTTING ON	2.00	3.00	2.50
☐ 40832		OUT OF MY HEAD AND BACK IN MY BED/OLD ROOSTER	2.00	3.00	2.50
☐ 40910		SPRING FEVER/GOD BLESS THE CHILDREN	2.00	3.00	2.50
☐ 40920		FROM SEVEN TILL TEN/YOU'RE THE REASON OUR KIDS ARE UGLY	2.00	3.00	2.50
☐ 40954		WE'VE COME A LONG WAY BABY/ I CAN'T FEEL YOU ANYMORE ..	2.00	3.00	2.50
☐ 41021		I CAN'T FEEL YOU ANYMORE/ TRUE LOVE NEEDS TO KEEP IN TOUCH	2.00	3.00	2.50
☐ 41129		I'VE GOT A PICTURE OF US ON MY MIND/I DON'T FEEL LIKE A MOVIE TONIGHT	2.00	3.00	2.50
☐ 41141		YOU KNOW JUST WHAT I'D DO/ THE SADNESS OF IT ALL ....:	2.00	3.00	2.50
☐ 41185		PREGNANT AGAIN/YOU'RE A CROSS I CAN'T BEAR	2.00	3.00	2.50
☐ 41250		NAKED IN THE RAIN/I SHOULD BE OVER YOU BY NOW	2.00	3.00	2.50
☐ 51015		CHEATIN' ON A CHEATER/ UNTIL I MET YOU	2.00	3.00	2.50
☐ 51050		LOVIN' WHAT YOUR LOVIN' DOES TO ME/SILENT PARTNERS	2.00	3.00	2.50
☐ 51058		SOMEBODY LED ME AWAY/ EVERYBODY'S LOOKIN' FOR SOMEBODY NEW	2.00	3.00	2.50
☐ 51114		I STILL BELIEVE IN WALTZES/ OH HONEY, OH BABE	2.00	3.00	2.50
☐ 51226		I LIE/IF I AIN'T GOT IT, YOU DON'T NEED IT	2.00	3.00	2.50
☐ 52059		MAKING LOVE FROM MEMORY/ DON'T IT FEEL GOOD	2.00	3.00	2.50
☐ 52158		BREAKIN' IT/THERE'S ALL KINDS OF SMOKE	2.00	3.00	2.50
☐ 52219		LYIN', CHEATIN', WOMAN CHASIN', HONKY TONKIN' WHISKEY DRINKIN' YOU/ STARLIGHT, STARBRIGHT	2.00	3.00	2.50
☐ 52289		WALKING WITH MY MEMORIES/ IT'S GONE	2.00	3.00	2.50
		LORETTA LYNN—EPs			
☐ 2726	*DECCA*	THE OTHER WOMAN	4.00	9.00	7.50
☐ 2793		THE END OF THE WORLD	4.00	9.00	7.50
☐ 2800		HAPPY BIRTHDAY	4.00	9.00	7.50
☐ 2784		WINE WOMAN AND SONG	4.00	9.00	7.50

			Current Price Range		P/Y AVG
☐3164		THE VERY BEST OF LORETTA AND CONWAY TWITTY	3.50	7.50	5.00
☐3190		DIAMOND DUO	3.50	7.50	5.00
☐3217		LORETTA	3.50	7.50	5.00
☐5148		LOOKIN' GOOD	3.50	7.50	5.00
☐5178		TWO'S A PARTY	3.50	7.50	5.00
☐5293		I LIE	3.50	7.50	5.00
☐5354		MAKING LOVE FROM MEMORY ..	3.50	7.50	5.00
☐5723		LYIN', CHEATIN', WOMAN CHASIN', HONKY TONKIN', WHISKEY DRINKIN' YOU	3.50	7.50	5.00

M

MADISONS

☐13312	*MGM*	CHERYL ANNE/ LOOKING FOR TRUE LOVE	7.00	14.00	12.50

MAD MILO

☐20018	*MILLION DOLLAR*	HAPPY NEW YEAR/ ELVIS FOR XMAS	12.00	29.00	25.00

JOHNNY MAESTRO
SEE: BROOKLYN BRIDGE, CRESTS

☐527	*COED*	SAY IT ISN'T SO/THE GREAT PHYSICIAN (Johnny Masters) ..	6.00	11.00	7.00
☐545		MODEL GIRL/ WE'VE GOT TO TELL HIM	3.50	6.00	4.35
☐549		WHAT A SURPRISE!/ THE WARNING VOICE	3.50	6.00	4.35
☐552		MR. HAPPINESS/TEST OF LOVE .	3.50	6.00	4.35
☐557		THE WAY YOU LOOK TONIGHT/ I.O.U.....................	4.00	7.00	4.85
☐562		BESAME BABY/IT MUST BE LOVE	4.00	7.00	4.85
☐987	*PARKWAY*	TRY ME/HEARTBURN	3.50	6.00	4.35
☐999		COME SEE ME/I CARE ABOUT YOU	3.50	6.00	4.35
☐118		MY TIME/IS IT YOU?	3.50	6.00	4.35
☐474	*UNITED ARTISTS*	BEFORE I LOVED HER/ FIFTY MILLION HEARTACHES .	6.00	11.00	7.00
☐25075	*APT*	SHE'S ALL MINE ALONE/PHONE BOOTH ON THE HIGHWAY	5.00	8.50	6.00
☐256	*CAMEO*	I'LL BE THERE/ OVER THE WEEKEND	5.00	8.50	6.00
☐305		LEAN ON ME/MAKE UP MY MIND	5.00	8.50	6.00

MAGNIFICENTS

☐183	*VEE JAY*	UP ON THE MOUNTAIN/ WHY DID SHE GO?	9.50	17.00	15.00
☐183		UP ON THE MOUNTAIN/ WHY DID SHE GO? (red wax) ...	20.00	33.00	30.00
☐208		CADDY BO/HICCUP............	17.00	29.00	25.00
☐235		OFF THE MOUNTAIN/LOST LOVER	17.00	29.00	25.00

MAJORS

☐855	*IMPERIAL*	A WONDERFUL DREAM/ TIME WILL TELL	3.25	5.50	4.00
☐5879		A LITTLE BIT NOW/ SHE'S A TROUBLEMAKER	3.25	5.50	4.00
☐5914		ANYTHING YOU CAN DO/ WHAT IN THE WORLD	3.25	5.50	4.00

			Current Price Range		P/Y AVG
☐5936		TRA-LA-LA/			
		WHAT HAVE YOU BEEN DOIN'?	3.25	5.50	4.00
☐5991		YOUR LIFE BEGINS/			
		WHICH WAY DID SHE GO?	3.25	5.50	4.00
☐6009		I`LL BE THERE/OOH WEE BABY ..	3.25	5.50	4.00
		MAJORS—ALBUMS			
☐922 (M)	*IMPERIAL*	MEET THE MAJORS	7.00	17.00	15.00
☐1222 (S)		MEET THE MAJORS	9.00	25.00	22.50

MAMAS AND PAPAS
SEE: CASS ELLIOT

☐4018	*DUNHILL*	GO WHERE YOU WANNA GO/			
		(DJ only)	3.25	5.50	4.00
☐4020		CALIFORNIA DREAMIN'/			
		SOMEDAY GROOVY	3.00	5.00	3.65
☐4026		MONDAY MONDAY/			
		GOT A FEELING	3.00	5.00	3.65
☐4031		I SAW HER AGAIN/			
		EVEN IF I COULD	3.00	5.00	3.65
☐4050		LOOK THROUGH MY WINDOW/			
		ONCE WAS A TIME I THOUGHT .	3.00	5.00	3.65
☐4057		WORDS OF LOVE/			
		DANCIN` IN THE STREET	3.00	5.00	3.65
☐4077		DEDICATED TO THE ONE I LOVE/			
		FREE ADVICE	3.00	5.00	3.65
☐4083		CREEQUE ALLEY/			
		DID YOU EVER WANT TO CRY? .	3.00	5.00	3.65
☐4099		TWELVE THIRTY/			
		STRAIGHT SHOOTER	2.75	4.50	3.25
☐4107		GLAD TO BE UNHAPPY/HEY GIRL	2.75	4.50	3.25
☐4113		DANCING BEAR/			
		JOHN`S MUSIC BOX	2.75	4.50	3.25
☐4125		SAFE IN MY GARDEN/TOO LATE .	2.75	4.50	3.25
☐4150		FOR THE LOVE OF IVY/			
		STRANGE YOUNG GIRLS	2.75	4.50	3.25
☐4171		DO YOU WANNA DANCE?/			
		MY GIRL	2.75	4.50	3.25
☐4301		STEP OUT/SHOOTING STAR	2.75	4.50	3.25
		MAMAS AND PAPAS—ALBUMS			
☐50006 (M)	*DUNHILL*	IF YOU CAN BELIEVE YOUR			
		EYES AND EARS	5.50	14.00	12.00
☐50006 (S)		IF YOU CAN BELIEVE YOUR			
		EYES AND EARS	6.00	15.00	13.50
☐50010 (M)		CASS. JOHN. MICHELLE. DENNY	5.50	14.00	12.00
☐50010 (S)		CASS. JOHN. MICHELLE. DENNY	6.00	15.00	13.50
☐50014 (M)		DELIVER	5.50	14.00	12.00
☐50014 (S)		DELIVER	6.00	15.00	13.50
☐50025 (S)		FAREWELL TO THE FIRST			
		GOLDEN ERA	5.00	12.00	10.00
☐50031 (S)		THE MAMAS AND THE PAPAS ...	5.00	12.00	10.00
☐50038 (S)		GOLDEN ERA, VOL. II	5.00	12.00	10.00

MANHATTAN TRANSFER

☐3277	*ATLANTIC*	CLAP YOUR HANDS/			
		SWEET TALKING GUY	3.00	4.75	3.00
☐3292		OPERATOR/			
		TUXEDO JUNCTION	3.00	4.75	3.00
☐3349		HELPLESS/			
		MY CAT FELL IN THE WELL ...	3.00	4.75	3.00
☐3374		CHANSON D`AMOUR/			
		POPSICLE TOES	3.00	4.75	3.00
☐3472		WHERE DID OUR LOVE GO/			
		SINGLE GIRL	3.00	4.75	3.00
☐3636		BIRDLAND/THE SHAKER SONG ..	3.00	4.75	3.00

			Current Price Range		P/Y AVG
☐3649		TWILIGHT ZONE/ TWILIGHT TONE/BODY AND SOUL	3.00	4.75	3.00
☐3756		NOTHIN/YOU CAN DO ABOUT IT/WACKY DUST	3.00	4.75	3.00
☐3772		TRICKLE TRICKLE/ FOREIGN AFFAIR	3.00	4.75	3.00
☐3816		BOY FROM NEW YORK CITY/ CONFIRMATION	3.00	4.75	3.00
☐3855		SMILE AGAIN/ UNTIL I MET YOU	3.00	4.75	3.00
☐3877		SPIES IN THE NIGHT/ KAFKA	3.00	4.75	3.00
☐4034		ROUTE 66/ ON THE BOULEVARD	3.00	4.75	3.00
☐7-89786		SPICE OF LIFE/ THE NIGHT THAT MONK RETURNED TO HEAVEN	3.00	4.75	3.00
☐7-89720		AMERICAN POP/ WHY NOT	3.00	4.75	3.00
☐n/a		MYSTERY/ GOODBYE LOVE	3.00	4.75	3.00
		MANHATTAN TRANSFER—ALBUMS			
☐18133	*ATLANTIC*	THE MANHATTAN TRANSFER	7.00	14.00	9.00
☐18183		COMING OUT	6.00	11.00	7.50
☐19163		PASTICHE	6.00	11.00	7.50
☐50540		THE MANHATTAN TRANSFER— LIVE	6.00	11.00	7.50
☐19258		EXTENSIONS	6.00	11.00	7.50
☐16036		MECCA FOR MODERNS	6.00	11.00	7.50
☐19319		THE BEST OF THE MANHATTAN TRANSFER	6.00	11.00	7.50
☐80104-1		BODIES AND SOULS	6.00	11.00	7.50

MANCHESTERS
FEATURED: DAVID GATES
SEE: BREAD

☐700	*VEE JAY*	I DON'T COME FROM ENGLAND/ DRAGON FLY	4.50	7.50	6.00

BARRY MANN

☐5002	*JDS*	A LOVE TO LAST A LIFETIME/ ALL THE THINGS YOU ARE	5.00	9.00	7.00
☐10143	*ABC- PARAMOUNT*	COUNTING TEARDROPS/ WAR PAINT	3.75	6.00	4.50
☐10180		HAPPY BIRTHDAY, BROKEN HEART/THE MILLIONAIRE	2.50	5.50	4.00
☐10237		WHO PUT THE BOMP (IN THE BOMP, BOMP, BOMP?)/ LOVE, TRUE LOVE	3.00	5.00	3.50
☐10263		LITTLE MISS U.S.A./ FIND ANOTHER FOOL	3.00	5.00	3.50
☐10356		HEY BABY, I'M DANCIN'/ LIKE I DON'T LOVE YOU	3.00	5.00	3.50
☐10380		BLESS YOU/TEENAGE HAS-BEEN	3.25	5.50	4.00
		BARRY MANN—ALBUMS			
☐399 (M)	*ABC- PARAMOUNT*	WHO PUT THE BOMP (IN THE BOMP, BOMP, BOMP?)	13.00	24.00	20.00
☐399 (S)		WHO PUT THE BOMP (IN THE BOMP, BOMP, BOMP?)	20.00	34.00	30.00

			Current Price Range		P/Y AVG

CARL MANN

☐502	JASON	GONNA ROCK AND ROLL TONIGHT/ ROCKIN' LOVE	34.00	54.00	48.00
☐3539	PHILLIPS INTERNATIONAL	MONA LISA/FOOLISH ONE	3.50	6.00	4.35
☐3546		PRETEND/ROCKIN' LOVE	3.50	6.00	4.35
☐3550		SOME ENCHANTED EVENING/ I CAN'T FORGET	3.50	6.00	4.35
☐3555		SOUTH OF THE BORDER/ I'M COMIN' HOME	3.50	6.00	4.35
☐3564		THE WAYWARD WIND/ BORN TO BE BAD	3.50	6.00	4.35
☐3569		I AIN'T GOT NO HOME/ IF I COULD CHANGE YOU	3.50	6.00	4.35
☐3579		WHEN I GROW TOO OLD TO DREAM/ MOUNTAIN DEW	3.50	6.00	4.35

CARL MANN—ALBUM

☐1960 (M)	PHILLIPS INTERNATIONAL	LIKE MANN	19.00	49.00	45.00

MANFRED MANN

☐2157	ASCOT	DO WAH DIDDY DIDDY/ WHAT YOU GONNA DO?	3.50	6.00	4.00
☐2165		SHA LA LA/JOHN HARDY	3.50	6.00	4.00
☐2170		COME TOMORROW/ WHAT DID I DO WRONG?	3.50	6.00	4.00
☐2184		MY LITTLE RED BOOK/ WHAT AM I DOING WRONG?	3.50	6.00	4.00
☐2194		IF YOU GOTTA GO, GO NOW/ ONE IN THE MIDDLE	3.50	6.00	4.00
☐2210		SHE NEEDS COMPANY/ HI LILI, HI LO	3.50	6.00	4.00
☐2241		I CAN'T BELIEVE WHAT YOU SAY/ MY LITTLE RED BOOK	3.50	6.00	4.00
☐55040	UNITED ARTISTS	PRETTY FLAMINGO/ YOU'RE STANDING BY	3.50	6.00	4.00
☐55066		WHEN WILL I BE LOVED?/ DO YOU HAVE TO DO THAT?	3.50	6.00	4.00
☐72607	MERCURY	JUST LIKE A WOMAN/ I WANNA BE RICH	3.50	6.00	5.00
☐72629		EACH AND EVERY DAY/ SEMI-DETACHED SUBURBAN MR. JONES	3.00	5.00	3.65
☐72675		HA HA, SAID THE CLOWN/ FEELING SO GOOD	3.00	5.00	3.65
☐72770		QUINN THE ESKIMO/ BY REQUEST-EDWIN GARVEY (original title)	3.50	5.00	4.35
☐72770		THE MIGHTY QUINN/ BY REQUEST-EDWIN GARVEY	3.00	5.00	3.65
☐72822		MY NAME IS JACK/ THERE IS A MAN	3.00	5.00	3.65
☐72879		FOX ON THE RUN/ TOO MANY PEOPLE	3.00	5.00	3.65
☐72921		RAGMUFFIN MAN/A B SIDE	3.00	5.00	3.65

MANFRED MANN-ALBUMS

☐10315 (M)	ASCOT	THE MANFRED MANN ALBUM	7.00	17.00	15.00
☐16015 (S)		THE MANFRED MANN ALBUM	9.00	25.00	22.50
☐13018 (M)		THE FIVE FACES OF MANFRED MANN	7.00	17.00	15.00
☐16018 (S)		THE FIVE FACES OF MANFRED MANN	9.00	25.00	22.50

			Current Price Range		P/Y AVG
☐ 13021 (M)		MY LITTLE RED BOOK OF WINNERS	7.00	17.00	15.00
☐ 16021 (S)		MY LITTLE RED BOOK OF WINNERS	9.00	25.00	22.50
☐ 13024 (M)		MANN MADE	6.00	15.00	13.50
☐ 16024 (S)		MANN MADE	8.00	21.00	18.00
☐ 3549 (M)	UNITED ARTISTS	PRETTY FLAMINGO	8.00	21.00	18.00
☐ 6549 (S)		PRETTY FLAMINGO	9.00	25.00	22.50
☐ 3551 (M)		MANFRED MANN'S GREATEST HITS	6.00	15.00	13.50
☐ 6551 (S)		MANFRED MANN'S GREATEST HITS	8.00	21.00	18.00

MANUEL AND THE RENEGADES

☐ 7000	PIPER	SURF WALK/WOODY WAGON	3.25	5.50	4.00
☐ 7001		REV-UP/TRANS-MISS-YEN	3.25	5.50	4.00

MARATHONS
SEE: JAYHAWKS, VIBRATIONS

☐ 5027	ARVEE	PEANUT BUTTER/TALKIN' TRASH	3.25	5.50	4.00
☐ 5038		TIGHT SWEATER/C. PERRY MERCY OF SCOTLAND YARD	3.25	5.50	4.00
☐ 5389	ARGO	PEANUT BUTTER/DOWN IN NEW ORLEANS	5.00	10.00	5.25

MARATHONS—ALBUM

☐ 428 (M)	ARVEE	PEANUT BUTTER	12.00	29.00	25.00

MARCELS

☐ 186	COLPIX	BLUE MOON/GOODBYE TO LOVE	3.50	6.00	4.35
☐ 196		SUMMERTIME/ TEETER TOTTER LOVE	4.00	7.00	4.65
☐ 606		YOU ARE MY SUNSHINE/ FIND ANOTHER FOOL	5.00	9.00	6.00
☐ 612		HEARTACHES/MY LOVE FOR YOU	3.50	6.00	4.35
☐ 617		MERRY TWIST-MAS/ DON'T CRY FOR ME THIS CHRISTMAS	3.50	6.00	4.35
☐ 624		MY MELANCHOLY BABY/ REALLY NEED YOUR LOVE	3.50	6.00	4.35
☐ 629		TWISTIN' FEVER/ FOOTPRINTS IN THE SAND	3.50	6.00	4.35
☐ 640		HOLD UP/FLOWERPOT	3.50	6.00	4.35
☐ 651		FRIENDLY LOANS/LOVED HER THE WHOLE WEEK THROUGH	3.50	6.00	4.35
☐ 665		ALL RIGHT, OKAY, YOU WIN/ LOLLIPOP BABY	3.50	6.00	4.35
☐ 683		THAT OLD BLACK MAGIC/DON'T TURN YOUR BACK ON ME	3.50	6.00	4.35
☐ 687		I WANNA BE THE LEADER/ GIVE ME BACK YOUR LOVE	3.50	6.00	4.35
☐ 694		ONE LAST KISS/ TEETER TOTTER LOVE	3.50	6.00	4.35
☐ 694		ONE LAST KISS/ YOU GOT TO BE SINCERE	3.50	6.00	4.35
☐ 47001	QUEEN BEE	IN THE STILL OF THE NIGHT/ HIGH ON A HILL	4.00	7.00	4.65
☐ 112	MONOGRAM	I'LL BE FOREVER LOVING YOU/ A FALLEN TEAR	3.50	6.00	4.35
☐ 113		OVER THE RAINBOW/ SWEET WAS THE WINE	3.50	6.00	4.35
☐ 115		TWO PEOPLE IN THE WORLD/ MOST OF ALL	3.50	6.00	4.35
☐ 324	OWL	PEACE OF MINDY/CRAZY BELLS	3.50	6.00	4.35

			Current Price Range		P/Y AVG
☐ 13711	ST. CLAIR	PEACE OF MIND/			
		THAT LUCKY OLD SUN	3.50	6.00	4.35
☐ HAM-100	KYRA	YOUR RED WAGON/COMES LOVE	3.25	5.50	4.00
		MARCELS—ALBUM			
☐ 416 (M)	COLPIX	BLUE MOON.................	25.00	57.00	35.00

(LITTLE) PEGGY MARCH

☐ 8107	RCA	LITTLE ME/PAGAN LOVE SONG ..	4.00	7.00	4.35
☐ 8139		I WILL FOLLOW HIM/			
		WIND-UP DOLL	3.00	5.00	3.65
☐ 8189		I WISH I WERE A PRINCESS/			
		MY TEENAGE CASTLE	3.00	5.00	3.65
☐ 8221		HELLO HEARTACHE, GOODBYE			
		LOVE/BOY CRAZY	3.00	5.00	3.65
☐ 8267		THE IMPOSSIBLE HAPPENED/			
		WATERFALL	3.00	5.00	3.65
☐ 8302		EVERY LITTLE MOVE YOU MAKE/			
		AFTER YOU	3.00	5.00	3.65
☐ 8357		LEAVE ME ALONE/TAKIN' THE			
		LONG WAY HOME	3.00	5.00	3.65
☐ 8418		OH MY, WHAT A GUY/ONLY YOU			
		COULD DO THAT TO MY HEART	3.00	5.00	3.65
☐ 8460		WATCH WHAT YOU DO WITH MY			
		BABY/CAN'T STOP			
		THINKING ABOUT HIM	3.00	5.00	3.65
☐ 8534		WHY CAN'T HE BE YOU/			
		LOSIN' MY TOUCH	3.00	5.00	3.65
☐ 8605		LET HER GO/YOUR GIRL	3.00	5.00	3.65
☐ 8710		HEAVEN FOR LOVERS/			
		HE COULDN'T CARE LESS	3.00	5.00	3.65
		(LITTLE) PEGGY MARCH—EP			
☐ 4376	RCA	I WISH I WERE A PRINCESS	5.50	11.00	9.00
		(LITTLE) PEGGY MARCH—ALBUMS			
☐ 2732 (M)	RCA	I WILL FOLLOW HIM	7.00	17.00	15.00
☐ 2732 (S)		I WILL FOLLOW HIM	9.00	25.00	22.50

LEE MARENO

☐ 103	NEW ART	GODDESS OF LOVE/HE'S GONE ..	8.25	14.00	12.00

ERNIE MARESCA

☐ 107	SEVILLE	I DON'T KNOW WHY/			
		LONESOME BLUES	3.75	6.00	4.50
☐ 117		SHOUT! SHOUT! (KNOCK			
		YOURSELF OUT)/CRYING LIKE			
		A BABY	3.25	5.50	4.00
☐ 119		DOWN ON THE BEACH/			
		MARY JANE	3.25	5.50	4.00
☐ 122		SOMETHING TO SHOUT ABOUT/			
		HOW MANY TIMES?	3.25	5.50	4.00
☐ 125		THE LOVE EXPRESS/LORELEI ...	3.25	5.50	4.00
☐ 129		THE ROVIN' KIND/			
		PLEASE BE FAIR	3.25	5.50	4.00
☐ 138		IT'S THEIR WORLD/			
		I CAN'T DANCE	3.25	5.50	4.00
☐ 5076	RUST	THE BEETLE DANCE/			
		THE THEME FROM LILLY, LILLY.	3.75	6.00	4.50
☐ 3345	LAURIE	THE GOOD LIFE/			
		A BUM CAN'T CRY	3.00	5.00	3.65
☐ 3371		MY SHADOW AND ME/MY SON ..	3.00	5.00	3.65
☐ 3447		THE NIGHT MY PAPA DIED/			
		WHAT IS A MARINE	3.00	5.00	3.65
☐ 3496		PEOPLE GET JEALOUS/			
		BLIND DATE	3.00	5.00	3.65
☐ 3519		THE SPIRIT OF WOODSTOCK/			
		WEB OF LOVE	3.00	5.00	3.65

			Current Price Range		P/Y AVG
		ERNIE MARESCA-ALBUMS			
☐77001 (M)	**SEVILLE**	SHOUT SHOUT (KNOCK YOURSELF OUT)	10.00	23.00	14.50
☐87001 (S)		SHOUT SHOUT (KNOCK YOUSELF OUT)	15.00	33.00	21.00

TONY MARESCO & THE DYNAMICS

☐569	**HERALD**	FOREVER LOVE/BETTY MY OWN .	20.00	41.00	37.50

THIS GROUP ALSO RECORDED AS "ANTHONY & THE SOPHOMORES"

MAR—KETS

☐501	**UNION**	SURFER'S STOMP/START	3.75	6.00	4.50
☐504		BALBOA BLUE/STOMPEDE	3.75	6.00	4.50
☐507		STOMPIN' ROOM ONLY/ CANADIAN SUNSET	3.75	6.00	4.40
☐55401	**LIBERTY**	SURFER'S STOMP/START	3.00	5.00	3.50
☐55443		BALBOA BLUE/STOMPEDE	3.00	5.00	3.50
☐55506		STOMPIN' ROOM ONLY/ CANADIAN SUNSET	3.00	5.00	3.50
☐5365	**WARNER BROTHERS**	WOODY WAGON/COBRA	3.00	5.00	3.50
☐5391		OUTER LIMITS/BELLA DALENA (original title)	4.50	7.50	6.00
☐5391		OUT OF LIMITS/BELLA DALENA .	2.75	4.50	3.00
☐5423		VANISHING POINT/BOREALIS ...	2.75	4.50	3.00
☐5468		LOOK FOR A STAR/ COME SEE. COME SKA	2.75	4.50	3.00
☐5641		MIAMI BLUES/NAPOLEON'S GOLD	2.75	4.50	3.00
☐5670		READY. STEADY. GO/ LADY IN THE CAGE	2.75	4.50	3.00

MAR—KETS—ALBUMS

☐3226 (M)	**LIBERTY**	SURFER'S STOMP.............	12.00	29.00	25.00
☐1870 (M)	**WORLD PACIFIC**	SUN POWER.................	9.50	17.50	15.00
☐21870 (S)		SUN POWER.................	9.50	17.50	15.00
☐1509 (M)	**WARNER BROTHERS**	TAKE TO WHEELS	7.00	12.00	10.00
☐1509 (S)		TAKE TO WHEELS	8.00	14.00	12.50
☐1537 (M)		OUT OF LIMITS	7.00	12.00	10.00
☐1537 (S)		OUT OF LIMITS	8.00	14.00	12.50

MARKSMEN (VENTURES)

☐6052	**BLUE HORIZON**	NIGHT RUN/SCRATCH	5.00	8.50	7.00

RITCHIE MARSH (SKY SAXON)
SEE: SEEDS

☐2203	**SHEPHERD**	THEY SAY DARLING/ I SWEAR THAT IT'S TRUE	9.00	17.00	15.00
☐412	**ROSCO**	THERE'S ONLY ONE GIRL/ WHAT CHANCE HAVE I	5.00	9.00	7.50
☐125	**ACAMA**	BABY BABY BABY/HALF ANGEL .	5.00	9.00	7.00
☐122	**AVA**	CRYING INSIDE MY HEART/ GOODBYE	5.00	9.00	7.00

MARTHA AND THE VANDELLAS

☐7011	**GORDY**	I'LL HAVE TO LET HIM GO/ MY BABY WON'T COME BACK .	4.50	7.50	6.00
☐7014		COME AND GET THESE MEMORIES/JEALOUS LOVER ..	3.25	5.50	4.00
☐7022		HEAT WAVE/A LOVE LIKE YOURS	3.25	5.50	4.00
☐7025		QUICKSAND/ DARLING, I HUM OUR SONG ...	3.25	5.50	4.00
☐7027		LIVE WIRE/OLD LOVE	3.25	5.50	4.00
☐7031		IN MY LONELY ROOM/ A TEAR FOR THE GIRL	3.25	5.50	4.00

MARVELETTES

By 1961, Berry Gordy's Motown Records had grown from a small wooden office in the Detroit squalor to a respectable entertainment venture. Gordy sought a girl group to add to his roster. He had already auditioned — and rejected — a group called the Primettes. (They would later become the Supremes.)

Gordy heard of a singing group at nearby Inkster High School. As the school was near his office, Gordy walked over one day to sit in at a talent show. The Marvelettes (all 17 years old) convinced Gordy with their interpretation of current rhythm-and-blues hits that they were the group he had been looking for. He spoke with them later and had them come to his office to audition.

The Marvelettes' first disc was "Please Mr. Postman". It hit number one on both the soul and rock charts. It was also later "covered" by such diverse talents as the Beatles and the Carpenters.

The Marvelettes' second single was the mediocre "Twistin' Postman", an attempt to cash in on the Twist craze going on at the time. But the Marvelettes shot back into the Top 20 with agressive, danceable songs like "Playboy" and "Beechwood 4-5789". In all, they scored eight Top 30 winners.

			Current Price Range		P/Y AVG
☐7033		DANCING IN THE STREET/ THERE HE IS	3.25	5.50	4.00
☐7036		WILD ONE/DANCING SLOW	3.25	5.50	4.00
☐7039		NOWHERE TO RUN/MOTORING	3.25	5.50	4.00
☐7045		YOU'VE BEEN IN LOVE TOO LONG/ LOVE	3.00	5.00	3.65
☐7048		MY BABY LOVES ME/NEVER, NEVER LEAVE YOUR BABY'S SIDE	3.00	5.00	3.65
☐7053		WHAT AM I GOING TO DO WITHOUT YOUR LOVE?/ GO AHEAD AND LAUGH	3.00	5.00	3.65
☐7056		I'M READY FOR LOVE/HE DOESN'T LOVE HER ANYMORE	3.00	5.00	3.65
☐7058		JIMMY MACK/ THIRD FINGER, LEFT HAND	3.00	5.00	3.65
☐7062		LOVE BUG, LEAVE MY HEART ALONE/THE WAY OUT	3.00	5.00	3.65
☐7067		HONEY CHILE/ SHOW ME THE WAY	3.00	5.00	3.65
☐7070		I PROMISE TO WAIT, MY LOVE/ FORGET-ME-NOT	3.00	5.00	3.65
☐7075		I CAN'T DANCE TO THAT MUSIC YOU'RE PLAYIN'/I TRIED	3.00	5.00	3.65
☐7080		SWEET DARLIN'/WITHOUT YOU	3.00	5.00	3.65
☐7085		(WE'VE GOT) HONEY LOVE/ I'M IN LOVE	3.00	5.00	3.65
☐7094		TAKING MY LOVE (AND LEAVING ME)/HEARTLESS	3.00	5.00	3.65
☐7098		I SHOULD BE PROUD/ LOVE, GUESS WHO	3.00	5.00	3.65
☐7103		I GOTTA LET YOU GO/ YOU'RE THE LOSER NOW	3.00	5.00	3.65
☐7110		BLESS YOU/HOPE I DON'T GET MY HEART BROKE	3.00	5.00	3.65
☐7113		IN AND OUT OF LOVE/YOUR LOVE MAKES IT ALL WORTHWHILE	3.00	5.00	3.65
☐7118		TEAR IT ON DOWN/ I WANT YOU BACK	3.00	5.00	3.65
		MARTHA AND THE VANDELLAS—ALBUMS			
☐902 (M)	GORDY	COME AND GET THESE MEMORIES	12.00	29.00	25.00
☐907 (M)		HEAT WAVE	10.00	25.00	22.50
☐915 (M)		DANCE PARTY	10.00	25.00	22.50
☐917 (M)		GREATEST HITS	8.00	21.00	18.00
☐920 (M)		WATCH OUT	7.00	17.00	15.00
☐925 (M)		LIVE	7.00	17.00	15.00
		JANIS MARTIN			
☐6491	RCA	DRUG STORE ROCK AND ROLL/ WILL YOU, WILLYUM?	13.00	25.00	14.50
☐6560		OOBY DOOBY/ ONE MORE YEAR TO GO	13.00	25.00	14.50
☐6652		MY BOY ELVIS/LITTLE BIT	13.00	25.00	14.50
☐6983		LOVE AND KISSES/ I'LL NEVER BE FREE	5.00	9.00	7.50
☐7318		BANG BANG/PLEASE BE MY LOVE	5.00	9.00	7.50
		JANIS MARTIN—EP			
☐4093	RCA	JUST SQUEEZE ME	19.00	34.00	30.00
		MARVELETTES			
☐54046	TAMLA	PLEASE MR. POSTMAN/ SO LONG BABY	3.25	5.50	4.00
☐54054		TWISTIN' POSTMAN/ I WANT A GUY	3.25	5.50	4.00

			Current Price Range		P/Y AVG
☐54060		PLAYBOY/ALL THE LOVE I`VE GOT.	3.25	5.50	4.00
☐54065		BEECHWOOD 4-5789/			
		SOMEDAY. SOMEWAY	3.25	5.50	4.00
☐54072		STRANGE I KNOW/TOO STRUNG			
		OUT TO BE STRUNG ALONG	3.00	5.00	3.65
☐54077		LOCKING UP MY HEART/FOREVER.	3.00	5.00	3.65
☐54082		MY DADDY KNOWS BEST/TIE A			
		STRING AROUND MY FINGER	3.00	5.00	3.65
☐54088		AS LONG AS I KNOW HE`S MINE/			
		LITTLE GIRL BLUE	3.00	5.00	3.65
☐54091		HE`S A GOOD GUY/			
		GODDESS OF LOVE	3.00	5.00	3.65
☐54097		YOU`RE MY REMEDY/A LITTLE			
		BIT OF SYMPATHY. A LITTLE			
		BIT OF LOVE	3.00	5.00	3.65
☐54105		TOO MANY FISH IN THE SEA/			
		A NEED FOR TEARS	3.00	5.00	3.65
☐54116		I`LL KEEP HOLDING ON/			
		NO TIME FOR TEARS	3.00	5.00	3.65
☐54120		DANGER HEARTBREAK AHEAD/			
		YOUR CHEATING WAYS	3.00	5.00	3.65
☐54126		DON`T MESS WITH BILL/			
		ANYTHING YOU WANNA DO	3.00	5.00	3.65
☐54131		YOU`RE THE ONE/PAPER BOY	3.00	5.00	3.65
☐54143		THE HUNTER GETS CAPTURED BY			
		THE GAME/I THINK I CAN			
		CHANGE YOU	3.00	5.00	3.65
☐54150		WHEN YOU`RE YOUNG AND IN			
		LOVE/THE DAY YOU TAKE ONE.			
		YOU HAVE TO TAKE THE OTHER	3.00	5.00	3.65
☐54158		MY BABY MUST BE A MAGICIAN/			
		I NEED SOMEONE	3.00	5.00	3.65
☐54166		HERE I AM BABY/			
		KEEP OFF. NO TRESPASSING	3.00	5.00	3.65
☐54171		DESTINATION: ANYWHERE/			
		WHAT`S EASY FOR TWO			
		IS SO HARD FOR ONE	3.00	5.00	3.65
☐54177		I`M GONNA HOLD ON LONG AS I			
		CAN/DON`T MAKE HURTING			
		ME A HABIT	3.00	5.00	3.65
☐54186		THAT`S HOW HEARTACHES ARE			
		MADE/RAINY MORNING	3.00	5.00	3.65
☐54198		MARIONETTE/AFTER ALL	3.00	5.00	3.65
☐54213		A BREATH TAKING GUY/YOU`RE			
		THE ONE FOR ME. BABY	3.00	5.00	3.65
		MARVELETTES—ALBUMS			
☐228 (M)	*TAMLA*	PLEASE MR. POSTMAN	13.50	35.00	30.00
☐228 (M)		THE MARVELETTES SING	12.00	29.00	25.00
☐231 (M)		PLAYBOY	9.00	25.00	22.50
☐237 (M)		MARVELOUS	9.00	25.00	22.50
☐243 (M)		ON STAGE	8.00	21.00	18.00
☐253 (M)		GREATEST HITS	8.00	21.00	18.00
☐274 (M)		THE MARVELETTES	7.00	17.00	15.00

MARVELS

☐1916	*WINN*	FOR SENTIMENTAL REASONS/			
		COME BACK	8.00	14.00	12.50

MASCOTS

☐107	*MERMAID*	BLUEBIRDS OVER THE MOUNTAIN/			
		TIMBERLANDS	12.00	19.00	17.50
☐206	*BLAST*	ONCE UPON A LOVE/			
		HEY LITTLE ANGEL	7.00	12.00	10.00

			Current Price Range		P/Y AVG

BONNIE JO MASON (CHER)

SEE: CHERILYN, SONNY AND CHER, CAESAR AND CLEO

| ☐ 1001 | **ANNETTE** | RINGO. I LOVE YOU/ BEATLE BLUES | 7.00 | 14.00 | 12.50 |

SAMMY MASTERS

☐ 1695	**4 STAR**	PINK CADILLAC/ SOME LIKE IT HOT	9.00	18.00	15.00
☐ 108	**LODE**	ROCKIN' RED WING/ LONELY WEEKEND	3.25	5.50	4.00
☐ 109		CHARLOTTE (IN THE PINK CORVETTE)/GOLDEN SLIPPERS	3.75	6.00	4.50
☐ 5102	**WARNER BROTHERS**	ROCKIN' RED WING/ LONELY WEEKEND	2.75	4.50	3.00
☐ 16123	**DOT**	CHARLOTTE (IN THE PINK CORVETTE)/GOLDEN SLIPPERS	2.75	4.50	3.00

MATADORS

FEATURED: JAN AND DEAN

☐ 698	**COLPIX**	ACE OF HEARTS/PERFIDIA	6.00	10.00	7.00
☐ 718		I'VE GOTTA DRIVE/LA CORRIDA	6.00	10.00	7.00
☐ 741		C'MON. LET YOURSELF GO (PT. 1)/(PT. 2)	6.00	10.00	7.00

JOHNNY MATHIS

☐ 40784	**COLUMBIA**	WONDERFUL WONDERFUL/ WHEN SUNNY GETS BLUE	2.75	4.50	3.00
☐ 40851		IT'S NOT FOR ME TO SAY/ WARM AND TENDER	2.75	4.50	3.00
☐ 40993		CHANCES ARE/ THE TWELFTH OF NEVER	2.75	4.50	3.00
☐ 41060		WILD IS THE WIND/ NO LOVE (BUT YOUR LOVE)	2.75	4.50	3.00
☐ 41082		COME TO ME/ WHEN I AM WITH YOU	2.75	4.50	3.00
☐ 41152		ALL THE TIME/ TEACHER TEACHER	2.75	4.50	3.00
☐ 41193		A CERTAIN SMILE/ LET IT RAIN	2.75	4.50	3.00
☐ 41253		CALL ME/ STAIRWAY TO THE SEA	2.75	4.50	3.00
☐ 41304		YOU ARE BEAUTIFUL/ LET'S LOVE	2.75	4.50	3.00
☐ 41355		SOMEONE/VERY MUCH IN LOVE	2.75	4.50	3.00
☐ 41410		SMALL WORLD/ YOU ARE EVERYTHING TO ME	2.75	4.50	3.00
☐ 41483		MISTY/ THE STORY OF OUR LOVE	2.75	4.50	3.00
☐ 41491		THE BEST OF EVERYTHING/ CHERIE	2.75	4.50	3.00
☐ 41583		STARBRIGHT/ALL IS WELL	2.75	4.50	3.00
☐ 41684		MARIA/HEY LOVE	2.50	4.00	3.00
☐ 41764		MY LOVE FOR YOU/ OH THAT FEELING	2.50	4.00	3.00
☐ 41866		HOW TO HANDLE A WOMAN/ WHILE YOU'RE YOUNG	2.50	4.00	3.00
☐ 41980		YOU SET MY HEART TO MUSIC/ JENNY	2.50	4.00	2.75
☐ 42005		SHOULD I WAIT/ OH HOW I TRY	2.50	4.00	2.75
☐ 42048		LAURIE. MY LOVE/ SHOULD I WAIT	2.25	3.75	2.75
☐ 42156		WASN'T THE SUMMER SHORT/ THERE YOU ARE	2.25	3.75	2.75

JOHNNY MATHIS

Johnny Mathis was born on September 30, 1935 in San Francisco, California. He first entered show business in 1956 and has been a favorite of young and old alike ever since. A few years ago, Johnny had his first top chart hit in twenty one years with Deniece Williams. Their rendition of "Too Much, Too Little, Too Late" earned then a Gold Record for their exceptional styling.

Johnny's "You Light Up My Life" marked his tenth Gold Album and his album "Johnny's Greatest Hits" remains the only Pop album to be on the charts for 490 consecutive weeks. In addition, his single "Simple" is high on the charts for 1984 proving his incredible popularity.

He prefers these days to spend time in New York City and finds time in his busy schedule to enjoy a little tennis, swimming, golfing or just reading at home. When pressed for a definitive answer, Johnny will admit that of all of his recordings "Misty" is his favorite. His fans find the decision even harder.

		Current Price Range		P/Y AVG
☐ 42238	CHRISTMAS EVE/			
	MY KIND OF CHRISTMAS	2.25	3.75	2.75
☐ 42261	SWEET THURSDAY/ONE LOOK . . .	2.25	3.75	2.75
☐ 42420	MARIANNA/UNACCUSTOMED AS I			
	AM	2.25	3.75	2.75
☐ 42509	I'LL NEVER BE LONELY AGAIN			
	THAT'S THE WAY IT IS	2.25	3.75	2.75
☐ 42582	GINA/I LOVE HER THAT'S WHY . .	2.25	3.75	2.75
☐ 42666	WHAT WILL MARY SAY/			
	QUIET GIRL	2.25	3.75	2.75
☐ 42799	EVERY STEP OF THE WAY/			
	NO MAN CAN STAND ALONE . .	2.25	3.75	2.75
☐ 42836	SOONER OR LATER/			
	IN WISCONSIN	2.25	3.75	2.75
☐ 42916	I'LL SEARCH MY HEART/			
	ALL THE SAD YOUNG MEN	2.25	3.75	2.75
☐ 44266	DON'T TALK TO ME/			
	MISTY ROSES	2.25	3.75	2.75
☐ 44257	AMONG THE FIRST TO KNOW/			
	LONG WINTER NIGHTS	2.25	3.75	2.50
☐ 44517	DON'T GO BREAKING MY HEART/			
	VENUS	2.25	3.75	2.50
☐ 44637	YOU MAKE ME THINK ABOUT			
	YOU/NIGHT DREAMS	2.25	3.75	2.50
☐ 44728	THE END OF THE WORLD/			
	59TH STREET BRIDGE SONG . . .	2.25	3.75	2.50
☐ 44837	I'LL NEVER FALL IN LOVE AGAIN			
	WHOEVER YOU ARE. I LOVE			
	YOU	2.25	3.75	2.50
☐ 44915	A TIME FOR US/			
	THE WORLD I THREW AWAY . . .	2.25	3.75	2.50
☐ 45022	MIDNIGHT COWBOY/WE	2.25	3.75	2.50
☐ 45035	GIVE ME YOUR LOVE FOR			
	CHRISTMAS/CALYPSO NOEL . .	2.25	3.75	2.50
☐ 45104	FOR ALL WE KNOW/			
	ODDS AND ENDS	2.25	3.75	2.50
☐ 45183	LAST TIME I SAW HER/			
	WHEREFOR AND WHY	2.25	3.75	2.50
☐ 45223	PIECES OF DREAMS/			
	DARLING LILY	2.25	3.75	2.50
☐ 45263	UNTIL IT'S TIME FOR YOU TO			
	GO/EVIL WAYS	2.25	3.75	2.50
☐ 45281	CHRISTMAS IS/			
	SIGN OF THE DOVE	2.25	3.75	2.50
☐ 45323	TEN TIMES FOREVER MORE	2.25	3.75	2.50
☐ 45371	EVIE/LOVE STORY	2.25	3.75	2.50
☐ 45415	FOR ALL WE KNOW/			
	LONG AGO AND FAR AWAY	2.25	3.75	2.50
☐ 45470	IF WE ONLY HAVE LOVE/			
	HOW CAN YOU MEND A BROKEN			
	HEART	2.25	3.75	2.50
☐ 45513	CHRISTMAS IS/			
	SIGN OF THE DOVE	2.25	3.75	2.50
☐ 45559	SOMETIMES/			
	MAKE IT EASY ON YOURSELF .	2.25	3.75	2.50
☐ 45635	SOUL AND INSPIRATION-JUST			
	ONCE IN MY LIFE/I	2.25	3.75	2.50
☐ 45729	TAKE GOOD CARE OF HER/			
	WALKING TALL	2.25	3.75	2.50
☐ 45777	HAPPY/SHOW AND TELL	2.25	3.75	2.50
☐ 45835	I'M COMING HOME/STOP LOOK			
	AND LISTEN TO YOUR HEART . .	2.25	3.75	2.50

			Current Price Range		P/Y AVG
☐45908		I JUST WANTED TO BE ME/ LIFE IS A SONG WORTH SINGING	2.25	3.75	2.50
☐45975		I'M STONE IN LOVE WITH YOU/SWEET CHILD	2.25	3.75	2.50
☐46048		HEART OF A WOMAN/ SAIL ON WHITE MOON	2.25	3.75	2.50
☐410090		I'M STONE IN LOVE WITH YOU/FOOLISH	2.25	3.75	2.50
☐10112		YOU'RE AS RIGHT AS RAIN/ THE GREATEST GIFT	2.25	3.25	2.50
☐10250		STARDUST/WHAT I DID FOR LOVE .	2.25	3.25	2.50
☐10291		MIDNIGHT BLUE/ONE DAY IN YOUR LIFE	2.25	3.25	2.50
☐10350		YELLOW ROSES ON HER GOWN/ EVERYTIME YOU TOUCH ME ..	2.25	3.25	2.50
☐10404		DO ME WRONG BUT DO ME/ SEND IN THE CLOWNS	2.25	3.25	2.50
☐10447		TURN THE LIGHTS DOWN/ WHEN A CHILD IS BORN	2.25	3.25	2.50
☐10496		LOVING YOU. LOSING YOU/ WORLD OF LAUGHTER	2.25	3.25	2.50
☐10574		ARIANNE/99 MILES FROM L.A. ...	2.25	3.25	2.50
☐10611		HOLD ME THRILL ME KISS ME...	2.25	3.25	2.50
☐10640		EVERY TIME YOU TOUCH ME/ WHEN A CHILD IS BORN	1.75	3.00	2.00
☐10693		TOO MUCH TOO LITTLE TOO LATE/I WROTE A SYMPHONY ON MY GUIATAR	1.75	3.00	2.00
☐10772		YOU'RE ALL I NEED TO GET BY/YOU'RE A SPECIAL PART OF ME	1.75	3.00	2.00
☐10826		I JUST CAN'T GET OVER YOU/THAT'S WHAT FRIENDS ARE FOR	1.75	3.00	2.00
☐10902		LAST TIME I FELT LIKE THIS/ AS TIME GOES BY	1.75	3.00	2.00
☐11001		BEGIN THE BEGUINE/ GONE. GONE. GONE	1.75	3.00	2.00
☐11091		NO ONE BUT THE ONE YOU LOVE .	1.75	3.00	2.00
☐11158		CHRISTMAS IN THE CITY OF ANGELS/THE VERY FIRST CHRISTMAS DAY	1.75	3.00	2.00
☐11313		THE LIGHTS OF RIO/ DIFFERENT KINDA DIFFERENT .	1.75	3.00	2.00
☐DJ-77	**MERCURY**	THE SHADOW OF YOUR SMILE/ THE SWEETHEART TREE	3.25	4.50	3.50
☐71202		MOONLIGHT MAGIC/ YOU DON'T CARE	3.25	4.50	3.50
☐71273		ONE LIFE/HARBOR OF LIFE	3.25	4.50	3.50
☐72184		YOUR TEENAGE DREAMS/ COME BACK	3.25	4.50	3.50
☐72217		HAVE REINDEER WILL TRAVEL/ LITTLE DRUMMER BOY	3.25	4.50	3.50
☐72229		BYE BYE BARBARA/ A GREAT NIGHT FOR CRYING ..	3.25	4.50	3.50
☐72263		THE FALL OF LOVE/NO MORE ...	3.25	4.50	3.50
☐72287		TASTE OF TEARS/ WHITE ROSES FROM A BLUE VALENTINE	3.25	4.50	3.50
☐72339		LISTEN LONELY GIRL/ ALL I WANTED	3.25	4.50	3.50
☐72432		DIANACITA/TAKE THE TIME	3.25	4.50	3.50
☐72464		SWEETHEART TREE/MIRAGE	3.25	4.50	3.50

			Current Price Range		P/Y AVG
☐72493		ON A CLEAR DAY YOU CAN SEE FOREVER/COME BACK TO ME .	3.25	4.50	3.50
☐72539		MOMENT TO MOMENT/ THE GLASS MOUNTAIN	3.25	4.50	3.50
☐72568		LOVE THEME FROM ''THE SANDPIPER''/SWEETHEART TREE	3.25	4.50	3.50
☐72610		IMPOSSIBLE MAN/SO NICE	3.25	4.50	3.50
☐72653		SATURDAY SUNSHINE/ TWO TICKETS AND A CANDY HEART	3.00	4.00	3.50

DINO MATTHEWS

☐16365	**DOT**	THAT GIRL THAT I LOVE/LENORE	11.00	19.00	17.50

NATHANIEL MAYER

☐542	**FORTUNE**	MY LAST DANCE WITH YOU/ MY LITTLE DARLING	3.25	5.50	4.00
☐545		VILLAGE OF LOVE/I WANT A WOMAN (also on Fortune 449) ..	3.00	5.00	3.50
☐550		WELL. I'VE GOT NEWS/ MR. SANTA CLAUS	3.00	5.00	3.50
☐554		I HAD A DREAM/ I'M NOT GONNA CRY	3.00	5.00	3.50
☐557		GOING BACK TO THE VILLAGE OF LOVE/MY LAST DANCE WITH YOU	3.00	5.00	3.50

NATHANIEL MAYER—ALBUM

☐8014 (M)	**FORTUNE**	GOING BACK TO THE VILLAGE OF LOVE	8.00	19.50	18.00

MC-5

☐1000	**AMG**	I CAN ONLY GIVE YOU EVERYTHING/ I JUST DON'T KNOW	11.00	19.00	17.50
☐1001		I CAN ONLY GIVE YOU EVERYTHING/ ONE OF THE GUYS	11.00	19.00	17.50
☐333	**A-SQUARE**	LOOKING AT YOU/BORDERLINE ..	8.00	14.00	12.50
☐45648	**ELEKTRA**	KICK OUT THE JAMS/ MOTOR CITY IS BURNING	3.25	5.50	4.00
☐2724		AMERICAN RUSH/ SHAKIN' STREET	3.00	5.00	3.50

MC-5—ALBUMS

☐74072 (S)	**ELEKTRA**	KICKIN' OUT THE JAMS	8.00	21.00	18.00
☐8247 (S)	**ATLANTIC**	BACK IN THE U.S.A.	5.50	14.00	12.00
☐8285 (S)		HIGH TIME	5.50	14.00	12.00

PAUL McCARTNEY
FEATURED: WINGS
SEE: COUNTRYHAMS, BEATLES

☐1829	**APPLE**	ANOTHER DAY/OH WOMAN. OH WHY (Paul McCartney)	3.00	5.00	3.65
☐1837		UNCLE ALBERT-ADMIRAL HALSEY/ TOO MANY PEOPLE (Paul and Linda McCartney)	3.00	5.00	3.65
☐1847		GIVE IRELAND BACK TO THE IRISH (PT. 2)	3.00	5.00	3.65
☐1851		MARY HAD A LITTLE LAMB/ LITTLE WOMAN LOVE	3.00	5.00	3.65
☐1857		HI HI HI/C MOON	2.75	4.50	3.25
☐1861		MY LOVE/THE MESS	2.75	4.50	3.25
☐1863		LIVE AND LET DIE/I LIE AROUND .	2.75	4.50	3.25

PAUL McCARTNEY

The day James Paul McCartney was born (June 18, 1942) in Liverpool, England, he was put into a "special" post-delivery room. Paul's mother was then head nurse at that hospital. The placement must have been an omen. A very special life was to lay ahead of James Paul.

Paul (he never used the name James) wanted to join a rock-and-roll group, as he was infatuated with American rock-and-roll during the mid-1950s. There was none in his neighborhood, but he heard of one a few blocks away. They were called the Quarrymen. Paul didn't attend Quarry Bank High (their home school) but did pester leader John Lennon enough to win a tryout. Lennon initially thought McCartney too young, but also felt he did resemble Elvis Presley somewhat.

With John Lennon as his writing partner, Paul McCartney helped compose some of the most enduring rock-music songs ever. One of his best-known Beatle songs was "Yesterday", which began as a ditty called "Scrambled Eggs".

McCartney later married American divorcee' Linda Eastman, their nuptials being said on March 12, 1969.

Paul confesses to being a workaholic and to this day records and tours practically without let-up.

Today, James Paul McCartney is the richest rock star in the world.

			Current Price Range		P/Y AVG
☐1869		HELEN WHEELS/			
		COUNTRY DREAMER	2.75	4.50	3.25
☐1871		JET/MAMUNIA	3.50	5.50	4.00
☐1871		JET/LET ME ROLL IT	2.75	4.50	3.25
☐1873		BAND ON THE RUN/NINETEEN			
		HUNDRED AND EIGHTY-FIVE ..	2.75	4.50	3.25
☐1875		JUNIOR'S FARM/SALLY G.	2.75	4.50	3.25
		CAPITOL SINGLES ARE WORTH UP TO $2.50 MINT			
		PAUL McCARTNEY AND WINGS—ALBUMS			
☐3363 (S)	*APPLE*	McCARTNEY	11.00	17.00	12.50
☐3375 (S)		RAM	11.00	17.00	12.50
☐3386 (S)		WILD LIFE	11.00	17.00	12.50
☐3409 (S)		RED ROSE SPEEDWAY	11.00	17.00	12.50
☐3415 (S)		BAND ON THE RUN	11.00	17.00	12.50

McCOYS
FEATURED: RICK DERRINGER

			Current Price Range		P/Y AVG
☐506	*BANG*	HANG ON SLOOPY/			
		I CAN'T EXPLAIN IT	3.00	5.00	3.65
☐511		FEVER/SORROW	3.00	5.00	3.65
☐516		UP AND DOWN/			
		IF I TELL YOU A LIE	3.00	5.00	3.65
☐522		COME ON LET'S GO/			
		LITTLE PEOPLE	3.00	5.00	3.65
☐527		(YOU MAKE ME FEEL) SO GOOD/			
		RUNAWAY	3.00	5.00	3.65
☐532		DON'T WORRY, MOTHER, YOUR			
		SON'S HEART IS PURE/KO-KO .	3.00	5.00	3.65
☐538		I GOT TO GO BACK/DYNAMITE ...	3.00	5.00	3.65
☐543		BEAT THE CLOCK/			
		LIKE YOU DO TO ME	3.00	5.00	3.65
☐549		SAY THOSE MAGIC WORDS/			
		I WONDER IF SHE			
		REMEMBERS ME	3.00	5.00	3.65
		McCOYS—ALBUMS			
☐212 (M)	*BANG*	HANG ON SLOOPY	8.00	21.00	18.00
☐213 (M)		YOU MAKE ME FEEL SO GOOD ...	7.00	17.00	15.00

GENE McDANIELS

			Current Price Range		P/Y AVG
☐55231	*LIBERTY*	IN TIMES LIKE THESE/			
		ONCE BEFORE	3.25	5.50	4.00
☐55265		FACTS OF LIFE/THE GREEN DOOR	3.25	5.50	4.00
☐55308		A HUNDRED POUNDS OF CLAY/			
		TAKE A CHANCE ON LOVE	3.00	5.00	3.65
☐55344		A TEAR/SHE'S COME BACK	3.00	5.00	3.65
☐55371		TOWER OF STRENGTH/			
		THE SECRET	3.00	5.00	3.65
☐55405		CHIP CHIP/ANOTHER TEAR FALLS.	3.00	5.00	3.65
☐55444		FUNNY/CHAPEL OF TEARS	3.00	5.00	3.65
☐55480		POINT OF NO RETURN/			
		WARMER THAN A WHISPER ...	3.00	5.00	3.65
☐55510		SPANISH LACE/			
		SOMEBODY'S WAITING	3.00	5.00	3.65
☐55541		CRY BABY CRY/THE PUZZLE	3.00	5.00	3.65
☐55597		IT'S A LONELY TOWN/			
		FALSE FRIENDS	3.00	5.00	3.65
		GENE McDANIELS—EP			
☐1014	*LIBERTY*	GENE McDANIELS	6.00	10.50	7.50
		GENE McDANIELS—ALBUMS			
☐3146 (M)	*LIBERTY*	IN TIMES LIKE THESE	8.00	21.00	18.00
☐7146 (S)		IN TIMES LIKE THESE	12.00	29.00	25.00
☐3175 (M)		SOMETIMES I'M HAPPY			
		(SOMETIMES I'M BLUE)	8.00	21.00	18.00

CLYDE McPHATTER

Durham, NC, was the birthplace of Clyde McPhatter in 1931. At a young age, he became a choir boy in his Baptist Church in Durham. Clyde and his family moved to New York City in 1943 and Clyde joined a church group there. When he was 19, he met Billy Ward. McPhatter joined Ward's Dominoes rhythm-and-blues group shortly after that. In 1951, the Dominoes' "Sixty Minute Man" became the first rhythm-and-blues group song to reach a mass audience.

In September of 1953, Clyde left to form his own group. He drew some singers from a gospel group and later helped form the Drifters. They signed with Atlantic Records in 1953 and cut their first hit of "Money Honey".

McPhatter was drafted into the Army in 1954. He soon began recording on Atlantic alone during his military leaves. His first major hit as a solo artist came in 1956 with the hauntingly beautiful "Treasure of Love". He scored big again in 1958 with "A Lover's Question". His second (and last) Top 10 hit came four years later with "Lover Please", written by Billy Swan ("I Can Help").

Clyde McPhatter died suddenly of a heart attack in New Jersey on June 13, 1972. He was 41 years old.

			Current Price Range		P/Y AVG
☐7175	(S)	SOMETIMES I'M HAPPY (SOMETIMES I'M BLUE)	9.00	25.00	22.50
☐3191	(M)	100 LBS. OF CLAY	7.00	17.00	15.00
☐7191	(S)	100 LBS. OF CLAY	8.00	21.00	18.00
☐3204	(M)	GENE McDANIELS SINGS MOVIE MEMORIES	7.00	17.00	15.00
☐7204	(S)	GENE McDANIELS SINGS MOVIE MEMORIES	8.00	21.00	18.00
☐3258	(M)	HIT AFTER HIT	7.00	17.00	15.00
☐7258	(S)	HIT AFTER HIT	8.00	21.00	18.00
☐3275	(M)	SPANISH LACE	7.00	17.00	15.00
☐7275	(S)	SPANISH LACE	8.00	21.00	18.00
☐3311	(M)	THE WONDERFUL WORLD OF GENE McDANIELS	6.00	15.00	13.50
☐7311	(S)	THE WONDERFUL WORLD OF GENE McDANIELS	7.00	17.00	15.00

DON McLEAN

☐50856	**UNITED ARTISTS**	AMERICAN PIE (PT. 1)/(PT. 2)	2.75	5.00	3.50
☐50887		CASTLES IN THE AIR/VINCENT	2.75	5.00	3.50
☐51100		BRONCO BILL'S LAMENT/ DREIDEL	2.75	5.00	3.50
☐541		SITTING ON TOP OF THE WORLD/ MULE SKINNER BLUES	2.75	5.00	3.50
☐579		LA LA LOVE YOU/ HOMELESS BROTHER	2.75	5.00	3.50
☐614		BIRTHDAY SONG/ WONDERFUL BABY	2.75	5.00	3.50
☐0284	**ARISTA**	THE STATUE/PRIME TIME	2.75	5.00	3.50

CLYDE McPHATTER
SEE: DRIFTERS

☐1070	**ATLANTIC**	EVERYONE'S LAUGHING/ HOT ZIGGITY	5.50	11.00	9.00
☐1077		I GOTTA HAVE YOU/LOVE HAS JOINED US TOGETHER	6.00	11.00	8.00
☐1081		SEVEN DAYS/ I'M NOT WORTHY OF YOU	5.00	10.50	7.50

FIRST-PRESSES OF THE ABOVE WERE ON A YELLOW-AND-BLACK LABEL

☐1092		TREASURE OF LOVE/ WHEN YOU'RE SINCERE	4.00	7.00	4.85
☐1106		THIRTY DAYS/ I'M LONELY TONIGHT	4.00	7.00	4.85
☐1117		WITHOUT LOVE (THERE IS NOTHING)/I MAKE BELIEVE	4.00	7.00	4.85
☐1133		JUST TO HOLD MY HAND/ NO MATTER WHAT	3.50	6.00	4.35
☐1149		LONG LONELY NIGHTS/ HEARTACHES	3.50	6.00	4.35
☐1158		ROCK AND CRY/YOU'LL BE THERE	3.25	5.50	4.00
☐1170		NO LOVE LIKE HER LOVE/ THAT'S ENOUGH FOR ME	3.25	5.50	4.00
☐1185		COME WHAT MAY/LET ME KNOW	3.25	5.50	4.00
☐1199		A LOVER'S QUESTION/ I CAN'T STAND UP ALONE	3.00	5.00	3.65
☐2018		LOVEY DOVEY/ MY ISLAND OF DREAMS	3.00	5.00	3.65
☐2028		SINCE YOU'VE BEEN GONE/ TRY, TRY BABY	3.00	5.00	3.65
☐2038		YOU WENT BACK ON YOUR WORD/ THERE YOU GO	3.00	5.00	3.65
☐2049		JUST GIVE ME A RING/ DON'T DOG ME	3.00	5.00	3.65

			Current Price Range		P/Y AVG
☐ 2060		LET THE BOOGIE WOOGIE ROLL/			
		DEEP SEA BALL	3.00	5.00	3.65
☐ 2082		IF I DIDN'T LOVE YOU LIKE I DO/			
		GO! YES, GO!	3.00	5.00	3.65
☐ 12780	**MGM**	I TOLD MYSELF A LIE/			
		THE MASQUERADE IS OVER	3.00	5.00	3.65
☐ 12816		TWICE AS NICE/WHERE DID I			
		MAKE MY MISTAKE?	3.00	5.00	3.65
☐ 12843		LET'S TRY AGAIN/BLESS YOU	3.00	5.00	3.65
☐ 12877		THINK ME A KISS/WHEN THE			
		RIGHT TIME COMES ALONG	3.00	5.00	3.65
☐ 12949		THIS IS NOT GOODBYE/			
		ONE RIGHT AFTER ANOTHER	3.00	5.00	3.65
☐ 12988		THE GLORY OF LOVE/			
		TAKE A STEP	3.00	5.00	3.65
☐ 71660	**MERCURY**	TA TA/I AIN'T GIVIN' UP NOTHIN'	3.00	5.00	3.65
☐ 71692		I JUST WANT TO LOVE YOU/			
		YOU'RE FOR ME	3.00	5.00	3.65
☐ 71740		ONE MORE CHANCE/BEFORE I			
		FALL IN LOVE AGAIN	3.00	5.00	3.65
☐ 71783		TOMORROW IS A-COMIN'/			
		I'LL LOVE YOU TILL THE			
		COWS COME HOME	3.00	5.00	3.65
☐ 71809		A WHOLE HEAP OF LOVE/			
		YOU'RE MOVIN' ME	3.00	5.00	3.65
☐ 71841		I NEVER KNEW/HAPPINESS	3.00	5.00	3.65
☐ 71868		YOUR SECOND CHOICE/			
		SAME TIME, SAME PLACE	3.00	5.00	3.65
☐ 71941		LOVER PLEASE/LET'S FORGET			
		ABOUT THE PAST	3.00	5.00	3.65
☐ 71987		LITTLE BITTY PRETTY ONE/			
		NEXT TO ME	3.00	5.00	3.65
☐ 72025		I DO BELIEVE/MAYBE	3.00	5.00	3.65
☐ 72051		THE BEST MAN CRIED/STOP	3.00	5.00	3.65
☐ 72166		SO CLOSE TO BEING IN LOVE/			
		FROM ONE TO ONE	3.00	5.00	3.65
☐ 72220		DEEP IN THE HEART OF HARLEM/			
		HAPPY GOOD TIMES	3.00	5.00	3.65
☐ 72253		IN MY TENAMENT/SECOND			
		WINDOW, SECOND FLOOR	3.00	5.00	3.65
☐ 72317		LUCILLE/BABY, BABY	3.00	5.00	3.65
☐ 72407		I FOUND MY LOVE/			
		CRYING WON'T HELP YOU NOW	3.00	5.00	3.65
		CLYDE McPHATTER—ALBUMS			
☐ 8024 (M)	**ATLANTIC**	LOVE BALLADS	17.00	39.00	35.00
☐ 8031 (M)		CLYDE	14.00	34.00	30.00
☐ 8077 (M)		THE BEST OF CLYDE McPHATTER	14.00	34.00	30.00
☐ 3775 (M)	**MGM**	LET'S START OVER AGAIN	8.00	21.00	18.00
☐ 3866 (M)		GREATEST HITS	8.00	21.00	18.00
☐ 3866 (S)		GREATEST HITS	9.00	25.00	22.50
☐ 20597 (M)	**MERCURY**	TA TA	7.00	17.00	15.00
☐ 60597 (S)		TA TA	8.00	21.00	18.00
☐ 20665 (M)		GOLDEN BLUES HITS	7.00	17.00	15.00
☐ 60665 (S)		GOLDEN BLUES HITS	8.00	21.00	18.00
☐ 20711 (M)		LOVER PLEASE	7.00	17.00	15.00
☐ 60711 (S)		LOVER PLEASE	8.00	21.00	18.00
☐ 20750 (M)		RHYTHM AND SOUL	7.00	17.00	15.00
☐ 60750 (S)		RHYTHM AND SOUL	8.00	21.00	18.00
☐ 20783 (M)		GREATEST HITS	7.00	17.00	15.00
☐ 70783 (S)		GREATEST HITS	8.00	21.00	18.00
☐ 20902 (M)		SONGS OF THE BIG CITY	6.00	15.00	13.50
☐ 60902 (S)		SONGS OF THE BIG CITY	7.00	17.00	15.00
☐ 20915 (M)		LIVE AT THE APOLLO	6.00	15.00	13.50
☐ 60915 (S)		LIVE AT THE APOLLO	7.00	17.00	15.00

			Current Price Range		P/Y AVG

LARRY MEADOWS

☐969	STRATOLITE	WE'RE THROUGH/PHYLLIS	8.50	17.50	15.00

MELANIE

☐167	BUDDAH	CANDLES IN THE RAIN/			
		LAY DOWN	2.25	4.50	3.00
☐186		STOP!/PEACE WILL COME	2.25	4.50	3.00
☐202		MERRY CHRISTMAS/			
		RUBY TUESDAY	2.25	4.50	3.00
☐224		WE DON'T KNOW WHERE WE'RE			
		GOING/THE GOOD BOOK	2.25	4.50	3.00
☐268		WHAT HAVE THEY DONE TO MY			
		SONG MA/NICKEL SONG	2.25	4.50	3.00
☐304		JOHNNY BOY/I'M BACK IN TOWN	2.25	4.50	3.00
☐4201	NEIGHBORHOOD	BRAND NEW KEY/SOME SAY	2.25	4.00	2.50
☐4-44524	COLUMBIA	GARDEN CITY/			
		WHY DIDN'T MY MOTHER TELL			
		ME	2.25	4.00	2.50

LATER SINGLES ARE WORTH UP TO $2.50 MINT

MELLO—KINGS

☐502	HERALD	TONITE-TONITE/DO BABY DO			
		(Mello-Tones)	22.00	40.00	36.00
☐502		TONITE-TONITE/DO BABY DO	6.00	10.00	7.00
☐507		CHAPEL ON THE HILL/			
		SASSAFRASS	5.00	9.00	6.00
☐511		BABY TELL ME/ONLY GIRL	5.00	9.00	6.00
☐518		VALERIE/SHE'S REAL COOL	5.00	9.00	6.00
☐536		RUNNING TO YOU/CHIP CHIP . . .	5.00	9.00	6.00
☐548		OUR LOVE IS BEAUTIFUL/			
		DEAR MR. JOCK	5.00	9.00	6.00
☐554		KID STUFF/I PROMISE	5.00	9.00	6.00
☐561		TILL THERE WERE NONE/PENNY .	5.00	9.00	6.00
☐567		LOVE AT FIRST SIGHT/			
		SHE'S REAL COOL	3.75	6.00	4.50

MELLO—KINGS—EP

| ☐451 | HERALD | THE FABULOUS MELLO KINGS . . . | 14.00 | 24.00 | 20.00 |

MELLO—KINGS—ALBUM

| ☐1013 (M) | HERALD | TONIGHT, TONIGHT . . . . | 34.00 | 79.00 | 75.00 |

MELLO—TONES

☐1001	FASCINATION	ROSIE LEE/I'LL NEVER			
		FALL IN LOVE AGAIN	12.00	21.00	18.00
☐1037	GEE	ROSIE LEE/I'LL NEVER			
		FALL IN LOVE AGAIN	4.50	7.50	6.00
☐1040		CA-SANDRA/RATTLESNAKE ROLL	4.50	7.50	6.00

THE MELLOWS

☐3008	CELESTE	AIN'T SHE GOT NERVE/			
		YOU'RE GONE	45.00	110.00	70.00
☐3009		WHEN THE LIGHTS ON ON			
		AGAIN/I'M GONNA PICK			
		YOUR TEETH WITH AN ICE PICK	45.00	110.00	70.00
☐3012		LUCKY GUY/MY DARLING	40.00	100.00	90.00
☐3014		I M YOURS/SWEET			
		LORRAINE	30.00	90.00	60.00

MEMORIES

| ☐101 | WAY-LIN | I PROMISE/LOVE BELLS . . . . | 17.00 | 36.00 | 32.00 |

MERSEYBEATS

| ☐1882 | FONTANA | MISTER MOONLIGHT/ | | | |
| | | I THINK OF YOU . . . . | 3.50 | 6.00 | 4.00 |

			Current Price Range		P/Y AVG
☐1905		DON'T TURN AROUND/			
		REALLY MYSTIFIED	3.50	6.00	4.00
☐1950		SEE ME BACK/LAST NIGHT	3.50	6.00	4.00
		MERSEYBEATS—ALBUM			
☐834 (M)	*ARC*				
	INTERNATIONAL	ENGLAND'S BEST SELLERS	7.00	17.00	15.00

JIM MESSINA AND THE JESTERS

☐705	*ULTIMA*	DRAG BIKE BOOGIE/A-RAB	8.25	14.00	12.00
☐101	*FEATURE*	PANTHER POUNCE/TIGER TAIL ..	5.50	11.00	9.00
☐98	*AUDIO FIDELITY*	THE BREEZE AND I/			
		STRANGE MAN	5.00	9.00	7.00
	JIM	**MESSINA AND THE JESTERS—ALBUM**			
☐7037 (S)	*AUDIO*				
	FIDELITY	THE DRAGSTERS	9.00	25.00	22.50

METROS

☐1502	*JUST*	LOOKIN'/ALL OF MY LIFE	8.50	17.00	15.00

MICKEY AND SYLVIA

☐102	*CAT*	FINE LOVE/SPEEDY LIFE	12.00	21.00	18.00
☐316	*RAINBOW*	I'M SO GLAD/			
		SE DEE BOOM RUN DUN	8.25	14.00	12.00
☐318		FOREVER AND A DAY/			
		RISE SALLY RISE	8.25	14.00	12.00
☐330		WHERE IS MY HONEY?/			
		SEEMS JUST LIKE YESTERDAY	8.25	14.00	12.00
☐0164	*GROOVE*	WALKING IN THE RAIN/			
		NO GOOD LOVER	5.50	11.00	9.00
☐0175		LOVE IS STRANGE/			
		I'M GOING HOME	5.00	9.00	7.00
☐0267	*VIK*	THERE OUGHT TO BE A LAW/			
		DEAREST	3.50	6.00	4.35
☐0280		LOVE WILL MAKE YOU FAIL IN			
		SCHOOL/TWO SHADOWS ON			
		YOUR WINDOW	3.50	6.00	4.35
☐0290		LET'S HAVE A PICNIC/			
		LOVE IS A TREASURE	3.50	6.00	4.35
☐0297		WHERE IS MY HONEY?/			
		THERE'LL BE NO BACKING OUT	3.50	6.00	4.35
☐0324		BEWILDERED/			
		ROCK AND STROLL ROOM	3.50	6.00	4.35
☐0334		IT'S YOU I LOVE/			
		TRUE, TRUE LOVE	3.50	6.00	4.35
☐7403	*RCA*	OH YEAH! UH HUH/			
		TO THE VALLEY	3.25	5.50	4.00
☐7774		SWEETER AS THE DAY GOES BY/			
		MOMMY OUT DE LIGHT	3.25	5.50	4.00
☐7811		WHAT SHOULD I DO?/			
		THIS IS MY STORY	3.25	5.50	4.00
☐7877		LOVE LESSON/			
		LOVE IS THE ONLY THING·.....	3.25	5.50	4.00
☐8517		GYPSY/			
		LET'S SHAKE SOME MORE	3.25	5.50	4.00
☐8582		FROM THE BEGINNING OF TIME/			
		FALLING IN LOVE	3.25	5.50	4.00
☐23000	*WILLOW*	BABY, YOU'RE SO FINE/			
		LOVEDROPS	3.25	5.50	4.00
☐23002		DARLING, I MISS YOU/			
		I'M GUILTY	3.25	5.50	4.00
☐23004		SINCE I FELL FOR YOU/			
		HE GAVE ME EVERYTHING	3.25	5.50	4.00
☐23006		LOVE IS STRANGE/			
		WALKING IN THE RAIN	3.00	5.00	3.85

			Current Price Range		P/Y AVG
		MICKEY AND SYLVIA—EPs			
☐ 18	*GROOVE*	LOVE IS STRANGE	9.50	17.00	15.00
☐ 262	*VIK*	MICKEY AND SYLVIA	8.25	14.00	12.00
		MICKEY AND SYLVIA—ALBUMS			
☐ 1102 (M)	*VIK*	NEW SOUNDS	13.50	34.00	30.00
☐ 0327 (M)	*RCA*	MICKEY AND SYLVIA DO IT AGAIN	9.00	25.00	22.50
☐ 863 (M)	*CAMDEN*	LOVE IS STRANGE	8.00	21.00	18.00
☐ 863 (S)		LOVE IS STRANGE	9.00	25.00	22.50

MIDNIGHTERS
FEATURED: HANK BALLARD
SEE: HANK BALLARD AND THE MIDNIGHTERS, ROYALS

			Current Price Range		P/Y AVG
☐ 12169	*FEDERAL*	WORK WITH ME ANNIE/ SINNER'S PRAYER	9.50	17.00	15.00
☐ 12177		GIVE IT UP/THAT WOMAN	8.25	14.00	12.00
☐ 12185		SEXY WAYS/DON'T SAY YOUR LAST GOODBYE	8.25	14.00	12.00
☐ 12195		ANNIE HAD A BABY/ SHE'S THE ONE	8.25	14.00	12.00
☐ 12200		ANNIE'S AUNT FANNIE/ CRAZY LOVING	7.00	13.00	11.00
☐ 12202		STINGY LITTLE THING/ TELL THEM	6.00	11.00	8.00
☐ 12205		MOONRISE/SHE'S THE ONE	6.00	11.00	8.00
☐ 12210		RING-A-LING-A-LING/ ASHAMED OF MYSELF	6.00	11.00	6.00
		FIRST-PRESSES OF THE ABOVE FEATURE A SILVER TOP			
☐ 12220		SWITCHIE WITCHIE TICHIE/ WHY ARE WE APART?	5.50	10.00	7.00
☐ 12224		HENRY'S GOT FLAT FEET/ WHATSOEVER YOU DO	5.50	10.00	7.00
☐ 12227		LOOK-A-HERE/IT'S LOVE BABY . .	5.50	10.00	7.00
☐ 12230		GIVE IT UP/THAT WOMAN	5.50	10.00	7.00
☐ 12240		THAT HOUSE ON THE HILL/ ROCK AND ROLL WEDDING	5.50	10.00	7.00
☐ 12243		DON'T CHANGE YOUR PRETTY WAYS/WE'LL NEVER MEET AGAIN	5.50	10.00	7.00
☐ 12251		SWEET MAMA DO RIGHT/ PARTNERS FOR LIFE	5.50	10.00	7.00
☐ 12260		ROCK GRANNY ROLL/ OPEN UP THE BACK DOOR	5.50	10.00	7.00
☐ 12270		TORE UP OVER YOU/ EARLY ONE MORNING	5.50	10.00	7.00
☐ 12285		COME ON AND GET IT/ I'LL BE HOME SOMEDAY	5.50	10.00	7.00
☐ 12288		LET ME HOLD YOUR HAND/ OOH BAH BABY	5.50	10.00	7.00
☐ 12293		IN THE DOORWAY CRYING/ E BASTI COSI	5.50	10.00	7.00
☐ 12299		IS YOUR LOVE SO REAL?/ OH. SO HAPPY	5.50	10.00	7.00
☐ 12305		LET 'EM ROLL/WHAT MADE YOU CHANGE YOUR MIND?	5.50	10.00	7.00
☐ 12317		DADDY'S LITTLE BABY/ STAY BY MY SIDE	5.50	10.00	7.00
☐ 12339		BABY PLEASE/OW-WOW-OO-WEE	5.50	10.00	7.00
☐ 12345		THE TWIST/TEARDROPS ON YOUR LETTER	12.00	21.00	18.00
		MIDNIGHTERS—EP			
☐ 333	*FEDERAL*	THE MIDNIGHTERS SING THEIR GREATEST HITS	25.00	50.00	35.00
		MIDNIGHTERS—10"			
☐ 90	*FEDERAL*	THE MIDNIGHTERS: THEIR GREATEST HITS	90.00	240.00	225.00

MIDNIGHTERS

The Royals formed in Detroit in 1952. At that time, they were all 16-year-old high school students. They soon secured a contract with Cincinnati's Federal Records. Their initial single was a Johnny Otis song, "Every Beat of My Heart". (In 1961, Gladys Knight and the Pips made it a major hit.) Six singles later, the Royals did the sexually oriented "Get It". By then, 1953 had arrived, and so had scrappy young Henry (Hank) Ballard, just 17 and bursting with talent and confidence.

A few months later, Hank wrote "Work With Me, Annie" (drawn from "Get It"). Most stations refused to play the record because of its erotic overtones. Etta James and the Peaches called it "Roll With Me, Henry" (after Ballard's first name). Then white singer Georgia Gibbs sang it as a well-laundered "Dance With Me, Henry". It became a million-seller early in 1955.

Shortly after that, the Royals changed their name to the Midnighters. (This was to avoid confusion with the Five Royales, another group on their label.)

Ballard later wrote and sang "Teardrops on Your Letter" in 1959. The B side was "The Twist," later copied by Chubby Checker and made the biggest dance hit of the 1960s.

			Current Price Range		P/Y AVG
MIDNIGHTERS—ALBUMS					
☐ 541 (M)	*FEDERAL*	THE MIDNIGHTERS	45.00	110.00	100.00
☐ 581 (M)		THE MIDNIGHTERS, VOL. II	40.00	96.00	90.00

MIKE AND THE UTOPIANS

☐ 574	*CEE-JAY*	ERLENE/I FOUND A PENNY	14.00	36.00	32.00

ON SOME COPIES, "I FOUND A PENNY" IS BILLED AS "I WISH," THE VALUE IS THE SAME

GARRY MILES
SEE: STATUES

☐ 55261	*LIBERTY*	LOOK FOR A STAR/ AFRAID OF LOVE	3.25	5.50	4.00
☐ 55279		DREAM GIRL/WISHING WELL ...	3.25	5.50	4.00
☐ 55363		LOVE AT FIRST SIGHT/ COMMANDMENTS OF LOVE ...	3.25	5.50	4.00
		GARRY MILES—EP			
☐ 1005	*LIBERTY*	LOOK FOR A STAR	5.50	11.00	9.00

GARRY MILLS

☐ 5674	*IMPERIAL*	LOOK FOR A STAR (PT. 1)/(PT. 2)	3.00	5.00	3.50

HAYLEY MILLS

☐ 385	*VISTA*	LET'S GET TOGETHER/ COBBLER, COBBLER	2.75	4.50	3.00
☐ 295		JOHNNY JINGO/ JEEPERS, CREEPERS	2.75	4.50	3.00
☐ 401		SIDE BY SIDE/DING DONG DING ..	2.75	4.50	3.00
☐ 408		CASTAWAY/SWEET RIVER	2.75	4.50	3.00
☐ 409		ENJOY IT/LET'S CLIMB	2.75	4.50	3.00
☐ 420		FLITTERIN'/BEAUTIFUL BEAULAH.	2.75	4.50	3.00
		HAYLEY MILLS—ALBUM			
☐ 3311 (M)	*BUENA VISTA*	LET'S GET TOGETHER	7.00	17.00	15.00

RONNIE MILSAP

☐ 5405	*WARNER BROTHERS*	IT WENT TO YOUR HEAD/ TOTAL DISASTER	5.00	9.00	7.00
☐ 12109	*SCEPTER*	LET'S GO GET STONED/ NEVER HAD IT SO GOOD	4.50	7.50	6.00
☐ 12127		WHEN IT COMES TO MY BABY/ A THOUSAND MILES FROM NOWHERE	4.00	7.00	4.85
☐ 12145		END OF THE WORLD/I SAW PITY IN THE FACE OF A FRIEND	4.00	7.00	4.85
☐ 12161		ANOTHER BRANCH FROM THE OLD TREE/AIN'T NO SOLE IN THESE OLD SHOES	3.50	6.00	4.35
☐ 12228		DO WHAT YOU GOTTA DO/ MR. MAILMAN	3.50	6.00	4.35
☐ 12246		NOTHING IS AS GOOD AS IT USED TO BE/DENVER	3.50	6.00	4.35
☐ 12272		WHAT'S YOUR NAME/LOVE WILL NEVER PASS US BY	4.00	7.00	4.85
☐ 2889	*CHIPS*	LOVING YOU IS A NATURAL THING/SO HUNG UP ON SYLVIA.	4.00	7.00	4.85
☐ 2987		A ROSE BY ANY OTHER NAME/ SERMONETTE	3.50	6.00	4.35

MINDBENDERS
SEE: WAYNE FONTANA AND THE MINDBENDERS

☐ 1541	*FONTANA*	A GROOVY KIND OF LOVE/ LOVE IS GOOD	2.75	4.50	3.00

			Current Price Range		P/Y AVG
☐ 1555		ASHES TO ASHES/YOU DON'T KNOW ABOUT LOVE	2.75	4.50	3.00
☐ 1571		I WANT HER, SHE WANTS ME/ MORNING AFTER	2.75	4.50	3.00
☑ 1620		BLESSED ARE THE LONELY/ YELLOW BRICK ROAD	2.75	4.50	3.00
		MINDBENDERS—ALBUMS			
☐ 27554 (M)	*FONTANA*	A GROOVY KIND OF LOVE	7.00	17.00	15.00
☐ 67554 (S)		A GROOVY KIND OF LOVE	8.00	21.00	18.00

SAL MINEO

☐ 9216	*EPIC*	START MOVIN'/LOVE AFFAIR ...	3.25	5.50	4.00
☐ 9227		LASTING LOVE/ YOU SHOULDN'T DO THAT	3.25	5.50	4.00
☐ 9246		PARTY TIME/ THE WORDS THAT I WHISPER .	3.25	5.50	4.00
☐ 9260		LITTLE PIGEON/CUTTIN' IN	3.25	5.50	4.00
☐ 9327		MAKE BELIEVE BABY/ YOUNG AS WE ARE	3.25	5.50	4.00
☐ 9345		I'LL NEVER BE MYSELF AGAIN/ WORDS THAT I WHISPER	3.25	5.50	4.00
		SAL MINEO—EPS			
☐ 7187	*EPIC*	SAL MINEO	4.50	8.00	6.50
☐ 7194		SAL	4.50	8.00	6.50
☐ 7195		SAL	4.50	8.00	6.50

MIRACLES

FEATURED: "SMOKEY" ROBINSON

☐ 1016	*END*	GOT A JOB/ MY MAMA DONE TOLD ME	14.00	24.00	20.00
☐ 1029		I CRY/MONEY	12.00	21.00	18.00
☐ 1084		I CRY/MONEY	12.00	24.00	20.00
☐ 1/2	*MOTOWN*	BAD GIRL/I LOVE YOU BABY	54.00	96.00	90.00
☐ 1734	*CHESS*	BAD GIRL/I LOVE YOUR BABY ...	5.50	11.00	9.00
☐ 1768		I NEED A CHANGE/ALL I WANT ..	7.00	13.00	11.00
☐ 54028	*TAMLA*	THE FEELING IS SO FINE/ WAY OVER THERE	52.00	96.00	90.00
☐ 54028		WAY OVER THERE/DEPEND ON ME	4.50	7.50	6.00
☐ 54034		SHOP AROUND/ WHO'S LOVIN' YOU	3.50	6.00	4.35
☐ 54036		AIN'T IT BABY/ THE ONLY ONE I LOVE	3.50	6.00	4.35
☐ 54044		MIGHTY GOOD LOVIN'/ BROKEN HEARTED	3.50	6.00	4.35
☐ 54048		EVERYBODY'S GOTTA PAY SOME DUES/I CAN'T BELIEVE	3.50	6.00	4.35
☐ 54053		WHAT'S SO GOOD ABOUT GOODBYE/I'VE BEEN SO GOOD TO YOU	3.50	6.00	4.35
☐ 54059		I'LL TRY SOMETHING NEW/YOU NEVER MISS A GOOD THING ...	3.50	6.00	4.35
☐ 54069		WAY OVER THERE/ IF YOUR MOTHER ONLY KNEW .	3.25	5.50	4.00
☐ 54073		YOU'VE REALLY GOT A HOLD ON ME/HAPPY LANDING	3.25	5.50	4.00
☐ 54078		I LOVE SHE CAN COUNT ON/ I CAN TAKE A HINT	3.25	5.50	4.00
☐ 54083		MICKEY'S MONKEY/WHATEVER MAKES YOU HAPPY	3.25	5.50	4.00
☐ 54089		I GOTTA DANCE TO KEEP FROM CRYING/SUCH IS LIFE, SUCH IS LIFE	3.25	5.50	4.00
☐ 54092		THE MAN IN YOU/ HEARTBREAK ROAD	3.25	5.50	4.00

			Current Price Range		P/Y AVG
☐54098		I LIKE IT LIKE THAT/ YOU'RE SO FINE AND SWEET ..	3.25	5.50	4.00
☐54102		THAT'S WHAT LOVE IS MADE OF/ WOULD I LOVE YOU	3.25	5.50	4.00
☐54109		COME ON, DO THE JERK/ BABY DON'T YOU GO	3.25	5.50	4.00
☐54113		OOH BABY BABY/ ALL THAT'S GOOD	3.25	5.50	4.00
☐54118		THE TRACKS OF MY TEARS/ A FORK IN THE ROAD	3.25	5.50	4.00
☐54123		MY GIRL HAS GONE/ SINCE YOU WON MY HEART ...	3.25	5.50	4.00
☐54127		GOING TO A GO GO/ CHOOSEY BEGGAR	3.00	5.00	3.65
☐54134		WHOLE LOT OF SHAKIN' IN MY HEART/OH, BE MY LOVE	3.00	5.00	3.65
☐54140		(COME 'ROUND HERE) I'M THE ONE YOU NEED/SAVE ME	3.00	5.00	3.65
☐54145		THE LOVE I SAW IN YOU WAS JUST A MIRAGE/ COME SPY WITH ME	3.00	5.00	3.65
☐54152		MORE LOVE/ I WEPT FOR YOU BABY	3.00	5.00	3.65
☐54159		I SECOND THAT EMOTION/ YOU MUST BE LOVE	3.00	5.00	3.65
☐54162		IF YOU CAN WANT/WHEN THE WORDS FROM YOUR HEART GET CAUGHT UP IN YOUR THROAT .	3.00	5.00	3.65
☐54167		YESTER LOVE/MUCH BETTER ...	3.00	5.00	3.65
☐54172		SPECIAL OCCASION/GIVE HER UP	3.00	5.00	3.65
☐54178		BABY, BABY DON'T CRY/YOUR MOTHER'S ONLY DAUGHTER ..	3.00	5.00	3.65
☐54183		DOGGONE RIGHT/ HERE I GO AGAIN	3.00	5.00	3.65
☐54184		ABRAHAM, MARTIN AND JOHN/ MUCH BETTER OFF	3.00	5.00	3.65
☐54189		POINT IT OUT/DARLING DEAR ...	3.00	5.00	3.65
☐54194		WHO'S GONNA TAKE THE BLAME?/ I GOTTA THING FOR YOU	3.00	5.00	3.65
☐54199		THE TEARS OF A CLOWN/ PROMISE ME	3.00	5.00	3.65

LATER TAMLA SINGLES ARE WORTH UP TO $2.50 MINT

MIRACLES—ALBUMS

☐220 (M)	*TAMLA*	HI, WE'RE THE MIRACLES	17.00	39.00	35.00
☐223 (M)		COOKIN' WITH THE MIRACLES ..	17.00	39.00	35.00
☐224 (M)		SHOP AROUND	14.50	34.00	30.00
☐230 (M)		I'LL TRY SOMETHING NEW	12.00	29.00	25.00
☐236 (M)		CHRISTMAS WITH THE MIRACLES.	12.00	29.00	25.00
☐238 (M)		THE FABULOUS MIRACLES	10.00	25.00	22.50
☐241 (M)		THE MIRACLES ON STAGE	10.00	25.00	22.50
☐245 (M)		DOIN' MICKEY'S MONKEY	10.00	25.00	22.50
☐245 (S)		DOIN' MICKEY'S MONKEY	14.00	34.00	30.00
☐254 (M)		THE MIRACLES' GREATEST HITS— FROM THE BEGINNING	7.00	17.00	15.00
☐254 (S)		THE THE MIRACLES' GREATEST HITS— FROM THE BEGINNING	9.00	25.00	22.50
☐267 (M)		GOING TO A GO-GO	7.00	17.00	15.00
☐267 (S)		GOING TO A GO-GO	9.00	25.00	22.50
☐271 (M)		AWAY WE A-GO-GO	6.00	15.00	13.50
☐271 (S)		AWAY WE A-GO-GO	8.00	21.00	18.00
☐276 (M)		MAKE IT HAPPEN.............	6.00	15.00	13.50
☐276 (S)		MAKE IT HAPPEN.............	8.00	21.00	18.00
☐276 (M)		TEARS OF A CLOWN (second title).	5.50	14.00	12.00

			Current Price Range		P/Y AVG
☐ 276 (S)		TEARS OF A CLOWN (second title) .	6.00	15.00	13.50
☐ 280 (M)		THE MIRACLES' GREATEST HITS, VOL. II	5.00	12.00	10.00
☐ 280 (S)		THE MIRACLES' GREATEST HITS, VOL. II	5.00	12.00	10.00

MISFITS

☐ 7-10	*ARIES*	MIDNIGHT STAR/I DON'T KNOW .	12.00	21.00	18.00

JONI MITCHELL

☐ 0906	*REPRISE*	BIG YELLOW TAXI/WOODSTOCK .	3.50	7.00	4.50
☐ 1049		CASE OF YOU/CALIFORNIA	3.50	7.00	4.50
☐ 1154		CHELSEA MORNING/ BOTH SIDES NOW	3.50	7.00	4.50
☐ 11010	*ASYLUM*	URGE FOR GOING/ YOU TURN ME ON	3.00	5.25	3.85
☐ 11029		COURT & SPARK/ RAISED ON ROBBERY	3.00	5.25	3.85
☐ 11034		JUST LIKE THIS TRAIN/HELP ME	3.00	5.25	3.85
☐ 11041		FREE MAN IN PARIS/ PEOPLE'S PARTIES	3.00	5.25	3.85
☐ 45244		CAREY/JERICHO	2.75	5.00	3.65
☐ 45298		BOHO DANCE/IN FRANCE THEY DANCE ON MAIN STREET	2.75	5.00	3.65
☐ 45377		BLUE MOTEL ROOM/COYOTE ...	2.75	5.00	3.65
☐ 45467		JERICHO/DREAMLAND	2.75	5.00	3.65
☐ 46506		DRY CLEANER FROM DES MOINES/ GOD MUST BE A BOOGIE MAN .	2.75	5.00	3.65
☐ 54221		BIG YELLOW TAXI/ RAINY NIGHT HOUSE	2.50	4.50	3.10

PAT MOLITERRI

☐ 414	*TEEN*	SAY THAT YOU LOVE ME/ THE U.S.A.	12.00	32.00	28.00

MONKEES

SEE: MICHAEL BLESSING, DAVEY JONES, MIKE NESMITH

☐ 1001	*COLGEMS*	LAST TRAIN TO CLARKSVILLE/ TAKE A GIANT STEP	3.00	5.00	3.65
☐ 1002		I'M A BELIEVER/(I'M NOT YOUR) STEPPING STONE	3.00	5.00	3.65
☐ 1004		A LITTLE BIT ME, A LITTLE BIT YOU/THE GIRL I KNEW SOMEWHERE	3.00	5.00	3.65
☐ 1007		PLEASANT VALLEY SUNDAY/ WORDS	3.00	5.00	3.65
☐ 1012		DAYDREAM BELIEVER/ GOIN' DOWN	3.00	5.00	3.65
☐ 1019		VALLERI/TAPIOCA TUNDRA	3.00	5.00	3.65
☐ 1023		D.W. WASHBURN/ IT'S NICE TO BE WITH YOU	3.00	5.00	3.65
☐ 1031		PORPOISE SONG/ AS WE GO ALONG	3.00	5.00	3.65
☐ 5000		TEAR DROP CITY/ A MAN WITHOUT A DREAM ...	3.00	5.00	3.65
☐ 5004		LISTEN TO THE BAND/ SOMEDAY MAN	3.00	5.00	3.65
☐ 5005		GOOD CLEAN FUN/ MOMMY DADDY	3.00	5.00	3.65
☐ 5011		OH MY MY/I LOVE YOU BETTER .	3.00	5.00	3.65

MONKEES—ALBUMS

☐ 101 (M)	*COLGEMS*	MEET THE MONKEES	6.00	15.00	13.50
☐ 101 (S)		MEET THE MONKEES	8.00	21.00	18.00
☐ 102 (M)		MORE OF THE MONKEES	6.00	15.00	13.50

			Current Price Range		P/Y AVG
□ 102 (S)		MORE OF THE MONKEES	8.00	21.00	18.00
□ 103 (M)		HEADQUARTERS	6.00	15.00	13.50
□ 103 (S)		HEADQUARTERS	8.00	21.00	18.00
□ 104 (M)		PISCES, AQUARIUS, CAPRICORN AND JONES, LTD	6.00	15.00	13.50
□ 104 (S)		PISCES, AQUARIUS, CAPRICORN AND JONES, LTD	8.00	17.00	15.00
□ 109 (M)		THE BIRDS, THE BEES, AND THE MONKEES	6.00	15.00	13.50
□ 104 (S)		THE BIRDS, THE BEES, AND THE MONKEES	8.00	17.00	15.00
□ 113 (S)		INSTANT REPLAY	12.00	24.00	20.00
□ 115 (S)		GREATEST HITS	10.00	20.00	17.50
□ 117 (S)		THE MONKEES PRESENT	9.00	25.00	22.50
□ 5008 (S)		HEAD (soundtrack)	30.00	50.00	40.00
□ 1001 (S)		A BARREL FULL OF MONKEES . . .	25.00	45.00	35.00

MONOTONES

□ 124	**MASCOT**	BOOK OF LOVE/ YOU NEVER LOVED ME	20.00	34.00	30.00
□ 5290	**ARGO**	BOOK OF LOVE/ YOU NEVER LOVED ME	5.00	9.00	7.00
□ 5301		TOM FOOLERY/ZOMBI	5.50	11.00	9.00
□ 5321		THE LEGEND OF SLEEPY HOLLOW/ SOFT SHADOWS	7.00	13.00	11.00
□ 5339		FOOLS WILL BE FOOLS/ TELL IT TO THE JUDGE	8.25	14.00	12.00
□ 735	**HULL**	READING THE BOOK OF LOVE/ DREAM	14.00	24.00	20.00
□ 743		DADDY'S HOME BUT MAMA'S GONE/TATTLETALE	12.00	21.00	18.00

CHRIS MONTEZ

□ 500	**MONOGRAM**	ALL YOU HAD TO DO (WAS TELL ME)/LOVE ME	3.75	6.50	5.00
□ 505		LET'S DANCE/YOU'RE THE ONE .	3.00	5.00	3.50
□ 507		SOME KINDA FUN/TELL ME	3.00	5.00	3.50
□ 508		ROCKIN' BLUES/ LET'S DO (THE LIMBO)	3.00	5.00	3.50
□ 513		MY BABY LOVES TO DANCE/ IN AN ENGLISH TOWNE	3.00	5.00	3.50
□ 517		ALL YOU HAD TO DO (WAS TELL ME)/LOVE ME (with Kathy Young)	3.25	5.50	4.00
□ 520		IT TAKES TWO/ SHOOT THAT CURL	3.00	5.00	3.50

CHRIS MONTEZ—ALBUM

□ 100 (M)	**MONOGRAM**	LET'S DANCE/SOME KINDA FUN .	12.00	21.00	18.00

MONTGOMERYS

□ 883	**AMY**	GOTTA MAKE A HIT RECORD/ PROMISE OF LOVE	14.00	34.00	30.00

MOODY BLUES
FEATURED: DENNY LAINE

□ 9726	**LONDON**	GO NOW!/LOSE YOUR MONEY . . .	3.50	6.00	4.00
□ 9764		FROM THE BOTTOM OF MY HEART/MY BABY'S GONE	3.50	6.00	4.00
□ 9799		YOU DON'T/EV'RY DAY	3.50	6.00	4.00
□ 9810		STOP!/BYE BYE BIRD	3.50	6.00	4.00
□ 20030		FLY ME HIGH/I REALLY HAVEN'T GOT THE TIME	3.50	6.00	4.00
□ 85023	**DERAM**	NIGHTS IN WHITE SATIN/CITIES .	3.00	5.00	3.65

MOONGLOWS

The quintet formed in 1951 in Louisville, Kentucky. They sang at parties, dances and small clubs but never bothered to settle on a permanent name. A year after they formed, the group became aware of the growing importance of Cleveland disc jockey Alan Freed, reportedly the first white radio personality to refuse to play white "cover" versions of hits made originally by black artists.

They visited Freed at the WJW studios in Cleveland, and Freed suggested they take on the name of the Moonglows. (Freed's radio program was called "Moondog's Rock and Roll Party".) Freed steered the Moonglows to a solitary single on Champagne, then five discs on the Chance label. He then negotiated a contract with the Chess label in Chicago. Supposedly Freed promised the Moonglows good airplay in return for inclusion of his name as a co-writer on their songs. Word has it that Freed never really wrote anything.

The Moonglows saw their biggest commercial success on Chess, although their original version of the classic "Sincerely" went to No. 1 as a "cover" version by the saccharine McGuire Sisters.

			Current Price Range		P/Y AVG
☐ 85028		TUESDAY AFTERNOON (FOREVER AFTERNOON) ANOTHER MORNING	3.00	5.00	3.65
☐ 85033		RIDE MY SEE SAW/ VOICES IN THE SKY	3.00	5.00	3.65
☐ 85044		NEVER COMES THE DAY/ SO DEEP WITHIN	3.00	5.00	3.65
☐ 67004	THRESHOLD	QUESTION/CANDLE OF LIFE	3.00	5.00	3.65
☐ 67006		THE STORY IN YOUR EYES/ MELANCHOLY ME	3.00	5.00	3.65
☐ 67009		ISN'T LIFE STRANGE/ AFTER YOU CAME	3.00	5.00	3.65
☐ 67012		I'M JUST A SINGER (IN A ROCK AND ROLL BAND)/FOR MY LADY	3.00	5.00	3.65

MOODY BLUES—ALBUMS

☐ 3428 (M)	LONDON	GO NOW!-MOODY BLUES #1	9.00	25.00	22.50
☐ 428 (S)		GO NOW!-MOODY BLUES #1	14.00	34.00	30.00
☐ 16012 (M)	DERAM	DAYS OF FUTURE PASSED	5.50	14.00	12.00
☐ 18012 (S)		DAYS OF FUTURE PASSED	5.00	17.00	15.00
☐ 18017 (S)		IN SEARCH OF THE LOST CHORD	5.50	14.00	12.00
☐ 18025 (S)		ON THE THRESHOLD OF A DREAM	5.50	14.00	12.00
☐ 18051 (S)		IN THE BEGINNING	5.50	14.00	12.00
☐ 1 (S)	THRESHOLD	TO OUR CHILDREN'S CHILDREN'S CHILDREN	5.50	14.00	12.00
☐ 3 (S)		A QUESTION OF BALANCE	5.50	14.00	12.00
☐ 5 (S)		EVERY GOOD BOY DESERVES FAVOUR	5.50	14.00	12.00
☐ 7 (S)		SEVENTH SOJOURN	5.50	14.00	12.00
☐ 12/13 (S)		THIS IS THE MOODY BLUES	5.50	14.00	12.00

MOONGLOWS
FEATURED: HARVEY FUGUA

☐ 7500	CHAMPAGNE	I JUST CAN'T TELL YOU NO LIE/ I'VE BEEN YOUR DOG	76.00	128.00	120.00
☐ 1147	CHANCE	WHISTLE MY LOVE/BABY PLEASE	110.00	190.00	180.00
☐ 1150		JUST A LONELY CHRISTMAS/ HEY SANTA CLAUS	160.00	265.00	250.00
☐ 1152		SECRET LOVE/REAL GONE MAMA	110.00	190.00	180.00
☐ 1156		I WAS WRONG/ OOH ROCKING DADDY	76.00	128.00	120.00
☐ 1161		219 TRAIN/MY GAL	160.00	265.00	250.00
☐ 1581	CHESS	SINCERELY/TEMPTING	9.50	17.00	15.00
☐ 1589		MOST OF ALL/SHE'S GONE	9.50	17.00	15.00
☐ 1598		FOOLISH ME/SLOW DOWN	8.25	14.00	12.00
☐ 1605		STARLITE/IN LOVE	8.25	14.00	12.00
☐ 1611		IN MY DIARY/LOVER, LOVE ME	8.25	14.00	12.00
☐ 1619		WE GO TOGETHER/ CHICKIE UM BAH	8.25	14.00	12.00
☐ 1629		SEE SAW/WHEN I'M WITH YOU	5.50	11.00	9.00
☐ 1646		OVER AND OVER AGAIN/ I KNEW FROM THE START	5.50	11.00	9.00
☐ 1651		PLEASE SEND ME SOMEONE TO LOVE/MR. ENGINEER	5.00	9.00	7.00
☐ 1661		DON'T SAY GOODBYE/I'M AFRAID THE MASQUERADE IS OVER	5.50	11.00	9.00
☐ 1699		CONFESS IT TO YOUR HEART/ THE BEATING OF MY HEART	5.00	9.00	7.00

FIRST-PRESSES OF THE ABOVE FEATURE A SILVER TOP

☐ 1681		TOO LATE/HERE I AM	5.00	8.50	6.50
☐ 1689		IN THE MIDDLE OF THE NIGHT/ THIS LOVE	5.00	8.50	6.50
☐ 1701		THIS LOVE/ SWEETER THAN WORDS	5.00	8.50	6.50

			Current Price Range		P/Y AVG
1705		TEN COMMANDMENTS OF LOVE/ MEAN OLD BLUES (Harvey)....	5.00	8.00	6.00
1713		I WANT SOMEBODY/ DA DA GOO GOO (Harvey)......	5.00	8.00	6.00
1717		I'LL NEVER STOP WANTING YOU/ LOVE IS A RIVER............	5.00	8.00	6.00
1738		UNEMPLOYMENT/MAMA LOOCIE	5.00	8.00	6.00
1749		OOH OUCH STOP!/BLUE SKIES (Harvey)...................	5.00	8.00	6.00
1770		JUNIOR/BEATNIK.............	5.00	8.00	6.00
1781		THE FIRST TIME/MAMA (Harvey).	5.00	8.00	6.00
1811		BLUE VELVET/PENNY ARCADE..	5.00	8.00	6.00
806	CHECKER	SO ALL ALONE/SHOO DO-BE DOO (Moonlighters)..............	12.00	20.00	15.00
813		NEW GAL/A HUG AND A KISS...	12.00	20.00	15.00
		MOONGLOWS—ALBUMS			
1430 (M)	CHESS	LOOK.......................	16.00	39.00	35.00
1471 (M)		THE BEST OF BOBBY LESTER AND THE MOONGLOWS..........	14.00	35.00	30.00

HARV MOORE

20	AMERICAN ARTS	I FEEL SO FINE/THE FAB FOUR..	18.00	34.00	30.00

VAN MORRISON
SEE: THEM

545	BANG	BROWN EYED GIRL/ GOODBYE BABY............	2.75	4.50	3.00
552		CHICK-A-BOOM/RO RO ROSEY..	2.75	4.50	3.00
585		MIDNIGHT SPECIAL/ SPANISH ROSE.............	2.75	4.50	3.00

WARNER BROTHERS SINGLES ARE WORTH UP TO $2.50 MINT

VAN MORRISON—ALBUMS

218 (M)	BANG	BLOWIN' YOUR MIND..........	8.00	21.00	18.00
218 (S)		BLOWIN' YOUR MIND..........	7.00	17.00	15.00
222 (S)		THE BEST OF VAN MORRISON...	7.00	17.00	15.00

MOTHERS OF INVENTION
FEATURED: FRANK ZAPPA
SEE: BABY RAY AND THE FERNS, BOB GUY, RON ROMAN, RUEBEN AND THE JETS, FRANK ZAPPA

10418	VERVE	HOW COULD I BE SUCH A FOOL/ HELP, I'M A ROCK..........	5.50	11.00	9.00
10458		WHO ARE THE BRAIN POLICE?/ TROUBLE COMIN' EVERY DAY.	5.00	9.00	7.00
10513		BIG LEG EMMA/WHO DON'T YOU DO ME RIGHT?.........	5.00	9.00	7.00
10570		MOTHER PEOPLE/ LONELY LITTLE GIRL........	4.50	7.50	6.00
840	BIZARRE	DOG BREATH/MY GUITAR......	4.50	7.50	6.00
967		WOULD YOU GO ALL THE WAY?/ TELL ME YOU LOVE ME......	4.50	7.50	6.00
1052		JUNIOR MINTZ BOOGIE/ TEARS BEGAN TO FALL.......	4.50	7.50	6.00
1127		EAT THAT QUESTION/CLERIUS AWREETUS-AWARIGHTUS....	4.50	7.50	6.00
		MOTHERS OF INVENTION—ALBUMS			
5005 (M)	VERVE	FREAK OUT...............	9.00	22.00	14.00
5005 (S)		FREAK OUT.................	10.00	27.00	17.00
5013 (M)		ABSOLUTELY FREE............	8.00	20.00	12.00
5013 (S)		ABSOLUTELY FREE............	9.00	22.00	14.00
5045 (M)		WE'RE ONLY IN IT FOR THE MONEY..............	8.00	20.00	12.00
5045 (S)		WE'RE ONLY IN IT FOR THE MONEY..............	9.00	22.00	14.00

			Current Price Range		P/Y AVG
☐ 5068 (S)			MOTHERMANIA: THE BEST OF THE MOTHERS	8.00 20.00	12.00
☐ 5074 (S)			MOTHERS	8.00 20.00	12.00
☐ 6356 (S)	*BIZARRE*		HOT RATS	8.00 20.00	12.00
☐ 6370 (S)			BURNT WEENIE SANDWICH	8.00 20.00	12.00
☐ 2028 (S)			WEASELS RIPPED MY FLESH	8.00 20.00	12.00
☐ 2042 (S)			LIVE-FILLMORE EAST-JUNE 1971	8.00 20.00	12.00
☐ 2075 (S)			JUST ANOTHER BAND FROM L.A..	8.00 20.00	12.00
☐ 2093 (S)			GRAND WAZOO	8.00 20.00	12.00

MOTOR CITY FIVE

☐ 1000	*AMG*		I CAN ONLY GIVE YOU EVERYTHING/ I JUST DON'T KNOW	7.00 14.00	9.50
☐ 1001			I CAN ONLY GIVE YOU EVERYTHING/ ONE OF THE GUYS	7.00 14.00	9.50
☐ 333	*A-2*		LOOKING AT YOU/BORDERLINE, (in the original pictorial sleeve) .	17.00 41.00	36.00
☐			LOOKING AT YOU/BORDERLINE (plain record)	7.00 17.00	16.00

THIS GROUP WAS OFTEN BILLED AS MC5

MUDCRUTCH (TOM PETTY AND THE HEARTBREAKERS)

☐ 40357	*SHELTER*		WILD EYES/DEPOT STREET	8.25 14.00	12.00

MUDDY WATERS
MUDDY WATERS—78's

☐ 1302	*ARISTOCRAT*		GYPSY WOMAN/ LITTLE ANNA MAE	12.00 24.00	20.00
☐ 1305			I CAN'T BE SATISFIED/ I FEEL LIKE GOING HOME	12.00 24.00	20.00
☐ 1306			TRAIN FARE HOME/ WHISKEY BLUES	12.00 24.00	20.00
☐ 1307			YOU'RE GONNA MISS ME/ MEAN RED SPIDER..........	9.00 18.00	15.00
☐ 1310			STREAMLINE WOMAN/ MUDDY JUMPS ONE.........	9.00 18.00	15.00
☐ 1311			LITTLE GENEVA/CANARY BIRD ..	9.00 18.00	15.00
☐ 406			SCREAMIN' AND CRYIN'/ WHERE'S MY WOMAN BLUES .	18.00 35.00	30.00
☐ 412			ROLLIN' AND TUMBLIN'/ PARTS 1 & 2	14.00 28.00	24.00
☐ 1426	*CHESS*		ROLLIN' STONE/WALKIN' BLUES	6.00 12.00	9.00
☐ 1434			YOU'RE GONNA NEED MY HELP/ SAD LETTER BLUES	5.00 10.00	7.00
☐ 1441			LOUISIANA BLUES/ EVANS SHUFFLE	5.00 10.00	7.00
☐ 1452			LONG DISTANCE CALL/ TOO YOUNG TO KNOW	5.00 10.00	7.00
☐ 1468			HONEY BEE/APPEALING BLUES ..	4.00 8.00	5.00
☐ 1480			MY FAULT/STILL A FOOL	5.00 10.00	5.00
☐ 1490			SHE MOVES ME/ EARLY MORNING BLUES	4.00 8.00	5.00
			MUDDY WATERS—45s		
☐ 1509			COUNTRY BOY/ALL NIGHT LONG	18.00 35.00	30.00
☐ 1514			PLEASE HAVE MERCY/ LOOKING FOR MY BABY	18.00 35.00	30.00
☐ 1526			STANDING AROUND CRYING/ GONE TO MAIN STREET	18.00 35.00	30.00
☐ 1537			SHE'S ALL RIGHT/SAD SAD DAY .	15.00 30.00	25.00
☐ 1542			WHO'S GONNA BE YOUR SWEET MAN/TURN THE LAMP DOWN LOW	13.00 26.00	21.00

		Current Price Range		P/Y AVG
☐ 1550	BLOW WIND BLOW/MAD LOVE ..	11.00	22.00	18.00
☐ 1560	I'M YOUR HOOCHIE COOCHIE MAN/SHE'S SO PRETTY	11.00	22.00	18.00
☐ 1571	JUST MAKE LOVE TO ME/ OH YEAH	6.00	12.00	9.00
☐ 1579	I'M READY/I DON'T KNOW WHY .	5.00	10.00	7.00
☐ 1585	I'M A NATURAL BORN LOVER/ LOVING MAN	5.00	10.00	7.00
☐ 1596	I WANT TO BE LOVED/MY EYES ..	4.00	8.00	5.00
☐ 1602	YOUNG FASHIONED WAYS/ MANNIS BOY	3.50	7.00	4.75
☐ 1612	SUGAR SWEET/ TROUBLE NO MORE	3.50	7.00	4.75
☐ 1620	FORTY DAYS & FORTY NIGHTS/ ALL ABOARD	3.50	7.00	4.75
☐ 1630	DON'T GO NO FURTHER/ DIAMONDS AT YOUR FEET	3.50	7.00	4.75
☐ 1644	JUST TO BE WITH YOU/ I GOT TO FIND MY BABY	3.50	7.00	4.75
☐ 1652	ROCK ME/ GOT MY MOJO WORKING	3.50	7.00	4.75
☐ 1667	GOOD NEWS/COME HOME BABY .	3.50	7.00	4.75
☐ 1680	EVIL/I LIVE THE LIFE I LOVE	3.50	7.00	4.75
☐ 1692	I WON'T GO/SHE'S GOT IT	3.50	7.00	4.75
☐ 1704	SHE'S 19 YEARS OLD/ CLOSE TO YOU	3.25	6.50	4.50
☐ 1718	WALKING THRU THE PARK/ MEAN MISTREATER	3.25	6.50	4.50
☐ 1724	CLOUDS IN MY HEART/OOH WEE	3.25	6.50	4.50
☐ 1733	TAKE THE BITTER WITH THE SWEET/SHE'S INTO SOMETHING	3.25	6.50	4.50
☐ 1739	TELL ME BABY/RECIPE FOR LOVE	3.25	6.50	4.50
☐ 1748	I FEEL SO GOOD/ WHEN I GET TO THINKING	3.25	6.50	4.50
☐ 1752	I'M YOUR DOCTOR/ READ WAY BACK	3.25	6.50	4.50
☐ 1758	LOVE AFFAIR/ LOOK WHAT YOU'VE DONE	3.25	6.50	4.50
☐ 1765	TIGER IN YOUR TANK MEANEST WOMAN	3.25	6.50	4.50
☐ 1774	WOMAN WANTED/ GO MY MOJO WORKING. PART 1	3.25	6.50	4.50
☐ 1796	LONESOME ROOM BLUES/ MESSIN' WITH THE MAN	3.25	6.50	4.50
☐ 1819	GOING HOME/TOUGH TIMES	2.75	5.25	3.75
☐ 1827	MUDDY WATERS TWIST/ YOU SHOOK ME	2.75	5.25	3.75
☐ 1839	YOU NEED LOVE/ LITTLE BROWN BIRD	2.75	5.25	3.75
☐ 1862	FIVE LONG YEARS/ TWENTY FOUR HOURS	2.75	5.25	3.75
☐ 1895	THE SAME THING/YOU CAN'T LOSE WHAT YOU NEVER HAD ..	2.75	5.25	3.75
☐ 1914	MY JOHN THE CONQUER ROOT/ SHORT DRESS WOMAN	2.50	5.00	3.50
☐ 1921	PUT ME IN YOUR LAY AWAY/ STILL A FOOL...............	2.75	5.25	3.75
☐ 1937	MY DOG CAN'T BARK/ I GOT A RICH MAN'S WOMAN ..	2.75	5.25	3.75
☐ 1973	HOOCHIE COOCHIE MAN/ CORINA. CORINA	2.75	5.25	3.75

			Current Price Range		P/Y AVG
		MUDDY WATERS—ALBUMS			
☐2210	**TESTAMENT**	DOWN ON STOVALL'S PLANTATION	7.00	15.00	12.00
☐2207		CHICAGO BLUES: THE BEGINNING	7.00	15.00	12.00
☐8202	**CHESS**	ROLLING STONE	5.00	10.00	7.00
☐8203		WIZARDS FROM THE SOUTHSIDE	5.00	10.00	7.00
☐4006		MUDDY WATERS, CHESS MASTERS, VOL. 2	7.00	15.00	12.00
☐1427		THE BEST OF MUDDY WATERS	20.00	45.00	37.50
☐1539		SAIL ON	10.00	20.00	16.00
☐1501		THE REAL FOLK BLUES	10.00	20.00	16.00
☐1511		MORE REAL FOLK BLUES	10.00	20.00	16.00
☐1483		FOLK SINGER	13.00	25.00	20.00
☐1533		BLUES FROM BIG BILL'S COPACABANA	10.00	20.00	16.00
☐3444	**BLUE SKY**	HARD AGAIN	5.00	10.00	7.00
☐34928		I'M READY	4.00	8.00	5.00
☐37064		KING BEE	4.00	8.00	5.00
		MARIA MULDAUR			
☐1183	**REPRISE**	MIDNIGHT AT THE OASIS/ ANY OLD TIME	3.00	5.50	3.85
☐1319		COOL RIVER/I'M A WOMAN	3.00	5.50	3.85
☐1331		OH PAPA/GRINGO EN MEXICO	3.00	5.50	3.85
☐1362		JON THE GENERATOR/ SWEET HARMONY	3.00	5.50	3.85
☐8580	**WARNER BROTHERS**	I'LL KEEP MY LIGHT/ MAKE LOVE TO THE MUSIC	2.50	4.50	3.10
☐49058		BIRDS FLY SOUTH	2.50	4.50	3.10

MARIA MULDAUR'S HIT, "MIDNIGHT AT THE OASIS," WAS REVIVED AS
A RADIO JINGLE ADVERTISING CAMPBELL'S SOUPS

		MURMAIDS			
☐628	**CHATTAHOOCHEE**	POPSICLES AND ICICLES/ BLUE DRESS	3.25	5.50	4.00
☐628		POPSICLES AND ICICLES/ HUNTINGTON FLATS	3.00	5.00	3.50
☐636		HEARTBREAK AHEAD/ HE'S GOOD TO ME	3.00	5.00	3.50
☐641		WILD AND WONDERFUL/ BULL TALK	3.00	5.00	3.50

		MUSIC EXPLOSION			
☐1404	**ATTACK**	LITTLE BLACK EGG/ STAY BY MY SIDE	5.00	9.00	6.00
☐3380	**LAURIE**	LITTLE BIT O' SOUL/ I SEE THE LIGHT	3.00	5.50	3.85
☐3400		SUNSHINE GAMES/ CAN'T STOP NOW	3.00	5.50	3.85
☐3414		HEARTS AND FLOWERS/ WE GOTTA GO HOME	3.00	5.50	3.85
☐3429		ROAD RUNNER/WHAT YOU WANT	3.00	5.50	3.85
☐3440		FLASH/WHERE ARE WE GOING?	3.00	5.50	3.85
☐3454		YES SIR/DAZZLING	3.00	5.50	3.85
☐3466		JACK IN THE BOX/REWIND	3.00	5.50	3.85
☐3479		CALL ME ANYTHING/ WHAT'S YOUR NAME?	3.00	5.50	3.85
☐3500		LITTLE BLACK EGG/ STAY BY MY SIDE	3.00	5.50	3.85
		MUSIC EXPLOSION—ALBUM			
☐2040 (S)	**LAURIE**	LITTLE BIT O'SOUL	7.00	17.00	15.00

			Current Price Range		P/Y AVG

MUSIC MACHINE

☐61	*ORIGINAL SOUND*	TALK TALK/COME ON IN	2.75	4.50	3.25
☐67		THE PEOPLE IN ME/			
		MASCULINE INTUITION	2.75	4.50	3.25
☐71		DOUBLE YELLOW LINE/			
		ABSOLUTELY POSITIVELY	2.75	4.50	3.25

MUSIC MACHINE—ALBUMS

☐5015 (M)	*ORIGINAL SOUND*	TURN ON THE MUSIC MACHINE ..	8.00	21.00	18.00
☐8875 (S)		TURN ON THE MUSIC MACHINE ..	12.00	28.00	25.00

MYSTERIANS
SEE: ? AND THE MYSTERIANS

☐040	*JOX*	IS IT A LIE?/			
		WHY SHOULD I LOVE YOU? ...	5.50	11.00	9.00

MYSTICS

☐3028	*LAURIE*	HUSHABYE/ADAM AND EVE	3.25	5.50	4.00
☐3038		DON'T TAKE THE STARS/			
		SO TENDERLY	3.75	6.50	5.00
☐3047		ALL THROUGH THE NIGHT/			
		I BEGIN (TO THINK OF			
		YOU AGAIN)................	3.75	6.50	5.00
☐3058		WHITE CLIFFS OF DOVER/			
		BLUE STAR	3.75	6.50	5.00
☐3086		STAR-CROSSED LOVERS/			
		GOODBYE MR. BLUES	3.25	5.50	4.00
☐3014		A SUNDAY KIND OF LOVE/			
		DARLING. I KNOW	3.75	6.50	5.00

N

NASHVILLE TEENS

☐9689	*LONDON*	TOBACCO ROAD/			
		I LIKE IT LIKE THAT	3.00	5.00	3.65
☐9712		T.N.T./GOGGLE EYE	3.00	5.00	3.65
☐9736		FIND MY WAY BACK HOME/			
		DEVIL-IN-LAW	3.00	5.00	3.65
☐13357	*MGM*	LITTLE BIRD/WATCHA GONNA DO	3.00	5.00	3.65
☐13406		I KNOW HOW IT FEELS TO BE			
		LOVED/SOON FORGOTTEN	3.00	5.00	3.65
☐13483		THE HARD WAY/UPSIDE DOWN ..	3.00	5.00	3.65

NASHVILLE TEENS—ALBUMS

☐3407 (M)	*LONDON*	TOBACCO ROAD..............	7.00	17.00	15.00
☐407 (S)		TOBACCO ROAD..............	8.00	21.00	18.00

JERRY NAYLOR

☐1118	*SKYLA*	STOP YOUR CRYING/			
		YOU'RE THIRTEEN	3.25	5.50	4.00
☐1123		JUDEE MALONE/I'M TIRED	3.00	5.00	3.50

NAZZ
FEATURED: ALICE COOPER

☐001	*VERY RECORD*	LAY DOWN AND DIE. GOODBYE/			
		WONDER WHO'S LOVING			
		HER NOW	65.00	120.00	110.00

JERRY NEAL (CAPEHART)

☐15810	*DOT*	SCRATCHIN'/I HATE RABBITS ...	12.00	21.00	18.00

			Current Price Range		P/Y AVG

NEIL AND JACK
FEATURED: NEIL DIAMOND

			Current Price Range		P/Y AVG
☐508	*DUEL*	YOU ARE MY LOVE AT LAST/ WHAT WILL I DO	12.00	21.00	18.00

RICKY NELSON

☐10047	*VERVE*	A TEENAGER'S ROMANCE/ I'M WALKIN'	4.50	7.50	6.00
☐10070		YOU'RE MY ONE AND ONLY LOVE/ HONEY ROCK	5.00	9.00	7.00
☐5463	*IMPERIAL*	BE BOP BABY/HAVE I TOLD YOU LATELY THAT I LOVE YOU? (black)	3.50	6.00	4.35
☐5463		BE BOP BABY/HAVE I TOLD YOU LATELY THAT I LOVE YOU? (maroon)	4.50	7.50	6.00
☐5483		STOOD UP/WAITIN' IN SCHOOL	3.50	6.00	4.35
☐5503		BELIEVE WHAT YOU SAY/ MY BUCKET'S GOT A HOLE IN IT	3.50	6.00	4.35
☐5528		POOR LITTLE FOOL/ DON'T LEAVE ME THIS WAY	3.50	6.00	4.35
☐5545		LONESOME TOWN/ I GOT A FEELING	3.50	6.00	4.35
☐5565		NEVER BE ANYONE ELSE BUT YOU/IT'S LATE	3.50	6.00	4.35
☐5595		SWEETER THAN YOU/ JUST A LITTLE TOO MUCH	3.50	6.00	4.35
☐5614		I WANNA BE LOVED/ MIGHTY GOOD	3.25	5.50	4.00
☐5663		YOUNG EMOTIONS/ RIGHT BY MY SIDE	3.25	5.50	4.00
☐5685		I'M NOT AFRAID/ YES SIR, THAT'S MY BABY	3.25	5.50	4.00
☐5707		YOU ARE THE ONLY ONE/ MILK COW BLUES	3.25	5.50	4.00
☐5741		TRAVELIN' MAN/ HELLO MARY LOU	3.25	5.50	4.00
☐5770		A WONDER LIKE YOU/EVERLOVIN'	3.25	5.50	4.00
☐5805		YOUNG WORLD/SUMMERTIME	3.25	5.50	4.00
☐5864		TEEN AGE IDOL/ I'VE GOT MY EYES ON YOU	3.25	5.50	4.00
☐5901		IT'S UP TO YOU/I NEED YOU	3.25	5.50	4.00
☐5910		THAT'S ALL/I'M IN LOVE AGAIN	3.25	5.50	4.00
☐5935		OLD ENOUGH TO LOVE/ IF YOU CAN'T ROCK ME	3.25	5.50	4.00
☐5958		A LONG VACATION/ MAD, MAD WORLD	3.25	5.50	4.00
☐5985		TIME AFTER TIME/ THERE'S NOT A MINUTE	3.25	5.50	4.00
☐66004		TODAY'S TEARDROPS/ THANK YOU DARLIN'	3.25	5.50	4.00
☐66017		CONGRATULATIONS/ ONE MINUTE TO ONE	3.25	5.50	4.00
☐66039		LUCKY STAR/ EVERYBODY BUT ME	3.25	5.50	4.00
☐31475	*DECCA*	YOU DON'T LOVE ME ANYMORE/ I GOT A WOMAN	3.25	5.50	4.00
☐31495		STRING ALONG/GYPSY WOMAN	3.00	5.00	3.65
☐31533		FOOLS RUSH IN/DOWN HOME	3.00	5.00	3.65
☐31574		FOR YOU/ THAT'S ALL SHE WROTE	3.00	5.00	3.65
☐31612		THE VERY THOUGHT OF YOU/ I WONDER	3.00	5.00	3.65

RICKY NELSON

Before instant rock stardom, Ricky Nelson was chiefly known as the cute, skinny kid on TV who said things like "I don't mess around, boy!" (He also occasionally beat upon his drum set for the cameras.) But that all changed in 1957 during a particular "Ozzie and Harriet" episode. The script had Nelson dressed as Elvis Presley for a costume party. As a joke, Ricky "sang" two lines from Presley's "Love Me Tender". The result was 10,000 letters in a week, almost all wanting to know if Ricky was going to make a real record.

Ozzie — Ricky's father — steered his young (born May 8, 1940) son to the Verve Records. There Ricky Nelson waxed a pair of singles; they both made the Top 20 overnight.

When Imperial Records' president Lew Chudd learned that Nelson had only a verbal contract with Verve, he persuaded Ozzie to sign his younger son to Imperial. Ricky then proceeded to record a dozen Top 10 winners for Imperial.

Ricky later signed with Decca, where his hits eventually declined. His last big winner was "Garden Party", an angry retort to his "fans" who booed him for playing current music at an oldies concert at Madison Square Garden.

He is no longer a major hitmaker; still, Nelson's impact on rock-and-roll cannot be denied. And he outsold everybody during the 1950s except Elvis and Pat Boone.

			Current Price Range		P/Y AVG
☐31656		THERE'S NOTHING I CAN SAY/ LONELY CORNER	3.00	5.00	3.65
☐31703		A HAPPY GUY/ DON'T BREATHE A WORD	3.00	5.00	3.65
☐31756		MEAN OLD WORLD/ WHEN THE CHIPS ARE DOWN	3.00	5.00	3.65
☐31800		YESTERDAY'S LOVE/ COME OUT DANCIN'	3.00	5.00	3.65
☐31845		LOVE AND KISSES/ SAY YOU LOVE ME	3.00	5.00	3.65
☐31900		YOUR KIND OF LOVIN'/ FIRE-BREATHIN' DRAGON	3.00	5.00	3.65
☐31956		LOUISIANA MAN/ YOU JUST CAN'T QUIT	3.00	5.00	3.65
☐32026		THINGS YOU GAVE ME/ALONE	3.00	5.00	3.65
☐32055		TAKE A BROKEN HEART/ THEY DON'T GIVE MEDALS	3.00	5.00	3.65
☐32120		I'M CALLED LONELY/ TAKE A CITY BRIDE	3.00	5.00	3.65
☐32176		SUZANNE ON A SUNDAY MORNING/MOONSHINE	3.00	5.00	3.65
☐32222		DREAM WEAVER/ BABY CLOSE ITS EYES	3.00	5.00	3.65
☐32284		PROMENADE IN GREEN/ DON'T BLAME IT ON YOUR WIFE	3.00	5.00	3.65
☐32298		DON'T MAKE PROMISES/ BAREFOOT BOY	3.00	5.00	3.65
☐32550		SHE BELONGS TO ME/PROMISES	3.00	5.00	3.65
☐32635		EASY TO BE FREE/COME ON IN	3.00	5.00	3.65
☐32676		I SHALL BE RELEASED/ IF YOU GOTTA, GO, GO NOW	3.00	5.00	3.65
☐32711		WE GOT SUCH A LONG WAY TO GO/ LOOK AT MARY	3.00	5.00	3.65
☐32739		HOW LONG?/DOWN ALONG THE BAYOU COUNTRY	3.00	5.00	3.65
☐32779		LIFE/CALIFORNIA	3.00	5.00	3.65
☐32860		SING ME A SONG/ THANK YOU, LORD	3.00	5.00	3.65
☐32906		LOVE MINUS ZERO-NO LIMIT/ GYPSY PILOT	3.00	5.00	3.65
☐32980		GARDEN PARTY/ SO LONG MAMA	2.75	4.75	3.50
☐40001	**MCA**	PALACE GUARD/A FLOWER OPENS GENTLY BY	2.75	4.75	3.50
☐40130		LIFESTREAM/EVIL WOMAN CHILD	2.75	4.75	3.50
☐40187		WINDFALL/LEGACY	2.75	4.75	3.50
☐40214		ONE NIGHT STAND/ LIFESTREAM	2.75	4.75	3.50
☐40392		LOUISIANA BELLE/TRY (TRY TO FALL IN LOVE)	2.75	4.75	3.50
☐40458		ROCK AND ROLL LADY/ FADE AWAY	2.75	4.75	3.50
		RICKY NELSON—EPs			
☐5048	*VERVE*	RICKY	16.00	29.00	25.00
☐153	*IMPERIAL*	RICKY	8.50	17.00	15.00
☐154		RICKY	9.50	17.00	15.00
☐155		RICKY	9.50	17.00	15.00
☐156		RICKY NELSON	8.25	14.00	12.00
☐157		RICKY NELSON	8.25	14.00	12.00
☐158		RICKY NELSON	8.25	14.00	12.00
☐159		RICKY SINGS AGAIN	7.00	13.00	11.00
☐160		RICKY SINGS AGAIN	7.00	13.00	11.00
☐161		RICKY SINGS AGAIN	7.00	13.00	11.00
☐162		SONGS BY RICKY	6.00	12.00	10.00

COLPIX, CP612, 45

IMPERIAL, LP9244

			Current Price Range		P/Y AVG
☐ 163		SONGS BY RICKY	6.00	12.00	10.00
☐ 164		SONGS BY RICKY	6.00	12.00	10.00
☐ 165		RICKY SINGS SPIRITUALS	5.00	11.00	9.00
		RICKY NELSON—ALBUMS			
☐ 2083 (M)	**VERVE**	TEEN TIME	29.00	66.00	60.00
☐ 9048 (M)	**IMPERIAL**	RICKY	17.00	39.00	35.00
☐ 9050 (M)		RICKY NELSON	12.00	29.00	25.00
☐ 9061 (M)		RICKY SINGS AGAIN	12.00	29.00	25.00
☐ 9082 (M)		SONGS BY RICKY	12.00	29.00	25.00
☐ 9122 (M)		MORE SONGS BY RICKY	10.00	25.00	22.50
☐ 9152 (M)		RICK IS 21	10.00	25.00	22.50
☐ 9167 (M)		ALBUM SEVEN BY RICK	10.00	25.00	22.50
☐ 9218 (M)		BEST SELLERS	8.00	21.00	18.00
☐ 9223 (M)		IT'S UP TO YOU	8.00	21.00	18.00
☐ 9232 (M)		MILLION SELLERS	8.00	21.00	18.00
☐ 9244 (M)		A LONG VACATION	8.00	21.00	18.00
☐ 9251 (M)		RICK NELSON SINGS FOR YOU	8.00	21.00	18.00
		STEREO REISSUES OF THE ABOVE HAVE HALF THE VALUE OF THE ORIGINAL MONO PRESSING			
☐ 4419 (M)	**DECCA**	FOR YOUR SWEET LOVE	7.00	17.00	15.00
☐ 74419 (S)		FOR YOUR SWEET LOVE	8.00	21.00	18.00
☐ 4479 (M)		RICK NELSON SINGS FOR YOU	7.00	17.00	15.00
☐ 74479 (S)		RICK NELSON SINGS FOR YOU	8.00	21.00	18.00
☐ 4559 (M)		THE VERY THOUGHT OF YOU	7.00	17.00	15.00
☐ 74459 (S)		THE VERY THOUGHT OF YOU	8.00	21.00	18.00
☐ 4608 (M)		SPOTLIGHT ON RICK	7.00	17.00	15.00
☐ 74608 (S)		SPOTLIGHT ON RICK	8.00	21.00	18.00
☐ 4660 (M)		BEST ALWAYS	7.00	17.00	15.00
☐ 74660 (S)		BEST ALWAYS	8.00	21.00	18.00
☐ 4678 (M)		LOVE AND KISSES	7.00	17.00	15.00
☐ 74678 (S)		LOVE AND KISSES	8.00	21.00	18.00
☐ 4837 (M)		BRIGHT LIGHTS AND COUNTRY MUSIC	7.00	17.00	15.00
☐ 74779 (S)		BRIGHT LIGHTS AND COUNTRY MUSIC	8.00	21.00	18.00
☐ 4837 (M)		COUNTRY FEVER	7.00	17.00	15.00
☐ 74837 (S)		COUNTRY FEVER	8.00	21.00	18.00
☐ 4944 (M)		ANOTHER SIDE OF RICK	7.00	17.00	15.00
☐ 74944 (S)		ANOTHER SIDE OF RICK	8.00	21.00	18.00
☐ 5014 (M)		PERSPECTIVE	7.00	17.00	15.00
☐ 75014 (S)		PERSPECTIVE	7.00	17.00	15.00
☐ 75162 (S)		RICK NELSON IN CONCERT	6.00	15.00	13.50
☐ 75236 (S)		RICK SINGS NELSON	6.00	15.00	13.50
☐ 75297 (S)		RUDY THE FIFTH	6.00	15.00	13.50
☐ 75391 (S)		GARDEN PARTY	6.00	15.00	13.50
☐ 3830 (S)	**MCA**	WINDFALL	6.00	15.00	13.50
☐ 4004 (S)		RICK NELSON COUNTRY	6.00	15.00	13.50

SANDY NELSON
SEE: RENEGADES

☐ 5	**ORIGINAL SOUND**	TEEN BEAT/BIG JUMP	3.50	6.00	4.35
☐ 5630	**IMPERIAL**	DRUM PARTY/ BIG NOISE FROM WINNETKA	3.25	5.50	4.00
☐ 5648		PARTY TIME/THE WIGGLE	3.25	5.50	4.00
☐ 5672		BOUNCY/LOST DREAMS	3.25	5.50	4.00
☐ 5708		COOL OPERATOR/JIVE TALK	3.25	5.50	4.00
☐ 5745		BIG NOISE FROM THE JUNGLE/ GET WITH IT	3.25	5.50	4.00
☐ 5775		LET THERE BE DRUMS/ QUITE A BEAT	3.00	5.00	3.65
☐ 5809		DRUMS ARE MY BEAT/ THE BIRTH OF THE BEAT	3.00	5.00	3.65
☐ 5829		DRUMMIN' UP A STORM/ DRUM STOMP	3.00	5.00	3.65

		Current Price Range		P/Y AVG
☐5860	ALL NIGHT LONG/ ROMPIN' AND STOMPIN'	3.00	5.00	3.65
☐5870	AND THEN THERE WERE DRUMS/ LIVE IT UP	3.00	5.00	3.65
☐5884	TEENAGE HOUSE PARTY/ DAY TRAIN	3.00	5.00	3.65
☐5904	LET THE FOUR WINDS BLOW/ BE BOP BABY	3.00	5.00	3.65
☐5932	OHH POO PAH DOO/FEEL SO GOOD	3.00	5.00	3.65
☐5940	YOU NAME IT/ALEXIS	3.00	5.00	3.65
☐5965	HERE WE GO AGAIN/JUST BULL	3.00	5.00	3.65
☐5988	CARAVAN/SANDY	3.00	5.00	3.65
☐66019	DRUM SHACK/KITTY'S THEME	3.00	5.00	3.65
☐66034	CASTLE ROCK/YOU DON'T SAY	3.00	5.00	3.65
☐66093	REACH FOR A STAR/CHOP CHOP	3.00	5.00	3.65
☐66127	DRUM A-GO-GO/CASHBAH	3.00	5.00	3.65
☐66017	LET THERE BE DRUMS '66/LAND OF A THOUSAND DRUMS	3.00	5.00	3.65
☐66146	A LOVER'S CONCERTO/ TREAT HER RIGHT	3.00	5.00	3.65
☐66209	PIPELINE/LET'S GO TRIPPIN'	3.50	5.75	4.00
☐66246	THE DRUMS GO ON/ LAWDY MISS CLAWDY	3.00	5.00	3.65
☐66253	PETER GUNN/ YOU GOT ME HUMMIN'	3.00	5.00	3.65
☐66284	MIDNIGHT MAGIC/ ALLIGATOR BOOGALOO	3.00	5.00	3.65
☐66350	REBIRTH OF THE BEAT/ THE LION IN WINTER	3.00	5.00	3.65
☐66375	MANHATTAN SPIRITUAL/ THE STRIPPER	3.00	5.00	3.65
☐66402	LET THERE BE DRUMS AND BRASS/LEAP FROG	3.00	5.00	3.65

SANDY NELSON—ALBUMS

			Current Price Range		P/Y AVG
☐9044 (M)	IMPERIAL	SANDY NELSON PLAYS TEEN BEAT	12.00	29.00	25.00
☐9136 (M)		HE'S A DRUMMER BOY	10.00	25.00	22.50
☐9159 (M)		LET THERE BE DRUMS	8.00	21.00	18.00
☐9168 (M)		DRUMS ARE MY BEAT	8.00	21.00	18.00
☐9198 (M)		DRUMMIN' UP A STORM	8.00	21.00	18.00
☐9203 (M)		ON THE WILD SIDE	8.00	21.00	18.00
☐9204 (M)		COMPELLING PERCUSSION-AND THEN THERE WERE DRUMS	8.00	21.00	18.00
☐9215 (M)		TEENAGE HOUSE PARTY	7.00	17.00	15.00
☐9224 (M)		THE BEST OF THE BEATS	7.00	17.00	15.00

STEREO REISSUES OF THE ABOVE HAVE HALF THE VALUE
OF THE ORIGINAL MONO PRESSINGS

		Current Price Range		P/Y AVG
☐9249 (M)	SANDY NELSON PLAYS	6.00	15.00	13.50
☐9258 (M)	BE TRUE TO YOUR SCHOOL	6.00	15.00	13.50
☐9278 (M)	TEEN BEAT '65	6.00	15.00	13.50
☐9283 (M)	DRUM DISCOTHEQUE	6.00	15.00	13.50

STEREO REISSUES OF THE ABOVE HAVE ⅔ THE VALUE
OF THE ORIGINAL MONO PRESSINGS

		Current Price Range		P/Y AVG
☐9298 (M)	BOSS BEAT	5.50	14.00	12.00
☐12298 (S)	BOSS BEAT	6.00	15.00	13.50
☐9314 (M)	SUPERDRUMS	5.50	14.00	12.00
☐12314 (S)	SUPERDRUMS	6.00	15.00	13.50
☐9329 (M)	BEAT THAT #!!@*DRUM	5.50	14.00	12.00
☐12329 (S)	BEAT THAT #!!@*DRUM	6.00	15.00	13.50
☐9367 (M)	BOOGALOO BEAT	5.50	14.00	12.00
☐12367 (S)	BOOGALOO BEAT	6.00	15.00	13.50
☐9400 (M)	ROCK AND ROLL REVIVAL	5.50	14.00	12.00
☐12400 (S)	ROCK AND ROLL REVIVAL	6.00	15.00	13.50
☐9451 (M)	GROOVY	5.50	14.00	12.00
☐12451 (S)	GROOVY	6.00	15.00	13.50

			Current Price Range		P/Y AVG

WILLIE NELSON
SEE: WAYLON JENNINGS AND WILLIE NELSON

☐ 45-628	**WILLIE NELSON**	NO PLACE FOR ME/LUMBERJACK	4.00	6.00	5.00
☐ 1084	**D**	THE STORM HAS JUST BEGUN/ MAN WITH THE BLUES	4.00	6.00	5.00
☐ 1131		WHAT A WAY TO LIVE/ MISERY MANSION	4.00	6.00	5.00
☐ 5702	**BETTY**	WHAT A WAY TO LIVE/ MISERY MANSION (reissue) ...	3.00	5.00	4.00
☐ 5703		THE STORM HAS JUST BEGUN/ MAN WITH THE BLUES (reissue)	3.00	5.00	4.00
☐ B-5000	**BELLAIRE**	NIGHT LIFE '76/ MAN WITH THE BLUES	2.25	4.50	3.00
☐ 55386	**LIBERTY**	THE PART WHERE I CRY/ MR. RECORD MAN	2.25	4.50	3.00
☐ 55403		CHAIN OF LOVE/WILLINGLY	2.25	4.50	3.00
☐ 55439		TOUCH ME/ WHERE MY HOUSE LIVES	2.25	4.50	3.00
☐ 55468		YOU DREAM ABOUT ME/ THIS IS MY DESTINY	2.25	4.50	3.00
☐ 55494		WAKE ME WHEN IT'S OVER/ THERE'S GONNA BE LOVE IN MY HOUSE TONIGHT	2.25	4.50	3.00
☐ 55532		HALF A MAN/THE LAST LETTER .	2.25	4.50	3.00
☐ 55591		TAKE MY WORD/ FEED IT A MEMORY	2.25	4.50	3.00
☐ 55638		YOU TOOK MY HAPPY AWAY/ HOW LONG IS FOREVER	2.25	4.50	3.00
☐ 55661		AM I BLUE/THERE'LL BE NO TEARDROPS TONIGHT ..	2.25	4.50	3.00
☐ 55697		RIVER BOY/OPPORTUNITY TO CRY	2.25	4.50	3.00
☐ 56143		RIGHT OR WRONG/I HOPE SO ...	2.25	4.50	3.00
☐ XW771-Y	**UNITED ARTISTS**	THE LAST LETTER/ THERE GOES A MAN	2.25	4.50	3.00
☐ XW1165		HELLO WALLS/THE LAST LETTER	2.25	4.50	3.00
☐ X1254-Y		BLUE MUST BE THE COLOR OF THE BLUES/THERE'LL BE NO TEARDROPS TONIGHT	2.25	4.50	3.00
☐ 45-855	**MONUMENT**	I NEVER CARED FOR YOU/ YOU LEFT ME	2.25	4.50	3.00
☐ WS4-03408		EVERYTHING'S BEAUTIFUL	2.25	4.50	3.00
☐ WS4-03781		YOU'RE GONNA LOVE YOURSELF IN THE MORNING	2.25	4.50	3.00
☐ 47-8484	**RCA**	PRETTY PAPER/WHAT A MERRY CHRISTMAS THIS COULD BE ..	2.25	4.50	3.00
☐ 47-8519		PERMANENTLY LONELY/ SHE'S NOT FOR YOU	2.25	4.50	3.00
☐ 47-8594		HEALING HANDS OF TIME/ ONE DAY AT A TIME	2.25	4.50	3.00
☐ 47-8682		AND SO WILL YOU MY LOVE/ I JUST CAN'T LET YOU SAY GOODBYE	2.25	4.50	3.00
☐ 47-8801		COLUMBUS STOCKADE BLUE/ HE SITS AT MY TABLE	2.25	4.50	3.00
☐ 47-8852		I'M STILL NOT OVER YOU/ I LOVE YOU BECAUSE	2.25	4.50	3.00
☐ 47-8933		SAN ANTONIO ROSE/ ONE IN A ROW	2.25	4.50	3.00
☐ 47-9029		PRETTY PAPER/WHAT A MERRY CHRISTMAS THIS WILL BE (reissue)	2.25	4.50	3.00
☐ 47-9100		THE PARTY'S OVER/MAKE WAY FOR A BETTER MAN	2.25	4.50	3.00

WILLIE NELSON

Born on April 30, 1933 in the small, farming town of Abbot, Texas, Willie Hugh Nelson and his older sister Bobbie were raised by their grandparents. Willie's grandmother wrote gospel songs and inspired young Willie to try his hand at them, too.

Shortly before he died, Willie's grandfather gave him his first guitar. At the tender age of ten, Willie was playing professionally in a Bohemian polka band making the princely sum of $8 a night. By thirteen, Willie had formed his own group much to his grandmother's disapproval.

Willie held a variety of jobs while trying to break into the glittery world of show business. In Nashville, the songwriter Hank Cochran heard Willie singing one night and signed him with Pamper Music Publishing Company. Ray Price then hired Willie as a bass player in his road show and adapted Willie's composition of "Night Life" as his theme song.

Eventually, Willie signed a recording contract of his own with Liberty Records and, later, RCA. In 1962, he hit the country charts with "Touch Me". He didn't return to the top ten until "Blue Eyes Crying In The Rain" in 1975. Since then, America has taken Willie Nelson to their national heart. His recordings are consistent best-sellers and he has ventured into movies as well.

				Current Price Range		P/Y AVG
☐ 47-9202			SOME OTHER WORLD BLACKJACK COUNTY CHAIN ..	2.25	4.50	3.00
☐ 47-9334			TO MAKE A LONG STORY SHORT/ SAN ANTONIO	2.25	4.50	3.00
☐ 47-9427			I'LL STAY AROUND/ LITTLE THINGS	2.25	4.50	3.00
☐ 47-9536			GOOD TIMES/DON'T YOU EVER GET TIRED OF HURTING ME ...	2.25	4.50	3.00
☐ 47-9605			SHE'S STILL GONE/ JOHNNY ONE TIME	2.25	4.50	3.00
☐ 47-9684			DON'T SAY LOVE OR NOTHING/ BRING ME SUNSHINE	2.25	4.50	3.00
☐ 47-0825			ONE IN A ROW/ GOOD TIMES (reissue)	2.25	4.50	3.00
☐ 47-9798			WHO DO I KNOW IN DALLAS/ ONCE MORE WITH FEELING ...	2.25	4.50	3.00
☐ 47-9903			LAYING MY BURDENS DOWN/ TRUTH NUMBER ONE	2.25	4.50	3.00
☐ 47-9931			PRETTY PAPER/WHAT A MERRY CHRISTMAS THIS COULD BE (reissue)	2.25	4.50	2.75
☐ 47-9951			I'M A MEMORY/I'M SO LONESOME I COULD CRY	2.25	4.50	2.75
☐ 47-9984			WHAT CAN YOU DO TO ME NOW/ KNEEL AT THE FEET OF JESUS .	2.25	4.50	2.75
☐ 0162			JIMMY'S ROAD/ NATURAL TO BE GONE	2.25	4.50	3.00
☐ 0542			YESTERDAY'S WINE/ ME AND PAUL	2.25	4.50	3.00
☐ 0635			THE WORDS DON'T THE PICTURE/ A MOMENT ISN'T VERY LONG .	2.25	4.50	3.00
☐ 0816			PHASES. STAGES. CIRCLES. CYCLES AND SCENES/ MOUNTAIN DEW	2.25	4.50	3.00
☐ 447-0891			THE PARTY'S OVER/ BRING ME SUNSHINE (reissue)	2.25	4.50	3.00
☐ 45-2968	*ATLANTIC*		SAD SONGS AND WALTZES/ SHOTGUN WILLIE	2.25	4.50	3.00
☐ 45-2979			STAY ALL NIGHT/ DEVIL IN A SLEEPING BAG	2.25	4.50	3.00
☐ 45-3008			HEAVEN AND HELL/I STILL CAN'T BELIEVE YOU'RE GONE	2.25	4.50	3.00
☐ 45-3020			BLOODY MARY MORNING/ PHASES AND STAGES	2.25	4.50	3.00
☐ 45-3228			PICK UP THE TEMPO/ SISTER'S COMING HOME	2.25	4.50	3.00
☐ 45-3334			HEAVEN AND HELL/I STILL CAN'T BELIEVE THAT YOU'RE GONE . .	2.25	4.50	3.00
☐ CY-4028			AFTER THE FIRE IS GONE/ WHISKEY RIVER	2.25	4.50	3.00
☐ OS-13178			SHOTGUN WILLIE/I STILL BELIEVE THAT YOU'RE GONE (reissue)	1.75	3.50	2.25
☐ OS-13179			BLOODY MARY MORNING/ AFTER THE FIRE IS GONE (reissue)	1.75	3.50	2.25
☐ 1961-7	*DOUBLE BAR*		PRIDE WINE AGAIN/IS THERE SOMETHING ON YOUR MIND ..	1.75	3.50	2.25
☐ 703	*LONE STAR*		WILL YOU REMEMBER ME/ END OF UNDERSTANDING	1.75	3.50	2.25
☐ 41313	*MCA-SONGIRD*		FAMILY BIBLE/IN GOD'S EYES ..	2.00	4.00	2.50
☐ 3-10176	*COLUMBIA*		BLUE EYES CRYING IN THE RAIN/ BANDERA	2.00	4.00	2.50
☐ 3-10275			REMEMBER ME/ TIME OF THE PREACHER	2.00	4.00	2.50

		Current Price Range		P/Y AVG
13-33326	BLUE EYES CRYING IN THE RAIN/ REMEMBER ME (reissue)	1.75	3.50	2.25
3-10327	I'D HAVE TO BE CRAZY/ AMAZING GRACE	1.75	3.50	2.25
3-10383	IF YOU'VE GOT THE MONEY I'VE GOT THE TIME/ THE SOUND IN YOUR MIND	1.75	3.50	2.25
3-10453	PRECIOUS MEMORIES/ UNCLOUDY DAY	1.75	3.50	2.25
13-33346	PRECIOUS MEMORIES/ UNCLOUDY DAY (reissue)	1.75	3.50	2.25
3-10480	LILY DALE/ PLEASE DON'T LEAVE ME	1.75	3.50	2.25
3-10588	I LOVE YOU A THOUSAND WAYS/ MOM AND DAD'S WALTZ	1.75	3.50	2.25
3-10704	GEORGIA ON MY MIND/ON THE SUNNY SIDE OF THE STREET	1.75	3.50	2.25
3-10834	UNCHAINED MELODY/ALL OF ME	1.75	3.25	2.00
3-10877	WHISKEY RIVER/ UNDER THE DOUBLE EAGLE	1.75	3.25	2.00
3-10929	SEPTEMBER SONG/DON'T GET AROUND MUCH MORE	1.75	4.25	2.00
3-11023	HEARTBREAK HOTEL/ SIOUX CITY SUE	1.75	3.25	2.00
13-33362	GEORGIA ON MY MIND/ BLUE SKIES (reissue)	1.75	3.25	2.00
1-11126	HELP ME MAKE IT THROUGH THE NIGHT/THE PILGRIM: CHAPTER 33	1.75	3.25	2.00
1-11186	MY HEROS HAVE ALWAYS BEEN COWBOYS	1.75	3.25	2.00
1-11257	MIDNIGHT RIDER/SO YOU THINK YOU'RE A COWBOY	1.75	3.25	2.00
1-11329	FADED LOVE/ THIS COLD WAR WITH YOU	1.75	3.25	2.00
1-11351	ON THE ROAD AGAIN	1.75	3.25	2.00
11-11405	DON'T YOU EVER GET TIRED OF HURTING ME/FUNNY HOW TIME SLIPS AWAY	1.75	3.25	2.00
11-14184	ANGEL FLYING TOO CLOSE TO THE GROUND/I GUESS I'VE COME TO LIVE HERE	1.75	3.25	2.00
13-33403	ALL OF ME/ WHISKEY RIVER (reissue)	1.75	3.25	2.00
13-33404	HELP ME MAKE IT THROUGH THE NIGHT/HEARTBREAT HOTEL (reissue)	1.75	3.25	2.00
11-020000	MONA LISA/TWINKLE. TWINKLE LITTLE STAR	1.75	3.25	2.00
18-02187	I'M GONNA SIT RIGHT DOWN AND WRITE MYSELF A LETTER/ OVER THE RAINBOW	1.75	3.25	2.00
18-02558	UNCLOUDY DAY/ HEARTACHES OF A FOOL	1.75	3.25	2.00
18-02681	OLD FRIENDS/WHEN A HOUSE IS NOT A HOME	1.75	3.25	2.00
53-02741	ALWAYS ON MY MIND/ THE PARTY'S OVER	1.75	3.25	2.00
18-03073	PERMANENTLY LONELY/ LET IT BE ME	1.75	3.25	2.00
13-03123	MONA LISA/ANGEL FLYING TOO CLOSE TO THE GROUND (reissue)	1.75	3.25	2.00

			Current Price Range		P/Y AVG
☐ 13-03124		MIDNIGHT RIDER/ HEARTBREAK HOTEL (reissue) .	1.75	3.25	2.00
☐ 38-03213		SLOWLY/BACK STREET AFFAIR .	1.75	3.25	2.00
☐ 38-03385		THE LAST THING I NEEDED/ OLD FORDS AND A NATURAL STONE	1.75	3.25	2.00
☐ 38-03674		LITTLE OLD FASHIONED KARMA/ BEER BARREL POLKA	1.75	3.25	2.00
☐ 34-03494	EPIC	REASONS TO QUIT/HALF A MAN .	1.75	3.25	2.00
☐ 34-03842		PONCHO AND LEFTY/ OPPORTUNITY TO CRY	1.75	3.25	2.00
		WILLIE NELSON—ALBUMS			
☐ LST-7238	LIBERTY	. . . AND THEN I WROTE	12.00	17.00	14.00
☐ LST-7308		HERE'S WILLIE NELSON	12.00	17.00	14.00
☐ LN-10013		COUNTRY WILLIE	10.00	15.00	12.00
☐ LN-10118		THE BEST OF WILLIE NELSON . . .	10.00	15.00	12.00
☐ SUS-5138	SUNSET	HELLO WALLS	9.00	13.00	11.00
☐ LA086-F	UNITED ARTISTS	THE BEST OF WILLIE NELSON . . .	8.00	11.00	8.00
☐ LA410-G		COUNTRY WILLIE	8.00	11.00	8.00
☐ LA574-H2		TEXAS COUNTRY	8.00	11.00	8.00
☐ LA930-H		THERE'LL BE NO TEARDDROPS TONIGHT	8.00	11.00	8.00
☐ SPC-3584	PICKWICK	HELLO WALLS (reissue)	8.00	11.00	8.00
☐ ACL-0326		COUNTRY WINNERS	8.00	11.00	8.00
☐ ACL-0705		SPOTLIGHT ON WILLIE NELSON . .	8.00	11.00	8.00
☐ ACL-7018		COLUMBUS STOCKADE BLUES . .	8.00	11.00	8.00
☐ SD-7262	ATLANTIC	SHOTGUN WILLIE	8.00	11.00	8.00
☐ SD-7291		PHASES AND STAGES	8.00	11.00	8.00
☐ LSP-3418	RCA	COUNTRY WILLIE— HIS OWN SONGS	8.00	11.00	8.00
☐ LSP-3528		COUNTRY FAVORITES — WILLIE NELSON STYLE	8.00	11.00	8.00
☐ LSP-3659		COUNTRY MUSIC CONCERR	8.00	11.00	8.00
☐ LSP-3748		MAY WAY FOR WILLIE NELSON . .	7.00	10.00	8.00
☐ LSP-3858		THE PARTY'S OVER	7.00	10.00	7.50
☐ LSP-3937		TEXAS IN MY SOUL	7.00	10.00	7.50
☐ LSP-4057		GOOD TIMES	7.00	10.00	7.50
☐ LSP-4111		MY OWN PECULIAR WAY	7.00	10.00	7.50
☐ LSP-4294		BOTH SIDES NOW	7.00	10.00	7.50
☐ LSP-4404		LAYING MY BURDENS DOWN	7.00	10.00	7.50
☐ LSP-4489		WILLIE NELSON AND FAMILY . . .	5.00	10.00	7.00
☐ LSP-4568		YESTERDAY'S WINE	5.00	10.00	7.00
☐ LSP-4653		THE WORDS DON'T FIT THE PICTURE	5.00	10.00	7.00
☐ ANLI-1102		YESTERDAY'S WINE (reissue) . . .	7.00	10.00	8.00
☐ ANLI-1487		WILLIE NELSONLIVE	5.00	9.00	7.00
☐ ANLI-2210		WILLIE	5.00	9.00	7.00
☐ ANLI-2686		BEFORE HIS TIME	5.00	9.00	7.00
☐ ANLI-3243		SWEET MEMORIES	5.00	9.00	7.00
☐ ANLI-4045		THE MINSTREL MAN	5.00	9.00	7.00
☐ ANLI-4420		THE BEST OF WILLIE	5.00	9.00	7.00
☐ KC-33482	COLUMBIA	RED HEADED STRANGER	4.05	10.00	6.50
☐ KC-34092		THE SOUND IN YOUR MIND	4.50	10.00	6.50
☐ KC-31122		THE TROUBLEMAKER	4.50	10.00	6.50
☐ KC-34695		TO LEFTY FROM WILLIE	4.50	10.00	6.50
☐ JC-35305		STARDUST	4.50	8.00	6.00
☐ KC2-36542		WILLIE AND FAMILY LIVE	4.50	8.00	6.00
☐ KC2-36188		ONE FOR THE ROAD	4.50	8.00	6.00
☐ JC-36188		WILLIE NELSON SINGS KRISTOFFERSON	4.50	8.00	6.00
☐ JC-36189		PAPER PAPER	4.50	8.00	6.00
☐ JS-36327		THE ELECTRIC HORSEMAN	4.50	8.00	6.00
☐ JC-36476		SAN ANTONIO ROSE	4.50	8.00	6.00

			Current Price Range		P/Y AVG
☐ S2-36752		HONEYSUCKLE ROSE	4.50	8.00	6.00
☐ FC-36883		SOMEWHERE OVER THE RAINBOW	4.50	8.00	6.00
☐ KC2-37542		WILLIE NELSON'S GREATEST HITS	4.50	8.00	6.00
☐ FC-37951		ALWAYS ON MY MIND	6.00	10.00	7.00
☐ PC-38013		OLD FRIENDS	4.50	8.00	5.00
☐ PC-38095		IN THE JAILHOUSE NOW	4.50	8.00	5.00
☐ QC-38248		TOUGHER THAN LEATHER	4.50	8.00	5.00

NEONS

☐ 444	**TETRA**	ANGEL FACE/KISS ME QUICKLY	7.00	13.00	11.00
☐ 4449		ROAD TO ROMANCE/ MY CHICKADEE	12.00	21.00	18.00

NERVOUS NORVUS
SEE: FOUR JOKERS

☐ 15470	**DOT**	TRANFUSION/DIG	4.00	6.50	5.00
☐ 15485		APE CALL/ WILD DOG OF KENTUCKY	4.50	7.50	6.00
☐ 15500		THE FANG/THE BULLFROG HOP	7.00	13.00	11.00
		THE ABOVE FIRST-ISSUES WERE ON A MAROON LABEL			
☐ 117	**EMBEE**	STONAGE WOO/I LIKE GIRLS	9.50	17.00	15.00

MIKE NESMITH
SEE: MICHAEL BLESSING, MONKEES

☐ 1001	**EDAN**	JUST A LITTLE LOVE/ CURSION TERRACE	22.00	38.00	27.00

NEWBEATS

☐ 1269	**HICKORY**	BREAD AND BUTTER/ TOUGH LITTLE BUGGY	3.00	5.00	3.65
☐ 1282		EVERYTHING'S ALRIGHT/ PINK DALLY RUE	3.00	5.00	3.65
☐ 1290		BREAK AWAY (FROM THAT BOY)/ HEY-O. DADDY-O	3.00	5.00	3.65
☐ 1305		THE BIRDS ARE FOR THE BEES/ BETTER WATCH YOUR STEP	3.00	5.00	3.65
☐ 1332		RUN BABY RUN/ MEAN WOOLIE WILLY	3.00	5.00	3.65
☐ 1336		SHAKE HANDS/ TOO SWEET TO BE FORGOTTEN	3.00	5.00	3.65
☐ 1408		BIRD DOG/EVIL EVA	3.00	5.00	3.65
☐ 1422		MY YESTERDAY LOVE/ PATENT ON LOVE	3.00	5.00	3.65
☐ 1436		SO FINE/TOP SECRET	3.00	5.00	3.65
☐ 1467		IT'S REALLY GOODBYE/ HIDE THE MOON	3.00	5.00	3.65
☐ 1485		YOU & ME/DON'T TURN LOOSE	2.75	4.50	3.00
☐ 1496		BAD DREAMS/THE SWINGER	3.00	5.00	3.65
		NEWBEATS—ALBUMS			
☐ 120 (M)	**HICKORY**	BREAD AND BUTTER	8.00	21.00	18.00
☐ 122 (M)		BIG BEAT SOUNDS	8.00	21.00	18.00
☐ 128 (M)		RUN BABY RUN	7.00	17.00	15.00

NICKY & THE NACKS

☐ 108	**BARRY**	THAT OLD BLACK MAGIC/ THE NIGHT	13.00	35.00	32.00

NICKIE AND THE NITELITES

☐ 55155	**BRUNSWICK**	TELL ME YOU CARE/I'M LONELY	12.00	21.00	18.00

NICKY AND THE NOBLES

☐ 1098	**END**	SCHOOL BELLS/ SCHOOL DAY CRUSH	5.50	11.00	9.00

			Current Price Range		P/Y AVG
☐5039	**GONE**	SCHOOL BELLS/			
		SCHOOL DAY CRUSH	4.50	7.50	6.00
☐1	**TIMES SQUARE**	TING-A-LING/			
		POOR ROCK 'N' ROLL	4.50	7.50	6.00
☐12		CRIME DON'T PAY/DARKNESS ..	4.50	7.50	6.00
☐33		WHY BE A FOOL/THE SEARCH ...	3.75	6.00	4.50
☐37		SCHOOL BELLS/			
		SCHOOL DAY CRUSH	3.75	6.00	4.50

NIGHTCRAWLERS

☐1012	**LEE**	LITTLE BLACK EGG/IF I WERE YOU	5.00	8.50	7.00
☐709	**KAPP**	LITTLE BLACK EGG/IF I WERE YOU	3.00	5.00	3.50
☐746		BASKET OF FLOWERS/			
		WASHBOARD	3.00	5.00	3.50
☐826		TODAY I'M HAPPY/			
		MY BUTTERFLY	3.00	5.00	3.50

NIGHTCRAWLERS—ALBUM

☐1520 (M)	**KAPP**	THE LITTLE BLACK EGG	9.00	25.00	22.50

NINO AND THE EBB TIDES

☐405	**RECORTE**	PUPPY LOVE/YOU MAKE ME			
		WANT TO ROCK AND ROLL	9.50	17.50	15.00
☐408		PURPLE SHADOWS/THE REAL			
		MEANING OF CHRISTMAS	12.00	21.00	18.00
☐409		I'M CONFESSIN'/			
		TELL THE WORLD I DO	9.50	17.50	15.00
☐123	**MR. PEEKE**	TONIGHT/NURSERY RHYMES ...	4.50	7.50	6.00
☐162	**MADISON**	THOSE OLDIES BUT GOODIES/			
		DON'T RUN AWAY	4.50	7.50	6.00
☐166		JUKE BOX SATURDAY NIGHT/			
		I'LL FALL IN LOVE	3.75	6.00	4.50

NITTY GRITTY DIRT BAND

☐55948	**LIBERTY**	BUY FOR ME THE RAIN/			
		CANDY MAN	3.25	5.50	4.00
☐55982		TRULY RIGHT/			
		THE TEDDY BEAR'S PICNIC ...	3.25	5.50	4.00
☐56045		THESE DAYS/COLLEGIANA	3.25	5.50	4.00
☐56134		SOME OF SHELLY'S BLUES/			
		YUKON RAILROAD	3.25	5.50	4.00
☐56197		RAVE ON/THE CURE	3.25	5.50	4.00
☐56159		MR. BOJANGLES/UNCLE CHARLIE			
		INTERVIEW #2 - SPANISH			
		FANDANGO	2.50	4.00	2.50

NITTY GRITTY DIRT BAND—ALBUMS

☐7501 (S)	**LIBERTY**	THE NITTY GRITTY DIRT BAND ...	8.00	21.00	18.00
☐7516 (S)		RICOCHET	7.00	17.00	15.00
☐7540 (S)		RARE JUNK	6.00	15.00	13.50
☐7611 (S)		ALIVE......................	6.00	15.00	13.50
☐7642 (S)		UNCLE CHARLIE AND HIS			
		DOG TEDDY	5.50	14.00	12.00

JACK NITZSCHE

☐20202	**REPRISE**	THE LONELY SURFER/			
		SONG FOR A SUMMER NIGHT ..	3.25	5.50	4.00
☐20225		RUMBLE/			
		THEME FOR A BROKEN HEART .	3.25	5.50	4.00
☐20262		THE LAST RACE/THE MAN WITH			
		THE GOLDEN ARM	3.25	5.50	4.00

JACK NITZSCHE—ALBUMS

☐6101 (M)	**REPRISE**	THE LONELY SURFER	8.00	21.00	18.00
☐6101 (S)		THE LONELY SURFER	12.00	29.00	25.00
☐6115 (M)		HITS OF THE BEATLES	8.00	21.00	18.00
☐6115 (S)		HITS OF THE BEATLES	9.00	25.00	22.50

			Current Price Range		P/Y AVG
☐ 6200 (M)		CHOPIN '66	7.00	17.00	15.00
☐ 6200 (S)		CHOPIN '66	8.00	21.00	18.00
☐ 2092 (M)		ST. GILES CRIPPLEGATE	7.00	17.00	15.00
☐ 2092 (S)		ST. GILES CRIPPLEGATE	8.00	21.00	18.00

NOBELLS

☐ 101	MAR	CRYING OVER YOU/SEARCHIN' FOR MY LOVE	13.00	31.00	27.00

NUTMEGS
SEE: RAJAHS

128	LANA	STORY UNTOLD/ BEAUTIFUL DREAMER	10.00	20.00	13.00
☐ 905	NIGHTRAIN	SHIFTING SANDS/ TAKE ME AND MAKE ME	6.00	10.00	6.50
☐ 162	PYRAMID	OVER THE RAINBOW/ IN THE STILL OF THE NIGHT ...	5.00	9.00	5.50
☐ 6	TIMES SQUARE	LET ME TELL YOU/HELLO	5.00	9.00	5.50
☐ 14		THE WAY LOVE SHOULD BE/ WIDE HOOP SKIRTS	5.00	8.50	6.50
☐ 27		DOWN IN MEXICO/ MY SWEET DREAMS	5.00	8.50	6.50
☐ 103		YOU'RE CRYING/WA-DO-WA	5.00	8.00	5.25

THE NYLONS

☐ C-323	CBS	SOME PEOPLE (SONG FOR SHEENAN)/MIRAGE	8.00	15.00	11.00

O

OASIS

☐ 11372	ARCADE	WHEN I WOKE UP THIS MORN-ING/MY IMAGINATION	8.00	15.00	11.00

OCTAVES

☐ 1001	VAL	MOMBO CAROLYN/ YOU'RE TOO YOUNG	8.50	18.00	16.00

OLYMPICS
SEE: MARATHONS, WALTER WARD AND THE CHALLENGERS

☐ 1508	DEMON	WESTERN MOVIES/WELL	3.50	6.00	4.35
☐ 1512		DANCE WITH THE TEACHER/ EV'RYBODY NEEDS LOVE	3.50	6.00	4.35
☐ 1514		CHICKEN/YOUR LOVE	3.50	6.00	4.35
☐ 562	ARVEE	(BABY) HULLY GULLY/ PRIVATE EYE	3.25	5.50	4.00
☐ 595		BIG BOY PETE/THE SLOP	3.25	5.50	4.00
☐ 5006		SHIMMY LIKE KATE/ WORKIN' HARD	3.25	5.50	4.00
☐ 5020		DANCE BY THE LIGHT OF THE MOON/DODGE CITY	3.25	5.50	4.00
☐ 5023		LITTLE PEDRO/BULL FIGHT	3.25	5.50	4.00
☐ 5031		DOOLEY/STAY WHERE YOU ARE .	3.25	5.50	4.00
☐ 5044		THE STOMP/ MASH THEM 'TATERS	3.25	5.50	4.00
☐ 5051		THE TWIST/EVERYBODY LIKES TO CHA CHA CHA	3.25	5.50	4.00
☐ 5056		BABY IT'S HOT/THE SCOTCH ...	3.00	5.00	3.65
☐ 5073		WHAT'D I SAY/(PT. 2)	3.00	5.00	3.65
☐ 6501		BIG BOY PETE '65/ STAY WHERE YOU ARE	3.00	5.00	3.65

			Current Price Range		P/Y AVG
☐ 1718	*TITAN*	CHICKEN/COOL SHORT	4.00	7.00	4.85
☐ 106	*TRI DISC*	THE BOUNCE/FIREWORKS	3.00	5.00	3.65
☐ 107		DANCIN' HOLIDAY/ DO THE SLAUSON SHUFFE	3.00	5.00	3.65
☐ 110		BOUNCE AGAIN/ A NEW DANCIN' PARTNER	3.00	5.00	3.65
☐ 112		THE BROKEN HIP/SO GOODBYE	3.00	5.00	3.65
☐ 104	*DUO DISC*	THE BOOGLER/(PT. 2)	3.25	5.50	4.00
☐ 105		RETURN OF BIG BOY PETE/ RETURN OF THE WATUSI	3.25	5.50	4.00
☐ 2010	*LOMA*	RAINING IN MY HEART/ I'M GOING HOME	3.00	5.00	3.65
☐ 2013		GOOD LOVIN'/OLYMPIC SHUFFLE	3.00	5.00	3.65
☐ 2017		BABY I'M YOURS/ NO MORE WILL I CRY	3.00	5.00	3.65
☐ 5504	*MIRWOOD*	SECRET AGENTS/WE GO TOGETHER (PRETTY BABY)	3.00	5.00	3.65
☐ 5513		MINE EXCLUSIVELY/ SECRET AGENTS	3.00	5.00	3.65
☐ 5523		BABY, DO THE PHILLY DOG/ WESTERN MOVIES	3.00	5.00	3.65
☐ 5529		I'LL DO A LITTLE BIT MORE/ THE SAME OLD THING	3.00	5.00	3.65
☐ 5533		HULLY GULLY/BIG BOY PETE	3.00	5.00	3.65
☐ 6003	*PARKWAY*	LOOKIN' FOR A LOVE/ GOOD TIMES	3.00	5.00	3.65
		OLYMPICS—EP			
☐ 423	*ARVEE*	DOIN' THE HULLY GULLY	8.25	14.00	12.00
		OLYMPICS—ALBUMS			
☐ 423 (M)	*ARVEE*	DOIN' THE HULLY GULLY	9.00	29.00	25.00
☐ 424 (M)		DANCE BY THE LIGHT OF THE MOON	8.00	21.00	18.00
☐ 429 (M)		PARTY TIME	8.00	21.00	18.00
☐ 1001 (M)	*TRI DISC*	DO THE BOUNCE	7.00	17.00	15.00
☐ 7003 (M)	*MIRWOOD*	SOMETHING OLD, SOMETHING NEW	5.50	14.00	12.00
		YOKO ONO			
☐ 1839	*APPLE*	MRS. LENNON/ MIDSUMMER NEW YORK	4.00	7.00	4.85
☐ 1853		NOW OR NEVER/MOVE ON FAST	4.00	7.00	4.85
☐ 1859		DEATH OF SANTANA/YANG YANG	4.00	7.00	4.85
☐ 1867		WOMAN POWER/MEN, MEN, MEN	5.00	8.50	6.00
		YOKO ONO—ALBUMS			
☐ 3373 (S)	*APPLE*	YOKO ONO/PLASTIC ONO BAND	9.00	23.00	14.00
☐ 3380 (S)		FLY	9.00	23.00	14.00
☐ 3399 (S)		APPROXIMATELY INFINITE UNIVERSE	10.00	26.00	17.00
☐ 3412 (S)		FEELING THE SPACE	10.00	26.00	17.00
		ROY ORBISON			
☐ 101	*JE-WEL*	OOBY DOOBY/ TRYING TO GET TO YOU	175.00	295.00	210.00

THE JE-WEL VERSION DIFFERS FROM THE SUN VERSION OF "OOBY DOOBY"
SEE SUN 45s

☐ 7381	*RCA*	SWEET AND INNOCENT/ SEEMS TO ME	8.25	14.00	12.00
☐ 7447		ALMOST EIGHTEEN/JOLIE	8.25	14.00	12.00
☐ 409	*MONUMENT*	PAPER BOY/WITH THE BUG	4.50	7.50	6.00
☐ 412		UP TOWN/PRETTY ONE	3.50	6.00	4.35
☐ 421		ONLY THE LONELY/HERE COMES THAT SONG AGAIN	3.25	5.50	4.00
☐ 425		BLUE ANGEL/ TODAY'S TEARDROPS	3.25	5.50	4.00

ROY ORBISON

Roy Orbison doesn't sing the blues; however, if anybody were born to sing them, it is he. During the late 1960s, Roy's string of hits subsided. His wife Claudette died in a motorcycle crash before Ray's eyes. Shortly after that, two of his three children perished in a house fire. In 1978, Orbison underwent open-heart surgery.

He was born on April 21, 1936, in the Texas town of Vernon. His family later moved to Wink, where Roy learned the guitar as he grew into adolescence. He attended North Texas State College. There classmate Pat Boone (the future superstar) encouraged geology-major Orbison to try for a singing career. Roy took Pat's advice.

He formed the Teen Kings, played some local gigs and cut a single on Je-Wel called "Ooby Dooby". (It was co-written by a college professor of English.) Soon Roy and his band landed a Sun Records contract. There they cut an updated version of "Ooby Dooby" and it became a moderate hit.

With no success on RCA, Roy eventually struck it rich on Monument Records. In all, he recorded nine Top 10 winners; two hit number one. Roy later signed with MGM but he was never able to recapture those days of glory on Monument when the hits flowed non-stop and all ahead appeared good.

			Current Price Range		P/Y AVG
433		I'M HURTIN'/			
		I CAN'T STOP LOVING YOU	3.25	5.50	4.00
438		RUNNING SCARED/LOVE HURTS .	3.00	5.25	3.85
447		CRYING/CANDY MAN	3.00	5.25	3.85
456		DREAM BABY/THE ACTRESS	3.00	5.25	3.85
461		THE CROWD/MAMA	3.00	5.25	3.85
467		LEAH/WORKIN' FOR THE MAN ..	3.00	5.25	3.85
806		IN DREAMS/SHAHDAROBA	3.00	5.25	3.85
815		FALLING/DISTANT DRUMS	3.00	5.25	3.85
824		MEAN WOMAN BLUES/			
		BLUE BAYOU	3.00	5.25	3.85
830		PRETTY PAPER/			
		BEAUTIFUL DREAMER	3.00	5.25	3.85
837		IT'S OVER/INDIAN WEDDING	3.00	5.25	3.85
861		OH, PRETTY WOMAN/			
		YO TE AMO MARIA	3.00	5.25	3.85
873		GOODNIGHT/ONLY WITH YOU ...	3.00	5.25	3.85
891		(SAY) YOU'RE MY GIRL/			
		SLEEPY HOLLOW	3.00	5.25	3.85
906		LET THE GOOD TIMES ROLL/			
		DISTANT DRUMS	3.00	5.25	3.85
939		LANA/OUR SUMMER SONG	3.00	5.25	3.85
8690		BELINDA/NO CHAIN AT ALL	3.00	5.25	3.85
200		(I'M A) SOUTHERN MAN/			
		BORN TO LOVE ME	3.00	5.25	3.85
215		DRIFTING AWAY/			
		UNDER SUSPICION	3.00	5.25	3.85
11386	**MGM**	RIDE AWAY/WONDERING	2.75	4.75	3.50
13410		CRAWLING BACK/IF YOU CAN'T			
		SAY SOMETHING NICE	2.75	4.75	3.50
13446		BREAKIN' UP IS BREAKIN' MY			
		HEART/WAIT	2.75	4.75	3.50
13498		TWINKLE TOES/			
		WHERE IS TOMORROW?	2.75	4.75	3.50
13549		TOO SOON TO KNOW/YOU'LL			
		NEVER BE SIXTEEN AGAIN	2.75	4.75	3.50
13634		COMMUNICATION BREAKDOWN/			
		GOING BACK TO GLORIA	2.75	4.75	3.50
13685		MEMORIES/SO GOOD	2.75	4.75	3.50
13759		SWEET DREAMS/			
		GOING BACK TO GLORIA	2.75	4.75	3.50
13760		THERE WON'T BE MANY COMING			
		HOME/YOU'LL NEVER			
		BE SIXTEEN AGAIN	2.75	4.75	3.50
13764		CRY SOFTLY, LONELY ONE/			
		PISTOLERO	2.75	4.75	3.50
13817		HERE COMES THE RAIN, BABY/			
		SHE	2.75	4.75	3.50
13889		BORN TO BE LOVED BY YOU/			
		SHY AWAY	2.75	4.75	3.50
13950		WALK ON/FLOWERS...........	2.75	4.75	3.50
13991		HEARTACHE/SUGARMAN	2.75	4.75	3.50
14039		SOUTHBOUND JERICHO			
		TURNPIKE/MY FRIEND	2.75	4.75	3.50
14079		PENNY ARCADE/			
		TENNESSEE OWNS MY SOUL ..	2.75	4.75	3.50
14105		SHE CHEATS ON ME/			
		HOW DO YOU START OVER? ...	2.75	4.75	3.50
14121		SO YOUNG/IF I HAD A			
		WOMAN LIKE YOU	2.75	4.75	3.50
14293		LAST NIGHT/CLOSE AGAIN	2.75	4.75	3.50
14358		CHANGES/GOD LOVE YOU	2.75	4.75	3.50
11413		REMEMBER THE GOOD/			
		HARLEM WOMAN	2.75	4.75	3.50

			Current Price Range		P/Y AVG
☐ 14441			MEMPHIS/I CAN READ		
			BETWEEN THE LINES	2.75	4.57	3.50
☐ 73652	**MERCURY**	HUNG UP ON YOU/			
			SPANISH NIGHTS	2.75	4.75	3.50
		ROY ORBISON—ALBUMS			
☐ 1260 (M)	**SUN**	ROY ORBISON AT THE			
			ROCKHOUSE	35.00	68.00	60.00
☐ 4002 (M)	**MONUMENT**	LONELY AND BLUE	17.00	39.00	35.00
☐ 14002 (S)		LONELY AND BLUE	22.00	65.00	60.00
☐ 4007 (M)		CRYING	10.00	25.00	22.50
☐ 14007 (S)		CRYING	19.00	39.00	35.00
☐ 4009 (M)		GREATEST HITS..............	10.00	25.00	22.50
☐ 14009 (S)		GREATEST HITS..............	17.00	39.00	35.00
☐ 8003 (M)		IN DREAMS	10.00	25.00	22.50
☐ 18003 (S)		IN DREAMS	17.00	39.00	35.00
☐ 8023 (M)		EARLY ORBISON	10.00	25.00	22.50
☐ 18023 (S)		EARLY ORBISON	15.00	34.00	30.00
☐ 8024 (M)		MORE OF ROY ORBISON'S			
			GREATEST HITS	10.00	25.00	22.50
☐ 18024 (S)		MORE OF ROY ORBISON'S			
			GREATEST HITS	15.00	34.00	30.00
☐ 8035 (M)		ORBISONGS..................	10.00	25.00	22.50
☐ 18035 (S)		ORBISONGS..................	15.00	34.00	30.00
☐ 8045 (M)		THE VERY BEST OF ROY ORBISON	8.00	21.00	18.00
☐ 18045 (S)		THE VERY BEST OF ROY ORBISON	12.00	29.00	25.00
☐ 4308 (M)	**MGM**	THERE IS ONLY ONE			
			ROY ORBISON	7.00	17.00	15.00
☐ 4308 (S)		THERE IS ONLY ONE			
			ROY ORBISON	9.00	25.00	22.50
☐ 4322 (M)		THE ORBISON WAY	7.00	17.00	15.00
☐ 4322 (S)		THE ORBISON WAY	9.00	25.00	22.50
☐ 4379 (M)	**MERCURY**	CLASSIC ROY ORBISON	6.00	15.00	13.50
☐ 4379 (S)		CLASSIC ROY ORBISON	7.00	17.00	15.00
☐ 4424 (M)		ROY ORBISON SINGS DON GIBSON.	6.00	15.00	13.50
☐ 4424 (S)		ROY ORBISON SINGS DON GIBSON.	7.00	17.00	15.00
☐ 4514 (M)		CRY SOFTLY. LONELY ONE	6.00	15.00	13.50
☐ 4514 (S)		CRY SOFTLY. LONELY ONE	7.00	17.00	15.00
☐ 4683 (S)		HANK WILLIAMS THE			
			ROY ORBISON WAY	5.50	14.00	12.00
☐ 4835 (S)		ROY ORBISON SINGS	5.50	14.00	12.00
☐ 4934 (S)		MILESTONES.................	5.50	14.00	12.00

ORIOLES
FEATURED: SONNY TILL
NOTE: PRIOR TO JUBILEE 5045, ORIOLES RELEASES WERE
AVAILABLE ONLY ON 78 RPM DISCS

☐ 5045	**JUBILEE**	OH HOLY NIGHT/			
			THE LORD'S PRAYER	120.00	235.00	150.00
☐ 5051		I MISS YOU SO/			
			YOU ARE MY FIRST LOVE	95.00	175.00	125.00
☐ 5055		PAL OF MINE/HAPPY GO LUCKY			
			LOCAL BLUES	95.00	175.00	125.00
☐ 5057		WOULD I LOVE YOU/			
			WHEN YOU'RE A LONG. LONG			
			WAY FROM HOME	95.00	175.00	125.00
☐ 5061		I'M JUST A FOOL IN LOVE/			
			HOLD ME! SQUEEZE ME!	95.00	175.00	125.00
☐ 5065		DON'T TELL HER WHAT'S			
			HAPPENED TO ME/			
			BABY. PLEASE DON'T GO	95.00	175.00	125.00
☐ 5071		WHEN YOU'RE NOT AROUND/			
			HOW BLIND CAN YOU BE?	95.00	175.00	125.00
☐ 5074		TRUST IN ME/SHRIMP BOATS ...	95.00	175.00	125.00

			Current Price Range		P/Y AVG
☐ 5082		IT'S OVER BECAUSE WE'RE THROUGH/WAITING	95.00	175.00	125.00
☐ 5084		GETTIN' TIRED, TIRED, TIRED/ BARFLY	95.00	175.00	125.00
☐ 5092		DON'T CRY BABY/SEE SEE RIDER	95.00	175.00	125.00
☐ 5102		YOU BELONG TO ME/I DON'T WANT TO TAKE A CHANCE	85.00	150.00	98.00
☐ 5107		TILL WHEN/I MISS YOU SO	85.00	150.00	98.00
☐ 5108		TEARDROPS ON MY PILLOW/ HOLD ME, THRILL ME, KISS ME	85.00	150.00	98.00
☐ 5115		BAD LITTLE GIRL/DEM DAYS (ARE GONE FOREVER)	85.00	150.00	98.00
☐ 5120		I COVER THE WATERFRONT/ ONE MORE TIME	85.00	150.00	98.00
☐ 5122		CRYING IN THE CHAPEL/DON'T YOU THINK I OUGHT TO KNOW	20.00	35.00	23.00
☐ 5127		IN THE MISSION OF ST. AUGUSTINE/WRITE AND TELL ME WHY	23.00	40.00	28.00
☐ 5134		THERE'S NO ONE BUT YOU/ ROBE OF CALVARY	23.00	40.00	28.00
☐ 5137		SECRET LOVE/ DON'T GO TO STRANGERS	23.00	40.00	28.00
☐ 5143		MAYBE YOU'LL BE THERE/ DROWNING EVERY HOPE I EVER HAD	23.00	39.00	27.00
☐ 5154		IN THE CHAPEL IN THE MOONLIGHT/THANK THE LORD! THANK THE LORD!	19.00	33.00	23.00
☐ 5161		IF YOU BELIEVE/LONGING	15.00	26.00	19.00
☐ 5172		RUNAROUND/COUNT YOUR BLESSINGS INSTEAD OF SHEEP	15.00	26.00	19.00
☐ 5177		I LOVE YOU MOSTLY/ FAIR EXCHANGE	15.00	26.00	19.00
☐ 5189		I NEED YOU BABY/THAT'S WHEN THE GOOD LORD WILL SMILE	15.00	26.00	19.00
☐ 5221		PLEASE SING MY BLUES TONIGHT/ MOODY OVER YOU	15.00	26.00	19.00
☐ 5231		ANGEL/DON'T GO TO STRANGERS	15.00	26.00	19.00
☐ 5363		TELL ME SO/AT NIGHT	5.50	10.50	9.00
☐ 5384		THE FIRST OF SUMMER/ COME ON HOME	5.50	10.50	9.00
☐ 6001		CRYING IN THE CHAPEL/ FORGIVE AND FORGET	3.25	5.50	4.00
☐ 196	**VEE JAY**	HAPPY TILL THE LETTER/ I JUST GOT LUCKY	9.50	17.00	15.00
☐ 228		FOR ALL WE KNOW/ NEVER LEAVE ME BABY	14.00	24.00	20.00
☐ 224		DIDN'T I SAY/SUGAR GIRL	23.00	45.00	27.00
		ORIOLES—EP			
☐ 5000	**JUBILEE**	THE ORIOLES	70.00	130.00	75.00

TONY ORLANDO

☐ 55299	**EPIC**	HAPPY TIMES ARE HERE TO STAY/WILL YOU LOVE ME TOMORROW (PROMO)	3.50	6.00	5.00
☐ 9441		HALFWAY TO PARADISE/ LONELY TOMORROWS	3.00	5.00	3.50
☐ 9452		BLESS YOU/AM I THE GUY	3.00	5.50	4.50
☐ 9476		HAPPY TIMES ARE HERE TO STAY/ LONELY AM I	3.00	5.00	3.50
☐ 9491		MY BABY'S A STRANGER/ TALKIN' ABOUT YOU	3.00	5.00	3.50

TONY ORLANDO

In 1958, a pleasant young man knocked on Don Kirshner's office door in New York's Brill Building. There stood Michael Anthony Orlando Cassivitis, age 14. (His birthdate was April 3, 1944.) Kirshner learned that Cassivitis had just quit school and was seeking employment as a demo singer. After a brief audition, Kirshner hired the lad.

Tony quit school after constantly falling asleep in class. Both parents worked nights and Tony was left to care for his severely retarded stepsister. The only way to keep her calm (and from going into convulsions) was for the boy to rock with her in a chair and sing. In this way, at least, he developed his singing talents.

As a demo singer, Tony did manage to cut one single of his own. But "Ding Dong" on a label called Milo went nowhere. Later, Don Kirshner allowed Tony to begin recording under his own (middle) name.

After a couple of top 40 hits, the magic of Tony Orlando faded. In 1969, he sang lead on "Make Believe", a Top 30 hit listed as being by Wind (but no such group existed). Of course, Tony Orlando gained worldwide fame during the 1970s as the lead singer of Dawn.

			Current Price Range		P/Y AVG
☐9502		I'D NEVER FIND ANOTHER YOU/LOVE ON YOUR LIPS	3.00	5.00	3.50
☐9519		CHILLS/AT THE EDGE OF TEARS .	3.00	5.00	3.50
☐9562		BEAUTIFUL DREAMER/LONELIEST	3.00	5.00	3.50
☐9570		SHIRLEY/JOANIE	3.00	5.00	3.50
☐9622		I'LL BE THERE/ WHAT AM I GONNA DO?	3.00	5.00	3.50
☐9668		SHE DOESN'T KNOW IT/ TELL ME WHAT CAN I DO	3.00	5.00	3.50
☐9715		TO WAIT FOR LOVE/ACCEPT IT ..	3.00	5.00	3.50
☐6376	**ATCO**	THINK BEFORE YOU ACT/SHE LOVES ME FOR WHAT I AM ...	3.00	5.00	3.50
☐471	**CAMEO**	SWEET, SWEET/MANUELITO	3.00	5.00	3.50
☐45542	**ELEKTRA**	A LOVER'S QUESTION/ I COUNT THE TEARS	2.00	3.00	2.50
☐45501		DON'T LET GO/BRING IT ON HOME TO ME	2.00	3.00	2.50
☐991	**CASSABLANCA**	SWEET FOR MY SWEET/ HIGH STEPPIN'	2.00	3.00	2.50
☐967		THEY'RE PLAYING OUR SONG/ MOONLIGHT	2.00	3.00	2.50
☐2249		PULLIN' TOGETHER/ SHE ALWAYS KNEW	2.00	3.00	2.50
☐2002	**TRIAD**	CLOSE YOUR EYES/WHAT'S A LITTLE LOVE BETWEEN FRIENDS	2.00	3.00	2.50

TONY ORLANDO AND DAWN

☐903	**B LL**	CANDIDA/LOOK AT	2.00	3.00	2.50
☐938		KNOCK THREE TIMES/HOME	2.00	3.00	2.50
☐970		I PLAY AND SING/GET OUT FROM WHERE WE ARE	2.00	3.00	2.50
☐45107		SUMMER SAND/SWEET SOFT SOUNDS OF LOVE	2.00	3.00	2.50
☐45175		RUNAWAY, HAPPY TOGETHER/ DON'T ACT LIKE A BABY	2.00	3.00	2.50
☐45225		VAYA CON DIOS (PROMO)	2.00	3.00	2.50
☐45285		YOU'RE A LADY/IN THE PARK ...	2.00	3.00	2.50
☐45318		TIE A YELLOW RIBBON/I CAN'T BELIEVE HOW MUCH I LOVE YOU	2.00	3.00	2.50
☐45374		SWEET GYPSY ROSE/SPARK OF LOVE IS KINDLIN'	2.00	3.00	2.50
☐45424		STRAWBERRY PATCH/ UKYLELE MAN	2.00	3.00	2.50
☐45450		IT ONLY HURTS WHEN I TRY TO SMILE/SWEET SUMMER DAYS	2.00	3.00	2.50
☐45601		STEPPIN' OUT, GONNA BOOGIE TONIGHT/SHE CAN'T HOLD A CANDLE TO YOU	2.00	3.00	2.50
☐45620		LOOK IN MY EYES PRETTY WOMAN/ MY LOVE HAS NO PRIDE	2.00	3.00	2.50
☐45240	**ELEKTRA**	HE DON'T LOVE YOU/ PICK IT UP	2.00	3.00	2.50
☐45260		MORNIN' BEAUTIFUL/ DANCE ROSIE DANCE	2.00	3.00	2.50
☐45302		CUPID/YOU'RE GROWIN' ON ME .	2.00	3.00	2.50
☐45319		MIDNIGHT LOVE AFFAIR/ SELFISH ONE	2.00	3.00	2.50
☐45387		SING/SWEET ON CANDY	2.00	3.00	2.50
☐0105	**ARISTA**	GIMME A GOOD OLE MAMMY SONG/LITTLE HEADS IN BUNKBEDS	2.00	3.00	2.50
☐0156		SKYBIRD/THAT'S THE WAY A WALLFLOWER GROWS	2.00	3.00	2.50

			Current Price Range		P/Y AVG
		TONY ORLANDO—ALBUMS			
☐3808 (M)	**EPIC**	BLESS YOU	17.00	29.00	25.00
☐611 (S)		BLESS YOU	20.00	40.00	35.00
		ORLONS			
☐198	**CAMEO**	HEART DARLING ANGEL/ I'LL BE TRUE	4.50	7.50	6.00
☐211		MR. 21/PLEASE LET IT BE ME	4.50	7.50	6.00
☐218		THE WAH WATUSI/HOLIDAY HILL	3.00	5.00	3.65
☐231		DON'T HANG UP/ THE CONSERVATIVE	3.00	5.00	3.65
☐243		SOUTH STREET/ THEM TERRIBLE BOOTS	3.00	5.00	3.65
☐257		NOT ME/MY BEST FRIEND	3.00	5.00	3.65
☐273		CROSSFIRE!/IT'S NO BIG THING	3.00	5.00	3.65
☐287		BON-DOO-WAH/DON'T THROW YOUR LOVE AWAY	3.00	5.00	3.65
☐295		SHIMMY SHIMMY/ EVERYTHING NICE	3.00	5.00	3.65
☐319		RULES OF LOVE/ HEARTBREAK HOTEL	3.00	5.00	3.65
☐332		KNOCK KNOCK (WHO'S THERE?)/ GOIN' PLACES	3.00	5.00	3.65
☐346		I AIN'T COMING BACK/ ENVY (IN MY EYES)	3.00	5.00	3.65
☐352		COME ON DOWN, BABY/ I AIN'T COMING BACK	3.00	5.00	3.65
☐372		DON'T YOU WANT MY LOVIN'?/ I CAN'T TAKE IT	3.00	5.00	3.65
☐384		NO LOVE BUT YOUR LOVE/ ENVY (IN MY EYES)	3.00	5.00	3.65
		ORLONS—ALBUMS			
☐1033 (M)	**CAMEO**	ALL THE HITS	7.00	17.00	15.00
☐1041 (M)		SOUTH STREET	6.00	15.00	13.50
☐1054 (M)		NOT ME	6.00	15.00	13.50
☐1061 (M)		BIGGESST HITS	5.50	14.00	12.00
☐1067 (M)		GOLDEN HITS	5.50	14.00	12.00
☐1073 (M)		DOWN MEMORY LANE	4.50	14.00	12.00
		MILT OSHINS			
☐169	**PELVIS**	ALL ABOUT ELVIS (PT. 1)/(PT. 2)	13.00	35.00	32.00
		GILBERT O'SULLIVAN			
☐3602	**MAM**	NOTHING RHYMED/ EVERYBODY KNOWS	2.75	5.00	3.50
☐3613		I DON'T KNOW WHAT TO DO/ WE WILL	2.50	4.50	3.00
☐3619		ALONE AGAIN/SAVE IT	2.25	4.00	2.50
☐3626		CLAIR/OOH-WAKKA-DOO	2.25	4.00	2.50
☐3629		A VERY EXTRAORDINARY SORT OF GIRL/GET DOWN	2.50	4.50	3.00
☐3633		GOOD COMPANY/OOH BABY	2.50	4.50	3.00
☐3636		HAPPINESS IS ME & YOU/ BREAKFAST, DINNER & TEA	2.75	5.00	3.50
☐3642		YOU ARE YOU/ TO CUT A LONG STORY SHORT	2.50	4.50	3.00

LATER MAM SINGLES ARE WORTH UP TO $3.00 MINT

OUR GANG
FEATURED: LEON RUSSELL, DEAN TORRENCE

☐001	**BR'ER BIRD**	SUMMERTIME, SUMMERTIME THEME FROM LEON'S GARAGE	40.00	65.00	60.00

			Current Price Range		P/Y AVG

OUTSIDERS

			Current Price Range		P/Y AVG
☐5573	CAPITOL	TIME WON'T LET ME/ WAS IT REALLY REAL?	3.00	5.00	3.65
☐5646		GIRL IN LOVE/ WHAT MAKES YOU SO BAD?	3.00	5.00	3.65
☐5701		RESPECTABLE/ LOST IN MY WORLD	3.00	5.00	3.65
☐5759		HELP ME GIRL/YOU GOTTA LOOK	3.00	5.00	3.65
☐5843		I'LL GIVE YOU TIME/ I'M NOT TRYIN' TO HURT YOU	3.00	5.00	3.65
☐5892		I JUST CAN'T SEE YOU ANYMORE/ GOTTA LEAVE US ALONE	3.00	5.00	3.65
☐5995		AND NOW YOU WANT MY SYMPATHY/I'LL SEE YOU IN THE SUMMERTIME	3.00	5.00	3.65
☐2055		LITTLE BIT OF LOVIN'/ I WILL LOVE YOU	3.00	5.00	3.65
☐2216		OH, HOW IT HURTS/ WE AIN'T GONNA MAKE IT	3.00	5.00	3.65

OUTSIDERS—ALBUMS

☐2501 (M)	CAPITOL	TIME WON'T LET ME	8.25	14.00	12.00
☐2501 (S)		TIME WON'T LET ME	9.50	17.00	15.00
☐2568 (M)		ALBUM #2	8.25	14.00	12.00
☐2568 (S)		ALBUM #2	9.50	17.00	15.00

OXFORD CIRCLE

☐002	WORLD UNITED	FOOLISH WOMAN/ MIND DESTRUCTION	13.00	35.00	30.00

P

JIMMY PAGE
SEE: LED ZEPPLIN

☐533	FONTANA	SHE JUST SATISFIES/ KEEP MOVING	55.00	98.00	90.00

PAGEANTS

☐3013	GOLDSIC	HAPPY TOGETHER/ WHY DID YOU GO	16.00	35.00	32.00

PALISADES
FEATURED: CAROLE KING

☐4401	CHAIRMAN	MAKE THE NIGHT A LITTLE LONGER/IT'S HEAVEN BEING WITH YOU	9.50	17.00	15.00

PARAGONS

☐215	WINLEY	FLORENCE/ HEY LITTLE SCHOOL GIRL	5.00	9.00	7.50
☐220		LET'S START OVER AGAIN/ STICK WITH ME BABY	5.00	9.00	7.00
☐223		TWO HEARTS ARE BETTER THAN ONE/GIVE ME LOVE	4.50	8.00	6.50
☐227		TWILIGHT/THE VOWS OF LOVE	4.50	8.00	6.00
☐236		DARLING I LOVE YOU/DOLL BABY	4.50	8.00	6.00
☐240		SO YOU WILL KNOW/DOLL BABY	4.00	7.00	4.85
☐250		JUST A MEMORY/ KNEEL AND PRAY	4.00	7.00	4.85
☐1102	MUSICRAFT	BLUE VELVET/WEDDING BELLS	4.00	7.00	4.85
☐3001	MUSIC CLEF	TIME AFTER TIME/ BABY, TAKE MY HAND	4.00	7.00	4.85

PENGUINS

In 1954, high school student Cleve Duncan decided to form a rhythm-and-blues quartet. Soon after that, he met a boyhood friend, Curtis Williams. (They had drifted apart during their junior-high years.) Curtis told Cleve of a song he had composed called "Earth Angel". It had been written by Williams for his girl friend. Duncan then asked Cleve to join his group.

They needed a name and later chose the title Penguins. At that time, Kools cigarettes featured a penguin on their packet. This supposedly inspired the name.

During the summer of 1954, the Penguins rehearsed "Earth Angel" in a backyard garage in Los Angeles. They then decided to try to get on record.

They tried out at Dootone Records in South Los Angeles and made it. They first recorded a song called "Ain't No News Today", which went nowhere. Dootsie Williams (Dootone's owner) then assigned the group an uptempo song called "Hey Senorita". Dootsie recorded the song and put "Earth Angel" on the B side. The song was poorly engineered and was recorded in about 10 minutes.

"Earth Angel" became one of the first rhythm-and-blues group records to ever break the national Top 10. It proved to be the Penguins only chart hit as well.

			Current Price Range		P/Y AVG
☐500	TAP	IF/HEY BABY	3.50	6.00	4.35
☐503		IN THE MIDST OF THE NIGHT/ BEGIN THE BEGUINE	3.50	6.00	4.35
☐504		THESE ARE THE THINGS I LOVE/ IF YOU LOVE ME	3.50	6.00	4.35
☐9	TIMES SQUARE	DON'T CRY BABY/ SO YOU WILL KNOW	5.00	8.50	7.00

PARAGONS—ALBUM

☐8002 (M)	RARE BIRD	SIMPLY THE PARAGONS	9.00	25.00	22.50

PARAMOUNTS

☐524	CARLTON	TRYING/GIRL FRIEND	5.50	11.00	9.00
☐16201	DOT	WHEN YOU DANCE/ YOU'RE SEVENTEEN	5.50	11.00	9.00
☐1099	EMBER	SHEDDING TEARDROPS/ IN A DREAM	5.00	12.00	10.00
☐3201	LAURIE	JUST TO BE WITH YOU/ ONE MORE FOR THE ROAD . . .	5.00	9.00	7.00

PAUL AND PAULA
SEE: JILL AND RAY

☐40084	PHILIPS	HEY PAULA/BOBBY IS THE ONE .	2.75	4.50	3.00
☐40096		YOUNG LOVERS/BA-HAY-BE	2.75	4.50	3.00
☐40114		FIRST QUARREL/ SCHOOL IS THRU	2.75	4.50	3.00
☐40130		SOMETHING OLD. SOMETHING. NEW/FLIPPED OVER YOU	2.75	4.50	3.00
☐40158		HOLIDAY FOR TEENS/ HOLIDAY HOOTENANNY	2.75	4.50	3.00
☐40168		CRAZY LITTLE THINGS/WE'LL NEVER BREAK UP FOR GOOD . .	2.75	4.50	3.00
☐40209		DARLIN'/THE YOUNG YEARS	2.75	4.50	3.00
☐40234		NO OTHER BABY/ TOO DARK TO SEE	2.75	4.50	3.00
☐40268		TRUE LOVE/ ANY WAY YOU WANT ME	2.75	4.50	3.00
☐40296		DEAR PAUL/ALL THE LOVE	2.75	4.50	3.00
☐40352		ALL I WANT IS YOU/ THE BEGINNING OF LOVE	2.75	4.50	3.00

PAUL AND PAULA—ALBUMS

☐200078 (M)	PHILIPS	PAUL AND PAULA SING FOR YOUNG LOVERS	7.00	17.00	15.00
☐600078 (S)		PAUL AND PAULA SING FOR YOUNG LOVERS	9.00	25.00	22.50
☐200101 (M)		HOLIDAY FOR TEENS	7.00	17.00	15.00
☐600101 (S)		HOLIDAY FOR TEENS	9.00	25.00	22.50

GARY PAXTON

☐44108	GARPAX	YOUR PAST IS BACK AGAIN/ DUAL HUMP CAMEL NAMED ROBERT E. LEE	3.25	5.50	4.00
☐44177		HOW TO BE A FOOL/ THE SCAVENGER	3.25	5.50	4.00
☐8691	FELSTED	KANSAS CITY/SWEET SENORITA FROM SANTA FE	3.25	5.50	4.00
☐55584	LIBERTY	SPOOKY MOVIES (PT. 1)/(PT. 2) .	3.00	5.00	3.50
☐5208	LONDON	SUPER TORQUE/ CUTE LITTLE COLT	3.00	5.00	3.50

PENGUINS

☐345	DOOTONE	AIN'T NO NEWS TODAY/ WHEN I AM GONE	55.00	98.00	90.00

			Current Price Range		P/Y AVG
☐348		EARTH ANGEL/HEY SENORITA (red label)	11.00	21.00	18.00
☐348		EARTH ANGEL/HEY SENORITA (maroon label)	8.25	14.00	12.00
☐348		EARTH ANGEL/HEY SENORITA (blue label)	8.25	14.00	12.00
☐348		EARTH ANGEL/HEY SENORITA (black label)	7.00	13.00	11.00
☐353		LOVE WILL MAKE YOUR MIND GO WILD/OOKEY OOK	11.00	21.00	18.00
☐362		BABY, LET'S MAKE SOME LOVE/ KISS A FOOL GOODBYE	9.50	17.00	15.00
☐428	DOOTO	THAT'S HOW MUCH I NEED YOU/ BE MY LOVIN' BABY	3.75	6.00	4.50
☐432		SWEET LOVE/LET ME MAKE UP YOUR MIND	3.50	6.00	4.35
☐435		IF YOU'RE MINE/ DO NOT PRETEND	3.50	6.00	4.35
☐451		TO KEEP OUR LOVE/MY HEART (Cleve and the Radiants)	3.50	6.00	4.35
☐456		YOU'RE AN ANGEL/ MR. JUNKMAN	3.50	6.00	4.35
☐70610	MERCURY	BE MINE OR BE A FOOL/ DON'T DO IT	12.00	24.00	16.00
☐70654		IT ONLY HAPPENS WITH YOU/ WALKIN' DOWN BROADWAY	12.00	24.00	16.00
☐70703		DEVIL THAT I SEE/PROMISES, PROMISES, PROMISES	12.00	24.00	16.00
☐70762		A CHRISTMAS PRAYER/ JINGLE JANGLE	12.00	24.00	16.00
☐70799		SHE'S GONE, GONE/MY TROUBLES ARE NOT AT AN END	12.00	24.00	16.00
☐70943		EARTH ANGEL/ICE	8.25	14.00	12.00
☐71033		COOL COOL BABY/ WILL YOU BE MINE?	8.25	14.00	12.00
☐90076	WING	DEALER IN DREAMS/ PEACE OF MIND	7.00	13.00	11.00
☐119	ELDO	TO KEEP OUR LOVE/ UNIVERSAL TWIST	7.00	13.00	11.00
☐1132	ATLANTIC	PLEDGE OF LOVE/ I KNEW I'D FALL IN LOVE	8.25	14.00	12.00
☐001	SUN STATE	BELIEVE ME/THE PONY ROCK	8.25	14.00	12.00
☐27	ORIGINAL SOUND	MEMORIES OF EL MONTE/ BE MINE	5.50	10.50	9.00
		THE ABOVE WAS WRITTEN BY FRANK ZAPPA			
☐54		HEAVENLY ANGEL/ BIG BOBO'S PARTY	4.50	7.50	6.00
☐7023	POWER	EARTH ANGEL/HEY SENORITA (outtakes)	5.50	11.00	9.00
		PENGUINS—EPs			
☐201	DOOTO	THE PENGUINS	12.00	25.00	20.00
☐241		THE COOL, COOL PENGUINS	10.00	20.00	17.50
☐243		THE COOL, COOL PENGUINS	10.00	20.00	17.50
☐244		THE COOL, COOL PENGUINS	10.00	20.00	17.50
		PENGUINS—ALBUM			
☐242 (M)	DOOTO	THE COOL, COOL PENGUINS	20.00	40.00	35.00

PENTAGONS

☐100	FLEET INTERNATIONAL	TO BE LOVED/ DOWN AT THE BEACH	8.25	14.00	12.00

			Current Price Range		P/Y AVG
☐ 1337	**DONNA**	TO BE LOVED (FOREVER)/ DOWN AT THE BEACH	3.25	5.50	4.00
☐ 1344		FOR A LOVE THAT IS MINE/I LIKE THE WAY YOU LOOK AT ME	3.25	5.50	4.00
☐ 1201	**JAMIE**	I WONDER/SHE'S MINE	3.25	5.50	4.00
☐ 1210		UNTIL THEN/I'M IN LOVE	3.25	5.50	4.00

PEPE & THE ASTROS

			Current Price Range		P/Y AVG
☐ 554	**SWAMI**	NOW AIN'T THAT A SHAME/ JUDY, MY LOVE	14.00	35.00	32.00

CARL PERKINS

			Current Price Range		P/Y AVG
☐ 501	**FLIP**	MOVIE MAGG/TURN AROUND	190.00	315.00	300.00
☐ 224	**SUN**	LET THE JUKE BOX KEEP ON PLAYING/GONE GONE GONE	34.00	54.00	48.00
☐ 234		BLUE SUEDE SHOES/ HONEY DON'T	5.00	8.50	7.00
☐ 243		BOPPIN' THE BLUES/ ALL MAMA'S CHILDREN	4.50	7.50	6.00
☐ 249		DIXIE FRIED/ I'M SORRY I'M NOT SORRY	4.50	7.50	6.00
☐ 261		YOUR TRUE LOVE/MATCHBOX	4.50	7.50	6.00
☐ 274		FOREVER YOURS/THAT'S RIGHT	4.50	7.50	6.00
☐ 287		GLAD ALL OVER/ LEND ME YOUR COMB	4.50	7.50	6.00
☐ 41131	**COLUMBIA**	PINK PEDAL PUSHERS/ JIVE AFTER FIVE	4.50	7.50	6.00
☐ 41207		LEVI JACKET/ POP, LET ME HAVE THE CAR	4.50	7.50	6.00
☐ 41296		Y-O-U/THIS LIFE I LEAD	4.50	7.50	6.00
☐ 41379		POINTED TOE SHOES/ HIGHWAY OF LOVE	4.50	7.50	6.00
☐ 41449		ONE TICKET TO LONELINESS/ I DON'T SEE ME IN YOUR ARMS ANYMORE	3.75	6.00	4.50
☐ 41651		L-O-V-E-V-I-L-L-E/TOO MUCH FOR A MAN TO UNDERSTAND	3.75	6.00	4.50
☐ 41825		JUST FOR YOU/ HONEY, 'CAUSE I LOVE YOU	3.75	6.00	4.50
☐ 42061		ANY WAY THE WIND BLOWS/ THE UNHAPPY GIRLS	3.75	6.00	4.50
☐ 42405		HOLLYWOOD CITY/ THE FOOL I USED TO BE	3.75	6.00	4.50
☐ 42514		TWISTER SISTER/HAMBONE	2.25	5.50	4.00
☐ 42753		FORGET ME NEXT TIME AROUND/ I JUST GOT BACK FROM THERE	3.25	5.50	4.00
☐ 44883		FOR YOUR LOVE/ FOUR LETTER WORD	3.25	5.50	4.00
☐ 45107		ALL MAMA'S CHILDREN/ STEP ASIDE	3.00	5.00	3.50
☐ 45253		WHAT EVERY LITTLE BOY OUGHT TO KNOW/JUST AS LONG	3.00	5.00	3.50
☐ 45347		ME WITHOUT YOU/ RED HEADED WOMAN	3.00	5.00	3.50
☐ 45466		COTTON TOP/ABOUT ALL I CAN GIVE YOU IS LOVE	3.00	5.00	3.50
☐ 45582		TAKE ME BACK TO MEMPHIS/ HIGH ON LOVE	3.00	5.00	3.50
☐ 45694		SOMEDAY/THE TRIP	3.00	5.00	3.50
☐ 31548	**DECCA**	HELP ME FIND MY BABY/ FOR A LITTLE WHILE	3.00	5.50	3.50
☐ 31591		AFTER SUNDOWN/ I WOULDN'T HAVE YOU	3.00	5.00	3.50

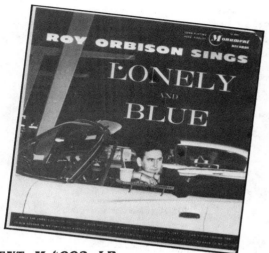

MONUMENT, M 4002, LP

SUN, 1225, LP

			Current Price Range		P/Y AVG
☐31709		LET MY BABY BE/ THE MONKEYSHINE	3.00	5.00	3.50
☐31786		ONE OF THESE DAYS/ MAMA OF MY SONG	3.00	5.00	3.50
☐505	*DOLLIE*	COUNTRY BOY'S DREAM/ IF I COULD COME BACK	3.25	5.50	4.00
☐508		SHINE, SHINE, SHINE/ ALMOST LOVE	3.25	5.50	4.00
☐512		WITHOUT YOU/YOU CAN TAKE THE BOY OUT OF THE COUNTRY	3.25	5.50	4.00
☐514		BACK TO TENNESSEE/ MY OLD HOME TOWN	3.25	5.50	4.00
☐73393	*MERCURY*	HELP ME DREAM/YOU TORE MY HEAVEN ALL TO HELL	3.00	5.00	3.50
☐73425		(LET'S GET) DIXIE FRIED/ ONE MORE LOSER GOIN' HOME	3.00	5.00	3.50
☐73653		YOU'LL ALWAYS BE A LADY TO ME/LOW CLASS	3.00	5.00	3.50
☐73690		THE E.P. EXPRESS/ BIG BAD BLUES	3.00	5.00	3.50
☐102	*SUEDE*	ROCK-A-BILLY FEVER/TILL YOU GET THROUGH WITH ME	3.00	5.00	3.50
		CARL PERKINS—EPs			
☐115	*SUN*	CARL PERKINS	22.00	40.00	36.00
☐12341	*COLUMBIA*	WHOLE LOTTA SHAKIN'	20.00	34.00	30.00
		CARL PERKINS—ALBUMS			
☐1225 (M)	*SUN*	DANCE ALBUM (shoes on cover)	88.00	190.00	180.00
☐1225 (M)		TEEN BEAT-THE BEST OF CARL PERKINS (without shoes)	68.00	160.00	150.00
☐1234 (M)	*COLUMBIA*	WHOLE LOTTA SHAKIN'	40.00	98.00	90.00
☐4001 (M)	*DOLLIE*	COUNTRY BOY'S DREAM	10.00	25.00	22.50
☐1691 (S)	*MERCURY*	MY KIND OF COUNTRY	5.50	14.00	12.00
		PERSIANS			
☐114	*RSVP*	TEARS OF LOVE/DANCE NOW	6.00	12.00	10.00
☐1	*GOLDISC*	TEARDROPS ARE FALLING/ VAULT OF MEMORIES	5.00	9.00	7.00
☐17		WHEN YOU SAID LET'S GET MARRIED/LET'S MONKEY AROUND	4.50	7.50	6.00
☐601	*PAGEANT*	GET AHOLD OF YOUSELF/ THE STEADY KIND	3.75	6.00	4.50
☐1813	*GOLD EAGLE*	GEE WHAT A GIRL/ LOVE ME TONIGHT	3.75	6.00	4.50
		PERSONALITIES			
☐1002	*SAFARI*	YOURS TO COMMAND/ WOE WOE BABY	12.00	35.00	30.00
		THE PERSUASIONS			
☐103	*BLUE SKY*	FOR YOUR LOVE/ IN THE STILL OF THE NIGHT	12.00	24.00	16.00
☐171 ☐(DJ COPY)	*KING TUT*	THE SUN/THE ABC'S OF LOVE	18.00	36.00	23.00
☐40118 ☐(PROMO COPY)	*MCA*	LOVE YOU MOST OF ALL/ LOVE MOST OF ALL	10.00	19.00	13.00
☐977 ☐(PROMO COPY)	*REPRISE*	WITHOUT A SONG/ WITHOUT A SONG	13.00	25.00	18.00

			Current Price Range		P/Y AVG

PETER AND GORDON
FEATURED: PETER ASHER

			Current Price Range		P/Y AVG
☐5175	*CAPITOL*	A WORLD WITHOUT LOVE/ IF I WERE YOU	3.00	5.50	3.85
☐5211		NOBODY I KNOW/YOU DON'T HAVE TO TELL ME	3.00	5.50	3.85
☐5272		I DON'T WANT TO SEE YOU AGAIN/ I WOULD BUY YOU PRESENTS ..	3.00	5.50	3.85
☐5335		I GO TO PIECES/LOVE ME BABY ..	3.00	5.50	3.85
☐5406		TRUE LOVE WAYS/IF YOU WISH .	3.00	5.50	3.85
☐5461		TO KNOW YOU IS TO LOVE YOU/ I TOLD YOU SO	3.00	5.50	3.85
☐5532		DON'T PITY ME/ CRYING IN THE RAIN	3.00	5.50	3.85
☐5579		WOMAN/ WRONG FROM THE START	3.00	5.50	3.85
☐5650		THERE'S NO LIVING WITHOUT YOUR LOVING/STRANGER WITH A BLACK DOVE	3.00	5.50	3.85
☐5684		TO SHOW I LOVE YOU/ START TRYING SOMEONE ELSE	3.00	5.50	3.85
☐5740		LADY GODIVA/ YOU'VE HAD BETTER TIMES ..	3.00	5.50	3.85
☐5808		KNIGHT IN RUSTY ARMOR/ FLOWER LADY	3.00	5.50	3.85
☐5864		SUNDAY FOR TEA/ HURTIN' IS LOVIN'	3.00	5.50	3.85
☐5919		THE JOKERS/ RED, CREAM AND VELVET	3.00	5.50	3.85
☐2071		NEVER EVER/GREENER DAYS ...	3.00	5.50	3.85
☐2214		SIPPIN' MY WINE/ YOU'VE HAD BETTER DAYS ...	3.00	5.50	3.85
☐2544		I CAN REMEMBER/ HARD TIMES, RAINY DAY	3.00	5.50	3.85

PETER AND GORDON—ALBUMS

			Current Price Range		P/Y AVG
☐2115 (M)	*CAPITOL*	A WORLD WITHOUT LOVE	7.00	17.00	15.00
☐2115 (S)		A WORLD WITHOUT LOVE	8.00	21.00	18.00
☐2220 (M)		I DON'T WANT TO SEE YOU AGAIN	7.00	17.00	15.00
☐2220 (S)		I DON'T WANT TO SEE YOU AGAIN	8.00	21.00	18.00
☐2324 (M)		I GO TO PIECES	7.00	17.00	15.00
☐2324 (S)		I GO TO PIECES	8.00	21.00	18.00
☐2368 (M)		TRUE LOVE WAYS	7.00	17.00	15.00
☐2368 (S)		TRUE LOVE WAYS	8.00	21.00	18.00
☐2430 (M)		PETER AND GORDON SING AND PLAY THE HITS OF NASHVILLE, TENNESSEE	7.00	17.00	15.00
☐2430 (S)		PETER AND GORDON SING AND PLAY THE HITS OF NASHVILLE, TENNESSEE	8.00	21.00	18.00
☐2477 (M)		WOMAN.....................	6.00	15.00	13.50
☐2477 (S)		WOMAN	7.00	17.00	15.00
☐2549 (M)		THE BEST OF PETER AND GORDON	6.00	15.00	13.50
☐2549 (S)		THE BEST OF PETER AND GORDON	7.00	17.00	15.00
☐2664 (M)		LADY GODIVA	6.00	15.00	13.50
☐2664 (S)		LADY GODIVA	7.00	17.00	15.00
☐2729 (M)		KNIGHT IN RUSTY ARMOR	6.00	15.00	13.50
☐2729 (S)		KNIGHT IN RUSTY ARMOR	7.00	17.00	15.00
☐2747 (M)		IN LONDON FOR TEA	6.00	15.00	13.50
☐2747 (S)		IN LONDON FOR TEA	6.00	15.00	13.50
☐2882 (M)		HOT, COLD AND CUSTARD	6.00	15.00	13.50
☐2882 (S)		HOT, COLD AND CUSTARD	5.50	17.00	12.00

PAUL PETERSON

			Current Price Range		P/Y AVG
☐620	*COLPIX*	SHE CAN'T FIND HER KEYS/ VERY UNLIKELY	3.00	5.00	3.65

			Current Price Range		P/Y AVG
☐ 532		KEEP YOUR LOVE LOCKED/ EVERYTHING TO ANYONE YOU LOVE	3.00	5.00	3.65
☐ 649		LOLLIPOPS AND ROSES/ PLEASE MR. SUN	3.00	5.00	3.65
☐ 663		MY DAD/LITTLE BOY SAD	3.00	5.00	3.65
☐ 676		AMY/GOODY GOODY	3.00	5.00	3.65
☐ 697		GIRLS IN THE SUMMERTIME/ MAMA, YOUR LITTLE BOY FELL	3.00	5.00	3.65
☐ 707		THE CHEER LEADER/POLKA DOTS AND MOON BEAMS	3.00	5.00	3.65
☐ 720		SHE RIDES WITH ME/ POOREST BOY IN TOWN	5.50	11.00	9.00
☐ 730		HEY THERE, BEAUTIFUL/ WHERE IS SHE?	3.00	5.00	3.65
☐ 763		LITTLE DREAMER/HAPPY	3.00	5.00	3.65
☐ 1108	*MOTOWN*	DON'T LET IT HAPPEN TO US/ CHAINED	3.00	5.00	3.65
☐ 1129		LITTLE BIT FOR SANDY/YOUR LOVE'S GOT ME BURNING ALIVE	3.00	5.00	3.65
		PRODUCER ON COLPIX 720: BRIAN WILSON			
		PAUL PETERSON—ALBUMS			
☐ 429 (M)	*COLPIX*	LILLIPOPS AND ROSES	7.00	17.00	15.00
☐ 429 (S)		LILLIPOPS AND ROSES	9.00	25.00	22.50
☐ 442 (M)		MY DAD	7.00	17.00	15.00
☐ 442 (S)		MY DAD	9.00	25.00	22.50

RAY PETERSON

			Current Price Range		P/Y AVG
☐ 7098	*RCA*	FEVER/ WE'RE OLD ENOUGH TO CRY	3.50	6.00	4.35
☐ 7165		LET'S TRY ROMANCE/ SHIRLEY PURLY	3.50	6.00	4.35
☐ 7255		SUDDENLY/TAIL LIGHT	3.50	6.00	4.35
☐ 7303		MY BLUE-EYED BABY/PATRICIA	3.50	6.00	4.35
☐ 7336		DREAM WAY/I'LL ALWAYS WANT YOU NEAR	3.50	6.00	4.35
☐ 7404		RICHER THAN I/ LOVE IS A WOMAN	3.50	6.00	4.35
☐ 7513		THE WONDER OF YOU/I'M GONE	3.25	5.50	4.00
☐ 7578		MY BLUE ANGEL/ COME AND GET IT	3.25	5.50	4.00
☐ 7635		GOODNIGHT MY LOVE/WHAT DO YOU WANT TO MAKE THOSE EYES AT ME FOR?	3.25	5.50	4.00
☐ 7703		ANSWER ME MY LOVE/WHAT DO YOU WANT TO MAKE THOSE EYES AT ME FOR?	3.25	5.50	4.00
☐ 7745		TELL LAURA I LOVE HER/ WEDDING DAY	3.25	5.50	4.00
☐ 7779		TEENAGE HEARTACHE/ I'LL ALWAYS WANT YOU NEAR	3.25	5.50	4.00
☐ 7845		MY BLUE ANGEL/I'M TIRED	3.00	5.00	3.65
☐ 8333		THE WONDER OF YOU/I'M GONE	3.00	5.00	3.65
☐ 2002	*DUNES*	CORINNA, CORINNA/BE MY GIRL	3.25	5.50	4.00
☐ 2004		SWEET LITTLE KATHY/ YOU DIDN'T CARE	3.25	5.50	4.00
☐ 2006		MISSING YOU/YOU THRILL ME	3.25	5.50	4.00
☐ 2009		I COULD HAVE LOVED YOU SO WELL/WHY DON'T YOU WRITE ME	3.25	5.50	4.00
☐ 2013		YOU KNOW ME MUCH TOO WELL/ YOU DIDN'T CARE	3.25	5.50	4.00
☐ 2018		IF ONLY TOMORROW/ YOU DIDN'T CARE	3.00	5.00	3.65

			Current Price Range		P/Y AVG
☐2019		IS IT WRONG?/SLOWLY	3.00	5.00	3.65
☐2022		I'M NOT JIMMY/			
		A LOVE TO REMEMBER	3.00	5.00	3.65
☐2024		WHERE ARE YOU?/			
		DEEP ARE THE ROOTS	3.00	5.00	3.65
☐2025		GIVE US YOUR BLESSING/			
		WITHOUT LOVE	3.00	5.00	3.65
☐2027		BE MY GIRL/I FORGOT			
		WHAT IT WAS LIKE	3.00	5.00	3.65
☐2030		SWEET LITTLE KATHY/PROMISES			
		YOU MADE ARE BROKEN	3.00	5.00	3.50
☐13269	**MGM**	IF YOU WERE HERE/OH NO!	3.00	5.00	3.65
☐13299		ACROSS THE STREET/			
		WHEN I STOP DREAMING	3.00	5.00	3.65
☐13330		UNCHAINED MELODY/			
		THAT'S ALL	3.00	5.00	3.65
☐13336		A HOUSE WITHOUT WINDOWS/			
		I WISH I COULD SAY NO TO YOU.	3.00	5.00	3.65
☐13388		I'M ONLY HUMAN/			
		ONE LONESOME ROSE	3.00	5.00	3.65
☐13436		EVERYBODY/LOVE HURTS	3.00	5.00	3.65
☐13508		I'M GONNA CHANGE			
		EVERYTHING/AMANDA	3.00	5.00	3.65
☐13564		WHOLE WORLD GOIN' CRAZY/			
		JUST ONE SMILE	3.00	5.00	3.65
☐0811	**REPRISE**	TOGETHER/			
		LOVE RULES THE WORLD	3.00	5.00	3.65
☐55249	**UNI**	OKLAHOMA CITY BLUES/LOVE			
		THE UNDERSTANDING WAY ...	3.00	5.00	3.65
☐55268		TELL LAURA I LOVE HER/			
		TO WAIT FOR LOVE	3.00	5.00	3.65
☐55275		FEVER/CHANGES	3.00	5.00	3.65
☐32861	**DECCA**	THERE'S A BETTER WAY/			
		STAMP OUT LONLINESS	3.00	5.00	3.65

RAY PETERSON—EP

☐4367	**RCA**	TELL LAURA I LOVE HER	7.00	17.00	15.00

RAY PETERSON—ALBUMS

☐2297 (M)	**RCA**	TELL LAURA I LOVE HER	9.00	25.00	22.50
☐2297 (S)		TELL LAURA I LOVE HER	17.00	39.00	35.00
☐4250 (M)	**MGM**	THE VERY BEST OF			
		RAY PETERSON	7.00	17.00	15.00
☐4260 (S)		THE VERY BEST OF			
		RAY PETERSON	9.00	25.00	22.50
☐4277 (M)		THE OTHER SIDE OF			
		RAY PETERSON	6.00	15.00	13.50
☐4277 (S)		THE OTHER SIDE OF			
		RAY PETERSON	8.00	21.00	18.00
☐75307 (S)	**DECCA**	RAY PETERSON COUNTRY	6.00	15.00	13.50

NORMAN PETTY TRIO
GUITAR: BUDDY HOLLY

☐41039	**COLUMBIA**	MOONDREAMS/TOY BOY	14.00	24.00	20.00

TOM PETTY AND THE HEARTBREAKERS
SEE: MUDCRUTCH

☐62007	**SHELTER**	AMERICAN GIRL/LUNA	3.00	5.00	3.50
☐62008		BREAKDOWN/FOOLED AGAIN ...	2.75	4.50	3.00
☐62010		I NEED TO KNOW/			
		NO SECOND THOUGHTS	2.75	4.50	3.00
☐62011		LISTEN TO HER HEART/I DON'T			
		KNOW WHAT TO SAY TO YOU ..	2.75	4.50	3.00

			Current Price Range		P/Y AVG

PHAETONS
FEATURED: DEAN TORRENCE

| ☐103 | *SAHARA* | THE BEATLE WALK/FRANTIC .... | 4.00 | 6.50 | 5.00 |

PHAROAHS

| ☐201 | *CLASS* | TEENAGER'S LOVE SONG/WATUSI | 15.00 | 29.00 | 25.00 |

PHAROS
PRODUCER: BRUCE JOHNSON

| ☐1327 | *DONNA* | TENDER TOUCH/HEADS UP, HIGH HOPES OVER YOU ...... | 5.00 | 9.00 | 7.50 |
| ☐4208 | *DEL-FI* | RHYTHM SURFER/PINTOR ...... | 4.00 | 6.50 | 5.00 |

PHIL PHILLIPS

☐711	*KHOURY'S*	SEA OF LOVE/JUELLA	39.00	68.00	60.00
☐71465	*MERCURY*	SEA OF LOVE/JUELLA	2.75	4.50	3.00
☐71531		TAKE THIS HEART/VERDIE MAE .	2.75	4.50	3.00
☐71611		YOUR TRUE LOVE ONCE MORE/ WHAT WILL I TELL MY HEART?	2.75	4.50	3.00
☐71657		NOBODY KNOWS AND NOBODY CARES/COME BACK, MY DARLING	2.75	4.50	3.00

BOBBY "BORIS" PICKET

☐44167	*GARPAX*	MONSTER MASH/ MONSTER MASH PARTY	3.50	6.00	4.00
☐44171		MONSTER'S HOLIDAY/ MONSTER MOTION	3.50	6.00	4.00
☐44175		GRADUATION DAY/ THE HUMPTY DUMPTY	3.50	6.00	4.00
☐724		I CAN'T STOP/I'M DOWN TO MY LAST HEARTBREAK	3.50	6.00	4.00
☐5063	*CAPITOL*	SIMON THE SENSIBLE SURFER/ SIMON SAYS "SO WHAT!" ...	3.50	6.00	4.00
☐8312	*RCA*	SMOKE, SMOKE, SMOKE/ GOTTA LEAVE THIS TOWN	3.50	6.00	4.00
☐8459		MONSTER SWIM/ THE WEREWOLF WATUSI	3.50	6.00	4.00

BOBBY "BORIS" PICKET—ALBUM

| ☐57001 (M) | *GARPAX* | MONSTER MASH.............. | 8.50 | 21.00 | 18.00 |
| ☐67001 (S) | | MONSTER MASH.............. | 12.00 | 29.00 | 25.00 |

WILSON PICKETT

☐501	*CORRECTONE*	MY HEART BELONGS TO YOU/ LET ME BE YOUR BOY	8.25	14.00	12.00
☐9113	*CUB*	MY HEART BELONGS TO YOU/ LET ME BE YOUR BOY	5.50	11.00	9.00
☐713	*DOUBLE L*	IF YOU NEED ME/ BABY CALL ON ME	3.25	5.50	4.00
☐717		IT'S TOO LATE/ I'M GONNA LOVE YOU	3.25	5.50	4.00
☐724		I'M DOWN TO MY LAST HEARTBREAK/I CAN'T STOP ..	3.25	5.50	4.00

ATLANTIC SINGLES ARE WORTH UP TO $2.00 MINT

WILSON PICKETT—ALBUM

| ☐2300 (M) | *DOUBLE L* | IT'S TOO LATE .... | 9.00 | 25.00 | 22.50 |

VITO PICONE
SEE ELEGANTS

| ☐103 | *ADMIRAL* | I LIKE TO RUN/THE SONG FROM MOULIN ROUGE .... | 5.50 | 11.00 | 9.00 |
| ☐302 | | STILL WATERS RUN DEEP/ BOLT OF LIGHTNING .... | 5.50 | 11.00 | 9.00 |

			Current Price Range		P/Y AVG

PILTDOWN MEN

☐4414	CAPITOL	BRONTOSAURUS STOMP/ McDONALD'S CAVE	3.50	6.00	4.35
☐4460		PILTDOWN RIDES AGAIN/ BUBBLES IN THE TAR	3.50	6.00	4.35
☐4501		GOODNIGHT MRS. FLINTSTONE/ THE GREAT IMPOSTER	3.50	6.00	4.35
☐4851		FOSSIL ROCK/GARGANTUA	3.50	6.00	4.35
☐4703		BIG LIZARD/A PRETTY GIRL IS LIKE A MELODY	3.50	6.00	4.35
☐4875		NIGHT SURFIN'/ TEQUILA BOSSA NOVA	3.50	6.00	4.35

PINK FLOYD

☐333	TOWER	ARNOLD LAYNE/ CANDY AND A CURRANT BUN .	4.50	7.50	6.00
☐356		SEE EMILY PLAY/SCARECROW ..	4.50	7.50	6.00
☐378		THE GNONE/FLAMING	4.50	7.50	6.00
☐440		LET THERE BE MORE LIGHT/ REMEMBER A DAY	4.50	7.50	6.00
☐3391	CAPITOL	STAY/FREE FOUR	3.75	6.00	4.50
☐3609	HARVEST	MONEY/ANY COLOUR YOU LIKE .	2.75	4.50	3.00
☐3832		US AND THEM/TIME	2.75	4.50	3.00

PINK FLOYD—ALBUMS

☐5093 (S)	TOWER	PINK FLOYD.................	17.00	29.00	25.00
☐5131 (S)		SAUCERFUL OF SECRETS	17.00	29.00	25.00

HARVEST ALBUMS ARE WORTH UP TO $10.00 MINT

GENE PITNEY
SEE: BILLY BRYAN

☐25002	FESTIVAL	PLEASE COME BACK/ I'LL FIND YOU	10.00	18.00	11.00
☐1002	MUSICOR	LOVE MY LIFE AWAY/ I LAUGHED SO HARD I CRIED ..	3.50	6.00	4.35
☐1006		LOUISIANA MAMA/ TAKE ME TONIGHT	5.00	9.00	6.00
☐1009		TOWN WITHOUT PITY/ AIR MAIL SPECIAL DELIVERY ..	3.25	5.50	4.00
☐1011		EVERY BREATH I TAKE/ MR. MOON, MR. CUPID AND I .	3.25	5.50	4.00
☐1020		LIBERTY VALANCE/ TAKE IT LIKE A MAN	3.00	5.00	3.65
☐1022		ONLY LOVE CAN BREAK A HEART/ IF I DIDN'T HAVE A DIME	3.00	5.00	3.65
☐1026		HALF HEAVEN-HALF HEARTACHE/ TOWER TALL	3.00	5.00	3.65
☐1028		MECCA/TEARDROP BY TEARDROP	3.00	5.00	3.65
☐1032		TRUE LOVE NEVER RUNS SMOOTH/ DONNA MEANS HEARTBREAK .	3.00	5.00	3.65
☐1034		TWENTY-FOUR HOURS FROM TULSA/LONELY NIGHT DREAMS	3.00	5.00	3.65
☐1036		THAT GIRL BELONGS TO YESTERDAY/WHO NEEDS IT? .	3.00	5.00	3.65
☐1038		YESTERDAY'S HERO/ CORNFLOWER BLUE	3.00	5.00	3.65
☐1040		IT HURTS TO BE IN LOVE/HAWAII	3.00	5.00	3.65
☐1045		I'M GONNA BE STRONG/ ALLADIN'S LAMP	3.00	5.00	3.65
☐1045		I'M GONNA BE STRONG/ DEESE DOMANI	3.00	5.00	3.65
☐1070		I MUST BE SEEING THINGS/ MARIANNE	3.00	5.00	3.65

			Current Price Range		P/Y AVG
☐ 1093		LAST CHANCE TO TURN AROUND/ SAVE YOUR LOVE	3.00	5.00	3.65
☐ 1103		LOOKING THROUGH THE EYES OF LOVE/THERE'S NO LIVIN' WITHOUT YOUR LOVIN'	3.00	5.00	3.65
☐ 1130		PRINCESS IN RAGS/AMORE MIO .	3.00	5.00	3.65
☐ 1150		JOJAS MUERTAS/ ME VOY PARA EL CAMPO	3.50	6.00	4.35
☐ 1155		NESSUNO MI PUO GUIDICARE/ LEI MI ASPETTA	3.50	6.00	4.35
☐ 1171		BACKSTAGE/BLUE COLOR	3.00	5.00	3.65
☐ 1200		THE BOSS'S DAUGHTER/ COLD LIGHT OF DAY	3.25	5.50	4.00
☐ 1219		JUST ONE SMILE/INNAMORATO .	3.00	5.00	3.65
☐ 1233		I'M GONNA LISTEN TO ME/ FOR ME THIS IS HAPPY	3.00	5.00	3.65
☐ 1234		DON'T MEAN TO BE A PREACHER/ ANIMAL CRACKERS	3.00	5.00	3.65
☐ 1235		FLOWER GIRL/ ANIMAL CRACKERS	3.00	5.00	3.65
☐ 1245		WHERE DID THE MAGIC GO?/ TREMBLIN'	3.00	5.00	3.65
☐ 1252		SOMETHING'S GOTTEN HOLD OF MY HEART/BUILDING UP MY DREAM WORLD	3.00	5.00	3.65
☐ 1299		THE MORE I SAW OF HER/ WON'T TAKE LONG	3.00	5.00	3.65
☐ 1306		SHE'S A HEARTBREAKER/ CONQUISTADOR	3.00	5.00	3.65
☐ 1308		LONELY DRIFTER/SOMEWHERE IN THE COUNTRY	3.00	5.00	3.65
☐ 1331		BILLY YOU'RE MY KIND OF WOMAN/HATE	3.00	5.00	3.65
☐ 1358		MARIA ELENA/THE FRENCH HORN	3.00	5.00	3.65
☐ 1361		CALIFORNIA/ PLAYING GAMES FOR LOVE . . .	3.00	5.00	3.65
☐ 1384		SHE LETS HER HAIR DOWN/ I REMEMBER	3.00	5.00	3.65
☐ 1394		ALL YOUNG WOMAN/ I REMEMBER	3.00	5.00	3.65
☐ 1405		THINK OF US/ A STREET CALLED HOP	3.00	5.00	3.65
☐ 1419		SHADY LADY/ BILLY YOU'RE MY FRIEND	3.00	5.00	3.65
☐ 1439		HIGHER AND HIGHER/ BEAUTIFUL SOUNDS	3.00	5.00	3.65
☐ 1442		GENE ARE YOU THERE/ A THOUSAND ARMS	3.00	5.00	3.65
☐ 1453		I JUST CAN'T HELP MYSELF/ BEAUTIFUL SOUNDS	3.00	5.00	3.65
☐ 1461		SUMMERTIME DREAMIN'/ A THOUSAND ARMS	3.00	5.00	3.65
☐ 1474		RUN, RUN ROADRUNNER/ SHADY LADY	3.00	5.00	3.65
☐ 50332		DEDICATION	3.00	5.00	3.65
☐ 50461	*EPIC*	IT'S OVER/IT'S OVER MEDLEY . .	3.00	5.00	3.65
		GENE PITNEY—ALBUMS			
☐ 2001 (M)	*MUSICOR*	THE MANY SIDES OF GENE PITNEY	8.00	21.00	18.00
☐ 3001 (S)		THE MANY SIDES OF GENE PITNEY	12.00	29.00	25.00
☐ 2003 (M)		ONLY LOVE CAN BREAK A HEART	7.00	17.00	15.00
☐ 3003 (S)		ONLY LOVE CAN BREAK A HEART	9.00	25.00	22.50
☐ 2004 (M)		GENE PITNEY SINGS JUST FOR YOU	7.00	17.00	15.00

			Current Price Range		P/Y AVG
3004 (S)		GENE PITNEY SINGS JUST FOR YOU	9.00	25.00	22.50
2005 (M)		WORLD WIDE WINNERS	6.00	15.00	13.50
3005 (S)		WORLD WIDE WINNERS	8.00	21.00	18.00
2006 (M)		BLUE GENE	6.00	15.00	13.50
3006 (S)		BLUE GENE	8.00	21.00	18.00
2007 (M)		GENE PITNEY MEETS THE FAIR YOUNG LADIES OF FOLKLAND .	6.00	15.00	13.50
3007 (S)		GENE PITNEY MEETS THE FAIR YOUNG LADIES OF FOLKLAND .	8.00	21.00	18.00
2008 (M)		GENE PITNEY'S BIG SIXTEEN	5.50	14.00	12.00
3008 (S)		GENE PITNEY'S BIG SIXTEEN	7.00	17.00	15.00
2015 (M)		GENE ITALIANO	6.00	15.00	13.50
3015 (S)		GENE ITALIANO	8.00	21.00	18.00
2019 (M)		IT HURTS TO BE IN LOVE	5.50	14.00	12.00
3019 (S)		IT HURTS TO BE IN LOVE	7.00	17.00	15.00
2043 (M)		MORE BIG SIXTEEN, VOL. II	5.50	14.00	12.00
3043 (S)		MORE BIG SIXTEEN, VOL. II	7.00	17.00	15.00
2044 (M)		GEORGE JONES AND GENE PITNEY .	5.50	14.00	12.00
3044 (S)		GEORGE JONES AND GENE PITNEY .	7.00	17.00	15.00
2056 (M)		I MUST BE SEEING THINGS	5.50	14.00	12.00
3056 (S)		I MUST BE SEEING THINGS	7.00	17.00	15.00
2065 (M)		IT'S COUNTRY TIME AGAIN	5.50	14.00	12.00
3065 (S)		IT'S COUNTRY TIME AGAIN	7.00	17.00	15.00
2069 (M)		LOOKING THROUGH THE EYES OF LOVE	5.50	14.00	12.00
3069 (S)		LOOKING THROUGH THE EYES OF LOVE	7.00	17.00	15.00
2072 (M)		GENE PITNEY ESPANOL	6.00	15.00	13.50
3072 (S)		GENE PITNEY ESPANOL	6.00	15.00	13.50
2077 (M)		BEING TOGETHER (with Melba Montgomery)	6.00	15.00	13.50
3077 (S)		BEING TOGETHER (with Melba Montgomery)	6.00	15.00	13.50
2085 (M)		BIG SIXTEEN, VOL. III	6.00	15.00	13.50
3085 (S)		BIG SIXTEEN, VOL. III	5.50	14.00	12.00
2095 (M)		BACKSTAGE (I'M LONELY)	6.00	15.00	13.50
3095 (S)		BACKSTAGE (I'M LONELY)	5.50	14.00	12.00
2102 (M)		GREATEST HITS OF ALL TIME . . .	7.00	17.00	15.00
3102 (S)		GREATEST HITS OF ALL TIME . . .	5.50	14.00	12.00

LATER MUSICOR ALBUMS ARE WORTH UP TO $5.00 MINT

PLANETS

4551	ROULETTE	YOU ARE MY SUNSHINE/ MR. MOON	8.00	19.00	16.00

ROBERT PLANT
SEE: LED ZEPPLIN

43967	COLUMBIA	YOU BETTER RUN/ EVERYBODY'S GONNA SAY . . .	34.00	54.00	48.00

PLATTERS

12153	FEDERAL	GIVE THANKS/HEY NOW	55.00	98.00	90.00
12164		I'LL CRY WHEN YOU'RE GONE/ I NEED YOU ALL THE TIME	55.00	98.00	90.00
12181		ROSES OF PICARDY/ BEER BARREL BOOGIE	90.00	160.00	150.00
12188		TELL THE WORLD/ LOVE ALL NIGHT	12.00	21.00	18.00
12198		SHAKE IT UP MAMBO/ VOO-VEE-AH-BEE	12.00	21.00	18.00
12204		MAGGIE DOESN'T WORK HERE ANYMORE/TAKE ME BACK, TAKE ME BACK	12.00	21.00	18.00

			Current Price Range		P/Y AVG
☐ 12244		ONLY YOU/YOU MADE ME CRY ..	65.00	118.00	110.00
☐ 12250		TELL THE WORLD/			
		I NEED YOU ALL THE TIME	9.50	17.00	15.00
☐ 12271		GIVE THANKS/			
		I NEED YOU ALL THE TIME	9.50	17.00	15.00
☐ 4733	*KING*	PLEASE HAVE MERCY/			
		OOCHI PACHI	14.00	24.00	20.00
☐ 4752		MY NAME AIN'T ANNIE/			
		LET'S BABALU (Linda Hayes			
		and the Platters).............	14.00	24.00	20.00
☐ 7012	*POWER*	ONLY YOU/YOU MADE ME CRY ..	7.00	13.00	11.00
☐ 70633	*MERCURY*	ONLY YOU/			
		BARK, BATTLE AND BALL	4.50	7.50	6.00
☐ 70753		THE GREAT PRETENDER/			
		I'M JUST A DANCING PARTNER	4.50	7.50	6.00
☐ 70819		THE MAGIC TOUCH/			
		WINNER TAKE ALL	4.50	7.50	6.00
☐ 70893		MY PRAYER HEAVEN ON EARTH .	4.50	7.50	6.00
☐ 70948		YOU'LL NEVER NEVER KNOW/			
		IT ISN'T RIGHT	3.75	6.00	4.50
☐ 71011		ON MY WORD OF HONOR/			
		ONE IN A MILLION	3.75	6.00	4.50
☐ 71032		I'M SORRY/HE'S MINE	3.75	6.00	4.50
☐ 71093		MY DREAM/I WANNA	3.75	6.00	4.50
☐ 71184		ONLY BECAUSE/			
		THE MYSTERY OF YOU	3.50	6.00	4.35
☐ 71264		HELPLESS/INDIFF'RENT	3.50	6.00	4.35
☐ 71289		TWILIGHT TIME/OUT OF MY MIND.	3.50	6.00	4.35
☐ 71320		YOU'RE MAKING A MISTAKE/			
		MY OLD FLAME	3.50	6.00	4.35
☐ 71353		I WISH/IT'S RAINING OUTSIDE ..	3.50	6.00	4.35
☐ 71383		SMOKE GETS IN YOUR EYES/			
		NO MATTER WHAT YOU ARE ..	3.25	5.50	4.00
☐ 71427		ENCHANTED/			
		THE SOUND AND THE FURY ...	3.25	5.50	4.00
☐ 71467		REMEMBER WHEN/			
		LOVE OF A LIFETIME	3.25	5.50	4.00
☐ 71502		WHERE/WISH IT WERE ME	3.25	5.50	4.00
☐ 71538		MY SECRET/			
		WHAT DOES IT MATTER?	3.25	5.50	4.00
☐ 71563		HARBOR LIGHTS/SLEEPY LAGOON	3.25	5.50	4.00
☐ 71624		EBB TIDE/APPLE BLOSSOM TIME	3.00	5.00	3.65
☐ 71656		RED SAILS IN THE SUNSET/			
		SAD RIVER	3.00	5.00	3.65
☐ 71697		TO EACH HIS OWN/DOWN THE			
		RIVER OF DREAMS	3.00	5.00	3.65
☐ 71749		IF I DIDN'T CARE/TRUE LOVER ..	3.00	5.00	3.65
☐ 71791		TREES/IMMORTAL LOVE	3.00	5.00	3.65
☐ 71847		I'LL NEVER SMILE AGAIN/			
		YOU DON'T SAY	3.00	5.00	3.65
☐ 71904		SONG FOR THE LONELY/			
		YOU'LL NEVER KNOW	3.00	5.00	3.65
☐ 71921		IT'S MAGIC/			
		REACHING FOR A STAR	3.00	5.00	3.65
☐ 71986		MORE THAN YOU KNOW/			
		EVERY LITTLE MOMENT	3.00	5.00	3.65
☐ 72060		MEMORIES/HEARTBREAK	3.00	5.00	3.65
☐ 72107		ONCE IN A WHILE/			
		I'LL SEE YOU IN MY DREAMS .	3.00	5.00	3.65
☐ 72129		HERE COMES HEAVEN AGAIN/			
		STRANGERS	3.00	5.00	3.65
☐ 72194		CUANDO CALIENTE EL SOL/			
		VIV JU JUY	3.00	5.00	3.65

MUSIC O DISC, MDS 1002, LP

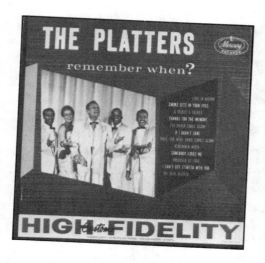

MERCURY, MG20410, LP

			Current Price Range		P/Y AVG
☐72242		ROW THE BOAT ASHORE/			
		JAVA JIVE	3.00	5.00	3.65
☐72305		SINCERELY/P.S., I LOVE YOU . . .	3.00	5.00	3.65
☐72359		LOVE ME TENDER/			
		LITTLE THINGS MEAN A LOT . .	3.00	5.00	3.65

MUSICOR SINGLES ARE WORTH UP TO $1.75 MINT

PLATTERS—EPs

			Current Price Range		P/Y AVG
☐FEP 378	FEDERAL	THE PLATTERS SING FOR ONLY			
		YOU	75.00	120.00	95.00
☐378	KING	THE PLATTERS	17.00	29.00	25.00
☐651		THE PLATTERS	23.00	40.00	36.00
☐3336	MERCURY	THE PLATTERS	9.50	17.00	15.00
☐3341		THE FLYING PLATTERS	8.25	14.00	12.00
☐3343		THE PLATTERS	6.00	12.00	8.00
☐3344		THE PLATTERS	6.00	12.00	8.00
☐3345		THE PLATTERS	6.00	12.00	8.00
☐3353		THE FLYING PLATTERS	6.00	12.00	8.00
☐3354		THE FLYING PLATTERS	6.00	12.00	8.00
☐3355		THE FLYING PLATTERS	6.00	12.00	8.00
☐3393		TWILIGHT TIME	6.00	12.00	8.00
☐4029		ENCORE OF GOLDEN HITS	5.00	9.00	7.00
☐4030		ENCORE OF GOLDEN HITS	5.00	9.00	7.00

PLATTERS—ALBUMS

			Current Price Range		P/Y AVG
☐549 (M)	FEDERAL	THE PLATTERS	46.00	98.00	90.00
☐549 (M)	KING	THE PLATTERS	40.00	98.00	90.00
☐20146 (M)	MERCURY	THE PLATTERS	13.50	34.00	30.00
☐20216 (M)		THE PLATTERS, VOL. II	12.00	29.00	25.00
☐20298 (M)		THE FLYING PLATTERS	12.00	29.00	25.00
☐20366 (M)		THE FLYING PLATTERS			
		AROUND THE WORLD	10.00	25.00	22.50
☐60043 (S)		THE FLYING PLATTERS			
		AROUND THE WORLD	14.00	34.00	30.00
☐20410 (M)		REMEMBER WHEN	10.00	25.00	22.50
☐60087 (S)		REMEMBER WHEN	14.00	34.00	30.00
☐20472 (M)		ENCORE OF GOLDEN HITS	8.00	21.00	18.00
☐60243 (S)		ENCORE OF GOLDEN HITS	12.00	29.00	25.00
☐20481 (M)		REFLECTIONS	9.00	21.00	18.00
☐60160 (S)		RELFECTIONS	12.00	29.00	25.00
☐20589 (M)		THE PLATTERS	7.00	17.00	15.00
☐60254 (S)		THE PLATTERS	9.00	25.00	22.50
☐20591 (M)		MORE ENCORE OF GOLDEN HITS .	7.00	17.00	15.00
☐60252 (S)		MORE ENCORE OF GOLDEN HITS .	9.00	25.00	22.50
☐20669 (M)		SONG FOR THE LONELY	7.00	17.00	15.00
☐60669 (S)		SONG FOR THE LONELY	9.00	25.00	22.50
☐20693 (M)		ENCORE OF GOLDEN HITS			
		OF THE GROUPS	7.00	17.00	15.00
☐60893 (S)		ENCORE OF GOLDEN HITS			
		OF THE GROUPS	9.00	25.00	22.50
☐20759 (M)		MOONLIGHT MEMORIES	7.00	17.00	15.00
☐60759 (S)		MOONLIGHT MEMORIES	8.00	21.00	18.00
☐20782 (M)		THE PLATTERS ALL-TIME			
		MOVIE HITS	7.00	17.00	15.00
☐60782 (S)		THE PLATTERS SING ALL-TIME			
		MOVIE HITS	8.00	21.00	18.00
☐20808 (M)		THE PLATTERS SING LATINO	5.50	14.00	12.00
☐60808 (S)		THE PLATTERS SING LATINO	7.00	17.00	15.00
☐20841 (M)		CHRISTMAS WITH THE PLATTERS	5.50	14.00	12.00
☐60841 (S)		CHRISTMAS WITH THE PLATTERS	7.00	17.00	15.00
☐20983 (M)		NEW SOUL OF THE PLATTERS . . .	5.50	14.00	12.00
☐60983 (S)		NEW SOUL OF THE PLATTERS . . .	7.00	17.00	15.00

PLAYMATES

			Current Price Range		P/Y AVG
☐4003	ROULETTE	BAREFOOT GIRL/PRETTY WOMAN	3.50	6.00	4.35
☐4022		DARLING IT'S WONDERFUL/			
		ISLAND GIRL	3.50	6.00	4.35

			Current Price Range		P/Y AVG
☐ 4022		DARLING IT'S WONDERFUL/ MAGIC SHOES	3.50	6.00	4.35
☐ 4037		JO-ANN/YOU CAN'T STOP ME FROM DREAMING	3.25	5.50	4.00
☐ 4056		LET'S BE LOVERS/ GIVE ME ANOTHER CHANCE	3.25	5.50	4.00
☐ 4072		DON'T GO HOME/CAN'T YOU GET IT THROUGH YOUR HEAD?	3.25	5.50	4.00
☐ 4100		THE DAY I DIED/WHILE THE RECORD GOES AROUND	3.25	5.50	4.00
☐ 4115		BEEP BEEP/YOUR LOVE	3.25	5.50	4.00
☐ 4126		STAR LOVE/THE THING-A-MA-JIG	3.25	5.50	4.00
☐ 4160		WHAT IS LOVE?/I AM	3.25	5.50	4.00
☐ 4200		FIRST LOVE/A CIU-E	3.25	5.50	4.00
☐ 4211		ON THE BEACH/THE SONG EVERYBODY'S SINGING	3.25	5.50	4.00
☐ 4227		THESE THINGS I OFFER YOU/ SECOND CHANCE	3.25	5.50	4.00
☐ 4252		OUR WEDDING DAY/ PARADE OF PRETTY GIRLS	3.25	5.50	4.00
☐ 4276		WAIT FOR ME/ THE EYES OF AN ANGEL	3.25	5.50	4.00
☐ 4322		LITTLE MISS STUCK-UP/ REAL LIFE	3.25	5.50	4.00
☐ 4370		TELL ME WHAT SHE SAID/ COWBOYS NEVER CRY	3.25	5.50	4.00
☐ 4393		WIMOWEH/ONE LITTLE KISS	3.25	5.50	4.00
☐ 4432		KEEP YOU HANDS IN YOUR POCKETS/THE COP ON THE BEAT	3.25	5.50	4.00
☐ 4464		WHAT A FUNNY WAY TO SHOW IT/ PETTICOATS FLY	3.25	5.50	4.00
☐ 10422	*ABC-PARAMOUNT*	JUST A LITTLE BIT/ "A" MY NAME IS ALICE	3.00	5.00	3.65
☐ 10468		SHE NEVER LOOKD BETTER/ BUT NOT THROUGH TEARS	3.00	5.00	3.65
☐ 10492		CROSS MY FINGERS/ I'LL NEVER GET OVER YOU	3.00	5.00	3.65
☐ 10522		THE GUY BEHIND THE WHEEL/ THE ONLY GUY LEFT ON THE CORNER	3.00	5.00	3.65
☐ 760	*COLPIX*	PIECE OF THE SKY/ FIDDLER ON THE ROOF	3.00	5.00	3.65
☐ 769		ONE BY ONE THE ROSES DIED/ SPANISH PERFUME	3.00	5.00	3.65

PLAYMATES—ALBUMS

☐ 25002 (M)	*ROULETTE*	CALYPSO	9.00	25.00	22.50
☐ 25043 (M)		ROCK AND ROLL RECORD HOP	8.00	21.00	18.00
☐ 25068 (M)		CUTTIN' CAPERS	8.00	21.00	18.00
☐ 25068 (S)		CUTTIN' CAPERS	12.00	29.00	25.00
☐ 25084 (M)		BROADWAY SHOW STOPPERS	7.00	17.00	15.00
☐ 25139 (S)		BROADWAY SHOW STOPPERS	9.00	25.00	22.50
☐ 25139 (M)		WAIT FOR ME	7.00	17.00	15.00
☐ 25139 (S)		WAIT FOR ME	9.00	25.00	22.50

PLEDGES
SEE: SKIP AND FLIP

☐ 3517	*REV*	BERMUDA SHORTS/BETTY JEAN	5.00	9.00	7.00

PONI-TAILS

☐ 9846	*ABC-PARAMOUNT*	IT'S JUST MY LUCK TO BE FIFTEEN/WILD EYES AND TENDER LIPS	5.00	9.00	6.50

			Current Price Range		P/Y AVG
☐9934		BORN TOO LATE/COME ON, JOEY, DANCE WITH ME	4.00	7.00	4.85
☐9969		SEVEN MINUTES IN HEAVEN/ CLOSE FRIENDS	3.50	6.00	4.35
☐9995		FATHER TIME/EARLY TO BED . . .	3.25	5.50	4.00
☐10027		MOODY/OO-PAH POLKA	3.25	5.50	4.00
☐10047		I'LL BE SEEING YOU/ I'LL KEEP TRYIN'	3.25	5.50	4.00
☐10077		BEFORE WE SAY GOODNIGHT/ COME BE MY LOVE	3.25	5.50	4.00
☐10014		WHO, WHEN AND WHY/ OH, MY, YOU	3.25	5.50	4.00

PORTRAITS

☐928	SIDEWALK	A MILLION TO ONE/ LET'S TELL THE WORLD	5.50	11.00	9.00
☐935		OVER THE RAINBOW/ RUNAROUND GIRL	5.50	11.00	9.00

SANDY POWELL

☐557	HERALD	PISTOL PACKIN' MAMA/BON BON	25.00	46.00	42.00

PREMIERS

☐615	FARON	FARMER JOHN/DUFFY'S BLUES .	4.50	7.50	6.00

ELVIS PRESLEY

☐209	SUN	THAT'S ALL RIGHT/ BLUE MOON OF KENTUCKY . . .	200.00	390.00	270.00
☐210		GOOD ROCKIN' TONIGHT/I DON'T CARE IF THE SUN DON'T SHINE	185.00	325.00	225.00
☐215		MILKCOW BLUES BOOGIE/ YOU'RE A HEARTBREAKER	275.00	450.00	310.00
☐217		BABY LET'S PLAY HOUSE/ I'M LEFT, YOUR RIGHT, SHE'S GONE	150.00	275.00	190.00
☐223		MYSTERY TRAIN/I FORGOT TO REMEMBER TO FORGET	140.00	260.00	185.00
☐6357	RCA	MYSTERY TRAIN/I FORGOT TO REMEMBER TO FORGET	16.00	29.00	19.50
☐6380		THAT'S ALL RIGHT/ BLUE MOON OF KENTUCKY . . .	16.00	29.00	19.50
☐6381		GOOD ROCKIN' TONIGHT/I DON'T CARE IF THE SUN DON'T SHINE	16.00	29.00	19.50
☐6382		MILKCOW BLUES BOOGIE/ YOU'RE A HEARTBREAKER	16.00	29.00	19.50
☐6383		BABY LET'S PLAY HOUSE/ I'M LEFT, YOU'RE RIGHT, SHE'S GONE	16.00	29.00	19.50
☐6420		HEARTBREAK HOTEL/ I WAS THE ONE	6.00	10.00	7.00
☐6540		I WANT YOU, I NEED YOU, I LOVE YOU/MY BABY LEFT ME	6.00	10.00	7.00
☐6604		DON'T BE CRUEL/HOUND DOG . .	5.00	9.00	6.50
☐6636		BLUE SUEDE SHOES/ TUTTI FRUITTI	16.00	29.00	19.50
☐6637		I GOT A WOMAN/ I'M COUNTIN' ON YOU	16.00	29.00	19.50
☐6638		I'M GONNA SIT RIGHT DOWN AND CRY OVER YOU/I'LL NEVER LET YOU GO	16.00	29.00	19.50
☐6639		TRYIN' TO GET TO YOU/ I LOVE YOU BECAUSE	16.00	29.00	19.50
☐6640		BLUE MOON/JUST BECAUSE	16.00	29.00	19.50
☐6641		MONEY HONEY/ ONE-SIDED LOVE AFFAIR	16.00	29.00	19.50

		Current Price Range		P/Y AVG
☐6642	SHAKE, RATTLE AND ROLL/			
	LAWDY MISS CLAWDY	16.00	29.00	19.50
☐6643	LOVE ME TENDER/			
	ANYWAY YOU WANT ME	5.00	9.00	6.00
☐6800	TOO MUCH/PLAYING FOR KEEPS	5.00	9.00	6.00
☐6870	ALL SHOOK UP/THAT'S WHEN			
	YOUR HEARTACHES BEGIN ...	5.00	9.00	6.00
☐7000	TEDDY BEAR/LOVING YOU	5.00	9.00	6.00
☐7035	JAILHOUSE ROCK/			
	TREAT ME NICE	5.50	9.00	6.00
☐7150	DON'T/I BEG OF YOU	5.00	9.00	6.00
☐7240	WEAR MY RING AROUND YOUR			
	NECK/DONCHA THINK			
	IT'S TIME	5.00	9.00	6.00
☐7280	HARD HEADED WOMAN/			
	DON'T ASK ME WHY	5.00	9.00	6.00
☐7410	ONE NIGHT/I GOT STUNG	5.00	9.00	6.00
☐7506	A FOOL SUCH AS I/			
	I NEED YOUR LOVE TONIGHT ..	4.00	7.00	4.85
☐7600	A BIG HUNK O' LOVE/			
	MY WISH CAME TRUE	4.00	7.00	4.85
☐7740	STUCK ON YOU/			
	FAME AND FORTUNE	3.50	6.00	4.35
☐7740	STUCK ON YOU/FAME AND			
	FORTUNE (stereo single)	80.00	150.00	100.00
☐7777	IT'S NOW OR NEVER/			
	A MESS OF BLUES	3.50	6.00	4.35
☐7777	IT'S NOW OR NEVER/			
	A MESS OF BLUES			
	(stereo single)	80.00	150.00	100.00
☐7810	ARE YOU LONESOME TONIGHT?/			
	I GOTTA KNOW	3.50	6.00	4.35
☐7810	ARE YOU LONESOME TONIGHT?/			
	I GOTTA KNOW (stereo single) ..	80.00	150.00	100.00
☐7850	SURRENDER/LONELY MAN	3.50	6.00	4.35
☐7850	SURRENDER/LONELY MAN			
	(stereo single)	110.00	200.00	130.00
☐7880	I FEEL SO BAD/			
	WILD IN THE COUNTRY	3.50	6.00	4.35
☐7880	I FEEL SO BAD/WILD IN THE			
	COUNTRY (stereo single)	100.00	200.00	130.00
☐7908	HIS LATEST FLAME/			
	LITTLE SISTER	3.25	5.50	4.00
☐7968	CAN'T HELP FALLING IN LOVE/			
	ROCK-A-HULA-BABY	3.25	5.50	4.00
☐7992	GOOD LUCK CHARM/ANYTHING			
	THAT'S A PART OF YOU	3.25	5.50	4.00
☐8041	SHE'S NOT YOU/JUST TELL HER			
	JIM SAID HELLO	3.25	5.50	4.00
☐8100	RETURN TO SENDER/			
	WHERE DO YOU COME FROM? .	3.25	5.50	4.00
☐8134	ONE BROKEN HEART FOR SALE/			
	THEY REMIND ME TOO MUCH			
	OF YOU	3.25	5.50	4.00
☐8188	DEVIL IN DISGUISE/			
	PLEASE DON'T DRAG THAT			
	STING AROUND	3.25	5.50	4.00
☐8243	BOSSA NOVA BABY/WITCHCRAFT .	3.75	5.50	4.25
☐8307	KISSIN' COUSINS/IT HURTS ME .	3.25	5.50	4.00
☐8360	WHAT'D I SAY/VIVA LAS VEGAS .	3.25	5.50	4.00
☐8400	SUCH A NIGHT/NEVER ENDING ..	3.25	5.50	4.00
☐8440	ASK ME/			
	AIN'T THAT LOVING YOU BABY	3.25	5.50	4.00
☐8500	DO THE CLAM/YOU'LL BE GONE .	3.25	5.50	4.00

		Current Price Range		P/Y AVG
☐8585	(SUCH AN) EASY QUESTION/			
	IT FEELS SO RIGHT	3.25	5.50	4.00
☐8657	I'M YOURS/IT'S A LONG, LONELY			
	HIGHWAY	3.25	5.50	4.00
☐8740	TELL ME WHY/BLUE RIDER	3.25	5.50	4.00
☐8780	FRANKIE AND JOHNNY/PLEASE			
	DON'T STOP LOVING ME	3.25	5.50	4.00
☐8870	LOVE LETTERS/COME WHAT MAY.	3.25	5.50	4.00
☐8941	ALL THAT I AM/SPINOUT	5.00	9.00	6.00
☐8950	IF EVERYDAY WAS LIKE			
	CHRISTMAS/HOW WOULD YOU			
	LIKE TO BE?	3.75	5.50	4.25
☐9056	INDESCRIBABLY BLUE/			
	FOOLS FALL IN LOVE	3.25	5.50	4.00
☐9115	LONG LEGGED GIRL/THAT'S			
	SOMEONE YOU NEVER FORGET	3.25	5.50	4.00
☐9287	THERE'S ALWAYS ME/JUDY	3.25	5.50	4.00
☐9341	BIG BOSS MAN/			
	YOU DON'T KNOW ME	3.25	5.50	4.00
☐94258	GUITAR MAN/			
	HIGH HEELED SNEAKERS	3.25	5.50	4.00
☐9465	U.S. MALE/STAY AWAY JOE	3.25	5.50	4.00
☐9547	LET YOURSELF GO/YOUR TIME			
	HASN'T COME YET BABY	3.25	5.50	4.00
☐9600	YOU'LL NEVER WALK ALONE/			
	WE CALL ON HIM	3.25	5.50	4.00
☐9610	A LITTLE LESS CONVERSATION/			
	ALMOST IN LOVE	3.25	5.50	4.00
☐9670	IF I CAN DREAM/			
	EDGE OF REALITY	3.00	5.00	3.65
☐9731	MEMORIES/CHARRO	3.00	5.00	3.65
☐9741	IN THE GHETTO/ANY DAY NOW ..	3.00	5.00	3.65
☐9747	CLEAN UP YOUR OWN BACK YARD/			
	THE FAIR IS MOVING ON	3.00	5.00	3.65
☐9764	SUSPICIOUS MINDS/			
	YOU'LL THINK OF ME	3.00	5.00	3.65
☐9768	DON'T CRY DADDY/			
	RUBBERNECKIN'	3.00	5.00	3.65
☐9791	KENTUCKY RAIN/			
	MY LITTLE FRIEND	3.00	5.00	3.65
☐9835	THE WONDER OF YOU/			
	MAMA LIKED THE ROSES	3.00	5.00	3.65
☐9873	I'VE LOST YOU/			
	THE NEXT STEP IS LOVE	3.00	5.00	3.65
☐9916	YOU DON'T HAVE TO SAY YOU			
	LOVE ME/PATCH IT UP	3.00	5.00	3.65
☐9960	I REALLY DON'T WANT TO KNOW/			
	THERE GOES MY EVERYTHING .	3.00	5.00	3.65
☐9980	WHERE DID THEY GO, LORD?/			
	RAGS TO RICHES	3.00	5.00	3.65
☐9985	LIFE/ONLY BELIEVE	3.00	5.00	3.65
☐9998	I'M LEAVIN'/HEART OF ROME ...	3.00	5.00	3.65
☐1017	IT'S ONLY LOVE/			
	THE SOUND OF YOUR CRY	3.00	5.00	3.65
☐0619	UNTIL IT'S TIME FOR YOU TO GO/			
	WE CAN MAKE THE MORNING .	3.00	5.00	3.65
☐0672	AN AMERICAN TRILOGY/			
	THE FIRST TIME I EVER			
	SAW YOUR FACE	3.00	5.00	3.65
☐0769	BURNING LOVE/			
	IT'S A MATTER OF TIME	2.75	4.50	3.25
☐0815	SEPARATE WAYS/			
	ALWAYS ON MY MIND	2.75	4.50	3.25
☐0910	STEAMROLLER BLUES/FOOL	2.75	4.50	3.25

RCA VICTOR, LSP-3921

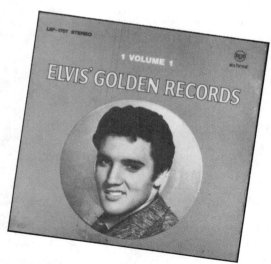

RCA, LSP-1707

			Current Price Range		P/Y AVG
☐ 0088		RAISED ON ROCK/ FOR OL' TIME SAKE	2.75	4.50	3.25
☐ 0196		I'VE GOT A THING ABOUT YOU BABY/TAKE GOOD CARE OF HER	2.75	4.50	3.25
☐ 0280		IF YOU TALK IN YOUR SLEEP/ HELP ME	2.75	4.50	3.25
☐ 10074		PROMISED LAND/IT'S MIDNIGHT	2.75	4.50	3.25
☐ 10191		MY BOY/THINKING ABOUT YOU .	2.75	4.50	3.25
☐ 10278		T-R-O-U-B-L-E/MR. SONGMAN ..	2.75	4.50	3.25
☐ 10401		BRINGING IT BACK/ PIECES OF MY LIFE	2.75	4.50	3.25
☐ 10601		HURT/FOR THE HEART	2.75	4.50	3.25
☐ 10857		MOODY BLUE/ SHE THINKS I STILL CARE	2.75	4.50	3.25
		ELVIS PRESLEY—GOLD STANDARD SINGLES			
☐ 0639	*RCA*	KISS ME QUICK/SUSPICION	3.25	5.50	4.00
☐ 0643		CRYING IN THE CHAPEL/ I BELIEVE IN THE MAN IN THE SKY	3.00	5.00	3.50
☐ 0647		BLUE CHRISTMAS/SANTA CLAUS IS BACK IN TOWN	4.50	7.50	6.00
☐ 0650		PUPPET ON A STRING/ WOODEN HEART	2.75	4.50	3.00
☐ 0651		JOSHUA FIT THE BATTLE/ KNOWN ONLY TO HIM	4.50	7.50	6.00
☐ 0652		SWING DOWN SWEET CHARIOT/ MILKY WHITE WAY	4.50	7.50	6.00
☐ 0720		BLUE CHRISTMAS/ WOODEN HEART	3.25	5.50	4.00
☐ 0130		HOW GREAT THOU ART/ HIS HAND IN MINE	8.25	14.00	12.00
		ELVIS PRESLEY—EPs			
☐ 1254	*RCA*	ELVIS PRESLEY (double-pocket) ..	95.00	165.00	150.00
☐ 747		ELVIS PRESLEY	12.00	25.00	18.00
☐ 821		HEARTBREAK HOTEL...........	14.00	27.00	20.00
☐ 830		ELVIS PRESLEY	14.00	27.00	20.00
☐ 940		THE REAL ELVIS	14.00	27.00	20.00
☐ 965		ANYWAY YOU WANT ME	14.00	27.00	20.00
☐ 4006		LOVE ME TENDER	12.00	25.00	18.00
☐ 992		ELVIS, VOL. I...............	12.00	25.00	18.00
☐ 993		ELVIS, VOL. II	14.00	27.00	20.00
☐ 994		STRICTLY ELVIS	14.00	27.00	20.00
☐ 1-1515		LOVING YOU, VOL. I	14.00	27.00	20.00
☐ 2-1515		LOVING YOU, VOL. II	14.00	27.00	20.00
☐ 4041		JUST FOR YOU	14.00	27.00	20.00
☐ 4054		PEACE IN THE VALLEY	12.00	25.00	18.00
☐ 4108		ELVIS SINGS CHRISTMAS SONGS	14.00	27.00	20.00
☐ 4114		JAILHOUSE ROCK	14.00	27.00	20.00
☐ 4319		KING CREOLE, VOL. I	14.00	27.00	20.00
☐ 4321		KING CREOLE, VOL. II	14.00	27.00	20.00
☐ 4325		ELVIS SAILS	27.00	48.00	42.00
☐ 4340		CHRISTMAS WITH ELVIS	14.00	27.00	20.00
☐ 4368		FOLLOW THAT DREAM	8.25	14.00	12.00
☐ 4371		KID GALAHAD	8.25	14.00	12.00
☐ 4382		EASY COME, EASY GO	9.50	18.00	15.00
☐ 4383		TICKLE ME..................	9.50	18.00	15.00
☐ 5088		A TOUCH OF GOLD, VOL. I (maroon label)	35.00	56.00	48.00
☐ 5088		A TOUCH OF GOLD, VOL. I (black label)	12.00	25.00	18.00
☐ 5120		THE REAL ELVIS (reissue) (maroon label)	35.00	54.00	48.00
☐ 5120		THE REAL ELVIS (reissue) (black label)	9.50	15.00	12.00

			Current Price Range		P/Y AVG
☐5121		PEACE IN THE VALLEY (reissue) (maroon label)	35.00	54.00	48.00
☐5151		PEACE IN THE VALLEY (reissue) (black label)	11.00	21.00	12.50
☐5122		KING CREOLE, VOL. I (reissue) (maroon label)	40.00	75.00	45.00
☐5122		KING CREOLE, VOL. I (reissue) (black label)	11.00	21.00	12.50
☐5101		A TOUCH OF GOLD, VOL. II (maroon label)	40.00	75.00	45.00
☐5101		A TOUCH OF GOLD, VOL. II (black label)	14.00	29.00	18.00
☐5141		A TOUCH OF GOLD, VOL. II (maroon label)	40.00	75.00	45.00
☐5141		A TOUCH OF GOLD, VOL. III (black label)	14.00	29.00	18.00
☐5157		ELVIS SAILS (reissue) (maroon label)	48.00	89.00	55.00
☐5157		ELVIS SAILS (reissue) (maroon label)	14.00	29.00	18.00

ELVIS PRESLEY—COMPACT 33's

			Current Price Range		P/Y AVG
☐37-7850	*RCA*	SURRENDER/LONELY MAN	55.00	130.00	80.00
☐37-7880		I FEEL SO BAD/ WILD IN THE COUNTRY	85.00	185.00	125.00
☐37-7908		HIS LATEST FLAME/ LITTLE SISTER	85.00	185.00	125.00
☐37-7968		CAN'T HELP FALLING IN LOVE/ ROCK-A-HULA BABY	85.00	185.00	125.00
☐37-7992		GOOD LUCK CHARM/ANYTHING THAT'S PART OF YOU	85.00	185.00	125.00
☐37-8041		SHE'S NOT YOU/JUST TELL HER JIM SAID HELLO	100.00	250.00	170.00
☐37-8100		RETURN TO SENDER/ WHERE DO YOU COME FROM? .	100.00	250.00	170.00

ELVIS PRESLEY-ALBUMS

THE ALBUMS BELOW WERE FIRST ISSUED ONLY IN MONO

			Current Price Range		P/Y AVG
☐1254 (M)	*RCA*	ELVIS PRESLEY	30.00	62.00	40.00
☐1382 (M)		ELVIS.	30.00	62.00	40.00
☐1515 (M)		LOVING YOU	20.00	40.00	28.00
☐1035 (M)		ELVIS' CHRISTMAS ALBUM (double-pocket)	80.00	195.00	130.00
☐1707 (M)		ELVIS' GOLDEN RECORDS	20.00	40.00	28.00
☐1884 (M)		KING CREOLE.	20.00	40.00	28.00
☐1951 (M)		ELVIS' CHRISTMAS ALBUM (reissue) (photo on back)	20.00	40.00	28.00
☐1990 (M)		FOR LP FANS ONLY	27.00	58.00	40.00
☐2011 (M)		A DATE WITH ELVIS (double pocket)	37.00	85.00	58.00
☐2011 (M)		A DATE WITH ELVIS (single pocket)	20.00	40.00	28.00
☐2075		ELVIS' GOLDEN RECORDS, VOL. II	20.00	40.00	28.00

THE ALBUMS BELOW HAVE EQUIVALENT VALUE IN MONO AND STEREO

			Current Price Range		P/Y AVG
☐2231 (M)		ELVIS IS BACK	20.00	40.00	28.00
☐2256 (M)		G.I. BLUES	20.00	40.00	28.00
☐2328 (M)		HIS HAND IN MINE	14.00	31.00	21.00
☐2370 (M)		SOMETHING FOR EVERYBODY . . .	20.00	40.00	28.00
☐2436 (M)		BLUE HAWAII	20.00	40.00	28.00
☐2523 (M)		POT LUCK	20.00	40.00	28.00
☐2621 (M)		GIRLS! GIRLS! GIRLS!	20.00	40.00	28.00
☐2697 (M)		IT HAPPENED AT THE WORLD'S FAIR	20.00	40.00	28.00
☐2697 (M)		FUN IN ACAPULCO	17.00	37.00	25.00
☐2765 (M)		ELVIS' GOLDEN RECORDS, VOL. II	17.00	37.00	25.00

			Current Price Range		P/Y AVG
☐2894 (M)		KISSIN' COUSINS	17.00	37.00	25.00
☐2999 (M)		ROUSTABOUT	17.00	37.00	25.00
☐3338 (M)		GIRL HAPPY	17.00	37.00	25.00
☐3450 (M)		ELVIS FOR EVERYONE	17.00	37.00	25.00
☐3468 (M)		HARUM SCARUM			
		(with photo enclosed)	35.00	65.00	40.00
☐3553 (M)		FRANKIE AND JOHNNY	20.00	40.00	28.00
☐3643 (M)		PARADISE, HAWAIIAN STYLE	17.00	37.00	25.00
☐3702 (M)		SPINOUT	20.00	40.00	28.00
☐3758 (M)		HOW GREAT THOU ART	17.00	37.00	25.00
☐3787 (M)		DOUBLE TROUBLE	17.00	37.00	25.00
		THE ALBUMS BELOW HAVE A HIGHER VALUE IN MONO			
☐3893 (M)		CLAMBAKE	45.00	105.00	70.00
☐3893 (S)		CLAMBAKE	20.00	40.00	28.00
☐3921 (M)		ELVIS' GOLDEN RECORDS,			
		VOL. IV	100.00	250.00	170.00
☐3921 (S)		ELVIS' GOLDEN RECORDS,			
		VOL. IV	20.00	40.00	28.00
☐3989 (M)		SPEEDWAY	350.00	850.00	595.00
☐3989 (S)		SPEEDWAY	20.00	40.00	28.00

JOHNNY PRESTON

☐71474	**MERCURY**	RUNNING BEAR/			
		MY HEART KNOWS	3.25	5.50	4.00
☐71528		CRADLE OF LOVE/CITY OF TEARS	3.25	5.50	4.00
☐71651		FEEL SO FINE/I'M STARTING			
		TO GO STEADY	3.25	5.50	4.00
☐71691		UP IN THE AIR/CHARMING BILLY	3.25	5.50	4.00
☐71728		ROCK AND ROLL GUITAR/			
		NEW BABY FOR CHRISTMAS	3.25	5.50	4.00
☐71761		LEAVE MY KITTEN ALONE/			
		TOKEN OF LOVE	3.00	5.00	3.65
☐71803		I FEEL GOOD/WILLY WALK	3.00	5.00	3.65
☐71865		SHE ONCE BELONGED TO ME/			
		LET THEM TALK	3.00	5.00	3.65
☐71908		FREE ME/KISSIN' TREE	3.00	5.00	3.65
☐71951		BROKEN HEARTS ANONYMOUS/			
		LET'S LEAVE IT THAT WAY	3.00	5.00	3.65
☐72049		LET THE BIG BOSS MAN/			
		THE DAY AFTER FOREVER	3.00	5.00	3.65
☐1201	**HALLWAY**	ALL AROUND THE WORLD/			
		JUST PLAIN HURT	3.00	5.00	3.65
☐1204		WILLIE AND THE HAND JIVE/			
		I'VE GOT MY EYES ON YOU	3.00	5.00	3.65
☐101	**TCF HALL**	RUNNING BEAR '65/DEDICATED			
		TO THE ONE I LOVE	3.00	5.00	3.65
☐120		GOOD GOOD LOVIN'/			
		I'M ASKING FORGIVENESS	3.00	5.00	3.65
		JOHNNY PESTON—EP			
☐3397	**MERCURY**	RUNNING BEAR	7.00	13.00	11.00
		JOHNNY PRESTON—ALBUMS			
☐20592 (M)		RUNNING BEAR	16.00	39.00	35.00
☐60592 (S)		RUNNING BEAR	24.00	58.00	50.00
☐20609 (M)		COME ROCK WITH ME	12.00	29.00	25.00
☐60609 (S)		COME ROCK WITH ME	16.00	39.00	35.00

LLOYD PRICE

☐428	**SPECIALTY**	LAWDY MISS CLAWDY/MAILMAN			
		BLUES (Fats Domino on piano)	6.00	12.00	8.50
☐440		OOH OOH OOH/RESTLESS HEART	5.50	10.00	7.00
☐452		AIN'T IT A SHAME/			
		TELL ME PRETTY BABY	5.50	10.00	7.00
☐457		SO LONG/			
		WHAT'S THE MATTER NOW	5.50	10.00	7.00

		Current Price Range		P/Y AVG
☐463	WHERE YOU AT?/BABY DON'T TURN YOUR BACK ON ME	5.50	10.00	7.00
☐471	I WISH YOUR PICTURE WAS YOU/ FROG LEGS	5.50	10.00	7.00
☐483	LET ME COME HOME BABY/ TOO LATE FOR TEARS	5.50	10.00	7.00
☐494	WALKIN' THE TRACK/JIMMIE LEE.	5.50	10.00	7.00
☐535	CHEE KOO BABY/OO EE BABY ...	5.50	10.00	7.00
☐540	LORD LORD, AMEN/TRYING TO FIND SOMEONE TO LOVE	5.50	10.00	7.00
☐571	I YI YI GOMEN-A-SAL (I'M SORRY)/WOE HO HO	5.00	9.00	6.00
☐576	ROCK 'N' DANCE/ COUNTRY BOY ROCK	5.00	9.00	6.00
☐582	FORGIVE ME CLAWDY/ I'M GLAD GLAD	5.00	9.00	6.00
☐602	BABY PLEASE COME HOME/ BREAKING MY HEART (ALL OVER AGAIN)...........	4.00	7.00	4.85

FIRST-PRESSES OF THE ABOVE FEATURE A WAVY YELLOW CENTER LINE

☐301	**KRC** LONELY CHAIR/ THE CHICKEN AND THE BOP ...	4.00	7.00	4.85
☐303	HELLO LITTLE GIRL/GEORGIANA .	4.00	7.00	4.85
☐305	TO LOVE AND BE LOVED/ HOW MANY TIMES?	4.00	7.00	4.85
☐587	JUST BECAUSE/WHY	20.00	38.00	23.00
☐9792	**ABC-PARAMOUNT** JUST BECAUSE/WHY	3.50	6.00	4.35
☐9972	STAGGER LEE/YOU NEED LOVE ..	3.50	6.00	4.35
☐9997	WHERE WERE YOU (ON YOUR WEDDING DAY?)/ IS IT REALLY LOVE	3.50	6.00	4.35
☐10018	PERSONALITY/HAVE YOU EVER HAD THE BLUES?	3.50	6.00	4.35
☐10032	I'M GONNA GET MARRIED/ THREE LITTLE PIGS	3.50	6.00	4.35
☐10062	COME INTO MY HEART/ WON'TCHA COME HOME	3.25	5.50	4.00
☐10075	LADY LUCK/NEVER LET ME GO ..	3.25	5.50	4.00
☐10102	NO IF'S-NO AND'S/FOR LOVE ...	3.25	5.50	4.00
☐10123	QUESTION/ IF I LOOK A LITTLE BLUE	3.25	5.50	4.00
☐10139	JUST CALL ME/ WHO COULD HAVE TOLD YOU ..	3.00	5.00	3.65
☐10162	(YOU BETTER) KNOW WHAT YOU'RE DOING/THAT'S WHY TEARS COME AND GO	3.00	5.00	3.65
☐10177	I MADE YOU CRY/BOO HOO	3.00	5.00	3.65
☐10197	SAY I'M THE ONE/100%	3.00	5.00	3.65
☐10206	CHANTILLY LACE/ STRING OF PEARLS	3.00	5.00	3.65
☐10221	I AIN'T GIVIN' UP NOTHIN'/ MARY AND MAN-O	3.00	5.00	3.65
☐10229	TALK TO ME/ I COVER THE WATERFRONT ...	3.00	5.00	3.65
☐10288	'NOTHER FAIRY TALE/ BE A LEADER	3.00	5.00	3.65
☐10299	TWISTIN' THE BLUES/ POPEYE'S IRRESISTABLE YOU .	3.00	5.00	3.65
☐10342	COUNTERFEIL FRIENDS/ YOUR PICTURE	3.00	5.00	3.65
☐10372	UNDER YOUR SPELL AGAIN/ HAPPY BIRTHDAY MAM	3.00	5.00	3.65
☐10412	WHO'S SORRY NOW/HELLO BILL	3.00	5.00	3.65

			Current Price Range		P/Y AVG
		LLOYD PRICE—EPs			
☐ A-272	**ABC-PARAMOUNT**	THE EXCITING LLOYD PRICE	6.00	11.00	9.00
☐ B-272		THE EXCITING LLOYD PRICE	6.00	11.00	9.00
☐ C-272		THE EXCITING LLOYD PRICE	6.00	11.00	9.00
☐ 315		MR. PERSONALITY SINGS THE BLUES	5.50	11.00	9.00
		LLOYD PRICE—ALBUMS			
☐ 227 (M)	**ABC-PARAMOUNT**	THE EXCITING LLOYD PRICE	11.00	26.00	17.00
☐ 297 (M)		MR. PERSONALITY	9.00	22.00	14.00
☐ 315 (M)		MR. PERSONALITY SINGS THE BLUES	8.00	18.00	12.00
☐ 324 (M)		MR. PERSONALITY'S BIG 15	8.00	18.00	12.00
☐ 346 (M)		FANTASTIC LLOYD PRICE	8.00	18.00	12.00
☐ 366 (M)		LLOYD PRICE SINGS THE MILLION SELLERS	8.00	18.00	12.00
☐ 382 (M)		COOKIN'	7.00	16.00	10.50
		PRIMETTES (SUPREMES)			
☐ 120	**LUPINE**	TEARS OF SORROW/PRETTY BABY	26.00	46.00	42.00
		PRISONAIRES			
☐ 186	**SUN**	JUST WALKIN' IN THE RAIN/ BABY PLEASE	22.00	40.00	36.00
☐ 189		MY GOD IS REAL/ SOFTLY AND TENDERLY	17.00	30.00	25.00
☐ 191		A PRISONER'S PRAYER/I KNOW .	26.00	46.00	42.00
☐ 207		THERE IS LOVE IN YOU/ WHAT'LL YOU DO NEXT	190.00	310.00	300.00
		P. J. PROBY			
☐ 714	**SURFSIDE**	YOU GOT ME CRYING/ I NEED LOVE	5.00	8.50	7.00
☐ 9688	**LONDON**	HOLD ME/ THE TIP OF MY FINGERS	3.50	6.00	4.35
☐ 9705		TOGETHER/ SWEET AND TENDER ROMANCE	3.50	6.00	4.35
☐ 55367	**LIBERTY**	TRY TO FORGET HER/ THERE STANDS THE ONE	3.50	6.00	4.35
☐ 55505		THE OTHER SIDE OF TOWN/ WATCH ME WALK AWAY	3.50	6.00	4.35
☐ 55588		I CAN'T TAKE IT LIKE YOU CAN/ SO DO I	3.50	6.00	4.35
☐ 55757		SOMEWHERE/JUST LIKE HIM ...	3.25	5.50	4.00
☐ 55777		ROCKIN' PNEUMONIA/ I APOLOGIZE	3.25	5.50	4.00
☐ 55791		MISSION BELL/STAGGER LEE ...	3.25	5.50	4.00
☐ 55850		MARIA/GOOD THINGS ARE COMING MY WAY	3.25	5.50	4.00
☐ 55875		MY PRAYER/WICKED WOMAN ...	3.25	5.50	4.00
☐ 55936		NIKI HOKEY/GOOD THINGS ARE COMING MY WAY	3.25	5.50	4.00
☐ 55974		WORK WITH ME ANNIE/ YOU CAN'T COME HOME	3.25	5.50	4.00
☐ 55989		JUST HOLDING ON/ BUTTERFLY HIGH	3.25	5.50	4.00
☐ 56031		IT'S YOUR TURN TODAY/ I APOLOGIZE, BABY	3.25	5.50	4.00
☐ 56051		WHAT'S WRONG WITH MY WORLD?/TURN HER AWAY ...	3.25	5.50	4.00
☐ 56079		ROCKIN' PNEUMONIA/ JUST CALL, I'LL BE THERE ...	3.25	5.50	4.00

			Current Price Range		P/Y AVG

P. J. PROBY—ALBUMS

			Current Price Range		P/Y AVG
☐3406 (M)	LIBERTY	SOMEWHERE	8.00	21.00	18.00
☐7406 (S)		SOMEWHERE	9.00	25.00	22.50
☐3421 (M)		P. J. PROBY	8.00	21.00	18.00
☐7421 (S)		P. J. PROBY	9.00	25.00	22.50
☐3497 (M)		ENIGMA	7.00	17.00	15.00
☐7497 (S)		ENIGMA	8.00	21.00	18.00
☐3561 (M)		WHAT'S WRONG WITH MY WORLD?	7.00	17.00	15.00
☐7561 (S)		WHAT'S WRONG WITH MY WORLD?	8.00	21.00	18.00

ROD PRINCE

☐2140	COMET	MY STAR ALL ALONE/ RAINBOW OF LOVE	8.00	19.00	16.00

PYRAMIDS

☐13001	BEST	PYRAMID STOMP/PAUL	3.75	6.00	4.50
☐13002		PENETRATION/ HERE COMES MARSHA	3.00	5.00	3.50
☐13005	CEDWICKE	MIDNIGHT RUN/ CUSTOM CARAVAN	3.00	5.00	3.50
☐13006		CONTACT/PRESSURE	3.00	5.00	3.50

PYRAMIDS—ALBUM

☐1001 (M)	BEST	PENETRATION	13.00	24.00	20.00

Q

SUZI QUATRO

☐4512	RAK	ROLLING STONE/ BRAIN CONFUSION (by Susie Quatro)	7.00	13.00	11.00
☐45401	BELL	48 CRASH/(DJ)	3.25	5.50	4.00
☐45477		ALL SHOOK UP/ GLYCERINE QUEEN	3.00	5.00	3.50
☐45609		DEVIL GATE DRIVE/ IN THE MORNING	3.25	5.50	4.00
☐45615		KEEP A KNOCKIN'/(DJ)	3.00	5.00	3.50
☐16053	BIG TREE	CAN THE CAN/ DON'T MESS AROUND	3.00	5.00	3.50
☐0106	ARISTA	YOUR MAMA WON'T LIKE ME/ PETER, PETER	3.00	5.00	3.50

SUZI QUATRO—ALBUMS

☐1302 (S)	BELL	SUZI QUATRO	7.00	17.00	15.00
☐1313 (S)		QUATRO	7.00	17.00	15.00
☐4035 (S)	ARISTA	YOUR MAMA WON'T LIKE ME	6.00	15.00	13.50

QUEEN
SEE: LARRY LUREX, SMILE

☐45863	ELEKTRA	KEEP YOURSELF ALIVE/ SON AND DAUGHTER	5.00	8.50	7.00
☐45884		LIAR/(DJ)	4.50	7.50	6.00
☐45891		SEVEN SEAS OF RHYE/ SEE WHAT A FOOL I'VE BEEN	3.75	6.00	4.50
☐45226		KILLER QUEEN/ FLICK OF THE WRIST	2.50	4.50	3.00
☐45268		KEEP YOURSELF ALIVE/ LILY OF THE VALLEY- GOD SAVE THE QUEEN	3.25	5.50	4.00

LATER QUEEN SINGLES ARE WORTH UP TO $2.25 MINT

			Current Price Range		P/Y AVG

? AND THE MYSTERIANS
SEE: MYSTERIANS

			Current Price Range		P/Y AVG
☐ 102	**PA-GO-GO**	96 TEARS/MIDNIGHT HOUR	26.00	46.00	42.00
☐ 441		I NEED SOMEBODY/"8" TEEN . .	9.50	17.00	15.00
☐ 467		CAN'T GET ENOUGH OF YOU, BABY/SMOKES	5.50	11.00	9.00
☐ 479		GIRL (YOU CAPTIVATE ME)/ GOT TO	5.50	11.00	9.00
☐ 496		DO SOMETHING TO ME/ LOVE ME BABY	5.50	11.00	9.00
☐ 428	**CAMEO**	96 TEARS/MIDNIGHT HOUR	3.00	5.00	3.65
☐ 441		I NEED SOMEBODY/"8" TEN . . .	3.00	5.00	3.65
☐ 467		CAN'T GET ENOUGH OF YOU, BABY/SMOKES	3.00	5.00	3.65
☐ 479		GIRL (YOU CAPTIVATE ME)/ GOT TO	3.00	5.00	3.65
☐ 496		DO SOMETHING TO ME/ LOVE ME BABY	3.00	5.00	3.65

? AND THE MYSTERIANS—ALBUMS

☐ 2004 (M)	**CAMEO**	96 TEARS	7.00	17.00	15.00
☐ 2004 (S)		96 TEARS	8.00	21.00	18.00
☐ 2006 (M)		ACTION	7.00	17.00	15.00
☐ 2006 (S)		ACTION	8.00	21.00	18.00

QUICK
FEATURED: ERIC CARMEN
SEE: CHOIR

☐ 10516	**EPIC**	AIN'T NOTHING' GONNA STOP ME/ SOUTHERN COMFORT	7.00	13.00	11.00

QUIN-TONES

☐ 1009	**GEE**	STRANGE AS IT SEEMS/ I'M WILLING	85.00	150.00	100.00
☐ 1685	**CHESS**	I TRY SO HARD/DING DONG	5.50	11.00	9.00
☐ 108	**RED TOP**	DOWN THE AISLE OF LOVE/ PLEASE DEAR	7.00	13.00	11.00
☐ 321	**HUNT**	DOWN THE AISLE OF LOVE/ PLEASE DEAR	4.50	7.50	6.00
☐ 322		WHAT AM I TO DO?/ THERE'LL BE NO SORROW	4.50	7.50	6.00

EDDIE QUINTEROS

☐ 7009	**BRENT**	COME DANCE WITH ME/VIVIAN .	5.00	9.00	7.00
☐ 7012		LOOKIN' FOR MY BABY/ PLEASE DON'T GO	5.00	9.00	7.00
☐ 7014		SLOW DOWN SANDY/LINDA LOU .	6.00	11.00	9.00

QUOTATIONS

☐ 1003	**DOWNSTAIRS**	NIGHT/WHY DO YOU DO ME LIKE YOU DO	3.00	6.00	5.00
☐ 10245	**VERVE**	IMAGINATION/ALA MEN SY	7.50	12.00	10.00
☐ 10252		THIS LOVE OF MINE/WE'LL REACH HEAVEN TOGETHER . . .	7.50	12.00	10.00
☐ 10261		SEE YOU IN SEPTEMBER/ SUMMERTIME GOODBYES	7.50	12.00	10.00
☐ 107	**DE VENUS**	IT CAN HAPPEN TO YOU/ I DON'T HAVE TO WORRY	3.00	6.00	5.00

R

			Current Price Range		P/Y AVG

RACHEL AND THE REVOLVERS
PRODUCER: BRIAN WILSON

☐16392	DOT	THE REVO-LUTION/NUMBER ONE	11.00	21.00	18.00

RAINBO
FEATURED: SISSY SPACEK

☐7030	ROULETTE	C'MON TEACH ME TO LIVE/ JOHN, YOU WENT TOO FAR THIS TIME	5.00	9.00	7.00

RAINDROPS
FEATURED: JEFF BARRY, ELLIE GREENWICH

☐5444	JUBILEE	WHAT A GUY/ IT'S SO WONDERFUL	3.25	5.50	4.00
☐5455		THE KIND OF BOY YOU CAN'T FORGET/EVEN THOUGH YOU CAN'T DANCE	3.25	5.50	4.00
☐5466		THAT BOY JOHN/HANKY PANKY .	3.25	5.50	4.00
☐5469		BOOK OF LOVE/I WON'T CRY	3.25	5.50	4.00
☐5475		LET'S GET TOGETHER/ YOU GOT WANT I LIKE	3.25	5.50	4.00
☐5487		ONE MORE TEAR/ ANOTHER BOY LIKE MINE	3.25	5.50	4.00
☐5497		DON'T LET GO/ MY MAMA DON'T LIKE HIM . . .	3.25	5.50	4.00

RAINDROPS—ALBUMS

☐5023 (M)	JUBILEE	RAINDROPS	9.00	25.00	22.50
☐5023 (S)		RAINDROPS	12.00	25.00	22.50

RAINY DAZE

☐404	CHICKORY	THAT ACAPULCO GOLD/ IN MY MIND LIVES A FOREST . .	5.50	11.00	9.00
☐55002	UNI	THAT ACAPULCO GOLD/ IN MY MIND LIVES A FOREST . .	3.00	5.00	3.85
☐55011		DISCOUNT CITY/ GOOD MORNING, MR. SMITH . .	3.00	5.00	3.85
☐55026		BLOOD OF OBLIVION/STOP SIGN .	3.00	5.00	3.85
☐279	WHITE WHALE	MY DOOR IS ALWAYS OPEN/ MAKE ME LAUGH	3.00	5.00	3.85

RAINY DAZE—ALBUM

☐73002 (S)	UNI	THAT ACAPULCO GOLD	7.00	17.00	15.00

RAJAHS (NUTMEGS)

☐7805	KLIK	I FELL IN LOVE/SHIFTING SANDS	15.00	30.00	25.00

RALLY PACKS
FEATURED: JAN AND DEAN

☐66035	IMPERIAL	MOVE OUT LITTLE MUSTANG/ BUCKET SEATS	6.00	11.00	9.00

RAN-DELLS

☐4403	CHAIRMAN	MARTIAN HOP/ FORGIVE ME DARLING	3.00	5.00	3.50
☐4407		SOUND OF THE SUN/ COME ON AND LOVE ME TOO . .	3.00	5.00	3.50

			Current Price Range		P/Y AVG

RANDY AND THE RAINBOWS
SEE: DIALTONES

☐5059	*RUST*	DENISE/COME BACK	2.75	4.50	3.00
☐5073		WHY DO KIDS GROW UP?/			
		SHE'S MY ANGEL	3.00	5.00	3.50
☐5080		DRY YOUR EYES/			
		HAPPY TEENAGER	3.00	5.00	3.50
☐5091		LITTLE STAR/SHARIN'	3.25	5.50	4.00
☐5101		JOYRIDE/LITTLE HOT ROD SUZIE	3.00	5.00	3.50
☐4001	*MIKE*	LOVELY LIES/			
		I'LL FORGET HER TOMORROW	3.25	5.50	4.00
☐4004		QUARTER TO 3/HE'S A FUGITIVE	3.25	5.50	4.00
☐535	*B.T. PUPPY*	I'LL BE SEEING YOU/			
		OH, TO GET AWAY	3.00	5.00	3.50

KEN RANK

☐2194	*FENTON*	TWIN CITY SAUCER/KEN'S THING	12.00	24.00	20.00

THE SECOND SIDE OF THIS DISC IS NOT BY KEN RANK

RASCALS
SEE YOUNG RASCALS

RASPBERRIES
FEATURED: ERIC CARMEN

☐3280	*CAPITOL*	DON'T WANT TO SAY GOODBYE/			
		ROCK AND ROLL MAMA	3.00	5.00	3.50
☐3348		GO ALL THE WAY/			
		WITH YOU IN MY LIFE	2.75	4.50	3.00
☐3473		I WANNA BE WITH YOU/			
		GOIN' NOWHERE	2.75	4.50	3.00
☐3546		LET'S PRETEND/			
		EVERY WAY I CAN	2.75	4.50	3.00
☐3610		TONIGHT/HARD TO GET			
		OVER A HEARTBREAK	2.75	4.50	3.00
☐3765		I'M A ROCKER/MONEY DOWN	2.75	4.50	3.00
☐3826		ECSTACY/			
		DON'T WANNA SAY GOODBYE	2.75	4.50	3.00
☐3885		DRIVIN' AROUND/			
		MIGHT AS WELL	2.75	4.50	3.00
☐3946		OVERNIGHT SENSATION (HIT			
		RECORD)/HANDS ON YOU	2.75	4.50	3.00
☐4001		THE PARTY'S OVER/			
		CRUISIN' MUSIC	2.75	4.50	3.00

RASPBERRIES—ALBUMS

☐11036 (S)	*CAPITOL*	RASPBERRIES	5.50	11.00	9.00
☐11123 (S)		FRESH	5.50	11.00	9.00
☐11220 (S)		SIDE 3	5.50	11.00	9.00
☐11329 (S)		STARTING OVER	7.00	11.00	9.00
☐11542 (S)		RASPBERRIES' BEST	5.50	11.00	9.00

RATIONALS

☐101	*A-SQUARE*	LOOK WHAT YOU'RE DOIN'/			
		GAVE MY NAME	6.00	11.00	8.00
☐103		LITTLE GIRLS CRY/FEELIN' LOST	6.00	11.00	8.00
☐104		RESPECT/LEAVIN' HERE	6.00	11.00	8.00
☐107		I NEED YOU/OUT IN THE STREETS	5.00	9.00	7.00

LOU RAWLS

☐702	*SHAR-DEE*	MY HEART BELONGS TO YOU/			
		LOVE, LOVE, LOVE	3.75	6.00	4.50
☐705		KIDDIO/WALKIN' (FOR MILES)	3.75	6.00	4.50

			Current Price Range		P/Y AVG
☐305	*CANDIX*	IN MY LITTLE BLACK BOOK/JUST THOUGHT YOU'D LIKE TO KNOW	3.25	5.50	4.00
☐312		WHEN WE GET OLD/80 WAYS ...	3.25	5.50	4.00

RAY & THE DARCHAES

☐202	*BUZZY*	THERE WILL ALWAYS BE/ DARLING FOREVER	8.25	18.00	16.00

RAYS

☐1613	*CHESS*	TIPPITY TOP/MOO-GOO-GAI-PAN .	11.00	21.00	18.00
☐1678		HOW LONG MUST I WAIT?/ SECOND FIDDLE	9.50	17.00	15.00
☐102	*XYZ*	SILHOUETTES/DADDY COOL	14.00	24.00	20.00
☐605		MEDITERRANEAN MOON/ IT'S A CRYIN' SHAME	3.00	5.00	3.50
☐607		MAGIC MOON/LOUIE HOO HOO ..	3.00	5.00	3.50
☐117	*CAMEO*	SILHOUETTES/DADDY COOL	3.25	5.50	4.00
☐128		TRIANGLE/RENDEZVOUS	3.25	5.50	4.00
☐133		RAGS TO RICHES/ THE MAN ABOVE	3.25	5.50	4.00

RAYS—EP

☐5120	*CHESS*	THE RAYS	9.50	17.00	15.00

REBELS

SEE: BUFFALO REBELS, ROCKIN' REBELS

☐0094	*MARLEE*	WILD WEEKEND/ WILD WEEKEND CHA CHA	9.50	17.00	15.00
☐4125	*SWAN*	WILD WEEKEND/ WILD WEEKEND CHA CHA	3.00	5.00	3.50

EIVETS REDNOW (STEVIE WONDER)

☐7076	*GORDY*	ALFIE/MORE THAN A DREAM ...	3.00	5.00	3.50

REDWOODS

☐9947	*EPIC*	SHAKE SHAKE SHERRY/ THE MEMORY LINGERS ON ...	6.00	11.00	7.00
☐9473		NEVER TAKE IT AWAY/ UNEMPLOYMENT INSURANCE .	6.00	11.00	7.00
☐9505		WHERE YOU USED TO BE/ PLEASE MR. SCIENTIST	6.00	11.00	7.00

DENNY REED

☐1024	*MCI*	A TEENAGER FEELS IT TOO/ HOT WATER	8.25	14.00	12.00
☐3007	*TREY*	A TEENAGER FEELS IT TOO/ HOT WATER	3.25	5.50	4.00
☐3014		LITTLE LONELY BLUEBIRD/ NO ONE CARES	3.25	5.50	4.00

REFLECTIONS

☐9	*GOLDEN WORLD*	ROMEO AND JULIET/CAN'T YOU TELL BY THE LOOK IN MY EYES	3.00	5.00	3.65
☐12		LIKE COLUMBUS DID/ LONELY GIRL	3.00	5.00	3.65
☐15		TALKIN' 'BOUT MY GIRL/ OOWEE WOW	3.00	5.00	3.65
☐16		DON'T DO THAT TO ME/ A HENPECKED GUY	3.00	5.00	3.65
☐19		YOU'RE MY BABY/ SHABBY LITTLE HUT	3.00	5.00	3.65
☐20		POOR MAN'S SON/ COMIN' AT YOU	3.00	5.00	3.65

			Current Price Range		P/Y AVG

REFLECTIONS—ALBUM

| ☐ 300 (M) | GOLDEN WORLD | JUST LIKE ROMEO AND JULIET .. | 9.00 | 25.00 | 22.50 |

REGENTS

SEE: DESIRES, LITTLE DAVID, RUNAROUNDS

☐ 1002	COUSINS	BARBARA-ANN/I`M SO LONELY .	40.00	70.00	44.00
☐ 1065	GEE	BARBARA-ANN/I`M SO LONELY .	3.25	5.50	4.00
☐ 1071		RUNAROUND/			
		LAURA MY DARLING	3.25	5.50	4.00
☐ 1073		DON`T BE A FOOL/LIAR	3.25	5.50	4.00
☐ 1075		LONESOME BOY/OH BABY	3.25	5.50	4.00

REGENTS—ALBUMS

| ☐ 706 (M) | GEE | BARBARA-ANN .... | 14.00 | 35.00 | 30.00 |
| ☐ 706 (S) | | BARABARA-ANN .... | 19.00 | 49.00 | 45.00 |

RELATIONS

| ☐ 703 | KAPE | TOO PROUD TO LET YOU KNOW/ WHAT DID I DO WRONG ...... | 2.00 | 3.50 | 2.75 |

KEITH RELF

SEE: YARDBIRDS

| ☐ 10044 | EPIC | MR. ZERO/KNOWING .... | 5.00 | 9.00 | 6.00 |
| ☐ 10110 | | SHAPES IN MY MIND/ BLUE SANDS .... | 5.00 | 9.00 | 6.00 |

RENEGADES

FEATURED: BRUCE JOHNSTON, SANDY NELSON, KIM FOWLEY

| ☐ 537 | AMERICAN INTERNATIONAL | CHARGE!/GERONIMO .... | 8.25 | 14.00 | 12.00 |

REPARTA AND THE DELRONS

☐ 1036	WORLD ARTISTS	WHENEVER A TEENAGER CRIES/ HE`S MY GUY	3.25	5.50	4.00
☐ 1051		TOMMY/MAMA DON`T ALLOW ..	3.25	5.50	4.00
☐ 1062		THE BOY I LOVE/ I FOUND MY PLACE	3.25	5.50	4.00
☐ 1075		HE`S THE GREATEST/ SUMMER THOUGHTS	3.25	5.50	4.00

REPARTA AND THE DELRONS—ALBUM

| ☐ 2006 (M) | WORLD ARTISTS | WHENEVER A TEENAGER CRIES .. | 10.00 | 25.00 | 22.50 |

REUNION

| ☐ SR-45-18A | STARLIGHT | HEART OF SATURDAY NIGHT/ DRIFT AWAY .... | 10.00 | 19.00 | 13.00 |
| ☐ SR-45-17B | | LEAN ON ME/SLIPPING INTO DARKNESS .... | 10.00 | 19.00 | 13.00 |

REVALATIONS

| ☐ 45-15 | STARLIGHT RECORDS | HIGHER AND HIGHER/ SPANISH HARLEM .... | 4.00 | 6.00 | 4.50 |
| ☐ 45-16 | | LOVE POTION NO. 9/ DON`T LOOK BACK .... | 4.00 | 6.00 | 4.50 |

PAUL REVERE AND THE RAIDERS

☐ 106	GARDENA	BEATNIK STICKS/ORBIT	9.50	17.00	15.00
☐ 115		PAUL REVERE`S RIDE/ UNFINISHED 5TH	8.25	14.00	12.00
☐ 116		LIKE LONG HAIR/SHARON	6.00	12.00	8.00
☐ 118		LIKE CHARLESTON/ MIDNIGHT RIDE	5.50	10.00	7.00
☐ 124		ALL NIGHT LONG/GROOVY	5.50	10.00	7.00

			Current Price Range		P/Y AVG
☐ 127		LIKE BLUEGRASS/LEATHERNECK	5.50	10.00	7.00
☐ 131		SHAKE IT UP (PT. 1)(PT. 2)	5.50	10.00	7.00
☐ 137		TALL COOL ONE/ROAD RUNNER .	5.50	10.00	7.00
☐ 807	JERDEN	SO FINE/BLUES STAY AWAY	11.00	21.00	18.00
☐ 101	SANDE	LOUIE LOUIE/NIGHT TRAIN	8.25	17.00	15.00
☐ 42813	COLUMBIA	LOUIE LOUIE/NIGHT TRAIN	3.50	6.00	4.35
☐ 43008		HAVE LOVE, WILL TRAVEL/ LOUIE GO HOME	3.50	6.00	4.35
☐ 43114		OVE YOU/SWIM	3.50	6.00	4.35
☐ 43273		OO POO PAH DO/SOMETIMES ...	3.50	6.00	4.35
☐ 43375		STEPPIN' OUT/BLUE FOX	3.25	5.50	4.00
☐ 43461		JUST LIKE ME/B.F.D.R.F. BLUES	3.00	5.00	3.65
☐ 43356		KICKS/SHAKE IT UP	3.00	5.00	3.65
☐ 43678		HUNGRY/THERE SHE GOES	3.00	5.00	3.65
☐ 43810		THE GREAT AIRPLANE STRIKE/ IN MY COMMUNITY	3.00	5.00	3.65
☐ 43907		GOOD THING/UNDECIDED MAN ..	3.00	5.00	3.65
☐ 44018		UPS AND DOWNS/LESLIE	3.00	5.00	3.65
☐ 44094		HIM OR ME-WHAT'S IT GONNA BE/LEGEND OF PAUL REVERE .	3.00	5.00	3.65
☐ 44227		I HAD A DREAM/ UPON YOUR LEAVING	3.00	5.00	3.65
☐ 44335		PEACE OF MIND/ DO UNTO OTHERS	3.00	5.00	3.65
☐ 44444		TOO MUCH TALK/HAPPENING '68	3.00	5.00	3.65
☐ 44553		DON'T TAKE IT SO HARD/ OBSERVATION FROM FLIGHT 285	3.00	5.00	3.65
☐ 44655		CINDERELLA SUNSHINE/ IT'S HAPPENING	3.00	5.00	3.65
☐ 44744		MR. SUN, MR. MOON/ WITHOUT YOU	3.00	5.00	3.65
☐ 44854		LE ME/I DON'T KNOW	3.00	5.00	3.65
☐ 44970		WE GOTTA ALL GET TOGETHER/ FRANKFORT SIDE STREET	3.00	5.00	3.65
☐ 45082		JUST SEVENTEEN/SORCERESS WITH BLUE EYES	3.00	5.00	3.65
☐ 45150		MOVIN' ON/INTERLUDE (TO BE FORGOTTEN)	3.00	5.00	3.65
☐ 45332		INDIAN RESERVATION/ TERRY'S TUNE	2.75	4.75	3.50
☐ 45453		BIRDS OF A FEATHER/ THE TURKEY	2.75	4.75	3.50
☐ 45535		COUNTRY WINE/ IT'S HARD GETTING UP TODAY .	2.75	4.75	3.50
☐ 45601		POWDER BLUE MERCEDES QUEEN/ GOLDEN GIRLS SOMETIMES ...	2.75	4.75	3.50
☐ 45688		SONG SELLER/A SIMPLE SONG ..	2.75	4.75	3.50
☐ 45759		LOVE MUSIC/GOODBYE #9	2.75	4.75	3.50
☐ 45898		ALL OVER YOU/ SEABOARD LINE BOOGIE	2.75	4.75	3.50
☐ 10126		YOUR LOVE (IS THE ONLY LOVE)/ GONNA HAVE A GOOD TIME ...	2.75	4.75	3.50
☐ 2281	20th CENTURY	THE BRITISH ARE COMING/ SURRENDER AT APPOMATOX ..	2.75	4.75	3.50
☐ 6248	DRIVE	AIN'T NOTHING WRONG/ YOUNG ENOUGH TO CRY	2.75	4.75	3.50

PAUL REVERE AND THE RAIDERS—ALBUMS

☐ 1000 (M)	GARDENA	LIKE LONG HAIR	37.00	98.00	90.00
☐ 7004 (M)	JERDEN	IN THE BEGINNING	10.00	25.00	22.50
☐ 1001 (M)	SANDE	PAUL REVERE AND THE RAIDERS	49.00	130.00	120.00
☐ 2307 (M)	COLUMBIA	HERE THEY COME	7.00	17.00	15.00

			Current Price Range		P/Y AVG
☐ 9107 (S)		HERE THEY COME	9.00	25.00	22.50
☐ 2451 (M)		JUST LIKE US	6.00	15.00	13.50
☐ 9251 (S)		JUST LIKE US	10.00	17.00	15.00
☐ 2508 (M)		MIDNIGHT RIDE	7.00	13.00	11.00
☐ 9308 (S)		MIDNIGHT RIDE	10.00	17.00	15.00
☐ 2595 (M)		THE SPIRIT OF '67	7.00	13.00	11.00
☐ 9395 (S)		THE SPIRIT OF '67	10.00	17.00	15.00
☐ 2662 (M)		GREATEST HITS	6.00	11.00	9.00
☐ 9462 (S)		GREATEST HITS	8.50	14.00	12.00
☐ 2721 (M)		REVOLUTION	6.00	11.00	9.00
☐ 9521 (S)		REVOLUTION	7.00	13.00	11.00
☐ 2755 (M)		A CHRISTMAS PRESENT AND PAST	7.00	13.00	11.00
☐ 9555 (S)		A CHRISTMAS PRESENT AND PAST	6.00	11.00	9.00
☐ 2805 (M)		GOIN' TO MEMPHIS	7.00	13.00	11.00
☐ 9605 (S)		GOIN' TO MEMPHIS	6.00	11.00	11.00
☐ 9665 (S)		SOMETHING HAPPENING	5.50	11.00	9.00
☐ 9753 (S)		HARD AND HEAVY WITH MARSHMALLOW	5.50	11.00	9.00
☐ 9905 (S)		ALIAS PINK FUZZ	5.50	11.00	9.00
☐ 9964 (S)		COLLAGE (Raiders)	5.50	11.00	9.00

JODY REYNOLDS

			Current Price Range		P/Y AVG
☐ 1507	DEMON	ENDLESS SLEEP/TIGHT CAPRIS	3.25	5.50	4.00
☐ 1509		FIRE OF LOVE/DAISY MAE	3.25	5.50	4.00
☐ 1511		CLOSIN' IN/ELOPE WITH ME	3.25	5.50	4.00
☐ 1515		GOLDEN IDOL/BEULAH LEE	3.25	5.50	4.00
☐ 1519		PLEASE REMEMBER/THE STORM	3.25	5.50	4.00
☐ 7042	BRENT	RAGGEDY ANN/THE GIRL FROM KING MARIE	3.25	5.50	4.00

CHARLIE RICH
SEE: BOBBY SHERIDAN

			Current Price Range		P/Y AVG
☐ 3532	PHILLIPS INTERNATIONAL	WHIRLWIND/PHILADELPHIA BABY	7.00	13.00	11.00
☐ 3542		BIG MAN/REBOUND	5.00	8.00	7.00
☐ 3552		LONELY WEEKENDS/ EVERYTHING I DO IS WRONG	3.25	5.00	4.00
☐ 3560		GONNA BE WAITING/ SCHOOL DAYS	3.75	6.00	4.50
☐ 3562		STAY/ON MY KNEES	3.75	6.00	4.50
☐ 3566		WHO WILL THE NEXT FOOL BE?/ CAUGHT IN THE MIDDLE	3.75	6.00	4.50
☐ 3572		JUST A LITTLE SWEET/ IT'S TOO LATE	3.75	6.00	4.50
☐ 3584		THERE'S ANOTHER PLACE I CAN'T GO/I NEED YOUR LOVE	3.75	6.00	4.50
☐ 580020	GROOVE	SHE LOVED EVERYBODY BUT ME/ THE GRASS IS ALWAYS GREENER	3.00	5.00	3.50
☐ 580035		THE WAYS OF A WOMAN IN LOVE/ MOUNTAIN DEW	3.00	5.00	3.50
☐ 1993	SMASH	MOHAIR SAM/I WASHED MY HANDS IN MUDDY WATER	2.75	4.50	3.00
☐ 2012		THE DANCE OF LOVE/ I CAN'T GO ON	2.75	4.50	3.00
☐ 2022		SOMETHING JUST CAME OVER ME/HAWG JAW	2.75	4.50	3.00
☐ 2038		TEARS AGO/NO HOME	2.75	4.50	3.00

CHARLIE RICH—ALBUMS

			Current Price Range		P/Y AVG
☐ 1970 (M)	PHILLIPS INTERNATIONAL	LONELY WEEKENDS	42.00	100.00	65.00

			Current Price Range		P/Y AVG
☐ 27070 (M)	**SMASH**	MANY NEW SIDES OF CHARLIE RICH	7.00	17.00	15.00
☐ 67070 (S)		MANY NEW SIDES OF CHARLIE RICH	8.00	21.00	18.00

CLIFF RICHARD

☐ 4086	**LABEL**	MOVE IT/HIGH CLASS BABY	2.75	4.50	3.10
☐ 4154	**CAPITOL**	LIVIN' LOVIN' DOLL/STEADY WITH YOU	2.75	4.00	3.10
☐ 45-10042	**ABC PARAMOUNT**	LIVING DOLL/APRON STRINGS ..	2.75	4.00	3.10
☐ 45-10066		TRAVELLIN' LIGHT/DYNAMITE ..	2.75	4.00	3.10
☐ 45-10083		A VOICE IN THE WILDERNESS/DON'T BE MAD AT ME	2.75	4.00	3.10
☐ 45-10109		FALL IN LOVE WITH YOU/CHOPPIN' 'N' CHANGIN'	2.75	4.00	3.10
☐ 45-10136		PLEASE DON'T TEASE/WHERE IS MY HEART	2.75	4.00	3.10
☐ 45-10175		"D" IN LOVE/CATCH ME I'M FALLING	2.75	4.00	3.10
☐ 45-10195		THEME FOR A DREAM/MUMBLIN' MOSIE	2.75	4.00	3.10
☐ 45-31-1	**BIG TOP**	THE YOUNG ONES/WE SAY YEAH	2.75	4.00	3.10
☐ 45-16399	**DOT**	IT'S WONDERFUL TO BE YOUNG/GOT A FUNNY FEELING	2.75	4.00	3.10
☐ 5-9597	**EPIC**	LUCKY LIPS/THE NEXT TIME	2.50	3.75	2.75
☐ 5-9633		IT'S ALL IN THE GAME/I'M LOOKING OUT OF THE WINDOW	2.50	3.75	2.75
☐ 5-9670		I'M THE LONELY ONE/I ONLY HAVE EYES FOR YOU ..	2.50	3.75	2.75
☐ 5-9691		BACHELOR BOY/TRUE TRUE LOVIN'	2.50	3.75	2.75
☐ 5-9737		I DON'T WANNA LOVE YOU/LOOK IN MY EYES, MARIA	2.50	3.75	2.75
☐ 5-9757		THE MINUTE YOU'RE GONE/AGAIN	2.50	3.75	2.75
☐ 5-9810		I COULD EASILY FALL/ON MY WORD	2.50	3.75	2.75
☐ 5-9839		THE TWELFTH OF NEVER/PARADISE LOST	2.50	3.75	2.75
☐ 5-9867		WIND ME UP/THE EYE OF THE NEEDLE	2.50	3.75	2.75
☐ 5-10018		BLUE TURNS TO GREY/I'LL WALK ALONE	2.50	3.75	2.75
☐ 5-10070		VISIONS/QUANDO, QUANDO, QUANDO ..	2.50	3.75	2.75
☐ 5-10101		TIME DRAGS BY/LA LA LA SONG	2.50	3.75	2.75
☐ 5-10178	**UNI**	HEARTBEAT/IT'S ALL OVER	2.25	3.50	2.50
☐ 55061		ALL MY LOVE/OUR STORY BOOK	2.25	3.50	2.50
☐ 55069		CONGRATULATOINS/HIGH 'N' DRY	2.25	3.50	2.50
☐ 55145		THE DAY I MET MARIE/SWEET LITTLE JESUS BOY	2.25	3.50	2.50
☐ L-601	**LIGHT**	TWO A PENNY/I'LL LOVE YOU FOREVER TODAY	2.25	3.50	2.50
☐ 7734	**WARNER BROS. SEVEN ARTS**	THROW DOWN THE LINE/REFLECTIONS	2.25	3.50	2.50

			Current Price Range		P/Y AVG
☐ MN-1211	**MONUMENT**	GOODBYE SAM, HELLO SAMANTHA/YOU NEVER CAN TELL	2.25	3.50	2.50
☐ MN-1229		I AIN'T GOT TIME ANYMORE MONDAY COMES TOO SOON	2.25	3.50	2.50
☐ SAA-703	**SIRE**	LIVING IN HARMONY/JESUS	2.25	3.50	2.50
☐ SAA-707		POWER TO ALL OUR FRIENDS/ COME BACK BILLIE JO	2.25	3.50	2.50
☐ PIC-40531	**ROCKET**	MISS YOU NIGHTS/LOVE ENOUGH	2.25	3.50	2.50
☐ PIC-40574		DEVIL WOMAN/ LOVE ON (SHINE ON)	2.25	3.50	2.50
☐ PIC-40652		I CAN'T ASK FOR ANYMORE THAN YOU/JUNIOR COWBOY	2.25	3.50	2.50
☐ PIC-40724		DON'T TURN THE LIGHT OUT/ NOTHING LEFT FOR ME TO SAY	2.25	3.50	2.50
☐ PIC-40771		TRY A SMILE/ YOU'VE GOT ME WONDERING	2.25	3.50	2.50
☐ YB-11463		GREEN LIGHT/NEEDING A FRIEND	2.25	3.50	2.50
☐ 8025	**EMI AMERICA**	WE DON'T TALK ANYMORE/ COUNT ME OUT	2.25	3.50	2.50
☐ 8035		CARRIE/LANGUAGE OF LOVE	2.25	3.50	2.50
☐ 8057		DREAMING/DYNAMITE	2.25	3.50	2.50
☐ 8068		A LITTLE IN LOVE/EVERYMAN	2.25	3.50	2.50
☐ 8076		GIVE A LITTLE BIT MORE/ KEEP ON LOOKING	2.25	3.50	2.50
☐ A-8095		WIRED FOR SOUND/HOLD ON	2.25	3.50	2.50
☐ A-8103		DADDY'S HOME/SUMMER RAIN	2.25	3.50	2.50
☐ B-8135		THE ONLY WAY OUT/ BE IN MY HEART	2.25	3.50	2.50
☐ B-8149		LITTLE TOWN/BE IN MY HEART	2.25	3.50	2.50
☐ B-8180		NEVER SAY DIE (GIVE A LITTLE BIT MORE)/FRONT PAGE	2.25	3.50	2.50
		CLIFF RICHARD—EPS			
☐ 001	**UNI**	TWO A PENNY	3.25	5.50	4.00
☐ 101	**LIGHT**	TWO A PENNY	3.25	5.50	4.00
☐ 102		HIS LAND	3.25	5.50	4.00
		CLIFF RICHARD—ALBUMS			
☐ 321	**ABC-PARAMONT**	CLIFF SINGS	3.50	7.50	5.00
☐ 391		LISTEN TO CLIFF	3.50	7.50	5.00
☐ 3473	**DOT**	WONDERFUL TO BE YOUNG	3.50	7.50	5.00
☐ 24063	**EPIC**	HITS FROM THE SOUNDTRACK OF SUMMER HOLIDAY	3.50	10.00	6.00
☐ 24089		IT'S ALL IN THE GAME	3.50	7.50	5.00
☐ 24115		CLIFF RICHARD IN SPAIN	3.50	7.50	5.00
☐ 24145		SWINGER'S PARADISE	3.50	7.50	5.00
☐ LS-5530	**LIGHT**	TWO A PENNY	3.50	7.50	5.00
☐ LS-5532		HIS LAND	3.50	7.50	5.00
☐ 8507	**WORD**	GOOD NEWS	3.50	7.50	5.00
☐ 2210	**ROCKET**	I'M NEARLY FAMOUS	3.50	7.50	5.00
☐ 2268		EVERY FACE TELLS A STORY	3.50	7.50	5.00
☐ 1-2958		GREEN LIGHT	3.50	7.50	5.00
☐ 17018	**EMI AMERICA**	WE DON'T TALK ANYMORE	3.50	7.50	5.00
☐ 17039		I'M NO HERO	3.50	7.50	5.00
☐ 17059		WIRED FOR SOUND	3.50	7.50	5.00
☐ 16220		GREEN LIGHT (REISSUE)	3.50	7.50	5.00
☐ 16221		I'M NEARLY FAMOUS (REISSUE)	3.50	7.50	5.00
☐ 16253		EVERY FACE TELLS A STORY (REISSUE)	3.50	7.50	5.00
☐ 17081		NOW YOU SEE ME, NOW YOU DON'T	3.50	7.50	5.00
☐ 17105		GIVE A LITTLE BIT MORE	3.50	7.50	5.00

CLIFF RICHARD

Cliff Richard was born Harry Webb on October 14, 1940 in Lucknow, India. In 1948, he moved to England with his parents and attended school in Cheshunt, Hertfordshire where he devoted most of his time to athletics.

Upon leaving school and armed only with a second-hand guitar, Cliff formed his own group and started to look for work in and around London.

In 1958, Cliff and his group The Drifters (later changed to The Shadows) made a private recording and sent it to Norrie Paramor. This led to the release of "Move It" and spurred Cliff's career onward.

Since then, Cliff has starred in many motion pictures, plays, TV shows; received numerous platinum, gold and silver discs and is consistently ranked as a favorite in annual music polls.

In 1976, his "I'm Nearly Famous" album gave him the break he needed in the United States. The year 1978 marked Cliff Richard's twentieth year in show business and to celebrate, he and The Shadows reunited for a two week event at The London Palladium.

			Current Price Range		P/Y AVG

RIGHTEOUS BROTHERS

			Current Price Range		P/Y AVG
☐215	*MOONGLOW*	LITTLE LATIN LUPE LU/ I'M SO LONELY	3.50	6.00	4.35
☐220		I NEED A GIRL/HOT TAMALE (Bobby Hatfield)	3.50	6.00	4.35
☐223		MY BABY/FEE-FI-FIDDLY-I-OH	3.50	6.00	4.35
☐224		KO KO JOE/B FLAT BLUES	3.50	6.00	4.35
☐231		TRY TO FIND ANOTHER MAN/ I STILL LOVE YOU	3.50	6.00	4.35
☐234		BRING YOUR LOVE TO ME/ IF YOU'RE LYING YOU'LL BE CRYING	3.50	6.00	4.35
☐235		THIS LITTLE GIRL OF MINE/ IF YOU'RE LYING YOU'LL BE CRYING	3.50	6.00	4.35
☐238		FANNIE MAE/ BRING YOUR LOVE TO ME	3.50	6.00	4.35
☐239		YOU CAN HAVE HER/ LOVE OR MAGIC	3.25	5.50	4.00
☐242		JUSTINE/IN THAT GREAT GETTIN' UP MORNIN'	3.25	5.50	4.00
☐243		FOR YOUR LOVE/ GOTTA TELL YOU HOW I FEEL	3.25	5.50	4.00
☐244		GEORGIA ON MY MIND/ MY TEARS WILL GO AWAY	3.25	5.50	4.00
☐245		I NEED A GIRL/ BRING YOUR LOVE TO ME	2.75	4.50	3.00
☐124	*PHILLES*	YOU'VE LOST THAT LOVIN' FEELIN'	3.50	6.00	4.35
☐127		JUST ONCE IN MY LIFE/ THE BLUES	3.50	6.00	4.35
☐129		UNCHAINED MELODY/ HUNG ON YOU	3.50	6.00	4.35
☐130		EBB TIDE/FOR SENTIMENTAL REASONS	3.50	6.00	4.35
☐132		WHITE CLIFFS OF DOVER/ SHE'S MINE, ALL MINE	8.00	13.00	6.75
☐10383	*VERVE*	(YOU'RE MY) SOUL AND INSPIRATION/B SIDE BLUES	3.00	5.00	3.65
☐10403		RAT RACE/GREEN ONIONS	3.00	5.00	3.65
☐10406		HE/HE WILL BREAK YOUR HEART	3.00	5.00	3.65
☐10425		SOMETHING'S SO WRONG/THIS IS A LOVE SONG (Bill Medley)	3.00	5.00	3.65
☐10430		GO AHEAD AND CRY/ THINGS DIDN'T GO YOUR WAY	3.00	5.00	3.65
☐10449		ON THIS SIDE OF GOODBYE/ A MAN WITHOUT A DREAM	3.00	5.00	3.65
☐10479		ALONG CAME JONES/ JIMMY'S BLUES	3.00	5.00	3.65
☐10507		MELANCHOLY MUSIC MAN/ DON'T GIVE UP ON ME	3.00	5.00	3.65
☐10551		STRANDED IN THE MIDDLE OF NO PLACE/BEEN SO NICE	3.00	5.00	3.65
☐10569		THAT LUCKY OLD SUN/ MY DARLING CLEMENTINE	3.00	5.00	3.65
☐10577		HERE I AM/SO MANY LONELY NIGHTS AHEAD	3.00	5.00	3.65
☐10637		LET THE GOOD TIMES ROLL/ YOU'VE LOST THAT LOVIN' FEELIN'	3.00	5.00	3.65
☐10648		AND THE PARTY GOES ON/ WOMAN, MAN NEEDS YA	3.00	5.00	3.65
☐10649		GOOD N'UFF/PO' FOLKS	3.00	5.00	3.65

GEE, GLP 706

MGM, VERVE, VK-10383

			Current Price Range		P/Y AVG
☐7002	**HAVEN**	ROCK AND ROLL HEAVEN/ I JUST WANNA BE ME	2.75	4.75	3.50
☐7004		GIVE IT TO THE PEOPLE/ LOVE IS NOT A DIRTY WORD	2.75	4.75	3.50
☐7006		DREAM ON/ DOCTOR ROCK AND ROLL	2.75	4.75	3.50
☐7011		HIGH BLOOD PRESSURE/ NEVER SAY I LOVE YOU	2.75	4.75	3.50
☐7014		YOUNG BLOOD/SUBSTITUTE	2.75	4.75	3.50
		RIGHTEOUS BROTHERS—EP			
☐1004	**MOONGLOW**	GREATEST HITS	10.00	17.00	12.00
		RIGHTEOUS BROTHERS—ALBUMS			
☐1001 (M)	**MOONGLOW**	RIGHT NOW	8.00	21.00	18.00
☐1002 (M)		SOME BLUE-EYED SOUL	8.00	21.00	18.00
☐1003 (M)		THIS IS THE RIGHTEOUS BROTHERS	8.00	21.00	18.00
☐1004 (M)		BEST OF THE RIGHTEOUS BROTHERS	8.00	21.00	18.00
☐4007 (M)	**PHILLES**	YOU'VE LOST THAT LOVIN' FEELIN'	15.00	25.00	18.00
☐4008 (M)		JUST ONCE IN MY LIFE	15.00	25.00	18.00
☐4009 (M)		BACK TO BACK	15.00	25.00	18.00
☐5004 (M)	**VERVE**	GO AHEAD AND CRY	6.00	17.00	15.00
☐5004 (S)		GO AHEAD AND CRY	8.00	21.00	18.00
☐5010 (M)		SAYIN' SOMETHIN'	7.00	17.00	15.00
☐5010 (S)		SAYIN' SOMETHIN'	8.00	21.00	18.00
☐5020 (M)		THE RIGHTEOUS BROTHERS' GREATEST HITS	6.00	15.00	13.50
☐5020 (S)		THE RIGHTEOUS BROTHERS' GREATEST HITS	7.00	17.00	15.00
☐5051 (S)		RIGHTEOUS BROTHERS STANDARDS	5.50	14.00	12.00
☐5058 (S)		ONE FOR THE ROAD	5.50	14.00	12.00
☐5071 (S)		GREATEST HITS, VOL. II	5.50	14.00	12.00
☐9201 (S)	**HAVEN**	GIVE IT TO THE PEOPLE	5.00	14.00	10.00
☐9203 (S)		THE SONS OF MRS. RIGHTEOUS	5.00	14.00	10.00

RINKY-DINKS
FEATURED: BOBBY DARIN

☐6121	**ATCO**	EARLY IN THE MORNING/ NOW WE'RE ONE	4.50	7.50	6.00
☐6128		MIGHTY MIGHTY MAN/ YOU'RE MINE	5.50	10.50	9.00

BILLY RILEY

☐245	**SUN**	TROUBLE BOUND/ ROCK WITH ME BABY	20.00	35.00	23.00
☐260		FLYIN' SAUCERS ROCK & ROLL/ I WANT YOU BABY	20.00	35.00	23.00
☐277		RED HOT/PEARLY LEF	6.00	11.00	6.85
☐289		WOULDN'T YOU KNOW/ BABY PLEASE DON'T GO	6.00	11.00	6.85
☐313		DOWN BY THE RIVERSIDE/ NO NAME GIRL (Bill Riley)	4.00	7.00	4.85
☐322		GOT THE WATER BOILING/ ONE MORE TIME (Bill Riley)	10.00	19.00	11.50

RIP CHORDS
FEATURED: BRUCEJOHNSTON, TERRY MELCHER (BRUCE AND TERRY)

☐42687	**COLUMBIA**	HERE I STAND/KAREN	3.75	6.00	4.50
☐42812		GONE/SHE THINKS I STILL CARE	3.75	5.50	4.50
☐42921		HEY LITTLE COBRA/THE QUEEN	3.00	5.00	3.50
☐43035		THREE WINDOW COUPE/ HOT ROD U.S.A.	3.00	5.00	3.50

			Current Price Range		P/Y AVG
☐ 43039		ONE-PIECE TOPLESS BATHING SUIT/AH-WAHINI	3.25	5.50	4.00
☐ 43221		DON'T BE SCARED/BUNNY HILL .	3.25	5.50	4.00

RIP CHORDS—ALBUMS

☐ 2151 (M)	**COLUMBIA**	HEY LITTLE COBRA	9.00	25.00	22.50
☐ 8951 (S)		HEY LITTLE COBRA	14.00	35.00	30.00
☐ 2216 (M)		THREE WINDOW COUPE	9.00	25.00	22.50
☐ 9016 (S)		THREE WINDOW COUPE	14.00	35.00	30.00

RITUALS
FEATURED: ARNIE GINSBERG (OF JAN AND ARNIE)
PRODUCER: BRUCE JOHNSTON

☐ 120	**ARWIN**	GIRL IN ZANZIBAR/GUITARRO . . .	7.50	13.00	11.00
☐ 127		THIS IS PARADISE/GONE	7.50	13.00	11.00
☐ 128		SURFERS RULE/GONE	5.50	11.00	9.00

JOHNNY RIVERS

☐ 5026	**GONE**	BABY COME BACK/ LONG, LONG WALK	8.25	14.00	12.00
☐ 9047	**CUB**	EVERY DAY/ DARLING, TALK TO ME	5.50	11.00	9.00
☐ 9058		ANSWER ME, MY LOVE/ THE CUSTOMARY THING	5.50	11.00	9.00
☐ 239	**DEE DEE**	THAT'S MY BABE/ YOUR FIRST AND LAST LOVE . .	5.50	11.00	9.00
☐ 3037	**ERA**	CALL ME/ANDERSONVILLE	5.00	9.00	7.00
☐ 2033	**GUYDEN**	YOU'RE THE ONE/ HOLE IN THE GROUND	4.00	9.00	7.00
☐ 1070	**CHANCELLOR**	KNOCK THREE TIMES/ I GET SO DOGGONE LONESOME	4.50	7.00	6.00
☐ 1096		BLUE SKIES/ THAT SHOULD BE ME	4.50	7.00	6.00
☐ 1108		TO BE LOVED/TOO GOOD TO LAST	3.75	5.50	4.50
☐ 4850	**CAPITOL**	LONG BLACK VEIL/ THIS COULD BE THE ONE	3.75	5.50	4.50
☐ 4913		IF YOU WANT IT I'VE GOT IT/ MY HEART IS IN YOUR HANDS .	3.75	5.50	4.50
☐ 5232		LONG BLACK VEIL/ DON'T LOOK NOW	3.25	5.50	4.00
☐ 13266	**MGM**	ANSWER ME, MY LOVE/ THE CUSTOMARY THING	3.25	5.50	4.00
☐ 62425	**CORAL**	THAT'S MY BABE/ YOUR FIRST AND LAST LOVE . .	3.25	5.50	4.00
☐ 4565	**ROULETTE**	BABY COME BACK/ LONG, LONG WALK	3.25	5.50	4.00
☐ 66032	**IMPERIAL**	MEMPHIS/IT WOULDN'T HAPPEN WITH ME .	3.00	5.00	3.65
☐ 66056		MAYBELLENE/ WALK MYSELF ON HOME	3.00	5.00	3.65
☐ 66075		MOUNTAIN OF LOVE/ MOODY RIVER	3.00	5.00	3.65
☐ 66087		MIDNIGHT SPECIAL/CUPID	3.00	5.00	3.65
☐ 66112		SEVENTH SUN/ UN-SQUARE DANCE	3.00	5.00	3.65
☐ 66133		WHERE HAVE ALL THE FLOWERS GONE/LOVE ME WHILE YOU CAN	3.00	5.00	3.65
☐ 66144		UNDER YOUR SPELL AGAIN/ LONG TIME MAN	3.00	5.00	3.65
☐ 66159		SECRET AGENT MAN/YOU DIG . .	3.00	5.00	3.65
☐ 66175		(I WASHED MY HANDS IN) MUDDY WATER/ROOGALATOR	3.00	5.00	3.65
☐ 66205		POOR SIDE OF TOWN/ A MAN CAN CRY	3.00	5.00	3.65

			Current Price Range		P/Y AVG
☐66227		BABY, I NEED YOUR LOVIN'/ GETTIN' READY FOR TOMORROW	3.00	5.00	3.65
☐66244		THE TRACKS OF MY TEARS/ REWIND MEDLEY	3.00	5.00	3.65
☐66267		SUMMER RAIN/ MEMORY OF THE COMING GOOD	3.00	5.00	3.65
☐66286		LOOK TO YOUR SOUL/ SOMETHING STRANGE	2.75	4.75	3.50
☐66335		RIGHT RELATIONS/A BETTER LIFE.	2.75	4.75	3.50
☐66360		THESE ARE NOT MY PEOPLE/ GOING BACK TO BIG SUR	2.75	4.75	3.50
☐66386		MUDDY RIVER/RESSURECTION ..	2.75	4.75	3.50
☐66418		ONE WOMAN/ODE TO JOHN LEE .	2.75	4.75	3.50
☐66448		INTO THE MYSTIC/ JESUS WAS A SOUL MAN	2.75	4.75	3.50
☐66453		FIRE AND RAIN/APPLE TREE	2.75	4.75	3.50
		JOHNNY RIVERS—ALBUMS			
☐2161 (M)	**CAPITOL**	THE SENSATIONAL JOHNNY RIVERS	9.00	25.00	22.50
☐9264 (M)	**IMPERIAL**	JOHNNY RIVERS AT THE WHISKEY A-GO-GO	7.00	17.00	15.00
☐12664 (S)		JOHNNY RIVERS AT THE WHISKEY A-GO-GO	8.00	21.00	18.00
☐9274 (M)		HERE WE A-GO-GO AGAIN	7.00	17.00	15.00
☐12274 (S)		HERE WE A-GO-GO AGAIN	8.00	21.00	18.00
☐9280 (M)		IN ACTION	7.00	17.00	15.00
☐12280 (S)		IN ACTION	8.00	21.00	18.00
☐9284 (M)		MEANWHILE BACK AT THE WHISKEY A-GO-GO	7.00	17.00	15.00
☐12284 (S)		MEANWHILE BACK AT THE WHISKEY A-GO-GO	8.00	21.00	18.00
☐9239 (M)		JOHNNY RIVERS ROCKS THE FOLK	7.00	17.00	15.00
☐12293 (S)		JOHNNY RIVERS ROCKS THE FOLK	8.00	21.00	18.00
☐9307 (M)		AND I KNOW YOU WANNA DANCE	7.00	17.00	15.00
☐12037 (S)		AND I KNOW YOU WANNA DANCE	8.00	21.00	18.00
☐9324 (M)		JOHNNY RIVERS' GOLDEN HITS .	6.00	15.00	13.50
☐12324 (S)		JOHNNY RIVERS' GOLDEN HITS .	6.00	15.00	13.50
☐9334 (M)		CHANGES	6.00	15.00	13.50
☐12334 (S)		CHANGES	5.50	14.00	12.00
☐9341 (M)		REWIND....................	6.00	15.00	13.50
☐12341 (S)		REWIND....................	5.50	14.00	12.00
☐12372 (S)		REALIZATION................	5.00	12.00	10.00
		RIVIERAS			
☐503	**COED**	COUNT EVERY STAR/ TRUE LOVE IS HARD TO FIND ..	5.00	8.50	7.00
☐508		MOONLIGHT SERENADE/ NEITHER RAIN NOR SNOW	4.50	7.50	6.00
☐513		OUR LOVE/MIDNIGHT FLYER	4.50	7.50	6.00
☐522		SINCE I MADE YOU CRY/ ELEVENTH HOUR MELODY	4.50	7.50	6.00
☐529		MOONLIGHT COCKTAILS/ BLESSINGS OF LOVE	4.50	7.50	6.00
☐538		MY FRIEND/GREAT BIG EYES ...	3.75	6.00	4.50
☐542		STAY IN MY HEART/ EASY TO REMEMBER	3.75	6.00	4.50
☐551		ELDORADO/REFRIGERATOR	3.25	5.50	4.00
☐592		MOONLIGHT COCKTAILS/ MIDNIGHT FLYER	3.00	5.00	3.50
		RIVIERAS			
☐1401	**RIVIERA**	CALIFORNIA SUN/ H.B. GOOSE STEP	3.25	5.50	4.00

			Current Price Range		P/Y AVG
☐ 1402		LITTLE DONNA/ LET'S HAVE A PARTY	3.25	5.50	4.00
☐ 1403		ROCKIN' ROBIN/BATTLE LINE	3.25	5.50	4.00
☐ 1405		WHOLE LOTTA SHAKIN'/RIP IT UP.	3.25	5.50	4.00
☐ 1406		LET'S GO TO HAWAII/ LAKEVIEW LANE	3.25	5.50	4.00

RIVIERAS—ALBUMS

☐ 701 (M)	RIVIERA	CAMPUS PARTY	12.00	29.00	25.00
☐ 102 (M)	U.S.A.	LET'S HAVE A PARTY	12.00	29.00	25.00

RIVINGTONS
SEE: 4 AFTER 5's

☐ 55427	LIBERTY	PAPA OOM MOW MOW/ DEEP WATER	3.75	6.00	4.50
☐ 55513		KICKAPOO JOY JUICE/ MY REWARD	4.50	7.50	6.00
☐ 55528		MAMA OOM MOW MOW/WAITING	4.50	7.50	6.00
☐ 55553		THE BIRD'S THE WORD/ I'M LOSING MY GRIP	3.75	6.00	4.50
☐ 55585		THE SHAKY BIRD (PT. 1)/(PT. 2) .	4.50	7.50	6.00
☐ 55610		CHERRY/LITTLE SALLY WALKER	17.00	29.00	25.00
☐ 55671		WEEJEE WALK/FAIRY TALES	3.75	6.00	4.50

RIVINGTONS—ALBUMS

☐ 3282 (M)	LIBERTY	DOIN' THE BIRD	9.00	25.00	22.50
☐ 7282 (S)		DOIN' THE BIRD	14.00	34.00	30.00

ROBBINS AND PAXTON
FEATURED: GARY "FLIP" PAXTON

☐ 704	RORI	TEEN ANGEL/STRANGE RAIN	4.50	7.50	6.00

ROBERT AND JOHNNY

☐ 1038	OLD TOWN	BABY COME HOME/DON'T DO IT .	4.50	7.50	6.00
☐ 1043		BROKEN HEARTED MAN/ INDIAN MARRIAGE	4.50	7.50	6.00
☐ 1047		WE BELONG TOGETHER/ WALKIN' IN THE RAIN	4.00	7.00	4.85
☐ 1052		I KNOW/MARRY ME	4.00	7.00	4.85
☐ 1052		I BELIEVE IN YOU/MARRY ME	4.00	7.00	4.85
☐ 1058		ETERNITY WITH YOU/ I'M TRULY TRULY YOURS	4.00	7.00	4.85
☐ 1065		GIVE ME THE KEY TO YOUR HEART/TRULY IN LOVE	3.25	5.50	4.00
☐ 1068		DREAM GIRL/OH MY LOVE	3.25	5.50	4.00
☐ 1072		WEAR THIS RING/BAD DAN	3.25	5.50	4.00
☐ 1086		WE BELONG TOGETHER/ IN THE RAIN	2.75	4.50	3.00
☐ 1100		PLEASE BE MINE/YOU'RE MINE .	3.00	5.00	3.50
☐ 1108		TOGETHERNESS/I GOT YOU	3.00	5.00	3.50
☐ 1117		WEAR THIS RING/ BROKEN HEARTED MAN	2.75	4.50	3.00

ROBINS
SEE: COASTERS

☐ 106	CROWN	I MADE A VOW/ DOUBLE CROSSIN' BABY	46.00	80.00	72.00
☐ 120		KEY TO MY HEART/ ALL I DO IS ROCK	50.00	98.00	90.00
☐ 12100	FEDERAL	SATURDAY NIGHT DADDY/ MAINLINER	25.00	130.00	120.00
☐ 5175	RCA	A FOOL SUCH AS I/MY HEART'S THE BIGGEST FOOL ..	80.00	140.00	105.00
☐ 5271		OH WHY/ALL NIGHT BABY	80.00	140.00	105.00
☐ 5434		HOW WOULD YOU KNOW?/ LET'S GO TO THE DANCE	80.00	140.00	105.00
☐ 5489		TEN DAYS IN JAIL/ EMPTY BOTTLES	25.00	42.00	36.00

			Current Price Range		P/Y AVG
☐ 5564		GET IT OFF YOUR MIND/ DON'T STOP NOW	30.00	48.00	42.00
☐ 5564	**SPARK**	RIOT IN CELL BLOCK #9/WRAP IT UP (silver-top label)	23.00	35.00	30.00
☐ 107		LOOP DE LOOP MAMBO/FRAMED	23.00	35.00	30.00
☐ 110		IF TEARDROPS WERE KISSES/ WHADAYA WANT?	24.00	40.00	36.00
☐ 113		ONE KISS/I LOVE PARIS	14.00	24.00	20.00
☐ 116		I MUST BE DREAMIN'/ THE HATCHET MAN	9.50	18.00	15.00
☐ 122		SMOKEY JOE'S CAFE/ JUST LIKE A FOOL	9.50	18.00	15.00
☐ 6059	**ATCO**	SMOKEY JOE'S CAFE/JUST LIKE A FOOL (maroon label)	5.50	11.00	9.00
☐ 200	**WHIPPET**	CHERRY LIPS/ OUT OF THE PICTURE	4.50	'7.50	6.00
☐ 201		HURT ME/MERRY GO ROCK	4.50	7.50	6.00
☐ 203		SINCE I FIRST MET YOU/ THAT OLD BLACK MAGIC	4.50	7.50	6.00
☐ 206		A FOOL IN LOVE/ALL OF A SUDDEN MY HEART SINGS	4.50	7.50	6.00
☐ 208		EVERY NIGHT/ WHERE'S THE FIRE?	4.00	7.00	4.85
☐ 211		IN MY DREAMS/ KEEP YOUR MIND ON ME	4.00	7.00	4.85
☐ 212		SNOWBALL/YOU WANTED FUN . .	4.00	7.00	4.85
☐ 5001	**ARVEE**	JUST LIKE THAT/ WHOLE LOT IMAGINATION	4.00	7.00	4.85
☐ 5013		LIVE WIRE SUZIE/OH NO	4.00	7.00	4.85
☐ 2001	**KNIGHT**	A QUARTER TO TWELVE/ PRETTY LITTLE DOLLY	3.25	5.50	4.00
☐ 2008		A LITTLE BIRD TOLD ME/ IT'S NEVER TOO LATE	3.25	5.50	4.00

ROBINS—ALBUM

☐ 703 (M)	**WHIPPET**	ROCK 'N ROLL WITH THE ROBINS	35.00	82.00	75.00

ROCK-A-TEENS

☐ 3515	**DORAN**	WOO-HOO/UNTRUE	19.00	29.00	25.00
☐ 4192	**ROULETTE**	WOO-HOO/UNTRUE	3.25	5.50	4.00
☐ 4217		TWANGY/DOGGONE IT BABY	3.25	5.50	4.00

ROCK-A-TEENS—ALBUMS

☐ 25109 (M)	**ROULETTE**	WOO-HOO	25.00	60.00	40.00
☐ 25109 (S)		WOO-HOO	40.00	75.00	55.00

ROCKATONES WITH LARRY DOWD

☐ 6009	**SPINNING**	PINK CADILLAC/ BLUE SWINGIN' MAMA	14.00	35.00	32.00

ROCKIN' REBELS

SEE: BUFFALO REBELS, HOT TODDYS, REBELS

☐ 4140	**SWAN**	ROCKIN' CRICKETS/ HULLY GULLY ROCK	3.25	5.50	4.00
☐ 4150		ANOTHER WILD WEEKEND/ HAPPY POPCORN	3.25	5.50	4.00

ROCKIN' REBELS—ALBUM

☐ 509 (M)	**SWAN**	WILD WEEKEND	17.00	39.00	35.00

ROCKIN' RONALD AND THE REBELS

RONNIE HAWKINS AND THE HAWKS

☐ 1043	**END**	KANSAS CITY/CUTTIN' OUT	5.00	8.50	7.00

JIMMIE RODGERS

☐ 4015	**ROULETTE**	HONEYCOMB/THEIR HEARTS WERE FULL OF SPRING	3.25	5.50	4.00
☐ 4031		KISSES SWEETER THAN WINE/ BETTER LOVED YOU'LL NEVER BE	3.00	5.00	3.50

			Current Price Range		P/Y AVG
☐ 4045		UH-OH. I'M FALLING IN LOVE AGAIN/THE LONG HOT SUMMER	3.00	5.00	3.50
☐ 4070		SECRETLY/MAKE ME A MIRACLE	3.00	5.00	3.50
☐ 4090		ARE YOU REALLY MINE/ THE WIZARD	3.00	5.00	3.50
☐ 4116		BIMBOMBEY/ YOU UNDERSTAND ME	3.00	5.00	3.50
☐ 4129		I'M NEVER GONNA TELL/ BECAUSE THEY'RE YOUNG	2.75	4.50	3.00
☐ 4158		RING-A-LING-A-LARIO/ WONDERFUL YOU	2.75	4.00	3.50
☐ 4191		TUCUMCARI/THE NIGHT YOU BECAME SEVENTEEN	2.75	4.50	3.00
☐ 4205		IT'S CHRISTMAS ONCE AGAIN/ WISTFUL WILLIE	3.00	5.00	3.50
☐ 4218		T. L. C. (TENDER LOVE AND CARE)/WALTZING MATILDA	2.75	4.50	3.00
☐ 4234		JUST A CLOSER WALK WITH THEE/ JOSHUA FIT THE BATTLE OF JERICHO	2.75	4.50	3.00
☐ 4260		THE WRECK OF THE JOHN B/ A LITTLE GIRL IN BOSTON	2.75	4.50	3.00
☐ 4293		WOMAN FROM LIBERIA/ COME ALONG JULIE5	3.00	5.00	3.50
☐ 4318		WHEN LOVE IS YOUNG/ THE LITTLE SHEPHERD FROM KINGDOM COME	3.00	5.00	3.65
☐ 4349		EVERYTIME MY HEART SINGS/ I'M ON MY WAY	3.00	5.00	3.65
☐ 4371		I'M GOIN' HOME/ JOHN BROWN'S BABY	3.00	5.00	3.65
☐ 4384		A LITTLE DOG CRIED/ ENGLISH COUNTRY GARDEN	3.00	5.00	3.65
☐ 4439		YOU ARE EVERYTHING TO ME/ WANDERIN' EYES	3.00	5.00	3.65
☐ 16378	DOT	NO ONE WILL EVER KNOW/ BECAUSE	2.75	4.50	3.25
☐ 16407		RAINBOW AT MIDNIGHT/ RHUMBA BOOGIE	2.75	4.50	3.25
☐ 16428		I'LL NEVER STAND IN YOUR WAY/ AFRAID	2.75	4.50	3.25
☐ 16450		FACE IN THE CROWD/ LONELY TEARS	2.75	4.50	3.25
☐ 16467		(I DON'T KNOW WHY) I JUST DO/ LOAD 'EM UP (AND KEEP ON STEPPIN')	2.75	4.50	3.25
☐ 16490		POOR LITTLE RAGGEDY ANN/ I'M GONNA BE THE WINNER	2.75	4.50	3.25
☐ 16527		TWO-TEN. SIX-EIGHTEEN/ THE BANANA BOAT SONG	3.00	5.00	3.25
☐ 16561		TOGETHER/MAMA WAS A COTTON PICKER	3.00	5.00	3.25
☐ 16595		THE WORLD I USED TO KNOW/ I FORGOT MORE THAN YOU'LL EVER KNOW	3.00	5.00	3.25
☐ 16653		WATER BOY/SOMEPLACE GREEN	3.00	5.00	3.25
☐ 16673		TWO TICKETS/BELL WITCH	3.00	5.00	3.25
☐ 16694		STRANGERS/BON SOIR. MADAMOISELLE	3.00	5.00	3.25
☐ 16826		A FALLEN STAR/ BROTHER. WHERE ARE YOU?	3.00	5.00	3.25
☐ 16861		IT'S OVER/ ANITA. YOU'RE DREAMING	3.00	5.00	3.25
☐ 16871		BYE BYE LOVE/HOLLOW WORDS	3.00	5.00	3.25

			Current Price Range		P/Y AVG
☐ 25453 (S)		NO ONE WILL EVER KNOW	8.00	21.00	18.00
☐ 3496 (M)		FOLK CONCERT	5.50	14.00	12.00
☐ 25496 (S)		FOLK CONCERT	7.00	17.00	15.00
☐ 3502 (M)		MY FAVORITE HYMNS	5.50	14.00	12.00
☐ 25502 (S)		MY FAVORITE HYMNS	7.00	17.00	15.00
☐ 3525 (M)		HONEYCOMB/ KISSES SWEETER THAN WINE	5.50	14.00	12.00
☐ 25525 (S)		HONEYCOMB/ KISSES SWEETER THAN WINE	7.00	17.00	15.00

TOMMY ROE
SEE: ROEMANS

☐ 1018	JUDD	CAVEMAN/I GOTTA GIRL	9.50	17.00	15.00
☐ 1022		SHEILA/PRETTY GIRL	21.00	35.00	30.00
☐ 10329	ABC-PARAMOUNT	SHELIA/SAVE YOUR KISSES (Different Version)	3.00	5.00	3.50
☐ 10362		SUSIE DARLIN'/PIDDLE DE PAT	3.25	5.50	4.00
☐ 10379		TOWN CRIER/RAINBOW	3.25	5.50	4.00
☐ 10389		DON'T CRY DONNA/ GONNA TAKE A CHANCE	3.25	5.50	4.00
☐ 10423		THE FOLK SINGER/COUNT ON ME	3.25	5.50	4.00
☐ 10454		KISS AND RUN/ WHAT MAKES THE BLUES	3.25	5.50	4.00
☐ 10478		EVERYBODY/ SORRY I'M LATE, LISA	3.00	5.00	3.65
☐ 10515		COME ON/THERE WILL BE BETTER YEARS	3.00	5.00	3.65
☐ 10543		CAROL/BE A GOOD LITTLE GIRL	3.00	5.00	3.65
☐ 10604		PARTY GIRL/OH, HOW COULD I LOVE YOU	3.00	5.00	3.65
☐ 10762		SWEET PEA/MUCH MORE LOVE	3.00	5.00	3.65
☐ 10853		HOORAY FOR HAZEL/ NEED YOUR LOVE	3.00	5.00	3.65
☐ 10888		IT'S NOW WINTER'S DAY/ KICK ME, CHARLIE	3.00	5.00	3.65
☐ 10908		SING ALONG WITH ME/ NIGHTTIME	3.00	5.00	3.65
☐ 10945		LITTLE MISS SUNSHINE/ THE YOU I NEED	3.00	5.00	3.65
☐ 11164		DIZZY/THE YOU I NEED	3.00	5.00	3.65
☐ 11211		HEATHER HONEY/ MONEY IS MY PAY	3.00	5.00	3.65
☐ 11229		JACK AND JILL/TIP TOE TINA	3.00	5.00	3.65
☐ 11247		JAM UP AND JELLY TIGHT/ MOONTALK	2.75	4.50	3.25
☐ 11258		STIR IT UP AND SERVE IT	2.75	4.50	3.25
☐ 11266		PEARL/A DOLLAR'S WORTH OF PENNIES	2.75	4.50	3.25
☐ 11273		WE CAN MAKE MUSIC/ GOTTA KEEP ROLLING ALONG	2.75	4.50	3.25
☐ 11281		KING OF FOOLS/ BRUSH A LITTLE SUNSHINE	2.75	4.50	3.25
☐ 11287		LITTLE MISS GOODIE TWO SHOES/TRAFFIC JAM	2.75	4.50	3.25
☐ 11293		PISTOL LEGGED WOMAN/ KING OF FOOLS	2.75	4.50	3.25
☐ 11307		STAGGER LEE/ BACK STREETS AND ALLEYS	2.75	4.50	3.25

TOMMY ROE—ALBUMS

☐ 432 (M)	ABC-PARAMOUNT	SHEILA	8.00	21.00	18.00
☐ 432 (S)		SHEILA	12.00	29.00	25.00
☐ 467 (M)		SOMETHING FOR EVERYBODY	8.00	21.00	18.00

ROULETTE SR 25109

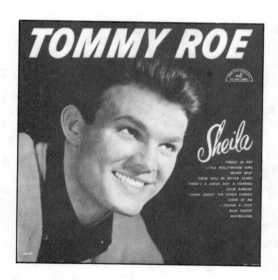

ABC-PARAMOUNT, ABC-432, LP

			Current Price Range		P/Y AVG
☐467 (S)		SOMETHING FOR EVERYBODY ...	12.00	29.00	25.00
☐575 (M)		SWEET PEA	7.00	17.00	15.00
☐575 (S)		SWEET PEA	9.00	25.00	22.50
☐594 (M)		IT'S NOW WINTER'S DAY	7.00	17.00	15.00
☐594 (S)		IT'S NOW WINTER'S DAY	9.00	21.00	18.00
☐610 (S)		PHANTASY	7.00	17.00	15.00
☐683 (S)		DIZZY	5.00	12.00	10.00
☐700 (S)		12 IN A ROE (greatest hits)	5.00	12.00	10.00
☐714 (S)		WE CAN MAKE MUSIC	4.00	12.00	10.00
☐732 (S)		BEGINNINGS	4.00	12.00	10.00
☐762 (S)		TOMMY ROE'S 16 GREATEST HITS	5.00	12.00	10.00

ROEMANS
FEATURED: TOMMY ROE

☐10583	ABC-PARAMOUNT	GIVE ME A CHANCE/YOUR FRIEND	3.00	5.00	3.65
☐10671		MISERLOU/DON'T	3.00	5.00	3.65
☐10723		UNIVERSAL SOLDIER/ LOST LITTLE GIRL	3.00	5.00	3.65
☐10757		LISTEN TO ME/ YOU MAKE ME FEEL GOOD	3.00	5.00	3.65
☐10814		LOVE (THAT'S ALL I WANT)/ WHEN THE SUN SHINES IN THE MORNIN'	3.00	5.00	3.65
☐10871		PLEASING YOU PLEASES ME/ ALL THE GOOD THINGS	3.00	5.00	3.65

KENNETH ROGERS (KENNY ROGERS)

☐454	CARLTON	THAT CRAZY FEELING/ WE'LL ALWAYS HAVE EACH OTHER	8.25	14.00	12.00
☐468		I'VE GOT A LOT TO LEARN/ FOR YOU ALONE	8.25	14.00	12.00
☐102	KEN-LEE	JOLE BLON/LONELY	12.00	21.00	18.00
☐72545	MERCURY	HERE'S THAT RAINY DAY/ TAKE LIFE IN STRIDE	4.50	7.50	6.00

KENNY ROGERS AND THE FIRST EDITION

☐0625	REPRISE	TELL IT ALL BROTHER/ JUST REMEMBER YOU'RE MY SUNSHINE	3.25	5.50	4.00
☐0628		I FOUND A REASON/ TICKET TO NOWHERE	3.25	5.50	4.00
☐0655		JUST DROPPED IN (TO SEE WHAT CONDITION MY CONDITION WAS IN)/SHADOW IN THE CORNER OF YOUR MIND	3.00	5.00	3.65
☐0638		DREAM ON/ONLY ME	3.00	5.00	3.65
☐0693		LOOK AROUND, I'LL BE THERE/ CHARLIE THE FER' DE LANCE	3.00	5.00	3.65
☐0773		IF I COULD ONLY CHANGE YOUR MIND/MY THOUGHTS ARE WITH YOU	3.00	5.00	3.65
☐0799		BUT YOU KNOW I LOVE YOU/ HOME MADE LIES	3.00	5.00	3.65
☐0822		GOOD TIME LIBERATOR/ ONCE AGAIN SHE'S ALL ALONE	3.00	5.00	3.65
☐0829		RUBY, DON'T TAKE YOUR LOVE TO TOWN/GIRL, GET AHOLD OF YOURSELF	3.00	5.00	3.65
☐0854		RUBEN JAMES/SUNSHINE	3.00	5.00	3.65
☐0888		SOMETHING'S BURNIN'/ MAMA'S WAITING	3.00	5.00	3.65

			Current Price Range		P/Y AVG
☐0923		TELL IT ALL BROTHER/JUST REMEMBER YOU'RE MY SUNSHINE	3.00	5.00	3.65
☐0953		HEED THE CALL/ STRANGER IN MY PLACE	3.00	5.00	3.65
☐0999		SOMEONE WHO CARES/ MISSION OF SAN NEHRO	3.00	5.00	3.65
☐1018		TAKE MY HAND/ ALL GOD'S LONELY CHILDREN .	3.00	5.00	3.65
☐1053		WHAT AM I GONNA DO?/ WHERE DOES ROSIE GO?	3.00	5.00	3.65
☐1069		SCHOOL TEACHER/ TRIGGER-HAPPY KID	3.00	5.00	3.65
☐1001	*JOLLY ROGERS*	LADY, PLAY YOUR SYMPATHY/ THERE'S AN OLD MAN IN OUR TOWN	3.25	5.50	4.00
☐1003		THE FIRST TIME/INDIAN JOE	3.25	5.50	4.00
☐1004		SHE THINKS I STILL CARE/TODAY I STARTED LOVING YOU AGAIN	3.25	5.50	4.00
☐1005		GALLOP COUNTY TRAIN/ LENA LOOKIE	3.25	5.50	4.00
☐1006		SOMETHING ABOUT YOUR SONG/ WHATCHA GONNA DO?	3.25	5.50	4.00
☐1007		MAKIN' MUSIC FOR MONEY/ STRANGER IN MY PLACE	3.25	5.50	4.00
		KENNY ROGERS AND THE FIRST EDITION—ALBUMS			
☐6276 (M)	*REPRISE*	THE FIRST EDITION	8.00	21.00	18.00
☐6276 (S)		THE FIRST EDITION	7.00	17.00	15.00
☐6328 (S)		THE FIRST EDITION OF '69	7.00	17.00	15.00
☐6352 (S)		RUBY, DON'T TAKE YOUR LOVE TO TOWN	6.00	15.00	13.50
☐6385 (S)		SOMETHING'S BURNIN'	6.00	15.00	13.50
☐6412 (S)		TELL IT ALL BROTHER	6.00	15.00	13.50
☐6437 (S)		GREATEST HITS.	5.50	14.00	12.00
☐6476 (S)		THE BALLAD OF CALICO	5.50	14.00	12.00
☐2039 (S)		TRANSITION	5.50	14.00	12.00
☐5003 (S)	*JOLLY ROGERS*	ROLLIN'	5.50	14.00	12.00
☐5004 (S)		MONUMENTAL	5.50	14.00	12.00
		TIMMY ROGERS			
☐116	*CAMEO*	BACK TO SCHOOL AGAIN/ I'VE GOT A DOG WHO LOVES ME.	3.25	5.50	4.00
☐131		TAKE ME TO YOUR LEADER/ FLA-GA-LA-PA	3.25	5.50	4.00
		ROGUES			
		PRODUCER: BRUCE JOHNSTON			
☐43190	*COLUMBIA*	EVERYDAY/ROGUE'S REEF	3.25	5.50	4.00
☐43253		COME ON LET'S GO/ ROGUE'S REEF, (PT. 2)	3.75	6.00	4.50
		ROLLERS			
☐55303	*LIBERTY*	BONNEVILLE/ GOT MY EYE ON YOU	3.25	5.50	4.00
☐55320		THE CONTINENTAL WALK/ I WANT YOU SO	3.00	5.00	3.50
☐55357		BOUNCE/TEENAGER'S WALTZ . . .	3.00	5.00	3.50
		ROLLING STONES			
☐9641	*LONDON*	STONED/I WANNA BE YOUR MAN (DJ only)	90.00	150.00	108.00
☐9657		NOT FADE AWAY/ I WANNA BE YOUR MAN	4.50	8.00	6.50

		Current Price Range		P/Y AVG
☐9682	TELL ME/I JUST WANT TO MAKE LOVE TO YOU	4.50	7.50	6.00
☐9687	IT'S ALL OVER NOW/ GOOD TIMES, BAD TIMES	4.50	7.50	6.00
☐9708	TIME IS ON MY SIDE/ CONGRATULATIONS	4.00	7.00	4.85
☐9725	HEART OF STONE/ WHAT A SHAME	4.00	7.00	4.85
☐9741	THE LAST TIME/PLAY WITH FIRE	4.00	7.00	4.85
☐9766	SATISFACTION/ UNDER ASSISTANT WEST COAST PROMOTION MAN	3.50	6.00	4.00
☐9792	GET OFF MY CLOUD/I'M FREE . . .	3.50	6.00	4.00
☐9808	AS TEARS GO BY/ GOTTA GET AWAY	3.50	6.00	4.00
☐9823	19TH NERVOUS BREAKDOWN/ SAD DAY	3.50	6.00	4.00
☐901	PAINT IT, BLACK/STUPID GIRL . .	3.50	6.00	4.00
☐902	MOTHER'S LITTLE HELPER/ LADY JANE	3.50	6.00	4.00
☐903	HAVE YOU SEEN YOUR MOTHER, BABY, STANDING IN THE SHADOW/WHO'S DRIVING YOUR PLANE	3.50	6.00	4.00
☐904	RUBY TUESDAY/LET'S SPEND THE NIGHT TOGETHER	3.50	6.00	4.00
☐905	DANDELION/WE LOVE YOU	3.50	6.00	4.00
☐906	SHE'S A RAINBOW/2,000 LIGHT YEARS FROM HOME	3.50	6.00	4.00
☐907	IN ANOTHER LAND/THE LANTERN (Bill Wyman)	4.00	7.00	4.85
☐908	JUMPIN' JACK FLASH/ CHILD OF THE MOON	3.00	5.00	3.50
☐909	STREET FIGHTING MAN/ NO EXPECTATIONS	3.75	6.00	4.50
☐910	HONKY TONK WOMEN/YOU CAN'T ALWAYS GET WHAT YOU WANT	3.00	5.00	3.50
☐19100	**ROLLING STONES** BROWN SUGAR/BITCH	2.75	4.50	3.00
☐19101	WILD HORSES/SWAY	2.75	4.50	3.00
☐19103	TUMBLING DICE/ SWEET BLACK ANGEL	2.75	4.50	3.00
☐19104	HAPPY/ALL DOWN THE LINE	2.75	4.50	3.00
☐19105	ANGIE/SILVER TRAIN	2.75	4.50	3.00
☐19109	DOO DOO DOO DOO DOO (HEARTBREAKER)/ DANCING WITH MR. D	2.75	4.50	3.00
☐19301	IT'S ONLY ROCK 'N ROLL (BUT I LIKE IT)/THROUGH THE LONELY NIGHTS	2.75	4.50	3.00
☐19302	AIN'T TOO PROUD TO BEG/ DANCE LITTLE SISTER	2.75	4.50	3.00
☐19304	FOOL TO CRY/CRAZY MAMA	3.25	5.50	4.00
☐19304	FOOL TO CRY/HOT STUFF	2.50	4.00	2.50

LATER ROLLING STONES SINGLES ARE WORTH UP TO $1.75 MINT

ROLLING STONES—ALBUMS

☐3375 (M)	**LONDON** THE ROLLING STONES	15.00	30.00	19.00
☐3402 (M)	12x5	13.00	24.00	16.00
☐3420 (M)	THE ROLLING STONES NOW	13.00	24.00	16.00
☐3429 (M)	OUT OF OUR HEADS	13.00	24.00	16.00
☐3451 (M)	DECEMBER'S CHILDREN	13.00	24.00	16.00
☐3476 (M)	AFTERMATH	11.00	20.00	13.50
☐3493 (M)	GOT LIVE IF YOU WANT IT	11.00	20.00	13.50

RONETTES

Ronnie and Estelle Bennett, two New York City sisters, formed a group in 1959 with their first cousin, Nedra Talley. They spent much after-school time (they were in junior high at the time) rehearsing a tight, sexy, "little girl" sound. During the early 1960s they began getting gigs at such places as the Peppermint Lounge, where they worked as a warmup act for Joey Dee and the Starliters.

In 1963 record-production genius Phil Spector was in New York in search of new talent. Impressed with the trio, Spector signed the girls (who had recorded flops on Colpix and May) to his red-hot Philles label. By the end of the summer, the Ronettes were rapidly climbing the charts with "Be My Baby", a song that went all the way to No. 2. This was followed by such later hits as "Baby, I Love You", "(The Best Part Of) Breakin' Up", "Do I Love You" and the now-classic "Walking In the Rain".

In 1968 Phil Spector married Ronnie Bennett, but they were divorced six years later.

			Current Price Range		P/Y AVG
☐ 3499 (M)		BETWEEN THE BUTTONS	11.00	20.00	13.50
☐ 3509 (M)		FLOWERS	11.00	20.00	13.50
STEREO COPIES OF THE ABOVE ALBUMS ARE WORTH HALF OF THE MONO PRESSINGS					
☐ NPS-1 (S)		BIG HITS	11.00	20.00	13.50
☐ NPS-2 (S)		THEIR SATANIC MAJESTIES' REQUEST (with 3-D cover)	17.00	29.00	25.00
☐ NPS-3 (S)		THROUGH THE PAST DARKLY . . .	9.00	15.00	11.00
☐ 539 (S)		BEGGAR'S BANQUET	9.00	15.00	11.00
☐ NPS-4 (S)		LET IT BLEED	9.00	15.00	11.00
☐ NPS-5 (S)		GET HER YA-YA'S OUT	9.00	15.00	11.00
☐ NPS-6/7 (S)		HOT ROCKS (1964-71)	9.00	15.00	11.00
☐ 2900 (S)		EXILE ON MAIN STREET	9.00	15.00	11.00
☐ 59100 (S)		STICKY FINGERS	9.00	15.00	11.00
☐ 59101 (S)		GOAT'S HEAD SOUP	9.00	15.00	11.00
☐ 79102 (S)		MADE IN THE SHADE	9.00	15.00	11.00
☐ 79104 (S)		BLACK AND BLUE	9.00	15.00	11.00

RON ROMAN (FRANK ZAPPA)
SEE: MOTHERS OF INVENTION

☐ 101	**DAANI**	LOVE OF MY LIFE/TELL ME	24.00	42.00	36.00

RONETTES
SEE: RONNIE AND THE RELATIVES, RONNIE SPECTOR, VERONICA

☐ 646	**COLPIX**	I'M GONNA QUIT WHILE I'M AHEAD/I'M ON THE WAGON . . .	12.00	21.00	18.00
☐ 114	**MAY**	SILHOUETTES/YOU BET I WOULD .	9.50	21.00	18.00
☐ 138		GOOD GIRLS/MEMORY	9.50	21.00	18.00
☐ 116	**PHILLES**	BE MY BABY/ TEDESCO AND PITTMAN	3.50	5.75	4.35
☐ 118		BABY, I LOVE YOU/ MISS JOAN AND MR. SAM	3.50	5.75	4.35
☐ 120		(THE BEST PART OF) BREAKIN' UP/BIG RED	3.50	5.75	4.35
☐ 121		DO I LOVE YOU/BEBE AND SUSU .	3.50	5.75	4.35
☐ 123		WALKING IN THE RAIN/ HOW DOES IT FEEL?	3.50	5.75	4.35
☐ 126		BORN TO BE TOGETHER/ BLUES FOR MY BABY	3.75	6.00	4.50
☐ 128		IS THIS WHAT I GET FOR LOVING YOU?/OH, I LOVE YOU	3.75	6.00	4.50
☐ 133		I CAN HEAR MUSIC/ WHEN I SAW YOU	4.50	7.50	6.00
☐ 1046	**DIMENSION**	HE DID IT/RECIPE FOR LOVE	12.00	21.00	18.00
☐ 1040	**A&M**	YOU CAME, YOU SAW, YOU CONQUERED/OH, I LOVE YOU .	5.00	8.50	7.00
☐ 384	**BUDDAH**	LOVER, LOVER/ GO OUT AND GET IT	4.50	7.50	6.00
☐ 408		I WISH I NEVER SAW THE SUNSHINE/I WONDER WHAT HE'S DOING	3.75	6.00	4.50
☐ 3010	**UNICAL**	YA GOTTA TAKE A CHANCE/ YA GOTTA TAKE A CHANCE (instrumental)	3.25	5.50	4.00

RONETTES—ALBUMS

☐ 486 (M)	**COLPIX**	THE RONETTES FEATURING VERONICA	35.00	70.00	60.00
☐ 4006 (M)	**PHILLES**	PRESENTING THE FABULOUS RONETTES	40.00	80.00	75.00
☐ 4006 (S)		PRESENTING THE FABULOUS RONETTES	45.00	118.00	110.00

RONNIE & THE DELAIRES

☐ 62404	**CORAL**	MY FUNNY VALENTINE/THE DRAG	8.25	21.00	18.00

LONDON, 45-9808, 45

PHILLES, PHLP-4006, LP

			Current Price Range		P/Y AVG

RONNIE AND THE RELATIVES (RONETTES)

☐481	COLPIX	SWEET SIXTEEN/I WANT A BOY .	12.00	21.00	18.00
☐111	MAY	MY GUIDING ANGEL/I'M GONNA QUIT WHILE I'M AHEAD	17.00	29.00	25.00

RONNY AND THE DAYTONAS

☐481	MALA	G.T.O./HOT ROD BABY	3.00	5.00	3.65
☐490		CALIFORNIA BOUND/ HEY LITTLE GIRL	3.00	5.00	3.65
☐492		BUCKET "T"/LITTLE RAIL JOB . .	3.00	5.00	3.65
☐497		LITTLE SCRAMBLER/ TEENAGE YEARS	3.00	5.00	3.65
☐503		NO WHEELS/BEACH BOY	3.00	5.00	3.65
☐513		SANDY (vocal)/ SANDY (instrumental)	3.00	5.00	3.65
☐525		GOODBYE BABY/ SOMEBODY TO LOVE ME	3.00	5.00	3.65
☐531		ANTIQUE '32 STUDEBAKER DICTATOR COUPE/ THEN THE RAINS CAME	3.00	5.00	3.65
☐542		I'LL THINK OF SUMMER/ LITTLE SCRAMBLER	3.00	5.00	3.65

RONNY AND THE DAYTONAS—ALBUMS

☐4001 (M)	MALA	G.T.O.	8.00	21.00	18.00
☐4002 (M)		SANDY	8.00	21.00	18.00

ROOMATES
SEE: CATHY JEAN AND THE ROOMATES

☐008	VALMOR	GLORY OF LOVE/NEVER KNEW . .	3.25	5.50	4.00
☐13		MY FOOLISH HEART/MY KISSES FOR YOUR THOUGHTS	3.25	5.50	4.00
☐40105	PHILIPS	ANSWER ME, MY LOVE/GEE	3.00	5.00	3.50
☐40153		THE NEARNESS OF YOU/ PLEASE DON'T CHEAT ON ME .	3.00	5.00	3.50
☐40161		THE NEARNESS OF YOU/ PLEASE DON'T CHEAT ON ME .	3.00	5.00	3.50

LINDA RONSTADT
SEE: STONE PONEYS

☐1003	CAPITOL	LIVING LIKE A FOOL/ HE DARK THE SUN	3.00	5.00	3.75
☐5838		ALL THE BEAUTIFUL THINGS/ SWEET SUMMER BLUE AND GOLD	5.00	9.00	7.00
☐5910		EVERGREEN/ONE FOR ALL	5.00	9.00	7.00
☐2004		DIFFERENT DRUM/I'VE GOT TO KNOW (Stone Poneys)	3.00	5.00	3.50
☐2110		UP TO MY NECK IN MUDDY WATER/CARNIVAL BEAT (Stone Poneys)	3.25	5.50	4.00
☐2195		SOME OF SHELLY'S BLUES/ HOBO (MORNING GLORY)	3.00	5.00	3.50
☐2438		DOLPHINS/LONG WAY AROUND .	3.00	5.00	3.50
☐2767		WILL YOU LOVE ME TOMORROW/ LOVESICK BLUES	3.00	5.00	3.50
☐2846		LONG LONG TIME/NOBODYS	2.75	5.50	3.00
☐3021		(SHE'S A) VERY LOVELY WOMAN/ LONG WAY AROUND	2.75	4.50	3.00
☐3210		I FALL TO PIECES/CAN IT BE TRUE	2.75	4.50	3.00
☐3273		ROCK ME ON THE WATER/ CRAZY ARMS	2.75	4.50	3.00

LATER CAPITOL SINGLES ARE WORTH UP TO $1.75 MINT

☐2846		LONG, LONG TIME/ NOBODY'S	3.00	5.05	3.75

LINDA RONSTADT

The queen of the rock world was born in Tucson, AZ, on July 15, 1946. Linda began singing at a young age and played a guitar for a short time. During high school, she and some family members appeared on Tucson TV as a singing group. Linda Ronstadt finished high school in 1964 as a chubby bleached blonde.

She enrolled at the University of Arizona, stayed one semester, quit, and took off for Los Angeles in hopes of establishing herself as a singer. A lone single on Sidewalk Records failed. Ms. Ronstadt later drifted into the Stone Poneys, a folk-rock group. After two flop Capitol singles, the Stone Poneys were offered a song called "Different Drum". It had been written by Monkee Mike Nesmith. The Stone Poneys then struck it big with "Different Drum". Later releases did little and the trio went their separate ways.

Linda became a solo artist once again. On Capitol, she recorded excellent singles like "Some of Shelley's Blues" (another Nesmith number) and Fred Neil's "Dolphins". None sold.

In 1970, she hit with "Long Long Time", but again fell from public attention with lesser follow-ups. Linda later switched to Asylum Records but owed Capitol one more album. From that obligatory LP came her first real winner, "You're No Good", a song first done in 1963 by Betty Everett.

			Current Price Range		P/Y AVG
☐3990		YOU'RE NO GOOD/ I CAN'T HELP IT	3.00	5.00	3.75
☐4050		WHEN WILL I BE LOVED/ IT DOESN'T MATTER ANYMORE	3.00	5.00	3.75
☐45271	**ASYLUM**	LOVE IS A ROSE/ SILVER BLUE	2.50	4.00	2.75
☐45295		TRACKS OF MY TEARS	2.50	4.00	2.75
☐45340		THAT'LL BE THE DAY/ TRY ME AGAIN	2.50	4.00	2.75
☐45361		SOMEONE TO LAY DOWN BESIDE ME/CRAZY	2.50	4.00	2.75
☐45431		BLUE BAYOU/ MAYBE I'M RIGHT	2.50	4.00	2.75
☐45438		IT'S SO EASY	2.50	4.00	2.75
☐45462		POOR POOR PITIFUL ME/ SIMPLE MAN, SIMPLE DREAMS	2.50	4.00	2.75
☐45464		LAGO AZUL/BLUE BAYOU	2.25	3.75	2.50
☐45519		BACK IN THE U.S.A./ WHITE RHYTHM AND BLUES ..	2.25	3.75	2.50
☐45546		OOH BABY BABY/ BLOWIN' AWAY	2.25	3.75	2.50
☐46011		JUST ONE LOOK	2.25	3.75	2.50
☐46034		ALLISON/ALL THAT YOU DREAM	2.25	3.75	2.50
☐46602		HOW DO I MAKE YOU/ RAMBLER GAMBLER	2.25	3.75	2.50
☐46624		HURT SO BAD/ JUSTINE	2.25	3.75	2.50
☐46654		I CAN'T LET GO/ LOOK OUT FOR MY LOVE	2.25	3.75	2.50
☐12103		GET CLOSER/ SOMETIMES YOU JUST CAN'T WIN	2.25	3.75	2.50
☐69853		I KNEW YOU WHEN/ TALK TO ME OF MENDOCINO ..	2.25	3.75	2.50
☐69383		EASY FOR YOU TO SAY/ MR. RADIO	2.25	3.75	2.50
☐69780		WHAT'S NEW/ CRAZY HE CALLS ME	2.25	3.75	2.50
☐11026	**ELEKTRA**	LOVE HAS NO PRIDE/ I CAN ALMOST SEE IT	2.25	3.75	2.50
☐45479		TUMBLING DICE/ I NEVER WILL MARRY	2.25	3.75	2.50
☐937	**SIDEWALK**	EVERYBODY HAS THEIR OWN IDEAS/SO FINE	9.50	18.00	15.00
		LINDA RONSTADT—ALBUMS			
☐208	**CAPITOL**	HAND SOWN . . . HOME GROWN .	6.00	11.00	7.50
☐407		SILK PURSE	6.00	11.00	7.50
☐635		LINDA RONSTADT	6.00	11.00	7.50
☐11269		DIFFERENT DRUM	6.00	11.00	7.50
☐11358		HEART LIKE A WHEEL	6.00	11.00	7.50
☐11629		A RETROSPECTIVE	6.00	11.00	7.50
☐16130		HAND SOWN . . . HAND GROWN (REISSUE)	5.00	10.00	6.50
☐16131		SILK PURSE (REISSUE)	5.00	10.00	6.50
☐16132		LINDA RONSTADT (REISSUE)	5.00	10.00	6.50
☐5064	**ASYLUM**	DON'T CRY NOW	5.00	9.00	6.00
☐1054		PRISONER IN DISGUISE	5.00	9.00	6.00
☐1072		HASTEN DOWN THE WIND	5.00	9.00	6.00
☐1092		GREATEST HITS	5.00	9.00	6.00
☐104		SIMPLE DREAMS	5.00	9.00	6.00
☐155		LIVING IN THE U.S.A.	5.00	9.00	6.00
☐510		MAD LOVE	5.00	9.00	6.00
☐516		GREATEST HITS OF VO. 2	5.00	9.00	6.00
☐540		KEEPING OUT OF MISCHIEF	5.00	9.00	6.00

			Current Price Range		P/Y AVG
☐60185		GET CLOSER	5.00	9.00	6.00
☐60260		WHAT'S NEW	5.00	9.00	6.00
☐601	**ELEKTRA**	PIRATES OF PENZANCE	5.00	10.00	7.00

ROSIE AND THE ORIGINALS

☐1011	**HIGHLAND**	ANGEL BABY/GIVE ME LOVE	3.00	5.00	3.50
☐1025		ANGEL FROM ABOVE/			
		WHY DID YOU LEAVE ME?	5.00	9.00	7.00
☐1031		LONELY BLUE NIGHTS/			
		WE'LL HAVE A CHANCE	8.25	14.00	12.00
☐55205	**BRUNSWICK**	LONELY BLUE NIGHTS/			
		WE'LL HAVE A CHANCE (Rosie)	3.75	6.00	4.50
☐55213		MY DARLIN' FOREVER/			
		THE TIME IS NEAR (Rosie)	4.50	7.50	6.00

ROSIE—ALBUM

☐54102 (M)	**BRUNSWICK**	LONELY BLUE NIGHTS	14.00	34.00	30.00

ROXY & THE DAYCHORDS

☐46	**DONEL**	MARY LOU/I'M SO IN LOVE	14.00	36.00	32.00

ROYAL DRIFTERS

☐506	**TEEN**	LITTLE LINDA	14.00	34.50	30.50

ROYALS
SEE: HANK BALLARD AND THE MIDNIGHTERS, MIDNIGHTERS

☐12064	**FEDERAL**	EVERY BEAT OF MY HEART/			
		ALL NIGHT LONG	80.00	140.00	103.00
☐12077		STARTING FROM TONIGHT/			
		I KNOW I LOVE YOU SO	80.00	140.00	103.00
☐12088		MOONRISE/FIFTH ST. BLUES ...	80.00	140.00	103.00
☐12098		A LOVE IN MY HEART/			
		I'LL NEVER LET HER GO	80.00	140.00	103.00
☐12113		ARE YOU FORGETTING/			
		WHAT DID I DO	80.00	140.00	103.00
☐12121		THE SHRINE OF ST. CECELIA/			
		I FEEL SO BLUE	27.00	50.00	32.00
☐12133		GET IT/NO IT AIN'T	27.00	50.00	32.00
☐12150		I FEEL THAT-A WAY/			
		HELLO MISS FINE	27.00	50.00	32.00
☐12160		SOMEONE LIKE YOU/THAT'S IT ..	27.00	50.00	32.00
☐12169		WORK WITH ME ANNIE/			
		UNTIL I DIE	23.00	40.00	27.00
☐12177		GIVE IT UP/THAT WOMAN	23.00	40.00	27.00

ROYAL TEENS

☐113	**POWER**	SITTIN' WITH MY BABY/			
		MAD GASS	14.00	24.00	20.00
☐215		SHORT SHORTS/PLANET ROCK ...	21.00	34.00	30.00
☐9882	**ABC- PARAMOUNT**	SHORT SHORTS/PLANET ROCK ..	4.00	7.00	4.65
☐9918		BIG NAME BUTTON/SHAM ROCK .	4.00	7.00	4.65
☐9945		HARVEY'S TO A GIRL FRIEND/			
		HANGIN' ROUND	3.50	6.00	4.35
☐9955		MY KIND OF DREAM/			
		OPEN THE DOOR	3.50	6.00	4.35
☐4261	**CAPITOL**	BELIEVE ME/LITTLE CRICKET ...	3.50	6.00	4.35
☐4335		THE MOON'S NOT MEANT FOR			
		LOVERS/WAS IT A DREAM? ...	3.75	6.00	4.50
☐4402		IT'S THE TALK OF THE TOWN/			
		WITH YOU	3.75	6.00	4.50
☐111	**MIGHTY**	ROYAL BLUES/LEOTARDS	3.25	5.50	4.00
☐111		I'LL NOT BE THE ONE (TO SAY			
		GOODBYE)/ROYAL BLUE	3.25	5.50	4.00
☐112		CAVE MAN/WOUNDED HEART ...	3.25	5.50	4.00

			Current Price Range		P/Y AVG
☐ 1415	**ALL NEW**	SHORT SHORT TWIST/ ROYAL TWIST	4.50	7.50	6.00
☐ 5418	**JUBILEE**	SHORT SHORT TWIST/ ROYAL TWIST	3.25	5.50	4.00
☐ 4200	**SWAN**	I'LL LOVE YOU TILL THE END OF TIME/(PT. 2)	3.25	5.50	4.00
☐ 101	**BLUE JAY**	I'LL LOVE YOU TILL THE END OF TIME/(PT. 2) (Blue Tones) ..	3.25	5.50	4.00

RUBEN AND THE JETS
FEATURED: FRANK ZAPPA

☐ 10632	**VERVE**	JELLY ROLL GUM DROP/ ANYWAY THE WIND BLOWS ...	5.00	9.00	7.00
☐ 73381	**MERCURY**	IF I COULD BE YOUR LOVE AGAIN/ WEDDING BELLS	4.50	7.50	6.00

RUBEN AND THE JETS—ALBUM

☐ 5055 (S)	**VERVE**	CRUISIN' WITH RUBEN AND THE JETS	12.00	21.00	18.00

RUMBLERS

☐ 1026	**HIGHLAND**	INTERSECTION/STOMPING TIME .	5.50	11.00	9.00
☐ 103	**DOWNEY**	BOSS/ I DON'T NEED YOU NO MORE ..	4.50	8.00	6.00
☐ 106		BOSS STRIKES BACK/SORRY ...	3.75	6.00	4.50
☐ 107		ANGRY SEA/BUGGED	3.75	6.00	4.50
☐ 111		IT'S A GASS/TOOTENANNY	3.25	5.50	4.00
☐ 114		HIGH OCTANE/NIGHT SCENE ...	3.25	5.50	4.00
☐ 127		SOULFUL JERK/HEY-DID-A-DA-DA	3.25	5.50	4.00
☐ 16421	**DOT**	BOSS/ I DON'T NEED YOU NO MORE ..	3.00	5.00	3.50
☐ 16455		BOSS STRIKES BACK/SORRY ...	3.00	5.00	3.50
☐ 18292		IT'S A GASS/TOOTENANNY	3.00	5.00	3.50

RUMBLERS—ALBUMS

☐ 1001 (M)	**DOWNEY**	BOSS!	14.50	34.00	30.00
☐ 1001 (S)		BOSS!	22.00	56.00	50.00
☐ 3509 (M)	**DOT**	BOSS!	8.00	21.00	18.00
☐ 22509 (S)		BOSS!	12.00	29.00	25.00

RUNAROUNDS (REGENTS)

☐ 1004	**COUSINS**	MASHED POTATO MARY/ I'M ALL ALONE	8.25	14.00	12.00
☐ 116	**KC**	UNBELIEVABLE/ HOORAY FOR LOVE	5.00	9.00	7.00
☐ 8704	**FELSTED**	CARRIE (YOU'RE AN ANGEL)/ SEND HER BACK	4.50	7.50	6.00
☐ 5644	**CAPITOL**	PERFECT WOMAN/ YOU'RE A DRAG	3.00	7.50	5.00

TODD RUNDGREN

☐ 0003	**BEARSVILLE**	I SAW THE LIGHT/MARLENE	8.25	21.00	18.00
		THIS INITIAL PRESSING WAS ISSUED ON BLUE VINYL, IN VERY LIMITED NUMBERS			
☐ 0003		I SAW THE LIGHT/ MARLENE (black vinyl)	2.50	4.50	3.00
☐ 0007		WOLFMAN JACK/ COULDN'T I JUST TELL YOU ...	2.75	5.00	3.50
☐ 0009		COLD MORNING LIGHT/ HELLO IT'S ME	2.75	5.00	3.50
☐ 0015		SOMETIMES/ DOES ANYBODY LOVE YOU	2.75	5.00	3.50
☐ 0020		HEAVY METAL KIDS/ A DREAM GOES ON FOREVER ..	2.75	5.00	3.50

LATER BEARSVILLE SINGLES ARE WORTH UP TO $2.75 MINT

BOBBY RYDELL

He began life as Robert Lewis Ridarelli in Philadelphia, PA, on April 26, 1942. As a young TV watcher, he delighted in mimicking the personalities that flickered on his home screen. Bobby's interests turned to music at a young age. He became a competent drummer by age 6, and was appearing in local clubs a year later.

Before he entered junior high school, Bobby had become a drumming regular on Paul Whiteman's TV show. It was Whiteman who suggested to Ridarelli that he shorten his name to something simplier and more commercial.

Bobby joined Rocco and the Saints (Frankie Avalon's first group; he played trumpet) during high school. Rydell was later tagged to be a solo act when it was discovered that he could sing well. He signed to a pair of small labels — Venise and Veko — before going with Cameo Records. There he recored a fine "do-wop" disc called "Please Don't Be Mad". When this failed, he tried again with "All I Want is You". This also died.

Rydell found his third attempt the charm with "Kissin' Time", a 1959 winner and the first of eleven Top 20 hits on Cameo. During the mid-1960s, his career declined, thanks in part to the "British invasion" of that period.

			Current Price Range		P/Y AVG

LEON RUSSELL

☐4049	**ROULETTE**	HONKY TONK WOMAN/RAINBOW AT MIDNIGHT (by Lee Russell) .	5.50	11.00	9.00
☐7325	**SHELTER**	TIGHT ROPE/THIS MASQUERADE	2.75	4.50	3.00
☐7328		SLIPPING INTO CHRISTMAS/ CHRISTMAS IN CHICAGO	3.00	5.00	3.50
☐7337		QUEEN OF THE ROLLER DERBY/ ROLL AWAY THE STONE	2.75	4.50	3.00
☐40210		IF I WERE A CARPENTER/ WILD HORSES	2.75	4.50	3.00
☐40277		TIME FOR LOVE/ LEAVING WHIPPORWILL	2.75	4.50	3.00
☐40378		LADY BLUE/ LAYING RIGHT HERE IN HEAVEN	2.50	4.00	2.50
☐40483		BACK TO THE ISLAND/ LITTLE HIDEAWAY	2.50	4.00	2.50

BOBBY RYDELL

☐201	**VENISE**	FATTY FATTY/HAPPY HAPPY	12.00	21.00	18.00
☐731	**VEKO**	FATTY FATTY/DREAM AGE	8.25	14.00	12.00
☐160	**CAMEO**	PLEASE DON'T BE MAD/ MAKIN' TIME	14.00	24.00	20.00
☐164		ALL I WANT IS YOU/ FOR YOU, FOR YOU	9.50	17.00	15.00
☐167		KISSIN' TIME/ YOU'll NEVER TAME ME	3.50	6.00	4.35
☐169		WE GOT LOVE/I DIG GIRLS	3.50	6.00	4.35
☐171		WILD ONE/ITTY BITTY GIRL	3.50	6.00	4.35
☐175		SWINGIN' SCHOOL/DING A LING .	3.50	6.00	4.35
☐179		VOLARE/I'LL DO IT AGAIN	3.25	5.50	4.00
☐182		SWAY/GROOVY TONIGHT	3.25	5.50	4.00
☐186		GOOD TIME BABY/CHERIE	3.25	5.50	4.00
☐190		THAT OLD BLACK MAGIC/ DON'T BE AFRAID	3.20	5.50	4.00
☐192		THE FISH/THE THIRD HOUSE . . .	3.25	5.50	4.00
☐201		I WANNA THANK YOU/ THE DOOR TO PARADISE	3.25	5.50	4.00
☐209		I'VE GOT BONNIE/LOSE HER	3.25	5.50	4.50
☐217		I'LL NEVER DANCE AGAIN/ GEE, IT'S WONDERFUL	3.25	5.50	4.00
☐228		THE CHA-CHA-CHA/ THE BEST MAN CRIED	3.25	5.50	4.00
☐242		BUTTERFLY BABY/LOVE IS BLIND.	3.00	5.00	3.65
☐252		WILDWOOD DAYS/ WILL YOU BE MY BABY	3.00	5.00	3.65
☐265		LITTLE QUEENIE/ THE WOODPECKER SONG	3.00	5.00	3.65
☐272		LET'S MAKE LOVE TONIGHT/ CHILDHOOD SWEETHEART	3.00	5.00	3.65
☐280		FORGET HIM/ LOVE, LOVE, GO AWAY	3.00	5.00	3.65
☐309		MAKE ME FORGET/LITTLE GIRL, I'VE HAD A BUSY DAY	3.00	5.00	3.65
☐320		A WORLD WITHOUT LOVE/ OUR FADED LOVE	3.00	5.00	3.65
☐361		CIAO CIAO BAMBINO/ VOCE DE LA NOTTE	3.25	5.50	4.00
☐1070		FORGET HIM/ A MESSAGE FROM BOBBY	2.75	4.50	3.25
☐5305	**CAPITOL**	I JUST CAN'T SAY GOODBYE/TWO IS THE LONELIEST NUMBER . . .	3.00	5.00	3.65
☐5352		DIANA/STRANGER IN THE WORLD	3.00	5.00	3.65
☐5436		SIDESHOW/THE JOKER.	3.00	5.00	3.65
☐5513		IT TAKES TWO/WHEN I SEE THAT GIRL OF MINE	3.00	5.00	3.65

			Current Price Range		P/Y AVG
☐5556		ROSES IN THE SNOW/			
		THE WORD FOR TODAY	3.00	5.00	3.65
☐5696		SHE WAS THE GIRL/NOT YOU ...	3.00	5.00	3.65
☐5780		YOU GOTTA ENJOY JOY/			
		OPEN FOR BUSINESS AS USUAL	3.00	5.00	3.65
☐0656	*REPRISE*	THE LOVIN' THINGS/			
		IT'S GETTING BETTER	3.00	5.00	3.65
☐0684		THE RIVER IS WIDE/			
		ABSENCE MAKES THE HEART			
		GROW FONDER	3.00	5.00	3.65
☐0751		EVERY LITTLE BIT HURTS/			
		TIME AND CHANGES	3.00	5.00	3.65
☐9892	*RCA*	CHAPEL ON THE HILL/			
		IT MUST BE LOVE	3.00	5.00	3.65
		BOBBY RYDELL—ALBUMS			
☐1006 (M)	*CAMEO*	WE GOT LOVE	12.00	29.00	25.00
☐1007 (M)		BOBBY SINGS	12.00	29.00	25.00
☐1009 (M)		BIGGEST HITS	9.00	25.00	22.50
☐1010 (M)		BOBBY RYDELL SALUTES THE			
		GREAT ONES	9.00	25.00	22.50
☐1011 (M)		RYDELL AT THE COPA	8.00	21.00	18.00
☐1019 (M)		ALL THE HITS BY BOBBY RYDELL	8.00	21.00	18.00
☐1028 (M)		BIGGEST HITS, VOL. II	8.00	21.00	18.00
☐1040 (M)		ALL THE HITS BY BOBBY RYDELL,			
		VOL. II	8.00	21.00	18.00
☐1043 (M)		BYE BYE BIRDIE	8.00	21.00	18.00
☐1055 (M)		WILD (WOOD) DAYS	7.00	17.00	15.00
☐1055 (S)		WILD (WOOD) DAYS	9.00	25.00	22.50
☐1070 (M)		TOP HITS OF '63	7.00	17.00	15.00
☐1070 (S)		TOP HITS OF '63	8.00	21.00	18.00
☐1080 (M)		FORGET HIM	7.00	17.00	15.00
☐1080 (S)		FORGET HIM	8.00	21.00	18.00
☐2001 (M)		16 GOLDEN HITS	7.00	17.00	15.00
☐2001 (S)		16 GOLDEN HITS	8.00	17.00	15.00
☐4017 (M)		AN ERA REBORN	6.00	15.00	13.50
☐4017 (M)		AN ERA REBORN	7.00	17.00	15.00
☐2281 (S)	*CAPITOL*	SOMEBODY LOVES YOU	5.50	15.00	13.50

BOBBY RYDELL AND CHUBBY CHECKER

☐205	*CAMEO*	JINGLE BELL ROCK/			
		JINGLE BELL IMITATIONS	2.75	4.50	3.00
☐214		TEACH ME TO TWIST/			
		SWINGIN' TOGETHER	3.00	5.00	3.50
		BOBBY RYDELL AND CHUBBY CHECKER—ALBUM			
☐1013 (M)	*CAMEO*	BOBBY RYDELL AND			
		CHUBBY CHECKER	7.00	12.00	10.00

MITCH RYDER AND THE DETROIT WHEELS
SEE: BILLY AND THE RIVIERAS

☐801	*NEW VOICE*	I NEED HELP/I HOPE	3.50	6.00	4.35
☐806		JENNY TAKE A RIDE!/BABY JANE	3.00	5.00	3.65
☐808		LITTLE LATIN LUPE LU/I HOPE ..	3.00	5.00	3.65
☐811		BREAK OUT/I NEED HELP	3.00	5.00	3.65
☐814		TAKIN' ALL I CAN GET/			
		YOU GET YOUR KICKS	3.00	5.00	3.65
☐817		DEVIL WITH A BLUE DRESS ON/			
		I HAD IT TWICE	3.00	5.00	3.65
☐820		SOCK IT TO ME BABY!/			
		I NEVER HAD IT BETTER	3.00	5.00	3.65
☐822		TOO MANY FISH IN THE SEA/			
		ONE GRAIN OF SAND	3.00	5.00	3.65
☐824		JOY/I'D RATHER GO TO JAIL	3.00	5.00	3.65
☐826		YOU ARE MY SUNSHINE/			
		WILD CHILD	3.00	5.00	3.65

			Current Price Range		P/Y AVG
☐828		COME SEE ABOUT ME/ FACE IN THE CROWD	3.00	5.00	3.65
☐830		RUBY BABY-PEACHES ON A CHERRY TREE/ YOU GET YOUR KICKS	3.00	5.00	3.65

MITCH RIDER AND THE DETROIT WHEELS—ALBUMS

			Current Price Range		P/Y AVG
☐2000 (M)	*NEW VOICE*	JENNY TAKE A RIDE	7.00	17.00	15.00
☐2000 (S)		JENNY TAKE A RIDE	8.00	21.00	18.00
☐2002 (M)		BREAKOUT....................	7.00	17.00	15.00
☐2002 (S)		BREAKOUT....................	8.00	21.00	18.00
☐2003 (M)		SOCK IT TO ME	6.00	15.00	13.50
☐2003 (S)		SOCK IT TO ME	7.00	17.00	15.00
☐2004 (M)		ALL MITCH RYDER HITS	6.00	15.00	13.50
☐2004 (S)		ALL MITCH RYDER HITS	7.00	17.00	15.00
☐2005 (S)	*NEW VOICE*	NEW MITCH RYDER SINGS THE HITS	6.00	15.00	13.50

MITCH RYDER

☐901	*DYNO VOICE*	WHAT NOW MY LOVE/ BLESSING IN DISGUISE	2.75	4.50	3.00
☐905		PERSONALITY-CHANTILLY LACE/ I MAKE A FOOL OF MYSELF ...	2.75	4.50	3.00
☐916		THE LIGHTS OF NIGHT/ I NEED LOVING YOU	2.75	4.50	3.00
☐934		RING YOUR BELL/BABY I NEED YOUR LOVING— THEME FOR MITCH	2.75	4.50	3.00

MITCH RYDER—ALBUMS

☐31901	*DYNO VOICE*	WHAT NOW MY LOVE	5.50	14.00	12.00
☐31901 (S)		WHAT NOW MY LOVE	6.00	15.00	13.50

S

JOHNNY SABER & THE PASSIONS

☐103	*ADONIS*	DOLLY IN A TOYSHOP/ WISH IT COULD BE ME	13.00	33.00	28.00

SAFARIS

☐101	*ELDO*	IMAGE OF A GIRL/ 4 STEPS TO LOVE	3.50	6.00	4.35
☐105		GIRL WITH THE STORY IN HER EYES/SUMMER NIGHTS	3.50	6.00	4.35
☐110		IN THE STILL OF THE NIGHT/ SHADOWS	3.50	6.00	4.35
☐113		SOLDIER OF FORTUNE/ GARDEN OF LOVE	3.50	6.00	4.35

SAGITTARIUS
FEATURED: BRUCE JOHNSTON, TERRY MELCHER (BRUCE AND TERRY), GARY USHER, GLEN CAMPBELL

☐44163	*COLUMBIA*	MY WORLD FELL DOWN/LIBRA ..	3.25	5.50	4.00
☐44289		HOTEL INDISCREET/VIRGO	3.25	5.50	4.00
☐44398		ANOTHER TIME/PISCES	3.25	5.50	4.00
☐105	*TOGETHER*	IN MY ROOM/NAVAJO GIRL	3.00	5.00	3.50
☐122		I CAN STILL SEE YOUR FACE/ I GUESS THE LORD MUST BE IN NEW YORK CITY	3.00	5.00	3.50

			Current Price Range		P/Y AVG
		SAGITTARIUS—ALBUMS			
☐ 9644 (S)	*COLUMBIA*	PRESENT TENSE	7.00	17.00	15.00
☐ 1002 (S)	*TOGETHER*	THE BLUE MARBLE	8.00	21.00	18.00
		DOUG SAHM			
		SEE: SIR DOUGLAS QUINTET			
☐ 107	*HARLEM*	WHY OH WHY/			
		IF YOU EVER NEED ME	8.25	14.00	12.00
☐ 625	*SWINGIN'*	WHY OH WHY/			
		IF YOU EVER NEED ME	5.50	11.00	9.00
☐ 3505	*PERSONALITY*	BABY, WHAT'S ON YOUR MIND?/			
		CRAZY, CRAZY FEELING	5.50	11.00	9.00
☐ 212	*RENNER*	MAKES NO DIFFERENCE/BIG HAT	5.50	11.00	9.00
☐ 215		BABY, WHAT'S ON YOUR MIND?/			
		CRAZY, CRAZY FEELING	5.00	9.00	7.00
☐ 226		JUST BECAUSE/			
		TWO HEARTS IN LOVE	5.00	9.00	7.00
☐ 240		LUCKY ME/A YEAR AGO TODAY . .	5.00	9.00	7.00
		SAM THE SHAM AND THE PHAROAHS			
☐ 2982	*TUPELO*	BETTY AND DUPREE/MAN CHILD	9.50	17.00	15.00
☐ 001	*DINGO*	HAUNTED HOUSE/HOW DOES			
		A CHEATING WOMAN FEEL? . . .	8.25	14.00	12.00
☐ 905	*XL*	THE SIGNIFYING MONKEY/			
		JUIMONOS	8.25	14.00	12.00
☐ 906		WOOLY BULLY/			
		AIN'T GONNA MOVE	21.00	34.00	30.00
☐ 13322	*MGM*	WOOLY BULLY/			
		AIN'T GONNA MOVE	3.25	5.50	4.00
☐ 13364		JU JU HAND/BIG CITY LIGHTS . . .	3.25	5.50	4.00
☐ 13397		RING DANG DOO/DON'T TRY IT . .	3.25	5.50	4.00
☐ 13452		RED HOT/A LONG LONG WAY	3.25	5.50	4.00
☐ 13506		LIL' RED RIDING HOOD/			
		LOVE ME LIKE BEFORE	3.00	5.00	3.65
☐ 13851		THE HAIR ON MY CHINNY CHIN			
		CHIN/THE OUT CROWD	3.00	5.00	3.65
☐ 13649		HOW DO YOU CATCH A GIRL?/			
		THE LOVE YOU LEFT BEHIND . .	3.00	5.00	3.65
☐ 13713		OH THAT'S GOOD, NO THAT'S			
		BAD/TAKE WHAT YOU CAN GET	3.00	5.00	3.65
☐ 13747		BLACK SHEEP/			
		MY DAY'S GONNA COME	3.00	5.00	3.65
☐ 13803		BANNED IN BOSTON/			
		MONEY'S MY PROBLEM	3.00	5.00	3.65
☐ 13863		YAKETY YAK/			
		LET YOUR LOVE LIGHT SHINE .	3.00	5.00	3.65
☐ 13920		OLD McDONALD HAS A BOOGALOO			
		FARM/I NEVER HAD NO ONE . .	3.00	5.00	3.65
☐ 13972		I COULDN'T SPELL !!*@!/			
		THE DOWN HOME SPIRIT	3.00	5.00	3.65
		SAM THE SHAM AND THE PHAROAHS—ALBUMS			
☐ 4297 (M)	*MGM*	WOOLY BULLY	7.00	17.00	15.00
☐ 4297 (S)		WOOLY BULLY	9.00	25.00	22.50
☐ 4314 (M)		THEIR SECOND ALBUM	7.00	17.00	15.00
☐ 4314 (S)		THEIR SECOND ALBUM	9.00	25.00	22.50
☐ 4347 (M)		ON TOUR	6.00	15.00	13.50
☐ 4347 (S)		ON TOUR	8.00	21.00	18.00
☐ 4407 (M)		LIL' RED RIDING HOOD	6.00	15.00	13.50
☐ 4407 (S)		LIL' RED RIDING HOOD	8.00	21.00	18.00
☐ 4422 (M)		THE BEST OF SAM THE SHAM			
		AND THE PHAROAHS	6.00	15.00	13.50
☐ 4422 (S)		THE BEST OF SAM THE SHAM			
		AND THE PHAROAHS	8.00	17.00	15.00
☐ 4479 (S)		NEFERTITI	6.00	15.00	13.50

			Current Price Range		P/Y AVG
☐4479 (S)		THE SAM THE SHAM REVUE			
		(same as above)	6.00	15.00	13.50
☐4526 (S)		TEN OF PENTACLES.	6.00	15.00	13.50
☐8271	ATLANTIC	HARD AND HEAVY			
		(without Pharoahs).	7.00	17.00	15.00

BOBBY SANDERS

☐618	KAYBO	I'M ON MY WAY/IT WAS YOU . . .	9.00	19.00	16.00

TOMMY SANDS

☐3639	CAPITOL	TEEN-AGE CRUSH/			
		HEP DEE HOOTIE	3.50	6.00	4.35
☐3690		RING-A-DING-A DING/			
		MY LOVE SONG	3.50	6.00	4.35
☐3723		GOIN' STEADY/RING MY PHONE .	3.50	6.00	4.35
☐3743		LET ME BE LOVED/			
		FANTASTICALLY FOOLISH	3.50	6.00	4.35
☐3810		A SWINGIN' ROMANCE/			
		MAN, LIKE WOW	3.50	6.00	4.35
☐3867		SING BOY SING/			
		CRAZY 'CAUSE I LOVE YOU . . .	3.25	5.50	4.00
☐3953		TEENAGE DOLL/HAWAIIAN ROCK	3.25	5.50	4.00
☐3985		AFTER THE SENIOR PROM/			
		BIG DATE	3.25	5.50	4.00
☐4036		BLUE RIBBON BABY/			
		I LOVE YOU BECAUSE	3.25	5.50	4.00
☐4082		THE WORRYIN' KIND/			
		BIGGER THAN TEXAS	3.25	5.50	4.00
☐4259		I'LL BE SEEING YOU/			
		THAT'S THE WAY I AM	3.25	5.50	4.00
☐4316		YOU HOLD THE FUTURE/			
		I GOTTA HAVE YOU	3.25	5.50	4.00
☐4321		SINNER MAN/			
		BRING ME YOUR LOVE	3.25	5.50	4.00
☐4366		THAT'S LOVE/CROSSROADS	3.25	5.50	4.00
☐4407		THE OLD OAKEN BUCKET/THESE			
		ARE THE THINGS YOU ARE	3.25	5.50	4.00
☐4470		DOCTOR HEARTACHE/ON AND ON	3.25	5.50	4.00

TOMMY SANDS—EPs

☐1-848	CAPITOL	STEADY DATE WITH			
		TOMMY SANDS	5.50	11.00	9.00
☐2-848		STEADY DATE WITH			
		TOMMY SANDS	5.50	11.00	9.00
☐3-848		STEADY DATE WITH			
		TOMMY SANDS	5.50	11.00	9.00
☐1-851		TEENAGE CRUSH	5.00	9.00	7.00
☐1-929		SING BOY SING	4.50	7.50	6.00
☐2-929		SING BOY SING	3.25	7.50	6.00
☐3-929		SING BOY SING	4.50	7.50	6.00
☐1-1123		THIS THING CALLED LOVE	4.50	7.50	6.00

TOMMY SANDS—ALBUMS

☐848 (M)	CAPITOL	STEADY DATE WITH			
		TOMMY SANDS	9.00	25.00	22.50
☐1109 (M)		TEENAGE ROCK	9.00	25.00	22.50
☐1081 (M)		SANDS STORM	9.00	25.00	22.50
☐1123 (M)		THIS THING CALLED LOVE	7.00	17.00	15.00
☐1123 (S)		THIS THING CALLED LOVE	9.00	25.00	22.50
☐1239 (M)		WHEN I'M THINKING OF YOU	6.00	15.00	13.50
☐1239 (S)		WHEN I'M THINKING OF YOU	8.00	21.00	18.00
☐1364 (M)		SANDS AT THE SANDS	6.00	11.00	9.00
☐1364 (S)		SANDS AT THE SANDS	8.25	14.00	12.00
☐1426 (M)		DREAM WITH ME.	6.00	11.00	9.00
☐1426 (S)		DREAM WITH ME.	8.25	14.00	12.00

TOMMY SANDS

Tommy Sands first saw life on August 27, 1937, in Chicago, Illinois. Influenced by his piano-playing father, young Sands started singing before he reached his tenth birthday. While he had first learned music on the piano, Tommy later took up the guitar.

The family moved to Houston, Texas. Tommy Sands, then a twelve-year-old seventh grader, landed a job as an afternoon disc jockey on a small Houston radio station. He worked there until his graduation from high school in 1955. Tommy soon left Houston and made appearances on Tennessee Ernie Ford's television show.

Sands' career blossomed when he landed the part of a rock-and-roll singer on NBC's "Kraft Television Theater" in 1957. The show on which Tommy appeared was called "The Singing Idol", and the twenty-year-old rocker sang two songs, "Hep Dee Hootie" and "Teenage Crush". Response to Sands' appearance was so great that Capitol Records signed him to record "Teenage Crush" immediately. The song became a smash and Tommy Sands' only million-seller.

			Current Price Range		P/Y AVG
		SANTO AND JOHNNY			
☐ 103	**CANADIAN-**				
	AMERICAN	SLEEP WALK/ALL NIGHT DINER	3.50	6.00	4.35
☐ 107		TEAR DROP/			
		THE LONG WAY HOME	3.50	6.00	4.35
☐ 111		CARAVAN/SUMMERTIME	3.25	5.50	4.00
☐ 115		THE BREEZE AND I/LAZY DAY . . .	3.25	5.50	4.00
☐ 118		LOVE LOST/ANNIE	3.25	5.50	4.00
☐ 120		TWISTIN' BELLS/BULLSEYE	3.25	5.50	4.00
☐ 124		HOP SCOTCH/SEA SHELLS	3.00	5.00	3.65
☐ 128		THEME FROM ''COME			
		SEPTEMBER''/THE LONG			
		WALK HOME	3.00	5.00	3.65
☐ 131		BIRMINGHAM/THE MOUSE	3.00	5.00	3.65
☐ 132		TWISTIN' BELLS/CHRISTMAS			
		DAY (with Linda Scott)	3.00	5.00	3.65
☐ 137		SPANISH HARLEM/			
		STAGE TO CIMARRON	3.00	5.00	3.65
☐ 141		STEP ASIDE/THREE CABALLEROS	3.00	5.00	3.65
☐ 144		MISERLOU/TOKYO TWILIGHT . . .	3.00	5.00	3.65
☐ 148		MANHATTAN/TWISTIN' BELLS . .	3.00	5.00	3.65
☐ 155		MANHATTAN SPIRITUAL/			
		THE WANDERING SEA	3.00	5.00	3.65
☐ 164		IN THE STILL OF THE NIGHT/			
		SONG FOR ROSEMARY	3.00	5.00	3.65
☐ 167		A THOUSAND MILES AWAY/			
		ROAD BLOCK	3.00	5.00	3.65
☐ 182		GOLDFINGER/SLEEP WALK	3.00	5.00	3.65
☐ 189		BRAZILIAN SUMMER/			
		MUCHO TEMPO	3.00	5.00	3.65
		SANTO AND JOHNNY—ALBUMS			
☐ 1001 (M)	**CANADIAN-**				
	AMERICAN	SANTO AND JOHNNY	12.00	29.00	25.00
☐ 1002 (M)		ENCORE	9.00	25.00	22.50
☐ 1002 (S)		ENCORE	14.00	34.00	30.00
☐ 1004 (M)		HAWAII	8.00	21.00	18.00
☐ 1004 (S)		HAWAII	12.00	29.00	25.00
☐ 1006 (M)		COME ON IN	7.00	17.00	15.00
☐ 1006 (S)		COME ON IN	9.00	25.00	22.50
☐ 1011 (M)		OFF SHORE	7.00	17.00	15.00
☐ 1011 (S)		OFF SHORE	9.00	25.00	22.50
☐ 1014 (M)		IN THE STILL OF THE NIGHT	7.00	17.00	15.00
☐ 1014 (S)		IN THE STILL OF THE NIGHT	9.00	25.00	22.50
☐ 1016 (M)		WISH YOU WERE HERE	7.00	17.00	15.00
☐ 1016 (S)		WISH YOU WERE HERE	9.00	25.00	22.50
☐ 1017 (M)		THE BEATLES' GREATEST HITS . .	7.00	17.00	15.00
☐ 1017 (S)		THE BEETLES' GREATEST HITS . .	9.00	25.00	22.50
☐ 1018 (M)		MUCHO	7.00	15.00	13.50
☐ 1018 (S)		MUCHO	8.00	21.00	18.00
		SAPPHIRES			
☐ R-100	**RAVIN'**	SO MUCH IN LOVE/SH-BOOM . . .	5.00	10.00	7.00
☐ 4143	**SWAN**	YOUR TRUE LOVE/			
		WHERE IS JOHNNY NOW?	3.75	6.00	4.50
☐ 4162		WHO DO YOU LOVE/OH SO SOON .	3.50	5.50	4.00
☐ 4177		I'VE GOT MINE, YOU BETTER GET			
		YOURS/I FOUND OUT TOO LATE	3.50	5.50	4.00
☐ 4148		GOTTA BE MORE THAN FRIENDS/			
		SONG FROM MOULIN ROUGE . .	3.50	5.50	4.00
		SAPPHIRES—ALBUM			
☐ 513 (M)	**SWAN**	WHO DO YOU LOVE	12.00	29.00	25.00

CARLTON, STLP 12 / 107

AMY, 8003-M, LP

			Current Price Range		P/Y AVG

MIKE SARNE

☐72071	CAPITOL (CANADIAN LABEL)	MY BABY'S CRAZY 'BOUT ELVIS/ JUST FOR KICKS	12.00	29.00	25.00

PETER SARSTEDT

☐77911	WORLD PACIFIC	WHERE DO YOU GO TO, MY LOVELY/I AM A CATHEDRAL	2.75	5.50	4.00

SKY SAXON
SEE: RITCHIE MARSH, SEEDS

☐777	CONQUEST	THEY SAY/GO AHEAD AND CRY	5.50	11.00	9.00

SCARLETS (PRE-FIVE SATINS)

☐128	RED ROBIN	DEAR ONE/I'VE LOST	29.00	48.00	42.00
☐133		LOVE DOLL/DARLING I'M YOURS	48.00	80.00	72.00
☐135		TRUE LOVE/CRY BABY	48.00	80.00	72.00
☐138		KISS ME/INDIAN RIVER	60.00	104.00	95.00
☐7905	KLIK	SHE'S GONE (WITH THE WIND)/ THE VOICE (Fred Parris and the Scarlets)	22.00	40.00	36.00

JACK SCOTT

☐9818	ABC-PARAMOUNT	BABY SHE'S GONE/YOU CAN BET YOUR BOTTOM DOLLAR	25.00	50.00	36.00
☐9860		TWO TIMIN' WOMAN/ I NEED YOUR LOVE	34.00	54.00	48.00
☐10843		BEFORE THE BIRD FLIES/INSANE	16.00	30.00	25.00
☐462	CARLTON	MY TRUE LOVE/LEROY	4.50	7.50	6.00
☐483		WITH YOUR LOVE/GERALDINE	4.50	7.50	6.00
☐493		GOODBYE BABY/SAVE MY SOUL	4.00	7.00	4.85
☐504		I NEVER FELT LIKE THIS/BELLA	4.00	7.00	4.85
☐514		THE WAY I WALK/MIDGIE	4.00	7.00	4.85
☐519		THERE COMES A TIME/ BABY MARIE	4.00	7.00	4.85
☐209	GUARANTEED	WHAT AM I LIVING FOR?/ INDIANA WALTZ	5.50	11.00	9.00
☐211		GO WILD, LITTLE SADIE/ NO ONE WILL EVER KNOW	9.50	17.00	15.00
☐2028	TOP RANK	WHAT IN THE WORLD'S COME OVER YOU?/BABY, BABY	3.25	5.50	4.00
☐2041		BURNING BRIDGES/ OH LITTLE ONE	3.25	5.50	4.00
☐2055		IT ONLY HAPPENED YESTERDAY/ COOL WATER	3.25	5.50	4.00
☐2075		PATSY/OLD TIME RELIGION	3.00	5.00	3.50
☐2093		IS THERE SOMETHING ON YOUR MIND?/FOUND A WOMAN	3.00	5.00	3.50
☐4554	CAPITOL	A LITTLE FEELING CALLED LOVE/ NOW THAT	5.00	9.00	6.00
☐4597		MY DREAM COME TRUE/ STRANGE DESIRE	5.00	9.00	6.00
☐4637		STEPS 1 AND 2/ ONE OF THESE DAYS	5.00	9.00	6.00
☐4689		CRY, CRY, CRY/GRIZZLY BEAR	5.00	9.00	6.00
☐4738		THE PART WHERE I CRY/ YOU ONLY SEE WHAT YOU WANT TO SEE	5.00	9.00	6.00
☐4796		SAD STORY/I CAN'T HOLD YOUR LETTERS (IN MY ARMS)	4.00	7.00	4.50
☐4855		IF ONLY/GREEN, GREEN VALLEY	4.00	7.00	4.50

			Current Price Range		P/Y AVG
☐4903		STRANGERS/LAUGH AND THE WORLD LAUGHS WITH YOU ...	4.00	7.00	4.50
☐4955		ALL IS SEE IS BLUE/ME-O MY-O .	4.00	7.00	4.50
☐0027	GROOVE	THERE'S TROUBLE BREWING/ JINGLE BELL SLIDE	4.00	7.00	4.50
☐0031		I KNEW YOU FIRST/BLUE SKIES .	4.00	7.00	4.50
☐0037		WIGGLE ON OUT/WHAT A WONDERFUL NIGHT OUT	4.00	7.00	4.50
☐0042		THOU SHALT NOT STEAL/ I PRAYED FOR AN ANGEL	4.00	7.00	4.50
☐0049		TALL TALES/FLAKEY JOHN	4.00	7.00	4.50
☐8505	RCA	I DON'T BELIEVE IN TEA LEAVES/ SEPARATION'S NOW GRANTED	3.50	6.00	4.35
☐8685		LOOKING FOR LINDA/ I HOPE, I THINK, I WISH	3.50	6.00	4.35
☐8724		DON'T HUSH THE LAUGHTER/ LET'S LEARN TO LIVE AND LOVE AGAIN	3.50	6.00	4.35
☐5606	JUBILEE	MY SPECIAL ANGEL/ I KEEP CHANGING MY MIND ...	3.50	6.00	4.35
☐17475	DOT	MAY YOU NEVER BE ALONE/ FACE TO THE WALL	3.25	5.50	4.00
☐17504		YOU'RE JUST GETTING BETTER/ WALK THROUGH MY MIND	3.25	5.50	4.00
		JACK SCOTT—EPs			
☐1070	CARLTON	JACK SCOTT	12.00	21.00	18.00
☐1071		JACK SCOTT	12.00	21.00	18.00
☐1072		JACK SCOTT SINGS	12.00	21.00	18.00
☐1073		STARRING JACK SCOTT	12.00	21.00	18.00
☐1001	TOP RANK	WHAT IN THE WORLD'S COME OVER YOU?	14.00	24.00	20.00
		JACK SCOTT—ALBUMS			
☐107 (M)	CARLTON	JACK SCOTT	39.00	98.00	90.00
☐107 (S)		JACK SCOTT	50.00	130.00	120.00
☐122 (M)		WHAT AM I LIVING FOR?........	34.00	80.00	75.00
☐122 (S)		WHAT AM I LIVING FOR?........	45.00	110.00	100.00
☐319 (M)		I REMEMBER HANK WILLIAMS ..	29.00	65.00	60.00
☐619 (S)		I REMEMBER HANK WILLIAMS ..	34.00	80.00	75.00
☐326 (M)		WHAT IN THE WORLD'S COME OVER YOU?	29.00	65.00	60.00
☐626 (S)		WHAT IN THE WORLD'S COME OVER YOU?	34.00	80.00	75.00
☐348 (M)		THE SPIRIT MOVES ME	29.00	65.00	60.00
☐648 (S)		THE SPIRIT MOVES ME	34.00	80.00	75.00
☐2035 (M)	CAPITOL	BURNING BRIDGES	17.00	39.00	35.00
☐2035 (S)		BURNING BRIDGES	19.50	50.00	45.00

JOEL SCOTT

☐101	PHILLES	HERE I STAND/ YOU'RE MY ONLY LOVE	5.00	9.00	7.00

LINDA SCOTT

☐123	CANADIAN-AMERICAN	I'VE TOLD EVERY LITTLE STAR/ THREE GUESSES	3.00	5.00	3.50
☐127		DON'T BET MONEY HONEY/ STARLIGHT, STARBRIGHT	3.00	5.00	3.50
☐129		I DON'T KNOW WHY/ IT'S ALL BECAUSE	3.00	5.00	3.50
☐132		CHRISTMAS DAY/TWISTIN' BELLS (with Santo and Johnny) .	3.00	5.00	3.50
☐133		COUNT EVERY STAR/ LAND OF STARS	3.00	5.00	3.50
☐134		BERMUDA/LONELY FOR YOU ...	3.00	5.00	3.50

			Current Price Range		P/Y AVG
☐ 101	**CONGRESS**	YESIREE/TOWN CRIER	2.75	4.50	3.00
☐ 103		NEVER IN A MILLION YEARS/ THROUGH THE SUMMER	2.75	4.50	3.00
☐ 106		I LEFT MY HEART IN THE BALCONY/LOPSIDED LOVE AFFAIR	2.75	4.50	3.00
☐ 108		LONELIEST GIRL IN TOWN/ I'M SO AFRAID OF LOSING YOU	2.75	4.50	3.00
☐ 110		AIN'T THAT FUN/ SIT RIGHT DOWN AND WRITE MYSELF A LETTER	2.75	4.50	3.00
☐ 200		LET'S FALL IN LOVE/ I KNOW YOU KNOW IT	2.75	4.50	3.00
☐ 204		WHO'S BEEN SLEEPING IN MY BED/MY HEART	2.75	4.50	3.00
☐ 209		EVERYBODY STOPPED/ I ENVY YOU	2.75	4.50	3.00
☐ 610	**KAPP**	THIS IS MY PRAYER/ THAT OLD FEELING	2.75	4.50	3.00
☐ 641		IF I LOVE AGAIN/PATCH IT UP ...	2.75	4.50	3.00
☐ 677		I'LL SEE YOU IN MY DREAMS/ DON'T LOSE YOUR HEAD	2.75	4.50	3.00
☐ 713		YOU BABY/ I CAN'T GET THROUGH TO YOU	2.75	4.50	3.00
		LINDA SCOTT—ALBUMS			
☐ 1005 (M)	**CANADIAN- AMERICAN**	STARLIGHT, STARBRIGHT	9.00	25.00	22.50
☐ 1005 (S)		STARLIGHT, STARBRIGHT	14.00	34.00	30.00
☐ 1007 (M)		GREAT SCOTT- HER GREATEST HITS	9.00	25.00	22.50
☐ 1007 (S)		GREAT SCOTT- HER GREATEST HITS	14.00	34.00	30.00
☐ 1424 (M)	**KAPP**	HEY, LOOK AT ME NOW	8.00	21.00	18.00

RODNEY SCOTT

☐ 225	**CANNON**	GRANNY WENT ROCKIN'/ BITTER TEARS	80.00	180.00	120.00

WALTER SCOTT
SEE: THE GUISE AND BOB KUBAN AND THE IN-MEN

☐ 111	**MUSICLAND**	JUST YOU WAIT/SILLY GIRL	2.00	7.00	4.00
☐ WW259	**WHITE WHALE**	JUST YOU WAIT/ SILLY GIRL (REISSUE)	2.00	7.00	4.00
☐ V-131	**VANESSA**	THERE'LL ALWAYS BE A LOVE SONG/THE CHEATER	2.00	7.00	4.00
		WALTER SCOTT—ALBUMS			
☐ n/a	**MUSICLAND**	GREAT SCOTT	3.00	8.00	5.00
☐ WWS-7131(S)	**WHITE WHALE**	WALTER SCOTT	3.00	8.00	5.00

SEALS AND CROFTS
SEE: CHAMPS, JIMMY SEALS

☐ 208	**T. A.**	RIDIN' THUMB/(DJ)	3.75	6.00	4.50
☐ 210		ROBIN/GABRIEL GO ON HOME ...	3.75	6.00	4.50
☐ 7536	**WARNER BROTHERS**	WHEN I MEET THEM/IRISH LINEN	3.00	5.00	3.50
		SEALS AND CROFTS—ALBUM			
☐ 5004 (S)	**T. A.**	DOWN HOME	7.00	17.00	15.00

JIMMY SEALS (PRE-SEALS AND CROFTS)

☐ 9153	**CHALLENGE**	WISH FOR YOU, WANT FOR YOU, WAIT FOR YOU/ RUNAWAY HEART	5.00	9.00	6.00
☐ 9200		LADY HEARTBREAK/GROUNDED .	5.00	9.00	6.00

			Current Price Range		P/Y AVG
☐59270		EVERYBODY'S DOIN' THE JERK/ WA-HOO	5.00	9.00	6.00

SEARCHERS

☐55646	**LIBERTY**	SUGAR AND SPICE/ SAINTS AND SINNERS	4.50	7.50	6.00
☐55689		SUGAR AND SPICE/ SAINTS AND SINNERS	3.75	6.00	4.50
☐27	**KAPP**	LOVE POTION NUMBER NINE/ HI-HEEL SNEALERS	3.25	5.50	4.00
☐49		BUMBLE BEE/A TEAR FELL	3.25	5.50	4.00
☐577		NEEDLES AND PINS/ AIN'T THAT JUST LIKE ME	3.25	5.50	4.00
☐593		DON'T THROW YOUR LOVE AWAY/ I PRETEND I'M WITH YOU	3.25	5.50	4.00
☐609		SOME DAY WE'RE GONNA LOVE AGAIN/NO ONE ELSE COULD LOVE ME	3.25	5.50	4.00
☐618		WHEN YOU WALK IN THE ROOM/ I'LL BE MISSING YOU	3.25	5.50	4.00
☐644		WHAT HAVE THEY DONE TO THE RAIN?/THIS FEELING INSIDE	3.25	5.50	4.00
☐658		GOODBYE MY LOVER GOODBYE/ TILL I MEET YOU	3.00	5.00	3.65
☐686		HE'S GOT NO LOVE/SO FAR AWAY	3.00	5.00	3.65
☐706		YOU CAN'T LIE TO A LIAR/ DON'T KNOW WHY	3.00	5.00	3.65
☐729		TAKE ME FOR WHAT I'M WORTH/ TOO MANY MILES	3.00	5.00	3.65
☐783		HAVE YOU EVER LOVED SOMEBODY?/IT'S JUST THE WAY	3.00	5.00	3.65
☐811		LOVERS/ POPCORN DOUBLE FEATURE	3.00	5.00	3.65
☐72172	**MERCURY**	SWEETS FOR MY SWEET/ IT'S ALL BEEN A DREAM	3.00	5.00	3.65
☐72390		AIN'T THAT JUST LIKE ME/ I CAN TELL	3.00	5.00	3.65

SEARCHERS—ALBUMS

☐3363 (M)	**KAPP**	NEEDLES AND PINS	9.00	25.00	22.50
☐3412 (M)		THE NEW SEARCHERS' LP	9.00	25.00	22.50
☐1409 (M)		THIS IS US	8.00	21.00	18.00
☐1449 (M)		SEARCHERS NO. 4	8.00	21.00	18.00
☐1477 (M)		TAKE ME FOR WHAT I'M WORTH	8.00	21.00	18.00
☐20914 (M)	**MERCURY**	HEAR! HEAR!	8.00	21.00	18.00
☐60914 (S)		HEAR! HEAR!	9.00	25.00	22.50
☐20994 (M)		SEARCHERS MEET THE RATTLES	7.00	17.00	15.00
☐60994 (S)		SEARCHERS MEET THE RATTLES	8.00	21.00	18.00

NEIL SEDAKA
SEE: TOKENS

☐30520	**DECCA**	LAURA LEE/SNOWTIME	17.00	29.00	25.00
☐133	**LEGION**	RING-A-ROCKIN'/ FLY DON'T FLY ON ME	17.00	29.00	25.00
☐2004	**GUYDEN**	RING-A-ROCKIN'/ FLY DON'T FLY ON ME	12.00	21.00	18.00
☐7408	**RCA**	THE DIARY/NO VACANCY	3.50	6.00	4.35
☐7473		I GO APE/MOON OF GOLD	3.50	6.00	4.35
☐7530		YOU GOTTA LEARN YOUR RHYTHM AND BLUES/CRYING MY HEART OUT FOR YOU	4.00	7.00	4.85
☐7597		OH! CAROL/ONE WAY TICKET	3.25	5.50	4.00
☐7709		STAIRWAY TO HEAVEN/ FORTY WINKS AWAY	3.25	5.50	4.00

			Current Price Range		P/Y AVG
☐7781		YOU MEAN EVERYTHING TO ME/			
		RUN SAMPSON RUN	3.25	5.50	4.00
☐7829		CALENDAR GIRL/			
		THE SAME OLD FOOL	3.25	5.50	4.00
☐7874		LITTLE DEVIL/			
		I MUST BE DREAMING	3.25	5.50	4.00
☐7922		SWEET LITTLE YOU/			
		I FOUND MY WORLD IN YOU ...	3.50	6.00	4.35
☐7957		HAPPY BIRTHDAY, SWEET			
		SIXTEEN/DON'T LEAD ME ON .	3.25	5.50	4.00
☐8007		KING OF CLOWNS/			
		WALK WITH ME	3.25	5.50	4.00
☐8046		BREAKING UP IS HARD TO DO/			
		AS LONG AS I LIVE	3.25	5.50	4.00
☐8086		NEXT DOOR TO AN ANGEL/			
		I BELONG TO YOU	3.25	5.50	4.00
☐8137		ALICE IN WONDERLAND/			
		CIRCULATE	3.25	5.50	4.00
☐8169		LET'S GO STEADY AGAIN/			
		WAITING FOR NEVER	3.25	5.50	4.00
☐8209		THE DREAMER/			
		LOOK INSIDE YOUR HEART	3.00	5.00	3.65
☐8254		BAD GIRL/			
		WAIT 'TIL YOU SEE MY BABY ..	3.00	5.00	3.65
☐8341		THE CLOSEST THING TO HEAVEN/			
		WITHOUT A SONG	3.00	5.00	3.65
☐8382		SUNNY/SHE'LL NEVER BE YOU ..	3.00	5.00	3.65
☐8453		I HOPE HE BREAKS YOUR HEART/			
		TOO LATE	3.00	5.00	3.65
☐8511		LET THE PEOPLE TALK/			
		IN THE CHAPEL WITH YOU	3.00	5.00	3.65
☐8637		THE WORLD THROUGH A TEAR/			
		HIGH ON A MOUNTAIN	3.00	5.00	3.65
☐8737		THE ANSWER TO MY PRAYER/			
		BLUE BOY	3.00	5.00	3.65
☐8844		THE ANSWER LIES WITHIN/			
		GROWN UP GAMES	3.00	5.00	3.65
☐9004		WE CAN MAKE IT IF WE TRY/			
		TOO LATE	3.00	5.00	3.65
☐623	**PYRAMID**	OH DELILAH/NEIL'S TWIST	4.50	7.50	6.00
☐005	**SGC**	STAR CROSSED LOVERS/			
		WE HAD A GOOD THING GOIN' .	3.75	6.00	4.50
☐008		RAINY JANE/JEANNINE	3.75	6.00	4.50
☐14564	**MGM**	STANDING ON THE INSIDE/			
		LET DADDY KNOW	3.00	5.00	3.50
☐14661		ALONE IN NEW YORK IN THE RAIN/			
		SUSPICIONS	3.00	5.00	3.50
		NEIL SEDAKA—ALBUMS			
☐2035 (M)	**RCA**	NEIL SEDAKA			
		(ROCK WITH SEDAKA)	9.00	25.00	22.50
☐2035 (S)		NEIL SEDAKA			
		(ROCK WITH SEDAKA)	17.00	39.00	35.00
☐2317 (M)		CIRCULATE	7.00	25.00	22.50
☐2317 (S)		CIRCULATE	14.00	24.00	20.00
☐2421 (M)		LITTLE DEVIL................	9.00	25.00	22.50
☐2421 (S)		LITTLE DEVIL................	14.00	34.00	30.00
☐2627 (M)		NEIL SEDAKA SINGS HIS			
		GREATEST HITS	7.00	17.00	15.00
☐2627 (S)		NEIL SEDAKA SINGS HIS			
		GREATEST HITS	9.00	25.00	22.50

			Current Price Range		P/Y AVG

SEEDS

FEATURED: SKY SAXON
SEE: RITCHIE MARSH, SKY SAXON

			Current	Price Range	P/Y AVG
☐354	GNP-CRESCENDO	I CAN'T SEEM TO MAKE YOU MINE/I TELL MYSELF	3.75	6.00	4.50
☐354		I CAN'T SEEM TO MAKE YOU MINE/DAISY ME	3.25	5.50	4.00
☐372		PUSHIN' TOO HARD/ TRY TO UNDERSTAND	3.25	5.50	4.00
☐383		MR. FARMER/NO ESCAPE	3.25	5.50	4.00
☐394		A THOUSAND SHADOWS/MARCH OF THE FLOWER CHILDREN ...	3.25	5.50	4.00
☐398		THE WIND BLOWS YOUR HAIR/ SIX DREAMS	3.75	6.00	4.50
☐408		900 MILLION PEOPLE DAILY/ (MAKING LOVE) SATISFY YOU .	3.75	6.00	4.50

SEEDS—ALBUMS

☐2023 (M)	GNP-CRESCENDO	THE SEEDS	9.00	23.00	14.00
☐2033 (M)		A WEB OF SOUND	8.00	19.00	12.00
☐2038 (M)		FUTURE.....................	8.00	19.00	12.00
☐2040 (M)		A SPOONFUL OF SEEDY BLUES (Sky Saxon's Blues Band)	8.00	19.00	12.00
☐4043 (S)		MERLIN'S MUSIC BOX	8.00	19.00	12.00

BOB SEGER

☐1013	HIDEOUT	EAST SIDE STORY (vocal)/ EAST SIDE STORY (instrumental)	8.00	14.00	12.00
☐438	CAMEO	EAST SIDE STORY (vocal)/ EAST SIDE STORY (instrumental)	3.75	6.00	4.50
☐444		SOCK IT TO ME, SANTA/ FLORIDA TIME	3.75	6.00	4.50
☐465		CHAIN SMOKIN'/ PERSECUTION SMITH	3.75	6.00	4.50
☐473		VAGRANT WINTER/VERY FEW ...	3.75	6.00	4.50
☐494		HEAVY MUSIC (PT. 1)/(PT. 2) ...	3.75	6.00	4.50
☐1117	REPRISE	TURN ON YOUR LOVE LIGHT/ WHO DO YOU LOVE?	3.25	5.50	4.00
☐1143		ROSALIE/NEON SKY	3.25	5.50	4.00
☐1079	PALLADIUM	IF I WERE A CARPENTER/ JESSE JAMES	3.00	5.00	3.65
☐1143		ROSALIE/NEON SKY	3.00	5.00	3.65
☐1171		NEED YA/SEEN A LOT OF FLOORS	3.00	5.00	3.65
☐1205		GET OUT OF DENVER/ LONG SONG COMIN'	3.00	5.00	3.65
☐1316		THIS OLD HOUSE/UMC	3.00	5.00	3.65

BOB SEGER—ALBUMS

☐1106 (S)	PALLADIUM	SMOKIN' O.P.'S	7.00	17.00	15.00
☐2126 (S)		BACK IN '72.................	7.00	17.00	15.00

BOB SEGER SYSTEM

☐2143	CAPITOL	2 PLUS 2 EQUALS WHAT?/ DEATH ROW	3.25	5.50	4.00
☐2297		RAMBLIN' GAMBLIN' MAN/ TALES OF LUCY BLUE	3.00	5.00	3.50
☐2480		IVORY/THE LAST SONG	3.00	5.00	3.50
☐2576		NOAH/LENNIE JOHNSON	2.75	4.50	3.00
☐2640		LONELY MAN/INNERVENUS EYES	2.75	4.50	3.00
☐2748		LUCIFER/BIG RIVER	2.75	4.50	3.00
☐3187		LOOKIN' BACK/HIGHWAY CHILD .	2.75	4.50	3.00
☐4062		BEAUTIFUL LOSER/FINE MEMORY	2.75	4.50	3.00
☐4116		KATMANDU/BLACK NIGHT	2.75	4.50	3.00

LATER CAPITOL SINGLES ARE WORTH UP TO $2.75 MINT

			Current Price Range		P/Y AVG
		BOB SEGER SYSTEM—ALBUMS			
☐ 172 (S)	*CAPITOL*	RAMBLIN' GAMBLIN' MAN	6.00	18.00	13.50
☐ 236 (S)		NOAH	5.50	14.00	12.00
☐ 499 (S)		MONGREL	5.50	14.00	12.00
☐ 731 (S)		BRAND NEW DAY	5.50	14.00	12.00
		RONNIE SELF			
☐ 45-9714	*ABC-PARAMOUNT*	PRETTY BAD BLUES/THREE HEARTS LATER (promo)	25.00	50.00	40.00
☐ 40989	*COLUMBIA*	AIN'T I'M A DOG/ROCKY ROAD BLUES	9.50	17.00	15.00
☐ 41101		BOP-A-LENA/I AIN'T GOIN' NOWHERE	4.50	7.50	6.00
☐ 41166		BIG BLON' BABY/DATE BAIT	8.25	14.00	12.00
☐ 30958	*DECCA*	THIS MUST BE THE PLACE/BIG TOWN	3.50	6.00	4.35
☐ 31131		I'VE BEEN THERE/SO HIGH	3.50	6.00	4.35
☐ 31351		SOME THINGS YOU CAN'T CHANGE/INSTANT MAN	3.50	6.00	4.35
☐ 31431		OH ME, OH MY/PAST, PRESENT AND FUTURE	3.50	6.00	4.35
☐ 546	*KAPP*	BLESS MY BROKEN HEART/HOUDINE	3.00	5.00	3.50
		RONNIE SELF—EP			
☐ 2149	*COLUMBIA*	AIN'T I'M A DOG	32.00	60.00	36.00
		TOMMY SENA			
☐ 905	*VALMONT*	THE WOBBLE/ONIONS REMIND ME OF YOU	12.00	27.00	24.00
		SHADOWS OF KNIGHT			
☐ 6634	*ATCO*	GLORIA 69/SPANIARD AT MY DOOR	3.00	6.50	5.50
☐ 520	*TEAM*	SHAKE/FROM WAY OUT TO WAY IN	3.00	5.00	3.75
☐ 116	*DUNWICH*	GLORIA/SPANIARD AT MY DOOR	3.00	5.00	3.50
☐ 122		OH YEAH/LIGHT BULB BLUES	3.00	5.00	3.50
☐ 128		BAD LITTLE WOMAN/GOSPEL ZONE	3.00	5.00	3.50
☐ 141		I'M GONNA MAKE YOU MINE/I'LL MAKE YOU SORRY	3.00	5.00	3.50
☐ 151		THE BEHEMOTH/WILLIE JEAN	3.00	5.00	3.50
		SHADOWS OF KNIGHT—ALBUMS			
☐ 666 (M)	*DUNWICH*	GLORIA	7.00	12.00	10.00
☐ 666 (S)		GLORIA	9.00	17.00	15.00
☐ 667 (M)		BACK DOOR MEN	7.00	12.00	10.00
☐ 667 (S)		BACK DOOR MEN	9.00	17.00	15.00
		SHA NA NA			
☐ 507	*KAMA SUTRA*	PAY DAY	3.75	7.00	5.50
☐ 522		YAKETY-YAK/ONLY ONE SONG	3.50	6.50	5.00
☐ 528		I WONDER WHY/TOP 40	3.50	6.50	5.00
☐ 592		MAYBE I'M OLD FASHIONED/STROLL ALL NIGHT	3.50	6.50	5.00
☐ 602		JUST LIKE ROMEO & JULIET	3.50	6.50	5.00
☐ 909	*RSO*	ROCK 'N' ROLL IS HERE TO STAY/GREASED LIGHTNIN' (second side by John Travolta; both numbers from movie ''Grease'')	2.50	4.00	2.50
		SHANGRI-LAS			
☐ 1866	*SMASH*	SIMON SAYS/SIMON SPEAKS	4.50	7.50	6.00
☐ 4006	*SPOKANE*	WISHING WELL/HATE TO SAY I TOLD YOU SO	5.00	9.00	7.00
☐ 1291	*SCEPTER*	WISHING WELL/HATE TO SAY I TOLD YOU SO	3.75	6.00	4.50

			Current Price Range		P/Y AVG
☐ 10-008	**RED BIRD**	REMEMBER (WALKIN' IN THE SAND)/ IT'S EASIER TO CRY	3.25	5.50	4.00
☐ 10-014		LEADER OF THE PACK/ WHAT IS LOVE	3.25	5.50	4.00
☐ 10-018		GIVE HIM A GREAT BIG KISS/ TWIST AND SHOUT	3.25	5.50	4.00
☐ 10-019		MAYBE/SHOUT	3.25	5.50	4.00
☐ 10-025		OUT IN THE STREETS/THE BOY ..	3.25	5.50	4.00
☐ 10-030		GIVE US YOUR BLESSINGS/ ONLY HEAVEN KNOWS	3.25	5.50	4.00
☐ 10-036		RIGHT NOW AND NOT LATER/ TRAIN FROM KANSAS CITY ...	3.25	5.50	4.00
☐ 10-043		I CAN NEVER GO HOME ANYMORE/BULLDOG	3.25	5.50	4.00
☐ 10-048		LONG LIVE OUR LOVE/ SOPHISTICATED BOOM BOOM .	3.25	5.50	4.00
☐ 10-053		HE CRIED/DRESSED IN BLACK ..	3.25	5.50	4.00
☐ 10-068		PAST, PRESENT AND FUTURE/ PARADISE	3.25	5.50	4.00
☐ 72645	**MERCURY**	THE SWEET SOUND OF SUMMER/I'LL NEVER LEARN .	3.00	5.00	3.65
☐ 72670		TAKE THE TIME/FOOTSTEPS ON THE ROOF	3.00	5.00	3.65

SHANGRI-LAS—ALBUMS

☐ 101 (M)	**RED BIRD**	LEADER OF THE PACK	8.00	21.00	18.00
☐ 104 (M)		SHANGRI-LAS '65	12.00	29.00	25.00
☐ 104 (M)		I CAN NEVER GO HOME ANYMORE (reissue of above)	8.00	21.00	18.00
☐ 21099 (M)	**MERCURY**	GOLDEN HITS OF THE SHANGRI-LAS	7.00	17.00	15.00
☐ 61099 (S)		GOLDEN HITS OF THE SHANGRI-LAS	8.00	21.00	18.00

DEL SHANNON

☐ 3067	**BIG TOP**	RUNAWAY/JODY	3.25	5.50	4.00
☐ 3075		HATS OFF TO LARRY/ DON'T GILD THE LILY, LILY ...	3.25	5.50	4.00
☐ 3083		SO LONG BABY/THE ANSWER TO EVERYTHING	3.25	5.50	4.00
☐ 3091		HEY! LITTLE GIRL/I WON'T CARE ANYMORE	3.25	5.50	4.00
☐ 3098		GINNY IN THE MIRROR/I WON'T BE THERE	3.25	5.50	4.00
☐ 3112		CRY MYSELF TO SLEEP/ I'M GONNA MOVE ON	3.50	6.00	4.35
☐ 3117		THE SWISS MAID/YOU NEVER TALKED ABOUT ME	3.25	5.50	4.00
☐ 3131		LITTLE TOWN FLIRT/ THE WAMBOO	3.25	5.50	4.00
☐ 3143		TWO KINDS OF TEARDROPS/ KELLY	3.25	5.50	4.00
☐ 3152		FROM ME TO YOU/ TWO SILHOUETTES	6.00	11.00	7.00
☐ 501	**BERLEE**	SUE'S GOTTA BE MINE/ NOW SHE'S GONE	3.50	6.00	4.35
☐ 502		THAT'S THE WAY LOVE IS/ TIME OF THE DAY	3.50	6.00	4.35
☐ 897	**AMY**	STAINS ON MY LETTER/ MARY JANE	3.50	6.00	4.35
☐ 905		HANDY MAN/GIVE HER LOTS OF LOVIN'	3.25	5.50	4.00
☐ 911		DO YOU WANT TO DANCE/ THIS IS ALL I HAVE TO GIVE ...	3.25	5.50	4.00

			Current Price Range		P/Y AVG
☐915		KEEP SEARCHIN'/			
		BROKEN PROMISES	3.25	5.50	4.00
☐919		STRANGER IN TOWN/OVER YOU .	3.25	5.50	4.00
☐925		BREAK UP/WHY DON'T YOU TELL			
		HIM	3.50	6.00	4.35
☐937		SHE STILL REMEMBERS TONY/			
		MOVE IT OVER	3.50	6.00	4.35
☐55866	**LIBERTY**	THE BIG HURT/I GOT IT BAD	3.25	5.50	4.00
☐55889		FOR A LITTLE WHILE/			
		HEY LITTLE STAR	3.25	5.50	4.00
☐55894		SHOW ME/NEVER THOUGHT			
		I COULD	3.25	5.50	4.00
☐55904		UNDER MY THUMB/			
		SHE WAS MINE	3.25	5.50	4.00
☐55939		WHAT MAKES YOU RUN/SHE ...	3.25	5.50	4.00
☐55961		LED ALONG/I CAN'T BE TRUE ...	3.25	5.50	4.00
☐55993		YOU CHEATED/RUN AWAY	3.25	5.50	4.00
☐56018		THINKIN' OF YOU/			
		RUNNIN' ON BACK	3.25	5.50	4.00
☐56036		GEMINI/MAGICAL MUSICAL BOX	3.25	5.50	4.00
☐56070		RAINDROPS/YOU DON'T LOVE ME	3.25	5.50	4.00
☐4193	**DUNHILL**	COME BACK TO ME/			
		SWEET MARY LOU	3.00	5.00	3.65
☐4224		SISTER ISABELLE/			
		COLORADO RAIN	3.00	5.00	3.65
☐21	**ISLAND**	TELL HER NO/RESTLESS	3.00	5.00	3.65
☐38		CRY BABY CRY/			
		IN MY ARMS AGAIN	3.00	5.00	3.65
		DEL SHANNON—ALBUMS			
☐1303 (M)	**BIG TOP**	RUNAWAY	25.00	50.00	35.00
☐1308 (M)		LITTLE TOWN FLIRT	12.00	29.00	25.00
☐8003 (M)		HANDY MAN	9.00	25.00	22.50
☐8003 (S)		HANDY MAN	14.00	34.00	30.00
☐8004 (M)		DEL SHANNON SINGS HANK			
		WILLIAMS	7.00	17.00	15.00
☐8004 (S)		DEL SHANNON SINGS HANK			
		WILLIAMS	9.00	25.00	22.50
☐8006 (M)		1,661 SECONDS OF DEL SHANNON	7.00	17.00	15.00
☐8006 (S)		1,661 SECONDS OF DEL SHANNON	9.00	25.00	22.50
☐3435	**LIBERTY**	THIS IS MY BAG	6.00	15.00	13.50
☐7453 (S)		THIS IS MY BAG	8.00	21.00	18.00
☐3479 (M)		TOTAL COMMITMENT	6.00	15.00	13.50
☐7479 (S)		TOTAL COMMITMENT	8.00	21.00	18.00
☐8539 (S)		THE FURTHER ADVENTURES OF			
		CHARLES WESTOVER	5.50	14.00	12.00
☐3824	**DOT**	THE BEST OF DEL SHANNON	5.50	14.00	12.00
☐25824 (S)		THE BEST OF DEL SHANNON	5.50	14.00	12.00
☐151 (S)	**UNITED ARTISTS**	LIVE IN ENGLAND	4.50	11.50	9.50

JACKIE SHANNON (JACKIE DeSHANNON)

☐290	**SAGE**	JUST ANOTHER LIE/			
		CAJUN BLUES	5.50	11.00	9.00
☐15928	**DOT**	JUST ANOTHER LIE/			
		CAJUN BLUES	3.75	6.00	4.50
☐330	**SAND**	TROUBLE/LIES	5.50	11.00	9.00
☐15980	**DOT**	TROUBLE/LIES	3.75	11.00	4.50

THE SHARKS QUINTET

☐1129	**BROADCAST**	BLUEBERRY HILL/I LOVE YOU			
		FOR SENTIMENTAL REASONS .	25.00	55.00	36.00
☐1128	**BROADWAY**	I'LL BE HOME/SHIRLEY	25.00	55.00	36.00

			Current Price Range		P/Y AVG

SHARON MARIE

☐5064	CAPITOL	SUMMERTIME/ RUNAROUND LOVER	24.00	46.00	42.00
☐5195		THINKIN' ABOUT YOU BABY/ STORY OF MY LIFE	22.00	44.00	40.00

DEE DEE SHARP

☐212	CAMEO	MASHED POTATO TIME/ SET MY HEART AT EASE	3.25	5.50	4.00
☐219		GRAVY/BABY CAKES	3.25	5.50	4.00
☐230		RIDE!/THE NIGHT	3.25	5.50	4.00
☐244		DO THE BIRD/LOVER BOY	3.25	5.50	4.00
☐260		ROCK ME IN THE CRADLE OF LOVE/YOU'LL NEVER BE MINE	3.00	5.00	3.65
☐274		WILD!/WHY DONCHA ASK ME . . .	3.00	5.00	3.65
☐296		WHERE DID I GO WRONG?/ WILLYAM, WILLYAM	3.00	5.00	3.65
☐329	CAMEO	NEVER PICK A PRETTY BOY/ HE'S NO ORDINARY GUY	3.00	5.00	3.65
☐335		DEEP DARK SECRET/GOOD	3.00	5.00	3.65
☐347		TO KNOW HIM IS TO LOVE HIM/THERE AIN'T NOTHIN' I WOULDN'T DO FOR YOU	3.00	5.00	3.65
☐357		LET'S TWINE/THAT'S WHAT MY MAMA SAID	3.00	5.00	3.65
☐375		I REALLY LOVE YOU/STANDING IN THE NEED OF LOVE	3.00	5.00	3.65
☐382		IT'S A FUNNY SITUATION/ THERE AIN'T I NOTHIN' I WOULDN'T DO FOR YOU	3.00	5.00	3.65

DEE DEE SHARP—ALBUMS

☐1018 (M)	CAMEO	IT'S MASHED POTATO TIME	7.00	17.00	15.00
☐1022 (M)		SONGS OF FAITH	7.00	17.00	15.00
☐1027 (M)		ALL THE HITS	7.00	17.00	15.00
☐1032 (M)		ALL THE HITS BY DEE DEE SHARP	6.00	15.00	13.50
☐1032 (S)		ALL THE HITS BY DEE DEE SHARP	8.00	21.00	18.00
☐1050 (M)		DO THE BIRD	6.00	15.00	13.50
☐1050 (S)		DO THE BIRD	8.00	21.00	18.00
☐1062 (M)		BIGGEST HITS	5.50	14.00	12.00
☐1062 (S)		BIGGEST HITS	7.00	17.00	15.00
☐1074 (M)		DOWN MEMORY LANE	5.50	14.00	12.00
☐1074 (S)		DOWN MEMORY LANE	7.00	17.00	15.00
☐2002 (M)		18 GOLDEN HITS	5.00	12.00	10.00
☐2002 (S)		18 GOLDEN HITS	6.00	15.00	13.50

SHELLS

☐104	JOHNSON	BABY OH BABY/WHAT'S IN AN ANGEL'S EYES	5.00	9.00	7.00
☐104		BABY OH BABY/ANGEL EYES . . .	4.50	7.50	6.00
☐106		PLEADING NO MORE/CAN'T SAY GOODBYE	17.00	29.00	25.00
☐107		EXPLAIN IT TO ME/ AN ISLAND UNKNOWN	9.00	15.00	11.00
☐109		BETTER FORGET HIM/ CAN'T TAKE IT	9.00	15.00	11.00
☐110		IN THE DIM LIGHT OF THE DARK/ O-MI YUM-MI YUM-MI	9.00	15.00	11.00
☐112		SWEETEST ONE/BABY, WALK ON IN	9.50	17.50	15.00
☐119		DEEP IN MY HEART/(IT'S A) HAPPY HOLIDAY	6.00	12.00	8.00
☐120		A TOAST TO YOUR BIRTHDAY/ THE DRIVE	6.00	12.00	8.00
☐127		ON MY HONOR/MY ROYAL LOVE .	6.00	12.00	8.00

			Current Price Range		P/Y AVG
☐009		MY CHERIE/EXPLAIN IT TO ME ..	3.75	6.00	4.50
☐106	JUANITA	PLEADING NO MORE/			
		DON'T SAY GOODBYE	12.00	21.00	18.00
☐1022	END	SIPPIN' SODA/PRETTY LITTLE			
		GIRL	25.00	48.00	42.00
☐1050		WHISPERING WINGS/			
		SHOOMA DOM DOM	21.00	34.00	30.00
☐5103	GONE	SIPPIN' SODA/PRETTY LITTLE			
		GIRL	14.00	24.00	20.00
☐4156	ROULETTE	SHE WASN'T MEANT FOR ME/			
		THE THIEF	3.75	6.00	4.50
☐912	JOSIE	OUR WEDDING DAY/DEEP			
		IN MY HEART	5.50	11.00	9.00
		SHELLS—ALBUM			
☐1619 (M)	JOHNSON	THE GREATEST HITS OF			
		THE SHELLS	15.00	40.00	22.50

GARY SHELTON

☐143	MARK	STOP THE WORLD/GOODBYE			
		LITTLE DARLIN'	45.00	100.00	67.00

SHEP AND THE LIMELITES
SEE: HEARTBEATS

☐25039	APT	TOO YOUNG TO WED/TWO LOVING			
		HEARTS (Shane Sheppard)	5.50	11.00	9.00
☐25046		I'M SO LONELY (WHAT CAN I			
		DO?)/ONE WEEK FROM TODAY	8.25	14.00	12.00
☐740	HULL	DADDY'S HOME/THIS I KNOW ...	3.25	5.50	4.00
☐742		READY FOR YOUR LOVE/YOU'LL			
		BE SORRY	3.25	5.50	4.00
☐747		THREE STEPS FROM THE ALTAR/			
		OH, WHAT A FEELING	3.25	5.50	4.00
☐748		OUR ANNIVERSARY/WHO TOLD			
		THE SANDMAN	3.25	5.50	4.00
☐751		WHAT DID DADDY DO?/			
		TEACH ME HOW TO TWIST	3.50	6.00	4.35
☐753		EVERYTHING IS GOING TO BE			
		ALRIGHT/GEE, BABY, WHAT			
		ABOUT YOU?	3.50	6.00	4.35
☐756		REMEMBER BABY/THE MONKEY .	3.50	6.00	4.35
☐757		IT'S ALL OVER NOW/STICK BY ME	3.50	6.00	4.35
☐759		STEAL AWAY (WITH YOUR BABY)/			
		FOR YOU, MY LOVE	3.50	6.00	4.35
☐761		EASY TO REMEMBER/WHY, WHY			
		DON'T YOU BELIEVE ME?	3.50	6.00	4.35
☐767		I'M ALL ALONE/WHY DID YOU			
		FALL FOR ME?	3.50	6.00	4.35
☐770		YOU BETTER BELIEVE/			
		PARTY FOR TWO	3.50	6.00	4.35
☐772		I'M A HURTIN' INSIDE/IN CASE			
		I FORGET	3.50	6.00	4.35
		SHEP AND THE LIMELITES—ALBUM			
☐25350 (M)	ROULETTE	OUR ANNIVERSARY	14.00	34.00	30.00

BOBBY SHERIDAN (CHARLIE RICH)

☐354	SUN	RED MAN/SAD NEWS	4.00	7.00	5.50

MIKE SHERIDAN

☐902	LIVERPOOL SOUND	IN LOVE/PLEASE MR. POSTMAN .	28.00	56.00	50.00

TONY SHERIDAN AND THE BEAT BROTHERS (BEATLES)

☐31382	DECCA	MY BONNIE/THE SAINTS			
		(DJ copy) (pink)	450.00	800.00	550.00

			Current Price Range		P/Y AVG
☐31382		MY BONNIE/THE SAINTS (regular release) (black)	900.00	1700.00	1100.00

SHERRYS

☐2068	GUYDEN	POP POP POP-PIE/ YOUR HAND IN MINE	3.00	5.00	3.50
☐2077		SLOP TIME/LET'S STOMP AGAIN	3.00	5.00	3.50
☐2094		THAT BOY OF MINE/ MONK,MONK, MONKEY	3.00	5.00	3.50
		SHERRYS—ALBUM			
☐503 (M)	GUYDEN	AT THE HOP WITH SHERRYS	9.00	25.00	22.50

SHERWOODS

☐16540	DOT	COLD & FROSTY MORNING/ TRUE LOVE WAS BORN	8.50	19.00	16.00

SHIELDS

☐513	TENDER	YOU CHEATED/THAT'S THE WAY IT'S GONNA BE	9.50	17.50	15.00
☐518		NATURE BOY/I'M SORRY NOW . .	12.00	21.00	18.00
☐521		PLAY THE GAME FAIR/FARE THEE WELL, MY LOVE	12.00	21.00	18.00
☐15805	DOT	YOU CHEATED/THAT'S THE WAY IT'S GONNA BE	3.25	5.50	4.00
☐15856		NATURE BOY/I'M SORRY NOW . .	3.25	5.50	4.00
☐15940		PLAY THE GAME FAIR/FARE THEE WELL, MY LOVE	3.25	5.50	4.00
☐100	FALCON	THE GIRL AROUND THE CORNER/ YOU'LL BE COMING HOME SOON	12.00	21.00	18.00
☐1013	TRANSCONTI- NENTAL	THE GIRL AROUND THE CORNER/ YOU'LL BE COMING HOME SOON	8.25	14.00	12.00

BILLY SHIELDS (TONY ORLANDO)

☐304	HARBOUR	I WAS A BOY/MOMENTS FROM NOW, TOMORROW	6.00	11.00	9.00

SHIRELLES

☐6112	TIARA	I MET HIM ON A SUNDAY/I WANT YOU TO BE MY BOYFRIEND . . .	60.00	110.00	71.00
☐30588	DECCA	I MET HIM ON A SUNDAY/I WANT YOU TO BE MY BOYFRIEND . . .	5.00	9.00	6.00
☐30669		MY LOVE IS A CHARM/SLOP TIME.	6.00	12.00	8.00
☐30761		I GOT THE MESSAGE/STOP ME . .	6.00	12.00	8.00
☐1203	SCEPTER	DEDICATED TO THE ONE I LOVE/ LOOK-A-HERE BABY	3.50	6.00	4.00
☐1205		A TEARDROP AND A LOLLIPOP/ DOIN' THE RONDE	4.00	7.00	4.85
☐1207		PLEASE BE MY BOYFRIEND/ I SAW A TEAR	4.00	7.00	4.85
☐1208		TONIGHT'S THE NIGHT/ THE DANCE IS OVER	3.25	5.50	4.00
☐1211		WILL YOU LOVE ME TOMORROW/ BOYS	3.25	5.50	4.00
☐1217		MAMA SAID/BLUE HOLIDAY	3.25	5.50	4.00
☐1220		A THING OF THE PAST/WHAT A SWEET THING THAT WAS	3.25	5.50	4.00
☐1223		BIG JOHN/TWENTY-ONE	3.25	5.50	4.00
☐1227		BABY IT'S YOU/ THE THINGS I WANT TO HEAR .	3.25	5.50	4.00
☐1228		SOLDIER BOY/ LOVE IS A SWINGIN' THING . . .	3.25	5.50	4.00
☐1234		WELCOME HOME BABY/MAMA, HERE COMES THE BRIDE	3.00	5.00	3.65

			Current Price Range		P/Y AVG
☐ 1237		STOP THE MUSIC/IT'S LOVE THAT REALLY COUNTS ..	3.00	5.00	3.65
☐ 1243		EVERYBODY LOVES A LOVER/ I DON'T THINK SO	3.00	5.00	3.65
☐ 1248		FOOLISH LITTLE GIRL/ NOT FOR ALL THE MONEY	3.00	5.00	3.65
☐ 1255		DON'T SAY GOODNIGHT AND MEAN GOODBYE/I DIDN'T MEAN TO HURT YOU	3.00	5.00	3.65
☐ 1259		WHAT DOES A GIRL DO?/ DON'T LET IT HAPPEN TO US ..	3.00	5.00	3.65
☐ 1260		IT'S A MAD. MAD. MAD. MAD. MAD WORLD/31 FLAVORS	3.25	5.50	4.00
☐ 1264		TONIGHT YOU'RE GONNA FALL IN LOVE WITH ME/20TH CENTURY ROCK AND ROLL	3.00	5.00	3.65
☐ 1267		SHA-LA-LA/ HIS LIPS GET IN THE WAY	3.50	5.50	4.00
☐ 1278		THANK YOU BABY/DOOMSDAY ..	3.00	5.00	3.65
☐ 1284		MAYBE TONIGHT/LOST LOVE . . .	3.00	5.00	3.65
☐ 1292		ARE YOU STILL MY BABY/ I SAW A TEAR	3.00	5.00	3.65
☐ 12101		EVERYBODY'S GOIN' MAD/ MARCH (YOU'LL BE SORRY) . . .	3.00	5.00	3.65
☐ 12114		MY HEART BELONGS TO YOU/ LOVE THAT MAN	3.00	5.00	3.65
☐ 12123		(MAMA) MY SOLDIER BOY IS COMING HOME/SOLDIER BOY .	3.00	5.00	3.65
☐ 12132		I MET HIM ON A SUNDAY '66/ LOVE THAT MAN	3.00	5.00	3.65
☐ 12150		QUE SERA SERA/ TILL MY BABY COMES HOME ..	3.00	5.00	3.65
☐ 12162		SHADES OF BLUE/ LOOKING AROUND	3.00	5.00	3.65
☐ 12162		SHADES OF BLUE/WHEN THE BOYS TALK ABOUT THE GIRLS .	3.00	5.00	3.65
☐ 12162		SHADES OF BLUE/ AFTER MIDNIGHT	3.00	5.00	3.65
☐ 12178		TEASIN' ME/LOOK AWAY	3.00	5.00	3.65
☐ 12185		DON'T GO HOME (MY LITTLE DARLIN')/NOBODY'S BABY AFTER YOU	3.00	5.00	3.65
☐ 12192		TOO MUCH OF A GOOD THING/ BRIGHT SHINY COLORS	3.00	5.00	3.65
☐ 12198		LAST MINUTE MIRACLE/ NO DOUBT ABOUT IT	3.00	5.00	3.65
☐ 12209		WILD AND SWEET/WAIT TILL I HAVE THE SIGNAL	3.00	5.00	3.65
☐ 12217		HIPPIE WALK(PT. 1)/(PT. 2)	3.00	5.00	3.65
		SHIRELLES—ALBUMS			
☐ 501 (M)	SCEPTER	TONIGHT'S THE NIGHT	14.00	34.00	30.00
☐ 502 (M)		SHIRELLES SING TO TRUMPETS AND STRINGS	12.00	29.00	25.00
☐ 504 (M)		BABY IT'S YOU	9.00	21.00	18.00
☐ 505 (M)		SHIRELLES AND KING CURTIS GIVE A TWIST PARTY	8.00	21.00	18.00
☐ 507 (M)		GREATEST HITS.	8.00	21.00	18.00
☐ 511 (M)		FOOLISH LITTLE GIRL	8.00	21.00	18.00
☐ 514 (M)		THE SHIRELLES SING THEIR SONGS IN THE GREAT MOVIE "IT'S A MAD. MAD. MAD. MAD. MAD WORLD" AND OTHERS	7.00	25.00	22.50
☐ 516 (M)		THE SHIRELLES SING THE GOLDEN OLDIES	7.00	25.00	22.50

			Current Price Range		P/Y AVG
☐ 560 (M)		GREATEST HITS, VOL. II	6.00	15.00	13.50
☐ 560 (S)		GREATEST HITS, VOL. II	7.00	17.00	15.00
☐ 562 (S)		SPONTANEOUS COMBUSTION . . .	5.50	14.00	12.00
☐ 599 (S)		REMEMBER WHEN	5.50	14.00	12.00

SHIRLEY AND LEE

☐ 3152	*ALADDIN*	I'M GONE/SWEETHEARTS	34.00	49.00	45.00
☐ 3175		SHIRLEY COME BACK TO ME/			
		BABY	28.00	48.00	42.00
☐ 3192		SHIRLEY'S BACK/SO IN LOVE . . .	20.00	34.00	30.00
☐ 3205		THE PROPOSAL/			
		TWO HAPPY PEOPLE	20.00	34.00	30.00
☐ 3222		LEE GOOFED/WHY DID I?	14.00	24.00	20.00
☐ 3244		CONFESSING/KEEP ON	9.50	17.50	15.00
☐ 3258		COMIN' OVER/TAKES MONEY . . .	9.50	17.50	15.00
☐ 3289		FEEL SO GOOD/YOU'LL BE			
		THINKING OF ME	9.50	21.00	18.00
☐ 3302		I'LL DO IT/LEE'S DREAM	8.25	14.00	12.00
☐ 3313		THAT'S WHAT I'LL DO/			
		A LITTLE WORD	8.25	14.00	12.00
☐ 3325		LET THE GOOD TIMES ROLL/			
		DO YOU MEAN HURT ME?	5.00	9.00	7.00
☐ 3338		I FEEL GOOD/			
		NOW THAT IT'S OVER	4.75	8.00	6.00
☐ 3362		WHEN I SAW YOU/			
		THAT'S WHAT I WANNA DO . . .	4.75	8.00	6.00
☐ 3369		I WANT TO DANCE/MARRY ME . .	4.75	8.00	6.00
☐ 3380		ROCK ALL NITE/DON'T YOU			
		KNOW I LOVE YOU	4.75	8.00	6.00
☐ 3390		ROCKIN' WITH THE CLOCK/			
		THE FLIRT	4.75	8.00	6.00
☐ 3405		I'LL THRILL YOU/			
		LOVE NO ONE BUT YOU	4.75	8.00	6.00
☐ 3418		DON'T LEAVE ME HERE TO CRY/			
		EVERYONE'S ROCKIN'	4.75	8.00	6.00
☐ 3432		ALL I WANT TO DO IS CRY/COME			
		ON AND HAVE YOUR FUN	4.50	7.50	6.00
☐ 3455		WHEN DAY IS DONE/TRUE LOVE .	4.50	7.50	6.00

SHIRLEY AND LEE—ALBUMS

☐ 807 (M)	*ALADDIN*	LET THE GOOD TIMES ROLL	50.00	130.00	120.00
☐ 2028 (M)	*WARWICK*	LET THE GOOD TIMES ROLL	34.00	82.00	75.00
☐ 9179 (M)	*IMPERIAL*	LET THE GOOD TIMES ROLL	17.00	39.00	35.00
☐ 4023 (M)	*SCORE*	LET THE GOOD TIMES ROLL	12.00	29.00	25.00

PAUL SIMON

SEE: SIMON AND GARFUNKEL, TOM AND JERRY, PAUL KANE,
JERRY LANDIS, TRUE TAYLOR, TICO AND THE TRIUMPHS

☐ 10197	*COLUMBIA*	GONE AT LAST/TAKE ME TO THE			
		MARDI GRAS	2.75	4.75	3.50
☐ 10270		SOME FOLKS/50 WAYS TO LEAVE			
		YOUR LOVER	2.75	4.75	3.50
☐ 45638		DUNCAN/RUN THAT BODY DOWN	2.75	4.75	3.50
☐ 45859		KODACHROME/TENDERNESS . . .	2.25	4.00	2.50
☐ 45900		ONE MAN'S CEILING/			
		AMERICAN TUNE	2.50	4.50	3.00
☐ 45585		ME & JULIO DOWN BY THE			
		SCHOOLYARD/			
		CONGRATULATIONS	2.25	4.00	2.50
☐ 45547		MOTHER & CHILD REUNION/			
		PARANOIA BLUES	2.25	3.00	1.50
☐ 10332		STILL CRAZY AFTER ALL THESE			
		YEARS/I DO IT FOR YOUR LOVE	2.25	3.00	1.50
☐ 10630		SLIP SLIDIN' AWAY/SOMETHING			
		SO RIGHT	2.25	3.00	1.50

			Current Price Range		P/Y AVG
☐45907		LOVES ME LIKE A ROCK/LEARN HOW TO FALL	2.25	3.00	1.50
☐10711		HAVE A GOOD TIME/STRANDED IN A LIMOUSINE	2.25	3.00	1.50

SIMON AND GARFUNKEL

			Current Price Range		P/Y AVG
☐43396	COLUMBIA	SOUNDS OF SILENCE/WE'VE GOT A GROOVY THING GOIN'	3.00	5.00	3.65
☐43511		HOMEWARD BOUND/LEAVES THAT ARE GREEN	3.00	5.00	3.65
☐43617		I AM A ROCK/FLOWERS NEVER BEND WITH THE RAINFALL	3.00	5.00	3.65
☐43728		DANGLING CONVERSATION/BIG BRIGHT GREEN PLEASURE MACHINE	3.00	5.00	3.65
☐43873		A HAZY SHADE OF WINTER/FOR EMILY, WHEREVER I MAY FIND HER	3.00	5.00	3.65
☐44046		AT THE ZOO/59TH STREET BRIDGE SONG (FEELIN' GROOVY)	3.00	5.00	3.65
☐44232		FAKIN' IT/YOU DON'T KNOW WHERE YOUR INTEREST LIES	3.00	5.00	3.65
☐44465		SCARBOROUGH FAIR/ APRIL COME SHE WILL	3.00	5.00	3.65
☐44465		SCARBOROUGH FAIR/CANTICLE	3.00	5.00	3.65
☐44511		MRS. ROBINSON/OLD FRIENDS-BOOKENDS	3.00	5.00	3.65
☐44785		THE BOXER/BABY DRIVER	3.00	5.00	3.65
☐45079		BRIDGE OVER TROUBLED WATER/ KEEP THE CUSTOMER SATISFIED	3.00	5.00	3.65
☐45133		CECELIA/THE ONLY LIVING BOY IN NEW YORK CITY	3.00	5.00	3.65
☐45237		EL CONDOR PASA/WHY DON'T YOU WRITE ME?	2.75	4.50	3.00
☐45663		FOR EMILY, WHEREVER I MAY FIND HER/AMERICA	2.75	4.50	3.00
☐10230		MY LITTLE TOWN/RAG DOLL-YOU'RE KIND	2.50	4.50	2.50

SIMON AND GARFUNKEL—ALBUMS

			Current Price Range		P/Y AVG
☐3059 (S)	PICKWICK	HIT SOUNDS OF SIMON AND GARFUNKEL (pre-Columbia material)	17.00	39.00	35.00
☐2249 (M)	COLUMBIA	WEDNESDAY MORNING, 3 A.M.	6.00	15.00	13.50
☐9049 (S)		WEDNESDAY MORNING, 3 A.M.	8.00	21.00	18.00
☐2469 (M)		SOUNDS OF SILENCE	6.00	15.00	13.50
☐9269 (S)		SOUNDS OF SILENCE	7.00	17.00	15.00
☐2563 (M)		PARSLEY, SAGE, ROSEMARY & THYME	6.00	15.00	13.50
☐9363 (S)		PARSLEY, SAGE, ROSEMARY & THYME	7.00	17.00	15.00
☐9529 (S)		BOOKENDS	5.50	14.00	12.00
☐9914 (S)		BRIDGE OVER TROUBLED WATER	5.50	14.00	12.00
☐31350 (S)		GREATEST HITS	5.50	14.00	12.00

SIMON SISTERS
FEATURED: CARLY SIMON

			Current Price Range		P/Y AVG
☐586	KAPP	WINKIN' BLINKIN' AND NOD/ SO GLAD I'M HERE	3.00	5.00	3.50
☐624		CUDDLE BUG/NO ONE TO TALK MY TROUBLES TO	3.25	5.50	4.00

SIMON SISTERS—ALBUMS

			Current Price Range		P/Y AVG
☐1359 (M)	KAPP	SIMON SISTERS	9.00	25.00	22.50

			Current Price Range		P/Y AVG
☐21539 (S)	COLUMBIA	THE SIMON SISTERS SING FOR CHILDREN	7.00	17.00	15.00

SIR DOUGLAS QUINTET
SEE: DOUG SAHM

☐8308	TRIBE	SHE'S ABOUT A MOVER/WE'LL TAKE OUR LAST WALK TONIGHT	3.00	5.00	3.65
☐8310		THE TRACKER/BLUE NORTHER	3.00	5.00	3.65
☐8312		THE STORY OF JOHN HARDY/ IN TIME	3.00	5.00	3.65
☐8314		THE RAINS CAME/BACON FAT	3.00	5.00	3.65
☐8317		QUARTER TO THREE/SHE'S GOTTA BE BOSS	3.00	5.00	3.65
☐40676	PHILIPS RECORDS	WHAT ABOUT TOMORROW?/ A NICE SONG	3.00	5.00	3.65

SINGLES ON SMASH ARE WORTH UP TO $2.75 MINT
SIR DOUGLAS QUINTET—ALBUMS

☐37001 (M)	TRIBE	BEST OF THE SIR DOUGLAS QUINTET	8.00	21.00	18.00
☐47001 (S)		BEST OF THE SIR DOUGLAS QUINTET	9.00	25.00	22.50

SIXPENCE (STRAWBERRY ALARM CLOCK)

☐1025	IMPACT	YOU'RE THE LOVE/WHAT TO DO	7.00	13.00	11.00

SIX TEENS

☐311	FLIP	DON'T WORRY ABOUT A THING/ FOREVER MORE (Sweeteens)	17.00	29.00	25.00
☐315		A CASUAL LOOK/TEEN AGE PROMISE	4.00	7.00	4.85
☐317		AFAR INTO THE NIGHT/SEND ME FLOWERS	4.00	7.00	4.85
☐320		ONLY JIM/MY SPECIAL GUY	4.00	7.00	4.85
☐322		ARROW OF LOVE/WAS IT A DREAM OF MINE?	4.00	7.00	4.85
☐326		BABY YOU'RE DYNAMITE/ MY SURPRISE	4.00	7.00	4.85
☐329		MY SECRET/STOP PLAYING PING PONG (WITH MY HEART)	4.00	7.00	4.85
☐333		DANNY/LOVE'S FUNNY THAT WAY	4.00	7.00	4.85
☐338		OH, IT'S CRAZY/BABY-O	4.00	7.00	4.85
☐346		HEAVEN KNOWS I LOVE YOU/ WHY DO I GO TO SCHOOL?	4.00	7.00	4.85
☐350		SO HAPPY/THAT WONDERFUL SECRET OF LOVE	4.00	7.00	4.85
☐351		A LITTLE PRAYER/SUDDENLY IN JAIL	4.00	7.00	4.85

SKARLETTONES

☐1053	EMBER	WILL YOU DREAM/ DO YOU REMEMBER	12.00	32.00	28.00

SKIP AND FLIP
FEATURED: GARY "FLIP" PAXTON
SEE: GARY AND CLYDE, PLEDGES, ROBBINS AND PAXTON

☐7002	BRENT	IT WAS I/LUNCH HOUR	3.25	5.50	4.00
☐7005		FANCY NANCY/IT COULD BE	3.25	5.50	4.00
☐7010		CHERRY PIE/CRYIN' OVER YOU	3.25	5.50	4.00
☐7013		TEENAGE HONEYMOON/HULLY GULLY CHA CHA CHA	3.25	5.50	4.00
☐7017		WILLOW TREE/GREEN DOOR	3.25	5.50	4.00
☐1031	TIME	BETTY JEAN/DOUBT	5.00	10.00	6.00

			Current Price Range		P/Y AVG
☐ 2325	**CALIFORNIA**	TOSSIN' AND TURNIN'/ EVERYDAY I HAVE TO CRY	3.50	6.00	4.35

SKYLINERS
FEATURED: JIMMIE BEAUMONT

☐ 103	**CALICO**	SINCE I DON'T HAVE YOU/ ONE NIGHT, ONE NIGHT	3.50	6.00	4.35
☐ 106		THIS I SWEAR/TOMORROW	3.50	6.00	4.35
☐ 109		IT HAPPENED TODAY/ LONELY WAY	3.50	6.00	4.35
☐ 114		HOW MUCH/LORRAINE FROM SPAIN	3.50	6.00	4.35
☐ 117		PENNIES FROM HEAVEN/I'LL BE SEEING YOU	3.50	6.00	4.35
☐ 120		BELIEVE ME/HAPPY TIME	3.50	6.00	4.35
☐ 188	**COLPIX**	I'LL CLOSE MY EYES/ THE DOOR IS STILL OPEN	3.25	5.50	4.00
☐ 613		CLOSE YOUR EYES/OUR LOVE WILL LAST	3.25	5.50	4.00
☐ 215	**CAMEO**	EVERYONE BUT YOU/THREE COINS IN THE FOUNTAIN	3.25	5.50	4.00
☐ 104	**VISCOUNT**	TELL ME/COMES LOVE	3.25	5.50	4.00
☐ 6270	**ATCO**	SINCE I FELL FOR YOU/I'D DIE ..	3.25	5.50	4.00
☐ 1046	**MOTOWN**	SINCE I FELL FOR YOU/I'D DIE ..	3.25	5.50	4.00
☐ 5506	**JUBILEE**	THE LOSER/EVERYTHING IS FINE	3.25	5.50	4.00
☐ 5512		WHO DO YOU LOVE?/GET YOURSELF A BABY	3.25	5.50	4.00
☐ 5520		I RUN TO YOU/DON'T HURT ME. BABY	3.25	5.50	4.00
☐ 6520	**DRIVE**	THE DAY THE CLOWN CRIED/ OUR DAY IS HERE	3.25	5.50	4.00
☐ 496	**DOC**	I CAN'T SLEEP/WHY SHOULD YOU TAUNT ME?	3.25	5.50	4.00

SKYLINERS—ALBUMS

☐ 3000 (M)	**CALICO**	SKYLINERS	19.50	50.00	45.00
☐ 5010 (M)	**ORIGINAL SOUND**	SINCE I DON'T HAVE YOU	8.00	21.00	18.00

SLADES

☐ 500	**DOMINO**	YOU CHEATED/THE WADDLE	4.00	8.00	5.50
☐ 800		YOU GAMBLED/NO TIME	4.00	8.00	5.50
☐ 901		JUST YOU/IT'S BETTER TO LOVE	4.00	8.00	5.50
☐ 1000		SUMMERTIME/YOU MUST TRY ..	4.00	8.00	5.50

SMALL FACES
FEATURED: STEVE MARRIOTT

☐ 8949	**RCA**	ALL OR NOTHING/ UNDERSTANDING	5.50	11.00	9.00
☐ 9055		MY MIND'S EYE/I CAN'T DANCE WITH YOU	5.50	11.00	9.00
☐ 9794	**PRESS**	WHATCHA' GONNA DO ABOUT IT?/WHAT'S A MATTER. BABY?	5.00	9.00	6.00
☐ 9826		SHA-LA-LA-LA-LEE/GROW YOUR OWN	5.00	9.00	6.00
☐ 5007		ALMOST GROWN/HEY GIRL	5.00	9.00	6.00
☐ 501	**IMMEDIATE**	ITCHYKOO PARK/I'M ONLY DREAMING	3.25	5.50	4.00
☐ 5003		TIN SOLDIER/I FEEL MUCH BETTER	3.25	5.50	4.00
☐ 5007		ROLLIN' OVER/LAZY SUNDAY ...	3.25	5.50	4.00
☐ 5009		UNIVERSAL/DONKEY RIDES	3.25	5.50	4.00
☐ 5012		MAD JOHN/THE JOURNEY	3.25	5.50	4.00

		Current Price Range		P/Y AVG

| ☐5014 | | AFTERGLOW OF YOUR LOVE/ WHAM BAM, THANK YOU MA'AM | 3.25 | 5.50 | 4.00 |

SMALL FACES—ALBUMS

☐52001 (M)	*IMMEDIATE*	THERE ARE BUT FOUR SMALL FACES	7.00	17.00	15.00
☐52002 (S)		THERE ARE BUT FOUR SMALL FACES	8.00	21.00	18.00
☐52008 (S)		OGDEN'S NUT GONE FLAKE TOBACCO	7.00	17.00	15.00

SMILE (PRE-QUEEN)

| ☐72977 | *MERCURY* | EARTH/STEP ON ME | 17.00 | 29.00 | 25.00 |

HUEY "PIANO" SMITH AND THE CLOWNS

☐521	*ACE*	LITTLE LIZA JANE/ EVERYBODY'S WAILIN'	4.50	7.50	6.00
☐530		ROCKIN' PNEUMONIA AND THE BOOGIE WOOGIE FLU (PT. 1)/(PT. 2)	3.75	6.00	4.50
☐538		JUST A LONELY CLOWN/ FREE, SINGLE AND DISENGAGED	3.75	6.00	4.50
☐545		DON'T YOU JUST KNOW IT/ HIGH BLOOD PRESSURE	3.25	5.50	4.00
☐548		HAVIN' A GOOD TIME/ WE LIKE BIRDLAND	3.75	6.00	4.50
☐533		DON'T YOU KNOW YOCKOMO/ WELL, I'LL BE JOHN BROWN	3.25	5.50	4.00
☐562		WOULD YOU BELIEVE IT (I HAVE A COLD)/GENEVIEVE	3.25	5.50	4.00
☐571		TU-BER-CU-LUCAS AND THE SINUS BLUES/ DEAREST DARLING	3.25	5.50	4.00
☐584		BEATNIK BLUES/ FOR CRYIN' OUT LOUD	3.25	5.50	4.00
☐638		SHE GOT LOW DOWN/ MEAN, MEAN MAN	3.25	5.50	4.00
☐639		LITTLE LIZA JANE/ROCKIN' PNEUMONIA AND THE BOOGIE WOOGIE FLU	3.00	5.00	3.50
☐649		POP-EYE/SCALDED DOG	3.00	5.00	3.50
☐672		SOMEBODY TOLD IT/ EVERY ONCE IN A WHILE	3.00	5.00	3.50
☐8002		TALK TO ME BABY/IF IT AIN'T ONE THING IT'S ANOTHER	3.00	5.00	3.50
☐8008		LET'S BRING 'EM BACK AGAIN/ QUIET AS IT'S KEPT	3.00	5.00	3.50

HUEY "PIANO" SMITH AND THE CLOWNS—EP

| ☐104 | *ACE* | HAVING FUN WITH HUEY "PIANO" SMITH | 9.50 | 17.00 | 15.00 |

HUEY "PIANO" SMITH AND THE CLOWNS—ALBUMS

☐1004 (M)	*ACE*	HAVING A GOOD TIME	24.00	56.00	50.00
☐1015 (M)		FOR DANCING	24.00	56.00	50.00
☐1027 (M)		'TWAS THE NIGHT BEFORE CHRISTMAS	19.00	50.00	45.00
☐2021 (M)		ROCK 'N ROLL REVIVAL	10.00	25.00	22.50
☐418 (M)	*GRAND PRIX*	HUEY "PIANO" SMITH	8.00	21.00	18.00

PATTI SMITH

| ☐601 | *MER* | HEY JOE/PISS FACTORY | 17.00 | 42.00 | 38.00 |

A RARE INSTANCE OF A RECORDING ISSUED AS A LIMITED EDITION. ONLY 1,600 COPIES WERE PRESSED. LATER, A REGULAR NON-LIMITED VERSION OF THIS DISC WAS ISSUED BY SIRE. IT HAS CONSIDERABLY LESS VALUE

			Current Price Range		P/Y AVG

RAY SMITH

			Current Price Range		P/Y AVG
☐298	SUN	RIGHT BEHIND YOU BABY/ SO YOUNG	5.00	9.00	7.00
☐308		WHY, WHY, WHY/ YOU MADE A HIT	4.50	7.50	6.00
☐319		ROCKIN' BANDIT/SAIL AWAY	4.50	7.50	6.00
☐372		TRAVELIN' SALESMAN/I WON'T MISS YOU (TILL YOU'RE GONE)	3.25	5.50	4.00
☐375		CANDY DOLL/HEY, BOSS MAN	3.75	5.50	4.00
☐610		SHAKE AROUND/ WILLING AND READY	3.00	5.00	3.50
☐579	VEE JAY	ROBBIN' THE CRADLE/ ROCKIN' ROBIN	3.75	6.00	4.50
☐1016	JUDD	ROCKIN' LITTLE ANGEL/ THAT'S ALL RIGHT	3.50	6.00	4.65
☐1017		PUT YOUR ARMS AROUND ME HONEY/MARIA ELENA	3.50	6.00	4.65
☐1019		ONE WONDERFUL LOVE/ MAKES ME FEEL GOOD	3.50	6.00	4.65
☐1021		BLONDE HAIR, BLUE EYES/ YOU DON'T WANT ME	3.50	6.00	4.65
☐6901	CELEBRITY CIRCLE	I WALK THE LINE/ FOOL NUMBER ONE	3.00	5.00	3.50
☐351	BC	I GUESS I BETTER MOVE ALONG/ FOUR SEASONS OF MY LIFE	3.00	5.00	3.50
☐4100		WALK ON BY/DID HE HURT YOU ALL THAT BAD?	3.00	5.00	3.50
☐7130		LET THE FOUR WINDS BLOW/ I'M IN LOVE AGAIN	3.00	5.00	3.50
☐5371	WARNER BROTHERS	TURN OVER A NEW LEAF/ I'M SNOWED	3.00	5.00	3.50
☐1787	SMASH	ROOM 503/THOSE FOUR PRECIOUS YEARS	3.00	5.00	3.50
☐1055	ZIRKON	TURN ON THE MOONLIGHT/AFTER THIS NIGHT IS THROUGH	3.00	5.00	3.50
☐003	INFINITY	TURN ON THE MOONLIGHT/AFTER THIS NIGHT IS THROUGH	3.00	5.00	3.50
☐007		LET YOURSELF GO/ JOHNNY THE HUMMER	3.00	5.00	3.50
☐9020	TOLLIE	DID WE HAVE A PARTY/HERE COMES MY BABY BACK AGAIN	3.50	6.00	4.35
☐193	DIAMOND	EVERYBODY'S GOIN' SOMEWHERE/AU GO GO GO	3.00	5.00	3.50

RAY SMITH—ALBUMS

			Current Price Range		P/Y AVG
☐701 (M)	JUDD	TRAVELIN' WITH RAY	40.00	98.00	90.00
☐1737 (M)	COLUMBIA	RAY SMITH'S GREATEST HITS	7.00	17.00	15.00
☐8737 (S)		RAY SMITH'S GREATEST HITS	8.00	21.00	18.00

WARREN SMITH

			Current Price Range		P/Y AVG
☐239	SUN	ROCK 'N ROLL RUBY/I'D RATHER BE SAFE THAN SORRY	14.00	25.00	16.50
☐250		UBANGI STOMP/BLACK JACK DAVID	9.00	18.00	13.00
☐268		SO LONG I'M GONE/ MISS FROGGIE	8.00	15.00	10.00
☐286		I'VE GOT LOVE IF YOU WANT IT/ I FEEL IN LOVE	6.50	12.00	8.00
☐314		SWEET, SWEET GIRL/GOODBYE MR. LOVE	5.00	9.00	6.25
☐55248	LIBERTY	CAVE IN/I DON'T BELIEVE I'LL FALL IN LOVE TODAY	3.50	6.00	4.35
☐55302		A WHOLE LOT OF NOTHIN'/ODDS AND ENDS (BITS AND PIECES)	3.50	6.00	4.35

			Current Price Range		P/Y AVG
☐ 55336		OLD LONESOME FEELING/ CALL OF THE WILD	3.50	6.00	4.35
☐ 55361		WHY BABY WHY/WHY I´M WALKING (with Shirley Collie) . .	3.50	6.00	4.35
☐ 55409		BAD NEWS GETS AROUND/FIVE MINUTES OF THE LATEST BLUES	3.25	5.50	4.00
☐ 55575		BOOK OF BROKEN HEARTS/ 160 POUNDS OF HURT	3.25	5.50	4.00
		WARREN SMITH—ALBUMS			
☐ 3199 (M)	**LIBERTY**	THE FIRST COUNTRY COLLECTION OF WARREN SMITH	5.50	14.00	12.00
☐ 7199 (S)		THE FIRST COUNTRY COLLECTION OF WARREN SMITH	7.00	17.00	15.00

RONNY SOMMERS (SONNY BONO)
SEE: SONNY AND CHER, CAESAR AND CLEO

☐ 1001	**SWAMI**	DON´T SHAKE MY TREE/ (MAMA) COME GET YOUR BABY BOY	4.50	7.50	6.00

SOLITAIRES

☐ 1000	**OLD TOWN**	WONDER WHY/BLUE VALENTINE	23.00	38.00	28.00
☐ 1000		WONDER WHY/BLUE VALENTINE (red wax)	52.00	98.00	90.00
☐ 1006		PLEASE REMEMBER MY HEART/ SOUTH OF THE BORDER	26.00	46.00	42.00
☐ 1008		CHANCES I´VE TAKEN/LONELY . .	46.00	80.00	72.00
☐ 1010		GIRL OF MINE/I DON´T STAND A GHOST OF A CHANCE	29.00	47.00	42.00
☐ 1012		WHAT DID SHE SAY?/MY DEAR . .	17.00	29.00	25.00
☐ 1014		THE WEDDING/DON´T FALL IN LOVE	9.50	17.00	15.00
☐ 1015		MAGIC ROSE/LATER FOR YOU BABY	21.00	35.00	30.00
☐ 1019		FINE LITTLE GIRL/THE HONEYMOON	21.00	35.00	30.00
☐ 1026		YOU´VE SINNED/YOU´RE BACK WITH ME	15.00	25.00	19.00
☐ 1032		GIVE ME ONE MORE CHANCE/ NOTHING LIKE A LITTLE LOVE .	15.00	25.00	19.00
☐ 1034		WALKING ALONG/PLEASE KISS THIS LETTER	20.00	34.00	30.00
☐ 1044		I REALLY LOVE YOU SO/ THRILL OF LOVE	15.00	25.00	19.00
☐ 1049		WALKIN´ AND TALKIN´/NO MORE SORROWS	15.00	25.00	19.00
☐ 1059		PLEASE REMEMBER MY HEART/ BIG MARY´S HOUSE	15.00	25.00	19.00
☐ 1066		EMBRACEABLE YOU/ROUND GOES MY HEART	15.00	25.00	19.00
☐ 1071		LIGHT A CANDLE IN THE CHAPEL/HELPLESS	15.00	25.00	19.00
☐ 1096	**OLD TOWN**	LONESOME LOVER/PRETTY THING	15.00	25.00	19.00
☐ 1139		HONEY BABE/THE TIME IS HERE .	12.00	21.00	18.00
☐ 5316	**ARGO**	WALKING ALONG/PLEASE KISS THIS LETTER	9.50	17.00	15.00
☐ 13221	**MGM**	FOOL THAT I AM/FAIR WEATHER LOVER	4.50	7.50	6.00
☐ 4549	**ROULETTE**	THROUGH A LONG AND SLEEPLESS NIGHT/ WHAT WOULD YOU SAY?	4.50	7.50	6.00

			Current Price Range		P/Y AVG

SONNY

SEE: DON CHRISTY, RON SOMMERS, SONNY AND CHER

☐6369	**ATCO**	LAUGH AT ME/GIP TONY	3.00	5.00	3.65
☐6386		THE REVOLUTION KIND/GEORGIA AND JOHN QUETZAL	3.00	5.00	3.65
☐6505		I TOLD MY GIRL TO GO AWAY/ MISTY ROSES	3.00	5.00	3.65
☐6531		MY BEST FRIEND'S GIRL IS OUT OF SIGHT/ PAMMIE'S ON A BUMMER	3.00	5.00	3.65

SONNY AND CHER

SEE: CAESAR AND CLEO, CHER, CHERILYN, DON CHRISTY, BONNIE JO MASON, RONNY SOMMERS, SONNY

☐6345	**ATCO**	JUST YOU/SING C'EST LA VIE . . .	3.00	5.00	3.65
☐6359		I GOT YOU BABE/IT'S GONNA RAIN	3.00	5.00	3.65
☐6381		BUT YOU'RE MINE/HELLO	3.00	5.00	3.65
☐6395		WHAT NOW MY LOVE/I LOOK FOR YOU	3.00	5.00	3.65
☐6420		HAVE I STAYED TOO LONG/ LEAVE ME BE	3.00	5.00	3.65
☐6440		LITTLE MAN/MONDAY	3.00	5.00	3.65
☐6461		THE BEAT GOES ON/LOVE DON'T COME	3.00	5.00	3.65
☐6480		A BEAUTIFUL STORY/PODUNK . .	3.00	5.00	3.65
☐6486		PLASTIC MAN/IT'S THE LITTLE THINGS	3.00	5.00	3.65
☐6507		IT'S THE LITTLE THINGS/ DON'T TALK TO STRANGERS . .	3.00	5.00	3.65
☐6541		GOOD COMBINATION/YOU AND ME	3.00	5.00	3.65
☐6555		I WOULD MARRY YOU TODAY/ CIRCUS	3.00	5.00	3.65
☐6605		YOU GOTTA HAVE A THING OF YOUR OWN/ I GOT YOU BABE . .	3.00	5.00	3.65
☐6683		YOU'RE A FRIEND OF MINE/I WOULD MARRY YOU TODAY . . .	3.00	5.00	3.65
☐6758		GET IT TOGETHER/HOLD ME TIGHTER	3.00	5.00	3.65

SONNY AND CHER—ALBUMS

☐6177 (M)	**REPRISE**	BABY DON'T GO	7.00	17.00	15.00
☐6177 (S)		BABY DON'T GO	8.00	21.00	18.00
☐177 (S)	**ATCO**	LOOK AT US	6.00	15.00	13.50
☐183 (S)		THE WONDROUS WORLD OF SONNY AND CHER	6.00	15.00	13.50
☐203 (S)		IN CASE YOU'RE IN LOVE	6.00	15.00	13.50
☐214 (S)		GOOD TIMES (soundtrack)	6.00	15.00	13.50
☐219 (S)		THE BEST OF SONNY AND CHER .	6.00	15.00	13.50

DAVID SOUL

☐13510	**MGM**	I WILL WARM YOUR HEART/COVERED MAN	3.25	5.50	4.00
☐13589		WAS I EVER SO YOUNG/BEFORE .	3.25	5.50	4.00
☐13842		NO ONE'S GONNA CRY/QUIET KIND OF HATE	3.25	5.50	4.00
☐45129	**PRIVATE STOCK**	DON'T GIVE UP ON US/ BLACK BEAN SOUP	2.50	4.50	3.00
☐45150		GOING IN WITH MY EYES OPEN/TOPANGA	2.75	4.50	3.00
☐45163		SILVER LADY/HERE COMES THE RAIN	2.75	4.50	3.00

			Current Price Range		P/Y AVG

JIMMY SOUL

☐3300	**S.P.Q.R.**	TWISTIN' MATILDA/			
		I CAN'T HOLD OUT ANY LONGER	3.00	5.00	3.50
☐3302		WHEN MATILDA COMES BACK/			
		SOME KINDA NUT	3.00	5.00	3.50
☐3305		IF YOU WANNA BE HAPPY/DON'T			
		RELEASE ME	2.75	4.50	3.00
☐3310		TREAT 'EM TOUGH/			
		CHURCH STREET IN THE			
		SUMMERTIME	2.75	4.50	3.00
☐3312		EVERYBODY'S GONE APE/			
		GO 'WAY, CHRISTINA	2.75	4.50	3.00
		JIMMY SOUL—ALBUM			
☐16001 (M)	**S.P.Q.R.**	IF YOU WANNA BE HAPPY	9.00	25.00	22.50

SPANIELS

☐CBR101	**CANTERBURY**	SHE SANG TO ME; DANNY BOY/			
		PEACE OF MIND	70.00	150.00	115.00
☐101	**VEE JAY**	BABY IT'S YOU/BOUNCE	215.00	365.00	350.00
☐103		THE BELLS RING OUT/			
		HOUSECLEANING	46.00	78.00	72.00
☐103		THE BELLS RING OUT/			
		HOUSECLEANING (red wax) ...	100.00	190.00	180.00
☐107		GOODNIGHT SWEETHEART			
		GOODNIGHT/YOU DON'T			
		MOVE ME	14.00	24.00	20.00
☐107		GOODNIGHT SWEETHEART			
		GOODNIGHT/YOU DON'T MOVE			
		ME (red wax)	52.00	94.00	88.00
☐116		LET'S MAKE UP/PLAY IT COOL ..	17.00	29.00	25.00
☐131		DO-WAH/DON' CHA GO	17.00	29.00	25.00
☐154		PAINTED PICTURE/HEY SISTER			
		LIZZIE	12.00	21.00	18.00
☐178		FALSE LOVE/DO YOU REALLY ...	12.00	21.00	18.00
☐189		DEAR HEART/WHY WON'T YOU			
		DANCE?	17.00	29.00	25.00
☐202		SINCE I FELL FOR YOU/BABY,			
		COME ALONG WITH ME	17.00	29.00	25.00
☐229		YOU GIVE ME PEACE OF MIND/			
		PLEASE DON'T TEASE	8.25	14.00	12.00
☐246		EVERYONE'S LAUGHING/I.O.U. ..	7.00	13.00	11.00
☐257		I NEED YOUR KISSES/YOU'RE			
		GONNA CRY	8.25	14.00	12.00
☐264		I LOST YOU/CRAZEE BABY	8.25	14.00	12.00
☐278		TINA/GREAT GOOGLEY MOO	17.00	29.00	25.00
☐290		STORMY WEATHER/HERE IS WHY			
		I LOVE YOU	8.25	14.00	12.00
☐301		BABY, IT'S YOU/HEART AND			
		SOUL	8.25	14.00	12.00
☐310		TREES/I LIKE IT LIKE THAT	7.50	13.50	10.00
☐328		100 YEARS FROM TODAY/			
		THESE THREE WORDS	7.50	15.00	10.00
☐342		PEOPLE WILL SAY WE'RE IN			
		LOVE/THE BELLS RING OUT ...	7.50	13.50	10.00
☐350		I KNOW/BUS FARE HOME	7.50	13.50	10.00
☐1411	**CHANCE**	BABY, IT'S YOU/BOUNCE			
		(red wax)	78.00	130.00	120.00
☐124	**NEPTUNE**	FOR SENTIMENTAL REASONS/			
		MEEK MAN	8.25	14.00	12.00
☐711	**DOUBLE-L**	I KNOW, I KNOW/JEALOUS HEART	7.50	13.50	10.00
☐720		FOR SENTIMENTAL REASONS/			
		MIRACLES	7.50	13.50	10.00
☐001	**NORTH AMERICAN**	FAIRY TALES/JEALOUS HEART ..	5.00	8.00	6.00

			Current Price Range		P/Y AVG
☐002		LONELY MAN/STAND IN LINE ...	5.00	8.00	6.00
☐3114		COME BACK TO THESE ARMS/ MONEY BLUES	5.00	8.00	6.00
☐172	*CALLA*	FAIRY TALES/JEALOUS HEART ..	4.50	7.50	6.00
		SPANIELS—ALBUMS			
☐1002 (M)	*VEE JAY*	GOODNIGHT, IT'S TIME TO GO ...	40.00	98.00	90.00
☐1024 (M)		THE SPANIELS	24.00	55.00	50.00
☐137 (M)	*LOST NITE*	THE SPANIELS	7.00	17.00	15.00

SPARROW (STEPPENWOLF)

☐72203	*CAPITOL OF COLUMBIA*	IF YOU DON'T WANT MY LOVE IT'S BEEN ONE OF THOSE DAYS TODAY	8.25	14.00	12.00
☐72210		I'LL BE THE BOY/DREAM ON DREAMER	8.25	14.00	12.00
☐72229		OUR LOVE HAS PASSED/ SPARROWS AND DAISIES	7.00	13.00	11.00
☐72257		HARD TIMES WITH THE LAW/ MEET ME AFTER FOUR	8.25	14.00	12.00
☐43755	*COLUMBIA*	TOMORROW'S SHIP/ ISN'T IT STRANGE?	5.00	9.00	7.00
☐43960		GREEN BOTTLE LOVER/DOWN GOES YOUR LOVE LIFE	5.00	9.00	7.00

THE SPARROWS QUARTET

☐3001	*DELTONE*	I LOVE YOU SO MUCH I COULD DIE/PLEASE COME BACK TO ME	11.00	21.00	14.00
☐J-3020	*JET REC. CO.*	THE CHRISTMAS SONG/ HE IS MY FRIEND	10.00	19.00	13.00

RONNIE SPECTOR
SEE: RONETTES, VERONICA

☐1832	*APPLE*	TRY SOME, BUY SOME/ TANDOORI CHICKEN	3.25	5.50	4.00
☐0409	*WARNER- SPECTOR*	WHEN I SAW YOU/PARADISE ...	3.25	5.50	4.00

SPECTORS THREE
PRODUCER: PHIL SPECTOR

☐3001	*TREY*	I KNOW WHY/I REALLY DO	5.00	9.00	7.00
☐3005		MY HEART STOOD STILL/ MR. ROBIN	5.00	9.00	7.00

SPIDERS
FEATURED: ALICE COOPER

☐003	*SANTA CRUZ*	DON'T BLOW YOUR MIND/ NO PRICE TAG	50.00	100.00	63.00

SPIRALS

☐1719	*SMASH*	FOREVER & A DAY/PLEASE BE MY LOVE	12.00	24.00	20.00

SPRING (HONEYS)
PRODUCER: BRIAN WILSON
SEE: AMERICAN SPRING

☐50848	*UNITED ARTISTS*	NOW THAT EVERYTHING'S BEEN SAID/AWAKE	6.00	12.00	8.00
☐50907		GOOD TIME/SWEET MOUNTAIN ..	6.00	12.00	8.00

BRUCE SPRINGSTEEN

"I was really nowhere as a kid!" — *Bruce Springsteen*

And he wasn't. Springsteen attended a Catholic elementary school where, as a third-grader, he was once stuffed into a trash can by an angry nun. ("That's where you belong, Bruce Springsteen!") At home, Bruce was constantly at odds with his parents' ideals and philosophies. Springsteen was painfully shy and had few close pals.

During junior high, Bruce became involved with rock-and-roll music and bought an $18 guitar. As a high-school sophomore, he formed a rock band called Castile, which became Child, then Steel Mill. Springsteen grew shoulder-length hair, which his teachers at Freehold (NJ) High denounced in class. Bruce barely graduated in 1967 (he was born September 19, 1949) and split for New York City the next day.

Springsteen later returned to New Jersey. He formed Dr. Zoom and the Sonic Boom and began playing gigs at nearby Asbury Park. His band also played prisons and mental institutions. "Once at a mental hospital, a guy spent twenty minutes introducing us," Bruce recalls. "He kept saying we were better than the Beatles. Then the doctors came and took him away."

He lived above a surfboard shop, learned to drive at 19, and eventually signed with Columbia in 1972. Today the Boss is America's top solo concert draw. A great showman.

			Current Price Range		P/Y AVG

SPRINGFIELDS
FEATURED: DUSTY SPRINGFIELD

			Current Price Range		P/Y AVG
☐ 40038	PHILIPS	SILVER THREADS AND GOLDEN NEEDLES/AUNT RHODY	3.00	5.00	3.65
☐ 40072		DEAR HEARTS AND GENTLE PEOPLE/GOTTA TRAVEL ON	3.00	5.00	3.65
☐ 40099		FOGGY MOUNTAIN TOP/ISLAND OF DREAMS	3.00	5.00	3.65
☐ 40121		SAY I WON'T BE THERE/ LITTLE BOAT	3.00	5.00	3.65
☐ 40162		LITTLE BY LITTLE/WAF-WOOF	3.00	5.00	3.65
		SPRINGFIELDS—ALBUMS			
☐ 200052 (M)	PHILIPS	SILVER THREADS AND GOLDEN NEEDLES	7.00	17.00	15.00
☐ 600052 (S)		SILVER THREADS AND GOLDEN NEEDLES	8.00	21.00	18.00
☐ 200076 (M)		FOLK SONGS FROM THE HILLS	6.00	15.00	13.50
☐ 600076 (S)		FOLK SONGS FROM THE HILLS	7.00	17.00	15.00

BRUCE SPRINGSTEEN

☐ 45805	COLUMBIA	BLINDED BY THE LIGHT/ THE ANGEL	26.00	46.00	42.00
☐ 45864		FOR YOU/SPIRIT IN THE NIGHT	22.00	40.00	36.00
☐ 10209		BORN TO RUN/MEETING ACROSS THE RIVER	3.00	5.00	3.50
☐ 10274		TENTH AVENUE FREEZE-OUT/SHE'S THE ONE	3.25	4.00	
☐ 10763		PROVE IT ALL NIGHT/FACTORY	2.75	4.50	3.00
☐ 10801		BADLANDS/STREETS OF FIRE	2.75	4.50	3.00
		COLUMBIA ALBUMS ARE WORTH UP TO $10.00 MINT			

TERRY STAFFORD

☐ 101	CRUSADE	SUSPICION/JUDY	3.00	5.00	3.50
☐ 105		I'LL TOUCH A STAR/PLAYING WITH FIRE	3.00	5.00	3.50
☐ 109		FOLLOW THE RAINBOW/ARE YOU A FOOL LIKE ME?	3.00	5.00	3.50
☐ 110		A LITTLE BIT BETTER/HOPING	3.00	5.00	3.50
☐ 914	SIDEWALK	THE JOKE'S ON ME/A STEP OR TWO BEHIND YOU	3.25	5.50	4.00
		TERRY STAFFORD—ALBUMS			
☐ 1001 (M)	CRUSADE	SUSPICION	9.00	25.00	22.50
☐ 1001 (S)		SUSPICION	14.00	34.00	30.00

STANDELLS
FEATURED: LARRY TAMBLYN

☐ 61000	SUNSET	OOH POO PAH DOO/ HELP YOURSELF	8.25	14.00	12.00
☐ 55680	LIBERTY	PEPPERMINT BEATLES/ THE SHAKE	5.50	11.00	9.00
☐ 55722		I'LL GO CRAZY/HELP YOURSELF	5.50	11.00	9.00
☐ 55743		LINDA LOU/SO FINE	5.00	9.00	7.00
☐ 185	TOWER	DIRTY WATER/RORI	3.50	6.00	4.00
☐ 257		SOMETIMES GOOD GUYS DON'T WEAR WHITE/WHY DID YOU HURT ME	3.50	6.00	4.00
☐ 282		WHY PICK ON ME?/MR. NOBODY	3.50	6.00	4.00
☐ 310		POOR SHELL OF A MAN/TRY IT	3.50	6.00	4.00
☐ 312		DON'T TELL ME WHAT TO DO/ WHEN I WAS A COWBOY	3.50	6.00	4.00
☐ 314		RIOT ON SUNSET STRIP/BLACK HEARTED WOMAN	3.50	6.00	4.00
☐ 348		CAN'T HELP BUT LOVE YOU/ NINETY-NINE-AND-A-HALF	3.50	6.00	4.00

			Current Price Range		P/Y AVG
☐398		ANIMAL GIRL/SOUL DRIPPIN` ...	3.50	6.00	4.50

STANDELLS—ALBUMS

			Current Price Range		P/Y AVG
☐5027 (M)	**TOWER**	DIRTY WATER	8.00	21.00	18.00
☐5027 (S)		DIRTY WATER	10.00	29.00	25.00
☐5044 (M)		WHY PICK ON ME?	7.00	17.00	15.00
☐5044 (S)		WHY PICK ON ME?	9.00	25.00	22.50
☐5049 (M)		HOT ONES	7.00	17.00	15.00
☐5049 (S)		HOT ONES	8.00	21.00	18.00
☐5098 (M)		TRY IT	7.00	17.00	15.00
☐5098 (S)		TRY IT	8.00	21.00	18.00
☐1186 (M)	**SUNSET**	LIVE AND OUT OF SIGHT	7.00	17.00	15.00
☐5136 (S)		LIVE AND OUT OF SIGHT	8.00	21.00	18.00
☐3384 (M)	**LIBERTY**	THE STANDELLS IN PERSON AT P.J.`S	14.00	34.00	30.00
☐7384 (S)		THE STANDELLS IN PERSON AT P.J.`S	17.00	40.00	35.00

RAY STANLEY
GUITAR: EDDIE COCHRAN

			Current Price Range		P/Y AVG
☐011	**ZEPHYR**	PUSHIN`/MARKET PLACE	12.00	29.00	25.00
☐012		MY LOVIN` BABY/LOVE CHARMS	12.00	29.00	25.00

RINGO STARR
SEE: BEATLES

			Current Price Range		P/Y AVG
☐2969	**APPLE**	BEAUCOUPS OF BLUES/COOCHY COOCHY	3.50	6.00	4.00
☐1831		IT DON`T COME EASY/EARLY 1970	3.00	5.00	3.65
☐1849		BACK OFF BOOGALOO/BLIND MAN	3.00	5.00	3.65
☐1865		PHOTOGRAPH/DOWN AND OUT	3.00	5.00	3.65
☐1870		YOU`RE SIXTEEN/DEVIL WOMAN	3.00	5.00	3.65
☐1872		OH MY MY/STEP LIGHTLY	3.00	5.00	3.65
☐1876		ONLY YOU/CALL ME	3.00	5.00	3.65
☐1880		NO-NO SONG/SNOOKEROO	3.00	5.00	3.65
☐1882		IT`S ALL DOWN TO GOODNIGHT VIENNA/OH-WEE	3.00	5.00	3.65
☐3361	**ATLANTIC**	A DOSE OF ROCK AND ROLL/CRYIN`	3.00	5.00	3.65
☐3371		HEY BABY/LADY GAYE	3.00	5.00	3.65
☐3429		JUST A DREAM/WINGS	3.00	5.00	3.65

RINGO STARR—ALBUMS

			Current Price Range		P/Y AVG
☐3365 (S)	**APPLE**	SENTIMENTAL JOURNEY	7.00	15.00	9.00
☐3368 (S)		BEAUCOUPS OF BLUES	6.00	13.00	8.50
☐3413 (S)		RINGO	6.00	13.00	8.50
☐3417 (S)		GOODNIGHT VIENNA	6.00	13.00	8.50
☐3422 (S)		BLAST FROM YOUR PAST (greatest hits)	6.00	13.00	8.50
☐18193 (S)	**ATLANTIC**	ROTOGRAVURE	6.00	13.00	8.50
☐19108 (S)		RINGO IV	6.00	13.00	8.50

STATENS

			Current Price Range		P/Y AVG
☐8011	**MARK-X**	THAT CERTAIN KIND/SUMMERTIME IS TIME FOR LOVE	12.00	24.00	20.00

STEPPENWOLF
SEE: SPARROW

			Current Price Range		P/Y AVG
☐4109	**DUNHILL**	A GIRL I KNOW/THE OSTRICH	3.25	5.50	4.00
☐4123		SOOKIE SOOKIE/TAKE WHAT YOU NEED	3.25	4.50	4.00
☐4138		BORN TO BE WILD/EVERYBODY`S NEXT ONE	3.00	5.00	3.35
☐4160		MAGIC CARPET RIDE/SOOKIE SOOKIE	3.00	5.00	3.35

			Current Price Range		P/Y AVG
☐4182		ROCK ME/JUPITER CHILD	2.75	4.50	3.25
☐4192		IT'S NEVER TOO LATE/			
		HAPPY BIRTHDAY	2.75	4.50	3.25
☐4205		MOVE OVER/POWER PLAY	2.75	4.50	3.25
☐4221		MONSTER/BERRY RIDES AGAIN .	2.75	4.50	3.25
☐4234		HEY LAWDY MAMA/TWISTED ...	2.75	4.50	3.25
☐4248		SCREAMIN' NIGHT HOG/			
		CORRINA CORRINA	2.75	4.50	3.25
☐4261		WHO NEEDS YA/EARSCHPLITTEN			
		LOUDENBOOMER	2.75	4.50	3.25
☐4269		SNOW BLIND FRIEND/			
		HIPPO STOMP	2.75	4.50	3.25
☐4283		RIDE WITH ME/BLACK PIT	2.75	4.50	3.25
☐4283		RIDE WITH ME/FOR MADMEN			
		ONLY	2.75	4.50	3.25
☐4292		FOR LADIES ONLY/SPARKLE EYES	2.75	4.50	3.25
		STEPPENWOLF—ALBUMS			
☐50029 (S)	*DUNHILL*	STEPPENWOLF	6.00	13.00	8.50
☐50037 (S)		STEPPENWOLF THE SECOND	6.00	13.00	8.50
☐50053 (S)		AT YOUR BIRTHDAY PARTY	6.00	13.00	8.50
☐50060 (S)		EARLY STEPPENWOLF	6.00	13.00	8.50
☐50066 (S)		MONSTER	6.00	13.00	8.50
☐50075 (S)		STEPPENWOLF LIVE	6.00	13.00	8.50
☐50090 (S)		STEPPENWOLF 7	6.00	13.00	8.50
☐50099 (S)		STEPPENWOLF GOLD—THEIR			
		GREATEST HITS	6.00	13.00	8.50

CAT STEVENS

			Current Price Range		P/Y AVG
☐5872	*DERAM*	PORTOBELLO ROAD/I LOVE MY			
		DOG	3.50	6.00	4.35
☐7505		MATTHEW AND SON/GRANNY ...	3.50	6.00	4.35
☐85006		SCHOOL IS OUT/I'M GONNA GET			
		ME A GUN	3.50	6.00	4.35
☐85015		BAD NIGHT/LAUGHING APPLE ...	3.50	6.00	4.35
		CAT STEVENS—ALBUMS			
☐18005 (S)	*DERAM*	MATTHEW AND SON/			
		NEW MASTERS	8.00	21.00	18.00
☐18061 (S)		VERY YOUNG AND EARLY SONGS	7.00	17.00	15.00

CONNIE STEVENS

			Current Price Range		P/Y AVG
☐5092	*WARNER BROTHERS*	WHY DO I CRY FOR JOEY?/			
		APOLLO	3.75	6.00	4.50
☐5137		SIXTEEN REASONS/			
		LITTLE SISTER	3.25	5.50	4.00
☐5159		TOO YOUNG TO GO STEADY/			
		A LITTLE KISS	3.25	5.50	4.00
☐5232		THE GREENWOOD TREE/IF YOU			
		DON'T SOMEBODY ELSE WILL .	3.25	5.50	4.00
☐5217		MAKE-BELIEVE LOVER/			
		AND THIS IS MINE	3.25	5.50	4.00
☐5265		WHY'D YOU WANNA MAKE ME			
		CRY/JUST ONE KISS	3.25	5.50	4.00
☐5289		MR. SONGWRITER/			
		I COULDN'T SAY NO	3.25	5.50	4.00
☐5318		NOBODY'S LONESOME FOR ME/			
		HEY GOOD LOOKIN'	3.25	5.50	4.00
☐5380		THERE GOES YOUR GUY/			
		LITTLE MISSUNDERSTOOD	3.25	5.50	4.00
		CONNIE STEVENS—ALBUMS			
☐1208 (M)	*WARNER BROTHERS*	CONCHETTA	9.00	25.00	22.50
☐1382 (M)		CONNIE STEVENS (FROM			
		"HAWAIIAN EYE")	8.00	21.00	18.00

			Current Price Range		P/Y AVG
☐ 1382 (S)		CONNIE STEVENS (FROM "HAWAIIAN EYE")	12.00	29.00	25.00
☐ 1431 (M)		CONNIE STEVENS	8.00	21.00	18.00
☐ 1431 (S)		CONNIE STEVENS	12.00	29.00	25.00
☐ 1460 (M)		THE HANK WILLIAMS SONG BOOK	7.00	17.00	15.00
☐ 1460 (S)		THE HANK WILLIAMS SONG BOOK	9.00	25.00	22.50

RAY STEVENS

			Current Price Range		P/Y AVG
☐ 108	PREP	RANG TANG DING DONG/ SILVER BRACELET	4.50	7.50	6.00
☐ 122		FIVE MORE STEPS/TINGLE	4.50	7.50	6.00
☐ 4101	CAPITOL	THE CLOWN/SCHOOL	4.50	7.50	6.00
☐ 031	NRC	HIGH SCHOOL YEARBOOK/ TRULY TRUE	4.00	7.00	4.85
☐ 042		MY HEART CRIES FOR YOU/WHAT WOULD I DO WITHOUT YOU? ..	4.00	7.00	4.85
☐ 057		SERGEANT PRESTON OF THE YUKON/WHO DO YOU LOVE? ..	4.00	7.00	4.85
☐ 063		WHITE CHRISTMAS/ HAPPY BLUE YEAR	4.00	7.00	4.85
☐ 71843	MERCURY	JEREMIAH PEABODY'S POLY UNSATURATED, QUICK DISSOLVING, FAST ACTING, PLEASANT TASTING GREEN AND PURPLE PILLS/TEEN YEARS ..	3.00	5.00	3.50
☐ 71888		SCRATCH MY BACK/WHEN YOU WISH UPON A STAR	4.50	7.50	3.50
☐ 71966		AHAB THE ARAB/ IT'S BEEN SO LONG	2.25	4.50	3.00
☐ 72039		FURTHER MORE/SATURDAY NIGHT AT THE MOVIES	2.25	4.50	3.00
☐ 72058		SANTA CLAUS IS WATCHING YOU/LOVED AND LOST	2.25	4.50	3.00
☐ 72098		FUNNY MAN/JUST ONE OF LIFE'S LITTLE TRAGEDIES	2.25	4.50	3.00
☐ 72125		HARRY THE HAIRY APE/ LITTLE STONE STATUE	2.25	4.50	3.00
☐ 72189		SPEED BALL/IT'S PARTY TIME ..	2.25	4.50	3.00
☐ 72255		BUTCH BARBARIAN/ DON'T SAY ANYTHING	2.25	4.50	3.00
☐ 72307		BUBBLE GUM THE BUBBLE DANCER/LAUGHING OVER MY GRAVE	2.25	4.50	3.00
☐ 72382		ROCKIN' TEENAGE MUMMIES/IT ONLY HURTS WHEN I LOVE ...	2.25	4.50	3.00
☐ 72430		MR. BAKER THE UNDERTAKER/ THE OLD ENGLIGH SURFER ...	2.25	4.50	3.00
☐ 911	MONUMENT	A-B-C/PARTY PEOPLE	2.25	4.50	3.00
☐ 927		MAKE A FEW MEMORIES/ DEVIL MAY CARE	2.25	4.50	3.00
☐ 946		FREDDY FEELGOOD/THERE'S ONE IN EVERY CROWD	2.25	4.50	3.00
☐ 1001		MARY MY SECRETARY/ ANSWER ME, MY LOVE	2.25	4.50	3.00
☐ 1048		UNWIND/FOR HE'S A JOLLY GOOD FELLOW	2.00	4.00	2.50
☐ 1083		MR. BUSINESSMAN/ FACE THE MUSIC	2.00	4.00	2.50
☐ 1099		THE GREAT ESCAPE/ ISN'T IT LONELY TOGETHER ...	2.00	4.00	2.50
☐ 1131		GITARZAN/BAGPIPES— THAT'S MY BAG	2.00	4.00	2.50
☐ 1150		ALONG CAME JONES/ YAKETY YAK	2.00	4.00	2.50

			Current Price Range		P/Y AVG
☐1163		SUNDAY MORNIN' COMIN' DOWN/ THE MINORITY	2.00	4.00	2.50
☐1171		HAVE A LITTLE TALK WITH MYSELF/THE LITTLE WOMAN	2.00	4.00	2.50
☐1187		THE FOOL ON THE HILL/I'LL BE YOUR BABY TONIGHT	2.00	4.00	2.50

RAY STEVENS—ALBUMS

☐20732 (M)	MERCURY	1,837 SECONDS OF HUMOR	7.00	17.00	15.00
☐60732 (S)		1,837 SECONDS OF HUMOR	8.00	25.00	22.50
☐20732 (M)		AHAB THE ARAB (later title)	5.00	15.00	13.50
☐60732 (S)		AHAB THE ARAB (later title)	7.00	21.00	18.00
☐20828 (M)		THIS IS RAY STEVENS	5.00	15.00	13.50
☐60828 (S)		THIS IS RAY STEVENS	7.00	21.00	18.00
☐61262 (S)		THE BEST OF RAY STEVENS	7.00	17.00	15.00
☐18102 (S)	MONUMENT	EVEN STEVENS	5.00	12.00	10.00
☐18115 (S)		GITARZAN	5.00	12.00	10.00

ROD STEWART
SEE: PYTHON LEE JACKSON

☐8722	PRESS	GOOD MORNING, LITTLE SCHOOLGIRL/I'M GONNA MOVE TO THE OUTSKIRTS OF TOWN	9.00	16.00	14.00
☐73009	MERCURY	HANDBAGS AND GLADRAGS/ AN OLD RAINCOAT WON'T LET YOU DOWN	3.75	6.00	4.50
☐73031		HANDBAGS AND GLADRAGS/ MAN OF CONSTANT SORROW	3.25	5.50	4.00
☐73095		IT'S ALL OVER NOW/(DJ)	3.25	5.50	4.00
☐73115		ONLY A HALO/(DJ)	3.25	5.50	4.00
☐73156		CUT ACROSS SHORTY/ GASOLINE ALLEY	3.25	5.50	4.00
☐73175		LADY DAY/MY WAY OF GIVING	3.25	5.50	4.00
☐73196		COUNTRY COMFORT/ GASOLINE ALLEY	3.00	5.00	3.50
☐73224		MAGGIE MAY/ REASON TO BELIEVE	2.50	4.50	3.00
☐73244		(I KNOW) I'M LOSING YOU/ MANDOLIN WIND	2.50	4.50	3.00
☐73330		YOU WEAR IT WELL/TRUE BLUE	2.50	4.50	3.00
☐73344		ANGEL/LOST PARAGUAYOS	2.50	4.50	3.00
☐73412		TWISTING THE NIGHT AWAY/ TRUE BLUE-LADY DAY	2.50	4.50	3.00
☐73426		OH NO! NOT MY BABY/JODIE	2.75	4.50	3.00
☐73636		MINE FOR ME/FAREWELL	2.75	4.50	3.00
☐73660		SAILOR/LET ME BE YOUR CAR	3.00	5.00	3.50
☐73802		WHAT'S MADE MILWAUKEE FAMOUS/EVERY PICTURE TELLS A STORY	3.00	5.00	3.50

MERCURY ALBUMS ARE WORTH UP TO $10.00 MINT

STONE PONEYS

☐937	SIDEWALK	SO FINE/EVERYBODY HAS THEIR OWN IDEAS	4.50	7.50	5.50
☐2004	CAPITOL	DIFFERENT DRUM/I'VE GOT TO KNOW	4.00	7.00	5.00
☐2110		UP TO MY NECK IN HIGH MUDDY WATER/CARNIVAL BEAR	4.00	7.00	5.00

STONE PONEYS—ALBUMS

☐2666	CAPITOL	THE STONE PONEY'S	12.50	20.00	15.00
☐2763		EVERGREEN VOL. 2	10.00	17.50	12.50
☐2863		EVERGREEN VOL. 3	10.00	17.50	12.50
☐11383		BEGINNINGS	7.50	15.00	10.50
☐3298	PICKWICK	STONEY END	7.00	12.00	9.75

ROD STEWART

North London, England, was Rod's birthplace. The year was 1945, the date January 10th. Restless in classrooms as a child, Stewart found soccer and music his two main interests outside the halls of learning. He became such a skilled soccer player that he signed with a semi-pro team as a teenager.

Shortly before soccer training camp opened, though, Rod and another British singer (Wizz Jones) departed to travel throughout England and, later, Europe. For two years the pair sang and played the banjo in pubs. When Stewart returned to his hometown, he supported himself at times by working as a freelance gravedigger.

Rod became frustrated with blues music and drifted through a series of British r & b bands. Among these were Jimmy Powell and the Dimensions, Python Lee Jackson, the Hoochie Coochie Men (Stewart shared vocals with an also unknown named Long John Baldry), Steam Packet, the Shotgun Express and the Jeff Beck Group.

He fronted the group Faces (formerly the Small Faces of "Itchykoo Park" fame). Rod then signed with Mercury Records as a soloist. In 1971 he hit pay dirt with his first number — one winner, "Maggie May"/"Reason to Believe." Since then, he hasn't looked back. Despite a number of personal problems with his girl friends and excess drinking, Rod Stewart still ranks as one of the most important rock figures of the day.

			Current Price Range		P/Y AVG

GALE STORM

			Current Price Range		P/Y AVG
☐15412	DOT	I HEAR YOU KNOCKING/ NEVER LEAVE ME	3.25	5.50	4.00
☐15436		TEEN AGE PRAYER/ MEMORIES ARE MADE OF THIS	3.25	5.50	4.00
☐15448		WHY DO FOOLS FALL IN LOVE/ I WALK ALONE	3.25	5.50	4.00
☐15458		IVORY TOWER/ I AIN'T GONNA WORRY	3.25	5.50	4.00
☐15474		TELL ME WHY/ DON'T TREAT ME THAT WAY ..	3.25	5.50	4.00
☐15492		NOW IS THE HOUR/A HEART WITHOUT A SWEETHEART	3.25	5.50	4.00
☐15493		A CASUAL LOOK/ COTTON PICKIN' KISSES	3.25	5.50	4.00
☐15539		LUCKY LIPS/ ON TREASURE ISLAND	3.25	5.50	4.00
☐15558		DARK MOON/A LITTLE TOO LATE	3.25	5.50	4.00
☐15606		LOVE BY THE JUKEBOX LIGHT/ ON MY MIND AGAIN	3.25	5.50	4.00

GALE STORM—EPs

☐1050	DOT	GALE STORM	5.50	11.00	9.00
☐1051		GALE STORM	5.50	11.00	9.00
☐1052		GALE STORM	5.50	11.00	9.00
☐1074		GALE'S GREAT HITS	5.50	11.00	9.00

GALE STORM—ALBUMS

☐3011 (M)	DOT	GALE STORM	9.00	25.00	22.50
☐3017 (M)		SENTIMENTAL ME	9.00	25.00	22.50
☐3098 (M)		GALE STORM HITS	9.00	25.00	22.50
☐3197 (M)		SOFTLY AND TENDERLY	6.00	15.00	13.50
☐25197 (S)		SOFTLY AND TENDERLY	9.00	25.00	22.50

STORYTELLERS

☐500	STACK	YOU PLAYED ME A FOOL/ HEY BABY	8.50	18.00	16.00

THREE DIFFERENT NON-RELATED GROUPS USED THE NAME STORYTELLERS IN THE LATE '50's AND '60's. ONLY ONE RECORDED FOR STACK LABEL

STRANGELOVES

☐4192	SWAN	I'M ON FIRE/LOVE, LOVE (THAT'S ALL I WANT FROM YOU)	3.25	5.50	4.00
☐501	BANG	I WANT CANDY/ IT'S ABOUT MY BABY	2.50	4.00	2.50
☐508		CARA-LIN/(ROLL ON) MISSISSIPPI	2.50	4.00	2.50
☐514		NIGHT TIME/RHYTHM OF LOVE ..	2.50	4.00	2.50
☐524		HAND JIVE/I GOTTA DANCE	2.50	4.00	2.50
☐544		QUARTER TO THREE/ JUST THE WAY YOU ARE	2.50	4.00	2.50

STRANGELOVES—ALBUM

☐211 (M)	BANG	I WANT CANDY	7.00	17.00	15.00

STRAWBERRY ALARM CLOCK
SEE: SIXPENCE

☐373	ALL AMERICAN	INCENSE AND PEPPERMINTS/ BIRDMAN OF ALKATRASH	9.50	17.00	15.00
☐55018	UNI	INCENSE AND PEPPERMINTS/ BIRDMAN OF ALKATRASH	2.75	4.50	3.25
☐55046		TOMORROW/BIRDS IN MY TREE .	2.75	4.50	3.25
☐55055		SIT WITH THE GURU/PRETTY SONG FROM PSYCH-OUT	2.75	4.50	3.25
☐55076		BAREFOOT IN BALTIMORE/ ANGRY YOUNG MAN	2.75	4.50	3.25
☐55093		SEA SHELL/PAXTON'S BACK STREET CARNIVAL	2.75	4.50	3.25

			Current Price Range		P/Y AVG
☐55113		STAND BY/MISS ATTRACTION ..	2.75	4.50	3.25
☐55125		GOOD MORNING STARSHINE/			
		ME AND THE TOWNSHIP	2.75	4.50	3.25
☐55158		DESIREE/CHANGES	2.75	4.50	3.25
☐55185		STARTING OUT THE DAY/			
		SMALL PACKAGE	2.75	4.50	3.25
☐55190		I CLIMBED THE MOUNTAIN/			
		THREE	2.75	4.50	3.25
☐55218		CALIFORNIA DAY/THREE	2.75	4.50	3.25
☐55241		GIRL FROM THE CITY/THREE	2.75	4.50	3.25
		STRAWBERRY ALARM CLOCK—ALBUMS			
☐73014 (S)	*UNI*	INCENSE AND PEPPERMINTS	6.00	13.00	8.50
☐73025 (S)		WAKE UP—IT'S TOMORROW	6.00	13.00	8.50
☐73035 (S)		THE WORLD IN A SEA SHELL	6.00	13.00	8.50
☐73054 (S)		GOOD MORNING STARSHINE	6.00	13.00	8.50
☐73074 (S)		THE BEST OF THE STRAWBERRY			
		ALARM CLOCK	5.00	12.00	10.00

BARRETT STRONG

☐54027	*TAMLA*	MONEY/OH, I APOLOGIZE	14.00	24.00	20.00
☐54029		YOU KNOWS WHAT TO DO/			
		YES NO MAYBE SO	5.50	11.00	9.00
☐54033		WHIRLWIND/I'M GONNA CRY ...	4.50	8.00	6.50
☐54035		MONEY AND ME/YOU GOT			
		WHAT IT TAKES	4.50	8.00	6.50
☐54043		MISERY/TWO WRONGS DON'T			
		MAKE A RIGHT	4.50	8.00	6.00
		THE ABOVE PRICES APPLY TO FIRST-PRESS TAMLA LABELS WITH LINES			
☐1111	*ANNA*	MONEY/OH, I APOLOGIZE	3.25	5.50	4.00
☐1116		YOU KNOWS WHAT I WANT TO			
		DO/YES, NO, MAYBE SO	3.25	5.50	4.00

GENE SUMMERS

☐100	*JAN*	SCHOOL OF ROCK 'N ROLL/			
		STRAIGHT SKIRT	12.00	21.00	18.00
☐102		GOTTA LOTTA THAT/NERVOUS ..	12.00	21.00	18.00

SUNDIALS

☐2065	*GUYDEN*	CHAPEL OF LOVE/			
		WHETHER TO RESIST	14.00	34.00	28.00

SUNNY & THE HORIZONS

☐1013	*LUXOR*	BECAUSE THEY TELL ME/			
		NATURE'S CREATION	17.00	39.00	35.00

SUNRAYS

☐5253	*WARNER BROTHERS*	TALK TO HIM/GIDEON..........	5.00	9.00	7.00
☐101	*TOWER*	CAR PARTY/OUT OF GAS	4.50	8.00	6.00
☐148		I LIVE FOR THE SUN/			
		BYE BABY BYE	3.25	5.50	4.00
☐191		ANDREA/YOU DON'T PLEASE ME	3.25	5.50	4.00
☐224		STILL/WHEN YOU'RE NOT HERE .	3.25	5.50	4.00
☐256		DON'T TAKE YOURSELF TOO			
		SERIOUSLY/I LOOK, BABY,			
		BUT I CAN'T SEE	3.25	5.50	4.00
☐290		HI, HOW ARE YOU/			
		JUST 'ROUND THE RIVER BEND	3.25	5.50	4.00
☐340		LOADED WITH LOVE/TIME	3.25	5.50	4.00
		SUNRAYS—ALBUM			
☐5017 (M)	*TOWER*	ANDREA...................	12.00	14.00	25.00

			Current Price Range		P/Y AVG

SUPREMES
FEATURED: DIANA ROSS
SEE: FLORENCE BALLARD, PRIMETTES

			Current Price Range		P/Y AVG
☐ 54038	**TAMLA**	I WANT A GUY/NEVER AGAIN ...	17.00	29.00	25.00
☐ 54045		BUTTERED POPCORN/ WHO'S LOVING YOU	14.00	24.00	20.00
		THE ABOVE PRICES APPLY TO FIRST-PRESS TAMLA LABELS WITH LINES			
☐ 1027	**MOTOWN**	YOUR HEART BELONGS TO ME/ (HE'S) SEVENTEEN	4.50	7.50	6.00
☐ 1034		LET ME GO THE RIGHT WAY/ TIME CHANGES THINGS	4.50	7.50	6.00
☐ 1040		YOU BRING BACK MEMORIES/ MY HEART CAN'T TAKE IT NO MORE	3.75	6.00	4.50
☐ 1044		A BREATH-TAKING GUY/ ROCK AND ROLL BANJO BAND .	3.25	5.50	4.00
☐ 1051		WHEN THE LOVELIGHT STARTS SHINING THROUGH HIS EYES/ STANDING AT THE CROSSROADS OF LOVE	3.00	5.00	3.50
☐ 1054		RUN, RUN, RUN/I'M GIVING YOU YOUR FREEDOM ..	3.00	5.00	3.50
☐ 1060		WHERE DID OUR LOVE GO?/ HE MEANS THE WORLD TO ME .	2.75	4.50	3.00
☐ 1066		BABY LOVE/ASK ANY GIRL	2.75	4.50	3.00
☐ 1068		COME SEE ABOUT ME/ ALWAYS IN MY HEART	2.75	4.50	3.00
☐ 1074		STOP! IN THE NAME OF LOVE/ I'M IN LOVE AGAIN	2.75	4.50	3.00
☐ 1075		BACK IN MY ARMS AGAIN/ WHISPER YOU LOVE ME, BOY .	2.75	4.50	3.00
☐ 1080		NOTHING BUT HEARTACHES/ HE HOLDS HIS OWN	2.75	4.50	3.00
☐ 1083		I HEAR A SYMPHONY/WHO COULD EVER DOUBT MY LOVE .	2.75	4.50	3.00
☐ 1085		CHILDREN'S CHRISTMAS SONG/ TWINKLE TWINKLE LITTLE ME .	3.00	5.00	3.50
☐ 1089		MY WORLD IS EMPTY WITHOUT YOU/EVERYTHING IS GOOD ABOUT YOU	2.75	4.50	3.00
☐ 1094		LOVE IS LIKE AN ITCHING IN MY HEART/HE'S ALL I GOT	2.75	4.50	3.00
☐ 1097		YOU CAN'T HURRY LOVE/ PUT YOURSELF IN MY PLACE ..	2.75	4.50	3.00
☐ 1101		YOU KEEP ME HANGIN' ON/ REMOVE THIS DOUBT	2.75	4.50	3.00
☐ 1103		LOVE IS HERE AND NOW YOU'RE GONE/THERE'S NO STOPPING US NOW	2.75	4.50	3.00
☐ 1107		THE HAPPENING/ ALL I KNOW ABOUT YOU	2.75	4.50	3.00
☐ 1111		REFLECTIONS/GOING DOWN FOR THE THIRD TIME	2.75	4.50	3.00
☐ 1116		IN AND OUT OF LOVE/I GUESS I'LL ALWAYS LOVE YOU	2.75	4.50	3.00
☐ 1122		FOREVER CAME TODAY/ TIME CHANGES THINGS	2.75	4.50	3.00
☐ 1126		SOME THINGS YOU NEVER GET USED TO/YOU'VE BEEN SO WONDERFUL TO ME	2.75	4.50	3.00
☐ 1135		LOVE CHILD/ WILL THIS BE THE DAY	2.75	4.50	3.00
☐ 1139		I'M LIVIN' IN SHAME/I'M SO GLAD I GOT SOMEBODY	2.75	4.50	3.00

			Current Price Range		P/Y AVG
☐ 1146		THE COMPOSER/THE BEGINNING OF THE END	2.75	4.50	3.00
☐ 1148		NO MATTER WHAT SIGN YOU ARE/ THE YOUNG FOLKS	2.75	4.50	3.00
☐ 1156		SOMEDAY WE'LL BE TOGETHER/ HE'S MY SUNNY BOY	2.75	4.50	3.00

LATER MOTOWN SINGLES ARE WORTH UP TO $2.25 MINT

SUPREMES—ALBUMS

			Current Price Range		P/Y AVG
☐ 606 (M)	*MOTOWN*	MEET THE SUPREMES (girls on stools)	34.00	82.00	75.00
☐ 606 (M)		MEET THE SUPREMES (girls' faces)	19.00	34.00	30.00
☐ 621 (M)		WHERE DID OUR LOVE GO?	7.00	17.00	15.00
☐ 623 (M)		A BIT OF LIVERPOOL	7.00	17.00	15.00
☐ 625 (M)		THE SUPREMES SING COUNTRY, WESTERN AND POP	7.00	17.00	15.00
☐ 625 (S)		THE SUPREMES SING COUNTRY, WESTERN AND POP	9.00	25.00	22.50
☐ 627 (M)		MORE HITS BY THE SUPREMES . .	6.00	15.00	13.50
☐ 627 (S)		MORE HITS BY THE SUPREMES . .	8.00	21.00	18.00
☐ 629 (M)		WE REMEMBER SAM COOKE	6.00	15.00	13.50
☐ 629 (S)		WE REMEMBER SAM COOKE	8.00	21.00	18.00
☐ 636 (M)		AT THE COPA	5.50	14.00	12.00
☐ 636 (S)		AT THE COPA	7.00	17.00	15.00
☐ 638 (M)		MERRY CHRISTMAS	6.00	15.00	13.50
☐ 638 (S)		MERRY CHRISTMAS	7.00	17.00	15.00
☐ 643 (M)		I HEAR A SYMPHONY	5.50	14.00	12.00
☐ 643 (S)		I HEAR A SYMPHONY	5.50	14.00	12.00
☐ 649 (M)		SUPREMES A-GO-GO	5.50	14.00	12.00
☐ 649 (S)		SUPREMES A-GO-GO	5.50	14.00	12.00
☐ 659 (M)		THE SUPREMES SING ROGERS AND HART	6.00	15.00	13.50
☐ 659 (S)		THE SUPREMES SING ROGERS AND HART	5.50	14.00	12.00
☐ 663 (M)		GREATEST HITS.	7.00	17.00	15.00
☐ 663 (S)		GREATEST HITS.	5.00	12.00	10.00
☐ 665 (M)		REFLECTIONS	7.00	17.00	15.00
☐ 665 (S)		REFLECTIONS	5.00	12.00	10.00

SURFARIS

			Current Price Range		P/Y AVG
☐ 11/12	*DFS*	WIPEOUT/SURFER JOE	45.00	78.00	72.00
☐ 50	*PRINCESS*	WIPEOUT/SURFER JOE	14.00	36.00	30.00
☐ 16479	*DOT*	WIPEOUT/SURFER JOE	3.50	6.00	4.00
☐ 16966		SHOW BIZ/CHICAGO GREEN	3.50	6.00	4.00
☐ 31538	*DECCA*	POINT PANIC/WAIKIKI RUN	3.50	6.00	4.00
☐ 31561		SANTA'S SPEED SHOP/ SURFER'S CHRISTMAS LIST . .	3.50	6.00	4.00
☐ 31581		SCATTER SHIELD/I WANNA TAKE A TRIP TO THE ISLANDS	3.50	6.00	4.00
☐ 31641		BOSS BARRACUDA/DUNE BUGGY	3.50	6.00	4.00
☐ 31682		HOT ROD HIGH/KAREN	3.50	6.00	4.00
☐ 31731		BEAT '65/BLACK DENIM	3.50	6.00	4.00
☐ 31784		SOMETHIN' ELSE/ THEME OF THE BATTLE MAIDEN	3.00	5.00	3.50
☐ 31835		CATCH A LITTLE RIDE WITH ME/ DON'T HURT MY LITTLE SISTER.	3.00	5.00	3.50
☐ 31954		HEY JOE (WHERE ARE YOU GOING?/SO GET OUT	3.00	5.00	3.50
☐ 32003		WIPE OUT/I'M A HOG FOR YOU . .	2.75	4.50	3.00

SURFARIS—ALBUMS

			Current Price Range		P/Y AVG
☐ 3535 (M)	*DOT*	WIPE OUT	8.00	21.00	18.00
☐ 25535 (S)		WIPE OUT	12.00	29.00	25.00
☐ 4470 (M)	*DECCA*	THE SURFARIS	8.00	21.00	18.00
☐ 74470 (S)		THE SURFARIS	12.00	29.00	25.00

			Current Price Range		P/Y AVG
☐ 4487 (M)		HIT CITY '64	8.00	17.00	15.00
☐ 74487 (S)		HIT CITY '64	9.00	25.00	22.50
☐ 4560 (M)		FUN CITY, U.S.A.	7.00	17.00	15.00
☐ 74560 (S)		FUN CITY, U.S.A.	9.00	25.00	22.50
☐ 4614 (M)		HIT CITY '65	7.00	17.00	15.00
☐ 74614 (S)		HIT CITY '65	9.00	25.00	22.50
☐ 4683 (M)		IT AIN'T ME BABE	7.00	17.00	15.00
☐ 73683 (S)		IT AIN'T ME BABE	8.00	21.00	18.00

SURFETTES
FEATURED: CAROL CONNORS

☐ 3001	**MUSTANG**	SAMMY THE SIDEWALK SURFER/ BLUE SURF	5.00	9.00	7.00

SURVIVORS (BEACH BOYS)

☐ 5120	**CAPITOL**	PAMELA JEAN/AFTER THE GAME	55.00	100.00	72.00

SWALLOWS

☐ 4458	**KING**	DEAREST/WILL YOU BE MINE ...	128.00	215.00	200.00
☐ 4466		SINCE YOU'VE BEEN AWAY/ WISHING FOR YOU	128.00	215.00	200.00
☐ 4501		ETERNALLY/IT AIN'T THE MEAT .	78.00	130.00	120.00
☐ 4501		ETERNALLY/IT AIN'T THE MEAT (blue wax)	160.00	265.00	250.00
☐ 4515		TELL ME WHY/ ROLL, ROLL, PRETTY BABY ...	50.00	80.00	72.00
☐ 4525		BESIDE YOU/YOU LEFT ME......	50.00	80.00	72.00
☐ 4533		I ONLY HAVE EYES FOR YOU/ YOU WALKED IN	78.00	130.00	120.00
☐ 4579		WHERE DO I GO FROM HERE?/ PLEASE BABY PLEASE	34.00	54.00	48.00
☐ 4612		OUR LOVE IS DYING/LAUGH	34.00	54.00	48.00
☐ 4632		NOBODY'S LOVIN' ME/ BICYCLE TILLIE	26.00	48.00	42.00
☐ 4656		TRUST ME/PLEADING BLUES ...	26.00	48.00	42.00
☐ 4676		I'LL BE WAITING/ IT FEELS SO GOOD	26.00	48.00	42.00
☐ 104	**AFTER HOURS**	MY BABY/GOOD TIME GIRLS	92.00	160.00	150.00
☐ 12319	**FEDERAL**	ANGEL BABY/OH LONESOME ME	9.50	17.00	15.00
☐ 12328		ROCK-A-BYE BABY ROCK	8.25	14.00	12.00
☐ 12329		BESIDE YOU/LAUGHING BOY	8.25	14.00	12.00
☐ 12333		ITCHY TWITCHY FEELING/ WHO KNOWS, DO YOU?	5.50	11.00	9.00
☐ 2023	**GUYDEN**	YOU MUST TRY/HOW LONG MUST A FOOL GO ON?	5.50	11.00	9.00

SWEET

☐ 45126	**BELL**	CO-CO/BURN IT DOWN	3.50	6.00	4.00
☐ 45184		POPPA JOE/JEANNIE...........	3.50	6.00	4.00
☐ 45251		LITTLE WILLY/ MAN FROM MECCA	3.00	5.00	3.50
☐ 45361		BLOCKBUSTER/ NEED A LOT OF LOVIN'	3.00	5.00	3.50
☐ 45408		NEW YORK CONNECTION/ WIGWAM BAM	3.00	5.00	3.50
☐ 4055	**CAPITOL**	BALLROOM BLITZ/RESTLESS ...	3.00	5.00	3.25
☐ 4157		FOX ON THE RUN/ BURN ON THE FLAME	3.00	5.00	3.25
☐ 4220		ACTION/MEDUSSA	3.00	5.00	3.25
☐ 4429		FEVER OF LOVE/ HEARTBREAK TODAY	3.00	5.00	3.25
☐ 4454		FUNK IT UP (DAVID'S SONG)/ STAIRWAY TO THE STARS	3.00	5.00	3.25

			Current Price Range		P/Y AVG
☐ 4599		LOVE IS LIKE OXYGEN/			
		COVER GIRL	3.00	5.00	3.25
☐ 4610		CALIFORNIA NIGHTS/			
		A GIRL LIKE YOU	3.00	5.00	3.25
☐ 4730		MOTHER EARTH/WHY DON'T YOU.	3.00	5.00	3.25
☐ 4908		WATERS EDGE/SIXTIES MAN ...	2.50	4.00	2.50
		SWEET—ALBUMS			
☐ 1125 (S)	**BELL**	SWEET......................	7.00	17.00	15.00
☐ 11395 (S)	**CAPITOL**	DESOLATION BOULEVARD.......	5.50	14.00	12.00
☐ 11496 (S)		GIVE US A WINK	5.50	14.00	12.00
☐ 11636 (S)		OFF THE RECORD	5.00	12.00	10.00
☐ 11744 (S)		LEVEL-HEADED	5.00	12.00	10.00

SWINGING BLUE JEANS

☐ 66021	**IMPERIAL**	HIPPY HIPPY SHAKE/			
		NOW I MUST GO	3.25	5.50	4.00
☐ 66030		GOOD GOLLY MISS MOLLY/			
		SHAKING FEELING	3.25	5.50	4.00
☐ 66049		YOU'RE NO GOOD/			
		SHAKE, RATTLE AND ROLL ...	3.25	5.50	4.00
☐ 66059		TUTTI FRUITTI/			
		PROMISE YOU'LL TELL HER ...	3.25	5.50	4.00
☐ 66154		DON'T MAKE ME OVER/			
		WHAT CAN I DO TODAY?	3.25	5.50	4.00
☐ 66225		RUMORS, GOSSIP, WORDS UNTRUE/NOW THE			
		SUMMER'S GONE	3.25	5.50	4.00
☐ 66255		SOMETHING'S COMING ALONG/			
		TREMBLIN'	3.25	5.50	4.00
		SWINGING BLUE JEANS—ALBUMS			
☐ 9261 (M)	**IMPERIAL**	HIPPY HIPPY SHAKE	7.00	17.00	15.00
☐ 12261 (S)		HIPPY HIPPY SHAKE	9.00	25.00	22.50

SWINGIN' MEDALLIONS

☐ 002	**4 SALE**	DOUBLE SHOT/			
		HERE IT COMES AGAIN	8.25	14.00	12.00
☐ 2033	**SMASH**	DOUBLE SHOT (OF MY BABY'S LOVE)/HERE IT COMES AGAIN .	2.75	4.50	3.00
☐ 2050		SHE DRIVES ME OUT OF MY MIND/YOU GOTTA HAVE FAITH	2.75	4.50	3.00
		SWINGIN' MEDALLIONS—ALBUMS			
☐ 27083 (M)	**SMASH**	DOUBLE SHOT	7.00	17.00	15.00
☐ 67083 (S)		DOUBLE SHOT	8.00	21.00	18.00

SYNDICATE OF SOUND

☐ 503	**SCARLET**	TELL THE WORLD/			
		PREPARE FOR LOVE	5.50	11.00	9.00
☐ 4304	**DEL-FI**	TELL THE WORLD/			
		PREPARE FOR LOVE	3.75	6.00	4.50
☐ 228	**HUSH**	LITTLE GIRL/YOU	8.25	14.00	12.00
☐ 640	**BELL**	LITTLE GIRL/YOU	3.50	6.00	4.00
☐ 646		RUMORS/THE UPPER HAND	3.50	6.00	4.00
☐ 655		GOOD TIME MUSIC/KEEP IT UP ..	3.50	6.00	4.00
☐ 666		MARY/THAT KIND OF MAN	3.50	6.00	4.00
☐ 2426	**CAPITOL**	CHANGE THE WORLD/ YOU'RE LOOKING FINE	3.50	6.00	4.00
☐ 156	**BUDDAH**	BROWN PAPER BAG/ REVERB BEAT	3.50	6.00	4.00
☐ 183		THE FIRST TO LOVE YOU/MEXICO	3.50	6.00	4.00
		SYNDICATE OF SOUND—ALBUMS			
☐ 6001 (M)	**BELL**	LITTLE GIRL.................	6.00	15.00	13.50
☐ 6001 (S)		LITTLE GIRL.................	7.00	17.00	15.00

T

			Current Price Range		P/Y AVG

MARC TANNO

| ☐501 | **WHALE** | DEAR ABBY/ANGEL . . . . | 8.50 | 18.00 | 16.00 |

TASSELS

☐117	**MADISON**	TO A SOLDIER BOY/ THE BOY FOR ME	3.50	6.00	4.00
☐121		TO A YOUNG LOVER/ MY GUY AND I	3.50	6.00	4.00
☐11	**GOLDISC**	THE TWELFTH OF NEVER/ SINCE YOU WENT AWAY	3.50	6.00	4.00

JAMES TAYLOR

☐1805	**APPLE**	CAROLINA IN MY MIND/ SOMETHING'S WRONG	3.00	5.00	3.65
☐201	**EUPHORIA**	BRIGHTEN YOUR DAY WITH MY DAY/THE ZOO	3.50	6.00	4.00
☐45880	**ELEKTRA**	GROWNUP/MOCKINGBIRD	3.00	5.00	3.65
☐7135	**WARNER BROTHERS**	SWEET BABY JAMES/ LONG AGO & FAR AWAY	3.00	5.00	3.65
☐7387		SWEET BABY JAMES/ SUITE FOR 20G	3.00	5.00	3.65
☐7423		FIRE & RAIN/ ANYWHERE LIKE HEAVEN	3.00	5.00	3.65

LATER WARNER BROTHERS SINGLES ARE WORTH UP TO $2.25 MINT

TRUE TAYLOR (PAUL SIMON)

| ☐614 | **BIG** | TRUE OR FALSE/TEENAGE FOOL . | 21.00 | 34.00 | 30.00 |

TEARDROPS (FOUR PREPS)

☐766	**JOSIE**	THE STARS ARE OUT TONIGHT/ OH! STOP IT	27.00	46.00	42.00
☐771		MY HEART/OOH BABY	57.00	102.00	95.00
☐856		WE WON'T TELL/AL CLAIRE DE LUNA PORTO FORTUNA	5.00	9.00	7.00
☐862		CRY NO MORE/ YOU'RE MY HOLLYWOOD STAR	4.50	7.50	6.00
☐873		ALWAYS YOU/ DADDY'S LITTLE GIRL	4.50	7.50	6.00

TEDDY BEARS
FEATURED: PHIL SPECTOR

☐503	**DORE**	TO KNOW HIM, IS TO LOVE HIM/ DON'T YOU WORRY MY PRETTY PET	3.25	6.00	4.50
☐520		WONDERFUL, LOVEABLE YOU/ TILL YOU'LL BE MINE	5.00	9.00	7.00
☐5562	**IMPERIAL**	OH WHY/ I DON'T NEED YOU ANYMORE .	4.50	7.50	6.00
☐5581		IF YOU ONLY KNEW/ YOU SAID GOODBYE	5.50	7.50	6.00
☐5594		DON'T GO AWAY/ SEVEN LONELY DAYS	5.50	7.50	6.00

TEDDY BEARS—ALBUMS

| ☐9067 (M) | **IMPERIAL** | TEDDY BEARS . . . . | 29.00 | 66.00 | 60.00 |
| ☐12067 (S) | | TEDDY BEARS . . . . | 66.00 | 162.00 | 150.00 |

			Current Price Range		P/Y AVG

TEENAGERS

SEE: FRANKIE LYMON AND THE TEENAGERS

☐4086	*ROULETTE*	MY BROKEN HEART/			
		MAMA WANNA ROCK	4.50	7.50	6.00
☐42054	*COLUMBIA*	WHAT'S ON YOUR MIND?/			
		THE DRAW	3.75	6.00	4.50
☐43094		SOMEWHERE/			
		SWEET AND LOVELY	3.75	6.00	4.50
☐1071	*END*	TONIGHT'S THE NIGHT/CRYING .	3.75	6.00	4.50
☐1076		CAN YOU TELL ME?/			
		A LITTLE WISER NOW	3.75	6.00	4.50

TEENAGERS—EP

☐602	*GEE*	THE TEENAGERS GO ROMANTIC .	9.50	17.00	15.00

TEEN ANGELS

☐388	*SUN*	AIN'T GONNA LET YOU BREAK MY			
		HEART/TELL ME MY LOVE	12.00	24.00	20.00

TEMPTATIONS

☐5	*MIRACLE*	OH MOTHER OF MINE/			
		ROMANCE WITHOUT FINANCE .	8.25	14.00	12.00
☐12		YOUR WONDERFUL LOVE/			
		CHECK YOURSELF	7.00	13.00	11.00
☐7001	*GORDY*	DREAM COME TRUE/			
		ISN'T SHE PRETTY	4.00	7.00	4.85
☐7010		PARADISE/SLOW DOWN HEART .	4.00	7.00	4.85
☐7015		THE FURTHER YOU LOOK/			
		I WANT A LOVE I CAN SEE	4.00	7.00	4.85
☐7020		MAY I HAVE THIS DANCE?/			
		FAREWELL MY LOVE	4.00	7.00	4.85
☐7028		THE WAY YOU DO THE THINGS			
		YOU DO/JUST LET ME KNOW ..	3.00	5.00	3.65
☐7030		KEEP ME/MIDNIGHT JOURNEY ..	3.50	5.50	4.00
☐7032		I'LL BE IN TROUBLE/			
		THE GIRL'S ALRIGHT WITH ME	3.00	5.00	3.65
☐7035		GIRL (WHY YOU WANNA MAKE ME			
		BLUE?)/BABY, BABY,			
		I NEED YOU	3.00	5.00	3.65
☐7038		MY GIRL/NOBODY BUT MY BABY	3.00	5.00	3.65
☐7040		IT'S GROWING/WHAT LOVE			
		HAS JOINED TOGETHER	3.00	5.00	3.65
☐7043		SINCE I LOST MY BABY/			
		YOU'VE GOT TO EARN IT	3.00	5.00	3.65
☐7047		MY BABY/DON'T LOOK BACK ...	3.00	5.00	3.65
☐7049		GET READY/FADING AWAY	3.00	5.00	3.65
☐7054		AIN'T TOO PROUD TO BEG/			
		YOU'LL LOSE A PRECIOUS LOVE	3.00	5.00	3.65
☐7055		BEAUTY IS ONLY SKIN DEEP/			
		YOU'RE NOT AN ORDINARY GIRL	3.00	5.00	3.65
☐7057		(I KNOW) I'M LOSING YOU/I			
		COULDN'T CRY IF I WANTED TO	3.00	5.00	3.65
☐7061		ALL I NEED/			
		SORRY IS A SORRY WORD	3.00	5.00	3.65
☐7063		YOU'RE MY EVERYTHING/			
		I'VE BEEN GOOD TO YOU	3.00	5.00	3.65
☐7065		(LONELINESS MADE ME REALIZE)			
		IT'S YOU THAT I NEED/			
		DON'T SEND ME AWAY	3.00	5.00	3.65
☐7068		I WISH IT WOULD RAIN/			
		I TRULY TRULY BELIEVE	3.00	5.00	3.65
☐7072		I COULD NEVER LOVE ANOTHER			
		(AFTER LOVING YOU)/GONNA			
		GIVE HER ALL THE LOVE I GOT .	3.00	5.00	3.65

		Current Price Range		P/Y AVG
☐7074	PLEASE RETURN YOUR LOVE TO ME/HOW CAN I FORGET	3.00	5.00	3.65
☐7081	CLOUD NINE/WHY DID SHE HAVE TO LEAVE ME?	3.00	5.00	3.65
☐7082	RUDOLPH THE RED NOSED REINDEER/SILENT NIGHT	3.00	5.00	3.65
☐7084	RUNAWAY CHILD. RUNNING WILD/I NEED YOUR LOVE	3.00	5.00	3.65
☐7086	DON'T LET THE JONESES GET YOU DOWN/SINCE I'VE LOST YOU . .	3.00	5.00	3.65
☐7093	I CAN'T GET NEXT TO YOU/ RUNNING AWAY AIN'T GONNA HELP YOU	3.00	5.00	3.65
☐7096	PSYCHEDELIC SHACK/ THAT'S THE WAY LOVE IS	3.00	5.00	3.65
☐7099	BALL OF CONFUSION/ IT'S SUMMER	3.00	5.00	3.65
☐7102	UNGENA ZA ULIMWENGU (UNITE THE WORLD)/ HUM ALONG AND DANCE	3.00	5.00	3.65
☐7015	JUST MY IMAGINATION RUNNING AWAY WITH ME)/ YOU MAKE YOUR OWN HEAVEN AND HELL RIGHT HERE ON EARTH	3.00	5.00	3.65
☐7109	IT'S SUMMER/I'M THE EXCEPTION TO THE RULE	3.00	5.00	3.65
☐7111	SUPERSTAR (REMEMBER HOW YOU GOT WHERE YOU ARE)/ GONNA KEEP ON TRYIN' TILL I WIN YOUR LOVE	3.00	5.00	3.65
☐7115	TAKE A LOOK AROUND/SMOOTH SAILING (FROM NOW ON)	3.00	5.00	3.65
☐7119	MOTHER NATURE/FUNKY MUSIC SHONUFF TURNS ME ON	3.00	5.00	3.65
☐7121	PAPA WAS A ROLLIN' STONE/ PAPPA WAS A ROLLIN' STONE (instrumental)	2.75	4.50	3.25
☐7126	MASTERPIECE/MASTERPIECE (instrumental)	2.75	4.50	3.25
☐7129	THE PLASTIC MAN/ HURRY TOMORROW	2.75	4.50	3.25
☐7131	HEY. GIRL (I LIKE YOUR STYLE)/ MA	2.75	4.50	3.25
☐7133	LET YOU HAIR DOWN/ AIN'T NO JUSTICE	2.75	4.50	3.25
☐7135	HEAVENLY/ZOOM	2.75	4.50	3.25
☐7136	YOU'VE GOT MY SOUL ON FIRE/ I NEED YOU	2.75	4.50	3.25
☐7138	HAPPY PEOPLE/HAPPY PEOPLE (instrumental)	2.75	4.50	3.25
☐7142	SHAKEY GROUND/ I'M A BACHELOR	2.75	4.50	3.25
☐7144	GLASS HOUSE/THE PROPHET . . .	2.75	4.50	3.25
☐7146	KEEP HOLDING ON/WHAT YOU NEED MOST (I DO BEST OF ALL)	2.75	4.50	3.25
☐7150	UP THE CREEK (WITHOUT A PADDLE)/ DARLING, STAND BY ME	2.75	4.50	3.25
☐7152	WHO ARE YOU?/LET ME COUNT THE WAYS (I LOVE YOU)	2.75	4.50	3.25

TEMPTATIONS—ALBUMS

☐911 (M)	**GORDY**	MEET THE TEMPTATIONS	8.00	21.00	18.00
☐911 (S)		MEET THE TEMPTATIONS	12.00	29.00	25.00

			Current Price Range		P/Y AVG
☐912 (M)		THE TEMPTATIONS SING SMOKEY.	7.00	17.00	15.00
☐912 (S)		THE TEMPTATIONS SING SMOKEY.	9.00	25.00	22.50
☐914 (M)		TEMPTIN' TEMPTATIONS	7.00	17.00	15.00
☐914 (S)		TEMPTIN' TEMPTATIONS	9.00	21.00	18.00
☐918 (M)		GETTIN' READY	7.00	17.00	15.00
☐918 (S)		GETTIN' READY	9.00	.21.00	18.00
☐919 (M)		GREATEST HITS.	6.00	15.00	13.50
☐919 (S)		GREATEST HITS.	7.00	17.00	15.00
☐921 (M)		LIVE.	6.00	15.00	13.50
☐921 (S)		LIVE.	7.00	17.00	15.00
☐922 (M)		WITH A LOT O' SOUL	5.50	14.00	12.00
☐922 (S)		WITH A LOT O' SOUL	6.00	15.00	13.50
☐924 (M)		IN A MELLOW MOOD	5.50	14.00	12.00
☐924 (S)		IN A MELLOW MOOD	5.50	14.00	12.00
☐927 (M)		THE TEMPTATIONS WISH IT WOULD RAIN	6.00	15.00	13.50
☐927 (S)		THE TEMPTATIONS WISH IT WOULD RAIN	5.50	14.00	12.00
☐933 (S)		TV SHOW	5.00	12.00	10.00
☐938 (S)		LIVE AT THE COPA.	5.00	12.00	10.00
☐939 (S)		CLOUD NINE	5.00	12.00	10.00
☐947 (S)		PSYCHEDELIC SHACK	5.00	12.00	10.00
☐949 (S)		PUZZLE PEOPLE	5.00	12.00	10.00
☐953 (S)		LIVE AT LONDON'S TALK OF THE TOWN	5.00	12.00	10.00
☐954 (S)		GREATEST HITS. VOL. II	5.00	12.00	10.00

TEMPTATIONS

☐3001	GOLDISC	BARBARA/SOMEDAY	3.50	6.00	4.35
☐3007		LETTER OF DEVOTION/ FICKLE LITTLE GIRL	3.50	6.00	4.35
☐3019		BALLAD OF LOVE/TONIGHT MY HEART SHE IS CRYING	3.50	6.00	4.35

TENDERTONES

☐713	DUCKY	JUST FOR A LITTLE WHILE/ I LOVE YOU SO	14.00	34.00	30.00

TERRACE TONES

☐25016	APT	WORDS OF WISDOM/ THE RIDE OF PAUL REVERE . . .	12.00	21.00	18.00

TEX & THE CHEX

☐2116	ATLANTIC	MY LOVE/I DO LOVE YOU	12.00	26.00	22.00

CHUCK THARP
FEATURED: FIREBALLS

☐0012	LUCKY	LONG LONG PONYTAIL/ LET THERE BE LOVE	14.00	23.00	16.50
☐77020	JARO	LONG LONG PONYTAIL/ LET THERE BE LOVE	14.00	23.00	16.50

VIC THOMAS

☐40183	PHILLIPS	NAPOLEON BONAPARTE/ MARIANNE	14.00	32.00	28.00

THYME

☐201	A-SQUARE	SHAME. SHAME/SOMEHOW	5.50	10.00	7.00
☐202		TIME OF THE SEASON/ I FOUND A LOVE	5.50	10.00	7.00

TICO AND THE TRIUMPHS
FEATURED: PAUL SIMON

☐169	MADISON	MOTORCYCLE/ I DON'T BELIEVE THEM	9.50	17.00	15.00

			Current Price Range		P/Y AVG
☐835	**AMY**	MOTORCYCLE/			
		I DON'T BELIEVE THEM	8.25	14.00	12.00
☐845		EXPRESS TRAIN/WILDFLOWER	5.00	9.00	7.00
☐860		CRY, LITTLE BOY, CRY/			
		GET UP AND DO THE WONDER	5.00	9.00	7.00
☐876		CARDS OF LOVE/NOISE	8.25	14.00	12.00

JOHNNY TILLOTSON

			Current Price Range		P/Y AVG
☐1353	**CADENCE**	DREAMY EYES/			
		WELL, I'M YOUR MAN	4.00	7.00	4.85
☐1364		TRUE TRUE HAPPINESS/			
		LOVE IS BLIND	4.00	7.00	4.85
☐1372		WHY DO I LOVE YOU SO/			
		NEVER LET ME GO	4.00	7.00	4.85
☐1377		EARTH ANGEL/			
		PLEDGING MY LOVE	4.00	7.00	4.85
☐1384		POETRY IN MOTION/			
		PRINCESS, PRINCESS	3.50	6.00	4.35
☐1391		JIMMY'S GIRL/			
		HIS TRUE LOVE SAID GOODBYE	3.50	6.00	4.35
☐1404		WITHOUT YOU/CUTIE PIE	3.50	6.00	4.35
☐1409		DREAMY EYES/			
		WELL, I'M YOUR MAN	3.50	6.00	4.35
☐1418		IT KEEPS RIGHT ON A-HURTIN'/			
		SHE GAVE SWEET LOVE TO ME	3.25	5.50	4.00
☐1424		SEND ME THE PILLOW YOU			
		DREAM ON/WHAT'LL I DO?	3.25	5.50	4.00
☐1432		I CAN'T HELP IT/			
		I'M SO LONESOME I COULD CRY	3.25	5.50	4.00
☐1437		YOU CAN NEVER STOP ME LOVING			
		YOU/JUDY JUDY JUDY	3.25	5.50	4.00
☐1441		FUNNY HOW THE TIME SLIPS			
		AWAY/GOOD YEAR FOR GIRLS	3.25	5.50	4.00
☐13181	**MGM**	TALK BACK, TREMBLING LIPS/			
		ANOTHER YOU	3.00	5.00	3.65
☐13193		WORRIED GUY/			
		PLEASE DON'T GO AWAY	3.00	5.00	3.65
☐13232		I RISE, I FALL/			
		I'M WATCHING MY WATCH	3.00	5.00	3.65
☐13255		WORRY/SUFFERIN'			
		FROM A HEARTACHE	3.00	5.00	3.65
☐13284		SHE UNDERSTANDS ME/			
		TOMORROW	3.00	5.00	3.65
☐13316		ANGEL/LITTLE BOY	3.00	5.00	3.65
☐13344		THEN I'LL COUNT AGAIN/			
		ONE'S YOURS, ONE'S MINE	3.00	5.00	3.65
☐13376		HEARTACHES BY THE NUMBER/			
		YOUR MEM'RY COMES ALONG	3.00	5.00	3.65
☐13408		OUR WORLD/(WAIT TILL			
		YOU SEE) MY GIDGET	3.50	6.00	4.00
☐13445		I NEVER LOVED YOU ANYWAY/			
		HELLO ENEMY	3.00	5.00	3.65
☐13499		ME, MYSELF AND I/			
		COUNTRY BOY, COUNTRY BOY	3.00	5.00	3.65
☐13519		NO LOVE AT ALL/			
		WHAT AM I GONNA DO	3.00	5.00	3.65
☐13598		OPEN UP YOUR HEART/			
		BABY'S GONE	3.00	5.00	3.65
☐13598		OPEN UP YOUR HEART/			
		MORE THAN BEFORE	3.00	5.00	3.65
☐13633		CHRISTMAS COUNTRY STYLE/			
		CHRISTMAS IS THE BEST			
		OF ALL	3.00	5.00	3.65

			Current Price Range		P/Y AVG
☐ 13684		STRANGE THINGS HAPPEN/ TOMMY JONES	2.75	4.50	3.00
☐ 13738		DON'T TELL ME IT'S RAINING/ TAKIN' IT EASY	2.75	4.50	3.00
☐ 13829		COUNTING MY TEARDROPS/ YOU'RE THE REASON	2.75	4.50	3.00
☐ 13888		IT KEEPS RIGHT ON A-HURTIN'/ I CAN SPOT A CHEATER	2.50	4.00	2.50
☐ 13924		I HAVEN'T BEGUN TO LOVE YOU YET/I CAN SPOT A CHEATER ..	2.50	4.00	2.50
☐ 13977		A LETTER TO EMILY/ YOUR MEM'RY COMES ALONG	2.50	4.00	2.50
		JOHNNY TILLOTSON—EP			
☐ 114	**CADENCE**	JOHNNY TILLOTSON	8.25	14.00	12.00
		JOHNNY TILLOTSON—ALBUMS			
☐ 3052 (M)	**CADENCE**	JOHNNY TILLOTSON'S BEST	14.00	34.00	30.00
☐ 25052 (S)		JOHNNY TILLOTSON'S BEST	19.00	50.00	45.00
☐ 3058 (M)		IT KEEPS RIGHT ON A-HURTIN' ..	8.00	21.00	18.00
☐ 25058 (S)		IT KEEPS RIGHT ON A-HURTIN' ..	9.00	25.00	22.50
☐ 3067 (M)		YOU CAN NEVER STOP ME LOVING YOU	8.00	21.00	18.00
☐ 25067 (S)		YOU CAN NEVER STOP ME LOVING YOU	9.00	25.00	22.50
☐ 4188 (M)	**MGM**	TALK BACK TREMBLING LIPS ...	7.00	17.00	15.00
☐ 4188 (S)		TALK BACK TREMBLING LIPS ...	8.00	21.00	18.00
☐ 4224 (M)		THE TILLOTSON TOUCH	7.00	17.00	15.00
☐ 4224 (S)		THE TILLOTSON TOUCH	8.00	21.00	18.00
☐ 4270 (M)		SHE UNDERSTANDS ME	7.00	17.00	15.00
☐ 4270 (S)		SHE UNDERSTANDS ME	8.00	21.00	18.00
☐ 4328 (M)		JOHNNY TILLOTSON SINGS OUR WORLD	7.00	17.00	15.00
☐ 4328 (S)		JOHNNY TILLOTSON SINGS OUR WORLD	8.00	21.00	18.00
☐ 4395 (M)		NO LOVE AT ALL	6.00	15.00	13.50
☐ 4395 (S)		NO LOVE AT ALL	7.00	17.00	15.00
☐ 4402 (M)		CHRISTMAS TOUCH	6.00	15.00	13.50
☐ 4402 (S)		CHRISTMAS TOUCH	7.00	17.00	15.00
☐ 4532 (M)		THE BEST OF JOHNNY TILLOTSON	6.00	15.00	13.50
☐ 4532 (S)		THE BEST OF JOHNNY TILLOTSON	7.00	15.00	
☐ 4814 (S)		THE VERY BEST OF JOHNNY TILLOTSON	5.50	14.00	12.00

TIMETONES

☐ 26	**TIMES SQ.**	SUNDAY KIND OF LOVE/ ANGELS IN THE SKY	16.00	37.00	24.00

TODAY & TOMORROW

☐ 812	**NOOSE**	DOOLEY SWINGS (PT. 1)/(PT. 2) .	8.50	24.00	20.00

TOM AND JERRY (SIMON AND GARFUNKEL)

☐ 613	**BIG**	HEY, SCHOOLGIRL/DANCIN' WILD	8.25	14.00	12.00
☐ 616		OUR SONG/TWO TEENAGERS ...	9.50	17.00	15.00
☐ 618		THAT'S MY STORY/ DON'T SAY GOODBYE	9.50	17.00	15.00
☐ 621		BABY TALK/TWO TEENAGERS ...	12.00	21.00	18.00
☐ 319	**HUNT**	THAT'S MY STORY/ DON'T SAY GOODBYE	12.00	21.00	18.00
☐ 120	**BELL**	BABY TALK/I'M GOING TO GET MARRIED (Ronnie Lawrence)...	14.00	24.00	20.00
☐ 1094	**EMBER**	I'M LONESOME/LOOKING AT YOU	21.00	34.00	30.00
☐ 71930	**MERCURY**	I'LL DROWN IN MY TEARS/ THE FRENCH TWIST	17.00	29.00	25.00
☐ 5167	**KING**	HEY, SCHOOLGIRL/DANCIN' WILD	8.25	14.00	12.00
☐ 10363	**ABC-**				

			Current Price Range		P/Y AVG
	PARAMOUNT	SURRENDER, PLEASE			
		SURRENDER/FIGHTING MAD ..	9.50	17.00	15.00
☐ 10788		THAT'S MY STORY/			
		TIA-JUANA BLUES	8.25	14.00	12.00

TONY AND THE RAINDROPS

☐609	**CHESAPEAKE**	OUR LOVE IS OVER/			
		WHILE WALKING	7.00	18.00	16.00

TORNADOES

☐9561	**LONDON**	TELSTAR/JUNGLE FEVER	3.00	5.00	3.65
☐9579		LIKE LOCOMOTION/			
		GLOBETROTTIN'	3.00	5.00	3.65
☐9581		RIDIN' THE WIND/			
		THE BREEZE AND I	3.00	5.00	3.65
☐9599		LIFE ON VENUS/ROBOT	3.00	5.00	3.65
		TORNADOES—ALBUM			
☐3279 (M)	**LONDON**	TELSTAR	8.00	21.00	18.00

TORNADOES
SEE: HOLLYWOOD TORNADOES

☐100	**AERTAUN**	BUSTIN' SURFBOARDS/			
		BEYOND THE SURF	3.50	6.00	4.35
☐103		PHANTOM SURFER/			
		SHOOTIN' BEAVERS	3.50	6.00	4.35
		TORNADOES—ALBUM			
☐4005 (M)	**JOSIE**	BUSTIN' SURFBOARDS	14.00	34.00	30.00

TOWNSMEN

☐1340	**J.P.**	I CAN'T GO/			
		THAT'S ALL I'LL EVER NEED ..	12.00	34.00	28.00
☐6202	**JOEY**	MOONLIGHT WAS MADE FOR			
		LOVERS/I'M IN THE MOOD			
		FOR LOVE	7.00	17.00	15.00

TRADE WINDS (VIDELS)

☐10-020	**RED BIRD**	NEW YORK'S A LONELY TOWN/			
		CLUB SEVENTEEN	3.25	5.50	4.00
☐10-028		ROCK AND ROLL SHOW IN TOWN/			
		GIRL FROM GREENWICH			
		VILLAGE	3.25	5.50	4.00
☐10-033		SUMMERTIME GIRL/			
		THE PARTY STARTS AT NINE ..	3.25	5.50	4.00
☐212	**KAMA SUTRA**	MIND EXCURSION/			
		LITTLE SUSAN'S DREAMIN' ...	3.00	5.00	3.65
☐218		I BELIEVE IN HER/			
		CATCH ME IN THE MEADOW ...	3.00	5.00	3.65
☐234		MIND EXCURSION/			
		ONLY WHEN I'M DREAMIN' ...	3.00	5.00	3.65
		TRADE WINDS (VIDELS)—ALBUM			
☐8057 (M)	**KAMA SUTRA**	EXCURSIONS	7.00	17.00	15.00
☐8057 (S)		EXCURSIONS	8.00	21.00	18.00

TRASHMEN

☐4002	**GARRETT**	SURFIN' BIRD/KING OF THE SURF.	3.25	5.50	4.00
☐4003		BIRD DANCE BEAT/A-BONE	3.25	5.50	4.00
☐4005		ON THE MOVE/BAD NEWS	3.25	5.50	4.00
☐4010		PEPPERMINT MAN/			
		NEW GENERATION	3.25	5.50	4.00
		TRASHMEN—ALBUM			
☐200 (M)	**SOMA**	SURFIN' BIRD	12.00	29.00	25.00

			Current Price Range		P/Y AVG

TREBLE CHORDS

			Current Price Range		P/Y AVG
☐31015	*DECCA*	MY LITTLE GIRL/TERESA	13.00	29.00	25.00

TREMELOES

☐10075	*EPIC*	GOOD DAY SUNSHINE/ WHAT A STATE I'M IN	3.00	5.00	3.50
☐10139		HERE COMES MY BABY/ GENTLEMAN OF PLEASURE . . .	2.75	4.50	3.00
☐10184		SILENCE IS GOLDEN/ LET YOUR HAIR HANG DOWN . .	2.75	4.50	3.00
☐10233		EVEN THE BAD TIMES ARE GOOD/ JENNY'S ALL RIGHT	2.75	4.50	3.00
☐10293		SUDDENLY YOU LOVE ME/ SUDDENLY WINTER	2.75	4.50	3.00
☐10328		GIRL FROM NOWHERE/ HELULE HELULE	2.75	4.50	3.00
☐10376		ALL THE WORLD TO ME/ MY LITTLE LADY	2.75	4.50	3.00
☐10437		I SHALL BE RELEASED/ MISS MY BABY	2.75	4.50	3.00
☐10682		ME AND MY LIFE/TRY ME	2.75	4.50	3.00

TREMELOES—ALBUMS

☐24310 (M)	*EPIC*	HERE COMES MY BABY	7.00	17.00	15.00
☐26310 (S)		HERE COMES MY BABY	6.00	15.00	13.50
☐24326 (M)		EVEN THE BAD TIMES ARE GOOD .	7.00	17.00	15.00
☐26326 (S)		EVEN THE BAD TIMES ARE GOOD .	6.00	15.00	13.50
☐24363 (M)		SUDDENLY YOU LOVE ME	8.00	21.00	18.00
☐26363 (S)		SUDDENLY YOU LOVE ME	6.00	15.00	13.50
☐26388 (S)		WORLD EXPLOSION '58/'68	5.50	14.00	12.00

TRIUMPHS
FEATURED: B. J. THOMAS

☐1788	*DANTE*	I KNOW IT'S WRONG/ THE LAZY MAN	8.25	14.00	12.00

TROGGS

☐6415	*ATCO*	WITH A GIRL LIKE YOU/ I WANT YOU	3.75	6.00	4.50
☐6415		WILD THING/ WITH A GIRL LIKE YOU	3.00	5.00	3.65
☐6444		I CAN'T CONTROL MYSELF/ GONNA MAKE YOU MINE	3.00	5.00	3.65
☐1548	*FONTANA*	WILD THING/FROM HOME	3.00	5.00	3.65
☐1552		WITH A GIRL LIKE YOU/ I WANT YOU	3.00	5.00	3.65
☐1557		I CAN'T CONTROL MYSELF/ GONNA MAKE YOU MINE	3.00	5.00	3.65
☐1576		GIVE IT TO ME/YOU'RE LYING	3.00	5.00	3.65
☐1585		ANY WAY YOU WANT ME/ 6-5-4-3-2-1	3.00	5.00	3.65
☐1607		LOVE IS ALL AROUND/ WHEN WILL THE RAIN COME? .	3.00	5.00	3.65
☐1622		YOU CAN CRY IF YOU WANT TO/ THERE'S SOMETHING ABOUT YOU	3.00	5.00	3.65
☐1630		SURPRISE, SURPRISE (I NEED YOU)/COUSIN JANE	3.00	5.00	3.65
☐1634		SAY DARLIN'/HIP HIP HOORAY . .	3.00	5.00	3.65
☐21026	*PAGE ONE*	EVIL WOMAN/HEADS OR TAILS . .	3.00	5.00	3.65
☐21030		EASY LOVIN'/ GIVE ME SOMETHING	3.00	5.00	3.65
☐21032		LOVER/COME NOW	3.00	5.00	3.65
☐21035		THE RAVER/YOU	3.00	5.00	3.65

			Current Price Range		P/Y AVG
		TROGGS—ALBUMS			
☐ 193 (M)	**ATCO**	WILD THING..................	8.00	21.00	18.00
☐ 193 (S)		WILD THING..................	9.00	25.00	22.50
☐ 67556 (S)	**FONTANA**	WILD THING..................	7.00	17.00	15.00
☐ 67576 (S)		LOVE IS ALL AROUND..........	6.00	15.00	13.50
		TROPHIES			
☐ 9133	**CHALLENGE**	DOGGONE IT/DESIRE...........	14.00	34.00	30.00
		TURBANS			
☐ 209	**MONEY**	THE NEST IS WARM/ TICK TOCK AWOO...........	14.00	24.00	20.00
☐ 211		WHEN I RETURN/EMILY (Turks)..	14.00	24.00	20.00
☐ 458	**HERALD**	WHEN YOU DANCE/ LET ME SHOW YOU..........	5.00	9.00	7.00
☐ 469		SISTER SOOKEY/ I'LL ALWAYS WATCH OVER YOU	5.50	11.00	9.00
☐ 478		I'M NOBODY'S/B-I-N-G-O......	5.50	11.00	9.00
☐ 486		IT WAS A NIGHT LIKE THIS/ ALL OF MY LOVE............	5.50	11.00	9.00
☐ 495		VALLEY OF LOVE/BYE AND BYE.	5.50	11.00	9.00
☐ 510		CONGRATULATIONS/ THE WADDA-DO............	5.50	11.00	9.00
☐ 115	**RED TOP**	I PROMISE YOU LOVE/ CURFEW TIME.............	5.00	9.00	7.00
☐ 4281	**ROULETTE**	DIAMONDS AND PEARLS/ BAD MAN.................	4.50	7.50	6.00
☐ 4326		I'M NOT YOUR FOOL ANYMORE/ THREE FRIENDS............	4.50	7.50	6.00
☐ 820	**PARKWAY**	WHEN YOU DANCE/ GOLDEN RINGS.............	3.25	5.50	4.00
☐ 5807	**IMPERIAL**	SIX QUESTIONS/THE LAMENT OF SILVER GULCH..........	3.25	5.50	4.50
☐ 5828		THIS IS MY STORY/ CLICKY CLICKY CLACK.......	3.75	5.50	4.50
☐ 5847		I WONDER/THE DAMAGE IS DONE	3.75	5.50	4.50
		JOE TURNER			
☐ 939	**ATLANTIC**	CHAINS OF LOVE/AFTER MY LAUGHTER CAME TEARS.....	11.00	20.00	13.50
☐ 949		BUMP MISS SUSIE/ THE CHILL IS ON...........	9.00	16.00	11.00
☐ 960		SWEET SIXTEEN/ I'LL NEVER STOP LOVING YOU.	9.00	16.00	11.00
☐ 970		DON'T YOU CRY/ POOR LOVER'S BLUES.......	8.00	15.00	10.00
☐ 982		STILL IN LOVE/ BABY, I STILL WANT YOU....	8.00	15.00	10.00
☐ 1001		HONEY HUSH/CRAWDAD HOLE..	8.00	15.00	10.00
☐ 1016		TV MAMA/ OKE-SHE-MOKE-SHE-POP....	6.00	12.00	6.00
☐ 1026		SHAKE, RATTLE AND ROLL/ YOU KNOW I LOVE YOU......	6.00	12.00	8.00
☐ 1040		MARRIED WOMAN/ WELL AT RIGHT............	5.50	10.00	7.00
☐ 1053		FLIP, FLOP AND FLY/TI-RI-LEE..	5.50	10.00	7.00
☐ 1069		MIDNIGHT CANNONBALL/ HIDE AND SEEK.............	5.00	10.00	7.00
☐ 1080		THE CHICKEN AND THE HAWK/ MORNING NOON AND NIGHT..	5.50	10.00	7.00
		FIRST-PRESSES OF THE ABOVE ARE ON THE YELLOW-AND-BLACK LABEL			
☐ 1088		CORRINE CORRINA/ BOOGIE WOOGIE COUNTRY GIRL.	5.00	9.00	6.00

			Current Price Range		P/Y AVG
☐1100		LIPSTICK, POWDER AND PAINT/ ROCK A WHILE	5.00	9.00	6.00
☐1122		MIDNIGHT SPECIAL TRAIN/ FEELING HAPPY	5.00	9.00	6.00
☐1131		RED SAILS IN THE SUNSET/ AFTER AWHILE	5.00	9.00	6.00
☐1146		LOVE ROLLER COASTER/ WORLD OF TROUBLE	4.00	8.00	4.85
☐1155		TROUBLE IN MIND/I NEED A GIRL	4.00	8.00	4.85
☐1167	ATLANTIC	WEE BABY BLUES/ TEEN AGE LETTER	3.25	5.50	4.00
☐1184		BLUES IN THE NIGHT/ JUMP FOR JOY	3.25	5.50	4.00
☐2034		LOVE, OH CARELESS LOVE/ GOT YOU ON MY MIND	3.25	5.50	4.00
☐2054		CHAINS OF LOVE/ MY LITTLE HONEY DRIPPER ...	3.00	5.00	3.50
☐2072		SWEET SUE/ MY REASON FOR LIVING	3.00	5.00	3.50
		JOE TURNER—EPs			
☐536	ATLANTIC	JOE TURNER SINGS	8.25	14.00	12.00
☐565		JOE TURNER	7.00	13.00	11.00
☐606		ROCK WITH JOE TURNER	5.50	11.00	9.00
		JOE TURNER—ALBUMS			
☐1234 (M)	ATLANTIC	BOSS OF THE BLUES	17.00	39.00	35.00
☐1332 (M)		BIG JOE RIDES AGAIN	14.00	34.00	30.00
☐8005 (M)		JOE TURNER	12.00	29.00	25.00
☐8023 (M)		JUMPIN' THE BLUES	9.00	25.00	22.50
☐8033 (M)		BIG JOE IS HERE	9.00	25.00	22.50
☐8081 (M)		THE BEST OF JOE TURNER	9.00	25.00	22.50

SAMMY TURNER

☐3007	BIG TOP	SWEET ANNIE LAURIE/ THUNDERBOLT	3.25	5.50	4.00
☐3016		LAVENDER BLUE/ WRAPPED UP IN A DREAM	3.00	5.00	3.50
☐3032		PARADISE/I'D BE A FOOL AGAIN .	3.00	5.00	3.50
☐3029		ALWAYS/SYMPHONY	3.00	5.00	3.50
☐3038		I WANT TO BE LOVE/ GOODNIGHT IRENE	3.00	5.00	3.50
☐3049		FOOLS FALL IN LOVE/ STAY, MY LOVE	3.00	5.00	3.50
☐3089		RAINCOAT IN THE RIVER/FALLING	5.00	9.00	7.00
☐1055	MOTOWN	ONLY YOU/RIGHT NOW	2.75	4.50	3.00
		SAMMY TURNER—ALBUMS			
☐1301 (M)	BIG TOP	LAVENDER BLUE MOODS	8.00	21.00	18.00
☐1301 (S)		LAVENDER BLUE MOODS	12.00	29.00	25.00

TURTLES
FEATURED: FLO AND EDDIE
SEE: CROSSFIRES

☐222	WHITE WHALE	IT AIN'T ME BABE/ ALMOST THERE	3.00	5.00	3.65
☐224		LET ME BE/ STAR SPANGLED HEAVEN	3.00	5.00	3.65
☐227		YOU BABY/WANDERIN' KIND ...	3.00	5.00	3.65
☐231		GRIM REAPER OF LOVE/ COME BACK	3.00	5.00	3.65
☐234		OUTSIDE CHANCE/ WE'LL MEET AGAIN	3.00	5.00	3.65
☐238		CAN I GET TO KNOW YOU BETTER?/LIKE THE SEASONS .	3.00	5.00	3.65

			Current Price Range		P/Y AVG
☐244		HAPPY TOGETHER/			
		LIKE THE SEASONS	3.00	5.00	3.65
☐249		SHE'D RATHER BE WITH ME/			
		THE WALKING SONG	3.00	5.00	3.65
☐251		GUIDE FOR THE MARRIED MAN/			
		THINK I'LL RUN AWAY	3.00	5.00	3.65
☐254		YOU KNOW WHAT I MEAN/RUGS			
		OF WOODS AND FLOWERS	3.00	5.00	3.65
☐260		SHE'S MY GIRL/			
		CHICKEN LITTLE WAS RIGHT . .	3.00	5.00	3.65
☐264		SOUND ASLEEP/			
		UMBASSA THE DRAGON	3.00	5.00	3.65
☐273		THE STORY OF ROCK AND ROLL/			
		CAN'T YOU HEAR THE COWS? .	3.00	5.00	3.65
☐276		ELENORE/SURFER DAN	2.75	4.50	3.25
☐292		YOU SHOWED ME/BUZZ SAW . . .	2.75	4.50	3.25
☐308		YOU DON'T HAVE TO WALK IN THE			
		RAIN/COME OVER	2.75	4.50	3.25
☐326		LOVE IN THE CITY/BACHELOR . . .	2.75	4.50	3.25
☐334		LADY-O/			
		SOMEWHERE FRIDAY NITE	2.75	4.50	3.25
☐341		WE AIN'T GONNA PARTY NO			
		MORE/WHO WOULD EVER			
		THINK THAT I WOULD MARRY			
		MARGARET?	2.75	4.50	3.25
☐350		IS IT ANY WONDER?/			
		WANDERIN' KIND	2.75	4.50	3.25
☐355		EVE OF DESTRUCTION/			
		WANDERIN' KIND	2.75	4.50	3.25
☐364		ME ABOUT YOU/			
		THINK I'LL RUN AWAY	2.75	4.50	3.25

TURTLES—ALBUMS

☐111 (M)	**WHITE WHALE**	IT AIN'T ME BABE	8.00	21.00	18.00
☐7111 (S)		IT AIN'T ME BABE	9.00	25.00	22.50
☐112 (M)		YOU BABY	8.00	21.00	18.00
☐7112 (S)		YOU BABY	9.00	25.00	22.50
☐114 (M)		HAPPY TOGETHER	7.00	17.00	15.00
☐7114 (S)		HAPPY TOGETHER	8.00	21.00	18.00
☐115 (M)		GOLDEN HITS OF THE TURTLES . .	6.00	15.00	13.50
☐7115 (S)		GOLDEN HITS OF THE TURTLES . .	7.00	17.00	15.00
☐7118 (S)		THE BATTLE OF THE BANDS	5.50	14.00	12.00
☐7124 (S)		TURTLE SOUP	5.50	14.00	12.00
☐7127 (S)		MORE GOLDEN HITS	5.50	14.00	12.00
☐7133 (S)		WOODEN HEADS	5.50	14.00	12.00

CONWAY TWITTY

☐71086	**MERCURY**	I NEED YOUR LOVIN'/			
		BORN TO SING THE BLUES	9.50	17.00	15.00
☐71384		DOUBLE TALK BABY/WHY CAN'T I			
		GET THROUGH TO YOU	12.00	21.00	18.00
☐12677	**MGM**	IT'S ONLY MAKE BELIEVE/			
		I'LL TRY	3.50	6.00	4.35
☐12748		THE STORY OF MY LOVE/			
		MAKE ME KNOW YOU'RE MINE	3.50	6.00	4.35
☐12785		HEY LITTLE LUCY/			
		WHEN I'M NOT WITH YOU	3.50	6.00	4.35
☐12804		MONA LISA/HEAVENLY	3.50	6.00	4.35
☐12826		DANNY BOY/			
		HALFWAY TO HEAVEN	3.50	6.00	4.35
☐12857		LONELY BLUE BOY/			
		STAR SPANGLED HEAVEN	3.50	6.00	4.35
☐12886		WHAT AM I LIVING FOR?/			
		THE HURT IN MY HEART	3.50	6.00	4.35

PICKWICK, POA 061, LP

MGM, #3744, LP

			Current Price Range		P/Y AVG
☐ 12918		TELL ME ONE MORE TIME/ WHAT A DREAM	3.50	6.00	4.35
☐ 12911		IS A BLUE BIRD BLUE/ SHE'S MINE	3.50	6.00	4.35
☐ 12943		I NEED YOU SO/TEASIN'	3.25	5.50	4.00
☐ 12962		WHOLE LOT OF SHAKIN' GOING ON/THE FLAME	3.25	5.50	4.00
☐ 12969		C'EST SI BON/ DON'T YOU DARE LET ME DOWN	3.25	5.50	4.00
☐ 12998		THE NEXT KISS (IS THE LAST GOODBYE)/MAN ALONE	3.25	5.50	4.00
☐ 13011		A MILLION TEARDROPS/ I'M IN A BLUE, BLUE MOOD . . .	3.25	5.50	4.00
☐ 13034		IT'S DRIVIN' ME WILD/ SWEET SORROW	3.25	5.50	4.00
☐ 13050		TOWER OF TEARS/ PORTRAIT OF A FOOL	3.25	5.50	4.00
☐ 13072		COMFY 'N COZY/ A LITTLE PIECE OF MY HEART .	3.25	5.50	4.00
☐ 13089		THERE'S SOMETHING ON YOUR MIND/UNCHAINED MELODY . .	3.25	5.50	4.00
☐ 13112		THE PICKUP/ I HOPE, I THINK/I WISH	3.25	5.50	4.00
☐ 13149		GOT MY MOJO WORKING/ SHE AIN'T NO ANGEL	3.25	5.50	4.00
		CONWAY TWITTY—EPs			
☐ 14408	**MGM**	HEY MISS RUBY/TALK ON BY . . .	3.00	5.00	3.50
☐ 1623		IT'S ONLY MAKE BELIEVE	9.50	17.00	15.00
☐ 1640		CONWAY TWITTY SINGS	8.25	14.00	12.00
☐ 1641		CONWAY TWITTY SINGS	8.25	14.00	12.00
☐ 1642		CONWAY TWITTY SINGS	8.25	14.00	12.00
☐ 1678		SATURDAY NIGHT WITH CONWAY TWITTY	7.50	13.50	10.00
☐ 1679		SATURDAY NIGHT WITH CONWAY TWITTY	7.50	13.50	10.00
☐ 1680		SATURDAY NIGHT WITH CONWAY TWITTY	7.50	13.50	10.00
☐ 1071		LONELY BLUE BOY	7.50	13.50	10.00
		CONWAY TWITTY—ALBUMS			
☐ 3744 (M)	**MGM**	CONWAY TWITTY SINGS	14.00	34.00	30.00
☐ 3744 (S)		CONWAY TWITTY SINGS	23.00	50.00	45.00
☐ 3786 (M)		SATURDAY NIGHT WITH CONWAY TWITTY	12.00	34.00	25.00
☐ 3786 (S)		SATURDAY NIGHT WITH CONWAY TWITTY	18.00	39.00	35.00
☐ 3818 (M)		LONELY BLUE BOY	12.00	29.00	25.00
☐ 3818 (S)		LONELY BLUE BOY	18.00	39.00	35.00
☐ 3849 (M)		CONWAY TWITTY'S GREATEST HITS	12.00	29.00	25.00
☐ 3849 (S)		CONWAY TWITTY'S GREATEST HITS	18.00	39.00	35.00
☐ 3907 (M)		ROCK AND ROLL STORY	10.00	25.00	22.50
☐ 3907 (S)		ROCK AND ROLL STORY	14.00	34.00	30.00
☐ 3943 (M)		THE CONWAY TWITTY TOUCH . . .	8.00	21.00	18.00
☐ 3943 (S)		THE CONWAY TWITTY TOUCH . . .	12.00	29.00	25.00
☐ 4019 (M)		CONWAY TWITTY SINGS	8.00	21.00	18.00
☐ 4019 (S)		CONWAY TWITTY SINGS	12.00	29.00	25.00
☐ 4089 (M)		R & B '63	7.00	17.00	15.00
☐ 4089 (S)		R & B '63	9.00	25.00	22.50
☐ 4217 (M)		CONWAY TWITTY HITS THE ROAD	7.00	17.00	15.00
☐ 4217 (S)		CONWAY TWITTY HITS THE ROAD	9.00	21.00	18.00

U

			Current Price Range		P/Y AVG

UNDERDOGS
FEATURED: BOB SEGER

			Current Price Range		P/Y AVG
☐ 1001	**HIDEOUT**	THE MAN IN THE GLASS/ JUDY BE MINE	5.00	9.00	6.00
☐ 1004		DON'T PRETEND/LITTLE GIRL ...	5.00	9.00	6.00
☐ 1011		SUNRISE/ GET DOWN ON YOUR KNEES ...	5.00	9.00	6.00

UNIT FOUR PLUS TWO

☐ 9732	**LONDON**	SORROW AND PAIN/ WOMAN FROM LIBERIA	3.25	5.50	4.00
☐ 9751		CONCRETE AND CLAY/ WILD AS THE WIND	3.25	5.50	4.00
☐ 9751		CONCRETE AND CLAY/ WHEN I FALL IN LOVE	3.00	5.00	3.50
☐ 9761		YOU'VE NEVER BEEN IN LOVE LIKE THIS BEFORE/TELL SOMEBODY YOU KNOW	3.00	5.00	3.50
☐ 9790		STOP WASTING YOUR TIME/HARK	3.00	5.00	3.50

UNIT FOUR PLUS TWO—ALBUM

☐ 3427 (M)	**LONDON**	UNIT FOUR PLUS TWO	8.25	17.00	15.00
☐ 427 (S)		UNIT FOUR PLUS TWO	12.00	21.00	18.00

UNTOUCHABLES

☐ 128	**MADISON**	POOR BOY NEEDS A PREACHER/ NEW FAD	5.00	9.00	7.00
☐ 134		GOODNIGHT SWEETHEART GOODNIGHT/VICKIE LEE	4.50	7.50	6.00
☐ 139		SIXTY MINUTE MAN/ EVERYBODY'S LAUGHIN'	4.50	7.50	6.00
☐ 147		RAISIN' SUGAR CANE/ DO YOUR BEST	4.50	7.50	6.00
☐ 55335	**LIBERTY**	YOU'RE ON TOP/LOVELY DEE ...	4.50	750	6.00
☐ 55423		PAPA/MEDICINE MAN..........	3.75	6.00	4.50

GARY USHER
PRODUCER: BRIAN WILSON

☐ 5128	**CAPITOL**	THE BEETLE/JODY	5.50	11.00	9.00
☐ 5193		SACRAMENTO/ THAT'S THE WAY I FEEL	9.50	17.00	15.00
☐ 16518	**DOT**	THREE SURFER BOYS/ THE MILKY WAY	8.25	14.00	12.00

V

VAL-CHORDS

☐ 104	**GAMETIME**	YOU'RE LAUGHING AT ME/ CANDY STORE LOVE	8.50	18.00	16.00

RITCHIE VALENS
SEE: ARVEE ALLENS

☐ 4106	**DEL-FI**	COME ON, LET'S GO/FRAMED ...	5.00	9.00	7.00
☐ 4110		DONNA/LA BAMBA	3.75	6.00	4.50

			Current Price Range		P/Y AVG
☐ 4114		THAT'S MY LITTLE SUZIE/			
		IN A TURKISH TOWN	3.75	6.00	4.50
☐ 4117		LITTLE GIRL/			
		WE BELONG TOGETHER	4.50	7.50	6.00
☐ 4128		STAY BESIDE ME/			
		BIG BABY BLUES	4.50	7.50	6.00
☐ 4133		CRY, CRY, CRY/			
		PADDIWACK SONG	4.50	7.50	6.00
		RITCHIE VALENS—EPs			
☐ 101	*DEL-FI*	RITCHIE VALENS..............	16.00	30.00	19.00
☐ 111		RITCHIE VALENS..............	16.00	30.00	19.00
		RITCHIE VALENS—ALBUMS			
☐ 1201 (M)	*DEL-FI*	RITCHIE VALENS..............	19.00	50.00	45.00
☐ 1206 (M)		RITCHIE....................	23.00	55.00	50.00
☐ 1214 (M)		IN CONCERT AT			
		PACOIMA JR. HIGH	45.00	110.00	65.00
☐ 1225 (M)		HIS GREATEST HITS	12.00	29.00	25.00
☐ 1247 (M)		GREATEST HITS, VOL. II	22.00	55.00	50.00

FRANKIE VALLEY (VALLI)

☐ 1234	*CORONA*	MY MOTHER'S EYES/			
		THE LAUGH'S ON ME	100.00	195.00	180.00

FRANKY VALLEY AND THE TRAVELERS (VALLI)

☐ 70381	*MERCURY*	FORGIVE AND FORGET/			
		SOMEBODY ELSE TOOK			
		HER NAME	39.00	68.00	60.00

FRANKIE VALLE AND THE ROMANS (FOUR SEASONS)

☐ 3012	*CINDY*	COME SI BELLA/REAL	39.00	68.00	60.00

FRANKIE VALLY (VALLI)

☐ 30994	*DECCA*	PLEASE TAKE A CHANCE/			
		IT MAY BE WRONG	39.00	68.00	60.00

BOBBY VEE

☐ 1110	*SOMA*	SUZIE BABY/FLYIN' HIGH	21.00	34.00	30.00
☐ 55208	*LIBERTY*	SUZIE BABY/FLYIN' HIGH	5.50	11.00	9.00
☐ 55234		WHAT DO YOU WANT/			
		MY LOVE LOVES ME	5.00	9.00	7.00
☐ 55251		ONE LAST KISS/LAURIE	5.00	9.00	7.00
☐ 55270		DEVIL OR ANGEL/			
		SINCE I MET YOU BABY	3.50	6.00	4.00
☐ 55287		RUBBER BALL/EVERYDAY	3.50	6.00	4.00
☐ 55296		STAYIN' IN/			
		MORE THAN I CAN SAY	3.50	6.00	4.00
☐ 55325		HOW MANY TEARS/BABY FACE .	3.50	6.00	4.00
☐ 55354		TAKE GOOD CARE OF MY BABY/			
		BASHFUL BOB	3.50	6.00	4.00
☐ 55388		RUN TO HIM/			
		WALKIN' WITH MY ANGEL	3.50	6.00	4.00
☐ 55419		PLEASE DON'T ASK ABOUT			
		BARBARA/I CAN'T SAY			
		GOODBYE	3.50	6.00	4.00
☐ 55451		SHARING YOU/			
		IN MY BABY'S EYES	3.50	6.00	4.00
☐ 55479		PUNISH HER/SOMEDAY			
		(with the Crickets)	3.50	6.00	4.00
☐ 55517		CHRISTMAS VACATION/			
		A NOT SO MERRY CHRISTMAS .	4.00	7.00	4.85
☐ 55521		THE NIGHT HAS A THOUSAND			
		EYES/ANONYMOUS PHONE			
		CALL	3.00	5.00	3.65

DEL-FI, DF-4117, 45

CAPITOL, EAP 3-764

			Current Price Range		P/Y AVG
☐55530		CHARMS/BOBBY TOMORROW ...	3.00	5.00	3.65
☐55581		BE TRUE TO YOURSELF/			
		A LETTER FROM BETTY	3.00	5.00	3.65
☐55636		YESTERDAY AND YOU/			
		NEVER LOVE A ROBIN	3.00	5.00	3.65
☐55654		STRANGER IN YOUR ARMS/1963	3.00	5.00	3.65
☐55670		I'LL MAKE YOU MINE/			
		SHE'S SORRY	3.00	5.00	3.65
☐55700		HICKORY, DICK AND DOC/I WISH			
		YOU WERE MINE AGAIN	3.00	5.00	3.65
☐55726		WHERE IS SHE/			
		HOW TO MAKE A FAREWELL ..	3.00	5.00	3.65
☐55751		EV'RY LITTLE BIT HURTS/			
		PRETEND YOU DON'T SEE HER .	3.00	5.00	3.65
☐55761		CROSS MY HEART/			
		THIS IS THE END	3.00	5.00	3.65
☐55790		YOU WON'T FORGET ME/			
		KEEP ON TRYING	3.00	5.00	3.65
☐55828		RUN LIKE THE DEVIL/			
		TAKE A LOOK AROUND ME	3.00	5.00	3.65
☐55843		THE STORY OF MY LIFE/			
		HIGH COIN	3.00	5.00	3.65
☐55877		LOOK AT ME GIRL/BUTTERFLY ..	3.00	5.00	3.65
☐55877		LOOK AT ME GIRL/SAVE A LOVE .	3.00	5.00	3.65
☐55921		HERE TODAY/BEFORE YOU GO ...	3.00	5.00	3.65
☐55964		COME BACK WHEN YOU GROW			
		UP/SWAHILI SERENADE	3.00	5.00	3.50
☐55964		COME BACK WHEN YOU GROW			
		UP/THAT'S ALL IN THE PAST ..	3.00	5.00	3.65
☐56009		BEAUTIFUL PEOPLE/			
		I MAY BE GONE	3.00	5.00	3.65
☐56014		MAYBE JUST TODAY/			
		YOU'RE A BIG GIRL NOW	3.00	5.00	3.65
☐56033		MY GIRL-HEY GIRL/			
		JUST KEEP IT UP	3.00	5.00	3.65
☐56057		DO WHAT YOU GOTTA DO/			
		THANK YOU	3.00	5.00	3.65
☐56080		SOMEONE TO LOVE/THANK YOU .	3.00	5.00	3.65
☐56096		JENNY CAME TO ME/			
		SANTA CRUZ	3.00	5.00	3.65
☐56124		LET'S CALL IT A DAY GIRL/I'M			
		GONNA MAKE IT UP TO YOU ...	3.00	5.00	3.65
☐56149		ELECTIC TRAINS AND NOW/			
		IN AND OUT OF LOVE	3.00	5.00	3.65
☐56178		NO OBLIGATIONS/			
		WOMAN IN MY LIFE	3.00	5.00	3.65
☐56208		SWEET SWEETHEART/			
		ROCK 'N ROLL MUSIC AND YOU	3.00	5.00	3.65
		BOBBY VEE—EPs			
☐1006	*LIBERTY*	DEVIL OR ANGEL	9.50	17.00	15.00
☐1010		BOBBY VEE'S HITS	8.25	14.00	12.00
☐1013		BOBBY VEE	8.25	14.00	12.00
		BOBBY VEE—ALBUMS			
☐3165 (M)	*LIBERTY*	DEVIL OR ANGEL	14.00	34.00	30.00
☐7165 (S)		DEVIL OR ANGEL	19.00	50.00	45.00
☐3181 (M)		BOBBY VEE	12.00	29.00	25.00
☐7181 (S)		BOBBY VEE	17.00	39.00	35.00
☐3186 (M)		WITH STRINGS AND THINGS	9.00	25.00	22.50
☐7186 (S)		WITH STRINGS AND THINGS	14.00	34.00	30.00
☐3205 (M)		HITS OF THE ROCKIN' 50'S	8.00	21.00	18.00
☐7205 (S)		HITS OF THE ROCKIN' 50'S	12.00	29.00	25.00
☐3211 (M)		TAKE GOOD CARE OF MY BABY ..	8.00	21.00	18.00
☐7211 (S)		TAKE GOOD CARE OF MY BABY ..	12.00	29.00	25.00
☐3228 (M)		BOBBY VEE MEETS THE CRICKETS	8.00	21.00	18.00

			Current Price Range		P/Y AVG
☐ 7228 (S)		BOBBY VEE MEETS THE CRICKETS	12.00	29.00	25.00
☐ 3232 (M)		A BOBBY VEE RECORDING SESSION	7.00	17.00	15.00
☐ 7232 (S)		A BOBBY VEE RECORDING SESSION	9.00	25.00	22.50
☐ 3245 (M)		GOLDEN GREATS	7.00	17.00	15.00
☐ 7245 (S)		GOLDEN GREATS	9.00	25.00	22.50
☐ 3267 (M)		MERRY CHRISTMAS FROM BOBBY VEE	7.00	17.00	15.00
☐ 7267 (S)		MERRY CHRISTMAS FROM BOBBY VEE	9.00	25.00	22.50
☐ 3285 (M)		THE NIGHT HAS A THOUSAND EYES	7.00	17.00	15.00
☐ 7285 (S)		THE NIGHT HAS A THOUSAND EYES	9.00	25.00	22.50
☐ 3289 (M)		BOBBY VEE MEETS THE VENTURES	7.00	17.00	15.00
☐ 7289 (S)		BOBBY VEE MEETS THE VENTURES	9.00	25.00	22.50
☐ 3336 (M)		I REMEMBER BUDDY HOLLY	8.00	21.00	18.00
☐ 7336 (S)		I REMEMBER BUDDY HOLLY	12.00	29.00	25.00
☐ 3352 (M)		THE NEW SOUND FROM ENGLAND	7.00	17.00	15.00
☐ 7352 (S)		THE NEW SOUND FROM ENGLAND	8.00	25.00	22.50
☐ 3385 (M)		30 BIG HITS FROM THE '60s	7.00	17.00	15.00
☐ 7385 (S)		30 BIG HITS FROM THE '60s	9.00	25.00	22.50
☐ 3393 (M)		LIVE ON TOUR	7.00	17.00	15.00
☐ 7393 (S)		LIVE ON TOUR	8.00	21.00	18.00
☐ 3464 (M)		GOLDEN GREATS, VOL. II	7.00	17.00	15.00
☐ 7464 (S)		GOLDEN GREATS, VOL. II	8.00	21.00	18.00
☐ 3480 (M)		LOOK AT ME GIRL	7.00	17.00	15.00
☐ 7480 (S)		LOOK AT ME GIRL	7.00	17.00	15.00
☐ 3534 (M)		COME BACK WHEN YOU GROW UP	7.00	17.00	15.00
☐ 7534 (S)		COME BACK WHEN YOU GROW UP	6.00	15.00	13.50
☐ 7554 (S)		JUST TODAY	5.50	14.00	12.00
☐ 7592 (S)		DO WHAT YOU GOTTA DO	5.50	14.00	12.00
☐ 7612 (S)		GATES, GRILLES AND RAILINGS	5.50	14.00	12.00

VENTURES
SEE: MARKSMEN

☐ 100	**BLUE HORIZON**	THE REAL McCOY/ COOKIES AND COKE	5.50	11.00	9.00
☐ 101		WALK-DON'T RUN/HOME	8.25	14.00	12.00
☐ 25	**DOLTON**	WALK-DON'T RUN/HOME	3.00	5.00	3.65
☐ 28		PERFIDIA/NO TRESPASSING	3.00	5.00	3.65
☐ 32		RAM-BUNK-SHUSH/ LONELY HEART	3.00	5.00	3.65
☐ 41		LULLABY OF THE LEAVES/ GINCHY	2.75	4.50	3.25
☐ 44		(THEME FROM) SILVER CITY/ BLUER THAN BLUE	2.75	4.50	3.25
☐ 47		BLUE MOON/LADY OF SPAIN	2.75	4.50	3.25
☐ 50		YELLOW JACKET/GENESIS	2.75	4.50	3.25
☐ 55		INSTANT MASHED/MY BONNIE	2.75	4.50	3.25
☐ 60		LOLITA YA-YA/LUCILLE	2.75	4.50	3.25
☐ 67		THE 2,000 POUND BEE (PT. 1)/ (PT. 2)	2.75	4.50	3.25
☐ 68		SKIP TO M'LIMBO/ EL CUMBANCHERO	2.75	4.50	3.25
☐ 78		THE NINTH WAVE/ DAMAGED GOODS	2.75	4.50	3.25
☐ 85		THE CHASE/THE SAVAGE	2.75	4.50	3.25
☐ 91		JOURNEY TO THE STARS/ WALKIN' WITH PLUTO	2.75	4.50	3.25
☐ 94		FUGITIVE/SCRATCHIN'	2.75	4.50	3.25

			Current Price Range		P/Y AVG
☐96		WALK-DON'T RUN '64/			
		THE CRUEL SEA	2.75	4.50	3.25
☐300		SLAUGHTER ON TENTH AVENUE/			
		RAP CITY	2.75	4.50	3.25
☐303		DIAMOND HEAD/LONELY GIRL	2.75	4.50	3.25
☐306		PEDAL PUSHER/			
		THE SWINGIN' CREEPER	2.75	4.50	3.25
☐308		BIRD ROCKERS/			
		TEN SECONDS TO HEAVEN	2.75	4.50	3.25
☐311		LA BAMBA/GEMINI	2.75	4.50	3.25
☐312		SLEIGH RIDE/SNOW FLAKES	2.75	4.50	3.25
☐316		SECRET AGENT MAN/007-11	2.75	4.50	3.25
☐320		BLUE STAR/COMIN' HOME BABY . .	2.75	4.50	3.25
☐321		ARABESQUE/GINZA LIGHTS	2.75	4.50	3.25
☐323		GREEN HORNET THEME/			
		FUZZY AND WILD	2.75	4.50	3.25
☐325		WILD THING/PENETRATION	2.75	4.50	3.25
☐327		THEME FROM ''THE WILD			
		ANGELS''/KICKSTAND	2.75	4.50	3.25
		LIBERTY SINGLES ARE WORTH UP TO $1.75 MINT			
		VENTURES—EP			
☐503	*DOLTON*	WALK-DON'T RUN	5.50	11.00	9.00
		VENTURES—ALBUMS			
☐2003 (M)	*DOLTON*	WALK-DON'T RUN	8.00	21.00	18.00
☐8003 (S)		WALK-DON'T RUN	12.00	29.00	25.00
☐2004 (M)		THE VENTURES	8.00	21.00	18.00
☐8004 (S)		THE VENTURES	12.00	29.00	25.00
☐2006 (M)		ANOTHER SMASH	7.00	17.00	15.00
☐8006 (S)		ANOTHER SMASH	9.00	25.00	22.50
☐2008 (M)		THE COLORFUL VENTURES	7.00	17.00	15.00
☐8008 (S)		THE COLORFUL VENTURES	9.00	25.00	22.50
☐2010 (M)		TWIST WITH THE VENTURES	7.00	17.00	15.00
☐8010 (S)		TWIST WITH THE VENTURES	8.00	21.00	18.00
☐2010 (M)		DANCE! (second title)	6.00	15.00	13.50
☐8010 (S)		DANCE! (second title)	7.00	17.00	15.00
☐2014 (M)		THE VENTURES' TWIST PARTY,			
		VOL. II	7.00	17.00	15.00
☐8014 (S)		THE VENTURE'S TWIST PARTY,			
		VOL. II	8.00	21.00	18.00
☐2014 (M)		DANCE WITH THE VENTURES			
		(second title)	6.00	15.00	13.50
☐8014 (S)		DANCE WITH THE VENTURES			
		(second title)	7.00	17.00	15.00
☐2016 (M)		MASHED POTATOES AND GRAVY . .	7.00	17.00	15.00
☐8016 (S)		MASHED POTATOES AND GRAVY . .	8.00	21.00	18.00
☐2016 (M)		THE VENTURES' BEACH PARTY			
		(second title)	6.00	15.00	13.50
☐8016 (S)		THE VENTURES' BEACH PARTY			
		(second title)	7.00	17.00	15.00
☐2017 (M)		GOING TO THE VENTURES' DANCE			
		PARTY	7.00	17.00	15.00
☐8017 (S)		GOING TO THE VENTURES' DANCE			
		PARTY	8.00	21.00	18.00
☐2019 (M)		THE VENTURES PLAY TELSTAR			
		(THE LONELY BULL)	6.00	15.00	13.50
☐8019 (S)		THE VENTURES PLAY TELSTAR			
		(THE LONELY BULL)	7.00	17.00	15.00
☐2022 (M)		SURFING	6.00	15.00	13.50
☐8022 (S)		SURFING	7.00	17.00	15.00
☐2023 (M)		THE VENTURES PLAY THE			
		COUNTRY CLASSICS	6.00	15.00	13.50
☐8023 (S)		THE VENTURES PLAY THE			
		COUNTRY CLASSICS	7.00	17.00	15.00
☐2024 (M)		LET'S GO!	6.00	14.00	12.00

			Current Price Range		P/Y AVG
☐ 8024 (S)		LET'S GO!	7.00	17.00	15.00
☐ 2027 (M)		THE VENTURES IN SPACE	6.00	14.00	12.00
☐ 8027 (S)		THE VENTURES IN SPACE	7.00	17.00	15.00
☐ 2029 (M)		THE FABULOUS VENTURES	6.00	14.00	12.00
☐ 8029 (S)		THE FABULOUS VENTURES	7.00	17.00	15.00
☐ 2031 (M)		WALK, DON'T RUN, VOL. II	5.00	14.00	12.00
☐ 8031 (S)		WALK, DON'T RUN, VOL. II	6.00	15.00	13.50
☐ 2033 (M)		THE VENTURES KNOCK ME OUT	5.00	14.00	12.00
☐ 8033 (S)		THE VENTURES KNOCK ME OUT	6.00	15.00	13.50
☐ 2035 (M)		ON STAGE	5.00	12.00	10.00
☐ 8035 (S)		ON STAGE	6.00	15.00	13.50
☐ 2037 (M)		THE VENTURES A GO-GO	5.00	12.00	10.00
☐ 8037 (S)		THE VENTURES A GO-GO	6.00	15.00	13.50
☐ 2038 (M)		THE VENTURES' CHRISTMAS ALBUM	5.00	12.00	10.00
☐ 8038 (S)		THE VENTURES' CHRISTMAS ALBUM	6.00	15.00	13.50
☐ 2040 (M)		WHERE THE ACTION IS	5.00	12.00	10.00
☐ 8040 (S)		WHERE THE ACTION IS	6.00	14.00	12.00
☐ 2042 (M)		VENTURES	5.25	12.00	10.00
☐ 8042 (S)		VENTURES	5.25	14.00	12.00
☐ 2042 (M)		BATMAN THEME (second title)	5.25	12.50	8.50
☐ 8042 (S)		BATMAN THEME (second title)	5.25	12.50	8.50
☐ 2045 (M)		GO WITH THE VENTURES!	5.25	12.50	8.50
☐ 8045 (S)		GO WITH THE VENTURES!	5.25	12.50	8.50
☐ 2047 (M)		WILD THINGS!	5.25	12.50	8.50
☐ 8047 (S)		WILD THINGS!	5.25	12.50	8.50
☐ 2050 (M)		GUITAR FREAKOUT	5.25	12.50	8.50
☐ 8050 (S)		GUITAR FREAKOUT	5.25	12.50	8.50

VERDICTS

☐ 103	EAST COAST	MUMMY'S BALL/ MY LIFE'S DESIRE	5.75	12.00	10.00

VIDELS
SEE: TRADE WINDS

☐ 5004	JDS	MR. LONELY/I'LL FORGET YOU	4.00	7.00	4.85
☐ 5005		NOW THAT SUMMER IS HERE/ SHE'S NOT COMING HOME	4.00	7.00	4.85
☐ 361	KAPP	I'LL KEEP WAITING/ STREETS OF LOVE	3.50	6.00	4.35
☐ 495		A LETTER FROM ANNE/ THIS YEAR'S MISTER NEW	3.50	6.00	4.35
☐ 203	MEDIEVAL	BE MY GIRL/ A PLACE IN MY HEART	3.50	6.00	4.35
☐ 2000	RHODY	BE MY GIRL/ A PLACE IN MY HEART	3.50	6.00	4.35
☐ 117	MUSICNOTE	WE BELONG TOGETHER/ IT'S ALL OVER	3.50	6.00	4.35

GENE VINCENT
FEATURED: THE BLUE CAPS

☐ 3450	CAPITOL	BE-BOP-A-LULU/WOMAN LOVE	5.00	9.00	6.50
☐ 3530		RACE WITH THE DEVIL/ GONNA BACK UP BABY	6.00	12.00	8.50
☐ 3558		BLUEJEAN BOP/ WHO SLAPPED JOHN	5.50	10.00	7.00
☐ 3617		CRAZY LEGS/IMPORTANT WORDS	5.50	10.00	7.00
☐ 3678		FIVE DAYS, FIVE DAYS/ BI-BICKEY-BI-BO-BO-GO	5.50	10.00	7.00
☐ 3763		LOTTA LOVIN'/WEAR MY RING	5.50	10.00	7.00
☐ 3839		DANCE TO THE BOP/I GOT IT	5.00	9.00	6.00
☐ 3874		WALKIN' HOME FROM SCHOOL/ I GOT A BABY	5.00	9.00	6.00

			Current Price Range		P/Y AVG
☐ 3959		BABY BLUE/TRUE TO YOU	5.00	9.00	6.00
☐ 4010		ROCKY ROAD BLUES/			
		YES, I LOVE YOU BABY	5.00	9.00	6.00
☐ 4051		LITTLE LOVER/GIT IT	5.00	9.00	6.00
☐ 4105		BE BOP BOOGIE BABY/SAY MAMA.	5.00	9.00	6.00
☐ 4153		WHO'S PUSHIN' YOUR SWING?/			
		OVER THE RAINBOW	5.00	9.00	6.00
☐ 4237		RIGHT NOW/			
		THE NIGHT IS SO LONELY	5.00	9.00	6.00
☐ 4313		WILD CAT/RIGHT HERE ON EARTH.	5.00	9.00	6.00
☐ 4442		ANNA-ANNABELLE/			
		PISTOL PACKIN' MAMA	5.00	9.00	6.00
☐ 4525		IF YOU WANT MY LOVIN'/			
		MISTER LONELINESS	5.00	9.00	6.00
☐ 4665		LUCKY STAR/			
		BABY DON'T BELIEVE HIM	5.00	9.00	6.00
☐ 59337	*CHALLENGE*	BIRD DOGGIN'/			
		AIN'T THAT TOO MUCH	3.50	6.00	4.35
☐ 59347		I'VE GOT MY EYES ON YOU/			
		LONELY STREET	3.50	6.00	4.35
☐ 59365		BORN TO BE A ROLLING STONE/			
		HURTING FOR YOU BABY	3.50	6.00	4.35
☐ 100	*PLAYGROUND*	STORY OF THE ROCKERS/			
		PICKIN' POPPIES	25.00	45.00	27.00
☐ 6001	*FOREVER*	STORY OF THE ROCKERS/			
		PICKIN' POPPIES	4.00	7.00	4.50
☐ 514	*KAMA SUTRA*	SUNSHINE/GEESE	3.50	5.50	4.00
☐ 518		THE DAY THE WORLD TURNED			
		BLUE/HIGH ON LIFE	3.50	5.50	4.00
		GENE VINCENT—EPs			
☐ 1-764	*CAPITOL*	BLUEJEAN BOP	17.00	30.00	19.00
☐ 2-764		BLUEJEAN BOP	17.00	30.00	19.00
☐ 3-764		BLUEJEAN BOP	17.00	30.00	19.00
☐ 1-811		GENE VINCENT AND HIS			
		BLUE CAPS	17.00	30.00	19.00
☐ 2-811		GENE VINCENT AND HIS			
		BLUE CAPS	17.00	30.00	19.00
☐ 3-811		GENE VINCENT AND HIS			
		BLUE CAPS	17.00	30.00	19.00
☐ 1-970		GENE VINCENT ROCKS	17.00	30.00	19.00
☐ 2-970		GENE VINCENT ROCKS	17.00	30.00	19.00
☐ 3-970		GENE VINCENT ROCKS	17.00	30.00	19.00
☐ 985		HOT ROD GANG (soundtrack) ...	30.00	60.00	36.00
☐ 1-1059		A GENE VINCENT RECORD DATE .	17.00	30.00	19.00
☐ 2-1059		A GENE VINCENT RECORD DATE .	17.00	30.00	19.00
☐ 3-1059		A GENE VINCENT RECORD DATE .	17.00	30.00	19.00
		GENE VINCENT—ALBUMS			
☐ 764 (M)	*CAPITOL*	BLUEJEAN BOP	46.00	110.00	100.00
☐ 811 (M)		GENE VINCENT AND HIS			
		BLUE CAPS	35.00	80.00	75.00
☐ 970 (M)		GENE VINCENT ROCKS AND THE			
		BLUE CAPS ROLL	35.00	80.00	75.00
☐ 1059 (M)		A GENE VINCENT RECORD DATE .	35.00	80.00	75.00
☐ 1207 (M)		SOUNDS LIKE GENE VINCENT ...	24.00	55.00	50.00
☐ 1342 (M)		CRAZY TIMES	24.00	55.00	50.00
☐ 1342 (S)		CRAZY TIMES	35.00	80.00	75.00
☐ 102 (S)	*DANDELION*	I'M BACK AND I'M PROUD	10.00	20.00	12.00
☐ 2019 (S)	*KAMA SUTRA*	GENE VINCENT	10.00	20.00	12.00
☐ 2027 (S)		THE DAY THE WORLD TURNED			
		BLUE	10.00	20.00	12.00

BOBBY VINTON

☐ 50	*ALPINE*	YOU'LL NEVER FORGET/			
		FIRST IMPRESSION	6.00	12.00	8.00

			Current Price Range		P/Y AVG
☐59		THE SHIEK/A FRESHMAN AND A SOPHOMORE	6.00	12.00	8.00
☐121	**DIAMOND**	I LOVE YOU THE WAY YOU ARE/ YOU'RE MY GIRL	4.00	7.00	4.85
☐9417	**EPIC**	TORNADO/POSIN'	4.00	7.00	4.85
☐9440		CORRINA, CORRINA/ LITTLE LOVELY ONE	4.00	7.00	4.85
☐9469		WELL, I ASK YA/HIP-SWINGING, HIGH-STEPPING DRUM MAJORETTE	4.00	7.00	4.85
☐9509		ROSES ARE RED (MY LOVE)/ YOU AND I	3.00	5.00	3.65
☐9532		RAIN, RAIN, GO AWAY/ OVER AND OVER	3.00	5.00	3.65
☐9561		TROUBLE IS MY MIDDLE NAME/ LET'S KISS AND MAKE UP	3.00	5.00	3.65
☐9577		OVER THE MOUNTAIN (ACROSS THE SEA)/FADED PICTURES	3.00	5.00	3.65
☐9593		BLUE ON BLUE/ THOSE LITTLE THINGS	3.00	5.00	3.65
☐9614		BLUE VELVET/IS THERE A PLACE	3.00	5.00	3.65
☐9638		THERE! I'VE SAID IT AGAIN/ THE GIRL WITH THE BOW IN HER HAIR	3.00	5.00	3.65
☐9662		MY HEART BELONGS TO ONLY YOU/WARM AND TENDER	3.00	5.00	3.65
☐9687		TELL ME WHY/REMEMBERING	3.00	5.00	3.65
☐9705		CLINGING VINE/IMAGINATION IS A MAGIC DREAM	3.00	5.00	3.65
☐9730		MR. LONELY/ IT'S BETTER TO HAVE LOVED	3.00	5.00	3.65
☐9741		DEAREST SANTA/THE BELL THAT COULDN'T JINGLE	3.00	5.00	3.65
☐9768		L-O-N-E-L-Y/GRADUATION TEARS	3.00	5.00	3.65
☐9791		LONG, LONELY NIGHTS/SATIN	3.00	5.00	3.65
☐9814		THEME FROM ''HARLOWE''/ IF I SHOULD USE YOU LOVE	3.00	5.00	3.65
☐9846		WHAT COLOR (IS A MAN?)/ LOVE OR INFATUATION	3.00	5.00	3.65
☐9869		SATIN PILLOWS/CARELESS	3.00	5.00	3.65
☐9894		TEARS/GO AWAY, PAIN	3.00	5.00	3.65
☐10014		DUM-DE-DA/BLUE CLARINET	3.00	5.00	3.65
☐10048		PETTICOAT WHITE (SUMMER SKY BLUE)/ALL THE KING'S HORSES	3.00	5.00	3.65
☐10090		COMING HOME SOLDIER/DON'T LET MY MARY GO AROUND	3.00	5.00	3.65
☐10136		FOR HE'S A JOLLY GOOD FELLOW/ SWEET MARIA	3.00	5.00	3.65
☐10168		RED ROSES FOR MOM/ COLLEGE TOWN	3.00	5.00	3.65
☐10228		PLEASE LOVE ME FOREVER/ MISS AMERICA	3.00	5.00	3.65
☐10266		JUST AS MUCH AS EVER/ ANOTHER MEMORY	3.00	5.00	3.65
☐10305		TAKE GOOD CARE OF MY BABY/ STRANGE SENSATIONS	3.00	5.00	3.65
☐10350		HALFWAY TO PARADISE/ (MY LITTLE) CHRISTIE	3.00	5.00	3.65
☐10397		I LOVE HOW YOU LOVE ME/ LITTLE BAREFOOT BOY	3.00	5.00	3.65
☐10461		TO KNOW YOU IS TO LOVE YOU/ THE BEAT OF MY HEART	3.00	5.00	3.65

			Current Price Range		P/Y AVG
☐ 10485		THE DAYS OF SAND AND SHOVELS/SO MANY LONELY GIRLS	3.00	5.00	3.65
☐ 10554		FOR ALL WE KNOW/ WHERE IS LOVE?	3.00	5.00	3.65
☐ 10576		MY ELUSIVE DREAMS/ OVER AND OVER	3.00	5.00	3.65
☐ 10629		NO ARMS CAN EVER HOLD YOU/ I'VE GOT THAT LOVIN' FEELING (BACK AGAIN)	3.00	5.00	3.65

LATER EPIC SINGLES ARE WORTH UP TO $1.75 MINT

BOBBY VINTON—ALBUMS

☐ 3727 (M)	*EPIC*	DANCING AT THE HOP	8.00	21.00	18.00
☐ 579 (S)		DANCING AT THE HOP	12.00	29.00	25.00
☐ 3780 (M)		YOUNG MAN WITH A BIG BAND	8.00	21.00	18.00
☐ 597 (S)		YOUNG MAN WITH A BIG BAND	12.00	29.00	25.00
☐ 24020 (M)		ROSES ARE RED	7.00	17.00	15.00
☐ 26020 (S)		ROSES ARE RED	9.00	25.00	22.50
☐ 24035 (M)		BOBBY VINTON SINGS THE BIG ONES	7.00	17.00	15.00
☐ 26035 (S)		BOBBY VINTON SINGS THE BIG ONES	9.00	25.00	22.50
☐ 24068 (M)		BLUE VELVET	6.00	15.00	13.50
☐ 26068 (S)		BLUE VELVET	8.00	21.00	18.00
☐ 24081 (M)		THERE! I'VE SAID IT AGAIN	6.00	15.00	13.50
☐ 26081 (S)		THERE! I'VE SAID IT AGAIN	8.00	21.00	18.00
☐ 24098 (M)		BOBBY VINTON'S GREATEST HITS	5.50	14.00	12.00
☐ 26098 (S)		BOBBY VINTON'S GREATEST HITS	7.00	17.00	15.00
☐ 24113 (M)		TELL ME WHY	5.50	14.00	12.00
☐ 26113 (S)		TELL ME WHY	7.00	17.00	15.00
☐ 24122 (M)		A VERY MERRY CHRISTMAS	6.00	15.00	13.50
☐ 26122 (S)		A VERY MERRY CHRISTMAS	8.00	21.00	18.00
☐ 24136 (M)		MR. LONELY	6.00	12.00	10.00
☐ 26136 (S)		MR. LONELY	7.00	13.00	11.00
☐ 24182 (M)		SATIN PILLOWS	6.00	12.00	10.00
☐ 26182 (S)		SATIN PILLOWS	6.00	12.00	10.00
☐ 24187 (M)		MORE OF BOBBY'S GREATEST HITS	6.00	12.00	10.00
☐ 24187 (S)		MORE OF BOBBY'S GREATEST HITS	5.50	11.00	9.00

LATER EPIC ALBUMS ARE WORTH UP TO $6.00 MINT

VIRTUES

☐ 12475	*LYCO—TONE*	SO MUCH IN LOVE/GLORIA	6.00	11.00	8.00
☐ 501	*SURE*	GUITAR BOOGIE SHUFFLE/ GUITAR IN ORBIT	8.25	14.00	12.00
☐ 1733		GUITAR BOOGIE SHUFFLE TWIST/ GUITAR BOOGIE STOMP	3.75	6.00	4.50
☐ 1779		TELSTAR GUITAR/ JERSEY BOUNCE	3.25	5.50	4.00
☐ 324	*HUNT*	GUITAR BOOGIE SHUFFLE/ GUITAR IN ORBIT	3.00	5.00	3.50
☐ 327		SHUFFLIN' ALONG/FLIPPIN' IN	3.00	5.00	3.50
☐ 328		VIRTUES' BOOGIE WOOGIE/ PICKIN' THE STROLL	3.00	5.00	3.50
☐ 331		BLUES IN THE CELLAR/ VAYA CON DIOS	3.00	5.00	3.50
☐ 10071	*ABC-PARAMOUNT*	BLUES IN THE CELLAR/ VAYA CON DIOS	2.75	4.50	3.00
☐ 2505	*HIGHLAND*	BYE BYE BLUES/HAPPY GUITAR	2.75	4.50	3.00
☐ 603	*VIRNON*	GUITAR BOOGIE TWIST/ GUITAR SHIMMY	2.75	4.50	3.00

			Current Price Range		P/Y AVG
☐ 123	**WYNNE**	HIGHLAND GUITAR/			
		PICKIN' PLANKIN' BOOGIE	2.75	4.50	3.00
		VIRTUES—ALBUMS			
☐ 1061 (M)	**STRAND**	GUITAR BOOGIE SHUFFLE	9.00	25.00	22.50
☐ 1061 (S)		GUITAR BOOGIE SHUFFLE	12.00	27.00	25.00
☐ 111 (M)	**WYNNE**	GUITAR BOOGIE SHUGGLE	7.00	17.00	15.00

VISCOUNTS

☐ 123	**MADISON**	HARLEM NOCTURNE/DIG	3.25	5.50	4.00
☐ 129		CHUG-A-LUG/THE TOUCH	3.25	5.50	4.00
☐ 133		NIGHT TRAIN/SUMMERTIME	3.25	5.50	4.00
☐ 140		WABASH BLUES/SO SLOW......	3.25	5.50	4.00
☐ 940	**AMY**	HARLEM NOCTURNE/DIG	3.25	5.50	4.00
☐ 949		NIGHT TRAIN/WHEN THE SAINTS			
		GO MARCHING IN	3.25	5.50	4.00
		VISCOUNTS—ALBUMS			
☐ 1001 (M)	**MADISON**	THE VISCOUNTS	12.00	29.00	25.00
☐ 8008 (M)	**AMY**	HARLEM NOCTURNE	8.00	21.00	18.00
☐ 8008 (S)		HARLEM NOCTURNE	12.00	29.00	25.00

VISUALS

☐ 115	**POPLAR**	MAYBE YOU/SUBMARINE RACE .	9.50	23.00	20.00
☐ 117		BOY, GIRL & DREAM/MY JUANITA	9.50	23.00	20.00
☐ 121		PLEASE DON'T BE MAD AT ME/			
		BLUE ENOUGH	14.00	30.00	26.00

VITO AND THE SALUTATIONS

☐ 5002	**KRAN**	HEY, HEY BABY/YOUR WAY	17.00	29.00	25.00
☐ 583	**HERALD**	UNCHAINED MELODY/			
		HEY, HEY BABY	4.25	7.50	6.00
☐ 586		EENIE MEENIE/			
		EXTRAORDINARY GIRL	4.25	7.50	6.00
☐ 5009	**RAYNA**	GLORIA/			
		LET'S UNTWIST THE TWIST ...	5.00	9.00	7.00
☐ 1008	**WELLS**	CAN I DEPEND ON YOU?/			
		LIVERPOOL BOUND	4.50	7.50	6.00
☐ 1010		DON'T COUNT ON ME/DAY-O	4.50	7.50	6.00
☐ 5106	**RUST**	CAN I DEPEND ON YOU/			
		HELLO DOLLY	3.75	6.00	4.50
☐ 60020	**BOOM**	BRING BACK YESTERDAY/			
		I WANT YOU TO BE MY BABY ..	3.75	6.00	4.50
☐ 1320	**REGINA**	GIRLS I KNOW/GET A JOB	3.75	6.00	4.50
☐ 1001	**RED BOY**	SO WONDERFUL (MY LOVE)/			
		I'D BEST BE GOING	4.50	7.50	6.00
☐ 103	**SANDBAG**	SO WONDERFUL (MY LOVE)/			
		I'D BEST BE GOING	3.75	6.00	4.50
☐ 25079	**APT**	WALKIN'/HIGH NOON	3.25	5.50	4.00
☐ 104	**CRYSTAL BALL**	UNCHAINED MELODY/SO MUCH .	3.00	5.00	3.50

VOGUES

☐ 15798	**DOT**	LOVE'S A FUNNY LITTLE GAME/			
		WHICH WITCH DOCTOR	3.25	5.50	4.00
☐ 15859		FALLING STAR/TRY, BABY, TRY .	3.25	5.50	4.00
☐ 1029	**ASTRA**	YOU'RE THE ONE/			
		GOODNIGHT MY LOVE	12.00	24.00	20.00
☐ 229	**BLUE STAR**	YOU'RE THE ONE/SOME WORDS .	8.25	14.00	12.00
☐ 229	**CO & CE**	YOU'RE THE ONE/SOME WORDS .	3.00	5.00	3.25
☐ 232		FIVE O'CLOCK WORLD/			
		NOTHING TO OFFER YOU	3.00	5.00	3.25
☐ 234		MAGIC TOWN/HUMPTY DUMPTY	3.00	5.00	3.25
☐ 238		THE LAND OF MILK AND HONEY/			
		TRUE LOVERS	3.00	5.00	3.25

			Current Price Range		P/Y AVG
☐240		PLEASE, MR. SUN/ DON'T BLAME THE RAIN	3.00	5.00	3.25
☐242		THAT'S THE TUNE/ MIDNIGHT DREAMS	3.00	5.00	3.25
☐244		SUMMER AFTERNOON/ TAKE A CHANCE ON ME BABY .	3.00	5.00	3.25
☐246		LOVERS OF THE WORLD, UNITE/ BRIGHTER DAYS	3.00	5.00	3.25
☐13813	*MGM*	LOVERS OF THE WORLD, UNITE/ BRIGHTER DAYS	3.00	5.00	3.25

REPRISE SINGLES ARE WORTH UP TO $2.25 MINT

VOGUES—ALBUMS

☐1228 (M)	*CO & CE*	MEET THE VOGUES	6.00	15.00	13.50
☐1228 (S)		MEET THE VOGUES	7.00	17.00	15.00
☐1229 (M)		YOU'RE THE ONE.............	5.00	14.00	12.00
☐1229 (S)		YOU'RE THE ONE.............	6.00	15.00	13.50
☐1230 (M)		FIVE O'CLOCK WORLD.........	5.00	12.00	10.00
☐1230 (S)		FIVE O'CLOCK WORLD.........	5.00	14.00	12.00

W

WAILERS

☐518	*GOLDEN CREST*	TALL COOL ONE/ROAD RUNNER (1959-photo on label)	3.75	6.00	4.50
☐518		TALL COOL ONE/ROAD RUNNER (1964-plain label)............	3.00	5.00	3.50
☐526		MAU MAU/DIRTY ROBBER	2.75	4.50	3.00
☐532		WAILIN'/SHANGHIED	2.75	4.50	3.00
☐545		SCRATCHIN'/LUCILLE	2.75	4.50	3.00
☐591		BEAT GUITAR/MAU MAU	2.75	4.50	3.00
☐6	*ETIQUETTE*	WE'RE GOIN' SURFIN'/ SHAKEDOWN	2.75	4.50	3.00
☐21		OUT OF OUR TREE/I GOT ME	2.75	4.50	3.00
☐66045	*IMPERIAL*	MASHY/ON THE ROCKS	2.75	4.50	3.00

WAILERS—ALBUMS

☐3075 (M)	*GOLDEN CREST*	THE FABULOUS WAILERS	12.00	29.00	25.00
☐1	*ETIQUETTE*	THE FABULOUS WAILERS AT THE CASTLE	10.00	25.00	22.50
☐22		WAILERS AND COMPANY	8.00	21.00	18.00
☐26		OUT OF OUR TREE	8.00	21.00	18.00

WALKER BROTHERS
SEE: NEWPORTERS

☐1952	*SMASH*	PRETTY GIRLS EVERYWHERE/ DOIN' THE JERK	3.25	5.50	4.00
☐1976		SEVENTH DAWN/LOVE HER	3.25	5.50	4.00
☐2000		MAKE IT EASY ON YOURSELF/ DO THE JERK	3.25	5.50	4.00
☐2009		MAKE IT EASY ON YOURSELF/ BUT I DO	3.00	5.00	3.65
☐2016		MY SHIP IS COMIN' IN/ YOU'RE ALL AROUND ME	3.00	5.00	3.65
☐2032		THE SUN AIN'T GONNA SHINE (ANYMORE)/AFTER THE LIGHTS GO OUT	3.00	5.00	3.65
☐2048		YOU DON'T HAVE TO TELL ME BABY/THE YOUNG MAN CRIED	3.00	5.00	3.65

			Current Price Range		P/Y AVG
☐ 2063		ANOTHER TEAR FALLS/SADDEST NIGHT IN THE WORLD	3.00	5.00	3.65

WALKER BROTHERS—ALBUMS

☐ 27076 (M)	*SMASH*	INTRODUCING THE WALKER BROTHERS	7.00	17.00	15.00
☐ 67076 (S)		INTRODUCING THE WALKER BROTHERS	8.00	21.00	18.00
☐ 27082 (M)		THE SUN AIN'T GONNA SHINE ANYMORE	7.00	17.00	15.00
☐ 67082 (S)		THE SUN AIN'T GONNA SHINE ANYMORE	8.00	21.00	18.00

BILLY WARD AND HIS DOMINOES

☐ 29933	*DECCA*	ST. THERESE OF THE ROSES/ HOME IS WHERE YOU HANG YOUR HEART	4.50	8.00	6.00
☐ 30043		WILL YOU REMEMBER/COME ON, SNAKE, LET'S CRAWL	5.00	9.00	7.00
☐ 30149		EVERMORE/HALF A LOVE.	5.00	9.00	7.00
☐ 30199		'TIL KINGDOM COME/ ROCK PLYMOUTH ROCK	5.00	9.00	7.00
☐ 30420		TO EACH HIS OWN/I DON'T STAND A GHOST OF A CHANCE WITH YOU	4.50	7.50	6.00
☐ 30514		SEPTEMBER SONG/WHEN THE SAINTS GO MARCHING IN	4.50	7.50	6.00
☐ 55071	*LIBERTY*	STAR DUST/LUCINDA	3.50	6.00	4.35
☐ 55099		DEEP PURPLE/DO IT AGAIN	3.50	6.00	4.35
☐ 55111		SOMEONE GREATER THAN I/ MY PROUDEST POSSESSION . .	3.50	6.00	4.35
☐ 55126		SWEETER AS THE YEARS GO BY/ SOLITUDE	3.50	6.00	4.35
☐ 55136		JENNIE LEE/ MUSIC, MAESTRO, PLEASE . . .	3.50	6.00	4.35
☐ 55181		PLEASE DON'T SAY NO/ BEHAVE, HULA GIRL	3.50	6.00	4.35
☐ K-12063	*KING*	O HOLY NIGHT/WHAT ARE YOU DOING NEW YEAR'S EVE	3.50	6.00	4.35
☐ 10,128	**ABC- PARAMOUNT**	YOU'RE MINE/ THE WORLD IS WAITING FOR THE SUNRISE	3.50	6.00	4.35

BILLY WARD AND HIS DOMINOES—EPs

☐ 2549	*DECCA*	BILLY WARD AND THE DOMINOES	12.00	21.00	18.00
☐ 1-3056	*LIBERTY*	SEA OF GLASS.	6.00	12.00	8.00
☐ 2-3056		SEA OF GLASS.	6.00	12.00	8.00
☐ 3-3056		SEA OF GLASS.	6.00	12.00	8.00
☐ 1-2083		YOURS FOREVER	6.00	12.00	8.00
☐ 2-2083		YOURS FOREVER	6.00	12.00	8.00
☐ 3-3083		YOURS FOREVER	6.00	12.00	8.00

BILLY WARD AND HIS DOMINOES—ALBUMS

☐ 8621 (M)	*DECCA*	BILLY WARD AND HIS DOMINOES	40.00	98.00	90.00
☐ 3056 (M)	*LIBERTY*	SEA OF GLASS.	12.00	29.00	25.00
☐ 3083 (M)		YOURS FOREVER	10.00	25.00	22.50
☐ 3113 (M)		PAGAN LOVE SONG	8.00	21.00	18.00
☐ 7113 (S)		PAGAN LOVE SONG	12.00	29.00	25.00

DALE WARD
SEE: CRESCENDOS

☐ 16520	*DOT*	LETTER FROM SHERRY/OH JULIE	3.00	5.00	3.50
☐ 16590		CRYING FOR LAURA/ I'VE GOT A GIRL FRIEND	2.75	4.50	3.00
☐ 16632		I'LL NEVER LOVE AGAIN/ YOUNG LOVERS AFTER MIDNIGHT	2.75	4.50	3.00

			Current Price Range		P/Y AVG
☐ 16672		ONE LAST KISS, CHERIE/			
		THE FORTUNE	2.75	4.50	3.00
☐ 118	**BOYD**	BIG DALE TWIST/			
		HERE'S YOUR HAT	2.75	4.50	3.00
☐ 150		SHAKE, RATTLE AND ROLL/			
		YOU GOTTA LET ME KNOW	3.00	5.00	3.50
☐ 152		LIVING ON COAL/I TRIED	2.75	4.50	3.00

WALTER WARD AND THE CHALLENGERS (OLYMPICS)

☐ 1002	**MELATONE**	I CAN TELL/THE MAMBO BEAT . .	26.00	46.00	42.00

DIONNE WARWICK

☐ 1239	**SCEPTER**	DON'T MAKE ME OVER	3.50	6.50	4.75
☐ 1253		PLEASE MAKE HIM LOVE ME/			
		MAKE THE MUSIC PLAY	3.50	6.50	4.75
☐ 1247		THIS EMPTY PLACE/			
		WISHIN' & HOPIN'	3.50	6.50	4.75
☐ 1274		ANY OLD TIME OF DAY/			
		WALK ON BY	3.50	6.50	4.75
☐ 1282		A HOUSE IS NOT A HOME/YOU'LL			
		NEVER GET TO HEAVEN	3.25	6.00	4.50
☐ 1294		YOU CAN HAVE HIM/			
		IS THERE ANOTHER WAY	3.25	6.00	4.50
☐ 1298		DON'T SAY I DIDN'T TELL YOU SO/			
		WHO CAN I TURN TO	3.25	6.00	4.50

AFTER THIS SERIES OF RECORDINGS, SCEPTER CHANGED ITS NUMBERING SYSTEM TO 5-DIGIT INSTEAD OF 4-DIGIT SERIAL NUMBERS. THIS MAKES IT APPEAR THAT A VAST LENGTH OF TIME ELAPSED BETWEEN THE DISCS, BUT ACTUALLY IT DID NOT

THOMAS WAYNE

☐ 109	**FERNWOOD**	TRAGEDY/SATURDAY DATE	3.50	6.00	4.35
☐ 111		ETERNALLY/			
		SCANDALIZING MY NAME	3.50	6.00	4.35
☐ 113		GONNA BE WAITIN'/			
		JUST BEYOND	3.50	6.00	4.35
☐ 122		THE GIRL NEXT DOOR/			
		BECAUSE OF YOU	3.50	6.00	4.35
☐ 71454	**MERCURY**	YOU'RE THE ONE THAT DONE IT/			
		THIS TIME	15.00	24.00	20.00

WEBS
FEATURED: BOBBY GOLDSBORO

☐ 9004	**LITE**	BLUE SKIES/			
		LOST (CRICKET IN MY EAR) . . .	5.00	9.00	7.00

MARY WELLS

☐ 1003	**MOTOWN**	BYE BYE BABY/			
		PLEASE FORGIVE ME	4.50	7.50	6.00
☐ 1011		I DON'T WANT TO TAKE A			
		CHANCE/I'M SO SORRY	3.75	6.00	4.50
☐ 1016		COME TO ME/STRANGE LOVE . . .	4.50	7.50	6.00
☐ 1024		THE ONE WHO REALLY LOVES			
		YOU/I'M GONNA STAY	3.25	5.50	4.00
☐ 1032		YOU BEAT ME TO THE PUNCH/			
		OLD LOVE	3.25	5.50	4.00
☐ 1035		TWO LOVERS/OPERATOR	3.25	5.50	4.00
☐ 1039		LAUGHING BOY/TWO WRONGS			
		DON'T MAKE A RIGHT	3.25	5.50	4.00
☐ 1042		YOUR OLD STANDBY/WHAT LOVE			
		HAS JOINED TOGETHER	3.25	5.50	4.00
☐ 1048		YOU LOST THE SWEETEST BOY/			
		WHAT'S EASY FOR TWO IS			
		HARD FOR ONE	3.25	5.50	4.00

			Current Price Range		P/Y AVG
☐ 1056		MY GUY/OH LITTLE BOY (WHAT DID YOU DO TO ME)	3.25	5.50	4.00
☐ 1057		ONCE UPON A TIME/WHAT'S THE MATTER WITH YOU BABY (with Marvin Gaye)	3.25	5.50	4.00
		MARY WELLS—ALBUMS			
☐ 600 (M)	*MOTOWN*	BYE BYE BABY	14.00	34.00	30.00
☐ 605 (M)		ONE WHO REALLY LOVES YOU . . .	9.00	25.00	22.50
☐ 607 (M)		TWO LOVERS	8.00	21.00	18.00
☐ 607 (S)		TWO LOVERS	12.00	29.00	25.00
☐ 611 (M)		LIVE ON STAGE	7.00	17.00	15.00
☐ 611 (S)		LIVE ON STAGE	9.00	25.00	22.50
☐ 616 (M)		MARY WELLS GREATEST HITS . .	7.00	17.00	15.00
☐ 616 (S)		MERY WELLS GREATEST HITS . . .	9.00	25.00	22.50
☐ 617 (M)		MARY WELLS SINGS ''MY GUY''	7.00	17.00	15.00
☐ 617 (S)		MARY WELLS SINGS ''MY GUY''	8.00	21.00	18.00
☐ 653 (M)		VINTAGE STOCK	6.00	15.00	13.50
☐ 653 (S)		VINTAGE STOCK	7.00	17.00	15.00

WHEELERS

☐ 107	*CENCO*	ONCE I HAD A GIRL/ SHINE 'EM ON	12.00	25.00	22.00

WHIRLWINDS

☐ 40139	*PHILLIPS*	AFTER THE PARTY/HEARTBEAT (DJ copy)	13.00	34.00	30.00
☐		AFTER THE PARTY/HEARTBEAT (commercial copy)	9.00	21.00	17.00
☐ 2052	*GUYDEN*	THE MOUNTAIN/ANGEL LOVE . . .	4.50	11.00	9.00

IAN WHITCOMB

☐ 120	*TOWER*	THIS SPORTING LIFE/FIZZ	3.50	6.00	4.35
☐ 134		YOU TURN ME ON/ POOR BUT HONEST	3.25	5.50	4.00
☐ 155		N-E-R-V-O-U-S/THE END	3.25	5.50	4.00
☐ 170		18 WHITCOMB STREET/FIZZ	3.25	5.50	4.00
☐ 189		BE MY BABY/ NO TEARS FOR JOHNNY	3.25	5.50	4.00
☐ 192		HIGH BLOOD PRESSURE/ GOOD HARD ROCK	3.25	5.50	4.00
☐ 251		YOU WON'T SEE ME/PLEASE DON'T LEAVE ME ON THE SHELF	3.25	5.50	4.00
☐ 274		WHERE DID ROBINSON CRUSOE GO WITH FRIDAY ON SATURDY NIGHT/POOR LITTLE BIRD	3.25	5.50	4.00
		IAN WHITCOMB—ALBUMS			
☐ 5004 (M)	*TOWER*	YOU TURN ME ON	7.00	17.00	15.00
☐ 5004 (S)		YOU TURN ME ON	9.00	25.00	22.50
☐ 5042 (M)		IAN WHITCOMB'S MOD, MOD MUSIC HALL	9.00	17.00	15.00
☐ 5042 (S)		IAN WHITCOMB'S MOD, MOD MUSIC HALL	8.00	21.00	18.00
☐ 5071 (S)		YELLOW UNDERGROUND	7.00	17.00	15.00
☐ 5100 (S)		ROCK ME SOME ROCK	8.00	21.00	18.00

WHO

FEATURED: ROGER DATRY, PETER TOWNSEND, KEITH MOON
SEE: HIGH NUMBERS, ROGER DALTRY

☐ 31725	*DECCA*	I CAN'T EXPLAIN/ BALD HEADED WOMAN	4.50	7.50	6.00
☐ 31801		ANYWAY, ANYWHERE, ANYHOW/ DADDY ROLLING STONE	5.00	9.00	7.00
☐ 31801		ANYWAY, ANYWHERE, ANYHOW/ ANYTIME YOU WANT ME	4.50	7.50	6.00

			Current Price Range		P/Y AVG
☐ 31877		MY GENERATION/ OUT IN THE STREET	3.25	5.50	4.00
☐ 31988		THE KIDS ARE ALRIGHT/ A LEGAL MATTER	3.75	6.00	4.50
☐ 32058		I'M A BOY/IN THE CITY	3.75	6.00	4.50
☐ 32114		HAPPY JACK/WHISKEY MAN	2.75	4.50	3.00
☐ 32156		PICTURES OF LILY/ DOCTOR, DOCTOR	3.00	5.00	3.65
☐ 32206		I CAN SEE FOR MILES/ MARY-ANNE WITH THE SHAKEY HANDS	3.00	5.00	3.65
☐ 32288		CALL ME LIGHTNING/ DR. JEKYLL AND MR. HYDE ...	3.00	5.00	3.65
☐ 32362		MAGIC BUS/SOMEONE'S CRYING	3.00	5.00	3.65
☐ 32465		PINBALL WIZARD/DOGS, (PT. 1) .	3.00	5.00	3.65
☐ 32519		I'M FREE/ WE'RE NOT GONNA TAKE IT ...	3.00	5.00	3.65
☐ 32670		THE SEEKER/HERE FOR MORE ...	3.00	5.00	3.65
☐ 32708		SUMMERTIME BLUES/ HEAVEN AND HELL	2.75	4.50	3.00
☐ 32729		SEE ME, FEEL ME/ OVERTURE FROM TOMMY	2.75	4.50	3.00
☐ 32737		SUBSTITUTE/YOUNG MAN BLUES.	3.25	5.50	4.00
☐ 32856		WON'T GET FOOLED AGAIN/ I DON'T EVEN KNOW MYSELF .	2.75	4.50	3.00
☐ 32888		BEHIND BLUE EYES/MY WIFE ...	2.75	4.50	3.00
☐ 32983		RELAY/WASPMAN	2.75	4.50	3.00

MCA SINGLES ARE WORTH UP TO $2.25 MINT

WHO—ALBUMS

☐ 4664 (M)	DECCA	THE WHO SINGS "MY GENERATION"	8.00	21.00	18.00
☐ 74664 (S)		THE WHO SINGS "MY GENERATION"	12.00	29.00	25.00
☐ 4892 (M)		HAPPY JACK	8.00	21.00	18.00
☐ 74892 (S)		HAPPY JACK	9.00	25.00	22.50
☐ 4950 (M)		THE WHO SELL OUT	7.00	17.00	15.00
☐ 74950 (S)		THE WHO SELL OUT	8.00	21.00	18.00
☐ 75064 (S)		MAGIC BUS	6.00	15.00	13.50
☐ 79175 (S)		LIVE AT LEEDS	6.00	15.00	13.50
☐ 79182 (S)		WHO'S NEXT	6.00	15.00	13.50
☐ 79184 (S)		MEATY, BEATY, BIG & BOUNCY (greatest hits)	6.00	15.00	13.50
☐ 7205 (S)		TOMMY	6.00	15.00	13.50

WHYTE BOOTS

☐ 40422	PHILLIPS	LET NO ONE/NIGHTMARE	14.00	34.00	29.00

ANN WILSON AND THE DAYBREAKS
SEE: HEART

☐ 1311	TOPAZ	STANDIN' WATCHIN' YOU/ WONDER HOW I MANAGED	5.00	9.00	7.00
☐ 1312		THROUGH EYES AND GLASS/ I'M GONNA DRINK MY HURT AWAY	5.00	9.00	7.00

BRIAN WILSON
SEE: BEACH BOYS

☐ 5610	CAPITOL	CAROLINE, NO/ SUMMER MEANS NEW LOVE ..	3.25	5.50	4.00

			Current Price Range		P/Y AVG

JACKIE WILSON

☐55024	**BRUNSWICK**	REET PETITE/BY THE LIGHT OF THE SILVERY MOON	5.00	9.00	6.00
☐55052		TO BE LOVED/ COME BACK TO ME	4.00	7.00	4.85
☐55070		AS LONG AS I LIVE/ I'M WANDERIN'	4.00	7.00	4.85
☐55086		WE HAVE LOVE/ SINGING A SONG	3.50	6.00	4.35
☐55105		LONELY TEARDROPS/IN THE BLUE OF THE EVENING	3.50	6.00	4.35
☐55121		THAT'S WHY/LOVE IS ALL	3.50	6.00	4.35
☐55136		I'LL BE SATISFIED/ASK	3.50	6.00	4.35
☐55149		YOU BETTER KNOW IT/ NEVER GO AWAY	3.25	5.50	4.00
☐55165		TALK THAT TALK/ ONLY YOU AND ONLY ME	3.25	5.50	4.00
☐55166		NIGHT/DOGGIN' AROUND	3.25	5.20	4.00
☐55167		ALL MY LOVE/A WOMAN, A LOVER, A FRIEND	3.25	5.50	4.00
☐55170		ALONE AT LAST/ AM I THE MAN?	3.25	5.50	4.00
☐55201		MY EMPTY ARMS/ TEAR OF THE YEAR	3.25	5.50	4.00
☐55208		PLEASE TELL ME WHY/ YOUR ONE AND ONLY LOVE	3.00	5.00	3.65
☐55216		I'M COMING ON BACK TO YOU/ LONELY LIFE	3.00	5.00	3.65
☐55219		YEARS FROM NOW/YOU DON'T KNOW WHAT IT MEANS	3.00	5.00	3.65
☐55220		THE WAY I AM/MY HEART BELONGS TO ONLY YOU	3.00	5.00	3.65
☐55221		THE GREATEST HURT/ THERE'LL BE NO NEXT TIME	3.00	5.00	3.65
☐55225		HEARTS/SING	3.00	5.00	3.65
☐55229		I JUST CAN'T HELP IT/ MY TALE OF WOE	3.00	5.00	3.65
☐55233		FOREVER AND A DAY/ BABY THAT'S ALL	3.00	5.00	3.65
☐55236		WHAT AM I GONNA DO WITHOUT YOU?/A GIRL NAMED TAMIKO	3.50	5.50	4.00
☐55239		BABY WORKOUT/ I'M GOING CRAZY	3.00	5.00	3.65
☐55243		SHAKE A HAND/SAY I DO	3.00	5.00	3.65
☐55246		SHAKE! SHAKE! SHAKE!/ HE'S A FOOL	2.75	4.50	3.25
☐55250		BABY GET IT/THE NEW BREED	2.75	4.50	3.25
☐55254		O HOLY NIGHT/SILENT NIGHT	2.75	4.50	3.25
☐55260		I'M TRAVELIN' ON/ HAUNTED HOUSE	2.75	4.50	3.25
☐55263		CALL HER UP/KICKAPOO	2.75	4.50	3.25
☐55266		BIG BOSS LINE/BE MY GIRL	2.75	4.50	3.25
☐55269		SQUEEZE HER-TEASE HER/ GIVE ME BACK MY HEART	2.75	4.50	3.25
☐55273		SHE'S ALL RIGHT/WATCH OUT	2.75	4.50	3.25
☐55277		DANNY BOY/SOUL TIME	2.75	4.50	3.25
☐55280		NO PITY (IN THE NAKED CITY/ I'M SO LONELY	2.75	4.50	3.25
☐55283		I BELIEVE I'LL LOVE ON/ LONELY TEARDROPS	2.75	4.50	3.25
☐55287		THINK TWICE/PLEASE DON'T HURT ME (with LaVern Baker)	2.75	4.50	3.25
☐55289		I'VE GOT TO GET BACK/3 DAYS, 1 HOUR, 30 MINUTES	2.75	4.50	3.25

			Current Price Range		P/Y AVG
☐55290		BRAND NEW THING/ SOUL GALORE	2.75	4.50	3.25
☐55294		BE MY LOVE/I BELIEVE	2.75	4.50	3.25
☐55300		WHISPERS/ THE FAIREST OF THEM ALL . . .	2.75	4.50	3.25
☐55309		I DON'T WANT TO LOSE YOU/ JUST BE SINCERE	2.75	4.50	3.25
☐55321		I'VE LOST YOU/ THOSE HEARTACHES	2.75	4.50	3.25
☐55336		(YOUR LOVE KEEPS LIFTING ME) HIGHER AND HIGHER/ I'M THE ONE TO DO IT	2.75	4.50	3.25
☐55345		SINCE YOU SHOWED ME HOW TO BE HAPPY/ THE WHO WHO SONG	2.75	4.50	3.25
☐55365		FOR YOUR PRECIOUS LOVE/ UPTIGHT (with Count Basie)	2.75	4.50	3.25
☐55373		CHAIN GANG/FUNKY BROADWAY (with Count Basie)	2.75	4.50	3.25
☐55381		I GET THE SWEETEST FEELING/ NOTHING BUT HEARTACHES . .	2.75	4.50	3.25
☐55392		FOR ONCE IN MY LIFE/YOU BROUGHT ABOUT A CHANGE IN ME	2.75	4.50	3.25
☐55402		I STILL LOVE YOU/ HUM DE DUM DE DO	2.75	4.50	5.25
☐55418		HELPLESS/DO IT THE RIGHT WAY	2.75	4.50	3.25
☐55423		WITH THESE HANDS/WHY DON'T YOU (DO YOUR THING)	2.75	4.50	3.25
☐55435		LET THIS BE A LETTER (TO MY BABY)/DIDN'T I	2.75	4.50	3.25
☐55443		THIS LOVE IS REAL/ LOVE UPRISING	2.75	4.50	3.25
☐55449		SAY YOU WILL/THIS GUY'S IN LOVE WITH YOU	2.75	4.50	3.25
☐55461		LOVE IS FUNNY THAT WAY/ TRY IT AGAIN	2.75	4.50	3.25
☐55467		YOU GOT ME WALKING/ THE FOUNTAIN	2.75	4.50	3.25
☐55475		THE GIRL TURNED ME ON/ FOREVER AND A DAY	2.75	4.50	3.25
☐55480		YOU LEFT THE FIRE BURNING/ WHAT A LOVELY WAY	2.75	4.50	3.25
☐55490		BEAUTIFUL DAY/WHAT' CHA GONNA DO ABOUT LOVE	2.75	4.50	3.25
☐55499		NO MORE GOODBYES/ SING A LITTLE SONG	2.75	4.50	3.25
☐55504		IT'S ALL OVER/SHAKE A LEG . . .	2.75	4.50	3.25
☐55536		NOBODY BUT YOU/ I'VE LEARNED ABOUT LIFE	2.50	4.00	2.50
		JACKIE WILSON—EPs			
☐71040	**BRUNSWICK**	THE VERSATILE JACKIE WILSON .	8.25	14.00	12.00
☐71042		JUMPIN' JACK	7.00	13.00	11.00
☐71045		THAT'S WHY	7.00	13.00	11.00
☐71046		TALK THAT TALK	7.00	13.00	11.00
☐71047		MR. EXCITEMENT	7.00	13.00	11.00
☐71048		JACKIE WILSON	5.50	11.00	9.00
☐71049		JACKIE WILSON	5.50	11.00	9.00
		JACKIE WILSON—ALBUMS			
☐54042 (M)	**BRUNSWICK**	HE'S SO FINE	19.00	50.00	45.00
☐54045 (M)		LONELY TEARDROPS	17.00	39.00	35.00
☐54050 (M)		SO MUCH	12.00	29.00	25.00
☐754050 (S)		SO MUCH	17.00	39.00	35.00
☐54055 (M)		JACKIE SINGS THE BLUES	9.00	25.00	22.50

			Current Price Range		P/Y AVG
☐754055 (S)		JACKIE SINGS THE BLUES	14.00	24.00	20.00
☐54058 (M)		MY GOLDEN FAVORITES	9.00	25.00	22.50
☐754058 (S)		MY GOLDEN FAVORITES	14.00	34.00	30.00
☐54059 (M)		A WOMAN, A LOVER, A FRIEND ..	9.00	25.00	22.50
☐754059 (S)		A WOMAN, A LOVER, A FRIEND ..	14.00	34.00	30.00
☐54100 (M)		YOU AIN'T HEARD NOTHIN' YET .	8.00	21.00	18.00
☐754100 (S)		YOU AIN'T HEARD NOTHIN' YET .	12.00	29.00	25.00
☐54101 (M)		BY SPECIAL REQUEST..........	8.00	21.00	18.00
☐754101 (S)		BY SPECIAL REQUEST..........	12.00	29.00	25.00
☐54105 (M)		BODY AND SOUL	7.00	17.00	15.00
☐754105 (S)		BODY AND SOUL	8.00	25.00	22.50
☐54106 (M)		THE WORLD'S GREATEST MELODIES	7.00	17.00	15.00
☐754106 (S)		THE WORLD'S GREATEST MELODIES	9.00	25.00	22.50
☐54108 (M)		AT THE COPA	6.00	15.00	13.50
☐754108 (S)		AT THE COPA	8.00	21.00	18.00
☐54110 (M)		BABY WORKOUT	6.00	15.00	13.50
☐754110 (S)		BABY WORKOUT	7.00	17.00	15.00
☐54112 (M)		MERRY CHRISTMAS FROM JACKIE WILSON	6.00	15.00	13.50
☐754112 (S)		MERRY CHRISTMAS FROM JACKIE WILSON	7.00	17.00	15.00
☐54115 (M)		MY GOLDEN FAVORITES, VOL. II .	7.00	17.00	15.00
☐754115 (S)		MY GOLDEN FAVORITES, VOL. II .	8.00	21.00	18.00
☐54117 (M)		SOMETHIN' ELSE	6.00	15.00	13.50
☐754117 (S)		SOMETHIN' ELSE	7.00	17.00	15.00
☐54118 (M)		SOUL TIME	6.00	15.00	13.50
☐754118 (S)		SOUL TIME	7.00	17.00	15.00
☐54120 (M)		SOUL GALORE	6.00	15.00	13.50
☐754120 (S)		SOUL GALORE	7.00	17.00	15.00
☐54112 (M)		WHISPERS....................	6.00	15.00	13.50
☐754112 (S)		WHISPERS....................	7.00	17.00	15.00
☐54130 (M)		HIGHER AND HIGHER	6.00	15.00	13.50
☐754130 (S)		HIGHER AND HIGHER	7.00	17.00	15.00
☐54138 (M)		I GET THE SWEETEST FEELING ..	5.50	14.00	12.00
☐754138 (S)		I GET THE SWEETEST FEELING ..	6.00	15.00	13.50
☐54140 (M)		GREATEST HITS...............	5.50	14.00	12.00
☐754140 (S)		GREATEST HITS...............	6.00	15.00	13.50

LATER ALBUMS ARE WORTH UP TO $10.00 MINT

J. FRANK WILSON
FEATURED: CAVALIERS

☐722	**LE CAM**	LAST KISS/CARLA	14.00	24.00	20.00
☐761	**TAMARA**	LAST KISS/ THAT'S HOW MUCH I LOVE YOU	9.50	17.00	15.00

LE CAM AND TAMARA VERSIONS OF "LAST KISS" DIFFER

☐923	**JOSIE**	LAST KISS/ THAT'S HOW MUCH I LOVE YOU	3.25	5.50	4.00
☐924		TEARS OF HAPPINESS/ SUMMERTIME (Cavaliers)	3.25	5.50	4.00
☐926		HEY LITTLE ONE/SPEAK TO ME ..	3.25	5.50	4.00
☐929		SIX BOYS/SAY IT NOW	3.25	5.50	4.00
☐931		DREAMS OF A FOOL/ OPEN YOUR EYES	3.25	5.50	4.00
☐938		FORGET ME NOT/A WHITE SPORT COAT AND A PINK CARNATION .	3.25	5.50	4.00

J. FRANK WILSON—ALBUM

☐4006 (M)	**JOSIE**	LAST KISS...................	8.00	21.00	18.00
☐4006 (S)		LAST KISS...................	12.00	29.00	25.00

PEANUTS WILSON

☐55039	**BRUNSWICK**	CAST IRON ARM	16.00	55.00	50.00

			Current Price Range		P/Y AVG

WINDS IN THE WILLOW—ALBUM
FEATURED: DEBBIE HARRY

| ☐2956 (S) | CAPITOL | WIND IN THE WILLOWS . . . . | 24.00 | 55.00 | 50.00 |

WIND
FEATURED: TONY ORLANDO

| ☐200 | LIFE | MAKE BELIEVE/ GROVIN' WITH MR. BLOE . . . . . | 3.00 | 6.00 | 5.00 |
| ☐202 | | TEENY BOPPER/ I'LL HOLD OUT MY HAND . . . . . | 3.00 | 6.00 | 5.00 |

STEVIE WONDER
SEE: EIVETS REDNOW

☐54061	TAMLA	I CALL IT PRETTY MUSIC (BUT OLD PEOPLE CALL IT THE BLUES) (PT. 1)/(PT. 2)	5.50	11.00	9.00
☐54070		LA LA LA LA LA/ LITTLE WATER BOY	5.00	9.00	7.00
☐54074		CONTRACT ON LOVE/SUNSET . . .	5.00	9.00	7.00
☐54080		FINGERTIPS (PT. 1)/(PT. 2)	3.25	5.50	4.00
☐54086		WORKOUT STEVIE, WORKOUT/ MONKEY TALK	3.25	5.50	4.00
☐54090		CASTLES IN THE SAND/ TO THANK YOU	3.25	5.50	4.00
☐54096		HEY HARMONICA MAN/ THIS LITTLE GIRL	3.25	5.50	4.00
☐54103		SAD BOY/HAPPY STREET	3.25	5.50	4.00
☐54114		TEARS IN VAIN/ KISS ME, BABY	3.00	5.00	3.50
☐54119		HIGH HEEL SNEAKERS/ MUSIC NOTES	3.00	5.00	3.50
☐54124		UPTIGHT (EVERYTHING'S ALRIGHT)/PURPLE RAINDROPS	2.75	5.00	3.00
☐54130		NOTHING'S TOO GOOD FOR MY BABY/WITH A CHILD'S HEART	2.75	5.00	3.00
☐54136		BLOWIN' IN THE WIND/AIN'T THAT ASKING FOR TROUBLE . .	2.75	5.00	3.00
☐54139		A PLACE IN THE SUN/SYLVIA . . .	2.75	5.00	3.00
☐54142		SOMEDAY AT CHRISTMAS/THE MIRACLE OF CHRISTMAS	3.25	5.50	4.00
☐54147		TRAVELIN' MAN/HEY LOVE	2.75	4.50	3.00
☐54151		I WAS MADE TO LOVE HER/ HOLD ME	2.75	4.50	3.00
☐54157		I'M WONDERING/EVERY TIME I SEE YOU I GO WILD	2.50	4.00	2.50
☐54165		SHOO-BE-DOO-BE-DOO-DA-DAY/ WHY DON'T YOU LEAVE ME TO LOVE?	2.50	4.00	2.50
☐54168		YOU MET YOUR MATCH/MY GIRL	2.50	4.00	2.50
☐54174		FOR ONCE IN MY LIFE/ ANGIE GIRL	2.50	4.00	2.50
☐54180		MY CHERIE AMOUR/ I DON'T KNOW WHY.	2.50	4.00	2.50
☐54188		YESTER-ME, YESTER-YOU, YESTERDAY/I'D BE A FOOL RIGHT NOW	2.50	4.00	2.50
☐54191		NEVER HAD A DREAM COME TRUE/SOMEBODY KNOWS, SOMEBODY CARES	2.50	4.00	2.50
☐54196		SIGNED, SEALED, DELIVERED, I'M YOURS/I'M MORE THAN HAPPY	2.50	4.00	2.50
☐54200		HEAVEN HELP US ALL/ I GOTTA HAVE A SONG	2.50	4.00	2.50

DECCA, DL 79184

EPIC, 5-10094

			Current Price Range		P/Y AVG
☐ 54202		WE CAN WORK IT OUT/NEVER DREAMED YOU'D LEAVE ME IN SUMMER	2.50	4.00	2.50
☐ 54208		IF YOU REALLY LOVE ME/ THINK OF ME AS YOUR SOLDIER	2.50	4.00	2.50
☐ 54214		WHAT CHRISTMAS MEANS TO ME/BEDTIME FOR TOYS	2.75	4.50	3.00
☐ 54216		SUPERWOMAN (WHERE WERE YOU WHEN I NEEDED YOU)/I LOVE EVERY LITTLE THING ABOUT YOU	2.50	4.00	2.50
☐ 54223		KEEP ON RUNNING/EVIL	2.50	4.00	2.50

LATER TAMLA SINGLES ARE WORTH UP TO $1.75 MINT

STEVIE WONDER—ALBUMS

☐ 232 (M)	*TAMLA*	TRIBUTE TO UNCLE RAY	9.00	25.00	22.50
☐ 233 (M)		JAZZ SOUL	9.00	25.00	22.50
☐ 240 (M)		THE 12-YEAR-OLD GENIUS	8.00	21.00	18.00
☐ 248 (M)		WORKOUT STEVIE, WORKOUT ...	7.00	17.00	15.00
☐ 250 (M)		WITH A SONG IN MY HEART	7.00	17.00	15.00
☐ 255 (M)		STEVIE AT THE BEACH	7.00	17.00	15.00
☐ 268 (M)		UPTIGHT	7.00	17.00	15.00
☐ 268 (S)		UPTIGHT	9.00	25.00	22.50
☐ 272 (M)		DOWN TO EARTH	7.00	17.00	15.00
☐ 272 (S)		DOWN TO EARTH	9.00	25.00	22.50
☐ 279 (M)		I WAS MADE TO LOVE HER	7.00	17.00	15.00
☐ 279 (S)		I WAS MADE TO LOVE HER	8.00	21.00	18.00
☐ 282 (M)		GREATEST HITS..............	6.00	15.00	13.50
☐ 282 (S)		GREATEST HITS..............	7.00	17.00	15.00
☐ 291 (S)		FOR ONCE IN MY LIFE	6.00	15.00	13.50
☐ 296 (S)		MY CHERIE AMOUR............	6.00	15.00	13.50
☐ 298 (S)		STEVIE WONDER LIVE	6.00	15.00	13.50
☐ 304 (S)		SIGNED, SEALED AND DELIVERED	5.50	14.00	12.00
☐ 308 (S)		WHERE I'M COMING FROM	5.50	14.00	12.00
☐ 313 (S)		GREATEST HITS, VOL. II	5.50	14.00	12.00

LATER ALBUMS ARE WORTH UP TO $7.50 MINT

YARDBIRDS
SEE: LED ZEPPELIN, KEITH RELF

☐ 9709	*EPIC*	I WISH YOU WOULD/ A CERTAIN GIRL.............	12.00	21.00	18.00
☐ 9709		I WISH YOU WOULD/ I AIN'T GOT YOU	12.00	21.00	18.00
☐ 9790		FOR YOUR LOVE/GOT TO HURRY .	3.50	6.00	4.35
☐ 9823		HEART FULL OF SOUL/ STEELED BLUES	3.50	6.00	4.35
☐ 9857		I'M A MAN/STILL I'M SAD	3.50	6.00	4.35
☐ 9891		SHAPES OF THINGS/ I'M NOT TALKING	5.50	11.00	9.00
☐ 10006		SHAPES OF THINGS/ NEW YORK CITY BLUES	3.50	6.00	4.35
☐ 10006		SHAPES OF THINGS/YOU'RE A BETTER MAN THAN I	3.50	6.00	4.35
☐ 10035		OVER UNDER SIDEWAYS DOWN/ JEFF'S BOOGIE	3.50	6.00	4.35
☐ 10094		HAPPENINGS TEN YEARS TIME AGO/THE NAZZ ARE BLUE	3.50	6.00	4.35
☐ 10094		HAPPENINGS TEN YEARS TIME AGO/PSYCHO DAISIES	3.50	6.00	4.35
☐ 10156		LITTLE GAMES/PUZZLES	4.00	7.00	4.85

			Current Price Range		P/Y AVG
☐ 10204		HA HA SAID THE CLOWN/ TINKER, TAILOR, SOLDIER, SAILOR	4.00	7.00	4.85
☐ 10248		TEN LITTLE INDIANS/ DRINKIN' MUDDY WATER	4.50	7.50	6.00
☐ 10303		GOODNIGHT SWEET JOSEPHINE/ THINK ABOUT IT	5.00	9.00	7.00

YARDBIRDS—ALBUMS

☐ 24167 (M)	*EPIC*	FOR YOUR LOVE	9.00	25.00	22.50
☐ 26167 (S)		FOR YOUR LOVE	12.00	29.00	25.00
☐ 24177 (M)		HAVING A RAVE-UP WITH THE YARDBIRDS	9.00	25.00	22.50
☐ 26177 (S)		HAVING A RAVE-UP WITH THE YARDBIRDS	12.00	29.00	25.00
☐ 24210 (M)		OVER UNDER SIDEWAYS DOWN	9.00	25.00	22.50
☐ 26210 (S)		OVER UNDER SIDEWAYS DOWN	12.00	29.00	25.00
☐ 24246 (M)		GREATEST HITS	9.00	25.00	22.50
☐ 26246 (S)		GREATEST HITS	12.00	29.00	25.00
☐ 24313 (M)		LITTLE GAMES	12.00	29.00	25.00
☐ 26313 (S)		LITTLE GAMES	14.00	34.00	30.00
☐ 30615 (S)		LIVE YARDBIRDS FEATURING JIMMY PAGE	24.00	55.00	50.00

YESTERDAY'S TODAY

☐ 1B	*STARLIGHT*	ONE MINT JULEP/ PAPA WAS A ROLLING STONE	9.00	17.00	13.00
☐ 2A		WHO'S THAT KNOCKING/ THERE AIN'T NO SUNSHINE	9.00	16.00	12.00

YOUNG RASCALS
SEE: FELIX AND THE ESCORTS

☐ 2312	*ATLANTIC*	I AIN'T GONNA EAT OUT MY HEART ANYMORE/SLOW DOWN	2.75	4.50	3.00
☐ 2321		GOOD LOVIN'/MUSTANG SALLY	2.75	4.50	3.00
☐ 2338		YOU BETTER RUN/ LOVE IS A BEAUTIFUL THING	2.75	4.50	3.00
☐ 2353		COME ON UP/ WHAT IS THE REASON?	2.75	4.50	3.00
☐ 2377		I'VE BEEN LONELY TOO LONG/ IF YOU KNEW	2.75	4.50	3.00
☐ 2401		GROOVIN'/SUENO	2.75	4.50	3.00
☐ 2424		A GIRL LIKE YOU/IT'S LOVE	2.75	4.50	3.00
☐ 2428		GROOVIN' (Italian)/GROOVIN' (Spanish)	3.00	5.00	3.50
☐ 2438		HOW CAN I BE SURE?/ I'M SO HAPPY	2.75	4.50	3.00
☐ 2463		IT'S WONDERFUL/OF COURSE	2.75	4.50	3.00

THE FOLLOWING SINGLES ARE LISTED AS BEING THE RASCALS

☐ 2493		A BEAUTIFUL MORNING/ RAINY DAY	2.50	4.00	2.50
☐ 2537		PEOPLE GOT TO BE FREE/ MY WORLD	2.50	4.00	2.50
☐ 2584		A RAY OF HOPE/ ANY DANCE'LL DO	2.50	4.00	2.50
☐ 2599		HEAVEN/BABY, I'M BLUE	2.50	4.00	2.50
☐ 2634		SEE/AWAY AWAY	2.50	4.00	2.50
☐ 2664		CARRY ME BACK/REAL THING	2.50	4.00	2.50
☐ 2695		HOLD ON/I BELIEVE	2.50	4.00	2.50
☐ 2743		GLORY GLORY/YOU DON'T KNOW	2.50	4.00	2.50
☐ 2773		ALMOST HOME/RIGHT ON	2.50	4.00	2.50

YOUNG RASCALS—ALBUMS

☐ 8123 (M)	*ATLANTIC*	THE YOUNG RASCALS	6.00	15.00	13.50
☐ 8123 (S)		THE YOUNG RASCALS	7.00	17.00	15.00
☐ 8134 (M)		COLLECTIONS	6.00	15.00	13.50

			Current Price Range		P/Y AVG
☐ 8134 (S)		COLLECTIONS	7.00	17.00	15.00
☐ 8148 (M)		GROOVIN'	7.00	17.00	15.00
☐ 8148 (S)		GROOVIN'	6.00	15.00	13.50
☐ 8169 (S)		ONCE UPON A DREAM	5.00	12.00	10.00
☐ 8190 (S)		TIME PEACE-THE RASCALS' GREATEST HITS	5.00	12.00	10.00

YOUNG RASCALS
SEE: FELIX AND THE ESCORTS

☐ 2312	ATLANTIC	I AIN'T GONNA EAT OUT MY HEART ANYMORE/SLOW DOWN	2.75	4.50	3.00
☐ 2321		GOOD LOVIN'/MUSTANG SALLY	2.75	4.50	3.00
☐ 2338		YOU BETTER RUN/ LOVE IS A BEAUTIFUL THING	2.75	4.50	3.00
☐ 2353		COME ON UP/ WHAT IS THE REASON?	2.75	4.50	3.00
☐ 2377		I'VE BEEN LONELY TOO LONG/ IF YOU KNEW	2.75	4.50	3.00
☐ 2401		GROOVIN'/SUENO	2.75	4.50	3.00
☐ 2424		A GIRL LIKE YOU/IT'S LOVE	2.75	4.50	3.00
☐ 2428		GROOVIN' (Italian)/GROOVIN' (Spanish)	3.00	5.00	3.50
☐ 2438		HOW CAN I BE SURE?/ I'M SO HAPPY	2.75	4.50	3.00
☐ 2463		IT'S WONDERFUL/OF COURSE	2.75	4.50	3.00
		THE FOLLOWING SINGLES ARE LISTED AS BEING THE RASCALS			
☐ 2493		A BEAUTIFUL MORNING/ RAINY DAY	2.50	4.00	2.50
☐ 2537		PEOPLE GOT TO BE FREE/ MY WORLD	2.50	4.00	2.50
☐ 2584		A RAY OF HOPE/ ANY DANCE'LL DO	2.50	4.00	2.50
☐ 2599		HEAVEN/BABY, I'M BLUE	2.50	4.00	2.50
☐ 2634		SEE/AWAY AWAY	2.50	4.00	2.50
☐ 2664		CARRY ME BACK/REAL THING	2.50	4.00	2.50
☐ 2695		HOLD ON/I BELIEVE	2.50	4.00	2.50
☐ 2743		GLORY GLORY/YOU DON'T KNOW	2.50	4.00	2.50
☐ 2773		ALMOST HOME/RIGHT ON	2.50	4.00	2.50
		YOUNG RASCALS—ALBUMS			
☐ 8123 (M)	ATLANTIC	THE YOUNG RASCALS	6.00	15.00	13.50
☐ 8123 (S)		THE YOUNG RASCALS	7.00	17.00	15.00
☐ 8134 (M)		COLLECTIONS	6.00	15.00	13.50
☐ 8134 (S)		COLLECTIONS	7.00	17.00	15.00
☐ 8148 (M)		GROOVIN'	7.00	17.00	15.00
☐ 8148 (S)		GROOVIN'	6.00	15.00	13.50
☐ 8169 (S)		ONCE UPON A DREAM	5.00	12.00	10.00
☐ 8190 (S)		TIME PEACE-THE RASCALS' GREATEST HITS	5.00	12.00	10.00

YOUNGTONES

☐ 104	X-TRA	IT'S OVER NOW/YOU I ADORE	25.00	47.00	31.00
☐ 110		BY THE CANDLEGLOW/PATRICIA	25.00	47.00	31.00
☐ 120		CAN I COME OVER?/GONNA GET TOGETHER AGAIN	25.00	47.00	31.00

Z

JOHN ZACHERLE

☐ 130	CAMEO	DINNER WITH DRAC (PT. 1)/ (PT. 2)	3.00	5.00	3.50
☐ 139		LUNCH WITH MOTHER GOOSE/ 82 TOMBSTONES	3.25	5.50	4.00

			Current Price Range		P/Y AVG
☐ 145		I WAS A TEENAGE CAVEMAN/ DUMMY DOLL	3.25	5.50	4.00
☐ 853	*PARKWAY*	DINNER WITH DRAC/ HURRY BURY HARRY	3.00	5.00	3.50
☐ 45013	*ELEKTRA*	COOLEST LITTLE MONSTER/ RING-A-DING ORANGOUTANG ..	3.25	5.50	4.00

JOHN ZACHERLE—ALBUMS

☐ 7018 (M)	*PARKWAY*	MONSTER MASH..............	9.00	25.00	22.50
☐ 7023 (M)		SCARY TALES	8.00	21.00	18.00
☐ 190 (M)	*ELEKTRA*	SPOOK ALONG WITH ZACHERLE .	6.00	15.00	13.50
☐ 7190 (S)		SPOOK ALONG WITH ZACHERLE .	7.00	17.00	15.00

ZAGER AND EVANS

☐ 8082	*TRUTH*	IN THE YEAR 2525/LITTLE KIDS .	8.25	17.00	15.00

FRANK ZAPPA

SEE: BABY RAY AND THE FERNS, BOB GUY, HEARTBREAKERS, MOTHER OF INVENTION, RON ROMAN, RUBEN AND THE JETS

☐ 889	*BIZARRE*	LITTLE UMBRELLAS/ PEACHES EN REGALIA	3.25	5.50	4.00
☐ 967		WOULD YOU GO ALL THE WAY FOR THE U.S.A./TELL ME YOU LOVE ME	3.25	5.50	4.00
☐ 58057	*UNITED ARTISTS*	MAGIC FINGERS/ DADDY, DADDY, DADDY	3.25	5.50	4.00
☐ 1312	*DISCREET*	DON'T EAT THE YELLOW SNOW/ COSMIK DEBRIS	5.00	8.00	6.00
☐ 214		SHE'S MINE/BICYCLE RIDE	5.00	8.00	6.00
☐ 215		DON'T MISS THE BOAT/ YES MY LOVE	5.00	8.00	6.00
☐ 5006	*ROTATE*	THERE'S SOMETHING ABOUT YOU/SHE'S LOST YOU	5.00	8.00	6.00
☐ 5009		WONDER WHAT I'M GONNA DO/ LET ME LOVE YOU BABY	5.00	8.00	6.00

FRANK ZAPPA— ALBUMS

☐ 8741 (M)	*VERVE*	LUMPY GRAVY	8.00	21.00	18.00
☐ 8741 (S)		LUMPY GRAVY	9.00	25.00	22.50
☐ 6356 (S)	*BIZARRE*	HOT RATS	8.00	21.00	18.00
☐ 2030 (S)		CHUNGA'S REVENGE	8.00	21.00	18.00
☐ 2094 (S)		WAKA/JAWAKA-HOT RATS......	7.00	17.00	15.00
☐ 2175 (S)	*DISCREET*	APOSTROPHE (')	6.00	15.00	9.50
☐ 2202 (S)		ROXY AND ELSEWHERE	6.00	15.00	9.50
☐ 2216 (S)		ONE SIZE FITS ALL	6.00	15.00	9.50
☐ 2234 (S)		BONGO FURY.................	6.00	15.00	9.50
☐ 2289 (S)		APOSTROPHE (') (second issue) ..	6.00	15.00	9.50
☐ 2290 (S)		ZAPPA IN NEW YORK...........	6.00	15.00	9.50
☐ 2291 (S)		STUDIO TAN	6.00	15.00	9.50

ZEBULONS

☐ 9069	*CUB*	FALLING WATER/ WO-HO-LA-TEE-DA	12.00	24.00	20.00

BEN ZEPPA

☐ 577	*SPECIALTY*	A FOOLISH FOOL/BABY I NEED (TING A LING)	21.00	34.00	30.00
☐ 278	*TOP (EP)*	WHY DO FOOLS FALL IN LOVE (+ various artists and songs) ..	9.50	17.00	15.00
☐ 1042	*ERA*	TOPSY TURVY/MOM AND DAD ...	4.50	7.00	6.00
☐ 1000	*HUSH*	YOUNG HEARTACHES/ RIDIN' HERD	3.75	6.00	4.50

ZIGGY & THE ZEU

☐ 5011	*ZEU*	COME GO WITH ME/ LITTLE STAR	9.50	23.00	21.50

			Current Price Range		P/Y AVG

THE ZIRCONS

| ☐ CS-1030 | **COOL SOUND** | (I HEAR) SILVER BELLS/ YOU ARE MY SUNSHINE ...... | 18.00 | 35.00 | 22.00 |

ZOMBIES

☐ 9695	**PARROT**	SHE'S NOT THERE/YOU MAKE ME FEEL SO GOOD	3.25	5.50	4.00
☐ 9723		TELL HER NO/LEAVE ME BE	3.25	5.50	4.00
☐ 9747		SHE'S COMING HOME/ I MUST MOVE	3.25	5.50	4.00
☐ 9769		I WANT YOU BACK AGAIN/ ONCE UPON A TIME	3.25	5.50	4.00
☐ 9797		JUST OUT OF REACH/ REMEMBER YOU	3.25	5.50	4.00
☐ 9821		DON'T GO AWAY/ IS THIS THE DREAM?	3.00	5.00	3.50
☐ 3004		HOW WE WERE BEFORE/ INDICATION	3.00	5.00	3.50
☐ 1604	**DATE**	TIME OF THE SEASON/ I'LL CALL YOU MINE	3.25	5.50	4.00
☐ 1612		THIS WILL BE YOUR YEAR/ BUTCHER'S TALE	3.00	5.00	3.50
☐ 1628		TIME OF THE SEASON/ FRIENDS OF MINE	2.75	4.50	3.00
☐ 1644		CONVERSATION ON FLORAL STREET/IMAGINE THE SWAN ..	2.75	4.50	3.00
☐ 1648		IF IT DON'T WORK OUT/ DON'T CRY FOR ME	2.75	4.50	3.00

ZOMBIES—ALBUMS

☐ 61001 (M)	**PARROT**	ZOMBIES	8.00	21.00	18.00
☐ 71001 (S)		ZOMBIES	9.00	25.00	22.50
☐ 4013 (S)	**DATE**	ODYSSEY AND ORACLE	7.00	17.00	15.00
☐ 32861 (S)	**EPIC**	TIME OF THE ZOMBIES	6.00	15.00	13.50

THE MOTOWN SINGLES DISCOGRAPHY

MIRACLES

| ☐ 1/2 | BAD GIRL/I LOVE YOUR BABY ALSO RELEASED AS MOTOWN 2207 | 50.00 | 98.00 | 70.00 |

SATINTONES

| ☐ 1000 | MY BELOVED/SUGAR DADDY | 20.00 | 35.00 | 23.00 |

EUGENE REMUS

| ☐ 1001 | YOU NEVER MISS A GOOD THING/GOTTA HAVE YOUR LOVIN' .... | 19.00 | 33.00 | 23.00 |

POPCORN AND THE MOHAWKS

| ☐ 1002 | CUSTER'S LAST MAN/ SHIMMY GULLY .... | 11.00 | 20.00 | 13.50 |

MARY WELLS

| ☐ 1003 | BYE BYE BABY/ PLEASE FORGIVE ME ..... | 4.50 | 7.50 | 6.00 |

SHERRI TAYLOR AND SINGIN' SAMMY WARD

| ☐ 1004 | LOVER/THAT'S WHY I LOVE YOU SO MUCH .... | 10.00 | 17.00 | 13.00 |

		Current Price Range		P/Y AVG

HENRY LUMPKIN

☐ 1005   I'VE GOT A NOTION/WE REALLY LOVE EACH OTHER   8.25   14.00   12.00

SATINTONES

☐ 1006   A LOVE THAT CAN NEVER BE/ ANGEL 37.00   62.00   44.00

SATINTONES

☐ 1006   A LOVE THAT CAN NEVER BE/ TOMORROW AND ALWAYS   37.00   62.00   44.00

DEBBIE DEAN

☐ 1007   DON'T LET HIM SHOP AROUND/A NEW GIRL 7.00   13.00   11.00

CONTOURS

☐ 1008   WHOLE LOTTA WOMAN/ COME ON AND BE MINE . . .   7.00   13.00   11.00

RICHARD WYLIE

☐ 1009   MONEY/I'LL BE AROUND . . .   8.00   15.00   10.00

SATINTONES

☐ 1010   I KNOW HOW IT FEELS/ MY KIND OF LOVE 37.00   60.00   44.00

MARY WELLS

☐ 1011   I DON'T WANT TO TAKE A CHANCE/I'M SO SORRY . .   3.75   6.00   4.50

CONTOURS

☐ 1012   THE STRETCH/FUNNY 5.50   11.00   9.00

HENRY LUMPKIN

☐ 1013   DON'T LEAVE ME/ WHAT IS A MAN 7.00   14.00   9.00

DEBBIE DEAN

☐ 1014   BUT I'M AFRAID/ ITTY BITTY PITY LOVE 6.00   12.00   10.00

GOLDEN HARMONIERS

☐ 1015   PRECIOUS MEMORIES/ I'M BOUND 6.00   12.00   10.00

MARY WELLS

☐ 1016   COME TO ME/STRANGE LOVE   4.50   7.50   6.00

☐ 1017   UNISSUED

☐ 1018   UNISSUED

POPCORN AND THE MOHAWKS

☐ 1019   REAL GOOD LOVING/ HAVE I THE RIGHT? 6.00   12.00   10.00

SATINTONES

☐ 1020   ZING! WENT THE STINGS OF MY HEART/FADED LETTER   11.00   20.00   13.50

EDDIE HOLLAND

☐ 1021   JAMIE/TAKE A CHANCE 3.00   5.00   3.50

		Current Price Range		P/Y AVG
□ 1022	**TWISTIN' KINGS** CHRISTMAS TWIST/ WHITE HOUSE TWIST	5.00	9.00	6.00
□ 1023	**TWISTIN' KINGS** CONGO TWIST/(PT. 1)/ (PT. 2)	5.00	9.00	6.00
□ 1024	**MARY WELLS** THE ONE WHO REALLY LOVES YOU/I'M GONNA STAY ...	3.25	5.50	4.00
□ 1025	**DEBBIE DEAN** EVERYBODY'S TALKING ABOUT MY BABY/I CRIED ALL NIGHT	3.75	6.00	4.50
□ 1026	**EDDIE HOLLAND** YOU DESERVE WHAT YOU GOT/LAST NIGHT I HAD A VISION	3.00	5.00	3.50
□ 1027	**SUPREMES** YOUR HEART BELONGS TO ME/(HE'S) SEVENTEEN ..	4.50	7.50	6.00
□ 1028	**HERMAN GRIFFIN** UPTIGHT/ SLEEP (LITTLE ONE)	4.00	7.00	4.85
□ 1029	**HENRY LUMPKIN** MO JO HANNA/ BREAK DOWN AND SING ..	4.00	7.00	4.85
□ 1030	**EDDIE HOLLAND** WHAT ABOUT ME/ IF CLEOPATRA TOOK A CHANCE	3.00	5.00	3.50
□ 1031	**EDDIE HOLLAND** IF IT'S LOVE/ IT'S NOT TOO LATE	3.00	5.00	3.50
□ 1032	**MARY WELLS** YOU BEAT ME TO THE PUNCH/OLD LOVE	3.25	5.50	4.00
□ 1033	UNISSUED			
□ 1034	**SUPREMES** LET ME GO THE RIGHT WAY/ TIME CHANGES THINGS ..	4.50	7.50	6.00
□ 1035	**MARY WELLS** TWO LOVERS/OPERATOR ...	3.25	5.50	4.00
□ 1036	**EDDIE HOLLAND** DARLING, I HUM OUR SONG/ JUST A FEW MORE DAYS .	3.00	5.00	3.50

		Current Price Range		P/Y AVG

LINDA GRINER
☐ 1037   GOODBYE CRUEL LOVE/ ENVIOUS 4.00   7.00   4.85

AMOS MILBURN
☐ 1038   I'LL MAKE IT UP TO YOU/ SOMEHOW 5.00   9.00   6.00

MARY WELLS
☐ 1039   LAUGHING BOY/ TWO WRONGS DON'T MAKE A RIGHT 3.25   5.50   4.00

SUPREMES
☐ 1040   MY HEART CAN'T TAKE IT NO MORE/YOU BRING BACK MEMORIES 3.75   6.00   4.50

CONNIE VAN DYKE
☐ 1041   IT HURT ME TOO/OH FREDDIE   4.00   7.00   4.85

MARY WELLS
☐ 1042   YOUR OLD STANDBY/ WHAT LOVE HAS JOINED TOGETHER 3.25   5.50   4.00

EDDIE HOLLAND
☐ 1043   BABY SHAKE/BRENDA 3.00   5.00   3.50

SUPREMES
☐ 1044   A BREATH-TAKING GUY/ ROCK AND ROLL BANJO MAN 3.25   5.50   4.00

HOLLAND AND DOZIER
☐ 1045   WHAT COMES UP MUST COME DOWN/COME ON HOME 3.50   6.00   4.00

SKYLINERS
☐ 1046   SINCE I FELL FOR YOU/ I'D DIE 3.25   5.50   4.00

MORROCCO MUZIK
☐ 1047   BACK TO SCHOOL AGAIN/ PIG KNUCKLES 5.00   9.00   6.00

MARY WELLS
☐ 1048   YOU LOST THE SWEETEST BOY/WHAT'S EASY FOR TWO IS HARD FOR ONE ...   3.25   5.50   4.00

EDDIE HOLLAND
☐ 1049   I'M ON THE OUTSIDE LOOKING IN/I COULDN'T CRY IF I WANTED TO 3.00   5.00   3.50

CAROLYN CRAWFORD
☐ 1050   FORGET ABOUT ME/ DEVIL IN HIS EYES 4.00   7.00   4.85

		Current Price Range		P/Y AVG

SUPREMES
☐ 1051 WHEN THE LOVELIGHT STARS SHINING THROUGH HIS EYES/STANDING AT THE CROSSROADS OF LOVE — 3.00 — 5.00 — 3.50

EDDIE HOLLAND
☐ 1052 LEAVING HERE/BRENDA .... — 3.00 — 5.00 — 3.50

BOBBY BREEN
☐ 1053 HOW CAN WE TELL HIM/ BETTER LATE THAN NEVER — 3.50 — 6.00 — 4.35

SUPREMES
☐ 1054 RUN, RUN, RUN/I'M GIVING YOU YOUR FREEDOM ..... — 3.00 — 5.00 — 3.50

SAMMY TURNER
☐ 1055 ONLY YOU/RIGHT NOW .... — 2.75 — 4.50 — 3.00

MARY WELLS
☐ 1056 MY GUY/ OH LITTLE BOY ... — 3.25 — 5.50 — 4.00

MARY WELLS AND MARVIN GAYE
☐ 1057 ONCE UPON A TIME/ WHAT'S THE MATTER WITH YOU BABY .... — 3.25 — 5.50 — 4.00

EDDIE HOLLAND
☐ 1058 JUST AIN'T ENOUGH LOVE/ LAST NIGHT I HAD A VISION .... — 3.00 — 5.00 — 3.50

BOBBY BREEN
☐ 1059 YOU'RE JUST LIKE YOU/ HERE COMES THAT HEARTACHE .... — 3.50 — 6.00 — 4.35

SUPREMES
☐ 1060 WHERE DID OUR LOVE GO?/ HE MEANS THE WORLD TO ME .... — 2.75 — 4.50 — 3.00

☐ 1061 UNISSUED

FOUR TOPS
☐ 1062 BABY I NEED YOUR LOVING/ CALL ON ME .... — 2.75 — 4.50 — 3.00

EDDIE HOLLAND
☐ 1063 CANDY TO ME/IF YOU DON'T WANT MY LOVE .... — 3.00 — 5.00 — 3.50

CAROLYN CRAWFORD
☐ 1064 I'LL COME RUNNING/MY SMILE IS JUST A FROWN . — 3.50 — 6.00 — 4.35

☐ 1065 UNISSUED

SUPREMES
☐ 1066 BABY LOVE/ASK ANY GIRL .. — 2.75 — 4.50 — 3.00

		Current Price Range		P/Y AVG
☐ 1067	**SPINNERS** SWEET THING/HOW CAN I? .	3.00	5.00	3.50
☐ 1068	**SUPREMES** COME SEE ABOUT ME/ ALWAYS IN MY HEART ...	2.75	4.50	3.00
☐ 1069	**FOUR TOPS** WITHOUT THE ONE YOU LOVE/LOVE HAS GONE ...	2.75	4.50	3.00
☐ 1070	**CAROLYN CRAWFORD** MY HEART/WHEN SOMEONE'S GOOD TO YOU	3.50	6.00	4.35
☐ 1071	**TONY MARTIN** OUR RHAPSODY/TALKIN' TO YOUR PICTURE	3.50	6.00	4.35
☐ 1072	**CHOKER CAMPBELL** COME SEE ABOUT ME/ PRIDE AND JOY	3.50	6.00	4.35
☐ 1073	**FOUR TOPS** ASK THE LONELY/ WHERE DID YOU GO?	2.75	4.50	3.00
☐ 1074	**SUPREMES** STOP! IN THE NAME OF LOVE/ I'M IN LOVE AGAIN	2.75	4.50	3.00
☐ 1075	**SUPREMES** BACK IN MY ARMS AGAIN/ WHISPER YOU LOVE ME, BOY	2.75	4.50	3.00
☐ 1076	**FOUR TOPS** I CAN'T HELP MYSELF/ SAD SOUVENIRS	2.75	4.50	3.00
☐ 1077	**BILLY ECKSTINE** DOWN TO EARTH/ HAD YOU BEEN AROUND ..	4.00	7.00	4.85
☐ 1078	**SPINNERS** I'LL ALWAYS LOVE YOU/ TOMORROW MAY NEVER COME	3.00	5.00	3.65
☐ 1079	UNISSUED			
☐ 1080	**SUPREMES** NOTHING BUT HEARTACHES/ HE HOLDS HIS OWN	2.75	4.50	3.00
☐ 1081	**FOUR TOPS** IT'S THE SAME OLD SONG/ YOUR LOVE IS AMAZING ..	2.75	4.50	3.00
☐ 1082	**TONY MARTIN** TWO OF US/THE BIGGER YOUR HEART IS	3.25	5.50	4.00

		Current Price Range		P/Y AVG

SUPREMES
☐ 1083 I HEAR A SYMPHONY/ WHO COULD EVER DOUBT MY LOVE 2.75 4.50 3.00

FOUR TOPS
☐ 1084 SOMETHING ABOUT YOU/ DARLING I HUM OUR SONG 2.75 4.50 3.00

SUPREMES
☐ 1085 CHILDREN'S CHRISTMAS SONG/TWINKLE TWINKLE LITTLE ME 3.00 5.00 3.50

TAMMI TERRELL
☐ 1086 I CAN'T BELIEVE YOU LOVE ME/HOLD ON, OH MY DARLING 3.00 5.00 3.65

BARBARA McNAIR
☐ 1087 TOUCH OF TIME/YOU'RE GONNA LOVE MY BABY ... 5.00 9.00 6.00

TONY MARTIN
☐ 1088 SPANISH ROSE/ ASK ANY MAN 3.50 6.00 4.35

SUPREMES
☐ 1089 MY WORK IS EMPTY WITHOUT YOU/ EVERYTHING IS GOOD ABOUT YOU 2.75 4.50 3.00

FOUR TOPS
☐ 1090 SHAKE ME, WAKE ME/JUST AS LONG AS YOU NEED ME 2.75 4.50 3.00

BILLY ECKSTINE
☐ 1091 WISH YOU WERE HERE/ SLENDER THREAD 4.00 7.00 4.85

CONNIE HAINES
☐ 1092 WHAT'S EASY FOR TWO IS HARD FOR ONE/ EVERYTHING IS GOOD ABOUT YOU 3.50 6.00 4.35

SPINNERS
☐ 1093 TRULY YOURS/ WHERE IS THAT GIRL? ... 3.00 5.00 3.65

SUPREMES
☐ 1094 LOVE IS LIKE AN ITCHING IN MY HEART/HE'S ALL I GOT 2.75 4.50 3.00

TAMMI TERRELL
☐ 1095 COME ON AND SEE ME/ BABY DON'TCHA WORRY . 3.00 5.00 3.65

		Current Price Range		P/Y AVG

FOUR TOPS
☐ 1096 LOVING YOU IS SWEETER THAN EVER/I LIKE EVERYTHING ABOUT YOU . 2.75 4.50 3.00

SUPREMES
☐ 1097 YOU CAN'T HURRY LOVE/ PUT YOURSELF IN MY PLACE 2.75 4.50 3.00

FOUR TOPS
☐ 1098 REACH OUT, I'LL BE THERE/ UNTIL YOU LOVE SOMEONE 2.75 4.50 3.00

BARBARA McNAIR
☐ 1099 WHAT A DAY/EVERYTHING IS GOOD ABOUT YOU 4.00 7.00 4.65

BILLY ECKSTINE
☐ 1100 A WARMER WORLD/ AND THERE YOU WERE . . . 4.00 6.00 4.65

SUPREMES
☐ 1101 YOU KEEP ME HANGIN' ON/ REMOVE THIS DOUBT 2.75 4.50 3.00

FOUR TOPS
☐ 1102 STANDING IN THE SHADOWS OF LOVE/SINCE YOU'VE BEEN GONE 2.75 4.50 3.00

SUPREMES
☐ 1103 LOVE IS HERE AND NOW YOU'RE GONE/THERE'S NO STOPPING US NOW 2.75 4.50 3.00

FOUR TOPS
☐ 1104 BERNADETTE/ I GOT A FEELING 2.75 4.50 3.00

BILLY ECKSTINE
☐ 1105 I WONDER WHY (NOBODY LOVES ME)/I'VE BEEN BLESSED 3.50 6.00 4.35

BARBARA McNAIR
☐ 1106 MY WORLD IS EMPTY WITHOUT YOU/HERE I AM, BABY 3.50 6.00 4.35

SUPREMES
☐ 1107 THE HAPPENING/ ALL I KNOW ABOUT YOU . . 2.75 4.50 3.00

PAUL PETERSON
☐ 1108 DON'T LET IT HAPPEN TO US/ CHAINED 3.00 5.00 3.65

SPINNERS
☐ 1109 FOR ALL WE KNOW/ CROSS MY HEART 3.00 5.00 3.65

		Current Price Range		P/Y AVG

FOUR TOPS

☐ 1110 SEVEN ROOMS OF GLOOM/
I'LL TURN TO STONE 2.75 4.50 3.00

DIANA ROSS AND THE SUPREMES

☐ 1111 REFLECTIONS/GOING ON FOR
THE THIRD TIME 2.75 4.50 3.00

☐ 1112 UNISSUED

FOUR TOPS

☐ 1113 YOU KEEP RUNNING AWAY/IF
YOU DON'T WANT MY LOVE 2.75 4.50 3.00

CHRIS CLARK

☐ 1114 FROM HEAD TO TOE/
BEGINNING OF THE END ... 3.50 6.00 4.00

TAMMI TERRELL

☐ 1115 WHAT A GOOD MAN HE IS/
THERE ARE THINGS 3.50 6.00 4.00

DIANA ROSS AND THE SUPREMES

☐ 1116 IN AND OUT OF LOVE/
I GUESS I'LL ALWAYS
LOVE YOU 2.75 4.50 3.00

THE ONES

☐ 1117 YOU HAVEN'T SEEN MY
LOVE/HAPPY DAY 3.50 6.00 4.00

CHUCK JACKSON

☐ 1118 THE MAN IN YOU/
GIRLS, GIRLS, GIRLS 3.00 5.00 3.50

FOUR TOPS

☐ 1069 WALK AWAY RENEE/
YOUR LOVE IS WONDERFUL 2.75 4.50 3.00

BILLY ECKSTINE

☐ 1120 IS ANYONE HERE GOING MY
WAY?/THANK YOU, LOVE . 3.50 6.00 4.00

CHRIS CLARK

☐ 1121 BEGINNING OF THE END/
WHISPER YOU LOVE TO
ME, BOY 3.50 6.00 4.00

DIANA ROSS AND THE SUPREMES

☐ 1122 FOREVER CAME TODAY/
TIME CHANGES THINGS .. 2.75 4.50 3.00

BARBARA McNAIR

☐ 1123 FOR ONCE IN MY LIFE/
WHERE WOULD I BE
WITHOUT YOU? 3.75 6.50 4.35

FOUR TOPS

☐ 1124 IF I WERE A CARPENTER/
WONDERFUL BABY 2.75 4.50 3.00

☐ 1125 UNISSUED

		Current Price Range		P/Y AVG

DIANA ROSS AND THE SUPREMES

☐ 1126 SOME THINGS YOU NEVER GET USED TO/YOU'VE BEEN SO WONDERFUL TO ME 2.75 4.50 3.00

FOUR TOPS

☐ 1127 YESTERDAY'S DREAMS/ FOR ONCE IN MY LIFE 2.75 4.50 3.00

MARVIN GAYE AND GLADYS KNIGHT AND THE PIPS

☐ 1128 JUST A CLOSER WALK WITH THEE/HIS EYE IS ON THE SPARROW 3.50 6.00 4.35

PAUL PETERSON

☐ 1129 LITTLE BIT FOR SANDY/ YOUR LOVE'S GOT ME BURNING ALIVE 3.00 5.00 3.65

THE ONES

☐ 1130 DON'T LET ME LOSE THIS DREAM/I'VE BEEN GOOD TO YOU 3.25 5.50 4.00

BILLY ECKSTINE

☐ 1131 FOR LOVE OF IVY/A WOMAN 3.25 5.50 4.00

FOUR TOPS

☐ 1132 I'M IN A DIFFERENT WORLD/ REMEMBER WHEN 2.75 4.50 3.00

BARBARA McNAIR

☐ 1133 YOU COULD NEVER LOVE HIM/FANCY PASSES 3.25 5.50 4.00

BLINKY

☐ 1134 I WOULDN'T CHANGE THE MAN HE IS/I'LL ALWAYS LOVE YOU 3.25 5.50 4.00

DIANA ROSS AND THE SUPREMES

☐ 1135 LOVE CHILD/ WILL THIS BE THE DAY? .. 2.75 4.50 3.00

SPINNERS

☐ 1136 I JUST CAN'T HELP BUT FEEL THE PAIN/BAD BAD WEATHER 3.25 5.50 4.00

DIANA ROSS AND THE SUPREMES AND THE TEMPTATIONS

☐ 1137 I'M GONNA MAKE YOU LOVE ME/A PLACE IN THE SUN . 2.75 4.50 3.00

TAMMI TERRELL

☐ 1138 THIS OLD HEART OF MINE/ JUST TOO MUCH TO HOPE FOR 3.00 5.00 3.65

		Current Price Range		P/Y AVG

DIANA ROSS AND THE SUPREMES

☐ 1139   I'M LIVIN' IN SHAME/ I'M SO GLAD I GOT SOMEBODY 2.75   4.50   3.00

DAVID RUFFIN

☐ 1140   MY WHOLE WORLD ENDED THE MOMENT YOU LEFT ME/I'VE GOT TO FIND MYSELF A BRAND NEW BABY 3.25   5.50   4.00

SOUPY SALES

☐ 1141   MUCK ARTY PARK/GREEN GROW THE LILACS 3.25   5.50   4.00

DIANA ROSS AND THE SUPREMES AND THE TEMPTATIONS

☐ 1142   I'LL TRY SOMETHING NEW/ THE WAY YOU DO THE THINGS YOU DO 2.75   4.50   3.00

☐ 1143   UNISSUED

CHUCK JACKSON

☐ 1144   YOUR WONDERFUL LOVE/ ARE YOU LONELY FOR ME BABY 3.00   5.00   3.50

☐ 1145   UNISSUED

DIANA ROSS AND THE SUPREMES

☐ 1146   THE COMPOSER/THE BEGINNING OF THE END ..   2.75   4.50   3.00

FOUR TOPS

☐ 1147   WHAT IS A MAN?/DON'T BRING BACK MEMORIES ..   2.75   4.50   3.00

DIANA ROSS AND THE SUPREMES

☐ 1148   NO MATTER WHAT SIGN YOU ARE/THE YOUNG FOLKS ..   2.75   4.50   3.00

DAVID RUFFIN

☐ 1149   I'VE LOST EVERYTHING I EVER LOVED/WE'LL HAVE A GOOD THING GOING ON .   3.25   5.50   4.00

☐ 1150   UNISSUED

CAPTAIN ZAP AND THE MOTOWN CUT-UPS

☐ 1151   LUNEY TAKE-OFF/ LUNEY LANDING 3.25   5.50   4.00

CHUCK JACKSON

☐ 1152   HONEY COME BACK/ WHAT AM I GONNA DO WITHOUT YOU? 3.00   5.00   3.50

		Current Price Range		P/Y AVG

DIANA ROSS AND THE SUPREMES AND THE TEMPTATIONS

☐1153 THE WEIGHT/ FOR BETTER OR WORSE .. 2.75 4.50 3.00

JOE HARNELL

☐1154 MIDNIGHT COWBOY/GREEN GROW THE LILACS 3.25 5.50 4.00

☐1155 UNISSUED

DIANA ROSS AND THE SUPREMES

☐1156 SOMEDAY WE'LL BE TOGETHER/HE'S MY SUNNY BOY 2.75 4.50 3.00

LATER MOTOWN SINGLES ARE WORTH UP TO $2.50 MINT

THE PHILLES RECORDS DISCOGRAPHY

SINGLES

CRYSTALS

☐100 THERE'S NO OTHER (LIKE MY BABY) 4.50 7.50 6.00

JOEL SCOTT

☐101 HERE I STAND 5.00 9.00 7.00

CRYSTALS

☐102 UPTOWN 4.50 7.50 6.00

ALI HASSAN

☐103 CHOP STICKS............. 5.00 9.00 7.00

STEVE DOUGLAS

☐104 YES SIR, THAT'S MY BABY . 5.50 11.00 9.00

CRYSTALS

☐105 HE HIT ME (AND IT FELT LIKE A KISS)............ 5.50 11.00 9.00

CRYSTALS

☐106 HE'S A REBEL 3.25 5.50 4.00

BOB B. SOXX AND THE BLUE JEANS

☐107 ZIP-A-DEE DOO-DAH 3.25 5.50 4.00

ALLEY CATS

☐108 PUDDIN' N' TAIN 4.50 7.50 6.00

CRYSTALS

☐109 HE'S SURE THE BOY I LOVE . 3.25 5.50 4.00

BOB B. SOXX AND THE BLUE JEANS

☐110 WHY DO LOVERS BREAK EACH OTHER'S HEARTS? . 3.25 5.50 4.00

		Current Price Range		P/Y AVG
	CRYSTALS			
☐111	DO THE SCREW	220.00	365.00	350.00
	DARLENE LOVE			
☐111	(TODAY I MET) THE BOY I'M GONNA MARRY	5.50	11.00	9.00
	CRYSTALS			
☐112	DA DO RON RON	3.25	5.50	4.00
	BOB B. SOXX AND THE BLUE JEANS			
☐113	NOT TOO YOUNG TO GET MARRIED	3.25	5.50	4.00
	DARLENE LOVE			
☐114	WAIT 'TIL MY BOBBY GETS HOME	3.25	5.50	4.00
	CRYSTALS			
☐115	THEN HE KISSED ME	3.25	5.50	4.00
	RONETTES			
☐116	BE MY BABY	3.50	5.75	4.35
	DARLENE LOVE			
☐117	A FINE, FINE BOY.	3.25	5.50	4.00
	RONETTES			
☐118	BABY, I LOVE YOU	3.50	5.75	4.35
	CRYSTALS			
☐119X	LITTLE BOY	3.75	6.00	4.50
	DARLENE LOVE			
☐119	CHRISTMAS (BABY, PLEASE COME HOME)	5.50	11.00	9.00
	RONETTES			
☐120	(THE BEST PART OF) BREAKIN' UP	3.25	5.50	4.00
	RONETTES			
☐121	DO I LOVE YOU	3.50	5.75	4.35
	CRYSTALS			
☐122	ALL GROWN UP	3.75	6.00	4.50
	DARLENE LOVE			
☐123	HE'S A QUIET GUY	24.00	40.00	36.00
	RONETTES			
☐123	WALKING IN THE RAIN	3.50	5.75	4.35
	RIGHTEOUS BROTHERS			
☐124	YOU'VE LOST THAT LOVIN' FEELIN'	3.50	6.00	4.35
	DARLENE LOVE			
☐125	WINTER WONDERLAND	4.50	7.50	6.00
	RONETTES			
☐126	BORN TO BE TOGETHER	3.75	6.00	4.50

		Current Price Range		P/Y AVG

RIGHTEOUS BROTHERS

| ☐ 127 | JUST ONCE IN MY LIFE . . . . . | 3.50 | 6.00 | 4.35 |

RONETTES

| ☐ 128 | IS THIS WHAT I GET FOR LOVING YOU? . . . . | 3.75 | 6.00 | 4.50 |

RIGHTEOUS BROTHERS

| ☐ 130 | EBB TIDE . . . . | 3.50 | 6.00 | 4.35 |

IKE AND TINA TURNER

| ☐ 131 | RIVER DEEP — MOUNTAIN HIGH . . . . | 5.00 | 9.00 | 6.00 |

RIGHTEOUS BROTHERS

| ☐ 132 | THE WHITE CLIFFS OF DOVER | 8.00 | 13.00 | 6.75 |

RONETTES

| ☐ 133 | I CAN HEAR MUSIC . . . . | 4.00 | 7.50 | 6.00 |

IKE AND TINA TURNER

| ☐ 134 | A MAN IS A MAN IS A MAN . . | 5.00 | 9.00 | 6.00 |

IKE AND TINA TURNER

| ☐ 135 | I'LL NEVER NEED MORE THAN THIS . . . . | 5.00 | 9.00 | 6.00 |

IKE AND TINA TURNER

| ☐ 136 | HOLD ON BABY . . . . | 4.50 | 7.50 | 6.00 |

ALBUMS

CRYSTALS

☐ 4001	TWIST UPTOWN	34.00	50.00	45.00
☐ 4001	HE'S A REBEL	34.00	50.00	45.00
☐ 4003	THE CRYSTALS SING THE GREATEST HITS, VOL. 1 . .	26.00	46.00	42.00

RONETTES

| ☐ 4006 | PRESENTING THE FABULOUS RONETTES (FEATURING VERONICA) . . . . | 40.00 | 80.00 | 75.00 |

RIGHTEOUS BROTHERS

☐ 4007	YOU'VE LOST THAT LOVIN' FEELIN'	15.00	25.00	18.00
☐ 4008	JUST ONCE IN MY LIFE	15.00	25.00	18.00
☐ 4009	BACK TO BACK	15.00	25.00	18.00

IKE AND TINA TURNER

| ☐ 4011 | RIVER DEEP — MOUNTAIN HIGH . . . . | 50.00 | 100.00 | 72.00 |

VARIOUS ARTISTS

| ☐ 4005 | A CHRISTMAS GIFT FOR YOU | 20.00 | 36.00 | 21.50 |

SUN RECORDS SINGLES DISCOGRAPHY

		Current Price Range		P/Y AVG

JACKIE BOY AND LITTLE WALTER
☐ 174 SELLIN' MY WHISKEY/
BLUES IN MY CONDITION . 120.00 230.00 145.00
KNOWN ONLY TO EXIST ON ACETATE

JOHNNY LONDON
☐ 175 DRIVIN' SLOW/FLAT TIRE .. 60.00 110.00 63.00

WALTER BRADFORD AND THE BIG CITY FOUR
☐ 176 DREARY NIGHT/NUTHIN'
BUT THE BLUES 60.00 110.00 71.00

HANDY JACKSON
☐ 177 GOT MY APPLICATION BABY/
TROUBLE (WILL BRING
YOU DOWN) 50.00 100.00 63.00

JOE HILL LOUIS
☐ 178 WE ALL GOTTA GO
SOMETIME/SHE MAY
BE YOURS 50.00 100.00 63.00

WILLIE NIX-THE MEMPHIS BLUES BOY
☐ 179 SEEMS LIKE A MILLION
YEARS/BARBER SHOP
BOOGIE 45.00 80.00 53.00
THE FIRST SIX SUN SINGLES WERE PRESSED ONLY ON 78 RPM

JIMMY AND WALTER
☐ 180 EASY/BEFORE LONG 90.00 170.00 105.00

RUFUS "HOUND DOG" THOMAS, JR.
☐ 181 BEARCAT (THE ANSWER TO
HOUND DOG)/WALKIN'
IN THE RAIN 25.00 45.00 31.00
LATER PRESSINGS OMITTED "THE ANSWER TO HOUND DOG"

DUSTY BROOKS AND HIS TONES
☐ 182 TEARS AND WINE/
HEAVEN OR FIRE 37.00 59.00 42.00

D. A. HUNT
☐ 183 LONESOME OL' JAIL/
GREYHOUND BLUES 250.00 450.00 285.00
NOT KNOWN IF 45 RPM EXISTS; 78 PRICE WOULD BE HALF OF ABOVE

BIG MEMPHIS MARAINEY-ONZIE HORNE COMBO
☐ 184 CALL ME ANYTHING BUT
CALL ME/NO MEANS NO .. 110.00 200.00 125.00

JIMMY DEBERRY
☐ 185 TAKE A LITTLE CHANCE/
TIME HAS MADE A CHANGE 60.00 115.00 75.00

PRISONAIRES
☐ 186 JUST WALKIN' IN THE RAIN/
BABY PLEASE 28.00 50.00 32.00

		Current Price Range		P/Y AVG

LITTLE JUNIOR'S BLUE FLAMES

☐187 FEELIN' GOOD/FUSSIN' AND
FIGHTIN' BLUES 18.00 33.00 19.00

RUFUS THOMAS, JR.

☐188 TIGER MAN (KING OF THE
JUNGLE)/SAVE THAT
MONEY 24.00 41.00 28.00

PRISONAIRES

☐189 MY GOD IS REAL/
SOFTLY AND TENDERLY .. 20.00 37.00 23.00

RIPLEY COTTON CHOPPERS

☐190 SILVER BELLS/
BLUES WALTZ 100.00 190.00 125.00
"HILLBILLY" STAMPED IN RED ON LABEL

PRISONAIRES

☐191 A PRISONER'S PRAYER/
I KNOW 37.00 72.00 37.00

LITTLE JUNIOR'S BLUE FLAMES

☐192 MYSTERY TRAIN/
LOVE MY BABY 16.00 31.00 19.00

DOCTOR ROSS

☐193 COME BACK BABY/
CHICAGO BREAKDOWN ... 52.00 95.00 62.00

LITTLE MILTON

☐194 BEGGIN' MY BABY/
SOMEBODY TOLD ME 20.00 35.00 23.00

BILLY "THE KID" EMERSON

☐195 NO TEASING AROUND/
IF LOVIN' IS BELIEVING .. 24.00 42.00 28.00

HOT SHOT LOVE

☐196 WOLF CALL BOOGIE/
HARMONICA JAM 110.00 200.00 125.00

EARL PETERSON-MICHIGAN'S SINGING COWBOY

☐197 BOOGIE BLUES/IN THE DARK 30.00 55.00 36.00
"HILLBILLY" STAMPED IN RED ON LABEL

HOWARD SERATT

☐198 TROUBLESOME WATERS/
I MUST BE SAVED 115.00 210.00 125.00

JAMES COTTON

☐199 MY BABY/
STRAIGHTEN UP BABY ... 75.00 140.00 90.00

LITTLE MILTON

☐200 IF YOU LOVE ME/
ALONE AND BLUE 25.00 47.00 28.00

HARDROCK GUNTER

☐201 GONNA DANCE ALL NIGHT/
FALLEN ANGEL 105.00 185.00 125.00

		Current Price Range		P/Y AVG

DOUG POINDEXTER AND STARLITE WRANGLERS

☐ 202   MY KIND OF CARRYIN' ON/
NOW SHE CARES NO
MORE FOR ME 95.00   160.00   105.00
"HILLBILLY" STAMPED IN RED ON LABEL

BILLY (THE KID) EMERSON

☐ 203   I'M NOT GOING HOME/
THE WOODCHUCK 50.00   90.00   52.00

RAYMOND HILL

☐ 204   BOURBON STREET JUMP/
THE SNUGGLE 45.00   85.00   52.00

HARMONICA FRANK

☐ 205   ROCKIN' CHAIR DADDY/
THE GREAT MEDICAL
MENAGERIST 185.00   300.00   215.00

JAMES COTTON

☐ 206   HOLD ME IN YOUR ARMS/
COTTON CROP BLUES 100.00   190.00   125.00

PRISONAIRES

☐ 207   THERE IS LOVE IN YOU/
WHAT'LL YOU DO NEXT . . 220.00   370.00   265.00

BUDDY CUNNINGHAM

☐ 208   RIGHT OR WRONG/
WHO DO I CRY 38.00   60.00   42.00

ELVIS PRESLEY-SCOTTY AND BILL

☐ 209   THAT'S ALL RIGHT/BLUE
MOON OF KENTUCKY 200.00   390.00   270.00

ELVIS PRESLEY-SCOTTY AND BILL

☐ 210   GOOD ROCKIN' TONIGHT/
I DON'T CARE IF THE
SUN DON'T SHINE 185.00   325.00   225.00

MALCOLM YELVINGTON AND STAR RHYTHM BOYS

☐ 211   DRINKIN' WINE SPODEE-O-
DEE/JUST ROLLING ALONG   24.00   39.00   28.00

DOCTOR ROSS

☐ 212   THE BOOGIE DISEASE/
JUKE BOX BOOGIE 100.00   185.00   125.00

THE JONES BROTHERS

☐ 213   EVERY NIGHT/
LOOK TO JESUS 190.00   345.00   215.00
NOT KNOWN IF 45 RPM EXISTS; 78 PRICES WOULD BE LESS THAN
HALF OF THOSE LISTED ABOVE

BILLY (THE KID) EMERSON

☐ 214   MOVE BABY MOVE/WHEN IT
RAINS IT POURS 23.00   41.00   28.00

ELVIS PRESLEY-SCOTTY AND BILL

☐ 215   MILKCOW BLUES BOOGIE/
YOU'RE A HEARTBREAKER   275.00   450.00   310.00

		Current Price Range		P/Y AVG

SLIM RHODES
☐216 DON'T BELIEVE/
UNCERTAIN LOVE 23.00   41.00   28.00

ELVIS PRESLEY-SCOTTY AND BILL
☐217 BABY LET'S PLAY HOUSE/
I'M LEFT, YOU'RE RIGHT,
SHE'S GONE 150.00   275.00   190.00

SAMMY LEWIS-WILLIE JOHNSON COMBO
☐218 SO LONG BABY/
I FEEL SO WORRIED 14.00   21.00   14.50

BILLY "THE KID" EMERSON
☐219 RED HOT/NO GREATER LOVE   20.00   35.00   23.00

LITTLE MILTON
☐220 LOOKIN' FOR MY BABY/
HOMESICK FOR MY BABY .   60.00   115.00   73.00

JOHNNY CASH AND THE TENNESSEE TWO
☐221 HEY PORTER/CRY! CRY! CRY!   5.00   9.00   7.00

THE FIVE TINOS
☐222 SITTING BY MY WINDOW/
DON'T DO THAT 125.00   235.00   150.00

ELVIS PRESLEY-SCOTTY AND BILL
☐223 MYSTERY TRAIN/I FORGOT
TO REMEMBER TO FORGET   140.00   260.00   185.00

CARL PERKINS
☐224 LET THE JUKE BOX KEEP ON
PLAYING/GONE GONE
GONE 34.00   50.00   45.00

SLIM RHODES
☐225 THE HOUSE OF SIN/ARE YOU
ASHAMED OF ME 17.00   32.00   19.00

EDDIE SNOW
☐226 AIN'T THAT RIGHT/BRING
YOUR LOVE BACK HOME . .   23.00   41.00   27.00

ROSCOE GORDON
☐227 JUST LOVE ME BABY/
WEEPING BLUES 14.00   24.00   17.00
ALSO RELEASED ON FLIP 227 WITH SAME VALUE

SMOKEY JOE
☐228 THE SIGNIFYING MONKEY/
LISTEN TO ME BABY 10.00   19.00   13.00
ALSO RELEASED ON FLIP 228; DOUBLE VALUE FROM ABOVE

MAGGIE SUE WIMBERLY
☐229 HOW LONG/DAYDREAMS
COME TRUE 11.00   19.00   13.00

		Current Price Range		P/Y AVG

THE MILLER SISTERS
☐230 THERE'S NO RIGHT WAY TO DO ME WRONG/YOU CAN TELL ME 25.00 43.00 28.00
ALSO RELEASED ON FLIP 230 WITH SAME VALUE

CHARLIE FEATHERS
☐231 DEFROST YOUR HEART/ WEDDING GOWN OF WHITE 115.00 225.00 150.00
ALSO RELEASED ON FLIP 231 WITH SAME VALUE

JOHNNY CASH
☐232 FOLSOM PRISON BLUES/ SO DOGGONE LONESOME . 4.50 7.50 6.00

BILLY "THE KID" EMERSON
☐233 LITTLE FINE HEALTHY THING/ SOMETHING FOR NOTHING 8.00 15.00 10.00

CARL PERKINS
☐234 BLUE SUEDE SHOES/ HONEY DON'T 5.00 9.00 7.00

CARL PERKINS
☐235 SURE TO FALL/TENNESSEE . (UNISSUED)

JIMMY HAGGETT
☐236 NO MORE/THEY CALL OUR LOVE A SIN 185.00 335.00 210.00

ROSCO GORDON
☐237 ''THE CHICKEN'' (DANCE WITH YOU)/LOVE FOR YOU BABY 6.00 11.00 7.00
ALSO RELEASED ON FLIP 237 WITH SAME VALUE

SLIM RHODES
☐238 GONNA ROMP AND STOMP/ BAD GIRL 14.00 25.00 16.50

WARREN SMITH
☐239 ROCK 'N' ROLL RUBY/ I'D RATHER BE SAFE THAN SORRY 14.00 25.00 16.50

JACK EARLS AND THE JIMBOS
☐240 SLOW DOWN/A FOOL FOR LOVIN' YOU 12.00 21.00 18.00

JOHNNY CASH AND THE TENNESSEE TWO
☐241 I WALK THE LINE/ GET RHYTHM 3.25 5.50 4.00

ROY ORBISON AND THE TEEN KINGS
☐242 OOBY DOOBY/GO, GO, GO ... 8.25 14.00 12.00

CARL PERKINS
☐243 BOPPIN' THE BLUES/ ALL MAMA'S CHILDREN .. 4.50 7.50 6.00

		Current Price Range		P/Y AVG

JEAN CHAPEL

☐244   I WON'T BE ROCKIN' TONIGHT/WELCOME TO THE CLUB 5.00   9.00   6.00

BILLY RILEY

☐245   TROUBLE BOUND/ ROCK WITH ME BABY 20.00   35.00   23.00

MALCOLM YELVINGTON

☐246   ROCKIN' WITH MY BABY/ IT'S ME BABY 14.00   26.00   16.50

SONNY BURGESS

☐247   RED HEADED WOMAN/ WE WANNA BOOGIE 11.00   20.00   13.50

RHYTHM ROCKERS

☐248   FIDDLE BOP/JUKE BOX, HELP ME FIND MY BABY 10.00   19.00   13.25

CARL PERKINS

☐249   DIXIE FRIED/I'M SORRY, I'M NOT SORRY 4.60   7.50   6.00

WARREN SMITH

☐250   UBANGI STOMP/ BLACK JACK DAVID 9.00   18.00   13.00

ROY ORBISON-TEEN KINGS

☐251   ROCKHOUSE/ YOU'RE MY BABY 8.25   17.00   15.00

☐252   UNISSUED . . . .

BARBARA PITMAN

☐253   I NEED A MAN/NO MATTER WHO'S TO BLAME 6.00   11.00   7.00

RAY HARRIS

☐254   COME ON LITTLE MAMA/ WHERE'D YOU STAY LAST NIGHT 23.00   39.00   28.00

MILLER SISTERS

☐255   TEN CATS DOWN/ FINDERS KEEPERS 23.00   39.00   28.00

SLIM RHODES FEATURING SANDY BROOKS

☐256   TAKE AND GIVE/ DO WHAT I DO 6.00   12.00   8.00

ROSCO GORDON

☐257   SHOOBIE OOBIE/ CHEESE AND CRACKERS . .   3.50   6.50   4.65

JOHNNY CASH AND THE TENNESSEE TWO

☐258   TRAIN OF LOVE/ THERE YOU GO 3.25   6.00   4.00

JERRY LEE LEWIS

☐259   CRAZY ARMS/ END OF THE ROAD 8.25   14.00   12.00

		Current Price Range		P/Y AVG

BILLY RILEY AND HIS LITTLE GREEN MEN

☐260 FLYIN' SAUCERS ROCK & ROLL/I WANT YOU BABY . — 20.00 — 38.00 — 23.00

CARL PERKINS

☐261 YOUR TRUE LOVE/ MATCHBOX .... — 4.50 — 7.50 — 6.00

ERNIE CHAFFIN

☐262 LONESOME FOR MY BABY/ FEELIN' LOW .... — 4.00 — 7.00 — 4.35

SONNY BURGESS

☐263 RESTLESS/ AIN'T GOT A THING ...... — 9.00 — 17.00 — 10.00

GLENN HONEYCUTT

☐264 I'LL BE AROUND/ I'LL WAIT FOREVER ...... — 5.00 — 9.00 — 6.00

ROY ORBISON AND THE ROSES

☐265 DEVIL DOLL/ SWEET AND EASY .... — 6.00 — 12.00 — 8.00

JOHNNY CASH AND THE TENNESSEE TWO

☐266 NEXT IN LINE/ DON'T MAKE ME GO ..... — 3.25 — 5.50 — 4.00

JERRY LEE LEWIS

☐267 WHOLE LOT OF SHAKIN' GOING ON/IT'LL BE ME ... — 4.50 — 7.50 — 6.00

WARREN SMITH

☐268 SO LONG I'M GONE/ MISS FROGGIE .... — 8.00 — 15.00 — 10.00

WAKE AND DICK THE COLLEGE KIDS

☐269 BOP BOP BABY/DON'T NEED YOUR LOVIN' BABY ...... — 5.00 — 9.00 — 6.00

JIM WILLIAMS

☐270 PLEASE DON'T CRY OVER ME/ THAT DEPENDS ON YOU .. — 3.50 — 6.00 — 4.35

RUDI RICHARDSON

☐271 FOOL'S HALL OF FAME/ WHY SHOULD I CRY ..... — 3.50 — 6.00 — 4.35

RAY HARRIS

☐272 GREENBACK DOLLAR, WATCH AND CHAIN/ FOOLISH HEART .... — 12.00 — 21.00 — 13.50

MACK SELF

☐273 EASY TO LOVE/EVERY DAY . — 3.50 — 6.00 — 4.35

CARL PERKINS

☐274 FOREVER YOURS/ THAT'S RIGHT .... — 4.50 — 7.50 — 6.00

		Current Price Range		P/Y AVG
ERNIE CHAFFIN				
☐275 I'M LONESOME/ LAUGHIN' AND JOKIN' ...		3.50	6.00	4.35
EDWIN BRUCE				
☐276 ROCK BOPPIN' BABY/ MORE THAN YESTERDAY .		3.50	6.00	4.35
BILLY RILEY-LITTLE GREEN MEN				
☐277 RED HOT/PEARLY LEE		6.00	11.00	6.85
TOMMY BLAKE-RHYTHM REBELS				
☐278 FLAT FOOT SAM/ LORDY HOODY		6.00	10.00	6.85
JOHNNY CASH AND THE TENNESSEE TWO				
☐279 HOME OF THE BLUES/ GIVE MY LOVE TO ROSE ..		3.25	5.50	4.00
DICKEY LEE AND THE COLLEGIATES				
☐280 MEMORIES NEW GROW OLD/ GOOD LOVIN'		4.00	7.00	4.85
JERRY LEE LEWIS				
☐281 GREAT BALLS OF FIRE/ YOU WIN AGAIN		2.50	7.50	6.00
DICK PENNER				
☐282 YOUR HONEY LOVE/ CINDY LOU		6.00	10.00	6.85
JOHNNY CASH AND THE TENNESSEE TWO				
☐283 BALLAD OF A TEENAGE QUEEN/BIG RIVER		3.00	5.00	3.50
ROY ORBISON				
☐284 CHICKEN-HEARTED/ I LIKE LOVE		6.50	12.00	8.00
SONNY BURGESS				
☐285 MY BUCKET'S GOT A HOLE IN IT/SWEET MISERY		6.50	12.00	8.00
WARREN SMITH				
☐286 I'VE GOT LOVE IF YOU WANT IT/I FEEL IN LOVE		6.50	12.00	8.00
CARL PERKINS				
☐287 GLAD ALL OVER/ LEND ME YOUR COMB		4.50	7.50	6.00
JERRY LEE LEWIS				
☐288 BREATHLESS/ DOWN THE LINE		3.75	6.00	4.50
BILLY RILEY-THE LITTLE GREEN MEN				
☐289 WOULDN'T YOU KNOW/ BABY PLEASE DON'T GO ..		6.00	11.00	7.00
RUDY GRAYZELL				
☐290 JUDY/I THINK OF YOU		6.00	11.00	7.00

		Current Price Range		P/Y AVG

JACK CLEMENT
☐291 TEN YEARS/
YOUR LOVER BOY 3.50 6.00 4.00

EDWIN BRUCE
☐292 SWEET WOMAN/
PART OF MY LIFE 5.00 9.00 6.00

THE SUN-RAYS
☐293 THE LONELY HOURS/
LOVE IS A STRANGER 3.75 6.50 4.35

MAGEL FRIESMAN
☐294 I FEEL SO BLUE/
MEMORIES OF YOU 3.75 6.75 4.35

JOHNNY CASH AND THE TENNESSEE TWO
☐295 GUESS THINGS HAPPEN THAT
WAY/COME IN STRANGER 3.00 5.00 3.50

JERRY LEE LEWIS
☐296 HIGH SCHOOL CONFIDENTIAL/
FOOLS LIKE ME 3.75 6.00 4.50

DICKEY LEE
☐297 FOOL, FOOL, FOOL/
DREAMY NIGHTS 3.50 5.75 4.25

RAY SMITH
☐298 RIGHT BEHIND YOU BABY/
SO YOUNG 5.00 8.50 7.00

GENE SIMMONS
☐299 DRINKIN' WINE/
I DONE TOLD YOU 16.00 30.00 19.00
THIS WAS NOT THE GENE SIMMONS OF "KISS"

TOMMY BLAKE
☐300 SWEETIE PIE/I DIG YOU BABY 85.00 150.00 105.00

GEORGE AND LOUIS
☐301 THE RETURN OF JERRY LEE/
LEWIS BOOGIE 5.00 9.00 6.00

JOHNNY CASH AND THE TENNESSEE TWO
☐302 THE WAYS OF A WOMAN IN
LOVE/YOU'RE THE
NEAREST THING TO
HEAVEN 3.00 5.00 3.50

JERRY LEE LEWIS
☐303 BREAK-UP/I'LL MAKE IT ALL
UP TO YOU 3.25 5.50 4.00

SONNY BURGESS
☐304 ITCHY/THUNDERBIRD 14.00 29.00 18.00

ROSCO GORDON
☐305 SALLY JO/TORRO 3.50 6.00 4.35

		Current Price Range		P/Y AVG
	JIMMY ISLE			
☐306	I'VE BEEN WAITING/ DIAMOND RING	3.50	6.00	4.35
	ERNIE CHAFFIN			
☐307	MY LOVE FOR YOU/ BORN TO LOSE	3.25	5.50	4.00
	RAY SMITH			
☐308	WHY, WHY, WHY/ YOU MADE A HIT	4.50	7.50	6.00
	JOHNNY CASH AND THE TENNESSEE TWO			
☐309	IT'S JUST ABOUT TIME/ I JUST THOUGHT YOU'D LIKE TO KNOW	3.00	5.00	3.50
	VERNON TAYLOR			
☐310	BREEZE/TODAY IS BLUE DAY	3.50	6.00	4.35
	JACK CLEMENT			
☐311	THE BLACK HAIRED MAN/ WRONG	3.25	5.50	4.00
	JERRY LEE LEWIS			
☐312	I'LL SAIL MY SHIP ALONE/ IT HURT ME SO	3.25	5.50	4.00
	BILL RILEY			
☐313	DOWN BY THE RIVERSIDE/ NO NAME GIRL	4.00	7.00	4.85
	WARREN SMITH			
☐314	SWEET, SWEET GIRL/ GOODBYE MR. LOVE	5.00	9.00	6.25
	ONIE WHEELER			
☐315	JUMP RIGHT OUT OF THIS JUKE BOX/TELL 'EM OFF .	5.00	9.00	6.25
	JOHNNY CASH AND THE TENNESSEE TWO			
☐316	THANKS A LOT/LUTHER PLAYED THE BOOGIE	3.00	5.00	3.50
	JERRY LEE LEWIS			
☐317	LOVIN' UP A STORM/ BIG BLON' BABY	3.25	5.50	4.00
	JIMMY ISLE			
☐318	TIME WILL TELL/ WITHOUT A LOVE	3.50	6.00	4.35
	RAY SMITH			
☐319	ROCKIN' BANDIT/SAIL AWAY	4.50	7.50	6.00
	ERNIE CHAFFIN			
☐320	DON'T EVER LEAVE ME/ MIRACLE OF YOU	3.50	6.00	4.35
	JOHNNY CASH AND THE TENNESSEE TWO			
☐321	KATY TOO/I FORGOT TO REMEMBER TO FORGET ...	3.00	5.00	3.50

		Current Price Range		P/Y AVG
☐322	**BILL RILEY** GOT THE WATER BOILING/ ONE MORE TIME	10.00	19.00	11.50
☐323	**ALTON AND JIMMY** HAVE FAITH IN MY LOVE/NO MORE CRYING THE BLUES	6.00	11.00	7.00
☐324	**JERRY LEE LEWIS** LET'S TALK ABOUT US/ BALLAD OF BILLY JOE	3.25	5.50	4.00
☐325	**VERNON TAYLOR** MYSTERY TRAIN/SWEET AND EASY TO LOVE	6.00	11.00	7.00
☐326	**JERRY McGILL AND THE TOP COATS** I WANNA MAKE SWEET LOVE/ LOVE STRUCK	5.00	9.00	6.00
☐327	**JOHNNY POWERS** WITH YOUR LOVE, WITH YOUR KISS/BE MINE, ALL MINE	11.00	20.00	13.00
☐328	**SHERRY CRANE** WILLIE, WILLIE/ WINNIE THE PARAKEET ...	3.50	6.00	4.00
☐329	**WILL MERCER** YOU'RE JUST MY KIND/ BALLAD OF ST. MARKS ...	3.50	6.00	4.00
☐330	**JERRY LEE LEWIS** LITTLE QUEENIE/ I COULD NEVER BE ASHAMED OF YOU	3.25	5.50	4.00
☐331	**JOHNNY CASH AND THE TENNESSEE TWO** GOODBYE, LITTLE DARLING/ YOU TELL ME	3.00	5.00	3.50
☐332	**JIMMY ISLE** WHAT A LIFE/TOGETHER ...	3.00	5.00	3.65
☐333	**RAY B. ANTHONY** ALICE BLUE GOWN/ ST. LOUIS BLUES	3.00	5.00	3.65
☐334	**JOHNNY CASH AND THE TENNESSEE TWO** STRAIGHT A'S IN LOVE/ I LOVE YOU BECAUSE	3.00	5.00	3.50
☐335	**TRACY PENDARVIS AND THE SWAMPERS** A THOUSAND GUITARS/ IS IT TOO LATE	3.00	5.00	3.65
☐336	**MACK OWEN** WALKIN' AND TALKIN'/ SOMEBODY JUST LIKE YOU	3.00	5.00	3.65

		Current Price Range		P/Y AVG

JERRY LEE LEWIS
☐ 337 OLD BLACK JOE/
BABY, BABY BYE BYE 3.25 5.50 4.00

PAUL RICKY
☐ 338 LEGEND OF THE BIG STEEPLE/
BROKEN HEARTED WILLIE . 3.00 5.00 3.65

RAYBURN ANTHONY
☐ 339 THERE'S NO TOMORROW/
WHOSE GONNA SHINE
YOUR PRETTY LITTLE FEET 3.00 5.00 3.65

BILL JOHNSON
☐ 340 BOBALOO/BAD TIMES AHEAD 3.00 5.00 3.65

SONNY WILSON
☐ 341 THE GREAT PRETENDER/I'M
GONNA TAKE A WALK 3.00 5.00 3.65

BOBBIE JEAN
☐ 342 YOU BURNED THE BRIDGES/
CHEATERS NEVER WIN ... 3.00 5.00 3.65

JOHNNY CASH AND THE TENNESSEE TWO
☐ 343 DOWN THE STREET TO 301/
THE STORY OF A BROKEN
HEART 3.00 5.00 3.50

JERRY LEE LEWIS
☐ 344 JOHN HENRY/HANG UP MY
ROCK AND ROLL SHOES .. 3.25 5.50 4.00

TRACY PENDARVIS
☐ 345 IS IT ME/SOUTHBOUND LINE 3.50 6.00 4.35

BILL STRENGTH
☐ 346 I GUESS I'D BETTER GO/
SENORITA 3.25 5.50 4.00

JOHNNY CASH AND THE TENNESSEE TWO
☐ 347 MEAN EYED CAT/
PORT OF LONELY HEARTS . 3.00 5.00 3.50

LANCE ROBERTS
☐ 348 THE GOOD GUY ALWAYS
WINS/THE TIME IS RIGHT . 3.00 5.00 3.65

TONY ROSSINI
☐ 349 I GOTTA KNOW WHERE I
STAND/IS IT TOO LATE ... 3.00 5.00 3.65

THE ROCKIN' STOCKINGS
☐ 350 YULESVILLE U.S.A./ROCKIN'
OLD LANG SYNE 3.50 6.00 4.35

IRA JAY II
☐ 351 YOU DON'T LOVE ME/
MORE THAN ANYTHING ... 3.00 5.00 3.65

		Current Price Range		P/Y AVG

JERRY LEE LEWIS
☐ 352 WHEN I GET PAID/LOVE
MADE A FOOL OF ME 3.25 5.50 4.00

ROY ORBISON
☐ 353 DEVIL DOLL/SWEET AND
EASY TO LOVE 6.00 11.00 6.85

BOBBY SHERIDAN
☐ 354 RED MAN/SAD NEWS 4.00 7.00 4.35
BOBBY SHERIDAN WAS REALLY CHARLIE RICH

JOHNNY CASH AND THE TENNESSEE TWO
☐ 355 OH, LONESOME ME/
LIFE GOES ON 3.00 5.00 3.50

JERRY LEE LEWIS
☐ 356 WHAT'D I SAY/
LIVIN' LOVIN' WRECK 3.00 5.00 3.50
☐ 357 UNISSUED ....

GEORGE KLEIN
☐ 358 U. T. PARTY (PT. 1)/(PT. 2) . 3.00 5.00 3.65

TRACY PENDARVIS
☐ 359 BELL OF THE SUWANEE/
ETERNALLY 3.00 5.00 3.65

WADE CAGLE AND THE ESCORTS
☐ 360 GROOVEY TRAIN/
HIGHLAND ROCK 3.50 6.00 4.35

ANITA WOOD
☐ 361 I'LL WAIT FOREVER/I CAN'T
SHOW HOW I FEEL 3.00 5.00 3.65

HAROLD DORMAN
☐ 362 THERE THEY GO/
I'LL STICK BY YOU 4.00 7.00 4.85

JOHNNY CASH AND THE TENNESSEE TWO
☐ 363 MY TREASURE/SUGAR TIME 3.00 5.00 3.50

JERRY LEE LEWIS
☐ 364 IT WON'T HAPPEN WITH ME/
COLD, COLD HEART 3.00 5.00 3.50

SHIRLEY SISK
☐ 365 I FORGOT TO REMEMBER TO
FORGET/OTHER SIDE 3.00 5.00 3.65

TONY ROSSINI
☐ 366 WELL I ASK YA/DARLENA .. 3.00 5.00 3.65

JERRY LEE LEWIS
☐ 367 SAVE THE LAST DANCE FOR
ME/AS LONG AS I LIVE ... 3.00 5.00 3.50

DON HOSEA
☐ 368 SINCE I MET YOU/
U HUH UNH 3.00 5.00 3.65

		Current Price Range		P/Y AVG

BOBBY WOOD

☐369 EVERYBODY'S SEARCHIN'/ HUMAN EMOTIONS 3.25 5.50 4.00

HAROLD DORMAN

☐370 UNCLE JONAH'S PLACE/ JUST ONE STEP 4.00 7.00 4.85

JERRY LEE LEWIS

☐371 MONEY/BOBBIE B 3.00 5.00 3.50

RAY SMITH

☐372 TRAVELIN' SALESMAN/ I WON'T MISS YOU (TIL YOU'RE GONE) 3.25 5.50 4.00

RAYBURN ANTHONY

☐373 HOW WELL I KNOW/ BIG DREAM 3.00 5.00 3.65

JERRY LEE LEWIS

☐374 I'VE BEEN TWISTIN'/ RAMBLIN' ROSE 3.00 5.00 3.50

RAY SMITH

☐375 CANDY DOLL/ HEY, BOSS MAN 3.25 5.50 4.00

JOHNNY CASH AND THE TENNESSEE TWO

☐376 BLUE TRAIN/BORN TO LOSE . 3.00 5.00 3.50

HAROLD DORMAN

☐377 WAIT TIL' SATURDAY NIGHT/ IN THE BEGINNING 4.00 7.00 4.85

TONY ROSSINI

☐378 (MEET ME) AFTER SCHOOL/ JUST AROUND THE CORNER 3.00 5.00 3.65

JERRY LEE LEWIS

☐379 SWEET LITTLE SIXTEEN/ HOW'S MY EX TREATING YOU? 3.00 5.00 3.50

TONY ROSSINI AND THE CHIPPERS

☐380 YOU MAKE IT SOUND SO EASY/NEW GIRL IN TOWN 3.00 5.00 3.65

THE FOUR UPSETTERS

☐381 CRAZY ARMS/ MIDNIGHT SOIREE 3.00 5.00 3.65

JERRY LEE LEWIS

☐382 GOOD GOLLY, MISS MOLLY/ I CAN'T TRUST ME (IN YOUR ARMS) 3.00 5.00 3.50

☐383 UNISSUED ....

		Current Price Range		P/Y AVG

JERRY LEE LEWIS
| ☐384 | TEENAGE LETTER/SEASONS OF MY HEART (with Linda Gail Lewis) .... | 3.00 | 5.00 | 3.50 |
| ☐385 | UNISSUED .... | | | |

THE FOUR UPSETTERS
| ☐386 | WABASH CANNONBALL/ SURFIN' CALLIOPE ...... | 3.00 | 5.00 | 3.65 |

TONY ROSSINI
| ☐387 | MOVED TO KANSAS CITY/ NOBODY .... | 3.00 | 5.00 | 3.65 |

THE TEENANGELS
| ☐388 | AIN'T GONNA LET YOU/TELL ME MY LOVE (dj only)..... | 12.00 | 24.00 | 13.50 |

BILLY ADAMS
| ☐389 | BETTY AND DUPREE/ GOT MY MOJO WORKIN' .. | 3.00 | 5.00 | 3.65 |

BILL YATES AND HIS T-BIRDS
| ☐390 | DON'T STEP ON MY DOG/ STOP, WAIT, LISTEN ..... | 3.00 | 5.00 | 3.65 |

BILLY ADAMS
| ☐391 | TROUBLE IN MIND/LOOKIN' FOR MARY ANN .... | 3.00 | 5.00 | 3.65 |

JOHNNY CASH
| ☐392 | WIDE OPEN ROAD/ BELSHAZAR .... | 3.00 | 5.00 | 3.50 |

SMOKEY JOE
| ☐393 | SIGNIFYING MONKEY/ LISTEN TO ME BABY ..... | 5.00 | 10.00 | 6.85 |

BILLY ADAMS
| ☐394 | RECONSIDER BABY/ RUBY JANE .... | 3.00 | 5.00 | 3.65 |

RANDY AND THE RADIANTS
| ☐395 | PEEK-A-BOO/ MOUNTAIN HIGH .... | 3.00 | 5.00 | 3.65 |

JERRY LEE LEWIS
| ☐396 | CARRY ME BACK TO OLD VIRGINIA/I KNOW WHAT IT MEANS .... | 3.00 | 5.00 | 3.50 |

GORGEOUS BILL
| ☐397 | CARLEEN/TOO LATE TO RIGHT MY WRONG .... | 3.00 | 5.00 | 3.65 |

RANDY AND THE RADIANTS
| ☐398 | MY WAYS OF THINKING/ TRUTH FROM MY EYES ... | 3.00 | 5.00 | 3.65 |

BILL YATES
| ☐399 | BIG, BIG WORLD/I DROPPED MY M AND M'S .... | 3.00 | 5.00 | 3.65 |

		Current Price Range		P/Y AVG

THE JESTERS
| ☐400 | MY BABE/CADILLAC MAN . . | 5.00 | 10.00 | 6.00 |

BILLY ADAMS
| ☐401 | OPEN THE DOOR RICHARD/ ROCK ME BABY . . . . | 3.00 | 5.00 | 3.65 |

DANE STINIT
| ☐402 | DON'T KNOCK WHAT YOU DON'T UNDERSTAND/ ALWAYS ON THE GO . . . . . | 3.00 | 5.00 | 3.65 |

DAVID HOUSTON
| ☐403 | SHERRY'S LIPS/ MISS BROWN . . . . | 3.50 | 6.00 | 4.35 |

THE CLIMATES
| ☐404 | NO YOU FOR ME/ BREAKING UP AGAIN . . . . . | 3.00 | 5.00 | 3.65 |

DANE STINIT
| ☐405 | SWEET COUNTRY GIRL/ THAT MUDDY OLE RIVER . . | 3.00 | 5.00 | 3.65 |

GOSPEL SERIES: BROTHER JAMES ANDERSON
| ☐406 | I'M GONNA MOVE IN THE ROOM WITH THE LORD/MY SOUL NEEDS RESTING . . . | 4.00 | 7.00 | 4.85 |

"LOAD OF MISCHIEF"
| ☐407 | BACK IN MY ARMS AGAIN/ I'M A LOVER . . . . | 4.00 | 7.00 | 4.85 |

ROCK MEMORABILIA

Almost evey rock enthusiast accumulates souvenirs or memorabilia. Those who consider themselves collectors, usually interested in a single group or artist, look beyond the common store items and seek out the items most desirable to complete their collections. Press kits, ticket stubs, tour books and candid unpublished photographs are examples. All of these are found on the collector market, through the advertisements appearing in music magazines and fanzines. All the artists have their fan clubs, and the fan club bulletins do carry ads from persons who want to buy, sell, or exchange. Some extremely unique items can be found in this fashion, as well as by visiting record collector shows.

Posters are among the favorites. While they are hardly ever of the "limited edition" variety, many are scarce and can attain a surprising value. Numerous different posters exist for all the major rock stars and their values vary from one to another. When a poster is called *commercial,* it was intended to be sold to the public, and is found in stores. A promotional poster is designed to promote with which the artist was connected, an LP album, single recording, or concert tour. These are displayed in record shops and elsewhere. As a rule the promotional posters are more scarce. An advanced collector does not limit himself to the domestic versions but gets those issued for use in Italy, Holland, Germany, Japan and elsewhere. These are often more valuable, either from having been printed in lower quantities or simply not reaching the U.S. in large numbers. Today they are somewhat more obtainable than in the past, as each foreign country has its collectors who are anxious to exchange with, or sell to those in the U.S. The variations that exist from one printing of a poster to another are also of great interest to advanced collectors.

When a poster has a name, such as David Bowie's "China Girl," this is almost always the name of an LP album being promoted by the poster. It can be assumed to be contemporary in age with that LP. In such instances the poster is an enlargement of the picture appearing on the LP sleeve, though the wording may be arranged or styled differently. If the picture is different, there may be a small inset illustration of the LP sleeve. The size of a poster is important in determining its value, as the same poster may have been issued in different sizes. There is no standard size for either commercial or promotional posters, but the promotionals vary the most in size. They will be found from 12″ x 18″ up to 60″ x 48″ and all sizes between. Thus it you find an advertisement stating simply "Duran Duran poster," without details, size is questionable. There are also such things as bootleg posters.

Press kits are issued by the recording companies or management companies to whom artists are contracted. They are more scarce than posters as they are not intended for a large distribution. Press kits are given away to the news media and record stores. Most press kits contain one photo. Accompanying the photo is a brief biography, sometimes only one page but running to as much as ten or a dozen pages. The biography contains essential facts that an editor would want to know and it includes only a minimum amount of what could be called "advertising copy." It is presumed that the editor or his reporters would want to do their own story and refer to the press kit only for dates, names, statistics, etc. These press kits are kept on file by the media and used for years, or until a new one is issued for that group or artist. Sometimes a press kit is not "general," but relates to a given event such as the release of a new LP, a motion picture, or a tour. In that case there will be special information which could be used by an editor in reviewing the LP, motion picture, or concert performance. The press kit is also "required reading" for any reporter assigned to interview the artist. It gives him a good insight into the appropriate questions to ask.

The photo in a press kit (or photos as the case may be) will be loose, as the intention is to publish it. When the photo is missing, the press kit has little or no collector value. Most press kits are just folders but some are a bit more elaborate. There is seldom any attempt to make them really showy, as the people to whom they are directed are not the fans themselves. The best feature of press kits is that you always get an original photo with them. Publicists are careful to avoid sending out a photo which editors might already have on file.

Tour books, of which a few are listed below, comprise another very popular element of the rock memorabilia hobby. These are soft covered, fairly thin, illustrated with color photos and of course a full color cover. They are issued in conjunction with a specific concert tour made by the group or artist involved, and are available for sale at the concerts. While it is true that many thousands of fans attend each concert, the overall distribution of the average tour book is still more limited than a book released into book stores. As the book is not reissued, it has a short life-span and it definitely can achieve a scarcity factor after a few years have passed.

A tour program is different than a tour book. It is sometimes given away free to those attending a concert, or, if sold, the price is very low. It gives essential facts along with some photographs but a large part of the tour program consists of advertisements from local merchants and other businesses in the area. These, too, are collectible.

Candid photographs are very popular as memorabilia, but as they tend to sell for uniform prices of $1 to $2 each we have not included them in the following listings. Rather than buying them, most collectors prefer to trade prints of photos they have taken for photos taken by other collectors. Before attending a concert, the photo enthusiasts should check to determine if photographic equipment is being permitted on the grounds.

Price Range

ABBA

☐	MAGAZINE, issue of Record World, October 1979, with cover photo and article on them...	4.00	5.00
☐	PICTURE SLEEVE from 45 r.p.m. (no record), Knowing Me..........	.50	.75
☐	POSTER, group picture, commercial, 21x30".....................	4.50	6.00

AC/DC

☐	POSTER, AC/DC in Concert with white snake, German promotional, 24x33"...	6.00	8.00
☐	POSTER, Back in Black, U.S. promotional, 24x24".................	3.50	4.50
☐	POSTER, Flick of the Switch, promotional, 24x24".................	6.00	8.00
☐	POSTER, For Those About to Rock, gold color, promotional, 18x27".....	3.50	4.50
☐	POSTER, Let There Be Rock, concert picture, U.S. promotional, 24x24".	4.50	6.00

ADAM ANT

☐	POSTER, Friend or Foe, 24x35"................................	4.00	5.00
☐	POSTER, Kings of the Wild Frontier/Ant Invasion, tour, 24x36"........	9.00	12.00
☐	TICKET STUB, Radio City Music Hall, New York City, 1984...........	2.00	2.50

ADAMS, BRYAN

☐	POSTER, Cuts Like a Knife, promotional, 24x24".................	4.50	6.00

AEROSMITH

☐	POSTER, Coming Soon to Madison Square Garden, tour, 20x30".......	7.00	10.00
☐	POSTER, Toys in the Attic, blue/red/green, tour, 26x45"............	9.00	12.00
☐	TOUR BOOK, 1979...	4.00	5.00

ALABAMA

☐	POSTER, Roll On, U.S. promotional, 24x36".....................	6.00	8.00

ALLMAN, GREG

☐	POSTER, picture playing guitar, black and white, commercial, 28x38"...	4.50	6.00

AMERICAN HOT WAX

☐	POSTER, O.S.T. Marquee, promotional, 28x40"..................	7.00	10.00

Price Range

APRIL WINE
☐ POSTER, Animal Grace, promotional, 24x36"...................... 5.00   7.00

ASIA
☐ POSTER, serpent album cover, promotional, 24x36"............... 6.00   8.00

BEEFHEART
☐ PRESS KIT, Shiny Beast, two pictures and a three page biography...... 5.00   7.00

BEE GEES
☐ POSTER, Sgt. Pepper's Lonely Hearts Club Band, 24x36"............. 4.00   5.00

BENATAR, PAT
☐ POSTER, Get Nervous, promotional, 24x24"...................... 9.00   12.00
☐ POSTER, Live From Earth, promotional, 24x24".................... 9.00   12.00

BIG COUNTRY
☐ POSTER, The Crossing, promotional, 24x36"..................... 5.00   7.00

BLACK SABBATH
☐ POSTER, Born Again, red and blue, promotional, 23x23"............ 5.00   7.00
☐ POSTER, Live Evil, promotional, 23x23"........................ 5.00   7.00
☐ POSTER, Mob Rules, promotional, 23x24"....................... 6.00   8.00
☐ TICKET STUB, Tempe, Arizona, 1980.......................... 2.50   3.50
☐ TOUR BOOK, Mob Rules, 1982................................ 3.00   4.00

BLONDIE
☐ TOUR BOOK, 1979, color photos.............................. 8.00   11.00
☐ BUMPER STICKER, Eat to the Beat............................. 2.00   3.00
☐ BUTTON, Best of Blondie.................................... 2.00   3.00
☐ BUTTON, square, Autoamerican, 2"............................ 3.00   4.00
☐ CALENDAR, Autoamerican, 1981.............................. 3.00   4.00
☐ POSTER, Deborah Harry topless wearing white shorts............... 6.00   8.00
☐ POSTER, Koo Koo, promotional, 36x36"........................ 7.00   10.00
☐ PRESS KIT, Autoamerican, custom folder, one photo plus three page
    biography... 10.00   15.00
☐ TOUR PROGRAM, Parallel Lines, 1979......................... 6.00   8.00

BLUE OYSTER CULT
☐ TOUR BOOK, Cultosaurus, 1980.............................. 3.00   4.00

BLUE THUNDER
☐ POSTER, for video cassette, 41x27".......................... 4.50   6.00

BOFILL, ANGELA
☐ POSTER, Teaser, promotional, 17x22"......................... 4.50   6.00

BOSTON
☐ TOUR BOOK, Debut Album Tour, 1978.......................... 4.50   6.00

BOWIE, DAVID
☐ BOOK, David Bowie by Vivian Claire, 80 pages, 1977.............. 20.00   25.00
☐ BOOK, David Bowie: A Chronology by Kevin Cann, paperback, 240
    pages.. 8.00   11.00

Price Range

☐ BOOK, David Bowie Black Book by Miles (author who uses no last name),
paperback.. 12.00 15.00
☐ BOOKLET, Rotterdam 1983, 26 pages with vinyl flexi record inserted.... 9.00 12.00
☐ POSTER, China Girl, promotional color poster, 36x36"................ 5.00 7.00
☐ POSTER, Gigolo, Italian, 55x40"................................... 18.00 23.00
☐ POSTER, Just a Gigolo, promotional, 27x41"........................ 11.00 15.00
☐ POSTER, Let's Dance, blow-up from LP cover, 36x36"................ 5.00 7.00

BROWNE, JACKSON

☐ POSTER, artist's sketch on textured paper, 40x30"................. 4.50 6.00
☐ POSTER, Hold Out, promotional, 48x48"............................ 13.00 18.00

CARMEN, ERIC

☐ PRESS KIT, Tonight, one page and a two page biography............. 6.00 8.00

CARNES, KIM

☐ POSTER, for video cassette, 18x12"............................... 2.50 3.50

CARS

☐ POSTER, Heartbeat City, promotional, 27x40"...................... 7.00 10.00
☐ POSTER, Shake it Up, promotional, 48x48"......................... 13.00 18.00

CHAPIN, HARRY

☐ POSTER, Living Room Suite, promotional, 24x24"................... 9.00 12.00
Harry Chapin died in an auto crash in 1981.

CHARLIE DANIELS BAND

☐ POSTER, High Lonesome, 22x32"................................... 4.00 5.00

CHEAP TRICK

☐ POSTER, New York is in For a Cheap Trick, tour, 1978, 18x25"....... 10.00 14.00
☐ POSTER, New York's Finest, tour, May 24 and 25, year unspecified,
20x30".. 8.00 11.00

CHER

☐ BOOK, Cher by Vicki Pellagrino, paperback, 1975.................. 3.00 4.00
☐ POSTER, Prisoner, 23x35"... 7.00 10.00

CHICAGO

☐ TICKET STUB, Berkeley, California, 1971.......................... 3.50 4.50

CLAPTON, ERIC

☐ BOOK, Eric Clapton Deluxe, paperback, 156 pages................. 10.00 14.00
☐ POSTER, Money and Cigarettes, promotional, 24x24"............... 4.50 6.00

CLASH

☐ POSTER, Bond's International Casino, black and white, promotional,
23x36".. 7.00 10.00
☐ POSTER, Combat Rock, 48x32"..................................... 9.00 12.00
☐ POSTER, Sandinista, red and black, tour, French, 15x22".......... 7.00 10.00

COOLIDGE, RITA

☐ POSTER, Satisfied, 24x36".. 4.00 5.00

COOPER, ALICE

☐ BOOK, Alice Cooper by Steve Demorest, paperback, 1974........... 9.00 12.00

	Price Range	
☐ TOUR BOOK, From the Inside...................................	6.00	8.00

COSTELLO, ELVIS

☐ HANDBILL, Grand Ole Opry Concert, 1982......................	1.00	1.50
☐ POSTCARD, Imperial Bedroom, issued in Great Britain..............	4.50	6.00
☐ POSTER, Almost Blue, 23x23"...................................	11.00	14.00
☐ POSTER, Bottom Line, concert, December 13 and 14, year unspecified, 24x34"..	11.00	15.00
☐ POSTER, Musician #60, promotional, 17x22".....................	6.00	8.00
☐ POSTER, Punch the Clock, blue and brown, promotional, 36x40".......	13.00	18.00
☐ POSTER, Taking Liberties, 36x36"...............................	13.00	17.00
☐ T-SHIRT, My Aim is True from tour, said to be only 500 made, called "official tour t-shirt"..	15.00	20.00

COUGAR, JOHN

☐ POSTER, Authority Song, U.S. promotional, 24x30"................	6.00	8.00
☐ PRESS KIT, American Fool, one picture and a three page biography.....	6.00	8.00
☐ TOUR BOOK, American Fool, 1982.............................	7.00	10.00

CREAM

☐ TICKET STUB, Fillmore East, 1968.............................	23.00	30.00

CROSBY, STILLS, NASH AND YOUNG

☐ BOOK, The Authorized Biography by Dave Zimmer and Henry Diltz, paperback, 256 pages.......................................	11.00	15.00
☐ POSTER, 1982 tour, 18x31"....................................	5.00	7.00

CROSS, CHRISTOPHER

☐ POSTER, Another Page, promotional, 27x37".....................	6.00	8.00

CULTURE CLUB

☐ BOOK, Boy George by Merle Ginsberg, paperback, 191 pages.........	2.50	3.50
☐ BOOK, Boy George and Culture Club by Maria David, clothbound.......	7.00	10.00
☐ BOOK, Boy George and The Culture Club by Jo Dietrich, paperback.....	3.50	4.50
☐ BOOK, Boy George: Today's #1 Sensation by Scott Cohen, paperback, 158 pages..	2.50	3.50
☐ POSTER, Louisville Concert, April 15 but year not specified, 14x22"....	5.00	7.00
☐ TICKET STUB, Chicago, 1983..................................	3.00	3.50

DALTRY, ROGER

☐ POSTER, Pace International, has number 3077 and date 1975, issued in Scotland, 24x37"..	20.00	30.00
☐ POSTER, Parting Should Be Painless, U.S. promotional, 24x30".......	5.00	7.00

DEBURGH, CHRIS

☐ POSTER, Man on the Line, U.S. promotional, 24x30"...............	4.50	6.00

DEEP PURPLE

☐ BOOK, Deep Purple: Heavy Metal Photo Book by Chris Welch, paperback.	12.00	16.00

DERRINGER, RICK

☐ POSTER, Sweet Evil, promotional, 12x20".......................	4.50	6.00

DIRE STRAITS

☐ PRESS KIT, Making Moves, one picture and a three page biography.....	6.00	8.00

Price Range

DOLBY, THOMAS

☐ POSTER, On the Cover of The Rolling Stone, U.S. promotional, 24x30"..   4.50   6.00

DOOBIE BROTHERS

☐ TOUR BOOK, Farewell Tour, 1982............................   7.00   10.00

DOORS, THE

☐ BOOK, Jim Morrison and The Doors by Mike Jahn, an unauthorized
biography, 95 pages, 1969..................................   10.00   15.00
☐ BOOK, The Doors by John Tobler and Andrew Doe, paperback, 127
pages. 10.00   13.00
☐ POSTER, Alive She Cried, promotional, 24x24"..................   5.00   7.00
☐ TICKET STUB, Whisky-a-Go-Go, Los Angeles, 1967..............   45.00   57.00

DURAN DURAN

☐ BOOK, Duran Duran in Japan, authorship uncredited, mainly photos, 100
pages, published in Japan....................................   11.00   15.00
☐ BOOK, Duran Duran Lyric Book, paperback.....................   6.00   8.00
☐ BOOK, Duran Duran Scrapbook Volume Two, paperback...........   6.00   8.00
☐ BOOK, Duran Duran Scrapbook Volume Three, paperback.........   6.00   8.00
☐ BOOK, Inside Duran Duran by Robyn Flans, paperback, 64 pages......   4.50   6.00
☐ BOOK, Rio, paperback, 32 pages..............................   5.00   7.00
☐ POSTER, promotional, from Rolling Stone magazine, 19x23"........   5.00   7.00
☐ POSTER, Seven and the Ragged Tiger, promotional, 24x36".........   5.00   7.00
☐ POSTER, wall display that folds in half, 12x22", 1984..............   8.00   10.00

EAGLES

☐ POSTER, Eagles' Greatest Hits, promotional, 24x24"...............   7.00   10.00

EASTON, SHEENA

☐ POSTER, Best Kept Secret, 24x36"............................   6.00   8.00
☐ TOUR BOOK, On Tour, 1982..................................   7.00   10.00

EDMUNDS, DAVE

☐ POSTER, Information, 36x20".................................   3.00   4.00

ELECTRIC LIGHT ORCHESTRA

☐ BOOK, Electric Light Orchestra Story by Bev Bevan, clothbound, 176
pages, published in Australia.................................   10.00   13.00

ENGLISH BEAT

☐ TOUR BOOK, Special Beat Service, 1982.......................   7.00   10.00

EURYTHMICS

☐ BOOK, The Eurythmics in Their Own Words, paperback, centerfold poster
of Annie and Dave...   7.00   10.00

FAITHFUL MARIA

☐ POSTER, A Child's Adventure, promotional, 18x27"..............   5.00   7.00

FLEETWOOD MAC

☐ POSTER, Mirage, promotional, 24x48".........................   6.00   8.00
☐ TOUR BOOK, Rumors, 1975...................................   5.00   7.00

FLYING BURRITO BROTHERS

☐ PRESS KIT, one picture and a two page biography................   5.00   7.00

	Price Range	

FOGELBERG, DAN
☐ POSTER, Greatest Hits, promotional, 36x36"...................... 5.00 7.00

FOREIGNER
☐ TOUR BOOK, 1980... 6.00 8.00

FRAMPTON, PETER
☐ POSTER, Art of Control, promotional, 24x36"..................... 3.50 4.50
☐ PRESS KIT, I'm in You, two pictures plus biography................ 6.00 8.00

GARCIA, JERRY
☐ POSTER, Cats Under the Stars, promotional, 24x36"............... 5.00 7.00

GENESIS
☐ POSTER, Mountain Dew, U.S. promotional, 17x22"................. 2.50 3.50

J. GEILS BAND
☐ POSTER, for video cassette, 18x12"............................. 2.50 3.50

GILMORE, DAVID
☐ POSTER, About Face, promotional, 33x48"....................... 7.00 10.00

GO-GOS
☐ POSTER, Talk Show, promotional, 24x36"........................ 6.00 8.00
☐ TOUR BOOK, 1982 U.S. Vacation Tour........................... 4.00 5.00

GRATEFUL DEAD
☐ TICKET STUB, Fillmore Auditorium, San Francisco, 1966............ 37.00 46.00

HALL and OATS
☐ POSTER, Lexington tour, February 20 but year not specified, 14x23".... 5.00 7.00

HELIX
☐ POSTER, No Rest For the Wicked, promotional, 24x30"............. 3.50 4.50

HENDRIX, JIMI
☐ BOOK, Hendrix: An Illustrated Biography by Victor Sampson, paperback,
125 pages.. 10.00 14.00

HENDRIX, NONA
☐ POSTER, Art of Defense, promotional, 18x28".................... 4.50 6.00

HIATT, JOHN
☐ POSTER, Two Bit Monsters, 24x24"............................. 4.00 5.00

HOLLIES
☐ PRESS KIT, What Goes Around, one picture and a four page biography... 6.00 8.00

HOLLY, BUDDY
☐ BOOK, The Buddy Holly Collector's Guide by Bill Griggs and Jim Black,
paperback.. 6.00 8.00
☐ TICKET STUB, Clear Lake, Iowa, 1959........................... 100.00 125.00

HOLMES, RUPERT
☐ POSTER, Partners in Crime, 24x24"............................. 3.00 4.00

HUMAN LEAGUE
☐ POSTER, Hysteria, promotional, 24x48"......................... 4.50 6.00

Price Range

HUMBLE PIE
☐ POSTER, Go For the Throat, 24x24".............................. 3.00 4.00

IAN, JANIS
☐ POSTER, Restless Eyes, 23x23".................................. 3.00 4.00

IDOL, BILLY
☐ POSTER, full length color, 35x27".............................. 4.50 6.00
☐ PRESS KIT, Rebel Yell, one picture and a three page biography........ 7.00 10.00

IRON MAIDEN
☐ TOUR BOOK, Number of the Beast, 1982.......................... 7.00 10.00

JACKSON, MICHAEL
☐ BOOK, Body and Soul by Geoff Brown, paperback, 128 pages......... 9.00 12.00
☐ BOOK, Soul of the Jackson Five by James Gregory, paperback, 1973.... 4.00 5.00
☐ POSTER, The Making of Thriller, 36x24"......................... 4.50 6.00

JAGGER, MICK
☐ BOOK, Mick Jagger by J. Marks, paperback, 1973................. 4.00 5.00

JARREAU, AL
☐ TOUR BOOK, Breakin' Away, 1982................................ 5.00 7.00

JEFFERSON AIRPLANE
☐ POSTER, Surrealistic Pillow, black and white, 43x33"............... 15.00 20.00

JETHRO TULL
☐ TOUR BOOK, ''A'' tour.. 6.00 8.00
☐ TOUR BOOK, 1979 tour... 6.00 8.00

JETT, JOHN
☐ POSTER, full length with guitar, 35x24"......................... 3.50 4.50

JOEL, BILLY
☐ PRESS KIT, Innocent Man, one picture and a ten page biography....... 6.00 8.00
☐ TOUR BOOK, Behind the Nylon Curtain, 1982.................... 8.00 11.00

ELTON JOHN
☐ BOOK, Elton John by Cathi Stern, paperback, 1975................ 4.00 5.00
☐ BOOK, Elton John Anthology, paperback, 208 pages............... 11.00 14.00
☐ PROGRAM, 1972 concert tour.................................... 11.00 14.00
☐ TOUR BOOK, Jump Up, 1982.................................... 6.00 8.00
☐ TOUR BOOK, Louder Than Concorde, 1976...................... 7.00 10.00

JONES, GRACE
☐ POSTER, Warm Leatherette, promotional, 24x36"................. 6.00 8.00

JONES, HOWARD
☐ POSTER, Human Liberation, promotional, 24x36"................. 3.50 4.50

JOPLIN, JANIS
☐ BOOK, Going Down with Janis by Peggy Caserta, paperback, 1973..... 6.00 8.00

JUDAS PRIEST
☐ BOOK, Judas Priest: The Early Years by Milton Okun, paperback, 103 pages. 8.00 10.00

		Price Range	
☐ POSTER, Louisville concert 1981, 23x17"......................		7.00	10.00
☐ TOUR BOOK, Point of Entry.....................................		6.00	8.00
☐ TOUR BOOK, Screaming for Vengeance, 1982....................		11.00	15.00

KINKS

☐ PRESS KIT, State of Confusion, two pictures and a five page biography..		6.00	8.00

KISS

☐ PRESS KIT, fold open with color photos and biographies, 1974.........		20.00	25.00

KNACK

☐ POSTER, Get the Knack, promotional, 20x30"....................		4.50	6.00

LARSON, NICOLETTE

☐ POSTER, Nick of Time, 23x23".................................		3.00	4.00

LAUPER, CYNDI

☐ POSTER, She is So Unusual, promotional, 36x38".................		9.00	12.00

LED ZEPPELIN

☐ BOOK, Led Zeppelin: Heavy Metal Photo Book by Chris Welch, paperback...		11.00	14.00
☐ TICKET STUB, Houston, Texas, 1976...........................		13.00	18.00

LITTLE FEAT

☐ POSTER, Time Loves A Hero, 32x23"..........................		2.00	3.00

MANCHESTER, MELISSA

☐ POSTER, Working Girl, 22x37"................................		4.00	5.00

MEN AT WORK

☐ POSTER, Cargo, 33x48"....................................		6.00	8.00

MISSING PERSON

☐ POSTER, Rhyme and Reason, U.S. promotional, 24x36"............		4.50	6.00

MITCHELL, JONI

☐ POSTER, Mingus, 24x36"....................................		3.00	4.00

MONKEES

☐ BOOK, The Monkees by Gene Fawcett and Howard Liss, paperback, 1966..		9.00	12.00

MOODY BLUES

☐ PROGRAM for 1978 tour, color..............................		9.00	12.00
☐ POSTER, Past Present and Future, 32x22"......................		11.00	14.00
☐ TOUR BOOK, Octave, 1978..................................		5.00	7.00

MOTHERS OF INVENTION

☐ POSTER, The Mothers of Invention This Week, apparently for concert but does not further specify, 24x36".............................		35.00	45.00

MOTLEY CRUE

☐ POSTER for Lexington concert, also features Ozzy Osbourne and Wasted, 14x22"..		7.00	10.00

MOTT THE HOOPLE

☐ PRESS KIT, four CBS network pictures from the 1970s plus a biography.		20.00	27.00

Price Range

NENA

☐ POSTER, 99 Luftballoons, promotional, 24x36", ''Luft'' is German for
''air.''.. 5.00   7.00

NEWTON-JOHN, OLIVIA

☐ CALENDAR, Twist of Fate, 1984, 16x25"........................ 5.00   7.00
☐ POSTER, In Concert, double sided videodisc poster, 11x33".......... 3.50   5.00
☐ POSTER, Two of a Kind, 24x36"............................... 5.00   7.00
☐ Same as above, 27x41"..................................... 5.75   7.00
☐ TOUR BOOK, Physical, 1982.................................. 4.00   5.00

NEW YORK DOLLS

☐ PRESS KIT, Nasty, in custom folder with twenty pages of interviews,
1973.. 40.00   55.00

NICKS, STEVIE

☐ PIN, Wild Heart, 14K gold lapel pin, promotional item from her 1983 tour. 275.00   325.00
☐ POSTER, Wild Heart, textured paper, 21x30".................... 8.00   11.00
☐ PRINT, Rhiannon, color print of Stevie Nicks painting, also has poem
about her song ''Rhiannon'' with story of her friend Robin, limited edition
but no information available on specific total, 12x14", 1982.......... 75.00   100.00
☐ RING, Wild Heart, 14K gold women's ring made as promotional item for
the Stevie Nicks tour of 1983, said to have been given away to members
of her entourage without any offered for public sale................. 300.00   350.00

NUGENT, TED

☐ PRESS KIT, Epic, one picture and a biography.................... 15.00   20.00

OCASEK, RICK

☐ POSTER, Beatitude, promotional, 24x24"....................... 3.50   4.50

OINGO BOINGO

☐ POSTER, Nothing to Fear, promotional, 24x36"................... 4.50   6.00

OSBOURNE, OZZY

☐ BOOK, Ozzy Osbourne Heavy Metal Photo Book by Chris Charlesworth,
paperback.. 13.00   16.00
☐ POSTCARD, Barking at the Moon, 6x8"......................... 2.00   2.50

PARKER, GRAHAM

☐ PRESS KIT, Another Gray Area, one picture and a two page biography... 5.00   7.00

PETTY, TOM

☐ TOUR BOOK, Damn the Torpedos, 1980.......................... 3.00   4.00

PINK FLOYD

☐ POSTER, The Wall, 40x27"................................... 9.00   12.00
☐ TICKET STUB, Marquee Club, London, 1968...................... 32.00   40.00

PLANT, ROBERT

☐ POSTER, Pictures at Eleven, 36x36".......................... 4.00   5.00
☐ TOUR BOOK, Principle of Moments............................ 6.00   8.00

POINTER SISTERS

☐ POSTER, Break Out, U.S. promotional, 24x30".................. 3.50   4.50

Price Range

POLICE

☐ BOOK, Ghost in the Machine, paperback............................. 6.00 8.00
☐ BOOK, The Police Chronicles by Philip Kamin and Peter Goddard, 127 pages............................. 9.00 12.00
☐ POSTER, Synchronicity, 24x36"............................. 4.50 6.00
☐ POSTER, Synchronicity II, 24x24"............................. 4.50 6.00
☐ POSTER, Synchronicity 83............................. 4.50 6.00

PRETENDERS

☐ PRESS KIT, Learning to Crawl, one picture and a two page biography.... 5.00 7.00

PRETTY THINGS

☐ PRESS KIT, Savage Eye, one picture and an eight page biography...... 6.00 8.00

QUATRO, SUZI

☐ POSTER, If You Knew Suzi, 24x36"............................. 4.00 5.00

QUEEN

☐ POSTER, Hot Space, issued in Great Britain, 60x40"............... 11.00 14.00
☐ PRESS KIT, Live Killers, five pictures plus biographies............... 15.00 20.00

QUIET RIOT

☐ POSTER, Freedom Hall concert, December 29, 1983, 14x22"........... 6.00 8.00

RAINBOW

☐ POSTER, Difficult to Cure, promotional, 22x30"................... 4.50 6.00
☐ TOUR BOOK, Straight Between the Eyes, 1982.................... 7.00 10.00

REAL LIFE

☐ POSTER, Send Me An Angel, promotional, 24x36"................. 4.50 6.00

REDDY, HELEN

☐ PICTURE SLEEVE from 45 r.p.m. (no record), Candle of Water......... .50 .75

REED, LOU

☐ PRESS KIT, New Sensation, one picture and a ten page biography...... 6.00 8.00

REFLEX

☐ POSTER, Politics of Dancing, promotional, 20x24"................. 3.50 4.50

R.E.M.

☐ POSTER, The Reckoning, U.S. promotional, 24x36"................ 3.50 4.50

REO SPEEDWAGON

☐ TOUR BOOK, Nine Lives, 1979.................................. 4.00 5.00

RICHIE, LIONEL

☐ POSTER, close-up with inset of LP covers, 36x24"................. 4.50 6.00

ROCKPILE

☐ POSTER, Seconds of Pleasure, tour, 36x36"...................... 11.00 15.00

ROLLING STONES

☐ BOOK, Rolling Stones: An Unauthorized Biography by David Dalton, paperback, 128 pages............................. 6.00 8.00
☐ BOOK, Rolling Stones From A to Z by Sue Weiner and Lisa Howard, paperback, 149 pages............................. 10.00 13.00
☐ POSTER, Gimme Shelter, promotional for motion picture, 18x26"........ 6.00 8.00

	Price Range	
☐ POSTER, Tattoo You, promotional, 23x22″	6.00	8.00
☐ POSTER, 1970 United Kingdom Tour, 20x30″	13.00	18.00
☐ POSTER, 1976 European Tour, 20x28″	9.00	12.00
☐ PRESS KIT, Some Girls, in folder with stickers and five pictures	30.00	40.00

RONSTADT, LINDA

☐ POSTER, Get Closer, promotional, 24x39″	5.00	7.00

ROSS, DIANA

☐ TICKET STUB, Oakland Coliseum, 1979	4.00	5.00

ROTTEN, JOHNNY

☐ PRESS KIT, one picture plus four page biography	6.00	8.00

RUSH

☐ TOUR BOOK, Signals, 1983	6.00	8.00

SCAGGS, BOZ

☐ POSTER, Silk Degrees, tour, 20x30″	9.00	12.00

SCORPIONS

☐ TOUR BOOK, Blackout, 1982	4.00	5.00

SEGER, BOB

☐ POSTER, Nine Tonight, 30x20″	5.00	7.00

SHA NA NA

☐ TOUR BOOK, Grease for Peace, 1982	4.00	5.00

The "Grease" referred to is the Broadway musical (later motion picture) starring John Travolta and Newton-John.

SIMON, CARLY

☐ PRESS KIT, Come Upstairs, one picture and a two page biography	6.00	8.00

SIMON, PAUL

☐ POSTER, Hearts and Bones, U.S. promotional, 36x36″	5.00	7.00
☐ POSTER, One Trick Pony, 23x35″	6.00	8.00

SLICK, GRACE

☐ POSTER, Software, U.S. promotional, 24x30″	3.50	4.50

SNOW, PHOEBE

☐ POSTER, Never Letting Go, tour, 20x30″	7.00	10.00

SOFT CELL

☐ POSTER, Art of Falling Apart, promotional, 24x24″	3.50	4.50

SPINAL TAP

☐ POSTER, This is Spinal Tap, promotional, 27x40″	7.00	10.00

SPLIT ENZ

☐ PRESS KIT, Conflicting Emotions	7.00	10.00

SPRINGFIELD, RICK

☐ FIGURE, cardboard stand-up promoting Hard to Hold, 24″ tall	6.00	8.00
☐ NAPKINS, set of paper napkins promoting Hard to Hold	2.00	2.50
☐ POSTER, Hard to Hold, for video cassette, 35x23″	4.50	6.00

	Price Range	
☐ POSTER, Success Hasn't Spoiled Me Yet, promotional, 24x24"	4.50	6.00
☐ TOUR BOOK, Sweat for Success, 1982	6.00	8.00

SPRINGSTEEN, BRUCE

☐ BACKSTAGE PASS for 1980 tour	7.00	10.00
☐ POSTER, Born in the U.S.A., pictures LP cover with ad for LP, 44x36"	9.00	12.00
☐ TOUR BOOK, The River, undated	6.00	8.00

STEELY DAN

☐ POSTER, Gaucho, 23x35"	3.00	4.00

STEWART, ROD

☐ POSTER, Camouflage, 60x48"	7.00	10.00
☐ TOUR BOOK, Footloose and Fancy Free	6.00	8.00
☐ TOUR BOOK, United States/Canadian tour, 1982	7.00	10.00

STRAY CATS

☐ POSTER, Built For Speed, 36x24"	4.50	6.00
☐ POSTER, Rant and Rave, promotional, 24x36"	4.50	6.00

STYX

☐ PRESS KIT, Caught in the Act	6.00	8.00

SUPERTRAMP

☐ PRESS KIT, Famous Last Words, one picture and a biography in a folder.	7.00	10.00
☐ TOUR BOOK, Breakfast	6.00	8.00

SWEET, RACHEL

☐ POSTER, Fool Around, tour, 24x33"	7.00	10.00

TALKING HEADS

☐ PRESS KIT, More Songs, one picture and three pages of biographies	10.00	15.00

TANGERINE DREAM

☐ PRESS KIT for North American tour	10.00	13.00

TAYLOR, JAMES

☐ POSTER, untitled, 24x34"	4.00	5.00
☐ TICKET STUB, Hartford Coliseum, Connecticut, 1974	4.00	5.00

THOROUGHGOOD, GEORGE

☐ TOUR BOOK, Bad to the Bone, 1982	8.00	11.00

TOWNSHEND, PETER

☐ BOOK, Through the Eyes of Peter Townshend, paperback, 113 pages with illustrations, 1974	9.00	12.00

TUFF DARTS

☐ PRESS KIT for their first album, 1978	10.00	15.00

TURNER, TINA

☐ POSTER, Private Dancer, 36x24"	4.50	6.00

UTOPIA

☐ POSTER, Deface the Music, promotional, 24x24"	5.00	7.00

VAN HALEN

☐ BOOK, Van Halen: Metal Mania by David Lee Roth, paperback	7.00	10.00

	Price Range	
☐ POSTER, Diver Down, red and white, U.S. promotional, 35x35"........	7.00	10.00
☐ TOUR BOOK, Women and Children First, 1980.....................	6.00	8.00
☐ TOUR BOOK, World Tour, 1979...............................	6.00	8.00

VEE, BOBBY

| ☐ PICTURE SLEEVE from 45 r.p.m. (no record), Rubber Ball............ | 2.00 | 3.00 |

VILLAGE PEOPLE

| ☐ POSTER, Go West, 23x35".................................. | 4.00 | 5.00 |

THE WHO

☐ POSTER, Face Dancing, orange and black, promotional, 24x30".......	5.00	7.00
☐ POSTER, It's Hard, issued in Great Britain, 60x40"................	4.50	6.00
☐ TICKET STUB, Metropolitan Opera, New York, year unspecified........	38.00	48.00

YOUNG, NEIL

| ☐ POSTER, Rust Never Sleeps, promotional, 27x41"................. | 11.00 | 15.00 |

ZAPPA, FRANK

| ☐ BOOK, 1980 Fall Tour...................................... | 9.00 | 12.00 |

ZEVON, WARREN

| ☐ POSTER, Excitable Boy, 23x35"............................... | 7.00 | 10.00 |

ZZ TOP

| ☐ KEYCHAIN, chrome plated................................... | 9.00 | 11.00 |

THE OFFICIAL PRICE GUIDES TO:

☐	465-8	**American Silver & Silver Plate** 4th Ed.	10.95
☐	482-8	**Antique Clocks** 3rd Ed.	10.95
☐	283-3	**Antique & Modern Dolls** 3rd Ed.	10.95
☐	287-6	**Antique & Modern Firearms** 6th Ed.	11.95
☐	271-X	**Antiques & Other Collectibles** 6th Ed.	9.95
☐	289-2	**Antique Jewelry** 5th Ed.	11.95
☐	270-1	**Beer Cans & Collectibles,** 3rd Ed.	7.95
☐	262-0	**Bottles Old & New** 9th Ed.	10.95
☐	255-8	**Carnival Glass** 1st Ed.	10.95
☐	453-4	**Collectible Cameras** 2nd Ed.	10.95
☐	277-9	**Collectibles of the Third Reich** 2nd Ed.	10.95
☐	454-2	**Collectible Toys** 2nd Ed.	9.95
☐	490-9	**Collector Cars** 6th Ed.	11.95
☐	267-1	**Collector Handguns** 3rd Ed.	11.95
☐	459-3	**Collector Knives** 7th Ed.	10.95
☐	266-3	**Collector Plates** 4th Ed.	11.95
☐	476-3	**Collector Prints** 6th Ed.	11.95
☐	489-5	**Comic Books & Collectibles** 8th Ed.	9.95
☐	433-X	**Depression Glass** 1st Ed.	9.95
☐	472-0	**Glassware** 2nd Ed.	10.95
☐	492-5	**Hummel Figurines & Plates** 5th Ed.	9.95
☐	451-8	**Kitchen Collectibles** 2nd Ed.	10.95
☐	460-7	**Military Collectibles** 4th Ed.	10.95
☐	268-X	**Music Collectibles** 5th Ed.	11.95
☐	491-7	**Old Books & Autographs** 6th Ed.	10.95
☐	452-6	**Oriental Collectibles** 2nd Ed.	11.95
☐	461-5	**Paper Collectibles** 4th Ed.	10.95
☐	276-0	**Pottery & Porcelain** 5th Ed.	11.95
☐	263-9	**Radio, T.V. & Movie Memorabilia** 2nd Ed.	11.95
☐	288-4	**Records** 7th Ed.	10.95
☐	485-2	**Royal Doulton** 4th Ed.	10.95
☐	418-6	**Science Fiction & Fantasy Collectibles** 1st Ed.	9.95
☐	477-1	**Wicker** 3rd Ed.	10.95

THE OFFICIAL:

☐	369-4	**Guide to Buying & Selling Antiques** 1st Ed.	9.95
☐	448-8	**Identification Guide to Gunmarks** 2nd Ed.	9.95
☐	412-7	**Identification Guide to Pottery & Porcelain** 1st Ed.	9.95
☐	415-1	**Identification Guide to Victorian Furniture** 1st Ed.	9.95

THE OFFICIAL (POCKET SIZE) PRICE GUIDES TO:

☐	473-9	**Antiques & Flea Markets** 3rd Ed.	3.95
☐	442-9	**Antique Jewelry** 2nd Ed.	3.95
☐	264-7	**Baseball Cards** 5th Ed.	4.95
☐	488-7	**Bottles** 2nd Ed.	4.95
☐	468-2	**Cars & Trucks** 2nd Ed.	4.95
☐	260-4	**Collectible Americana** 1st Ed.	4.95
☐	294-9	**Collectible Records** 3rd Ed.	4.95
☐	469-0	**Collector Guns** 2nd Ed.	4.95
☐	474-7	**Comic Books** 3rd Ed.	3.95
☐	486-0	**Dolls** 3rd Ed.	4.95
☐	292-2	**Football Cards** 5th Ed.	4.95
☐	258-2	**Glassware** 2nd Ed.	4.95
☐	487-9	**Hummels** 3rd Ed.	4.95
☐	441-0	**Military Collectibles** 2nd Ed.	3.95
☐	480-1	**Paperbacks & Magazines** 3rd Ed.	4.95
☐	443-7	**Pocket Knives** 2nd Ed.	3.95
☐	479-8	**Scouting Collectibles** 3rd Ed.	4.95
☐	439-9	**Sports Collectibles** 2nd Ed.	3.95
☐	494-1	**Star Trek/Star Wars Collectibles** 3rd Ed.	3.95
☐	493-3	**Toys** 3rd Ed.	4.95

THE OFFICIAL BLACKBOOK PRICE GUIDES TO:

☐	284-1	**U.S. Coins** 24th Ed.	3.95
☐	286-8	**U.S. Paper Money** 18th Ed.	3.95
☐	285-X	**U.S. Postage Stamps** 8th Ed.	3.95

THE OFFICIAL INVESTORS GUIDE TO BUYING & SELLING:

☐	496-8	**Gold, Silver and Diamonds** 2nd Ed.	9.95
☐	497-6	**Gold Coins** 2nd Ed.	9.95
☐	498-4	**Silver Coins** 2nd Ed.	9.95
☐	499-2	**Silver Dollars** 2nd Ed.	9.95

TOTAL	

SEE REVERSE SIDE FOR ORDERING INSTRUCTIONS